Criminal Law

WITHDRAWN

137 Stamford Street
London SE1 9NN
librarywaterloo@bpp.com
020 7633 4397

D0185584

BPP University College

080845

foundations series

Written with learning in mind, these texts allow students to gain a solid understanding of the law. Each book presents the subject clearly and accessibly for effective and satisfying study.

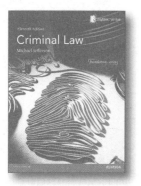

The Foundations series comes with MyLawChamber which provides online study support through: the interactive Pearson eText, Case Navigator, practice questions, online glossary and legal updates, all located at **www.mylawchamber.co.uk**.

Available from all good
bookshops or order online at:
www.pearsoned.co.uk/law

PEARSON

Eleventh Edition

Criminal Law

MICHAEL JEFFERSON
MA (Oxon), BCL
Senior Lecturer
University of Sheffield

PEARSON

Harlow, England • London • New York • Boston • San Francisco • Toronto • Sydney • Auckland • Singapore • Hong Kong
Tokyo • Seoul • Taipei • New Delhi • Cape Town • São Paulo • Mexico City • Madrid • Amsterdam • Munich • Paris • Milan

Pearson Education Limited
Edinburgh Gate
Harlow CM20 2JE
United Kingdom
Tel: +44 (0)1279 623623
Web: www.pearson.com/uk

First published 1992 (print)
Sixth edition published 2003 (print)
Seventh edition published 2006 (print)
Eighth edition published 2007 (print)
Ninth edition published 2009 (print)
Tenth edition published 2011 (print)
Eleventh edition published 2013 (print and electronic)

© Pearson Education Limited 1992, 2011 (print)
© Pearson Education Limited 2013 (print and electronic)

The right of Michael Jefferson to be identified as author of this work has been asserted
by him in accordance with the Copyright, Designs and Patents Act 1988.

The print publication is protected by copyright. Prior to any prohibited reproduction, storage
in a retrieval system, distribution or transmission in any form or by any means, electronic,
mechanical, recording or otherwise, permission should be obtained from the publisher or,
where applicable, a licence permitting restricted copying in the United Kingdom should
be obtained from the Copyright Licensing Agency Ltd, Saffron House, 6–10 Kirby Street,
London EC1N 8TS.

The ePublication is protected by copyright and must not be copied, reproduced,
transferred, distributed, leased, licensed or publicly performed or used in any way except
as specifically permitted in writing by the publishers, as allowed under the terms and
conditions under which it was purchased, or as strictly permitted by applicable copyright
law. Any unauthorised distribution or use of this text may be a direct infringement of the
author's and the publishers' rights and those responsible may be liable in law accordingly.

Contains public sector information licensed under the Open Government Licence (OGL) v1.0.
www.nationalarchives.gov.uk/doc/open-government-licence.

The screenshots in this book are reprinted by permission of Microsoft Corporation.

Pearson Education is not responsible for the content of third-party internet sites.

ISBN: 978-1-4479-2332-9 (print)
      978-1-4479-2333-6 (PDF)
      978-1-4479-2339-8 (eText)

British Library Cataloguing-in-Publication Data
A catalogue record for the print edition is available from the British Library

Library of Congress Cataloging-in-Publication Data
A catalog record for the print edition is available from the Library of Congress

10 9 8 7 6 5 4 3 2 1
16 15 14 13

Cover photo: © Motoring Picture Library/Alamy

Print edition typeset in 9/12pt Stone Serif by 35
Print edition printed and bound by Ashford Colour Press Ltd., Gosport

NOTE THAT ANY PAGE CROSS REFERENCES REFER TO THE PRINT EDITION

Brief contents

Contents

premium
mylawchamber
unrivalled support for legal education

Join over 5,000 law students succeeding with MyLawChamber

Visit **www.mylawchamber.co.uk** to access a wealth of tools to help you develop and test your knowledge of criminal law, strengthening your understanding so you can excel.

 The Pearson eText is a fully searchable, interactive version of *Criminal Law*. You can make notes in it, highlight it, bookmark it, even link to online sources – helping you get more out of studying and revision. The Pearson eText is linked to the learning tools you'll find in MyLawChamber.

- Interactive multiple choice questions to test your understanding of each topic
- Practice exam questions with guidance to hone your exam technique
- Annotated weblinks to help you read more widely around the subject and really impress your lecturers
- Glossary flashcards to test yourself on legal terms and definitions
- Legal newsfeed to help you read more widely, stay right up to date with the law and impress examiners
- Legal updates to help you stay up to date with the law and impress examiners

 Case Navigator provides in-depth analysis of the leading cases in criminal law, improving your case-reading skills and understanding of how the law is applied.

 Explore the world of **Virtual Lawyer** and develop your skills in answering legal problem questions as you apply your knowledge of the law to a range of interactive scenarios.

Use the access card at the back of the book to activate MyLawChamber. Online purchase is also available at **www.mylawchamber.co.uk/register**.

Lecturers *Teach your course, your way.*

MyLawChamber is a powerful teaching tool which you can use to assess your students, and improve their understanding.

 Make the interactive Pearson eText a 'live' teaching resource by annotating with your own commentary, links to external sources, critique, or updates to the law and share with your students.

 Set quizzes and mini-assessments using the bank of over 450 multiple-choice questions to gauge your students' understanding.

 Use Case Navigator, a case reading resource we offer in conjunction with LexisNexis, to assign student seminar work.

 Virtual Lawyer is an engaging way to help your students develop their problem-solving skills through scenario-based learning.

For information about teaching support materials, please contact your local Pearson sales consultant or visit **www.mylawchamber.co.uk**.

The regularly maintained MyLawChamber site provides the following features:

- Search tool to help locate specific items of content.
- Online help and support to assist with website usage and troubleshooting.

Case Navigator access is included with your mylawchamber premium registration. The LexisNexis element of Case Navigator is only available to those who currently subscribe to LexisNexis Butterworths online.

Preface

This book is written for LLB, CPE/Graduate Diploma in Law and BA students sitting examinations on English criminal law in their first or second year whether in England and Wales or outside the jurisdiction. It is hoped that persons with little or no access to law libraries will find the text helpful. The text is also useful for those studying for other qualifications by private study including distance learning. Extracts of law reform reports may be of especial use to such students.

The book, which is analytical in nature, includes those areas of substantive criminal law which are traditionally covered on a criminal law course, and those topics are presented in the way in which English law subjects are normally taught. Criminal law is fast-moving and fast-growing, and there has to be some selection among topics.

Criminal Law can be approached in different ways such as political, feminist, theoretical, and other standpoints may be taken. The focus in this book is on the rules of criminal law and criticism of them. It will quickly become obvious that the law is contingent, historical, and in many ways controversial. There is no vast eternal plan. English criminal law is replete with inconsistencies, and this book reflects those issues. Students must grapple with such difficulties, for a superficial treatment will lead to wrong law and low marks. Attention is focused on what is sometimes called the 'internal critique of the law', in order that such inconsistencies are brought out, and on those areas which present difficulties. This is a common approach in UK Law Schools, but it is well worth considering the approach which your tutors use. There are many areas of controversy such as the definition of offences such as rape, murder and theft and the width of defences such as duress and loss of control. Indeed, controversy rages over whether an element of a crime is a part of the offence or part of the defence. The best example is consent in rape. Is it part of the offence or part of the defence? Students should not think that understanding criminal law consists solely of learning legal rules and knowing how to apply them to the facts. In legal jargon this is a 'black-letter' approach to the subject and one which has not been in common use in England and Wales for perhaps 40 years.

The arrangement of topics may differ from the order in which the subjects are taught on your course. However, for the assistance of those familiar with older editions, because of the House of Lords' decision in *G* (2004) some rearrangement of topics was made in a previous edition. In particular, the consideration of intention and recklessness in the context of murder and criminal damage respectively has been abolished. This 'unique selling point' of the text was intended to encourage readers to focus their minds on the results that the accused had to intend or on to which he had to be reckless. For example, as an examiner I saw too many students writing: 'the *mens rea* for murder is intent'. Besides being incorrect (if it were true, an intent say to touch would be malice aforethought, the mental element of murder), the statement reveals an ignorance as to how precisely the elements of a crime are defined. Whether this experiment was successful is for others to judge. As things are now, namely the law has returned to the pre-*Caldwell* position, opportunity was taken to reorder the book. This reordering is maintained in the current edition.

Among differences from other textbooks are the following:

(a) There is a concentration on one or two topics which have been unjustifiably neglected in recent years in comparison with some other matters. Offences of strict liability are instanced. Some issues which this book considers have over the past 25 years come to the fore: corporate criminal liability is one obvious instance.

(b) Emphasis is laid on suggestions for reform and on criticism both of individual decisions and the ambit of offences. Criminal law needs to be evaluated and criticised. Proposals contained in Law Commission Consultation Papers and Reports are analysed. It is in the context particularly of reform that the European Convention on Human Rights is looked at. Some attempt is made to uncover the underlying purposes behind offences: if that purpose is not served by current law, reform is due.

(c) There is some reference to Commonwealth and US cases and commentators.

(d) The student is introduced to some of the concepts of theoretical criminal law, such as the distinction between excuses and justifications. There is a growing body of academic criticism and this book introduces the reader to some of the major issues. There is discussion of gender issues, particularly in the law concerned with battered women. This is not, however, a book on criminal law theory. Readers are referred to the further reading at the end of each chapter.

(e) I hope that values and policies underlying the rules of criminal law are brought out.

This book deals with, as stated earlier, substantive criminal law; that is, it is concerned with the question of whether an accused is guilty of a particular offence. It does not deal with the following, all of which are important topics in their own right.

(a) *Bringing the accused to trial* and *procedure at trial*. Such topics are generally covered in courses of varying names such as English Legal System, Criminal Justice, and Criminal Process. Arrest may be dealt with in constitutional or public law. Similarly excluded are the choice of charges, the workings of the police, the Crown Prosecution Service, the Director of Public Prosecutions, plea bargaining, and the investigation of crime, including forensic jurisprudence.

(b) *Sentence*. The methods of disposal after trial are usually dealt with, if at all, in criminology or perhaps jurisprudence courses. Why people commit offences is also part of criminology. Victimology is also not part of substantive criminal law.

(c) *Evidence*. The opening chapter of this book looks at the evidential and legal burdens of proof so that readers can understand the terms when they meet them in, for example, Chapter 9, which deals with the defences of insanity, diminished responsibility and automatism. The remainder of the law of evidence is for a course on evidence.

(d) *Public order*. Criminal law can be seen as a way in which the state controls citizens and how officials control state officers. Offences against public order are usually covered by courses on public law.

All these excluded topics are interesting in their own right. For example, why was the Commissioner of Police for the Metropolis charged with endangering the public contrary to s 3 of the Health and Safety at Work Act 1971 rather than murder, when his officers put seven bullets into the head of the Brazilian Jean Charles de Menezes at Stockwell underground station in south London in 2005?

The remainder of a possibly very wide course forms substantive criminal law. It is that area of law which has to be applied by the triers of fact, the jury in the Crown Court and the justices of the peace in the magistrates' courts, in order to determine whether the accused is guilty. (It should be noted immediately that the topics selected for inclusion in this book are, as stated above, those normally taught on a criminal law course and not necessarily those such as motoring offences most often met in practice.) A jury may have to determine whether the accused is to be convicted of murder or whether he has the defence of loss of control. Substantive criminal law is concerned with *what* has to be shown in order to find the accused guilty or not. *How* a matter of substantive criminal law is to be proved is part of the law of evidence. A person may confess to murder, have the crime proved against him in court, and so on. Those matters are ones of evidence. What has to be proved is part of substantive law. If when reading substantive criminal law you find difficulty accepting what it is said the accused thought or did, don't worry: assume that the prosecution has proved to the satisfaction of the triers of fact what the accused did or thought.

This book is part of the *Foundation Studies in Law* Series and has a Companion Website at: **www.mylawchamber.co.uk/jefferson**.

Errors and omissions are my own.

When originally submitted to the publishers, this book was written in what I considered to be a non-sexist style. However, to conform to series style, the traditional use of 'he' to refer to both sexes was reverted to at editing stage.

I would like to thank Christine Statham, the publisher, and editors and proofreaders at Pearson for their professionalism and patience, and the anonymous students who read the book with 'student eyes' on the text.

Michael Jefferson
February 2013

Guided tour

Aims and objectives at the start of each chapter help focus your learning before you begin.

1

Introduction to criminal law

Aims and objectives

After reading this chapter you will understand and be able to critique:

- the basic principles of criminal law
- the Human Rights Act 1998 insofar as it affects criminal liability
- the definition of crimes
- the differences between civil and criminal law
- the hierarchy of criminal courts and the doctrine of precedent in criminal law
- the courts' interpretation of statutes imposing criminal liability
- the classifications of crimes and the powers of the courts to create offences
- the burden of proof in criminal law
- codification of criminal law

Case summaries highlight the facts and key legal principles of essential cases that you need to be aware of in your study of tort law.

Deller (1952) 36 Cr App R 184 (CCA)

The accused was charged with what was then false pretences and is now fraud by false representation contrary to s 2 of the Fraud Act 2006. When he took his car in for a trade-in, he represented that there was no money owing on it. He believed that there were payments outstanding. It looked as if he had made a false pretence. In fact the loan on the car was void and in law did not exist. Therefore, he did not owe any money. His representation turned out to be true, though he mistakenly believed it to be false. The Court of Criminal Appeal quashed his conviction. The prosecution had failed to prove that the pretence was false.

One is not guilty of an offence simply because one believes oneself to be guilty. The prosecution must prove the whole of the *actus reus* and, on the facts, one element was missing. *Deller* can stand for the proposition that one is not guilty for having guilty thoughts. *Mens rea* alone is insufficient. The accused did intend to make a false representation but that representation turned out to be true. Therefore, all the elements of the offence were not fulfilled. The charge nowadays would be one of attempted fraud under the Criminal Attempts Act 1981.

The case always contrasted with *Deller* is *Dadson*. The distinction between the two authorities is often stated to be that in *Deller* there was an absence of an element of the offence whereas in *Dadson* there was an absence of an element of a defence. This

---

Examples throughout illustrate possible case scenarios to explain how the law operates in practice and help you understand complex legal processes.

Legal burden

Example

On whom is the burden of proof in the following defences: loss of control; duress; insanity; and diminished responsibility?

The answers are respectively: prosecution; prosecution; defence; and defence. With regard to diminished responsibility, s 2(2) of the Homicide Act 1957 expressly places the burden on the accused. Parliament can do anything and therefore it can place the burden of proof on the accused. Where the onus is on the accused, she must prove that she has the defence on the balance of probabilities, the civil law standard of proof. With regard to loss of control and duress, the burden is on the prosecution, as it normally is, and they

25

Marginal cross-references direct you to other places in the text where the same subject is discussed, helping you to make connections and understand how the material fits together.

See p 67 later in this chapter for a more detailed explanation of omission.

prove the whole of the *actus reus*. To call self-defence a 'defence' is a misnomer if by the term is meant a third concept beyond *actus reus* and *mens rea*. Nevertheless, the accused bears the evidential burden.

Some offences can be committed by a failure to act, and others such as possessing cannabis are status or state of affairs ones. It is difficult to describe these offences as 'conduct' ones. Omission involves the opposite, a lack of conduct.

Causation

There is no more intractable problem in the law than causation (Criminal Law and Penal Methods Reform Committee, South Australia, Fourth Report, *The Substantive Criminal Law*, 1977, 50, quoted in E. Colvin 'Causation in criminal law' (1989) 1 Bond LR 253).

Questions of causation arise in many different legal contexts and no single theory of causation will provide a ready-made answer to the question whether [the accused's] action is to be treated as the cause or a cause of some ensuing event. The approach must necessarily be pragmatic . . . (Lord Bridge in ***Attorney-General of Hong Kong v Tse Hung-lit*** [1986] 1 AC 876 (PC)).

The law in deciding questions of causation selects one or more causes out of the total sum of conditions according to the purpose in hand . . . (McGarvie and O'Bryan JJ in ***Demirian*** [1989] VR 97, 110).

Figures and diagrams are used to strengthen your understanding of complex legal processes in tort law.

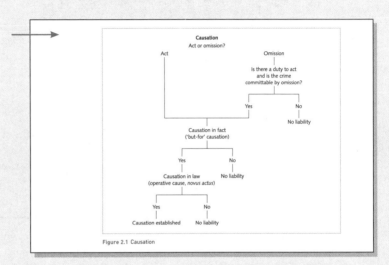

Figure 2.1 Causation

Chapter summaries located at the end of each chapter draw together the key points that you should be aware of following your reading, and provide a useful check for revision.

Summary

- *Introduction*: Criminal law is concerned with forbidding various forms of behaviour, whether that consists of acts, omissions or states of affairs. These are called *actus reus* or the external element(s) of offences. When added to the *mens rea*, there is an offence (though note Chapter 4 on strict liability); there may also be a defence.
- *Some problems*: The *actus reus* must not be read as meaning solely the conduct of the accused: it can, for example, cover the behaviour of the victim. An illustration is rape, which includes lack of consent by the alleged victim. Similarly, when considering defences, it is difficult to match some defences with the analysis of *actus reus*; *mens rea*; and defence. Some defences, for example mistake, seem not to be separate at all from the offence: they are not a third ingredient. Rather they negate either the *actus reus* or *mens*

Suggestions for **Further reading** at the end of each chapter encourage you to delve deeper into the topic and read those articles which help you to gain higher marks in both exams and assessments.

Further reading

Alldridge, P. 'What's wrong with the traditional criminal law course?' [1990] 10 LS 38

Ashworth, A. 'Is the criminal law a lost cause?' [2000] 116 LQR 228

Ashworth, A. 'The Human Rights Act and the substantive criminal law: a non-minimalist view' [2000] Crim LR 564

Ashworth, A. Case comment on *Attorney-General's Reference (No. 4 of 2002)* [2005] Crim LR 215

Ashworth, A. 'Conceptions of overcriminalization' [2008] 5 Ohio St J Crim L 407

Ashworth, A. and Blake, M. 'The presumption of innocence in criminal law' [1996] Crim LR 306

Ashworth, A. and Zedner, L. 'Defending the criminal law: reflections on the changing character of crime' [2008] 2 Crim Law and Philos 21

Bennion, F. 'Codification of the criminal law — Part 2. The technique of codification' [1986] Crim LR 295

Bingham, Lord 'A criminal code: must we wait forever?' [1998] Crim LR 694

Bowles, R., Faure, M. and Garoupa, N. 'The scope of the criminal law and criminal sanctions: An economic view and policy implications' [2008] 35 JLS 389

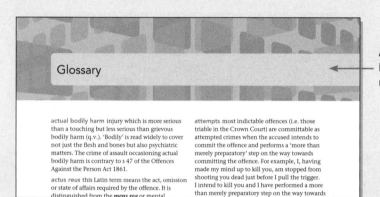

an unlawful act. If the unlawful act is a crime, the offence is one contrary to the Criminal Law Act 1977, s 1(1), as amended. There are one or two common law conspiracy offences, the main one being conspiracy to defraud: one can be guilty of this offence even though the object is not in itself criminal.

constructive manslaughter a person is guilty of this form of **manslaughter** if she kills as a result of committing a crime which is seen objectively as being dangerous. The term 'dangerous' in this context means: one which 'all sober and reasonable people would inevitably recognise must subject the other person to, at least, the risk of some harm resulting therefrom, albeit not serious harm' (per Edmund Davies LJ, *Church*

destroys or damages property *whether belonging to another or not*, intending to destroy or damage property or being reckless as to whether property is destroyed or damaged. Criminal damage by fire should be charged as **arson**: see s 1(3) of the 1971 Act.

deception misrepresentation, fraud, telling lies. See also **fraud**.

diminished responsibility this defence found in s 2(1) of the Homicide Act 1957 as inserted by the Coroners and Justice Act 2009 has the effect of reducing murder to (voluntary) manslaughter. It comprises three elements: (i) an abnormality of mental functioning, which arises from 'a recognised medical condition'; (ii) this must substantially impair the accused's ability to do

Reference sections have a stepped coloured tab to allow you to navigate quickly to key information within the text.

Glossary

A full **Glossary** located at the back of the book can be used throughout your reading to clarify unfamiliar terms.

actual bodily harm injury which is more serious than a touching but less serious than grievous bodily harm (q.v.). 'Bodily' is read widely to cover not just the flesh and bones but also psychiatric matters. The crime of assault occasioning actual bodily harm is contrary to s 47 of the Offences Against the Person Act 1861.

actus reus this Latin term means the act, omission or state of affairs required by the offence. It is distinguished from the ***mens rea*** or mental

attempts most indictable offences (i.e. those triable in the Crown Court) are committable as attempted crimes when the accused intends to commit the offence and performs a 'more than merely preparatory' step on the way towards committing the offence. For example, I, having made my mind up to kill you, am stopped from shooting you dead just before I pull the trigger. I intend to kill you and I have performed a more than merely preparatory step on the way towards

---

Visit **www.mylawchamber.co.uk** to access a wealth of tools to help you develop and test your knowledge of criminal law, strengthening your understanding so you can excel.

 The Pearson eText is a fully searchable, interactive version of *Criminal Law*. You can make notes in it, highlight it, bookmark it, even link to online sources – helping you get more out of studying and revision.

- Interactive multiple choice questions to test your understanding of each topic
- Practice exam questions with guidance to hone your exam technique
- Annotated weblinks to help you read more widely around the subject and really impress your lecturers
- Glossary flashcards to test yourself on legal terms and definitions
- Legal newsfeed to help you read more widely, stay right up to date with the law and impress examiners
- Legal updates to help you stay up to date with the law and impress examiners

 Case Navigator provides in-depth analysis of the leading cases in criminal law, improving your case-reading skills and understanding of how the law is applied.

VL Explore the world of **Virtual Lawyer** and develop your skills in answering legal problem questions as you apply your knowledge of the law to a range of interactive scenarios.

Use the access card at the back of the book to activate MyLawChamber. Online purchase is also available at **www.mylawchamber.co.uk/register**.

Table of cases

 mylawchamber

Case Navigator provides in-depth analysis of the leading cases in criminal law, improving your case-reading skills and understanding of how the law is applied.

Visit **www.mylawchamber.co.uk** to access unique online support:

- **Direct deep links** to the core cases in criminal law
- **Short introductions** provide guidance on what you should look out for while reading the case
- **Questions** help you to test your understanding of the case, and provide feedback on what you should have grasped
- **Summaries** contextualise the case and point you to further reading so that you are fully prepared for seminars and discussions

Case Navigator cases are highlighted **in bold** below.

Case Navigator access is included with your mylawchamber premium registration. The LexisNexis element of Case Navigator is only available to those who currently subscribe to LexisNexis Butterworths online.

Case Navigator cases are highlighted in bold.

For ease of reference this table of cases includes authorities from different jurisdictions. Reference is to readily accessible series.

Table of Legislation

Part 1

Preliminary matters

1   Introduction to criminal law

1

Introduction to criminal law

Aims and objectives

After reading this chapter you will understand and be able to critique:

- the basic principles of criminal law
- the Human Rights Act 1998 insofar as it affects criminal liability
- the definition of crimes
- the differences between civil and criminal law
- the hierarchy of criminal courts and the doctrine of precedent in criminal law
- the courts' interpretation of statutes imposing criminal liability
- the classifications of crimes and the powers of the courts to create offences
- the burden of proof in criminal law
- codification of criminal law

The fundamental principles of criminal liability

As stated in the preface, criminal law may be approached in several different ways. This book deals with how the various crimes and defences are defined and subjects them to criticism. Before, however, offences and defences are dealt with, various preliminary matters must be understood. Part of that understanding is, if there is to be any criminal law at all, how it would look in a more perfect world. From knowing fundamental principles, one can see how the law should be reformed.

There are some five million crimes notified to the police each year. *Crime in England and Wales* is published quarterly. The latest figures, for the year ending June 2010, are 4,339,000. The British Crime Survey, which includes unreported and unrecorded crimes, estimated that there were 9.6 million offences in 2009–10, a statistic which continues to decline and which was down by nine per cent on the previous year and is half the figure it was in 1995. The British Crime Survey, like police statistics, is an undercount because it does not include, for instance, victimless and corporate crimes and those surveyed might not know whether an event constitutes an offence or not. The 2001 Survey estimated that only half of crimes are reported to the police and the proportion may be less than that. Perhaps one in thirty crimes leads to a conviction, though many people are cautioned.

Most of these crimes are committed by men and boys. Offences against property comprise some 75 per cent, of which half involve theft.

Violent crimes make up five per cent. Violent crimes decreased by eight per cent in 2007–08 and six per cent in 2008–09, according to the British Crime Survey. There is a public fear in some cities such as London, Manchester and Nottingham of gun and knife crime by young males (but these crimes are still well below the level of 1995, the peak year), and non-violent offences are decreasing. Contrary therefore to the popular view the number of crimes committed is not rising year on year, but what is increasing is the number of offences created by Parliament. Fear of crime is a significant restriction on freedom of movement, despite the fact that the number of offences has declined drastically since the mid-1990s.

Criminal law can be seen as a series, perhaps not a system, of rules aimed at controlling misconduct, and contrary to expectation criminal law is often not certain or consistent. From the other end of the telescope criminal law also controls the behaviour of those involved in the criminal justice system such as the police and judges. It ensures that the stigma of a conviction is attached only to those to whom it should be attached. To see a course on criminal law as one designed only to see whether a rule applies to a given set of facts is a narrow-minded approach.

Criminal law was for many years regarded as undeveloped in terms of theory. The jury's verdict – guilty or not guilty – cannot be explored. Jury instructions are not precedents. It was not until 1907 that there was a Court of Criminal Appeal (now the Court of Appeal (Criminal Division)) and until 1960 appeals to the House of Lords (now the Supreme Court) were few. Until the mid-1960s textbooks for both students and practitioners were largely lists of rules with authorities. Since then there has been an exponential growth in academic interest and analysis, including theoretical works. Despite this development and perhaps because of it, a substantial amount of criminal law is unclear. Should the person who attempts to kill but fails be treated in the same manner as one who succeeds? Why is murder more serious than manslaughter? Is sexual intercourse part of life or part of a crime? Accordingly rules, principles and policies have to be investigated. Attention in this book is focused on those offences normally discussed in a criminal law course, but there are thousands of others and no one book can deal with all of them. This book deals with the criminal law of England and Wales: each state has its own penal law, for example each of the 50 United States has its own laws, as does the federal state. This law is contingent historically and currently (dependent for example on the government of the day and media interest) and therefore differs across the world. Nevertheless, in the Anglophone world certain principles apply but there are often exceptions.

Which principles are to be considered when looking at criminal law? As already stated, the criminal law is often unclear and sometimes inconsistent. Some argue that there are no principles, and certainly Parliament is subject to few international or other constraints when making law; others argue that such principles as exist are subject to large exceptions. Since Parliament theoretically can do anything, for example order the French to kill all their blue-eyed boys, it can make anything into a crime. Of course theory and practice are not the same, and indeed in theory there may be restrictions imposed by human rights conventions. See the discussion of the European Convention on Human Rights (ECHR), below.

In his book *Philosophy of Criminal Law* (Rowman & Littlefield, 1987), the American legal theorist Douglas Husak postulates eight principles of liberal philosophy underlying US criminal law. They are generally based on the autonomy of the individual. The accused is taken, unless the facts demonstrate otherwise, to be responsible for his crimes. They can be taken to represent aspirations of some of those involved in creating, applying and teaching criminal law in the UK and elsewhere. These principles are not constrained by country, time or politics. It should, however, be stressed that these principles are not always applied. Parliament is rarely concerned with these general principles of criminal law. It may, for example, try to prohibit an activity which many people indulge in on an almost daily basis such as speeding on motorways. It presumably saw criminal law as being the most efficient means of bearing down on speeding, despite the fact that many do not see conviction for this crime as containing stigma. Judges may be influenced by their desire to put those who have done bad things behind bars rather than apply the law consistently.

Why criminalisation takes place is an important area of study. Criminal law cannot be divorced from its political, sociological and economic context. Some control of the creation of new offences and the increase in width of old ones is provided by the ECHR; its influence as yet has been minimal but may increase in the next few years.

Legality

This principle is that persons must not be held to be criminally liable without there first being a law so holding (see also below). It prevents arbitrary state power. Husak derives four subsidiary conditions: (a) laws must not be vague; (b) the legislature must not create offences to cover wrongdoing retrospectively; (c) the judiciary must not create new offences; and perhaps (d) criminal statutes should be strictly construed. (Others derive different sub-rules: for example, laws must be published and laws must not be impossible to obey.) English law does not adopt the first subsidiary principle, and the others are doubtful. For example, it could be said that in *Preddy* [1996] AC 815 the House of Lords strictly construed the Theft Act 1968 (with the effect that mortgage fraudsters were not convicted of a deception offence), whereas the House has at times extended the criminal law by defining statutory offences broadly, as occurred in *Hinks* [2001] 2 AC 241 where 'appropriation' in the same Act was read broadly to cover a gift.

Many of the offences have uncertain boundaries. For example, murder is a very serious crime, but the state of mind needed for it has been the subject of change over the past 60 years. As a matter of parliamentary sovereignty, the government acting through Parliament can create laws which apply retroactively. Judges are not consistent in their interpretation of statutes, but have more or less given up the privilege of law-making (see further below).

Judges in what is now the Supreme Court have extended liability in several cases, yet in *Clegg* [1995] 1 AC 482 the House of Lords refused to change the law of self-defence in favour of the accused. The accused was a soldier in Northern Ireland who shot a person in a car which had been taken by a joyrider. He alleged that he thought she was part of a terrorist gang, though it must be said that she posed no danger to him or his colleagues. The Lords held that he was guilty of murder. Their Lordships rejected the contention that he should be guilty of manslaughter, not murder, when the force used in self-defence was excessive. They did so with regret but said that any reform was for Parliament. In *Ireland; Burstow* [1998] AC 147, two conjoined cases involving stalking, the Lords, disregarding the learning of centuries, extended assault to cover frightening by words including words spoken over the phone. In *R* [1992] 1 AC 599 the Lords in effect retrospectively abolished the long-standing immunity of the husband on a charge of rape of his wife, a breach of the principle of strict construction of penal statutes and of the principle against retroactivity, though its reasoning was that the exemption did not exist at the time of the accused's act. However, decisions of the House of Lords (now the Supreme Court) are not uniformly in favour of widening criminal liability and when in *C* v *DPP* the Divisional Court abrogated the principle that children aged over 10 but under 14 were not guilty unless they had mischievous discretion, the House restored the previous law ([1996] 1 AC 1). Similarly, in *GG* [2008] UKHL 17 it was held that the offence of conspiracy to defraud did not extend to a price-fixing arrangement because for several hundred years this common law crime had not been used against such agreements.

Both offences and defences are subject to change, with the result that a person would be guilty one day, but not guilty on the next because of a change in the law made by the judiciary. If the accused in *R* v *R* (above), the case involving the marital immunity in rape, often known as 'marital rape', had asked a lawyer for advice whether he would be guilty, the reply before the case would have been in the negative. Such rulings were not predictable. The contrary argument is that expressed by Lord Keith in *R* (above): 'The common law is capable of evolving in the light of changing social, economic and cultural developments.' Changing the common law keeps it up to date.

As can be seen from this discussion, criminal law does not always consist of hard and fast rules, and the extension of the law to previously exempt categories is inconsistent with Article 7(1) of the ECHR, to which the UK is a signatory. Article 7 of the ECHR is an embodiment of the principle of legality. It provides that no one can be convicted of an offence which was not an offence at the time when the act or omission allegedly constituting the crime was committed. Article 7 was applied in *GG*, above. The Human Rights Act 1998 obliges the courts to give effect to the ECHR. Currently it remains uncertain what will be the full effect of the statute. It is suggested that it may affect strict liability, the age of consent to sexual activities, insanity and self-defence, but as yet English criminal courts have been tentative in their approach to construing the definitional elements of offences in conformity with the Convention. The general judicial view seems to be that as a rule the *substantive* law is largely unaffected. See the discussion of the Human Rights Act 1998 later in this chapter.

The courts must construe statutes and interpret the common law consistently with the Convention and can issue declarations of incompatibility if a statute is inconsistent with the provisions of the Convention. The Convention must be read in accordance with modern conditions. Therefore, what was once Convention law need not be so now, and authorities are not to be used as precedents. An example is *Sutherland* v *UK* [1998] EHRLR 117. The European Court of Human Rights ruled that a ban on male homosexual behaviour until the age of 18 when male heterosexuals were legally permitted to have sexual intercourse from 16 was a breach of Article 8(1), the right to respect for private life, despite the fact that other Convention decisions supported the ban.

Article 7 can be used to prevent a court from making a statutory offence have retrospective effect. It would also seem on its face to ban, for example, the penalisation of marital rape as occurred in *R*. However, the European Court of Human Rights by a majority ruled in *SW* v *United Kingdom* [1996] 1 FLR 434, which is *R* before that Court, that 'however clearly drafted a legal provision may be, in any system of law, including criminal law, there is an inevitable element of judicial interpretation'. Article 7 did not prohibit the clarification of the law over time and the final abolition of the marital immunity in rape constituted a gradual clarification. What the Lords had done in *R* was to declare that the marital exemption had disappeared over time; Article 7 permitted them to do so because there was no retroactivity. As the Court put it:

> The essentially debasing character of rape is so manifest that the result of the decisions of the Court of Appeal and the House of Lords cannot be said to be at variance with the object

and purpose of Article 7 of the Convention, namely to ensure that no one should be subjected to arbitrary prosecution, conviction or punishment. What is more, the abandonment of the unacceptable idea of a husband being immune against prosecution . . . was in conformity not only with a civilised concept of marriage but also, and above all, with the fundamental objectives of the Convention, the very essence of which is respect for human dignity . . .

However, while the gradual clarification doctrine may be acceptable, it cannot be said that the law was as clear in 1970 as in 1990, yet a husband was found guilty in 2004 of raping his wife in 1970: *C* [2004] 1 WLR 2098 (CA). The decision does appear to be a retrospective one. The Supreme Court in *Norris* [2010] 2 AC 487 distinguished *SW v UK* on the grounds that the extension of conspiracy to defraud to price-fixing agreements was not reasonably foreseeable in light of several hundred years of development of this common law offence.

In *Misra* [2005] 1 WLR 1 the Court of Appeal said:

Vague laws which purport to create criminal liability are undesirable, and in extreme cases . . . their very vagueness may make it impossible to identify the conduct which is prohibited by a criminal sanction. . . . That said, however, the requirement is for sufficient rather than absolute certainty.

It was held that the crime of gross negligence manslaughter, which is discussed in Chapter 12, did not contravene Article 7.

Another aspect of Article 7 is that it appears to prohibit the restriction of defences. If so, cases such as *Gotts* [1992] 2 AC 412 (HL), the authority on whether duress is a defence to attempted murder, are incorrect. It should be noted that there is an exception to non-retrospectivity. This occurs where the act 'was criminal according to the general principles of law recognised by civilised nations'. This exception was held in *C*, above, to cover the judicial abolition of the marital immunity from conviction for rape. Judge LJ said:

Article 7(2) provides ample justification for a husband's trial and punishment for the rape of his wife, according to the general principles recognised by civilised nations. Indeed, . . . it would be surprising to discover that the law in any civilised country protected a woman from rape, with the solitary and glaring exception of rape by a man who had promised to love and comfort her.

UK jurisprudence on Article 7 so far is disappointing to those who expected the Human Rights Act 1998 to restrain judicial legislation. *C* so demonstrates. In *Rimmington* [2006] 1 AC 459 the House of Lords did, however, amend the common law crime of public nuisance to bring it into line with Article 7. The Lords found that they had no common law powers to abolish offences, but they could overrule cases to bring the common law into line with Article 7. *C* is inconsistent with *Rimmington* where Lord Bingham stressed that: 'There are two guiding principles: no one should be punished under a law unless it is sufficiently clear and certain to enable him to know what conduct is forbidden before he does it; and no one should be punished for any act which was not clearly and ascertainably punishable when the act was done.' The second principle is contrary to the ratio of *C*. *C*, however, may be upheld on the basis provided by the European Court in *SW* v *UK*, namely, that what the accused did was 'criminal according to the general principles of law recognised by civilised nations', as Article 7(2) ECHR states. *Rimmington* is also authority for the proposition that the crime of causing a public nuisance was not too vague to satisfy Article 6. As that Court said in *Kokkinakis* v *Greece* (1993) 17 EHRR 397, 'where the individual can know from the wording of the relevant provision and, if need be, with the assistance of the courts' interpretation of it, what acts and omissions will make him liable', then Article 7 is satisfied but Article 7 is breached if 'the criminal law [is] extensively construed to the accused's detriment, for instance by analogy'.

Actus reus

The accused is guilty only if he has acted or has brought about a state of affairs (*actus reus*). He is not liable for just being as he is (e.g. poor, black). People are not punished for mere thoughts. The nearest English law has come to penalising people for thinking is one form of treason, encompassing the Queen's death, and conspiracy. Partly on account of this principle there have arisen problems about the scope of criminal liability for omissions (see Chapter 2), attempts (see Chapter 10), and involuntary acts (see automatism in Chapter 9).

Mens rea

A mental state, *mens rea*, is required in almost all serious crimes. This state of mind is sometimes known as the fault or mental element. People should not be punished unless they are at fault. Only people who act intentionally or who knowingly run a risk are at fault. Justice is not done if persons are punished when they have not acted culpably. Criminal responsibility is largely founded on moral culpability. There are, however, many exceptions: strict liability offences minor or serious do not require *mens rea* as to one or more parts of the *actus reus* (see Chapter 4). It has been questioned whether negligence is properly to be classified as a state of mind. It is sometimes argued that an accused should not be guilty when he is not blameworthy and offences which do so convict him should be abrogated.

Take care when translating *mens rea*. The common translation is 'guilty mind', but there need be nothing criminal or otherwise wrongful about what the accused's state of mind is, yet that may still be a *mens rea*. For example, in theft part of the *mens rea* is intention permanently to deprive, but there is nothing inherently wrongful about this state of mind. The honest shopper who takes a tin from the supermarket shelf has this state of mind just as much as the dishonest thief.

Concurrence

In English law the basic rule is that the *actus reus* and *mens rea* must be simultaneous. There are several exceptions discussed in Chapter 3.

Harm

In many offences a person or thing is harmed. In murder someone is killed; in criminal damage property is destroyed or damaged. One purpose of the law is to allow people to act free from harm. Aggressors are to be deterred. As the European Court of Human Rights stated in *Laskey* **v** *United Kingdom* (1997) 24 EHRR 39, a case involving sado-masochism by male homosexuals: 'one of the roles which the state is unquestionably entitled to undertake is to seek to regulate, through the operation of the criminal law, activities which involve the infliction of physical harm'. There are, however, different opinions at times whether something constitutes a harm. In *Laskey*, above, the sado-masochist homosexuals would no doubt have said that they were not harming anyone, whereas the Lords held them to be guilty of causing harm.

There are several offences which are not predicated on harm to others. The Terrorism Act 2006 creates the offence of glorifying terrorism, a vague term, but one which does not require any victim to be injured or killed. No one need be harmed in the inchoate offences (Chapter 10), and there is argument about so-called 'victimless offences' such as possessing marijuana. If one does not wear a seatbelt and, as a result, one is more seriously injured than otherwise, one becomes a burden to others. An alternative view is to contend that the state has an interest in the well-being of its citizens (see N. Lacey, *State Punishment* (Routledge, 1988), in which Lacey argues in favour of a concept of 'welfare': the state is entitled to intervene to provide for the physical welfare of its citizens by such means as ordering the wearing of seatbelts and penalising violations). Moreover, health costs and absences from work are prevented by such means. Some harms may be trivial; others may be serious, for example pollution. One aim of the criminal law is to prevent certain harms such as interferences with the person or property by penalising infractions.

Some academics also derive a principle of proportionality. In other words, some crimes are more serious than others. For example, murder is more serious than assault occasioning actual bodily harm. Therefore, murder should be punished more severely than actual bodily harm. Perhaps linked closely with this principle is that of fair labelling; namely, that the name given to the crime should correspond to the wrong encapsulated by the offence.

Insofar as criminal law has paradigmatic crimes, an offence comprising harm and intent constitutes the paradigm. Murder consists of harm, death, coupled with the intent to kill or the intent to cause grievous bodily harm; rape in part is comprised of penetration of certain orifices (the harm) and intent to penetrate; theft in part is the harm of appropriating property belonging to another and the intent to deprive the other of that property permanently. Many offences such as criminal damage may, however, be committed either intentionally or recklessly; and many offences do not require any harm to be caused, for instance careless driving. Indeed that crime is an illustration of both the lack of harm and the lack of intent: negligence suffices.

Jurisprudential discussion of the 'harm' principle over the past 60 years is extensive. Some jurists have sought to justify offences based on morality or offensiveness. Readers are referred to the Further reading at the end of this chapter for discussion.

Causation

In result crimes it must be proved that the accused committed the *actus reus* (see Chapter 2). It is not always clear who caused an event. **Causation** in pollution and driving cases seems to be wider than the doctrine found elsewhere in criminal law. Transferred malice can be seen as exceptional: the accused intends to harm one person but harms another. There are also difficulties with omissions (Chapter 2).

Defences

These are examined in Chapters 7–9.

Proof (beyond reasonable doubt)

This is dealt with in this chapter. All the elements of the offence charged must be proved **beyond reasonable doubt**. What has to be proved varies from crime to crime, and that may change from time to time. For example, since 1994 men can be the victims of rape; before then only women could be.

The principles of criminal law and criminalisation

Alan Norrie summarised these norms in *Crime, Reason and History* (2nd edn, Butterworths, 2001) 10: 'Criminal law is, at heart, a practical application of liberal political philosophy.' These principles restrain the power of the state expressed through its agencies, such as the police and the judiciary. Without them criminal law would have no bounds and the powers of the agents of the state would be limitless. The democratic enactment of offences justifies the use of state power to punish lawbreakers. Punishment after conviction is a substantial power in the hands of the state and may take the form of imprisonment, which deprives the offender of his freedom. There is attached to all serious and some less serious crimes the stigma of being convicted. Most people shun murderers and rapists. The principles also allow citizens, to some degree, to be able to foresee whether their conduct will be criminal or not. In *Jackson* (1994) *The Independent*, 25 May, the Court of Appeal said that legal certainty was a fundamental principle of criminal law. One may criticise criminal law textbooks for being positivistic, that is, describing the law as it exists (in all its detail), but one would surely not wish to be convicted because some people say that what one has done is not in line with their moral stance. Liability should not depend on 'speculation or inquiry' or the politics of the moment. Even the 'bad man' ought to know whether he is breaking the criminal law. (See below for judicial interpretation of statutes.)

The principles are not, however, uniformly applied. The American jurist, Oliver Wendell Holmes, formulated the aphorism that the life of the law has been experience, not logic. Criminal law is an exemplar of this proposition. It is not consistent or logical, as this book demonstrates. Much of the law is complex, sometimes needlessly, as the chapter on non-fatal offences demonstrates. In reading this book you may consider that there is little which can be said of the general principles said by Husak to underlie criminal law. Students who start on criminal law courses are often of the belief that they know a good deal about the subject, but find difficulty with the course because they are not prepared for a mass of difficult law, such as that on intent. There is a trend towards consistency, encouraged by the Law Commission, but the government has not felt the need to reform the law, even when such reform would save money.

While these principles inform the substance of the law, they do not delimitate its width. That width is sometimes a matter of history. For example, the law on dangerous dogs is a response to a small number of horrific attacks by certain breeds on children. Whether behaviour is criminal should be a matter of policy, and the state's making behaviour criminal needs justification. Most would agree that murder and rape are not good things. Some attempt to consider when criminal liability should be imposed must be made because otherwise criminal law's condemnatory function is undermined. Moreover, in a democracy there must be some control over the agents of the state who could otherwise use the strongest of state sanctions against trivial offenders.

The most authoritative exposition of the aims of criminal law from a liberal viewpoint is the *Report of the (Wolfenden) Committee on Homosexual Offences and Prostitution*, Cmnd 247, 1957, which led to the decriminalisation of adult male homosexual practices in private. Criminal law existed:

> . . . to preserve public order and decency, to protect the citizen from what is injurious and to provide sufficient safeguards against exploitation or corruption of others . . . It is not . . . the function of the law to intervene in the private lives of citizens . . . further than is necessary to carry out [these] purposes . . . (paras 13–14).

 It can be argued that the majority of the House of Lords in *Brown* [1994] AC 212, discussed in Chapter 13, broke these principles when they penalised homosexual sado-masochism.

The reduction of the age of consent for male homosexuals from 21 to 18 came into force when the Criminal Justice and Public Order Act 1994 received Royal Assent (3 November 1994). The then difference in the age of consent for heterosexual (16) and homosexual intercourse (18) was condemned by the European Court of Human Rights as being contrary to Article 8 of the Convention, respect for private life, and contrary to the parasitic Article 14, non-discrimination: *Sutherland* v *United Kingdom* [1998] EHRLR 117. The Sexual Offences (Amendment) Act 2000 reduced the age to 16. The Wolfenden Committee's main contention was that the criminal law should not be used to enforce the morality even of a majority of the members of society. Lord Hobhouse (dissenting) in *Hinks* [2001] 2 AC 241 (HL), where the majority held that one can appropriate an item by receiving it as a gift and potentially be guilty of theft, stated: 'To treat otherwise lawful conduct as criminal merely because it is open to . . . disapprobation [by ordinary right-thinking citizens] would be contrary to principle and open to the objection that it fails to achieve the objective and transparent certainty required of the criminal law by the principles basic to human rights.' On the facts, the majority held, the donee was guilty of theft from the donor when she dishonestly received gifts of money.

The US Model Penal Code, which seeks to encapsulate best practice in state jurisdictions, famously states that the criminal law has five aims (spelling anglicised):

(a) to forbid and prevent conduct which unjustifiably and inexcusably inflicts or threatens to inflict harm to public interests;

(b) to subject to public control persons whose conduct indicates that they are disposed to commit crimes;

(c) to safeguard conduct that is without fault from condemnation as criminal;

(d) to give fair warning of the nature of the conduct declared to be an offence;

(e) to differentiate on reasonable grounds between serious and minor offences.

The phrase 'unjustifiably and inexcusably' in (a) refer to defences, which are discussed in Chapters 7–9 and, in respect of a defence which applies to murder, loss of control, Chapter 11. It is worth comparing these aims with current English law. For example, do strict offences (see Chapter 4) offend principle (c)?

As the Commentaries explain, this part of the Code 'undertakes to state the most pervasive general objectives of the Code'. It is also meant to control official discretion and to aid interpretation of the Code. Some of these principles are broken by current English law, which does not have any written aims. For example, maliciously inflicting grievous bodily harm is a more serious offence than occasioning actual bodily harm, yet both have the same maximum punishment. Sometimes the principles conflict, and there may be disagreement about the scope of each principle. The Court of Appeal in *Kingston* [1994] QB 81, in a passage which was not criticised by the House of Lords (discussed in Chapter 8 below under the heading of Involuntary intoxication), said that 'the purpose of the criminal law is to inhibit, by proscription and by penal sanction, antisocial acts which individuals may otherwise commit'. Unfortunately the common law has not developed principles such as those found in the Model Penal Code. The same is true of Parliament. Therefore, one cannot draw in advance the line between criminalising conduct and not doing so. Criminal law sets norms, standards of behaviour, to which natural and juristic persons must conform. Largely it tells people what not to do, not what they should do.

It is highly important that criminal law is kept within bounds. Police resources would be even more stretched than at present if the law were widened unnecessarily, and the powers of arrest and prosecution could become more arbitrary than they are at present. Criminal law is a strong form of state control. After all, people can be deprived of their liberty for life. There is stigma attached to a conviction. One's name may be in the local paper even for trivial offences. Society condemns a person for offending. For these reasons citizens must know which conduct is criminally unlawful. Areas of law such as dishonesty, conspiracy to corrupt public morals, and intent where the definition is not clear are scrutinised in this book, as are occasions when judges are seen to 'stretch' the law to cover 'manifestly guilty' persons who are charged with the wrong offence. A case on insider trading provides useful material for discussion. Until Parliament penalised the use of confidential information to buy shares at a low price there was no offence directed specifically at this form of behaviour. This way of making money was acceptable to those who did it. Does the insider trader's conduct fall within the scope of criminal law adumbrated by the Wolfenden Committee? Within Husak's fifth principle, harm, who is harmed? The reader is invited to consider what would happen if there was no criminal law. Indeed, as a general rule misappropriating confidential information is not a crime. Not all offences are serious socially or economically, and sometimes it might be better to use training and administrative measures rather than criminal sanctions. Governments of all persuasions seem to have a tendency to criminalise behaviour which they cannot control otherwise, even when there is no consensus in society that certain forms of conduct should be visited by penal sanctions. Criminal law has developed in a piecemeal fashion without regard to theory. Some laws epitomise kneejerk reaction to perceived crises such as dangerous dogs, stalking, raves, anti-roads protesters and 'hippie' convoys. In the jargon such offences are 'historically contingent': their arrival on the scene marks some kind of campaign, not rational and principled inquiry. As can be seen, modern criminal law is vast in scope. It covers both serious and non-serious offences by individuals, and is also used as a means of regulating business.

Furthermore, Parliament, while rarely abolishing offences, also creates new offences, with the consequence that the boundaries of criminal law are ever widening. There were some 7,000 offences in 1980. The current figure seems to be about 11,000: see *Independent*, p. 1, 16 August 2006. It was estimated that the government created 3,023 crimes from 1997 to 2006. Senior members of the police have called for the decriminalisation of the possession and inhalation of so-called soft drugs such as cannabis. In a rational system of law, if one wanted to penalise the possession of drugs, one might start with criminalising alcohol (look at any volume of the Criminal Appeal Reports for what people do when drunk), or if one wanted to stop violence, one might easily conclude that boxing should be illegal. After all, politicians, and to some extent judges, make law (we no longer believe the fairy tale that judges do not make law) and they have their own predilections and are subject to moral panics. In a Written Answer the then Minister of State at the Home Office, Lord Williams of Mostyn, stated that new offences 'should be created only when absolutely necessary' (*Hansard*, HL Deb, 18 June 1999, WA 57). That pledge is not honoured. In summary, the creation of new law by Parliament may depend on politics, not principle. It is interesting to see how much parliamentary time can be given to a subject in the news such as, say, dangerous dogs, whereas no time can be found to enact well-considered proposals for law reform, such as those put forward by the Law Commission, discussed below.

Human Rights Act 1998

This statute does not entrench the European Convention on Human Rights into UK law: it is not a constitution or a higher law. What the Act does is to oblige courts to interpret legislation in accordance with the Convention 'so far as . . . possible' (s 3(1)). Moreover, decisions of the European Court of Human Rights are not binding on English courts. If the impugned statute cannot be so construed, the High Court (and the Court of Appeal and the Supreme Court) is to make a declaration of incompatibility. That declaration does not, however, affect the validity of the statute (s 4(1)). Parliament then has the option of deciding whether to amend the law or not. This power has not so far been used in a substantive criminal case. Public bodies, a term which includes courts, must act consistently with the Convention (s 6). The Act does not only permit the accused to argue that certain offences are contrary to the statute but it also allows a victim to argue that the state has not protected his rights. An example of the latter method is the law relating to a parent's chastisement of his child. The state's protection of the child leads to a narrowing of the circumstances in which a child could be punished by his parent (or other person *in loco parentis*). Similarly, if a signatory state were to punish rape only when the victim resisted, the law would be in breach of Article 8 of the Convention, the right to respect for private life. It should be noted that the Convention also obliges states to create new laws. Article 3, for example, obliges states to create laws to prevent inhuman and degrading treatment.

It should be noted that the 1998 Act does not directly apply to the common law. A way to avoid this non-application is as follows. Take insanity as an example. Current law may be incompatible with the Convention. Article 5 stipulates that everyone has a right to liberty and to security of the person. If a verdict of insanity would be inconsistent with the Convention, then since the courts are public bodies, they must act in conformity with it. In *H* [2002] 2 Cr App R (S) 59 the Court of Appeal accepted that using s 6 of the Human Rights Act 1998 was a legitimate way of proceeding.

It is suggested that in the next few years the following areas of criminal law which form part of this book may be affected by the ECHR: the defence of self-defence/prevention of crime (by Article 2, right to life), strict liability (by Article 3, right not to be subjected to inhuman and degrading punishment: Arden J writing extrajudicially in [1999] Crim LR 439 thought that the courts could create a defence of due diligence but UK courts have not gone so far as yet in criminal law), insanity (by Article 5, above), strict liability and burden of proof (by Article 7, right to a fair hearing and presumption of innocence), conspiracy to defraud, corrupt public morals and outrage public decency and offences of dishonesty (by Article 7, non-retroactivity), and consent to non-fatal and sexual offences and offences of dishonesty (by Article 8, respect for private life). As an illustration the defence of prevention of crime seems to fall foul of Article 2 (and in the view of the writer does fall foul of it) because (a) killing in defence of property is not justifiable under the Convention and (b) case law, including *McCann v United Kingdom* (1995) 21 EHRR 97, which involved soldiers of the UK security services (the SAS) shooting dead members of the Provisional IRA in Gibraltar, demands a belief based on reasonable grounds whereas in present English law an honest belief suffices.

Much of the case law at present deals with Article 6, the right to a fair trial, which to a large extent is outside the scope of this book, but it is mentioned where relevant such as in the discussion of the burden of proof. Article 6 does not affect the fairness of the substantive offence: see for example *MM* [2011] EWCA Crim 1291. Most claims that English law breached the Convention have failed so far. For example, prohibiting the possession of marijuana is not a breach of the right to manifest one's religion and the criminalisation of the taking of indecent photographs does not interfere with the rights to private life or freedom of expression. It should be noted that the Convention is interpreted in the light of current social conditions. Therefore old precedents may no longer be of value. Some of the Articles of the Convention have been mentioned above when discussing the principle of legality, and the ECHR is mentioned in this book at the appropriate places.

The 1998 Act does not affect the right to petition the European Court of Human Rights but Article 34 of the Convention provides that domestic remedies must be exhausted first. Therefore, an applicant must use the English courts first.

If a court considers that an English precedent is inconsistent with the Convention, it should follow the case and give leave to appeal: *Lambeth London Borough Council* v *Kay* [2006] 4 All ER 128 (HL).

Attempted definitions of a crime

Definitions are said to be unfashionable, but without them the reader may be misled into thinking that a violation of one of the Ten Commandments is *per se* a crime or that a breach of contract is a crime. There have been several attempts at defining crimes, most of which are to the effect that a crime may give rise to criminal proceedings which may lead to punishment. Blackstone wrote that a crime was 'a violation of the public rights and duties due to the whole community considered as a community'. This definition came from the mid-eighteenth century from one of the leading commentators on English law.

The House of Lords, the highest English tribunal for most criminal law purposes (now the Supreme Court), essayed a definition in *Board of Trade* v *Owen* [1957] AC 602: 'an unlawful act or default which is an offence against the public and renders the person guilty of the act liable to legal punishment'. Such a definition tells us nothing about why conduct is made criminal. A crime may cause less harm than a tort or breach of contract. If an employer dismisses employees in breach of their contracts, loss is caused to them, their families, local shops and so on, but punches in a pub car park at closing time may not even cause bruises except to self-esteem.

One of the leading writers on criminal law, Glanville Williams, in 'The definition of a crime' [1955] CLP 107 stated that a crime was 'a legal wrong that can be followed by criminal proceedings which may result in punishment', while a leading American, H.M. Hart, in 'The aims of the criminal law' (1958) 23 L & CP 401 at 405 considered that a crime is 'conduct which . . . will incur a formal and solemn pronouncement of the moral condemnation of the community'. Therefore, criminal law is imbued with symbolism: a convicted accused is condemned by the state and that condemnation has a public aspect. Such a definition may be rejected on the basis that some offences may not be morally wrong, yet they are crimes.

It should be noted that these definitions do not say that a penalty must follow after conviction and that there is no necessity that crimes are always prosecuted and even if the accused is prosecuted, he may escape conviction. For example, breaches of safety legislation are often dealt with administratively without recourse to enforcing criminal law. Compliance with the law and not punishment for breach is the driving force.

By enacting a law, Parliament is seen to be doing something about a social problem. Parliament may convert a tort into a crime or what was previously lawful into one, or it may make lawful that which was previously illegal. Moreover, it is not always clear why an offence has been created. Sometimes it seems simpler to institute an offence than to do anything else.

The more modern definitions are admittedly circular and do not lay down rules on what types of behaviour should be criminalised. Criminal procedure defines what is criminal law. Unfortunately, we do not know whether criminal proceedings are needed until we know that the criminal law has been broken. The definitions do not resolve doubt whether a matter is civil or criminal. Further, knowing that there are procedural differences between criminal and civil law does not justify distinguishing the two types of law in terms of substance. Williams noted that he could give only a list of factors indicating on which side of the line an issue fell, but sometimes features indicating criminal law had to be balanced against factors indicating civil law. Nevertheless, in most instances the criminal law is like an elephant: we know it when we see it. Card, Cross and Jones: *Criminal Law* (OUP, 2012), pp. 1–2, state: '. . . a crime is a legal wrong . . . the principal legal consequence of a crime is that the offender . . . is prosecuted by or in the name of the State.' Accordingly there must be (a) some wrongdoing, or indeed a wrongful situation; (b) 'a legal wrong'; (c) a wrong where the state in whichever guise intervenes to punish the wrongdoer; and (d) a remedy for the wrong in terms of punishment. Punishment marks out or stigmatises the defendant as a criminal.

Take, for example, the offence of theft. The accused has stolen something. The state has decreed that this wrongdoing is punishable, the prosecution proves that the accused committed the offence beyond reasonable doubt, and the accused receives a sentence such as a fine or imprisonment. The victim of the offence normally gets nothing out of the criminal justice system either from the state or from the accused, though there are exceptions, such as a restitution order of the thing stolen under s 28 of the Theft Act 1968 or in some cases money from the Criminal Injuries Compensation Authority. The accused may be prosecuted either at the instance of the state (normally the Crown Prosecution Service or the Director of Public Prosecutions, the DPP) or by private individuals or com-

See page 550 (Chapter 15) for the definition of theft.

panies, such as when a high-street shop prosecutes for shoplifting. On the definition given earlier, theft is a crime because it may be followed by criminal proceedings.

The wrong must be a legal wrong. This phrase points to one of the differences between criminal law and morals (or what the majority of society thinks). A crime is a breach of the criminal law, whether that law was laid down by Parliament or the courts. It need not be a moral wrong, a breach of a duty imposed by an ethical system. Criminal law covers a vast range of situations not all of which are condemned as breaches of morals. For example, euthanasia as when a daughter kills her terminally ill mother who is suffering great pain is not seen by everyone as morally wrong, but it is a breach of one of the criminal laws: it is murder. Taking food to feed a starving baby is theft. Morality can, however, be taken into account at the sentencing stage. No doubt a person who stole to feed a starving child would receive less punishment than one who stole to satisfy greed. Indeed, many crimes have no moral content whatsoever. Drivers in the UK drive on a side of the road different from that in the USA and continental Europe but there is no morality behind the difference. While not all crimes are breaches of all forms of morality, similarly not all moral wrongs are crimes. Selfishness, lying, breaking promises and adultery may be morally wrong, but they are not crimes. Yet, the same event may be both a crime and a moral wrong. Rape is a crime, and presumably most people would also say that rape is morally wrong. Therefore, although crime and morality are not the same, there are some areas of overlap.

It is sometimes said that a crime affects the public and civil law affects one person, but this proposition is easily disproved. For example, a fight between two people in a pub car park may lead to injuries such as cuts, bruises and perhaps concussion. These injuries constitute one or more non-fatal offences. It cannot be said that the public is affected. However, an oil spillage will affect many more people than a punch-up in a car park despite its being a tort.

Just as some aspects of morality change, so does the criminal law. The usual example is homosexuality. Until quite recently it was an offence among consenting males, of whatever age, to perform homosexual acts. In 1967 Parliament changed the law to make homosexual activities in private between two men over 21 lawful. The age was reduced to

18 in 1994 and later to 16. It should be noted that these changes in the law can be consistent with the ECHR. The Convention is a living document which has to be interpreted as society now exists and not as how matters were at the time of its drafting. Generally speaking, homosexuality was illegal in the states which signed the Convention in the 1950s and the European Commission on Human Rights permitted such laws. However, just as national laws have changed, so has the interpretation of the Convention with the result that states can, for instance, no longer lay down separate ages of consent for heterosexual and homosexual intercourse. Similarly, heterosexual buggery was illegal until 3 November 1994, since when it has been lawful, subject to conditions: both partners had to be over 18 and the activity had to take place in private and be consensual. (Lesbianism has never been a crime though sometimes indecent assault charges were brought. It is unlikely that charges will be brought nowadays.) In a different area of criminal law, dishonesty under the Theft Acts, the courts have said that juries can take into account current standards of behaviour. It could be that a jury in 1973 would not convict on the same facts on which a jury would convict now. An example might be the practice of asking for more shares than one had money to pay for at the time when the shares would be allotted in the expectation that the full amount of shares requested would not be allocated to the accused so that he would have sufficient money to pay for the shares which he did obtain. In this way he would get the shares he really wanted. If he had just put in for that number, he would not have got all of them in the event of oversubscription. Which forms of behaviour are criminal is a matter for Parliament and the courts. Sometimes coverage is non-existent. If I misappropriate trade secrets, I am not guilty of theft. Sometimes coverage is only partial. If I tell lies to have sexual intercourse, I am not guilty of rape, unless I lie about the nature or purpose of the act or my identity. If I tell lies to gain an item of property, I may be guilty of fraud.

One aspect of the problem is that Parliament and the courts create offences of enormous width with the result that acts of vastly different depravity are included within the same offence. Two illustrations suffice. In manslaughter the crime covers misconduct on the border of murder (and even acts which not much more than 35 years ago would have been murder) as well as the scenario where there is a brief fist-fight, the victim is punched, falls on the ground, hits his head on a brick by mischance, and dies. The best-known example is, however, murder, which covers the worst terrorist outrage and the most compassionate mercy-killing.

There is also the fact that the criminal law is changed only slowly and partially by Parliament to reflect social developments. There was no Computer Misuse Act until 1990. The language both in judge-made and Parliament-made criminal law may be out of date. 'Malice aforethought', the state of mind required for murder, is not based on spite or premeditated killing. Similarly the term 'maliciously' in the Offences Against the Person Act 1861 was badly chosen, for there is no need for malice. Some areas of the law have been updated and the language modernised in recent years, for example theft, criminal damage, but some parts use old-fashioned vocabulary. Since the development of the law has been piecemeal over centuries it is not surprising that there is no single definition which encapsulates why this conduct is a crime and that conduct is not.

Parliament has not defined a crime. There is, however, a provision now found in s 18(1)(a) of the Senior Courts Act 1981 (previously called the Supreme Court Act 1981) by which subject to exceptions there is no appeal from the High Court to the Court of Appeal (Civil Division) in any 'criminal cause or matter'. Cases, the principal one being ***Amand v Home Secretary and Minister of Defence of the Royal Netherlands Government*** [1943] AC 147 (HL), decide that if the proceedings may lead to punishment, they constitute a criminal cause or matter. Even if Parliament did define a crime, that definition would now be subject to the ECHR.

Article 6(2) of the ECHR applies only to persons 'charged with a criminal offence'. It gives greater protection to those accused of crimes than to defendants in civil cases. For example, the accused is subject to the presumption of innocence and must be provided with a lawyer free of charge if he cannot afford one. If Article 6(2) applies, the protection it provides applies in whichever court the case is heard, even a civil one. The definition of 'criminal offence' is an autonomous one, not tied to that found in national law. The nature of the proceedings, the severity of the penalty (such as imprisonment) and the classification by national law are all taken into account, but the first consideration is the most vital. An example is *Benham* v *UK* (1996) 22 EHRR 293 (ECHR). The accused was put into prison when bailiffs could not find goods of sufficient value to pay his community charge ('poll tax'). English law says that such proceedings, although they take place in the magistrates' court, are civil in nature: as the ECHR put it, 'The purpose of the detention was to coerce the appellant into paying the tax owed, rather than to punish him for not having paid it.' Nevertheless, the Court held that the proceedings were criminal ones and, therefore, Article 6 of the Convention applied. The nature of the proceedings was very important. The proceedings were brought by a public authority and had a punitive element in that the magistrates could commit to prison and the defendant could be imprisoned for a maximum of three months. (The European Court called this maximum 'relatively severe'.) The classification according to English domestic law was not decisive. *Benham* was distinguished by the House of Lords in *Clingham* v *Royal Borough of Kensington and Chelsea* [2003] 1 AC 787. The making of an anti-social behaviour order was a civil law matter, though a breach of it led to proceedings of a criminal nature: there was no penalty until that stage. Then there is a penalty of up to five years' imprisonment. As yet, the European Court of Human Rights and the English courts have not been divided as to whether there is or is not a 'criminal offence'. There will be more jurisprudence on this issue over time.

Differences between criminal and civil law

Modern legal systems throughout the world distinguish between civil and criminal law, and England and Wales is no different. One might assume that a breach of criminal law would necessarily be more serious than a breach of civil law but that does not necessarily follow. Criminal and civil law do not necessarily differ in the sorts of behaviour they are intended to control. The same act can be both a crime and a tort. If I assault you, I am guilty of a crime and a tort. If the bus driver who drove you home this evening carelessly crashed and you were injured, there may be several crimes relating to the driving and the harm as well as tort and a breach of contract by the bus company to transport you safely.

However, there are important differences in some respects which may be listed thus:

(a) *The courts are not the same.* In civil law the two courts which are the first to hear cases are the High Court and the county court. The basic division remains that the High Court hears cases involving high monetary amounts, the county court hears the rest. Under the wing of the county court exists the small claims court, the jurisdiction of which is limited. Appeals are to the Court of Appeal (Civil Division) and thence to the Supreme Court. There is also a possibility of a reference from any of these courts to the Court of Justice of the European Union (CJEU) on a matter of EU law.

Courts which hear matters first (courts of first instance) are the Crown Court and the magistrates' courts. In both courts most defendants plead guilty. There is appeal to the Divisional Court or Court of Appeal (Criminal Division), with most appeals from magistrates going to the Crown Court. The final appeal court is the Supreme Court. It was not until 1960 that the House of Lords, now the Supreme Court, gained its present full appellate jurisdiction in criminal matters. Criminal law has hardly been touched by European Union law, but that law does now, for example, affect the law on fisheries.

(b) *The terminology is different.* In criminal law the prosecution prosecutes the accused (or defendant). In civil law the claimant sues the defendant.

(c) *The outcome is different.* In civil law if the claimant wins, he usually receives damages or an injunction. Damages at civil law may well exceed criminal law fines. In criminal law the accused, if guilty, is (usually though not always) sentenced. The aim of civil law is normally to compensate the victim, whereas in criminal law punishment is the objective. There are several exceptions. The accused may be ordered to restore the stolen item (Theft Act 1968, s 28) or any item taken (Police (Property) Act 1897, s 1), or to compensate the victim (Powers of Criminal Courts (Sentencing) Act 2000, s 130), but although compensation orders are often made in magistrates' courts, in most criminal cases the victim receives nothing from the offender. Moreover, convictions usually bear a greater stigma than do unsuccessful civil law claims or defences. Because punishment is not a necessary consequence of conviction, it is suggested that criminal law and punishment are not as inextricably linked as some believe.

(d) *Procedural matters differ.* It is normally the state which prosecutes, whereas it is private individuals or companies which sue, and the Crown can commute a sentence in criminal law but not in civil law. Another distinction is that once started, criminal proceedings cannot be stopped except by the Attorney-General issuing what is called a *nolle prosequi* ('do not prosecute'), whereas civil proceedings can be settled at any time by the parties. The defendant can be compelled to give evidence in a civil but not a criminal matter. It may be said that the state has an interest in criminal proceedings which the wishes of the non-state parties cannot override.

(e) *Breach of the criminal law is a symbol of state power.* Conviction communicates the state's displeasure at certain forms of conduct. Being found civilly liable does not serve this purpose.

(f) *The victim does not play a large role in substantive criminal law,* whereas the claimant has the leading role in civil law.

In general a prosecution is no bar to civil proceedings, and vice versa. There are exceptionally provisions found in ss 44–45 of the Offences Against the Person Act 1861 which stipulate that a civil action for assault or battery may not be brought when the accused has been tried in a magistrates' court and has either obtained a certificate of dismissal of the complaint or been punished.

Hierarchy of the criminal courts: the appeal system

After the decision is taken in which court the case is to be heard, the accused is in time tried, unless diverted to another criminal procedure. The process of appeal depends on whether the case was tried in the magistrates' court or at the Crown Court. The final Anglo-Welsh court on criminal matters is the Supreme Court.

Magistrates' courts

There are two possible routes of appeal. The usual one is to the Crown Court, which for this purpose is composed of a judge and (usually) two magistrates. Only the accused can appeal, and the grounds are (a) on the points of fact or law against conviction, or (b) against sentence. The first ground may be used only if the accused pleaded not guilty. The format is a rehearing, that is, a new trial (a trial *de novo*). The alternative appeal is to the Divisional Court of the Queen's Bench Division of the High Court. The appeal is called 'by way of case stated'. Either side may appeal, but the grounds are solely (a) on a point of law, or (b) that the magistrates exceeded their jurisdiction. If the prosecution succeeds, the magistrates are directed to convict and give the appropriate sentence. There is also an appeal by way of case stated from the Crown Court to the Divisional Court. Appeal from the Divisional Court is to the Supreme Court. Either side may appeal, but only on points of law. There are two other prerequisites: the Divisional Court must certify that the point is of general public importance and either that Court or the Supreme Court must grant leave to appeal.

Crown Court

Appeals from this Court lie to the Court of Appeal (Criminal Division). Appeal against conviction lies on the ground that the conviction was 'unsafe'. It does not matter that the accused might nevertheless have been found guilty by the jury. Only the accused may appeal. The appeal may be against conviction on a point of law, or against conviction on a point of fact or mixed law and fact, or against sentence. Retrials are a growing phenomenon. Under the Criminal Justice Act 1972, s 36, the Attorney-General may refer a point of law to have the matter clarified. If the court decides that the Crown Court should have convicted, the accused's acquittal is not affected.

Appeal from the Court of Appeal is to the Supreme Court. The point must be one of law, and either side may appeal. Again there are two requirements: the Court of Appeal must certify that there is a point of law of general public importance, and either that court or the Supreme Court must grant leave. An example of a reference is ***Attorney-General's Reference (No. 1 of 1988)*** [1989] AC 971 (HL), which is discussed below.

Precedent in criminal law

Decisions of magistrates' courts are not binding on any court. Decisions of the Crown Court are not binding, though judges may well follow them if they know of them. Such decisions are rarely reported, but see Chapter 14 on rape for modern exceptions. Decisions of the Divisional Court and Court of Appeal (Criminal Division) bind courts below them in the hierarchy (see previous section). It is said, but not always adopted, that the Court of Appeal (Criminal Division) will not adhere as closely to its previous decisions as the civil side does because of its supposed bias in favour of the accused, in favour of liberty: *Gould* [1968] 2 QB 65. It seems that a five-person court can overrule a three-person court.

The Supreme Court binds courts below it. Since 1966 it has not been bound by its own decisions: *Practice Statement* [1966] 1 WLR 1234. However, that Practice Statement declares that the House of Lords, now the Supreme Court, will take into account the especial need for certainty in the criminal law. That is, in criminal law matters more than civil law ones it will strive not to depart from its previous judgments. The effect of the Practice Statement is that their Lordships seek to uphold previous decisions under which people have been convicted, even though the result is unjust. However, the House of Lords on one occasion very rapidly did just that, overruling its decision on impossible attempts in *Anderton* v *Ryan* [1985] AC 560 in *Shivpuri* [1987] AC 1. These cases, which concern 'impossible' attempts, are discussed in Chapter 10 under the heading The abolition of the defence of impossibility.

See pp 424–27 (Chapter 10) for a detailed explanation of impossible attempts.

It is uncertain whether a lower court is bound by the court immediately above it or by the court above that one. On the civil side the former rule applies.

In criminal cases the Court of Appeal has stated that it is bound by earlier Court of Appeal decisions and not by the advice of the Privy Council: *Campbell* [1997] 1 Cr App R 199. The rule is otherwise in the civil law, and there is no apparent reason for the difference. However, recently the Court of Appeal has, amazingly to some, followed the advice of the Privy Council and not the decision of the Lords: see *James* [2006] EWCA Crim 14 on now-abolished defence of provocation. The court stressed the following: there were nine Law Lords in the Privy Council; the majority explicitly said that their advice was the law of England; and the majority constituted more than half the Law Lords.

In terms of orthodox theory of precedent there are doubts about the precedential value of Attorney-General's References, but they have been treated as being equivalent to authorities from the courts in which they were heard.

English 'courts should, in the absence of some special circumstances, follow any clear and constant jurisprudence of the European Court of Human Rights' (per Lord Nicholls in *Kay* v *London Borough of Lambeth* [2006] UKHL 10), unless there is a domestic precedent, in which case the court should apply the precedent, give its view and give leave of appeal: see Lord Bingham in the same case at [43].

The interpretation of criminal statutes

Most criminal law is statute-based. Since statutes do not apply automatically, someone has to explain their width to the triers of fact, whether Justices of the Peace (or district judges (magistrates' court)) in the Magistrates' Courts or juries in the Crown Court, in order that they can apply the law to the facts. Moreover, Parliament often omits fundamental matters such as which party bears the burden of proof and what the *mens rea*, if any, is. Sometimes too statutes become outdated by technology. The judge is in a difficult position. He has to apply the law impartially but he forms part of the state order, part of the mechanism for repressing crime. There is still room for judicial creativity, for Parliament cannot legislate for every eventuality.

It used to be said that in England criminal law should be construed strictly, or at least in favour of the accused (sometimes put as 'in favour of liberty'). That is, criminal statutes had to be read narrowly so as to cover only those areas where it was clear that Parliament wanted the law to apply. There seem to be several reasons why such a view was taken. In the era of capital punishment it did not appear just to hang a person when Parliament had not expressly laid down a rule which covered the situation. In the time when parliamentary intervention was rare, and even today murder is a common law offence, judges said that the law they made was the epitome of reason, and any changes made by Parliament should be narrowly read. Lord Reid stated in *Sweet* v *Parsley* [1970] AC 132 (HL), one of the major authorities in the law relating to strict liability (see Chapter 4): 'It is a universal principle that if a penal provision is reasonably capable of two interpretations, that interpretation which is most favourable to the accused must be adopted.'

Modern-day judges seem at times to have gone to the other extreme: 'Here is a naughty or nasty person; he ought to be guilty of something; therefore let's make him guilty of something.' The lawyers had nevertheless by the middle of the twentieth century adopted what is called the literal approach to the construction of statutes. *Fisher v Bell* [1961] 1 QB 394 exemplifies this literal rule. A shopkeeper was charged with the offence of offering a flick-knife for sale when he had displayed it in his window. Parliament had decided that flick-knives were dangerous and it wanted them not to be sold. One might have thought that the Divisional Court would reason like this: 'A flick-knife is dangerous; a person who puts one into his shop window wishes to sell a dangerous item; therefore he is guilty of offering that knife for sale.' However, Lord Parker CJ ruled that what the shopkeeper had done was not to offer the knife for sale, but to invite passers-by to come into the shop and offer to buy it, therefore the accused was not guilty. His method of analysis is sometimes known as 'conceptual'. He worked from one category to the next with the result that the accused was set free (to the evident chagrin of Parliament, which changed the law the following year: the accused would now be guilty). Besides issues of sovereignty of Parliament, there was no compulsion on Lord Parker CJ to adopt the categories of contract law in criminal law, but his use of such categories demonstrates how statutes can be interpreted to convict or acquit the accused. For a House of Lords decision applying the literal rule, see *Bentham* [2005] 1 WLR 1057. It was held that the accused did not have 'in his possession, an imitation firearm' when he pointed his fingers under his jacket at the time of a robbery. He did not possess his own fingers within the meaning of the statute.

The Lords took a different approach with regard to criminal statutes. In *Attorney-General's Reference (No. 1 of 1988)*, above, it adopted what is called the 'purposive' approach. Lord Lowry said that judges should use the context of the offence in the statute in order to effect Parliament's purpose. The case involved insider dealing. The accused had received confidential information about prices of shares. A company was on the point of being taken over. He was charged with obtaining such information. The trial judge ruled that he had not obtained the information 'by purpose and effort'. He had simply received it while talking to a person from a merchant bank. The Attorney-General referred the matter to the Court of Appeal and it went to the Lords, the principal speech being delivered by Lord Lowry. He said:

(a) The dictionary definition of 'obtained' covered both getting possession by effort and acquiring (with or without effort). In other words, there were two meanings of 'obtained' in ordinary language. The former was the primary meaning, the latter the secondary one.

(b) The principle about the strict construction of penal statutes applied only in cases of real doubt. It was not sufficient that there was an ambiguity.

(c) The question therefore was whether Parliament intended to use the word in its primary or secondary meaning. Only if it was the latter was the accused guilty. The undesirability of the information being used did not depend on whether the accused had acquired it effortfully or effortlessly. The White Paper on which the relevant statute was based contemplated the mischief as being the possession of the information, not the mode of acquisition. The act of procuring is not the *actus reus*: why should the accused be prohibited from using only some of the confidential information? 'The object of the legislation must be partially defeated if the narrow meaning of "obtained" is adopted.' The narrow meaning would also lead to fine distinctions.

The contrary arguments were rebutted. 'Obtain' can mean 'obtain by endeavour' in some statutes, but that meaning does not apply in all contexts. The case was not one of a proper meaning and a loose (or inaccurate) one: it was of a primary and secondary meaning, both of which were correct. Accordingly, the wider meaning was adopted, with the effect that those who received snippets of confidential information from insider-traders were liable, and the matter should not have been withdrawn from the jury.

There is a tension between the freedom of the individual and not letting the 'obviously guilty' go. Part of this tension was noted by Professor Ashworth, 'Interpreting criminal statutes: a crisis of legality?' (1991) 107 LQR 419 at 443–444:

> If one of the aims of the criminal law is to convict those who culpably cause harm, this constitutes a policy goal which should form part of the doctrine of criminal law and which may properly enter into decisions on interpretation. The claim here is not that criminal laws should be extended retrospectively to citizens' conduct, but rather that people who knowingly 'sail close to the wind' should not be surprised if the law is interpreted so as to include their conduct.

Furthermore:

> To aim for maximum certainty in all these cases might minimise judicial discretion (and with it discriminatory practices and casual inconsistency), but it might equally lead to inflexible provisions which fail to draw distinctions in fair places and which result in the acquittal of some persons who should be convicted.

The strict construction of criminal statutes imposing liability never extended to defences, few of which are statutory. The Law Commission, always ready to reduce the width of fault terms, especially recklessness, continues to propose that some defences should not be defined in statute, in order to allow for judicial development. One must not be misled by such protestations. It is as easy to find examples of courts narrowing defences (e.g. duress) as it is to see their widening them (e.g. *Clinton* [2012] EWCA Crim 2 on the defence of loss of control).

As on the civil side, criminal courts may look at *Hansard* and law reform reports to find the mischief that an Act of Parliament was designed to fill but cannot use them to determine the width of the statutory words where there is no ambiguity, obscurity or absurdity: *Pepper v Hart* [1993] AC 593 (HL). There is recent authority that this rule should not be used to extend criminal liability when the words of the statute on their own are not such that the accused is guilty: *Thet v DPP* [2007] 2 All ER 425 (DC). However, *Thet v DPP* was distinguished in *Tabnack* [2007] 2 Cr App R 34. It was said that *Thet* applied when the prosecution sought to rely on parliamentary debates, not where the defence did.

Classification of offences by origin: can judges make new criminal laws?

Common law crimes are those created by judges, such as murder (see Chapter 11). Statutory offences are those created by Parliament, such as criminal damage (see Chapter 18). The vast majority of offences nowadays are statutory ones. Parliament often creates offences; it rarely unmakes them.

Judges have renounced the power to make new criminal offences: *Knuller (Publishing, Printing and Promotions) Ltd v DPP* [1973] AC 435 and *DPP v Withers* [1975] AC 842, both decisions of the House of Lords on conspiracy. A more recent Lords authority is *Jones* [2006] UKHL 16. This abnegation contrasts sharply with the strongly expressed view of the same court in the conspiracy to corrupt public morals authority of *Shaw v DPP* [1962] AC 220, a case involving the publication of the names, addresses and sexual services of female prostitutes, that 'there remains in the courts of law a residual power to enforce the supreme and fundamental purpose of the law to conserve not only the safety and order but also the moral welfare of the state'. The case involved a controversial social problem, and a matter on which Parliament had had its say only a short while previously. On both counts the Lords should not have intervened. *Shaw v DPP* was a breach of the principle of legality discussed at the start of this chapter. Lord Reid's dissent is a clear statement of constitutional principle that: 'Parliament is . . . the only proper place to settle the criminal law's purview.' There is nowadays little doubt that there exists a crime of outraging public decency, but that determination took 30 years after *Shaw* to occur.

The Court of Appeal, while saying that it was not doing so, reasserted the power to create new crimes when it held in *R* [1991] 2 All ER 257 that husbands were liable when they had sexual intercourse with their wives without their consent. The judgment was upheld by the House of Lords ([1992] 1 AC 599), despite the fact that since the early eighteenth century at the latest the general rule had been that a husband was exempt from conviction for rape of his wife. The removal of exceptions is equivalent to creating new offences, and both lead to uncertainty in the law. Compare the stance of Lord Reid in *Shaw*: '[w]here Parliament fears to tread it is not for the Courts to rush in.' *Shaw* and *Knuller* are presumably wrong now that the courts in England have been given the duty to apply the ECHR by the Human Rights Act 1998. The House of Lords authority discussed next was also decided before the 1998 statute came into force, but this time the principles are not affected.

C v DPP [1996] 1 AC 1 (HL) concerns the former doctrine that children aged 10–14 were presumed not to be capable of committing crimes unless the prosecution proved that the accused knew that what she was doing was seriously wrong. Lord Lowry laid down five principles:

(1) If the solution is doubtful, the judges should beware of imposing their own remedy; (2) caution should prevail if Parliament has rejected opportunities of clearing up a known difficulty or has legislated while leaving the difficulty untouched; (3) disputed matters of social policy are less suitable areas for judicial intervention than purely legal problems; (4) fundamental legal doctrines should not be lightly set aside; (5) judges should not make a change unless they can achieve finality and certainty.

For all these reasons Lord Lowry rejected a lower court's attempt to abolish the rebuttable presumption that children aged over 10 but under 14 are legally incapable of committing crimes. (It was for similar reasons that in *Clegg* [1995] 1 AC 482 the House denied a defence of excessive self-defence because the decision to reduce the offence from murder to manslaughter in such circumstances was one for Parliament, though Lord Lloyd was willing to change the law, even where questions of social policy are involved.) Parliament in fact changed the law in the Coroners and Justice Act 2009 to give in some instances a partial defence to excessive force used in self-defence through the new defence of loss of control.

Cases such as *Shaw* would not survive the application of Lord Lowry's five principles: at least principle (3) was broken. It is interesting to compare these guidelines with recent judge-made changes in the law. For example, the reader is invited to consider how many of them were breached when the House of Lords abolished the husband's immunity in rape (*R* [1992] 1 AC 599). This decision was not foreseeable in, say, 1970. It has to be said that the major judicial changes to the law in the last 40 years would probably not all fall foul of these guidelines. The various attempts to define intention and recklessness, discussed in Chapter 3, would be permissible under them.

Power in the judges to create new offences is not needed in a democracy, and the judiciary realises that it should not in theory invent new criminal laws. That is the reason why in *R* the Lords maintained that it was not doing so. Courts do not have the socio-economic information which Parliament has when deciding to enact Bills, for example England has no 'Brandeis' brief which the USA has to decide the effect of decisions either way, though the growing practice in some areas of law to have a barrister briefed as *amicus curiae* (literally 'friend of the court') may go some way to remedy this lack, and they do not have the power to supervise the implementation of their judgments which Parliament has in order to implement statutes. Parliament does not always pass statutes on controversial matters and some statutes are not drafted well or integrated into existing law, but the constitutional theory is plain: Parliament enacts laws and the courts apply them. This doctrine of parliamentary legislative sovereignty is under attack in European Union matters, but in criminal law the thesis stands. Parliament, moreover, can legislate whenever it wishes and in such manner as the government of the day thinks fit. It does not have to wait for the point to be brought before it by the prosecution as the courts do. Parliament can therefore enact statutes directed at evils, mischiefs, if the government so wishes. For example, it fairly quickly passed the Prohibition of Female Circumcision Act 1985 (replaced by the Female Genital Mutilation Act 2003), the Computer Misuse Act 1990 and the Theft (Amendment) Act 1996. To allow the judiciary, which is not democratically accountable, to invent new offences gives it too much power.

Sometimes, however, Parliament does not act and the courts may, often reluctantly, decide as a result to change the law. Lord Millett in *K* [2002] 1 AC 462 (HL), a case on the now-repealed law of indecent assault (but the principle still stands), made a heartfelt plea:

> ... The age of consent has long since ceased to reflect ordinary life, and in this respect Parliament has signally failed to discharge its responsibility for keeping the criminal law in touch with the needs of society. I am persuaded that the piecemeal introduction of the various elements of s 14 [of the Sexual Offences Act 1956, the crime of indecent assault, since repealed], coupled with the persistent failure of Parliament to rationalise this branch of the law even to the extent of removing absurdities which the courts have identified, means that we ought not to strain after internal coherence even in a single offence. Injustice is too high a price to pay for consistency.

The general acceptance by the judges that they are constitutionally unable to create new crimes does not extend to two matters. The first is that they can apply present law to new circumstances though the line between not creating new crimes and extending old ones may be narrow. There are offences under ss 23–24 of the Offences Against the Person Act 1861 of administering a noxious thing to a person. If the accused made up a bag containing glue and invited his best friend to sniff it, the court would have to decide whether the glue was a noxious thing and whether, if so, it was administered within the meaning of the statute. The law is already in existence but the problem is new. (For a statute dealing with selling glue-sniffing kits, see the Intoxicating Substances (Supply) Act 1985: English courts could not have phrased the crime in the way Parliament did.) A similar decision was reached by the House of Lords in *Ireland; Burstow*, the cases on stalking mentioned above, where it was held that although the drafter of the 1861 statute did not have psychiatric harm in mind, the statute was to be interpreted according to modern definitions and therefore 'harm' included 'psychiatric harm'. In the jargon of the law the 1861 Act is 'ever-speaking'. Secondly, the judges have not eschewed the creation of new defences. The development of the defence of duress of circumstances (see Chapter 7) has partly undercut the previous general non-recognition of necessity as a defence.

The Law Commission proposed in its Report No. 218, *Legislating the Criminal Code – Offences against the Person and General Principles*, 1993, to endorse the judicial creation and development of defences 'either to recognise changing circumstances or to piece out unjustified gaps in the existing defences' (para. 27.8). Perhaps the ability to create new defences should be restricted to excuses (see Chapter 7), where one is looking at the mental state of the accused, not at whether his behaviour was justified. The law should lay down what is justified.

The enactment of the draft Criminal Code (see later in this chapter) would not abolish common law offences. Wide offences such as public nuisance and conspiracy to defraud would remain.

Evidential and legal burdens of proof

English criminal law to a large extent gives the accused the benefit of the doubt (the work of Ashworth and Blake cited in the Further Reading section does, however, demonstrate that 40 per cent of the offences triable on indictment reverse the presumption of innocence; the authors write of the casual manner in which Parliament has placed the burden of persuasion on the accused). Triers of fact, whether juries, magistrates or district judges (magistrates' court), are to convict only if they are sure of the accused's guilt. Punishment should be applied only when it is certain that the accused committed the offence. The principle and exceptions to it are noted in this section.

There is a distinction between the evidential and legal **burden of proof**. The difference may be illustrated by reference to **automatism** (see Chapter 9). Before the accused can rely on this defence, he must put forward some evidence that he was acting automatically when he, say, hit his lover over the head with a heavy ashtray. The evidence might consist of a witness's saying that he saw what happened or a psychiatrist's report. In legal terms he has to adduce or lead evidence. If he does not adduce such evidence, his plea will fail at that stage and the prosecution does not have to lead evidence that his plea ought not to succeed. If he does, the prosecution has to disprove that he was acting automatically. His burden is called the evidential burden of proof. The prosecution's burden is the legal one.

For more on automatism as a defence, see Chapter 9. This is illustrated in Figure 9.3.

Evidential burden

The evidential burden means that the accused has to adduce evidence that may raise a doubt in the minds of reasonable jurors. In most offences the Crown does not need to negative any defence the accused might have. It has to show the *actus reus* and *mens rea*, if any. If the defendant wishes to rely on a defence, he must raise it and show evidence in support.

Legal burden

Example

On whom is the burden of proof in the following defences: loss of control; duress; insanity; and diminished responsibility?

The answers are respectively: prosecution; prosecution; defence; and defence. With regard to diminished responsibility, s 2(2) of the Homicide Act 1957 expressly places the burden on the accused. Parliament can do anything and therefore it can place the burden of proof on the accused. Where the onus is on the accused, she must prove that she has the defence on the balance of probabilities, the civil law standard of proof. With regard to loss of control and duress, the burden is on the prosecution, as it normally is, and they must disprove both defences beyond reasonable doubt, the criminal law standard of proof. Insanity is anomalous: the burden is on the accused as a matter of common law. The 'basic' case on insanity, **M'Naghten** (1843) [1843–60] All ER Rep 229, has as part of its main rule 'every man is presumed to be sane . . . until the contrary is proved to [the jury's] satisfaction . . .'.

Insanity and diminished responsibility are the exceptional defences. For all other defences commonly met on a criminal law course the burden is on the prosecution and they must disprove the defence beyond reasonable doubt. Therefore, calling something a defence does *not* ordinarily mean the burden of proof is on the defence. Be very careful about saying that the prosecution must show/prove/establish something – most often this is *not* the case.

In most areas of the criminal law the prosecution must prove both the *actus reus* and the *mens rea* 'beyond reasonable doubt'. That means that the triers of fact (jury or magistrates) must be sure that the accused was guilty. If authority is needed for this proposition, it may be found in the famous speech of Viscount Simon in **Mancini v DPP** [1942] AC 1 (HL), which changed previous law:

> No matter what the charge or where the trial the principle that the prosecution must prove the guilt of the prisoner [the old-fashioned word for the accused] is part of the common law of England and no attempt to whittle it down can be entertained.

The 'Golden Thread' of English criminal law is the duty of the prosecution to prove guilt beyond a reasonable doubt. As regards the decision of **Mancini v DPP**, J.C. Smith wrote ('The presumption of innocence' (1987) 38 NILQ 223 at 224): 'Never, in my opinion, has the House of Lords done more noble a deed in the field of criminal law than on that day.' A more modern statement is that of Hodgson LJ in **More** [1987] 1 WLR 1578 (CA): 'The prosecution's first task is to satisfy each juror . . . that every ingredient of the offence has been made out.' The same principle applies to most defences. The prosecution has, for example, to disprove duress and self-defence.

To this principle there are three, perhaps four, exceptions. These exceptions have come in for criticism. Article 6(2) of the ECHR states that anyone 'charged with a criminal offence shall be presumed innocent until proved guilty according to the law'. The jurisprudence of the European Court of Human Rights is unhelpful to the accused: no challenge to placing the burden on defendants has so far been successful. However, the House of Lords by a majority of four to one ruled in **Lambert** [2002] 2 AC 545, in reliance on Article 6(2), that the phrase 'it shall be a defence for the accused to prove . . .' in s 28(2) of the Misuse of Drugs Act 1971 was to be interpreted contrary to previous authorities as imposing only an evidential burden on the accused. This is a remarkable interpretation, despite the presumption of innocence found in Article 6(2). It was unclear at the time whether or not this decision changed all other reverse onus decisions. It is thought not. Lord Steyn expressly spoke to that effect and no one disagreed. However, the Divisional Court in **L v DPP** [2003] QB 137 decided that placing the burden on the accused to prove that he had a good reason or lawful authority to carry a lock-knife in a public place once the prosecution had proved that he did possess that type of knife in a public place did not contravene Article 6(2). The court said that it was not disproportionate to place the onus on the accused.

There has been something of a retreat from **Lambert** and the current position is that reverse burdens of proof can be justified under Article 6(2). In **Johnstone** [2003] 1 WLR

1736 (HL) Lord Nicholls said: 'The court will reach a different conclusion from the legislature [as to the reverse burden] only when it is apparent the legislature has attached insufficient importance to the fundamental right of an individual to be presumed innocent until proven guilty.' The Court of Appeal followed *Johnstone* in preference to *Lambert* in *Attorney-General's Reference (No. 4 of 2004)* [2005] 1 WLR 2819 (CA) as being the later authority. The case provides a list of factors. On appeal, where the case is also known as *Sheldrake*, [2005] 1 AC 264 the Lords said that the true question for each offence was whether a reverse burden was consistent with a fair trial. They resurrected *Lambert*, holding that due deference should be paid to the fact that Parliament has imposed onus on the accused. Previous cases mentioned in the previous paragraph were approved. The law was summarised by Lord Bingham:

> relevant to any judgment on reasonableness or proportionality will be the opportunity given to the defendant to rebut the presumption, maintenance of the rights of the defendant, flexibility in the application of the presumption, retention by the court of a power to assess the evidence, the importance of what is at stake and the difficulty which a prosecution may face in the absence of a presumption.

He added:

> It is repugnant to the ordinary notions of fairness for a prosecutor to accuse a defendant of a crime and for the defendant to be then required to disprove the accusation on pain of conviction and punishment if he fails to do so.

In one of the latest authorities, *Webster* [2010] EWCA Crim 2819, the accused was charged under the Prevention of Corruption Act 1916, s 2. This provision places the legal burden of proof on the accused to show that if he made a cash gift, it was not for a corrupt purpose. The Court held that the legal burden was in accord with previous authorities to be read down to become an evidential burden. It is nowadays difficult but not impossible for the courts to hold placing the legal burden on the accused to prove an essential fact in the offence is the correct interpretation.

Insanity

For the accused to have this defence he must show that he was insane at the time of the offence. The standard of proof is on the 'balance of probabilities'. That phrase means in effect that if it is more likely than not that the accused was insane, he has the defence. This standard was stated in cases such as *Sodeman v R* [1936] 2 All ER 1138, a decision of the Privy Council (PC) which has been accepted as stating English law. The legal reason assigned for this exception is that every person is presumed to be sane; therefore, the accused must prove insanity: *M'Naghten* (1843) [1843–60] All ER Rep 229. The effect is that if the jurors are not certain either way, the accused does not have this defence. The principal justification for reversing the burden of proof is that the accused has some particular knowledge. For instance, in the crime of possessing articles for suspected terrorist purposes, the defendant has to prove that the articles were not for a terrorist purpose; that information is within his knowledge. In *DPP, ex parte Kebilene* [2000] 2 AC 326 (HL) Lord Hope referred to the nature of the threat (e.g. terrorism) which the statutory provision is designed to combat. Lord Steyn, with whom Lords Slynn and Cooke agreed, said that the reverse burden of proof found in the Prevention of Terrorism Act 1989 could be read as merely placing the evidential burden on the accused.

For more on insanity as a defence, see Chapter 9. This is illustrated in Figure 9.1.

Parliament's expressly placing the burden on the accused

As stated in Viscount Simon's speech in **Mancini v DPP**, quoted above, the general rule about onus of proof is a matter of the common law. Parliament can alter the burden by statute and has done so on several occasions. The following are examples. Section 4(1) of the Explosive Substances Act 1883 affords a defence if the accused is able to prove that he made the material for a lawful purpose. By s 2(2) of the Homicide Act 1957 the accused must prove that he has the defence of diminished responsibility. This reverse burden of proof does not violate Article 6(1) of the European Convention on Human Rights. One problem with s 2(2) occurs when the defence of diminished responsibility and loss of control (which is defined in the Coroner and Justice Act 2009) are pleaded together. The prosecution has to disprove loss of control and the defence has to prove diminished responsibility. Yet both may arise out of the same facts. By s 1 of the Prevention of Crime Act 1953, the accused has a defence if he can show that he had lawful authority or reasonable excuse to carry an offensive weapon. By s 6 of the Public Order Act 1986 which defines riot:

For more on the defence of diminished responsibility, see Chapter 9. This is illustrated in Figure 9.2.

> . . . a person whose awareness is impaired by intoxication shall be taken to be aware of that which he would be aware if not intoxicated, unless he shows either that his intoxication was not self-induced or that it was caused solely by the taking or administering of a substance in the course of medical treatment.

'Shows' was meant to place the legal burden on the accused, but it could be read as placing only the evidential burden on him. The Law Commission proposed in its Report No. 229, *Legislating the Criminal Code: Intoxication and Criminal Liability*, 1995, that the burden should be placed on the prosecution.

Following **Lambert** presumably many legal burdens placed on the defence when an element of the offence is under discussion should now be read as imposing only evidential burdens. While these provisions are seen as exceptional, that perception is not necessarily true. Andrew Ashworth ('Is criminal law a lost cause?' (2000) 116 LQR 225 at 228) reported the outcome of a survey he carried out of crimes created in 1997. He found that 'the bulk of new offences is characterised by . . . reverse onus provisions for exculpation. [Such a feature lies] a considerable distance from the conception of criminal law held by many university teachers and criminal practitioners. Indeed [it is] inconsistent with prominent elements of English criminal law – . . . that . . . the prosecution bears the burden of proving guilt.' Where Parliament places the burden of proof on the accused, the standard of proof is on the balance of probabilities, unless Parliament states otherwise.

'Exception, exemption, proviso, excuse or qualification' in a statutory offence

Example

Imagine a statute is passed that says:

> The Firearms Act 2011 makes it an offence to possess a firearm, even one which does not work, subject to this exception: 'It shall not be an offence if the firearm is an antique.'

The burden of proof, it is suggested, is on the accused because this exemption creates an exception to the rule that the defendant is liable for possessing a firearm. See **Edwards** [1975] QB 27 (CA). Where the onus is on the accused, the standard of proof is the civil law one of the balance of probabilities and not the normal criminal law one of 'beyond reasonable doubt'.

The Court of Appeal in *Edwards* [1975] QB 27 said that the burden lay on the accused when Parliament had enacted offences 'which prohibit the doing of an act save in specified circumstances or by persons of specified classes or with specified qualifications or with the licence or permission of specified authorities'. This rule, which the Court of Appeal had treated as being one of law, was in truth a guide to construction for 'each case must turn upon the construction of the particular legislation'.

The rule in *Edwards* in any case suffered from the defect that it did not rest on a solid distinction between the definition of the offence and the exception to that definition. For instance, suppose that there is a law providing that 'no one shall enter the County of North Yorkshire without a passport'. This law could be rephrased as 'no one shall enter the County of North Yorkshire, except when that person has obtained a passport'. The two versions mean the same thing, but if the rule in *Edwards* were correct, the accused would have to prove that he had a passport in the second version, whereas in the first version the prosecution would have to disprove that he did have a passport. The illustration shows how absurd *Edwards* was. One can reformulate offence and defence into a narrow offence.

The same rule applies whether trial is on indictment or summary: that is, whether in the Crown Court or in the Magistrates' Courts. If the former, *Edwards* applies. If the latter, s 101 of the Magistrates' Courts Act 1980 stipulates that:

> Where the defendant . . . relies for his defence on any exception, exemption, proviso, excuse or qualification . . . , the burden of proving the exception [etc] shall be on him.

It might also be argued that since Parliament did not determine which party should bear the burden of proof, Parliament impliedly left the onus on the prosecution as a matter of the law of evidence.

Lord Steyn in *Lambert* expressly stated that the revision of the law found in that case did not affect the law laid down in *Edwards*.

Autrefois acquit and autrefois convict

It may be that the burden of proof lies on the accused to prove that he has been previously acquitted or convicted in a criminal trial.

Two matters concerning the burden of proof

(a) Before 1935 it was said that where the accused had caused the victim's death, he had to show that he did not have the *mens rea* for murder. This burden was placed on the prosecution in *Woolmington* v *DPP* [1935] AC 462 (HL).

> Throughout the web of the English criminal law one golden thread is always to be seen, that is the duty of the prosecution to prove the prisoner's guilt.

Those words of Lord Sankey have often been repeated, but they do not explain why the 'golden thread' does not run through insanity and the statutory exceptions. The contrary argument, which is not tied to murder, is that the accused is best placed to explain his conduct. If, for instance, the victim is shot dead by a bullet from a smoking gun held by the accused, who coveted his wife, one might say that to put the burden of proof onto the prosecution is absurd. No doubt the triers of fact take a robust view on such facts.

(b) Under the influence of *DPP* v *Smith* [1961] AC 290 (HL) it was thought that a person intended to do what the natural consequences of his behaviour were. In legal terms a man was presumed to intend the natural consequences of his behaviour. If this presumption was ever irrebuttable, s 8 of the Criminal Justice Act 1967 abolished it.

> A court or jury in determining whether a person has committed an offence (a) shall not be bound in law to infer that he intended or foresaw a result of his actions by reason only of its being a natural and probable consequence of those actions, but (b) shall decide whether he did intend or foresee that result by reference to all the evidence, drawing such inferences from the evidence as appear properly in the circumstances.

Section 8 deals with *how* to prove intention or foresight. It deals with the law of evidence or procedure. It is not concerned with the substantive criminal law, which is the subject of this book. Therefore, it does not affect the substantive law of murder. One might have expected that since s 8 does not affect the substantive law of murder, the ruling in *DPP* v *Smith* that the *mens rea* for murder includes what a reasonable person in the position of the accused would have foreseen would continue to apply after the 1957 Act, but in fact courts quickly held that this part of *DPP* v *Smith* was overruled by s 8. This surprising stance on s 8 continues to be taken, as can be seen in the decision of the Lords in *Woollin* [1999] AC 82.

The section applies only to the accused's intention or foresight. Beyond those states of mind the common law governs. Section 8 is stated to apply to intention and foresight of results, but the same rule applies at common law to circumstances: *DPP* v *Morgan* [1976] AC 182 (HL), the classic authority on mistake of fact as a defence. It does not apply where the accused does not have to intend or foresee a consequence. In manslaughter by gross negligence the accused is guilty whether or not he realised that death might result. The same is true of crimes of negligence. As a result of judicial construction s 8 does not apply where the accused was intoxicated. The section refers to the jury's taking into account 'all the evidence'. The House of Lords in *DPP* v *Majewsk* [1977] AC 443 determined that 'all the evidence' meant 'all the legally relevant evidence'. Since intoxication is no defence to so-called basic intent offences it is not part of the evidence with regard to the offences.

Criminal law reform, the Law Commission, and the draft Criminal Code

The Criminal Law Revision Committee was the first body to take on reform, doing sterling work on the first Theft Act (1968). The Law Commission, which was established in 1965, has taken over its role in criminal law and has promoted several major reforms over the last 40 and more years, such as the Criminal Damage Act 1971. Its approach was summarised in Report No. 228, *Conspiracy to Defraud*, 1994, para. 1.18:

> The Commission has seen codification of the criminal law as a central feature of [its] work . . . The criminal law controls the exercise of state power against citizens, and the protection of citizens against unlawful behaviour, and it is important that its rules should be determined by Parliament and not by the sometimes haphazard methods of common law. This can be achieved only if the law is put into statutory form in a comprehensive manner. It is also important from the standpoints of efficiency, economy and the proper administration of justice that the law should be stated in clear and easily accessible terms.

The point about the common law may be expressed more strongly as a constitutional principle: in modern times a law should be created by a democratic body, not by an undemocratic judge.

Buxton J said extra-judicially ('The Human Rights Act and the substantive criminal law' [2000] Crim LR 331): '. . . the present jumble of ancient statutes, more modern accretions to them, and the acres of judicial pronouncements should be replaced by a criminal code that would set out the criminal law in rational, accessible and modern language'. Arden J wrote to similar effect in 'Criminal law at the crossroads: the impact of human rights from the Law Commission's perspective and the need for a code' [1999] Crim LR 439: the criminal law should be 'well considered, consistent, coherent and modern', not as it is, 'seriously defective and out of date'. She correctly added that political will is needed.

The Report, *A Criminal Code for England and Wales* (Law Com. No. 177), was published in 1989. A team of three academics had drawn up the preliminary version in *Codification of the Criminal Law: A Report to the Law Commission* Law (Com. No. 143, 1985). To emphasise that it is not part of English law but is a body of rules which may in the future be enacted, it is called the draft Criminal Code in this book. The Report consists of a draft Bill, examples of the application of the Bill, and a commentary. General principles are found in Part I of the draft Code. Part II deals with particular offences. The general principles apply to all offences treated in the Code and those created afterwards, including those crimes such as road traffic offences not contained in Part II. It was expected that some crimes not in Part II would in time be embodied in it, but that some areas of law, such as road traffic offences, would continue to be treated separately because of convenience to the users of legislation. If enacted, the Code would apply to 90 per cent of all indictable offences. It is fairly comprehensive of earlier work of the Commission in areas such as criminal damage, attempts and forgery. The law is not simply restated. There are amendments aimed at clarifying and reforming some parts of the law. For example, the proposals of law reform institutions such as the Criminal Law Revision Committee are incorporated. However, the Commission on this occasion did not incorporate all the amendments it thought were called for in criminal law, for example in relation to the liability of accomplices. The Commission took the view that such changes were for Parliament. It hoped that the draft Code's enactment would reduce the length of trials and appeals and improve access to and understanding of the criminal law. The themes of the draft Code were stated to be accessibility, comprehensibility, consistency and certainty. The need for certainty remains of especial importance in the criminal law, which regulates, in part, the relationship between the citizen and the state.

The draft Code came under criticism on several grounds. Under whatever type of Code people in England and Wales live, there will be difficulties of access and coverage. Even with computer monitors it is unlikely that everyone all the time will have access to all the law on a certain topic, and because of the flexibility of the language it may be impossible to tell whether a person is guilty of an offence until he has been tried. If a law bans vehicles from parks, is a child's bicycle, a unicycle, a horse, a horse and cart, a vehicle? The malleability of English language will be reflected in any penal code. The draft Code may, however, be criticised on other grounds. Not all offences are included. Road traffic offences constitute the main omission. (It must be questioned why a serious offence such as causing death by dangerous driving is not to be included, especially when many minor offences are.) Also excluded are *inter alia* drugs offences, many highly specific crimes such as offences in sports stadia, and crimes concerned with companies. The Commission considered that it would inconvenience users to have such crimes dealt with in the Code, for users would wish to see the excluded parts of the law contained in separate statutes. However, it may be argued that it would be best to have all crimes in one place. The draft

Code is not a reforming instrument. Some parts are revised in accordance with recommendations (above), but others which have not been subject to proposals are left unreformed. The draft Code remains open to judicial interpretation on key terms such as intention, and the possibility of inconsistent verdicts on dishonesty in theft remains. The choices of the Commission between different views of the law were not always justified by the members. If one form of recklessness is preferred to another in the interests of consistency, it would be just as consistent to choose the second form over the first. The choice should be justified on policy grounds. Those values need to be articulated and applied.

At present the development of criminal law is ill-disciplined. Nevertheless, the attempt to cut out anomalies, put the law into the form it would have been in had the recommendations of reform bodies been enacted, and restate the law in authoritative form is worthwhile. What the draft Code should not do is to lead to preferring the formal virtues of a code to principles of justice. It is no use having an accessible code, a comprehensive code, a consistent code, a certain code, if the values it contains do not strike a balance between social protection and the liberty of the individual. The formal virtues show where the line between the two is: they do not draw it for us. Moreover, the great argument against codification, that it puts the law into a straitjacket, misses the point when it is understood that constitutionally the role of judges in criminal law is not to make law, for that is Parliament's task. If Parliament fears to tread, even more strongly the courts should fear to tread. It is suggested that since the coming into force of the Human Rights Act 1998 the need for codification is even stronger than before. The Commission has sought to make its recommendations consonant with the ECHR. However, Parliament and the Home Secretaries for some years rarely listened to the Law Commission's criminal law reports, but more recently they have used the Commission's reports, though sometimes they have cherrypicked, as with the one on murder and manslaughter.

Changes from present law

The changes which were proposed in the draft Code, if it were ever to become law, are dealt with in the appropriate place. The following details the changes which affect criminal liability. As can be seen, the draft Code was both a restatement of then existing law and a revision of some parts of law. It was criticised for attempting to do both, and while there is a reason behind the proposed changes, which were found in the reports of law reform bodies, the recommended reforms do look arbitrary from a reformist viewpoint.

(a) *Burden of proof.* The evidential burden in relation to the defence of involuntary intoxication is placed on the accused.

(b) *Minimum fault element.* Unless Parliament ordains differently, the accused will not be guilty unless he adverted to the risk ('subjective recklessness'). The Law Commission used to be strong upholders of the doctrine of 'subjectivism'. An accused was not guilty when he intended to commit the crime or if he knew that he ran the risk of a certain result occurring. In fact the Commission has never fully debated the merits or otherwise of subjectivism as the base line for criminal liability. Since 1989, the Law Commission has sometimes resiled from this proposition. It proposed a new offence of killing by gross carelessness (and a similar offence for companies), recommended that only reasonable mistakes as to consent should give the accused a defence to rape and indecent assault (which indeed became the law as a result of the Sexual Offences Act 2003 but it is doubtful if those who voted in favour of the Bill had the Commission's arguments in mind), and in its Report No. 229 on intoxication has gone back on its proposal in Consultation Paper No. 127, *Intoxication and Criminal Liability*, 1993, to afford a defence of drunkenness whenever the defendant did not have the state of mind required in the definition of the crime.

(c) *Defences.* Mistake is to be a defence to all crimes where the accused honestly erred. Reasonableness is not demanded. The law on insanity is completely redrafted. There are changes in the law of duress and intoxication.

(d) *Vicarious and corporate liability.* The doctrine of delegation is abolished. The law on corporations is modified. The law on organisational liability for manslaughter was altered by statute in 2007.

(e) *Participation.* Recklessness as to circumstances will be sufficient if sufficient for the principal crime. A person will be exempt if he acts 'with the purpose of avoiding or limiting any harmful consequences of the offence and without the purpose of furthering its commission'.

(f) *Inchoate offences.* The law on so-called 'double inchoate' law is rationalised. Recklessness as to circumstances will be part of the fault element if it is sufficient for the full offence. There will be liability for conspiracy with one's spouse, the victim, and a child under 10.

(g) *Offences against the person.* The law is substantially revised. The Home Office unusually published a Consultation Paper in 1998 called *Violence: Reforming the Offences against the Person Act 1861*, with a view to reforming non-fatal offences but at the time of writing there has been no progress. This area of law is perhaps the most in need of modernisation.

(h) *Sexual offences.* There are some changes but the Sexual Offences Act 2003 and various statutory and judicial changes in the period 1989–2003 have rendered the recommendations somewhat superfluous.

Subjective recklessness is explained in Chapter 3 (pp 107–11).

(i) *Theft and other property offences.* Very minor alterations.

The flow of papers and reports from the Law Commission has continued unabated. Reports enacted are those which led to the abolition of the year-and-a-day rule in homicide and to the penalisation of mortgage fraudsters. Because of the perceived lack of parliamentary time the Law Commission proposed not to have the Code enacted in one statute but to put forward Bills dealing with various areas which will in the end be consolidated into a code. The approach has been criticised as selective. The first tranche is the Criminal Law Bill found in Report No. 218, *Legislating the Criminal Code – Offences against the Person and General Principles*, 1993. The Home Office consultation paper mentioned above contains the non-fatal offences part of this Report, together with a draft Bill, but the part on general matters is omitted. Later Reports also contain Bills ready for enactment. The government has not enacted any part of the draft Criminal Code.

As the former chair of the Law Commission, Brooke J, said in (1994) 158 JP 345, much criminal law 'is a disgrace, when judged in terms of simplicity, clarity and accessibility'. Money is being wasted and justice denied because of uncertainties in the law. As Henry LJ said in *Lynsey* [1995] 2 Cr App R 667 (CA) in the context of non-fatal offences, courts have better things to do than to administer bad laws. These words were echoed by Brooke LJ in *Baker* [1997] Crim LR 497 (CA). Brooke J was still in charge of the Law Commission when it put forward the second instalment of its attempt to have enacted parts of the 1989 draft Code when it stated that its aim especially in the criminal law was 'to make the law simpler, fairer and cheaper to use': *Legislating the Criminal Code: Intoxication and Criminal*

Liability, Report No. 229, 1995, para. 1.3. The text of this book demonstrates the truth of his statement.

The Law Commission announced in 2008 that it no longer intended to complete the criminal law codification project but it did intend to return to it at some future time. The reasons given for not proceeding were: 'the complexity of the common law, the increased pace of legislation, layers of legislation on a topic being placed one on another with bewildering speed, and the influence of European legislation'. Since 2002 the Commission has been working on seven parts which would revise the 1989 Draft Criminal Code: external elements especially causation, fault, parties to crime, incapacity and mental disorder, defences, preliminary offences and proof. Work has proceeded slowly because of other projects: partial defences to murder, assisting and encouraging crime, and non-accidental death or serious injury to children, among others. Consultation papers and reports have been published and there have been some successes, for example the Fraud Act 2006, but the government, despite saying in *Criminal Justice: The Way Ahead*, Home Office, 2001, that it favoured a criminal code, is not giving a lead. It preferred to legislate on matters of media concern rather than law reform in the round: that is why the archaic Offences Against the Person Act 1861 remains unrevised. What the government seemed to be doing was to pick and choose among the reforms while enacting its own views, as can be seen for example in the Coroners and Justice Act 2009: the law of diminished responsibility was revised but the Commission's recommendation that the defence should encompass developmental immaturity was not. The current coalition government seems to be of the same persuasion, and the possibility of a Code continues to diminish.

The Law Commission proposed in its Consultation Paper No. 195 *Criminal Liability in Regulatory Contexts*, 2010, that criminal law should be used only as a last resort and should be made only by statute and not by secondary legislation. The government rejected these recommendations and the Law Commission decided not to proceed.

The next part of this book, General Principles, outlines that area of criminal law which is often called 'the general part'. It is sometimes contended that there is no such concept as 'the general part', merely a wilderness of single instances. Whether there is or is not one is for debate, but the distinction between the general principles and specific offences helps to organise material. One does not need, for example, to repeat the law on duress or accessorial liability each time an offence is mentioned.

Summary

This chapter is concerned with introducing the reader to possible definitions of substantive criminal law and the distinctions between civil and criminal law and to the basic principles or building blocks of the law, in particular the concepts of *actus reus*, *mens rea* and defence, concepts which underlie most of the remainder of the book (see especially Chapters 2–4 and 7–9).

● *Fundamental principles of criminal law*: Using the approach of Husak in his *Philosophy of Criminal Law* the author guides the reader through the principal constraints on the law of crime: legality, *actus reus*, *mens rea*, concurrence (usually known in England and Wales as 'contemporaneity'), harm, causation, defences, and proof beyond reasonable doubt). Many of these elements such as *actus reus*, *mens rea* and defences are discussed at length in later chapters but here the focus is on legality, particularly in the context of Article 7(1) of the European Convention on Human Rights (ECHR).

- *Human Rights Act 1998*: This statute 'brings home' particularly those human rights found in the European Convention. The Act has not had a major effect so far (e.g. it is not contrary to the Convention to have offences of strict liability: see Chapter 4 for the meaning of such crimes) but it could greatly affect current definitions of offences and defences, for example the law on consent may be contrary to Article 8, respect for private life, and insanity looks certain to be contrary to Article 5, the right to liberty.

- *Attempted definitions of a crime*: Over the years various definitions of a 'crime' have been made but the standard definition is the circular one of 'a legal wrong that can be followed by criminal proceedings which may result in punishment' (Glanville Williams).

- *Differences between criminal and civil law*: among differences are terminology, courts, procedure and outcome of trials.

- *Hierarchy of courts*: The vast majority of criminal law cases start in the magistrates' courts where cases are heard by magistrates or by district judges (magistrates' court), who were previously called 'stipendiaries'; only the very serious offences are heard in the Crown Court, where the decision is taken by the jury after hearing the judge's instruction. Appeals from the Crown Court lie to the Court of Appeal and thence to the Supreme Court.

- *Precedent in criminal law*: The normal rules of precedent exist in criminal law except that the Court of Appeal (Criminal Division) does not consider itself as bound by its predecessors' decisions as does the Civil Division. Recently the Court of Appeal decided to follow a Privy Council case in preference to a House of Lords (now the Supreme Court) one.

- *The interpretation of criminal law statutes*: It is sometimes said that statutes creating offences are read in favour of liberty; that is, in favour of the accused. However, many cases may be found which go the other way, i.e. convict the 'manifestly guilty' even when the statute could be construed in favour of the accused.

- *Classification of offences*: There are several methods of classifying crimes, including by their source (statutory or common law).

- *May judges create crimes?* The short answer in the last quarter of a century is 'No, but they may apply the law to new scenarios.' The virtual ban on creating offences, however, does not apply to new defences and the development of duress of circumstances exemplifies how new defences can be created.

- *Proof*: In criminal law the burden of proof normally rests on the prosecution and the standard of proof is that the Crown must prove each element of the offence beyond reasonable doubt. Indeed, this principle applies even to defences: for most defences the prosecution must disprove each element beyond reasonable doubt. Therefore, in respect even of defences the accused does not need to prove anything: he or she is afforded the defence if the prosecution cannot disprove beyond reasonable doubt that he or she has the defence. However, since Parliament can do anything, it can put the burden of proof on to the defendant, both with regard to offences and defences. For example, Parliament has placed the burden on the accused to prove that he or she falls within the defence of diminished responsibility. Whenever the burden is on the accused, the standard of proof is the civil law one of 'on the balance of probabilities'. There is one exceptional defence, insanity, where the burden lies on the accused as a matter of common law and the reason behind this rule seems to be that everyone is presumed to be sane: therefore, the accused must prove that he or she was insane.

Wherever the burden in criminal law is on the accused, there is the possibility of conflict with Article 6(2) of the ECHR, the presumption of innocence, and English courts including the House of Lords have struggled to fit situations where the burden is on the accused with the ECHR.

- *The draft Criminal Code*: The Law Commission published the *draft* Criminal Code in 1989. It has not been enacted. The Law Commission currently sees no prospect of Parliament's enacting the whole of it in one go but has published several consultation papers and reports on various aspects of criminal law since 1989 and it hopes that these smaller tranches will be enacted and will over time form a code.

References

Reports

Home Office, *Criminal Justice: The Way Ahead* (2001)

Home Office, *Crime in England & Wales 2008/09* (2009)

Law Commission Consultation Paper no. 127, *Intoxication and Criminal Liability* (1993)

Law Commission Consultation Paper no. 195, *Criminal Liability in a Regulatory Context* (2010)

Law Commission Report no. 143, *Criminal Law: Codification of the Criminal Law – A Report to the Law Commission* (1985)

Law Commission Report no. 177, *A Criminal Code for England and Wales* (1989)

Law Commission Report no. 218, *Legislating the Criminal Code – Offences against the Person and General Principles* (1993)

Law Commission Report no. 228, *Conspiracy to Defraud* (1994)

Law Commission Report no. 229, *Legislating the Criminal Code: Intoxication and Criminal Responsibility* (1995)

Report of the Committee on Homosexual Offences and Prostitution (Wolfenden), Cmnd 247 (1957)

Books

Card, R., Cross, R. and Jones, P.A. *Criminal Law*, 20th edn (Oxford University Press, 2012)

Husak, D.N. *Philosophy of Criminal Law* (Rowman & Littlefield, 1987)

Lacey, N. *State Punishment* (Routledge, 1988)

Norrie, A. *Crime, Reason and History*, 2nd edn (Butterworths, 2001)

Journals

Arden, M. 'Criminal law at the crossroads: the impact of human rights from the Law Commission's perspective and the need for a code' [1999] Crim LR 439

Ashworth, A. 'Interpreting criminal statutes: a crisis of legality?' (1991) 107 LQR 419

Ashworth, A. 'Is criminal law a lost cause?' (2000) 116 LQR 225

Buxton, R. 'The Human Rights Act and the substantive criminal law' [2000] Crim LR 331

Hart, H.M. 'The aims of the criminal law' (1958) 23 L & CP 401

Smith, J.C. 'The presumption of innocence' (1987) 38 NILQ 223

Williams, G. 'The definition of a crime' [1955] CLP 107

Further reading

Alldridge, P. 'What's wrong with the traditional criminal law course?' (1990) 10 LS 38

Ashworth, A. 'Is the criminal law a lost cause?' (2000) 116 LQR 228

Ashworth, A. 'The Human Rights Act and the substantive criminal law: a non-minimalist view' [2000] Crim LR 564

Ashworth, A. Case comment on *Attorney-General's Reference (No. 4 of 2002)* [2005] Crim LR 215

Ashworth, A. 'Conceptions of overcriminalization' (2008) 5 Ohio St J Crim L 407

Ashworth, A. and Blake, M. 'The presumption of innocence in criminal law' [1996] Crim LR 306

Ashworth, A. and Zedner, L. 'Defending the criminal law: reflections on the changing character of crime' (2008) 2 Crim Law and Philos 21

Bennion, F. 'Codification of the criminal law – Part 2: The technique of codification' [1986] Crim LR 295

Bingham, Lord 'A criminal code: must we wait forever?' [1998] Crim LR 694

Bowles, R., Faure, M. and Garoupa, N. 'The scope of the criminal law and criminal sanctions: An economic view and policy implications' (2008) 35 JLS 389

Brownsword, R. 'Who says penal statutes are construed restrictively?' (1977) 28 NILQ 73

Burca, G. de and Gardner, S. 'The codification of the criminal law' (1990) 10 OJLS 559

Chalmers, J. and Leverick, F. 'Fair labelling in criminal law' (2008) 71 MLR 217

Dennis, I. 'The critical condition of criminal law' [1997] CLP 213

Doran, S. 'Alternative defences' [1991] Crim LR 878

Duff, A. 'Theorising criminal law' (2005) 25 OJLS 353

Duff, R.A. 'Theories of criminal law' *Stanford Encyclopaedia of Philosophy* (available online to UK higher and further education institutions)

Duff, R.A. 'Crime, prohibition, and punishment' (2002) 19 J Applied Phil 97

Duff, R.A. 'Towards a Theory of Criminal Law?' (2010) LXXXIV *Proceedings of the Aristotelian Supplementary Volume* 1

Duff, R.A., Farmer, L., Marshall, S.E., Renzo, M. and Tadros, V. (eds) *The Boundaries of the Criminal Law* (Oxford University Press, 2010)

Edwards, J. 'Coming clean about the criminal law' (2011) 5 Crim Law and Philos 315

Etherton, J. 'Law reform in England and Wales: a shattered dream or triumph of political vision?' (2008) 73 *Amicus Curiae* 3

Farmer, L. 'The obsession with definition' (1996) 5 *Social and Legal Studies* 57–73

Farmer, L. 'Constructing a criminal code' (2009) 20 CLF 139

Ferzan, F.F. 'The structure of criminal law' (2009) 28 *Criminal Justice Ethics* 223

Fletcher, G. 'Criminal theory in the twentieth century' (2001) 2 Theoretical Issues L 265

Hamer, D. 'A dynamic reconstruction of the presumption of innocence' (2011) 31 OJLS 417

Husak, D. 'The criminal law as a last resort' (2004) 24 OJLS 207

Husak, D. 'Crimes outside the core' (2004) 39 Tulsa L Rev 755

Husak, D. 'Why criminal law: a question of content?' (2008) 2 Crim Law and Philos 99

Husak, D. 'Repaying the scholar's compliment' (2010) 1 Jerusalem Rev Legal Studs 48

Jefferson, M. 'Regulation, business, and criminal liability' (2011) 75 JCL 37

Lacey, N. 'Historicising criminalisation: conceptual and empirical issues' (2009) 76 MLR 936

Lamond, G. 'What is a crime?' (2007) 27 OJLS 609

Lavery, J. 'Codification of the Criminal Law: An attainable idea?' (2010) 74 JCL 557

Law Commission of Canada *What is a Crime?* Discussion paper (2003)

Leader-Elliott, I. 'A critical reading of RA Duff, *Answering for Crime*' (2010) 31 Adel LR 47

Melissaris, E. 'Toward a political theory of criminal law: A critical Rawlsian account' (2012) 13 New Crim LR 122

Moore, M.S. 'A tale of two theories' (2009) 28 Crim Justice Ethics 27

Roberts, P. 'Philosophy, Feinberg, codification and consent' (2001) 5 Buff Crim LR 173

Robinson, P.H. *Structure and Function in Criminal Law* (Clarendon, 1997)

Rogers, J. 'Applying the doctrine of positive obligations to domestic substantive criminal law in domestic proceedings' [2003] Crim LR 690

Schünemann, B. 'Alternative project for a European criminal law and procedure' (2007) 18 Crim LF 227

Shiner, R.A. 'Theorizing criminal law reform' (2009) 3 Crim Law and Phil 167

Smith, A.T.H. 'The case for a Code' [1986] Crim LR 285

Smith, A.T.H. 'Criminal law: the future' [2004] Crim LR 971

Spencer, J.R. 'The drafting of criminal legislation: need it be so impenetrable?' Judicial Studies Board, 12th Annual Lecture, 13 March 2008

Stevenson, K. and Harris, C. 'Inaccessible and unknowable: accretion and uncertainty in modern criminal law' (2008) 29 Liv LR 247

Tierney, S. and Tadros, V. 'The presumption of innocence and the Human Rights Act' (2004) 67 MLR 402

Toulson, R. 'Forty years on: what progress in delivering accessible and principled criminal law?' [2006] Stat LR 61

Tur, R.H.S. 'Two theories of criminal law' (2003) 56 SMULR 797

White, R.M. 'Civil penalties: oxymoron, chimera and stealth sanction' (2010) 126 LQR 593

Williams, G. 'The definition of crime' (1955) 8 CLP 107. (For a criticism of his definition of a crime, see J. Dine [1994] JBL 325.)

Williams, G. 'The logic of exceptions' [1988] CLJ 261

For a critique of criminal law as a rational and principled enterprise see A. Norrie, *Crime, Reason and History*, 2nd edn (Butterworths 2001). He argues that in criminal law 'the "extraordinary" is as much the norm as the ordinary' (p. 7) and that English criminal law is a product of the epoch in which we live (p. 8). There is also a good discussion of what he calls 'orthodox subjectivism' and its rivals such as practical indifference. See also the collection edited by S. Shute and A.P. Simester, *Criminal Law Theory: Doctrines of the General Part* (Oxford University Press, 2002).

For more discussion of harm and morality in criminal law see P. Devlin, *The Enforcement of Morals* (Oxford University Press, 1965). H.L.A. Hart, *Law, Liberty and Morality* (Oxford University Press, 1963), and the sequence of books by J. Feinberg, *Harm to Others* (Oxford University Press, 1984), *Harm to Self* (Oxford University Press, 1986), *Harmless Wrongdoing* (Oxford University Press, 1988), and *Offense to Others* (Oxford University Press, 1985).

Visit **www.mylawchamber.co.uk** to access tools to help you develop and test your knowledge of criminal law, including interactive multiple choice questions, practice exam questions with guidance, annotated weblinks, glossary flashcards, legal newsfeed and legal updates.

Use Case Navigator to read in full some of the key cases referenced in this chapter with commentary and questions:

R v *Brown* [1994] 1 AC 212
R v *Hinks* [2001] 2 AC 241, [2000] 3 WLR 1590
R v *Ireland and Burstow* [1998] AC 147
R v *Woollin* [1999] AC 82

Part 2

General principles

2

Actus reus

Aims and objectives

After reading this chapter you will understand and be able to critique:

- the definition of *actus reus* and its explanatory power
- the difference between conduct and result crimes
- the principles of causation
- the ways in which a person may be criminally liable for omitting to do something

Introduction

Example

Deirdre provides Victor with heroin. It is Victor's first time injecting this drug. Deirdre demonstrates how to tie a tourniquet on Victor's arm and prepares the heroin for injection. Victor, a man aged 25 and of normal intelligence, injects himself and dies. Has Deirdre caused Victor's death?

The resounding answer for the House of Lords in *Kennedy (No. 2)* [2008] 1 AC 269 (HL), and contrary to a string of previous Court of Appeal authorities is 'No!' The victim has made a free, deliberate and informed decision to take the drug and that decision prevents liability in the supplier.

It should be noted that so-called 'drugs manslaughter' cases since *Kennedy (No. 2)* have loyally followed the authority, but there is a suggestion that the accused could be liable for a form of manslaughter called gross negligence manslaughter. This form of manslaughter is discussed in Chapter 12. It has to be said that with regard to this suggestion there remains the difficulty with causation.

The general aim of the criminal law is to forbid certain types of conduct, but in most serious crimes the accused must also have been legally at fault. Offences therefore have two sides: conduct and fault. The 'conduct' requirement means that an accused is not criminally liable for merely thinking about committing a crime. Sometimes defences such as lack of consent are seen as failures to prove one or other of these ingredients. However, some defences cannot easily be seen as negating either conduct or fault. For the purpose of examining and explaining criminal law, it has become orthodox in the twenty-first century to divide the constituent elements of a crime into these two parts, which are called *actus reus* (the conduct element in the definition of the crime) and *mens rea* (the mental element in the definition of the crime). Both ingredients must be present. If one crashes into one's neighbour's car, one is not necessarily guilty of criminal damage. If one does so intentionally or recklessly, one is. In criminal damage one is guilty only if one has the requisite state of mind, the *mens rea* or 'fault element', as the Law Commission draft Criminal Code (Law Com. No. 177, 1989), cl 6, calls it. The *actus reus* is called the 'external element', which is the heading to cl 15.

The *mens rea* is the state of mind, or in the case of negligence the failure to attain a certain standard of behaviour, which the definition requires before the accused can be convicted. The *actus reus* is sometimes defined negatively as the remainder of the offence once the *mens rea* has been subtracted.

● Since there may be a defence which is not defined in terms of vitiating the *mens rea* or *actus reus* or both, it may be better to regard the *actus reus* as the act (such as causing death in murder), the omission (as in not displaying a valid tax disc), or the state of affairs (as in possessing a controlled drug) rather than negatively.

● In most offences both must exist. Crimes where there is no *mens rea* as to one or more parts of the *actus reus* are called strict offences (see Chapter 4).

● Usually the *actus reus* and *mens rea* must be contemporaneous (see Chapter 3).

● The two parts do not exist separately. The *mens rea* qualifies the *actus reus*. For example, in the offence of rape, the accused among other matters must intend sexual intercourse with a woman or a man, and know that the victim does not consent. The 'sexual intercourse', 'woman' or 'man' and 'consent' points constitute the *actus reus*. The intention, recklessness and other relevant states of mind are designated the *mens rea* of the offences. To find out which mental element is required in relation to each element of the *actus reus* is a task for the law student, for each external element may have a different *mens rea* attached to it.

● There are difficulties in dividing all elements of a crime into *mens rea* and *actus reus*. The element of possessing a proscribed drug looks like *actus reus*, but it hides an aspect of *mens rea*: one does not possess something unless one knows one possesses it, and knowledge is part of *mens rea*. This difficulty is explored in the next section (Some problems) of this book.

The terms '*actus reus*' and '*mens rea*' are purely shorthand, useful for exposition. They are convenient for lawyers. This point was well put a long time ago by Rollin Perkins ('A rationale of *mens rea*' (1939) 52 Harv LR 905):

> Some years ago the *mens rea* doctrine was criticized on the ground that the Latin phrase is 'misleading'. If the words '*mens rea*' were to be regarded as self-explanatory they would be open to this objection, but they are to be considered merely as a convenient label attached to any psychical fact sufficient for criminal guilt . . . This includes a field too complex for any brief self-explanatory phrase, and since it is important to have some sort of dialectic shorthand to express the idea, this time-honored label will do as well as any. (American spelling retained)

To what extent these elements must be shown to exist, if at all, depends on an analysis of the particular offence with which the accused is charged. Moreover, whether an element of an offence is classified as *actus reus* or *mens rea* does not normally matter for in either case the accused is not guilty. One exception is the doctrine of procuring the *actus reus* of a crime discussed in Chapter 5, but that doctrine may not survive challenge in the Supreme Court.

There are also problems with the effect of mistake as to *actus reus* and *mens rea*. Normally even an unreasonable mistake exculpates, but if the crime is one of negligence, the accused has a defence only if the mistake was made on reasonable grounds.

Since the terms are legal ones, there is no need to use them before laypeople. Lord Diplock deprecated their use in court in **Miller** [1983] 2 AC 161 (HL), a leading authority on omissions discussed below.

> It would . . . be conducive to clarity of analysis of the ingredients of a crime that is created by statute, as are the great majority of criminal offences today, if we were to avoid bad Latin and instead to think and speak . . . about the conduct of the accused and his state of mind at the time of that conduct, instead of speaking about actus reus and mens rea.

His wish was granted in the draft Criminal Code. However, not only has the Code not been enacted but also there is more usage of the term in the courts today than there was three decades ago when Lord Diplock made his remarks, no doubt because practitioners were once students who were taught these terms. Certainly the terms could be dropped. Their use can be illustrated thus:

Murder: *actus reus* (in part) = causing death
           mens rea (in part) = intentionally causing death or serious bodily harm

The terms *actus reus* and *mens rea* need not be used. One could just say that murder was defined in part as causing death with the intention to cause death or to cause grievous bodily harm. Since the terms are used in courts and the academic world of law, they are utilised in this book as a handy way of distinguishing the accused's behaviour and the circumstances and consequences of the offence from his state of mind.

Some problems

(a) There are difficulties in defining the *actus reus* as the offence minus the *mens rea*. The *actus reus* of an offence may go beyond what the accused did. The *actus reus* can cover the mental state of the victim. In rape the victim must not be consenting. The victim's consent is a state of mind, but not the accused's state of mind. It is also arguable that in some crimes it is unclear whether something constitutes the *actus reus* or *mens rea*. In the offence of driving without due care and attention, is the element 'without due care and attention' a state of mind? It could be said that it means 'carelessly'. If negligence ('without due care and attention') is a state of mind (see Chapter 3), the element is *mens rea*. It might be said, however, that the phrase qualifies 'driving'. One is driving in such a manner that the driving falls short of the standard of due care and attention. One can only possess something such as a controlled drug if one knows one possesses it: the accused's state of mind is part of the *actus reus*. Whether touching is 'sexual' depends in part on the purpose for which the accused touches. It does not matter whether knowledge is part of the *mens rea* or *actus reus*. The prosecution has to prove it no matter how commentators define it. One form of aggravated burglary occurs when the accused has with him a weapon of offence. Whether an article is one of offence depends on the accused's intention. The *actus reus* includes the accused's state of mind. The division into *actus reus* and *mens rea* may not always be clear-cut.

In some offences it is only the *mens rea* which is wrongful – the *actus reus* is perfectly innocent. A good illustration is theft. If the accused picks a tin of beans from a supermarket shelf, there is nothing wrong in what he has done: most people act similarly indeed every day. However, the addition of (part of) the *mens rea*, dishonesty, converts the *actus reus* into a crime. If only for this reason, readers should not translate *actus reus* as 'guilty act'. There may be nothing 'guilty' about it.

Some defences also create difficulties. In duress the accused seems to have the intention to commit the crime and to have caused it, but he has a defence. This defence goes beyond *mens rea* and *actus reus*. Some defences are not failures to show *actus reus* and *mens rea*. Where does automatism fit? It could be a denial of the *actus reus*: the accused was not in truth 'driving' because he was being attacked by a swarm of bees, an example given a new lease of life in **Bell** [1984] 3 All ER 842 (CA). It could be a denial of *mens rea*: when attacked by bees he has no state of mind (there could be a problem with strict offences in this regard). It could even be what might be called a true defence: he was driving and he knew he was driving badly, but he has the defence of automatism. Another view is to say that the correct analysis is that before the stages of *actus reus* and *mens rea* are reached, it must be shown that the accused loses control of his bodily movements. In most cases control is not at issue, and unless the accused raises doubt about his control, the prosecution need not prove affirmatively that he was in control. If, however, he was being attacked by a swarm of bees with the result that he was not in charge of his vehicle, he will be acquitted unless the prosecution can disprove his evidence. This ingredient is sometimes phrased as: was the accused acting voluntarily? He is not acting voluntarily if he is being attacked by bees. It should be noted that this type of involuntariness is different from that in duress, where the accused's behaviour is determined by threat which obliges the accused to act in a certain way. In automatism the accused's voluntary conduct is negated by loss of conscious control. In duress the accused may have conscious control over his movements but his acts are directed by coercion.

Because the relationship between automatism and the definition of an offence is not yet solved, automatism cannot be neatly fitted into the distinction between justifications and excuses noted in Chapter 7. For further discussion of automatism see Chapter 9.

(b) The *actus reus* differs from crime to crime. In burglary the accused (for example) must enter a building or part of a building without the consent of the owner. In theft the defendant must appropriate property belonging to another. To say that all crimes have an *actus reus* does not inform us what that *actus reus* is in each offence. One has to look at each offence to determine what the *actus reus* is. One *actus reus* may suffice for several offences. In murder, manslaughter and other homicide offences the accused must cause the victim's death. The *actus reus* may also cover how a situation arose. Criminal damage caused by fire constitutes the offence of arson (Criminal Damage Act 1971, s 1(3)).

(c) As stated above, *actus reus* is not just a 'guilty act', as students sometimes say. It can cover a state of affairs, such as having with one articles for use in burglaries, being in possession of a controlled drug or of an article for use in the case of fraud (contrary to the Fraud Act 2006, s 6), membership of a proscribed terrorist organisation, and an omission (see below). The difference between these forms of behaviour may not be clearcut, and one may have difficulty distinguishing between acts and omissions, when one is guilty if one acts but not guilty if one fails to act (see **Fagan v MPC** [1969]

1 QB 439 (DC), discussed later in this chapter). Is drink-driving an act or is it a state of affairs? Also included in the *actus reus* are the legally relevant circumstances. In bigamy the accused must already be married. In rape the sexual intercourse must be without the consent of the victim.

(d) The *actus reus* must be proved. **Deller** is the authority normally given to illustrate this proposition.

Deller (1952) 36 Cr App R 184 (CCA)

The accused was charged with what was then false pretences and is now fraud by false representation contrary to s 2 of the Fraud Act 2006. When he took his car in for a trade-in, he represented that there was no money owing on it. He believed that there were payments outstanding. It looked as if he had made a false pretence. In fact the loan on the car was void and in law did not exist. Therefore, he did not owe any money. His representation turned out to be true, though he mistakenly believed it to be false. The Court of Criminal Appeal quashed his conviction. The prosecution had failed to prove that the pretence was false.

One is not guilty of an offence simply because one believes oneself to be guilty. The prosecution must prove the whole of the *actus reus* and, on the facts, one element was missing. **Deller** can stand for the proposition that one is not guilty for having guilty thoughts. *Mens rea* alone is insufficient. The accused did intend to make a false representation but that representation turned out to be true. Therefore, all the elements of the offence were not fulfilled. The charge nowadays would be one of attempted fraud under the Criminal Attempts Act 1981.

The case always contrasted with **Deller** is **Dadson**. The distinction between the two authorities is often stated to be that in **Deller** there was an absence of an element of the offence whereas in **Dadson** there was an absence of an element of a defence. This distinction is crucial, for the accused was not guilty in **Deller** but was guilty in **Dadson**.

Dadson (1850) 4 Cox CC 358 (CCR)

A constable was guarding a copse from which wood had been stolen on several occasions in the past. The constable saw the victim come out of the copse carrying wood. The wood had been stolen by the victim. He shot at the victim, who was injured. He was charged with shooting with intent to cause grievous bodily harm. At that time it was thought lawful for a constable to shoot an escaping felon. Stealing wood became a felony only if a person had two previous convictions, which the victim had. The constable did not know that the victim had the prior convictions. The constable was found guilty. In the Court for Crown Cases Reserved, where judges gathered to discuss points of criminal law, it was held that an accused did not have a defence unless he was aware of the facts justifying the defence at the time of the offence. (The conviction seems to be in line with policy, for persons should ask questions first and shoot later.)

The actual result in **Dadson** is now governed by s 24(4) of the Police and Criminal Evidence Act 1984 (PACE) (though cf. J.C. Smith's commentary on **Chapman v DPP** [1988] Crim LR 843), which deals with arrestable offences. The accused no longer needs reasonable grounds for suspecting that the victim has committed an offence when he uses force to effect the arrest, if the victim in fact was committing one when arrested (though the arrest might still be unlawful because it cannot be stated what the grounds of arrest were at the time under s 28). Nevertheless the principle stands elsewhere: to have a defence the accused must know the circumstances which justify his conduct.

Dadson is authority for the proposition that circumstances of justification are treated as part of the mental element, not as part of the *actus reus*. The accused must know of the circumstances of justification to obtain a defence. Accordingly, the accused is guilty of battery if he trips up the thief of a book from the library but does not know of the theft.

It has often been suggested that *Dadson* is wrong. The victim was a felon and therefore it was lawful to use deadly force to arrest him. He was not doing anything forbidden by law. There was no *actus reus* and the case is on all fours with *Deller*. The court, however, held that the accused was guilty unless he knew that the victim was a felon: there was no need for the court so to rule; it could have held that the accused had a defence if the victim was in fact a felon. If *Dadson* is wrong, there would be no gap in the law, for nowadays the accused would be guilty of the attempt to commit the offence.

Dadson is preserved by the Criminal Law Bill attached to Report No. 218, 1993. The policy behind *Dadson* was aptly and succinctly stated in para. 39.11 of the Report: 'citizens who react unreasonably to circumstances should not be exculpated by accidents of facts of which they were unaware.'

(e) There are times when a person other than the accused committed the *actus reus* but the accused is nevertheless guilty of the offence of which the other party committed the *actus reus*. The obvious example is vicarious liability, discussed in Chapter 6.

(f) The *actus reus* may help to prove the *mens rea*. If the accused stabs his victim through the heart at close range, there is some evidence that the accused had the *mens rea* of murder.

'Conduct' and 'result' crimes

It is becoming usual to divide offences into 'conduct' and 'result' offences. **Conduct crimes** are those where only the forbidden conduct need be proved: no harm need be caused. An example is dangerous driving, contrary to s 2 of the Road Traffic Act 1988 (as amended), which provides in relation to the *actus reus* that a person is guilty when he is 'driving a mechanically propelled vehicle on a road'. One does not have to show that anything else occurred. The accused is guilty if he drove a motor vehicle dangerously on a road. There need be no harmful consequences, such as the accused drove a car on a public road so dangerously that someone was knocked down. In perjury the accused is guilty if he makes a statement on oath, knowing or believing it to be false. The outcome of the case need not be affected. Perjury is therefore a conduct crime. In **result crimes**, because a forbidden consequence is part of the *actus reus*, the specified harm must be shown. In murder someone must be killed. The forbidden result must be caused.

With regard to conduct crimes, there is no problem normally with causation, since no result need be proved. In result crimes the accused must be proved to have caused the prohibited consequence. In s 1 of the Road Traffic Act 1988 (as amended), the prosecution must show that the accused drove dangerously and thereby occasioned the death of a person. (For causation generally, see below.)

One issue which has arisen in result crimes occurs where the definition of those offences contains the concept of unlawfulness. As late as **Albert v Lavin** [1981] 1 All ER 628 the Divisional Court thought that this word emphasised that the outcome of what would otherwise be crimes could be lawful. In murder, for instance, one is not guilty if one killed by performing service as public executioner or in self-defence. Such a defence would arise whether or not the word 'unlawfully' appeared in the definition of the offence. However, both **Kimber** [1983] 1 WLR 1118 (CA), where the issue of consent in the then existing crime of indecent assault was under discussion, and **Williams** [1987] 3 All ER 411 (CA), one of the major cases on self-defence, decided that 'unlawfully' is part of the *actus reus* (see Chapter 8 for the effect). This means that matters such as self-defence form part of the *actus reus*. If the accused falls within the boundaries of self-defence, the prosecution has failed to prove the whole of the *actus reus*. To call self-defence a 'defence' is a misnomer if by the term is meant a third concept beyond *actus reus* and *mens rea*. Nevertheless, the accused bears the evidential burden.

See p 67 later in this chapter for a more detailed explanation of omission.

Some offences can be committed by a failure to act, and others such as possessing cannabis are status or state of affairs ones. It is difficult to describe these offences as 'conduct' ones. Omission involves the opposite, a lack of conduct.

Causation

There is no more intractable problem in the law than causation (Criminal Law and Penal Methods Reform Committee, South Australia, Fourth Report, *The Substantive Criminal Law*, 1977, 50, quoted in E. Colvin 'Causation in criminal law' (1989) 1 Bond LR 253).

> Questions of causation arise in many different legal contexts and no single theory of causation will provide a ready-made answer to the question whether [the accused's] action is to be treated as the cause or a cause of some ensuing event. The approach must necessarily be pragmatic . . . (Lord Bridge in **Attorney-General of Hong Kong v Tse Hung-lit** [1986] 1 AC 876 (PC)).
>
> The law in deciding questions of causation selects one or more causes out of the total sum of conditions according to the purpose in hand . . . (McGarvie and O'Bryan JJ in **Demirian** [1989] VR 97, 110).

Introduction

 Causation is in some sense a difficult area of the law (Figure 2.1), yet according to the Court of Appeal in **Cato** [1976] 1 WLR 110, **Pagett** (1983) 76 Cr App R 279 and **Cheshire** [1991] 1 WLR 844 the issue of factual cause is largely one for the jury once the court has determined that there is sufficient evidence to be left to them, and since 'cause' is an ordinary English word, in most cases no direction need be given. As Lord Salmon put it in the pollution case of **Alphacell Ltd v Woodward** [1972] AC 824 (HL) in a passage approved by the House of Lords in another pollution authority, **Environment Agency v Empress Car Co (Abertillery) Ltd** [1999] 2 AC 22, 'What or who has caused a certain event to occur is essentially a practical question of fact which can best be answered by ordinary common sense rather than by abstract metaphysical theory.' Nevertheless, as Lord Hoffmann in the **Empress** case recognised, there are principles of law involved too, and some of these may be complicated. Moreover, there is not one single rule applicable to all issues of causation. As Lord Bingham put it in **Kennedy (No. 2)** [2008] 1 AC 269 (HL), the major recent authority on causation:

'. . . causation is not a single, unvarying concept to be mechanically applied without regard to the context in which the question happens.' The answer may depend on the question asked. Whether a person caused pollution and whether he caused a death may require different rules of attribution. A third party's intervention may prevent the latter being guilty but not the former. Doctors may give evidence of what they consider to be the cause, but the decision is for the jury. Similarly, whether an organisation had caused effluent to enter a river is a question of fact.

In the *Empress* case the Lords held that the magistrates were entitled to find that the defendants had caused pollution to a river. Only if the act of the third party was 'extraordinary' and not 'a matter of ordinary occurrence' were the defendants not liable. They had built a tank for diesel oil in a place where the oil would flow into a river if someone turned a tap. Someone did. The failure to install a lock on the tank caused the pollution. This case has come in for strong criticism because the 'free, deliberate and informed' act of a third party had released the oil: this act would seem to be a *novus actus interveniens*, a concept which is discussed below, but the phrase basically means that the accused is held not to have caused the prohibited result. It seems very strange to have an accused's criminal liability depend on the act of an unknown third party, who was after all a vandal. *Empress* is confined to instances of pollution: *Kennedy (No. 2)*, discussed below. An alternative view is to say that their Lordships were wrong because they hardly dealt with the standard authorities on causation: the installation of the tank was merely the setting for the

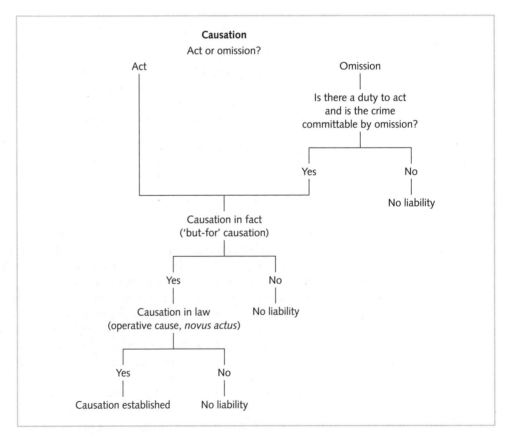

Figure 2.1 Causation

pollution, not the cause of it. The cause was the 'free, deliberate and informed' act of a third party. On ordinary principles, that should have broken the chain of causation.

The issue of legal causation can be withdrawn from the jury when the judge decides that the accused's act or omission was not the legal cause. The courts have readily stated what is and what is not a cause. There are principles of law operating. These principles may not cohere into doctrine, for the courts may increase or review their scope in order to catch or exculpate the accused. If a lorry driver falls asleep at the wheel and kills a motorist, is he liable or the employer who insures him to drive, or even the capitalist system which obliges him to work? (For the law on causation for secondary offences see Chapter 5.)

Cases on causation tend to arise in homicide, but the principles are applicable generally to result crimes, including strict offences, though pollution may be an exception.

It is not true to say that causation is always required. Some crimes ('conduct crimes', see above) do not require a consequence to be caused, and some crimes which are result crimes do not require causation. A person is vicariously liable, that is, criminally responsible for another's act, even though he did not occasion the wrongful act: the courts look for both 'but-for' causation (e.g. the victim would not have died but for the accused's shooting him – this aspect is sometimes called 'causation-in-fact') and legal causation (i.e. does the law attribute this cause to this defendant?). If the 'but-for' test were used alone, it would pick up too many accuseds. For example, if I am shot by a bank robber, I would not have been shot if I had stayed in bed. One would not say that my failure to stay in bed caused the shooting. Common sense comes into play in the jury's decision. In most scenarios it is evident as a matter of common sense that the accused caused the crime, for instance, by pulling the trigger. When there is no difficulty in determining causation, no direction is given. In some instances it is not simple to determine who caused death. If a person refuses a life-saving blood transfusion, one could contend that he caused his own death. The judges look further and give a direction on causation which potentially inculpates the accused who so injured the victim that he had to choose between a transfusion and death. It must be noted that there can be more than one cause of a consequence. In criminal law the inquiry is whether this accused contributed more than negligibly to the result, not whether or not there was any other significant contribution.

If the accused did not in fact cause the result, he is not guilty of the principal offence. In *White* [1910] 2 KB 124, the accused put potassium cyanide into lemonade, intending to kill his victim. She died, not through drinking the poison, but from natural causes. Therefore the accused had not caused her death, despite what he intended and did. The charge should be one of attempted murder. Similar is *Shoukatellie v R* [1962] AC 81 (PC), where the intended victim had died before the accused struck what would otherwise have been a fatal blow. A case which demonstrates 'but-for' causation is the South Australian Supreme Court one of *Hallett* [1969] SASR 141. The victim had allegedly made a homosexual advance to the accused while they were drinking on a beach at night. The accused beat him up, leaving him unconscious. The tide came in and drowned him. The accused had caused his death: but for what the accused had done the victim would not have drowned. He would not have been guilty, had there been a tsunami. In *Dyson* [1908] 2 KB 959 the Court of Criminal Appeal held that the accused had caused the victim's death even though the latter would shortly afterwards have died of meningitis. The former had accelerated his death.

As part of the 'but-for' test one should always remember *Dalloway* (1847) 3 Cox CC 273 in which Erle J directed the jury that the accused must have been able to prevent the crime. On the facts the accused did not cause the death of a child, whom he ran over. He was careless because he did not have the reins in his hands, but his negligent driving did not cause death. The victim would have died anyway under the wheels of the cart for even had the defendant been driving properly, there was nothing he could have done to prevent the accident. Despite the accused's negligence, the child still would have died. In modern terms an accused is not guilty of causing death by dangerous driving if, though he is driving dangerously, a child unexpectedly dashes out and is killed under the car's wheels. Causation is lacking. A modern application of *Dalloway* is *Marchant* [2004] 1 WLR 442 (CA). The accused, the driver of an agricultural vehicle with a grab unit at the front, was not guilty of causing death by dangerous driving when a motor cyclist impaled himself on a metre-long spike on the grab unit. The spike was not covered by a guard. The court held that, even if it had been, the collision would still have occurred; and the driver's appeal was allowed. One phrase sometimes used is that the accused's act must be the *sine qua non* (a precondition) of the death. As we shall see, even if it can be said that the accused did in fact cause the death, he may not be responsible in criminal law for it because, for example, there was in the Court of Criminal Appeal's words in *Jordan* (1956) 40 Cr App R 152 'palpably wrong' medical treatment, breaking the chain of causation and rendering the accused not liable. Accordingly, there are two stages: factual causation and legal causation. Proving factual or 'but-for' causation does not prove legal causation. Legal causation is concerned with whether criminal responsibility can fairly be ascribed to the accused.

The same rules apply in both murder and manslaughter as well as causing death by dangerous driving. In these crimes part of the *actus reus* is 'causing death'. Since it is certain that we are all going to die one day, the *actus reus* is better expressed as the accused accelerating death. Since the acceleration of death is the kingpin, it does not matter that the victim was suffering from a terminal illness, such as cancer: *Adams* [1957] Crim LR 365 (Devlin J). In the words of Lord Widgery CJ in *Cato* (above), 'It was sufficient if the prosecution could establish that it was a cause, provided it was a cause outside the *de minimis* range and effectively bearing on the acceleration of the moment of the victim's death.' (*De minimis* means so trivial that no account should be taken of it: *De minimis non curat lex*, the law is not conceived with trifles.)

Another result flowing from the definition, though not one totally accepted by Devlin J in *Adams*, is that a doctor who gives pain-killing drugs to a dying patient performs this part of the *actus reus* of murder if those drugs incidentally shorten life by a more than trifling period. If a doctor prescribes pain-killers in order to accelerate death, there is no problem. He has caused the patient's death. This is so despite any request from the patient and the severity of the pain. One might argue that the doctor should have a defence of necessity, or perhaps his motive should exculpate him. The law remains uncertain. There seems to be a move towards giving a doctor a defence when even though he knows that the treatment will accelerate death, he believes that he is undertaking the correct treatment to reduce pain. See the trial of *Moor* [2000] Crim LR 31 before Hooper J discussed by Arlidge, 'The trial of Dr David Moor' [2000] Crim LR 31.

It is also uncertain whether, if this rule restricted to doctors exists, the civil case of *Re A* [2001] Fam 147 (CA) has affected it. The surgeons realised that separating conjoined twins would kill one of them. Two of the Lords Justices stated that once a jury found that the doctors knew that it was (virtually) certain that one twin would die, they intended to kill. (Of course, normally a doctor will not have the *mens rea* for murder.) It may be that a trifling acceleration is insufficient. Devlin J said in *Adams* that an acceleration of death by 'minutes, hours or even, perhaps, days' by pain-killing drugs is not a cause of death. Incidental acceleration of death as a result of pain-killing drugs does not constitute a cause for the purposes of criminal law. It is certainly arguable that Devlin J confused motive (the desire to stop the patient suffering unbelievable pain) with causation. Surely he would not have said the same about an accused who was not a doctor who fed her mother death-accelerating, pain-killing tablets to receive her inheritance 'perhaps days' earlier than she would otherwise have done? Devlin J emphasised that cause was a matter of common sense to be determined by the jury. It 'means nothing philosophical or technical or scientific'.

Again, because the accused must be shown only to have caused death, it does not matter which of his acts caused death as long as one did. In *Attorney-General's Reference (No. 4 of 1980)* [1981] 2 All ER 617 (CA) the accused pushed the victim backwards, strangled her and cut her throat, but was guilty whichever act caused death. (In light of the requirement of contemporaneity of *mens rea* and *actus reus*, we must assume that the accused had *mens rea* throughout the series of acts unless all the acts can be regarded as the same transaction. The concept of an indivisible transaction is discussed below. The case was not decided on that basis, which would convict him if he had the *mens rea* at the time of the first attack and thereafter thought he was disposing of a corpse which in fact was a live body.) If the accused did not have *mens rea* at the start of the series of acts or throughout them, he is acquitted. If, however, the prosecution cannot prove beyond reasonable doubt that the accused's blow caused the victim's death when there were two blows from different persons, either of which might have occasioned death, the accused is not guilty: *Dyos* [1979] Crim LR 660 (Old Bailey). The prosecution could not prove that it was the accused's blow which caused the victim's death.

It is not essential that the accused's act is the sole, major or even a substantial cause of death: *Pagett*, above. In *Benge* (1865) 176 ER 665 the accused, a foreman of a platelaying gang, was guilty of manslaughter through his carelessness even though others had contributed to the victims' death. It was irrelevant that no one would have been killed if others had acted differently. (The others such as the train-driver and a signalman could also have been liable for manslaughter because they too had significantly contributed to the victims' death.) The term 'substantial' means only that the cause must be more than *de minimis*: *Notman* [1994] Crim LR 518 (CA). Therefore, it is not a misdirection to use 'substantial' in this sense. The same court held in *Kimsey* [1996] Crim LR 35, which involved racing cars along a public road, that while the term 'substantial' could be used, it was a dangerous expression in that it might lead the jury to think that the cause really had to be substantial. What it really means is that the accused's conduct had to be more than *de minimis*, which the trial judge correctly translated as 'slight or trifling'. Similarly in *Cheshire*, above, the same court emphasised that the act of the accused need not be the sole or main cause of death. It is sufficient if his act contributed significantly to the victim's demise. 'Significantly' simply meant 'more than negligibly'. Therefore, there was no requirement to show that the defendant's act was the dominant or even substantial cause of death. The victim was shot in the thigh and stomach by the accused. A tracheotomy was performed in order to allow him to breathe. He died from the narrowing of the windpipe at the operation scar. Despite the hospital's failure to diagnose what was wrong with the victim, the accused's acts still contributed significantly to the victim's death. It can be argued that the facts of *Cheshire* resemble those of *Jordan*. The injuries continued to exist but they did not threaten the victim's life, and the hospital had been negligent. The distinction resides in the grossness of the doctors' negligence in *Jordan*, which broke the chain of causation.

In *Armstrong* [1989] Crim LR 149, a Crown Court decision, the accused supplied the victim with heroin and the means of injecting it. The case proceeded on the basis that the victim injected himself. Evidence showed that the death was caused primarily by the victim's drinking a lethal amount of alcohol. The heroin was not a significant enough cause of death. (Experts were unsure whether heroin accelerated death appreciably: the case may therefore be authority for the proposition that in causation, *de minimis* applies.) It is possible that *Armstrong* is out of line with **Blaue** [1975] 3 All ER 446 (CA) discussed below. In

Armstrong the victim was under the influence of drugs. Why did not the accused take his victim as he found him? Compare also *Cato* above (which was distinguished in *Armstrong*) where the Court of Appeal looked for 'a cause' in a heroin-related death, not for 'but-for' causation in order to convict the accused of manslaughter. Again the court stressed that the issue was not one of substantial causation. In *Armstrong* the accused supplied the victim with the heroin and the means of injecting it but was found not guilty. In *Cato* the victim supplied the drug and mixed it, yet the accused was found guilty. On this analysis the cases look the wrong way round! In fact the distinction according to the courts resides in the identity of the person who injected the drug.

Normally, if the accused was the factual cause of death, he is also the legal cause. There are, however, some circumstances where this conclusion cannot always be drawn, and these form the subject of the next section of this chapter.

Finally, it should be noted that when the courts are dealing with causation, particularly legal causation, they are not really asking: Did this accused cause the death? They are asking: Is it fair to attribute the death to this accused? Questions of attribution are ones of morality, not of fact.

Some special problems in causation

(a) *Novus actus interveniens*

> ### Example
> Alf beats up Betty and leaves her on a beach.
> Scenario 1: she is left below the high water mark, the tide comes in and she drowns. Is Alf guilty of murder?
> Scenario 2: would it make a difference if she was left ABOVE the high water mark, and it was a tsunami and not the tide which had killed her?
> This is a straightforward instance of causation. The principal rule is that the accused must be the cause in fact and in law. Using the 'but-for' test, in both scenarios but for his leaving her on the beach she would not have drowned. However, in the first situation drowning by the tide is reasonably foreseeable and provided the accused did intend to kill or cause very serious harm ('malice aforethought') when he beat her up, he is guilty of murder. In the second scenario, the tsunami was not reasonably foreseeable and the accused is not guilty of murder, even if he did have the mental element for that offence.

This Latin phrase has become a legal term. What it means is that the intervening 'act was so independent of the act of the accused that it should be regarded in law as the cause of the victim's death to the exclusion of the act of the accused' (*per* Robert Goff LJ in *Pagett* (1983) 76 Cr App R 279 (CA)). When some event breaks the chain of causation, that is called a *novus actus interveniens*. The accused's conduct was no longer the operating cause of death, but merely part of the history. The judge noted that academic commentators spoke of the chain of causation being broken where the intervention was 'free, deliberate and informed'. Such intervention must be abnormal. In water cases the damage done by vandals has rendered factory owners not liable for polluting rivers. An example taken from the South Australian Full Court case of *Hallett* [1969] SASR 141 is of a victim left unconscious above the highwater mark who was drowned by the tide. If, however, the victim had been left unconscious below that mark and had drowned, the accused who had left him unconscious would be liable when the incoming tide overwhelmed him.

The problem is illustrated by **Pagett**. The police shot and killed a girl being used as a shield by the accused. The court held that their action in shooting her was instinctive, was a reasonable act of self-defence or indeed self-preservation and was reasonably foreseeable. Alternatively, the shooting was an act done to prevent crime. Therefore, her death was attributable to the accused, who had shot at the police. It was as if the accused had pushed the victim under a tube train. In legal jargon the chain of causation might not broken by the police's shooting of the victim. What the police did was instinctive; therefore, it was not 'free, deliberate and informed'. (Cf. **Empress**, where, despite the oil's release being caused by an unknown third party, the company was still liable. **Pagett** reiterates orthodox law; **Empress** is out of line.) Whether the police had a hand in the victim's death was therefore irrelevant. Had the police shot the victim dead in a grossly negligent fashion, then the chain of causation might have been broken. Similarly, a reasonable act of self-preservation, such as trying to escape from the accused's violence, will not break the chain of causation: see (b) 'The "escape" cases', below. It is interesting to note that in the civil action relating to **Pagett** reported in the *Guardian*, 4 December 1990, the police marksmen were held liable for negligence. They did not know that the victim was the defendant's former girlfriend; they ignored her mother's advice; there was no supervision of armed officers; the officer in charge had no experience of sieges; the officers could not see where the victim was standing because there was no light on the floors of the flats where the deceased was killed.

Of course the police were not on trial in **Pagett** itself, just as the doctors were not in **Malcherek** [1981] 1 WLR 690 (CA) in which the position of the negligent doctors was not discussed. In **Malcherek** it could also be said that the doctors' intervention, the turning off of the life-support system, was free, deliberate and informed. Both cases demonstrate how in criminal law there can be more than one cause. The fact that the police were negligent for the purposes of civil law did not of itself affect the accused's guilt in criminal law. (See also (f) 'Contributory negligence', below.) In **Pagett**, the human shield case, the marksmen acted instinctively to preserve their own lives. Though they were the immediate cause of death, the defendant was held to have been the legal cause of death. Even if the shooting of the victim was unlawful, it appears that he would still be criminally liable because he also unlawfully caused the death.

The basic rule is that the accused escapes liability only if the supervening event was highly abnormal or, put differently, unforeseeable or if there has occurred what has become known as 'free, deliberate and informed' intervention. The phrase is that of Hart and Honoré in the second edition of their treatise *Causation in the Law* (OUP, 1985). The law is unclear but in the context of *novus actus* it appears to be that 'free, deliberate and informed' intervention by the victim or a third party is not in itself sufficient to ground liability in the accused. The reasonable foreseeability test is often used. In **Girdler** [2010] EWCA Crim 2666 the accused crashed into a taxi, forcing it broadside on to the traffic; the deceased drove into the taxi, killing himself. Was the accused guilty of causing death by dangerous driving? The court held that the accused was guilty if 'it could reasonably have been anticipated that a fatal collision might occur in the circumstances . . .'. A retrial was ordered.

Where the concept of foreseeability is used, the test is an objective one. The accused's characteristics, such as youth, stupidity or gender, are not taken into account: **Marjoram** [2000] Crim LR 372 (CA). Lord Parker CJ in **Smith** [1959] 2 QB 35 in the Courts-Martial Appeal Court (nowadays called the Court Martial Appeal Court) said that:

> Only if the second cause is so overwhelming as to make the original wound merely part of the history can it be said that the death does not flow from the wound.

Otherwise, the accused's act will remain the effective or operative cause. On the facts of *Smith* the accused was guilty despite the 'thoroughly bad' treatment and despite the victim's good chance of recovery before that treatment. There were two concurrent causes of death, but because the wound made by the accused's stabbing the victim was still operative, the accused had caused his death. The jury does not choose which is the dominant cause. It answers the question whether the accused's acts contributed significantly to the death.

Smith was applied in *Gowans* [2003] EWCA Crim 3935. The defendants robbed a pizza delivery man. They put him into a coma. While in hospital he contracted septicaemia and died. The source of the infection was unknown. Evidence was led that the victim's condition required treatment which carried a risk of life-threatening infections. Kay LJ held that the jury had been directed properly. The attack made the victim vulnerable to infections; therefore, the death was attributable to the defendants. It would have been different if the attack was in the words of *Smith* 'merely the setting in which another cause operates'.

Another illustration is *Dear* [1996] Crim LR 595 (CA). The accused heard that the victim had sexually interfered with his young daughter. He slashed him repeatedly with a knife. The victim died from his wounds two days later. The accused argued that the chain of causation had been broken either by the victim's reopening his wounds (i.e. he committed suicide) or by failure to stop the blood from flowing. The court held that the injuries caused by the accused remained the operating and significant cause of death, whether or not the victim had reopened the wound. As long as the accused's acts had contributed significantly to the victim's death, the questions of whether the victim had acted in a negligent or grossly negligent manner or whether the intervening behaviour of the victim was foreseeable were irrelevant. It may be argued that if it were true that the victim did reopen his wounds, his behaviour was, in the words of *Roberts* (1971) 56 Cr App R 95 (CA), 'daft' and the accused should not have been convicted: suicide was not reasonably foreseeable. *Roberts* is discussed at (b) below. If the argument is accepted that as long as the accused's acts contributed significantly to the victim's death, the accused is liable, the law has moved on, for the previous law was that the chain of causation was broken when the victim's behaviour was not reasonably foreseeable. The contrary contention is that the accused must take his victim as he finds him, as noted at (e) 'The accused must take his victim as he finds him', below. If taking one's victim as one finds him means 'taking the whole of the victim including his mental state as one finds him', there is no scope for *Roberts*, for unreasonable behaviour (to escape, for instance) is part of the whole man. The rules can lead to different results. For example, if the accused sexually assaults the victim and the latter runs across a busy road and is killed, the facts look like a *Roberts* scenario: the accused is guilty if the victim's actions were reasonably foreseeable. If, however, the victim was suffering mental anguish at the time of the assault, the case resembles *Blaue* and the accused is guilty whether or not the death was reasonably foreseeable. Which rule applied was not discussed in *Dear*. In fact *Dear* is an unsatisfactory decision. The court said that 'the concepts of *novus actus interveniens* and foreseeability' should not 'invade the criminal law', yet these concepts have been used for many years.

For a case where it was suggested that suicide could be triggered by the accused's wounding the victim, who was mentally fragile, see *Dhaliwal* [2006] EWCA Crim 1139, also known as *D*. The discussion was *obiter*. Further discussion of this case is in Chapter 12 on manslaughter.

The chain of causation is also broken by a completely voluntary act of the victim. This principle was, however, not applied by the Court of Appeal in *Kennedy* [1999] Crim LR 65, a much criticised decision. The accused prepared for the victim a syringe containing heroin and water. The victim knew the contents of the syringe and injected herself. She died. The court held that the accused had caused the victim's death and that he was guilty of manslaughter. The court stressed that the accused supplied the drug to the victim for immediate use. These facts constituted encouragement to the victim to inject herself. (The position, the court thought, would have been different if the supply was for later use and therefore there was no encouragement.) What it should have said was that the voluntary act of the victim was a *novus actus*; therefore, the accused did not cause the victim's death. What he did was to bring about the facts which were the setting for the death but, leaving aside cases on pollution, that is not sufficient to constitute a cause of death. This case looks like one where the judges considered the accused to be morally at fault and so they made him legally guilty.

Kennedy was referred by the Criminal Cases Review Commission to the Court of Appeal where it is reported as *Kennedy (No. 2)* [2005] 1 WLR 2159. The judgment of Lord Woolf CJ was very strange. He said that the parties were 'jointly engaged in administering the heroin' and therefore the accused caused the victim's death. This was novel law. Fortunately, the House of Lords strongly reasserted the primacy of the principle of 'free, deliberate and informed' intervention of the victim.

The House emphatically restored orthodoxy in *Kennedy (No. 2)* [2008] 1 AC 269. The facts are those of the *Kennedy* case mentioned above. The Court of Appeal asked the following question of general public importance: 'When is it appropriate to find someone guilty of manslaughter where that person has been involved in the supply of a . . . controlled drug, which is then freely and voluntarily self-administered by the person to whom it was supplied, and the administration then causes his death?' The Lords strongly and unanimously replied in a speech delivered by Lord Bingham: 'In the case of a fully informed and responsible adult, never'! The heroin was prepared by the accused and he passed the syringe to the victim, who then voluntarily self-administered the drug. The chain of causation was broken. Although scenarios existed where the accused could be said to have been jointly engaged in administering heroin, on the facts the accused had supplied the drug to the victim, who had a free choice whether to inject or not. There was no joint administration: 'the deceased . . . had a choice, knowing the facts, whether to inject himself or not. The heroin was, as the certified question correctly recognises, self-administered, not jointly administered.' Indeed, the Law Lords restricted liability in joint administration cases to rare facts: they overruled *Rogers* [2003] 1 WLR 1374, where the accused had tied the tourniquet on the victim's arm and the victim had then self-administered the injection. If such a case cannot be seen as one on joint administration, it will be seldom that there can be liability of the accused when he jointly administered the drug. Their Lordships did not deal with the strength of the drugs he was given or whether he could not 'just say no' to the drugs because he was an addict (in which case it is arguable that the taking of the drugs was not free or voluntary).

The House, while not wishing 'to throw any doubt' on the authority, also took the opportunity to restrict the *Empress* case, above, to facts involving environmental offences. In Lord Bingham's words, the case does not 'lay down any general rules governing causation in criminal law'. Again, orthodoxy has been restored, but with a policy-based exception: 'causation is not a single, unvarying concept to be mechanically applied without regard to the context in which the question arises.' There is therefore some room for argument as to whether the general *Kennedy (No. 2)* principle or the *Empress* exception applies. Indeed, there is some possibility of further debate because the Lords did not define why drugs manslaughter cases fall within the orthodox rule.

An example of 'free, deliberate and informed' intervention occurred in *Latif* [1996] 1 WLR 104 (HL). The accused was charged with importing heroin into the UK. The drugs were given to a British customs officer in Pakistan and he brought them into the jurisdiction.

The House of Lords held that the accused who had arranged for the heroin to be passed to a US Drugs Enforcement Administration officer who then passed them to the British officer was not guilty of the full offence, though he might have been guilty of the attempt to commit the full offence. Lord Steyn stated: 'The general principle is that the free, deliberate and informed intervention of a second person, who intends to exploit the situation created by the first, but is not acting in concert with him, is held to relieve the first actor of criminal responsibility.' The words from 'the free . . .' onwards are those of Hart and Honoré in *Causation in the Law*, though Lord Steyn omitted 'normally' before 'relieves'. This decision is inconsistent with the House of Lords ruling in the *Empress* case. In the latter case the act of a vandal should have broken the chain of causation. Instead the Lords held the defendants were liable for the vandal's act because such behaviour was not unforeseeable. Lord Nicholls in *Empress* may have confused the law on natural occurrences (where the test is one of reasonable foreseeability) and the law on third parties (where the test is one that 'free, deliberate and informed intervention' breaks the chain of causation). As stated above, the Lords in *Kennedy (No. 2)* restricted *Empress* to environmental offences.

An illustration of this area of law is medical malpractice. Beldam LJ in *Cheshire*, above, said that only 'in the most extraordinary and unusual case' would negligent treatment, even if the immediate cause of death, be so independent of the acts of the accused that it could be regarded in law as the cause of the victim's death to the exclusion of the accused's acts. The maltreatment must be 'so potent in causing death that [the jury] regard the contribution made by his acts as insignificant'. Medical negligence by itself will not break the chain of causation. It does so only if it is so 'extraordinary' that the maltreatment made the accused's acts insignificant in causing death. (This rule would seem to be one which protects medical staff from the consequences of their carelessness.) The jury should look at the consequences of the treatment, and not at its degree of fault. In *Cheshire* the trial judge had directed the jury in terms of the recklessness of the treatment. He should have instructed them to consider whether it was the cause of death to the exclusion of the accused's acts. The Court of Appeal's test may be difficult to apply. The jurors have to use their judgment to determine whether or not the carelessness was 'so potent', and on the same facts different juries may disagree, with the result that one defendant is guilty of murder or manslaughter, whereas another is acquitted. Similar criticism may be made of 'so independent' and 'extraordinary'. The issue becomes one of normative attributions, not 'but-for' causation. A further criticism of *Cheshire* is that at the time of the victim's death, the acts of the accused no longer were 'potent' enough to cause death. As the court said, it was the negligent treatment which was the 'immediate' cause of death. Nevertheless, the accused was guilty. Furthermore, the accused shot the victim in the chest and leg; death was caused by a reaction to the insertion of a tube in his windpipe to aid breathing. The immediate cause of death, therefore, was not the accused's act, yet the accused was guilty because he had made a 'significant contribution' to the death.

One of the rare instances where medical mistreatment did break the chain of causation was in the following case, *Jordan*.

Jordan (1956) 40 Cr App R 152 (CCA)

The accused stabbed the victim, but the wound had largely healed. However, while undergoing treatment, the victim was injected with a drug and a large quantity of liquid, and died. The accused was not guilty of murder, because the treatment was so abnormal and so negligent ('palpably wrong', according to Lord Parker CJ) that the wound was merely the scene of the cause of death, not the cause itself.

Jordan has been called 'a very particular case depending upon its exact facts': *Blaue*, above. This was an attempt to distinguish *Jordan* out of existence. In *Malcherek*, above, the court said that if it were obliged to choose between *Jordan* and *Smith*, it would choose the latter; it did, however, recognise that both cases remained good law. *Jordan* is therefore the exceptional case. Only if, as occurred in *Jordan*, the treatment was 'palpably wrong' will it be a *novus actus interveniens*. (It should be noted that the medical treatment in *Smith* was said to be 'thoroughly bad', which seems the same as 'palpably wrong', yet in *Smith* the accused was convicted.) *Jordan* has been criticised for placing emphasis on the actions of the medical staff when it is the accused, and not the staff, who is on trial. *Jordan* is not too dissimilar from *Cheshire*, yet in the latter case the accused was convicted but not in the former. Presumably the question to be asked after *Cheshire* should be phrased as not 'Was the treatment palpably wrong?' but 'Was it so independent of the acts of the accused and so potent in causing death that the contribution of those acts was insignificant?'

The basic rule in *Smith*, that medical mistreatment does not break the chain of causation, was applied in *Cheshire*, above. Similarly, in *Mellor* [1996] 2 Cr App R 245 (CA) the accused was guilty when the elderly victim of his beating up died of aspiration pneumonia, even though there had been a 90 per cent chance of his survival if he had been given oxygen, the correct treatment on the day that he died. The court held that the prosecution did not have to prove that the medical maltreatment was not a significant cause of death; it had to prove that what the accused did was a significant contribution to the death. *Cheshire* was followed: despite the fact that there seemed to be medical negligence, the accused was guilty. In the New Zealand High Court case of *Kirikiri* [1982] 2 NZLR 648 the accused *inter alia* battered his wife's face with a rifle. To help her breathe a plastic pipe was inserted by the hospital through her neck into her windpipe. Somehow the pipe became dislodged and the victim died. Jeffries J in the High Court applied *Smith*. The original wound was still the operating cause: 'death can properly be said to be the result of the wound, albeit that some other cause of death is also operating', as Lord Parker CJ put it in *Smith*.

An interesting application is *Malcherek*, where the doctors turned off the life-support system of patients who were already brain-dead. (Presumably the same applies to patients in a persistent vegetative state.) This act was held not to be the operative cause of death. The assault which put the victim into hospital was. Lord Lane CJ thought it bizarre to say that a doctor who was doing his or her best to save life was the cause of the victim's death. The courts seem to be pulling the law on causation to exculpate doctors and the police in order to catch the attacker.

If a pre-existing medical condition of the victim cannot be treated because of the accused's injuring him, the accused remains liable for his death unless, it seems, the refusal to operate was 'extraordinary and unusual': *McKechnie* (1992) 94 Cr App R 51 (CA). The victim's ulcer would have been treated, had he not been put into hospital by the accused beating him over the head with a TV set. It was immaterial whether the lack of treatment was correct, provided that it was reasonable as it was on the facts: the doctors thought the victim might die under anaesthesia. The case illustrates the principle that a person's death may have more than one cause. Alternatively, one might say that the immediate cause of death was the refusal to operate, but the operative cause of that immediate cause was what the accused did.

An interesting comparison is with the law relating to refusal of medical treatment. The accused takes the risk that the victim will not undergo treatment, but not of independent and potent maltreatment. A case like *McKechnie* is also important for demonstrating that an accused can be held to be the cause of a consequence even though he did not cause the death in medical terms. The medical cause was a duodenal ulcer which burst. The accused has no control over the doctor, yet liability can turn on the doctor's competence.

Finally on medical treatment, attention should be drawn to the issue of the competence of the doctors. If the victim dies through their gross negligence, is it just to say that the accused contributed significantly to the death and therefore he or she is guilty of murder or manslaughter? In any case, even if not guilty of a fatal offence, he will be guilty of a non-fatal offence.

One fact-situation which has not yet troubled the English courts is whether an omission by a third party may constitute a *novus actus*. It is thought that such an omission does not break the chain of causation because the accused's act remains a significant contribution to the death or injury. The third party may also be guilty of an offence, depending on the facts.

Students should not get too worked up about this area of law. The Latin term *novus actus interveniens* is merely shorthand for a full statement of the law. As the Court of Appeal said in **Kennedy** [1999] Crim LR 65: 'Whether one talks of *novus actus interveniens* or simply in terms of causation . . . the critical question to which the jury must direct its mind, where (as in the instant case) there is an act causative of death performed by in this case the deceased himself, is whether the defendant can be said to be jointly responsible for the carrying out of that act.' The same applies where a third party jointly performs an act leading to death.

(b) The 'escape' cases

These, sometimes known as 'fight or flight' cases, are illustrative of the problem of *novus actus interveniens*. The accused is guilty when the victim is killed trying to escape, unless the escape was not foreseeable by a reasonable person. There are several cases, the principal English one being **Mackie** (1973) 57 Cr App R 453 (CA). A three-year-old boy fell downstairs and died in an attempt to escape a thrashing. The accused was found guilty of manslaughter. See also the discussion of **Roberts** (1971) 56 Cr App R 95(CA) in the context of assault occasioning actual bodily harm, below. In **Roberts** the escape by a girl from a moving car (she suffered concussion and abrasions and had to stay in hospital for three days) as a result of sexual advances made by the accused was said to break the chain of causation only when it was voluntary and 'daft'. If 'the victim does something so "daft" . . . that no reasonable person could be expected to foresee it . . . then, it is really occasioned by a voluntary act on the part of the victim'. If the act is reasonably foreseeable the chain of causation is not broken. However, in some of the cases on drugs where the accused supplies the victim with heroin and paraphernalia, he has been held liable despite the victim's injection being voluntary, as we have seen. The accused was guilty if the escape was the 'natural result of what the alleged assailant said and did in the sense that it was something that could reasonably have been foreseen as the consequence of what he was doing or saying'.

Roch LJ in **Marjoram**, above, approved the *ratio* of **Roberts**. The chain of causation is broken only if the victim does something so unexpected that it is 'daft'. The Court of Appeal in **Evans** [1992] Crim LR 659 seems to have been asking for the escape to be a 'natural consequence' of the accused's behaviour. In **Corbett** [1996] Crim LR 594 (CA), the victim was a man with both learning difficulties and an alcohol problem. He argued with the accused with whom he had been drinking all day. The accused head-butted him without of course intending to kill him, and as he fled he fell into the gutter. He was struck and killed by a passing car. The accused argued that the jury should have been instructed to inquire whether the death of the victim was the natural consequence of his conduct and that he should have been acquitted if that death was not the natural consequence. The court also followed **Roberts**. As long as what the victim did was within the range of foreseeable actions, the chain of causation remained unbroken. Only if the victim's act was 'daft' was the chain broken. His disability and intoxication did not make his reaction daft. The prosecution did not have to prove that the death of the victim was *the* natural consequence of the accused's conduct. Accordingly, the accused's appeal was dismissed.

It is suggested that there are strong *dicta* in **Environment Agency v Empress Car Co (Abertillery) Ltd** [1999] 2 AC 22 (HL), discussed above, which should lead to the demise of the 'foreseeability' test. Lord Clyde stated (and Lord Hoffmann spoke to similar effect):

> In deciding whether some particular factor has played so important a part that any activity by the defendant should be seen as entirely superseded as a causative element, it is not a consideration of the foreseeability, or reasonable foreseeability, of the extraneous factor which seems to me to be appropriate, but rather its unnatural, extraordinary or unusual character.

It may be that the House of Lords was restricting its remarks to pollution cases (indeed, the Lords seem to be striving to prevent pollution). Lord Hoffmann in **Empress** said that when determining causation, the purpose of the law has to be ascertained. The purpose in this case was to stop pollution entering controlled waters. Therefore, a company which played a part in the pollution caused that event (as did the third party who opened the tap, thereby allowing diesel to run into a river). Normally one would expect the intervention of a third party to break the chain of causation. On the facts it was not extraordinary that an unknown third party would turn the tap on a tank containing diesel, allowing the fuel to pollute a river. Looking at the issue from a different angle, a third party could make the accused guilty of a crime by choosing to cause pollution. (Does a householder cause burglary by owning a home? It is foreseeable that burglary may take place in houses including this one.) And it may be hard to distinguish unforeseeable and extraordinary occurrences contrary to the view of the House of Lords. If **Empress** is correct, the intervention of a third party, including the victim, would not break the chain of causation except in extraordinary circumstances even when that third party acted in a 'free, deliberate and informed' manner. Such extensions to the law should not be made *ad hoc*, and require justifying.

There is no need to give an instruction on the test in **Roberts** where the facts do not call for it. For example, in **Notman** [1994] Crim LR 518 (CA), the accused, who had been banned from a shop, created a disturbance with others in it. A constable put out his foot to stop the accused charging at him and sustained an injury to his ankle. The accused was guilty of assault occasioning actual bodily harm. The case was an easy one, not requiring an elaborate direction on causation: the injury was caused by the defendant or it was not.

Whichever test English law adopts, the law will be flexible. Judges will be able to use concepts such as 'daft' and 'foreseeable' to convict those whom they wish to find guilty and to exonerate those whom they do not. In the **Roberts** case the victim jumped out of a car which was travelling fairly slowly when the accused tried to take off her coat as part of a sexual attack. If the vehicle had been travelling fast, it is thought that in the words of the court her jumping out would have been 'daft'. The result is that victims ought not to try to escape from sexual assault when the vehicle is being driven quickly, but are at liberty to escape from a slow-moving car. Yet in both situations the factual cause of the attempted escape is the accused's act, and the question whether the accused is guilty becomes one of legal policy. In terms of policy, the accused, it might be argued, should be guilty, no matter how fast the vehicle is going, for women should have the right to escape from sexual assaults in all situations and it is neither unforeseeable nor daft that they should do so.

It should also be stated that the reasonably foreseeable test in **Roberts** is out of line with the operative cause test in **Smith**, above, and that the court made no reference to **Smith**. Certainly English judges, who may not have seen that they were faced in the cases with different tests, have not chosen which one should govern. Indeed, in **Williams** [1992] 1 WLR 380 (CA), Stuart-Smith LJ said that the accused was guilty if the deceased victim's attempted escape from a moving car travelling at some 30 mph was 'proportionate to the threat, that is to say, that it was within the ambit of reasonableness and not so daft as to make it his own voluntary act which amounted to a *novus actus interveniens'*. In judging whether the victim acted reasonably in trying to flee from an attempted robbery, the jury were to take into account 'any particular characteristic of the victim and the fact that in the agony of the moment he may act without thought and deliberation'. (Similar is **Marjoram**, above.) **Williams** was followed in **Lewis** [2010] EWCA Crim 151. The accused was driving in the early morning when a group of students crossed the road in front of him. One of them struck his car. The accused got out, pushing one of the students, a woman. Her brother, the victim, then intervened. The accused chased him into the road, where he was killed by a car. The trial judge asked the jury whether the running away might have been one of the responses to be expected of the victim. The Court of Appeal ruled that in an escape case it had to be proved that but for the accused's act the victim would not have tried to flee the scene and therefore death would not have occurred. The Court approved the judge's use of ordinary language to explain the legal test of reasonable foreseeability and they opined that the tests of 'wholly disproportionate' and 'daft' were the same as that test.

While the jury is to bear in mind the victim's characteristics, they must not take into consideration the accused's characteristics. The test is a 'reasonable person' one, not one which, as in the new defence of loss of control which in 2010 replaced provocation, involves a reasonable or ordinary person imbued with most of the characteristics of the accused. Presumably characteristics include both characteristics which are visible (e.g. gender) and those which are not (e.g. mental illness). The law remains uncertain.

There may be a difference between a range-of-reasonable-responses test as in this case and a no-reasonable-man-could-be-expected-to-foresee-the-victim's-act test in **Roberts**. On the facts of **Williams**, though the conviction for manslaughter was quashed, it is not easy to see whether the victim acted reasonably. He was dead, and the three defendants' statements were not uniform as to the threat which they made to him. Without knowing the nature of the threat, the jury could not say whether the reaction was daft or proportionate. The contrast with cases concerned with the rule that one takes one's victim as one finds him is obvious. In the latter type of case one does not inquire whether the victim's behaviour, such as refusing a blood transfusion, was 'daft', whereas in the escape cases an overreaction caused by the accused's overtimidity breaks the chain of causation.

(c) Indivisible transactions

The general rule is that 'the intent and the act must both concur to constitute the crime': **Fowler v Padget** (1798) 101 ER 1103, 1106 (Kenyon CJ). There is no defence where a series of actions culminate in death and are classified by the court as being inseparable. (See also the section on contemporaneity.) The authority establishing this point was **Thabo Meli v R** [1954] 1 All ER 373. The acts of rendering the victim unconscious and pushing him over a cliff at the bottom of which he died of exposure were classified by the Privy Council as being indivisible. The accused were guilty of murder even though the actual cause of death was not their act. That case was followed in **Church** [1966] 1 QB 59 by the Court of Criminal Appeal. Unlike in **Thabo Meli** there was no antecedent plan – to throw the female victim into the river – but **Thabo Meli** was extended from murder to manslaughter. **Thabo Meli** was also followed in **Moore** [1975] Crim LR 229 (CA), where the defendants apparently intended only to assault, not to kill. The first accused had a grudge against the victim and arranged a meeting with him. The second defendant accompanied the first. They took with them breeze-blocks, a plastic bag and a length of rope. The victim got into a van and the first accused knocked him unconscious with a truncheon. The first defendant thought he had killed him. He weighted him with the breeze-blocks and threw him into a harbour, where he died of drowning. Both defendants were found guilty of murder.

A case which applied the *Thabo Meli* principle was *Le Brun* [1992] QB 61 (CA). During an argument the accused struck his wife on the jaw, causing her to sink to her knees. He dropped her while trying to drag her into the house. She died of a fractured skull. The accused had battered her but did not intend seriously to hurt her. He had not dropped her intentionally. The court held that he had caused her death and took the view that the blow, dropping the victim, and the death were all part of the same transaction. Accordingly, the principle of indivisible transactions applies outside of the area of disposal of a supposed corpse. Under *Thabo Meli* it was sufficient that the accused had the *mens rea* of the crime, in this case manslaughter, at the start of the sequence of events. Alternatively the court adopted the first principle stated above, that when the accused dropped his wife there was no break in the chain of causation which prevented the blow being the cause of death. Death was reasonably foreseeable. The court thought that if the accused had been trying to help his wife into the house to make her better, the dropping might have been a *novus actus interveniens*. As things were, his action was an attempt to conceal his attack on her, or the completion of his argument with her. On this point the court confused motive and causation. It said that if the accused had a good motive, seeking medical help, he was not liable because he did not cause her death; if, however, he picked her up with a bad motive, such as concealing his attack on her, he was guilty, for then he would have caused her death. The reasoning makes the accused's state of mind relevant to causation but the rule is that causation forms part of the *actus reus*. (Presumably he was also guilty of gross negligence manslaughter. His dropping of her was grossly negligent, if the jury so held. If this supposition is correct, there was no need to argue about the intention to batter and the cause of death being separate in time, for under this type of manslaughter they were contemporaneous.)

Current authorities are concerned with homicide, but the principles apply to other offences.

(d) Refusal of medical treatment

An old case is *Holland* (1841) 2 Mood & R 351. The victim refused treatment for a wound to the finger and died of tetanus. The accused was convicted of murder at Liverpool Assizes on the grounds that the wound was the ultimate cause of death. The same applies where the victim will not undergo treatment for religious or psychological reasons. The most authoritative case is *Blaue*, above, where a Jehovah's Witness refused a blood transfusion. The Court of Appeal held that the accused must take his victim as he finds him (see (e) below), a proposition similar to the eggshell skull rule in tort. Therefore, it was the stab wound which caused the victim's death. Lawton LJ said: 'The fact that the victim refused to stop this end coming about did not break the causal connection between the act and death.' The court rejected the argument that since medical treatment had improved in the years since *Holland*, the law in that case had also changed. It might be said that *Blaue* exemplifies English law's policy of religious freedom. It is not to the point that the victim's refusal was unreasonable. This rule distinguishes this area of law from the 'escape cases' discussed above. To make the attacker guilty of murder, could the victim refuse to have a tourniquet applied, an unlikely but possible scenario? Why should an accused be guilty of murder when the victim unreasonably refuses to seek medical attention? Why is the refusal not a *novus actus interveniens* when very poor treatment may be? Should the accused

be guilty even though he did not foresee, and a reasonable person would not have foreseen, the refusal? Why should liability for homicide depend on whether the victim refuses
to look after himself?

(e) The accused must take his victim as he finds him

> ### Example
>
> Celia attacks David with a broom handle. She hits him over the head and he dies.
> Unknown to everyone including the accused and deceased he had a thin skull; he would
> not have died if his skull had been of normal thickness. She is charged with his man-
> slaughter. Did she cause his death?
>
> Here the principle to apply is that the accused must take his victim as he finds her;
> indeed, this principle is often known as the 'thin-skull' rule. If one applies this principle,
> Celia does cause David's death. *Blaue* [1975] 3 All ER 446 (CA) is the obvious authority,
> though it does deal with religion and not physical fragility. (Jehovah's Witness refused
> a blood transfusion in accordance with the tenets of her religion. HELD: her attacker
> caused her death even though he did not know of her religion and reasonable people
> would not have reasonably foreseen (without knowing of her religion) that she would have
> refused a transfusion.)
>
> It should be noted that the principle may lead to different results from the one stated
> under *novus actus interveniens*, above. It may well not be reasonably foreseeable that the
> victim had a thin skull.
>
> This type of homicide where the accused does not have the *mens rea* for murder
> is known as manslaughter and it is a form of manslaughter called unlawful act (or
> constructive) manslaughter.

This rule of causation is sometimes called the **'eggshell skull' rule** (also known as the thin-
skull rule) and is the same as in tort. If, for example, the victim had a thin skull and no one
including the accused knew of this fact, if the victim dies as a result of the accused's hitting
her over the head with a baseball bat but she would not have died, had she not had a thin
skull, then the accused is deemed to be responsible for the death, even though he did not
know of the thinness of the skull (and even though a reasonable person would not have
known). As we can see from *Blaue*, the case of the Jehovah's Witness who refused a blood
transfusion in conformity with her religion, the rule is not restricted to physical condition
(such as haemophilia) but most situations will in practice involve the physical well-being
of the victim where she is in a poor state of health. Presumably the rule may be extended
to a situation where a woman, on being raped, kills herself: see also *Dear*, discussed above.
Certainly the accused must act at his peril where the victim has a pre-existing mental condition such as depression. It is questionable whether or not the principle applies where
it is a third party who is the immediate cause of death, such as would happen where an
infant's parent or guardian who was a Jehovah's Witness refused a blood transfusion for
him. If the principle in *Blaue* is not applied because it leads to unfair outcomes, the
accused is still guilty of attempted murder and wounding with intent to cause grievous
bodily harm. For criticism of *Blaue* see Glanville Williams' casenote [1976] CLJ 15 where
he said that the authorities *Blaue* applied were out of date because they came from an era
when medical treatment was dangerous and that it was absurd to punish an accused for
homicide when the victim had unreasonably refused treatment. Contrariwise, freedom
of religion is one of the rights under the European Convention on Human Rights (see

Chapter 1), and it can be argued that the refusal of a transfusion is not a *novus actus* because the victim did not act in a free, deliberate and informed way because the victim was subject to the demands of her religion.

A justification for the rule was put forward by McLachlin J in the Supreme Court of Canada in **Creighton** (1993) 105 DLR (4th) 632. She said that the eggshell skull rule 'requires aggressors, once embarked on their dangerous course of conduct which may foreseeably injure others, to take responsibility for all the consequences that ensue, even to death'. Current law stops the court, rightly many think, from investigating the merits of religious beliefs. Although the scenario is unlikely, if the victim refused a transfusion out of spite towards the accused, the latter would still on these principles have caused the death of the former.

It is arguable that, though the accused has factually caused death (because the transfusion issue would not otherwise have arisen), death ought not to be legally ascribed to him. Hart and Honoré, *Causation in the Law*, 2nd edn (OUP, 1985) 332, consider that a person who refuses a transfusion on religious grounds is not acting voluntarily because of the pressure of his religion. Therefore, they argue that the spiteful victim is acting voluntarily. They contend, as already indicated, that the chain of causation is broken by 'a free, deliberate and informed act of a human being' (at 136). The epithets are, it may be said, to some extent normative and not purely descriptive. 'Voluntary' and 'involuntary' are, however, chameleon words, and if the accused is deemed to take his victim as he finds him, why cannot he find him spiteful and so be guilty? Is a person of a certain religious persuasion acting freely if she refuses a blood transfusion? Applying **Cheshire** the eggshell skull is 'independent' of the act of the accused and the accused should have been guilty. Moreover, if the accused in **Blaue** had to take his victim as he found her, why does not the same rule apply to the speeding motorist who is sexually assaulting a passenger (see **Roberts**, above)? These rules, both of which turn on the victim's response, are inconsistent.

For this reason it is impossible to assert that there is a single doctrine of causation. An eggshell skull is not reasonably foreseeable. It may not be reasonably foreseeable for a woman to kill herself after being raped but, following **Blaue**, the rapist would be guilty of manslaughter. **Blaue** has the potential to swallow the rule in **Roberts**. One possibility is that the accused does not take a 'daft' victim as he finds him. An example would occur if the victim thought that cancer could be caught by breathing her cancerous attacker's exhalations. Another attempt to reconcile **Blaue** and **Roberts** is to say that in **Blaue** the victim refused to act whereas in **Roberts** the victim did act, and therefore the distinction turns on whether there is an act or an omission. Alternatively if the victim must react reasonably in escape cases, why not in cases of refusing treatment? A linked argument is that if a daft escape breaks the chain of causation, why does not a voluntary decision not to have a transfusion break it? Surely it would have been broken if the victim had refused treatment because she did not like the colour of the hospital walls? Another way of reconciling **Blaue** and **Roberts** is to argue that **Blaue** is a special case concerned with freedom of religion. See D. Klimchuk, 'Causation: thin skulls and equality' (1998) 11 Can JL&J 115. It is suggested that the 'take your victim' test should not apply where the outcome would offend common sense; therefore, if the victim has acted in a 'daft' manner the accused should not be guilty of the offence charged, though he may still be guilty of a lesser offence or of the attempt. It is also suggested that whether the victim has a weak heart, refuses blood transfusions and the like, does not affect the accused's moral culpability.

This area of law can be usefully compared with that of negligent medical treatment. The accused takes the doctor as he finds him; that is, the competence of the doctor is (normally) irrelevant to criminal liability, just as the victim's personality is immaterial.

(f) Contributory negligence

The fact that the victim was contributorily negligent in causing her own death does not absolve the accused from criminal liability. In **Swindall and Osborne** (1846) 2 Cox CC 141 the victim was run over and killed by one of the two defendants. The jury was instructed that it did not matter whether the deceased was deaf, drunk or careless and whether his being so contributed to his death. If, however, the **contributory negligence** is gross, the chain of causation may be broken, gross negligence being seen as a *novus actus* (see above).

Difficulties of proof in causation

One can see the difficulty in proving causation and the effect of such a failure in **Fisher**.

Fisher [1987] Crim LR 334 (CA)

The defendant, a nightclub bouncer, intervened in a fight involving the victim. The bouncer banged the victim's head several times on the stairs while dragging him down them. By the time they got to the bottom of the stairs, the victim was dead. If death was partly caused by dragging the victim downstairs the accused was guilty of manslaughter. If, however, the victim was killed by a blow landed by the accused in self-defence, he was not guilty. Since the prosecution could not prove the former, the Court of Appeal ruled that the accused was not guilty.

Similar is **Bunn** (1989) *The Times*, 11 May. The defendant hit the victim over the head with a snooker cue. Perhaps as a result, the victim developed a mental disease and committed suicide over three months later. The prosecution abandoned its case because it was not sure that a reasonable jury would convict because it was uncertain whether the blow caused the death. In **Evans** [1992] Crim LR 659 (CA), the Crown could not prove that the accused's behaviour caused the victim to jump out of the window to his death. Where the victim has committed suicide, it may be particularly problematic to attribute the victim's death to the accused.

Proposals for the reform of causation

In the Law Commission's draft Criminal Code, Law Com. No. 177, 1989, cl 17 reads in part:

1 . . . a person causes a result which is an element of an offence when . . .
   (a) he does an act which makes a more than negligible contribution to its occurrence; or
   (b) he omits to do an act which might prevent its occurrence and which he is under a duty to do according to the law relating to the offence.

2 A person does not cause a result where, after he does such an act or makes such an omission, an act or event occurs . . .
   (a) which is the immediate and sufficient cause of the result;
   (b) which he did not foresee, and
   (c) which could not in the circumstances reasonably have been foreseen.

In its commentary the Law Commission (p 188) showed that it wished to restate present law in relation to causation-in-fact, taking one's victim as one finds him, intervening acts including the escape cases, medical mistreatment including the principle in **Jordan**, above, and the refusal of treatment. The restatement does not readily demonstrate that the choice of the act is an essentially normative exercise, not a factual one. A cause is selected and attributed to the accused or it is not. Current law is sometimes criticised for not being a straightforward application of scientific principles, but it is doubtful that one could reach the stage where science alone solves causation problems. Causation-in-fact is not sufficient by itself, and to say that the accused caused something is not necessarily a statement of fact. One might say that the accused was guilty in *Smith* only because the brawl was in Germany, a fortuitous circumstance, where treatment was at that time poor, another fortuitous circumstance, and of course neither the UK nor the (then) West German government was put on trial for not providing a good standard of medical care. For criticism of the scope of cl 17(2) see Glanville Williams '*Finis* for *novus actus*' [1989] CLJ 391. Certainly phrases such as 'negligible' and 'immediate and sufficient' are open to interpretation.

Omission

Example

Eric, aged 35, has become a drug addict. He has lost his home, his wife and his children and has moved in with a fellow junkie, Freda. One evening he injects himself with heroin and becomes unconscious in her presence. Construct scenarios in which she will be subject to liability for failing to preserve his life.

1 She is his mother or other (close) relative. See the position of the male accused, the brother, in *Stone and Dobinson* [1977] QB 354 (CA).
2 She has undertaken a duty to act, as did the female defendant, the brother's mistress, in that case. She may, as in *Ruffell* [2003] EWCA Crim 122, have sought to revive him, put him next to a radiator and covered him with towels for warmth, and placed him by an open window so that he could breathe more easily.

While over the past forty or so years criminal liability for omissions has expanded through the creation of more instances of liability (cf. the dates of the major authorities such as *Dytham* [1969] QB 722 (CA) and *Miller* [1983] 2 AC 161 (HL)), there must still be a heading under which the accused fits and the crime must be one which may be committed by an omission. Note that to be guilty of any crime the accused must also have the requisite *mens rea* and that she must cause the requisite outcome such as death or injury.

One must be careful when translating *actus reus* into English. It looks like 'guilty act'. However, the accused may also be guilty when he fails or omits to do something (**omission**). If in orthodox theory the criminal law imposes a duty to act and the accused does not perform that act, he is guilty. There has to be a duty to act; otherwise all who did nothing would cause the *actus reus* to happen. English law traditionally does not always hold a person guilty for failing to act. There are exceptional cases where the accused is liable provided that he has the requisite *mens rea*. These exceptions have grown in recent years, and there is no closed list of exceptions, but the principle remains that generally a person is not guilty for omitting to do something.

Generations of law students have been thrilled by the spine-chilling tale of individuals watching a small child drown in an inch of water . . .

is how C. Ryan, *Criminal Law*, 4th edn (Blackstone Press, 1995) 45, put it. Yet a parent is guilty if he lets his child drown in such circumstances. (Whether a child would have the *actus reus* of murder if he let his parent drown in similar circumstances is more debatable.) It should not be thought that omissions are always less serious than commissions. Starving a person to death may be more morally unacceptable than mercy-killing. Nevertheless, Anglo-Welsh criminal law draws a distinction between an act (such as stabbing) and an omission (such as not feeding a baby). This distinction is based on the view that a hard-and-fast line can be drawn between an act and an omission, which was the prevalent view until recently among the judiciary: see Phillimore LJ in *Lowe* [1973] QB 702 (CA). The case is one on constructive manslaughter and the court held that the crime could be committed only when the accused acted, and not when he did not act but omitted to act.

The general rule is exemplified by *Wychavon DC* v *National Rivers Authority* [1993] 1 WLR 125 (DC). The Council was charged with causing polluted matter to enter any controlled water contrary to the Water Act 1989, s 107(1)(c). Watkins LJ held that failing to prevent or to take steps to clear a blockage in a system for which it was responsible did not constitute the offence. There was no positive or deliberate act which caused the sewage to enter the river. This decision turns on the construction of the statute, 'causes or knowingly permits': normally 'causes' does include both acts and omissions. (Possibly the case itself would nowadays be decided differently: see, *inter alia*, *National Rivers Authority* v *Yorkshire Water Services Ltd* [1995] 1 AC 444 (HL); however, the principle of no liability for omissions stands.) The position would have been different had the council been charged with knowingly permitting polluted matter to enter controlled waters: *Environment Agency* v *Empress Car Co (Abertillery) Ltd* [1999] 2 AC 22 (HL), discussed above under Causation. 'Mere tacit standing by and looking on' is not 'causing': *Price* v *Cromack* [1975] 1 WLR 988 (DC). One can permit something to happen by failing to prevent it. This aspect of the case falls within (b) below.

The established exceptions are now detailed. In all cases it must be remembered that the accused must also have the *mens rea* for the offence.

Points (a)–(d) detail offences which may be committed by an omission. Points (e)–(i) state when a person is under a duty to act in relation to those offences, which are normally committed by an act, but which are capable of being committed by an omission, failing to intervene. The list of situations where a legal duty to act is imposed is not closed: *Khan* [1998] Crim LR 830 (CA). It is normally said that it is for the judge to rule whether such a duty exists but in *Khan* it was held that whether a duty of care was owed by a drug dealer to his client was a matter of fact which depended on the circumstances. It is suggested that *Khan* is wrong. Juries cannot expand and contract the various duties to act.

(a) Because of legislative supremacy Parliament can change the general law that a person is not guilty for omitting to do something. Statute has created offences which can be committed only by omissions, such as dishonestly retaining a wrongful credit contrary to s 24A of the Theft Act 1968 as inserted by the Theft (Amendment) Act 1996, failing to prevent bribery by a person associated with a commercial organisation contrary to the Bribery Act 2010 (in force 1 July 2011), and failing to produce a breath specimen. Usually liability is imposed on a certain type of person, such as an occupier or a driver. A person may be guilty of the offence of failing to report a traffic accident in which he was involved and which caused injury or damage: Road Traffic Act 1988, s 170. A failure to look after one's child is an offence under the Children and Young Persons Act 1933, s 1(1). This is the crime of wilful neglect which is discussed in the next chapter. In each of these offences it should be noted on whom the duty is imposed: masters or seamen, drivers and parents. Passers-by are not liable. The duty is restricted to a certain class of persons. A failure to disclose information relating to terrorism is a crime contrary to the Terrorism Act 2000, s 20, if the information comes to the accused in the course of his trade, profession, business or employment and he does not disclose it to the police as soon as reasonably practicable. The width of the duty depends on construction and may include the whole world, as this statute demonstrates.

(b) In some offences the language of the statute can be read as imposing liability for not doing something. One permits one's drivers to break the law if one does not take reasonable steps to prevent breaches: *Vehicle Inspectorate* v *Nuttall* [1999] 1 WLR 629 (HL). One is guilty of handling by 'assisting in the retention' of stolen goods when one leaves stolen money in one's Post Office account: *Pitchley* (1972) 57 Cr App R 30 (CA). Similarly one can obstruct the highway by not removing a collapsed wall after being given notice to remove it: *Gully* v *Smith* (1883) 12 QBD 121. In *Firth* (1990) 91 Cr App R 217 (CA) a doctor deceived by non-disclosure of the true facts. Another case is *Shama* [1990] 1 WLR 661 (CA). The accused was guilty of the crime of falsifying a document required for an accounting purpose contrary to s 17(1)(a) of the Theft Act 1968 when he failed to fill in a form, it being his duty to do so. On the wording of the crime it is, however, difficult to say that he falsified a document when he did nothing. He would certainly on the wording have been found guilty, had he completed the form but failed to supply a material statement. What was wrong about the discussion was that the words do not penalise a person who has not completed the form at all. In *Greener* v *DPP* (1996) 160 JP 265 the Divisional Court held that the crime of allowing a dangerous dog to enter a place which is not a public place, but where it is not permitted to be, covered a failure by the accused to take adequate precautions to secure the dog to a chain with the effect that it broke out of his back garden and bit the face of a child who was in a garden nearby. Some verbs can therefore be read as including failures to act. See 'causing' in (c) below.

There are a couple of problematical cases. In *Speck* [1977] 2 All ER 859, the Court of Appeal held that the accused was guilty of gross indecency (since repealed) when he failed to prevent a child doing such an act with him and he did not move away. A young girl had placed her hand on his penis. He had an erection. He was found guilty under s 1 of the Indecency with Children Act 1960. That statute required an 'act of gross indecency'. The court decided that his failure to remove the girl's hand, an omission, was an invitation to her to undertake the act. Therefore, there was an act. This interpretation in view of the facts looks like stretching words to catch the accused. In *Yuthiwattana* (1984) 80 Cr App R 55, the Court of Appeal held that a failure to replace a key amounted to an act calculated to interfere with a tenant's peace and comfort contrary to the Protection from Eviction Act 1977, s 1(3). It may be that the court did not see the point at issue.

In *Ahmad* (1986) 84 Cr App R 64, the same court determined that failure to provide a bathroom was not an act calculated to interfere with peace and comfort. Failing to complete repairs was not an 'act'. The words in the statute creating the offence were clear, and statutes creating crimes should be strictly construed. If Parliament had wanted to include omissions, it should have said so. *Ahmad* would seem to lay down a general rule of criminal law that where a statute states 'act', that term cannot be construed as including an omission. For further discussion in the context of attempts see Chapter 10. The court in *Ahmad* distinguished *Miller* [1983] 2 AC 161 (HL), see below, on the grounds that *Miller* did not apply where a statute expressly required an act. The accused in *Ahmad* was under no duty to act as the accused was in *Miller* because by its words the statute did not impose such an obligation. However, if one uses the so-called 'continuing (or continuous) act' theory one can find support for convicting the accused in *Ahmad*. He is guilty if he intentionally does an act and fails to take reasonable measures to prevent the *actus reus*. The situation is deemed to be an intentional act. Accordingly it may depend on which theory of omissions one uses to see whether the accused is guilty. Lord Diplock in *Miller* chose the duty theory on the ground that it was simpler than the other to explain to juries. A different court might be persuaded to adopt the continuous act theory if it wished to convict the accused. However that may be, *Yuthiwattana* seems incorrect. Parliament stipulated 'act'. If what the accused did cannot sensibly be described as an 'act', he should not be guilty.

It is thought that some offences cannot be construed as imposing criminal liability for omissions. It is impossible to conceive of a person's committing robbery (s 8 of the Theft Act 1968) or burglary (s 9) by omission. One might have expected that it would be impossible to rape by omission because rape involves penetration, but the Privy Council held on appeal from New Zealand in *Kaitamaki v R* [1985] AC 147 that a man could rape when he did not withdraw on request. This advice related to the pre-2003 definition of rape but the same law continues to apply under the Sexual Offences Act 2003, for the accused is guilty only if he 'penetrates the vagina, anus or mouth of another person with his penis'. For further discussion see Chapter 14.

(c) Sometimes the courts construe common law or statutory offences as imposing liability for omissions. If one part of the *actus reus* of murder and manslaughter is 'causing death' (rather than 'killing' which seems more to require a positive act, though one can 'kill' by an omission), one can cause death by failing to prevent death occurring. For more on this see gross negligence manslaughter (Chapter 12), but unlawful act manslaughter cannot be committed by an omission: *Lowe* [1973] QB 702 (CA). 'Causing' is therefore sometimes read as requiring an act (see *Wychavon*, above) but sometimes as covering an omission. It is suggested that it is construed in the latter sense when the *actus reus* is defined solely in terms of 'causing' something to happen, but in the former sense the offence consists of 'causing or permitting'; 'permitting' covers a failure to act but here 'causing' does not. This was the view of the House of Lords in *Environment Agency v Empress Car Co (Abertillery) Ltd*, above.

Since death may be caused by omission, so also may the lesser statutory offence of causing grievous bodily harm with intent contrary to s 18 of the Offences Against the Person Act 1861. 'Inflict' and 'wound' are debatable. It used to be said that 'inflict' requires an assault, which apparently can be committed only by an act, but the House of Lords in *Wilson* [1984] AC 242 held that an assault was not an essential element in inflicting grievous bodily harm. It is not certain whether other non-fatal offences, be they common law or statutory, may be committed by omission. The Court of Appeal in *Fagan v MPC* [1969] 1 QB 439 held that a battery (and therefore too assault occasioning actual bodily harm which requires an assault or a battery) could not be committed by an omission (the case is now regarded as one which falls within (h) below, though the *ratio* of the court was that what the accused did when he unwittingly parked his car on a police officer's booted foot was an act, a continuing act, and not a failure to move the car) but in *DPP v K* [1990] 1 WLR 1067 the Divisional Court did not doubt that assault (a term which includes battery) occasioning actual bodily harm could be committed by failing to clean out a hand drier into which the accused had poured acid. The situation was analogous to setting a trap into which the victim fell. If liability for a battery needs an act, it is strange that the much more serious offence of murder can be committed by an act or omission. If one took this principle too far, one would undermine the general principle that one is not liable for omission. For that reason the courts' restriction that there has to be a duty impedes the development of liability for homicide where one has omitted to save the victim. There are also problems with the width of causation in such cases, in that potentially a lot of people could be guilty of homicide. A simpler example of a common law offence is cheating the Revenue by failing to provide a tax return: *Mavji* [1987] 2 All ER 758 (CA).

(d) A rare common law offence committable by omission is misprision of treason. If a person fails to report treason to the authorities, he is guilty of this crime. It is also a common law offence to fail to assist a constable when he calls for assistance. It is suggested that the accused would not be guilty if he had a lawful excuse or if helping was physically impossible. There are, therefore, very few common law offences of omission, and in practice neither of the two mentioned has been used for many years.

(e) Liability is imposed for failing to perform a duty one has undertaken voluntarily. The more one does, the more likely it is that one will be liable for an omission. In other words, no duty will arise if the accused refused to accept the obligation to take care of another but it will arise if he does so and performs it poorly. The old authority is *Instan* [1893] 1 QB 450, where a niece had failed in her duty to look after an aunt. Lord Coleridge in the Court for Crown Cases Reserved said that the accused:

> . . . was under a moral obligation to the deceased from which arose a legal duty towards her; that legal duty the prisoner has wilfully and deliberately left unperformed with the consequence that there has been an acceleration of the death of the deceased owing to the non-performance of that legal duty.

A more modern case with the same result is one which Lord Mustill in *Airedale NHS Trust v Bland* [1993] AC 789 (HL) called troubling. *Stone and Dobinson* [1977] QB 354 has grisly facts and an uncertain *ratio*. The Court of Appeal held a man and his mistress guilty of manslaughter when the victim died after they had failed to summon medical attention. The man was deaf, blind, and had learning difficulties; the woman was described as inadequate and ineffective. The man was the brother of the victim (liability, however, was not based by the court on the blood relationship). The victim gave the male accused £1.50 a week towards her rent, but liability was not based on contract, as to which, see (f) below. They lived in the same house. The female accused had tried to look after the victim by leaving food for her to eat, calling for a doctor and washing her. She, the court held, had thereby undertaken an obligation to care for the victim. (However, only if she had embarked on looking after the sister would she have been found guilty.) The victim had paid money towards the rent, but the case was not decided on the contractual approach noted below – and one cannot really see the court imposing liability on absent landlords to look after their tenants. Since the accused persons were, at the least, lacking in intelligence and could not use a telephone, presumably the law is that one must act as a reasonable person would have acted, not as a person of limited intelligence and so on would have acted. This point presumably applies to the remaining exceptions.

It is unclear law as to how the defendants could have terminated their duty to look after the deceased. Perhaps it would have been sufficient for one of them to inform the social worker who came to see the male accused's son. Moreover, the victim refused to eat properly and could not use a phone. Did this fact release the accused from their obligation? Certainly, according to current law the free, deliberate and informed conduct of the deceased would have broken the chain of causation (see the discussion of *Kennedy (No. 2)* above).

Moreover, had the female accused really undertaken to look after the victim? She had undertaken various tasks which had benefited the victim but there was no promise along the lines of: 'I will look after you.' Another criticism of *Stone and Dobinson* is that the female accused would not have been liable, had she done nothing: her doing a few things for the deceased made her liable. Does the law therefore encourage people *not* to volunteer? Finally, the defendants would not have been found guilty if they had refused to let the victim stay in their house. To make them guilty when they were doing their (inadequate) best seems almost cruel. The defendants could hardly look after themselves, never mind the male defendant's sister (or his mentally ill son).

A father was found not guilty in *Lowe*, above: Phillimore LJ drew a line for the purposes of the crime of unlawful act manslaughter between an omission, even a deliberate one, such as failing to call a doctor, and commission. The case has been criticised for drawing this distinction because it is not always clear what is an act and what is an omission. For example, if I stop feeding a patient from a naso-gastric tube, do I withdraw treatment or do I omit to feed? Morally, we might also agree that starving one's child to death may be worse than killing her in one blow, but the law's distinction is the other way round.

See Figure 12.3 in Chapter 12 for a diagram illustrating constructive (unlawful act) manslaughter.

A more recent case than *Stone and Dobinson* is *Ruffell* [2003] EWCA Crim 122. The victim had injected a mixture of cocaine and heroin at the accused's house. He had become ill during the night, lapsed into unconsciousness, and the accused had tried to revive him. The next morning the accused put the victim outside of his house where he died from opiate intoxication and hypothermia. It was held that the jury could on the facts find that the accused had assumed a duty of care. The victim was a guest in his house and the accused had tried to revive him by splashing water on his face, putting him next to a radiator for warmth, putting him by an open window for air, and covering him in towels.

This head of liability might be extended in the future to cover, for example, joint participation in dangerous sports such as potholing. The Court of Appeal in *Khan* [1998] Crim LR 830 left open the possibility of a drug dealer's owing a duty to summon medical assistance to a person who had fallen into a coma as a result of taking heroin he had supplied. One difficulty, which was not discussed, was whether a duty can arise out of an illegal situation. The defendants were guilty of supplying drugs, the victim of possessing them. It is suggested, however, that this obstacle is not insuperable. In other areas of law such as illegal contracts the courts do take account of unlawful behaviour. (*Khan* can also be seen as an application of the *Miller* principle discussed at (h) below.) The Court of Appeal held in *Sinclair* [1998] NLJ 1353 that an attempt to assist the victim does not *per se* give rise to liability. On the facts, however, the accused did owe a duty of care to the victim. Rose LJ said:

> . . . [the accused] was a close friend of the deceased for many years and the two had lived together almost as brothers. It was Sinclair who paid for and supplied the deceased with the first dose of methadone and helped him to obtain the second dose. He knew that the deceased was not an addict. He remained with the deceased throughout the period of his unconsciousness and, for a substantial period, was the only person with him. . . . [T]here was . . . material on which the jury . . . could have found that Sinclair owed the deceased a legal duty of care.

A person who came to the victim's house and prepared methadone, a controlled drug, did not owe him a duty of care even though he had made 'a desultory attempt to be of assistance' to the dying victim.

One problematical question concerns whether, and if so how, a person can give up a duty once he has undertaken it. Must one tell, for instance, the Department of Social Security that one is going to stop looking after an elderly relative several weeks in advance? Another question concerns how far, once one has voluntarily embarked on a duty, one must perform it. If the rescue of a fellow potholer is dangerous, must a person nevertheless attempt it? Is one obliged to spend all one's money looking after the relative? Is it sufficient merely to call for the doctor or must one provide the best expertise? If the answer is to do what is reasonable for the accused in all the circumstances including any risk of danger, *Stone and Dobinson* looks out of line, for they may have done the best they could. It is uncertain if the law is that the accused has to do what a reasonable person would have done, or that the reasonable person possesses the characteristics such as the lack of intelligence which afflicted the defendants in that case. Whichever rule it is, the court held that they fell short of the required standard.

(f) If one fails to perform a duty imposed by contract, one is guilty. The case always cited for this proposition is *Pittwood* (1902) 19 TLR 37 at Assizes. Wright J rejected the argument that the accused did not owe a duty to the victim, and spoke of 'gross and criminal negligence' when an employee of a railway company failed to open a level-crossing gate. He seemed to be implying that the case was not one for pure nonfeasance (not doing) but one of misfeasance (doing something wrongly). The accused opened the gate for road traffic. The victim's haywain came through and he was then killed because the accused had not closed the gate to trains. The accused therefore caused the accident through doing his job badly in not closing the gate having previously opened it. The contract need not be and was not in *Pittwood* owed to the victim. Presumably a lifeguard employed by a local authority at a pool or a seaside resort, or a doctor whether employed by the NHS or privately, would be guilty of manslaughter under this exception. This exception developed out of the one in (e) and *Instan* was cited as authority for liability arising *ex contractu*. It should be noted that *Pittwood* can nowadays be justified as a case falling within (h), below, creating a dangerous situation.

(g) Liability will be imposed if one fails to perform a duty imposed by law. Responsibility may arise out of a blood or marital relationship or be generated by common law in other ways. There is, for example, an offence called misconduct in public office. A police officer off duty was found guilty of this offence when he did not go to the rescue of a man being kicked to death by bouncers at a club: *Dytham* [1979] QB 722 (CA). The ambit of this duty is unclear. Does it apply to prison officers, doctors, nurses, St John Ambulance persons? Does it apply when the accused is not contractually bound to be on duty? *Dytham* suggests that the defendant will not be liable 'if the circumstances contain a greater danger than a man of ordinary firmness . . . may be expected to encounter'. Yet surely one would expect a police officer to go beyond what an ordinary person would do to save someone's life? In this era of AIDS would it be expected of anyone that he gives mouth to mouth resuscitation? There is as yet no solution to the problem of how much risk the accused has to run before he is absolved of the duty. *Dytham* also does not answer the question of whether a person is to be convicted when he starts out to help, finds the task too arduous, and stops. Does it matter that the intervention led others not to join in? A further criticism of *Dytham* is the difficulty in correctly labelling the accused's conduct. The facts do not in themselves suggest that he misconducted himself in a public office. An offence which looks closer to the facts is manslaughter, but there is a problem with causation. Not attempting to save the victim did not 'cause' the death of the victim: he would have died even if the constable were on holiday in Ibiza.

A more recent authority is *Singh* [1999] Crim LR 582 (CA). The appellant's father ran a boarding house. The appellant collected the rent and did the maintenance. While his father was away a complaint was made about a gas fire in one of the rooms. The appellant found nothing wrong. Ten days later another lodger in another room was killed by carbon monoxide poisoning. The court held that all of his roles had to be conglomerated and out of that conglomeration arose a duty of care. That duty could have been fulfilled by calling in expert help. But he had not done so. Therefore, by his omission he was guilty of gross negligence manslaughter. There was an obvious and serious risk of death, and the accused had caused the death. Causation in omissions is discussed below.

The main illustration of a duty imposed by law is the obligation of a parent to feed his young child. In *Gibbins and Proctor* (1918) 13 Cr App R 134, the Court of Criminal Appeal held the father guilty of murder when he starved his child to death. (The father's mistress was guilty under the principle in (e) above because she had accepted money to buy food.) This case demonstrates that an accused can be liable for an omission when he deliberately refused to act. Not all omissions signify a poor imagination or lack of sympathy. It is uncertain whether children owe reciprocal obligations to their parents. It is also unclear whether the father would have been guilty if the child had been a normal 16-year-old able to fend for himself. An old case is *Shepherd* (1862) 9 Cox CC 123 where it was held that a mother did not owe a duty to act to her 18-year-old daughter. There is old law that a brother does not owe a duty of care to his sister: *Smith* (1826) 172 ER 203. Much more recently it was held in *Evans* [2009] EWCA Crim 650 that a half-sister did not owe her half-sister a duty of care. It is uncertain whether students sharing a flat would be liable for failing to look after one of the flatmates. Liability may depend upon how close the relationship was. It is questionable whether the courts would find such a duty between cohabitees or even married couples living apart, but the exceptions for voluntary undertakings or contract could apply.

It is unclear how far 'special relationships' extend. In *Curtis* (1885) 15 Cox CC 746, a child died after a relieving officer failed to perform his duty under Victorian poor law to summon medical assistance to a child of destitute parents. He would have been convicted of manslaughter, had the judge not directed the jury that the accused did not cause the death of the victim (causation in omission offences is difficult: see below). Parents have been tried for manslaughter on the grounds that they wilfully refused to give their daughter insulin. Presumably the duty of parents covers guardians, though there is as yet no precedent.

A case to compare with *Curtis* is *Smith* [1979] Crim LR 251 (Crown Court). The wife refused to see a doctor after childbirth. She then gave permission for her husband to call a doctor, but she died. The husband was charged with manslaughter. The judge directed the jury that, if the wife was not too ill, she could direct her husband not to call the doctor. Thereby he would be released from his duty, which was not automatically imposed by virtue of their spousal relationship but which could be easily inferred from the facts, to take care of her. Exactly how persons can be released from their duty is debatable. *Smith* is not well reasoned. If the husband owed his wife no duty while she was mentally capable, it could be said that as she drew near death, she was no longer mentally capable and therefore the duty again arose. Moreover, if his duty only arose when she was no longer mentally capable, there was no proof that he had *caused* her death, and causation is part of the *actus reus* of any form of manslaughter.

Support for this principle of termination of duty comes *obiter* from the civil law authority of ***Airedale NHS Trust v Bland*** [1993] AC 789. The House of Lords, in an attempt to protect doctors from being convicted of murder when they turned off life-support systems, treated the withdrawal of food and drink and ventilation as omissions, likening them to their non-provision in the first place (the argument is that not feeding the patient simply restored him to the position he was in when he was brought into the hospital), though this is moot. Apparently this is also the view of the medical profession. Lord Goff, who drew a line between ending treatment (an act) and not continuing it (an omission), a distinction difficult to accept (see the speech of Lord Mustill, who considered that an act and an omission were 'indistinguishable' from an ethical viewpoint), said: 'the doctor is simply allowing his patient to die . . . and as a matter of general principle an omission such as this will not be unlawful unless it constitutes a breach of duty to the patient'. The cause of death was not the turning off of life-support but was the reason why the victim had to be placed on life-support in the first place. On the facts there was no breach because it was not in the patient's best interests to continue life-support treatment when there was no chance that he might recover. (It can hardly be said that not feeding him was in the patient's best interests.) Certainly the House of Lords condemned active steps to kill a patient (such as giving a lethal injection). It may be argued that the removing of a feeding tube or a ventilator is an active step, but *Bland* treats such a step as an omission: the doctors are omitting to supply food or an instrument for breathing. Yet, the House of Lords said that if the doctors' act had been performed by a stranger, that would have been an act! (It is thought that *Bland* does not breach Article 2 of the European Convention on Human Rights because while there is a right to life, there is no positive duty on the state to prolong life; there is no breach of Article 3, the prohibition of inhuman and degrading punishment, because the victim must be aware of the mistreatment. These points have been made in a civil case, ***NHS Trust A v M*** [2001] Fam 348 (High Court).)

While *Bland* is not a criminal case, there was some support in the speeches for the duty of care to be terminated by the patient himself and indeed by close relatives when the patient was incapable of appreciating the situation. It was suggested that continued treatment by the doctor contrary to the patient's wishes would be (at least) a battery, but that proposition has not yet been tested. It is uncertain whether this case can be applied generally. What if a person of sound mind tells his partner to let him die if at some time in the future he suffers from senile dementia? It is uncertain how far this case may be generalised so as to provide an endpoint to all duties to act, however arising. If a lifeguard has gone off duty and has been replaced but is still at the edge of the pool, is he divested of the duty of care? Is there a duty to act until the moment of the termination of his contract of employment? The cases are not helpful. There is no doubt that a parent has a duty to intervene if his or her child is drowning, but what if the parent is heavily pregnant? Is she released from her duty if she shouts for help? Alternatively, should we say that no duty arose on the facts? Again the authorities do not provide guidance. Does the duty end when the accused divorces his wife and the child goes to live with her? If he is on business in Paris, is he still responsible? It is thought that the duty terminates when the situation which gave rise to it terminates. Therefore, in answer to the last two questions the duty is expunged on divorce but not by a business trip.

The generally accepted basis for liability in (e)–(g) is that the accused is guilty because he and the victim were living together, or were connected in some way, which gave rise to the duty to take care of the victim. Contracts and blood relationships, for instance, are in themselves merely matters going towards proving the assumption of a duty. This basis explains how duties can end. A parent no longer owes a duty to a child who is, say, married and living away from home, even though the blood relationship continues to exist. This principle applies even though the child is a minor.

(h) If one unwittingly (i.e. without *mens rea*) creates a dangerous situation, one is under a duty to put it right: *Miller*, above (see also Chapter 3). A squatter who set fire to a mattress and walked away was held guilty of arson when he did nothing to put the fire out. It was his physical act which caused the fire originally. It was held that he was under a duty to act. The issue of withdrawal in the event of the task becoming too onerous was not discussed in *Miller*. The recent cases on the *Miller* principle are *DPP v Santana-Bermudez* [2004] Crim LR 471 (DC) and *Matthews* [2003] 2 Cr App R 461 (CA). In the former case the victim, a police officer, asked the accused to turn out his pockets, which he did. She then asked: 'Are you sure that you do not have any needles or sharps on you?' He said that he did not. She started searching him but pricked her finger on a syringe. The court found him guilty of assault occasioning actual bodily harm. His failure to inform her of the hypodermic was the *actus reus* of the offences. The accused owed a duty of care as laid down by *Miller* to his victim. In *Matthews* the accused pushed the victim into a river, not knowing that he could not swim. The victim drowned. When they did realise that he could not swim, they were under a duty to act as in *Miller* and, because they intended to kill or cause grievous bodily harm, they were guilty of murder.

It is uncertain whether an accused is guilty if it was his omission to act which led to the dangerous situation. If he fails to shore up a dangerous building, hears a cracking sound, sees children whom he hates playing where the building is going to fall, then decides not to warn them, arguably he is guilty of murder if a child is killed and he had malice aforethought, on the *Miller* principle, despite the fact that it was not his physical act which started the train of events which led to the child's death. He could have been found guilty under what might be called the reverse of *Thabo Meli v R* [1954] 1 WLR 228 (PC) (see Chapter 3). In the latter case an earlier *mens rea* was added to a later *actus reus*. In *Miller* an earlier *actus reus* could have been added to a later *mens rea*. *Speck*, above, is different. There the girl had initiated the touching, not the accused. *Gully v Smith*, above, could also be taken to illustrate this principle: the accused had adopted the nuisance by not removing it. *DPP v K* above is an illustration of the *Miller* principle. The accused had created a dangerous situation by putting acid into a hand dryer. He had then failed to remove it (or to warn that it was there).

One yet unresolved point is whether the principle in *Miller* applies where the original act is justified, such as when the accused acts lawfully in self-defence but then refuses to call the medical services.

If enacted, the draft Offences against the Person Bill attached to the Home Office Consultation Document, *Violence: Reforming the Offences against the Person Act 1861*, 1998, will put *Miller* into statutory form. The government, both the present Coalition one and the previous one, has, however, shown little interest in reforming this part of the law, which really does cry out for change.

(i) The general rule is that one is not liable for failing to intervene to prevent a crime. Mere presence at the scene of the offence does not entail liability. There is, however, an exception. Where a person has a right of control over the action of another he is liable for failing to exercise that control when the other commits an offence. *Tuck v Robson* [1970] 1 All ER 1171 (DC) exemplifies this situation. A landlord did not require his customers to leave after closing time. Perhaps surprisingly, failing to do so is not an offence. It is the customers who are guilty of the substantive offence of consuming alcohol after hours, but the Divisional Court held that the landlord was guilty of aiding and abetting the offence. Cases falling within this category often involve driving. The owner who is a passenger in a car may have a right of control over the driver. In *Halmo* [1941] 3 DLR 6 the Ontario Court of Appeal held that the accused was guilty of being a secondary party to manslaughter when he was in the car at the time when his drunken chauffeur killed the victim. In England the law extends to the right of an instructor to control a learner driver: *Rubie v Faulkner* [1940] 1 KB 571.

There is no reason to think that the list of circumstances in which a duty to act arises is closed. The development of the law on a step-by-step basis is not inconsistent with the European Convention on Human Rights (see Chapter 1).

The Court of Appeal held in *Khan*, above, that whether a duty of care arises out of a certain set of facts is a question for the jury. However, a later Court of Appeal ruled in *Singh*, above, that the crime was one for the judge. It is suggested that *Singh* represents the better view, because *Khan* might lead to a jury saying that because the victim is dead, there must have arisen a duty to prevent that death.

The draft Criminal Code, 1989, did not attempt to state when an accused was liable for omissions. The Law Commission preferred to leave this area of law for judicial development rather than for a statutory formulation. Therefore, both the list provided above and the recommendations of the Law Commission do not restrict the development of the law: the list is not closed. One might expect that not restricting situations in which criminal liability for omissions can be found would breach Article 7 of the European Convention on Human Rights, the principle of non-retroactivity, but the European Court of Human Rights has ruled that common law extensions to liability do not breach that Article: *SW v United Kingdom* [1996] 1 FLR 434, the case on the marital immunity to rape discussed in Chapter 1.

Causation in omissions

Even where there is potentially liability for an omission, it must be proved in result crimes that the accused 'caused' the omission which led to the harm. Proving causation may be difficult. For example, if a police constable stands by while a victim is kicked to death, does he 'cause' her death? 'But for' his non-intervention would the victim still be alive?

Morby (1882) 15 Cox CC 35 (CCR)

A child was dying of smallpox. The father refused to summon medical aid. He was a member of a sect called the 'Peculiar People' who believed that prayer and anointment were sufficient to cure illness. The doctor gave evidence that the chances of the boy's survival would have been increased had a doctor been summoned. The father was tried for manslaughter. The Court for Crown Cases Reserved agreed with the direction of Hawkins J. The question was whether the child's death was accelerated by the accused's neglect. Lord Coleridge said:

> [I]t is not enough to sustain the charge of manslaughter to know that the parent has neglected to use all reasonable means of saving the life of his child; it was necessary to show that what the parent neglected had the effect of shortening the child's life.

The prosecution had failed to prove beyond reasonable doubt that the child died because of neglect.

Therefore, the normal rules of factual and legal causation apply. The principal English theorists on this topic see no difference between acts and omissions: Hart and Honoré, *Causation in the Law*, 2nd edn (Clarendon Press, 1985) 5. As an example one can use the facts of **Pittwood**, above: the victim, the driver of the haycart, would not have been killed by the train, had the accused, the level-crossing gatekeeper, closed the gate. It is, however, sometimes argued that one cannot cause something by omission. If I watch my child drown, how have I occasioned its death? I did not push the child in; I did not even create the pond. My child would still have drowned, had I been in Italy rather than walking by the pond. One response is to say that what occurred is an exceptional deviation from the behaviour expected of a parent. This view is advanced by Hart and Honoré (at 37). English courts have not tackled this potential source of difficulty. One argument which might succeed is that with regard to acts the accused has more control over the effects than he has in relation to omissions. The accused, for instance, could have exerted control over his movements to stop him pushing his victim into a pond but may not be in a position to exert control when someone else has pushed a child into the water. Several people may be responsible for causing an omission.

The Law Commission in the draft Criminal Code proposed to replace the 'but-for' test in **Morby** with the rule that the accused would be guilty if he might have prevented the *actus reus*. The result would be to have liability for omissions in this respect to be wider than that for acts, which seems strange. Clause 17(1) states:

> . . . a person causes a result . . . when . . .
>
> (b) he omits to do an act which might prevent its occurrence and which he is under a duty to do according to the law relating to the offence.

The provision will ease the position of a court faced with a plea that the accused did not cause something by omitting to prevent it. No longer will 'but-for' causation be required as in an offence of commission. Therefore, proving causation will be easier for offences of omission than for offences of commission.

The policy behind general non-liability for omissions

There is a debate between those who wish to extend the law to cover criminal omissions and those who do not. This debate may be summed up by using the views of two protagonists. Professor Ashworth 'The scope of criminal liability for omissions' (1989) 105 LQR 424 argued in favour of mutual assistance that:

> [T]he general principle in criminal law should be that omissions liability should be possible if a duty is established, because in those circumstances there is no fundamental moral distinction between failing to perform an act with foreseen bad consequences and performing an act with identical foreseen bad consequences.

In his view life is of such a basic value that it must be preserved. The saving of life is a public good which outweighs the public good of liberty not to act. The behaviour of the non-rescuer is so reprehensible that criminal sanctions should be available. It has also been argued that since one of the aims of the criminal law is to improve standards of behaviour, liability for failing to attain those standards should be imposed. A person should rescue if there is no danger to him. It is the socially responsible thing to do. Other countries have laws in respect of failure to rescue. Those chasing the Princess of Wales through Paris when she was killed were charged with failing to assist a person in danger. William Wilson,

Criminal Law: Doctrine and Theory, 4th edn (Longman, 2011) 84, also pointed out that omissions may be morally worse than acts. 'What is morally worse/causally more significant: shooting a child to prevent the agony of her burning to death in a flaming inferno one is powerless to prevent, or failing to save a similar child from a similar fate by the simple mechanism of unlocking the door behind which she is trapped?'

It is not always easy to see the difference between an act and an omission. Does one fail to stop at a red light or does one drive through a red light? Glanville Williams responded, 'Criminal omissions – the conventional view' (1991) 107 LQR 86 in defence of individualism.

(a) There is a difference even on Ashworth's approach. Omissions give rise to liability only where there is a duty. No duty is needed for acts. (One could in the view of the author of this book invent one, but certainly the problem does not arise in positive acts: there is a duty not to commit murder. There is no need to refer to the duty.)

(b) There is a moral distinction between killing and letting die (except perhaps between parent and child). My shooting you with a gun is more blameworthy than my permitting you to starve to death. My pushing you overboard in the middle of the ocean is more reprehensible than my not rescuing you when a third party has pushed you in.

(c) It may be difficult to distinguish acts from omissions (for example, is disconnecting a drip-feed an act or omission?), but the problem is inherent in all moral principles.

(d) The criminal law should be directed at active wrongdoing. It is not well suited to getting people to do things. Moreover, obliging people to perform acts is secondary to the primary purpose of suppressing bad behaviour.

(e) Everyone could be liable for omissions. By not selling one's house and giving the proceeds to aid agencies, one has failed to prevent a famine in Sudan.

(f) It is unfair to label non-doers as wrongdoers where statutory language is couched in active terms.

(g) The police, Crown Prosecution Service, courts and prisons would be overwhelmed if criminal liability for omissions were the norm. The clash of values is between interpersonal duties and personal autonomy.

Moreover, people should not be obliged to act when they do not so wish, especially if acting involves the expenditure of time and effort, as it does in this area of law. They would have to change their lives to accommodate what others were doing. Making people liable for omissions would encourage others to interfere in matters which do not concern them. Should it really be the law that if one hears a baby crying in a locked house, one should break down the door to check that it is not being ill-treated? People should be allowed to put their own interests and the interests of those they hold dear above strangers. In terms of the principles discussed at the start of Chapter 1, judicial extension of legal duties to act is a breach of the principle of legality.

The orthodox statement that English criminal law does not oblige people to do good but only prevents them from behaving badly is under attack, but the principle survives.

Reform of liability for omissions

(See also under 'Causation in omissions', above.)

The law of omissions has developed over time without much regard for principle. The Criminal Law Revision Committee in its Fourteenth Report, *Offences Against the Person*, Cmnd 7844, 1980, paras 252–255, recommended that in such crimes liability for omissions should be imposed only for murder, manslaughter, causing serious injury with intent (which was to replace grievous bodily harm and wounding with intent), kidnapping and abduction and unlawful detention. (The common law was to be left free to develop *when* an accused was under a duty to act. As has been seen, the draft Criminal Code adopted the latter proposition.) Since an accused was not to be liable for more minor offences against the person, he was also not to be liable for criminal damage.

The Law Commission in the draft Criminal Code, 1989, proposed a general provision on omissions which would not be restricted to those recommended by the Criminal Law Revision Committee. 'Causing' criminal damage and 'causing' death are to be used as the redrafted *actus reus* of criminal damage and murder and manslaughter to avoid any problem that those offences could not be committed by omission (for example, it may be difficult as a matter of language to say that a father *killed* his daughter when he starved her to death). This proposal is very much on the lines of the present law. The policy of imposing liability for omissions only in major crimes was reiterated by the Law Commission in *Legislating the Criminal Code – Offences against the Person and General Principles*, Report No. 218, 1993. The Non-Fatal Offences against the Person Bill would if enacted not impose liability for omissions in respect of the proposed crimes of recklessly causing serious injury, intentionally or recklessly causing injury and assault. No list of duties to act was recommended. It would be left to the common law to determine when a duty arose. The 1993 Report also confirmed the **Miller** principle about supervening fault.

One would hope in a true reform of the law that the position would be clarified by express words imposing liability for omissions. It should, however, be emphasised that simply making explicit what is implicit will not resolve some of the concerns about liability for omissions. Whether a person watching a small child drown in an inch of water is criminally liable should be based on principle and policy. It is the values the criminal law ought to incorporate which should be discussed. This is the reason why liability for omissions remains a controversial topic. Although changing the law from 'damaging' to 'causing criminal damage' resolves one issue, it does not alter the fact that the question of causation is dealt with in the draft Code in what looks like an over-inclusive way. ('Might prevent': see above.) Whether present law is retained or the draft Code enacted, to revert to the start of this chapter, a definition of the *actus reus* in terms of physical or bodily movement is incorrect for it fails to deal with criminal liability for omissions. If one cannot define 'act', one cannot define 'omission to act'. Lord Mustill in **Bland** said that 'the current state of the law is unsatisfactory both morally and intellectually', and that the distinction between act and omission was dubious: do you agree?

Summary

- *Introduction*: Criminal law is concerned with forbidding various forms of behaviour, whether that consists of acts, omissions or states of affairs. These are called *actus reus* or the external element(s) of offences. When added to the *mens rea*, there is an offence (though note Chapter 4 on strict liability); there may also be a defence.

- *Some problems*: The *actus reus* must not be read as meaning solely the conduct of the accused: it can, for example, cover the behaviour of the victim. An illustration is rape, which includes lack of consent by the alleged victim. Similarly, when considering defences, it is difficult to match some defences with the analysis of *actus reus*; *mens rea*; and defence. Some defences, for example mistake, seem not to be separate at all from the offence: they are not a third ingredient. Rather they negate either the *actus reus* or *mens rea* or both. For example, mistake seems to exist as a failure to prove the offence. Duress can be seen, however, as a defence available as a third ingredient: the accused did the prohibited conduct and had the relevant state of mind but she had a defence because she was forced to do what she did.

Other problems include these. 'Actus' must not be translated as 'act' because it is wider than that; it covers 'non-acts', omissions. The *actus reus* varies from crime to crime: knowing that part of the *actus reus* for theft is 'property' does not help with the *actus reus* of murder. The *actus reus*, obviously, must be proved: for students, this proposition is to be taken as meaning that all elements of the *actus reus* (and *mens rea*) must be considered.

- *Conduct and result crimes*: A modern division of offences is into those where the prosecution must prove that the accused caused something to happen ('result' crimes) and ones where it does not ('conduct' crimes). The obvious example of the former is murder; it must be shown that the defendant caused the death of the victim. An example of the latter is dangerous driving: no one need be harmed, no damage to property need be occasioned.

  Compare the crime of causing death by dangerous driving. This is a result crime because a certain consequence, death, forms part of the *actus reus* of the offence.

- *Causation*: Causation is not a problem in conduct crimes, only in result crimes. English law divides causation into two parts: causation in fact and causation in law. The former, often known as 'but-for' causation, asks: but for the act of the accused, would the victim be dead (etc.); if so, the triers of fact consider the second issue, that of legal causation. Usually but not always the question at this stage is: did the accused contribute significantly to the death (etc.)? There are exceptional principles, particularly the one which states that 'the accused must take his victim as he finds him', a principle often called the thin-skull rule. An example from the cases is the refusal of a Jehovah's Witness to receive a blood transfusion. Not all the cases are straightforwardly reconcilable, but in general a *novus actus interveniens* will break the chain of causation. For example, if the victim makes a free, deliberate and informed act, the so-called chain of causation is broken. This long-accepted statement of the law has come under increasing strain in recent years, especially in relation to suppliers of drugs present at the death of the drug-taker, but authorities which are to the effect that the accused remains guilty even when the victim refuses medical treatment may be seen as similar.

- *Omissions*: The general rule of English law is that no defendant is criminally liable for failing to act. To this rule there are exceptions. The starting point is that since Parliament can do anything, it can make persons guilty for not doing something. An example is the crime of failing to report a road traffic accident. Sometimes verbs in the definition of crimes can be interpreted as including failures to act. For example, one can obstruct a highway by not removing a blockage which has occurred naturally. Common law crimes of omission are very rare: the most common one, though rarely prosecuted, is that of not assisting a constable on request. However, the main difficulty surrounds liability for omissions when there may or may not be a duty to act. The law has been developed rapidly over the last 30 years or so by the courts and current situations where there is a duty to act comprise blood relationships, contractual relationships (not necessarily just encompassing the two parties), voluntary assumption of a duty of care, statutory duties, and dangerous situations which the accused has created. Outside these situations the law remains obscure, for example does a supplier of drugs have a duty to take care of his or her customer? Similarly obscure are the issues: how far must one go to fulfil the duty? And may the victim release the accused from the duty? The law remains open-ended, a scenario which may be in breach of Article 7 of the ECHR, the principle of non-retroactivity.

- *Whether people ought to be liable for not doing something* has exercised the mind of legal theorists. The issue tends to crystallise as: is there a moral difference between killing and allowing to die? Arguments in favour of current law that liability arises when there is a duty to act but not otherwise include: why should anyone be obliged to act, particularly when to do so may be dangerous, as may occur when attempting to rescue a drowning child?

References

Reports

Criminal Law and Penal Methods Reform Committee, South Australia, 4th Report, *The Substantive Criminal Law* (1977)

Criminal Law Revision Committee 14th Report, *Offences Against the Person*, Cmnd 7844 (1980)

Home Office Consultation Document, *Violence: Reforming the Offences Against the Person Act 1861* (1998)

Law Commission Report no. 177, *A Criminal Code for England and Wales* (1989)

Law Commission Report no. 218, *Legislating the Criminal Code – Offences Against the Person* (1993)

Books

Hart, H.L.A. and Honoré, T. *Causation in the Law*, 2nd edn (Oxford University Press, 1985)

Ryan, C. *Criminal Law*, 4th edn (Blackstone Press, 1995)

Wilson, W. *Criminal Law: Doctrine and Theory*, 4th edn (Longman, 2011)

Journals

Arlidge, A. 'The trial of Dr David Moor' [2000] Crim LR 31

Ashworth, A. 'The scope of criminal liability for omissions' (1989) 105 LQR 424

Colvin, E. 'Causation in criminal law' (1989) 1 Bond LR 253

Klimchuk, D. 'Causation: thin skulls and equality' (1998) 11 Can JL&J 115

Perkins, R. 'A rationale of *mens rea*' (1939) 52 Harv LR 905

Smith, J.C. 'Comment' [1988] Crim LR 843

Williams, G. '*Finis* for *novus actus*' [1989] CLJ 391

Williams, G. 'Criminal omissions – the conventional view' (1991) 107 LQR 86

Further reading

Alexander, L. and Fessler, K.K. '"Moore or less" causation and responsibility' (2012) 6 Crim Law and Philos 81

Ashworth, A. 'Public duties and criminal omissions: Some unresolved questions' (2011) 1 *Journal of Commonwealth Criminal Law* 1

Baker, D.J. 'Omissions liability for homicide offences: reconciling *R v Kennedy* with *R v Evans*' (2010) 74 JCL 310

Busuttil, A. and McCall Smith, A. 'Flight, stress and homicide' (1990) 54 JCL 374

Chiao, V. 'Action and agency in the criminal law' (2009) 15 *Legal Theory* 1

Dingwall, G. and Gillespie, A.A. 'Reconsidering the good Samaritan: A duty to rescue?' (2008) 29 Cambrian LR 26

Finn, J. 'Culpable non-intervention: reconsidering the basis for party liability by o[...] 18 Crim LJ 90

Hogan, B. 'The *Dadson* principle' [1989] Crim LR 679

Horder, J. and McGowan, L. 'Manslaughter by causing another's suicide' [2006] Crim LR 235

Hughes, G. 'Criminal omissions' (1958) 67 Yale LJ 590

Leavens, A. 'A causation approach to criminal omissions' (1988) 76 Cal LR 547

McCutcheon, J.P. 'Omissions and criminal liability' (1993–5) xxviii–xxx IJ 54

McGee, A. 'Ending the life of the act/omission dispute: Causation in withholding and withdrawing life-sustaining measures' (2011) 31 LS 467

Moore, M. *Act and Crime* (Oxford University Press, 1993)

Moore, M. 'The metaphysics of causal intervention' (2000) 88 Cal LR 1

Norrie, A. 'A critique of criminal causation' (1991) 54 MLR 685

Ormerod, D. 'Manslaughter: Suicide resulting from prolonged abuse' [2006] Crim LR 923

Ormerod, D. Casenote on *Williams* [2011] Crim LR 474

Smith, J.C. 'Liability for omissions in the criminal law' (1984) 4 LS 88

Smith, P. 'Legal liability for criminal omissions' (2001) 5 Buff Crim LR 69

Spellman, S. and Kincannon, A. 'The relation between counterfactual "but for" and causal reasoning: experimental findings and implications for jurors' decisions' (2001) 64 *Law and Contemporary Problems* 241

Wilson, W. 'Murder by omission: Some observations on a mismatch between the general and specific part' (2010) 13 New Crim LR 1

The standard work on causation is Hart and Honoré, *Causation in the Law*, above. For a theoretical explanation of omissions, voluntariness and causation see W. Wilson, *Central Issues in Criminal Theory* (Hart, 2002), chs 3, 4, 6 respectively. For a brief and more up-to-date version of Tony Honoré's views, see 'Causation in the law', *Stanford Encyclopedia of Philosophy*, 2001.

Visit **www.mylawchamber.co.uk** to access tools to help you develop and test your knowledge of criminal law, including interactive multiple choice questions, practice exam questions with guidance, annotated weblinks, glossary flashcards, legal newsfeed and legal updates.

Use Case Navigator to read in full some of the key cases referenced in this chapter with commentary and questions:

R v *Blaue* [1976] 61 Cr App R 271
R v *Cheshire* [1991] 1 WLR 844
R v *Church* [1966] 1 QB 59, [1965] 2 WLR 1220
R v *Kennedy* [2007] UKHL 38

3

Mens rea

Aims and objectives

After reading this chapter you will understand and be able to critique:

● the definition of *mens rea*

● the part motive plays in criminal law

● the definitions of the principal mental element terms in criminal law, particularly intent and recklessness

● the application of liability for negligence in criminal law

● the use of the doctrine of transferred malice

● the rule that the *actus reus* and *mens rea* must occur simultaneously, with exceptions

Introduction

> There is no term fraught with greater ambiguity than that venerable Latin phrase that haunts Anglo-American criminal law: *mens rea*. (George Fletcher, *Rethinking Criminal Law* (Little, Brown & Co, 1978) 398)

Mens rea or the mental element in crime is one of the most important concepts of criminal law. In general terms, an accused is liable only if he has *mens rea*. This principle ensures that the accused is guilty only when he is at fault, and the lack of it in respect of one or more elements of the *actus reus* provides one of the planks of subjectivists' critique of strict liability (see the next chapter). The actual form of *mens rea* varies from crime to crime. Two types, intention and recklessness, are discussed fully below. These are the concepts most often used in modern law, but others such as 'maliciously' are also explored. Doctrinal discussion of these two fault elements has led to an overconcentration on those terms. Expressing mental elements in those terms in law reform projects has obscured the fact that present law is distinguished by a multitude of words indicating culpability. Lord Simon in **DPP for Northern Ireland v Lynch** [1975] AC 653 (HL) spoke of: 'will, volition, motive, purpose, object, view, specific intent or intention, wish, desire. . . .' and said that the terminology of criminal law was chaotic. Strict liability, where there is no *mens rea* as to one or more elements of the *actus reus*, forms the subject of the next chapter. The specific mental element for each offence is tackled in the relevant chapter. It should be noted that different parts of the *actus reus* may have different states of mind attached to them. Even strict offences have some mental element in their definition. The *mens rea* doctrine ensures that those who cause the *actus reus* are legally responsible for doing so. This chapter, besides dealing with other general forms of *mens rea* including negligence, considers several problems relating to *mens rea* such as the so-called doctrine of transferred malice and the issue of contemporaneity or concurrence, the principle that in English law the *mens rea* and *actus reus* have to coincide in time.

The state of mind of the accused is relevant in several areas of criminal law.

(a) The mental capacity of the accused may be investigated. For example, a child under 10 is never criminally liable (see Chapter 7).

(b) The mentally disordered state of mind may be looked at, for example in the defences of insanity and diminished responsibility (see Chapter 9).

(c) At times the state of mind is relevant to the question of voluntariness. Is the accused acting of his own free will? This issue is discussed in Chapters 2 and 9.

(d) The fourth meaning concerns the particular state of mind required in relation to the other ingredients of the offence. This is a definition of *mens rea*. Sometimes the *mens rea* is expressly stated; sometimes it is implicit in the definition of the offence.

The philosophical foundation for *mens rea* is that the accused can control his conduct. He can decide whether to engage in conduct which breaks the criminal law. On one approach the law is to prevent harmful behaviour. A person acting when he is in control of his movements and adverts to the possible harmful consequences of his behaviour is more culpable than someone who acts carelessly, and he is deserving of more punishment than a person who has so acted. He as an autonomous human being has chosen certain forms of behaviour and should be penalised and deterred. It is usually said that penalising conduct without *mens rea* is inefficacious and unjust, for example H. Packer 'Mens rea and the Supreme Court' [1962] Sup Ct Rev 107 at 109. The accused will not be deterred from behaving similarly again; others will not be deterred; the defendant is not necessarily a dangerous person who needs to be reformed; and two other bases of punishment, prevention and retribution, do not work. It is arguably unjust because it is wrong to impose the stigma of criminal conviction on someone who was not morally blameworthy.

As was seen in the previous chapter, the division between *actus reus* and *mens rea*, though convenient for exposition, is artificial and has been frowned on at the House of Lords level. Both terms continue to be used. They should be used in conjunction, for often the '*actus*' is not '*reus*' without a *mens rea*. For instance, in theft, the appropriation of property belonging to another, the *actus reus* is neutral without the addition of the mental element. If you take your spouse's car, you are not guilty of theft. It is the addition of the *mens rea*, dishonesty and the intention permanently to deprive, which converts the legally neutral activity into a crime. Some *actus reus* words, such as 'possessing' and 'permitting', have within them a *mens rea* element, for instance one cannot 'permit' something without knowing of its existence.

Definitions of *mens rea*

A literal translation of *mens rea* is 'guilty mind'. There is, however, no need for the accused to feel morally guilty or to know that what he is doing is morally culpable. Indeed, for many offences no moral fault need occur, yet the accused has the *mens rea*. As the Courts-Martial

Appeal Court said in **Dodman** [1998] 2 Cr App R 338: '*mens rea* does not . . . involve blame-worthiness'. The same applies *vice versa*: a person may be morally innocent but have *mens rea*. An example is an undercover police officer who joins a criminal gang. He is liable, for example, for conspiring to import drugs: **Yip Chiu-Cheung v R** [1995] 1 AC 111 (PC). Smith and Hogan, *Criminal Law*, 10th edn (Butterworths, 2002) 88 (not in the 13th edn now called *Smith and Hogan's Criminal Law* (Oxford University Press, 2011) by David Ormerod) provided a working definition:

> Intention, knowledge or recklessness with respect to all the elements of the offence *together with any ulterior intent which the definition of the crime requires*. [Italics in original.]

The phrase 'elements of the offence' is a reference to what those writers used to call 'all the consequences and circumstances of the accused's acts (or state of affairs) which constitute the *actus reus*'. As previously noted there are, however, many *mens rea* words in English law which are not intention, knowledge or recklessness. The term 'ulterior intent' will be discussed shortly.

An example of the application of this definition comes from rape, which can be rephrased thus. A man is guilty of rape if he has sexual intercourse whether vaginal, oral, or anal (*actus reus*), intending to have and knowing that it is unlawful sexual intercourse (*mens rea*) with a woman or a man (*actus reus*) knowing her to be a woman or knowing him to be a man (*mens rea*) who does not consent (*actus reus*), knowing that the victim does not consent or being aware that they may not consent (*mens rea*). It should be noted that using the term 'mind' as a translation of *mens* is incorrect if *mens rea* is used to denote not just states of mind but also negligence, which is the failure to achieve a certain standard. The modern phrase of 'fault element' is more successful at capturing this aspect of *mens rea* than is 'guilty mind'.

For the basic definition of rape, see p 532 (Chapter 14).

Whichever definition is used, it does not get us far towards knowing what the *mens rea* required for each crime is, for it varies from crime to crime just as the *actus reus* varies from crime to crime. Its meaning in each crime must be determined by looking at statutes and cases. *Mens rea* is at heart an analytical tool, not a prescriptive norm.

To repeat a point mentioned already, *mens rea* does not mean morally wrongful mind, just as 'maliciously' in criminal law does not mean 'spitefully'. One can have *mens rea* even if one believes one's act to be morally right, such as euthanasia: 'The criminal law represents an objective ethic which must sometimes oppose individual convictions of right' (J. Hall, *General Principles of Criminal Law*, 2nd edn (Bobbs-Merrill, 1968) 385). No *mens rea* term, not even the most currently used ones such as intention and recklessness, has been statutorily defined. One must, therefore, investigate the cases to see how judges have defined each mental state required by the offence's definition. Unfortunately, as Lord Simon put it in **DPP for Northern Ireland v Lynch** [1975] AC 653 (HL): 'A principal difficulty in this branch of the law is the chaotic terminology, whether in judgments [or] academic writings . . .'

Examples of *mens rea*

Murder is a common law offence. Its *mens rea*, called malice aforethought, is the intention to kill or commit grievous bodily harm (see this chapter and Chapter 11). In theft *mens rea* comprises two elements, dishonesty and intention permanently to deprive. Section 20 of the Offences Against the Person Act 1861 penalises the malicious infliction of grievous bodily harm. 'Maliciously' means intentionally or recklessly in the **Cunningham** sense

(*Cunningham* [1957] 2 QB 396 (CCA), on which see below). Section 18 of the same Act concerns among other things malicious wounding with intent to cause grievous bodily harm. Intention is the part of the *mens rea* in s 18. The phrase 'with intent' means that the *mens rea* is called 'ulterior intent' or 'further intent'. In s 20 the accused need foresee only some harm, whereas in s 18 he must intend grievous bodily harm. The difference between ss 18 and 20 is reflected in the maximum sentence of imprisonment, life and five years respectively.

Sometimes the mental element is not laid down by Parliament. Problems arise as to which *mens rea*, if any, is called for. Illustrations include bigamy contrary to s 57 of the Offences Against the Person Act 1861 and assault occasioning actual bodily harm contrary to s 47 of the same Act. Even modern statutes do not always expressly state the mental element required. Section 9(1)(a) of the Theft Act 1968 creates one form of burglary, entering a building as a trespasser with intent to do one or more of several offences such as theft. No *mens rea* is explicitly attached to 'entering a building as a trespasser'. Must the accused intend to enter a building as a trespasser or is it enough that he is aware that he may be entering as a trespasser?

One must be careful not to think that the *actus reus* and *mens rea* are coextensive. In murder the intent to cause serious harm is sufficient, whereas part of the *actus reus* is killing. In s 20 of the Offences Against the Person Act 1861 the *actus reus* is in part causing grievous bodily harm but the *mens rea* is intentionally or recklessly causing any physical harm, grievous or less. Where the mental element is not as extensive as the *actus reus*, the crime is sometimes called a 'half *mens rea*' one. Such offences are instances of constructive liability. The accused is guilty whether or not he intended to cause or was reckless as to causing grievous bodily harm. The name of the crime is something of a misnomer.

Even if one does know what the *mens rea* is, there are difficulties in knowing the width of those expressions. Fault element terms are defined below.

Summary

The notion that a court should not find a person guilty of an offence against the criminal law unless he has a blameworthy state of mind is common to all civilised penal systems. It is founded upon respect for the person and for the freedom of the human will? . . . [T]o be criminal, the wrongdoing must have been consciously committed. To subject the offender to punishment, a mental element as well as a physical element is an essential concomitant of the crime.

So said Dickson J in the Supreme Court of Canada in *Leary* v *R* (1977) 74 DLR (3rd) 103, 116. The next topic, motive, deals with a matter which looks like *mens rea* but is treated as not being relevant. Negligence is sometimes treated as *mens rea* and sometimes not, while the next chapter is the exception to Dickson J's rule.

Motive

Example

Do I have a defence if I rob a bank in order to buy a pain-killing drug for my mother who is in the terminal stages of cancer and the drugs do not work?

The short answer is: 'No!' Motive may be taken into account when sentencing but it is not a defence, and it is not a defence no matter how good the motive is. So, for example, a drugs prevention officer would be guilty of conspiracy to import controlled drugs if he agreed with a drugs supplier in Afghanistan to smuggle drugs into England and Wales in order to prevent the importation. However,

1 since Parliament can create offences as it pleases it may make motive relevant, as in racially motivated offences under the Crime and Disorder Act 1998; and
2 at times the courts have interpreted offences in such a way as to exculpate the accused, the obvious example being *Steane* [1947] KB 997 (CCA). The accused broadcast for the Nazis in the Second World War; he was threatened that if he did not, he and his family would be put into a concentration camp. He was found not guilty of 'doing acts likely to assist the enemy with intent to assist the enemy'. His broadcasts were likely to assist, but the court held that he did not intend to assist. Using the ordinary language definition of intent, he did intend to assist and therefore should have been found guilty. Instead the court took the view that he had not truly made his mind up to help the Nazis.

While the criminal law takes into account *mens rea*, as a general rule it disregards motive. The problem is therefore to distinguish motive from *mens rea*. An accused can have *mens rea* despite having a good motive. Therefore, *mens rea* does not mean a morally 'guilty mind'. It is often easy to state that the accused's ultimate purpose was the motive. Why did this woman steal a loaf of bread? She stole because she wanted to feed her starving children, or she was greedy, and so on. Why did this accused put a bomb on a plane? He did so in order to kill his wife or to claim the insurance, wishing to set up home with his mistress.

In *Mohan* [1976] QB 1, a case on the rarely charged offence of attempting by wanton driving to cause bodily harm to the victim, a police officer, the Court of Appeal said that intention connoted 'a decision to bring about . . . the commission of the offence . . . , no matter whether the accused desired that consequence of his act or not'. What the accused 'desired' is the motive for the crime. By definition it is irrelevant. A recent illustration is *A-G v Scotcher* [2005] 1 WLR 1867 (HL), where a juror was guilty of contempt of court even though she had disclosed jury deliberations in an effort to prevent a miscarriage of justice. Her good motive was no defence.

An example of a motive being irrelevant is the Privy Council case *Wai Yu-Tsang v R* [1992] 1 AC 269. The accused was convicted of conspiring to defraud when his motive was to stop a run on the bank at which he was the chief accountant. Lord Goff drew a line between 'underlying purpose' (motive) and 'immediate purpose' (intention). If his immediate purpose involved a crime, he was guilty despite his honourable underlying purpose. A more recent and English authority is *Hales* [2005] EWCA Crim 1118. The accused ran over and killed a policeman who was attempting to arrest him. Since he was 'prepared to kill to escape' (Keene LJ), he intended to kill. His motive, trying to escape, was immaterial to the offence charged. In *Sood* [1998] 2 Cr App R 355 the accused, a doctor, certified that he had seen the deceased on the day of her death. In fact he had not. What he did was in accordance with standard practice. The Court of Appeal held that he was guilty of wilfully and knowingly making a false declaration. His belief that the practice was acceptable was his motive. As the Court said, 'concepts of motive, blame and moral culpability' go to punishment, not to guilt. In *Yip Chiu-Cheung v R* [1995] 1 AC 111 the Privy Council advised that a person who was an undercover drugs enforcement officer would be guilty of conspiracy to traffic in drugs despite his good motive. This case is further discussed in Chapter 10, where it is noted that the Law Commission proposes to reverse it by legislation.

Sometimes, however, the courts have, it seems, interpreted offences as including motive. In **Steane** [1947] KB 997, a British national was forced by the Nazis to broadcast in favour of them under the threat of the concentration camp for his family and himself. He was charged under a wartime regulation which created the offence of 'doing acts likely to assist the enemy with intent to assist the enemy'. Did he intend to assist the enemy? Under the definition in **Mohan** he did intend to assist the enemy. He did not desire to do so. Indeed he was under pressure. The Court of Criminal Appeal quashed his conviction. Lord Goddard CJ held that the accused did not intend to aid the enemy. The outcome may be reconciled with general principles by holding that the accused was acting under duress. The Lord Chief Justice did not think that defence was available, but in the light of the present state of the law it seems that the accused would have this defence to the charge.

Steane is out of line with the general definition of intention (see below), though it well illustrates how courts sympathetic to the accused's plight can alter the meaning of intent by calling the accused's motive his 'intent'. Moreover, if the accused's good motive led to his conviction being quashed, any motive good or bad would give the accused a defence. In Glanville Williams's example, if the accused broadcast for the Nazis for a packet of cigarettes, the court ought consistently to hold that the accused did not intend to broadcast for the Nazis. A defence of **Steane** can, however, be put up based on the drafting of the crime. The regulation penalised 'doing acts likely to assist the enemy with intent to assist the enemy'. If motive was to be excluded, the law would have been drafted as 'intentionally doing acts likely to assist the enemy'. The actual phrasing left the way open for Lord Goddard CJ's judgment. It is to be expected that the drafting of wartime regulations will not be perfect. The result is still that there are two possible interpretations of intention in the criminal law, just as there are two if not three definitions of recklessness. Until the enactment of the draft Criminal Code or something similar, the problem of competing definitions will remain.

While **Steane** can be seen as a decision that motive was relevant, **Chandler v DPP** [1963] AC 763 (HL) is the classic authority exemplifying the opposite. A statute was phrased in such a way that motive appeared relevant but was construed as not requiring an investigation of motive. The defendants were charged with conspiring to enter a prohibited place 'for a purpose prejudicial to the safety of the state', contrary to s 1 of the Official Secrets Act 1911. They had held a protest at an airforce base and stopped planes landing or taking off for six hours in order to demonstrate against nuclear weapons. Lord Devlin said that if 'purpose' meant motive, a spy who gathered information for money would not be guilty; that interpretation could not be right. Lord Radcliffe, with the other Law Lords agreeing, held that the accused's immediate purpose was to block the airfield, which was prejudicial to the safety of the state. One did not have to inquire whether the defendants' long-term purpose was prejudicial or not. Both speeches led to the same conclusion that the appellants were guilty. However, there is a problem in the speeches which demonstrates the difficulty of differentiating *mens rea* (in this case 'purpose') from motive. What if a person entered the airfield to stop a plane with a bomb on board taking off? Lord Radcliffe said that preventing the plane's leaving was not the purpose of that person. The purpose was to save life; the prevention of take-off was the means to that end. Lord Devlin differed. The purpose was to prevent the take-off, but that purpose was not prejudicial to the safety of the state.

A cynic might argue, in conclusion, that the courts in these cases were simply giving vent to their prejudices. In one case the accused had a motive the judges approved, in the other they did not. A less cynical view would be to note how the courts can manipulate the law to exculpate defendants, should they so wish. Certainly by refusing to look at the defendants' purpose in *Chandler* the Lords did not have to get involved in political discussion of nuclear arms.

There are exceptions to the rule that motive is irrelevant. In blackmail, the accused has a defence if the demand was warranted. His belief that he has reasonable grounds for making the demand may be based on his motive. The 'racially motivated offence' created by the Crime and Disorder Act 1998 is a crime listed in that Act which was committed with a racial motive. For example, criminal damage is made a more serious offence than usual if the offence was motivated wholly or in part by hostility towards members of a certain racial group. Here motive is expressly made part of the definition of the offence. Elsewhere motive can be 'smuggled' into the law through concepts such as dishonesty in theft and the defence of necessity. Therefore, Parliament can make the law expressly or implicitly take motive into account.

The exclusion from consideration of motive, whether as part of the accused's fault element or as a separate defence, can be seen as part of the 'objectivisation' of criminal conduct. The accused's behaviour is extracted from its context, such as hunger and avarice in the examples given above.

Intent

Example

Imagine that Roger is a member of a terrorist organisation, the Northern England Radical Volunteer Echelon (NERVE). Consider his liability for murder in each of the following scenarios:

1 He plants a bomb in the bus station timed to explode in the rush hour, and kills four people.
2 He plants a bomb in the bus station timed to explode in the rush hour but phones a warning using a coded message. Normally the bus station would have been evacuated in time but unfortunately the bomb explodes early, killing four persons.
3 He plants a fake bomb in the bus station and the timer shows that it is due to explode in the rush hour. When a security guard finds the bomb, she calls out a warning. In the panic four people are trampled to death.

In the first scenario these facts constitute murder in a very straightforward way. There is no problem with causation and the accused seems to have made his mind up to kill or cause grievous bodily harm (GBH), the malice aforethought or mental element required for murder.

The second scenario is more complex. It does not look as if he had the *mens rea* for murder because he did not make his mind up to kill or cause GBH, though of course he has factually and legally caused the death of the victims. If we look at indirect intent, as in *Woollin* [1999] AC 82 (HL), the accused is guilty only if the jury draws the conclusion that the accused foresaw death or GBH as virtually certain and that outcome was in fact virtually certain. No one knows what goes on behind closed doors, the doors of the jury room, but on the facts the accused did not foresee death or GBH as virtually certain. Facts giving rise to an indirect or oblique intent scenario are rare. The bomb-on-a-plane illustration given in the text is one of them.

The third scenario is yet more complex, but since there is no intent to kill or cause GBH it cannot be murder; it also cannot be attempted murder because the sole fault element for that crime is the intent to kill. For (involuntary) manslaughter, see Chapter 12.

Make sure you learn the definition of 'indirect intent' found in *Woollin* and that you know when (and when not) to use it.

Intention is an often used word in the English language. Its meaning in law despite its importance as a fundamental concept is problematic, though less problematic than it used to be. The basic definition, its 'natural and ordinary' one, according to Robert Walker LJ in the civil case of *Re A* [2001] Fam 147 (CA), is 'purpose'. *Moloney* [1985] AC 905 (HL), besides confirming that malice aforethought has two forms and stating that the term malice aforethought is 'anachronistic and now wholly inappropriate', also determined that intention alone suffices. Foresight of consequences as probable was not sufficient. Foresight of even a virtually or highly probable consequence was neither intention nor the equivalent of intention after *Moloney*. However, 'intention' was not defined. Lord Bridge told judges that in most cases they could leave the definition to 'the jury's good sense'. For example, if the accused had a motive for killing the victim, cut her throat, and did know what the consequence of doing so would be, it is legitimate for the jury to say that he did intend to kill. In *Dudley and Stephens* (1884) 14 QBD 273 (CCR) the defendants did intend to kill the cabin boy, but the motive was to eat him in order to survive. They argued that their intention was to preserve their lives, but the court rejected that contention. They would have been happy not to kill if they could have survived otherwise, but they did make up their minds to kill the boy in order to feast off his body. More up to date is *Wright* [2000] Crim LR 928 (CA). The victim was found unconscious on the floor of his prison cell. The accused said that he had nothing to do with what had happened. Accordingly, either he had made up his mind to kill or he had not. There was no room for a direction on oblique intent (see below).

Intention covers the state of mind where the accused aims or decides to kill ('direct intent'). Accordingly, if the accused decides or sets out to achieve a result or if that consequence is his aim or purpose, he intends that outcome to occur. There was no attempt in *Moloney* or subsequent cases to overturn the concept of direct intent. As Lloyd LJ stated in *Walker and Hayles* (1990) 90 Cr App R 226 (CA), 'It has never been suggested that a man does not intend what he is trying to achieve.' Brennan J in *He Kaw Teh* (1985) 157 CLR 523 at 569 HCA gave this definition of this form of intent: 'Intent . . . connotes a decision to bring about a situation, so far as it is possible to do so, to bring about an act of a particular kind or a particular result.' If a section penalises 'purpose', that term means 'direct intent': *Zafar* [2008] EWCA Crim 184 ('possessing articles for a purpose connected with the commission, preparation or instigation of an act of terrorism' contrary to the Terrorism Act 2000, s 57).

Because in the usual run of cases intention is not defined and is left to the juries' good sense, there is room for the juries to define intent on the facts of each case not in a descriptive way ('this accused did intend this consequence because that was his state of mind') but in a moral one ('this accused is a terrorist and therefore he's a murderer'). This point is picked up below.

It is still intention even though he thought that the chance of the harm occurring was slight. Presumably, it is not intention if the accused knows that the result is impossible, but it will be if he has a direct intent but considers that the chance of his achieving his objective is low, as when he, being a poor shot, fires at a person many yards away

Since trial judges usually ought not to give any definition of intention, juries may reach different conclusions on the same facts, and the Court of Appeal is powerless to intervene. As Lord Bridge emphasised, 'intention' bears its ordinary meaning, whatever that is. Lord Scarman in *Hancock and Shankland* [1986] AC 455 (HL) said that jurors have to use their common sense to reach their decision. General guidelines could not replace the jury's use of common sense on the facts of each case. Accordingly, it can be said at this point in the analysis that intention as part of the law of murder does not bear and must not be given a technical meaning. Judges must not use synonyms such as purpose or aim. No doubt juries, however, will use such synonyms. Unless told differently they will apply ordinary language definitions.

It was sometimes said that intention in criminal law (though perhaps not in ordinary language) also covers the state of mind of a person who thinks it virtually certain that the victim will die, the usual example being a person who plants a bomb on a plane to recoup insurance money on the cargo. He does not want the passengers to die and will be very happy if they survive but he demonstrates that he does not put any value on life. This state of mind in relation to the passengers, which goes often by the term 'oblique intent', was called by Glanville Williams (who was the first to use it in criminal law) the 'side-effect' of the accused's intent ('Oblique intention' [1987] CLJ 417). The same writer in *Criminal Law: The General Part*, 2nd edn (Stevens, 1961) 40, stressed that 'mere philosophical doubt, or the intervention of extraordinary chance, is to be ignored'. In *MD* [2006] EWCA Crim 1991 oblique intent was said to be 'designed to help the prosecution fill a gap in the rare circumstances in which a defendant does an act which caused death without the purpose of killing or causing serious bodily harm, but in circumstances when death or serious bodily harm had been a virtual certainty (barring some unforeseen intervention) as a result of the defendant's action and the defendant had appreciated that such was the case.' This quote does correctly encapsulate the law.

A case law example of oblique intent is *Mohan* [1976] QB 1 (CA), mentioned in the Motive section, above. The case facts resemble those in *Hales*, above. In order to escape, the accused drove his car at a police officer. His purpose was to escape. The side-effect of his direct intent was an attempt to cause grievous bodily harm with intent to do some bodily harm. The constable might step aside but if he did not, he would be knocked down. In different words, the accused acted *in order to* escape. The italicised words show what his intent was and that the running down of the constable was not his intent. He did not drive as he did in order to run over the police officer. This mental element, foresight of a virtual certainty, is sometimes called 'oblique intent', though not all writers agree on its width. Moreover, not all commentators agree whether oblique intent is intent. If this form of intent is part of the *mens rea* of murder there may be difficult cases on the borderline between foresight of a virtual certainty and foresight of a consequence as highly probable, the latter not amounting to evidence of intent. (Students should be careful in their reading because the latter type of foresight is also sometimes called 'oblique intent'. 'Oblique intent' is also the term used for the state of mind which occurs when there is no possible way of achieving one's end, a breach of the law, without violating another law. For example, to shoot dead a rival the accused may have to shoot through a fixed window. The direct intent is to kill, the oblique to cause criminal damage.) 'Virtual' or moral certainty means 'certainty excepting the unforeseeable results of action', for example that all passengers survive the blast and the plane lands safely. It is unsatisfactory that depending on the author, different frames of mind are called by the same name.

Moreover, intention and foresight, even of a certainty, can be completely different concepts. By imbibing alcohol you may foresee a hangover as a certain result, but one would not say that you intend to have a hangover. C. Finkelstein wrote in 'No harm no foul? Objectivism and the law of attempts' (1999) 18 *Law and Philosophy* 69, 75: 'Oblique intention is not really any kind of intention at all. It is a label for a different sort of mental state altogether, namely foresight. . . . Calling it a species of intention is pure obfuscation.' Nevertheless, some commentators consider that direct intent and foresight of a virtual certainty cannot be distinguished; both are morally wrong in that both represent a complete disregard for human life.

To gain an appreciation of what intention does mean, one must consider five important cases: *Moloney*, the facts of which are stated in Chapter 11, *Hancock and Shankland*, *Nedrick* [1986] 1 WLR 1025, *Walker and Hayles* (1990) 90 Cr App R 226 (CA), a case which is less important now than it was originally, and *Woollin* [1999] AC 82. The exegesis below omits the history of the topic except in so far as a knowledge of earlier authorities is necessary to understand present law.

Moloney

Despite criticism of *Moloney* in *Hancock and Shankland*, it remains an important case for several reasons.

(a) It abolished the previous law whereby foresight of death or grievous bodily harm (GBH) was sufficient malice aforethought. It affirmed the view of Wien J in *Belfon* [1976] 3 All ER 46 (CA) on non-fatal offences that foresight was not part of intention. Foresight of the likelihood of injury is part of the evidence going towards proving intent, not a variety of intent itself. As Lord Hailsham put it: 'Foresight and foreseeability are not the same thing as intention.' Lord Bridge stressed that: 'No one has yet suggested that recklessness can furnish the necessary element in the crime of murder.' The contrary view, that in ordinary language foresight of a probability was intention, a view which had received support from at least one Law Lord, was rejected.

(b) The accused's foresight was, however, one part, but only one part, of the evidence which may be taken into account by the jury in determining whether the accused did intend to kill or cause grievous bodily harm. Accordingly, intent *may* be inferred from foresight, but proof of foresight, even of a virtual certainty, was not proof of intent. Juries did find difficulty with this notion and asked the trial judge for guidance in *Moloney*, *Hancock and Shankland* and *Nedrick*. It remains to be seen whether juries will require such help after *Woollin*.

(c) In order to avoid confusion in the minds of the jury there was no need, save in exceptional cases, for the judge to give a direction on the meaning of 'intent'. In this respect the House of Lords confirmed what had been the previous law: *Beer* (1976) 63 Cr App R 222 (CA), which the Privy Council had approved in *Leung Kam Kwok* v *R* (1984) 81 Cr App R 83. *Nedrick*, above, and other authorities have more recently upheld this proposition. Lord Bridge put it this way in *Moloney*:

> The golden rule should be that . . . the judge should avoid any elaboration or paraphrase of what is meant by intent and leave it to the jury's good sense to decide whether the accused acted with the necessary intent.

The exception was meant to deal with an instruction on natural consequences, but refer to *Hancock and Shankland*, below, for further elaboration of this point. On this point *Moloney* is as correct today as it was then. The 'golden rule' is: the jury should not be directed in *Moloney* and *Hancock and Shankland* terms unless there is evidence that the accused intended to do something other than the crime alleged. If the prosecution alleges that he intended to kill or commit GBH but the defendant denies that allegation, there is no need for elaboration. If, however, he says that he did not so intend but wanted to put a bomb onto a plane to claim insurance money, there is a need for a *Moloney/Hancock and Shankland* direction.

(d) In murder there was no requirement that the accused should 'aim' at the victim. There were *dicta* of Viscount Kilmuir in *DPP* v *Smith* [1961] AC 290 (HL) and of Lord Hailsham in *Hyam* v *DPP* [1975] AC 55 (HL) to the effect that the victim must be the target of the accused, but Lord Hailsham withdrew his remarks and the rest of the House of Lords agreed unanimously with his withdrawal. This concession left the way open for the conviction of the terrorist who planted a bomb, even though he did not direct the bomb at the actual victim.

(e) The House of Lords disapproved of Lord Hailsham's view in **Hyam** that an intention to expose a potential victim to a serious risk of grievous bodily harm was part of the *mens rea* of murder. The House of Lords thought that if this type of malice aforethought were accepted, reckless drivers who killed could be convicted of murder, a result which they abhorred.

(f) Their Lordships continued to distinguish intention from motive and desire. In Lord Bridge's 'homely example':

> A man who, at London airport, boards a plane which he knows to be bound for Manchester clearly intends to travel to Manchester even though Manchester is the last place he wants to be and his motive for boarding the plane is simply to escape pursuit.

(Lord Bridge said that getting on the Manchester plane 'conclusively demonstrates his intention to go there, because it is a moral certainty that that is where he will arrive'. This statement seems to mix up the concept of intention and that of deriving intent from foresight of a moral certainty. This point is discussed below, particularly in reference to **Woollin**.)

An even homelier example is: you may intend to go to the dentist without having the least desire to go to the dentist's. Indeed, it may terrify you to sit in the dentist's chair! The emotional reason – greed, jealousy, ambition and the like – behind the killing is disregarded. Only the intent to kill or to commit grievous bodily harm is considered.

A summary of **Moloney** would be that foresight and motive are not intention, and except in rare cases 'intention' should be left to the jury. The principal difficulty was to understand and apply some of Lord Bridge's phraseology. At one point of his speech – unfortunately an important point, for he was stating what judges ought to tell juries in exceptional cases – he used the term 'natural consequence'. Did the defendant foresee death or really serious harm as a natural consequence of his act and was it in fact a natural consequence? What he seemed to have meant is that a result will occur 'unless something unexpected supervenes to prevent it', as he put it elsewhere (in this sense 'natural' means the same as 'virtually certain'), but it could mean that the accused was guilty where the death was indeed a natural, i.e. direct, consequence, without that consequence being morally certain (or even highly likely) to occur. To use a commentator's illustration, 'Conception is a natural consequence of sexual intercourse but it is not necessarily probable' (Glanville Williams 'Oblique intention' [1987] CLJ 417). In this second sense 'natural' does not include a virtual certainty. The term 'morally certain' means unless something unexpected supervenes. In another place in his speech he stated that the accused is guilty only if he foresaw the probability of an outcome as little short of overwhelming. Lord Hailsham said the same in **Hyam** v **DPP**, above.

Another difficulty with the speech of Lord Bridge was that he referred when defining intent not only to foresight of natural consequences but also to the fact that the harm was a natural consequence. It is uncertain why that fact should be relevant to the accused's *mens rea*. Another problem with **Moloney** is that the accused did not foresee the risk of death or grievous bodily harm at all; therefore, anything said about foresight of consequences, natural or otherwise, was *obiter*. Lord Bridge used the example of a terrorist bomber who leaves a bomb which has not yet exploded. He intends to scare people and phones a warning to the police. The bomb squad is summoned. While attempting to defuse the bomb, a soldier is killed. Lord Bridge assumed that the crime was murder. However, it is suggested that the offence is manslaughter: the terrorist did not foresee death or GBH of the soldier as a virtually certain consequence.

Despite the confusion which *Moloney* occasioned, it remains a highly important decision for the clarification of the points noted above and after all it was on its facts a simple case. The question for the jury was one of fact: what was in the accused's mind when he pulled the trigger? If he knew that the gun was pointing at the stepfather's head, the jury, in the words of Lord Bridge, 'were bound to convict him of murder. If, on the other hand, they thought it might be true that, in the appellant's drunken condition and in the context of [the] ridiculous challenge, it never entered the appellant's head when he pulled the trigger that the gun was pointing at his [stepfather], he should have been acquitted of murder and convicted of manslaughter.' A *Moloney* direction was not relevant on the facts of *Moloney*!

Hancock and Shankland

The House of Lords picked up on this point in the next case in this sequence. This case involved two striking Welsh miners, who during the 1984–85 miners' strike pushed a concrete block over a parapet onto a motorway with the purpose of encouraging a working miner to stop work. The driver of the taxi in which the miner was being carried was killed. They were held by the jury to be guilty of murder, but the House of Lords disagreed. The leading speech was delivered by Lord Scarman. Like the House of Lords in *Moloney*, he distinguished the *mens rea* of intention from the evidence needed to prove it. In *Moloney* their Lordships had stated that the jurors had to ask themselves in the exceptional case where they had to consider such matters (in the normal run of cases it is obvious that, say, the defendant stabbed the victim, intending to kill or cause grievous bodily harm) whether the result was a natural outcome of the accused's act. Lord Scarman added to this question that the death or injury had also to be a probable consequence of the act. Otherwise, the defendant would be liable for mere direct consequences, whereas the true import of Lord Bridge's speech in *Moloney* was that the accused was liable only where the jury inferred intent from his foresight of a virtually certain consequence.

While not laying down the minimum amount of foresight a jury could take into account, Lord Scarman emphasised that it was for the jury to determine on the facts, including the accused's degree of foresight, whether he intended to kill or cause grievous bodily harm. The greater the degree of foresight, the more likely it was that the jury would reach the conclusion that the accused did have that intent. Lord Scarman said: 'If the likelihood that death or serious injury will result is high, the probability of that result may . . . be seen as overwhelmingly evidence of the existence of the intent to kill or injure.' However, the question remained one of evidence, not of substantive law. The issue for the jury in *Hancock and Shankland*, as in *Moloney*, was not a complex one: did they believe the prosecution's case or the defendants'? If the former was believed, the crime was murder; if the latter, the crime was manslaughter. The possibility of inconsistent verdicts remained: one jury might infer intent, another might not, from the same facts, yet the courts were powerless to intervene. Judgments on which side of the line something falls are difficult in law, but the problem is exacerbated in intention where the judge cannot instruct the jury as to the meaning of intent. Furthermore, Lord Scarman said that a jury could infer intention from a high probability, a lower test than Lord Bridge's one of virtual certainty.

Nedrick

Lord Scarman in **Hancock and Shankland** thought that guidelines had little place in criminal law, yet the Court of Appeal laid down such principles in **Nedrick**, above.

Nedrick [1986] 1 WLR 1025 (CA)

The accused poured paraffin through the letter box of a house and on to the front door. He set it alight. The house blazed up and a child was killed. He was convicted of murder after a direction by the trial judge which followed the pre-*Moloney* law laid down in **Hyam v DPP**, above, a case with similar facts (including transferred malice: see below) that foresight of grievous bodily harm was to be treated as an intention to cause it. (The case was heard before *Moloney*.) The Appeal Court allowed the appeal on the grounds that, following *Moloney*, foresight was not to be equated with intention. Foresight was merely a step on the way towards proving intent.

The court gave advice to trial judges as to how they should direct juries when the defendant does a dangerous act, as a result of which someone dies. As ever, it should be noted that if the accused had a direct intent to kill or commit grievous bodily harm, the judge should not refer to these guidelines. They are used only when the consequences which occurred were not the accused's purpose.

(a) A person could intend to kill or cause grievous bodily harm even though he did not desire that result.

(b) The more probable that consequence was, the more likely it was that the accused foresaw it; and if the consequence was foreseen, the greater the probability was that the accused intended it. (This statement follows **Hancock and Shankland** if it means that a jury may infer intent from foresight of a virtual certainty. If, however, it means that an accused intends something when he foresees the consequence as virtually certain, it is inconsistent with *Moloney*.)

(c) If the accused did not foresee death or grievous bodily harm he did not intend it.

(d) If the accused did foresee it, but thought that the risk of it occurring was slight, the jury could easily conclude that he did not intend it.

(e) If the accused realised that death or serious injury was a virtual certainty ('barring some unforeseen intervention'), the jury might find it easy to infer that he intended that consequence. In this regard the court approved Lord Bridge's phrases in *Moloney* that the result has to be a 'moral certainty' or 'little short of overwhelming'. This proposition may be paraphrased in this way. In life few things are certain. Unforeseen circumstances may arise which prevent something happening. Passengers may live when a bomb explodes on a plane at 30,000 feet but barring unforeseen circumstances they will die. The bomber can still intend to kill even though he realises that there is a very slight possibility of the passengers surviving. This type of foresight is thus different from foresight of something occurring as a (very) high probability. On the facts of **Nedrick**, the outcome is that the accused did not have the requisite intent for murder because he did not foresee death or grievous bodily harm as a virtual certainty; therefore, intent could not be inferred.

(If the jury is entitled to infer intention from foresight of a virtual certainty, logically intention cannot include foresight of a virtual certainty.)

The Court of Appeal concluded, in a couple of sentences in which it came near to proclaiming that foresight of a virtual certainty is a form of intent, that:

> Where a man realises that it is for all practical purposes inevitable that his actions will result in death or serious harm, the inference may be irresistible that he intended that result, however little he may have desired or wished it to happen. The decision is one for the jury to be reached upon a consideration of all the evidence.

This quote may not be consistent with *Hancock and Shankland*, which is not necessarily restricted to deriving intent from foresight of virtual certainty, but may include deriving intent from a lesser degree of foresight than foresight of a virtual certainty. The Court of Appeal did, however, purport to apply that authority. *Nedrick* emphasised that not even foresight of a virtually certain consequence constitutes intention. In other words, foresight of a virtual certainty is not in itself intent but only part of the evidence as to whether the accused did intend the prohibited outcome. This ruling was not absolutely clear in *Moloney* where the question for the Lords was whether the *mens rea* for murder was established by proof of foresight 'that death or serious harm would probably occur'. The House rejected such foresight as malice aforethought. The guidelines are inconsistent with the speech of Lord Scarman in *Hancock and Shankland*, where he deprecated the use of guidelines. Lord Lane CJ, the leading member of the court in *Nedrick*, later said extrajudicially that he could not have been as clear as he would have liked because he was faced with two Lords' decisions.

The Court of Appeal in *Ward* (1987) 85 Cr App R 71 reiterated the view taken in all authorities that except in difficult cases only a simple direction of an intent was necessary: there was no need for an instruction on the difference between wanting and intending, unless such a distinction was called for by the facts. Another example is *Fallon* [1994] Crim LR 519. The prosecution alleged that the accused intended to kill a constable who was searching him by firing a pistol. The accused contended that the shooting was accidental. The Court of Appeal held that on these facts either the shooting was deliberate or it was not. In neither case did the defendant's foresight enter into the matter. Therefore, the trial judge was wrong to direct the jury as to foresight.

Walker and Hayles

The fourth case involved defendants who threw their victim from a third-floor balcony. They were tried for attempted murder. The sole mental element for that offence is the intention to kill. The Court of Appeal said:

(a) echoing *Belfon*, above, that ordinary people find no difficulty in knowing what intent means; the core meaning of intent is 'purpose'. In the words of the court: 'It has never been suggested that a man does not intend what he is trying to achieve.' It was only in rare cases that an elaborate direction on intent was needed. The exceptional case is one where the accused achieves a result which he did not try to obtain. A request from the jury for such an instruction does not make the case into an exceptional one;

(b) it was not a misdirection for a judge to direct that a very high degree of probability of a result happening was required, provided that intention remained a matter for the jury and that the line between intent and recklessness was drawn. Foresight was not to be equated with intent. However, it was better to use the phrase 'virtual certainty', as *Nedrick* had done. Again the court stressed that foresight of a virtually certain consequence was not intent.

In effect the court equated 'virtual certainty' and 'a very high degree of probability'. Yet there is a substantial difference between a virtual certainty and a high probability. If something is virtually certain, it is almost inevitable that it will occur. If an event will highly probably occur, it is only highly likely that it will. The two concepts are not the same. As the bomb-on-the-plane hypothetical illustration shows, because of chance occurrences, for example, few results are certain. An assassin can intend to kill an emperor, even though at the last second the empress leans across and takes the full force of the bullet. Foresight of a very high degree of probability looks like the *mens rea* of one form of manslaughter. As a result juries might have been uncertain as to what is the minimum degree of foresight needed before they may infer intent from foresight. Can one infer intent when the accused foresaw a result as probable, likely, on the cards, and so on? Perhaps judges should use the formulation of Lord Lane CJ in *Nedrick*: did the accused think that the consequence – death or grievous bodily harm – was 'inevitable'? Indeed Lord Lane CJ, the principal judge in *Nedrick*, said in the House of Lords' debate on the Nathan Report (*Report of the Select Committee of the House of Lords on Murder and Life Imprisonment*, 1989) that he did not consider virtual certainty and high probability as covering the same ground. Otherwise, jurors in some cases might think that a virtual certainty is required, while in others they may believe that it is sufficient that the result was very likely. *Walker and Hayles* was not a helpful decision in elucidating intention and (b) above is wrong after *Woollin*. The defendants would nowadays be guilty of manslaughter and not of murder.

Woollin

Woollin [1999] 1 AC 82 (HL)

The accused's baby began to choke on some food. The accused became angry and threw the baby towards his pram, which was against a wall. The baby's head hit the wall or possibly the floor. The baby died. At the trial for murder the accused alleged that he did not intend to cause death or grievous bodily harm. The prosecution did not seek to prove that he did. The judge ruled that the jury could infer intent if the defendant foresaw serious harm as a 'substantial risk' of his actions. The jury convicted. The Court of Appeal dismissed the appeal, but the House of Lords allowed it because the conviction was unsafe.

The principal speech was delivered by Lord Steyn.

(a) The judge's reference to 'substantial risk' was wrong. He had blurred the distinction between intent and recklessness. The accused was guilty of manslaughter, not of murder.

(b) *Nedrick* was correct in holding that the prosecution had to prove foresight of a virtual certainty before the jury might find that the accused intended a consequence. In different words, references to 'high probability' and other degrees of likelihood are incorrect. While *Woollin* did not expressly overrule *Walker and Hayles*, that authority must be taken to have been overruled.

(c) A judge should not direct a jury as to foresight where the accused did desire a result. In that situation no definition of intent should be given to the jury, who in accordance with *Moloney* have to use their good sense to determine whether or not the accused did intend to kill or cause GBH. A post-*Woollin* illustration is *Hales* [2005] EWCA Crim 1118, above. The accused drove his car at a policeman in order to escape. He either intended to kill or he did not. There was no space for a direction about foresight.

For further details of *Hales*, see the start of this section on intention. A *Nedrick* direction was needed only when the accused 'may not have had the desire to achieve that result'.

(d) Lord Lane CJ was, however, wrong in *Nedrick* to refer to how probable the consequences were (which is a matter of *actus reus*) and to whether the accused foresaw that consequence. These issues were unhelpful to the jury.

(e) Lord Lane's direction in *Nedrick*, which Lord Steyn thought was of 'valuable assistance to trial judges', was modified. He had said: 'the jury should be directed that they are not entitled to infer the necessary intention unless they feel sure that death or serious injury was a virtual certainty.' The Lords stated that 'infer' should be replaced by 'find'. ('Infer', as used in *Nedrick*, is also the language of the Criminal Justice Act 1967, s 8, that: 'A . . . jury . . . shall not be bound in law to infer that [the accused] intended . . . a result of his actions by reason only of its being a natural and probable consequence of those actions . . .') A terrorist who does not foresee the death of a bomb disposal expert as a virtually certain consequence of planting a bomb is not guilty of murder, contrary to the opinion of Lord Bridge in *Moloney*.

(f) There has been debate about whether Lord Scarman in *Hancock and Shankland* meant that a jury could find intent when the evidence disclosed something less than foresight of a virtual certainty. The House of Lords in *Woollin* stated that since Lord Scarman had approved everything which Lord Bridge said in *Moloney* except the reference to 'natural consequences', he had approved the minimum threshold of foresight of a virtual certainty (or otherwise put, where the probability of a consequence's occurring is little short of overwhelming) for finding intent.

(g) *Hancock and Shankland* did not rule out the framing of model directions.

(h) *Nedrick* is consistent with s 8 of the Criminal Justice Act 1967 because the jury has to take all the evidence into account.

(i) The Court of Appeal has been wrong to distinguish between cases where the only evidence is that of the accused and of the consequence (where *Nedrick* was necessary) and cases in which there was other evidence (where a *Nedrick* instruction was not necessary).

(j) Lord Steyn said that the definition of intent may vary throughout the criminal law. This aspect is dealt with below.

The major clarification lies in (e), above. Lord Steyn thought that he was merely clarifying the law, but on the most common interpretation of *Woollin* he was changing it. No longer is foresight just evidence of intent. The jury may now find intent from foresight of a virtual certainty. One interpretation of this phrase is that there are again two forms of intent for murder and most other crimes of intent. First, there is direct intent, where 'intent' means 'aim', 'purpose' or 'desire'; secondly, there is oblique intent, where the accused foresaw a consequence as virtually certain. This approach is that there is a change in substantive law. It is not that the second state of mind is a way of showing that the accused had the intent, but that there is a separate form of intent. The law would be clear and there would be no problem of inferring one state of mind from another state of mind. This interpretation comes from the substitution of 'find' for 'infer' in (e), the approval of Lord Bridge's speech in *Moloney* that if a person foresees the probability of a consequence as little short of overwhelming, this 'will suffice to *establish* the necessary intent', and the statement by Lord Steyn that the effect of *Nedrick* was that 'a result foreseen as virtually certain is an intended result'.

The alternative view is that the second state of mind is still only evidence of the first frame of mind. Foresight of a virtual certainty is not a definition of intent, only evidence from which a jury may, but need not, find intent. This interpretation is supported by the approval of the rest of Lord Lane's sentence, quoted above, that the inference of intent '*may* be irresistible'. There is nothing here about 'must be irresistible', even if one substitutes 'finding' for 'inference'. The jury may hold, therefore, that a consequence foreseen by the accused as virtually certain is not intended by him though presumably in most cases it will be so. Had Lord Steyn wished to change the law he would have said that a jury *must* find intent, not that they were entitled to find intent. The problem is that Lord Steyn and the rest of the Law Lords do not seem to understand that there is a difference between foresight being intent and foresight being evidence of intent. Authorities such as **Moloney** and **Hancock and Shankland** were not overruled as being inconsistent with **Woollin**.

In the year or two following **Woollin** it was suggested that **Woollin** took the former approach: the accused does have intent if he foresees a result as a virtually certain consequence. This outcome would certainly clarify the law, as Lord Steyn desired. It was also the approach taken in the first Court of Appeal decision after **Woollin**: **Re A (Children) (Conjoined Twins: Medical Treatment)** [2001] Fam 147 (CA), a civil case. Surgeons separating conjoined twins intended to kill when they foresaw the death of one as a virtually certain consequence. There was no discussion of whether on the facts a jury would be 'entitled to find' intent. Ward LJ said: 'The test . . . is . . . whether . . . the doctors recognise that death or serious harm will be virtually certain (barring some unforeseen intervention) to result from carrying out this operation. If so, the doctors intend to kill or to do that serious harm . . .' Brooke LJ spoke to similar effect and therefore there was a majority in favour of equating the two states of mind. Robert Walker LJ, however, said that despite the death of one twin being certain, the doctors did not intend for death because that was not their purpose.

There is, however, strong recent contrary authority in the form of **Matthews** [2003] 2 Cr App R 461 (CA), in which **Re A** was not mentioned: foresight of virtual certainty remains evidence of intent and is not, *per se*, intent. The defendants had thrown the victim into a river despite his telling them he could not swim. He drowned. They did not desire his death; they did not make up their minds to kill him. They were convicted of murder at first instance. While the trial judge had equated foresight of a virtual certainty with intent, the Court of Appeal held that the jury would have been sure that the defendants knew of the virtual certainty on the facts that the victim would die and that the jury would have found that the defendants intended to kill. However, the model direction given in **Nedrick** and amended in **Woollin** ('infer' becoming 'find') was not a rule of substantive law but one of evidence. As pointed out by the court on the facts of certain cases such as **Matthews**, the line between a rule of substantive law and one of evidence is not wide: it was very easy, perhaps irresistible, for the jury to find intent when the accused threw the victim, who they knew could not swim, into a river. On the facts it was just about impossible for the jury not to find that the defendant foresaw the victim's death as a virtual certainty.

This line of reasoning was adopted in later cases such as **Stringer** [2008] EWCA Crim 1322. The accused set light to an accelerant at the foot of the house stairs. The victim, who was wearing earphones, did not wake up and died in the fire. The court said that: '. . . it was a virtual certainty that someone in the house would suffer really serious harm or death . . . It would be wholly unrealistic to imagine all the occupants escaping from the house by jumping from the upstairs windows without any of them suffering any serious harm.' It continued by stating that the accused '*must have* [emphasis added] appreciated . . . it was overwhelming' and the conclusion that he had the necessary intent '*was bound to* follow' [emphasis added]. It would be more difficult for a jury to find intent when the accused acted for a good purpose. It must be remembered that it is only rarely that a *Woollin* direction is needed.

Summary

If the accused *did* intend to kill or commit GBH, that is the end of the question: *Woollin* is irrelevant. The trial judge in such cases should steer the jury away from 'the chameleon-like concepts of . . . foresight of consequences and awareness of risk' (*Wright* [2000] EWCA Crim 28). One may encapsulate the law by saying, as did *Matthews*, that jurors 'are not entitled to find the necessary intention unless they [feel] sure that death or serious bodily harm was a virtual certainty as a result of [the accused's] actions and that [he] appreciated that this was the case'. Even then the jurors may reject the evidence and hold that he did not intend the consequence.

Criticism

Moloney and its progeny do not reflect creditably on English law. Lord Bingham CJ in 'Lord Chief Justice calls for a criminal code' (1998) 148 NLJ 1134 stated: 'even the most breathless admirer of the common law must regard it as a reproach that after seven hundred years of judicial decision-making our highest tribunal should have been called upon time and time again in recent years to consider the mental ingredients of murder, the oldest and most serious of crimes.' Why cannot the judiciary define the core concept in this extremely serious case? Juries may acquit or convict on the same facts. Because there is no set definition, unmeritorious defendants may win appeals against judges' directions when they might not have been able to even bring an appeal had the law been clear. C.M.V. Clarkson's criticism of *Moloney et al.* remains apposite:

> A concept such as 'dishonesty' involves value judgments . . . and the jury, as the mouthpiece of community values, is probably the most appropriate body to express such judgments. But the same is not true of intention . . . In the interests of certainty and predictability it is surely for *the law* to determine what intention means . . . The House of Lords, by leaving intention undefined, is trying to retain maximum flexibility so that juries do not have to resort to perverse verdicts to convict those felt deserving of conviction. Many . . . terrorist bombers who do not necessarily mean to kill . . . could escape liability for murder if a clear and narrow definition of intention were laid down . . . This is an intolerable position inviting prejudice, discrimination and abuse. It involves the abandoning of all standards in an area of law where it is crucial that standards be clearly laid down. (*Understanding Criminal Law* (Fontana, 1987) 62)

Slightly different words appear in the fourth edition (Thomson, 2005) 61–3. There is nothing to stop a jury from, as it were, taking the law into its own hands and convicting defendants of murder even though they did not purposely seek to kill or cause grievous bodily harm.

The next criticism has often been made. If one is dealing with oblique intent, by definition there is no direct intent. Therefore, 'purpose', 'aim', 'decision' and the like are not oblique intent. Moreover, as a general rule motive or desire is irrelevant to guilt; therefore, they too cannot constitute oblique intent. Since aim, purpose, decision, motive and desire are ruled out, what is the ingredient which juries use to determine whether what the accused foresaw as a virtually certain consequence converts such a state of mind into intent? In other words, one state of mind, intent, cannot be inferred from another, foresight of a virtual certainty.

What about where the accused knew that a result was virtually certain to occur but intended the opposite? For example, assume that I am a novice at archery and I expect to miss the target on most occasions; nevertheless, I do intend to hit the target, even though I know that it is virtually certain that I will miss it. Yet after *Woollin* the courts could say that I intend to hit (desire or purpose) and at the same time I intend to miss (my foresight of a virtual certainty). The outcome is illogical!

Criticism may also be directed at the width of oblique intent. This point is very well put by S. Uniacke 'Was Mary's death murder?' (2001) 9 Medical LR 208, 217: '. . . to regard all killing that is foreseen by the actor as a virtual certainty as intended killing seems to include too much. For instance, if my car brakes fail I might deliberately swerve onto the footpath, foreseeing that I will kill one person who would not be able to get out of the way in time, rather than steer a straight course and run into a group of school children on a pedestrian crossing.'

Another criticism is that in present law the accused may be guilty if he foresees a consequence as a virtual certainty. In addition, there is the statement that the result must actually be a virtually certain consequence before the accused can be guilty. This objective test is inconsistent with the subjective nature of intent. If the terrorist plants a bomb, knowing that it is virtually certain that a person will be killed, why should it affect liability that a bomb-proof barrier has been erected that day between the bomb and the intended victim? His state of mind has not changed. All that has changed is something external to him.

As J. Stannard wrote in *Recent Developments in Criminal Law* (SLS, 1988) 38, malice aforethought is a confusing area because the courts are shifting the boundaries to catch persons whom they wish to be convicted of murder, while exculpating others. There is tension in the law. Some people wish the law to be flexible, to have in the words of Jeremy Horder ('Intention in criminal law: a rejoinder' (1995) 58 MLR 678) 'moral elbowroom' within which the jury can work. The contrary approach is that since murder is a particularly serious crime, it must be defined exactly: in other words, whether a person is convicted of murder should not depend on the jury's likes and dislikes. What a jury does is to consider the accused's moral sense; it should, however, according to *Woollin* consider which particular degree of foresight the accused had when he acted.

The main problem involves terrorists. Lord Bridge in *Moloney*, as we have seen, gave the illustration of a bomber who gave a warning. Is he guilty of murdering the bomb disposal expert whom he expected to be called in? Lord Bridge seems to think he is, as did Lord Hope in *Woollin*, but on his definition the bomber did not have malice aforethought. There is neither the desire or aim to cause death or serious injury nor foresight of death or serious harm as virtually certain. The position remains the same after *Woollin*: death or grievous bodily harm is not foreseen as a virtually certain consequence but there is no statutory list of factors which a jury must take into account when determining from the fact that the accused did foresee a consequence as virtually certain that he did also intend it. The courts wish to make terrorists guilty of murder, but exculpate persons like Moloney from that charge. However, terrorists could be found guilty of manslaughter and sentenced to life imprisonment, thereby maintaining a 'pure' concept of intention. Moreover, if the concept of intent is being expanded and contracted to reach a desirable outcome, why was Mrs Hyam found guilty of murder? Perhaps as suggested by C. Fennell 'Intention in murder: chaos, confusion and complexity' (1990) 41 NILQ 325 at 337–338 there should be an offence of second degree murder if the accused was aware of the risk of death or intended to cause fear. This proposal would catch terrorists who took a risk that someone might be killed or seriously injured.

It is unfortunate that the modern definition of intent has largely been laid down in murder cases. The result may have been 'pulled' by the facts, yet the law in these cases applies throughout the criminal law. If one looks at Lord Bridge's example in *Moloney* of a terrorist who plants a bomb and gives a warning, he foresees that someone may seek to defuse it but he does not foresee death or serious harm as being virtually certain. Bomb disposal experts do not become bomb disposal experts by getting killed or injured! Yet Lord Bridge would convict the terrorist of murder if the expert died. The difficulty lies in reconciling the core meaning of murder as deliberate killing and the need to satisfy public opinion that those who take a risk and kill (such as terrorists) are guilty of murder. The desire to convict terrorists of murder 'pulls' the law one way; the desire not to convict doctors of murder pulls it another way. In *Moor* [2000] Crim LR 31, noted below, the trial judge in a case of a doctor's prescribing pain-killing drugs to a patient he believed to be terminally ill directed the jury in terms of direct intent but failed to mention foresight of a virtually certain consequence, oblique intent. Yet had he done so, a jury should have found that the doctor knew that acceleration of death was virtually certain.

Intent is a real problem for judges and juries. Judges have to use ordinary English words so that juries understand the instruction, but 'intention' continues to elude clear judicial definition.

Does the definition of 'intent' in murder extend throughout the criminal law?

The House of Lords in *Moloney* and *Hancock and Shankland* did not restrict its remarks to murder. Its definition has been applied generally. In *AMK (Property Management) Ltd* [1985] Crim LR 600, the Court of Appeal applied this law to the offence under s 1(3) of the Protection from Eviction Act 1977: doing acts calculated to interfere with the peace or comfort of a residential occupier with intent to cause him to give up occupation. (See, however, below.) In *Bryson* [1985] Crim LR 669, the same court applied the law to wounding with intent to do grievous bodily harm, contrary to the Offences Against the Person Act 1861, s 18, when the accused drove at and knocked down four men celebrating the forthcoming wedding of one of their group. As we have seen, *Walker and Hayles*, above, involved attempted murder, where the sole *mens rea* is the intent to kill. The Court of Appeal of Northern Ireland held in *Murphy* [1993] NI 57 that 'common sense, reality and experience' led to the conclusion that when the IRA launched rockets and fired rifles at police stations they did intend to kill. No warning was given, and the weapons used were not ones for destroying buildings. Presumably the definition applies also where the term 'intent' does not stand alone in the definition of the offence but the crime is stated in terms of 'intentionally or recklessly' such as criminal damage. In these situations, however, the definition of intent is less important than in the three crimes just mentioned where the accused is not guilty if he acts recklessly.

In *Woollin* the House of Lords confined its remarks to murder. If *Woollin* does not apply, the problem is to discover which test does apply. Perhaps in relation to the crime of attempt only direct intent suffices with regard to consequences. That is, the accused's aim must be to cause the forbidden result; it is not sufficient that he foresaw it as a virtually certain consequence.

In *Moloney* the Lords approved *Steane* [1947] KB 997, where the Court of Criminal Appeal laid down a narrower definition of intent. As a result, there is no one definition which applies across the criminal law. The accused was convicted of doing acts likely to assist the enemy when he did a broadcast for the Nazis in order to save his family from the concentration camp. The court quashed the conviction. It held that his intention was to save his family, that intent was not part of the *mens rea* of the crime; therefore, he did not intend to assist the enemy. The accused did not desire to help the Nazis, but current law is to the effect that the desire or motive of the defendant is immaterial to 'intent'. One can intend something without desiring it: **Mohan**, above, and **Nedrick**, the relevant part of which is quoted above. The accused's good motive, protecting his family, is irrelevant. Similarly, a bad motive, say, a wish to get rid of a wife in favour of a younger person, is immaterial. For more on 'desire' see Motive, above. Under the **Moloney** approach surely he did foresee that it was (at least) virtually certain that he would be helping the enemy, and a jury could infer that he did intend to aid. Moreover, Lord Bridge in **Moloney** said that the accused intended to go to Manchester if the sole way he could escape the police was to go there, 'even though Manchester is the last place he wants to be'. **Steane** looks like a case of narrowing the law to exculpate the accused. The court wished to ensure that the accused's conviction could not be upheld, and to do so it manipulated the meaning of intention. It was able to do that because there is no one definition of intent which is accepted for all offences. **Steane** confuses an already confused area and should be overruled. **Steane** is also inconsistent with modern cases on duress which hold that that defence does not operate to negate intent. The accused did intend, but he has a defence.

Refer back in this chapter for a discussion of the *Steane* case. Note how a definition may vary from offence to offence.

More recently in the civil case of **Airedale NHS Trust v Bland** [1993] AC 789 (HL) Lord Goff said that it was an 'established rule' that a doctor could prescribe painkilling drugs knowing that they would shorten life, yet not be guilty of murder. **Re A**, above, the case of the conjoined twins, is similar: the surgeons knew that on separation one of the twins would die, but the Court of Appeal struggled to find a rule or rules which would exculpate doctors if they were put on trial. **Moor**, cited above, is a criminal case of a doctor's accelerating death but being found not guilty. The trial judge, Hooper J, said: 'a person intends to kill another person if he does an act . . . for the purpose of killing that person. If [the accused] thought . . . that it was only highly probable that death would follow . . . , then the prosecution would not have proved that he intended to kill . . .' This looks like the judge saying that proper treatment, including providing pain-killing drugs which incidentally shorten life, does not constitute an intent to murder. If so this defence needs public discussion. An alternative view is to say that the judge was laying down an unacknowledged new defence to murder available only to those providing medical treatment. Again, if we have such a defence, public debate beforehand is vital in a democracy.

The type of intention in **Steane**, sometimes called 'direct intent', may apply elsewhere. In the well-known case of **Ahlers** [1915] 1 KB 616 (CCA) the court held that a German consul was not guilty of treason when he assisted fellow nationals to return to their native land. He did not intend to aid the UK's enemies, merely to perform his consular duties. Applying modern law, the accused should have been found guilty. Alternatively, a different definition of intent, namely 'purpose', applies to this offence. Some statutes seem to require a certain purpose. In burglary, one form of the crime is trespassory entry with intent to commit one of a list of offences. It must be that intent in this context means 'purpose'. In blackmail the accused must act with 'intent' to gain or to cause loss. 'Intent' means direct intent. Similarly in the Protection from Eviction Act 1977, mentioned above, 'intent' means 'purpose' and the accused is not liable if he did not act with the purpose of getting the tenant out, even if he foresaw it as virtually certain that that result would occur. In the crime of using or threatening violence for the purpose of securing entry into premises only direct intent suffices. In such cases oblique intent will not suffice. The point is that **Steane** is not an isolated decision and **Moloney et al.** do not apply to all 'intent' crimes. There is debate among academics as to whether and if so which crimes are satisfied only when the accused acted with direct intent.

Proposals for defining intention

The *Report of the Select Committee of the House of Lords on Murder and Life Imprisonment* (HL Paper 78–1, 1989) and the Law Commission's Report, *A Criminal Code for England and Wales* (Law Com. No. 177, 1989) both recommended that foresight by the accused of a virtual certainty should amount to intention. The enactment of this recommendation would mean that foresight would again be part of substantive law, not merely part of evidence. The Law Commission stated that 'intention' should be defined in the interests of clarity and consistency. The Select Committee also wished to abolish the head of malice aforethought which is the intent to cause grievous bodily harm, and replace it by the intent to cause serious personal harm, being aware that death may be caused. The Select Committee approved, therefore, cl 54(1) of the draft Criminal Code, which states:

[a] person is guilty of murder if he causes the death of another –
(a) intending to cause death; or
(b) intending to cause serious personal harm and being aware that he may cause death.

The definition was approved by Lord Steyn in **Powell; English** [1998] AC 147 (HL). In his view, 'the present definition of the mental element of murder results in defendants being classified as murderers who are in truth not murderers'. 'Being aware' connotes subjective knowledge. It would not be sufficient that a reasonable person would have known but the accused did not. It may be that the test will be hard to apply. Furthermore, there seems to be little, if any, moral difference between intending to cause serious harm being aware that one may cause death and simply being aware that one may cause death. Both states of mind are ones of taking a risk, recklessness.

Intention is defined by cl 18(b) as covering both direct intent and oblique intent:

[a] person acts 'intentionally' with respect to . . .
(ii) a result when he acts either in order to bring it about or being aware that it will occur in the ordinary course of events.

Intention is therefore to be defined as to go beyond direct intent, something which it does not do in ordinary language. The accused in **Steane** would be guilty. The Law Commission thought that this change was demanded by justice. It would exclude foresight of anything less than a virtual certainty. This definition received the approval of Lord Lane CJ in the debate on the Select Committee's Report. Clause 18(b) would not cover the terrorist who plants a bomb intending to damage property and cause fear but not to kill or injure. Professor Smith criticised the width of the formulation. He wanted it to cover the terrorist who knows that half of his bombs will not explode. 'In the ordinary course of events' he is not virtually certain that a victim will die. He proposed to redraft (ii) as including the situation where 'his purpose is to cause some other result and he knows that, if he succeeds, his act will, in the ordinary course of events, cause that result' ([1990] Crim LR 85).

The Law Commission accepted this revision in *Legislating the Criminal Code – Offences against the Person and General Principles*, Law Com. No. 218, 1993. Clause 1(a) of the Criminal Law Bill attached to the Report states:

A person acts 'intentionally' with respect to a result when –

(i)   it is his purpose to cause it, or

(ii) although it is not his purpose to cause that result, he knows that it would occur in the ordinary course of events if he were to succeed in his purpose of causing some other result.

The replacement of 'in order to' with 'purpose' was thought to aid clarity; 'knows' replaced 'is aware' because the Law Commission thought that the awareness connoted a less clear appreciation than knowledge; and knowledge is linked to purpose, unlike in the draft Criminal Code, in order to disabuse people that intention might cover recklessness. The Law Commission rejected extending intention to awareness of any degree of probability less than virtual certainty. Such forethought would constitute recklessness. Therefore, the word used is 'would'. The accused has to know that an event would definitely occur unless something extraordinary occurred. The boundary between the concepts of intent and recklessness would be clearly drawn. Had the draft been 'he knows that it *might* occur', that state of mind is recklessness.

The Law Commission published its Report no. 306, *Murder, Manslaughter and Infanticide* in 2006. It is based on its Consultation Paper of 2005, *A New Homicide Act for England and Wales?* The Commission's view was that the mental element for first degree murder should be intent to kill and intent to cause serious injury, being aware that one's conduct involves a serious risk of causing death. Second degree murder would also comprise states of mind defined in terms of intent: intent to cause serious injury, and intent to cause injury, fear of injury or a risk of injury, being aware that one's conduct involves a serious risk of death. Therefore, intent would remain the *mens rea* of murder but there would be gradations in murder dependent on the state of mind of the accused.

The Commission was then faced with defining 'intent'. It had postulated two definitions in the Consultation Paper but having determined that current law could not to be left to common law, it decided to codify current law (though no supporting argument was given in the Report as to why the common law had to be codified) and it decided not to provide an extended meaning, which had been one of the options canvassed in the Paper. The revised definition is set out in para. 3.27:

1   A person should be taken to intend a result if he or she acts in order to bring it about.

2   In cases where the judge believes that justice may not be done unless an expanded understanding of intention is given, the jury should be directed as follows: an intention to bring about a result may be found if it is shown that the defendant thought that the result was a virtually certain consequence of his or her action.

This definition therefore covers an accused in this situation (para. 3.13):

D is in the process of stealing V's car. V leaps onto the car bonnet to deter D from driving off. D accelerates to 100 miles per hour and V falls off the car. The fall kills V. D claims he did not intend to kill V or cause V serious injury but was simply determined to escape come what may.

Common law leaves this issue to the jury, and if enacted, the recommendations in the Report would do similarly. It should also be remembered that as is the case with current law, it will be rare for a judge to give a 'virtually certain' instruction: normally, only the first direction ('in order to bring it about') will be needed, which again is the same as current law. Incidentally, the Law Commission opines that the jury would find intent in the example given (see para. 3.14) but it remains the case that the issue is one for the jury. The Commission also clarified that a person thinks a consequence is virtually certain to occur 'so long as he or she thinks that it will be virtually certain *if they do as they mean to do.*

For example, if someone plants a bomb on a plane intending to detonate it when the plane is in mid-air, given that they mean to detonate it, they can be taken to foresee the deaths of the passengers if they realise that the home-made bomb is unreliable and might fail to detonate as planned' (footnote 9 on p. 56). The Commission recognises that their proposed approach leaves discretion in the juries' hands but says (at para. 3.21): '. . . it is sometimes necessary and desirable that juries should have the element of discretion if the alternative is a more complex set of legal rules that they must apply. It is the price of avoiding complexity.' The Commission also thought that the current definition of intent had not caused any difficulties for juries.

Whatever happens, 'it is in the interests of clarity and the consistent application of criminal law to define intention', as the Law Commission put it (at 193). Present law lacks that clarity. As Stanley Yeo wrote in *Fault in Homicide* (Federation Press, 1997) 50: 'The law lacks a clear definition of intention which is a gross failure on the part of the English courts given the pivotal role that this concept plays in determining culpability for murder and, indeed, for many other offences.'

Summarising, under present law a person who kills foreseeing death or grievous bodily harm as virtually certain may be a murderer. Under the reformed scheme he would be a murderer.

Recklessness

Example

A girl, aged 14, tired, hungry and with learning difficulties, sets fire to a shed after pouring flammable liquid (white spirit) around. Is she guilty of arson?

Arson is criminal damage by fire (see Chapter 18). These are the facts of *Elliott v C* [1983] 1 WLR 939 (DC). Before *G* [2004] AC 1034 (HL) she was liable, as the court held in *Elliott v C*, applying *Caldwell* [1982] AC 341 (HL): she had given no thought to an obvious and serious risk of criminal damage. The reason why she had given no thought, for example her age, her 'backwardness', as the court put it, was irrelevant. After *G*, however, she is not liable. She did not herself foresee the risk of damage. Her learning difficulties, etc., explain why she did not foresee that risk.

G [2004] AC 1034

Avid readers of this textbook will have noted the downgrading of *Caldwell* [1982] AC 341 from 'the most important case' in Anglo-Welsh criminal law to 'for a decade thought to be the most important case'. The Lords have now overruled *Caldwell*, making it in practice one of the least important cases in Anglo-Welsh criminal law. Nevertheless, the 20 or so years of *Caldwell* remain significant theoretically and even after its demise the law of objective **recklessness** remains of importance, as will shortly be explained.

Facts and decision

Like *Caldwell* the facts of *G* are simple. Two boys, aged 11 and 12, set fire to some newspapers in the backyard of a shop. They threw the lit papers under a rubbish bin. The fire spread to the shop and some £1 million worth of damage was caused. The boys were charged with arson contrary to s 1(1) and (3) of the Criminal Damage Act 1971. They were found guilty at first instance, the trial judge directing the jury in accordance with *Caldwell*. The Lords overruled *Caldwell* and held that the boys were not guilty of arson. They did not foresee criminal damage. The House adopted the Law Commission's draft Criminal Code (Report No. 177, 1989) definition:

See Chapter 18 for more information on the relationship between arson and the Criminal Damage Act 1971.

A person acts recklessly . . . with respect to
(i) a circumstance when he is aware of a risk that it exists or will exist;
(ii) a result when he is aware of a risk that it will occur,
a result when he is aware of a risk that it will occur, and it is, in the circumstance known to him, unreasonable to take the risk.

Actually there is one way in which the boys could have been convicted of arson. If they adverted to the risk that by throwing lit newspapers they would set fire to rubbish underneath the bin, then this would set fire to the bin itself, and then they would be reckless as to criminal damage (to the bin), and as this fire caused damage to the shop, then they should have been convicted of arson to the shop.

What did *Caldwell* decide?

Caldwell held that for the purposes of s 1 of the Criminal Damage Act 1971 a person acted recklessly if (1) there was an obvious (and serious) risk of damage and either (2a) he gave no thought to the possibility of such a risk or (2b) he recognised that there was a risk but nevertheless went ahead. This is a short form of the definition given by Lord Diplock and for a full exegesis of this definition the reader is advised to read pp. 118–26 of the sixth edition of *Criminal Law*. (2b) is sometimes known as 'subjective recklessness' – did this accused foresee the relevant risk? This type of recklessness has existed for more than a century and the principal authority remains *Cunningham* [1957] 2 QB 396 (CCA). The words used were: 'The accused has foreseen that the particular kind of harm might be done and yet has gone on to take the risk of it.' (2a) is objective recklessness: might a reasonable person foresee a risk of some harm occurring? *G* overruled (2a), often known as *Caldwell* recklessness. Subjective recklessness (2b) remains. Since the boys did not foresee the risk of damage, they were not guilty of arson.

For a short while in the years following *Caldwell* objective recklessness was taken to apply to all offences of recklessness unless Parliament had otherwise ordained: *Seymour* [1983] 2 AC 493 (HL) *per* Lord Roskill. Offences committed maliciously, which means, as *Cunningham* held, 'intentionally or recklessly', constituted the main example of offences where Parliament had otherwise ordained, and subjective recklessness continued to apply to such offences: see *Savage* [1992] 1 AC 699 (HL). However, even crimes such as rape, which at that time included the mental element of committing sexual intercourse knowing that the victim did not consent or being reckless as to whether the victim consented or not, were held to be ones of objective recklessness: see *Pigg* [1982] 1 WLR 762 (CA). However, the courts began what might be called a retreat from *Caldwell*, holding that certain offences including rape were not crimes of objective recklessness. Parliament also abolished two of the principal crimes of objective recklessness, reckless driving and causing death by reckless driving (on which see *Lawrence* [1982] AC 510 (HL) and *Reid* [1992] 1 WLR 793 (HL)). By 2000 it was difficult to find a crime of objective recklessness other than criminal damage, but the astute knew of recklessly flying a microlight plane and recklessly misusing personal data contrary to the Data Protection Act 1984.

How far does *G* go?

All the Law Lords held that the interpretation by *Caldwell* of s 1 of the Criminal Damage Act 1971 was incorrect. Parliament did not intend to give a novel definition to recklessness when it replaced the crime of malicious damage with that of intentional or reckless criminal damage. Four of their Lordships also said that *Caldwell*, besides being legally wrong, was morally repugnant: as Lord Bingham put it, '. . . it is not clearly blameworthy to do something involving a risk of injury to another if . . . one genuinely does not perceive the risk'. Such a person may 'fairly be accused of stupidity or lack of imagination, but neither of those failings should expose him to conviction of serious crime or the risk of punishment . . . It is neither moral nor just to convict a defendant . . . on the strength of what someone else would have apprehended if the defendant himself had no such apprehension'. (Lord Bingham, however, cast no doubt on what is sometimes known as 'constructive recklessness', i.e. the deeming of the accused to be reckless when intoxicated by alcohol or drugs for crimes of basic intent in the defence of drunkenness: see *Majewski* [1977] AC 443(HL) and the part of *Caldwell* which deals with intoxication). Lord Bingham also disapproved of *Elliott* v *C* [1983] 1 WLR 939 (DC, a case where a tired, hungry and 'backward' 14-year-old girl was convicted of arson): 'It is neither moral or just to convict a defendant (least of all a child) on the strength of what someone would have apprehended if the defendant had no such apprehension.' The House could have restricted their speeches to overruling *Elliott* v *C* because the defendants were children, thereby preserving *Caldwell* for adults or at least non-disabled ones, as suggested by the question certified by the Court of Appeal, but they did not: both statutory interpretation and moral considerations required the overruling of *Caldwell*.

However, the doctrine of parliamentary supremacy should not be forgotten. At the time when the House of Lords in its judicial capacity was abolishing objective recklessness, the House of Lords in its legislative capacity and the House of Commons were passing the Sexual Offences Act 2003. Unreasonable belief in the victim's consent is no longer a defence. The statute is, depressingly but unsurprisingly, unclear about children as defendants. The first quote from Lord Bingham, above, continues: 'Such a person [i.e. an objectively reckless one] may fairly be accused of stupidity or lack of imagination, but neither of these failings should expose him to conviction of serious crime or the risk of punishment.' Rape is a serious crime; the maximum punishment is life imprisonment. Yet it can now be committed by a person who believed on unreasonable grounds in the consent of the victim. Parliament has not heeded *G*. The then Home Secretary was pleased with the revised definition of rape, and there is something, indeed quite a bit, to be said in favour of objective recklessness in sexual offences but it is disappointing to see the arguments of academic commentators not being taken into account by Parliament on such an important issue. It will be interesting to see how the courts deal with boys of 11 and 12 years of age who are charged with rape and who contend that they gave no thought as to whether or not the victim was consenting or believed that the victim was consenting when a reasonable person would not have so believed. *Elliott* v *C* produced a disastrous outcome; surely we should be able to prevent similar injustices to children. It was as recent as 1998 that the doctrine of mischievous discretion was abolished.

Outstanding issues

(a) Lord Bingham said: 'I wish to make it as plain as I can that I am not addressing the meaning of "reckless" in any other statutory or common law context.' This proposition is very much akin to that of Lord Steyn in **Woollin** [1999] 1 AC 82 (HL) that the definition he gave for intent in murder was not necessarily the one which applied throughout criminal law. This method of proceeding is unacceptable in a mature system of law. Can it really be true that **Caldwell** is abolished for criminal damage but not for other offences of objective recklessness such as recklessly flying a microlight? Lord Bingham stated that a person was reckless as to a circumstance when 'he is aware of a risk that it exists or will exist' and that a person is reckless as to a consequence if 'he is aware of a risk that it will occur'. These are standard definitions of subjective recklessness as to a circumstance and as to a consequence and are generalisable throughout criminal law but he prefaced these definitions by saying that they applied for the purposes of the Criminal Damage Act 1971.

In **B** [2000] 2 AC 428 (HL) in the context of strict liability a different formulation was made. In the context of sexual offences at least, if the accused has not thought about a circumstance, such as the consent of the victim, then he is guilty unless he believes that the circumstance does not exist. It is, it must be said, difficult to envisage someone who is not thinking about a circumstance but who at the same time genuinely believes that it does not exist. Perhaps an example might be this: Y and Z have been lovers for several years; Y does not on this occasion think about whether Z is consenting or not but, if asked, would say that he believes that his partner is consenting because he or she has always consented before. If this example is correct, Y is not guilty of rape as it was then defined under both **G** and **B**. If, however, Y and Z have not been in a long-term relationship but this is the first occasion of sexual intercourse, then if Y gave no thought to whether Z was consenting or not, he is not guilty under **G** but is under **B**.

Five Law Lords in **G** dealt with statutory interpretation, four of them with the lack of moral culpability of inadvertent recklessness. That leaves one Lord who did not treat of the moral dimension. This was Lord Rodger. He said that objective recklessness was a possible ground of liability for some offences. If **Caldwell** is overruled in relation to criminal damage but **Caldwell** is so morally repugnant that four Law Lords say that it should not be part of a civilised system of law, what scope is there for Lord Rodger's exception? It is highly tentatively suggested that what he may have had in mind was the previous offence of reckless driving. Here the recklessness is not as to a consequence or as to a circumstance but as to the *manner* in which the act, driving, was performed. Lord Bingham said: '. . . I would wish to throw no doubt on the decisions of this House in **Lawrence** and **Reid**.' If there are offences where recklessness is as to the way in which the act is done, it may be that the mental element is one of objective recklessness. This issue will have to be settled in the future.

It would seem that the lower courts take **G** to apply to all offences. In **A-G's Reference (No. 3 of 2003)** [2004] EWCA Crim 868 the subjective test was applied to the common law crime of misconduct in a public office. In **Heard** [2007] EWCA Crim 125 it was said that recklessness in criminal law had the meaning attached to it in **G**. However, the House did not in **G** overrule cases which had held that **Caldwell** applied to various offences such as recklessly flying a microlight plane. If **Caldwell** continues to apply to such offences, there are very few of them. All major crimes of recklessness are nowadays ones of subjective recklessness,

(b) Cases like **G** and **B** indicate a return to subjective *mens rea*. It should be noted that nothing in **G** affects gross negligence manslaughter. The House of Lords in **Adomako** [1995] 1 AC 171 reestablished manslaughter by gross negligence, reviving the pre-*Caldwell* law (see Chapter 12). Similarly, nothing in *G* affects duress, whether by threats or circumstances. The Court of Appeal in *Graham* [1982] 1 WLR 294, which was approved by the Lords in *Howe* [1987] AC 417, held that in duress the accused's belief in the existence of the threat had to be based on reasonable grounds. Lord Steyn in *G* opined that *Graham* and *Howe* were correct. There is some contrary authority, *Martin* [2000] 2 Cr App R 42 (CA): see Chapter 7 for further details. *Martin*, as is demonstrated there, is incorrect. *G* also does not affect the law of intoxication. A drunken accused is guilty of recklessly causing the *actus reus* if he was very drunk, even though he did not foresee the outcome. This type of recklessness is sometimes known as 'constructive recklessness'. For more on intoxication, see Chapter 8.

(c) In both subjective and objective recklessness there exists the prerequisite that the accused's behaviour must not be justifiable. If the conduct is justified, there is no recklessness. For example, if a car driver swerves to avoid a child and as a result crashes into a van, on a charge of criminal damage to the van the driver is not reckless because his action was justified, even if he foresaw that some criminal damage might be caused to the van. At this stage the test is objective even in subjective recklessness: whether the accused thought his conduct was justified is irrelevant.

(d) Insofar as *Cunningham* and *G* have different definitions of subjective recklessness, it is suggested that it is the latter definition which applies. The House of Lords in *G* rather than using the earlier definition relied on the Law Commission's proposed definition and not on *Cunningham* and *G* is a decision of the highest authority. When in *Brady* [2006] EWCA Crim 2413 the accused sought to argue in a non-fatal offence case that recklessness required that there had to be an obvious and serious risk of harm, the court held that it did not. Foresight by the accused of a risk of some harm was sufficient – the risk did not have to be an 'obvious and serious' risk of some harm.

Some criticisms of objective recklessness

(a) *The viewpoint of legal authority*. When Parliament enacted the Criminal Damage Act 1971 it did not intend to change the law. It simply intended to replace the old-fashioned term of 'maliciously' with the modern term of 'recklessly'. Lord Diplock thought otherwise, but was wrong. The Act is based on a Report by the Law Commission, *Offences of Damage to Property*, Report No. 29, 1970, which wished the Act to do the same. The Court of Appeal in *Briggs* [1977] 1 WLR 605, *Parker* [1977] Crim LR 102 and *Stephenson* [1979] QB 695 did not attempt to state the law of recklessness in criminal damage in any way other than that underlying the proposals of the Law Commission and the 1971 Act. Criminal law previously drew the line for most serious offences between advertently taking a risk (guilty) and inadvertently doing so (innocent). *Caldwell* runs these morally different states of mind together. There is little support for *Caldwell* in the earlier law. For example, the Lords in *Andrews v DPP* [1937] AC 576 equated recklessness and gross negligence, postulating an objective standard of behaviour, but that case occurred before the law's terms were settled.

(b) It is often said that criminal law is based on choice. An accused should be guilty only if he had a choice to commit the crime. Choice includes a conscious decision to run the risk of causing harm. In other words, subjective recklessness is acceptable. However, if the accused does not consider whether harm may be caused, he had not chosen to break the law.

(c) ***Caldwell*** made people guilty who previously were not: they were careless but under ***Caldwell*** were reckless. (Incidentally the job of the prosecution was thereby facilitated.) The Supreme Court of Canada in ***Sansregret v R*** (1985) 17 DLR (4th) 577 said that negligence should not be confused with recklessness.

> Negligence is tested by the objective standard of the reasonable man. A departure from his accustomed sober behaviour by an act or omission which reveals less than reasonable care will involve liability at civil law but forms no basis for the imposition of criminal penalties . . . [R]ecklessness, to form part of the criminal *mens rea*, must have an element of the subjective. It is found in the attitude of one who, aware that there is danger that his conduct could bring about the result prohibited by the criminal law, nevertheless persists, despite the risk. . . . It is in this sense that the term 'recklessness' is used in the criminal law and it is clearly distinct from the concept of civil negligence.

(d) One of the theories of punishment is specific deterrence: an accused must be deterred by punishment from committing an offence. However, if he does not advert to the risk of harm, he cannot be deterred.

It is an issue of policy whether people who gave no thought to a risk should be criminally liable. Lord Diplock did not think that the law should distinguish between the two states of mind, being aware and taking a chance on the one hand and not being aware on the other. In his view both were equally culpable frames of mind. People are blamed for not taking care. If a scaffolder drops a piece of equipment carelessly, he would be blamed if the equipment hit someone in the street on the head. After all, punishment of such careless people may make them take care next time. The Lords in ***Reid*** [1992] 1 WLR 793 adopted this view too. Indeed, Lord Keith said that ***Cunningham*** recklessness was hard to apply. His proposition is difficult to accept, for thousands of juries have over the years used the subjective definition without question. Academic commentators have, on the whole, rejected his approach. S. France 'Reckless approach to liability' (1988) 18 VUWLR 141 at 152–153 made the point:

> The real dangers of ***Caldwell*** lie in its potential to bring the might of the criminal law into the ordinary situations of life by equating acts of negligence with deliberate wilful acts of malice . . . Such acts do not involve consciously dangerous antisocial activity.

Do we really want the accused guilty of arson in ***Elliott v C*** [1983] 1 WLR 939 (DC)? The accused was 14, tired, hungry and had learning difficulties. She set fire to a shed after sprinkling a flammable liquid around; and was found guilty of arson. She did not choose to break the law, and she lacked the capacity to realise that what she was doing was dangerous. It was not that her actions showed an indifference to the harm she caused but that she was not capable of foreseeing any risk because of her learning difficulties.

Legal policy also comes to the fore when one considers the thrusts of ***Caldwell*** and ***B v DPP*** [2000] 2 AC 428 (HL). The latter states that a person is not liable for an offence which for many years had been a crime of strict liability: *mens rea* in the sense of knowledge as to the age of the victim is needed; however, ***Caldwell*** stated that for offences of objective recklessness knowledge is not needed.

Reform

Both before and after ***Caldwell*** law reform bodies have recommended continuing with the ***Cunningham*** definition. The Law Commission in *The Mental Element in Crime*, Report

No. 89, 1978, the Criminal Law Revision Committee's Fourteenth Report, *Offences Against the Person*, Cmnd 7844, 1980, and the draft Criminal Code (Law Com. No. 177, 1989), all adopted the *Cunningham* approach. Lord Diplock did not refer to any English proposals. The sole law reform matter he looked at was the US Model Penal Code, and even then he did so selectively. Academic comment supported a return to *Cunningham*, which is thought to be easy to apply, instead of *Caldwell*, which was thought to be hard for juries and judges to understand. Recklessness would need a definition because without one a jury might think that recklessness and negligence were the same. The draft Code, cl 18(c), defined 'recklessly' in relation to offences contained in the Code thus:

A person acts 'recklessly' with respect to –
(i)   a circumstance when he is aware of a risk that it exists or will exist;
(ii) a result when he is aware of a risk that it will occur;
and it is, in the circumstances known to him, unreasonable to take the risk . . .

(The same definition occurs in *Legislating the Criminal Code – Offences Against the Person and General Principles*, Law Com. No. 218, 1993, and is the one adopted by the House of Lords in *G*.) Recklessness defined in this way would be the minimum level of fault in Code offences, unless otherwise provided (cl 20(1)). The Law Commission stated that cl 8(c) is to the same effect as the definition it proposed in its 1978 Report, *The Mental Element in Crime* (p 193). The Commission thought that a person should be liable only if he consciously took a risk, and it preferred to adopt the subjectivist approach, while leaving it open to Parliament to enact *Caldwell*, should it so wish. If the accused is unaware of the risk, the inadvertence is negligence and not part of the Code.

There are two or three distinctions between *Cunningham* and the draft Code. First, there is no reference in *Cunningham* to the justifiability of the risk, but that omission is soon remedied. If the risk is justified, it remained the case that the accused was not reckless under the *Cunningham* definition. Secondly, *Cunningham* did not refer to risks as to circumstances but the draft Code does. Thirdly, *Cunningham* refers to foresight of this *type* of harm whereas the draft Code refers to the actual harm caused, and in this respect the *Cunningham* definition appears wider than that in the draft Code. The House of Lords in *G* referred to the definition in the draft Code rather than that in *Cunningham*; it is likely that English law prefers the former to the latter for all crimes including non-fatal ones.

The Lords in *Reid* [1992] 1 WLR 793 spoke to the effect that the person who gave no thought to the possibility of harm or substantial damage when driving a car was just as blameworthy as someone who did consider the risk. The reader is invited to consider whether she or he agrees. The Lords stated also that the former (lack of a) state of mind constituted *mens rea*. Lord Keith said: 'Inadvertence to risk is no less a state of mind than is disregard of a recognised risk.' Lord Diplock in *Caldwell* stated that it required 'meticulous analysis' to distinguish between an accused who foresees a risk and one who ought to have foreseen one. Do you agree?

'Knowingly'

Parliament sometimes uses this word to impose a requirement of *mens rea*. For example, a person is guilty of handling only if he knows or believes the goods to be stolen. Where the definition of the offence does not include 'knowing', the courts sometimes read it in (see Chapter 4 on strict offences).

The criminal courts recognise several degrees of knowledge.

(a) *Actual knowledge*. The principal authority is **Roper v Taylor's Central Garages (Exeter) Ltd** [1951] 2 TLR 284 (DC). Devlin J said that this type of knowledge is when the accused knows for a fact that something exists or is true.

(b) *Wilful blindness*. Devlin J in **Roper** called this state of mind 'knowledge in the second degree'. Lord Bridge in **Westminster CC v Croyalgrange Ltd** [1986] 1 WLR 674 (HL) said that knowledge could be based 'on evidence that the defendant had deliberately shut his eyes to the obvious or refrained from enquiring because he suspected the truth but did not want to have his suspicions confirmed'. Although Lord Bridge spoke of 'inference', it is arguable that the rule is one of law: **Roper**, above.

(c) *Constructive knowledge*. Again this term was expanded in **Roper**. This degree of knowledge occurs when the accused ought as a reasonable person to have made inquiries. This is negligence (see below).

The first type is always covered by 'knowing' or 'knowingly'. The second type is usually covered, but not always. In handling, wilful blindness is not sufficient (see Chapter 17). The third is rare in traditional criminal law (see **Flintshire CC v Reynolds** [2006] EWHC 195 (Admin): 'constructive knowledge is not enough to demonstrate that something has been done knowingly in the context of a criminal statute' (per Smith LJ)) but arises when Parliament creates an offence where the accused had reasonable cause to believe. An example is s 25 of the Firearms Act 1968. A person is guilty of an offence if he sells a firearm or ammunition to anyone who he knows or has reasonable cause to believe is drunk. A more recent example comes from the Protection from Harassment Act 1997. A person is guilty if he ought to have known that his conduct would harass the victim.

A person does not know that he has something if he has forgotten about it: **Russell** (1984) 81 Cr App R 315 (CA). It may be, however, that an accused continues to know something if he has the capacity to remember the relevant information: **Bello** (1978) 67 Cr App R 288 (CA).

Under the draft Criminal Code, cl 18:

A person acts . . . knowingly with respect to a circumstance not only when he is aware that it exists or will exist, but also when he avoids taking steps that might confirm his belief that it exists or will exist.

'Wilful blindness' is therefore to be covered by 'knowingly'.

'Wilfully'

Like 'knowingly', 'wilfully' is a term which normally gives rise to *mens rea*. The principal authority is **Sheppard** [1981] AC 394 (HL). By s 1(1) of the Children and Young Persons Act 1933:

[I]f any person who has attained the age of sixteen years and has custody, charge, or care of any child or young person under that age, wilfully assaults, ill-treats, neglects, abandons, or exposes him . . . in a manner likely to cause him unnecessary suffering or injury to health . . . that person shall be guilty . . .

Lord Diplock said that 'wilfully' connoted usually intention or recklessness in relation to 'assaults, ill-treats . . . , abandons or exposes'. It did not simply mean that the accused had to act voluntarily. Cases which are to the effect that 'wilfully' is simply a synonym for 'voluntarily' may need revision after **Sheppard**. Since voluntary conduct is implied into offences, saying that 'wilfully' means 'voluntarily' leads to the proposition that 'wilfully' means nothing or perhaps Parliament was expressing what was already implied. However, in relation to neglect, which was in issue in **Sheppard**, he held that the failure to summon a doctor with the result that the child died:

> . . . could not be properly described as 'wilful' unless the parent either (1) had directed his mind to the question whether there was some risk . . . that the child's health might suffer unless he were examined by a doctor . . . , and had made a conscious decision . . . to refrain from arranging for such medical examination, or (2) had so refrained because he did not care whether the child might be in need of medical treatment or not.

Lord Diplock confined himself to 'wilfully' in conjunction with omission, but the case is read as applying to the five actions stated in s 1(1) as well: **Daniels** [2008] EWCA Crim 2360, a case also known as **D**. This explanation reads like the equivalent of recklessness **Caldwell**-style in the era before **G** [2004] 1 AC 1034. Unlike in **Caldwell**, however, Lord Diplock stated that defendants who acted 'through ignorance or lack of intelligence' were not wilful. Since the overruling of **Caldwell** the Court of Appeal in **A-G's Reference (No. 3 of 2003)**, above, said that subjective recklessness is the test to apply and therefore Lord Diplock's 'speech in **Sheppard** should now be interpreted to exclude objective recklessness from the definition of "wilfulness"'. 'Wilfully' is not a 'fault term' within the draft Criminal Code. Therefore, it is not defined therein.

While normally 'wilfully' is a *mens rea* word, the courts have at times held that 'wilfully' governs one part of the *actus reus* but not another part. If one wilfully destroys an oak which is subject to a tree preservation order, one is guilty if one knows that one is chopping down a tree; one need not know that there is a preservation order attached to it: **Maidstone BC v Mortimer** [1980] 3 All ER 502 (DC). One need not, therefore, in this crime be wilful as to all parts of the *actus reus*. For this reason the offence is one of strict liability, a topic discussed in the next chapter. A contrasting case is **Willmott v Atack** [1977] QB 498 (DC). An accused is guilty of wilfully obstructing a constable only if he knows he is obstructing the officer. It is not sufficient that he performs an act which obstructs her.

Negligence

Offences of negligence such as careless driving are not seen by all academics as pukka. Professor Hogan wrote: 'Stupidity does not seem . . . to be an adequate basis for offences which society regards very seriously' ('Strict liability' [1978] Crim LR 593). Glanville Williams in *Criminal Law: The General Part*, 2nd edn (Stevens, 1961) 122, added: 'Some people are born feckless, clumsy, thoughtless, inattentive, irresponsible, with a bad memory and a slow "reaction time". With the best will in the world, we all of us at some times in our lives make negligent mistakes. It is hard to see how justice (as distinct from some utilitarian reason) requires mistakes to be punished.' These defects are not morally blame-worthy. Moreover, criminal law is the state's most serious method of obliging people not to do things, yet, if they cannot stop themselves doing so because, for example, they are careless, how will the penalties of the law stop them? Nevertheless, utilitarians reason that sanctions against crimes of negligence may oblige persons to think before acting. Unreasonable behaviour should be subject to penal sanctions. The careless are blame-worthy. There are indeed many statutory offences of negligence, most of which are minor, just as there are many statutory crimes of strict liability.

George Fletcher wrote: 'Negligence is suspect as a deviation from the paradigm of intentional criminality' ('The theory of criminal negligence: a comparative analysis' (1971) 119 U Pa LR 401 at 403). What are the problems with the law?

1 When one moves from intention and subjective recklessness to negligence the focus moves from conscious activity to inadvertence. Few authorities discuss the definition of negligence, but what it means is this. The accused has failed to attain the objective standard required by the criminal law. One argument against negligence as a basis for imposing criminal law liability is that the accused is judged by an objective criterion, not by his state of mind. For example, in **Bannister** [2009] EWCA Crim 1571 it was held that the test of a competent and careful (i.e. non-negligent) driver was an objective one and no account should be taken of the fact that the accused was a police officer with an advanced driving certificate. Similarly, there is no reduced standard for learner drivers. Yet even this standard is subject to exceptions. In **RSPCA v C** [2006] EWHC 1069 (Admin) it was held that whether a girl of 15 was negligent in not taking an injured pet to a vet was to be assessed by the standards of a reasonable person of her age. A statutory exception would seem to be the Sexual Offences Act 2003 whereby whether the accused is to be taken as having been negligent as to the victim's consent is judged by reference to all the circumstances including presumably the accused's own perceptions of the risk of lack of consent.

In the context of manslaughter by gross negligence the Court of Appeal in **Attorney-General's Reference (No. 2 of 1999)** [2000] QB 796 emphasised in a passage approved by the Divisional Court in **DPP ex p Jones** [2000] IRLR 373 that the test for negligence was objective and no evidence need be led of the accused's state of mind. Negligence as a standard of liability is not built on individual culpability. Therefore it should not be used to impose criminal sanctions. The contrary argument is that negligence connotes that the accused ought to have been aware of an unjustifiable risk of harm. In England it is accepted that liability for negligence imposes an objective standard: did this accused fall short of the standard required of a reasonable person?

'The underlying rationale of subjectivism appears to be that it allows punishment only where a person exercised some choice and that it prevents the natural converse, the punishment of those who had no choice' (C. Wells 'Swatting the subjectivist bug' [1982] Crim LR 209 at 212). A subjectivist would say that a person should not be convicted if she was not capable of changing her behaviour to stop committing an offence. Criticism of negligence might be reduced if a variable standard were adopted. A higher standard of liability might be imposed on a local authority or large firm than on a backward, tired and hungry 14-year-old. Even where the general standard is that of a reasonable person, a higher, that is, variable, standard is already imposed on a person who has special knowledge. Since the standard is variable upwards, why is it not variable downwards in relation to age, size, intelligence and the like? It might be asked whether a backward, tired and hungry 14-year-old deserved punishment even if a reasonable person would have deserved it. Furthermore, it is sometimes argued that liability should not be imposed where the accused did not have a fair opportunity to become aware of the risk. Did a backward, tired and hungry girl of 14 have such an opportunity?

Nevertheless, one may not always wish to exculpate some defendants despite their personal characteristics. Would one want to find a person not guilty of driving without due care and attention because she was young, tired and hungry and lacking in intelligence? Similarly one might wish, as the law does at present, to keep learner and experienced drivers to the same standard. It seems strange that the civil law should be more reflective of personal characteristics in this regard than criminal law (see the civil case of **BRB v Herrington** [1972] AC 877 (HL), on child trespassers). It should be remembered that the usual defences apply to offences of negligence, including ones based on mental capacity such as insanity and infancy. Even in relation to these offences the insane person is not treated as a sane one. The child of nine or eleven is not treated as a person of 35.

One of the strongest supporters of subjectivism in English law, J.C. Smith, wrote in 'Subjective or objective? The ups and downs of the test of criminal liability in England' [1981–82] Villanova LR 1179 at 1214 (spelling anglicised):

> [T]o support the subjectivist theory of criminal liability is not to deny that there is a place for offences where an objective test is justified, as with offences of negligence. For example, negligence is the appropriate criterion of liability in many regulatory offences, the very purpose of which is to ensure a high degree of care in the carrying out of certain activities like the sale of food and drugs, where negligence can be extremely harmful to the parties . . . Negligence is, of course, by definition, fault; but not every fault should entail liability. The process of the enforcement of the criminal law is costly and produces much pain . . . The onus of proof should be on the objectivist to show that we need criminal liability for negligence.

However, since Parliament may make new laws it may make new offences of negligence. Rape, a serious offence, is defined in the Sexual Offences Act 2003, s 1, as a crime where the accused 'does not reasonably believe' that the victim consents. This makes a serious offence into the crime of negligence. Similar is the crime of causing or allowing the death of or serious injury to a child or vulnerable adult contrary to s 5 of the Domestic Violence, Crime and Victims Act 2004 as amended in 2012.

2   Some commentators argue that *mens rea* denotes the accused's own state of mind. Falling short of a standard is not a state of mind. Therefore, negligence is not *mens rea*. This argument, however, is a definitional one: if one defined *mens rea* negatively as the offence less the *actus reus*, negligence would fall within this definition. It is also sometimes said that *mens rea* is a state of mind. If, however, one is acting negligently, by definition one does not have a state of mind or one has a blank state of mind. If one's mind is empty with regard to a risk, how can one be grossly negligent? When a mind is empty, it cannot be emptier. This criticism is met by the response that negligence is a failure to comply with an objective norm. One can fail to a greater or lesser extent.

The Court of Appeal in **Misra** [2005] 1 WLR 1 touched on the definitions of *mens rea* in the context of gross negligence manslaughter. It was said that *mens rea* meant either the accused's state of mind or 'the ingredient of fault or culpability required'. In the former sense negligence is not *mens rea*; in the latter sense it is. For the purposes of this crime negligence was the mental element.

3   Some commentators go further. They believe that the criminal law should punish only those who act knowingly, that is intentionally or subjectively recklessly. Negligence ought not to be *mens rea* because one does not advert to the consequences of one's behaviour. Perhaps the proposition may be differently put as: 'How can one have a wrongful state of mind, a *mens rea*, if one has no frame of mind at all?' One's mind is blank to the consequences when one acts negligently. Contrariwise negligence can be seen as liability based on fault just as intention and conscious recklessness are. The accused has not performed his duty because he was careless. He is at fault and is to be blamed. Ordinary people would, it is thought, hold a person to be at fault when he was

driving without lights in the middle of the night down an unlit portion of a motorway. It would not always be inquired whether he knew his lights had not been turned on. It may be socially useful to punish such a person. Furthermore, circumstances alter cases. G. Fletcher in *Rethinking Criminal Law* (Little, Brown & Co., 1978) uses this illustration: would one call negligent a person who threw a lighted match into a bucket containing liquid? Presumably one would if the bucket were at a petrol station, but not if it were under a drainpipe in a garden.

Another argument against negligence is that punishing people for acting carelessly would not deter them, though the issue is in doubt. Moreover, to say that people who are negligent are dangerous is over-inclusive. If that is so, why not abolish *mens rea* totally?

4 H.L.A. Hart argued that it was not unjust to individuals to convict them when they had acted negligently. Contrary to the view of most English academics, no line should be drawn between a person who foresaw the forbidden consequence and one who did not advert to it. The accused should be punished when he failed to pay attention to what he was doing or to examine the circumstances in which he found himself. Provided that his carelessness was unreasonable, he should be criminally liable. However, criminal law should not cover persons who could not have prevented the occurrence of the harm by reasonable care. Neither should the law cover people who because of mental deficiency could not take care in what they were doing (cf. *Elliott* v *C*, above). Children would be exculpated if they could not understand the consequences of their behaviour. Where the accused is guilty, he is criminally liable for failing to examine the situation in which he is and to assess the risk, and not for his state of mind in failing to advert to the consequences of his behaviour. In Hart's words, 'negligence does not consist in [a] blank state of mind but in . . . failure to take precautions against harm by examining the situation' (*Punishment and Responsibility* (Clarendon Press, 1968) 148). Accordingly Hart postulated a duty to take reasonable care against harm, and criminal law should be directed at careless people, not for their states of mind, but for getting into such mental states. The accused is therefore punished for failing to use his mental faculties such as judgment, which, if used, would have avoided harm.

Hart's thesis has been criticised on several grounds: (i) It does not explain why we punish those who intend more than those who are reckless, and those who are reckless more than those who are careless. (ii) The law does not look at whether the accused himself should have examined the situation, though perhaps it should. (iii) The negligent person, it is argued, does not deserve to be punished. There may, however, be other reasons for imposing liability.

5 One can argue that since the police and prosecuting authorities cannot cope with crimes of intention and recklessness, negligence should not be a basis of liability, at least until those authorities are given more resources.

6 Many offences can be committed intentionally or recklessly but not negligently. The wider the scope of recklessness, the less ground there is for negligence. When *Caldwell*, above, and *Lawrence* [1982] AC 510 (HL) expanded liability into part of the area previously covered by negligence, academic criticism focused on this extension. Lord Diplock's argument in *Caldwell* was that the person who acted without thinking was just as blameworthy as someone who thought about the risk but went ahead. In a modern society there is something to be said for penalising the careless, but to determine that they are just as culpable as those who advert to the risk is not a just assessment of the different states of mind, though reasonable people may disagree. *Caldwell* was 'departed from' by the House of Lords in *G* [2004] 1 AC 1034.

7 There is a type of manslaughter called manslaughter by gross negligence. It is one of the rare common law offences of negligence, albeit that the jury has to hold that the accused was not merely negligent but grossly so: *Large* [1939] 1 All ER 753 (CCA). The principal authority was *Andrews* v *DPP* [1937] AC 576 (HL) and is now *Adomako* [1995] 1 AC 171 (HL). Terminology in cases such as *Andrews*, where the House of Lords spoke of 'reckless' conduct as a synonym for grossly negligent behaviour, was inexact and not settled, but emphasis was laid on the grossness of the carelessness. Mere civil law negligence is insufficient. See Chapter 12 for this type of manslaughter. It should be noted that there is no crime of causing harm, even serious harm, in a grossly negligent manner.

The second common law offence of negligence is public nuisance. Employers are liable for the acts of their employees which have created a public nuisance. They need not know of those acts: it is sufficient that they ought reasonably to be aware of them. The Lords in *Rimmington* [2006] 1 AC 459 ruled that this definition stood after *G*. In other words the *mens rea* of negligence survived the revival of subjective recklessness.

8 Under statute there are offences where the accused is guilty if he inadvertently takes a risk. One such crime is selling a firearm to a person who the accused has reasonable cause to believe is drunk. Therefore, if the accused ought to have been aware that the accused was drunk, he is guilty.

The most common negligence offence is driving without due care and attention or without reasonable consideration for other road users (s 3 of the Road Traffic Act 1988 as substituted by s 2 of the Road Traffic Act 1991). It differed from the former offence of reckless driving ('reckless' then having its *Caldwell* definition) in that the accused is guilty even though the risk of harm was not serious. A similar offence is causing death by careless or inconsiderate driving contrary to s 28 of the Road Traffic Act 1988, inserted by the Road Safety Act 2006, s 20 (not in force at the time of writing). The offence of bigamy is treated as an offence of negligence because the alleged bigamist who makes a mistake that his former marriage was annulled or dissolved has a defence only if that mistake was based on reasonable grounds.

9 Where the offence is one of negligence, Parliament may give a special defence. The principal illustration is unlawful sexual intercourse with a mental defective, contrary to the now repealed s 7(1) of the Sexual Offences Act 1956. By s 7(2):

> [A] man is not guilty of an offence under this section, . . . if he does not know and has no reason to suspect her to be defective.

The defence was one of 'no negligence'. If the accused himself did not know and a person with his characteristics including mental ones would not have known that the woman was a defective, he has a defence. The test was therefore not a purely objective one, as can be seen from the words of s 7(2).

The wording of the defence defines what has to be shown. The Food Safety Act 1990, s 21(2), gives the accused a defence if he can prove both due diligence (i.e. no negligence) and that the defect was due to the act or default of a third party such as the manufacturer. The Trade Descriptions Act 1968, s 24(1)(b), gives a defence when 'he took all reasonable precautions and exercised all due diligence to avoid the commission of' one of several offences of strict liability. The Misuse of Drugs Act 1971, s 28(2), provides a defence for the accused to prove that 'he neither knew of nor suspected nor had reason to suspect the existence of some fact alleged by the prosecution', proof of the fact being necessary for conviction. The Lords ruled in *Lambert* [2002] 2 AC 545 that s 28(2) imposed only an evidential burden on the accused. It did so in reliance on the presumption of innocence found in Article 6(2) of the European Convention on

Human Rights. However, not all reverse onus provisions are now to be interpreted in a similar fashion. See Chapter 1 for further details.

It might also be that there is a defence at least to careless driving when the accused relied on instructions from someone else who was at fault in telling the driver to proceed. In **Thornton v Mitchell** [1940] 1 All ER 339 (KBD) a bus driver was acquitted of careless driving when he reversed his bus over a pedestrian, relying on signals from the conductor. Martin Wasik 'A learner's careless driving' [1982] Crim LR 411 argued that the same applied to a learner who obeyed the instructor's order.

10 *Reform.* The Law Commission in *Offences of Damage to Property*, Report No. 29, 1970, 44, stated that 'in the area of serious crime . . . the elements of intention, knowledge or recklessness have always been required as a basis of liability. The tendency is to extend this basis to a wider range of offences and to limit the area of offences where a lesser mental element [e.g. negligence] is required.' The Commission was in sympathy with this view. The efforts of law reform bodies over the last 40 years have been to promote a subjectivist approach in relation to serious offences. The draft Criminal Code, Law Com. No. 177, 1989, continued this process. Unless Parliament determined differently, recklessness in its subjective state would be the lowest culpable mental state for Code offences. Parliament, however, has chosen to follow a different route. In 2003 it made rape into an offence of negligence. Since rape is such a serious crime, the route is open to making more offences into ones of negligence, even very serious ones.

Some problems of *mens rea*

This section brings together difficulties in relation to the mental element which can be gleaned from this chapter and Chapter 2.

(a) There is no set terminology. Is gross negligence the same as recklessness?

(b) The boundaries of concepts may be highly imprecise. Is oblique intent part of intention or foresight? And what exactly is oblique intent? It is amazing that fundamental notions such as intention cannot be defined after hundreds of years.

(c) Terms may cover more than one mental state. **Caldwell** recklessness used to be the obvious example in that it covered both advertence and inadvertence. And is wilful blindness **Caldwell** recklessness?

(d) Older terms may require different definitions for each offence. There may be no set definition throughout criminal law. Stephen J in **Tolson** (1889) 23 QBD 168 at 187 (CCR), said: 'Malice means one thing in relation to murder, another in relation to the [long since repealed] Malicious Damage Act [1861], and a third in relation to libel, and so of fraud and negligence.'

(e) Some terms may be 'bent' to catch persons who ought to be caught but who are not caught under the usual width of the concept. The class of persons most obviously fitting within this kink in the law is terrorists.

(f) Where the accused has a defence such as prevention of crime it is difficult to describe his state of mind as a *mens rea*.

The draft Criminal Code, Law Com. No. 177, 1989, sought to avoid some of these difficulties by having consistent usage and certainty of meaning. *Mens rea*, to be called the fault element, consists of intention, knowledge and recklessness, unless Parliament ordains differently. By cl 19(1) '[A]n allegation in an indictment or information of knowledge or intention includes an allegation of recklessness.' The element of recklessness would be satisfied by intention or knowledge (cl 19(2)). The minimum fault element was to be recklessness (cl 20(1)).

Transferred malice

Examples

I attack you in your living room with a belt, intending to whip you. I miss and knock a vase of flowers off the coffee table. Which crimes, if any, am I guilty of?

If I've made you afraid, assault is a possible offence, but the question is really about transferred malice. 'Malice' can be transferred between person and person and thing and thing but not from person to thing or vice versa: see *Latimer* (1886) 17 QBD 359 (CCR). On the facts, therefore, it cannot be transferred between you and the vase: see *Pembliton* (1876) LR 2 CCR 119.

I don't in fact whip you, so no non-fatal offence such as wounding (intending to cause some harm) contrary to s 20 of the Offences against the Person Act 1861 applies but attempt to commit a non-fatal offence may occur on the facts as may a non-fatal crime of recklessness; similarly, one may damage the vase recklessly (see *G* [2004] AC 1034 (HL)), if one foresees damage.

A second example is provided by the facts of *Gnango* [2012] 1 AC 827 (Supreme Court). The accused and an unknown person wearing a bandana (he has come to be known as 'bandana man') shot at each other across a carpark. An innocent passerby was shot dead by bandana man. It did not matter in law that bandana man shot the victim dead when he was trying to kill the accused. Murder is the killing of a human being with malice aforethought (see Chapter 11) and that is what bandana man did. For the liability of the accused in being a secondary party to the killing, see Chapter 5.

In *Latimer* (1886) 17 QBD 359 the accused quarrelled with a person in a pub. He removed his belt and aimed a blow at him. The blow struck the victim, who was standing nearby. She was badly injured. The court held that the accused was guilty of unlawfully and maliciously wounding the victim. He had the *mens rea* and *actus reus* of the crime. He did not expect what occurred and in that sense the outcome was accidental, but the law holds him guilty under the doctrine of **transferred malice**. His mental state ('malice') is transferred. The doctrine is not restricted to crimes of malice or intent but extends to the transfer of the mental element however defined. A recent application of the principle is *Gnango* [2012] 1 AC 827. The victim was shot dead by a third party who was involved in a gunfight with the accused. The third party was guilty of murder by virtue of transferred malice: his intent to kill the accused was transferred to the victim.

In *McBride* v *Turnock* [1964] Crim LR 456 (DC) the accused struck at a person but hit a constable in the execution of his duty. He was guilty of the offence of assaulting a constable in the execution of his duty, an aggravated battery, even though his 'malice' was only as to common assault. Both crimes have the same *mens rea* because the accused is guilty of the aggravated offence even though he does not know that the person assaulted was a constable. The same principle applies to the crime of assaulting an officer of the court in the execution of his duty. Similarly if in *Latimer* it had been a father aiming at his daughter with his hand intending to effect reasonable chastisement and his hand hit her friend standing next to her, his defence would be transferred.

For the so-called doctrine to apply, the *mens rea* and *actus reus* must coincide (subject to the point in **McBride v Turnock**, above). In **Pembliton** (1876) LR 2 CCR 119, the accused was in a fight outside a pub. He broke a window with a stone. He was held by the Court for Crown Cases Reserved not to be guilty of malicious damage, the precursor of criminal damage. The accused did not have the *mens rea* of this offence. One could also charge attempted actual or grievous bodily harm, which captures what the accused meant to do better than criminal damage, which is the chance result of his actions. The basic point remained, that *mens rea* cannot be transferred across crimes.

Another restriction has been best stated by David Ormerod, *Smith and Hogan's Criminal Law*, 13th edn (Oxford University Press, 2011) 138 (footnote omitted):

> The intent which is transferred must be a *mens rea*, whether intention or recklessness. If D [the accused] shoots X with intent to kill because X is making a murderous attack on him and this is the only way in which he can preserve his own life, he does not intend an *actus reus* . . . for to kill in these circumstances is justified. If, however, D misses X and inadvertently kills V, an innocent bystander, he does so cause an *actus reus* . . . to transfer; the result which he intended was a perfectly lawful one.

It should be realised that in many instances one need not refer to this doctrine. One is guilty of recklessly damaging property if one throws a stone at a window of a pub belonging to the victim and the stone goes through the window, which is open, and breaks an optic belonging to the victim. If the stone happens to break a valuable vase left by a starving potter in payment for a meal, one is still guilty of criminal damage because property belonging to another has been destroyed or damaged. In murder one is guilty if one kills a human being. If one sets out to kill one person and accidentally kills another, one is guilty of murder. Malice aforethought covers intentionally killing a victim. It does not matter who the victim is, provided that the victim is in being at the time of the attack. For example, the stabbing of the accused's girlfriend caused the death of a baby which was born alive prematurely in **Attorney-General's Reference (No. 3 of 1994)** [1998] AC 245 (HL). The accused was not guilty of murder of the child. A foetus was held not to be part of the mother. Lord Mustill said:

> The defendant intended to commit and did commit an immediate crime of violence to the mother. He committed no relevant violence to the foetus, which was not a person, either at the time or in the future, and intended no harm to the foetus or to the human person which it would become. . . . I would not overstrain the idea of transferred malice by trying to make it fit the present case.

Malice was not to be transferred from the mother to the foetus and then from the foetus to the child (who would be a person in being for the purposes of the law of homicide only at some time in the future). It seems strange that there could be no transferred malice to make the accused guilty of murder, a homicide offence, yet he was convicted of manslaughter. An alternative approach is to say that the accused has a 'general intent' in relation to the property and the person. For these reasons the use of the doctrine is rare. Moreover, if the accused killed a victim, it does not matter in which way he killed him. If they are in an opera house and the accused shoots at the victim intending to kill him but the bullet hits a chandelier, which falls on the victim and kills him, the accused is guilty.

Transferred malice is restricted in participatory offences. If the acts of the principal offender go beyond the agreed plan, the accessory is not guilty to the offence which takes place. In **Leahy** [1985] Crim LR 99 (Crown Court), the accused told the principal offender to 'glass' X; the principal deliberately glassed Y. The accused was not guilty of counselling grievous bodily harm. The result is in accord with the ancient case of **Saunders and Archer** (1573) 75 ER 706. On the advice of the 'accessory', the principal gave his wife a poisoned apple intending to kill her. He stood by while his wife gave the apple to their child, who ate it and died. It was held that the 'accessory' was not guilty of being the secondary offender to the murder. There was a deliberate change from the plan agreed on. The case would have been one of transferred malice with the accessory now guilty if the killing of the child had been accidental in the sense that the principal could not have prevented it.

Reform of transferred malice

The Law Commission's draft Criminal Code (Law Com. No. 177, 1989) proposed to retain transferred malice for 'an attempt charge may be impossible (when it is not known until trial that the defendant claims to have X [the intended victim] and not Y [the actual victim] in contemplation); or inappropriate (as not describing the harm done adequately for labelling or sentencing purposes). Moreover, recklessness with respect to Y may be insufficient to establish the offence or incapable of being proved' (para. 8.57). Clause 24(1) of the draft Criminal Code provides:

> [I]n determining whether a person is guilty of an offence, his intention to cause, or his recklessness whether he causes, a result in relation to a person or thing capable of being the victim or subject matter of the offence shall be treated as an intention to cause or, as the case may be, recklessness whether he causes that result in relation to any person or thing affected by his conduct.

This clause is repeated in the Criminal Law Bill attached to the Law Commission Report No. 218, *Legislating the Criminal Code – Offences against the Person and General Principles*, 1993, with the replacement of 'recklessness' by 'awareness of a risk': cl 32(1). The change is because 'recklessness' in the Bill bears a specific meaning, but the Bill applies to other *mens rea* words. Clause 24(2) of the draft Criminal Code would codify the point made in *Smith and Hogan's Criminal Law* quoted above:

> Any defence on which a person might have relied in relation to a person or thing within his contemplation is open to him on a charge of the same offence in relation to a person or thing not within his contemplation.

This provision is now cl 32(3) of the Criminal Law Bill.

The term chosen by the Law Commission for this so-called doctrine is 'transferred fault', 'fault' being the Law Commission's term for *mens rea* or the mental element. The terminology is better chosen than the usual current one of transferred malice because it demonstrates that the law is not restricted to crimes in which the mental element is malice. Lord Mustill in **Attorney-General's Reference (No. 3 of 1994)**, above, called the doctrine of transferred malice a fiction and said that it had a misleading title, but 'one which is too firmly entrenched to be discarded'. Nevertheless, it has to be said that **Latimer**, above, reflects good sense. Surely one would not want the accused in that case to be not guilty. If a defendant kills or injures a human being, why should it matter that the human being so harmed was not the one aimed at? It is suggested that 'transferred fault' could in fact quite easily supplant 'transferred malice'. Perhaps a more modern name for the doctrine would make transferred malice more acceptable to Lord Mustill.

Contemporaneity

> ### Example
>
> You hate your neighbour and decide to kill him. One winter's day while driving your car on slippery roads you skid into him, killing him instantly. Are you guilty of murder?
>
> You intend to kill or cause grievous bodily harm at one time and do kill him at a later time but your *actus reus* and *mens rea* do not coincide in point of time, and you do not have both at the time when the neighbour dies. Therefore, you are not guilty of murder.
>
> The position is different if the two are contemporaneous. ***Thabo Meli v R*** [1954] 1 WLR 228 (PC) is illustrative. The two defendants assaulted the victim, intending to kill him; they thought he was dead and threw his supposed corpse over the edge of a cliff; in fact he was alive when thrown over but later died. The defendants were held to be guilty of murder. They intended to kill their (live) victim; the assault and the death (the attack and the attempt to hide the supposed corpse) were part of the same series of actions, part of the same transaction.

Consider this fact situation. The accused has decided to get rid of her partner. Before she can kill him intentionally, she accidentally runs him over and kills him. She has the *mens rea* for murder and she has caused his death. However, the *mens rea* and *actus reus* are not simultaneous and it would be unjust to convict her of murder. There are, however, situations where it is not unjust to convict. The principle is one of contemporaneity or, as some Americans call it, the union of *actus reus* and *mens rea*. Another example is the crime of burglary. One form of this offence is entry into a building or part of one with intent to commit one of four crimes. If the accused performs the *actus reus* and later decides to steal, etc., he is not guilty of this type of burglary. One could say that the principle is a flexible requirement or the number of exceptions has been growing.

See Chapter 8 for an in-depth discussion of Majewski in relation to the defence of intoxication.

(a) *The Dutch courage rule.* The accused who decides to commit a crime and gets into a drunken state to do so is guilty of the crime even though at the time of committing it he was so dead drunk that he was mindless, and without a '*mens*' one cannot have a *mens rea*. The Lords in **Attorney-General for Northern Ireland v Gallagher** [1963] AC 349 so decided.

 (b) Under **DPP v Majewski** [1977] AC 443 (HL) one is guilty of a crime of recklessly doing something if one commits the crime while under the influence of alcohol or drugs. The Lords decided as a matter of policy that recklessly getting drunk supplied the recklessness for the crime later committed. After **MPC v Caldwell**, above, there is no need for the **Majewski** approach for the defendant is deemed to be unaware of the risk of which ordinary people would have been aware at the time of the *actus reus*. On this view the mental element and the *actus reus* coincide. However, the use of the word 'deemed' should alert us to the fact that something strange is going on.

(c) *Continuing state of affairs.* In **Fagan v MPC** [1969] 1 QB 439 (DC), the accused accidentally drove onto a police officer's boot. The police officer pointed out what the accused had done. The accused deliberately left the wheel on the foot for a short while. There were various imprecations. The accused was convicted of a battery. **Fagan** demonstrates the strength of police boots – the constable suffered only two bruised toes after having a Mini parked on his foot – and the way in which the courts can stretch the law to catch the accused. The problem was that battery was thought (at that time) to be an offence which could not be committed by an omission, and leaving a car on a foot looks like an omission. The court held that the *actus reus* of battery can be a continuing act. That continuing act lasted until the accused realised what he had done and decided not to drive off. The accused continued to apply force by not removing the car, and he acted intentionally. In this way the *actus reus* and *mens rea* coincided. There is therefore no need for the mental element to accompany the *actus reus* throughout the sequence of events. Contemporaneity for a moment is sufficient. Moreover, since the *actus reus* is held to be continuing it is not difficult to hold that the two overlap in time at some point.

If **Fagan** is accepted as laying down a rule of law, there are extensive problems with its width. D. Husak, *Philosophy of Criminal Law* (Rowman & Littlefield, 1987) 178, suggests the following:

> Suppose the defendant manufactures cars and deliberately cuts corners by installing defective emergency brakes. A year later he notices one of his cars parked on a hill. Because the emergency brake is defective it rolls backwards and comes to rest on a policeman's foot. The defendant fails to assist the policeman for several moments, revelling in his suffering. Here the defendant initiated a causal chain culminating in harm. Is the sequence 'deemed' a 'single act' comparable to **Fagan**? There is no fact of the matter about how this question should be answered. [Spelling anglicised and footnote omitted.]

Fagan was said to have been decided on its own facts according to the House of Lords in **Miller** [1983] 2 AC 161, which is equivalent to saying that **Fagan** should not be followed. **Fagan** now falls within (d) below, causing a danger and intentionally not remedying it. **Fagan**, said the Lords, should be seen as a case in which the accused adopted his previous conduct. It is suggested that the *ratio* of **Fagan** should now be used only where the *actus reus* is of a continuing nature. By using the 'duty' approach courts can avoid the question of whether an *actus reus* is a continuing one or whether it is complete by the time there is *mens rea*.

(d) *The **Miller** principle.* In **Miller**, above, the House of Lords decided that a person who created a dangerous situation unwittingly and then realised what he had done was guilty if he failed to avert the prohibited consequence. This case is discussed above and in Chapter 2. It could have been treated as one of the exceptions to contemporaneity but instead was dealt with as a case where the common law imposed liability for omissions. The accused had a duty to act. The **Miller** principle is preserved in the draft Criminal Code, cl 23.

(e) *The principle established in **Thabo Meli** v R* [1954] 1 WLR 228 (PC). This situation is the opposite to **Fagan**. In **Thabo Meli** the *mens rea* preceded the *actus reus*. In **Fagan** the start of the *actus reus* preceded the *mens rea*. The facts of **Thabo Meli** were that the victim was beaten up and left for dead. His supposed corpse was thrown over a cliff, and he died of exposure. The Privy Council upheld the appellants' conviction for murder on the basis that the sequence of events constituted a series which could not be split into separate acts: 'It is too refined a ground of judgment to say that, because they were under a misapprehension at one stage and thought that their guilty purpose had been achieved before in fact it was achieved, therefore they are to escape the penalties of the law.' Although the defendants' plan to kill was completed at the time when they believed the victim to be dead and pushing what they believed to be a corpse over the cliff was part of the plan to get rid of the body, the whole sequence was deemed to be one act. The appellants could have been found guilty of attempted murder, but by holding as the Privy Council did, they were guilty of murder.

Thabo Meli was followed in **Church** [1966] 1 QB 59 by the Court of Criminal Appeal. There was no plan to kill but the accused thought he had killed his victim. He put her into a river, where she drowned. The conviction for manslaughter was upheld. The latest authority is *Le Brun* [1992] QB 61, which confirmed that the principle in *Thabo Meli* **v** *R* applied to manslaughter (where there was no plan to kill) just as it did to murder (where there was).

Le Brun [1992] QB 61(CA)

The accused struck his victim on the chin. She fell. In an attempt to conceal the battery he moved her. Her head accidentally struck the pavement. Her skull was fractured and she died. Lord Lane CJ in the Court of Appeal ruled that the unlawful application of force and the act which caused death were part of the same transaction. It did not matter that there was an appreciable time between the two events. The position was even more certain where the accused's subsequent actions were designed to conceal his earlier attack and the chain of causation (see Chapter 2) was unbroken.

The outcome would have been different if a passer-by had broken the chain of causation by the act of dropping the still-living victim's head onto the pavement. Perhaps it might be the law that the accused would not be guilty if he had been trying to drag the victim to hospital when she hit her head. The Court of Appeal in *Attorney-General's Reference (No. 4 of 1980)* [1981] 1 WLR 705 had previously some doubts whether the court was correct in **Church** to extend *Thabo Meli* to manslaughter. In the case the accused hit the victim. She fell down some steps and banged her head. The accused dragged her upstairs with a rope, drained off her blood, and dissected her. The problem was that it was impossible to state which act caused death. If it was uncertain to say which act caused death, it was impossible to say whether the accused had *mens rea* at the time of death. On the facts the accused had *mens rea* for manslaughter both (on normal principles) at the time of knocking her downstairs and (following *Thabo Meli*) when he cut her throat. There was a series of acts which could be viewed as one transaction; the accused had *mens rea* at some time in the transaction; therefore he was guilty. All cases on this topic have as yet concerned homicide but it is thought that the principle is not so restricted.

(f) *The rule in automatism.* As with regard to intoxication there is a principle in the defence of automatism that the accused will not receive the defence if he brought about the condition. It is as if the rule of contemporaneity applies to this defence. This was laid down in **Quick** [1973] QB 910 (CA), with the proviso that the condition had to be reasonably foreseeable. If it is reasonably foreseeable that the accused would fall into a state of automatism through failing to take prescribed drugs or regular meals, he could not have this defence. In **Bailey** [1983] 2 All ER 503, the Court of Appeal resiled from its position in **Quick**. The accused was not guilty if the accused himself did not foresee the consequences of his inaction, even if a reasonable person would have. **Quick** and **Bailey** should be compared with **Kay v Butterworth** (1945) 173 LT 191 (CA), where the problem was avoided. The accused fell asleep at the wheel and mowed down soldiers. He was held guilty of dangerous driving and careless driving, not for crashing into the soldiers when he was asleep but for not stopping to recover from tiredness after working in a munitions factory when he was still awake. This case is useful authority but useful to prosecutors only when the act can be described as a continuing one, as driving can be. It would have been different if he had become 'through no fault of his own . . . unconscious while driving, for example, by being struck by a stone, or being taken ill. . . .'.

(g) An accused is guilty if he with *mens rea* sets in train a course of events which will lead to the *actus reus* even though he no longer has *mens rea* when the *actus reus* occurs.

Where these exceptions do not apply, there must be contemporaneity. In ***Edwards v Ddin*** [1976] 1 WLR 942 (DC), the accused asked a garage attendant to fill up his tank. He intended to pay. When the petrol was in the tank, he dishonestly drove off without paying. By that time, under civil law, the petrol was his. He had not appropriated property belonging to another at the time when he had the *mens rea* because the property belonged to him. Therefore, he was not guilty of theft. There was no *actus reus* at the time of the *mens rea*. (Parliament intervened to create an offence to cover this situation. The offence is called making off without payment in s 3 of the Theft Act 1978, which is discussed in Chapter 16 below.)

Summary

- *Definition of* mens rea: *Mens rea* may be defined as 'the mental state which is required by the definition of the offence to accompany the act which produces or threatens harm' (S.H. Kadish).

- *Examples of* mens rea: The *mens rea* of murder, also known as malice aforethought, is in part composed of an intent to kill or commit grievous bodily harm. In theft, the mental element is 'dishonesty' and 'intention permanently to deprive'. The *mens rea*, like the *actus reus*, differs from crime to crime.

- *Motive*: In general the motive of the accused is irrelevant in criminal law. For instance, it does not matter if I kill you to get your money or your lover or if I do so in order to save you from a life filled with pain. Some offences do, however, make motive relevant in the sense that they are defined in such a way that the triers of fact have to consider the reason why the defendant behaved as she did. An illustration is blackmail. If the accused believed she was warranted in acting as she did, there is no offence and 'warranted' covers the accused's motive. Modern statutes sometimes make crimes more serious when the accused acted out of a certain motive, for example racially motivated crimes.

- *Intent*: The definition of intention is one basic to criminal law, partly because some offences may be committed only intentionally, but more fundamentally because intent is morally the worst state of mind with which one can act: for example murder is more serious than manslaughter, not because of the *actus reus* (which is the same), but because murder is committable only where the accused intends to kill or cause grievous bodily harm. It is usually easy to decide whether or not the accused intended a certain consequence. If she decided to kill, if her aim or purpose was to kill, if she made her mind up to kill, she intended to kill. This state of mind is sometimes known as 'direct intent'. If the accused did not decide to kill but foresaw death as a virtually certain consequence (and death actually was virtually certain), then the jury may but need not find that the accused intended to kill. Therefore, the fact that she did foresee death as virtually certain does not mean that she intended to kill; it means that she may have intended to kill, but the question is one of fact for the jury. After all, the law that a jury may find intent has as its corollary that the jury may decide not to find intent. This state of mind is often called 'oblique intent'. It is thought but not expressly determined that the definition of intent given in the previous paragraph applies throughout criminal law.

- *Recklessness*: Some crimes such as criminal damage may be committed intentionally and recklessly but not carelessly. Therefore, recklessness is distinguished from both intent and carelessness. The House of Lords has in the quite recent past returned to having one definition of recklessness for (at least most) crimes. If an accused foresees an outcome as possible, she is said to be reckless. This frame of mind is often known as 'subjective recklessness'. Current law is, therefore, that subjective recklessness applies in all crimes, unless Parliament otherwise ordains.

- *Knowingly*: 'Actual' knowledge is when the accused knows for a fact that something is true. Sometimes the law extends to 'wilful blindness': the accused shuts her eyes to the obvious. 'Constructive knowledge' is when a reasonable person would have known certain facts but the accused did not: sometimes the law stretches thus far.

- *Wilfully*: This term normally means 'intentionally or recklessly'.

- *Negligence*: Few serious crimes may be committed carelessly, the exception being manslaughter by gross negligence. Lesser crimes such as careless driving may be committed negligently. What negligence connotes is that the accused has fallen short of the standards of a reasonable person. Whether a person should be convicted for acting negligently remains contested, and with some exceptions the Law Commission strives to hold to the position that the minimum level for conviction for a serious offence is recklessness.

- *Transferred malice*: If one attacks one person but strikes another, one's intention ('malice') to assault the first is 'transferred' to the second. Similarly, an attack on one piece of property is transferable to other property. However, intent against a person is not transferable against property or vice versa.

- *Contemporaneity*: The general rule is that *actus reus* and *mens rea* must coincide in point of time. If I decide to kill you and then change my mind but then by chance I do kill you, perhaps by running you over, I am not guilty of murder. My *mens rea* and *actus reus* did not occur simultaneously. Sometimes the law regards not just a single point in time but the whole transaction, which may take place over a period. For example, I attack you and leave you for dead; you are not dead but you later die of exposure. Here, the attack and the death are seen in law as being indivisible and I will be guilty of murder or manslaughter depending on my *mens rea*.

References

Reports

Criminal Law Revision Committee Report no. 14, *Offences Against the Person*, Cmnd 7844 (1980)

Law Commission Consultation Paper no. 177, *A New Homicide Act for England and Wales?* (2005)

Law Commission Report no. 29, *Offences of Damage to Property* (1970)

Law Commission Report no. 89, *The Mental Element in Crime* (1978)

Law Commission Report no. 177, *A Criminal Code for England and Wales* (1989)

Law Commission Report no. 218, *Legislating the Criminal Code – Offences against the Person and General Principles* (1993)

Law Commission Report no. 306, *Murder, Manslaughter and Infanticide* (2006)

Report of the Select Committee of the House of Lords on Murder and Life Imprisonment (Nathan), HL Paper 78–1 (1989)

Books

Clarkson, C.M.V. *Understanding Criminal Law* (Fontana, 1987) and 4th edn (Thomson, 2005)

Fletcher, G. *Rethinking Criminal Law* (Little, Brown & Co., 1978)

Hall, J. *General Principles of Criminal Law*, 2nd edn (Bobbs–Merrill, 1968)

Hart, H.L.A. *Punishment and Responsibility* (Clarendon Press, 1968)

Husak, D.N. *Philosophy of Criminal Law* (Rowman & Littlefield, 1987)

Ormerod, D. *Smith and Hogan's Criminal Law*, 13th edn (Oxford University Press, 2011)

Smith, J.C. and Hogan, B. *Criminal Law*, 10th edn (Butterworths, 2002)

Stannard, J. *Recent Developments in Criminal Law* (SLS, 1988)

Williams, G. *Criminal Law: The General Part*, 2nd edn (Stevens, 1961)

Yeo, S. *Fault in Homicide* (Federation Press, 1997)

Journals

Fennell, C. 'Intention in murder: chaos, confusion and complexity' (1990) 41 NILQ 325

Finkelstein, C. 'No harm no foul? Objectivism and the law of attempts' (1999) 18 *Law and Philosophy* 69, 75

Fletcher, G. 'The theory of criminal negligence: a comparative analysis' (1971) 119 U Pa LR 401

France, S. 'Reckless approach to liability' (1988) 18 VUWLR 141

Hogan, B. 'Strict liability' [1978] Crim LR 593

Horder, J. 'Intention in criminal law: a rejoinder' (1995) 58 MLR 678

Kadish, S. 'The decline of innocence' [1968] CLJ 273

Packer, H. '*Mens rea* and the Supreme Court' [1962] Sup Ct Rev 107

Smith, J.C. 'Subjective or objective? The ups and downs of criminal liability in England' [1981–82] Villanova LR 1179

Uniacke, S. 'Was Mary's death murder?' (2001) 9 Medical LR 208, 217

Wasik, M. 'A learner's careless driving' [1982] Crim LR 411

Wells, C. 'Swatting the subjectivist bug' [1982] Crim LR 209

Williams, G. 'Oblique intention' [1987] CLJ 417

Further reading

Arlidge, A. 'The trial of Dr David Moor' [2000] Crim LR 31. (See also response by Sir John Smith, 'A comment on Dr Moor's case' (2000) Crim LR 41.)

Ashworth, A. and Mitchell, B. *Rethinking English Homicide Law* (Clarendon Press, 2000)

Binder, G. 'The rhetoric of motive and intent' (2002) 6 Buff Crim LR 1

Bohlander, M. 'Transferred malice and transferred defenses: A critique of the traditional doctrine and arguments for a change in paradigm' (2010) 13 New Crim LR 555

Brudner, A. 'Subjective fault for crime: a reinterpretation' (2008) 14 *Legal Theory* 1

Buxton, R. 'Some simple thoughts on intention' [1988] Crim LR 484

Chan, W. and Simester, A.P. 'Four functions of *mens rea*' [2011] CLJ 381

Chiu, E.M. 'The challenge of motive in criminal law' (2005) 8 Buff Crim LR 653

Ferzan, K.K. 'Beyond intention' (2008) 29 Cardozo L Rev 1147

Gledhill, K. 'Criminal carelessness' (2007) 157 NLJ 41

Halpin, A. 'The unlearned lessons of recklessness' in his *Definition in the Criminal Law* (Hart, 2008)

Horder, J. 'Transferred malice and the remoteness of unexpected outcomes' [2006] Crim LR 383

Kaveny, M.C. 'Inferring intention from foresight' (2004) 120 LQR 81

Keating, H. 'Reckless children' [2007] Crim LR 546

Kugler, I. 'Conditional oblique intention' [2004] Crim LR 284

Mitchell, B. 'Culpably indifferent murder' (1996) 25 A-ALR 64

Moore, M.S. and Hurd, H.M. 'Punishing the awkward, the stupid, the weak, and the selfish: The culpability of negligence' (2011) 5 Crim Law and Philos 147

Norrie, A. 'After Woollin' [1999] Crim LR 532

Norrie, A. 'Between orthodox subjectivism and moral contextualism' [2006] Crim LR 486

Patient, I.H.E. 'Transferred malice – a misleading misnomer' (1990) 54 JCL 116

Pedain, A. 'Intention and the terrorist example' [2003] Crim LR 579

Rubin, G.R. 'New light on Steane's case' (2003) 24 *Journal of Legal History* 143

Simester, A.P. 'Can negligence be culpable?' in J. Horder (ed.) *Oxford Essays in Jurisprudence*, 4th series (Oxford University Press, 2000)

Simons, K.W. 'Dimensions of negligence in criminal and tort law' (2002) 3 *Theoretical Inquiries L* 283

Stannard, J.E. 'Stretching out the *actus reus*' (1993–5) xxviii–xxx IJ 200

Tur, R.H.S. 'The doctor's defence' (2002) 69 Mount Sinai J of Medicine 317

Williams, G. 'The *mens rea* for murder: leave it alone' (1989) 105 LQR 387

Wilson, W. 'Doctrinal rationality after *Woollin*' (1999) 62 MLR 447

For a full-length treatment of fatal and non-fatal offences and the defences thereto, see B. Mitchell, *Law Relating to Violent Crime* (CLT Publishing, 1997). For an academic approach to *mens rea* see V. Tadros, *Criminal Responsibility* (Oxford University Press, 2005). For an attempt to define intent see I. Kugler, *Direct and Oblique Intention in the Criminal Law* (Ashgate, 2002). For a theoretical approach to intent see W. Wilson, *Central Issues in Criminal Theory* (Hart, 2002), ch. 5, and for good motives see A.J. Ashworth in A.P. Simester and A.T.H. Smith, *Harm and Culpability* (Clarendon Press, 1996). For a comment on carelessness in criminal law, see A.P. Simester in J. Horder (ed.), *Oxford Essays in Jurisprudence* (Clarendon Press, 2000).

Visit **www.mylawchamber.co.uk** to access tools to help you develop and test your knowledge of criminal law, including interactive multiple choice questions, practice exam questions with guidance, annotated weblinks, glossary flashcards, legal newsfeed and legal updates.

Use Case Navigator to read in full some of the key cases referenced in this chapter with commentary and questions:

DPP v *Majewski* [1976] UKHL 2
R v *Adomako* [1994] 3 WLR 288
R v *Church* [1996] 1 QB 59, [1965] 2 WLR 1220
R v *G and Another* [2003] UKHL 50
R v *Woollin* [1999] AC 82

4

Strict liability

Aims and objectives

After reading this chapter you will understand and be able to critique:

● the distinction between 'strict' and 'absolute' liability

● the 'situational liability' cases

● the guidelines on the use of strict liability

● the arguments for and against such liability

Introduction

> The contention that an injury can amount to a crime only when inflicted by intention is no provincial or transient notion. It is as universal and persistent in mature systems of law as belief in freedom of the human will and a consequent ability and duty of the normal individual to choose between good and evil. (US Supreme Court, *Morissette* v *United States* (1952) 342 US 246, 250)

In some offences the prosecution need not prove *mens rea* as to one or more elements of the *actus reus*. These crimes are known as ones of **strict liability**. Therefore, though there must always be an *actus reus*, there need not always be a mental element in relation to each part of the *actus reus*. For example, suppose that a statute forbids butchers to sell meat unfit for human consumption. If one does, the court may say that he or she is guilty even though he or she does not know that the meat is bad. There is then no *mens rea*, knowledge, as to the unfitness. However, presumably the butcher must know that the act being done is 'selling' and that what is being sold is meat. Accordingly, strict offences may well require *mens rea* as to some elements of the *actus reus*, and that is why strict liability means that there is no *mens rea* as to one (or more) elements of the *actus reus*. It does not mean that the prosecution is totally released from the duty of proving *mens rea*. This definition seems to be accepted by the courts: see Lord Edmund-Davies in *Lemon* [1979] AC 617 (HL).

There are thought to be perhaps 11,000 offences in English law. About half of these are strict ones. They are not strange interlopers but a large part of the fabric of criminal law. Strict offences committed feature largely in criminal prosecutions, and in magistrates' courts. More than half of the offences are strict. This surprising number is partly because many motoring crimes are strict, for example in speeding one is guilty even though one does not know one is breaking the speed limit. Many strict offences are concerned with regulating behaviour, and for this reason strict offences are often known as 'regulatory offences'. It must not be thought, however, that the harm resulting from strict offences is minor. An individual or company may have been guilty of such an offence after causing the death of dozens of people in a transport disaster.

The previous paragraph demonstrates that there is nothing peculiar in English law about strict offences. There are also some offences which are sometimes called 'half strict' or 'half *mens rea*' crimes. These are crimes in which the fault element does not or need not correspond to the external element. In assault occasioning actual bodily harm, the accused is guilty if he is reckless as to applying force (*mens rea*) but causes actual bodily harm (*actus reus*). In murder, death must be caused but the accused need intend only grievous bodily harm. Offences of strict liability are not isolated in the law. Indeed it may be said that few crimes can be defined in terms only of intentionally or recklessly committing the *actus reus*.

The effect of the Human Rights Act 1998 remains somewhat uncertain. One possibility is that offences of strict liability violate Article 3 of the European Convention on Human Rights, the right not to be punished in an inhuman or degrading manner, and Article 6(2), minimum rights in a criminal trial. If placing the burden on the accused is contrary to the Convention, so should strict offences be. In that event a court might write in a defence of due diligence. The European Court of Human Rights held in *Salabiaku v France* (1988) 13 EHRR 379 that strict offences were not forbidden by Article 6(2), which is part of the right to a fair trial, though evidential presumptions may be, particularly if they are irrebuttable. On the facts a French law placing the burden on the accused where the sentence was one of imprisonment was held not to breach Article 6(2), a perhaps surprising result. Again statute can set out the law including defences and Article 6(2) is not engaged.

Currently domestic law is in something of a state of flux because of two quite recent House of Lords decisions: *B v DPP* [2000] 2 AC 428 and *K* [2002] 1 AC 462. The effect that they have is not yet clear, but it appears that as a result (one cannot be precise because English courts have a tendency not to apply rules in the area of strict offences) and because of the Convention, courts will more rarely hold that an offence is strict than they have in the past, but that a crime can be held to be strict despite the enactment of the Human Rights Act 1998 and the two Lords cases: *Muhamad* [2003] QB 1031 (CA), which concerned the offence of materially contributing to, or increasing the extent of, insolvency by gambling. The court cited *Salabiaku*: '. . . the Contracting States may . . . penalise a simple or objective fact as such, irrespective of whether it results from criminal intent or from negligence.' In *Gemmell* [2003] Cr App R 23 (CA), Dyson LJ said: 'So far as Article 6 is concerned, the fairness of the substantive law of the Contracting States is not a matter for investigation. The content and interpretation of domestic substantive law is not engaged by Article 6.' The Divisional Court in *Barnfather v London Borough of Islington* [2003] 1 WLR 2318 held that Article 6(2) did not restrict the creation of strict offences by Parliament, and the same court in *R (on the Application of Grundy & Co. Excavations Ltd) v Halton Division Magistrates Court* [2003] EWHC 272 (Admin) similarly held that Article 6(2) did not affect substantive law.

The most recent major domestic authority is *G* [2009] 1 AC 92 (HL). The accused was charged with rape of a child under 13 contrary to s 5 of the Sexual Offences Act 2003. The Lords held that this offence was strict as to the age of the victim but that in this instance strict liability did not contravene the presumption of innocence found in Article 6(2). Again the House said that Article 6(2) was concerned with procedural fairness, not with substantive criminal law. The result was that a boy of 15 was convicted of a serious offence against a girl of 13 even though she had earlier lied to him about her age. The case went to the European Court as **G v UK**, Application no. 37334/08 of 2011, which determined that as has been consistently held, art 6 does not 'dictate the content of domestic criminal law'. Therefore, Parliament's decision not to insert a defence that the accused believed the victim to be aged over 13 despite the gravity of the offence did not breach Article 6. That Article did not oblige lawmakers to ensure that any crime or even any serious crime had *mens rea* or to provide for defences.

It is suggested that these courts acted too dismissively and the arguments will be raised again. It seems absurd that Article 6(2) comes into play when the burden of proving an element is on the accused but not when that element is totally removed in a strict liability offence!

Strict and absolute offences

In the past strict liability was often called 'absolute' liability. This phraseology is still sometimes used both in England and Wales and in the Commonwealth: see, for instance, the High Court of New Zealand in **Jackson v Attorney-General for and on behalf of the Department for Corrections** [2005] NZHC 377 and the Court of Appeal in **G**, above. Nowadays, however, it is common to say that strict offences are not absolute ones. Absolute liability means that the accused is guilty without any mental element at all and that he has no defence either at common law or under statute. Strict offences do need some type of mental state, as we have seen, and all the defences are available. For instance, a child under 10 cannot be convicted of a strict offence, just as he cannot be convicted of a crime of full *mens rea*.

Sometimes a special defence may be created by the statute which lays down the strict offence. In s 3 of the Food Act 1984 it is a defence for the accused to show that the adulteration of food was an 'unavoidable consequence of the process of . . . preparation'. The Lords in **Smedleys Ltd v Breed** [1974] AC 839, a case on the predecessor to the 1984 Act, the Food and Drugs Act 1955, held that the accused had no defence where they had taken all practicable precautions. The presence of a caterpillar in a tin of peas was not 'unavoidable'. This ruling would seem to accord with what Parliament wanted to happen. If Parliament knowingly creates a strict offence and then provides a defence, presumably it wants the defence to be narrowly construed so that it does not swallow the offence. Moreover, if it had wanted a defence of taking all practicable precautions, it would have said so. It did not. The word used was 'unavoidable' and it was not unavoidable to put a caterpillar into a tin.

Besides defences, the accused will not be convicted unless it can be shown that he was acting voluntarily. Sometimes this requirement is thought to be a separate defence, that of automatism, and it will be dealt with as such. Sometimes it is thought that the requirement of voluntary action is a part of a crime separate from *actus reus* and *mens rea*. Whichever it is, if the accused is not acting voluntarily in the sense that he has no control over his bodily movements, there can be no conviction. Three cases will make the point clearer:

Hill v Baxter [1958] 1 QB 277 (DC): *obiter*, a person who while driving is stung by a bee is not 'driving' for the purposes of the Road Traffic Acts when he crashes, and so cannot be found guilty of a crime involving driving, whether strict or otherwise.

Watmore v Jenkins [1962] 2 QB 572 (DC): a person who is unconscious during a diabetic episode is not acting voluntarily.

Bratty v Attorney-General for Northern Ireland [1963] AC 386: the House of Lords held that a man is not acting voluntarily when he is undergoing an epileptic fit, or at least those types of convulsions which involve jerky movements.

In those cases the accused cannot be said to have control over his actions, and the law does not permit a conviction in such circumstances. This proposition applies to strict offences. In the butcher illustration, the butcher would not be guilty of selling contaminated meat, a strict offence, if someone had clobbered him over the head with a blunt instrument and as a 'robot' the accused had 'sold' the meat. Just as the driver who is stung by a bee is not 'driving', so the butcher suffering from concussion is not 'selling'. For details of automatism as a general defence, see Chapter 9. This section merely makes the point that strict offences do require some mental activity. Therefore, even in strict offences, the prosecution must do more than simply prove that the defendant contrived the forbidden act, omission or state of affairs. And do not forget, as stated above, that the butcher will not be guilty of a strict offence if he has a defence. So if you threaten to shoot a butcher unless he sells bad meat to the next customer, he will have a defence even to a strict offence, that of duress.

Offences are therefore divided into three types: (a) *mens rea* ones; (b) strict ones; and (c) absolute ones: ***City of Sault Ste Marie*** [1978] 2 SCR 1299 (SCC). Absolute offences are discussed next.

The exceptional cases

The principal exception to the statement that the prosecution must show more than the *actus reus* even in strict offences is ***Larsonneur***, a decision of the Court of Criminal Appeal.

Larsonneur (1993) 24 Cr App R 74 (CCA)

The accused, Mme Larsonneur, came from France to England and was deported to Dublin. The Irish police sent her back. On arrival at Holyhead on Anglesey she was charged with being an illegal immigrant contrary to the Aliens Order 1920, which has since been repealed, in that she had been found in the UK and her presence there was illegal. Her appeal from conviction was dismissed.

She was guilty even though she had no choice as to whether she should come into the UK: she was guilty though faultless. The full facts disclose that the accused was partly to blame for her predicament, but the court did not take any fault into account.

This case has been constantly criticised by commentators:

(a) On the reasoning of the court, it would not have mattered whether the accused was drugged and taken to Wales, or forced to parachute into Holyhead. She would be guilty even though by no exercise of her will could she avoid entering the country. It is hard to see that she had any state of mind at all. She was liable for what she did, but her acts were done under the control of other people. One might compare her position with that of a farmer who sells adulterated milk, a strict offence. That person has a choice whether to sell any milk or not; Mme Larsonneur had no choice.

(b) The prosecution did not need to charge her with any offence. It is hard to see what benefit the UK derived from having her found guilty.

(c) It is arguable that there was no need to define the crime as one which did not require a blameworthy act. The crime could easily have been defined as being found in the UK, having willingly or knowingly entered the UK, and as the Order put it, being an alien to whom leave to land in the UK has been refused.

(d) The main judge in the case is generally reckoned to be the worst or second-worst criminal law judge of the twentieth century.

(e) Judges still continue to call strict offences 'absolute' ones, for example Auld LJ in *Loukes* [1996] 1 Cr App R 444 (CA). Where, however, the distinction has been noted, judges have strongly castigated absolute liability. In *Mayer v Marchant* (1973) 5 SASR 567 Zelling J called it a 'throwback to a highly primitive form of concept'.

For these reasons it is suggested that *Larsonneur* may not survive direct challenge in the Supreme Court.

It should be noted that Mme Larsonneur was sent to prison, unlike most strictly liable offenders, and that the conviction concerned a matter of her private life. Most strict crimes result in fines and are concerned with matters of business or motoring. For an academic comment supporting *Larsonneur*, see D. Lanham *'Larsonneur* revisited' [1976] Crim LR 276, an article which gives more facts about the case, enabling the reader to understand the outcome somewhat more easily than if one just considers the briefly reported case itself. He argues that the accused brought about the situation she found herself in but should have not been guilty had she been physically compelled to enter the UK if she did not culpably bring about the facts giving rise to the alleged offence.

Despite criticism of *Larsonneur*, which seemed to be highly exceptional and not to be followed, it was followed by the Divisional Court in *Winzar v Chief Constable of Kent* (1983) *The Times*, 28 March. The criminal responsibility in these cases is sometimes known as 'situational liability'; an alternative name is '**status offences**'.

Winzar v Chief Constable of Kent (1983) The Times, 28 March (DC)

> The accused was found guilty of being found drunk on the highway, despite being removed from a hospital to where he had been brought on a stretcher, the bearers believing that he was ill, and gently placed on the pavement by the police, contrary to s 12 of the Licensing Act 1872. He argued that he had not been found drunk on the highway because the police had carried him there. The court held that 'found drunk' meant 'perceived to be drunk'. The police perceived him to be drunk on the highway. Therefore, he was found drunk on the highway, and was accordingly guilty.

However, even if one accepts that 'found drunk' means 'perceived to be drunk' and does not involve *mens rea* on the part of the accused, surely he was perceived to be drunk in the hospital corridor, to which the police had been summoned. He was not on these facts perceived to be drunk at the later stage when he had been put onto the pavement. Accordingly he was not, contrary to the view of the court, perceived to be drunk when he was lying on the pavement, and even on the court's reasoning he ought not to have been guilty of being found drunk on a highway. He would have been guilty apparently if he had been thrown out of a speeding car onto the pavement! Alternatively, one might argue that he is really being punished for getting drunk, but that is no crime. If the accused is really being punished for getting drunk (what is sometimes known as 'preceding fault') or for not leaving the hospital despite numerous requests to do so, the law should say so. One can also blame Parliament for enacting a law which can be read as the court did in *Winzar*. As David Ormerod, *Smith and Hogan's Criminal Law*, 13th edn (Oxford University Press, 2011) 64 comments:

> Larsonneur and Winzar were convicted of offences the conviction of which was in fact procured by the police; and this seems peculiarly offensive [footnote omitted].

As might be expected, the police were not prosecuted for procuring the commission of the offences but this is what really happened. C.M.V. Clarkson, *Understanding Criminal Law*, 4th edn (Thomson, 2005) 47 takes a similar view:

> Our sense of justice would be outraged by a law that made it a crime to have measles – a condition one is powerless to prevent.

It is the 'impossible-to-prevent' point which goes against these two cases. Compulsion is no defence. The defendants were guilty even though they had no control over their actions at the time of the arrest. Despite the criticism of *Larsonneur* that the accused would have been guilty even if drugged and brought into the UK, it is suggested that even a court bound by *Larsonneur* and *Winzar* would distinguish those authorities when faced with a situation where at the barrel of a gun a person has been forced to enter the UK or has been forced out of his home and to lie down drunk on the pavement. Moreover, a court could hold the cases restricted to their particular facts and the Supreme Court of course is not bound by either case. Defences such as duress and, *a fortiori*, infancy apply even to absolute offences.

It remains to be seen whether such cases will survive testing under the European Convention on Human Rights.

Strict liability: the basics

Having clarified some issues, we can proceed to a discussion of strict offences.

Although there is some dispute as to which is the first crime of strict liability (see Singer 'The resurgence of *mens rea*: the rise and fall of strict criminal liability' (1989) 30 Boston College LR 377), *Woodrow* (1846) 153 ER 907 is generally treated as being the first one dealing with a statutory offence (certainly the common law crime of criminal libel was held to be strict before *Woodrow*). The accused was found guilty of possessing adulterated tobacco contrary to the Tobacco Act 1842, s 3, even though he did not know that there was something in the tobacco. *Woodrow* exemplifies one view of strict offences: that they form a sort of 'administrative criminal law', as Professor Leigh put it in his book *Strict and Vicarious Liability* (Sweet & Maxwell, 1982) 101. On this approach strict offences are not true crimes like murder but part of a system of regulation of activities, and this is why strict offences are sometimes called 'regulatory offences': they regulate enterprises for the public good. It should be mentioned that the legal thinking behind *Woodrow* seems to have been that in 1846 it had not been settled where the burden of proof should lie, and it did not seem unjust to place it on the accused, who after all had the tobacco in his possession.

Though regulation of undertakings sounds like a good thing, criticism of strict offences is strong. The basic argument is that strict liability sometimes punishes people who are not morally wrong. An example is *Sweet v Parsley*, a case which eventually reached the House of Lords, but the magistrates' court's decision is being considered here.

Sweet v Parsley [1970] AC 132 (HL)

Ms Sweet was a young teacher who worked in Oxford. She rented a farmhouse seven miles away in the countryside. She sublet the house to what the judges called 'beatniks' while she stayed in a flat in Oxford because her car (nick-named 'Young Maiden's Misery', because of its registration letters of YMM) had broken down. The beatniks smoked cannabis. She was found guilty of managing premises used for the purpose of smoking cannabis. She lost her job, even though she did not know that the sub-lessees were breaking the law and even though she had no control over them.

This case demonstrates that where one is convicted of a strict offence, one still suffers the social stigma of being branded a criminal and having one's name in the local newspaper. We shall see later what happened when Ms Sweet appealed.

Crimes which require *mens rea* and crimes which do not

Example

Suppose that Parliament creates an offence of causing or permitting a child under the age of 14 to masturbate oneself. The accused believes the child to be over 14 but he or she is in fact under 14. Does he have a defence?

The crime may be one of strict liability as to the age of the child, in which case he is liable; however, recent HL authorities in a similar area of law have held similar offences not to be strict: ***B v DPP*** [2000] 2 AC 428 and ***K*** [2002] 1 AC 462. These cases state that strict liability will not as a matter of constitutional propriety be implied unless it is necessary to do so. Accordingly, it is suggested that the offence is not one of strict liability and therefore the accused would have a defence if he was mistaken as to the age of the 'victim'. It is also suggested that if Parliament were to discover what the court had done, it would reverse the ruling (cf. the Sexual Offences Act 2003).

We come to the difficult problem of determining which crimes are strict as to one or more elements of the *actus reus* and which are crimes of full *mens rea*. There is no simple rule, but the law is not totally unpredictable.

(a) Generally speaking, all major crimes, especially those involving breaches of morality, require *mens rea*, for example rape, murder and theft. However, it must be said that the outcome of a violation of a rule in a strict offence may be extremely serious. A victim may be killed as a result of speeding, a strict offence.

(b) All common law crimes require *mens rea* except those listed below. Since no new common law offences can be created, this list is definitive.

   (i) *Public nuisance.* The case usually cited is ***Stephens*** (1866) LR 1 QB 702, but that case is really an authority on vicarious liability, and it may be that in modern times *mens rea* is needed for this offence. In the most recent authority, ***Shorrock*** [1993] 3 All ER 917 (CA), the court held that the accused need not know of the offence he had caused. It was sufficient that he ought to have known that a nuisance would result from his activity on the land.

   (ii) *Contempt of court.* The authority is ***Evening Standard Co. Ltd*** [1954] 1 QB 578. Parliament expressly recognised the 'strict liability rule', as it called this principle, when it created the Contempt of Court Act 1981.

   (iii) *The various forms of criminal libel.* All forms were said by Lord Salmon in ***Lemon***, above, to be strict. Certainly ***Lemon*** decided, Lords Diplock and Edmund-Davies dissenting, that in blasphemous libel there was no requirement of an intention to outrage Christians when publishing a poem depicting Christ as a homosexual, though there remained some *mens rea*, an intent to publish. Blasphemous libel was abolished by s 79 of the Criminal Justice and Immigration Act 2008, which came into force on 8 July 2008. Defamatory libel was abolished by the Coroners and Justice Act 2009. However, seditious libel may require *mens rea*: ***Bow Street Magistrates Court ex parte Choudhury*** [1991] 1 QB 429 (CA).

(iv) *Outraging public decency*. The Court of Appeal in *Gibson* [1990] 2 QB 619 applied *Lemon* from the cognate offence of blasphemous libel to this common law crime. A person is guilty whether or not he intends to corrupt or outrage public decency or is reckless as to whether he is corrupting or is outraging public decency. The Law Commission in its Consultation Paper No. 193, *Simplification of Criminal Law: Public Nuisance and Outraging Public Decency*, 2010, recommended that the crime should be enshrined in statute and that it should have a mental element of intention to or recklessness as to outrage, shock, or disgust ordinary people.

(c) Under statute much turns on the individual offence. One cannot state that if Parliament has omitted to mention *mens rea*, the court will or will not read it in. There is no authoritative guidance as to which factors are important. Lord Nicholls in *B v DPP* [2000] 2 AC 428 (HL) gave examples of these factors: 'the language used, the nature of the offence, the mischief sought to be prevented and any other circumstances that might assist in determining what intention was properly to be attributed to Parliament'. *B v DPP* reemphasised that there is a presumption of *mens rea*. It may take some years before the full effect of this authority is felt. Certainly it is less likely than before that a sex crime will be held to be a strict offence, but exceptions still arise, as in *Doring* [2002] Crim LR 817 (see below).

Many offences dealing with the welfare of the public do not require a mental element. Wright J in *Sherras v de Rutzen* [1895] 1 QB 918 (DC) said that such offences criminalised persons whose acts 'are not criminal in any real sense but are acts which in the public interest are prohibited under a penalty'. He instanced the possession of adulterated tobacco. This phrase continues to be used, for example by Lord Scarman and Viscount Dilhorne in *Alphacell Ltd v Woodward* [1972] AC 824 (HL). Another term is 'regulatory' offences. Unfortunately terms such as 'public interest' and 'regulatory' are conclusory rather than explanatory. They do not tell us which crimes are strict, which are not. There is no definition in statute or cases. The two other categories Wright J mentioned were public nuisance and 'cases in which, although the proceeding is criminal in form, it is really only a summary mode of enforcing a civil right', such as an unintentional trespass in pursuit of game. It must be added that not all regulatory offences are minor and subject only to minor penalties. Pollution of the environment, to use an illustration, is often seen as a regulatory offence but its consequences may be substantial, and the punishment can be substantial too.

These types of offences are sometimes called 'quasi-criminal', as, for instance, Lord Reid put it in *Warner v MPC* [1969] 2 AC 256 (HL), discussed below. However, the term is not very helpful: is selling bad meat a crime or a quasi-crime? Keeping to the point about public welfare offences, one can, however, state that the subject matter of some offences attracts strict liability more than do others. The selling of tainted food may well not require *mens rea*; for example *Parker v Alder* [1899] 1 QB 20, where the crime was one of selling bad milk, whereas bigamy is a crime requiring mental element: *Gould* [1968] 2 QB 65 (CA) overruling *Wheat and Stocks* [1921] 2 KB 119. Lord Diplock was to similar effect in *Sweet v Parsley* above, when he spoke of activities involving 'potential danger to public health, safety or morals'. The citizen had a choice whether or not to participate in these activities. If he did, he was subject to a higher duty of care than normal. 'An obligation to take whatever measure may be necessary to prevent the prohibited act, without regard to those considerations of cost or business practicability which play a part in the determination of what would be required of them in order to fulfil the ordinary common law duty of care.' In Lord Diplock's mind there were probably thoughts of butchers, pharmacists, milkmen. It should be mentioned that bigamy is sometimes seen as an offence contrary to morality, yet it is not a strict offence and, furthermore, murder involves actual danger to public health and safety, yet is not strict. What Lord Diplock seems to have meant is that there is a wide span of possible victims in strict crimes; any one of a million customers might suffer, for instance, if milk is contaminated.

(d) At least outside the area of food and drugs, the courts are often not willing to impose an unreasonable burden on the accused. In *Sherras v de Rutzen*, above, a pub landlord was held not to be guilty of supplying liquor to a constable on duty, contrary to s 16(2) of the Licensing Act 1872, because in the view of one of the two judges he had no easy way of checking whether the police constable was on or off duty. The contrasting case to *Sherras* is always *Cundy v Le Cocq* (1884) 13 QBD 207(DC), where a landlord was convicted under s 13 of the same Act of selling liquor to a drunk. One distinction between the two cases may be that a landlord can be expected to know that a drunk is indeed drunk. Accordingly, it can be said that the courts are generally reluctant to punish people when there is nothing they could have done to prevent it occurring: how can one report a road accident, when one does not know there has been one? In the Privy Council case of *Lim Chin Aik v R* [1963] AC 160, the accused could not easily find out that it was illegal for him to enter Singapore, punishment would serve no purpose, and so he was not guilty. He was not to be expected to check whether he was permitted to enter at all times. This reasoning has not always been followed; often persons are convicted despite their having taken all possible precautions. See, for example, *Smedleys Ltd v Breed*, above.

This attempted reconciliation of the famous cases of *Sherras* and *Cundy* does not explain everything. Two equally well-known cases are *Prince* (1875) LR 2 CCR 154 and *Hibbert* (1869) LR 1 CCR 184. Both cases are concerned with what became s 20 of the Sexual Offences Act 1956 (since repealed):

> It is an offence for a person acting without lawful authority or excuse to take an unmarried girl under the age of sixteen out of the possession of her parent or guardian against her will.

In *Prince* the accused believed the girl to be 18; she was in fact under 16 and he was found guilty (the majority, eight judges, said that the words of the statute were to be read literally, others (a minority of six) that taking the girl was immoral and wrongful and the accused (who in the words of Stephen J in *Tolson* (1889) 23 QBD 168 (CCR) could be likened to 'seducers and abductors', which it has to be said Mr Prince was not) acted at his peril, and one judge dissented), yet only six years earlier the same court, the Court for Crown Cases Reserved, had decided in *Hibbert* that an accused was not guilty when he did not know that the girl whom he had taken away was in the possession of her parents. Accordingly, s 20 had to be read in this way: the accused was guilty if he takes a girl, knowing her to be a girl, who is unmarried, knowing her to be unmarried, out of the possession of her parent or guardian, knowing her to have a parent or guardian, and she happened to be under 16. A solid distinction between these two cases has not been found. Perhaps the difference is that in *Hibbert* the accused did not intend to take the girl out of anyone's possession, whereas the accused in *Prince* did. Surely, though, the crime was not so defined. The age of the girl was a most material element. Mr Prince would not have been guilty if the girl was over 16. Moreover, if the accused was guilty even though he did not know the age, why was he not guilty when he had not even checked whether the girl had a father? It should be noted that the accused in *Prince* was guilty no matter how deeply he had inquired into the girl's age and no matter how reasonable his error as to her age was.

Prince was trenchantly criticised (*obiter*) in *B v DPP*, above, but it was not overruled and until it is, it remains authoritative on what was s 20 of the 1956 Act. *B v DPP* was not a case on s 20. However, as a result of the next two cases mentioned it is difficult to see *Prince* continuing to exist for much longer and since the repeal of s 20 of the Sexual Offences Act 1956 in 2003 its authority has been further reduced. Both decisions were made unanimously by the Lords.

B v DPP [2000] 2 AC 428 (HL)

The accused pressed a girl who was 13 to perform oral sex on him. She refused. He was charged with inciting a girl under 14 to commit an act of gross indecency contrary to the Indecency with Children Act 1960, an offence which was repealed and replaced by the Sexual Offences Act 2003. His defence was that he believed the girl to be over 14. The Divisional Court held that, as in *Prince* (above), liability as to the age of the girl was strict, and the conviction was affirmed. The Divisional Court reasoned that the purpose of the 1960 statute was to protect children under 14; therefore, it was immaterial that the accused was mistaken as to the age of the girl. (The age was raised to 16 by the Criminal Justice and Court Services Act 2000, s 39.)

The 1960 Act was enacted because a defendant was not guilty of indecent assault on a child when he did not use threats (assault) or force (battery). This aim would be undermined if the accused had a defence when he was mistaken as to age. Moreover, Parliament did sometimes provide defences based on such errors, but it did not do so for the offence of indecency with children. It should be noted that the 1960 Act created an offence of grave social stigma and with a maximum sentence of 10 years' imprisonment: the offence was not a regulatory one. Brooke LJ stated: 'Parliament continues to legislate in this area on an *ad hoc* piecemeal basis, and declines to set aside the time to make the necessary policy choices as to the *mens rea* requirement in relation to the changes in the law it enacts, let alone the many parts of the law it leaves unaltered. Hour after expensive hour has to be spent in the courts and elsewhere puzzling over these matters.' The court certified that a point of law of general public importance was involved, but refused leave to appeal.

The Lords overruled the Divisional Court and decided that the offence was not one of strict liability. It was held that the accused was not guilty if he made an honest mistake as to the girl's age. There was no special rule relating to age: the presumption of *mens rea* applied to all elements of offences. The mistake need not be one based on reasonable grounds. Lord Steyn spoke of the 'constitutional principle' that *mens rea* was to be presumed in a statute. Lord Nicholls applied the common law presumption that *mens rea* is part of a statutory offence unless Parliament has indicated otherwise, whether expressly or by necessary implication. Implication on reasonable grounds was not enough. The implication had to be 'compellingly clear'. This is a high hurdle to jump, and if correct, many of the other authorities were wrongly decided. (The other Law Lords spoke to similar effect. For example, Lord Hutton said that the implication that the statute ruled out *mens rea* had to be a '*necessary*' one (his emphasis).)

The fact that the offence was serious reinforced that presumption, as did the fact that the crime covered a wide range of facts from 'predatory approaches by a much older paedophile' to 'consensual sexual experimentation between precocious teenagers of whom the offender may be the younger of the two'. The fact that sometimes the offence was used to protect vulnerable children was not of itself sufficient to make the crime one of strict liability. Furthermore, it was uncertain whether or not strict liability would lead to better enforcement of the crime. He added that insofar as the reasoning in *Prince* was inconsistent with the *mens rea* principle, it was wrong; the presumption applied even when the accused's act was immoral; the displacement of the presumption must be made clearly; and it is not displaced by comparing two badly drafted sections. Lord Nicholls stressed that the decision was not restricted to cases where the age of the victim is an ingredient of the offence.

Lord Steyn said that the Lords in **Sweet v Parsley** may have expected that their decision would have overruled *Prince*. He said that that authority was 'was out of line with the modern trend in criminal law which is that a defendant should be judged on the facts as he believes them to be'. He added that *Prince* 'is a relic from an age dead and gone'. Any reform of the law was for Parliament, which despite the expert advice of the Criminal Law Revision Committee and the Law Commission over the years, had not acted decisively. In criticism it should be said that when Parliament re-enacted the crime which was at issue in *Prince*, it did so on the basis that *Prince* was authoritative.

B v DPP was applied in *K* [2002] 1 AC 462 (HL). There was no necessary implication that an accused was guilty of indecent assault on a victim aged under 16 when he honestly believed her to be over 16; she had also told him that she was 16. Both cases are concerned with mistakes as to age, as *Prince* was, but neither's *ratio* is so restricted. In criticism it must be said that when Parliament enacted the Sexual Offences Act 1956 it did not intend to affect *Prince*.

Both *B v DPP* and *K* are now subject to the Sexual Offences Act 2003 which provides that a mistake as to the age of a child is irrelevant if he is under 13 and, if the child is between 13 and 16, only mistakes made on reasonable grounds suffice. In relation to a child under 13, liability is now strict. Liability for those aged between 13 and 16 is arguably not strict because of the general rule in *B v DPP* and *K*. It would have been better for Parliament to have stated the law clearly in the 2003 Act. However, the cases remain authoritative as general statements on the law of strict liability. See, for example, *Kumar* [2004] EWCA Crim 3207 (buggery of a boy under 16 when the accused believed him to be over 16). Contrariwise, courts can still find that offences are ones of strict liability even after *B v DPP* and *K*: see, for example, *Corporation of London v Eurostar (UK) Ltd* [2004] EWHC 187 (Admin) where Article 4 of the Rabies (Importation of Dogs, Cats and other Mammals) Order 1974 was held to be strict as to the landing of an animal in great Britain. Henriques J said that the risk of bringing rabies into the country was so grave that the crime was a strict one; the accused company ran a transport business which gave rise to the possible entry of animals with rabies; therefore the offence was strict, although there was a defence of lawful authority or excuse. Both Lords Steyn and Bingham in *K* said that the presumption of *mens rea* was a constitutional principle.

A stronger case than *Hibbert* and *Sherras v de Rutzen* exemplifying the courts' implying a *mens rea* word into the statutory definition of a crime is *Harding v Price* [1948] 1 KB 695. The Divisional Court held that the accused was guilty of failing to report a road accident only if he knew that there had been one. The ruling is surprising when one realises that the statute at issue was the Road Traffic Act 1930. Parliament omitted 'knowingly' in that Act, whereas in the first statute dealing with the matter, the Motor Car Act 1903, the statute did contain this *mens rea* word. It would not be difficult for a court to hold that the omission was deliberate and that Parliament intended the offence to be strict. See also *Tolson* (1889) 23 QBD 168 where, as in

Prince, there was no *mens rea* word, yet the accused was not guilty. Wills J spoke to the effect that circumstances alter cases.

(e) Another helpful guide is that where the punishment for the crime is severe, there is at times a presumption that *mens rea* is required. Lord Nicholls in *B v DPP* said: 'The more serious the offence, the greater was the weight to be attached to the presumption, because the more severe was the punishment and the greater the stigma that accompanied a conviction.' Originally the crime discussed in *B v DPP* had a maximum sentence of two years but that was raised to 10. In *Crown Prosecution Service v M* [2009] EWCA Crim 2615 Rix LJ said of a crime, taking various articles into prison, with a ten years maximum sentence that: 'It is counter-intuitive to think that such an offence is one of absolute liability.'

This presumption, however, does not always take effect, for example on a second conviction for polluting a river, a strict offence, the accused may be sentenced to prison; similarly s 5(b) of the Dangerous Drugs Act 1965 created an offence with a maximum of 10 years' imprisonment, yet it was held to be strict. In *Howells* [1977] QB 614, the Court of Appeal held the crime of possessing a firearm to be strict (the accused believed the gun to be an antique, which it was not), yet the penalty was a maximum of five years. Inconsistencies continue to flourish. In *Blake* [1997] 1 WLR 1167 (CA) where the accused made a broadcast on a pirate radio station, a maximum sentence of two years made the offence 'truly criminal' but the court ruled that the offence was a strict one in light of the other indications; and in *Harrow London Borough Council v Shah* [1999] 2 Cr App R 457 (DC), where the crime was one of selling lottery tickets to a person under 16, the same maximum did *not* make the offences truly criminal. Accordingly, the mere fact that imprisonment is the sentence does not mean that the crime is a *mens rea* one: *Wells St Magistrates* [1986] 1 WLR 1046 (DC). This conclusion may not survive challenge under the Human Rights Act 1998. For example, as stated the maximum penalty in *Howells* was quite high, yet Parliament had not provided a due diligence defence. It is suggested that *Howells* may fall foul of Article 3 of the ECHR (inhuman or degrading treatment) or Article 6 (presumption of innocence) or both, though current case law is against a breach of the latter.

Too much should not be read into the severity of the maximum penalty. Since strict offences can also be committed intentionally, recklessly and negligently, the maximum is reserved for intentionally bringing about the *actus reus*. The sentence for a strict liability breach of the same offence may be minor: *Matudi* [2003] EWCA Crim 697.

(f) The words of the statute are sometimes interpreted as giving rise to strict liability. The following offer case law illustrations. Humphreys J in *Grade v DPP* [1942] 2 All ER 118 (DC) said that 'sell' does not require knowledge, but 'permit' does. In *Grade* the accused was charged with unlawfully presenting part of a new stage play before that part had been passed by the Lord Chamberlain, contrary to s 15 of the Theatres Act 1843, since abolished. A joke had been inserted into a music-hall revue *To See Such Fun* without the accused's knowledge, while he was away from the venue, and contrary to his instructions. Nevertheless, he was guilty.

In *James & Son Ltd v Smee* [1955] 1 QB 78 (DC) the offence of 'permitting' someone to use a vehicle which had defective brakes was held not to be a strict offence. The accused was guilty only if he knew that the brakes were faulty. However, the crime of permitting the use of a vehicle without insurance is a strict one: see, for example, *Braugh v Crago* [1975] RTR 453 and *Chief Constable of Norfolk v Fisher* [1992] RTR 6 (DC). In the latter case, which is also known as *DPP v Fisher*, *Newbury v Davies* [1974]

RTR 367 (DC) was distinguished. In **Newbury v Davies** the owner was found not guilty of the offence when he permitted use of a vehicle only on the express condition that the daughter arranged insurance cover. Since, subject to the obtaining of the licence, use was not permitted, use of the car without a licence was not permitted. In **Fisher**, which involved the same offence, the accused knew that a person was disqualified and allowed him to have the car only if he got someone else to drive. He did so, but that other was not insured. The owner was convicted. The distinction between the cases is weak. Surely it should be immaterial whether the condition not to drive without insurance was imposed directly as in **Newbury** or indirectly as in **Fisher**. At present therefore some 'permitting' offences are strict but others are not, a not very helpful conclusion but one based on the cases. It was suggested by Walker J in **Cambridgeshire County Council v Associated Lead Mills** [2005] EWHC 1627 (Admin) that the 'revitalisation' of the presumption against strict liability in **B v DPP** and **K**, both above, means that the authorities holding that 'permits' is a word importing strict liability are wrong.

'Uses' has been held to give rise to strict liability: **Green v Burnett** [1955] 1 QB 78 (DC). Therefore, using a vehicle with defective brakes is a strict offence but permitting or allowing a person to drive a car with defective brakes is not!

Even 'wilfully' has been read as not importing knowledge in relation to s 86(3) of the Police Act 1996, wilful obstruction of a police officer: **Rice v Connolly** [1966] 2 QB 414 (DC) and **Lewis v Cox** [1985] QB 509 (DC). However, the House of Lords held in **Sheppard** [1981] AC 394 that 'wilfully' in s 1 of the Children and Young Persons Act 1933, which creates the crime of wilful neglect of a child in such a manner that it is likely to cause unnecessary suffering or injury to health, meant both wilfully neglecting the child and knowing of the risk that the child's health might suffer or not knowing of the risk because the accused did not care whether or not the child needed medical treatment. Therefore, the crime was not one of strict liability but of objective recklessness. 'Procure' and probably 'suffer' also require *mens rea*. In all cases except one (**Brooks v Mason** [1902] 2 KB 743(DC)), 'knowingly' has been held to require *mens rea*. One cannot imagine that **Brooks v Mason** would ever be followed, particularly not after **B v DPP** and **K**.

(g) The fact that *mens rea* is required in one section of a statute but not in another does not mean that *mens rea* is not required in the latter: **Sherras** and **Lim Chin Aik**, **B v DPP**, all above. A similar case is one from New South Wales. In **Turnbull** (1944) 44 NSWLR 108, the phrase 'knowingly suffering' a girl under 18 to be in a house of ill-fame contrary to s 91D of the Crimes Act 1900 was read so that the accused was guilty only if he knew that the girl was under 18 (cf. **Prince** above). Contrary cases include **Cundy**, above, which was approved in **Hobbs v Winchester Corp** [1910] 2 KB 471 (CCA), and **Neville v Mavroghenis** [1984] Crim LR 42 (DC): in the latter case, which turned on s 13(4) of the Housing Act 1961, the court held that the subsection could be divided into two parts, one having 'knowingly' in it, the other not: the second part, being a landlord of rented premises which had defects, was held to be strict. Therefore, the accused was guilty even though he did not know of the defect. Somewhat similar is the statement of Lord Goff in **PSGB v Storkwain Ltd** [1986] 1 WLR 903 (HL) that in the Medicines Act 1968 Parliament had made it plain by the use or omission of a *mens rea* word which offence was strict and which was not. It must be said, however, that the presence or absence of a *mens rea* word is more dependent on the vagaries of draftsmanship than on forethought. For example, according to Lords Steyn and Hutton in **B v DPP**, while it can be said the Sexual Offences Act 1956 was aimed in part at protecting the vulnerable, that consolidation statute contained such a disparate mixture of crimes, that the fact that *mens rea* was stated in some sections but not in others did not mean the latter were offences of strict liability.

(h) The fact that there is a defence of due diligence is a good indication that the offence is strict. If the offence is not strict, there is no need for a 'no negligence' offence because the prosecution has to prove fault, negligence. Section 7(1) of the Children and Young Persons Act 1933 provides a defence of taking all reasonable precautions and exercising due diligence to the crime of selling tobacco to a child under 16.

The above guidelines are just that – guidelines, though subject to what the House of Lords said in *B v DPP* and *K*. It is easy to point to cases which are inconsistent. In the case of a crime created by Parliament, one has to look both at the words of the statute and at the intention of Parliament, as the courts put it. The words are important, for example if the Act says 'knowingly' it has to be proved that the accused acted knowingly: *Westminster CC v Croyalgrange Ltd* [1986] 1 WLR 674 (HL), knowingly permitting premises to be used as a sex establishment. Some judges have gone further and said that the requirement of *mens rea* is to be presumed when Parliament has omitted to state any. Brett MR in *Attorney-General v Bradlaugh* (1885) 14 QBD 689 said:

> It is contrary to the whole established law of England (unless the legislation on the subject has clearly enacted it) to say that a person can be guilty of a crime in England without a wrongful intent.

Similar sentiments abound, for example Cave J in *Tolson*, above, stated that the elimination of *mens rea* was:

> . . . so revolting to the moral sense that we ought to require the clearest and most indisputable evidence that such is the meaning of the Act.

In one of the most important cases on this topic, *Sweet v Parsley*, above, Lord Diplock went so far as to say that:

> The mere fact that Parliament has made the conduct a criminal offence gives rise to *some* implication about the mental element.

It is not difficult to find contrary sentiments. In *Mallinson v Carr* [1891] 1 QB 48, just two years after *Tolson*, the court held that a criminal statute was to be read literally and if no *mens rea* was stated, none was to be implied. Nevertheless, the strong modern trend as exemplified by *Sweet v Parsley*, *B v DPP* and *K* is that in the words of Lord Nicholls in the second case the presumption of *mens rea* in statutory offences could be displaced only by 'necessary implication' using 'compellingly clear evidence'. That evidence may sometimes be easy to find. The Sexual Offences (Amendment) Act 2000, s 3(1) (see now the Sexual Offences Act 2003), made it an offence to have sexual activity with a person under 18 if the accused was in a position of trust in relation to him. He had a defence if he proved that he did not know and could not reasonably have been expected to know that he was under 18. This defence would have no effect unless the offence were a strict one as to the age. Here is an example that Parliament on compellingly clear evidence intended this offence to be strict.

How the courts apply these guidelines

The reader, having grasped what has been said in the previous section, may be in some doubt as to how the law there stated is to be applied. This section examines several cases in order to show how the courts deal with this issue. **Whiteside v DPP** [2011] EWHC 3471 (Admin) exemplifies the current state of the law. The appellant was charged under s 172(3) of the Road Traffic Act 1988, failing to respond to a notification requiring driver details. His car was being driven at more than 70 m.p.h. and the notice obliged him to provide details of who the driver was. He did not personally receive the notice. He contended that he was not guilty, arguing that the offence was not one of strict liability. The Court held to the contrary. It distinguished **Sweet v Parsley**, above, as involving a more serious offence with greater sanctions than the one at issue; moreover, the statute provided various defences to the crime.

A relevant authority is **Bradish** [1990] 1 QB 981 (CA). The accused was found in possession of a canister which contained CS gas. He was charged with possessing a prohibited weapon contrary to s 5(1)(b) of the Firearms Act 1968. Did the accused have to know that what he was carrying was a CS gas canister? No mental element was stated in the paragraph. Auld J, giving the judgment of the Court, referred to **Warner v MPC** [1969] 2 AC 256 (HL) for the proposition that the dangerous subject matter of the crime, coupled with the plain words used, might well rebut the presumption of *mens rea*. In the Firearms Act 1968 there was no exception which gave the accused a defence if he could prove that he did not believe that the thing was dangerous as the defendant had under s 28(3) of the Misuse of Drugs Act 1971. Previous cases had held other parts of the 1968 Act to be strict. In **Howells** [1977] QB 614 (CA) and **Hussain** [1981] 1 WLR 416 (CA), s 1, possessing a firearm without a certificate was held to create a strict offence in light according to **Howells** of 'the clear intention of the Act'; in **Harrison** [1996] Crim LR 200 (CA), s 19, possessing a loaded shotgun in a public place, was held to be a crime of strict liability; while in **Pierre** [1963] Crim LR 513, s 17, using a firearm to resist arrest, was held to be strict. Auld J in **Bradish** said:

> The clear purpose of the firearms legislation is to impose a tight control on the use of highly dangerous weapons. To achieve effective control and to prevent the potentially disastrous consequences of their misuse strict liability is necessary, just as it is in the equally dangerous field of drugs . . . Given that s 1 has been held to create an offence of strict liability, this consideration applies *a fortiori* to s 5 which is concerned with more serious weapons, such as automatic handguns and machine guns, and imposes a higher maximum penalty.

He added: '. . . the possibilities and consequences of evasion would be too great for effective control' if the offence were other than one of strict liability, and 'to the argument that the innocent possessor or carrier of firearms or prohibited weapons . . . is at risk of unfair conviction . . . there has to be balanced the important public policy behind the legislation of protecting the public from the misuse of such dangerous weapons'.

These authorities were endorsed in **Deyemi** [2007] EWCA Crim 2060, a case on s 5(1)(b), in which it was held that the accused was strictly liable for possessing a stun gun, which he believed to be a torch and which looked like a torch. **B v DPP** and **K**, above, were held not to govern because they dealt with different statutes and the strict liability doctrine and its exceptions are based according to those House of Lords' decisions on statutory interpretation. The court certified a question for what is now the Supreme Court as to whether s 5(1)(b) created a strict offence and, if so, whether it contravened the ECHR. For the answer to the latter question, refer to the beginning of this chapter. **Zahid** [2010] EWCA Crim 2158 is one of the most recent of those authorities which consider strict liability in relation to firearms. The defendant was accused of possessing ammunition (bullets) designed to expand on impact contrary to s 5(1A)(f) of the Firearms Act 1968. The trial judge directed that the offence was one of strict liability, and the accused pleaded guilty. His appeal was rejected. The Court held that he had no defence when he said that he had found a package containing what he thought to be bolts or screws but which in fact contained two bullets. The so-called 'container' cases applied; that is, the accused did not have a defence if he knew he had a container but did not know its contents. This rule is often used in drugs cases. The cases of **Warner v MPC**, **Bradish** (which includes a discussion of **Howells**) and **Deyemi** were considered and applied. In relation to **K**, the Court of Appeal held without discussion that despite the constitutional principle laid down in that case, they were bound by precedents from the Court of Appeal itself. The Court refused leave to appeal, though certifying that there was a point of law of general public importance, and the Supreme Court refused an application for leave to appeal. **Zahid** was applied to another firearms offence, possessing an altered firearm (a sawn-off shotgun) without a firearms certificate, in **Gregory** [2011] EWCA Crim 1712.

The court in **Bradish** referred to decisions on other sections of the 1968 Act and to another dangerous matter, drugs. What is interesting in the light of other cases is that the court ruled that the severe penalty was a factor in treating the offence as strict, whereas in other cases judges have said that since the penalty was low the offence was a regulatory offence and so strict! A case for comparison is **Berry (No. 3)** [1995] 1 WLR 7 (CA). The accused was charged with making an explosive substance, electronic timers, contrary to s 4(1) of the Explosive Substances Act 1883. That section penalises a 'person who makes or knowingly has in his possession or under his control any explosive substance . . .'. The word 'knowingly' was not placed before 'makes' but the word was implied by the Court of Appeal. The court did not give a reason for not following the successful contentions in the firearms authorities. The court reasoned that the maker of the substance could be in no doubt that he had made it. In Lord Taylor CJ's judgment the addition of 'knowingly': '. . . simply emphasises that where possession or control is relied upon, the defendant must know the substance is in his possession, for example in his house or his car. No person who makes the substance can be unaware that he had done so.' The sentence, a maximum of 14 years, was not mentioned, and there was no reference to the need for 'tight control' of explosive devices.

Another illustration of judicial activity in a different area of strict offences is **Miller** [1975] 1 WLR 1222 (CA). The accused was charged with driving a vehicle on a road while disqualified. The defence was that he did not know that the place where he was driving was a 'road' within the meaning of the Road Traffic Acts. The Court of Appeal rejected his contention. First, while noting that the absence of the words 'knowingly' or 'negligently' in the relevant section was not conclusive, it was a factor; secondly, the crime was not a 'truly criminal' one, but rather the crime existed 'for safeguarding the safety of the public by prohibiting an act under sanction of a penalty'; and thirdly, previous authorities had treated the section as imposing strict liability. Accordingly the offence was strict in the light both of principle and precedent and the accused's mistake was irrelevant. A contrasting case is **Phekoo** [1981] 1 WLR 1117, where the Court of Appeal sifted through similar factors and reached the opposite conclusion. The accused had to believe that the persons to whom he was doing 'acts calculated to interfere with the peace or comfort of the residential occupier' with intent to cause them to give up occupation of the premises contrary to s 1(3) of the Protection from Eviction Act 1977 were indeed residential occupiers and not, for instance, squatters.

Another example of the court's inconsistency, this time at the House of Lords level, is provided by the contrast between **Warner v MPC** and **Sweet v Parsley**, both above. In **Warner** their Lordships, Lord Reid dissenting, held that possession of drugs contrary to the Drugs (Prevention of Misuse) Act 1964 was a partly strict offence. Lords Morris and Guest simply followed the wording of the Act. Lord Pearce considered the gravity of the evil, while he and Lord Wilberforce said that the offence was not really strict because the accused must know that he is possessing something, that is, the prosecution must prove that the accused knows that he is in possession of something, and if that matter turns out to be a forbidden drug, the crime is proved. (There has been since *Warner* a conviction for possessing cannabis resin when the accused had put it into his wallet two years earlier and had forgotten it: *Martindale* [1986] 1 WLR 1042 (CA).) The dissentient also looked at the seriousness of the offence but determined that because the crime was a grave one, *mens rea* was needed. *Warner* looks like a policy decision against drugs.

The arguments in *Warner* were in people's minds when *Sweet v Parsley* reached the Lords. The House persuaded itself that Ms Sweet was not concerned in the management of the farmhouse which was used for smoking cannabis. The case involved drugs, yet the Lords did not convict. Lord Reid repeated his stigma point from *Warner*: the crime was not strict because a person guilty of it suffered social stigma. *Mens rea* was to be presumed but that presumption could be rebutted. Whether it was not depended in part on whether the act was truly criminal or was criminal merely because public welfare so demanded. Lord Pearce said that the accused had no control over the people at the farmhouse and therefore should not be guilty. The House of Lords decided that, for the purposes of s 5(b) of the Dangerous Drugs Act 1965, the purpose mentioned had to be that of the manager of the premises. Here her purpose was not to provide premises to be used for the purpose of smoking cannabis. Her purpose was to provide a dwelling house for the 'beatniks'.

It is unclear whether Parliament really wished s 5(b) to be interpreted as their Lordships did. One reading of the statute was that Ms Sweet was concerned in the management of premises and those premises were used for the purpose of smoking cannabis. If that construction is correct Ms Sweet should have been found guilty. If you are a student in a hall of residence, imagine what your college authorities would think about that result! Certainly the Lords was anxious to exonerate Ms Sweet, and despite the strong vocabulary of the judgments, the case does not provide definite guidance for the future. *Sweet v Parsley* was seen as marking a change in attitude by the judges. If Parliament enacts legislation and is silent as to *mens rea*, that silence is presumed to mean that liability is not strict. The House did not overrule cases where liability had been held to be strict, so the presumption was rebuttable. As we shall see, later cases continue to impose strict liability, and indeed *Bradish* [1990] 1 QB 981 demonstrates the Court of Appeal's upholding strict liability post-*Sweet v Parsley*. Perhaps *Sweet* is authority for the proposition that since that decision the courts scrutinise all factors to see whether or not strict liability is justified: they do not impose strict liability without thinking, as they have sometimes appeared to do in the past. Parliament enacted the result in *Sweet* in s 8(d) of the Misuse of Drugs Act 1971, which requires the prosecution to prove that the defendant acted knowingly.

The law elsewhere has, however, not been clarified by Parliament, and the courts have been left to their own devices. The Law Commission in *The Mental Element in Crime*, Report No. 89, 1978, said the following about *Sweet* and *Warner*:

> [T]hese cases strikingly illustrate the difference of view and emphasis which can occur even in the highest judicial tribunal when dealing with the general problem of attributing an intention to Parliament with regard to the mental element (if any) in an offence when . . . Parliament has given no express indication of that intent.

Strict liability continues to pose questions in the highest judicial tribunal. In *Sheppard*, above, a bare majority determined that in the crime of wilful neglect the accused must realise that the child is in need of medical attention. The House was of the opinion that the courts were nowadays less likely to hold that an offence was a strict one than it had been in earlier years. Yet in the first case to reach their Lordships after *Sweet*, *Alphacell Ltd* v *Woodward* [1972] AC 842, the appellants were found guilty of causing effluent to enter a river from their factory, contrary to s 2(1)(a) of the Rivers (Prevention of Pollution) Act 1951, thereby showing that the House of Lords was still willing to impose strict liability. The appellants had caused the pollution through the design of the system for dealing with effluent. By building an overflow from their system to the river, they caused the effluent to enter this river when their system could not cope. Lords Wilberforce and Cross simply looked at the wording of the statute and gave a common-sense meaning to 'cause', a term which does not require *mens rea*. Viscount Dilhorne took into account the nature of the offence, but unlike Lord Wilberforce he emphasised that the section said 'causes or knowingly permits': it does not say 'knowingly causes or permits', that is, the position of the *mens rea* term was vital. If the paragraph had stated 'knowingly causes or permits', 'permits' would be otiose, because 'knowingly causes' includes 'knowingly permits'. Lord Salmon – a good name for a judge dealing with pollution – pointed out the grave social consequences which would follow if the offence were not one of strict liability: pollution would be unchecked if negligence had to be proved. He stated that if the defendant had not acted with *mens rea*, only a small fine need be imposed. He added: 'This [outcome] may be regarded as a not unfair hazard of carrying on a business which may cause pollution on the banks of a river.' In other words, firms who build factories on riversides act at their peril. As M. Cremona and J. Herring put it in *Criminal Law*, 2nd edn (Macmillan, 1998) 83 (not in 5th edn (Palgrave, 2007), by J. Herring):

> [I]t is a question, then, of weighing up different aspects of the public interest: in *Sweet* v *Parsley* the stigma of conviction was regarded as crucial: in *Alphacell Ltd* v *Woodward* the evidence of pollution was given greater weight. This was then reinforced by characterising the offence in the former case as 'truly criminal', and in the latter as 'quasi-criminal' . . .

Though the accused were found guilty in *Alphacell*, the House of Lords went out of its way to stress that other accused charged with the same offence were not totally defenceless. Lord Wilberforce stated that a defendant would have a defence if the act causing the pollution was that of a third party, Lord Pearson would have given a defence if the discharge of effluent was an Act of God or the result of interference by a trespasser, and Lord Cross said that there was a defence if the event was out of the defendants' control or beyond their foresight. There are cases showing that riparian factory owners are not guilty of causing pollution if the harm was caused by a vandal or by a lorry-driver spilling diesel oil.

In *B* v *DPP*, above, the House of Lords was divided whether or not interpreting the words of a statute so as to read in *mens rea* was effective in preventing the sexual abuse of children. Lord Hutton said: 'This purpose may be impeded if the happiness and stability of a child under 14 is harmed by the violation of his or her innocence by some act of gross indecency or incitement to gross indecency committed by a person who honestly believes that the child is older than 14', whereas Lord Nicholls stated: 'There is no general agreement that strict liability is necessary to the enforcement of the law protecting children in sexual matters.' Certainly *B* v *DPP* and *K* have been trenchantly criticised by commentators for not protecting children. Among the less condemnatory critiques is that of C.M.V. Clarkson, H. Keating and S.R. Cunningham, *Criminal Law: Text and Materials*, 7th edn (Sweet & Maxwell, 2010) at 200: '. . . the basis of . . . *K* is flawed. The effect of this case is that a middle-aged paedophile can escape liability for [the then existing crime of] an indecent assault on a girl under the age of 16 on the basis that he genuinely believed, albeit unreasonably, that she was 16. Surely, if older men want to have sex with "children" they should be under a duty to ensure that the person is at least 16 . . .'

Even in relation to sex crimes the courts still sometimes construe statutes to provide for strict liability. An example is *G* [2006] 1 WLR 2052. The Court of Appeal said that s 5 of the Sexual Offences Act 2003, rape of a child under 16, created an offence which was strict as to the age of the victim. The court said with reference to other sections of the Act that this was so 'by necessary implication', to use the words of Lord Steyn in *K*. Other nearby sections referred to a reasonable belief as to age, whereas s 5 did not. Therefore, the accused is guilty of this offence even if he believes on reasonable grounds that the child is older than 13. The HL [2008] UKHL 37 concentrated on the effect of the European Convention on Human Rights.

Doring [2002] Crim LR 817 (CA) distinguished *B v DPP* and *K* in effect. The Court of Appeal held, *obiter*, the offence of acting as a director of a company as an undischarged bankrupt and being concerned in the management of a company known by a prohibited name. Lord Steyn in *K* had said: '. . . the presumption [of *mens rea*] can only be displaced by specific language, i.e. an express provision or a necessary implication.' Yet the court looked beyond the language to the public interest, which after *B v DPP* and *K* they should not be doing. Buxton LJ said that *B v DPP* did not offset pre-existing jurisprudence which was to the effect that 'social policy and prudence' could displace the presumption of *mens rea*.

Brief mention should also be made of *Wings Ltd v Ellis* [1985] AC 272 (HL). The accused company was charged with making a false statement which it knew to be untrue, contrary to s 14(1)(a) of the Trade Descriptions Act 1968. It had published a false description in a travel brochure, realised the error, and corrected it, but someone had read an uncorrected brochure. The Lords decided that the company was guilty, holding that the outcome was in accord with the purpose of the statute. Accordingly strict liability was imposed, despite the accused doing its best to prevent anyone relying on the brochure to book a holiday.

Summary of strict liability

One may agree with Wright J in **Sherras v de Rutzen**, above: 'There are many cases on the subject and it is not very easy to reconcile them.'

One cannot always predict whether *mens rea* will be imported. It would be a good idea for Parliament to settle the law. The House of Lords in *B v DPP* and *K* has been placing the ball firmly in Parliament's court: offences will only be strict if Parliament expressly says so or if such is the necessary implication. One attempt at pulling together the considerations which may affect the courts was put forward by Lord Pearce in **Sweet v Parsley**, above:

> The nature of the crime, the punishment, the absence of social obloquy, the particular mischief and the field of activity in which it occurs, and the wording of the particular section and its context may show that Parliament intended that the act should be prevented by punishment regardless of intent or knowledge.

This *dictum* has been influential and was applied in, for example, **Phekoo** [1981] 1 WLR 1117, see above. Such considerations may override the presumption in **Sweet** that Parliament does not intend to create strict offences. A case illustrating the rebuttal of the presumption of *mens rea* is **PSGB v Logan** [1982] Crim LR 443 (Croydon Crown Court). The accused was charged with selling a medicinal product not on the general sale list without the transaction being supervised by a pharmacist, contrary to s 52 of the Medicines Act 1968. The judge said: 'Parliament intended to restrict sales of medicinal products in the interests of safety; the product could be locked away or the shop closed when the pharmacist was absent; the offence was not a truly criminal one: therefore, the crime was strict. Moreover, to say that strict offences involve matters of social concern is not to the point. Rape and murder, both *mens rea* crimes, are of social concern.'

It should be noted that when the courts declare that they are seeking the intention of Parliament they are not really doing so, for as a result of a self-denying ordinance they cannot readily have access to the best available material, *Hansard*, the reports of proceedings in Parliament, to discover what the true intention of Parliament is, unless the words creating the offence are ambiguous (*Pepper* v *Hart* [1993] AC 593(HL)); that is always provided that a body can have a state of mind. Often *Hansard* is not helpful. In *B* v *DPP*, above, Rougier J in the Divisional Court said that the need for *mens rea* was not discussed in either House and Lord Steyn in the House of Lords noted that the Report of the Criminal Law Revision Committee which led to the creation of the crime at issue also did not discuss it.

Reasons for strict liability

(a) If a person runs a business properly, the law should not be broken. If he commits the *actus reus* of a crime, he is running the business improperly. (However, not all strict offences involve businesses. The crime in *Prince* can be seen as one of public morality.)

(b) Certain activities must be prohibited in the interests of public well-being. Some of these are regulatory offences (called in the USA 'trader' offences), but some are not, especially drug offences. A utilitarian argument is sometimes advanced: there is a greater good in raising standards than in not convicting faultless people. *Yeandel* v *Fisher* [1966] 1 QB 440 (DC) illustrates the principle. Lord Parker said: 'Drugs are a great danger today and legislation has been tightening up the control of drugs.' The courts are looking for socially dangerous activities when they implement the doctrine of strict liability. So in *Searle* v *Randolph* [1972] Crim LR 779 the accused was guilty of possessing cannabis when he knew that he had a cigarette end, but not that it contained cannabis. Moreover, a regulatory offence may be more serious than a 'standard' crime. Leonard Leigh gave this example in his book *Strict and Vicarious Liability* (Sweet & Maxwell, 1982): '. . . is it clear that theft necessarily poses a graver violation of a basic rule than does the pollution of a beach in a resort which depends upon its summer trade for prosperity?'

As stated above, certain types of behaviour attract strict liability more than others, for example pollution (*Alphacell*, above), some licensee offences, such as serving alcohol to drunks (*Cundy* v *Le Cocq*, above), and anti-inflation crimes (*St Margaret's Trust* [1958] 2 All ER 289 (CCA)). As Donovan J put it in the last case:

> There would be little point in enacting that no one should breach the defences against a flood, and at the same time excusing anyone who did it innocently.

He said that there was no presumption of *mens rea*.

Similarly food legislation is often strict, for example *Pearks Gunston and Tee* v *Ward* [1902] 2 KB 1: selling food not of the quality demanded. Some road traffic offences are strict, such as driving on a road while disqualified (*Miller* [1975] 1 WLR 1222, above), but not all are. One has to know that there has been an accident before one can fail to report it: *Harding* v *Price*, above.

The following cases provide a selection of regulatory offences which have been held to be strict: being concerned in the organisation of a public musical entertainment (an acid house party) at a place for which no licence had been obtained: ***Chichester DC v Silvester*** (1992) *The Times*, 6 May (DC), the court so holding in view of the public mischief to be avoided, of risk to health and safety and of the lack of a *mens rea* word in the relevant sub-sub-paragraph when its sister sub-paragraph contained *mens rea* words; cutting trees in contravention of a preservation order, even though the statute contained the word 'wilfully': ***Maidstone BC v Mortimer*** [1980] 3 All ER 502 (DC); not sending a child to school regularly: ***Crump v Gilmore*** [1970] Crim LR 28 (CA); failing to give 28 days' notice of working with blue asbestos and failing to provide workers with protection against asbestos: ***Atkinson v Sir Alfred McAlpine & Son Ltd*** (1974) 16 KIR 220 (DC); executing unauthorised work on a listed building: ***Wells St Magistrates*** [1986] 1 WLR 1046 (DC). The accused need not know that the building was listed. Public concern over attacks by Rottweilers and pit bull terriers was one reason for deciding that the crime of being the owner of a dog which was dangerously out of control in a public place was a strict one: ***Bezzina*** [1994] 1 WLR 1057 (CA). The owner did not have to know that the dog might behave dangerously. *Bezzina* was followed by the Court of Appeal in ***Singh*** [2011] 5 July in relation to a person who was in charge of the dangerous dog but not the owner when he had lost control. He was liable even though the dog had escaped his control without his being at fault. Similarly, the accused need not know that he has allowed a dangerous dog to enter a prohibited place: ***Greener*** (1996) 160 JP 265. The Divisional Court held that if *mens rea* had to be proved, convictions would be almost impossible if the accused was not accompanying the dog. In both of the last two offences the courts did not accept the argument that a crime punishable by imprisonment could not be a strict offence. This principle extends beyond regulatory offences. In ***Densu*** [1998] 1 Cr App R 400 (CA) the accused was convicted of having with him an offensive weapon, even though he did not know its purpose. The article was a telescopic baton, but he thought it was an aerial.

As can be seen from the drugs cases, the principle in this section is not limited to what laypeople might not think of as being crimes, but extends to possessing an altered passport (***Chajutin v Whitehead*** [1938] 1 KB 306) and advertising for the return of goods 'no questions asked' (***Denham v Scott*** (1983) 77 Cr App R 210(DC)). The courts state that in relation to these offences they are not trying to penalise certain conduct but to prohibit it. For example, in the last-named decision the court said that no stigma attached to the accused who committed the crime: he had not read the advertisement; the deed was against public policy: the offence was not truly criminal, and the law would be impossible to enforce if the offence were a *mens rea* one. It was accordingly justifiable to impose strict liability.

(c) Difficulties of proof can be got round if the prosecution does not have to prove *mens rea*. Guilty people will not escape through lack of evidence. This factor has been mentioned in several cases, such as ***Maidstone BC v Mortimer***, above. This rationale applies especially to companies. One does not have to show, for instance, that one of the directors, the directing mind of the company, knew that his company was pouring effluent into a river.

(d) It is easier to enforce the law when *mens rea* is irrelevant than when the prosecution have to prove it. This reasoning was mentioned by the Privy Council in ***Lim Chin Aik*** [1963] AC 160, see above, and was approved by Lord Diplock in ***Sweet v Parsley*** above. An illustration of this way of thinking occurs in the following Privy Council case.

Gammon (Hong Kong) Ltd v *Attorney-General of Hong Kong* [1985] AC 1 (PC)

The defendants were charged with deviating in a material way from approved plans for a building, contrary to the Hong Kong Building Ordinance. They contended that they were not guilty because they did not know that the deviation was a material one. The Judicial Committee held that the offence did not require knowledge if the deviation was a material one and that the offence did not require knowledge of the materiality of the deviation from the plans. To make the offence strict meant that persons in the position of the accused would be obliged to exercise control and vigilance to stop the occurrence of the prohibited act. The purpose of the Ordinance was to regulate building sites which were dangerous to workers and the public. The public's protection would be seriously weakened if the offence were not strict. The aim of the offence was, *therefore*, to keep up standards and *mens rea* was irrelevant to that objective.

Gammon provides a good example of the present approach of English judges to analysing whether a crime is strict or not. First, Lord Scarman stated that there was a presumption of *mens rea*; secondly, this presumption may be displaced by considering the words and subject matter of the statute (in this case there was a 'social concern' in 'public safety'), and by investigating whether the act was 'truly criminal' (a tendentious phrase, it must be said) and whether strict liability would assist in preventing the forbidden act; thirdly, the maximum penalty was substantial, but that fact showed only the seriousness with which Hong Kong viewed lack of supervision on building sites.

Gammon, which is a Privy Council case, is subject to the House of Lords' rulings in *B* v *DPP* and *K* that the presumption of *mens rea* can be displaced only when Parliament has expressly said so or if the presumption is excluded by necessary implication. Moreover, do not all statutes reflect a 'social concern'? *Gammon* is often cited in the cases, for example *Bezzina*, above. An example is *Collett* [1994] Crim LR 607. Using land in contravention of a planning enforcement notice was a strict liability crime because the aim behind the relevant statute was to encourage users of land to check whether such notices were in force. Another example is *Brockley* (1994) 99 Cr App R 385 (CA). The law which prevented an undischarged bankrupt from being a company director was a matter of social concern. Otherwise he could escape the consequences of his insolvency by turning himself into a company. If the prosecution had to prove that the accused knew he was undischarged this would undermine Parliament's will. *Gammon* was applied on the basis that, in the words of Lord Scarman, 'the creation of strict liability will be effective to promote the objects of the statute by encouraging greater vigilance to prevent the commission of the prohibited acts'. Henry LJ said that it was 'unacceptable' for an irresponsible bankrupt to bury his head in the sand and thereby fail to establish his true status.

In *Blake* [1997] 1 WLR 1167 the Court of Appeal held that the crime of using apparatus for wireless telegraphy was a strict offence because to so hold would encourage radio operators to avoid committing the offence, and interfering with the emergency services and air traffic control was a matter of public safety, despite the fact that the offence was a truly criminal one because of the possibility of imprisonment. *Gammon* was applied. An illustration of the application of *Gammon* is *Jackson* [2006] EWCA Crim 2386, where it was held that flying a military plane below 100 feet is an offence of strict liability.

An application of *Gammon* is *Harrow London Borough Council* v *Shah* [1999] 2 Cr App R 457 (DC). The defendants were charged with selling National Lottery tickets to children under 16 contrary to s 13 of the National Lottery Act 1993. They believed on reasonable grounds that the purchaser was over 16 but he was in fact 13. In holding that this offence was strict as to the age, Mitchell J held that the offence was not a truly criminal offence (using the language of Wright J in *Sherras v de Rutzen* [1895] 1 QB 918 (DC) and of Lord Reid in *Sweet v Parsley* [1970] AC 132 (HL)), that gambling was an issue of social concern particularly in respect of those under 16, that the maximum penalty, two years, though severe, was not conclusive (it was three years in *Gammon*), and that attaching strict liability to this crime 'will unquestionably encourage greater vigilance in preventing the commission of the prohibited act'. In *Gammon* similarly the defendants could have prevented the commission of the offence by taking more care. Mitchell J added that no stigma attached to the offence, and that the defendants' belief could be taken into account when determining the sentence. In criticism surely Parliament intended this offence to be 'truly criminal' when it attached a maximum penalty of two years' imprisonment? In *Coventry City Council v Vassell* [2011] EWHC 1542 (Admin) the Court followed *Sweet v Parsley*, *Sherras v de Rutzen* and *Gammon* to hold that the crime alleged, failing to give prompt notification of a change in circumstances, was not strict.

Even after *B v DPP* and *K* English courts are applying *Gammon*. In *Muhamad*, above, the Court of Appeal cited *Gammon* when dealing with whether the offence of materially contributing to insolvency by gambling was strict. The maximum sentence was two years' imprisonment whereas the maximum for some other offences under the statute was ten years, and because of that the court was uncertain whether the offence was 'truly criminal'. The court then discussed *B v DPP*, holding that the language, maximum sentence and social concern led to the conclusion that the offence was strict.

Lord Scarman took a similar view of 'social concern' in *Wings Ltd v Ellis*, above. His approach was followed in *PSGB v Storkwain Ltd* and *Wells St Magistrates*, both above. In the former case, the accused supplied drugs on prescriptions purportedly signed by a doctor. In fact the prescriptions were forged. The defendants were found guilty by the Divisional Court, even though they were deceived, for the reasons advanced by Lord Scarman. On appeal the Lords confirmed the decision without mentioning *Gammon*. Indeed the House of Lords in *Storkwain* did not give much weight to the fact that the maximum penalty was two years' imprisonment or that the principle in favour of *mens rea* should have been weighed in the balance. It must be admitted that many traditional areas of criminal law, such as murder and rape, are also matters of social concern, yet they are not strict offences. The same applies to non-traditional areas, such as planning. Parliament is hardly likely to enact legislation which is not a matter of some social concern.

(e) Public disapproval of various forms of behaviour may be marked by the use of sanctions without proof of fault. Business people ought not to pollute rivers, and if they do, they should be made to pay.

(f) Strict liability deters others from committing the same offence.

(g) The doctrine obliges people to adopt high standards of care in their trades and other activities. Beldam LJ said in *Hallett Silberman Ltd v Cheshire CC* [1993] RTR 32 (DC): 'The reason for the creation of offences of strict liability is to put pressure on the thoughtless and inefficient to do their whole duty in the interests of public health or safety.' People do not like their names in the paper, so they will try hard to avoid contravening the public good. The fact that some people are convicted when they are blameless is outbalanced by the raising of standards generally. For example, in *Bezzina* the imposition of strict liability was justified by the court as a spur to owners taking more care of their dangerous dogs than before.

(h) Because of strict liability, courts are not overburdened with prosecutions seeking to prove petty violations.

(i) If a person creates a risk and takes a profit from that risk, he ought to be liable if the happening of that risk creates problems. This rationale was first advanced by Kennedy LJ in *Hobbs* v *Winchester Corp*, above. The pollution case of *Alphacell*, above, may provide an illustration of this principle. The accused could have established a back-up system for disposing of the effluent, but did not do so to save money. (This argument cannot be taken too far. It assumes that all business activities are run for profit, which is not necessarily so.)

These reasons demonstrate to some that strict offences are not always morally repugnant, and that it may sometimes be better to convict the innocent in order to prevent a large number undermining well-being than to let the blameless go. Some of these arguments do, however, prove too much. Surely convenience of lawyers in argument (h) ought not to outweigh the *mens rea* principle. If it did, why does murder have a *mens rea*? It would be easier to convict people of murder if the prosecution did not have to prove malice afore-thought, but murder is a crime which does require a mental element. Such arguments lead us into the next section.

Reasons why there should not be offences of strict liability

(a) As Dickson J said in the Supreme Court of Canada in *City of Sault Ste Marie* (1978) 85 DLR (3rd) 161, there is no evidence that standards are raised by strict liability. Similarly in *B* v *DPP*, above, Lord Nicholls stated that there was no general agreement whether strict liability was of use in preventing the sexual abuse of children. Moreover, a series of small fines is hardly a deterrent. Bad publicity may be a better method than strict liability for improving standards.

(b) It is morally wrong to punish people who have not voluntarily broken the law. These people are not blameworthy and should not be. Not all strict offences are so minor that it may be said that a small punishment for a violation of a law was ethically acceptable. For example, in *Prince*, above, the maximum sentence was two years' imprisonment, while in *Chajutin* v *Whitehead*, above, the accused was deported.

(c) Even if a person has taken all reasonable care, he is guilty, yet he does not deserve punishment. For example, in *Callow* v *Tillstone* (1900) 83 LT 411 (DC) a butcher was guilty of exposing for sale meat which was unfit for human consumption despite a veterinary surgeon's certifying it as sound. In *PSGB* v *Storkwain*, above, a pharmacist was guilty even though the prescription contained a forgery. He would have been guilty even if he had checked with the doctor. If there is no defence, why take any care at all? Furthermore, if the aim of strict liability law is to stop people being careless, a law of criminal negligence would do that and would do so directly and without any need for penalising the faultless.

(d) The laws on strict liability are not always vigorously enforced. Factory inspectors rarely prosecute until they have warned owners about breaches. Surely this type of rule is best enforced by a mechanism which is not the criminal law. In any event there should be controls over the discretion to prosecute. The argument that prosecutions are rarely brought unless the accused is at fault was said to be a weak one by the High Court in *Barnfather* v *London Borough of Islington*, above.

(e) Respect for the law is lessened because people who are not at fault are punished. A.A. Cuomo said in (1967) 40 S Cal LR 463, 518, strict liability 'can only breed frustration and disrespect for the law . . .'. The accused has a conviction, though not blameworthy.

(f) People (such as butchers, perhaps) would be put out of business if strict liability laws were always enforced. Such may not be what the public want. A person should not be forced to do something unreasonable. Making strict offences into cases of negligence would ensure that reasonable standards are maintained. However, as J. Brady put it, 'Strict liability offences: a justification' (1972) 8 Crim L Bull 217:

> First, there is little evidence to show that the effect of strict liability offences has been to make these socially beneficent enterprises less attractive. [Secondly], . . . a person who does not have the capacity to run (for example) a dairy in such a manner as to prevent the adulteration of milk is not to be protected on the sole ground that he is engaged in a 'socially beneficial' enterprise. An incompetent carrying on an enterprise in which there is the danger of widespread harm . . . is *not* engaged in a 'socially beneficial' enterprise.

(g) When a judge deals with a strict offence, he or she excludes from the jury all arguments about intention, recklessness and carelessness, yet such arguments are relevant to sentence. They are made to the judge after conviction. The judge decides as a matter of fact what the accused's state of mind was. It is, therefore, not true to say that strict liability saves time.

(h) Authorities tend not to prosecute for strict offences unless the accused, intentionally or subjectively, acted recklessly. Since *mens rea* is considered at the stage of the decision to prosecute, it should also be taken into account when crimes are created and defendants are tried.

(i) If one considers the theories of punishment, a person who breaks a rule of strict liability is not deterable individually and there is no general deterrence. He will not be reformed by a conviction, and he will not be incapacitated unless he is put into prison or his licence withdrawn, sanctions which may be disproportionate to the breach of the law.

The arguments for and against strict liability have to be balanced. The courts have not placed these arguments in any order of priority.

Suggestions for reform of the law relating to strict liability

(a) The fiction that Parliament intends offences to be strict or not is not helpful and should be abolished. As Jordan CJ put it in the New South Wales case of *Turnbull* (1944) 44 NSWLR 108, see above, if legislators knew that the courts would always read in *mens rea*, they would soon become accustomed to stating whether the offence was strict or not. The present situation leads to litigation and a multitude of reported cases, many of them irreconcilable. The Law Commission, in *The Mental Element in Crime*, Report No. 89, 1978, recommended the abolition of the fiction.

(b) One suggested reform is that all regulatory offences should be dealt with by tribunals, not courts. The accused would know that he was being tried for a public welfare violation, not for a crime. However, the effect of a tribunal appearance might be the same as court proceedings, for the accused would be held up to public display, and certainly some offences, especially drugs ones, cannot be taken out of the criminal law.

(c) In Report No. 89, 1978 (see above), the Law Commission recommended that strict offences should remain within the criminal law, but treated as crimes of negligence. This proposal is similar to the 'half-way house' idea of Lord Diplock in *Sweet v Parsley*, above. The burden of proof would be on the prosecution. For example, in *PSGB v Storkwain*, the pharmacist would not be guilty unless the prosecution proved that he did not check the doctor's signature on the prescription. One possible drawback of this suggestion is that the courts might impose a very high standard of care. In *Evans* [1963] 1 QB 412 (CCA) the accused, a learner driver, was charged with the offence of causing death by dangerous driving, an offence which has been repealed. Though he had been doing his best, he knocked a man down and killed him. The court found him guilty because he fell short of the standard expected of a good driver. This approach makes negligence little different from strict liability, though the charge would allow the accused to adduce evidence that he was not at fault.

In fact Parliament often does provide a defence to a strict offence. A recent example is found in the Bribery Act 2010. A strict crime is created, that of a commercial organisation's failing to prevent a person associated with it from bribing. However, that body has a defence if it has taken 'adequate procedures'.

(d) The onus of proof could be placed on the accused. The accused to have a defence would have to show that he or she did not have the *mens rea* for the offence and was not negligent. Lord Reid hinted at this reform in *Tesco Supermarkets Ltd v Nattrass* [1972] AC 153 (HL). This reasoning has some historical support. In *Grade v DPP* [1942] 2 All ER 118, Humphreys J treated *Sherras v de Rutzen* [1895] 1 QB 918 as a case where the accused had to show that he did not know that the constable was on duty. Day J in *Sherras* said that the omission of 'knowingly' shifted the burden. The same view was taken in *Harding v Price*, above, but was doubted in *Roper v Taylor's Central Garages (Exeter) Ltd* [1951] 2 TLR 284 (DC) and *Lim Chin Aik*, above, and was rejected by Lord Pearce in *Warner v MPC* [1969] 2 AC 256 (HL). More recently the House of Lords in *B v DPP*, above, also rejected this version of the 'half-way house'.

(e) One should look at each crime to see whether adequate reasons exist for retaining that offence as one of strict liability.

(f) Lord Reid in *Warner* was prepared to tolerate strict liability where people set themselves up in certain businesses such as pub landlords and butchers and where the penalties were minor and the stigma small. He thought that the doctrine could be tolerated only in order to protect the public, and he advocated a defence where 'the defect was truly latent so that no one could have discovered it'.

(g) Other commentators have proposed an exception for persons who are not careless (a 'no-negligence' defence). Such provisions are becoming common. In the Food Act 1984, ss 2–3, it is a defence to a charge of possessing contaminated food if the accused can show that the adulteration was unavoidable.

(h) One of the most interesting proposals is that of David Tench in his pamphlet *Towards a Middle System of Law* (Consumers' Association, 1981). He contends that it is not always necessary to make a crime of something that has to be forbidden or controlled.

Some forms of conduct such as murder and theft must remain offences, but others – not displaying a car licence, parking on a yellow line and the like – should become subject to a so-called 'civil penalty' and not subject to imprisonment or a fine. He writes:

> It surely is ridiculous for Parliament to go on legislating to make things criminal which no civilised individual really regards as criminal.

The proposal would save time and money. There would be no investigation and no need to go to court, and penalties could be fixed. He suggests that people may become more ready to obey the criminal law which remains. Into this middle system Tench would also put regulatory offences such as the one which affected the butcher in **Hobbs** v **Winchester Corp**, above, sexual and racial discrimination, tax penalties, picketing, and a new law on privacy. Tench would like the middle system of law to be dealt with by magistrates, who now try most strict offences. His idea has not been taken up. However, civil penalties are now used in the fields of direct taxation and VAT.

(i) Baroness Wootton of Abinger wrote in *Crime and the Criminal Law*, 2nd edn (Stevens, 1981), that crimes should contain no *mens rea*. The accused should be guilty not because he was at fault but because he had acted in a criminal way. She wanted strict offences to replace *mens rea* ones, leaving the fault element to become relevant only after conviction for sentencing purposes. In her view (at 46):

> If . . . the primary function of the Courts is conceived as the prevention of forbidden acts, there is little cause to be disturbed by the multiplication of offences of strict liability. If the law says that certain things are not to be done, it is illogical to confine this prohibition to occasions on which they are done from malice aforethought . . . A man is equally dead . . . whether he was stabbed or run over by a drunken motorist or an incompetent one.

In her view offenders should be treated (for instance taught to drive better), not punished.

The rejoinder to this attempted destruction of *mens rea* comes from the doyen of English criminal lawyers, J.C. Smith, in his essay 'Responsibility in criminal law' in P. Bean and B. Whynes (eds.), *Barbara Wootton* (Tavistock, 1986). Smith retorted:

(i) Blameless people who kill by accident deserve sympathy not stigma.

(ii) Wootton's view would stigmatise the blameless and place them in the same category as those who intentionally broke the law. People who have drugs planted on them should not be treated in the same way as those who intentionally hold large quantities of drugs.

(iii) If one looks at matters of fault at the sentencing stage, one does not get rid of the difficulty of determining degrees of fault.

(iv) Strict liability leads to the conviction of people like Mrs Tolson who was prosecuted for bigamy even though she thought that her husband was dead. She was found guilty by the trial judge and five out of 14 judges in the Court for Crown Cases Reserved (*Tolson* (1889) 23 QBD 168). She should not have been prosecuted at all, never mind convicted of a crime for which the maximum penalty was seven years' imprisonment.

(v) Wootton wanted the criminal law to prevent the recurrence of forbidden acts, but Mrs Tolson would not do what she had done again.

(vi) The work of the police and courts would be multiplied if all non-intentional breaches of the criminal law had to be prosecuted.

(vii) 'To remove the element of fault is to empty the law of moral content' (at 154).

It should be added that no amount of re-education could change the behaviour of some people convicted of strict offences. Would re-education help the landlord in **Cundy v Le Cocq**, above? To all appearances the drunk did not look drunk.

(j) The 1985 version of the draft Criminal Code, Law Commission, Report No. 143, provided in cl 24(1):

> Unless a contrary intention appears, a person does not commit a Code offence unless he acts intentionally, knowingly or recklessly in respect of each of its elements other than fault elements.

Therefore, if Parliament did indicate that an offence was strict that interpretation was to be adopted, but if Parliament did not so enact, the offence was to be a *mens rea* crime. The courts would be permitted to look only at 'the terms of enactment'. A similar provision appears in the 1989 version (Law Com. No. 177):

> Every offence requires a fault element of recklessness with respect to each of its elements, other than fault elements, unless otherwise provided (cl 20(1)).

Like the 1985 version, the 1989 one would not apply to offences existing before the Code ('pre-Code offences'). The examples given by the Law Commission are these (Law Com. No. 177, 157):

> Under clause 147 a person commits burglary if he enters a building as a trespasser intending to steal in the building. Nothing is said as to any fault required in respect of the fact that the entrant is a trespasser. The offence is committed only if the entrant knows that, or is reckless whether, he is trespassing.

The second example would reverse **Alphacell Ltd v Woodward**, above, prospectively:

> An offence of causing polluting matter to enter a watercourse is created after the Code comes into force. In the absence of provision to the contrary the offence requires (a) an intention to cause the matter to enter the watercourse or recklessness whether it will do so, and (b) knowledge that the matter is a pollutant or recklessness whether it is.

The Law Commission opined that cl 20 would clarify the 'regrettable' state of uncertainty in the law. It should be noted that cl 20 does not apply where Parliament has *expressly* or *impliedly* provided to the contrary. The rationale is that courts are constitutionally obliged to apply the law Parliament has decided whether that law is expressly or impliedly stated. The possibility of impliedly strict offences may still leave room for uncertainty.

(k) The Law Commission proposed in its Consultation Paper No. 195, *Criminal Liability in Regulatory Contexts*, 2010, that strict liability should no longer be used in respect of offences concerned with the regulation of businesses and therefore all such offences would prospectively have the mental element of 'recklessly' or 'knowingly' inserted into them, unless Parliament expressly stated otherwise. The effect would be that in this area of law strict offences would fade away. Criminal law should be used only when the activity was seriously reprehensible and stigma would result from a conviction. The Commission also criticised the lack of clarity in the law as to when fault terms would be used when Parliament had included no such term. This chapter demonstrates the difficulty of predicting how the courts will react. Finally, where the offence was a strict one, the Commission proposed that except perhaps for road traffic offences there should be a due diligence offence. The burden of proof would be on the accused but the standard of proof would be the civil law one.

Conclusions

Strict offences have been dealt with at length for several reasons.

(a) The mere fact that such crimes exist shows that the criminal law is not based on breaches of a moral code. A crime is what Parliament or in strict offences the judges say is a crime.

(b) From this proposition one can deduce that *mens rea* does not mean a malicious or guilty frame of mind. Morals and law form different sets of rules.

(c) Many crimes exist without there being any intentionally or recklessly caused act. *Mens rea* therefore need not exist in every crime in relation to each element of the *actus reus*. Such indeed is the definition of strict liability.

(d) The topic makes one look at the rationale of certain laws and of law in general. Should people be punished who are not consciously at fault? Can the criminal law be used to improve standards? Why are murder and polluting a river both crimes? Is the criminal law addressed to the citizen to make him or her change behaviour or is it addressed to the police, the Crown Prosecution Service and the judiciary to catch, prosecute and punish those breaching standards?

(e) The topic has links with other law subjects. For instance, if Parliament enacts that doing X is an offence, how can the courts say that only doing X knowingly is a crime in the light of the doctrine of parliamentary sovereignty? If one argues that Parliament passes statutes against the background of the common law, which has a presumption of *mens rea*, why does it often not state what the mental element is, and why does not the common law always introduce *mens rea*? Glanville Williams put it in this way in *Criminal Law: The General Part*, 2nd edn (Stevens, 1961) 260: 'The law of *mens rea* belongs to the general part of the criminal law, and it is not reasonable to expect Parliament every time it creates a new crime to enact it . . .'

(f) The law is not a set of rules to be learned by rote. Some matters are certain but at times law consists of principles to which differing weight is attached according to the circumstances. On particular facts it may be difficult to predict whether a court would decide that the offence was strict or not. Yet people are convicted and imprisoned on those decisions. The criminal law is not a game; nor is it an exact science. It constitutes part of everyday life, for example speeding, and affects people's lives and jobs. Indeed, for some people it *is* their job.

(g) Studies of the effects of strict liability laws do not affirmatively support those academics who wish to abolish the doctrine. Those involved in enforcing such rules do not always use the law as their first mode of attack. For example, in dealing with accidents at work the Health and Safety Inspectorate relies largely on persuasion, but the availability of strict offences helps inspectors to enforce the law when other means have failed. One can conclude from this illustration that there is a gap between law in theory and law in practice.

(h) The criminal law is only one way of controlling harmful activities. There are others such as warnings, supervision, inspection, seizure of equipment, persuasion, and giving no effect to the wrongful behaviour.

Finally, a comment from N. Lacey, C. Wells and O. Quick, *Reconstructing Criminal Law*, 4th edn (Cambridge University Press, 2010) 107: 'Instances of strict liability are . . . marginalised as exceptional, relatively non-serious and calling for special justification.' Yet as we have seen, about half of the criminal calendar consists of strict offences, and most crimes are strict. There is nothing marginal about strict liability. Some are grave, and as for justification, what do you think?

Summary

- *Strict and absolute offences*: Strict offences must be distinguished from absolute offences, which are ones where *mens rea* is lacking and to which there is no defence. However, the older cases use 'absolute liability' as a synonym for strict liability. Examples of absolute offences found by the courts are the former crime of being found in the UK illegally and the offence of being found drunk on the highway. A term used in the literature to mean absolute liability is 'situational liability'.

- *Strict liability and common law crimes*: Rarely at common law are crimes strict but the following are: public nuisance, contempt of court, criminal libel and outraging public decency.

- *Strict liability and statutory crimes*: Courts interpret statutes and often Parliament does not state the requisite *mens rea*. In that event, the judges look to 'the language used, the nature of the offence, the mischief sought to be prevented and any other circumstances that might assist in determining what intention was properly to be attributed to Parliament' (per Lord Nicholls in *B v DPP* [2000] 2 AC 428 (HL)). Also considered are whether the accused could have avoided committing the crime and whether the maximum sentence is severe. The fact that these considerations form guidelines only means that it is not always predictable how the courts will apply them. While the courts' views on strict offences have varied across the years, the current position is that there is quite a strong presumption that an offence is strict and usually *mens rea* is read in.

- *The arguments for and against strict liability*: There has been debate over the years as to whether strict liability is justified or not. Among arguments in favour are the ease of proof and the 'gadfly' contention, that is, that strict liability forces people to adopt high standards. The contrary approach includes the arguments that the criminal law should not apply to those who are not at fault and it should not apply to those who cannot be deterred.

- *Suggestions for reform*: Several proposals have been made for reform of the law. These include converting all strict offences into negligence-based ones and providing a defence of due diligence to all strict offences.

References

Reports

Law Commission Consultation Paper no. 195, *Criminal Liability in Regulatory Contexts* (2010)

Law Commission Consultation Paper no. 193, *Simplification of Criminal Law: Public Nuisance and Outraging Public Decency* (2010)

Law Commission Report no. 177, *A Criminal Code for England and Wales* (1989)

Law Commission Report no. 143, Criminal Law: *Codification of the Criminal Law – A Report to the Law Commission* (1985)

Law Commission Report no. 89, *The Mental Element in Crime* (1978)

Books

Bean, P. and Whynes, B. (eds.) *Barbara Wootton* (Tavistock, 1986)

Clarkson, C.M.V. *Understanding Criminal Law*, 4th edn (Thomson, 2005)

Clarkson, C.M.V., Keating, H. and Cunningham, S.R. *Criminal Law: Text and Materials*, 7th edn (Sweet & Maxwell, 2010)

Cremona, M. and Herring, J. *Criminal Law*, 2nd edn (Macmillan, 1998)

Herring, J. *Criminal Law*, 5th edn (Palgrave, 2007)

Lacey, N., Wells, C. and Quick, O. *Reconstructing Criminal Law*, 4th edn (Cambridge University Press, 2010)

Leigh, L. *Strict and Vicarious Liability* (Sweet & Maxwell, 1982)

Ormerod, D. *Smith and Hogan's Criminal Law*, 13th edn (Oxford University Press, 2011)

Tench, D. *Towards a Middle System of Law* (Consumers' Association, 1981)

Williams, G. *Criminal Law: The General Part*, 2nd edn (Stevens, 1961)

Wootton, Baroness *Crime and the Criminal Law*, 2nd edn (Stevens, 1981)

Journals

Brady, J. 'Strict liability offences: a justification' (1972) 8 Crim L Bull 217

Lanham, D. '*Larsonneur* revisited' [1976] Crim LR 276

Singer, R.C. 'The resurgence of *mens rea*: the rise and fall of strict criminal liability' (1989) 30 Boston College LR 377

Further reading

Ashworth, A. 'Should strict offences be removed from all imprisonable offences?' [2010] *Irish Jurist* 1

Brudner, A. 'Imprisonment and strict liability' (1990) 40 UTLJ 73

Cartwright, P. 'Unfair commercial practices and the future of criminal law' [2010] JBL 618

Editorial, 'The Policing and Crime Act 2009' [2010] Crim LR 91

Fitzpatrick, B. 'Strict liability: reverse burden and Article 6(2) of the European Convention on Human Rights' (2003) 67 JCL 363

Fitzpatrick, B. 'Strict liability and Article 6(2) of the European Convention on Human Rights' (2004) 68 JCL 11

Hamdani, A. 'Mens rea and the cost of ignorance' (2007) 93 Va L Rev 415

Hawthorne, R. 'Strict criminal liability: A principled approach' [2010] Cambridge Student LR 33

Horder, J. 'Strict liability, statutory construction and the spirit of liberty' (2002) 118 LQR 459

Horder, J. *Excusing Crime* (Oxford University Press, 2004) ch. 6

Jackson, B.S. '*Storkwain*: a case study in strict liability and self-regulation' [1991] Crim LR 892

Levenson, L.L. 'Good faith defenses: reshaping strict liability crimes' (1993) 78 Cornell LR 401

Manchester, C. 'Knowledge, due diligence and strict liability in regulatory offences' [2006] Crim LR 213

Moodie, R.A. 'Refulgent *mens rea* eclipsed' (1974–5) 6 NZULR 230

Parker, J.S. 'The economics of *mens rea*' (1993) 79 Virg LR 741

Prendergast, D. 'Strict liability and the presumption of mens rea after *CC v Ireland*' [2011] *Irish Jurist* 211

Reid, K. 'Strict liability: some principles for Parliament' (2008) 29 Stat LR 173

Richardson, G. 'Strict liability for regulatory crime: the empirical research' [1987] Crim LR 295

Simons, K.W. 'Criminal law: when is strict liability just?' (1997) 87 JCL & Crim 1075

Simons, K.W. 'Is strict liability in the grading of offences consistent with retributive desert?' (2012) 32 OJLS 445

Smith, J. and Pearson, A. 'The value of strict liability' [1969] Crim LR 5

Stanton-Ife, J. 'Strict liability: stigma and regret' (2007) 27 OJLS 151

The principal theoretical work is the series of essays in A.P. Simester (ed.), *Appraising Strict Liability* (Oxford University Press, 2005). An older account is L. Leigh, *Strict and Vicarious Liability* (Sweet & Maxwell, 1982).

Visit **www.mylawchamber.co.uk** to access tools to help you develop and test your knowledge of criminal law, including interactive multiple choice questions, practice exam questions with guidance, annotated weblinks, glossary flashcards, legal newsfeed and legal updates.

5

Principal parties and secondary offenders

Aims and objectives

After reading this chapter you will understand and be able to critique:

- the distinction between principal and secondary offenders and the relevance, if any, between those two types of criminals
- the meaning of aiding, abetting, counselling and procuring and wherein their differences lie
- the application of the joint enterprise doctrine and whether it is distinguishable from secondary parties' liability
- the effect the non-conviction of the perpetrator makes on the liability of the secondary offender
- the place of liability of 'victims' for their crimes
- the doctrine of innocent agency
- the effect of purported withdrawal on the secondary party's liability
- the law of assisting offenders and compounding arrestable offences

Introduction

Example

A mother and a father are in the room with their son. There are no other persons in the room. The son is stabbed to death. Is the father or mother or both guilty of murder?

'Neither!' is the short answer. Unless the prosecution can prove beyond reasonable doubt that one of them killed with the requisite mental element, then neither is guilty of murder. However,

1 if one of them did kill, and the other aided and abetted the killing, but it cannot be proved who did kill and who was the secondary party, then BOTH are guilty of murder and it need not be proved who did what;

2 Parliament enacted the Domestic Violence Crime and Victims Act 2004, which was extended in 2012 to cover serious injury, in an attempt to get round the problem demonstrated in the question. For further details, please see the text, but note that the offence is not one of murder.

The Judicial Studies Board's *Specimen Direction on Joint Responsibility* reads in part:

> Where a criminal offence is committed by two or more persons, each of them may play a different part, but if they are in it together as part of a joint plan or agreement to commit it, they are each guilty. The words 'plan' and 'agreement' do not mean that there has to be any formality about it. An agreement may arise on the spur of the moment. Nothing need be said at all. It can be made with a nod and a wink, or a knowing look. An agreement can be inferred from the behaviour of the parties.

The Judicial Studies Board provides trial judges with specimen instructions on the law to be given to juries. This area of law is often known as '**secondary participation**'.

Grundy is an illustration of this topic.

Grundy [1989] Crim LR 502 (CA)

Two accused were beating up a constable on the stairs up to an Indian restaurant. The first accused joined in after a few seconds. The constable suffered a broken nose and other injuries. All three were charged. The first accused was convicted of aiding (see below for definition) that offence.

The court held that the whole of the injuries suffered by the constable amounted to grievous bodily harm. The first accused was aiding the commission of the offence as soon as he joined in. It was therefore immaterial that he had joined in after the other defendants had begun to inflict the injuries and had already broken the officer's nose. The two other defendants were the principal offenders. Both were striking the officer. They perpetrated the harm. The first accused was the secondary offender or accessory to the injuries other than the broken nose. In *Grundy* the people who inflicted the harm were joint principals. A principal is defined as a person who commits or contributes to the *actus reus*. A secondary party or accessory is someone who encourages or helps the principal. These definitions, which are explained below, are subject to various exceptions such as the doctrine of innocent agency but in the general run of fact situations these definitions suffice.

Usually the secondary party is guilty only if a principal committed an offence with the requisite *actus reus* and *mens rea*, though no principal offender need have been identified, let alone tried and convicted. The principle is called 'derivative liability'. Modern law is moving away from this form of liability (see *Howe* [1987] AC 417 (HL), discussed below, and *DPP v K&B* [1997] 1 Cr App R 36 (DC), though the latter case may be explained as being an authority on procedure to which different principles may apply) but normally it still applies. As the Supreme Court of Victoria in *Demirian* [1989] VR 97, 116, said: 'The accessory may play a dominant, an equal or a subsidiary role in respect of the commission of the crime.' Mafia godfathers, for instance, may be more morally blameworthy than their minions who perform the act of killing.

Lord Goddard CJ in *Abbott* [1955] 2 QB 497 (CCA), which was distinguished in *Grundy*, noted the problem with persons jointly charged:

> If two people are jointly indicted for the commission of a crime and the evidence does not point to one rather than the other, and there is no evidence that they were acting in concert, the jury ought to return a verdict of not guilty in the case of both because the prosecution have not proved the case.

In *Aston* (1991) 94 Cr App R 180 the Court of Appeal quashed the appellants' convictions for cruelty and manslaughter because it could not be proved whether the victim's mother or a person who treated the victim as his own daughter caused the harm. Both of these persons, the appellants, had the opportunity of inflicting the fatal injury, but it could not be proved that this one rather than the other killed, that the two were acting in concert, that they had expressly or tacitly agreed that the victim should be injured, or that either had encouraged the other to inflict harm. There are several similar cases involving parents, such as *Lane* (1986) 82 Cr App R 5 (CA) and *Strudwick* (1994) 99 Cr App R 326 (CA) which followed both *Abbott* and *Lane*, and spouses or cohabitees: *Collins* v *Chief Constable of Merseyside* [1988] Crim LR 247 (DC), which also followed *Abbott* and *Lane*. Either of the appellants in *Collins* could have disconnected the meter from the electricity supply. There was no joint enterprise in these cases, and either could have acted without the other knowing. The law was neatly summarised in *Collins* thus: 'where two people were jointly indicted and the evidence did not point to one rather than the other, they both ought to be acquitted because the prosecution had not proved its case. The uncertainty could not be resolved by convicting both.' (See now the Domestic Violence, Crime and Victims Act 2004, as amended in 2012, s 5, below.) In summary, if the prosecution can prove that one of two persons was guilty, but cannot prove which one committed the offence, neither is guilty, unless it is shown that one was the principal, the other the accessory. In that situation it does not matter which was the principal, which the accessory.

If the triers of fact find that of the defendants one must be the principal and the other must be the accessory, the Accessories and Abettors Act 1861, s 8, deems the accessory to be the principal and so both are guilty. *Mohan* v *R* [1967] 2 AC 187 (PC) illustrates this proposition. Two defendants attacked their victim with cutlasses. It could not be proved who struck the fatal blow. Both were guilty of murder. Each had been encouraging the other. They both intended (at least) grievous bodily harm. It did not matter that they did not kill as a result of any agreement between them. In *Fitzgerald* [1992] Crim LR 660 (CA), which is similar to *Mohan* v *R*, either the accused set fire to a scooter by flicking matches out of the car he was driving or his passenger did so. He was either the principal offender or engaged in a joint unlawful enterprise. He could be convicted on either basis; similarly if he was either the principal or the accessory. In *Swindall* & *Osborne* (1846) 2 Cox CC 141 either the first defendant killed the victim by running him over, with the second accused being the accessory, or the second accused killed him, the first defendant being the accessory. Both parties were guilty where it was proved that each must be liable either as principal or accessory. This authority was applied in *Giannetto* [1997] 1 Cr App R 1 (CA). The accused had either killed his wife himself or he had hired another to do so. He was guilty of murder. Whether he participated as principal or as accessory was irrelevant. Provided he had the *mens rea* of murder or of being a secondary party to murder, he was guilty. This principle can apply to parents. In strict offences in such circumstances neither party is guilty unless the prosecution can show that he had the *mens rea* of being a secondary party: *Smith* v *Mellors* (1987) 84 Cr App R 279 (DC). On the facts each accused had to know that the other was over the limit when it could not be proved who was driving.

The Domestic Violence, Crime and Victims Act 2004 as amended by the Domestic Violence, Crime and Victims (Amendment) Act 2012 provides a partial solution to the difficulty of proving which of two or more defendants unlawfully attacked and seriously injured (for example caused brain damage or broken bones) or killed a child or vulnerable adult. 'Unlawfully' in the previous sentence is defined to include not just those who commit an offence but also those who cause death or serious physical injury but are not criminally responsible (for example because they have the defence of insanity). The crime is not restricted to family members or carers, but is expected to be applied where there has been history of abuse. The extension to serious physical injury was made by the 2012 Act and came into force on 2 July 2012. Unfortunately the crime does not yet have a short name. The offence is perhaps best dealt with through the facts of one of the principal authorities. On the facts of **Khan** [2009] 1 Cr App R 28 (CA) a wife killed by her husband was held to be a vulnerable adult. Four others in the household who knew of the violence from him to her in the previous three weeks were guilty of this offence, even though the killing was not foreseen and took place in the garage and even though the four accused were asleep at the time. The term 'household' is not intended to cover care homes or nurseries. The Act differs from the Law Commission Reports, *Children: Their Non-Accidental Death or Serious Injury (Criminal Trials)*, Law Com. Nos 279 and 282, 2003. It must be understood that the statute is not restricted to instances where it is unclear which of two or more defendants killed the victim. The statute creates an offence of causing the death of a child or other vulnerable person. The offence may be committed by a member of the protected individual's household or by a person who had frequent contact with the victim killing or failing to protect a member of the accused's household or from a known threat or from a threat which ought to have been known from another person in that household, and the accused did not take such steps as could reasonably be expected to protect the victim. What are reasonable steps will differ on the facts of each case but they may include informing the police or social services of abuse, phoning the NSPCC or Childline, and telling the family doctor or the school nurse. The killing of or injury to the victim must occur in circumstances in which the accused did foresee or ought to have foreseen a significant risk of serious physical harm. The steps that a person ought reasonably to have taken may depend on the mental capacity of the accused, for instance a person with learning difficulties may be expected to take fewer steps than a person without them. Although this is a serious offence akin to manslaughter or grievous bodily harm, negligence (and not even gross negligence) suffices as the mental element: the mental element extends to cases where the accused could reasonably be expected to be aware of the risk of death or serious physical injury to the victim. Note also that the definition encompasses people who would not owe a duty to act under omissions liability (see Chapter 2).

The maximum sentence is 14 years' imprisonment when the victim is killed and ten years when she is seriously injured. Between 2005 and 2010 the 2005 statute was successfully used against 31 defendants, including the killers of Baby P, who died as result of blows and neglect inflicted by his mother, her boyfriend, and his brother. As said, one perhaps minor matter is that the s 5 crime does not have a short name, such as, for example, murder, which is unfortunate. If it did, it would be better known to the public.

This chapter deals with participatory offences deriving from the common law. There are similar statutory provisions such as ones relating to terrorism. Unless Parliament excludes the possibility, one can be a secondary party to any offence: *Jefferson* [1994] 1 All ER 270 (CA). One can, for example, be an accomplice to an attempted offence, for an attempt is itself an offence.

Definitions and terminology

The principal is the person who commits the crime. The secondary party is the one who in some sense assists or encourages the principal. One must be a secondary party of an offence charged. One is, for example, an accomplice to murder and not simply an accomplice.

By the Accessories and Abettors Act 1861, s 8, as amended,

[W]hosoever shall aid, abet, counsel or procure the commission of any indictable offence shall be liable to be tried indicted and punished as a principal offender.

There is a similar provision for summary crimes: Magistrates' Courts Act 1980, s 44. Therefore, the accessory may be charged as a principal. The effect is stark. The person who encourages the principal offender to kill is guilty of the same crime as the killer. The practice should be to charge as an accessory in order to give the defendant detail of the accusation: *DPP for NI v Maxwell* [1978] 1 WLR 1350 (HL). However, this practice seems to be rarely adopted, and accessories are charged as principals. The practice was held not to be a breach of Article 6(3) of the European Convention on Human Rights in *Mercer* [2001] EWCA Crim 638, despite the Article's wording that an accused is entitled to be told 'in detail of the nature and cause of the accusation against him'. It was sufficient for the accused to be charged as one of three persons engaged in a joint enterprise (see below) when in fact he was the getaway driver.

The accomplice is subject to the same penalty as the principal, though the degree of participation may affect sentence. Exceptionally, the Road Traffic Offenders Act 1988, s 34(5), provides that disqualification of accessories is discretionary but disqualification of principals is mandatory. In the well-known case of *Craig and Bentley* (1952) *The Times*, 10–13 December, the accused who killed could not be hanged because he was under age. However, the secondary party is by s 8 liable to be punished as principal and was hanged, even though he did not fire the shot. (Bentley received a posthumous pardon in 1998.) It is arguable that while sometimes the accessory is worse than the principal (as when he is a 'godfather'); on the facts of this case – and perhaps of most – the accessory should not be punishable to the same extent as the principal, for he may be less culpable than the latter.

There is nowadays very little distinction between principals and accessories. 'The law no longer concerns itself with niceties of degrees of participation in crime' is how the Court of Appeal put it in *Cogan and Leak* [1976] QB 217, discussed below. The chief differences of substantive law are that one cannot be an accessory to an attempted crime, there are differences in the *mens rea* of principals and accessories, only a principal can be liable vicariously, sometimes only certain people can be guilty as principals (only a man may be convicted of rape as a principal but a woman may be convicted as an accessory), and the law on strict liability does not apply to accessories (see below). Beyond these matters the capacity in which the accused acted is irrelevant. Whether a person acted as accessory or joint principal is immaterial.

Terminology has changed since the older cases were reported. A principal in the first degree is nowadays the principal. A principal in the second degree is an aider, abettor and perhaps procurer. He assisted at the time when the offence was committed. An accessory before the fact was not present at the scene of the crime. He is now a counsellor, procurer or aider. An accessory after the fact, a person who assisted after the crime, was guilty of a crime now abolished. That offence has been partly replaced by s 4(1) ('impeding') and s 5(1) ('concealing and giving false information') of the Criminal Law Act 1967 (see below). Even though some terminology has been modernised, not all has been updated. The person in the street may have difficulty in defining 'abet'.

For more on impeding and concealing, see later in this chapter.

An accessory can be liable as a secondary party to a greater crime than that committed by the principal. The House of Lords so ruled in *Howe* [1987] AC 417, overruling *obiter* a previous Court of Appeal authority to the contrary. The main discussion of this case occurs in Chapter 7 under the heading of duress. Suffice it to say for present purposes that the law in *Howe* is sometimes criticised on the basis that it does not accord with the theory of derivative liability mentioned at the start of this chapter. What the accused is guilty of depends on his state of mind, not on the offence the principal committed. Accordingly a person may be guilty of aiding murder when the principal is guilty only of grievous bodily harm. *Howe* represents a break from the orthodox English theory of derivative liability:

there is no single principal offence to which the accused is a party. The more serious offence intended did not take place. By s 2(4) of the Homicide Act 1957 the defence of diminished responsibility for one party does not affect the liability of others. The same applies to another form of voluntary manslaughter, loss of self-control: Coroners and Justice Act 2009, s 54(8).

To be liable as an accomplice, the principal offence must have been committed. That is why secondary liability is sometimes said to be based on the principle of 'derivative liability'. The accomplice is not, generally speaking, liable unless the principal offender is. The secondary's liability derives from the principal's liability. The ancient authority for this proposition is *Vaux* (1591) 76 ER 992. If the principal offence has not been committed, there may still be conviction for one of the inchoate offences: incitement, attempt and conspiracy. If, therefore, a person advises on an offence, but the principal does not commit the offence, the person is not a counsellor, but an encourager or assister within the Serious Crime Act 2007. Both abetting and encouragement/assisting are based on one party's persuading another to do something. Current law has been criticised on the ground that basing liability of the secondary offender on the liability of the principal fails to support the policy of intervening before crimes have been committed.

Being an accomplice is not in itself an offence. There has to be a principal offence to which one is an accomplice. The charge is not, for instance, 'aiding and abetting' but 'aiding and abetting murder' (or theft, rape, and so on).

'Aid, abet, counsel or procure'

A secondary party is one who aids, abets, counsels or procures the commission of the offence. In *Bryce* [2004] 2 Cr App R 35 (CA), the facts of which are given below, it was said that 'the shades of difference between them are far from clear'. For that reason the charge often involves all four terms. These terms are said (wrongly in the light of history) to mean different things on the ground that 'Parliament would be wasting time in using four words where two or three would do': *Attorney-General's Reference (No. 1 of 1975)* [1975] QB 773 (CA), the principal authority. Unfortunately the court did not state in which respects the verbs differ and it is difficult to see how abetting adds anything not already covered by the other three terms.

(a) Aiding and abetting

In *Bentley* v *Mullen* [1986] RTR 7 the Divisional Court stated:

> As was pointed out in *A-G's Reference (No. 1 of 1975)* . . . , the words **'aiding'** and **'abetting'** have to be given their ordinary natural meaning. The natural meaning of 'aid' is to give help, support or assistance to and the natural meaning of 'abet' is to incite, instigate or encourage.

It was held that the accused, a driving instructor, aided and abetted the crime of failing to stop after an accident when he walked away with the driver and then both of them returned, hoping that the mess had been cleared and that they could drive away with no trouble. It is suggested that 'abet' does not have an ordinary meaning because it is no longer used in everyday language and the definition given in *Bentley* v *Mullen* also applies to 'counsel'. However, in *NCB* v *Gamble* [1959] 1 QB 11 (DC) and *Lynch* v *DPP for NI* [1975] AC 653 (HL), 'aid' and 'abet' were thought to be synonymous. In *NCB* v *Gamble* Devlin J said that counselling took place before the crime, whereas abetting occurred at the time of the offence, but this distinction seems to have disappeared over the last half-century. In *Lynch* 'aid and abet' were thought to be the same concept: 'aid' was the *actus reus* of that concept; 'abet' was the *mens rea*. No authority was supplied for this proposition. Under present law an aider is an accused who assists the principal offender, for instance by supplying a gun or metal-cutting equipment, and an abettor is the person who acts to incite, instigate or encourage the principal at the time of the offence. The Court of Appeal in *Giannetto* (above) both stated that abetting covered 'any involvement from mere encouragement upwards' and approved the trial judge's statement that patting a person on the back and saying 'oh, goody' constituted abetting if done and said in response to the principal saying 'I am going to murder your wife'.

The definition of abetting looks very much like counselling. In *Robinson v R* [2011] UKPC 3 on appeal from Bermuda Sir Anthony Hughes said that the meaning of 'abet' 'is encompassed . . . within "counsel" or "procure" and it may also be within "aid"'. The aider gives help or support to the principal such as occurs where the accused drives the principal to the scene of the crime. Aiding can take place before or during the crime. Devlin J in *NCB v Gamble* and Lord Lowry in the Northern Ireland Court of Criminal Appeal in *DPP for NI v Maxwell*, above, adopted similar definitions.

(b) Counselling

A counsellor is a person who before the commission of the offence (and often not at the scene of the offence) conspires to commit it, advises its commission or knowingly gives assistance to the principal: *DPP for NI v Maxwell* (HL). In *Luffmann* [2008] EWCA Crim 1752 the accused approached a third party and offered him money to kill the victim. These facts constituted counselling. Giving information to and urging the principal also fall within 'counselling'. The accused must be in contact with the principal, but there is no requirement that the accused did cause the principal offender to do the act: *Luffmann*. Therefore, a person can counsel the perpetrator even if the latter ignores the counselling or would have committed the crime in any case. Similarly, counselling occurs even though the principal had already decided to commit the offence.

The old distinction between abetting and **counselling** was that abetting took place at the time of the offence, whereas counselling occurred before. The requirement of presence at the crime seems to have disappeared, though it is still sometimes mentioned in the cases. In *Attorney-General v Able* [1984] 1 QB 795 (DC), a civil case, there was discussion of whether a person aided and abetted suicide by publishing a booklet about the various methods. Under old law the appropriate charge would have been counselling suicide, not aiding and abetting, because the writer would not have been present at the self-killing. Similarly in the civil case of *Gillick v West Norfolk and Wisbech AHA* [1986] AC 112 the Lords discussed *obiter* whether a doctor would be aiding and abetting sexual intercourse with a girl under 16, which is a crime, by prescribing contraceptives to her. If aiding and abetting are restricted to events at the time of the offence, it is very difficult to envisage a doctor being present at the time of the illegal sexual intercourse. Either the House of Lords should have been discussing counselling and procuring or the rule has disappeared. (Parliament has since specifically provided a doctor with a defence to being a secondary party in such circumstances: see Sexual Offences Act 2003, s 73.) In *Rook* [1993] 1 WLR 1005 the accused arranged the killing of the wife of one of his co-defendants. The Court of Appeal applied the same law on joint principals (see below) whether he was present or not. If presence at the scene of the crime is required, as it was at the time of *Bowker v Premier Drug Co Ltd* [1928] 1 KB 217, the 'scene' is construed broadly to include the place where the lookout man was. The suggestion remains, however, that this former rule no longer exists. (Cf. *Lynch* where the accused, who was guilty as aider and abettor, drove a terrorist gang to the scene of the offence.) If abetting means assistance at the time of the offence, it is likely that the accused is at the scene but he need not be. In abetting the accused and principal need not have agreed beforehand that the abettor should join in: *Mohan* v *R*, above.

(c) Procuring

Lord Widgery CJ in *Attorney-General's Reference (No. 1 of 1975)* said that 'procure' meant 'produce by endeavour'. (It is uncertain whether 'by endeavour' adds anything to 'produce'.) In other words, a procurer instigates or causes the crime. The instigation may take the form of persuasion or even threats. Despite this narrow ruling the Divisional Court in *Blakely* v *DPP* [1991] Crim LR 763 *obiter* gave a much wider meaning to 'procure'. The accused procures if he foresees something as a possible consequence of his behaviour. On the facts, the accused spiked the 'victim's' drink; the 'victim' drove away and was guilty of driving with excess alcohol; the accused could have been convicted of procuring this offence if the accused was aware that the 'victim' would drive with excess alcohol. If this is so, in **procuring** there is, contrary to previous authority, no need for the accused to cause the principal party to commit an offence. However, in *Marchant* [2004] 1 WLR 442 (CA) the accused, who directed the driver to drive on the road, was held to be not guilty of procuring death by dangerous driving when a motor cyclist drove on to a spike on the grab unit at the front of his agricultural vehicle. Driving the vehicle on a public road did not cause the death of the victim and the accused did not procure the driver to cause death. The next case illustrates the thrust of the law. In *Attorney-General's Reference (No. 1 of 1975)*, the Lord Chief Justice held the accused guilty of procuring the principal (who did not realise what was happening) to drive with a blood-alcohol concentration above the legal limit when he had laced his drink with alcohol. Hosts who give their guests lots of alcohol should be aware of this decision. Lord Widgery CJ considered that if the principal was aware that his drinks were being laced, the alleged accessory would probably not be guilty of procuring this offence because the principal's knowledge and his 'free, deliberate and informed' decision to drive off would break the chain of causation. It used to be said that procuring takes place before the commission of the principal offence, but there seems no reason why it cannot cover producing by endeavour at the time of the offence.

(d) 'Causal link'

In abetting and counselling it seems that there must be consensus between secondary party and principal; that is, the principal must be aware that he is being assisted or encouraged, though it need not be proved that he would not have committed the offence without the assistance or encouragement: *Calhaem* [1985] 1 QB 808. The Court of Appeal held that the accused was guilty of being a secondary party to murder when she hired a man to kill her rival in love, even though he had decided not to kill her but changed his mind when she screamed and he killed her.

In aiding there need be no consensus. The principal need not be (but can be) aware that he is being assisted. *Calhaem* was followed in *Luffmann*, above. Therefore, for counselling it need not be proved that the secondary party caused the principal to do as he did.

In procuring the secondary party must be proved to have caused the offence. For example, in *Attorney-General's Reference (No. 1 of 1975)* the accused was guilty of procuring the principal to drive with excess alcohol in his body when he surreptitiously laced his drinks. Lord Widgery CJ said: 'You cannot procure an offence unless there is a causal link between what you do and the commission of the offence.' Accordingly, the accused would not have been guilty of procuring driving with excess alcohol if the principal was already over the limit when he supplied him with alcohol. There need, however, be no communication, no consensus, between the parties. There is a statement in this case that usually in aiding, abetting and counselling the parties will have met, but a meeting is not a requirement of these offences. In procuring the parties need never have known each other and, as the facts show, the principal need not know that he is being helped to break the law, nor need he make up his mind to break the criminal law. It is suggested that whatever the mental element in the other forms of accomplice liability, one can procure an outcome only intentionally ('by endeavour').

In *Bryce* [2004] 2 Cr App R 35 the Court of Appeal held that in respect of all four types of secondary participation the accused had to have what Lord Widgery CJ called a 'causal link' with the principal. The accused drove the principal offender to a caravan near where the victim lived. The principal the next day killed the victim. It was held that there was a causal link with the effect that the accused was guilty of counselling the principal. It had been argued, particularly by Sir John Smith, that there did not need to be a causal link for counselling but this case holds that for all forms of participation there must be a causal nexus. That link is broken only by an 'overwhelming supervening event', relegating the accused's conduct to the mere setting for the offence. The law needs to be clarified.

(e) Framing the charge

The charge is generally one of 'aiding, abetting, counselling or procuring'. The accused is convicted if he participated in any of those ways: *Ferguson* v *Weaving* [1951] 1 KB 814 (DC). This is done because 'the shades of difference between [these terms] are far from clear': *Bryce*, above. One is a secondary party to the principal offence. One does not 'aid' in general but one aids a particular crime. Aiding (etc.) is not in itself a crime but a way in which a crime is committed.

Failure to act

The basic rule, as elsewhere in criminal law, is that an omission does not give rise to liability unless there is a duty to act. Presence at the scene of the principal offence does not necessarily mean that the accused is an accessory, though it may be evidence of encouragement. The old-established authority is *Coney* (1882) 8 QBD 534 (CCR), where standing watching a prize fight did not mean that the spectators were aiding an illegal boxing match. Hawkins J said that 'some active steps must be taken by word or action'. The accused would have been guilty had he cheered or applauded. Another old case is *Atkinson* (1869) 11 Cox CC 330. An employer was not guilty of being a secondary party to a riot by his employees when he did nothing to stop it. More recent is *Clarkson* [1971] 3 All ER 344 (CMAC) where drunken soldiers stood around while a girl was raped in a barracks. A perhaps worse case is the Ontario one of *Salajko* [1970] 1 Can CC 352 where the accused, who had his trousers around his ankles, watched a gang rape. There are several similar cases such as *Bland* [1988] Crim LR 41 (CA): the accused was not guilty of being a secondary party to the crime of unlawfully possessing controlled drugs by continuing to share a room with the principal offender after she found out about the drugs. It could not be inferred that she assisted him in his possession of the drugs. She would be guilty if she encouraged the principal or if she had a right of control (see below).

Accordingly, mere presence at the scene of the principal offence does not give rise to secondary liability, but it does not take much to move beyond mere presence into aiding. For example, in *Robinson* v *R* [2011] UKPC 3 on appeal from Bermuda the accused stood inside a room guarding a door while in that room twins were being beaten to death constituted aiding. Presence at a crime is therefore some evidence that the accused did encourage the principals: for example *Allen v Ireland* [1984] 1 WLR 903 (CA). A secret resolve to help one's friend in a fight is not sufficient: *Allan* [1965] 1 QB 130 (CCA). Accordingly there must be an act of encouragement or assistance (but see below for duty situations). A case drawing the line is *Wilcox v Jeffery* [1951] 1 All ER 464 (CCA) where the accused invited an alien saxophonist, Coleman Hawkins, into the UK contrary to the Aliens Order, met him at the airport, clapped his performance and wrote about him. He was guilty of aiding and abetting the breach of the Order by encouraging the principal party. Similar is *Ellis* [2008] EWCA Crim 886. Encouraging attackers is participating in crime; it would have been different if, as in *Clarkson*, the accused had simply stood around while the victim was being beaten up. *McCarry* [2009] EWCA Crim 1718 also draws the line. The accused was in the same car as the killer when the latter strangled the victim. There was evidence for the jury that he was a wilful participant, not a mere bystander.

There is, moreover, no need for the accused to be present at the scene of the principal offence: *JF Alford Transport Ltd* [1997] 2 Cr App R 326 (CA). In this case the accused, a company and its managers, were guilty of aiding and abetting employees to make false entries on tachograph records (which state how many miles the driver has driven in the day). They knew what the employees were doing. They had the legal right to stop them, but they had done nothing.

Omission is described in Chapter 2.

Where there is a duty to act in order to control the behaviour of the principal, the accused is guilty of being an accessory (provided the other elements are fulfilled) if he does nothing to prevent the occurrence of the crime. The accused must know that he had an opportunity of intervening to prevent the commission of the substantive crime: *Webster* [2006] EWCA Crim 415. In *Rubie v Faulkner* [1940] 1 KB 571, an instructor of a learner driver was convicted of aiding and abetting driving without due care and attention. There was no need for direct control over the steering wheel. Hilbery J said: '. . . the supervisor could see the driver was about to do the unlawful act of which he was convicted [careless driving] and the magistrates found that the supervisor remained passive . . . For him to refrain from doing anything when he could see that an unlawful act was about to be done, and his duty was to prevent an unlawful act, if he could, was for him to aid and abet.' In *Tuck v Robson* [1970] 1 All ER 1171 (DC), a pub landlord did not make his customers leave. He was convicted of aiding their consumption of alcohol after time. Simply calling 'Time, glasses please' and turning off the main lights did not serve to exonerate the landlord. Failure to prevent was also taken to be assistance or encouragement (that is, one need not prove that the accused's omission did in fact encourage or assist the principal) in *Du Cros v Lambourne* [1907] 1 KB 40 (DC), where the owner of the car, who was at the time of the principal offence a passenger, did not stop the driver from driving at a dangerous speed. (In fact it could not be proved who was driving. If the owner was driving, he was the principal offender. If he was the passenger, he had a right of control. Whichever seat he was in, he was guilty.) The same result occurs where, for example, a mother watches her husband killing their child. She has a duty to intervene. (A stranger has no such duty: see Chapter 2.) Similarly a police officer is under a duty to prevent another officer hitting a suspect: *Forman* [1988] Crim LR 677, a Crown Court decision of HHJ Woods.

The outcome in these cases would have been different if the accused had no right of control or duty to act. In that eventuality inactivity would not constitute being a secondary party. To secure a conviction, the prosecution would have to prove that the accused encouraged or assisted. For example, in *Du Cros v Lambourne* if the car had belonged to the other party, the accused would have had no right of control over it. As a passenger he would not have been guilty unless he authorised or encouraged the dangerous driving. Cases such as **Tuck v Robson** are getting a bit aged. Modern authorities are necessary to determine the scope of this exception to the general rule of non-liability for omissions.

The Law Commission's draft Criminal Code, Law Com. No. 177, 1989, would rationalise present law in cl 27(3) by creating a general principle. Assistance or encouragement includes assistance or encouragement arising from a failure by a person to take reasonable steps to exercise any authority or discharge any duty he has to control the relevant acts of the principal in order to prevent the commission of the offence.

Mens rea

A person is not liable as an accessory unless he has the required mental elements. These elements apply to all principal offences, including strict liability ones. There is therefore a difference between the *mens rea* of the secondary offence and that of the principal party. The Court of Appeal in **Rook**, above, which was approved in **Bryce**, above, stated that the mental element is the same for aiding, abetting, counselling and procuring. The law is relatively underdeveloped. The following strives to encapsulate it.

The accused must intend to do the act which constitutes the encouraging, advising or assisting. One authority among several is **Bryce**.

Intention to encourage, advise or assist

An accessory is guilty only if he did acts which he knew were capable of encouraging and assisting: **JF Alford Transport Ltd** (above). There is no need to prove that the accused intended that the crime be committed: **Rook**, above, which was endorsed in **Bryce**, above. Potter LJ said in **Bryce**: '. . . it is sufficient if the secondary party at the time of his actions . . . contemplates the commission of the offence, that is knows that it will be committed or realises that it is a real possibility that it will be committed.' As elsewhere in the criminal law motive is irrelevant. The principal authority is **NCB v Gamble**.

NCB v Gamble [1959] QB 11(DC)

An employee of the National Coal Board, the precursor of British Coal, was the weighbridge operator. He told a driver that his lorry was overladen. Driving an overladen vehicle is an offence. The driver said that he was prepared to take the risk of being caught and the employee gave him a weighbridge ticket, without which the driver could not have left the pit. Was the employee guilty of being a secondary party to the principal offence of driving an overladen lorry?

The Court held that he was. Devlin J said:

An indifference to the result of the crime does not of itself constitute negative abetting. If one man deliberately sells to another a gun to be used for murdering a third, he may be indifferent about whether the third man lives or dies and interested only in the cash profit to be made out of the sale, but he can still be an aider and abettor. To hold otherwise would be to negative the rule that *mens rea* is a matter of intent only and does not depend on desire or motive.

Since the employee had intentionally assisted the principal he was liable as accessory. The effect of **NCB v Gamble** should be noted. If the accused knows that the bag of sugar he has just sold to the principal may be used by him to cosh an old lady in a house in which the principal will be rummaging for money to steal, he will be guilty of being an accessory to aggravated burglary. His intention is not that the principal will cosh the old lady. He is happy to have made the sale and does not care how the principal will use the sugar. The principle also catches the landlord who sells alcohol to a man who he knows intends to drive.

There is no need for the accused's *purpose* to be the commission of the crime; oblique intent suffices, as was said in *JF Alford Transport Ltd*, above. It is the intent to aid, abet, counsel or procure which counts, and it has indeed at times been suggested that knowledge that acts may assist is sufficient for liability, though cases such as *Gamble* reject this approach. There is earlier authority for the proposition that it is not counselling or procuring when the accused hopes that the offence will not be committed, at least if the accused tries to stop the principal party committing the offence (cf. *Lynch v DPP for NI*, above, where the accused, who drove terrorists to a place where they murdered their victim, was guilty but it has to be said that he did not make strenuous efforts to prevent the killing). In *Fretwell* (1862) 9 Cox CC 471 (CCR), a lover gave his woman a drug to cause an abortion under threats of her suicide. He hoped that she would not take it but she did. She died. He was held not to be a secondary party to her suicide, which at that time was an offence. The case appears to be wrongly decided in the light of *NCB v Gamble* because it is one in which motive exonerated the accused: he did not wish to see her dead. It has been said in the civil case of *Attorney-General v Able* [1984] QB 795 (DC) to be restricted to its own facts. However, *Fretwell* was cited approvingly in *Gamble* for the proposition that knowingly supplying an article does not amount to an intent to aid, and it has not been overruled. In *Bryce*, above, the Court of Appeal reiterated the law that one could intend to assist a principal even though one intended to hinder his plans. The same was true in *Lynch*. In *Rook*, above, the Court of Appeal said that the accused was guilty even though it was not his intention that the principal offence was committed.

There is a statement in *NCB v Gamble* that an accessory is not liable if before delivery ownership passed and the accused was not aware of the illegal purpose until after ownership passed. (On the facts ownership of the coal passed when the employee gave the driver the ticket.) If this *dictum* were correct, and the law remains uncertain, then if the alleged accessory sold a gun to the principal but before handing it over found out that it was to be used to kill someone, he would not be guilty, whereas he would be guilty if he knew from the start of the transaction that the gun would be used to kill. Similarly, to use the facts of an early case, if the accused handed over the principal's jemmy to him, he would not be liable, for he was doing what in law he was obliged to do. It is suggested that this distinction does not serve any purpose. It is also not soundly based on civil law, as the Divisional Court seemed to think. An illegal contract is unenforceable no matter when the seller, the accessory, comes to know of the illegality. More recent is *Garrett v Arthur Churchill (Glass) Ltd* [1970] 1 QB 92 (CA). Lord Parker CJ said that the legal duty to hand the item over is subordinated to the public interest in preventing a crime being committed with the item.

This issue is dealt with in cl 27(6)(c) of the draft Criminal Code, where the accused is not guilty if he believes that he is under a legal obligation to do the act and acts 'without the purpose of furthering the commission of the offence'. A person supplying an article in the ordinary course of business would, therefore, not be liable.

Knowledge of 'the essential matters'

Lord Goddard CJ said in *Johnson v Youden* [1950] 1 KB 544 (DC), which was approved in *Churchill v Walton* [1967] 2 AC 224 (HL), a case on conspiracy, by the Privy Council in *Mok Wai Tak* v *R* [1990] 2 AC 333 and by the Court of Appeal in *Roberts* [1997] Crim LR 209, that:

> [B]efore a person can be convicted of aiding and abetting the commission of an offence he must at least know the essential matters which constitute that offence. He need not actually know that an offence has been committed, because he may not know that the facts constitute an offence and ignorance of the law is not a defence.

Solicitors were not guilty of conveying a house at a price above the maximum, when they did not know the price. While not pellucid, the phrase 'essential matters' seems to include the circumstances of the *actus reus*, any relevant consequences and perhaps the principal's fault element. The circumstances are the facts which give rise to the offence. If a person supplies a ladder, he is not guilty of aiding burglary unless he knows 'the facts [which] constitute the offence'. However, as Lord Goddard CJ said, the accused is guilty whether or not he knows that what he did constitutes a crime. 'Wilful blindness' is sufficient: *D Stanton & Sons Ltd* v *Webber* [1973] RTR 86 (DC) and *Roberts*, above.

It was said in *Carter* v *Richardson* [1976] Crim LR 190 (DC) that 'know the essential matters' extends to recklessness as to circumstances and wilful blindness as to a risk that the facts constituting the principal offence probably would occur (see Chapter 3). The supervisor of a learner driver was held to be guilty of abetting the learner to drive with a blood-alcohol concentration above the limit. He knew that the learner was above the limit, but *obiter* the court said that he would have been guilty if he thought that the driver was probably over the limit, the state of mind known as subjective recklessness. In *Blakely* v *DPP*, above, the accused's conviction for procuring a person to drive above that limit was quashed because the justices had used the *Caldwell* definition. The accused were the principal's mistress and a friend. They spiked his non-alcoholic drink with vodka in an attempt to prevent him driving back to his wife. In fact he drove off before they could tell him the truth. The Divisional Court said that the accused's knowledge that his act might help the commission of the principal offence was sufficient for aiding, abetting and counselling and probably for procuring. *Blakely* v *DPP* was approved in *Webster* [2006] EWCA Crim 415. Moses LJ said: 'It is the defendant's foresight that the principal was likely to commit the offence which must be proved and not merely that he ought to have foreseen that the principal was likely to commit the offence.'

It may be that *Blakely* is wider than *Carter* v *Richardson*. In the latter case the secondary party was reckless as to circumstances, namely the amount of alcohol in the blood, but was intentional as to encouraging this principal's driving, whereas in the former case she was reckless as to both and would have been convicted on a proper direction. If so, the spectre of liability of hosts at parties resurrects itself. He will be guilty of aiding drunk driving if he was aware that his conduct might encourage the commission of this offence. By definition, however, procuring requires that the accused must intend to bring about the principal offence. As the court said in *Blakely* v *DPP*: '. . . mere awareness that [the principal offence] might result would not suffice.' Nevertheless, while stating that *Caldwell* recklessness, which existed at that time, would also not suffice, it did not rule subjective recklessness out. If *Carter* v *Richardson* is correct it may apply only to strict offences.

The draft Criminal Code does not permit *Caldwell* recklessness and would confirm the court's view in *Blakely* v *DPP* that recklessness is defined in *Cunningham* terms. Clause 27(1)(b) would preserve recklessness as to circumstances, an outcome in accord with the present law of attempt, but there must be intent as to the principal's conduct: *Carter* v *Richardson* would be overruled.

Caldwell recklessness is described in Chapter 3. Compare with *Cunningham* recklessness.

The Divisional Court in *Blakely* v *DPP* said that in procuring and perhaps counselling and commanding it must be shown that the accused intended to bring about the principal offence and that the position might be different in relation to other forms of participation where the accused assisted the principal. In relation to forms of secondary participation such as counselling where the accused is encouraging the principal before the commission of the offence, the accused can hardly be said to 'know' the facts surrounding the crime. It is better to say that the accused must believe that action will occur which will give rise to an offence. It is difficult to square these authorities with the definition of procuring as 'produce by endeavour'. Procuring would seem to require intent alone.

An example of the requirement of knowledge is *Ferguson* v *Weaving* [1951] 1 KB 814 (DC). A pub landlady was not guilty of aiding and abetting the offence of consuming alcohol after hours when she did not know that the customers were so doing. This rule even applies to strict offences. In *Callow* v *Tillstone* (1900) 19 Cox CC 576 (QBD), a butcher was convicted of the strict offence of exposing unsound meat for sale. The vet who had examined the heifer at the butcher's request was not guilty of aiding and abetting the offence because he did not know of the unsoundness of the meat. He was not guilty even though he had performed his inspection carelessly. In terms of justice, the case looks topsy-turvy. The butcher who had done his best not to expose unsound meat for sale was guilty, while the vet, who was careless over such an important matter, was not guilty.

As stated above, knowledge of the 'essential matters' includes knowledge of the principal's *mens rea*. The accused does not aid murder if the principal does not possess malice aforethought.

Both intention to encourage or assist and knowledge (subject to *Carter* v *Richardson*) of the essential facts are necessary for conviction as an accessory. The width of these rules should be noted. If a person provides the principal with a room, turning a blind eye to the fact that the principal is going to set up girls in a brothel, he is guilty of being an accessory to living off the earnings of prostitutes. The question of whether a doctor who prescribes contraceptives to a girl under the age of 16 intends to aid and abet unlawful sexual intercourse has exercised minds. The House of Lords thought not in *Gillick* v *West Norfolk and Wisbech AHA* [1986] AC 112, a civil case, but the decision looks incorrect. It has been suggested that doctors are not guilty because of their good motive, despite the fact that elsewhere in the criminal law motive provides no defence. Another idea is that the defence of necessity applies. An alternative view is that 'intent' in this area of law means 'direct intent'. Since it was not the doctors' purpose to encourage unlawful sex, they are not accessories. Other authorities, however, do not restrict intent to purpose. If *Gillick* is correct, *Fretwell* (discussed above) may also be correct. In respect of secondary participation, where the *actus reus* is an omission, as in *Tuck* v *Robson* (above), the *mens rea* was stated in *JF Alford Transport Ltd* (above) as being: (i) knowledge that the principal was committing a crime; (ii) deliberately turning a blind eye to that crime; and (iii) knowledge that the principal was being encouraged to commit the crime.

Contemplation of a range of offences

It does not matter that the accessory does not know when and how the principal offence will take place: *Bullock* [1955] 1 WLR 1 (CCA). On the other hand, it is not sufficient that the principal is going to break the law *simpliciter*. In *Bainbridge* [1960] 1 QB 129 the accused thought that oxyacetylene equipment was to be used to cut up stolen goods. In fact it was used to break into the Midland Bank, Stoke Newington, London. The accused was not guilty. He would have been guilty if he knew that a burglary would take place but he did not know when or in which building (following *Bullock*).

After **Bainbridge** it was thought that the accused was guilty if he knew, in the words of Lord Parker CJ, that 'a crime of the type in question was intended'. This requirement is additional to 'knowledge of the essential matters'. The principal authority despite **Bainbridge** never being overruled and being an English case now is **DPP for NI v Maxwell**, above. Four Law Lords held that the same type of case test was to be widened. Lord Scarman adopted the formulation of Lord Lowry CJ in the Northern Irish Appeal Court. The guilt of the accessory springs 'from the fact that he contemplates the commission of one (or more) of a number of crimes by the principal and he intentionally lends his assistance in order that such a crime will be committed'. The accused is convicted of counselling the offence which actually occurs if he contemplated a range of offences and the actual offence which took place was one of those. **Maxwell** differs from **Bainbridge**, which it did not overrule, because (a) there is no need for knowledge; (b) the accused must foresee the offence committed; (c) the 'type' of offence is not relevant: one looks at the contemplated range of offences. The fifth Law Lord, Lord Hailsham, said 'bullet, bomb or incendiary device, indeed most if not all types of terrorist violence' gave rise to offences of the same type within **Bainbridge**. 'The fact that, in the event, the offence committed by the principals crystallised into one rather than the other of the possible alternatives within his contemplation only means that in the event he was an accessory to that specific offence rather than one of the others.'

As a result of the majority in **Maxwell**, the law can be stated thus:

(a) if the accused knows of the offence, he is liable as accessory;

(b) if the accused knows that one or more of a range of offences will take place, he is guilty if one or more of those offences occur;

(c) if the accused contemplated that one offence was to be committed, but another similar crime took place, he is not guilty. The result would have been different under **Bainbridge**;

(d) if the accused knows only the general class of offence, not the specific offence, it appears that he is guilty.

One issue raised but not resolved in **Maxwell** was: how far into the future does liability stretch? Is the accused guilty as an accessory to an offence 60 years in the future? It is suggested that criminal liability ought not to stretch so far, but the policy underlying accomplice liability, that of deterring those who encourage crime, may support a conviction. Contrariwise, it might be argued that 'supported' involves motive and it is sufficient if the accused knowingly assisted or encouraged the burglary and accordingly he is guilty.

Summary of the conduct and fault elements

In **Bryce**, above, the Court of Appeal summarised the law thus. To be guilty of aiding, abetting, counselling or procuring, the accused must be proved to have done:

(a) an act . . . which in fact assisted the later commission of the offence;

(b) . . . [the accused] did the act deliberately realising that it was capable of assisting the offence;

(c) . . . [the accused] at the time of doing the act contemplated the commission of the offence by . . . [the principal] i.e. he foresaw it as a 'real or substantial risk' or 'real possibility'; and

(d) . . . [the accused] when doing the act intended to assist the [principal] in what he was doing.

Joint enterprise liability

Example

Zac and Yvonne agree to burgle Xerxes' house. While doing so Xerxes disturbs them. Zac, who is in the kitchen, picks up a rolling pin and hits Xerxes over the head with it. Zac is guilty of murder. Has Yvonne committed any offence against the person?

'Murder!' Despite not dealing the fatal blow and therefore not having the *actus reus* of murder and not having the *mens rea* of murder, she is guilty of that offence and must be sentenced to life imprisonment. She took part in a joint criminal enterprise, burglary, and is liable for offences committed by the principal offender, even if that offence, here murder, was unforeseen by the secondary party, Yvonne, provided that the killer did not fundamentally depart from what was agreed. It is suggested that torture of Xerxes would be a fundamental difference but whether there is such a difference is a question of fact for the jury.

If two or more persons agree to carry out a common purpose, a joint venture or **joint enterprise**, the secondary party is liable for crimes committed by the principal in executing that purpose, even unforeseen ones, provided that there is not a 'fundamental difference' between the act agreed on and the act carried out. Such crimes are sometimes known as 'collateral offences'. He is guilty irrespective of the actual part he played in the venture. This doctrine means that where a member of an unlawful enterprise kills, members of the group can also be found guilty of murder even though they did not commit the *actus reus* of murder, provided that they foresaw that the principal offender might (not would) 'act with intent to kill *or* [emphasis added] to do GBH': *A, B, C, D* [2010] EWCA Crim 1622. This point marks a distinction between this form of liability and ordinary accessorial responsibility. In the latter the accused must have encouraged or assisted the principal in the commission of the offence. In the former the accused is guilty without encouragement or assistance. In *Baldessare* (1930) 29 Cox CC 193 (CCA), two defendants took a car. The first accused drove so recklessly that he killed someone. He was guilty of manslaughter. It was held that the common purpose was reckless driving. The second defendant was convicted of abetting manslaughter, even though the killing was not foreseen by him.

There has been a remarkable number of joint enterprise cases in recent years. Those mentioned in this section are selected ones which give rise to principles; a few have been chosen as factual illustrations of those principles. Often cases involve two parties who set out to burgle a house. One kills the occupier. The other is guilty of the murder if that crime was committed in pursuance of their common intent, the burglary. The violence need not be contemplated at the start of their venture. It does not matter that the principal cannot be identified: *Conroy*, unreported, 10 February 2000 (CA). Similarly, if there is spontaneous violence, that is, violence about which there was no plan (as distinguished from where there was a plan but one accused went beyond what was agreed), the question for the jury is whether the actions of the participants and what they knew led to the inference of a joint enterprise: *O'Flaherty* [2004] 2 Cr App R 315 (CA). On the facts there was evidence that one of the accused pursued the victim as part of a joint enterprise with others. When the others attacked and killed the victim, he was holding a cricket bat at the scene of the killing and was, it seems, encouraging them. The others, however, did not form part of the joint enterprise. They had originally been part of the group which attacked the victim but they did not join in the pursuit of him to a different place. That pursuit was not part of the joint plan. Therefore, there was no evidence that these two defendants were at the time of the killing part of the joint enterprise.

George [2011] All ER (D) 27 (May) is an example of cases on joint enterprise and illustrates two basic principles of the doctrine, the *mens rea* and the 'fundamental departure' rule. It involved a squat, drugs, alcohol and killing with a large knife. The killer was one of three defendants but it could not be proved which of the three stabbed the victim and the prosecution case was that there was a joint enterprise. The *mens rea* issue was whether the defendants did foresee that the murderer had the *mens rea* for murder. The Court held that foresight that the killer might use a knife almost inevitably proved that the killer would use it to kill or cause GBH. The Court added that on the facts the killer's possession of the knife was known to the others and therefore there was no fundamental departure from their plan.

If, however, there was no joint enterprise, but one of only two persons could have committed the offence, as we have seen neither is guilty if it cannot be proved which one did it. For example, in **Swallow v DPP** [1991] Crim LR 610 (DC), where the preventing of the recording of electricity by means of a black box had to have been done either by the landlord or by his wife, neither was to be convicted. Both would have been liable if both knew of the black box and the rest of the *mens rea* and *actus reus* existed. Similarly in **Petters** [1995] Crim LR 501 (CA) there was no joint enterprise where two persons had come separately to a car park and one of them had kicked the victim to death. They had not communicated to one another the fact that they had a common objective. Therefore, their conviction for manslaughter was quashed. The law is that separate actions by two defendants do not constitute a joint enterprise. They had to share a common purpose.

In **Gnango** [2010] EWCA Crim 1691 there was no joint enterprise where the accused and an unidentified man had been involved in an exchange of gunfire and the latter shot the victim dead. On appeal, **Gnango** [2011] UKSC 59 is the first Supreme Court authority on joint enterprise liability: for much more on this case, see the box below (pp. 189–90). In light of recent criticism of that doctrine, it is of assistance in delimiting the boundaries of joint criminal enterprise. Unfortunately, the facts are quite eccentric, so the case is not as helpful as one might have hoped. The accused and another (known as 'Bandana man' but who was never identified, let alone arrested or tried) were involved in a shoot-out in a public place. Bandana man killed the victim and *he* was guilty of murder by virtue of the doctrine of transferred malice. Was the accused guilty of murder via joint enterprise principles? A seven-person Supreme Court held that on these facts joint enterprise law did not apply because there was no common purpose. However, by a majority of six to one the Court held that the accused was guilty of murder. Four (Lords Phillips P, Judge CJ, Wilson and Dyson) so held because he was *aiding and abetting* Bandana man's murder; two (Lords Brown and Clarke) held that he was guilty of murder as a *joint principal* with Bandana man. The dissent on both points by Lord Kerr is well worth reading.

Joint enterprise differs from joint principalship liability. In the latter both defendants had the external and fault element for the principal offence. In the former only one accused did. It is the liability of the other accused which is at issue in this section. There is a debate, which is noted below, as to whether joint enterprise is merely one part of the law of accessorial liability or whether it constitutes a separate area. If the law is separate, the joint enterprise principle is that the accused is liable according to his own *mens rea*. Therefore, the principal may be a murderer, but the accused may be guilty only of manslaughter. If the accused is a true secondary party, he is liable as an accessory of the principal's actual offence. An example of this point is this: if two defendants have a common purpose, they are engaged in a joint enterprise; if, however, one accused spontaneously comes to the other's aid, there is no such venture but there could be a conviction in the ordinary way for secondary participation.

If, however, there is a joint enterprise, but one party intentionally goes beyond what was agreed, the accessory is not liable for the unforeseen circumstances. A blow with a knife is not within the contemplation of an accessory who expected a blow with a fist. Whether the principal exceeded the scope of the agreement is a question of fact. In *Davies v DPP* [1954] AC 378 (HL), there was a gang-fight on Clapham Common, London. The first accused stabbed the victim to death. The second accused, though a member of the same gang, did not know of the knife. The first accused was guilty of murder, but the second was not an accomplice to that offence. The use of the knife was not within his contemplation. Similarly, the abandonment of a car by the driver who has joy-ridden in it and left it in gear with the result that it mounted the pavement and killed a baby in a pram were not within the contemplation of the accused; the grossly negligent acts were not in pursuance of the joint enterprise (joy-riding) but beyond anything the accused contemplated as a real possibility: *Mahmood* [1994] Crim LR 368 (CA).

If the accused knows that the principal *will* commit an offence if need be to carry out their joint enterprise, he will be liable if the principal does carry out that offence: *Betts and Ridley* (1930) 22 Cr App R 148.

Powell; English now form the landmark authorities on joint enterprise. Two appeals were heard together by the Lords.

Powell; English [1998] AC 147 (HL)

In *Powell* the two defendants went to the home of a drug dealer in order to buy drugs. The dealer was shot dead, apparently by a third party. The defendants were convicted of murder on the basis that they knew that the third party was armed with a gun and foresaw that he might use it to kill or cause serious harm to the dealer. The House dismissed their appeals. In *English* the two defendants jointly attacked a police sergeant with wooden posts. A third person killed him with a knife. The defendants did not know that he had a knife. The first accused appealed against the judge's direction that he was guilty of murder if he had taken part in a joint unlawful enterprise, knowing that there was a substantial risk that the third person might kill or cause grievous bodily harm. The appeal was allowed.

The following propositions can be drawn from the speeches and later developments:

(a) 'A secondary party to a criminal enterprise may be criminally liable for a greater criminal offence committed by the primary offender of a type which the former foresaw but did not necessarily intend' (Lord Steyn). The Privy Council advice in both *Chan Wing-siu v R* [1985] AC 168 and *Hui Chi-ming v R* [1992] 1 AC 34 was approved. For this reason the defendants in *Powell* were guilty of murder. It should be noted that the secondary party has to be reckless both as to the *actus reus* of the principal crime and as to whether that *actus reus* would be caused by the principal with *mens rea*. Earlier cases seem to have required recklessness only as to the *actus reus*.

Why was the accessory liable for murder when he did not intend to kill or cause grievous bodily harm?

- First, the House of Lords in *Moloney* [1985] AC 905 and *Hancock and Shankland* [1986] AC 455 (which are discussed in Chapter 3 in relation to intent) did not lay down any rule as to accessories. Therefore, they are not authoritative on the law of what Lord Steyn called the 'accessory principle', namely that 'criminal liability is dependent on proof of subjective foresight on the part of a participant in the criminal enterprise that the primary offender might commit a greater offence'.

- Secondly, if the secondary party has a lesser *mens rea* than the principal offender, his liability is not a form of constructive liability. The Lords did not explain what it meant by 'constructive liability', but the best current illustration is constructive manslaughter. The accused is liable even though he did not foresee death or grievous bodily harm: it suffices that he foresaw a lesser crime such as battery.

- Thirdly, while it was accepted that it was anomalous that an accessory could be guilty of murder even though he was merely reckless as to death or grievous bodily harm, 'practical and policy considerations', as Lord Steyn put it, militate against the secondary party's not being convicted of murder. If intent was needed, it would be hard to prove, thereby undermining 'the utility of the accessory principle'. 'Experience has shown that joint criminal enterprises only too readily escalate into the commission of greater offences. In order to deal with this important social problem the accessory principle is needed and cannot be abolished or relaxed' (Lord Steyn). The public must be protected against gangs. Sir John Smith 'Criminal liability of accessories: law and law reform' (1997) 113 LQR 453 added: 'The accessory to murder . . . must be proved to have been reckless, not merely whether death might be caused, but whether murder might be committed; he must have been aware, not merely that death or grievous bodily harm might be caused, but that it might be caused intentionally . . .' Lord Steyn approved this passage in *Powell*; *English*, above. The argument to the contrary is that an accused who did not intend to kill or commit GBH is by definition not guilty of murder. He may have been reckless as to death or GBH but that is not sufficient *mens rea* for murder as a principal offender. Therefore, he should be convicted of manslaughter, because he has foreseen the risk that the principal might kill or commit GBH.

See Figure 12.3 on p 472 (Chapter 12) for a diagram illustrating constructive (unlawful act) manslaughter.

There is a strong dissent by Kirby J in the High Court of Australia case of *Clayton v R* [2006] HCA 58 on the point that accessories may be murderers without their having malice aforethought. He wished to 'restore greater concurrence between moral culpability and criminal responsibility' by replacing the 'seriously unprincipled' law that a secondary offender is liable for murder 'merely on the foresight of a possibility'.

(b) Lord Hutton stated in relation to the degree of foresight necessary for conviction: 'the secondary party is subject to criminal liability if he contemplated the act causing the death as a possible incident of the joint venture, unless the risk was so remote that the jury take the view that the secondary party genuinely dismissed it as altogether negligible.'

(c) As Lord Parker CJ said in *Anderson and Morris* [1966] 2 QB 110 (CCA), 'if one of the adventurers goes beyond what has been tacitly agreed as part of the common enterprise, his co-adventurer is not liable for the consequences of that unauthorised act'. There need be no tacit agreement; foresight suffices: *Hyde* [1991] 1 QB 134 (CA) was approved. It remains a question of fact whether the principal offender has acted in a fundamentally different manner from what was agreed: *Attorney-General's Reference (No. 3 of 2004)* [2006] Crim LR 63 (CA) among other cases. In this case the fundamental change was the use of a weapon to fire at the victim rather than near him.

The appellant in *English* fell within this principle. The use of the knife was in the words of Lord Hutton 'fundamentally different to the use of a wooden post', despite the fact that both could be used to cause serious injuries. The accused was not guilty of murder or manslaughter. Whether the principal acted beyond the scope of the joint enterprise is 'an issue of fact for the common sense of the jury' (Lord Hutton). Later Court of Appeal decisions including *Rafferty* [2007] EWCA Crim 1846 (the accused was not a secondary party when he contemplated a robbery and was absent from the scene at the time of the killing) and *Campbell* [2009] EWCA Crim 50 have uniformly applied this 'substantial deviation' law.

Some authorities before *Powell; English* had taken the view that if the principal offender had exceeded the limits as foreseen by the accused, the secondary party, the latter was guilty of a less serious offence than a principal. For example, if the principal went beyond the plan and killed, he was guilty of murder: the accessory was guilty of manslaughter. These earlier authorities must now be taken to be wrong. In *Mitchell* [1999] Crim LR 496 the Court of Appeal said *obiter* that a secondary party can no longer be convicted of manslaughter when the principal goes beyond the scope of the joint enterprise and is guilty of murder. However, if the principal intends a serious offence but the accessory contemplates only a minor one, then if the victim dies, the principal is guilty of murder but the accessory only of manslaughter.

An example given by the Northern Ireland Court of Criminal Appeal in *Gilmour* [2000] 2 Cr App R 407 was of two parties agreeing to carry out a conspiracy to post an incendiary bomb through a letter box. The principal intends death or serious injury; the accessory foresees superficial harm. The victim dies. The accessory is guilty of (being a secondary party to) manslaughter, not to murder. Lord Carswell CJ saw no 'convincing reason why a person acting as an accessory to a principal who carries out the very deed contemplated by both should not be guilty of the degree of offence appropriate to the interest with which he so acted'. This is not a deviation case (as in *Anderson and Morris*) but one of differing *mens rea*. The outcome is one which aligns the defendant's *mens rea* with the crime, which is praiseworthy, but one strange result should be noted. The accused in *English* foresaw grievous bodily harm but was not guilty; the accused in *Gilmour* did not foresee such harm, yet he is guilty! It may be that *Gilmour* and *Powell; English* are irreconcilable. *Powell; English* appears to hold that an accused can be guilty of the same crime as the principal or of nothing, whereas *Gilmour* permits the conviction for an offence lesser than the one committed by the principal.

There are different streams of authority. Cases such as *Day* [2001] Crim LR 984 (CA), *Gilmour, Stewart and Schofield* [1995] 3 All ER 159 (CA) and *Reid* (1975) 62 Cr App R 109 support the view that a secondary party can be guilty of (being an accessory to) a lesser offence such as manslaughter when the principal party is guilty of a more serious crime such as murder. In *Gilmour*, for example, the court distinguished cases such as *Anderson and Morris* and *English* as being ones where 'the principal departs from the contemplated joint enterprise and perpetrates a more serious act of a different kind unforeseen by the accessory. In such cases . . . the accessory is not liable at all for such unforeseen acts. It does not follow that the same result should follow where the principal carries out the very act contemplated by the accessory, though the latter does not realise that the principal intends a more serious consequence . . .' In such an event the accessory may be convicted of a lesser offence than that committed by the principal. *Carpenter* [2011] EWCA Crim 2568 confirms the line of cases (*Roberts* [2001] EWCA Crim 1594, a case which is also called *Day*, and *Yemoh* [2009] EWCA Crim 230) which hold that a member of a joint enterprise can be guilty of manslaughter when the killer is guilty of murder. This occurs where the person foresees that the killer will inflict harm less than death or GBH but that he will cause some harm. The killer acting with malice aforethought is guilty of murder and the person involved in the joint enterprise is guilty of manslaughter (and not, as had been argued, no offence).

A recent authority is *Carpenter*. The principal pleaded guilty to murder of the victim in a knife fight resulting from disagreements between two families. The Court held that the killer's mother could be convicted of manslaughter as an accessory to the murder by her son. *Roberts* (also known as *Day*) and *Yemoh* were approved. Manslaughter arises because the accused foresaw the risk of some injury but did not foresee death or serious harm. Anything that may have been said to the contrary in *Mendez* [2010] EWCA Crim 516 was not directed at the current issue and if it was (contrary to the Court's view), it was wrong.

Clarification from the Supreme Court would be helpful.

(d) In respect of a deviation from the venture Lord Hutton opined: 'if the weapon used by the primary party is different to, but as dangerous as, the weapon which the secondary party contemplated he might use, the secondary party should not escape liability for murder because of the difference in the weapon, for example, if he foresaw that the primary party might use a gun to kill and the latter used a knife to kill, or vice versa.'

Powell; English was applied by the Court of Appeal in *Uddin* [1999] QB 431. The accused had joined in an attack on another man who was having an argument with the driver of a car in which friends of the accused were. Six men in total had attacked the victim with poles or bars. The deceased was killed by a flick-knife wielded by one of the co-defendants. Apparently the accused did not know of the knife. He was convicted at first instance. The Court of Appeal allowed the appeal on the ground that the conviction was unsafe. The flick-knife's use was 'of a completely different type' from the use of poles. However, it ordered a retrial because the jury had not been directed as to the use of the knife by the killer and whether the accused was aware that the killer might use it. The reserved judgment of the court was delivered by Beldam LJ. He considered that *Powell; English* could not be directly applied to cases where there was 'spontaneous behaviour of a group of irrational individuals who jointly attack a common victim, each intending severally to inflict serious harm by any means at their disposal and giving no thought to the means by which the others will individually commit similar offences on the same person'. *Powell; English* was an authority on conduct performed as a result of a plan.

Beldam LJ laid down seven principles governing the type of case with which he was concerned. It must be stressed that the seven principles are just that: they are not rules of law (*O'Flaherty* [2004] 2 Cr App R 315 (CA), the facts and law of which are noted below). They are matters of evidence, not substantive law. The court stressed that they aimed to avoid 'the creation of a complex body of doctrine as to whether one weapon (for instance a knife) differs in character from another (for example a claw hammer) and which weapons are more likely to inflict fatal injury'.

(i) Where several persons join to attack a victim in circumstances which show that they intend to inflict serious harm and as a result of the attack the victim sustains fatal injury, they are jointly liable for murder, but if such injury inflicted with that intent is shown to have been caused solely by the actions of one participant of a type entirely different from actions which the others foresaw as part of the attack, only that participant is guilty of murder.

(ii) In deciding whether the actions are of such a different type the use by that party of a weapon is a significant factor. If the character of the weapon, for example its propensity to cause death, is different from any weapon used or contemplated by the others and if it is used with a specific intent to kill, the others are not responsible for the death unless it is proved that they knew or foresaw the likelihood of the use of such a weapon.

(iii) If some or all of the others are using weapons which could be regarded as equally likely to inflict fatal injury, the mere fact that a different weapon was used is immaterial.

(iv) If the jury concludes that the death of the victim was caused by the actions of one participant which can be said to be of a completely different type to those contemplated by the others, they are not to be regarded as parties to the death whether it amounts to murder or manslaughter. They may nevertheless be guilty of offences of wounding or inflicting grievous bodily harm with intent which they individually commit.

(v) If in the course of the concerted attack a weapon is produced by one of the participants and the others knowing that he has it in circumstances where he may use it in the course of the attack participate or continue to participate in the attack, they will be guilty of murder if the weapon is used to inflict a fatal wound.

(vi) In a case in which after a concerted attack it is proved that the victim died as a result of a wound with a lethal weapon, for example a stab wound, but the evidence does not establish which of the participants used the weapon, then if its use was foreseen by the participants in the attack they will all be guilty of murder notwithstanding that the particular participant who administered the fatal blow cannot be identified (see *Powell*). If, however, the circumstances do not show that the participants foresaw the use of a weapon of this type, none of them will be guilty of murder, though they may individually have committed offences in the course of the attack.

(vii) The mere fact that by attacking the victim together each of them had the intention to inflict serious harm on the victim is insufficient to make them responsible for the death of the victim caused by the use of a lethal weapon used by one of the participants with the same or shared intention.

The Court of Appeal in *O'Flaherty*, above, stated that whether weapons were of the same type was a matter for the jury. Therefore, the trial judge was correct in leaving to the jury whether a claw hammer, cricket bat and broken bottles were of the same type of weapon as a knife, with which the principal offender killed. *O'Flaherty* was followed by the Court of Appeal in *Mitchell* [2009] 1 Cr App R 31.

Powell; English, above, was also applied in *Greatrex* [1998] Crim LR 733 (CA). At least six men attacked the victim. One of them killed him with a metal bar. None of the others knew of the bar. The others were not guilty of murder because the principal had acted in a way fundamentally different from what was foreseen by the others. They foresaw the use of kicking but not of the metal bar. Therefore, despite the others' intent to cause serious injury, they were not guilty of murder or manslaughter, just as in the 1999 case of *Mitchell*, above. A retrial was ordered so that the jury could determine whether the hitting with the bar was fundamentally different from the kicking. In *Lewis* [2010] EWCA Crim 496 a more severe beating up (which led to death) was not fundamentally different from a beating up, whereas in *Jackson v R* [2009] UKPC 28 on appeal from Jamaica the Privy Council *obiter* considered that striking a cutting blow with a machete was fundamentally different from beating with the weapon's flat side. The decisions are particularly fact-sensitive. It should be noted that the 'fundamental difference' rule applies beyond joint enterprise to standard secondary parties law. For example, in *Luffmann*, above, the Court of Appeal said that the principal party would still be acting within the scope of the accused's counselling if the former killed the victim as a result of a robbery going wrong rather than as a result of being counselled by the accused to kill the victim.

As *Greatrex* illustrates, the issue whether the principal acted in a 'fundamentally different' way is one for the jury. Assume that in *Greatrex* the potential accessories agreed to kick the victim to death but before they could do so the principal shot and killed him. All the defendants intended to kill and one did kill. Why should it matter if the mode of killing was fundamentally different from that agreed on by the non-perpetrators of the killing?

The Lords reconsidered the 'fundamental difference' rule in **Rahman** [2009] 1 AC 129. A gang armed with wooden and metal poles set out to attack the victim. One participant killed the victim with a knife. Were the other members of the gang guilty as secondary parties to murder or was there a fundamental difference between what they intended and the principal's stabbing? The House held that the doctrine of 'fundamental difference' did not come into play simply because the accessories had a different state of mind from the killer at the time of the killing. Therefore, the secondary participants were guilty of murder in the normal way of accessories just as much as the person who knifed the victim to death. There is a helpful summary of the law provided by Lord Brown (at [68]):

> If B [the accessory] realises without agreeing to such conduct being used that A [the principal offender] may kill or intentionally inflict serious injury, but nevertheless continues to participate with A in the venture, that will amount to a sufficient mental element for B to be guilty of murder if A with the requisite intent, kills in the course of the venture unless (i) A suddenly produces and uses a weapon of which B knows nothing and which is more lethal than any weapon which B contemplates that A or any other participant may be carrying and (ii) for that reason A's act is to be regarded as fundamentally different from anything foreseen by B.

The first part of the quote is based on **Hyde**, above, and the second part (after 'unless') is derived from **Powell**; **English**, above. **Rahman** is now the principal authority on the 'fundamental difference' rule. It was, for example, applied in **Yemoh** [2009] EWCA Crim 230 where stabbing with a knife with a pointed blade was not fundamentally different from stabbing with a Stanley knife (a type of craft knife) as foreseen by the accused, though the issue remains one for the jury. Compare **Mendez** [2010] EWCA Crim 516: a stab in the heart was held to be fundamentally different from an attack comprising of knives, kicks, punches and the use of pieces of wood and metal bars. The court said that the paraphrase of 'fundamental difference' used by the trial judge in **Rahman** ('in a different league'), which the Lords had approved, was helpful to the jury when deciding whether the nature of the attack was fundamentally different from what had been foreseen. Stress was laid on the fact that juries had to determine the issue as a matter of common sense. The court stated that the issue was not a difficult one for juries to grasp and did not require 'expert evidence or minute calibration': a 'broad-brush' approach was to be used.

The accused may be convicted of being an accessory even though he does not approve of the action. In **Day** [2001] Crim LR 984 (CA) the accused contended that he did not approve of his co-defendants' kicking the deceased in the head. The court held that this lack of approval was irrelevant. He was guilty if he foresaw that the kicking might occur. Moreover, it was not necessary for him to foresee that death or GBH might occur from the kicking. His co-defendants were convicted of murder; he was convicted of manslaughter on the grounds that there was a 'joint enterprise at least to inflict some harm' and it did not matter that his co-defendants intended to inflict at least GBH.

For an explanation of negligence, see Chapter 3.

Throughout this law the secondary party is not liable if he ought to have been aware of the risk but was not. This principle applies even where the principal crime is one of negligence: **Reid** (1975) 62 Cr App R 109, *obiter*.

In *McKechnie* (1992) 94 Cr App R 51 (CA) one accused was acting in pursuance of a joint enterprise. He was provoked by the victim, whom he killed. It was held that his outburst meant that the other joint principals were not liable. The act of the killer was outside the common purpose of the others. However, the law is not clearly stated and appears irreconcilable with *Calhaem* [1985] 1 QB 808 (CA). One party went berserk and killed. Nevertheless, the accused was guilty of counselling the offence. Why did not the running amok break the chain of causation?

In the 2009 *Mitchell* case the Court of Appeal drew attention to the plethora of precedent which required trial judges to provide complex instructions to juries. For example, do the different words in respect of the fundamental difference rule in *Powell*; *English* and *Rahman* signify a shift in the law or are the words used merely synonyms?

Is joint enterprise part of secondary liability?

There is debate whether the law of joint enterprise is separate from secondary liability. This paragraph considers the arguments and the authorities. Most cases do not refer to any distinction. *Rook* [1993] 1 WLR 1005 (CA) expressly stated that the doctrine of joint enterprise applies whether the accused is present or not. It does not matter whether the assistance is given before or after the principal offence. In *Bryce*, above, the Court of Appeal applied the law on the *mens rea* on joint enterprise liability to a person who was not part of a joint enterprise. There are other authorities to this effect. *Stringer* [2011] EWCA Crim 1396 is a good first case for students to read on joint enterprise. Its facts read something like an episode of Channel 4's *Shameless* and both the case and the series were set on a Manchester council housing estate. The facts as accepted by the jury were that the principal killed a man nicknamed 'Bones' and indeed the Court referred throughout to his nickname. The question was whether the two defendants, father and son, were involved in a joint criminal venture with the killer. If so, they too were guilty of murder under the law of secondary participation.

The Court held:

1 secondary participation may occur before the moment of the commission of the principal offence. Of course a person who supplies the murder weapon may be just as guilty as one who applauds a murder;

2 there is no need except for procuring for the principal offence to be caused by the assistance or encouragement;

3 'There may be cases where any assistance or encouragement provided by D [the secondary party] is so distanced in time, place or circumstances from the conduct of P [the principal offender] that it would be unjust to regard P's act as done with D's encouragement or assistance.' On the facts the defendants were not too far removed in time and place from the killing;

4 'Joint enterprise is not a term of art.' It is not a separate doctrine, but part of the law of secondary participation. This ruling is in line with recent authorities.

However, there are contrary authorities. In *Stewart* [1995] 3 All ER 159 the Court of Appeal said that whereas an accessory is liable only for the secondary offence though he may be charged as a principal, a person who takes part in a joint enterprise does participate in the primary offence. The doctrine 'renders each of the parties to a joint enterprise liable for the acts done in the course of carrying out the joint enterprise'. The outcome is that counsellors and procurers are not engaged in a joint enterprise because they are not present when the principal offence is committed. The same court spoke to similar effect in *O'Brien* [1995] 2 Cr App R 649, which also held that on a charge of being an accessory to attempted murder of a policeman, it was sufficient that the accused knew the principal *might* kill; it did not have to be proved that he knew the principal *would* kill. The latest authority is *Bryce*, above. The Court of Appeal said that the joint enterprise doctrine differed from secondary participation because in the latter it was necessary to show an intent to assist the principal whereas in the former such an intent is not required. The court also said that those who assist at a 'preliminary stage' are accessories, whereas those who assist at the time of the offence are joint enterprise participants. While the cases do not descend to details, one difference seems to be in the *mens rea*. In a joint enterprise scenario the accused is guilty if he foresees that the principal may commit an offence, whereas in secondary participation he is guilty only if he knows the 'essential facts'. It is, however, suggested that the Court of Appeal's view is erroneous. The law on joint enterprise is truly part of accessorial liability. The joint venturer participates as an aider, etc. What distinguishes it from the law on secondary parties is that proof of guilt is easier when two or more persons are engaged in a joint enterprise than if they are not. Joint participation supplies the evidence of assisting and encouraging.

In *Reardon* [1999] Crim LR 392 the Court of Appeal approved the trial judge's direction that in a joint enterprise the accused was liable as secondary if he foresaw the principal offence 'as a strong possibility'. This statement is very much a direction used in the law of secondary participation without a joint enterprise. The court's mind was not on the current issues. But the law as stated in *Reardon* is inconsistent with *Stewart* and *O'Brien*. One criticism of *Reardon* is that there was no joint enterprise between the parties to kill the victims. Therefore, the court should not have been discussing joint enterprise. The High Court of Australia considered that the doctrine was separate in *McAuliffe* v *R* (1995) 69 ALJR 621 because to be liable in a joint enterprise one did not have to aid, abet, counsel or procure, but this proposition is wrong. This issue was not considered in *Powell*; *English*, but since all the speeches treat parties to a joint venture as accessories, it is suggested that they are against the principle stated in *Stewart*. The Court of Appeal in *Mendez*, above, also said that joint enterprise liability falls within the principles of secondary offences and is not a separate free-standing category of criminal responsibility. Similarly, in *A*, *B*, *C*, *D*, above, the Court of Appeal said: '. . . guilt based upon common enterprise is a form of *secondary* [their emphasis] liability.' Clarification is needed.

The argument that joint enterprise and liability as secondary parties are discrete doctrines is best put by A.P. Simester 'The mental element in complicity' (2006) 122 LQR 578, which is well worth studying.

Joint enterprise and the ECHR

The Court of Appeal in *Concannon* [2002] Crim LR 213 held that joint enterprise liability did not breach Article 6 of the European Convention on Human Rights, the provision on the right to a fair trial. The accused and the killer went to the flat of a drug-dealer, intending to rob him. The killer used a knife to kill the dealer. The jury convicted the accused of (being an accessory to) murder. The defence contended that the accused, who did not strike the fatal blow, should not be guilty of murder when he did not intend to kill or commit GBH. The court held that Article 6 applied to procedural, and not to substantive, matters. The law of joint enterprise may be unfair, but any change was for Parliament. Laws may be unfair. The doctrine of joint enterprise may be unfair, as may be the law of murder, but unfairness is not a ground for determining that a rule of substantive criminal law breaches Article 6.

Gnango [2012] 1 AC 827 Supreme Court

This case is the latest on joint enterprise and is of the highest authority. However, its facts are such that not much can be applied to other scenarios. The accused and a man wearing a bandana ('Bandana man') were involved in a shoot-out in which a woman was shot dead by the cross-fire from Bandana man. Bandana man was never arrested but the accused was. Was he guilty of any offence? The trial judge directed the jury that if the accused and Bandana man were acting together with a common purpose to commit an affray by shooting at each other, then if Bandana man killed the victim and the accused realised that Bandana man might kill someone with the *mens rea* of murder, he was guilty of murder too. The jury decided that the accused was guilty of murder, presumably on this basis, but the Court of Appeal allowed the appeal on the basis that no liability for joint enterprise arose on the facts. The case came before a seven-person Supreme Court. That Court restored the conviction.

Two matters are straightforward:

(i) if Bandana man were apprehended, he would be guilty of murder (as a principal offender): he fired the fatal shot;

(ii) transferred malice applies to accessories as well as principals. When Bandana man shot at the accused but killed the bystander, his 'malice' towards the accused was 'transferred' to the victim. Similarly, when D1 encourages D2 to kill V1 but D2 misses and kills V2, D1 is liable for being an accomplice to D1's murder of V2.

A third matter is perhaps less straightforward.

(iii) The Supreme Court was clear that the trial judge was wrong to direct the jury as to the accused and Bandana man's having a common purpose of committing an affray and that if Bandana man went beyond that joint enterprise and he killed the victim, they should convict the accused of being an accessory to murder. The Supreme Court basically said that the facts could not be cut up in this way. The accused and Bandana man had agreed to shoot at each other; in those circumstances both of them acted with the *mens rea* of murder, not just of affray.

The Supreme Court was divided.

(a) Six held that the accused was guilty of murder; one, Lord Kerr, dissented.

(b) Of the six, two, Lords Brown and Clarke, held that the accused was a joint principal with Bandana man. Lord Brown said that he was guilty of murder as a principal offender because he took part by agreement in unlawful violence designed to kill or seriously injure. He had the *actus reus* and *mens rea* of murder and was therefore guilty of murder. The same reasoning as applies to duels and prizefights applies to the killing of the woman. Lord Clarke reasoned similarly. When Bandana man and the accused agreed to a shoot-out, they were both guilty of murder as principals. The accused had agreed to take part in violence intended to cause death or grievous bodily harm and the victim's death occurred as a result. It did not matter that the killing was in fact by Bandana man because the accused was a joint principal in that killing.

The ruling that the accused was guilty as principal to murder was *obiter*.

(c) Four, Lords Phillips, Judge CJ, Wilson and Dyson, convicted the accused as a murderer via the accessory route, and their ruling was *ratio*. Their ruling was that he was the secondary party to Bandana man's murder of the woman. We can analyse the reasoning thus:

(i)   An accused can be liable as accessory even though he was the intended victim of the shot which killed the woman.

(ii) If the accused had aided Bandana man to shoot at himself, he was liable as a secondary party to the attempted murder of himself.

(iii) Since the accused was a secondary party to the attempted murder of himself, he was guilty of being a secondary party to the killing of the victim (by means of the doctrine of transferred malice) when she was murdered by Bandana man.

(iv) Having got so far, the judges were faced with a practical matter: the trial judge had ruled that the accused had not aided the murder of the victim because he did not actively encourage Bandana man to shoot at himself; therefore, the judge had not left aiding murder to the jury. Their Lordships held that the jury must have accepted that the accused aided Bandana man to shoot back at himself with Bandana man's having malice aforethought. Accordingly, there was no impediment to hold that he had aided Bandana man to commit murder. In that event the accused was the secondary party to murder and therefore in accord with normal principles he was liable to be tried, found guilty, and sentenced as a principal offender, that is, here as a murderer.

(d) Causation: some of their Lordships considered that the accused could be convicted via causation. He had caused Bandana man to shoot at him; when Bandana man did shoot back, he killed the victim. Therefore, the accused contributed to the victim's death and was guilty of murder as a principal. Lord Clarke thought that this route was a means to convict him of murder but since this route to conviction had not been put to the jury, the Supreme Court could not allow the appeal against the Court of Appeal's ruling on this basis. Lord Dyson argued thus:

(i) Bandana man's shooting at the victim broke the chain of causation from the accused's aiding Bandana man to cause the victim's death because he acted in a free, deliberate and informed way;

(ii) however, it was arguable that Bandana man's actions were not free, deliberate and informed because he acted in self-defence, but this argument was a weak one on the facts;

(iii) this reliance on free, deliberate and informed conduct broke down where the parties, Bandana man and the accused, were acting in concert;

(iv) in any case, the matter had not been put to the jury in this way and thus the accused's conviction for murder could not be upheld via this route.

Lord Kerr said that the accused could not be guilty via the causation route because Bandana man shot at him first; therefore, the accused's shooting did not cause Bandana man to shoot. Therefore, when Bandana man killed the victim, the accused did not significantly contribute to her death and therefore he was not guilty as a principal to murder.

Criticism of the joint principal route to conviction

To be guilty as a (joint) principal it is not sufficient that the accused took part by agreement in violence which was aimed at causing death or grievous bodily harm. The issue is whether he contributed to the victim's death. It is difficult to accept that he can be a principal offender when he did not commit at least part of the *actus reus*. Moreover, this issue was not put to the jury. Lord Kerr's dissent on this point is worth reading.

Criticism of the D's liability for murder as an accessory

(i) How can the jury's verdict support the step in the majority's thinking that there had been an agreement between Bandana man and the accused?

(ii) Even if we accept that the verdict did provide such support, that does not mean that the accused aided Bandana man to shoot him (and that Bandana man aided him to shoot him). The jury presumably convicted on the basis of the judge's instruction, and certainly did not convict for the reason stated by the majority.

The reform of joint enterprise

The Law Commission's 2006 proposals are noted below but the then government decided not to proceed with reforming the law only in the context of homicide: Ministry of Justice, *Murder, Manslaughter and Infanticide: Proposals for Reform of the Law*, 2009. The Court of Appeal in *Mitchell*, above, called for reform 'which would set out clear and simple principles easy for the jury to apply.'

The Eleventh Report of the Justice Committee, *Joint Enterprise*, 2012 is a brief exposition the law and criticisms of it, especially now that it is now so complex that juries cannot understand it. It calls for the Ministry of Justice to bring forward legislation on the topic (and to do so without completing a review of the law of homicide, which in any case the government does not intend to undertake) and in the meantime calls for the Director of Public Prosecutions to develop guidance on the charge of being a member of a joint enterprise, a call which has been accepted. Not surprisingly written evidence is divided into those who support the doctrine because their family members have been killed in a gang attack and those who are critical of it because it makes the people who do not stab or shoot guilty of murder when they did not intend to kill or cause GBH and they did not strike the fatal blow or shoot the lethal shot. It should be noted that the government said in evidence to the Committee that it will not implement the recommendations of Law Commission Report on *Participating in Crime* (2007), despite the fact that reform of the law would bring benefits, because the project was too big for enactment in the current Parliament.

Non-conviction of the principal offender

No *actus reus* and acquittal of principal

If the principal offender is not guilty because he did not perform the *actus reus*, the accessory is also not guilty. The authority is *Thornton v Mitchell* [1940] 1 All ER 339 (KBD). A bus conductor signalled to the driver to back up. Two pedestrians were knocked down. The driver was held not guilty of careless driving. He had driven with due care and attention because he had relied on the conductor's signals. There was therefore no *actus reus*. The conductor was held by the Divisional Court not to be guilty of aiding and abetting. There was no offence to which the alleged secondary party could be accessory. The law was pithily put by Avory J in *Morris v Tolman* [1923] 1 KB 166 (DC): 'A person cannot aid another in doing something which that other has not done.' The accused, the secondary party, was charged with abetting the owner of a vehicle, the alleged principal offender, to use it for a purpose for which it had not been licensed. The owner was the licence holder, and he had not used the vehicle. Therefore, the accused was not guilty of abetting the principal offence – there was no such principal offence. The doctrine of innocent agency cannot apply on the facts of *Thornton v Mitchell* because again there was no *actus reus* of which the conductor could be guilty (see below).

If, however, a principal is acquitted because evidence is not admissible against him (for example because it is hearsay), the accomplice may be guilty where evidence is admissible against him (for instance he has confessed).

Exemption from liability

A person may be convicted as accessory even though he cannot be guilty as principal. Even when a boy under 14 could not be guilty of rape, a law repealed in 1993, he could be guilty as accessory: *Eldershaw* (1828) 172 ER 472. A woman cannot be guilty as a rapist but she can as a secondary offender: *Ram and Ram* (1893) 17 Cox CC 609. More up to date was the charge of being an accessory to rape made against Rosemary West of 25 Cromwell Street, Gloucester, notoriety. She helped her husband Fred to kill women who stayed at their house.

So far the position of accessories where the principal is guilty has been dealt with. What if the principal is not guilty not because there is no *actus reus* but because he is exempt? In those circumstances the accessory is guilty. At one time a father could not be guilty of child-stealing. However, the accessory who helped the father in the snatch was guilty as a secondary party: *Austin* [1981] 1 All ER 374. The Court of Appeal held that the father had committed the offence but was exempt from prosecution. Thus, there was a crime to which the accused could be a secondary party. The wording of the statute was that a person who claimed a right to possession of the child should not 'be liable to be prosecuted'. The decision illustrates the principle of derivative liability.

Can a 'victim' be an accessory?

There is no general rule that a 'victim' cannot be an accessory to a crime. For instance, if the 'victim' encourages the accused to cause him serious harm, the victim is guilty of a participatory offence. Sometimes judges have held that when a statute is intended to protect persons, members of that class cannot be convicted as accessories. A girl under 16 could not be convicted of an offence involving unlawful sexual intercourse because the statute penalising such behaviour was passed to protect girls from themselves: *Tyrrell* [1894] 1 QB 710 (CCR). It is irrelevant whether she initiated the act. A similar case is *Whitehouse* [1977] QB 868 (CA). A girl of 15 was held to belong to a class protected by ss 10 and 11 of the then existing Sexual Offences Act 1956, which punished men for committing incest with their daughters. The outcome in *Whitehouse* was quickly changed by statute but the principle stands, as *Pickford* [1995] 1 Cr App R 420 (CA) demonstrates. *Tyrrell* was applied. A boy under 14 was the victim of the crime of incest with his mother. The stepfather was guilty of inciting (a crime which has been abolished but replaced with a similar offence) his wife to commit incest with his stepson but at that time could not have been found guilty of inciting his stepson to commit incest with his wife. He also could not have been found guilty of aiding and abetting his stepson to commit the crime of incest. At that time Parliament protected boys under 14 by ruling that such boys could not be guilty of committing crimes of sexual intercourse, a category which included incest. The rule was abolished in 1993 but the principle stands. There was no *actus reus*.

In *Congdon* (1990) 140 NLJ 1221 (Crown Court), it was held that a prostitute could not be convicted of abetting her husband (or any other pimp) to live on her earnings, an offence which could be committed only by a man. She was to be protected from his exploitation of her. The law applies whether or not the woman egged the man on. In other words, the woman need not in fact be the victim of the principal. It is sufficient that she fell within a class expressly or impliedly protected by Parliament. The offence of living off immoral earnings was abolished by the Sexual Offences Act 2003 but the principle remains.

It is uncertain how far this 'victim' doctrine goes. Sometimes it is said that it applies only to sexual offences. The decision in *Tyrrell* arguably turns very much on statutory interpretation but the principle has become a general one. Mental defectives form a protected class. It has been held that the immunity does not extend to a woman on whom an unlawful abortion is performed even though the woman cannot be convicted of using an instrument to procure her own abortion: *Sockett* (1908) 1 Cr App R 101 (CCA). If the argument is that the statute is not designed to protect women, the outcome is sound. If, however, the statute is aimed at backstreet abortionists, women do fall within the protected class, and the accused in *Sockett* ought not to have been found guilty as accessory. In *Brown* [1994] AC 212 (HL), discussed in depth in Chapter 13 on non-fatal offences, sado-masochists were convicted of aiding and abetting assaults on themselves. They were not 'victims' for the purpose of this rule. The persons who perpetrated what were held to be offences on them were guilty of committing crimes against the 'victims'. The same persons were not victims for one purpose but were for another!

It should be remembered that this exemption applies only to the statutorily protected victim, for example of the unlawful sexual intercourse. If a 15-year-old girl assists a man to have sexual intercourse with a girl aged 14, she is the secondary party, because she is not the victim. It is the girl aged 14 who is the victim – she is not guilty as accessory. (A prostitute can be convicted of living on the earnings of another prostitute.)

Innocent agency

Example

David sends a monkey through a small open window of a house belonging to Erica. He has trained the monkey to take shiny objects from rooms. The monkey picks up a ring and climbs back through the window and hands it to David. Is David guilty of burglary?

Burglary includes entering a house as trespasser and stealing: see s 9(1)(a) of the Theft Act 1968. The objection to a charge of burglary being successful is simply that David did not himself enter the building as a trespasser and steal the ring. However, the doctrine of innocent agency makes him guilty and does so whether the thing used to pick up the ring is a monkey, a small child or a hook. It has to be admitted that case law post the Act is rare but the statute was meant on this point simply to codify previous common law: see for example *Manley* (1844) 1 Cox CC 104 for an illustration of a child stealing money from a till at the behest of the accused.

Where the 'principal' performed the *actus reus* of an offence with the accused's assistance or encouragement, but where the 'principal' has a defence or lacks *mens rea*, the accused who would otherwise be the accessory is treated at times as if he were the principal. He stands in the shoes of the person who would otherwise be the principal offender. (A straightforward application of the principle of derivative liability would render the person who would otherwise be the secondary party not guilty.) If a postman delivers a parcel bomb, he is not guilty and no doubt most of us would not even think of charging him, but the person who sent the parcel will be liable as a principal offender. A simple example is *Tyler and Price* (1838) 172 ER 643. The person who told an insane person to kill someone was deemed to be the principal offender when he did so. A similar case is *Michael* (1840) 169 ER 487 (CCR). The accused gave a childminder a bottle of laudanum, a poison, intending her to give it to her child. She said it was medicine. In fact the childminder's child, aged five, gave it to the child, not knowing what the contents were. The child died. It was held that the childminder's child was the innocent agent. The accused was convicted of murder. (Had the otherwise innocent agent, the child, been over 10 and had that child known of the poison, the minor would have been the principal offender and the adult who provided the poison would have been the accessory.)

In *Manley* (1844) 1 Cox CC 104, the accused was the principal offender when he told a nine-year-old child to take money out of the father's till. The principle is not restricted to situations where the 'principal' has a defence such as insanity or infancy. It applies where the 'principal' does not have the *mens rea*. In *Stringer* (1991) 94 Cr App R 13, the accused dishonestly sent bogus invoices through a firm's accounting system with the result that money was transferred from the firm to him. It was held that it was he who had appropriated for the purposes of theft because he was responsible for the accounts staff appropriating what he intended to steal. The staff were innocent agents. He was the principal offender. *Stringer* accords with the older case of *Butt* (1884) 15 Cox CC 564. The accused is not liable as accessory because the alleged principal has committed no crime. A final illustration is where the accused persuaded another to steal a car from a garage. The person who innocently took the car is not guilty but the one who induced him to take it is guilty of burglary as a principal offender. A modern Australian authority is *Pinkstone v R* (2004) 219 CLR 444 (HCA). The accused sent prohibited drugs via an air courier. Kirby J quoted from Brooking JA in *Franklin* [2001] 3 VR 9, 21: 'The law regards the puppet master as causing the mischief done by the puppet.' The courier was the innocent agent: the firm delivered the drugs but the accused 'supplied' them within the meaning of the legislation.

As stated above, the doctrine of innocent agency does not apply where the accused cannot be said to have done the *actus reus*. In *Thornton v Mitchell*, above, the conductor could not be said to have committed the act of careless driving through the innocent agency of the actual driver because he was not driving at all. 'Driving' requires the accused himself personally to do the act. One does not drive a car when someone else's hands are on the wheel and feet are busy on the pedals. The problem is even clearer in bigamy. Take this situation. A man believes that his wife is dead but she is in fact alive. A woman knows that the wife is alive but persuades the man to re-marry. The husband is not guilty of bigamy because he does not have *mens rea*. Is he an innocent agent? If he were, the woman would be the principal. However, to hold so would mean that the woman had 'married' the man's second 'wife', but one woman cannot 'marry' another. The position is exacerbated if the woman is not already married. Bigamy requires the *actus reus* of 'being married, marries again', but on these facts the woman is not married. It is not possible to say that she, being married, married again. For a person to be liable as an accessory, moreover, the principal offence must have been committed. In the cases discussed in this paragraph there was no principal offender and under the derivative liability rule the accused should not have been convicted.

To this exception to the doctrine of innocent agency there is a sub-exception, which might be called the doctrine of 'semi-innocent agency'. It is uncertain how far this doctrine extends and whether it is restricted to sexual offences. It derives from two cases which the Law Commission in 1993 called 'lurid' and 'unforgettable'. In *Bourne* (1952) 36 Cr App R 125 (CCA), the accused forced his wife to have sexual intercourse with a dog. She probably had the defence of duress. There was therefore no principal offender. The husband was convicted of aiding and abetting, even though he was not physically capable of committing the offence as charged. The line between this case and *Thornton v Mitchell* seems to be that in *Bourne* there was an *actus reus*, bestiality, whereas in *Thornton v Mitchell* it was not an *actus reus* to drive a bus. In **Bourne** there was a perpetrator; in **Thornton v Mitchell** there was not. In **Bourne** there was a principal crime on which the secondary offence could be parasitic. In **Cogan and Leak** [1976] QB 217 (CA), the husband compelled his wife to have sexual intercourse with the accused, who believed that the wife was consenting. The accused's conviction for rape was quashed on appeal: there was no *mens rea* (cf. **Bourne** where there was an *actus reus*). The Court of Appeal held that the husband's conviction as a secondary party could stand. The derivative theory of secondary participation was not applied in this case. This part of **Cogan and Leak** remains good law even though the part discussed next is incorrect. A husband could not until recently be guilty of rape as principal. In **Cogan and Leak**, however, Lawton LJ went beyond **Bourne**. He also said that the husband became the principal to the crime of rape, an offence which he could then not commit as principal. If this case is correct, **Bourne** could have been decided similarly, notwithstanding the difficulty of finding a person guilty of an offence which he cannot physically commit. Moreover, the reasoning in **Cogan and Leak** could be applied to women. If one woman forces another to have intercourse with a man who does not know that the second woman was not consenting, is the first woman guilty of rape through the innocent agency of the second, even though only a man, because of the definition of the crime of rape (see Chapter 14), can be guilty as principal? Lawton LJ said in **Cogan and Leak** that 'convictions should not be upset because of mere technicalities of pleading', but what occurred in the law seems to be more than technical. The decision in **Cogan and Leak** that the accused can rape through the genitals of someone else does not seem correct in principle. If one cannot 'drive' through another, how can one have vaginal sex through another? It is hard to say that a person who stands around is engaged in intercourse. This is not to say that the husband should not be guilty of something. It is only by altering the derivative liability doctrine underlying secondary offences that the accused could be found guilty. Neither judgment provides much in the way of theoretical justification for liability. Take another illustration, provided by B. Mitchell, *Law Relating to Violent Crime* (CLT Publishing, 1997) 313:

> . . . A woman deceives another woman into visiting a man's house and, pointing a gun at both of them, orders him to rape the other woman. The man has a good defence to the charge of rape on the ground of duress . . . , and the woman cannot be convicted of rape as a principal (with the man being treated as the innocent agent) because of her sex. . . . It seems unsatisfactory that the woman can escape criminal liability because of these 'technicalities'.

In a footnote Mitchell adds: 'Obviously, she cannot be convicted as an accessory to rape because no offence of rape has been committed.'

In **Millward** (1994) 158 JP 1091 (CA) the accused had given his employee instructions to tow his trailer. The trailer's hitch was poorly maintained. The trailer became detached, hit a car and killed a passenger. The employee was acquitted of causing death by reckless driving (a crime now abolished). The accused was charged with procuring the crime. He argued that he could not be convicted of a secondary offence when there was no principal offence, since the employee's acquittal meant that there was no crime to which he could be a party. The court, however, rejected his appeal. Since in procuring there need be no joint intention between the parties, the accessory can be liable when the principal is acquitted because he does not have the mental element for the crime or because he has a defence personal to him, provided that there is an *actus reus*. The employee did not have the *mens rea* for the offence charged and was therefore not guilty. The *actus reus* was taking a defective vehicle on to a road so as to cause death. The accused had procured that *actus reus*. (However, it may be doubted that the accused had the *mens rea* of procuring.) The court distinguished **Thornton v Mitchell**, above. The driver was not guilty of careless driving when he reversed his bus on the accused's instructions and killed a pedestrian. He had no *actus reus*. Therefore, there was no *actus reus* which the accused could abet. In other words, the driving was not careless; there was no principal crime and the defendant could not be convicted of abetting something which was not a crime.

The court ruled that the case was on all fours with *Cogan and Leak*, above. Scott Baker J said:

> . . . it is the authority of *Cogan & Leak* that is relevant to the decision that we have to make. In this court's view, the *actus reus* in the present case was the taking of the vehicle in the defective condition on to the road so as to cause the death of the little boy. It was procured by this appellant. The requisite *mens rea* was . . . present . . . The appellant caused [the employee] to drive that vehicle in that condition just as Leak had caused Cogan to have sexual intercourse with his wife.

Mr Cogan believed that Mrs Leak was consenting to sex when she was not. Mr Leak was convicted of aiding and abetting rape. The court in *Cogan and Leak* said that the offence of rape had occurred, not just the *actus reus*, and the accused was an accessory to that offence, though the alleged perpetrator was not liable. In *Millward* the court said that the offence had not taken place but the *actus reus* had. (This is the same situation in theft as seen in *Cogan and Leak*, but the court in *Cogan and Leak* said that an offence and not merely the *actus reus* had occurred.) In this sense the cases are different and the rule is new. This development has been criticised for creating crimes where none existed before.

The court said in *Millward* that its new rule was one applying to procuring (and it may be that the rule is restricted to procuring) and that *Cogan and Leak* was essentially a case on procuring. The question may be asked whether the accused did procure at all. He did not produce the victim's death by endeavour. He was not trying to kill anyone. He was reckless as to whether death might occur, but recklessness is insufficient *mens rea* for procuring. Furthermore, it is uncertain whether the principle enunciated in this case applies to other modes of participation. The court emphasised that in procuring, the minds of the parties need not be as one. This distinction may place procuring in a different category from the others.

It should be emphasised that *Millward* breaks away from the doctrine of derivative liability underlying the present law. A person can now definitely procure an offence where the principal is not liable in situations where it can be said that the *actus reus* of a crime has occurred. *Millward* was approved *obiter* by the Court of Appeal in *Wheelhouse* [1994] Crim LR 756. The court said that the accused's use of a dupe to remove a car from a garage was an instance of *Millward*. Actually the case is one of innocent agency. There is no difficulty in saying the accused burgled, whereas in *Cogan and Leak* and *Millward* one cannot hold the accused to have raped or driven. It is, however, arguable that the accused can rape and drive through an agent. It seems that the doctrine of innocent agency was not discussed in *Millward*. It might also be inquired whether the accused in *Millward* had the *mens rea* to be an accessory. Did he know the essential matter that the hitch was poorly maintained? If not, he should not have been found guilty. Another criticism of *Millward* is that the rule is stated as one of procuring the *actus reus* of a crime. In the former crime of reckless driving the principal had to drive in such a way as to create an obvious and serious risk of causing physical injury. This element is part of the *actus reus*. Since the principal did not drive in such a manner, there was no *actus reus* to which the accused could be attached. Therefore, he should have been found not guilty. The same analysis, it is suggested, applies to dangerous driving.

Millward was applied in *DPP* v *K & B* [1997] 1 Cr App R 36 (DC). Two girls, the defendants, procured an unidentified boy who was older than 10 but younger than 14 and who may have had the then-existing defence of infancy, to have sexual intercourse with a girl of 14 without her consent, that is, subject to the defence of infancy he raped her. The Court held that the defendants were guilty of rape, even if the boy was not. The Court thought it possible that a woman who deceived a man into having sexual intercourse with another person could be convicted of the offence of rape despite the offence being restricted by Parliament to male offenders. As stated above, *DPP* v *K & B* is a breach of the derivative theory of liability for secondary participation.

It may be that cases like *Millward* and *DPP* v *K & B* are irreconcilable with the House of Lords' decision in *Powell; English*, above. The Lords said that the accused was guilty only if he realised that the principal may commit an offence with the appropriate *mens rea*. However, the defendants in *Millward* and *DPP* v *K & B* did not realise that. Possibly the cases may be reconciled by holding that *Millward* and *DPP* v *K & B* are cases on procuring to which different principles may apply. Another criticism of *Millward* and similar cases is that they in effect create new crimes, contrary to the principle that courts must not create new offences, as discussed in Chapter 1.

In *Pickford* [1995] 1 Cr App R 420 the Court of Appeal distinguished *Bourne* and *Cogan and Leak*. The court considered *obiter* what would have happened if a person had been charged with aiding and abetting a boy to commit incest with his mother. At that time boys under 14 were irrebuttably presumed not to be capable of committing crimes involving sexual intercourse. Laws J said that in *Bourne* and *Cogan and Leak*: 'the person who committed the act said to constitute the principal offence . . . was fully capable at law of committing the offence in question, but had a complete defence on the facts. These authorities do not support the proposition that where the principal offender lacks all legal capacity to commit the crime in question another may nevertheless be guilty of aiding and abetting him.'

Subject to the doctrine of innocent agency and cases such as *Cogan and Leak*, the principal offence must have been committed before the accused is guilty as an accessory, though the perpetrator need not have been convicted. Without a principal offender, the accused is not guilty: see *Morris* v *Tolman* [1923] 1 KB 166, where the employer was not guilty of using a commercial van for private purposes, for only the licensee could be guilty of this offence, but it was the employee of the licensee who had used the vehicle for a purpose not covered by the licence, and accordingly the employee was not guilty of aiding. There was no *actus reus*. The Court of Appeal in *Loukes* [1996] 1 Cr App R 444 applied *Thornton* v *Mitchell* and distinguished *Millward*. The accused was charged with being a secondary party to an offence of causing death by dangerous driving. The trial judge directed the jury to acquit the driver. The Court of Appeal held that since there was no primary offence, the accused could not be guilty of procuring that offence. There was no *actus reus* (obviousness to a competent driver that the car was dangerous) which the accused had procured (cf. *Millward*). The position would have been different, had the alleged principal offender been found not guilty on the ground that he lacked *mens rea*. In that event *Millward* would have applied, and the accused could have been found guilty of procuring the *actus reus*. As it was, the principal crime was a strict offence and *mens rea* was irrelevant. The court asked for Parliament to change the law. It could be argued that this principle hinders crime prevention, for the reason why the principal offence does not take place may be fortuitous.

The statutory crime of abetting suicide should be noted. There is no crime of suicide, but a person may be guilty of abetting suicide. Perhaps in reality 'abetting suicide' is best described as the principal offence and the abettor is in truth the principal. Similarly there is a crime of procuring the execution of a valuable security. In this context 'procuring' is the principal offence. The accessory would be guilty of procuring the procuring [*sic*] of the execution of a valuable security!

Withdrawal

English law grants a defence to secondary parties who withdraw before the commission of the full offence. One possible rationale is that the accused is given an incentive to prevent the crime; another is that the accused is less blameworthy than one who continues. For a modern view on the possible rationales see A.J. Ashworth's commentary on *O'Flaherty* [2004] Crim LR 751 (CA).

If in a case involving pre-planned violence the accused assists or encourages a person to commit an offence but withdraws before the crime takes place, he is not liable as a secondary party, provided that he expressly or impliedly communicates his repentance or revocation to, it is thought, all the principals, but may remain liable for conspiracy or for encouraging or assisting or for both offences. The accused must give 'clear warning' that he has withdrawn from the criminal enterprise: *Becerra* (1976) 62 Cr App R 212 (CA), which remains the leading case and has often been followed as in *Bryce*, above, and *Whitefield* (1984) 79 Cr App R 36 (CA). In the latter case the Court of Appeal allowed the accused's appeal when he had told his co-conspirators that he had decided to play no more part in the burglary of an adjoining flat. The accused must give 'unequivocal communication' of withdrawal. The Northern Irish Crown Court in *Stewart* [2009] NICC 19 approved *Becerra* in respect of its holding that when the offence was imminent, the accused had to 'countermand' the crime and that merely shouting 'Come on, let's go' was insufficient.

It is not enough to avoid culpability that the accused has said to himself that he will withdraw (*Rook* [1993] 1 WLR 1005, following *Whitefield*, where the Court of Appeal said: 'If . . . participation is confined to advice or encouragement [the alleged accessory] must at least communicate his change of mind to the other'), and according to *Becerra* it is insufficient to say 'let's go'. In *Rook* it was said that the accused had to communicate his withdrawal unequivocally. In *Baker* [1994] Crim LR 444 (CA) the words 'I'm not doing it' were held to be equivocal. They could mean, 'I will stay but not do anything after having struck my blows'. The accused had not demonstrated an effective withdrawal by his deeds or words. Similarly in *Nawaz* (1999) *Independent*, 19 May, simply saying that he had withdrawn from the joint enterprise was insufficient. His withdrawal had to be unequivocal, notified to the other participants and included some effort at dissuading the others from proceeding. Perhaps in *Becerra* and *Baker* withdrawal would have been effective only if the accused had sought to restrain the other defendants. If communication is possible, there is no need to go to the police. If no communication is possible, presumably the accused must contact the police. Glanville Williams, *Textbook of Criminal Law*, 2nd edn (Stevens, 1983) 127, quotes from a US case: 'A declared intent to withdraw from a conspiracy to dynamite a building is not enough if the fuse has been set. He must step on the fuse.' (Not in the 3rd edn, edited by Dennis Baker, 2012, Sweet & Maxwell.) Lloyd LJ in *Rook* said, *obiter*, that it was perhaps an effective withdrawal when the accused had done his best to step on the fuses. In other words, the accused must go beyond effectively communicating withdrawal: there must be a negating of the assistance.

The question whether the accused has withdrawn is one for the jury: *Grundy* [1977] Crim LR 543 (CA). In that case the accused gave two men information about a house which they later burgled. Two weeks before the commission of the crime, he had been trying to stop them. There was evidence of an effective withdrawal. It is arguable that on the facts of *Grundy*, as well as some other cases such as *Whitefield*, there should not have been a defence, since the information continued to be valuable after withdrawal. Nevertheless, the Court of Appeal in *O'Flaherty* approved both *Grundy* and *Whitefield*.

The Court of Appeal in *Perman* [1996] 1 Cr App R 24 thought that in a joint enterprise scenario the accused could not withdraw once the criminal activity had begun. The statement was *obiter*. The court postulated that what was thought to be withdrawal in such circumstances was in truth the principal's exceeding the scope of the joint enterprises so that the accused was no longer liable. The Northern Ireland Court of Appeal faced a similar problem in *Graham* [1996] NI 157. In a joint enterprise case it was insufficient to urge that the victim should not be killed. The court did not wish to state what was needed, so the case's value as a precedent is somewhat limited, but it was said *obiter* that even informing the police would probably not be a withdrawal if the perpetrators of the crime, here terrorist murderers, were close to committing the offence. Similarly in *Gallant* [2008] EWCA Crim 1111 merely walking away from a joint enterprise was insufficient to demonstrate withdrawal.

The Court of Appeal in *Mitchell* [1999] Crim LR 496 said without citing authority that communication of withdrawal, while necessary when violence was planned, was not a requirement for withdrawal when the violence was spontaneous. On the facts the court said that the accused had withdrawn when he stopped fighting, threw down the stick he was carrying and walked away. *Mitchell* may be criticised on the grounds that the accused did not seek to put an end to the encouragement he had previously given and that the law of joint enterprise is not based on distinguishing planned and spontaneous violence. In the Court of Appeal in *Robinson*, unreported, 3 February 2000, Otton LJ said that *Mitchell*, in which he had also given the leading judgment, was exceptional. Even when violence was spontaneous, withdrawal must be communicated to give the other the opportunity to desist 'unless it is not practicable or reasonable so to communicate as in . . . *Mitchell* where the accused threw down his weapon and moved away before the final and fatal blows were inflicted'. *Mitchell* was not a joint enterprise case but was applied to a joint enterprise in *O'Flaherty*, above. Two of the defendants who originally attacked the victim did not pursue him with the others into the next street. They did not communicate their withdrawal but simply did not pursue him. The Court of Appeal held, where there was spontaneous violence, there was no need to communicate withdrawal to the others. On this point *O'Flaherty* is contrary to *Robinson*.

Mantell LJ summarised the law in *O'Flaherty*:

> . . . mere repentance does not suffice. To disengage from an incident a person must do enough to demonstrate that he or she is withdrawing from the joint enterprise. This is ultimately a question of fact and degree for the jury. Account will be taken of *inter alia* the nature of the assistance and encouragement already given and how imminent the infliction of the fatal injury or injuries is, as well as the nature of the action said to constitute withdrawal.

Otway [2011] EWCA Crim 3 is one of a lengthy list of recent authorities on joint enterprise, but also exemplifies current law on this issue. The accused was the driver of a car in which the murderer was the passenger; the murderer shot the victim dead. The accused and the murderer were in a joint venture. The issue was whether the words 'Don't smoke him' were sufficient to constitute withdrawal from a joint enterprise. The trial judge directed the jury that: '. . . the withdrawal must be (1) real and effective and (2) it must be communicated . . . in good time.' The Court of Appeal approved the instruction, noting that it was not necessary for the accused 'to restrain the gunman'.

If the accused's repentance is not sincere, as when he has been caught by the police, he is still liable as a counsellor, and even as an abettor if he is still encouraging his partner, as was said to have occurred in the famous case of **Craig and Bentley** (1952) *The Times*, 10–13 December, above. (An alternative is to say that the first defendant went beyond the scope of their joint enterprise by killing a police officer and, therefore, the second defendant was not an accessory to murder.) If the accused is in police custody, he will remain liable for encouragement or assistance previously given: **Johnson and Jones** (1841) 174 ER 479. It is uncertain whether the defence is available when the accused is physically not in a position to countermand his help. Perhaps it should not be, for the help given to the principal remains of use to him.

The previous paragraph spoke of 'repentance', and some English cases do the same. All that that term means is that the accused has to withdraw effectively. There need be no true repentance.

If there is more than one principal offender, it is uncertain whether the accused can withdraw only by unequivocally notifying all of them or whether notice to one is sufficient. Case law on this point would be helpful.

The Law Commission's 2006 recommendations on complicity in murder and manslaughter

The Law Commission published its Report No. 304, *Murder, Manslaughter and Infanticide*, in 2006. In it it proposed that the accused would be liable as an accomplice to first or second degree murder (for details of these two recommended tiers of murder see Chapter 11) if:

> he or she (D) intended to assist or encourage the principal offender (P) to commit the relevant type of murder, (for example, D would be liable for a first degree murder committed by P if D intended that P should or foresaw that he or she might commit the conduct element of first degree murder with the required fault element of first degree murder) or D was engaged in a joint criminal venture with P and realised that P might commit the relevant offence of murder.

There would be no need for a common purpose agreed on by D and P beforehand to fall within the 'joint criminal venture' proposal; it would be sufficient that D was encouraging or assisting P to commit a crime. In this regard the statutory reformulation would be the same as currently exists at common law. The Commission opined (at para. 4.11) that: 'D carries the additional fault of being involved in a joint venture with P to commit a crime. Individuals who perform a criminal act in groups have been shown to be more disposed to act violently than those who act alone, and this can be taken to be common knowledge.' It should also be noted that D would be liable as an accomplice to first degree murder, even though he or she did not intend to kill or did not intend to cause serious injury being aware that there was a serious risk of death, the proposed mental states for first degree murder. In this respect D would as now be liable for first degree murder even though he or she did not have the *mens rea* for it, whereas the perpetrator (P) would of course have to have the requisite *mens rea*.

The Commission foreshadowed in the 2006 Report its 2007 Report *Participating in Crime*, which recommended defences of acting in order to prevent the commission of the crime and acting in order to prevent or limit the occurrence of harm, and these defences will apply to fatal offences as well as other crimes. In this respect the harshness of the current and proposed rule about complicity as a joint venturer in a first degree murder would be mitigated. Similarly, there may be circumstances in which the murder came to be committed which are 'too remote from what D anticipated to make it right to regard the murder as within the foreseen scope of the joint venture. The question will be a matter of fact and degree for the jury to decide' (para. 4.30, footnote omitted). The sentence for first degree murder whether committed by the principal or the secondary offender would be mandatory life imprisonment; for second degree murder it would be a discretionary life sentence.

This proposal would rectify the anomaly whereby if D and P were involved in a joint venture and P committed a murder which D did not foresee, D would escape all criminal liability. In the words of the Law Commission (para. 4.5): 'This treats D too generously if D was aware that P meant to do *some* harm to V [the victim], even if D did not realise that P might commit murder.'

In relation to manslaughter, the third tier of non-fatal offences, the Commission proposed that D should be liable for manslaughter if:

D and P were parties to a joint venture,

P committed the crime of first degree or second degree murder when fulfilling that common purpose,

D intended or foresaw that (non-serious) harm or the fear of harm might be caused by P, and

'a reasonable person in D's position, with D's knowledge of the relevant facts, would have foreseen an obvious risk of death or serious injury being caused by a party to the venture.' (para. 4.6)

This offence would be called 'manslaughter'. There was some argument in the Consultation Paper No. 177, *A New Homicide Act for England and Wales?*, 2005, which preceded this Report that the crime should be called 'complicity in an unlawful killing' but in its Report the Commission settled on manslaughter. The concept of a 'reasonable person in D's position' in the proposed definition would include D's age, but which other factors would be taken into account by the jury would be determined on a case-by-case basis.

The Law Commission's 2007 Report No. 306, *Participating in Crime*

The Commission's proposals in Report No. 306 were not intended to replace but to supplement those in the 2006 Report on complicity in murder. The 2007 Report may be seen as a partner to the Law Commission Report No. 300, *Inchoate Liability for Assisting and Encouraging Crime*, 2006. The relationship between inchoate offences and secondary offences forms the crux of the Report: without the recommendations on inchoate liability the proposals on secondary offences would not have seen the light of day. For that reason, the two Reports must be read together, and the Law Commission's view was that they stood together. The previous government took the view that they did not. It had already enacted the Serious Crime Act 2007, which replaced the common law inchoate offence of incitement. The Act is based on, but does not completely follow, Report No. 300.

Introduction

The Law Commission's Report focused on the situation where one party assists or encourages another to commit a crime, the principal offence, and that offence is completed. Where the principal offence is not completed, there is the possibility of inchoate liability at present for incitement to commit the principal offence, but when the principal offence is completed, secondary liability occurs, and the secondary offender is liable to be prosecuted as if she were a principal offender and is subject to the same potential punishment as the principal offender. Also included, at least arguably within secondary offending, is the doctrine of joint enterprise which occurs when the secondary party agrees to commit an offence with the principal party. These are the areas covered by the Report.

The starting point is the proposal in the 2006 Report to extend the law of inchoate liability. At that time there was such liability for encouraging the principal offender to commit the principal offence when that offence was not committed, but none such for assisting her to do so. The 2006 Report recommended that inchoate liability be extended to assistance. As the Law Commission puts it in para. 1.3 of the 2007 Report:

> This recommendation now enables the problem of secondary liability's scope to be addressed along with problems that have arisen in relation to the very nature of such liability, without the distraction of a simultaneous concern with the nature and scope of inchoate liability.

The effect of enacting both Reports, the Commission opined at para. 1.41, would result in 'a scheme whereby inchoate and secondary liability will support and supplement each other in a way that is rational and fair'. The new law would replace one which is 'permeated with uncertainty' (para. 1.12).

The defects of current law

The Report begins with a critique of current law, in particular how the secondary party may be liable for the crime the principal party has committed even though she did not personally commit that offence but merely aided, abetted, counselled or procured it, yet she is liable as if she did personally commit the offence. For example, the principal offender's *mens rea* for murder is the intent to kill or cause grievous bodily harm but the secondary party is liable for murder with a lesser *mens rea*, the belief that the principal may commit the offence. The Commission recommends that in order for there to be 'parity of culpability' between the principal and secondary offenders the latter should be convicted as a secondary offender only if she intended that the principal would commit the offence; otherwise, the person who is now the secondary offender would become guilty of the recommended offence of assisting or encouraging the principal offence. However, where there is a joint venture, the Commission's view is that the secondary party should be liable as such because she has agreed or did intend to join in the criminal venture, and that agreement or intent constitutes 'parity of culpability' with the principal offender: if, for example, the secondary party in a joint enterprise foresaw that the principal offender might kill, she is appropriately labelled as a murderer just as much as is the principal offender who did kill and did intend to kill. The Commission says at para. 1.23 that:

> ... the mere fact of agreement is sufficient to render D [the accused] liable for the agreed offence, with no requirement that D does anything further by way of encouragement or assistance. By contrast, where D and P [the principal offender] are not parties to a joint criminal venture, there must be a discrete act of encouragement or assistance.

For this reason, the draft Bill attached to the Report deals with joint ventures separately from other instances of secondary participation.

A second criticism the Commission has of secondary liability is the definition of the *mens rea* and the defences possibly available to the accused. The Commission does not comment on the law in depth in the main part of the Report, but it does in Annexe B when discussing the present law, and comment on the position is picked up below when the recommendations are discussed. In summary, there is debate as to whether or not the accused is guilty if she foresaw that the principal might (rather than *would*) commit the principal offence; there is also controversy as to when the accused is guilty or not guilty when the principal commits an offence which is different from that agreed, a so-called 'collateral' offence: is the collateral offence 'fundamentally different' from the crime agreed?; also debatable is the liability of the secondary party for a string of offences, for example, if she loans the principal a gun for use on one occasion, is she liable on each occasion the principal uses it to kill others? The Commission refers to other points of difficulty: when is the accused liable as a secondary offender when she stands by and omits to control the principal's commission of the principal offence? Is the accused not guilty if she performs a duty imposed on her by law? For example, in *NCB* v *Gamble* [1959] QB 11 (DC), Devlin J said that the accused was not criminally liable if she returned the jemmy in the following circumstances (Law Commission Report, para. 1.19): 'P [the principal offender] lends D [the potential secondary party] a jemmy. Later P demands the jemmy back. D knows that P intends to use the jemmy to burgle V's [the victim's] premises. D, who hates V, returns the jemmy so that P can commit the burglary. P commits the burglary.' Further issues are noted by the Commission. One is the scope of the doctrine of innocent agency when the vagaries of the English language can lead to difficulties. This problem is well put by the Commission at para. 1.29:

> The problem, actual or perceived, has arisen when the principal offence can be committed only by a person who meets a particular description and D [the person who would normally be the secondary offender] does not meet that description. For example, where D, who is not married, causes X [the person who normally would be the principal party], who is married, to 'marry' V [the victim] by falsely telling X that his wife has died. On one view, convicting D as a principal [as the doctrine of innocent agency would normally lead to] is illogical because the definition of bigamy stipulates that a principal offender can commit the offence only if he or she is already married.

Finally, and again to quote the Law Commission (para. 1.30):

> if D 'procures' the commission of a no-fault [strict liability] offence by P, P is guilty of the offence as a principal party and D is guilty as a secondary party. However, in our view, holding D liable for the offence as a secondary party does not accurately reflect the nature of D's wrongdoing. This is because in reality D commits the offence through P.

The Commission proposed a new offence to deal with this situation.

The proposals

The question then becomes one of how to deal with these issues. The 1993 Law Commission Consultation Paper, *Assisting and Encouraging Crime*, recommended the abolition of secondary offences. However, the Commission now proposes to retain the area of law but in a modified form, as it had already said in its 2006 Report. There are (para. 1.38):

> cases where D's culpability was such that D would be insufficiently condemned and labelled if he or she was convicted of merely assisting or encouraging the commission of the principal offence rather than convicted of the offence itself. The obvious case, particularly it is D who is the instigator, is where D assists or encourages P with the intention that P should commit the principal offence.

The other advantage of retaining secondary liability occurs when it is not possible to prove which party was the principal offender and which the secondary one: at present it is irrelevant if the accused was the principal or secondary offender provided she must be one or the other. Abolishing secondary liability in favour of (mere) assisting or encouraging would abrogate this forensic advantage.

The Commission's solutions to the problems around secondary liability are to be found in one of the draft Bills attached to the Report. The proposals are:

- a crime of assisting or encouraging the principal party (see the discussion of encouraging and assisting in the chapter on inchoate offences): the accused's *mens rea* would be that she intended (as defined in Chapter 3: see **Woollin** [1999] 1 AC 82 (HL)) the principal offence to be committed (clause 1);

- a crime whereby the accused would be liable for any crime, agreed or collateral, carried out during a criminal venture: the mens rea would be that the accused foresaw that the offence might be committed (clause 2).

There would also be a clause dealing with innocent agency and the current doctrine would be abolished. The Commission stated (para. 1.52):

> D would be liable for an offence as a principal offender if he or she intentionally causes P, an innocent agent, to commit the conduct element [i.e. the *actus reus*] of an offence but P does not commit the offence because P:
> 1 is under the age of 10 years;
> 2 has a defence of insanity; or
> 3 acts without the fault required to be convicted of the offence.

The Commission adds in the next paragraph that the recommendations 'would ensure that D could be convicted of a principal offence as a principal offender even if the offence can only be committed by a person who meets a particular description and D does not fit that description'. In this way the Commission deals with the illustration of the bachelor boy and bigamy mentioned above. The Commission also proposes to address the issue, also mentioned above, of the accused who currently is guilty of being a secondary party to a strict offence committed by the principal. Instead the accused will be guilty as a principal offender. One effect of the scheme is that procuring in the sense of intentionally *causing* the principal to commit the crime will no longer form part of *secondary* liability. Instead, the accused will be guilty as *principal*.

The Commission next proposes to refine the defences to the new offences. First, the **Tyrrell** exception discussed above is preserved. Clause 6 of the draft Bill will exculpate the accused (whether as a secondary party or as a principal offender through the doctrine of innocent agency) if the principal offence is aimed at protecting a class of persons and she falls within that class and she is the victim of the offence. Secondly, the Commission proposes a defence when the accused acts to prevent the commission of an offence or to prevent or limit the harm. The burden of proof in respect of this defence would lie on the accused, and it would be question for the jury as to whether the accused did act reasonably. The Commission provides the following example of the application of this defence in para. 1.59:

> D and P are at a pub after a football match and meet a rival gang of supporters. P, along with some others, plans to attack the rival gang and stab their most vocal member (V). D, who does not want V to be harmed, manages to persuade P and the others to damage an item of V's property instead. D is charged with encouraging P to commit criminal damage.

It would be for the jury to take all the facts into account, for example how serious was the harm prevented? Should the accused have called the police?

For the previous government's reply, see the Ministry of Justice's *Murder, Manslaughter and Infanticide: Proposals for Reform of the Law*, 2009.

Assisting an offender and compounding an arrestable offence

By s 4(1) of the Criminal Law Act 1967:

> [w]here a person has committed an arrestable offence, any other person who, knowing or believing him to be guilty of the offence or of some other arrestable offence, does without lawful authority or reasonable excuse any act with intent to impede his apprehension or prosecution shall be guilty of an offence . . .

It does not matter that the alleged principal offender has been acquitted (***Donald*** (1986) 83 Cr App R 49 (DC) *obiter* and ***Zaman*** [2010] EWCA Crim 209 as a matter of *ratio*), provided that in the accused's trial it can be proved that the accused was guilty. ***Saunders*** [2011] EWCA Crim 1571 confirms the law in ***Donald*** and ***Zaman***. This law applies even though the other party charged is acquitted in the same trial as that in which the accused is convicted.

It is uncertain whether the opening words refer solely to the perpetrator of the offence or whether the phrase covers an accessory.

The *actus reus* includes 'any act'. Obvious examples include shielding the principal, destroying evidence, telling lies to the police about the whereabouts of the principal and providing a getaway car or a passport. The accused need not in fact do something which assists the offender. It is sufficient that the act is done with the intent required. Since an act is required, an omission to inform the police of the whereabouts of the principal offender does not give rise to liability. The *mens rea* comprises the intention to impede and knowledge or belief. The phrase 'with intent to' may mean that only direct intent is included (see Chapter 2) and not even foresight that the act is a (virtually) certain consequence is sufficient. 'Knowing or believing' may cover wilful blindness but not, it is thought, recklessness (see further Chapter 3 for knowledge and wilful blindness). The same phrase occurs in the crime of handling, and precedents from that offence may be relevant to the interpretation of s 4(1). The accused need not know the identity of the principal: ***Brindley*** [1971] 2 QB 300 (CA). The defence of lawful authority will cover a decision by the Crown Prosecution Service to abandon a prosecution. It has been suggested that 'reasonable excuse' may include a wife helping her husband: see D. Ormerod, *Smith and Hogan's Criminal Law*, 13th edn (Oxford University Press, 2011) 251, n. 36. There is no liability for attempting this offence: Criminal Attempts Act 1981, s 1(4)(c).

The best known authority on s 4(1) is ***Sherif*** [2008] EWCA Crim 2653, which deals with the consequences of '21/7', 21 July 2005, a fortnight after the '7/7' terrorism attacks on London Underground and buses. On 21/7 the bombs failed to explode on three tube trains, a bus, and in a copse in London. Part of the case involved, for example, supplying a burka to a male attempted killer so that he could escape from Golders Green coach station to Birmingham.

By s 5(1) of the same Act:

> [w]here a person has committed an arrestable offence, any other person who, knowing or believing that the offence or some other arrestable offence has been committed, and that he has information which might be of material assistance in securing the prosecution or conviction of an offender for it, accepts or agrees to accept for not disclosing that information any consideration other than the making good of loss or injury caused by the offence, or the making of reasonable compensation for that loss or injury shall be liable . . .

The word 'consideration' is well known in the law of contract. It will certainly include money and benefits in kind. 'Knowing or believing' bears the same meaning as in s 4(1). There is no requirement of 'with intent to' in s 5(1). Like s 4(1) this offence cannot be attempted: Criminal Attempts Act 1981, s 1(4)(c). A person is not guilty of the s 5(1) offence simply by not reporting an arrestable offence but there is a common law offence, misprision of treason, for failing to report treason. No prosecution may be brought for this offence without the DPP's consent.

Summary

- *Definitions*: The principal offender is the one who commits the principal offence: he or she stabs the victim, burns the house down, rapes the complainant. Other people, accessories, accomplices, or secondary parties, may in various ways encourage or assist the principal. For example, they may hand over the knife, shout words of encouragement to the perpetrator of the arson on the house, or hold the victim down in the crime of rape. The accomplice is liable to the same maximum sentence as the principal, but his or her culpability will affect the sentence. The accomplice may be liable for being a secondary party to an offence more serious than that committed by the principal. The theory behind secondary offences is that the principal offence must have been committed before there can be a secondary offence: this is the doctrine of 'derivative liability'. For example, one cannot be an accessory to murder until the killing has taken place. (One may be guilty of conspiring to murder, incitement to murder or attempted murder if the killing has not yet taken place.) However, the theory of derivative liability is sometimes not followed.

  An aider is one who assists, helps or supports the principal party, as when he or she supplies a gun. An abettor would seem to be the same but perhaps the term is more apt to cover those who encourage, incite or instigate the commission of the principal offence. A counsellor is one who gives advice or assistance.

  It has to be said that the distinctions between these forms of secondary liability are hard to find or non-existent. However, there is one form of secondary liability which is more certainly defined than the other three and that is 'procuring'. A procurer is one who produces an outcome by 'endeavour', as the cases put it.

- *Failure to act*: Normally, as we saw in Chapter 2, there is no criminal responsibility for omissions, subject to the imposition of duties to act. One exception is where the accused, the secondary offender, has control over the perpetrator, as occurs when a driving instructor fails to control his or her learner.

- Mens rea: The mental element for accessories is complex but it may be stated as: (i) the intent to advise, assist or encourage; and (ii) knowledge of the 'essential matters' of the principal offence (though recklessness would also seem to suffice); and (iii) in cases where there is more than one offence within the accused's contemplation, knowledge that that offence may take place.

- *Joint enterprise liability*: In recent years some judges have taken the view that where two or more set out to commit a crime (e.g. burglary) and one of them goes further (and, for example, kills), there is a doctrine of joint enterprise separate from that of liability of accessories which governs the liability of the party who did not commit the principal offence (here, murder). The stance taken in this book is that there are not two separate doctrines but that joint enterprise is a subset of secondary liability, but differences reside, not in the substantive law, but in ease of proof.

- *Non-conviction of the principal*: Because secondary liability is based on the theory of derivative liability, difficulties are faced when the person who would otherwise be the principal is acquitted, is exempt from liability or did not commit the *actus reus*. If there is no *actus reus*, there can be no accessorial liability; if, however, the person who would otherwise be the principal party is exempt, there is an *actus reus* – it's just that the accused cannot be convicted of it – and therefore the accessory may be convicted.

- *May the victim be an accessory?* In general there is no problem. For example, if a masochist incites a sadist to perform sadistic acts on him or her, the masochist can be guilty of being an accomplice to the principal's crime. However, statutory crimes may be interpreted as protecting members of a certain class. In that event the person who would otherwise be the secondary offender is not liable because he or she is protected. The usual illustration is that of girls under 16 who encourage boys over 16 to have sexual intercourse with them; the girls form a specially protected class and are not liable as accessories to boys' crimes.

- *Innocent agency*: If the person who would otherwise be the principal is a child under 10 or insane, the accessory is deemed to be the principal. For example, if Peter helps Queenie to commit burglary, normally Peter is the accessory to Queenie's principal; if, however, she is insane, Peter as it were steps into her shoes and he becomes principal. In law Queenie is said to be the innocent agent.

- *Withdrawal*: There is a defence if the accused withdraws before the commission of the principal offence. The boundaries of the defence seem to vary with the facts. It may consist of simply communicating the fact of withdrawal, stopping the offence or informing the police.

- *Assisting an offender and compounding an arrestable offence*: The crime of being an accessory after the fact was abolished in 1967 and partly replaced by assisting an offender (to avoid apprehension or prosecution for an arrestable offence) and by not revealing information 'which might be of material assistance in securing the prosecution or conviction of an offender' for an arrestable offence in return for consideration such as money. The latter crime is known as 'compounding' or 'compounding an arrestable offence'.

References

Reports

Judicial Studies Board, *Specimen Direction on Joint Responsibility*

Justice Committee, Eleventh Report, *Joint Enterprise*, 2012. The Written Evidence has also been published. Graham Virgo's synopsis of criticisms of the law is something of a *tour de force* but all is worth reading, especially the letters from those imprisoned through the joint enterprise doctrine.

Law Commission Consultation Paper no. 131, *Assisting and Encouraging Crime* (1993)

Law Commission Consultation Paper no. 177, *A New Homicide Act for England and Wales?* (2005)

Law Commission Report no. 177, *A Criminal Code for England and Wales* (1989)

Law Commission Report nos. 279 and 282, *Children: Their Non-Accidental Death or Serious Injury (Criminal Trials)* (2003)

Law Commission Report no. 300, *Inchoate Liability for Assisting and Encouraging Crime* (2006)

Law Commission Report no. 304, *Murder, Manslaughter and Infanticide* (2006)

Law Commission Report no. 306, *Participating in Crime* (2007)

Ministry of Justice, *Murder, Manslaughter and Infanticide: Proposals for Reform of the Law* (2009)

Books

Baker, D. *Glanville Williams – Textbook of Criminal Law*, 3rd edn (Sweet & Maxwell, 2012)

Mitchell, B. *Law Relating to Violent Crime* (CLT Publishing, 1997)

Ormerod, D. *Smith and Hogan's Criminal Law*, 13th edn (Oxford University Press, 2011)

Williams, G. *Textbook of Criminal Law*, 2nd edn (Stevens, 1983)

Journals

Simester, A.P. 'The mental element in complicity' (2006) 122 LQR 578

Smith, J.C. 'Criminal liability of accessories: law and law reform' (1997) 113 LQR 453

Smith, J.C. 'Secondary participation in crime – can we do without it?' [1994] NLJ 679

Further reading

Beaumont, J. 'Abetting without a principal' (1977) 30 NILQ 1

Bohlander, M. 'The Sexual Offences Act 2003 – the *Tyrrell* principle – criminalizing the victims' [2005] Crim LR 701

Buxton, R. 'Complicity in the Criminal Code' (1969) 85 LQR 252

Buxton, R. 'Being an accessory to one's own murder' [2012] Crim LR 275

Clarkson, C.M.V. 'Complicity, *Powell* and manslaughter' [1998] Crim LR 556

Cunningham, S. 'Complicating complicity: Aiding and abetting causing death by dangerous driving in R v Martin' (2011) 74 MLR 767

Giles, M. 'Complicity – the problem of joint enterprise' [1990] Crim LR 383

Kadish, S.H. 'Reckless complicity' (1997) 87 JCL & Crim 369

Krebs, B. 'Joint criminal enterprise' (2010) 73 MLR 578

Lanham, D. 'Accomplices and withdrawal' (1981) 97 LQR 575

Lanham, D. 'Primary and derivative criminal liability – an Australian perspective' [2000] Crim LR 707

Mitchell, B. and Roberts, J.V. *Public Opinion and Sentencing for Murder: An Empirical Investigation of Public Knowledge and Attitudes in England and Wales* (Nuffield Foundation, 2010) (on joint enterprise killing)

Ormerod, D. 'Joint enterprise: in course of a joint enterprise to inflict unlawful violence the principal kills with an intention to kill which is unknown and unforeseen by a secondary party' [2007] Crim LR 721

Ormerod, D. Case comments on *Rahman* [2008] Crim LR 979, *Yemoh* [2009] Crim LR 888, *Lewis* [2010] Crim LR 870, *Mendez* [2010] Crim LR 874, and *Stringer* [2011] Crim LR 887

Smith, J.C. Commentary on *Wan* [1995] Crim LR 297

Smith, J.C. 'Joint enterprise and secondary liability' (1999) 50 NILQ 153

Smith, K.J.M. 'Complicity and causation' [1986] Crim LR 663

Smith, K.J.M. 'Withdrawal in complicity: a restatement of principles' [2001] Crim LR 769

Sullivan, G.R. 'Complicity for first degree murder and complicity in an unlawful killing' [2006] Crim LR 502

Sullivan, G.R. 'Inchoate liability for assisting and encouraging crime' [2006] Crim LR 1047

Sullivan G.R. 'Participation in crime: Law Com No. 305 – joint enterprise' [2008] Crim LR 19

Taylor, R. 'Procuring, causation, innocent agency and the Law Commission' [2008] Crim LR 32

Virgo, G. Casenote on *Grango* [2012] Crim LR 850

Williams, G. 'Which of you did it?' (1989) 52 MLR 179

Williams, G. 'Letting offences happen' [1990] Crim LR 780

Williams, G. 'Victims and other exempt parties in crime' (1990) 10 LS 245

Wilson, W. 'A rational scheme of liability for participating in crime' [2008] Crim LR 3

The principal work is K.J.M. Smith, *A Modern Treatise on the Law of Criminal Complicity* (Clarendon, 1991). A more theoretical approach is found in W. Wilson, *Central Issues in Criminal Theory* (Hart, 2002), ch. 7.

For the problem of parents and the like killing children, see the Law Commission's Report, *Children: Their Non-accidental Death or Serious Injury (Criminal Trials)*, Law Com. No. 282, 2003, which was preceded by a Consultative Report, Law Com. No. 279, 2003. The government did not faithfully carry out the Commission's recommendations in the Domestic Violence, Crime and Victims Act 2004.

For an Australian view, see New South Wales Law Reform Commission Report Paper 2, *Complicity* (2008)

Visit **www.mylawchamber.co.uk** to access tools to help you develop and test your knowledge of criminal law, including interactive multiple choice questions, practice exam questions with guidance, annotated weblinks, glossary flashcards, legal newsfeed and legal updates.

Use Case Navigator to read in full some of the key cases referenced in this chapter with commentary and questions:

R v Brown [1994] 1 AC 212
R v Rahman and Others [2008] UKHL 45

6

Vicarious and corporate liability

Aims and objectives

After reading this chapter you will understand and be able to critique:

- the doctrine of vicarious liability: when it applies and when it does not
- the doctrine of corporate liability and the crimes for which a company cannot be liable
- the Corporate Manslaughter and Corporate Homicide Act 2007

Introduction to vicarious liability

Example

The Metropolitan Police Act 1839 s 44 makes it an offence for an accused knowingly to permit prostitutes to gather in a place of refreshment. The accused was the owner of a cafe where prostitutes had gathered in the past. He instructed his manager not to allow them to do so and he put up notices in the cafe instructing prostitutes not to gather together there. Prostitutes did gather in the cafe nevertheless. Was the owner guilty under the 1844 statute?

These facts are based on *Allen* v *Whitehead* [1930] 1 KB 211 (DC). Despite the notices and the instruction the owner was vicariously liable for what his manager had done, knowingly permitting prostitutes to gather in a place of refreshment. He is liable for the acts and state of mind of another via the delegation principle and the *actus reus* and *mens rea* of the manager is attributed to the owner. Note that the doctrine applies despite the accused's telling the manager not to serve prostitutes and even when the employer had taken all practicable care to select a good employee to run the cafe.

In criminal law one person is not generally speaking liable for the crimes of another. This accords with Judaeo–Christian morality: why should a person be guilty of another's crimes? Normally only one person is criminally liable for acts or omissions. An example is the decision of the Lords in *Seaboard Offshore Ltd* v *Secretary of State for Transport* [1994] 2 All ER 99. After the Zeebrugge ferry disaster, in which almost 200 were killed when a roll-on roll-off ferry sank off the Belgian coast, a new crime was introduced, failure by the owner or charterer of a ship to take all reasonable steps to ensure that it is operated in a safe manner. 'Reasonable' is defined as 'reasonable for him to take in the circumstances of the case'. The House of Lords held that the crime did not permit **vicarious liability**, emphasis being put on the phrase 'for him'. Therefore, the shipowner or charterer was not guilty when the crew or officers of the company operated the ship in an unsafe way. The duty was personal to the owner or charterer. Lord Keith noted that it would have been strange if Parliament had imposed liability on owners and charterers for all actions of their subordinates including failures by cabin stewards to close portholes. There are exceptions, and those exceptions form the topic of vicarious liability.

There is a doctrine of the same name in the law of tort, but the width of the two sets of law is different. In tort employers are usually liable for the tort of their employees committed in the course of their employment. In criminal law liability is exceptional because as a general rule liability and therefore the stigma of being convicted of an offence is personal to the accused. The old case of *Huggins* (1730) 92 ER 518, where the accused, warden of the Fleet prison, London, was acquitted of murder when the victim's death had been caused by his incarceration in an unhealthy cell by a gaoler, exemplifies the distinction. The warden did not know of the facts. In tort he would be liable; in criminal law he was not guilty. The gaoler and the warden, in the words of the court, 'must each answer for their own acts and stand or fall by their own behaviour'. The next section deals with the exceptions where a person is vicariously liable.

The exceptions are aimed at obliging the accused to exercise control over others, but it may be unfair to penalise someone for what another has done and the accused may not be deterred in the future. The perpetrator will also be guilty of the offence either as a principal or as an accessory.

The exceptions

(a) At common law two offences give rise to vicarious liability. The exception of public nuisance was established in *Stephens* (1866) LR 1 QB 702. Since the aim of the prosecution was not to punish the accused but to prevent the continuation of the nuisance, the accused was guilty when his servants had dumped rubbish into a river and thereby obstructed navigation. The court argued that the proceedings were in substance civil in character: it was as if the civil law doctrine of vicarious liability applied. It is assumed that if the proceedings are in truth criminal, the doctrine may not apply. It is difficult to distinguish criminal and civil objectives. Vicarious liability applies even though the employee disobeyed the employers' orders not to commit the nuisance. Certainly *Stephens* is not applicable to statutory nuisances, where the accused is guilty only when the words of the statute so demand. The other common law crime importing vicarious liability is criminal libel: see *Holbrook* (1878) 4 QBD 42. The accused is liable for the acts of his employees in publishing a criminal libel only if he acted negligently: Libel Act 1843, s 7.

(b) Some statutes expressly make one party liable for the acts of another. For example, the Transport Act 1982, s 31, conclusively presumes that the owner of a vehicle was the driver at the time of the commission of certain offences, but the owner can avoid liability by proving that another person was driving without his consent. An accused, the licensee of premises, is guilty of a crime if either he or his servant sells intoxicating liquor to a person out of permitted hours.

(c) Sometimes Acts of Parliament are construed so as to make one person liable for the acts of another. For this reason the principle is sometimes known as 'extensive construction'. The Law Commission in its Consultation Paper No. 135, *Involuntary Manslaughter,*

1994, called it 'extended construction'. There is no need for the relationship to be that of employer and employee (see below). This type of liability arises where the duty is said to be absolute, that is, personal to the accused. He cannot escape responsibility for delegating the obligation to another. In this sense the liability of the accused is personal, not vicarious. This type of vicarious liability works only when the statute creates a strict offence. (If the offence is not strict, the fourth exception, below, may be applicable.) The principal is liable for the physical acts of his agent, but not for his mental element. In order to see whether this principle applies, the court in *Mousell Bros* v *LNWR* [1917] 2 KB 836 (KBD) held that the aim of the Act, its words, and the nature of the duty had to be investigated as well as 'the person upon whom it is imposed, the person for whom it would in ordinary circumstances be performed, and the person upon whom the penalty is imposed'. This is an example.

Duke of Leinster [1924] 1 KB 311

An undisclosed bankrupt was convicted under s 155 of the Bankruptcy Act 1914 of obtaining credit of more than £10 without disclosing his financial situation. He was guilty, even though he had told his agent not to obtain such credit.

Among words which have given rise to this form of vicarious liability is 'use'. Employers 'use' a vehicle when an employee or independent contractor drives it: *Green* v *Burnett* [1955] 1 QB 78 (DC) (using a motor vehicle with a defective brake) and *Hallett Silberman Ltd* v *Cheshire CC* [1993] RTR 32 (DC). Both the employers and the driver 'use' the vehicle. Another word so interpreted is 'sell'. Employers are guilty of selling something which it is unlawful to sell (such as cigarettes to a person under 16) when the actual sale is made by an employee: *Coppen* v *Moore (No. 2)* [1898] 2 QB 306 (QBD). It does not matter that the employers did not know of the sale (or use) and were not even in the country at the time. An alternative approach to cases such as this is to say that the employers are the legal owners of the items sold; only they can sell them; they sell through the medium of the sales assistants; therefore, they are directly, not vicariously, liable. Employers also possess an item though it is their employee who controls it in fact. They supply a video to underage persons and possess goods through their employees. The accused is deemed to have done the unlawful act despite not having been physically the actor. For example, a person, including a company, can cause pollution to enter a river, even though the individual who actually did pollute the river was an employee. Some activities, however, cannot be interpreted as making the employers or principals liable. It is thought that such persons do not 'drive' when it is their employee's or agent's hands which are on the steering wheel. (Compare *Thornton* v *Mitchell* [1940] 1 All ER 339 (KBD), discussed in the previous chapter.) There has been little discussion in the courts as to why some words are interpreted to impose liability and some are not.

Besides the restriction that the verb must as a matter of English language be referable to the accused, the act must be within the course of employment or agency. For example, if the employee of an estate agency takes an illegal premium for a tenancy, the employer is not liable because the employee has no authority to take one: *Barker* v *Levinson* [1951] 1 KB 342 (DC). Cf. cases such as *Coppen* v *Moore (No. 2)*, above, which involve doing an authorised act, selling, in an unauthorised manner. The taking of the premium was not a way of doing the job, whereas using a car is a way of doing it. As in tort law a defendant is liable even though the delegate acted contrary to instructions, as

Coppen v *Moore (No. 2)* illustrates. However, employers would not be using a vehicle when the accused was on a frolic of his own such as when he is driving his family to the seaside on a summer Sunday.

It should be noted that this extensive construction principle has been said not to apply to licensing offences: *McKenna* v *Harding* (1905) 69 JP 354. Also under this principle the verb or adverb must not import *mens rea* as, for instance, 'allowing' (see *DPP* v *Kellet* [1994] Crim LR 916 (DC) but cf. *Greener* (1996) 160 JP 265 (DC) which is *contra*) and 'knowingly' usually do. As *Coppen* v *Moore (No. 2)* demonstrates, the accused remains liable even though he has forbidden the employee to do the forbidden act, in this case to sell American ham as 'Scotch ham'. The House of Lords approved this principle in *Director General of Fair Trading* v *Pioneer Concrete (UK) Ltd* [1995] 1 AC 456, a case on contempt of court.

The ability to get at the owner is especially useful where there are several branches. Since the accused is not in direct control of each branch, he would not be liable if the prosecution had to prove that he knew of the wrongdoing. However, the view of Card, Cross and Jones, *Criminal Law*, 20th edn (Oxford University Press, 2012), 781, 818, should be mentioned:

> It seems that under the extensive construction principle only the act of the employee etc., and not his *mens rea*, can be imputed to the employer etc. The result is that the principle is limited to offences of strict liability.

It should be noted that this exception is not restricted to the employer/employee relationship but includes, for example, the co-licensee of a refreshment house: *Linnett* v *MPC* [1946] KB 290 (DC). Other instances include club committee members for bar staff, employers for sub-contractors, partners for partners, and principals for agents. The issue is whether one person had control over another.

It should also be noted that extensive construction is not in truth an instance of vicarious liability but of personal liability. The act of one person is treated as if it were the act of the accused.

(d) The fourth exception is the delegation principle, which may make the accused vicariously liable when the offence is a *mens rea* one. Unlike in the third exception *mens rea* is attributed to the employers, or principals, or other delegators. The employer is liable for breach of a duty which statute has placed on him. Without this doctrine defendants could escape criminal liability by delegating their duties and the criminal law would be rendered unenforceable. The main, perhaps sole, use of this doctrine is in relation to licensees, and the Court of Appeal in *St Regis Paper Co Ltd* [2012] 1 Cr App R 14 refused to extend the doctrine beyond licensing cases.

An authority is *Allen* v *Whitehead*.

Allen v *Whitehead* [1930] 1 KB 211(DC)

The accused employed a manager to run a cafe in London. He instructed him not to allow prostitutes to gather on the premises, and visited the cafe once or twice daily. On eight consecutive days prostitutes stayed there from 8 p.m. to 4 a.m. He was held to be guilty of knowingly permitting prostitutes to remain in a place of refreshment, contrary to s 44 of the Metropolitan Police Act 1839. He was guilty even though his manager had flouted his instructions, even though he had put up notices telling prostitutes not to sit in the cafe, and even though he did not know that prostitutes had gathered together. (The manager could be convicted of being an accessory.)

The delegator is convicted for not doing anything (an omission), and even if he forbade the act. Lord Hewart CJ said that if the accused was not guilty, 'this statute would be rendered nugatory'. If there is delegation the accused is guilty whether he is in the next room or in the next county. The accused is liable vicariously even for the acts of employees low in the hierarchy and even though he is well away from the premises.

The doctrine ensures that natural and juristic persons do not escape liability when they have delegated a duty to low-level workers but it should be noted that the doctrine applies even though the accused has taken great care in selecting his employees. Most cases in this area, including **Allen v Whitehead**, are concerned with keeping certain premises or licensing offences.

Sopp v Long [1970] 1 QB 518 (DC)

The accused was secretary to a firm which ran the station buffet at Windsor. The manageress gave a short measure of whisky. The accused was convicted under s 24(1) of the Weights and Measures Act 1963. He 'sold' the whisky, which was served by the person on the spot, to whom the running of the premises had been delegated.

If the third exception, extensive construction, applied to licensing offences, the position would have been that the licence-holder 'sold' within the meaning of the statute. *Sopp v Long* illustrates that the delegation principle applies to sub-delegates. If one person, the licensee, delegates the running of a restaurant to another who sub-delegates it to a third party, the licensee is liable by means of this principle for the acts of the third party.

To the delegation principle there are three restrictions:

(i) *The delegation must be complete*. The landmark case is the House of Lords authority of **Vane v Yiannopoullos**.

Vane v Yiannopoullos [1965] AC 486

The accused, a restaurateur, held a licence under which he could serve alcohol only to persons taking meals. He ordered his staff to stick to the terms of the licence. One waitress did not follow his instructions. By a three to two majority and with little enthusiasm for the doctrine, the House of Lords held that there was only a partial delegation, which was not sufficient for conviction. The accused was not on the floor where the alcohol was served, but was on the premises.

Power must be generally delegated: **Winson** [1969] 1 QB 371 (CA), following *dicta* of Lords Reid and Evershed, two of the majority in **Vane**. Accordingly, on the facts of **Allen v Whitehead**, above, if the accused has not delegated control fully, he will not be guilty of allowing prostitutes to gather, even if he ought to have known of their presence and even if he was in control.

The line between 'complete' or 'general' and 'partial' delegation may not be easy to draw on the facts of cases. The case to compare with **Vane** is **Howker v Robinson** [1972] 2 All ER 786 (DC). A licensee, the accused, delegated the running of the lounge bar to a barman, but kept control of the public bar. Alcohol was served to a person under 18. The licensee was held to be guilty. The facts do not look like complete delegation and the outcome appears inconsistent with **Vane**. **Howker** can be supported on the ground that the question of delegation is one of fact, and since the magistrates had held there to be full delegation, the Divisional Court simply confirmed that decision. Nevertheless, on the facts **Howker** looks like a case of partial delegation at best, with the barman in the lounge being exactly that, the barman and not the delegate with full authority, and so the licensee should not have been guilty vicariously. Moreover, even accepting that there had been only partial delegation would not have exculpated the accused. The sub-section under which the accused was charged did not only catch the 'servant' who sold alcohol to someone under age. It also applied to 'the holder of the licence', that is, to the accused in *Howker*. There was no need to stretch the facts to fit the doctrine because the accused was liable personally anyway. *Howker* v *Robinson* demonstrates that the delegation principle applies even when the employee himself would be liable and the purpose of the legislation thereby promoted.

While the court did not reason in this way, *Howker* was distinguished in *Bradshaw* v *Ewart-James* [1983] QB 671 (DC). The master of a ship set a course which complied with the Collision Regulations. He handed over the watch to the chief officer and left the bridge. While under that officer's charge the vessel was navigated in such a way that the Regulations were violated. The ship's master was held to be not guilty. One way of justifying that result is to say that a temporary delegation (as here where the accused was asleep) is not a complete delegation. Similarly, the court in *Howker* should not have held that there was a complete delegation.

(ii) *The delegation principle applies only to* mens rea *offences*. Lord Parker CJ in *Winson*, above, decided that the delegation principle did not apply where the principal offence was a strict one. If the offence is strict (where there is no *mens rea* attached to any element of the *actus reus*: see Chapter 4), the accused may be liable under the third exception. Accordingly, where there is full delegation, the defendant is liable for *mens rea* crimes. If there is only partial delegation, the accused who did not know of the facts is not liable under this principle but can be liable where the statute can be interpreted in such a way that it covers what he did.

(iii) *The delegate must have acted within the scope of his authority*. As with extensive construction the delegator is not liable if the delegate acted on an unauthorised project. He remains liable for the doing of an authorised act in an unauthorised manner.

Under the fourth exception, where the licensee is guilty (as the principal offender), the person who did the act is liable as an accessory. If the third exception applies, both parties may be liable as joint principals. For example, both the driver and his employers 'use' a vehicle or 'sell' hams.

The delegation doctrine applies only to natural persons. Therefore, a company cannot be liable under this principle.

One final point on the delegation doctrine is this. If there is full delegation, the employer is liable no matter how well he has chosen his subordinates. However, if the delegation is not complete, he is not liable no matter how badly he supervises his subordinates.

Vicarious liability and attempts; vicarious liability and secondary participation

See Chapter 10, Inchoate offences, for a definition of a crime of attempt. See Chapter 5 for an explanation of aiding and abetting. *Gardner* v *Ackroyd* [1952] 2 QB 743 (DC) held that there can be no vicarious liability for **attempting** an offence even when that crime is one which imposes vicarious liability when completed. Similarly, *Ferguson* v *Weaving* [1951] 1 KB 814 (DC) decided that the doctrine did not apply to **aiding and abetting** an offence, even though that offence imposed vicarious liability on the principal offender. To be guilty as a secondary offender the accused must know the essential facts constituting the offence, even a crime of strict liability. He would not know them if he were liable vicariously.

The rationale of vicarious liability

This section considers the arguments for and against vicarious liability.

The justification for this doctrine is social policy. The statute is made effective by vicarious liability. As Lord Reid said in **Vane v Yiannopoullos**, above:

> If there was no provision making the servant liable to prosecution it would be impossible to enforce the law adequately if it was necessary in every case to prove *mens rea* in the licence holder.

Lord Reid considered that the effect was to oblige employers to choose employees who took care. However, employers are liable whether or not they themselves took care in the selection of employees, where the delegation has been total. Defendants are guilty even if they have instructed their agents to comply with the law. A second reason is illustrated thus: if one makes the owner of the car liable to pay excess parking charges even though someone else left it too long at the meter, the police are saved time and money in getting the right person. A third reason is that the employers may have financially benefited from the wrongdoing.

The rationale of the law and a statement of doctrine of delegation were brought together by Lord Evershed in **Vane**:

> Where the scope and purpose of the relevant Act is the maintenance of proper and accepted standards of public order in licensed premises or other comparable establishments, there arises under the legislation what Channell J, in **Emary v Nolloth** [1903] 2 KB 264, called a 'quasi-criminal offence' which renders the licensee or proprietor criminally liable for the acts of his servants, though there may be no *mens rea* on his part. On the other hand, where the relevant legislation imports the word 'knowingly' . . . the result will be different . . . In the absence of proof of actual knowledge, nevertheless, the licensee or proprietor may be held liable if he is shown . . . effectively to have 'delegated' his proprietary or managerial functions.

The phrase 'quasi-criminal' offence was a popular one around the end of the nineteenth century in vicarious and corporate liability cases. The justification used by J. Edwards, *Mens Rea in Statutory Offences* (Macmillan, 1955) 243 is:

> [s]o long as the criminal law is used as a means to securing the legislative standard of correct trading, business and social welfare behaviour, it is legitimate to have recourse to the principle of vicarious liability.

For example, polluting streams is deleterious. It is beneficial to prevent effluent entering water. If employers were not liable for the acts of their employees in letting a stream become polluted, pollution would not be controlled – with disastrous consequences for life. The effectiveness of legislation is increased by vicarious liability and defendants are obliged to increase training, numbers of supervisory personnel and the checking of machinery. Similarly sales of adult videos to children would not be prevented if it had to be proved that directors knew the child's age: **Tesco Stores Ltd v Brent LBC** [1993] 2 All ER 718 (DC). It was held that the company 'supplied' a video to an underage child when it was sold by a shop assistant. She had reasonable grounds to believe that the child was under age. Her state of mind was imputed to her employers, who therefore had no defence that they neither knew nor had reasonable grounds for believing that the child was over age.

The contrary arguments may be summarised thus:

(a) It is a fundamental principle that criminal responsibility should be personal. Why should a blameless person be punished for something another has done? Devlin J put this well in **Reynolds v GH Austin & Sons Ltd** [1951] 2 KB 135 (DC): 'If a man is punished because of an act done by another, whom he cannot reasonably be expected to influence or control, the law is engaged, not in punishing thoughtlessness or inefficiency, and thereby promoting the welfare of the community, but in pouncing upon the most convenient victim.'

(b) The accused may be guilty despite his not knowing that any offence has been committed.

(c) He is guilty even though he has done his best to prevent the offence. For example, he may have told the employee not to do as he did.

(d) The argument that the effect of the statute would be minimised if the courts did not read in vicarious liability is a weak one. It is certainly not proved. It should be for Parliament, not the courts, to decide when a person is guilty of a crime. Another way of making the same point is that the doctrine is an invention of the courts. It is not for the judiciary to create new crimes. If Parliament did not state that an accused was guilty, the courts should not interfere. If parliamentary drafting is poor, the remedy does not lie in the hands of the courts. The reader may care to compare strict liability where sometimes the judges read in *mens rea* when Parliament has (perhaps at times through poor drafting) not expressly stated the requisite fault element.

(e) The doctrine of delegation has come in for particular criticism. If the accused remains on the premises and there is no complete delegation, he is not liable no matter how careless he has been in selecting the delegate. However, if the accused is off the premises and has completely delegated, he is liable even though he took all due care in appointing a subordinate. One effect of this argument is that restaurateurs and the like should delegate only partly. However, surely liability should not turn on whether delegation is complete or not because the restaurateur may be performing other jobs as an employer which call for his attention and one would not want him to stop doing these tasks in order to provide complete supervision at all times.

The strength of these arguments both pro and con turns on the facts of individual cases unless one believes that criminal law should apply only where the accused committed the *actus reus* and had the *mens rea* of the offence charged.

The Human Rights Act 1998 may in time affect the law of vicarious liability. Article 3 of the European Convention on Human Rights forbids inhuman or degrading punishment and here the accused is penalised for another's actions.

Reform

The latest Law Commission proposal comes in its Consultation Paper No. 195, *Criminal Liability in Regulatory Contexts*, 2010. It recommended that the 'antiquated' (para. 1.88) doctrine of delegation should be abolished. It provided the following illustration of the defect in the law: '. . . suppose X asks Y to run X's pub while X goes on a round-the-world cruise. In fact, Y turns the pub into an unlicensed lap dancing club and brothel. In this instance, Y can, of course, be convicted of running an unlicensed lap dancing club or brothel. However, the doctrine of delegation means that X can also be convicted of these offences, even if he or she had no reason whatsoever to think that Y would do as he or she did.' (para. 1.89, footnote omitted) The Commission also noted that the delegation doctrine applied even when the delegate had forbidden the delegatee doing the prohibited act. The Commission concluded that if there was a requirement for liability in such circumstances, there should be an offence of failing to prevent the offence being committed.

Corporate liability

This section deals with situations in which a company is liable criminally (**corporate liability**). Only companies can be liable in these ways, not partnerships or unincorporated associations. However, an association is liable if the statute punishes a 'person', unless the contrary intention appears.

For many years companies were not criminally liable. Part of the problem was that criminal law was designed for individual defendants. For example, companies cannot be physically brought before the courts and could not be hanged or put into prison. Over time most of these restrictions were abolished but companies still cannot be found guilty of murder because the sole sanction is life imprisonment and one cannot imprison an intangible entity. Problems did remain. *Mens rea* is the doctrine which deals with the fault of human beings, not artificial entities. The problem of affixing a company with *mens rea* is considered below. Reform in respect of killings (only) came about in the Corporate Manslaughter and Corporate Homicide Act 2007.

Corporate liability is particularly important because most defective products are put onto the market by, most pollution is caused by, most crashes occur in transport run by, and most accidents at work take place at sites occupied by companies. Lord Hoffmann in the Privy Council in a civil case (but the same principles apply in criminal law), *Meridian Global Funds Asia Ltd* v *Securities Commission* [1995] 2 AC 500, advised that whether a company was liable for a statutory offence depended on the terms of the enactment, its content and its policy. The issue was whether a company was liable for the acts of its senior investment managers done without its knowledge. The Judicial Committee decided that it was, after investigating the policy of the statute, which was to compel disclosure of the identity of persons who had acquired substantial security. In a company those persons were those who had the company's authority to acquire the security. Therefore, the company was liable. This case marked a break from earlier law.

There are several ways in which a company may be made liable. Each mode has separate rules. The person in the company who actually committed the offence is guilty as joint principal.

(a) A statute may impose liability on a company just as on anyone. If a statute penalises the occupier of premises, and a company is the occupier, the company is guilty. Statute imposes a duty on companies to ensure the health and safety of employees and sub-contractors, and a breach of this duty renders the company criminally liable. For example, in *Gateway Foodmarkets Ltd* [1997] 2 Cr App R 40 (CA) a company was liable when it failed to ensure the safety of a lift and an employee was killed. The statute may impose liability either expressly or by necessary implication. Similarly, the corporation as owner of the vehicle is guilty of various offences committed by the driver: Transport Act 1982, s 31 (see under vicarious liability). There used to be several difficulties facing a prosecution. A company could not be personally present in court; a company could not be committed for trial; and a company could not be hanged. These difficulties were in time evaded, and none poses a problem nowadays.

(b) If the offence is a strict one, such as public nuisance and criminal libel, there is no problem in imposing liability: *Great North of England Railway Co* (1846) 2 Cox CC 70. The company was liable for obstructing the highway while building a railway. Liability was therefore imposed for doing an act, not merely for omitting to act. Denman CJ said liability was imposed to deter the company.

(c) A company is liable for omissions. While there may be a conceptual difficulty in understanding how it is that a company can act, there is none in punishing a company for failing to act.

(d) A company is vicariously liable in the same way as a person. Corporate vicarious liability is of the same width as the vicarious liability of natural persons. At least in a small company there is a good deal of supervision over employees. Vicarious liability punishes failures to exercise care. The human actor (the employee) is seen as the company's agent. However, it should be noted that the company, just like a natural person, is liable even though it has not been at fault.

The company can be liable for crimes of *mens rea*. In *Mousell Bros v LNWR*, above, a company was guilty of fraudulently evading freight charges. A company will be liable for tax evasion, fencing machinery, not holding a car licence, selling contaminated food, and so on. In *Chuter v Freeth & Pocock Ltd* [1911] 2 KB 832, it was held that a company 'believes' through its agents. The rule applies even though the company has told the employee not to do the act: *Griffiths v Studebakers Ltd* [1924] 1 KB 103 (DC). However, if it requires a natural person to perform the prohibited activity, a corporation will not be vicariously liable even though a natural person would be so liable. For example, a company cannot drive a vehicle, though a natural person can. Therefore, a company cannot be found guilty of an offence which has 'drives' as part of the *actus reus*: see *Richmond-upon-Thames LBC v Pinn & Wheeler Ltd* [1989] Crim LR 510 (DC).

As in vicarious liability there is an exception to liability. The company is not liable vicariously for aiding and abetting. The corporation must have knowledge of the facts out of which the offence arises through a responsible agent, though it need not know that a crime has been committed: *John Henshall (Quarries) Ltd v Harvey* [1965] 2 QB 233 (DC).

It cannot be too strongly emphasised that when vicarious liability applies, the master (whether a natural or juristic person) is liable for the activities of *all* employees, even subordinate ones, and may be criticised on that basis. The doctrine, unlike the identification doctrine, below, is not limited to controlling officers: see *National Rivers Authority v Alfred McAlpine Homes (East) Ltd* (1994) 158 JP 628 (DC) and *Tesco Stores Ltd v Brent LBC*, above. In the former case a company was liable for causing polluted matter, wet cement, to enter controlled water, a stream, even though the pollution was actually caused by employees and the site manager who were not directing minds of the company. This point received the approval of the Lords in *Director General of Fair Trading v Pioneer Concrete (UK) Ltd*, above.

One might have expected cases such as *Tesco Stores Ltd v Brent LBC* to be resolved using the identification doctrine. As a result it cannot be said with any certainty whether a company will be liable for all employees vicariously as in this case or only where the individual is part of the directing mind and will of the company.

(e) There is a *dictum* in *Seaboard*, above, that a company would be liable for the crime of failing to ensure that a ship is operated safely if it had not provided a system for ensuring the safe operation. If this *dictum* is correct, a company would be liable even though the prosecution could not prove that any one natural person was at fault. If followed, the *dictum* would swallow up the identification doctrine, which is discussed next.

(f) Under the doctrine of identification (which is also known as the *alter ego* doctrine) the company is personally liable. It is not liable vicariously. It is deemed to have committed the offence by itself. A term which is coming to be used in this context is direct liability. The doctrine makes a company liable for *mens rea* offences. The knowledge of the person to whom full delegation is made is treated as being the knowledge of the company. Under this doctrine a company is liable even when a natural person would not be liable. The methods of founding corporate liability in (a)–(d) are the same as for natural persons but this head marks a break from orthodox theory and penalises companies as companies, not as substitutes for natural persons. Where vicarious liability applies, the company is liable no matter what the status of the employee but the identification thesis governs only when the employee is a controlling officer. This doctrine applies to statutory offences but there is authority, noted below, that it does not apply to common law crimes. It is dependent on statutory interpretation when the crime is statutory: *Meridian*, above (cf. extensive construction, also discussed above).

In what was until *Meridian* the principal authority, *Tesco Supermarkets Ltd* v *Nattrass* [1972] AC 153 (HL), Lord Reid stated the basis of the doctrine in this way:

> A living person has a mind which can have knowledge or intention or be negligent and has hands to carry out his intentions. A corporation has none of these: it must act through living persons. Then the person who acts is not speaking or acting for the company. He is acting as the company . . . He is not acting as a servant, representative, agent or delegate . . . If [his mind] is a guilty mind, then that guilt is the guilt of the company.

In *St Regis Paper Co Ltd* v *R*, above, the Court was at pains to emphasise that the basic rule of attribution in English law remained *Tesco* v *Nattrass*. *Meridian* is a rule used when determining the intention of a statute but it restates the law in *Tesco* v *Nattrass*; it does not replace it. Applying *Tesco* a technical manager at one of the defendant company's paper-mills was not a directing mind and will of the company when he falsely entered records required for controlling pollution. Therefore, the company was not liable for his acts.

A company, being a legal institution, cannot operate without human intervention. It cannot take action or have a state of mind. The principle, which is sometimes known as the *alter ego* doctrine, was established in a trilogy of cases from 1944. In *DPP* v *Kent & Sussex Contractors Ltd* [1944] KB 146 Macnaghten J said:

> If a responsible agent of the company puts forward on its behalf a document which he knows to be false and by which he intends to deceive, . . . his intention and belief must be imputed to the company.

That is, the acts of the controlling officer of the company are deemed to be those of the company. The same is true of the officer's state of mind. A company not being a natural person has no mind, but others' states of mind are attributed to it. In *Meridian*, above, Lord Hoffmann called the methods by which acts and states of mind are imputed to the company 'rules of attribution'. If there is no identifiable human actor, there is no liability under *Meridian*.

The decision in *Kent & Sussex* was approved in *ICR Haulage Ltd* [1944] KB 551 (CCA). A company was held liable for conspiracy, then a common law offence. A natural person cannot in general be liable vicariously for a common law crime (the exceptions are criminal libel and public nuisance), yet the company was liable. The court adopted the test of identification. The acts and state of mind of the managing director were held to be those of the company. Unlike the doctrine of delegation, there is no need for an absolute or personal duty to be delegated before the company is liable.

The next case was *Moore v I Bresler Ltd* [1944] 2 All ER 515 (DC). False returns were made to purchase-tax forms. The Divisional Court held that the acts of the company secretary and branch managers were to be treated as those of the company.

In *Meridian* Lord Hoffmann advised that the question whose act and state of mind was to be attributed to the company was answered 'by applying the usual canons of interpretation, taking into account the language of the rule (if it is a statute) and its content and policy'. This response was especially problematic in respect of common law crimes but later authority on corporate manslaughter (see below) is to the effect that common law crimes are still governed by *Tesco v Nattrass* and are not affected by *Meridian*, though there is civil law authority that *Meridian* is of general application. The law is now more uncertain than it was after *Tesco v Nattrass*, and it must be added that *Meridian* has not yet been applied in an English case, which may be surprising.

Moore raises the issue of whether the activities of all employees are deemed to be those of the company. Modern law used to stress that only acts of controlling officers were taken to be those of the company. The question was: how far down the chain of command do the courts go? The metaphor often used was 'brain' and 'hands', terms which derive from the civil law judgment of Denning LJ in *HL Bolton (Engineering) Co Ltd v TJ Graham & Sons Ltd* [1957] 1 QB 159 (CA). Under this anthropomorphic distinction, which Y.Z. Stern in 'Corporate criminal personal liability: who is the corporation?' (1987–88) 13 *Journal of Corporation Law* 125 at 130 called 'another plastic and useless description', the company was liable only for the forbidden acts or omissions of its 'brain', and not for those of its 'hands'. Leonard Leigh wrote ('By whom does a company permit?' (1966) 29 MLR 568): 'The "brains" and "hands" dichotomy essentially represents vivid journalism. It is not a substitute for analysis.' The cases, however, depend very much on the facts: one role in one company may be a 'brain' but a 'hand' in another. This point was emphasised in *Meridian* where Lord Hoffmann advised that the policy behind the statute had to be investigated to determine whether a certain person's acts and state of mind were to be attributed to the company. The use of the terms 'hand' and 'brain' is a distraction from this task. For example, in *Moore v I Bresler Ltd* the court was right in attributing the *mens rea* of the servant authorised to complete the returns to the company, but that ruling did not automatically apply to other crimes such as manslaughter, while *Tesco v Nattrass* turned on the words of the relevant statute and did not lay down a general rule. In *Worthy v Gordon Plant (Services) Ltd* [1989] RTR 7 (DC) the *actus reus* and *mens rea* of a traffic manager were imputed to a company. This case demonstrates that the identification doctrine is not limited to directors (as Lord Diplock thought in *Tesco v Nattrass*: see below) nor to employees of the company: the manager was self-employed; nevertheless, the company was liable. The following are examples of 'hands' on the facts of the case:

Depot manager: *Magna Plant v Mitchell* [1966] Crim LR 394 (DC).

Weighbridge manager: *John Henshall*, above.

Shop manager: *Tesco v Nattrass*, above.

Transport manager: *Readhead Freight Ltd v Shulman* [1988] Crim LR 696 (DC).

Ship's master: *P & O Ferries (Dover) Ltd* (1991) 93 Cr App R 72 (CA).

European Sales Manager of a company's aircraft division: *Redfern* [1993] Crim LR 43 (CA). The court said that the doctrine depended on the delegation of the true power of management, not of administrative or executive functions, no matter how important those functions were. The manager was four ranks below the chief executive.

In *Tesco* v *Nattrass* the manager was simply one manager out of some 800. The larger a company is, the easier it will be to say that a person is a 'hand'. It does seem unfair that a large company would escape liability when a smaller one would not. Lord Reid postulated that the test of identification applied where there was a substantial delegation of the functions of management. Only a few people such as the managing director and the members of the board are in such positions. The majority looked for those who 'represent the directing mind and will of the company and control what it does'. The phrase 'directing mind and will', which is often used nowadays, comes from a civil case, *Lennard's Carrying Co Ltd* v *Asiatic Petroleum Co Ltd* [1915] AC 705 (HL). Lord Hoffmann in *Meridian* advised that courts should not place too much emphasis on this phrase. Instead they should ask whether an individual's acts and state of mind were to be attributed to the company for the purpose of the relevant statute. Viscount Dilhorne in *Tesco* v *Nattrass* looked for someone 'in actual control of the operations of the company . . . and who is not responsible to another person . . . for the manner in which he discharges his duties . . .'. Lord Reid looked for the substance of the transaction, not just at the form as Lord Diplock did. He instanced 'the board of directors, the managing director and perhaps other superior officers . . . [who] . . . speak and act as the company'. Lord Diplock laid down an even narrower test, a mechanical one. Companies with so-called 'Table A' articles of association were liable only when the acts were performed by those persons mentioned in Table A, that is, the directors. Whichever test is adopted, *Kent & Sussex* looks wrong in relation to the transport manager. And it may be that *Moore* v *I Bresler Ltd* was incorrect before *Meridian* in respect of the branch managers. It is now correct as a matter of statutory construction. *Tesco* v *Nattrass* must now be seen as a case of statutory interpretation: *Meridian*. The manager was not a 'brain', for the purpose of the relevant statute. A manager may be a 'brain' for another purpose. *Tesco* v *Nattrass* is a poor decision in terms of controlling wrongdoing: perhaps *Meridian* heralds a new era. However, in criticism of *Meridian* it may be said that until a decision by the court one will not know whether a person's activities are to be attributed to the company.

One observation about *Tesco* v *Nattrass* should be made. The offence was a regulatory one. Corporate liability could have been based upon vicarious liability: there was no need to investigate the identification doctrine. Applying vicarious liability the company would have been liable for the acts of any of its employees including the store manager. It should not have made any difference that the offence was phrased in terms of an offence coupled with a defence that the accused had taken all due diligence to prevent the occurrence of the crime. (C. Wells 'Corporate liability for crime – *Tesco* v *Nattrass* on the danger list?' [1996] 1 *Archbold News* 5 at 6, called the decision 'bizarre'.)

An important application of the identification doctrine took place in *P & O European Ferries (Dover) Ltd*, above, but which is unreported on this point. The case arose out of the sinking of the *Herald of Free Enterprise* at Zeebrugge. The assistant bosun, who was asleep when the ship was leaving the harbour, and chief officer, who should have checked whether the bow doors were closed but could not because he was on the bridge, were not senior enough for their alleged carelessness to be deemed to be the carelessness of the company. The failure to prove carelessness against senior management despite the fact that the directors were warned of the dangers of sailing with the bow doors open meant that the trial of the company for manslaughter collapsed. The case makes one think about the reasoning behind the identification test and its width. If Lord Diplock's rule were adopted, companies would rarely be liable. Yet it could easily be said that the failures of the bosun and the chief officer demonstrated the company's failure to execute the performance of its duty not to kill or injure passengers and crew. Moreover, the Board of Directors did not wish to fit lights showing that the doors were open because they employed a man to check, but he was asleep and no cover was provided by the company. Indeed, the Board seemed complacent. In other words, the company was negligent. Furthermore, if the rationale of the doctrine is to deprive companies of profits made out of breaches of law, why is it that the doctrine is not applied to middle managers and below who have made profits for the company? It might be better to speak of control of the company rather than management, depending on how far one wanted the law to apply, as Woolf J did in *Essendon Engineering Co Ltd v Maile* [1982] RTR 260. It is the judge who decides whether a person is 'brain' or 'hand'.

P & O European Ferries (Dover) Ltd was a case on manslaughter, which is a common law crime. Therefore, *Meridian*, which talks about statutory interpretation, is not directly applicable. An exploration of corporate manslaughter before the statute amending the law occurred in *Attorney-General's Reference (No. 2 of 1999)* [2000] QB 796 (CA), a case on a railway crash in which seven people died. It was held that a company (and, as the Divisional Court held in *Rowley v DPP* [2003] EWHC 693 (Admin), a local authority) could not be liable for manslaughter by gross negligence unless a human defendant had been convicted of it. The identification doctrine remained the rule of attribution for this common law offence. The person who was the 'directing mind and will' within *Tesco v Nattrass* had to be liable first. The effect of adhering to *Tesco v Nattrass* is easy to uncover. If that doctrine requires a director to be criminally liable, in a larger company it will be almost impossible to make a director guilty. A director does not drive a train, a train driver does; but the gross negligence of the driver cannot be attributed to the company – he is too low in the hierarchy. However, it would be hard to show that a decision of a director had caused the death of passengers when the immediate cause was, for example, a driver passing a signal at red. Furthermore, Rose LJ in *Attorney-General's Reference (No. 2 of 1999)* said that 'it would bring the laws into disrepute if every act and state of mind of an individual employee was attributed to a company which was entirely blameless'; however, that is the doctrine in the English tort law of vicarious liability and it is the general rule of criminal liability in the USA.

There are two restrictions on the identification doctrine. First, it has been suggested that it applies only when a 'brain' is performing a managerial function. A company would not be liable in criminal law (even though it may be liable in tort) when its managing director ran someone over, because driving is not a managerial function. It is uncertain whether this proposition represents the law or not, but it is hard to believe that judges would find a company liable if its managing director stole an ashtray even if he was on a business trip. Secondly, the doctrine applies only where one or more 'brains' are individually liable. One cannot aggregate several directing minds and activities to make the company liable: *R v HM Coroner for East Kent, ex parte Spooner* (1989) 88 Cr App R 10 (DC). Each individual 'brain' has to be liable before the company can be convicted under the identification doctrine. In a large company, where decisions are often jointly made, it is unlikely that one controlling officer will have the requisite knowledge. In an era of large multinational companies neither the identification principle nor the delegation doctrine takes effect because of the need to delegate further and further down the corporate hierarchy to make the company work in a competitive marketplace. It is suggested that even if the aggregation doctrine were adopted, the law would not stretch to finding guilty a corporation which did not have a corporate policy on the relevant issue, such as safety at work. For this reason the defendant company in *P & O European Ferries (Dover) Ltd* (above) may still not have been guilty.

Limitations on liability

A company is not liable in certain situations:

(a) A company may be convicted only of offences punishable by a fine. It cannot be imprisoned or hanged. Therefore, it cannot be guilty of treason or murder, for how can one put a legal construct into prison? Since most offences are punishable nowadays by a fine or some other non-corporal method, this restriction is minimal. This exception was accepted in *ICR Haulage* and *P & O European Ferries (Dover) Ltd*, above, as was the second exception, though perjury was said to be arguable. The argument contrary to the view that a company can be convicted of only those offences which are punishable by fines is that there should be other sentences available, such as 'corporate probation' and dissolution of the company. Where the company cannot be found guilty of an offence because no sanction is available, other defendants may be guilty in the normal way. However, this chapter is devoted to corporate liability.

(b) It seems that there are several offences which cannot be committed by an employee within the scope of his employment. There is a *dictum* of Finlay J in *Cory Bros & Co* [1927] 1 KB 810 (Assizes) to the effect that perjury is one of those offences. However, this *dictum* may be wrong, for a director who perjures can be identified with the company. The argument to the contrary is, however, strong. Only the person who has been lawfully sworn can be guilty of perjury, and a company cannot lawfully be sworn. Other such offences include being a rogue and a vagabond, bigamy, incest and rape. These crimes may be called personal offences. A company cannot, for example, have sexual intercourse. However, a company can be liable as a company to those offences. An illustration is given by A. Reed and B. Fitzpatrick, *Criminal Law*, 3rd edn (Thomson, 2006) 168 (not in the 4th edn, 2009): 'If Z, the managing director of X Company Ltd, a film company, supervises the filming of intercourse between M, an 18-year-old male, with N, a 15-year-old girl, there is no reason why Z and hence the film company should not be convicted as secondary parties to the unlawful sexual intercourse.' (The crime is now sexual activity with a child under 16.) For most crimes such as theft and burglary there is no problem in finding the company liable. Lord Steyn in *Deutsche Genossenschaftsbank v Burnhope* [1995] 1 WLR 1580 (HL) gave an example: '. . . If the chairman of a company dishonestly instructs an innocent employee to enter [a] warehouse and remove a bag containing valuables, the company may be guilty of burglary.'

(c) In *Cory Bros*, above, it was said at Assizes that a corporation could not be tried for a crime of personal violence including manslaughter. The facts involved the electrocution of a miner during the 1926 general strike. That case was criticised in *ICR Haulage*, above. In *Northern Strip Mining Construction Co Ltd*, unreported, 1965, an Assizes case, a company was tried for manslaughter but the issue of the propriety of the indictment was not discussed and the firm was acquitted; in *ex parte Spooner*, above, Bingham LJ tentatively accepted that a company could be guilty of manslaughter.

The final breakthrough came in *P & O European Ferries (Dover) Ltd*, above; the Court of Appeal accepted this change in the law in *Attorney-General's Reference (No. 2 of 1999)*, above. This part is reported. The successor company of the firm which owned the *Herald of Free Enterprise* was held to be properly tried for manslaughter. However, in the unreported portion of the trial the prosecution case collapsed because it could not be proved that the actions of the controlling officers were objectively reckless. No reasonably prudent person occupying the positions of the individual members of senior staff would have recognised the risk to a ship leaving port as 'obvious and serious'. (See also the discussion of reckless and gross negligence manslaughter in Chapter 12, where it is pointed out that objective reckless manslaughter has been abolished.) This point was reached despite the inquiry of Sheen J into the capsize, which stated that managers should have been aware that there was a real risk of ferries leaving port with their door open and that there were no standing orders to cover closure of the bow doors. The directors had not applied their mind to the type of instructions they should give in order for the ship safely to leave the harbour. However, each person's 'sloppiness' as Sheen J called it could not be aggregated to make the company liable. There was no recklessness. The system of the ship had worked on over 60,000 sailings. The ship's officers testified that they had not thought about the risk; therefore, it could not have been an obvious one. The ferry had left harbour several times with its doors open, but there had been no incidents and neither the Department of Transport nor the insurers required a system of reporting to the captain that the doors were closed or the installation of lights in the bridge to show that they were. It is thought that the resurgence of gross negligence manslaughter would make no difference to the outcome. A reasonably skilled ship's officer would not have operated a different mode of sailing from a harbour. The case also illustrates the importance of corporate liability. Each year there are some 600–800 homicides. The sinking of the *Herald of Free Enterprise* caused some 30 per cent of those in 1988.

Despite the collapse of the case, *P & O European Ferries (Dover) Ltd* signified that a company may be liable for crimes of violence. The third exception has disappeared. Difficulties of proof will not arise in every case. The first company convicted of (common law) manslaughter was the one accused of causing the Lyme Bay canoe tragedy in which four school-age canoeists were killed: *OLL Ltd*, unreported, 9 December 1994. It was fined £60,000. The company was found guilty of manslaughter by gross negligence. The managing director, the controlling mind of the company, owed a duty of care to the company's clients and he knew that safety standards were low. The safety systems were not effective, he had been warned that deaths would occur without such systems in place, and he did not supervise his canoeing instructor. His knowledge was imputed to the company. It was easy to identify the managing director as the directing mind and will in such a small company. The effect of the fine was to put the company into liquidation. The difference from *P & O European Ferries (Dover) Ltd* seems to consist in the difference in size of the company.

The second company to be convicted of manslaughter was *Jackson Transport (Ossett) Ltd*, unreported, 19 September 1996 (Bradford Crown Court). The former managing director was the company's 'directing mind' and ran the business personally. The victim had died while cleaning chemicals from a road tanker. The company was convicted of gross negligence manslaughter (and the individual accused received a sentence of 12 months' imprisonment). The sole other convictions of common law manslaughter were of *English Brothers Ltd* (2001), *Teglgaard Hardwood Ltd* (2003), *Dennis Clothier and Sons Ltd* (2003), *Nationwide Heating Services Ltd* (2004) and *Keymark Services* (2006), all of which were small firms: a large company was never convicted of this offence. The fines, respectively, were: £15,000, £25,000, £25,000, £4,000, £90,000 (including for health and safety offences) and unknown. To use the first of these cases as an example: an employee was killed after a toxic chemical was sprayed in his face while he was cleaning chemical residues from a road tanker. He had not been supervised or trained and he was not provided with protective equipment. At the same time fines have been increasing for health and safety offences, undermining the arguments in favour of reforming the whole law of corporate liability, though manslaughter is a much more stigmatic crime than is a conviction for a health and safety offence. For statutory corporate manslaughter, see below.

In 1989 there were 143 deaths and 4,010 serious injuries on building sites. Many of these were caused in the same way, such as by the collapse of trenches or scaffolding. Therefore, persons in charge of such construction companies ought to foresee such occurrences. Companies can accordingly be made liable. A similar point can be made about the King's Cross Underground fire. Between 1956 and 1988 there were 46 escalator fires on the Tube, of which 32 had been caused by smoking. These figures are taken from D. Bergman 'Recklessness in the boardroom' (1990) 140 NLJ 1496 at 1501. He added:

> The tangle of the common law of manslaughter could be avoided in these situations if a new crime were created, whereby a director faced large fines and possible imprisonment if his failure to abide by his duties caused a person to die.

Bergman estimated in 'Weak on crime – weak on the causes of crime' [1997] 147 NLJ 1652 that there had been more than 10,000 workplace deaths in the previous 10 years. The Health and Safety Commission reported 212 deaths and 28,605 serious injuries at work (*Health and Safety Statistics 2005/06*, 2006).

The conviction in the Lyme Bay case, **OLL Ltd**, occurred because of the small size of the company. The managing director *was* the company. The salient point is that no medium or large company has yet been convicted.

It should be noted that the *ultra vires* doctrine does not operate in criminal law and that directors may be disqualified by a court under the Company Directors Disqualification Act 1986, s 2, if they mismanage the health and safety matters of a company. The first director to be imprisoned for manslaughter in relation to his business was Peter Kite, the managing director in **OLL Ltd**. He was sentenced to three years' imprisonment on four counts, to run concurrently but the sentence was reduced to two years on appeal.

Critique of the law

After transport and industrial disasters corporate liability reform is on the agenda, and the law is in a state of flux. The public perceives companies to be at fault in failing to prevent such incidents. No longer are these disasters seen as accidents (cf. the Aberfan disaster of over 45 years ago): they are viewed as foreseeable and preventable. Companies are seen to be culpable and there is a desire to transmute moral blameworthiness into criminal liability. The phrase 'corporate manslaughter' is now known to the man in the street.

One difficulty with making companies criminally responsible for their acts or omissions is that criminal law is founded on personal liability; another is that prosecuting authorities are slow to act on 'crime in the suites'. For example, deaths on construction sites rarely came in the past to the attention of the police, but were dealt with solely by the Health and Safety Executive. This attitude was criticised for failing to take seriously deaths at work. The position is changing. There are several reasons for imposing criminal liability on corporations. Companies would escape regulation by the criminal law if they were not liable, and regulation is at times a good thing. It obliges companies to adopt policies which lead to careful procedures. Only the company can remedy some of the things which led to the deaths. For example, only P & O could install lights to signify that the bow doors were closed. The assistant bosun could not. It may be procedurally convenient to prosecute the company. The company is more likely to be able to pay a fine than an individual. Shareholders may be encouraged to exercise control, and the company may be deprived of unjust enrichment through fines. Fines, however, must be set high enough to be more than the profit gained from the violation of the law; otherwise there would be no deterrence and fines could be seen as a business expense.

Punishing only natural persons would not strike at the cause of the wrongdoing: natural persons may be mere minions. Indeed the fault may be that of the company, not that of an individual. It is possible that the existence of corporate liability can help to prevent companies placing pressure on employees to break the law. Adverse publicity and fines may act as a deterrent. Indeed, bad publicity is likely to be more of a deterrent than fines, which are often paltry. Nevertheless, it must be admitted that the effect of adverse publicity on consumers is uncertain, though it must be stronger than would occur if only the individual wrongdoer were prosecuted. Public opinion may be in favour of imposing liability on a company the activities of which have led to a disaster. It is not in favour of imposing liability only on employees at the base of the corporate hierarchy, and where people are killed there is a growing feeling that corporations ought to be convicted of 'normal' crimes such as manslaughter and not just of health and safety offences. Companies are seen as the cause of deaths and injuries. They could have prevented the harm. It is often said that the police and Health and Safety Executive do not treat corporate offending as 'real' crime. The name of the offence may not reflect the wrongdoing, there may be inaction by the prosecuting authorities, and the fine may be derisory.

However, not all these arguments are strong. The amount of a fine is not proportionate to the amount of enrichment; fines affect companies differently from individuals; shareholders very rarely exercise control over firms; and the fine may be too paltry to deter. It is thought that corporate policy in large firms is not affected by the imposition of fines: Anon. 'Increasing community control over corporate crime – problem of sanctions' (1961) 71 Yale LJ 280 at 290. Of course, the fact that fines are incorrectly calibrated does not mean that corporations should go unpunished. Some corporations such as universities do not have shareholders. A.M. Polinsky and S. Shavell argue in 'Should employees be subject to fines and imprisonment given the existence of corporate liability?' (1993) 13 *International Review of Law and Economics* 239 at 255, that (a) a company's control over its employees will not be increased by the imposition of corporate liability because control is already executed to the socially optimal level, and (b) a company should not be liable to a greater extent than the harm it has caused because otherwise its production costs will increase, thereby depressing the optimal level of consumption. Certainly these arguments do not differentiate between 'brain' and 'hands' as the identification doctrine does. Despite the weakness of some arguments, J.A. Andrews made a sensible comment in [1973] Crim LR 91 at 94:

> Where we use the penal law to support fiscal, health and safety and other regulations, corporations must be brought within the system. On the other hand when we use the penal process to deter delinquency, we should recognise that companies are not delinquents, only people are.

Moreover, there are some states, such as Italy, which do not have corporate liability law. The argument is that corporations have no morality, no personality in that sense, which criminal law and punishment can change. Prosecuting the company alone may miss the individuals who caused the harm.

Non-governmental proposals for reform

Other reforms have been suggested. As early as 1948 Sir Roland Burrows wrote in 'The responsibility of corporations under English law' (1948) 1 *Journal of Criminal Science* 1 at 19: 'Restriction of activities and even extinction by forfeiture are neither impossible nor absurd.' Rodger Pannone, England's chief disaster lawyer, thought that a company should be made civilly liable for punitive damages. N.J. Reville 'Corporate manslaughter' [1989] LSG No. 37, 17 at 19, proposed massive fines. However, a massive fine may lead to liquidation, an outcome which may not be appropriate. At present fines may not deprive the company of its ill-gotten profits, and they may not be pitched high enough to deter. Gary Slapper in 'A safe place to work' [1992] LSG No. 37, 24, pointed out that when BP Ltd was fined £750,000 by a Scottish court in 1987, that sum was 0.05 per cent of the company's after-tax profits and was the equivalent of a fine of £7.50 on a person earning £15,000 per year. Nevertheless, post-2000 fines for health and safety offences may be substantial. Although the Court of Appeal reduced the fine on Balfour Beatty for the Hatfield rail crash by £2.5m, the fine was still £7.5m: **Balfour Beatty Rail Infrastructure Services Ltd** [2006] EWCA Crim 1586. It is the shareholders (and the customers) who suffer from fines. Shareholders simply do not exercise their company law rights to control corporate officers. Moreover, heavy fines may leave the company with not enough money to remedy the situation. Employees may have to be dismissed when no fault is attached to them.

David Bergman in his *Deaths at Work: Accidents or Corporate Crime* (WEA, 1991) suggested that prosecutions for death at the workplace should be tried only on indictment and that courts should be able to impose imprisonment on a director or manager by whose ineptitude a worker was killed or seriously injured. He has on several occasions over the years criticised the Health and Safety Executive for failing to pursue what in reality are cases of corporate manslaughter. Other sanctions have been suggested, such as the dissolution of the company, nationalisation, monitoring its activities, corporate probation (which means that professionals, such as accountants, supervise and monitor the company's activities), community service, preventing it from working in certain areas of business, prohibiting it from performing government contracts, publicising the breach of the law in some official way. The last method has been tried in the USA, but experience in that country demonstrates that close control over such advertising has to be exercised, otherwise the company publishes only in rarely read journals.

Research work would have to be done to see whether these methods would be effective. Prevention, such as training in health and safety or an increase in the numbers of Health and Safety inspectors, may be more helpful than criminal law, and criminal laws should be utilised to prevent harm. Laws made for individuals cannot always be easily applied to companies. Certainly at present there is an imbalance between prosecutions by the Crown Prosecution Service for minor shoplifting and non-prosecution by arms of the government for breaches of health and safety at work subordinate legislation and for pollution, where prosecution is seen as very much a last measure after various admonitions. If the criminal law has a part to play in tackling modern social problems such as pollution and food hygiene, the principles of corporate liability must be clear and enforced. Reform of both corporate liability and involuntary manslaughter is necessary. The difficulties in one are exacerbated by those in the other.

Despite the arguments outlined in this section, it is sometimes said that corporate liability serves no purpose. The authors of a well-known textbook, Smith and Hogan, *Criminal Law*, 10th edn (Butterworths, 2002) 206, wrote, as they did in previous editions: 'The necessity for corporate criminal liability awaits demonstration.' (This comment does not appear in the 13th edition, 2011, Oxford University Press, the third to be edited by D. Ormerod.) G.R. Sullivan commented in 'Expressing corporate guilt' (1995) 15 OJLS 281 at 289:

> If we were to follow Smith and Hogan, the myriad of regulatory laws relating to safety, pollution, hygiene etc. would be lifted off the backs of companies and confined to individuals. It

would be a deregulation beyond the imaginings of the most doctrinaire free-marketeer . . . It is in the enforcement of regulatory criminal law against limited companies that we must continue to seek the major improvements in standards of safety. [footnote omitted]

Corporate Manslaughter and Corporate Homicide Act 2007

Example

Coco Construction Corporation ('Coco'), a small company, is building a block of flats on a brownfield site. Coco's director of operations, who is a member of the Board, tells Dora, a construction worker, to build a trench into which the company will pour concrete as part of the foundations. She starts digging but comes across a cellar, falls into it and is killed. Is Coco liable for corporate manslaughter?

The Corporate Manslaughter and Corporate Homicide Act 2007, on which there has so far been no case law, replaced the common law of corporate liability when death was caused. In brief Coco is liable if its activities are organised by senior management in such a way that they constitute a substantial element in a gross breach of the duty of care it owed (for example) to its employees and death is caused by that breach. Terms such as 'senior management', 'duty' and 'gross' are defined in the Act and the triers of fact are told by the Act which factors they must and which factors they may consider when determining whether the breach was gross. Students must go through each element of the offence to determine whether the company is guilty of the offence. For example, on the facts there is no doubt that the director of operations forms part of 'senior management' within the Act.

Note that if Eric had been working with Dora and had fallen into the hole at the same time but had been injured and not killed, then the Act would not apply. The common law identification doctrine would apply instead: the principal authority on that doctrine is **Tesco Supermarkets Ltd v Nattrass** [1972] AC 153 (HL). It is easy to criticise the two coexisting layers of law on this account alone.

This statute deals in England and Wales with corporate liability for death. It replaces the common law, which is abolished. The offence is called corporate manslaughter in England and Wales (s 2(5)). Most provisions came into force on 6 April 2008. However, since it deals only with corporate liability for deaths, and not with corporate liability for example for injuries, to which the common law remains, there is the possibility of dual forms of liability. If a company causes the death of one person and injury to another through the same act of gross negligence, the death falls under the Act but the injury is subject to the common law. The common law applies even when the injured person would have died, had he not been saved by immediate paramedic intervention. According to the Health and Safety Commission's website there were 173 work-related deaths in 2011–12 (note that this figure excludes deaths by industrial diseases such as asbestosis and it is unclear how many work-related road traffic deaths are contained in the figures) but 114,000 injuries. It should be added that the Act is not limited to work-related deaths; it extends beyond corporations to many other organisations including partnerships, the police, and trade unions; and goes beyond firms killing their workers, extending to killing members of the public.

The Act is focused on the liabilities of bodies which fall within its scope. There is no liability imposed on directors and senior managers by the Act, and they remain liable for common law manslaughter by gross negligence. Indeed, every criminal statute imposes secondary liability unless Parliament otherwise ordains and in the Act Parliament has so ordained: s 18. These exclusions may be surprising, for it is directors and senior executives who conceive and implement policies, not the incorporeal organisation.

Section 1 of the Act reads in part:

(1) An organisation to which this section applies is guilty of an offence if the way in which its activities are managed or organised –
   (a) causes a person's death, and
   (b) amounts to a gross breach of a relevant duty of care owed by the organisation to the deceased.

The government anticipated that the widening of the concept of causation through *Environment Agency* v *Empress Car Co. (Abertillery) Ltd* [1999] 2 AC 22 (HL) and in the period leading up to the House of Lords' decision in *Kennedy (No. 2)* [2008] AC 269 (HL) (see Chapter 2 on causation) would obviate the need to refer to the doctrine of *novus actus interveniens* but the House has reverted to the previous law in *Kennedy (No. 2)*. Now that the law has reverted to its pre-*Empress* position, the problem is this: if the death is caused by the gross negligence of a junior employee, does the organisation also cause that death within s 1(1)(a)? If the act of the employee is voluntary, on normal principles she is liable and her act or failure to act breaks the chain of causation, unless the organisation's conduct also is a significant contribution to the killing. It would have been better to rephrase by adding 'and the organisation remains guilty despite the fact that the act or omission of an individual was the immediate cause of death'.

Section 1 continues:

(2) The organisations to which this section applies are –
   (a) a corporation;
   (b) a department or other body listed in Schedule 1;
   (c) a police force;
   (d) a partnership, or a trade union or employers' association, that is an employer.

It should be noted that while the Act's title refers to 'corporate' manslaughter, the statute is not restricted to companies. This is in line with the Home Office's Consultation Document, *Reforming the Law on Involuntary Manslaughter: The Government's Proposals*, 2000.

Section 1 goes on to provide:

(3) An organisation is guilty of an offence under this section only if the way in which its activities are managed or organised by its senior management is a substantial element in the breach referred to in subsection (1).

(4) For the purposes of this Act –
   (a) 'relevant duty of care' has the meaning given by section 2, read with sections 3 to 7;
   (b) a breach of a duty of care by an organisation is a 'gross' breach if the conduct alleged to amount to a breach of that duty falls far below what can reasonably be expected of the organisation in the circumstances;
   (c) 'senior management', in relation to an organisation, means the persons who play significant roles in –
      (i) the making of decisions about how the whole or a substantial part of its activities are to be managed or organised, or
      (ii) the actual managing or organising of the whole or a substantial part of those activities.

The use of the concept of 'senior management' calls into question how far the 2007 Act breaks, as it should do, from the previous law of identification, to which reference should be made. Certainly there is no requirement as at common law for one specific senior person to be at fault; in this sense aggregation is permissible under the 2007 Act. The concept ensures that the acts of lesser employees are not attributed to the organisation but it must be appreciated that it is senior management who lay down general policies on, for instance, recruitment of staff. In respect of the requirement of 'gross' breach, the question whether the organisation's behaviour fell far below that which could reasonably be expected in the circumstances is a question for the jury (cf. the leading authority on gross negligence manslaughter committed by a natural person, *Adomako* [1995] 1 AC 171) and it is uncertain just how far below the standard the body must go to be criminally liable. It is also unclear what 'in the circumstances' means: surely it cannot mean that an organisation is not grossly in breach of a duty when it decides not to comply with it because it is short of money and as a result someone is killed:

(6) An organisation that is guilty of corporate manslaughter . . . is liable on conviction on indictment to a fine.

Other remedies are noted below. Fines for health and safety violations have been increasing since the late 1990s and this rise has been endorsed by the Health and Safety Act 2008. The Sentencing Guidelines Council (SGC) in 2009 stated that fines under the 2007 Act should be 'measured in millions of pounds and should seldom be below £500,000', but this is a decrease from the original recommendation of 10 per cent of turnover. Fines elsewhere may be higher. For example, BP was fined $87 million (some £53 million) for not complying with safety laws at the Texas City oil refinery as a result of which 15 were killed. Fines for breaches of EU economic laws can be 10 per cent of turnover.

Section 2 reads in part:

(1) A 'relevant duty of care', in relation to an organisation, means any of the following duties owed by it under the law of negligence –
    (a) a duty owed to its employees or to other persons working for the organisation or performing services for it;
    (b) a duty owed as occupier of premises;
    (c) a duty owed in connection with –
        (i) the supply by the organisation of goods or services (whether for consideration or not),
        (ii) the carrying on by the organisation of any construction or maintenance operations,
        (iii) the carrying on by the organisation of any other activity on a commercial basis, or
        (iv) the use or keeping by the organisation of any plant, vehicle or other thing;
    (d) a duty owed to a person who, by reason of being a person within subsection (2), is someone for whose safety the organisation is responsible.

(3) Subsection (1) is subject to sections 3 to 7.

(4) A reference in subsection (1) to a duty owed under the law of negligence includes a reference to a duty that would be owed under the law of negligence but for any statutory provision under which liability is imposed in place of liability under that law.

(6) For the purposes of this Act there is to be disregarded –
    (a) any rule of the common law that has the effect of preventing a duty of care from being owed by one person to another by reason of the fact that they are jointly engaged in unlawful conduct;
    (b) any such rule that has the effect of preventing a duty of care from being owed to a person by reason of his acceptance of a risk of harm.

This subsection ensures that the tort doctrines of *volenti* and contributory negligence do not apply to the offence.

Section 3 exempts certain public functions from the coverage of the Act. It reads:

(1) Any duty of care owed by a public authority in respect of a decision as to matters of public policy (including in particular the allocation of public resources or the weighing of competing public interests) is not a 'relevant duty of care'.

(2) Any duty of care owed in respect of things done in the exercise of an exclusively public function is not a 'relevant duty of care' unless it falls within section 2(1)(a), (b) or (d).

(3) Any duty of care owed by a public authority in respect of inspections carried out in the exercise of a statutory function is not a 'relevant duty of care' unless it falls within section 2(1)(a) or (b).

(4) In this section –
'exclusively public function' means a function that falls within the prerogative of the Crown or is, by its nature, exercisable only with authority conferred –
(a) by the exercise of that prerogative, or
(b) by or under a statutory provision;
'statutory function' means a function conferred by or under a statutory provision.

Sections 4, 5 and 7 relate to military and police activities and child protection respectively, which do not fall within the ambit of this book. Section 6, which deals with emergencies, may, however, be of relevance:

(1) Any duty of care owed by an organisation within subsection (2) in respect of the way in which it responds to emergency circumstances is not a 'relevant duty of care' unless it falls within section 2(1)(a) or (b).

(2) The organisations within this subsection are –
(a) a fire and rescue authority in England and Wales . . .
(d) any other organisation providing a service of responding to emergency circumstances either –
(i) in pursuance of arrangements made with an organisation within paragraph (a) . . . or
(ii) (if not in pursuance of such arrangements) otherwise than on a commercial basis;
(e) a relevant NHS body;
(f) an organisation providing ambulance services in pursuance of arrangements –
(i) made by, or at the request of, a relevant NHS body, or
(ii) made with the Secretary of State or with the Welsh Ministers;
(g) an organisation providing services for the transport of organs, blood, equipment or personnel in pursuance of arrangements of the kind mentioned in paragraph (f);
(h) an organisation providing a rescue service;
(i) the armed forces.

(3) For the purposes of subsection (1), the way in which an organisation responds to emergency circumstances does not include the way in which –
(a) medical treatment is carried out, or
(b) decisions within subsection (4) are made.

(4) The decisions within this subsection are decisions as to the carrying out of medical treatment, other than decisions as to the order in which persons are to be given such treatment.

(5) Any duty of care owed in respect of the carrying out, or attempted carrying out, of a rescue operation at sea in emergency circumstances is not a 'relevant duty of care' unless it falls within section 2(1)(a) or (b).

(7) In this section –

'emergency circumstances' means circumstances that are present or imminent and –

(a) are causing, or are likely to cause, serious harm or a worsening of such harm, or

(b) are likely to cause the death of a person;

'medical treatment' includes any treatment or procedure of a medical or similar nature;

'relevant NHS body' means –

(a) a Strategic Health Authority, Primary Care Trust, NHS trust, Special Health Authority or NHS foundation trust in England . . .

'serious harm' means –

(a) serious injury to or the serious illness (including mental illness) of a person;

(b) serious harm to the environment (including the life and health of plants and animals);

(c) serious harm to any building or other property.

(8) A reference in this section to emergency circumstances includes a reference to circumstances that are believed to be emergency circumstances.

Section 8(1) defines gross breach for the jury:

This section applies where –

(a) it is established that an organisation owed a relevant duty of care to a person, and

(b) it falls to the jury to decide whether there was a gross breach of that duty.

(2) The jury must consider whether the evidence shows that the organisation failed to comply with any health and safety legislation that relates to the alleged breach, and if so –

(a) how serious that failure was;

(b) how much of a risk of death it posed.

(3) The jury may also –

(a) consider the extent to which the evidence shows that there were attitudes, policies, systems or accepted practices within the organisation that were likely to have encouraged any such failure as is mentioned in subsection (2), or to have produced tolerance of it;

(b) have regard to any health and safety guidance that relates to the alleged breach.

It is unclear why a jury *may* refer to policies and the like but *must* refer to health and safety legislation.

Section 8 continues:

(4) This section does not prevent the jury from having regard to any other matters they consider relevant.

(5) In this section 'health and safety guidance' means any code, guidance, manual or similar publication that is concerned with health and safety matters and is made or issued (under a statutory provision or otherwise) by an authority responsible for the enforcement of any health and safety legislation.

An example is a Code of Practice approved by the Health and Safety Commission.

Section 9 adds to the usual sanction of a fine the power to issue a remedial order:

(1) A court before which an organisation is convicted of corporate manslaughter . . . may make an order (a 'remedial order') requiring the organisation to take specified steps to remedy –

(a) the breach mentioned in section 1(1) ('the relevant breach');

(b) any matter that appears to the court to have resulted from the relevant breach and to have been a cause of the death;

(c) any deficiency, as regards health and safety matters, in the organisation's policies, systems or practices of which the relevant breach appears to the court to be an indication.

(2) A remedial order may be made only on an application by the prosecution specifying the terms of the proposed order.

Any such order must be on such terms (whether those proposed or others) as the court considers appropriate having regard to any representations made, and any evidence adduced, in relation to that matter by the prosecution or on behalf of the organisation.

(3) Before making an application for a remedial order the prosecution must consult such enforcement authority or authorities as it considers appropriate having regard to the nature of the relevant breach.

(4) A remedial order –
   (a) must specify a period within which the steps referred to in subsection (1) are to be taken;
   (b) may require the organisation to supply to an enforcement authority consulted under subsection (3), within a specified period, evidence that those steps have been taken.
   A period specified under this subsection may be extended or further extended by order of the court on an application made before the end of that period or extended period.

(5) An organisation that fails to comply with a remedial order is guilty of an offence, and liable on conviction on indictment to a fine.

Section 10 is new. It provides the court with a power to issue a publicity order:

(1) A court before which an organisation is convicted of corporate manslaughter or corporate homicide may make an order (a 'publicity order') requiring the organisation to publicise in a specified manner –
   (a) the fact that it has been convicted of the offence;
   (b) specified particulars of the offence;
   (c) the amount of any fine imposed;
   (d) the terms of any remedial order made.

(2) In deciding on the terms of a publicity order that it is proposing to make, the court must –
   (a) ascertain the views of such enforcement authority or authorities (if any) as it considers appropriate, and
   (b) have regard to any representations made by the prosecution or on behalf of the organisation.

(3) A publicity order –
   (a) must specify a period within which the requirements referred to in subsection (1) are to be complied with;
   (b) may require the organisation to supply to any enforcement authority whose views have been ascertained under subsection (2), within a specified period, evidence that those requirements have been complied with.

(4) An organisation that fails to comply with a publicity order is guilty of an offence, and liable on conviction on indictment to a fine.

The publicity order remedy was not in the original bill but was added in the House of Lords. The SGC has stated that the court should normally make such an order. Section 10 was brought into force on 15 February 2010.

Section 17 provides that prosecutions for corporate manslaughter cannot be brought without the consent of the DPP. This provision has been criticised for putting prosecutions into the hands of a government-appointed official. It is contrary to the recommendation of the Home Office Consultation Document, mentioned above, and the Law Commission Report No. 237, *Legislating the Criminal Code: Involuntary Manslaughter*, 1996, which is the basis for much of the statute.

The Act may not lead to many more prosecutions per year than there were before the Act (the Home Office suggested that one aim of the legislation was to increase prosecutions and in turn convictions) but it is the culmination of public concern over corporate failings that lead to death.

Cotswold Geotechnical (Holdings) Ltd [2011] All ER (D) 100 (May) (CA) is the well-known case in which for the first time a company was convicted of the offence under the Corporate Manslaughter and Corporate Homicide Act 2007 at first instance. This report is of the appeal, not against liability but against sentence. The Winchester Crown Court judge, Field J, had imposed a fine of £385,000 (to be paid over ten years so as not to make the company insolvent) and the question for the present Court was whether the sanction was manifestly excessive. The amount was considerable for a small business but below the Sentencing Guidelines which state that fines will 'seldom be less than £500,000 and may be measured in millions'. The Court of Appeal rejected the appeal on the basis that though the sum was 250 per cent of turnover, it was payable over ten years; and the fact that the company might have to be put into liquidation was unfortunate but inevitable when the company had acted in such a manner that it had caused death through a gross breach of duty by failing to adopt a safe system of work in that it did not secure the sides of trenches with the result that a pit had collapsed on a worker, a geologist taking soil samples, killing him: he suffered traumatic asphyxia and the authorities took two days to remove several tons of mud on top of him. The company had already been warned by a Health and Safety Executive officer that putting workers into unsupported trenches was illegal, but the sole director of the company had ignored the warning. Reputational damage to the company was also considerable. For a brief comment see G. Bastable, 'Corporate convictions' (2011) 175 JPN 237. It should be recalled that a principal reason for having the 2007 Act was the disparity that the previous law could catch small ('one man') companies but not large diffuse ones. However, the new Act was not tested because the company here was a very small one with just one director.

The second English firm to be convicted was Lion Steel Equipment Ltd, which pleaded guilty. The victim fell to his death through a fragile roof panel. It had been hoped that this case would settle the meaning of various phrases in the 2007 Act such as 'senior manager' because, unlike Cotswold, Lion Steel was a medium-sized firm and had 100 or so employees but the decision to plead guilty prevented the court from exploring these definitions. The firm was fined £480,000, a sum which took into account the fact that the company had pleaded guilty. It was ordered to pay the sum in four instalments of varying sizes between September 2012 and September 2015.

Summary

- *Vicarious liability*: Rarely in criminal law is one person liable for the crimes of another. The exceptions are:
  1 public nuisance and publishing a criminal libel;
  2 where Parliament expressly makes one person liable for another's conduct;
  3 where statutes are construed to the same effect through the doctrine of extensive construction, the most famous authority being *Coppen v Moore (No. 2)* [1898] 2 QB 306 (DC);

4 the delegation principle. This doctrine is subject to the restriction that the delegation must be complete (see *Vane* v *Yiannopoullos* [1965] AC 486 (HL)), the principle applies only to *mens rea* offences, and the delegate must have acted within the scope of his authority.

It should be noted that there can be no vicarious liability for attempted crimes or for secondary participation in crimes.

There has been a long-standing debate on whether it is acceptable to make one person liable for what another has done. The principal argument in favour is that without it criminal behaviour would occur unpunished; the principal argument to the contrary is that criminal liability should be *personal* to the accused.

- *Corporate liability*: companies may be criminally liable:
  1 statute may impose liability;
  2 companies are liable for strict liability offences;
  3 companies are liable for omissions in the normal way (see Chapter 2);
  4 vicarious liability applies to companies as it applies to natural persons;
  5 controversially, the doctrine of identification makes companies liable for the conduct and states of mind of high corporate officers: see *Tesco Supermarkets Ltd* v *Nattrass* [1972] AC 153 (HL) and for statutory offences see *Meridian Global Funds Asia Ltd* v *Securities Commission* [1995] 2 AC 500 (PC). There is debate as to how far down the corporate hierarchy one can go to make the company liable, and one of the main criticisms of this form of liability is that because more can be delegated down the chain of command in larger than in smaller companies, it is much more likely that smaller enterprises will be held criminally liable than larger ones.

There are some offences for which companies cannot be criminally liable. One such is murder. The sentence for murder must be life imprisonment and companies not being natural persons cannot be imprisoned. Rape is another example: a corporation cannot insert its penis into one or more of the victim's anus, mouth or vagina.

References

Reports

Home Office Consultation Paper, *Reforming the Law on Involuntary Manslaughter: The Government's Proposals* (2000)

Law Commission Consultation Paper no. 135, *Involuntary Manslaughter* (1994)

Law Commission Consultation Paper no. 195, *Criminal Liability in Regulatory Contexts*, 2010

Law Commission Report no. 237, *Legislating the Criminal Code: Involuntary Manslaughter* (1996)

Sentencing Guidelines Council, *Corporate Manslaughter and Health and Safety Offences Causing Death: Consultation Guideline* (2009)

Books

Bergman, D. *Deaths at Work: Accidents or Corporate Crime?* (WEA, 1991)

Card, R., Cross, P. and Jones, P.A. *Criminal Law*, 20th edn (Oxford University Press, 2012)

Edwards, J. *Mens Rea in Statutory Offences* (Macmillan, 1955)

Ormerod, D. *Smith and Hogan's Criminal Law*, 13th edn (Oxford University Press, 2011)

Reed, A. and Fitzpatrick, B. *Criminal Law*, 3rd edn (Thomson, 2006)

Reed, A. and Fitzpatrick, B. *Criminal Law*, 4th edn (Thomson, 2009)

Smith, J.C. and Hogan, B. *Criminal Law*, 10th edn (Butterworths, 2002)

Journals

Andrews, J.A. 'Reform in the law of corporate liability' [1973] Crim LR 91

Anon. 'Increasing community control over corporate crime – problem of sanctions' (1961) 71 Yale LJ 280

Bastable, G. 'Corporate convictions' [2011] 175 JPN 237

Bergman, D. 'Recklessness in the boardroom' [1990] 140 NLJ 1496

Bergman, D. 'Weak on crime – weak on the causes of crime' [1997] 147 NLJ 1652

Burrows, R. 'The responsibility of corporations under English law' (1948) 1 *Journal of Criminal Science* 1

Leigh, L.H. 'By whom does a company permit?' (1966) 29 MLR 568

Polinsky, A.M. and Shavell, S. 'Should employees be subject to fines and imprisonment given the existence of corporate liability?' (1993) 13 *International Review of Law and Economics* 239

Reville, N.J. 'Corporate manslaughter' (1989) LSG no. 37, 17

Slapper, G. 'A safe place to work' [1992] LSG no. 37, 27

Stern, Y.Z. 'Corporate criminal personal liability: Who is the corporation?' (1987–88) 13 *Journal of Corporation Law* 125

Sullivan, G.R. 'Expressing corporate guilt' (1995) 15 OJLS 281

Wells, C. 'Corporate liability for crime – *Tesco* v *Nattrass* on the danger list?' [1996] 1 *Archbold News* 5

Further reading

Almond, P. 'Public perceptions of work-related fatality cases' (2008) 48 BJ Crim 448

Almond, P. 'Understanding the seriousness of corporate crime: some lessons for the new "corporate manslaughter" offence' (2009) 9 *Criminology and Criminal Justice* 145

Almond, P. and Colover, S. 'Mediating punitiveness: Understanding public attitudes towards work-related fatality cases' (2010) 7 *European Journal of Criminology* 323

Belcher, A. 'Corporate killing as a corporate governance issue' (2002) 10 *Corporate Governance* 47

Bergman, D. *Deaths at Work: Accident or Corporate Crime* (WEA, 1991)

Cavanagh, N. 'Corporate criminal liability: An assessment of the models of fault' (2011) 75 JCL 414

Centre for Corporate Accountability/Disaster Action/Trades Union Congress, *Why we Need a New Corporate Killing Law* (2003)

Clarkson, C.M.V. 'Kicking corporate bodies and damning their souls' (1996) 59 MLR 557

Clarkson, C.M.V. 'Corporate culpability' [1998] 2 Web JCLI

Clarkson, C.M.V. 'Corporate manslaughter: yet more government proposals' [2005] Crim LR 677

Clough, J. 'Sentencing the corporate offender: the neglected dimension of corporate criminal liability' (2003) *Corporate Misconduct Ezine*

Clough, J. 'Bridging the theoretical gap: the search for a realist model of corporate criminal liability' (2007) 18 Crim LF 267

Colvin, E. 'Corporate personality and criminal responsibility' (1995) 6 *Criminal Law Forum* 1

Dan-Cohen, M. 'Sanctioning corporations' (2010–11) 19 JL & Policy 15

Dobson, A. 'Shifting sands: Multiple counts in prosecutions for corporate manslaughter' [2012] Crim LR 200

Ferran, E. 'Corporate attribution and the directing mind and will' (2011) 127 LQR 239

Field, S. and Jorg, N. 'Corporate liability and manslaughter: should we be going Dutch?' [1991] Crim LR 156

Field, S. and Jones, L. 'Death in the workplace: Who pays the price?' (2011) 32 Co Law 166

Fisse, B. and Braithwaite, J. 'The allocation of responsibility for corporate crime' (1988) 11 Sydney LR 468

Glasbeek, M. 'Shielded by law: why corporate wrongs and wrongdoers are privileged' [2002] UWSL Rev 1

Glazebrook, P. 'A better way of convicting businesses of avoidable deaths and injuries' (2002) 61 CLJ 405

Gobert, J. 'Corporate criminality: four models of fault' (1994) 14 LS 393

Gobert, J. 'Corporate criminality: new crimes for the times' [1994] Crim LR 722

Gobert, J. 'Controlling corporate criminality: penal sanctions and beyond' [1998] 2 Web JCLI

Gobert, J. 'Corporate killing at home and abroad – reflections on the government's proposals' (2002) 118 LQR 72

Gobert, J. and Punch, M. *Rethinking Corporate Crime* (Butterworths, 2003)

Griffin, S. 'Corporate manslaughter: a radical reform?' (2007) 71 JCL 151

Hill, J. 'Corporate criminal liability in Australia' [2003] JBL 1

Jefferson, M. 'Corporate criminal liability in the 1990s' (2000) 64 JCL 106

Jefferson, M. 'Corporate criminal liability: the problem of sanctions' (2001) 65 JCL 235

Jefferson, M. 'Regulation, business, and criminal liability' (2011) 75 JCL 37

Jones, L. 'Death in the workplace: Who pays the price?' (2011) 32 Co Law 166

Lee, I.B. 'Corporate Criminal Liability as Team Member Responsibility' (2011) 31 OJLS 755

Mays, R. 'The criminal liability of corporations and Scots law: learning the lessons of Anglo-American jurisprudence' [2000] Edin LR 46

Ormerod, D. and Taylor, R. 'The Corporate Manslaughter and Corporate Homicide Act 2007' [2008] Crim LR 589

Pace, P.J. 'Delegation – a doctrine in search of a definition' [1982] Crim LR 627

Punch, M. '(g.b.h.) grievous business harm: exploring corporate violence' (1995) 3 EJCPR 92

Sargeant, C. '"Two steps forward, one step back" – The cautionary tale of the Corporate Manslaughter and Corporate Homicide Act 2007' [2012] 1 *UK Law Students' Review* 1

Slapper, G. 'Corporate manslaughter: an examination of the determinants of prosecutorial policy' (1993) 2 *Social and Legal Studies* 423

Stessens, G. 'Corporate criminal liability – a comparative perspective' (1994) 43 ICLQ 493

Sullivan, G.R. 'The attribution of culpability to limited companies' [1996] CLJ 515

Swigert, V.L. and Farrell, R.A. 'Corporate homicide' (1980–81) 15 *Law Society Review* 161

Tombs, S. 'Law, resistance and reform: "regulating" safety crimes in the UK' (1995) 4 *Social and Legal Studies* 343

Wells, C. 'The decline and rise of English murder: corporate crime and individual responsibility' [1988] Crim LR 788

Wells, C. 'The criminal liability of corporations and their officers' (1990) 2 *Law for Business* 120

Wells, C. 'Culture, risk and criminal liability' [1993] Crim LR 551

Wells, C. 'Corporate manslaughter: a cultural and legal form' (1995) 6 *Criminal Law Forum* 45

Wells, C. 'Corporations and the risk of criminal liability' (1996) 10 *The Whistle* (Bulletin of Freedom to Care, available on www.freedomtocare.org/page165.htm)

Wells, C. 'The corporate manslaughter proposals: pragmatism, paradox and peninsularity' [1996] Crim LR 545

Wenham, D. 'Recent developments in corporate homicide' (2000) 29 ILJ 378

Wickens, R.J. and Wong, C.A. 'Confusion worse confounded: the end of the directing mind theory' [1997] JBL 524

Wilkinson, M. 'Corporate criminal liability: The move towards recognising genuine corporate fault' (2003) 9 Canterbury LR 142

Williams, G. '*Mens rea* and vicarious liability' [1956] CLP 57

Celia Wells has also had a book published, *Corporations and Criminal Responsibility*, 2nd edn (Clarendon, 2001). In it she argues that companies should be punished if they exhibit practical indifference to a risk. For some of her other work see I. Loveland (ed.), *Frontiers of Criminality* (Sweet & Maxwell, 1995). See also B. Fisse and J. Braithwaite, *Corporations, Crime and Responsibility* (CUP, 1993). Fisse's (and Braithwaite's) articles are legion and include 'Reconstructing corporate criminal law: deterrence, retribution, fault and sanction' (1983) 56 S Cal LR 1141; 'Corporate criminal responsibility' (1991) 15 Crim LJ 166; 'The attribution of criminal liability to corporations' (1991) 13 Syd LJ 277. For a practitioner text see A. Pinto and M. Evans, *Corporate Criminal Liability* (Sweet & Maxwell, 2003).

There are many excellent American articles which discuss corporate liability; the following is a selection from the past 25 years.

Barnard, J. 'Reintegrating shaming in corporate sentencing' (1999) 5 Cal L Rev 959

Beale, S.S. and Safwat, A.G. 'What developments in Western Europe tell us about American critiques of corporate criminal liability' (2004) 8 Buff Crim L Rev 89

Forschler, A. 'Corporate criminal intent – toward a better understanding of corporate misconduct' (1990) 78 Cal LR 1287

Hall, J.S. 'Corporate criminal liability' (1998) 35 Am Crim L Rev 549

Khanna, V.S. 'Corporate criminal liability: what purpose does it serve?' (1996) 109 Harv LR 1477

Khanna, V.S. 'Corporate crime liability: a political economy analysis', John M. Olin Centre for Law and Economics, University of Michigan, Paper no. 3–012 2012

Laufer, W.S. 'Corporate bodies and guilty minds' (1994) 43 Emory LJ 647

Lederman, E. 'Models for imposing corporate criminal liability' (2000) 4 *Buffalo Criminal Law Review* 642

Lott, J.R. 'Corporate criminal penalties' (1996) 17 *Managerial and Decision Economics* 349

Parker, J.S. 'Doctrine for construction: the case of corporate criminal liability' (1996) 17 *Managerial and Decision Economics* 381

Ragozino, A. 'Replacing the collective knowledge doctrine with a better theory for attributing corporate *mens rea*' (1995) 24 Southwestern LR 423

Ulen, T.S. 'The economics of corporate criminal liability' (1996) 17 *Managerial and Decision Economics* 351

Walsh, C. and Pyrich, A. 'Corporate compliance programs as a defense to corporate criminal liability: can a corporation save its soul?' (1995) 47 Rutgers LJ 605

For an Irish view see Law Reform Commission, *Consultation Paper on Corporate Killing*, LRC CP 26, 2003, and the *Report on Corporate Killing*, no. 77, 2005

For an Australian view see Tasmania Law Reform Institute, *Criminal Liability of Organizations*, Issues Paper no. 9, 2005, and the Report no. 9 of the same name, 2007.

Visit **www.mylawchamber.co.uk** to access tools to help you develop and test your knowledge of criminal law, including interactive multiple choice questions, practice exam questions with guidance, annotated weblinks, glossary flashcards, legal newsfeed and legal updates.

7

Infancy, duress, coercion, necessity, duress of circumstances

Aims and objectives

After reading this chapter you will understand and be able to critique:

- the differences between justification and excuse and how they may affect English law
- the application of the criminal law of infancy
- the law of duress (by threats), duress of circumstances, and marital coercion
- the definition of necessity, whether it is a defence, and differences from duress

Introduction to Chapters 7–9

This chapter and the next two deal with what are normally called 'general defences', those which apply to most if not all offences. The exception is diminished responsibility, which is a defence only to murder but is treated in this chapter because of its affinity with insanity. The defences in the present chapter are often known as true defences in that they do not negate the *actus reus* or *mens rea* but act as a third element. Other so-called defences such as automatism and mistake are seen as operating differently. They do negate the external or fault element. The list of defences is not closed and within the last quarter of a century a new defence, duress of circumstances, has arisen. Similarly, some legal philosophers have at times pushed for the introduction of new defences such as poverty in the 1960s.

These chapters deal with those defences normally taught on a criminal law course. It should be pointed out that in ordinary language the term 'defence' is often used in a wider sense than here to mean any way in which the accused did not commit the offence, for instance 'It wasn't me because I was in London when the offence was committed in Sheffield', defence known as alibi, a term meaning 'somewhere else'.

Introduction to defences

The criminal law is not based solely on a series of offences, which are concerned with preventing harms on pain of sanctions, but also on a number of defences which qualify the offences. As will be seen, some defences (such as self-defence) apply to all offences, while some defences apply only to some offences (e.g. diminished responsibility applies only to murder and reduces the offence to manslaughter; duress does *not* apply to murder, attempted murder and some forms of treason). One could analyse all offences into *actus reus* and *mens rea*, leaving no room for defences. Murder would become an unlawful killing with malice aforethought. If the accused killed in self-defence, it would not be murder because the killing was not unlawful. For the purposes of exposition, the style adopted in this book is that defences form a separate element. A killing in self-defence is not murder because even though the accused did kill and did intend to do so, he has a defence. This method facilitates learning, for there is no need to say whether a certain defence obviates *actus reus* or *mens rea* (or both) and there is no difficulty with stating the burden of proof. One can therefore look at offences and defences in this way: is there an *actus reus*? If so, is there the relevant *mens rea*? If so, does the accused have a defence? Some defences are specific to certain offences, the obvious one being loss of control, which is a defence only to murder. Sometimes it may be difficult to state whether some matter is a failure by the prosecution to prove part of the offence or whether it is a defence. In rape the consent of the victim is part of the definition of the crime. If the woman or man consents to sexual intercourse, the offence of rape has not taken place. If, however, one consents to what would otherwise be a battery when one is engaged in a sport, the consent of the victim seems more appropriately to be a defence and not a failure by the prosecution to prove all the elements of the crime. Seeing consent as a separate defence enables us to consider it as a whole and not independently in each offence.

Each defence has its own rules and should not be confused with any other. If there is a common theme, it is that there has to be some kind of aberration of mind, such as the chemical change in drunkenness, the lack of mental responsibility in infancy and perhaps in duress, or the falling below a mental level as in insanity. It appears common sense to say for instance that a person forced to commit a crime should have a defence and that a young child should not suffer punishment for having broken the criminal law when he did not know that what he was doing was morally wrong. Why punish people who cannot change?

As Jordan CJ put it in **Turnbull** (1944) 44 NSWLR 108:

> A person is never regarded as criminally liable for an act which, although physically the act of his body, was done while his mind was in so abnormal a state that it cannot be regarded as his act at all, e.g. if he was sleep-walking, or so young, or so insane, as to be incapable of knowing that he was acting or the nature and quality of his act.

It should be noted that although the matters in this and the next two chapters are called 'defences', the burden of proof in most of them lies on the prosecution, which must disprove the defence beyond reasonable doubt. The exceptions are insanity and diminished responsibility, where the defence must prove them affirmatively but only on the balance of probabilities.

It is at times difficult to say whether an element of a defence is truly a matter of the offence or the defence. In recent years controversy has centred on consent in rape. The definition, which is expounded on in Chapter 14, seems to treat consent as part of the offence, and this seems to be in accord with the fact that in most cases consensual sexual intercourse is not a crime. However, this approach is not always taken. The argument runs that the act of sexual intercourse always needs to be justified. Therefore, the element of consent is a defence because it makes non-criminal what is otherwise criminal.

Until recently defences were not categorised: they either applied or they did not. Nowadays various attempts have been made to classify defences. The chief modern classification or taxonomy distinguishes between justifications and excuses.

Justification and excuse

English law used to distinguish between **justification** and **excuse** in relation to killings. Some homicides were justified, some others were excused. The distinction came to have no relevance to the accused for, whichever class of killing took place, he was not guilty. Until the early nineteenth century the distinction had some importance. An excusable killing led to the murderer's goods being forfeited to the Crown. Forfeiture did not take place when the killing was justifiable. Recently, however, it has become usual in the USA to divide defences into those which provide a justification and those which excuse. The division is a tool of analysis. It could be used to see how defences should be extended or reduced. The principal commentator is G. Fletcher, *Rethinking Criminal Law* (Little, Brown & Co., 1978). Readers who find difficulty with the concepts of justification and excuse should look at the individual defences first and then return to this section.

Justification means that the defendant's action is not disapproved of, for example in self-defence, in the use of force to effect a lawful arrest, in consent, and in the lawful chastisement of a child. The accused is not blameworthy because it has been decided that what he did was permissible. The otherwise wrongful conduct is legitimised. The law does not seek to deter such behaviour: it does not seek to punish persons who engage in such conduct. Joshua Dressler put it this way ('Provocation: partial justification or partial excuse' (1988) 51 MLR 467, 468): 'There is a considerable moral difference between saying that an intentional killing is warranted (partially or fully), and saying that it is entirely wrong but that the actor is partially or wholly morally blameless for his wrongful conduct.' Perhaps another way of making the same point is to say that the accused when he is acting in, say, the prevention of crime, does not commit the *actus reus*. If the accused killed an assailant in the lawful prevention of the attack, he is not guilty of murder because there was no unlawful killing. He is not guilty because he does not fall within the prohibition when the crime is fully defined. Therefore, criminal law does not condemn what he has done. One does not look at this particular accused's state of mind. In justification defences, since the accused is seen not to have acted wrongly, rules on justification provide guidance for citizens. A person who has a defence of self-defence was not acting in breach of the criminal law. Therefore, others will not be in breach if they do as he did. In excuse defences, however, the behaviour of the defendant himself is investigated. He is not guilty because of some lack of blame attaching to him. Perhaps he has misperceived reality, and accordingly he is not fully responsible for his actions. He has acted wrongfully but his position was such that he is excused. An insane person is not blameworthy. On this basis, these defences would provide only an excuse: duress both by threats and of circumstances, intoxication, mistake, insanity, diminished responsibility, automatism, infancy and provocation. Defences such as loss of control and diminished responsibility do not totally exculpate the accused. They are sometimes called 'partial excuses'. For discussion of duress, loss of control and mistake, see later. Judges have spoken similarly. In **Harding** [1976] VR 129 Gowans J stated that duress 'is properly to be classed as a matter of excuse for what otherwise would be criminal conduct on account of the will or intent with which it was done'.

One omission from those lists is necessity. That defence could be treated either as justification or as excuse. It is suggested that it is a justification when the harm which the accused is threatened with is greater than the harm which he does. When the harm to be caused is equal to the crime which results one might say that the actor is excused but the action is not justified. Perhaps the same should be said of duress both by threats and of circumstances, provided that the offence committed was a lesser evil than the act threatened. It must be stated that at least with regard to duress and necessity their place in this scheme is not secure and may depend on the object to be achieved. If one says that the accused when under threat did what a reasonable person would have done because neither he nor that paragon could have resisted, the defence is excusatory. If one says that the defence is based on the accused's choosing the lesser evil, breaking a legal rule, it is justification. Killing two to save one may be excused; it cannot be justified. English law sees duress as excusatory. Dickson J said in the Supreme Court of Canada in *Perka v R* (1984) 13 DLR (4th) 1: 'praise is indeed not bestowed, but pardon is, when one does a wrongful act under pressure.' The present view of necessity is not always accepted. L. Vandervort 'Social justice in the modern regulatory state: duress, necessity and the consensual model in law' (1987) 6 Law & Phil 205 treats it as a defence of justification. The Law Commission in its 1993 Report No. 218 noted in this chapter seems to have viewed duress as excusatory (the mind was overcome) but necessity as justificatory (the choice was permissible). The difference between the two forms of necessity is that when it operates as a justification there has to be a choice of evils; there is no such requirement when it operates as an excuse. In turn, when it operates as an excuse the accused has acted or failed to act because of pressure exerted on him, but, when it operates as a justification, there is no such requirement: the accused then may act calmly and rationally. If duress were justificatory, many of the limitations on its application, such as duress is not a defence to murder, would disappear. One difficulty would be that politics would become part of the law because one would have to weigh up evils to determine which was the lesser one.

Mistake also poses a problem. If one accepts that mistake negatives *mens rea*, it is not truly a defence but a failure to prove all elements of the offence. If mistake is in some fashion a defence, the argument runs that the defendant is to be excused because he made a mistake. Professor Glanville Williams [1982] Crim LR 33 considered self-defence to be justified if the facts allowing force exist, but only excused if the accused wrongly believes that such facts exist. It is suggested that where the accused believes he is acting in self-defence but in fact is not, one may wish to say that if the mistake was reasonably made, he should have a defence, but if it was unreasonably made, he should not, for a person who makes an unreasonable mistake is still blameworthy. Present law, however, exculpates both: *Williams* [1987] 3 All ER 411 (CA). The theory could explain the difference between the need according to most authorities for a reasonable mistake in duress (an excuse) but the fact that an honest mistake suffices in self-defence (a justification), but if it is not certain whether a defence is an excuse or a justification, the distinction loses its basis as a tool of analysis.

Academics, particularly US ones, trying to utilise this division have come up with a small number of reasons why the dichotomy is helpful:

(a) Where the assailant's defence is a justificatory one, a person threatened by the conduct is not entitled to resist because the accused who is using or threatening force is acting in accordance with law, whereas if the defence is excusatory, he is entitled to resist. For example, one is not entitled to resist a constable's making a lawful arrest but one is entitled to resist an attack by an insane person, an automaton or a child because that person acts wrongly.

(b) Where the principal has a defence which is justificatory in nature, a party who assists the principal is entitled to give that help. The person who assists is behaving appropriately. It should not be criminal to act acceptably. However, if the defence is excusatory, the secondary party is liable. The fact that the defendant's act is excused does not necessitate that the helper's assistance is also excused. A person who helps another to batter a victim should be liable as accessory even when the other has a defence of automatism. A 'crime' has been committed; therefore, applying the theory of derivative liability (see Chapter 5) the secondary party can aid and abet that 'crime'. However, if the principal is justified in acting as he did, there is no principal offence to which an accessory can be a party.

(c) Where the accused has a justificatory defence, the courts do not have to prevent the behaviour recurring. Excusatory defences should lead to attempts to stop the behaviour recurring. This rationale would support the use of some kind of court-ordered supervision of those excused. This outcome may not be what an accused who is at present acquitted totally, say by reason of automatism, would desire. This third distinction may be only a definitional one, though it looks consequential.

Another distinction may be that the accused only has an excusatory defence when he is aware of the facts which give rise to the excuse, whereas in a justificatory defence the accused is relieved of responsibility even though he did not know the facts giving rise to the justification. One might add that if a defence is classified as justificatory, it should be available to all offences; however, one might argue that public policy might be to the effect that one may be excused from culpability for some offences but not for others. One may be excused from assault occasioning actual bodily harm but not from murder, for instance. Certainly it is difficult to understand the concept that one can be only partially justified in committing a crime. Therefore, if one kills, one should be acquitted, and not just guilty of manslaughter, when one's defence is justificatory. It has also been said that if the accused makes a mistake in respect of a justification, he has a defence if his error was honestly made, whereas in relation to an excuse the mistake must be one made on reasonable grounds.

The difference between justification and excuse is, it is suggested, most vital when considering reform of the law. In respect of one defence the (Irish) Law Reform Commission, *Homicide: The Plea of Provocation*, Consultation Paper 27 (2003) 105, put this very well:

> The contrasting rationales of justification and excuse . . . reflect competing policy objectives. On the one hand, there is a feeling that the criminal law should make allowance for the infirmities of human nature. On the other, there is the general expectation that members of society should exercise a minimum standard of self-control. The aspiration for set standards inspired by this expectation does not sit easily with the sense of empathy aroused by a concern for human weakness. . . . The defence of provocation represents a compromise between these competing policy goals; indeed elements of both justification and excuse are often intermingled in the plea. The recent history of the defence has however been shaped by excusatory considerations, with the result that the issue of justification has . . . been pushed to the background.

The principal English discussion occurs in Chapter 1 of J.C. Smith's *Justification and Excuse in the Criminal Law* (Stevens, 1989). He believes that the theory is helpful in relation to resistance by a person threatened by an attack. One can resist an attack by a nine-year-old (infancy is an excuse), but one cannot resist a lawful arrest because that arrest is justified. If the arrest is, however, taking place with force, surely one is entitled to resist the force when the police have made a mistake as to the identity of the person they are arresting. The outcome is the same whether the behaviour of the police is described as justified or excused. The second distinction, assisting the person who has a defence, works well, says Smith, at the extremes. A person who helps a nine-year-old child to kill is guilty through the doctrine of innocent agency, whereas a person who helps the police in making an arrest is not guilty of an offence even though the arrest is unlawful because no crime has taken place. However, in other cases the division into excuse and justification is unhelpful. If it is held that police who shot in order to effect an arrest are excused but not justified in their action, why should a person who assists them in making the arrest be guilty because the police were mistaken in thinking that the person they were arresting was a violent criminal? One should look at what he believed, not at what the police believed.

With regard to the distinction in relation to the awareness of the circumstances, Smith argues that whether the defendant must know of the circumstances which justify or excuse his conduct, as was ruled in **Dadson** (1850) 4 Cox CC 358 (CCR) in relation to the shooting of an escaping felon, is a matter of policy, and is not to be determined by inquiry whether the defence is justificatory or excusatory. **Dadson** is incorrect according to the theory, as the constable was preventing crime, a justificatory defence. He illustrates the point through the defence of infancy, which is excusatory. If a nine-year-old thinks he is 10, surely he is not to be convicted because he did not know of the excusatory circumstance that he is only nine. The outcome is a matter of law, and what the child believes is irrelevant. A similar argument demonstrates that even in a justificatory defence the accused must know of the circumstances which give rise to the defence. If Alf assists Beth in breaking into the Post Office which he runs, he is surely guilty even though Beth has unknown to him threatened his family that she will kill them unless he helps her.

The basic thrust of the late Professor Smith's commentary seems to be that the distinction is at times useful but should not be allowed to dictate a result which is contrary to common sense or policy. Where the outcome would be 'pernicious' or 'outrageous' the dichotomy must not be applied. As Smith wrote elsewhere, [1991] Crim LR 151, he is 'not persuaded that the reception of the theory into English law is either practicable or desirable . . .'. Another difficulty is knowing whether an accused has an excuse or whether the prosecution has failed to prove the *mens rea*. For example, there is recent authority holding that insanity is no defence to strict offences because it affects the *mens rea*. If so, insanity is in truth a failure by the prosecution to prove all the elements of the offence, and the distinction between excuse and justification is inapplicable. Another approach is to keep the two categories but to add to them. For example, insanity may be taken out of the classification and called a 'status' defence. The accused is not guilty not because she has an excuse or justification but because she is of such a status, insane, that she should not be tried; this status affords her a defence. Lack of age, the defence of infancy, discussed next, can also be seen as a status defence. Arguably, automatism can also be characterised as a status defence: the accused had the status of being an involuntary actor when she performed the *actus reus* of the offence. Similarly, some defences are ones which may be called 'procedural'. For example, even if one has both the conduct and fault elements of the crime which one was alleged to have committed, one may nevertheless have the defence of diplomatic immunity.

There are many American critiques of the dichotomy. A book of this nature cannot deal with all of them. A way into the literature is via T. Morawetz 'Reconstructing the criminal defenses: the significance of justification' (1986) 77 JCL & Crim 277. Despite such criticisms the terms are infiltrating into English criminal law discourse and were espoused by the Law Commission in the 1989 draft Criminal Code. Clause 45 (1) refers to 'Acts justified or excused by' law.

A one-sentence summary of the distinction is that the accused who has a justification has acted rightly; he who has an excuse acted under some kind of disability. Another one-sentence summary of the law is: 'English criminal law does not make any clear-cut distinction between a justification and an excuse.' (Per Brooke LJ in the civil case of **Re A (Children) (Conjoined Twins: Surgical Separation)** [2001] Fam 147.) Whether it should is for a book on criminal law theory.

Infancy

> **Example**
>
> A girl of nine misappropriates another child's trike. She gives it to her father. Is the child guilty of theft? Is the father guilty of handling?
>
> These facts are similar to **Walters v Lunt** (1951) 35 Cr App R 94 (DC), which demonstrates that when the child is under the age of criminal responsibility (10), she is not guilty of any offence (it may also be difficult to show that the child was dishonest, dishonesty being one of the ingredients of theft, though all the other elements of theft are present); because the child does not commit theft, the father is not guilty of handling because the trike is not 'stolen' for the purposes of that crime and therefore the prosecution cannot prove this element of the offence.

The law absolves infants under the **age** of 10 from responsibility for what would otherwise be criminal acts or omissions. The defence of infancy (sometimes called nonage) applies to all crimes including strict liability offences. Therefore, this defence is not based on the absence of the mental capacity to commit an offence. The policy appears to be that children cannot distinguish between (moral) right and wrong. It might be added that punishment would serve little purpose, for some minors would not be able to link the penalty with breach of the law and so would not be deterred for the future. However, since 1998, children aged 10 and upwards are treated as if they were adults for the purposes of criminal liability. There is a strong case that children of 10 should not be subject to criminal trial and sanctions on conviction because they do not have the mental capacity to understand what the consequences of their actions are.

(a) *Up to 10 (i.e. nine and below)*: A child cannot be convicted of any offence: Children and Young Persons Act 1933, s 50, as amended by the Act of the same name from 1963, s 16. Such person may, however, be subject to care proceedings in the youth court.

   One effect of infancy follows from the child's not being guilty. If an adult encourages a child to commit a crime and the child does perform the *actus reus*, the child is the innocent agent and the adult is deemed to be the principal offender. See Chapter 5. Moreover, since the child is not guilty of theft, the person who would otherwise be guilty of handling stolen goods is not guilty because the goods have not been stolen. In **Walters v Lunt** (1951) 35 Cr App R 94 (DC) a child of seven took another child's tricycle in circumstances in which, had he been adult, the act would have amounted to theft. Since he could not be convicted, the tricycle was not stolen and his parents could not be found guilty of the offence which is now called handling.

(b) *10 to 13 (inclusive)*: There was until 1998 a rebuttable presumption that the child cannot form *mens rea*. This presumption was rebutted by the prosecution showing that the accused had a 'mischievous discretion', that is, that the child knew that what he was doing was morally or seriously wrong. This law was approved in the White Paper, *Crime, Justice and Protecting the Public*, Cm 965, 1990. 'The [Labour] Government does not intend to change these arrangements which make proper allowance for the fact that children's understanding, knowledge and ability to reason are still developing.' The presumption no longer saved children from being hanged, but it remained as a protection for children. Each child had to be looked at individually.

The doctrine had been under attack for some time because of its differential application to children from good homes, who – knowing the difference between right and wrong – were more likely to be convicted than children from bad homes, and because – in an era of education for all – children did know when they were doing wrong. It has to be said, however, that in the words of Lord Lowry in *C v DPP* [1996] 1 AC 1 (HL), 'better formal education, and earlier sophistication, do not guarantee that the child will more readily distinguish right from wrong'. The Lords reinstated the law that proof that the child committed the *actus reus* did not in itself prove that he knew that his act was seriously wrong, no matter whether his act was horrifying or appraised as seriously wrong by ordinary people, and that proof that the child knew that what he was doing was naughty did not demonstrate that he knew that it was seriously wrong. However, the then-existing law was condemned *obiter* by several of their Lordships. Lord Jauncey was representative: 'It is almost an affront to common sense to presume that a boy of 12 or 13 who steals a high-powered motor car, damages other cars while driving it, knocks down a uniformed police officer and then runs away when stopped is unaware that he is doing wrong.' He (a Scottish judge) also noted that the presumption did not apply in Scotland.

The House of Lords in *C v DPP* called for parliamentary revision of the law, which happened with the Crime and Disorder Act 1998. The Law Commission in its draft Criminal Code, 1989, had earlier recommended no change because it did not wish to see the extension of the use of the criminal law to deal with children. European countries vary tremendously in the minimum age of criminal responsibility. It is seven in Cyprus, Ireland, Liechtenstein and Switzerland, but 16 in Andorra, Poland, Portugal and Spain, and 18 in Belgium and Luxembourg. There is no minimum age in the United Nations Convention on the Rights of the Child. The call in *C v DPP* was taken up by the government.

The Crime and Disorder Act 1998, s 34, abolished the rebuttable presumption that children aged 10–13 inclusive were not guilty of crimes unless, in addition to the *actus reus* and *mens rea*, the prosecution proved that they knew that what they were doing was seriously wrong. The Home Office's Consultation Paper, *Tackling Youth Crime*, 1997, proposed to abolish the presumption because:

(i)   a child over 10 can distinguish right from wrong in an age of universal compulsory education;

(ii) such a child no longer needs protection from state punishment because the youth court has many sentencing options;

(iii) the presumption was illogical in that it could be rebutted by showing that the accused was of normal mental development for a child of that age, yet it was presumed that the accused did not know right from wrong;

(iv) the interests of justice and the victim are not served by not convicting children;

(v) discontinuance of prosecution is not in the young offender's interests if it means that the opportunity is missed to take appropriate action to prevent reoffending; and

(vi) 'justice is best served by allowing courts to take account of the child's age and maturity at the point of sentence, not by binding them to presume that normal children are incapable of the most basic moral judgments'.

The White Paper, *No More Excuses*, Cm 3809, 1997, stressed that children of 10–14 do know the difference between naughtiness and serious wrongdoing and, therefore, the presumption was contrary to common sense. Moreover, excuses were not to be made for children who offend.

The general view is that the criminal liability of children aged 10–13 is now assimilated with that of older people. There was, however, a different view put forward by N. Walker 'The end of an old song' (1999) 149 NLJ 64. This held that while the presumption is abolished, children can still have a defence if they can show that they do not know that what they did was seriously wrong. It must be said that this is exactly what the White Paper rejected. For a case supporting Walker's views see *Crown Prosecution Service* v *P* [2007] EWHC 946 (Admin). However, in *T* [2008] EWCA Crim 815 the court rejected *CPS* v *P*, holding that s 34 of the Crime and Disorder Act 1998 abolished not just the rebuttable presumption of incapacity but the whole concept that a child aged 10–13 inclusive could not be guilty of any crime. This was confirmed by the House of Lords in *JTB* [2009] 1 AC 130, and the legal position is now clear.

Infancy and human rights

Setting the minimum age of criminal responsibility at 10 does not offend the European Convention on Human Rights. In *T* v *UK* [2000] Crim LR 187 the European Court of Human Rights held there was no 'common standard amongst the member states of the Council of Europe as to the minimum age of criminal responsibility. Even if England and Wales is among the few European jurisdictions to retain a low age of criminal responsibility, the age of ten cannot be said to be so young as to differ disproportionately from the age-limit followed by other European States.' Therefore, there was no breach of Article 3, which prohibits torture and inhuman or degrading treatment. The Court in *T* v *UK* did, however, say that: '. . . it is essential that a child charged with an offence is dealt with in a manner which takes full account of his age, level of maturity and intellectual and emotional capacities, and that steps are taken to promote his ability to understand and participate in the proceedings.' The Court held that the trial of the defendants in *T* v *UK* did breach Article 6 because the state had failed to ensure that the boys understood the nature of the criminal proceedings against them.

A Practice Direction *Crown Court (Trial of Children and Young Persons)* [2000] 1 Cr App R 483 was issued in an attempt to satisfy the demands of Article 6, but in *SC* v *UK* (2005) 40 EHRR 226 the European Court of Human Rights held that the changes did not ensure that young people always had the opportunity to take part in their trials in a meaningful fashion.

Duress

Example

Roland threatens to kneecap Steph and her young family unless she drives him and the bomb he is carrying to Tessa's house; he tells her that he wishes to blow up Tessa's house with her inside. She very reluctantly obeys and the bomb does explode, killing Tessa and her young family. May Steph have a defence of duress?

The defence of duress has been tightened in recent years by the House of Lords' decision in **Hasan** [2005] 2 AC 467 (also known as **Z**) but at no time has it provided a defence to murder. The classic authority underlying duress by threats, duress of circumstances and necessity is **Dudley and Stephens** (1884) 14 QBD 273 (CCR), which involved the killing of a cabin boy after their vessel *The Mignonette* had sunk. The killers were found guilty of murder despite the necessitous circumstances (basically, 'kill the weakest member of the crew and eat him or die'). In duress (by threats) the authority is the Privy Council one of **Abbott v R** [1977] AC 755 where the accused who had killed a woman by ramming a cutlass down her throat and burying her alive was found guilty of murder despite the fact that he was coerced into the killing by a gangland boss.

Note that duress does apply where the threat is to persons for whom the accused is responsible, as was said particularly in **Hasan**; therefore on the facts there is no problem with the threat being made not just to Steph but also to her young family; and note too that the threat must be one of death or serious injury, as it is here: see, for example, **Graham** [1982] 1 WLR 294 (CA).

The death of Tessa's family is attributed to Steph via the doctrine of transferred malice.

Introduction

The law of **duress** may be seen as the outcome of two conflicting principles. The first was put by Sir James Fitzjames Stephen in his *History of the Criminal Law of England* (Sweet & Maxwell, 1883) 107:

> It is, of course, a misfortune for a man that he should be placed between two fires but it would be a much greater misfortune for society at large if criminals could confer impunity upon their agents by threatening them with death or violence if they refused to execute their commands.

This sentiment was approved by the Court of Appeal in **Gotts** [1991] 2 All ER 1. This case reached the House of Lords, and that body's decision is discussed below. The law is there as a deterrent to people surrendering to threats. The contrasting rationale was adopted by another Court of Appeal in **Ortiz** (1986) 83 Cr App R 173:

> The essence of [this] defence is that the will of the subject of the threats is no longer entirely under his own control because of the fear engendered by those threats.

To convict persons in situations of duress would be inhumane. These people are blameless. Punishment would serve no purpose. A phrase sometimes used in this context is that the act of the accused was 'morally involuntary'. He could not help doing as he did, although his conduct was not truly involuntary because he had control over his limbs: indeed, he may well have both the *actus reus* and *mens rea* of the offence. If, however, one were to adopt the moral involuntariness rationale, some of the rules become suspect: why are threats to reveal financial or sexual misdeeds excluded?

The second rationale was adopted by the Law Commission in its Report No. 83, *Defences of General Application*, 1978. Duress was to be seen as a concession to human weakness: the accused had chosen one evil, the apparent breaking of the law, when faced with a choice of two evils, the second one being to suffer serious injury or death either personally or to a third party (see later for a possible qualification of this proposition). The Court of Appeal rephrased the 'choice-of-evils' rationale in **Abdul-Hussain** [1999] Crim LR 570 as the alleged crime must be 'a reasonable and proportionate response' to the threat. The Law Commission's view was accepted by the House of Lords in **Howe** [1987] AC 417. However, as the Court of Appeal pointed out in **Shepherd** (1988) 86 Cr App R 47, this rationale fails to reveal why duress is a defence, rather than a factor in mitigating sentence. It also does not explain why duress is not a defence to all crimes. (Compare loss of control, which to all crimes except murder is an element in mitigation of sentence, not a defence to the offence.) Recent authorities have the effect of reining in any expansion of the defence: see Lord Bingham in **Hasan** [2005] UKHL 25 who said that duress should not confer immunity on those society fears.

Duress and reasonableness

In the important case of *Graham* [1982] 1 WLR 294 (CA) the accused, a homosexual, lived with his wife and a man. He was taking drugs for anxiety. The other man, a violent person, was jealous of the wife. At that man's suggestion, the accused and that man killed the wife. The defendant's conviction for murder was upheld. The Court of Appeal determined that it did not matter that his fortitude had been weakened by drugs. A sober person would not have given way. The court held that the test of human weakness was: how would a sober and reasonable person with the accused's characteristics (race, sex, age, etc.) have reacted? (The reference to 'sober' is omitted when there is no evidence of intoxication. In fact in provocation (since repealed), from where this test derives, the accused had a defence if because of intoxication he believed that there was provocation but in fact there was none.) A reasonable, frail old person would not be expected to reach the standard of fortitude of a reasonable, strong young person. On the facts of *Graham*, the question was: how would a reasonable bisexual man have reacted? This test was imported from the now repealed defence of provocation and approved by the House of Lords in *Howe*, above. The major modern authority, *Hasan*, above, approved the law. As in the defence of loss of control (see Chapter 12), which to some degree replaced provocation, there is a subjective and an objective test. First, did he succumb? Secondly, might a reasonable person with his legally relevant characteristics have succumbed? The argument in favour of *Graham* runs thus. The accused has committed what would otherwise be an offence but has acted under duress. If a person of reasonable fortitude might have capitulated to the threat, and this accused did, then the accused is excused from liability.

In *Bowen* [1996] 2 Cr App R 157 the Court of Appeal garnered the following propositions in relation to the second issue from the cases (Stuart-Smith LJ at 166–167):

(1) The mere fact that the accused is more pliable, vulnerable, timid or susceptible to threats than a normal person are not characteristics with which it is legitimate to invest the reasonable/ordinary person for the purpose of considering the objective test.

(2) The defendant may be in a category of persons who the jury may think less able to resist pressure than people not within that category. Obvious examples are age, where a young person may well not be so robust as a mature one; possibly sex, though many women would doubtless consider they had as much moral courage to resist pressure as men; pregnancy, where there is added fear for the unborn child; serious physical disability, which may inhibit self-protection; recognised mental illness or psychiatric condition, such as post-traumatic stress disorder leading to learned helplessness.

(3) Characteristics which may be relevant in considering provocation, because they relate to the nature of the provocation itself, will not necessarily be relevant in cases of duress. Thus homosexuality may be relevant to provocation if the provocative words or conduct are related to this characteristic; it cannot be relevant in duress, since there is no reason to think that homosexuals are less robust in resisting threats of the kind that are relevant in duress cases.

(4) Characteristics due to self-induced abuse, such as alcohol, drugs or glue-sniffing, cannot be relevant.

It is uncertain why the court took the view that a 'recognised mental illness or psychiatric condition' was needed. This dictum was approved by the Court of Appeal in *Moseley*, unreported, 21 April 1999. One should focus on whether this accused was capable of resisting the threat. It is also uncertain why some characteristics listed in (2) may affect the standard of fortitude. It may be difficult to distinguish timidity arising from a mental illness (which may be taken into consideration) from timidity arising from the accused's character (which may not). Is a person suffering from 'serious physical disability', even one which may 'inhibit self-protection', to be expected to be able to resist pressure less than an able-bodied person? Furthermore, addictions, for example to alcohol, are excluded even though they constitute recognised mental illnesses. The reference, however, does ensure that abused people can adduce evidence as mitigation of sentence to show that their wills have been crushed: *Emery* (1993) 14 Cr App R (S) 394 (CA). Similarly, in *Antar* [2006] EWCA Crim 2708 evidence from a psychologist that the accused was suffering from learning difficulties and had more than the usual level of suggestiveness was admissible in determining whether the objective test as to reasonable steadfastness was satisfied.

The court in *Graham* stated that its test conformed with public policy. One might, however, say that the same threat may be more compelling when used against a weak person than a normal one. If the conceptual basis of duress is that individuals are not expected to resist extremely compelling threats, some persons are not as able to resist threats as others are. Yet the law demands that even timid persons conform to a high standard of behaviour: the law makes no concession to the weakness of timid persons. The fact is irrelevant that the accused was vulnerable (*Horne* [1994] Crim LR 584 (CA)), had a weak personality because of sexual abuse as a child (*Hurst* [1995] 1 Cr App R 82 (CA)), had suffered ill-treatment and violence (*Moseley*, unreported, 21 April 1999 (CA), which confirmed that for a mental characteristic to be included it had to be a medically recognised illness – here, learned helplessness caused by the accused's relationships with violent men), or that the accused is unstable with a 'grossly elevated neurotic state' (*Hegarty* [1994] Crim LR 353 (CA)). If these characteristics were to be included in the reasonable firmness test, they would undermine it. A person of reasonable firmness is by definition not one of little firmness. As the court said in *Horne*: 'A person of reasonable firmness is an average member of the public; not a hero necessarily, not a coward, just an average person.' It is fascinating to note that the mental instability of the accused in *Hegarty* had earlier provided him with a defence of diminished responsibility on a charge of murdering his wife. Omitting the reasonable steadfastness point in relation to duress is a misdirection.

Since the reasonable person is not drunk, the accused who is drunk is to be judged against the standards of the reasonable sober person. In *Graham* the accused had been taking valium and alcohol. The Court of Appeal held that the jury should disregard the fact that drugs or drink or both had reduced the accused's ability to resist the threats. His intoxicated state was not to be attributed to the reasonable person when judging how a reasonable person with his legally relevant characteristics might have reacted. The case of *Kingston* [1995] 2 AC 355 (HL) is a reminder of the possibility of involuntary intoxication. It could be that an accused whose drink has been spiked is to be judged against the standards of the reasonable involuntarily intoxicated person. Self-induced drug addiction was rejected as a relevant characteristic in *Flatt* [1996] Crim LR 576 (CA). The accused was addicted to crack cocaine. His addiction was not to be attributed to the 'person of reasonable firmness' when judging his resistance to a drug-dealer. The addiction was a self-induced state, not a characteristic. As a result, all self-induced characteristics are irrelevant. An alternative view is that such is a characteristic but it does not bear on the accused's liability to resist threats. Triers of fact may have difficulty envisaging what they are being asked to do, and they are not helped by the exclusion of evidence which would tend to show that the accused was not a person of reasonable firmness such as that he was weak, vulnerable or susceptible to threats.

Because duress is on most arguments an excuse and not a justification, one might expect the 'reasonable person' test to play a part and the theory is partly reflected in the case law. In *Graham* the court also ruled that the accused must have good cause for his belief, and that his belief must have been based on reasonable grounds. The accused would have no good cause for his belief if he did not think that the threat would be carried out. These objective tests were also approved in *Howe* and followed in *DPP* v *Davis* [1994] Crim LR 600 (DC) and *Abdul-Hussain* [1999] Crim LR 570 (CA). However, there is a contrary view, namely that in light of the onward march of subjectivism in the House of Lords (*K* [2002] 1 AC 462, *B* v *DPP* [2000] 2 AC 428, and *G* [2004] 1 AC 1034) there is no room for an objective element, the reasonableness of the mistake. Even before these authorities, in *Martin* [2000] 2 Cr App R 42 the Court of Appeal ruled that in relation to duress by threats the test of belief was subjective. The accused is to be judged according to the facts as they appeared to him. Mantell LJ noted the analogy between duress and mistake which Lord Lane CJ had mentioned in *Graham*. Since the test in mistake is subjective, so should it be in respect of both forms of duress. An alternative view is that this case is simply wrong! Part of the reasoning against *Martin* is this: duress is an excuse; therefore, what the accused had done under duress was wrong; therefore, he should have a defence only if he has a reasonable explanation for committing what would otherwise be a crime. In *Martin* Mantell LJ purported to follow his previous judgment in the duress of circumstances case of *Cairns* [1999] 2 Cr App R 137 (CA) but in fact he had used the objective test in that decision ('reasonably believed'). The Court of Appeal in *Safi* [2004] 1 Cr App R 14, a case involving hijacking, certified a question for the House of Lords whether the accused's belief was based on reasonable or (only) genuine grounds, but it did say that although the approval of *Graham* was *obiter*, the fact that the House of Lords had expressly confirmed this particular point meant that *Graham* should be followed unless it was overruled or reversed. The House refused leave to appeal. However, in *Hasan* [2005] 2 AC 467 the Lords held that the objective approach was correct. Lord Bingham said: '. . . there is no warrant for relaxing the requirement that the belief must be reasonable as well as genuine.' Therefore, *Martin* is wrong. It should be noted that, provided the accused reasonably believes that there is a threat, there need not actually be one.

If the accused had a reasonable belief in the threat, it need not be proved that the threat actually existed: *Cairns*. The victim spreadeagled himself on the accused's windscreen. The latter did not know who the former was and was frightened by the former's friend shouting. The accused drove on. When he slowed down for a speed hump, the victim fell under the car and suffered very serious injuries. It was held that it was sufficient that the accused believed on reasonable grounds that a threat of death or serious harm existed. There are, however, authorities to the contrary. In *Abdul-Hussain*, above, it was said that the danger must 'objectively' exist and this statement was approved by the Court of Appeal in *S* [2001] 1 WLR 2206. Unfortunately all these cases were heard in the same court, and the authorities are inconsistent.

If enacted the draft Criminal Code, Law Com. No. 177, 1989, cl 41(1), would reverse *Graham* by holding that any mistake, reasonable or not, would give rise to the defence ('a person who acts in the belief that a circumstance exists has any defence that he would have if the circumstance existed'), while cl 42(3) would take into account the accused's own capacity to resist. The Law Commission continues to approve of this proposed reform: Report No. 218, *Legislating The Criminal Law – Offences against the Person and General Principles*, 1993. The argument is that reasonableness relates to evidence, not to substantive law. Certainly, as said above, the objective test as to belief in *Graham* and *Howe* looks frail after the House of Lords' decisions in *B* v *DPP* [2000] 2 AC 428, *K* [2002] 1 AC 462 and *G* [2004] 1 AC 1034 which strongly support the subjective test of mistaken belief.

The question of reasonableness is sensible in the defence of loss of control because one is comparing the accused with a person of reasonable firmness sharing the accused's characteristics to see whether the hypothetical person would have done as the accused did. In duress, however, the events are not connected with the defendant's characteristics. They are foisted on him. On this approach the reasonableness test in duress does not bear the same function as in loss of control, and one might ask whether it is needed. It perhaps serves no purpose except to deny the defence to persons who ought to have it. Certainly loss of control and duress are not directly comparable defences. Loss of control is a defence only to murder, whereas duress is not a defence to that crime, and provocation is based on the loss of self-control, whereas the modern English view of duress is that it is based on a choice of evils, the accused breaking the law in order to escape a greater evil (the concession-to-human-frailty argument).

For a list of most of the limitations on the defence of duress see the judgment of Smith J in *Hurley and Murray* [1967] VR 526 and *Abdul-Hussain* [1999] Crim LR 570 (CA). The accused must know of the facts which give rise to this defence.

The effect of a successful plea of duress

The accused escapes conviction if the prosecution fails to disprove duress beyond reasonable doubt. There are *dicta* to the contrary in the dissenting speech of Lord Simon in *Lynch v DPP for Northern Ireland* [1975] AC 653 (HL) but they are wrong: see the House of Lords, *Howe*, above. The burden of proof for all defences lies on the prosecution, with one common law exception (insanity). Parliament may place the onus on the accused but has not done so in respect of duress (cf. diminished responsibility).

The burden of proof

There are several cases, such as *Gill* [1963] 1 WLR 841 (CCA), which state that the prosecution must disprove duress. For an Australian authority see *Smyth* [1963] VR 737. The judge must instruct the jury that the prosecution bears the burden. Contrary *dicta* in *Steane* [1947] KB 997 (CCA) are incorrect. *Lynch* finally settled the issue. The defendant, however, bears the evidential burden. He must lead evidence that his mind was affected by duress.

Duress, *actus reus* and *mens rea*

There are three theories as to how duress fits in with *actus reus* and *mens rea*:

(a) The accused had no *mens rea*. This approach would mean that duress would not be a defence to strict liability offences, contrary to the Divisional Court's ruling in *Eden DC v Braid* [1998] 12 May (DC). This approach was rejected by Lords Edmund-Davies and Kilbrandon in *Lynch*, above, the Northern Ireland Court of Criminal Appeal in *Fitzpatrick* [1977] NI 20, and the Lords in *Howe* [1987] AC 417, refusing to follow *dicta* of Lord Goddard CJ in *Bourne* (1952) 36 Cr App R 125 (CCA). A person acting under duress does nevertheless intend to act, knowing of the consequences, although his freedom of action is constrained by the coercive power of the duressor.

(b) The defendant did not act voluntarily because his will was overborne. But for the duress, he would not have committed the crime. Therefore, there is no *actus reus*. This viewpoint was rejected in *Lynch*. (Compare automatism where the accused does not act voluntarily, but in a different sense. The accused is not unconscious when he acts under duress.) The defendant acts under pressure but he is not forced by someone's hand to do as he did. He had a choice. Nevertheless, it is arguable contrary to *Lynch* that when he acts under duress, he is compelled to do so in a way not dissimilar from involuntary action. In relation to the 'overborne will' theory, it is suggested that there are pressures which overbear the will just as much as duress but which do not constitute duress or any other defence. For example, financial pressures may overbear the will but it is not a defence to say that the accused stole because his will was overborne by worries about the mortgage.

(c) The accused had both *actus reus* and *mens rea* but duress is the reason why he escapes conviction. This stance was seemingly accepted in *Lynch*, *Fitzpatrick* and *Howe*. In *Lynch* Lord Wilberforce said that the accused 'completes the act and knows that he is doing so; but the addition of the element of duress prevents the law from treating what he has done as a crime'. Lord Simon said: 'There are both *actus reus* and *mens rea* . . . duress is not inconsistent with act and will . . .' The accused's conduct is excused, even though he intended harm, because society stipulates that he could not have been expected to act otherwise: faced with a choice of two evils, he chose to break the law.

Whichever theory is correct, there must be an evidential basis for duress. In *O'Too*, unreported, 4 March 2004, the accused said that he associated with members of a criminal gang but not that he was a member of it. Since he was not a member of a gang, there was no room for duress based on the law stated in the next section. In *Giaquinto* [2001] EWCA Crim 2696 it was said that the judge should not leave the defence to the jury if the accused's evidence contradicted it.

Risk of being subjected to threats

In the mid-1970s the Northern Ireland Court of Criminal Appeal held that duress was not a defence where the accused voluntarily joined up with violent criminals and thereby exposed himself to the risk of being compelled by pressure of a violent kind to commit an offence: *Fitzpatrick*, above. The accused had joined a terrorist organisation, the IRA. The court held that he had no defence to a charge of robbery. The House of Lords refused leave to appeal; so the assumption was that the law was as the Northern Irish Court had stated. In *Howe*, above, Lord Hailsham approved *Fitzpatrick*. Since then English courts have adopted the doctrine: *Sharp* [1987] QB 853, *Shepherd*, above, and *Ali* [1995] Crim LR 303, noted below (all CA). There is no need for the defendant to join an organisation: it is sufficient if he joins a one-off conspiracy. *Hasan* [2005] 2 AC 467 (HL) is the most authoritative supporting case. An accused is liable when he 'voluntarily becomes or remains associated with others engaged in criminal activity in a situation in which he knows or ought reasonably to know that he may be the subject of compulsion . . .' (Lord Bingham). The case is not limited to gangs. The objective element in the formulation should be noted: 'ought reasonably'. Earlier cases such as *Sharp* which had used a subjective formula are wrong.

In *Ali* the accused, a heroin addict, was a dealer for the duressor. He used all of one batch for himself, thereby placing himself in debt to the duressor, who gave him a gun and told him to rob a bank or a building society: otherwise he would be killed. The court held that he could not rely on duress because he had voluntarily joined himself to a violent individual. A similar case is *Heath* [2000] Crim LR 109 (CA) where the accused became indebted to a drugs dealer and thereby accepted the risk that he might be threatened with violence if he did not act as a drugs carrier. The Court of Appeal held in *Lewis* (1993) 96 Cr App R 412 that for this rule to apply the criminal enterprise and the threat must not be too remote from each other. The accused took part in a robbery with the duressor. Both were imprisoned and the latter attacked the former while they were both in prison. The accused refused to give evidence against the duressor. The court held that he was not guilty of contempt of court. The robbery was too remote from the alleged offence. The Court of Appeal in *Sharp* stated that the accused must be an active member of the organisation at the time of the pressure for this rule to apply. The court in *Ali* [2008] EWCA Crim 716 held that while most threats of violence take place in criminal groups, the law is not restricted to groups: '... it is the risk of being subjected to compulsion by threats of violence that must be foreseen or foreseeable that is relevant, rather than the nature of the activity in which the threatener is engaged' (Dyson LJ).

The pressure on the accused must be one which took the form of violence or the threat of violence either to the accused or to a member of his immediate family: *Baker* [1999] 2 Cr App R 335 (CA). It may be that pressure on the accused via a threat to a third party is sufficient. This would make the law consistent with that on duress and duress of circumstances generally. *Baker* also illustrates the point that this exception is not limited to joining a criminal gang; it is sufficient to associate with violent people. The Lords in *Hasan* held that the accused was not afforded the defence when he voluntarily associated himself with violent people: there was no need for the prosecutor to prove that he knew he would be coerced to commit offences, much less that he knew he would be coerced to commit offences of the type which in fact occurred. Any suggestion to that effect in *Baker* was incorrect. The accused, held the House, had no defence when he knew, or ought reasonably to have known, that he might be subject to threats. Lord Bingham expressed the policy of the law: 'to discourage association with known criminals ... or their associates ...'.

Sometimes the judge can rule that the accused cannot rely on duress, as when he joins a terrorist organisation or a violent gang: *Baker*. Otherwise it is a question for the jury whether the accused accepted the risk of violence on joining the gang or criminal activity (*Baker*). In the 1995 *Ali* case the court said that this rule applied whenever the accused knew he would become part of a crime. He did not need to know which specific crime (e.g. robbery) he would be ordered to commit. The Lords approved this principle in *Hasan*.

The law on joining violent gangs ceases to apply when the accused has served his sentence and abandons a life of crime. A subsequent threat by a former conspirator will now lead to the accused's regaining the defence of duress.

The Court of Appeal in *Harmer* [2002] Crim LR 401 rejected an argument that the accused should have a defence of duress when he did not foresee that he might be asked to commit crimes, though he had foreseen that he might be subjected to violence. It was sufficient that he had voluntarily exposed himself to threats by becoming indebted to a drugs supplier. *Heath*, above, is similar.

One might argue that this limitation ought not to be part of the law. If the basis of the defence is that the accused's will was overborne, his will was overborne when he was obliged to commit a crime by the gang he had joined. Moreover, the behaviour the courts are aiming at is membership of bodies which carry out illegal actions. The defence of duress is not an apt place for the courts to punish this conduct. In *Lynch*, above, Lord Morris said that defendants must not put themselves under the sway of gangster tyrants. It is doubtful whether this restriction does in fact help to dissolve the subjugation of those who are under the sway of such tyrants. Should there be no concession to frailty if the accused has voluntarily assumed the risk of duress? Nevertheless, the Law Commission in its Report No. 218, *Legislating the Criminal Code: Offences against the Person and General Principles* of 1993 proposed that this rule should continue to apply.

The types of threat sufficient to raise this defence

(a) Threats of death or serious physical violence are sufficient. For example, a threat to cut up two girls on the streets of Salford was a sufficient menace in *Hudson and Taylor* [1971] 2 QB 202 (CA). The Privy Council in *Sephakela* v *R* [1954] Crim LR 723 restricted duress to these types of threat and the Court of Appeal in *A*, unreported, 12 May 2003, doubted whether the threat of a punch in the face was sufficient to give rise to this defence. Similarly in the duress of circumstances case of *New Forest Local Education Authority* v *E* [2007] EWHC 2584 (Admin) violence by a son to the accused, his mother, and her daughter was insufficient to constitute a threat of death or serious injury. 'Serious harm' has not been much discussed in the cases. In *Quayle* [2006] 1 WLR 3642 it was held that pain, even extreme neurological pain as a result of the amputation of a leg, was insufficient: death or serious injury was required. The avoidance of severe pain was not to be treated as the avoidance of a threat to life or serious injury. The Court of Appeal noted that pain involves 'a large element of subjectivity'. Therefore, taking cannabis to avoid pain remains an offence. It ought to bear the same meaning as grievous bodily harm, discussed in Chapter 13, a phrase which includes serious psychiatric injury but see (f) below. Where the threat is insufficient to give this defence, it is a mitigating factor in punishment.

(b) A threat to expose someone to a charge involving immorality is not enough; for example *Valderrama-Vega* [1985] Crim LR 220 (CA) involving homosexuality. Similarly, as occurred in that case a threat to make the accused lose money must be disregarded.

(c) Threats to property would seem not to be enough. In *M'Growther* (1746) 18 State Tr 391 the accused was guilty when friends of Bonnie Prince Charlie compelled him to join their rebellion under a threat among other things to steal his cattle. The Divisional Court held in *DPP* v *Milcoy* [1993] Crown Office Digest 200 that a threat by a cohabitee to his partner's pony and dogs did not give rise to a defence of duress.

(d) Threats of false imprisonment are almost certainly not enough (for example among recent cases *M(L)* [2011] 1 Cr App R 12 and *Dao* [2012] EWCA Crim 1717, both *obiter*), but there is a contrary *dictum* of Lord Goddard CJ in *Steane* [1947] KB 997. Modern cases refer only to death and serious injury. Moreover, modern law has become narrower after *Hasan*, above, and extending the defence to cover imprisonment would be a move contrary to this shift in policy.

(e) A threat to reveal the accused's financial position is insufficient: *Valderrama-Vega*, above. In *Lynch* Lord Simon said that a threat to bankrupt the accused's son was not a defence, for the law had to draw a line somewhere and this type of threat fell below that line.

(f) A threat of serious psychological harm is insufficient: *Baker* [1999] 2 Cr App R 335 (CA). This is an authority on duress of circumstances, but in this respect the same principles apply. The decision is out of line with those on the law of non-fatal offences where 'harm' does nowadays include psychological injury. See *Ireland; Burstow* [1998] AC 147 (HL). It is suggested that *Baker* is incorrect, for what difference is there between physical and psychological harm if both are severe? The Court of Appeal in *Shayler* [2001] 1 WLR 2206 said that duress existed to protect 'the physical and mental well-being of a person' but it cannot be said that the court was thinking of this issue when it did so. (The case is also one of duress of circumstances but the same principle applies.)

(g) There has to be a threat. Committing a crime because one believes one has no choice is not sufficient.

(h) Outside circumstances prompting suicidal tendencies were held in **Rodger** [1998] 1 Cr App R 143 (CA) not to constitute grounds giving rise to duress of circumstances. The law was that the threat had to be extraneous to the accused. The court said that to allow a defence of duress based on suicidal tendencies would give people a licence to commit crimes if they were vulnerable. The test for duress was an objective standard, not a subjective one. **Rodger** may be criticised on the ground that the reason why the defendants had such tendencies was because the Home Secretary had increased their sentences, an external cause, but the court said that the circumstances were 'solely' ones subjective to the defendants. The Home Secretary's decision was the background to the suicidal tendencies, not the legal cause of the desire to escape from prison.

It seems strange that if duress is based on the overborne-will theory, only one type of threat is considered sufficient to overbear the will, despite the fact that another type of threat has actually caused the accused to act as he did. If fear of force is the motivating factor, why are not other fears taken into account? If I steal to avoid bankruptcy, I have no defence. If I drive dangerously to avoid being raped, I have no defence.

In **Graham**, above, the Court of Appeal restricted its model direction to threats of death or serious physical injury. In **Abdul-Hussain**, above, the Court of Appeal spoke of 'death or serious injury'. Two cases on the analogous defence of duress of circumstances call for 'death or serious injury'/'death or serious bodily injury' (**Conway** [1989] QB 290 (CA)) and 'death or serious injury'/'death or serious physical injury' (**Martin** [1989] 1 All ER 652 (CA)). It is unclear whether the court definitely meant to exclude serious mental injury, a point not raised on the facts. The Law Commission in its 1993 Report No. 218 recommended that the restriction to death and serious injury should continue.

The threat that the accused perceived need not be one which in fact exists. It is sufficient that the accused believed on reasonable grounds that he had good cause to fear death or serious harm. In **Cairns**, above, a driver drove off with a youth on his car bonnet. He was frightened both of the youth, who had his face against the windscreen, and of the youth's friends who followed the car shouting and gesticulating. In fact they were trying to get the youth to climb off the car. The court held that it did not matter that there was in truth no threat: it was the accused's perception of the situation that counted.

The threat need not be the sole cause of the accused's acting as he did. The defence applies if he would not have committed the offence but for the threat: **Valderrama-Vega, Ortiz** (both above).

Threats to whom?

Successful applications of the defence in England have involved the accused or his close family. In **K** (1984) 78 Cr App R 82 (CA), the threat involved the defendant's mother. In **Wright** [2000] Crim LR 510 (CA) the threat was to the accused's boyfriend. The court held that the accused must reasonably regard herself responsible for the person threatened, and the Court of Appeal approved this limitation in **S** [2001] 1 WLR 2206, which is also known as **Shayler**. In **Ortiz**, above, the court assumed that a threat to a wife and child was sufficient, while in **Shepherd**, above, Mustill LJ did not refer to the fact that the threat was to the accused and her family. Lord Mackay in **Howe**, above, mentioned a close relation such as a 'well-loved child'. Rose LJ in **Abdul-Hussain**, above, spoke of 'imminent peril or death or serious injury to the defendant or those to whom he has responsibility'. This restriction comes from a specimen direction provided by the Judicial Studies Board ('person for whom [the accused] would reasonably regard himself as responsible').

Lord Bingham spoke to the same effect in *Hasan*, above. It is suggested that English law does not recognise such a restriction. The Supreme Court of Victoria went further in *Hurley and Murray* [1967] VR 526 to hold that the defence was available when the threat was to a mistress. In *DPP v Milcoy*, above, the court did not question that a threat to a cohabitee was sufficient. There would seem to be no stopping place despite the restriction in *Wright* and *S* to, as the latter case put it, 'a person or persons for whom he has responsibility or . . . persons for whom the situation makes him responsible'. As the Court of Appeal noted in *S*, *Pommell* [1995] 2 Cr App R 607 (CA) is at variance, because the threat was to kill various people not connected with the accused. A threat to a hostage unrelated to the accused would be sufficient. In duress of circumstances a threat to the accused or some other person is sufficient (*Conway* – threat to passenger in the accused's car, the parties not being related by blood, marriage or sex – and *Martin*, both above). If such a threat is sufficient in duress of circumstances, which applies the rules from duress, it should also be sufficient in duress itself. Moreover, as one of the doyens of US criminal law, R.M. Perkins, wrote: 'Impelled perpetration restated' (1981) 33 Hastings LJ 403:

> [a] person might be willing to chance that a threat to kill, if directed at that person, was only a bluff, but may not be willing to chance it if it was a threat to kill his or her spouse or child.

This argument may also apply to strangers. Surely reasonable people are concerned for the safety of others. The relationship between the accused and the person threatened can be taken into account when determining whether or not he could reasonably have resisted the threat. A threat to kill one's children may be more overwhelming than one to a stranger. It might be added that it is arguable whether an accused should be allowed to say that he injured a stranger in order to prevent injury to another stranger.

Opportunity to escape

Duress is not available if the accused could have avoided the threat without harm to himself or to others: *Heath* [2000] Crim LR 1011 (CA). The accused was ordered to help to transport drugs the next day or he would be harmed. It was held that he was given enough time to go to the police for protection or he could have moved into his relatives' house in Scotland. The court also said that the fact that the accused was a drug user and therefore unlikely to go to the police did not affect the law that he could have turned to the police in this situation. Similar is *Hasan*. Lord Bingham said: '. . . if the retribution threatened against the defendant or his family or a person for whom he reasonably feels responsible is not such as he reasonably expects to follow immediately or almost immediately . . . there may be little if any room for doubt that he could have taken evasive action, whether by going to the police or in some other way, to avoid the crime.' There must be no opportunity of putting oneself under effective official protection (as *Baker* shows: police protection might not have stopped the duressors to whom the duressees owed money for cannabis), such as that provided by the police and prison warders: *Lynch*, *Sharp*, both above. In *Gill*, above, the court considered that the accused would not have this defence if the threat was not to be carried out immediately because he could have sought police protection. The law seems to be that the accused is judged according to how a person of the same age and sex as him with his relevant characteristics would have reacted: *Baker* [1999] 2 Cr App R 335 (CA).

The modern view is that the accused may be afforded the defence if the threat is imminent; the threat need not be one which can be executed immediately: *Abdul-Hussain*, above. The defendants hijacked a plane to escape from Iraq. The rule now seems to be that it is sufficient that the threat was one which would probably be carried out in the near future; it does not matter that it was not one which could be carried out there and then. The defendants could successfully plead duress at a time earlier than a request for extradition from the state whose aircraft they hijacked. In **Eden DC v Braid**, above, Lord Bingham CJ spoke of the accused's having 'no other viable options'. In the well-known Irish case of **Attorney-General v Whelan** [1934] IR 518 Murnaghan J said: '. . . if there were reasonable opportunity for the will to reassert itself, no justification can be found in antecedent threat'. The Court of Appeal spoke to similar effect in **Abdul-Hussain**: 'The peril must operate on the mind of the defendant when he commits the otherwise criminal act, so as to overbear his will . . .' The Court of Appeal in **Hudson and Taylor**, however, held that the accused had the defence because police could not provide protection on all occasions. Girls in **Hudson** committed perjury 'by immediate and unavoidable pressure'. Lord Parker CJ said that it did not matter that the threat could not be carried out 'instantly, but after an interval'. As Lord Griffiths put it in **Howe**: 'If duress is introduced as a merciful concession to human frailty it seems hard to deny it to a man who knows full well that any official protection he may seek will not be effective to save him from the threat of death under which he has acted.' This statement is quite a strong one. It is not sufficient that the accused believes official protection will be ineffective: he must know 'full well' that it is so. It seems strange that the judiciary, one arm of the state, is saying that another arm of the state, the police, cannot protect the state's citizens. All the circumstances including the age of the accused have to be taken into account. On the facts it might be doubted that the threat would be put into place immediately.

Hudson and Taylor requires reconsideration in the light of **Cole** [1994] Crim LR 582 (CA) and **Hasan** (HL). The court in **Cole** held that there had to be a direct and immediate link between the threat and the crime. On the facts the crimes committed by the accused, robberies at building societies, in order to obtain money to repay lenders, were not closely enough linked to threats to himself, his girlfriend and their child. The threat was not specific enough. The court spoke of duress only applying when the duressor had nominated the crime. (This area of law may be one where duress of circumstances is different.) The concept of nomination may be difficult to apply: if I tell you to steal money, have I nominated the crime if you obtain the money by fraud?

The court is looking for a much more spontaneous reaction than occurred in **Hudson and Taylor**. Lord Bingham in **Hasan** stated that **Hudson and Taylor** was wrong: 'I cannot, consistently with principle, accept that a witness testifying in the Crown Court at Manchester has no opportunity to avoid complying with a threat incapable of execution then or there.' For a High Court of Australia view of **Hudson and Taylor** see **Taiapa v R** [2009] HCA 53. **Hudson and Taylor** was, however, applied by the Court of Appeal in **Abdul-Hussain**. Rose LJ said in chilling words: 'If Anne Frank had stolen a car to escape from Amsterdam and been charged with theft, the tenets of English law would not . . . have denied her a defence of duress of circumstances, on the ground that she should have waited for the Gestapo's knock on the door.' **Cole** was doubted: a spontaneous reaction was not needed. The same rule occurs in necessity: the threat need not be one which forced the accused to act immediately, as the facts of the civil case of **Re A** [2001] Fam 147, discussed below, illustrate. One twin would not cause the death of the other unless the surgeons operated immediately. It was sufficient that without separation fairly soon one twin would cause the other's death.

Once the threat is over, the accused must desist, for example **DPP v Davis**, above, where driving two miles to escape unwanted sexual advances with excess alcohol in the accused's blood ruled out the defence. Similar is the New South Wales case of **Lawrence**

[1980] NSWLR 122. The navigator of a ship was threatened with violence if he did not continue navigating. He had a reasonable opportunity to escape. Therefore, the threat no longer operated. In one of the latest English cases, *DPP v Tomkinson* [2001] RTR 583 (DC), the accused drove 72 miles to escape from her abusive husband. Her defence of duress of circumstances to a charge of driving with excess alcohol failed because she had driven further than necessary to escape the danger. A more recent authority is *DPP v Mullally* [2006] EWHC 3448 (Admin). The accused lost her defence of duress on a charge of driving with excess alcohol in her blood because she was being followed by the police.

Offences to which duress is not a defence

Duress does provide a defence to most crimes, such as perjury (*Hudson and Taylor*, above), contempt of court (*K*, above, and *Lewis*, above), what is now theft (*Gill*, above), possessing ammunition (*Subramaniam* [1956] 1 WLR 965 (PC)), hijacking (*Abdul-Hussain*) and what is now handling (the Irish authority of *Attorney-General v Whelan*, above). Note that one does not use gradations. One does not say that a threat of death alone is sufficient to give rise to a defence in a case of contempt, but one of serious harm suffices for, say, perjury. There are statements in the cases that duress is no defence to all felonies and no defence to robbery. This section considers those exceptions which are recognised in modern English law, though the fourth one has not been definitively established.

(a) According to *Abbott v R* [1977] AC 755, where the Privy Council split three to two, duress is no defence to the perpetrator of murder. The accused killed a British woman on the orders of a wicked individual. The victim among other things had a cutlass rammed down her throat and was buried alive. The Privy Council ruled that the accused had no defence even though he acted under pressure from a person who in English terms was a gangland boss. Lord Salmon bolstered his conclusion by reference to war criminals: they were not allowed to rely on duress or superior orders even though they might or would be shot if they disobeyed. He also referred to the speech in *Lynch*, above, of Lord Simon, who stated that if the defence were afforded, it would provide a charter for terrorists, gangleaders and kidnappers. Lord Simon's argument has since been undermined by the development of the rule relating to voluntary membership of criminal gangs: see above. *Abbott* was approved by the House of Lords in *Howe* (above). The accused had acted under the malign influence of one Murray. They had assaulted one person whom another killed; they were participants in that murder and actually killed another victim at Murray's order. The result is that the accused has no defence to murder even though he would have been killed had he not killed. The law that duress is no defence to murder remains as true today as it did more than 30 years ago: *Wilson* [2007] *The Times*, 6 June (Court of Appeal), in which it was held that the rule applied even to defendants who were children, though the court did express the view that the law was not perfect.

(b) *Howe* ruled that duress is no defence for accessories to murder. *Lynch*, above, was departed from. *Howe* applies in Canada: see *Sandham* 2009 CanLII 58605 (Supreme Court of Justice, Ontario). Lord Hailsham LC in *Howe* said:
   (i) the law had to protect the innocent;
   (ii) a person of ordinary fortitude was capable of heroism, that is, would sacrifice his life rather than take innocent life (Lord Hailsham noted that if the accused did kill, he could not rely on the principle that he was choosing the lesser evil, but as we have seen the English law of duress is not predicated on the 'lesser evil' principle);

(iii) the law should not protect cowards and poltroons;
(iv) conviction could be mitigated by administrative remedies, such as occurred in *Dudley and Stephens* (1884) 14 QBD 273 (CCR), on which see below. The prerogative of mercy could be used; the judge need not recommend a minimum length of life sentence; and the Parole Board could recommend release.

Lord Mackay emphasised that the law should not give anyone the power to choose who would survive. Lord Griffiths spoke of 'the special sanctity that the law attaches to human life'. Innocent life was to be protected even at the cost of the life of the accused or another. There are cases in other jurisdictions where duress has been held not to be a defence to secondary parties to murder such as *Brown* [1968] SASR 467 and *Harding* [1976] VR 129, and English institutional writers in the main supported the rule.

The House of Lords in *Howe* and law which fails to provide for a defence to murder may be criticised on several grounds:
(i) Circumstances may occur when a person of ordinary firmness would submit to threats. Why should a person suffer life imprisonment for not acting as a hero?
(ii) If the accused is ordered under threat of death to injure someone seriously, for example to kneecap him, and the victim dies, he is guilty of murder. The threat was: injure someone or be killed, and the accused has no defence. On a choice-of-evils approach the accused chose the lesser evil. What if the threat is to the accused's family? Is it really the legal position that the law encourages a person to stand by while his family is killed? The accused remains guilty of murder even if the victim refused a blood transfusion because he was a Jehovah's Witness. It seems harsh to convict the accused of murder in these circumstances.
(iii) The discretion not to prosecute does not always save the law from absurdity. The accused was prosecuted in *Anderton v Ryan* [1985] AC 560 (HL) even in circumstances in which the Law Commission predicted no prosecution would take place. The same could apply in duress.
(iv) The sole penalty for murder is life imprisonment. Duress cannot be taken into account in the sentence as it can in other offences. Surely it should be for the courts, and not for the executive, to decide the penalty?
(v) It is harsh to call a person who yielded to a threat to kill his family a coward and a poltroon. Would only a coward choose to kill a third party?
(vi) Lord Griffiths said that the Law Commission Report No. 83, *Defences of General Application*, 1978, had not been acted on by Parliament. Therefore, he thought Parliament did not wish to change the law. Yet if that were so, Parliament's inactivity must have shown also that it did not wish to abrogate *Lynch*, above, which only 12 years earlier had decided in the opposite manner to *Howe*.
(vii) The two cases relied on by the Lords are not strong. *Tyler* (1839) 172 ER 643 is out of date because it was considered at that time that duress was no defence at all. *Dudley and Stephens* concerned necessity not duress. The two defences are linked but not the same. For example, necessity is not a defence to theft but duress is. In a third case, *Kray* (1969) 53 Cr App R 569, the Court of Appeal had considered that duress was a defence to an accessory to murder but the relevant passage was omitted in the major series of law reports.
(viii) In *Howe* no one asked the question: if the would-be accused refused to kill and was killed, what is there to prevent the duressor from threatening someone else with death and so on? The law encourages the killing of two or more persons and discourages the killing of one. Not a happy outcome!

A useful comparison is with the IRA's use of 'proxy bombers' in Northern Ireland. The organisation might have gone on killing people until someone yielded and drove the explosives to a checkpoint. In fact the proxy bombers were not prosecuted. If they had been, they would have had no defence to murder.

(ix) The law is brought into disrepute in such circumstances. In the words of Lord Morris in *Lynch*, above: 'The law would be censorious and inhumane which did not recognise the appalling plight of a person who perhaps suddenly finds his life in jeopardy unless he submits and obeys.'

(x) The Lords in *Howe* referred to authorities on provocation (now the defence of loss of control) when approving the proposition that a duressee must act as a person of reasonable firmness might act. Yet provocation is a defence to murder but duress is not. Is a person who kills under provocation less morally blame-worthy than a person who kills under duress? It is suggested indeed that a person who kills under duress is *less* blameworthy than a person who kills as a result of loss of control.

(xi) The majority in *Abbott v R* refused to afford the accused a defence to a charge of murder on the ground that concerned citizens might believe that a 'not guilty' verdict implied that what the accused had done was the morally correct thing to do, but since duress is an excuse, a concession to human weakness, and not a justification, this argument is inappropriate. The accused is excused because of his weakness; his killing is not justified.

(xii) The departing from *Abbott v R* is a breach of Article 7 of the European Convention on Human Rights, the principle of non-retroactivity. The accused is guilty of an offence when he would not have been guilty before *Howe*.

(c) Lord Griffiths in *Howe* went further than his brethren. He suggested that duress was no defence not just to murder, being an accessory to murder and some forms of treason (see (d) below), but also to attempted murder. Lord Hailsham thought the law required reconsideration. Until 1996 the law was that, if the accused intended to kill and the victim died within a year and a day, the offence was murder. However, if the victim survived for longer but still died, a charge of murder was not possible, only a charge of attempted murder. Why should the date of death of the victim affect the position whether duress was available? The House of Lords by a three to two majority in *Gotts* [1992] 2 AC 412 accepted that duress was not a defence to attempted murder. (The case does not discuss s 18, but for the sake of elegance the law should be the same.) The accused's father threatened that unless the accused killed his mother, he would be shot. He stabbed but did not kill his mother. She might have died but for prompt treatment. Lord Lane CJ in the Court of Appeal rejected the argument that there was a distinction between murder and attempted murder with regard to duress. Early commentators did not distinguish the two, and there was no common law rule on the matter. The law ought to intervene. The Lord Chief Justice said in the Court of Appeal:

> One can imagine a situation where a man under duress fires a shotgun in order to kill two men standing together. He kills one and maims the other. It would seem strange if he were convicted as to one victim and acquitted altogether in relation to the other when the death of the one victim and the maiming of the other were caused by the very same act committed with the very same intent.

Innocence or guilt should not depend on chance. He suggested that the rule of attempted murder did not apply to conspiracy and incitement to murder because such offences were 'generally speaking' further away from the full offence than attempt;

anyway, wherever the line was drawn anomalies would arise. Lord Jauncey in the Lords said: '[a] man shooting to kill but missing a vital organ by a hair's breadth can justify his action no more than can the man who hits that organ. It is pure chance that the attempted murderer is not a murderer.' He added: 'The law regards the sanctity of human life and the protection thereof as of paramount importance.' He left open for future discussion whether the defence should be available for any serious crime. Duress would, however, mitigate the sentence. The minority, led by Lord Lowry, thought that duress was available. He argued that, wherever the line was drawn between offences to which duress is or is not a defence (for example, is duress a defence to conspiracy or incitement to murder?), there would be anomalies. He said:

> Attempted murder, however heinous we consider it, was a misdemeanour . . . [w]hen attempted murder became a felony, that crime, like many other serious felonies, continued to have available the defence of duress.

Gotts is open to criticism on several counts:

(i)   There are problems with other offences. Encouraging and assisting (which replaced the common law crime of incitement) and conspiracy are, like attempt, inchoate offences. Why should the defence apply to two but not to the third? What about other crimes such as arson with intent to endanger life? Lord Jauncey suggested that duress should not be available for 'all very serious crimes', a term which he did not define. Certainly before the abolition of the year-and-a-day rule it would have been anomalous if the accused who attacked the victim was guilty of murder if the victim died within a year and a day but not guilty of inflicting grievous bodily harm with intent if she survived longer. If duress is a defence to s 18 of the Offences Against the Person Act 1861, but not to murder, there is an inconsistency. Both offences have the mental element of an intent to commit grievous bodily harm. To rule out the defence for murder, but not for s 18, would be strange. Moreover, the difference between murder and s 18 may be fortuitous. Assume that the accused stabs his victim intending to kill. If the victim dies, that is murder: if, however, by the purest good fortune a superb surgeon is at hand and the victim does not die, that is not murder. Why should the distinction between conviction and acquittal depend on luck?

(ii) The defence of coercion (see next section) found in s 47 of the Criminal Justice Act 1925 is restricted. It does not apply to treason and murder, but is a defence to attempted murder. It is said that the draughtsman of the statute adopted the common law position for duress. Since coercion and duress are parallel defences, the same rule should apply in duress.

(iii) Nowhere is it suggested that attempted murder does not give rise to the defence, except for a Royal Commission of 1879 (C 2345).

(iv) Murder has a mandatory sentence. This penalty marks murder off from other crimes. Therefore, a line can be drawn between murder and other offences, and this line can separate murder and attempted murder in duress.

(v)   The dissentients expressed the view that if the accused formed an intent to kill under duress, he was not so immoral that the law should withdraw the defence from him.

(vi) Should a person who kills to save others be treated differently from one who kills to save himself? Arguably there is a moral distinction.

(vii) In criminal law chance does play a part in the definition of offences. If one drives badly but by luck kills no one, one is guilty of dangerous driving; if one by mischance happens to kill somebody, one is guilty of causing death by dangerous driving. The sentence for the latter crime is more serious than that for the former, but luck may be the factor which differentiates them. The same is true in ordinary life: I carelessly fall and no injury is caused; I carelessly fall and by ill luck I knock someone over. Only in the latter situation is a passer-by likely to think me at fault, but what I did and did carelessly is exactly the same. There is therefore no reason for treating murder and attempted murder in the same way. There is a whole literature on the part so-called 'moral luck' plays in criminal law. A way into the literature is A. Ashworth, 'Taking the consequences', in S. Shute, S. Gardner and J. Horder (eds), *Action and Value in the Criminal Law* (Oxford University Press, 1993).

(d) In *Ness* [2011] Crim LR 645, an unreported Crown Court decision from Newcastle, the defendants submitted that the defence of duress was available on a charge of conspiracy to murder. There is no authority on this issue. The trial judge held that while it was not a defence to murder and attempted murder, it is available on a charge of conspiracy to murder. This is in accord with the statement of the law in practitioner works as well as academic texts. The case comment by David Ormerod, the criminal law Law Commissioner, is worth reading for discussion of earlier case law and of the logic or lack of it of duress being a defence to one form of inchoate liability, conspiracy to murder, but not to another form, attempt to murder.

(e) There is doubt whether duress is a defence to treason. Lord Goddard CJ in *Steane*, above, said *obiter* that duress was not a defence but his statement may be *per incuriam*. *M'Growther*, above, and *Purdy* (1946) 10 JCL 182 (*obiter*), Oliver J instructing the jury, are *contra*, *Purdy* was not cited in *Steane* (and this despite the factual similarities), and Lord Morris in *Lynch* accepted that the *dictum* was incorrect. The phrasing of this exception has remained fairly constant: duress is a defence to 'some forms of treason'. The phrase was used in *Abdul-Hussain*, above. This phrase means that minor acts of treason do attract the defence. It may, however, be difficult to distinguish major and minor acts of assistance, and Nelson J in the Full Court of Victoria rejected the distinction in relation to those who help in a major way in a murder and those who act in a minor way: *Harding*, above. If duress is a defence, it will apply only if the accused escapes at the first opportunity: *Oldcastle* (1419) noted in 3 Co Inst 10, and apparently only if the accused does not engage in battle: *Axtell* (1660) 84 ER 1060.

As the Court of Appeal put it in *Abdul-Hussain*, above, which the same court approved in *S* [2001] 1 WLR 2206, a case also known as *Shayler*: '. . . the defence of duress, whether by threats or from circumstances, is generally available in relation to all substantive crimes, except murder, attempted murder and some forms of treason . . .'. For suggested reform of this topic, see below. Present law is a prime illustration of illogicality. Some judges, such as Lord Hailsham in *Howe*, are content to reject logic and consistency in favour of precedent but law reformers need not work within common law constraints. Law reforming should be on the side of Lord Bingham, who in *Hasan*, above, said that the argument for extending duress to murder was irresistible.

Should there be a general defence of duress?

Duress is much more commonly pleaded than it was at the time of *Hudson and Taylor* (1971) and the courts have taken a tough stance in recent years on the width of the defence: see the speeches of the House of Lords in *Hasan*. If the basis of duress is that the law regards self-preservation as excusing an otherwise criminal deed, duress should be a defence to all offences, and the exceptions abolished. This rationale has been given full rein in self-defence, which is a defence to all crimes including murder. (One difference is that in duress the victim is an innocent person but he is not in self-defence.) The law should not condemn people who act under a compulsion which they are unable to resist and should not demand standards of heroism from ordinary people such as the accused in *Gotts*. It is suggested that if persons act reasonably under pressure exerted by threats they should have a defence. A comparison with diminished responsibility, which is a defence to murder, is instructive. An abnormal person can rely on this defence, but a person, even a normal reasonable one, cannot have a defence of duress if he kills. To say that they are guilty but their sentences would be reduced, as Lords Keith and Templeman did in *Gotts*, does not meet this argument. And the sentence for murder, life imprisonment, is mandatory. Duress as mitigation not as exculpation has no effect. Moreover, the law's penalties do not work whether as retribution or deterrence in situations where the defence is potentially applicable.

The Law Commission, which has always been in favour of duress being a general defence and not merely a mitigating factor, in Report No. 83, *Defences of General Application*, 1978 (see above), put the following arguments against duress as a general defence:

(a) It is never justifiable to do wrong.

(b) It is not for the individual to balance the doing of wrong against the avoidance of harm to himself or others.

(c) Duress could be classified as merely the motive for committing a crime, and the criminal law does not take motive into account.

(d) The criminal law is itself a system of threats, and that structure would be undermined if some other system of threats were permitted.

(e) To allow the defence is to provide a charter for terrorists, kidnappers and others of that ilk.

See p 439 (Chapter 11) for an explanation of the mandatory sentence for murder.

Further arguments against duress may be advanced. Lord Morris in *Lynch* said that: 'Duress must never be allowed to be the easy answer of those who can devise no other explanation of their conduct . . .' It might be said that a person is at fault and worthy of punishment if he yields to a threat. Moreover, arguments in favour of duress may be false. The law would not act as a deterrent if duress were available for all offences including murder.

The 1978 Law Commission Report took into account these arguments and recommended as follows.

(a) Duress should be a defence available generally, i.e. it should apply to the then exceptions of treason and murder. The Law Commission did, however, recognise the sanctity of human life. (The 1989 version, below, preferred this recommendation but in the light of present law did not give the defence to murder and attempted murder. The Select Committee of the House of Lords on Murder and Life Imprisonment (HL Paper 78–1, 1989) recommended the abolition of the mandatory sentence for murder. Duress could then be taken into account in the sentence. This Committee under the chairmanship of Lord Nathan rejected the view that duress should reduce murder to manslaughter.)

(b) A threat of harm to the accused or another should be sufficient, but a threat to property would not. This recommendation would be in line with current law, which is to the effect that only threats to oneself or to a person for whom the accused 'would reasonably regard himself as responsible' would qualify: *Wright*, above, under 'threats to whom'.

(c) The mental element was to be that the accused believed:

... whether or not on reasonable grounds –

(a) that the harm threatened was death or serious personal injury (physical or mental);

(b) that the threat would be carried out immediately if he did not take the action in question or, if not immediately, before he could have any real opportunity of seeking official protection; and

(c) that there was no other way of avoiding or preventing the harm threatened.

This recommendation would reverse *Graham*, above, on reasonable belief. The Law Commission accepted this recommendation in the 1989 draft Criminal Code.

(d) The threat must be such that 'in all the circumstances of the case ... he could not reasonably have been expected to resist'. See also the section 'Reform proposals', below.

The Law Commission also recommended the abolition of the defence of marital coercion (see next section). These proposals formed part of cl 42 of the 1989 draft Criminal Code and cl 36(2)(b) of the Criminal Code Bill attached to Law Commission Paper No. 218, 1993. Parliament has not acted on either set of recommendations. The Commission in its 1993 Report considered that after the Lords in both *Howe* and *Gotts* had called for parliamentary intervention the time was ripe for Parliament to clarify the width of duress.

It should be noted that the proposals leave for the jury the odious task of balancing one harm against another, and juries might hold that murder is always so heinous that duress is no defence, so stultifying the first proposed reform. The jury will also have to put themselves in the position of a defendant with certain long-term characteristics. One suggested reform which was not proposed was to link the gravity of the threat with the heinousness of the crime: the greater the harm caused under duress, the greater the threat must be. In the 1970s in *Lynch v DPP for Northern Ireland* [1975] AC 653 (HL) and *Abbott v R* [1977] AC 755 (PC), both discussed above, there were *dicta* in favour of such an approach. If accepted, one effect would presumably be that there would be no restriction as to the nature of the evil threatened. A threat to imprison would be sufficient if the matter demanded were small. Such reform would bring duress into line with self-defence where there is no limit on the type of threat uttered or used. There could still be restrictions on the type of harm threatened (such as no defence where the harm was to be the loss of the accused's job) or the crime to be committed (for instance no defence to treason). The accused under the draft Criminal Code would not have the defence if he brought the circumstances of duress on himself.

Reform proposals

The Law Commission investigated duress in its Report No. 218, *Legislating the Criminal Code – Offences against the Person and General Principles*, Cm 2370, 1993. Clause 25 reads:

(1) No act of a person constitutes an offence if the act is done under duress by threats.

(2) A person does an act under duress by threats if he does it because he knows or believes –

(a) that a threat has been made to cause death or serious injury to himself or another if the act is not done, and

(b) that the threat will be carried out immediately if he does not do the act or, if not immediately, before he or that other can obtain effective official protection, and

(c) that there is no other way of preventing the threat being carried out, and the threat is one which in all the circumstances (including any of his personal characteristics that affect its gravity) he cannot reasonably be expected to resist. It is for the defendant to show that the reason for his act was such knowledge or belief as is mentioned in paragraphs (a) to (c).

(3) This section applies in relation to omissions as it applies in relation to acts.

(4) This section does not apply to a person who knowingly and without reasonable excuse exposed himself to the risk of the threat made or believed to have been made.

If the question arises whether a person knowingly and without reasonable excuse exposed himself to such a risk, it is for him to show that he did not.

Clause 26, which is in similar terms, deals with duress of circumstances. Because the clauses are so similarly phrased, they will not be separately discussed. The definition of duress of circumstances found in cl 26(2) was approved by the Court of Appeal in **Baker** [1999] 2 Cr App R 335. One development which occurred after the publication of the Report is **Cole** [1994] Crim LR 582 (CA), in which the court distinguished between the two types of duress by reference to whether the duressor nominated the crimes (threats) or not (circumstances). It is uncertain how far the duressor must nominate the crime. Certainly he need not specify any particular building society branch to hold up: **Ali** [1995] Crim LR 303 (CA). It is hard to believe that this distinction truly represents the law. Why is it duress by threats if I say 'Steal from shops', but duress by circumstances if I say 'Get me some money'? The proposals partly amend and partly encapsulate present law. For example, cl 25(2)(a) states that a threat to any third party (e.g. a hostage) will suffice. The Law Commission had been of the opinion in the Consultation Paper No. 122 which preceded the Report (they bear the same name) that the accused would not have the defence if he believed that official protection would not avail him (such as in **Hudson and Taylor** [1971] 2 QB 202 (CA)). This recommendation finds no place in the Report. There is no definition of 'effective'. Moreover, cl 25(2)(c) does not address the issue of a belief that official protection is not available (rather than that it is available but ineffective). The proposal, while presented as one which mirrors current law, may be in truth a widening of it in the accused's favour. No longer need he know full well, as Lord Griffiths put it in **Howe** [1987] AC 417 (HL), that protection is ineffective but he has the defence if he knows *or believes* it is.

One difference from present law is the extension of the defence to all offences including murder. This is a long-standing Law Commission commitment, and the House of Lords in **Hasan**, above, thought the extension to all crimes was 'irresistible'. If Parliament did not like this proposal, the Commission suggested that duress should reduce the crime to manslaughter. The Commonwealth of Australia in the Criminal Code Act 1995 allowed duress as a defence to murder.

Another change is the proposed abolition of the objective elements in **Graham** [1982] 1 WLR 294 (CA): was the accused compelled to act because, as a result of what he *reasonably* believed the other to have said or done, he had *good cause* to fear death or serious injury? The **Graham** test of reasonable steadfastness is to be abolished. Timidity can be considered. The accused is still, however, to be judged against a standard of a reasonable person. Therefore, a timid accused is judged according to the standard of a reasonable timid person. The Court of Appeal in **Baker** did not notice that the terms of reasonable belief and good cause to believe were not to be found in the proposed definition of duress of circumstances.

The Law Commission proposed a shift in the burden of proof in relation to cl 25(2) and (4) and considered that the shift would not breach Article 6(2) of the European Convention on Human Rights. The Commission seemed to have taken this view in order to make Parliament accept that duress should be available to murder. The reasons advanced for the amendment were that the facts giving rise to the duress were peculiarly within the ken of the accused and members of a violent gang could escape guilt if they concocted a story of compulsion. The law on violent gangs has not caused problems in the past and the 'peculiar knowledge' doctrine was exploded long ago in murder, and if it were to apply to duress, it should also apply to, say, provocation; the person who besides the accused had an inkling about what happened is dead. There is no stopping place with regard to the doctrine. If the accused kills, there may be no one else present as witness. The deceased has peculiar knowledge of the events, but the victim is dead. The Court of Criminal Appeal in *Spurge* [1961] 2 QB 205 strongly rejected the 'peculiar knowledge' doctrine in relation to provocation and self-defence. Duress is no different. The Law Commission opined that where the defence is part of one incident, the prosecution should shoulder the burden. So in self-defence the onus is on the Crown because the accused is reacting to the use or threat of force immediately, whereas in duress there is a gap between the threat and the otherwise wrongful action. However, in self-defence one can strike preemptively, and in duress the threat may be immediately linked with the act: 'do this now or I shall kill you now'. Furthermore, in duress of circumstances the threat will almost always be immediately linked to the act: 'unless I knock this person off the ladder, all of us will die in seconds'. The Commission has since resiled from its recommendation and it no longer wishes to place the legal burden on the accused. It is suggested that contrary to the Commission's view the proposal would breach Article 6(2), the presumption of innocence, because Article 6(2) does not permit legal burdens on the accused when to shift the onus is disproportionate. See also *Lambert* [2002] 2 AC 545 (HL), discussed in Chapter 1.

One aspect of the proposed definition should be noted. The recommendation confirms current law that only threats of death or serious injury suffice for duress. Some lesser threats, however, can overwhelm an ordinary mortal. Lord Simon, dissenting, in *Lynch v DPP for Northern Ireland* [1975] AC 653 (HL) stated:

> . . . a threat to property may, in certain circumstances, be as potent in overbearing the actor's wish not to perform the prohibited act as a threat of physical harm. For example, the threat may be to burn down his house unless the householder merely keeps watch against interruption while a crime is committed. Or a fugitive from justice may say, 'I have it in my power to make your son bankrupt. You can avoid that merely by driving me to the airport.' Would not many ordinary people yield to such threats, and act contrary to their wish not to perform an action prohibited by law?

The concession-to-human-frailty rationale would support such a rule though it has to be admitted that that basis has been undermined by the later House of Lords authorities, *Howe*, above, and *Gotts* [1992] 2 AC 412. Nevertheless, there is statutory support for a defence in such circumstances. The Criminal Damage Act 1971, s 5(2)(b), stipulates that if a person destroys or damages property 'in order to protect property belonging to another' he has a lawful excuse to the offence of criminal damage.

In *Hurley and Murray* [1967] VR 526, the Full Court of Victoria said that: 'The whole body of law relating to duress is in a very vague and unsatisfactory state . . .'. The law has since firmed up but it remains controversial. We have not heard the last of the reform of duress, but calls for changes, in *Hurst* [1995] 1 Cr App R 82 (CA), *Cole* [1994] Crim LR 582 (CA), *Baker*, and *Abdul-Hussain* [1999] Crim LR 570 (CA), remain unheeded by the government. The Court of Appeal noted in *Safi*, above, that Parliament seemed content to leave the development of the law to the judges.

The Law Commission's 2006 proposals

The Law Commission issued its Report No. 304 on *Murder, Manslaughter and Infanticide* in late 2006. In it it proposed that contrary to current law duress whether by threats or of circumstances should be a defence to first and second degree murder and to attempted murder. For first and second degree murders, see Chapter 11. The proposals are different from that contained in the Consultation Paper *A New Homicide Act for England and Wales?* of

2005, which had proposed that a successful defence of duress would reduce first to second degree murder, while also recommending that duress should be a full defence to second degree murder and attempted murder. It noted (para. 6.60) that current law provided a strange outcome in relation to excuses: '. . . in cases of [loss of control] and diminished responsibility, D has not killed in order to preserve innocent life and yet he or she has a partial excuse. By contrast, a person who pleads duress is one who sought to avoid the death of or serious physical harm to an innocent person (not necessarily him or herself) by doing no more than is required to avert the harm. Yet, [loss of control] and diminished responsibility excuse murder while duress does not' (footnote omitted).

The Commission strongly endorsed the rules as to the width of duress as a defence laid down in *Z* [2005] 1 WLR 1269 (CA), which is known as **Hasan** in the House of Lords, as to the risk of threat with the rider that the threat believed to exist would have to be one of death or life-threatening harm: at present it is sufficient that the threat was one of 'serious harm', whether the accused believed the threat to be life-threatening or not. It should be noted that whether harm is life-threatening or not turns in part on the victim's age and vulnerability; the Law Commission provides this example: '. . . a jury might well conclude that D reasonably believed that a threat of torture to his or her five-year-old child involved a risk of life-threatening harm while taking a different view if the threat of torture was directed at D's spouse' (para. 6.75). What is different from present law is the recommendation that in respect of these three offences the legal burden of proof should be on the accused (the standard of proof would be on the balance of probabilities). The Commission thought that changing the burden would not infringe Article 6(2) of the European Convention on Human Rights because that right was outweighed by Article 2's obligation on the state to protect its citizens from being killed.

The Law Commission rejected the proposal for a partial defence of duress in respect to first degree murder but a full defence as to second degree and attempted murder because of:

1 the wide difference in outcome dependent on whether the accused had the fault element for first degree murder;

2 the element of chance, which is illustrated by the following example (paras 6.26–6.27):

> D, under duress, shoots both V1 and V2 with intent to kill, killing V1 but not V2. . . . [If the Consultation Paper's recommendation had been adopted,] D would have a partial defence in relation to the killing of V1 but a full defence in relation to the attempted killing of V2. The element of chance in whether the full defence is or is not available, depending on whether D is successful in carrying out his instructions, makes this option an unattractive one.

3 The Commission was also strongly of the view that 'as a matter of principle' (para 6.28) duress should be a complete defence to first degree murder. To quote the Law Commission's Report No. 83 on *Defences of General Application*, 1977, para 2.43:

> where duress is so compelling that the defendant could not reasonably have been expected to resist it, . . . it would be . . . unjust that the defendant should suffer the stigma of a conviction even for manslaughter. We do not think that any social purpose is served by requiring the law to prescribe such standards of determination and heroism.

Moreover, what would be gained by punishing an accused in these circumstances? The Commission quoted the view of the Criminal Bar Association (para 6.51): '. . . if duress were not a complete defence to first degree murder, it would give the impression that, in law, "it is better to prevent the death of a stranger than to prevent the death of one's children".'

The Commission rejected any analogy with provocation (now loss of control) and diminished responsibility, which under the proposed scheme would be a defence only to first degree murder and would lead to a conviction for second degree murder. The Commission noted that sometimes duress but not provocation (now loss of control) or diminished responsibility came close to a justificatory defence and it gave the example, drawn from duress of circumstances, where one roped mountaineer cuts the rope to save his or her own life when had he or she not cut it, both would have died. It rejected the argument that a person who intentionally killed should not have a complete defence. It also rejected the proposition that killing in defence of self was in itself morally worse than killing in defence of others. It gave (para. 6.56) several examples in favour of not differentiating, including: 'An uncle threatened with death commits murder so that he can donate a kidney to his desperately ill nephew.' It rejected the argument that principal and secondary parties could be distinguished because an accomplice acting under duress may be just as culpable as a perpetrator. 'For example, a husband and his wife are told that their child will be killed unless they kill V who is the husband's brother. They agree that the wife will perpetrate the killing and the husband will keep watch. It would be wrong to afford the husband but not the wife a complete defence' (para. 6.57).

The Commission proposed tightening the defence by replacing the current requirement that the threat had to be one which would be carried out imminently to one which would be carried out immediately, thereby confirming the criticism in *Hasan* of *Hudson and Taylor*.

The Law Commission also proposed to retain the 'reasonable belief' limitation; that is, that the accused has to believe on reasonable grounds that a threat exists and that the threat will be put into effect: *Graham* above, approved by the House of Lords in *Howe*, above. The 1989 draft Criminal Code and the Law Commission's Report No. 218, *Legislating the Criminal Code: Offences against the Person and General Principles*, 1993, had previously called for a subjective test, as is the law in self-defence and provocation, but the 2006 Report distinguished those defences: in duress the accused would normally have time to think about the threat, whereas he or she would not in self-defence and provocation; furthermore, since in respect of theft and other offences the law is that there has to be reasonable belief, it would be anomalous if a subjective test were used in first and second degree murder and in attempted murder. However, 'we see no reason why the particular characteristics of D should not be capable of being taken into account in determining whether or not his or her belief was reasonably held. This would enable account to be taken of the age and vulnerability of D' (para. 6.81). It was further proposed that the law on duress should be brought into line with that on provocation (now loss of control) in respect of the 'reasonable firmness' criterion: 'the jury should be entitled to take into account all of the circumstances of D, including his or her age, other than those which bear on his or her capacity to withstand duress' (para. 6.84). This recommendation will lead to the reversal of *Bowen* above in relation to the three crimes of first degree murder, second degree murder and attempted murder: for the others *Bowen* would remain.

The government's response, the Ministry of Justice's Consultation Paper No. 19, *Murder, Manslaughter and Infanticide*, 2009, did not refer to the Law Commission's 2006 proposals.

Coercion

Coercion is a (rarely used) defence akin to duress but available only to married women. For that reason it may be called '**marital coercion**' to distinguish it from the defences of duress both by threats and of circumstances. Before 1925 a married woman had a defence if she committed a crime other than treason or murder in her husband's presence. One argument for this defence was that if the husband was convicted of a felony, a serious offence, he would not be hanged for a first offence because, if he could read a certain verse from the Bible (the 'neck' verse), he would not be executed (he received 'benefit of clergy', the argument being that at that time only clergymen could read and the royal courts did not have jurisdiction over ecclesiastics), whereas a woman, not being able to be a cleric, would be hanged. The argument against the existence of this defence was put with force in the American case of *US v de Quilfeldt* (1881) 5 F 276. Coercion was the 'relic of a belief in the ignorance and pusillanimity of women'.

The law is now stated in s 47 of the Criminal Justice Act 1925, which, however, does not define coercion:

> Any presumption of law that an offence committed by a wife in the presence of her husband is committed under the coercion of the husband is hereby abolished, but on a charge against a wife for any offence other than treason or murder, it shall be a good defence to prove that the offence was committed in the presence of, and under the coercion of, the husband.

The reversal of the burden of proof may be the sole reason why s 47 was enacted. It has been suggested that only the evidential burden was placed on the wife, but the cases do not so hold. The burden is on the balance of probabilities: *Richman* [1982] Crim LR 507 (Crown Court).

It is unknown which fact situations would give rise to this defence. It was at one time thought that coercion was simply the name for the defence of duress where the accused was a married woman. In other words, the boundaries of duress were the boundaries of coercion. The modern view is that coercion is wider than duress and would cover matters such as a threat by the husband not to buy food for his wife and children, a threat to desert the wife and a threat to bring a mistress into the matrimonial home. Since neither Parliament nor the common law had defined the term, Lord Simon in *Lynch v DPP for Northern Ireland* [1975] AC 653 (HL) said that coercion was 'used in its ordinary sense . . .'. It is not limited to threats. *Richman* held that there was no need for physical force. The Court of Appeal in *Ditta* [1988] Crim LR 43 rejected the defence when the wife was acting out of loyalty. The test for coercion in *Richman* was: did she act willingly? Coercion could be an overbearing of the will by moral means not amounting to physical force or the threat of such force. This test was approved by the Court of Appeal in *Shortland* [1996] 1 Cr App R 116. In *Ditta* the test was: 'Was she forced by her husband either by physical, moral, psychological or mental processes, to do what she would not otherwise have done?' In duress a threat to expose the accused's homosexuality is insufficient. Is a threat to reveal one's wife's lesbianism to the tabloid press such a threat as to fall within 'moral, psychological or mental' pressure? If the threat is of death or serious injury, both coercion and duress may be available, but it should be noted that coercion is narrower than duress in one respect: the 'crime' must take place in her husband's presence. The term 'presence' has not been the subject of authoritative guidance. In *Caroubi* (1912) 7 Cr App R 149 it was held that it was sufficient that the wife was within sight of the husband. Presence was not restricted to being next to the husband. In *Whelan* [1937] SASR 237 the court held that 'it is sufficient if the husband is in a situation where he is close enough to influence the wife in doing what he wants done, even if he is not physically present in the room'.

Ditta is an authoritative case. The third defendant was charged with being concerned in the importation of heroin. She contended that the second defendant, to whom she believed she was married, had prevailed upon her to strap the drug round her body while in a plane which was to land at Heathrow. The court held that the statute, which was in straightforward terms, did not provide a defence in such a situation. She had to prove that she was married to the coercer. The fact that she believed, even on reasonable grounds, that she was married to him was insufficient. (Compare duress where the accused has a defence if he believes on reasonable grounds that he was obliged to do as he did.) The court did not deal with the question whether a polygamous marriage would give rise to this defence, but the hint was that it would not. The court distinguished the defence of mistake to bigamy, which is available only when the accused erred on reasonable grounds, as being concerned with mistake as to a vital element of the offence, whereas in coercion the mistake was one to a defence. Therefore, if one believes on reasonable grounds that one's husband is dead, one is not guilty of the offence of bigamy, but if one believes on reasonable grounds that one is married one does not have the defence of coercion. Certainly a mistress does not have this defence.

As stated above, the Law Commission in 1978, 1989 and 1993 proposed the abolition of coercion. It does not accord with modern views of marriage and is gender-based. It might be thought surprising that it has survived for so long.

One matter of which readers should be aware is that judicial and academic terminology varies. Sometimes coercion like compulsion is used as a synonym for duress. Usually in modern times coercion means the separate defence under the 1925 statute.

Necessity and duress of circumstances

Introduction

If terrorists aim a plane at Canary Wharf in London, may the Army shoot it down?

Lord Goff in *Richards*, unreported, 10 July 1986 (HL) said: 'That there exists a defence of **necessity** at common law, which may . . . be invoked to justify what would otherwise be a trespass to land, is not in doubt. But the scope of the defence is by no means clear.' This statement was *obiter*, but gives a flavour of this topic. Lord Goff had developed his views by *Re F* [1990] 2 AC 1 (HL), a civil case. He stated that the defence did exist at common law to render lawful what would otherwise be criminal: (1) public necessity (e.g. to create a firebreak in the Great Fire of London); (2) private necessity (e.g. to cause criminal damage to a neighbour's property to save oneself from harm); and (3) 'action taken as a matter of necessity to assist another person without his consent'. His example of the third category was the dragging of a person from the path of an oncoming vehicle. He confined category (3) to cases where it was not practicable to communicate with the assisted person and the action was 'such as a reasonable person would in all the circumstances take, acting in the best interests of the assisted person'. The facts of *Re F* fell within the third category. A mentally ill patient could be sterilised when she lacked the capacity to consent provided that the operation was in her best interests. It is uncertain whether Lord Goff's classification is exhaustive.

Modern cases tend to assume that there is a defence. For example, in *S* [2009] EWCA Crim 85 it was held that necessity could be a defence to a charge of deploying unlicensed security guards to protect persons under immediate or imminent threat of death or serious injury from a major terrorist attack on an unspecified retail location. In *Hutchinson* v *Newbury Magistrates Court*, unreported, 9 October 2002, the Queen's Bench Division Administrative Court said that a successful plea required a reasonable and proportionate response to present danger and there had to be no other means of avoiding it. A similar formula was adopted by the same court in *DPP* v *Hicks*, unreported, 19 July 2002. There was no defence of necessity where the accused drove with excess alcohol in his blood to get a bottle of medicine from the chemist's because either there was no risk of serious harm to the child or using the medicine would not have alleviated the risk of harm. In *S* [2001] 1 WLR 2206 the Court of Appeal held the following to be the requirements for the defence: 'the act must be done only to prevent an act of greater evil: the evil must be directed towards the defendant or a person . . . for whom he has responsibility . . . ; the act must be reasonable and proportionate to the evil avoided.' The Administrative Court in *Pipe v DPP* [2012] All ER (D) 238 (May) ruled that (like duress) necessity is restricted to emergencies where there was a risk of death or serious injury. The accused's partner's son suffered a broken leg. The ambulance did not arrive and the accused drove the partner's son to hospital at speeds ranging up to 100 m.p.h. The Court quashed the decision of the magistrates because they had restricted the defence to life-threatening situations.

Recent cases have focused on necessity as a possible defence to taking illegal drugs such as marijuana to relieve the effects of debilitating injuries. In *Altham* [2006] EWCA Crim 7 it was held that the accused could not rely on Article 3 of the European Convention on Human Rights (no inhuman or degrading treatment) to bolster a defence of necessity because the accused's condition was not worsened by any state act. In *Quayle* [2006] 1 WLR 3642 (CA) it was held that there was no defence of necessity to taking cannabis to relieve pain. To allow the defence was incompatible with the statutory scheme for regulating illegal drugs. The court did not rule on what the law would have been, had there been no statute in the field. The court stressed that there was no overarching doctrine of necessity but only a wilderness of single instances. Those single cases were decided on their particular facts. Insofar as the defence existed it was akin to duress and was to be kept within the same boundaries as that defence as laid down in *Hasan* (above). The court certified a point of law of general public importance but refused leave to appeal. The court in *Quayle* also held that denying a defence on these facts was not in breach of Article 8 of the Convention.

In one of the latest cases on necessity as a choice-of-evils defence, *Jones v Gloucestershire Crown Prosecution Service* [2005] QB 259 (CA) the court held that when the accused thought he had the choice between committing a less serious crime and committing a more serious one and he chose the former, the latter had to be a crime according to English law. Therefore, when the defendants committed various offences at RAF Fulford in order, they contended, to prevent aggression by the UK and the USA against Iraq, they had no defence of necessity because there was no crime of aggression in English law, even if it were an offence in international law. The House of Lords spoke to similar effect: *Jones* [2006] UKHL 16.

In duress the accused has the choice of breaking the law or having evil done to him or another by a person. In necessity the defendant is in a similar position except that the choice is imposed on him by natural events or by other situations not constituting a threat by a person in the form of 'do this or else' (I will kill you, etc.). In *Howe*, above, the House of Lords considered duress to be a species of necessity. Yet duress generally is a defence, while necessity generally is not, as the Court of Appeal recently reiterated in *Rodger*, above, though several modern cases assume that there is such a defence. In *Cichon v DPP* [1994] Crim LR 918 the Divisional Court accepted the existence of this defence but held on the facts that Parliament had excluded it in relation to the crime of allowing a pit bull terrier to be in a public place without a muzzle by the wording of the offence. Parliament had created an offence for the safety of the public. That policy was not to be wrecked by an accused's reaching a decision that the removal of the muzzle outweighed the public's safety. It might be said that the muzzle's removal was the physical manifestation of the accused's good motive, the prevention of cruelty to the dog: the accused took it off because the dog had a cough. The reasoning of the court is weak. Necessity, when it exists, is a defence to all offences (except perhaps those to which duress is not a defence), including statutory offences. Parliament rarely states expressly that a certain defence applies to the crime it is creating. Perhaps the court would have allowed a defence of necessity if the accused had removed the muzzle so as to let the dog bite the arm of a person who was robbing a post office. Another way of reaching the same result would be to say that there was on the facts no defence of necessity because the crime was defined in terms of permitting a dangerous dog to be in a public place. The accused could have kept it in a private place until the cough was cured. In this way the possibility of the defence could have been accepted. *Cichon v DPP* also illustrated the difference between duress of circumstances and a true defence of necessity. The former defence applies only when the accused acts to prevent death or serious injury to a person, and a dog is not a person. Necessity is not so restricted and applies whenever a greater good is done, and on the facts there may have been a greater good. In *Rodger* the defendants broke out of prison because they had suicidal tendencies. The court treated duress of circumstances and necessity as being the same, but they are not. Even if breaking out of prison was a greater good than committing suicide, the defence was not one of necessity, but of duress of circumstances. They acted under a threat to their lives.

Accordingly, for example, a doctor cannot take blood from a non-consenting person in order to save someone's life. It is no defence, even though the action of the accused promoted a value higher than that which would be served by compliance with the law. The social cost may be less by providing a defence than by not so doing.

This section considers necessity and duress of circumstances. It is suggested that the rationales of these defences, if they are to be distinguished (case law as yet is unclear), differ. In necessity the accused chooses the lesser evil: the pressure need be irresistible. In duress of circumstances the accused acts because of pressure: he need not choose the lesser evil. Jeremy Horder in 'Self-defence, necessity and duress: understanding the relationship' (1998) 11 *Canadian Journal of Law and Jurisprudence* 143 put the distinction in this way:

> In necessity cases, the key issue is the *moral imperative* to act: what matters is whether in the circumstances it was morally imperative to act, even if this might involve the commission of wrongdoing, in order to negate or avoid some other evil. In duress cases, the key issue is the *personal sacrifice* [the accused] is being asked to make: should [the accused] be expected to make the personal sacrifice involved in refusing to give in to a coercive threat, rather than avoid implementation of the coercive threat by doing wrong?

It is suggested that contrary to the view of Lord Woolf CJ in *S*, above, there are differences. The juridical bases, threats in duress and choices of lesser evils in necessity, have been mentioned. As we shall see, the Court of Appeal in *Re A* [2001] Fam 147, a civil law case, permitted a defence of necessity to facts which constituted murder, had the case been a criminal one, at least on the particular facts of the case. Duress is not a defence to murder. Moreover, duress is restricted to threats of death or grievous bodily harm but it is suggested that necessity is not. Can one doubt that one may shoot down a plane seized by terrorists who intend to crash it into Canary Wharf? Finally, as *Re A* shows, necessity may create a duty to act; however, as the law currently stands, duress does not create such a duty. The House of Lords in *Shayler* [2003] 1 AC 247, which is the appeal from *S*, said that the Law Lords did not agree with all that was said in the Court of Appeal about necessity but unfortunately did not specify the precise points on which they disagreed.

Dudley and Stephens

The principal reason why necessity has not got off the ground as a defence is **Dudley and Stephens** (1884) 14 QBD 273 (CCR), one of the most celebrated cases of English criminal law. Four men were adrift in a boat. Two, after some days without food and water, said a prayer (not Grace!) and killed the weakest, Parker, the cabin boy. After a reference to a court of five judges, the accused were found guilty of murder and sentenced to be hanged. The sentence was, however, commuted to six months' imprisonment. (For more details of this and other similar occurrences, see the magnificent A.W.B. Simpson, *Cannibalism and the Common Law* (University of Chicago Press, 1984).)

Dudley and Stephens is a fascinating case. It is not certain whether the victim would have died anyway. Not long after he was killed, the survivors were rescued. The cabin boy was not bringing the accused nearer to death. The case was not one like the hypothetical one of two roped mountaineers; the lower one falls, dragging the upper one down; seconds before they both would have been killed, the upper one cuts the rope thereby accelerating the lower one's death. The lower person had no chance of surviving, come what may. On those facts the lower person was dragging the upper one to his death. Parker did not volunteer to die, and he might have lived, had he been allowed to eat one of the others. Furthermore, though the accused had no defence, it is not certain to what they had no defence. There are three views:

(a) **Dudley and Stephens** held that there is no general defence of necessity in criminal law. Lord Coleridge said that if necessity were allowed, it might become a smokescreen for 'unbridled passion and atrocious crime'. This approach constitutes the widest view of the *ratio*.

(b) Necessity is no defence to murder. This was the emphatic stance of the judge, Lord Coleridge. The House of Lords took this approach in **Howe**, above. This view allows **Dudley and Stephens** to be distinguished from cases shortly to be mentioned where necessity was a defence.

(c) The narrowest view is that on the facts necessity did not arise. Therefore, the court did not reject the defence either generally or specifically in relation to murder. Such was the approach of the Full Court of the Victoria Supreme Court in **Loughnan** [1981] VR 443. This case like many US ones dealt with a prisoner who escaped from jail to avoid being killed by other prisoners. The court held that in exceptional circumstances necessity afforded a defence. The conditions for the defence were: the crime must have been committed to avoid irreparable evil on the accused or on those he was under a duty to protect; the danger must be immediate; and the response must be proportionate to the danger. This approach derives support from the jury's special verdict that the accused would probably have died, had they not eaten the boy, but that verdict also stated that there was no real chance of surviving except by feasting on someone. If no necessity existed, everything said about the defence was *obiter*.

Whatever the true view of **Dudley and Stephens**, the case has impeded the rational development of the law. It should also be noted that:

1 The facts of the case were peculiar. There was an emergency. Action was needed immediately on the facts as the defendants judged them to be. It is sometimes said that to give a defence of necessity would be dangerous because it could be used as an easy excuse. However, there was nothing bogus about the facts of **Dudley and Stephens**. Even the relatives of the cabin boy did not think that the defendants were to blame. The dreadfulness

of the defendants' situation ought on this view to have given them an excuse. They were not arguing that the boy's life was of less value than theirs (a justificatory approach, if successful) but that they were not blameworthy because of the situation they found themselves in.

2   The courts are reluctant to grant a defence where there is some immorality. Lord Coleridge, giving the principal judgment, noted that the weakest had been selected for being killed, and he said that in circumstances such as those at issue people were under a duty to sacrifice their lives.

3   Because of the extremity of the situation, it was no deterrent to threaten punishment or, indeed, to hang the accused. By killing the victim, the accused gained at least several months of life, and on the facts they gained the rest of their natural lives. Had they not eaten the cabin boy, they might have died before they could have been rescued. 'The underlying rationale for permitting the necessity defence is that given the circumstances the usual purposes for meting punishment under the criminal law would not be served.' So wrote M.R. Conde (1981) 29 UCLA LR 409 (spelling anglicised). Even if the lack of a necessity defence is justifiable on the grounds that the criminal law exists to deter, that justification does not show why persons who acted as most would have done should be punished.

4   To convict in *Dudley and Stephens* was to adopt a standard above that of reasonable people, as the court noted. Surely criminal law should not be based on saintliness. Lord Hailsham, however, in *Howe*, above, did think that in such circumstances reasonable people would die. Criminal law might also be seen as providing support for the Judaeo-Christian ethic: Thou shalt not kill. Intentional killing is unacceptable. To provide a defence might lead some members of the public to believe that some forms of intentional killing were acceptable.

5   On the facts of *Dudley and Stephens* it might be argued that the two possible harms could not be balanced against each other. One cannot quantify a death. The accused made, in US jargon, an inexcusable choice. Different principles might apply where the defendant had brought about a lesser harm than the one threatened by natural occurrences.

6   In a similar situation a US court, the Circuit Court for the Eastern District of Pennsylvania, held in *US v Holmes* (1846) 26 Fed Cas 360 that there should be selection by lot. Selecting by lot would exculpate sailors who threw overboard passengers on an overloaded lifeboat. *Dudley and Stephens* is distinguishable as a case involving no selection by chance. Presumably those to be thrown overboard would in law not have a right to fight against being cast into the sea, though one would not expect a person who resisted to be prosecuted whether his resistance was successful or not. Incidentally that court sentenced the accused to six months' imprisonment, the same end-result as in *Dudley and Stephens*.

7   Other jurisdictions do have a defence of necessity. In *US v Ashton* (1834) 24 F Cas 873 a Massachusetts court held that a mutiny of sailors was justified when the ship was unseaworthy and the captain refused to enter port to make repairs. Punishing men for refusing to follow an order which would have led to their death was in the court's view wrong.

Perhaps Lord Coleridge would not have argued as he did had he known that the accused would really be hanged, though in the opinion of the writer credence should not be given to such a view in the light of the phrasing of his speech. Nevertheless, it should be remembered that from the viewpoint of precedent the case is not a House of Lords one.

Though the three judges said different things, Ward LJ sitting in the Court of Appeal in *Re A*, above, a civil case, said that in some circumstances necessity was a defence to murder. On the facts surgeons who separated conjoined twins were not guilty of murder even though they knew it was certain that one of the twins would die. Brooke LJ distinguished *Dudley and Stephens*. First, he said, the decision to kill the cabin boy was arbitrary but in *Re A* it was certain which twin would die. Secondly, Lord Coleridge in *Dudley and Stephens* said that if the criminal law gave the defendants a defence, there would be a total divorce of law and morality; however, in *Re A* some people would say that it was *not* immoral to kill the weaker twin to save the stronger one rather than letting them both die. The case at least in part turns on its own facts: the twin which died was bringing the other twin closer to death but the latter could survive on her own. In other words, if necessity has a 'lesser evil' rationale, it was a lesser evil to kill one twin than to let both die.

It is difficult to reconcile the judgments of the three Lords Justices in *Re A*. Brooke LJ was prepared on the facts to allow a defence of necessity. Necessity had three conditions: the act was needed to avoid 'inevitable and irreparable evil', the accused must do no more than was reasonably necessary to avoid the evil; and the evil done by him must not be disproportionate to the evil averted. What he failed to notice was that these three conditions were satisfied in *Dudley and Stephens*, who should therefore have had a defence. Instead he, along with his brethren, said that the sailors were rightly convicted. Walker LJ, *obiter*, thought that necessity should be extended to cover the present case but no further. Ward LJ permitted the defence but only in these circumstances: '. . . it must be impossible to preserve the life of X without bringing about the death of Y. . . . Y by his or her very continued existence will inevitably bring about the death of X within a short period of time, and . . . X is capable of living an independent life but Y is incapable under any circumstances . . . of viable independent existence.' Therefore, only Brooke LJ would have come to a conclusion different from Coleridge J in *Dudley and Stephens*.

Dudley and Stephens is also out of line with some Commonwealth authorities. In *Perka v R* (1984) 13 DLR (4th) 1 the Supreme Court of Canada ruled that the defendants had a defence, which the judges called an excuse, when they had taken their boat into the shelter of Canadian waters during a storm. They were charged with importing cannabis for the purposes of sale. It was in the words of Dickson J (later CJ), speaking for the majority, one of those 'urgent situations of clear and imminent peril when compliance with the law is demonstrably impossible'. There was no reasonable lawful alternative. Dickson J said that necessity 'rests on a realistic assessment of human weakness, recognizing that a liberal and humane criminal law cannot hold people to the strict obedience of laws in emergency situations where normal human instincts, whether of self-preservation or of altruism, overwhelmingly impel disobedience'. The judge stated that it did not matter that the accused were doing something unlawful, but that it would not amount to necessity if the accused's fault contributed to the emergency. *Perka v R* was distinguished by the Supreme Court of Canada in *Latimer v R* [2001] SCR 1. A father had no defence when he killed his quadriplegic daughter. He was not in imminent peril; he did have a reasonable alternative to breaking the law; and the harm inflicted was disproportionate to the harm avoided. Somewhat similarly in one Scottish case, *Tudhope v Grubb* 1983 SCCR 350, a sheriff held that necessity was a defence where the accused drove with excess alcohol in his blood to avoid an assault. Perhaps this case could be explained nowadays as an example of duress of circumstances, on which see below.

Beyond *Dudley and Stephens*, when does necessity provide or not provide a defence? The law, as a result of *Re A*, is in a state of flux. Development will happen case by case.

Necessity is sometimes a defence in specific instances. The law has a 'pebble-dash' approach. These instances are pebbles of the defence in a wall of no defence. Surely, however, one would not charge a prisoner with escaping from a burning jail, never mind convict him. As a US court put it: 'He is not to be hanged because he would not stay to be burnt' (*US* v *Kirby* (1869) 7 Wall 482). Even before the Abortion Act 1967, preservation of the woman's life was a defence to abortion: *Bourne* [1939] 1 KB 687 at the Old Bailey, the Central Criminal Court. *Bourne* may be seen as a case of what is sometimes called 'hidden necessity'. The accused, a surgeon, was charged with unlawfully using an instrument with intent to procure a miscarriage, contrary to s 58 of the Offences Against the Person Act 1861. The judge instructed the jury that the accused was not acting unlawfully if he acted bona fide to save the life of the woman, who was a 14-year-old rape victim. The use of the word 'unlawfully' allowed the judge, as it were, to smuggle in a defence. Other instances are jettisoning cargo (*Mouse's case* (1608) 77 ER 1341, a civil law authority) and taking an infected child through the streets to obtain medical advice (*Vantandillo* (1815) 105 ER 762). Cases such as *Bourne* could now be treated as ones of duress of circumstances (see below). Lord Goff's taxonomy in *Re F*, noted at the start of this section, does not cover *Bourne*.

Following *Buckoke* v *GLC* [1971] Ch 655 (CA), preservation of property or life is not a good defence to a charge of going through traffic lights at red, brought against firefighters, though Lord Denning MR did say that the accused were to be congratulated. (The law has since been changed to allow fire officers, the police and paramedics to go through red lights and to exceed the speed limit in an emergency.) According to the same judge in the civil case of *Southwark LBC* v *Williams* [1971] Ch 734 (CA) the defence does not extend to the homeless or the starving. Therefore, a homeless person cannot break into an empty house to squat, nor may a woman steal in order to feed her starving children. The common law of crime has always turned its back on a defence of 'economic necessity'. *Buckoke* and *Southwark LBC* would presumably now be subject to the defence of duress of circumstances. If, for instance, food was taken to prevent someone starving to death, the accused would have a defence; if, however, it was taken merely to cure hunger, the defence would not be available. To permit a defence of necessity in the circumstances noted in this paragraph would allow the accused to rely on motive. I took the food because my children were hungry. I stole; my motive, however, was good. If the court permitted motive to be impleaded, evidence such as the effect of capitalism would have to be adduced. It is also unclear why a shopkeeper should suffer for the consequences of the socio-economic milieu we live in.

At least one statute expressly provides a defence of necessity. Section 13 of the Bribery Act 2010 (in force 2011) provides a defence to a charge of bribery when the accused had out of necessity acted in the proper exercise of any function of the armed services when engaged on active service or in the proper exercise of any function of the intelligence services. The burden of proof is explicitly placed on the accused but in accord with the law in Chapter 1 that legal burden may be read down to mean an evidential burden. Some statutes may be read as covering situations of necessity. The most obvious illustration is the Criminal Damage Act 1971, s 5. This section defines a defence of 'lawful excuse'. That phrase covers the protection of property. Accordingly knocking down a home to create a firebreak – a necessitous situation – gives rise to a defence under statute just as it would at common law. Another example is s 50 of the Serious Crime Act 2007, which provides an exception from the crime of encouraging or assisting when the accused has acted reasonably.

Section 34(3) of the Road Traffic Act 1988 exempts a person from conviction for driving a vehicle elsewhere than on roads 'if he proves to the satisfaction of the court that it was driven in contravention of this section for the purpose of saving life or extinguishing fire or meeting any other like emergency'. There are other sections of like nature such as that in the Road Traffic Regulation Act 1984, s 87 (as amended) which exempts emergency vehicles from speed limits. Professor Smith's comment on **Wood v Richards** [1977] Crim LR 295 (DC), where the accused was convicted, should also be noted. On a charge of driving without due care and attention, a police officer hurrying to an emergency should have a defence: 'due care' means 'due in the circumstances'. However, it would not provide a defence where the constable was rushing to the police ball, even though he performed exactly the same act. There may well be other circumstances of concealed necessity under statute.

One boundary to the defence of necessity, and this is not certain, is that Parliament may have covered the area by statute and there is no room for the defence. Perhaps the best illustration is not an English authority but a US one. In **Commonwealth v Leno** (1993) 616 NE 2d 53 the Massachusetts court held that the defendants had no defence of necessity when they distributed clean hypodermics to intravenous drug users in an attempt to stop the spread of AIDS in this way. The legislature had enacted law about the illegal possession of drugs paraphernalia. The courts had to defer to the legislative policy. There is support for this rule in **Quayle**, above (no defence in a drugs case because Parliament had exhaustively covered the area) and **CS** [2012] EWCA Crim 389 (possible defence of necessity to a charge of child abduction because Parliament's legislative scheme did leave open the possibility of this defence).

Reforming necessity

Looking at the law one might expect that necessity should be made consistent with duress by affording a defence in similar circumstances. It is, however, sometimes argued that it is better to consider and then mitigate the penalty as occurred in **Dudley and Stephens**. There are, however, several arguments against this view. The penalty for murder is the mandatory life sentence. That punishment cannot be reduced by the court. It is also wrong to convict someone when he has acted properly, and the possibility of conviction may be a disincentive to acting in a correct way: one is stigmatised by a conviction and has a criminal record even if one gets an absolute discharge. Such arguments lead to the suggestion that if necessity is to have any effect in criminal law, it ought to be as a defence, and not as a mitigating factor.

In the late 1970s, however, the Law Commission in its Report No. 83 on *Defences of General Application*, above, came out strongly against this reasoning. There were two major recommendations. First, there should be no attempt by Parliament to establish this defence; secondly, insofar as the defence existed at common law, it should be abolished. The Law Commission argued that there was no need for the defence because it would cover so few eventualities; that the discretion not to prosecute would cover necessitous situations; that necessity could be taken into account during sentencing; and that in some offences there always is a specific defence such as 'without lawful excuse' which includes facts which would otherwise fall within a defence of necessity. This approach was open to criticism. If all aspects of the defence were abolished, what would be done with those cases where most people would agree that some defence should be available, for example emergency operations on children?

Surely there must be some kind of a defence in circumstances such as those which occurred in **Kitson** (1955) 39 Cr App R 66 (CCA), which is one of the more ludicrous cases in post-war English law. The passenger in a car, having taken drink, fell asleep. He awoke to find the driver gone and the car coasting downhill. He grabbed hold of the steering-wheel and in doing so prevented a crash. Surely he should be congratulated not prosecuted, in Lord Denning MR's terms quoted above. If prosecuted for driving while under the influence of drink, he should have a defence. Similarly, if a person breaks the speed limit to avoid an accident, a result which has been reached in New York: *People* v *Cataldo* (1970) 65 Misc 2d 286. It cannot be foreseen in which circumstances a plea of necessity will be raised. For this reason a general defence is needed. Surely it would be unjust to convict the prisoner who broke out of his burning cell. He is not acting of his own free will. Indeed, it would not be absurd to say that the policy of the law is to encourage conduct such as in *Kitson*. The arguments of the Law Commission may also be criticised. The lack of demand for a defence does not mean that the defence should not exist. A person who should not be convicted should not have to rely on executive discretion not to prosecute or on judicial discretion to impose a light sentence. The law should clearly state that he has a defence. Duress of circumstances, which developed after the Law Commission's Report, has partly but not completely answered this criticism. Finally, the fact that there are special defences tied to specific offences does not undermine the claim that there should be a general defence to fill in such gaps in the law as exist.

Duress of circumstances as a separate defence

These arguments suggest that there should be some defence. In recent times – and the law is not yet completely settled – the courts have shown themselves more amenable than previously in creating a defence in the normal haphazard common law way. The Court of Appeal in *Conway* [1989] QB 290 established a defence called 'duress of circumstances' and subsequent cases have confirmed its existence. The defendant was charged with reckless driving. He said that he had driven recklessly because he feared that two men who approached his car were going to kill his passenger. The court allowed his appeal. The judges held that the facts amounted to duress of circumstances; that duress was an example of necessity; and that whether duress of circumstances was called duress or necessity did not matter. It should be noted that the threat came from a human agency, not from, say, starvation, a natural cause, as in *Dudley and Stephens*, above. In terms of justification and excuse, duress of circumstances looks like a justification, whereas normally at least duress is an excuse.

The defence is restricted in the same way as duress: the defendant must act to avoid a threat of death or serious physical injury, as was said, for example, in *Abdul-Hussain* [1999] Crim LR 570 (CA) and *Quayle*, above. Therefore, a threat of psychological harm does not suffice: *Baker*, above; cf. the law of non-fatal offences, and it is uncertain whether the law on duress of circumstances should be brought into line with that of non-fatal offences: *DPP* v *Rogers* [1998] Crim LR 202 (DC), or he must act to avoid an honestly (see *Cairns*, above) imagined threat of the same; and he must act with the steadfastness reasonably to be expected of the ordinary citizen in the defendant's situation. That is, the tests in *Graham*, above, applied. The court certified that a point of law of general importance arose but the House of Lords refused leave to appeal. More recently, in *Hampshire County Council* v *E* [2007] EWHC 2584 (Admin) it was held that the objective tests were to be applied: may 'the failure of her son to attend regularly at school . . . be the result of reasonable fear on the respondent's part that if she tried to get him to school she or her daughter could be at risk of death or serious injury at his hands'? The objective requirement precludes the use of a subjective element, such as suicidal tendencies found in *Rodger* (above) and the pain supposed in *Quayle*. In *Quayle* one reason for the failure of the defence was that there was no imminent risk of death or serious injury from the pain. Another similarity is that duress of circumstances is not available when the accused could have done something other than break the law. In the Scottish case of *Moss* v *Howdle* 1997 SLT 782 the accused broke the speed limit in order to drive as quickly as possible to the nearest service station for medical attention for his passenger who had cried out in pain. The court denied the defence on the ground that there were alternatives such as stopping on the hard shoulder. *CS*, above, is the latest authority. Sir John Thomas, the President of the Queen's Bench Division, spoke for the Court of Appeal when he said that the accused had no defence of necessity/duress of circumstances. 'There was no reasonable belief that a threat [of death or serious injury] was imminent nor could it be said that a person was acting reasonably and proportionately by removing the child from the jurisdiction in order to prevent serious injury.'

The law on duress by threats as laid down in *Hasan*, above, therefore lays down the limits of duress of circumstances. One difference, however, which the Court of Appeal laid down in *Cole*, above, is that duress by threats occurred when the threatener nominated the crime (for instance perjury in *Hudson and Taylor*, above), whereas in duress by circumstances there was no such nomination. In *Cole* the moneylenders did not nominate robbery and therefore his defence could not be duress by threats. *Cole* holds that the two defences are related, but not overlapping. They should not be confused. The Court of Appeal in *Abdul-Hussain*, above, stated that *Cole* was wrong as to this distinction. Rose LJ said: 'We see no reason of principle or authority for distinguishing the two forms of duress . . . In particular, we do not read the court's judgment in *Cole* as seeking to draw any such distinction.' There must be, in his words, 'a close nexus between the threat and the criminal act' but there is no requirement of 'a virtually instantaneous reaction'. *Cole* laid down the rule that there had to be a direct and immediate connection between the peril and the crime. On the facts there was no such link because of a gap of one hour and 50 minutes between the crime, robbery at a building society, and payment of the money stolen there to a moneylender. It is suggested that on this point *Cole* is incorrect. The threat was an immediate one, never mind an imminent one, when the accused committed the robbery. One interesting consideration is that the defence of duress of circumstances was being created at the same time that the defence of duress by threats was being restricted by the imposition of new limits on the crimes to which it applies and the use of the three objective tests in *Graham*.

The Court of Appeal in *Conway* believed themselves bound by their decision in *Willer* (1986) 83 Cr App R 225 (CA), a case definitely not one concerned with duress by threats. The term 'duress of circumstances' was not used. The first use was in *Conway*. The accused in *Willer* was charged with reckless driving. He had driven very slowly along a pavement to avoid a gang of youths. The court held he was driving under duress, but in fact he was not. The youths did not impliedly order him: drive on the pavement or we shall beat you up. Indeed, they very much wanted him to stay where he was. The case was really one of necessity. As David Ormerod, *Smith and Hogan's Criminal Law*, 13th edn (Oxford University Press, 2011) 362, wrote: 'the court was simply allowing the defence of necessity . . . It should surely make no difference whether D [the accused] drove on the pavement to escape from the youths, or a herd of charging bulls, a runaway lorry, or a flood, if he did so in order to escape death or serious bodily harm.' A similar phrase appears in D. Ormerod (ed.), *Smith and Hogan, Criminal Law: Cases and Materials*, 10th edn (OUP, 2009) 472. Simon Brown J in *Martin* said that this defence arose from 'objective dangers' and only in 'extreme circumstances'.

These two cases, *Conway* and *Willer*, were followed in *Martin* [1989] 1 All ER 652, where the Court of Appeal drew the boundaries of the defence. The question to be asked was whether a person of reasonable firmness sharing the defendant's characteristics would have responded as the accused did. As in duress, the accused must reasonably believe that he has good cause to fear death or serious injury (the requirement of reasonableness as to belief was omitted by the Divisional Court in **DPP v Rogers** [1998] Crim LR 202, but is wrong in the light of **Howe** on duress and the earlier cases on duress of circumstances). These limits do not appear in necessity as a defence. The Divisional Court in **DPP v Harris** [1995] 1 Cr App R 170 said that the accused had to act reasonably and proportionately, as did the court in **Martin**. McCowan LJ thought *dubitante* that there did exist a defence of necessity but that it was not needed on a charge of driving without due care and attention because the term 'due' incorporated the span of the defence. The other judge considered that necessity was a defence to this crime. The court thought that it was not faced with a situation of necessity and considered that **Willer** was the same. Therefore, the case is not conclusive. However, if a disqualified driver takes his wife to hospital by car when she has had a heart attack in remote countryside the situation is not one of duress but of necessity.

The Court of Appeal in **Backshall** [1998] 1 WLR 1506 held, contrary to McCowan LJ, that duress of circumstances (which the courts called 'necessity') was a defence to driving without due care and attention and not part of the analysis of whether there was *due* attention. In other words the facts gave rise to an excuse, duress of circumstances; they did not result in the accused's not having the fault element as defined by the offence. It should be noted that in **Martin** the threat was that the threatener would kill herself unless the accused, who was disqualified, drove her son (his stepson) to work, that is, the threat was to harm the threatener herself and not as it always has been so far in duress to harm the accused or a third party. (A threat, 'I will blow myself up unless you commit perjury', ought, it is thought, to give rise to a defence of duress, provided of course that all the limits on duress are fulfilled.) Note that the threat to kill oneself, suicide, is not a crime, yet the defence was available. Actually the facts of **Martin** would seem to constitute a situation of duress by threats. The accused's wife was making a threat in the classic duress formula: 'break the law or I shall do so-and-so'. (It did not matter that the wife's threat, to kill herself, was lawful.) Compare **Willer**: the accused was not ordered to drive on the pavement or else he would be killed. Indeed the gang did not want him to drive on the paved area for by doing so he escaped their threats. Another issue raised by **Martin** is whether the threat must be an unlawful one. Suicide is no longer a crime under English law. The point was not discussed by the Court of Appeal. If **Cole**, above, is correct, **Martin** should indeed be treated as a case on duress by threats.

While **Backshall** held that duress of circumstances is a defence available to careless driving, rather than part of the offence itself, there is a situation where the facts giving rise to what would otherwise be a defence of duress of circumstances are taken into account when determining whether or not there is an offence. In crimes of subjective recklessness it has to be proved that the accused took a risk which a reasonable person would not have taken. In examining the gravity of the risk the triers of fact could say that a reasonable person must have taken the risk of causing harm in order to prevent a greater harm. If so, the accused is not guilty because the prosecution has failed to prove all the elements of the offence; it is not the case that all the ingredients have been proved but there is a defence. The threat which is the subject of the defence must be one which objectively menaces the accused or others and makes him immediately fear a danger. The fact that one's conscience tells one to break the criminal law is not such a threat. In **Blake v DPP** [1993] Crim LR 586 (DC) the appellant believed that the voice of God instructed him to write a quotation from the Bible on a concrete pillar near the Houses of Parliament as a protest against the first Gulf War. There was no immediate danger to himself or others, and his defence to a charge of criminal damage failed.

Willer was followed in **DPP v Bell** [1992] RTR 335 (DC), again a driving case. The accused was not guilty of driving with excess alcohol when he drove his car to escape a threat of serious injury to himself. A similar case was ***DPP v Whittle*** [1996] RTR 154 (CA). Once the threat is over, the accused must stop driving; if he does not, he will be guilty of this crime: ***DPP v Jones*** [1990] RTR 33 (DC), ***DPP v Mullally***, above, and ***Malcolm v DPP*** [2007] EWHC 363 (Admin).

The first cases on duress of circumstances involved motoring offences. There was never any real doubt that it applied to other crimes (such as hijacking: ***Abdul-Hussain***, above, and cultivating cannabis: ***Blythe*** (1998) *The Independent*, 4 April (Warrington Crown Court)) and ***Pommell*** [1995] 2 Cr App R 607 (CA) confirmed the general application of the defence subject to the same exceptions found in duress by threats. Accordingly the defence was available on the facts of ***Pommell*** to an accused who took a sub-machine gun from a friend of his who intended to kill persons who had murdered a friend of the friend. There was no relationship between the accused and these third parties and after ***Hasan***, ***Pommell*** may well be wrong on this point. The court also held that the objective limitations of duress by threats applied to this offence ('reasonable belief', 'good cause' and 'person of reasonable firmness') as well as the rules that the threat had to be one of death or serious injury and the accused had to go to the police as soon as he could: a delay could, however, be explained away. ***Pommell*** also illustrates the law that duress of circumstances need not come from natural circumstances but can arise from a human cause. The court stressed that necessity in its 'lesser evil' guise was not a defence, whereas duress of circumstances was. ***Pommell*** illustrates the difference between duress and necessity. There was no threat; therefore, the case could not have been one of duress, contrary to the thinking of the court. What the accused did was to take a weapon from the accused when the alternative was to allow the other to kill with it. These facts gave rise to a choice-of-evils defence. The accused had the choice of breaking the law, possessing a firearm without a licence, or allowing the other party to kill. He chose the lesser evil. Whether necessity should exist on these facts is a matter of policy, but a conviction on the facts might have sent wrong signals to the public.

As already stated, the accused must have a reasonable belief that he had good cause to fear the threat. The requirement of reasonable belief has at times been ignored, but to keep consistency with duress by threats, this condition must be retained. ***Howe*** and ***Hasan*** are after all House of Lords authorities.

Duress of circumstances and necessity

The present law was summed up in ***Conway***: 'It appears that it is still not clear whether there is a general defence of necessity or, if there is, what are the circumstances in which it is available.' But there are indications that necessity may shortly be recognised as a defence. ***Re A*** is especially significant in this regard. However, the judiciary still displays confusion about the legal foundations of duress and necessity. For example, as stated above, Lord Hailsham in ***Howe*** regarded duress as a species of necessity. And some say 'duress of circumstances' is another name for necessity. In ***Quayle*** the defence of duress of circumstances was said to be one of 'necessity by circumstances'.

A different view was put by C. Gearty, 'Necessity: a necessary defence in criminal law?' [1989] CLJ 357:

> Well-meaning people who think the world is fair believe a defence of necessity would make it fairer still. The judges, who know better, realise that it would parade for public view the inequalities and iniquities inherent in our affluence, without ever threatening to remove them – the Crown Court is hardly the place, after all, to abolish the law of property.

For this reason the hungry are not permitted to steal, the homeless to squat. He continued:

> Where does the defence go from here? After **Martin**, duress of circumstances would appear to have a general application across the law (other than murder, one presumes). It remains to be seen whether the courts will be so eager to apply it where the crime said to have been necessary is more gruesome than the motoring infractions (a wounding or kidnapping for example). And nowhere is it suggested that [the accused] should be required to choose the lesser evil – yet such utilitarian calculus is the essence of necessity. We are still some way from a defence that might stimulate the needy into approved banditry.

Present law has not reached the stage of balancing evils which some see as the conceptual basis of necessity, which indeed in the USA is sometimes known as 'choice of evils'. However, since it is a defence to use reasonable force to injure a person damaging property, it seems absurd not to give a defence to someone who steals property to feed a starving child. **Pommell** has been taken to be the start of the opening of the floodgates to a full-scale defence of necessity. In the view of the present writer **Pommell** does not go so far. Duress of circumstances remains restricted to the same requirements as apply to duress by threats. Theft and squatting are rarely excused by duress of threats; similarly they will rarely be excused by duress of circumstances. Necessity is distinguished from duress of circumstances by its rationale of the balance of evils. Duress of circumstances does not have the rationale: the will of the accused is overridden by the threat. Necessity is a justificatory defence, whereas duress of both forms is an excuse. In terms of the distinction explored at the start of this chapter an accused who acts under duress of either variety is excused but one who acts under necessity is justified.

Conway and *Martin* do, however, suggest that some of the older cases requiring a defence ought to be reviewed. Interestingly cases at present except *Cole*, above, where the defence failed are concerned with victimless offences but it is assumed that the defence is not so restricted.

In one instance Parliament has ruled out a defence of duress of circumstances. The Human Fertilisation and Embryology Act 1990, s 37, amends s 5(2) of the Abortion Act 1967, which now provides that anything done with intent to perform a miscarriage is unlawful unless authorised by s 1 of the 1967 statute, which requires a registered medical practitioner to perform the abortion.

The position taken in this book

1 There is a defence of duress (by threats).
2 While the defence is perhaps still in the process of emerging, there is a defence of duress of circumstances.
3 Necessity, which is to be distinguished from duress of circumstances, is an embryo defence ripe for development.

Reform of duress of circumstances and necessity

This area of the law would receive the imprimatur of the Law Commission if its draft Criminal Code, Law Com. No. 177, 1989, were enacted. Clause 43 aptly restates present law:

1 A person is not guilty of an offence ... when he does an act under duress of circumstances.

2 A person does an act under duress of circumstances if –

   (a) he does it because he knows or believes that it is immediately necessary to avoid death or serious personal harm to himself or another; and

   (b) the danger that he knows or believes to exist is such that in all the circumstances (including any of his personal characteristics that affect its gravity) he cannot reasonably be expected to act otherwise.

These recommendations find their most recent expression in the Law Commission Report No. 218, *Legislating the Criminal Code – Offences Against the Person and General Principles*, 1993, discussed under Duress, above. The 1993 definition would leave to the jury the question of whether the defendants in ***Dudley and Stephens*** had an excuse for killing the cabin boy. Clause 43(3) denies the defence to murder and attempted murder in order to keep the law consistent with ***Howe*** on duress. The Law Commission would have preferred the defence to apply generally. There are provisions dealing with the overlap between this defence and others. Clause 43(3)(b)(iii) states that the defence does not apply if the person 'has knowingly and without reasonable excuse exposed himself to the danger'. That approach is also taken in the USA in the Model Penal Code *Official Draft*, 1985, s 3.02(2) and at common law, for example ***State v Diana*** (1979) 604 P 2d 1312, a decision of the Washington Court of Appeals. US law differs, however, from even the proposed English law by balancing harms. The Model Penal Code, s 3.02(2), provides that 'the harm or evil sought to be avoided . . . is greater than that sought to be prevented', while ***State v Diana*** stipulated that 'necessity is available as a defence when the physical forces of nature or the pressure of circumstances cause the accused to take unlawful action to avoid a harm which social policy deems greater than the harm resulting from a violation of the law'. As Gearty, quoted above, wrote, English law has not adopted this utilitarian calculus. At present therefore the law of necessity is in a state of flux.

In the draft Criminal Code, 1989, the Law Commission did not define necessity but left it to judicial development. Similarly in the 1993 Report it did not propose to put necessity, if it existed, on a statutory footing. Case law had to develop before the defence could be encapsulated by Parliament. Necessity-as-justification is therefore not touched, whereas necessity-as-excuse (duress of circumstances) is to be encapsulated in a statute because of its resemblance to duress by threats. Who knows: before your exam the law may have changed again! The Australian states of Queensland and Western Australia provide a defence where a person acted or omitted to act 'under such circumstances of sudden or extraordinary emergency that an ordinary person possessing ordinary powers of self-control could not reasonably be expected to act otherwise' – and the sky has not fallen in.

Summary

- *Infancy*: Children under 10 may not be convicted of any offence; children above 10 may be convicted of any offence. The law or presumption that children aged 10–14 could not be convicted of any offence unless the prosecution could prove not just the *actus reus* and *mens rea* but also the fact that the child knew the conduct was seriously (or morally) wrong was abolished in 1998. However, it should be noted that the doctrine of *mens rea* will sometimes work in favour of children: they may not intend or foresee consequences when an adult in the same position would have so intended or foreseen.

- *Duress*: This defence, also known as duress by threats, is based on the thinking that people cannot be expected to resist threats of scrious harm of death to themselves and their loved ones (and quite possibly strangers). The basis is: 'do this or else', for example 'unless you commit the crime of theft, I will kill you'. The defence is quite circumscribed and the House of Lords in **Hasan** has recently reemphasised that the defence is a narrow one. Its limits are:

  1 there is no defence of duress to murder, attempted murder, and some forms of treason;
  2 the threat must be one of death or serious personal injury;
  3 it seems that the threat must be one against the accused or his or her family or perhaps someone with whom the defendant has a special relationship: it is, however, arguable that the threat could be against a stranger;
  4 the threat must be one which can immediately (read fairly broadly) be carried out: if there is an opportunity to escape, the duressee must use it; and for a similar reason, once the duress is over, the accused must desist from the criminal behaviour;
  5 the accused must act reasonably to avoid the threat: he or she must have acted like a sober and reasonable person might have behaved;
  6 the belief that he or she is threatened with death or serious harm must be based on reasonable grounds;
  7 the accused must have 'good cause to fear that if he did not so act [the duressor] would kill him or cause him serious personal injury' (**Graham** (1982) CA, approved by the House of Lords in **Howe** (1987)); and
  8 no defence is available if the accused voluntarily joined a criminal organisation which he or she knew or ought to have known would expose him or her to the risk that duress would be used.

- *Coercion*: This defence is similar to duress but is available only to a married woman. The wife must prove that she acted under the coercion and in the presence of her husband: Criminal Justice Act 1925, s 47. Note that the burden of proof is placed on the accused. It is thought that coercion has a wider meaning than duress and includes, for example, a threat by the husband to leave his wife; 'presence' is not limited to the wife being in the same room as the husband but extends to being in the husband's sight. The husband and wife must actually be married: a reasonable belief by the alleged wife that they are is insufficient.

- *Duress of circumstances*: Cases over the last 25 years have established a defence of this name. The defence is similar to duress in that the restrictions noted above in respect of duress also apply to duress of circumstances but the basic formulation differs from duress which, as stated, is in the form of 'do this or else' (e.g. 'do this crime or we will kneecap you!') whereas duress of circumstances takes the form of: 'there is an emergency and the accused has to escape it by breaking the law'. An example occurs where the driver of a car drives on the pavement to avoid masked gunmen: the gunmen are not saying: 'we will shoot you unless you break the law by driving on the pavement'.

- *Necessity*: Sometimes duress of circumstances is called necessity and sometimes necessity is called duress of circumstances. The view taken here is that duress of circumstances is similar to the defence of duress: they share the same limitations, for example neither is a defence to murder. Necessity differs in that it is a choice-of-evils defence without such boundaries; it can, therefore, be a defence to all crimes including murder. The status of this defence remains uncertain but there is a modern view that it does exist.

References

Reports

Home Office Consultation Paper, *Tackling Youth Crime* (1997)

Irish Law Reform Commission Consultation Paper no. 27, *Homicide: the Plea of Provocation* (2003)

Law Commission Consultation Paper no. 122, *Legislating the Criminal Code: Offences against the Person and General Principles* (1992)

Law Commission Consultation Paper no. 177, *A New Homicide Act for England and Wales?* (2005)

Law Commission Report no. 83, *Defences of General Application* (1978)

Law Commission Report no. 177, *A Criminal Code for England and Wales* (1989)

Law Commission Report no. 218, *Legislating the Criminal Code – Offences against the Person and General Principles* (1993)

Law Commission Report no. 304, *Murder, Manslaughter and Infanticide* (2006)

Ministry of Justice, Consultation Paper no. 19, *Murder, Manslaughter and Infanticide* (2009)

Model Penal Code (US), *Official Draft* (1985)

Report of the Select Committee of the House of Lords on Murder and Life Imprisonment (Nathan), HL Paper 78–1 (1989)

White Paper, *Crime, Justice and Protecting the Public*, Cm 965 (1990)

White Paper, *No More Excuses*, Cm 3809 (1997)

Books

Fletcher, G. *Rethinking Criminal Law* (Little, Brown & Co., 1978)

Ormerod, D. *Smith and Hogan's Criminal Law* 13th edn (Oxford University Press, 2011)

Shute, S., Gardner, S. and Horder, J. *Action and Value in the Criminal Law* (Oxford University Press, 1993)

Simpson, A.W.B. *Cannibalism and the Common Law* (University of Chicago Press, 1984)

Smith, J.C. *Justification and Excuse in the Criminal Law* (Stevens, 1989)

Smith, J.C. and Hogan, B. *Criminal Law: Cases and Materials* (ed. D. Ormerod), 10th edn (Oxford University Press, 2009)

Stephen, J.F. *History of the Criminal Law of England* (Sweet & Maxwell, 1883)

Journals

Dressler, J. 'Provocation: partial justification or partial excuse' (1988) 51 MLR 467

Gearty, C. 'Necessity: a necessary defence in criminal law?' [1989] CLJ 357

Horder, J. 'Self-defence, necessity and duress: understanding the relationship' (1998) 11 *Canadian Journal of Law and Philosophy* 143

Morawetz, T. 'Reconstructing the criminal defences: the significance of justification' (1986) 77 JCL & Crim 277

Ormerod, D. 'Duress: Conspiracy to murder' [2011] Crim LR 645 (comment on *Ness*, Crown Court)

Perkins, R.M. 'Impelled perpetration restated' (1981) 33 Hastings LJ 403

Stone, N. 'Old heads upon young shoulders: "compassion to human infirmity" following *R v JTB*' (2010) 32 JSWFL 287

Vandervort, L. 'Social justice in the modern regulatory state: duress, necessity and the consensual model in law' (1987) 6 Law & Phil 205

Walker, N. 'The end of an old song' (1999) 149 NLJ 64

Further reading

Alexander, A. 'Lesser evils: a closer look at the paradigmatic justification' (2005) 24 *Law and Philosophy* 611

Arthur, R. 'Rethinking the criminal responsibility of young people in England and Wales' (2012) 20 *European Journal of Crime, Criminal Law and Criminal Justice* 13

Ashworth, A. 'Murder: defence – young defendant – intention to kill – defendant's father instructing him to assist in murder' [2008] Crim LR 138

Baron, M. 'Justifications and excuses' (2005) 2 Ohio St J Crim L 387

Baron, M. 'Excuses, excuses' (2007) 1 Crim Law and Philos 21

Bennett, C. 'Excuses, justifications and the normability of expressive behaviour' (2012) 32 OJLS 563

Berman, M.N. 'Justification and excuse, law and morality' (2003) 53 Duke LJ 1

Bohlander, M. '*In extremis*: hijacked airplanes, "collateral damage" and the limits of criminal law' [2006] Crim LR 579

Cavadino, P. 'Goodbye *Doli*, must we leave you?' (1997) 9 *Child and Family Law Quarterly* 165

Centre for Crime and Justice Studies, *From Punishment to Problem Solving – A New Approach to Children in Trouble* (Centre for Crime and Justice Studies, 2006)

Chan, W. and Simester, S. 'Duress, necessity: How many defences?' (2006) 16 KCLJ 121

Cipriani, D. *Children's Rights and the Minimum Age of Criminal Responsibility* (Ashgate, 2009)

Clarkson, C.M.V. 'Necessary action: a new defence?' [2004] Crim LR 81

Crofts, T. '*Doli incapax*' (2003) *eLaw: Murdoch University Electronic Journal of Law*, Issue 3

De Girolani, M.O. 'Culpability in creating criminal necessity' [2008] Columbia Public Law and Legal Theory Working Papers, Paper 08151

Dennis, I.H. 'On necessity as a "defence to crime": possibilities, problems, and the limits of justification and excuse' (2009) 3 Crim Law and Philos 29

Dressler, J. 'Why keep the provocation defense? Some reflections on a difficult subject' (2002) 86 Minnesota LR 959

Duff, R.A. 'Rethinking justifications' (2004) 39 Tulsa L Rev 829

Duff, R.A. 'Excuses, moral and legal' (2007) 1 Crim Law and Philos 49

Elliott, C. 'Criminal responsibility and children: A new defence required to acknowledge the absence of capacity and choice' (2011) 75 JCL 289

Elliott, D.W. 'Necessity, duress and self-defence' [1989] Crim LR 611

Finkelstein, C. 'Excuses and dispositions in criminal law' (2002) 6 Buff Crim LR 317

Forsyth, M. 'The divorce or the marriage of morality and law? The defence of necessity in Pacific island countries' (2010) 21 CLF 121

Gardner, J. 'The gist of excuses' (1998) 1 *Buffalo Criminal Law Review* 575

Gardner, J. 'The logic of excuses and the rationality of emotions' (2009) 43 J Value Inquiry 315

Gillen, J. (Mr Justice) 'Age of criminal responsibility: the frontier between care and justice' [2007] *International Family Law Journal* 7

Goldson, B. 'Difficult to understand or defend: a reasoned case for raising the age of criminal responsibility' (2009) 48 Howard J 514

Hassemer, W. 'Justification and excuse in criminal law: Theses and comments' [1986] Brigham Young LR 573

Horder, J. 'Occupying the moral high ground? The Law Commission on duress' [1994] Crim LR 334

Horder, J. *Excusing Crimes* (Oxford University Press, 2004)

Jefferson, M. 'Householders and the use of force against intruders' (2005) 69 JCL 405

Kugler, I. 'Necessity as a justification in *Re A (Children)*' (2004) 68 J Crim L 440

Maher, G. 'Age and criminal responsibility' (2005) 2 Ohio SJ Crim L 493

Milhizer, E.R. 'Justification and excuse: What they were, what they are, and what they ought to be' (2004) 78 St John's LR 725

Naylor, M. 'Resistance is futile: Duress as a defence to intentional killing' [2006] Cambridge Student LR 24

Ormerod, D. 'Necessity of circumstances' [2006] Crim LR 151 (comment on *Quayle*)

Padfield, N. 'Duress, necessity and the Law Commission' [1992] Crim LR 778

Peiris, G.L. 'Duress, volition and criminal responsibility' [1998] A-ALR 182

Quigley, J. 'The common law's theory of criminal liability: A challenge from across the Atlantic' (1989–90) 11 Whittier LR 479

Reed, A. Case comment on *Nguyen* (2012) 76 JCL 377

Robinson, P. 'Objective versus subjective justification: a case study in function and form in constructing a system of criminal law theory' (2008) Public Law and Legal Theory Research Paper Series, Research Paper no. 08–23, University of Pennsylvania Law School

Rogers, J. 'Necessity, private defence and the killing of Mary' [2001] Crim LR 515

Royal College of Psychiatrists, *Child defendants*, Occasional Paper OP56, 2006

Smith, J.C. 'Official secrets' [2001] Crim LR 987 (comment on *S, also known as Shayler*)

Smith, K.J.M. 'Duress and steadfastness; in pursuit of the unintelligible' [2001] Crim LR 363

Tadros, V. 'The character of excuses' (2001) 21 OJLS 495

Tadros, V. *Criminal Responsibility* (Oxford University Press, 2005)

Thorburn, M. 'Justifications, powers, and authority' (2008) 117 Yale LJ 1070

Uniacke, S. 'Emotional excuses' (2007) 26 Law and Phil 95

Urbas, G. *The Age of Criminal Responsibility* (2000) Australian Institute of Criminology, Trends and Issues in Crime and Criminal Justice, No. 181

Walsh, C. 'Irrational presumptions of rationality and comprehension' [1998] 3 Web JCLI

Westen, P. 'An attitudinal theory of excuse' (2006) 25 *Law and Philosophy* 289

Westen, P. 'Offences and defences again' (2008) 28 OJLS 563

Westen, P. and Mangiafico, J. 'The criminal defense of duress: a justification, not an excuse – and why it matters' (2005) 6 Buff Crim L Rev 833

Williams, G. 'Offences and defences' (1982) 2 LS 233

Williams, G. 'The theory of excuses' [1982] Crim LR 732

Wilson, W. 'The filtering role of crisis in the constitution of criminal excuses' (2004) XVII Can J of L and Jurisprudence 387

Wilson, W. 'The structure of criminal defences' [2005] Crim LR 108

Yaffe, G. 'A procedural rationale for the necessity defense' (2009) 43 J Value Inquiry 369

For a symposium on *Re A (Children) (Conjoined Twins)* see (2001) 9 Medical LR 201

For a critique of excuses and justifications, see R.F. Schopp, *Justification: Defences and Just Convictions* (Cambridge University Press, 1998) or his article of the same name (1993) 24 Pacific LJ 1233. For an English approach to the same topic, see W. Wilson, *Central Issues in Criminal Theory* (Hart, 2002), chs 10–11

For the Scottish Law Commission's approach, see its *Report on Age of Criminal Responsibility*, Scot. Law Com. No. 185, 2002. Note that the age of responsibility was raised from eight to 12 by the Criminal Justice and Licensing (Scotland) Act 2010, s 52. For an Irish view, see Law Reform Commission, *Duress and Necessity*, Consultation Paper no. 39, 2006

Visit **www.mylawchamber.co.uk** to access tools to help you develop and test your knowledge of criminal law, including interactive multiple choice questions, practice exam questions with guidance, annotated weblinks, glossary flashcards, legal newsfeed and legal updates.

Use Case Navigator to read in full some of the key cases referenced in this chapter with commentary and questions:

R v G and Another [2003] UKHL 50
R v Graham [1982] 1 WLR 294

POWERED BY LexisNexis®

8

Mistake, intoxication, self-defence

Aims and objectives

After reading this chapter you will understand and be able to critique:

- the definitions of mistake and the application of the law of mistake of fact and mistake of law
- the law on self-defence and the prevention of crime, in particular the effect of mistake of fact and intoxication
- the defence of intoxication, whether self-induced or otherwise, when the intoxication is voluntary, and the purported distinction between specific and basic intent crimes

Mistake

Introduction

English law divides **mistake** as a defence in criminal law into two parts: mistake of law and mistake of fact. The general rule is that if the accused makes a mistake of law, he is guilty, whereas if he makes a mistake of fact, he is not. Unfortunately the law is more complex than these propositions allow. A preliminary point is that if an accused because of a 'disease of the mind' makes a mistake of law, he may have a defence of insanity. This defence is discussed in the next chapter.

Mistake and ignorance of law

In **Esop** (1836) 173 ER 203 the accused was convicted of an offence under English law, buggery; under his personal law no such offence existed. Accordingly, where the accused has the relevant *actus reus* and *mens rea* for the crime, he is guilty even though he did not know that the *actus reus* was forbidden by the criminal law. He was mistaken as to the rules of English law. Moreover, ignorance of the law is no defence: **Bailey** (1800) 168 ER 657. The accused was convicted of a crime which Parliament had created while he was on the high seas, and there was no way of finding out that a law had been enacted. The case has been taken to hold that impossibility is no defence. However, it may be that **Bailey** should be read differently. The case was referred to all the judges. They recommended a pardon. Since at that time a pardon was the sole way of reversing the first instance decision, it may be that they disagreed with the proposition that ignorance of the law was no defence. *Bailey* has nevertheless been treated as deciding that, and the rule has been accepted in, for example, *Carter* v *McLaren* (1871) LR 2 Sc & D 120. The rule was stated by the Court of Appeal in *Lightfoot* (1993) 97 Cr App R 24: '. . . Knowledge of the law . . . is irrelevant . . . The fact that a man does not know what is criminal and what is not . . . cannot save him from conviction if what he does, coupled with the state of his mind, satisfies all the elements of the crime of which he is accused.' An illustration is *Broad* [1997] Crim LR 666 (CA). The defendants were convicted even though they were ignorant of the law. They did not know that what they were making was a proscribed drug. Certainly it is not always easy to discover that a Bill has been enacted or that a statute has come into force. If the accused believes that he is using force to prevent a crime, but there is no such crime, he has made a mistake as to the law and has no defence. Similarly in *Christian* v *R* [2006] UKPC 47 it was held that the defendants were guilty of various crimes of sexual abuse including rape even though there were no books of statutes on the island of Pitcairn.

An illustration of a mistake of law is *Hipperson* v *DPP*, unreported, 3 July 1996 (DC). The defendants had used bolt-cutters to break through the perimeter fence of the Atomic Weapons Establishment, Aldermaston, where the UK's atomic deterrent is produced. They contended that they had a defence to criminal damage in that they were acting to prevent genocide or conspiracy to commit genocide. However, the definition of genocide in the UK is restricted to acting 'with intent to destroy in whole or in part a national, ethnical, racial or religious group as such', and does not extend, as the defendants submitted, to the destruction in whole or in part of the human race. Therefore, the defendants had made a mistake of law and had no defence.

The rule that ignorance of the law is no defence is supported by the arguments that if it were a defence, the floodgates would open and the courts would be swamped by bogus claims of ignorance, people would not try and find out what the law is; 'floodgates' is a weak argument against justice and it would be impossible for the prosecution to show that the accused was truly ignorant of the law. However, it has to be said that no person could know all possible offences, and it may well be unjust to convict a person when only a few people would know of the crime. Judges, lawyers and law students in their professional lives are not expected to know all crimes. Surely ordinary citizens should not be!

There is no defence if the accused consulted a lawyer who stated that their activity was not a crime when it was: *Shaw* v *DPP* [1962] AC 220 (HL). The defendants wanted to know whether publishing a list of prostitutes and their services, *The Ladies' Directory*, was lawful. The Lords held they were guilty of conspiracy despite the legal advice that they had been given. *A fortiori* reliance on legal advice from a paralegal provides no answer: *Brockley* [1994] Crim LR 671 (CA).

Reliance on local authority or police advice is also no defence: *Cambridgeshire and Isle of Ely CC* v *Rust* [1972] 2 QB 426. The Divisional Court directed magistrates to convict the accused of the crime of setting up a stall on a highway without lawful excuse, even though he had sought advice and had paid rates on the stall to the local council. It is arguable that mistake of law should be a defence if the accused tried to find out the law or relied on official advice. He attempted to comply with the law, but failed. It is doubtful whether convicting him serves any purpose other than preventing bogus defences, and the triers of fact could do that: finding flimsy defences to be untrue is part of their role. At present reliance on official advice does not exculpate, but only mitigates the sentence, for example *Howell* v *Falmouth Boat Construction Co* [1951] AC 837 (HL), *obiter*, and *Surrey CC* v *Battersby* [1965] 2 QB 194 (DC). The latter case involved a crime of undertaking childcare without informing the council that the children were to spend more than a month in the house.

She had taken advice that she was not guilty of the offence because no one period extended beyond a month because the parents took the children away at certain weekends. She was held to be guilty. Breaks counted only if a fresh arrangement were made after the break. One might have thought that the Divisional Court might have held that penal statutes should be construed in favour of the accused. To grant her an absolute discharge does not resolve the issue. She had acted in good faith; she was a proper person to take care of the children; and she had taken the advice of the council, the same council which prosecuted her, and the council should have known the law it was administering. No advantage was gained from stigmatising the accused as a criminal, and the outcome may be to bring the legal system into disrepute.

There has been some indication in the cases that where an accused relies on official advice, it is an abuse of authority for the body which gave the advice to prosecute, and while no defence is afforded, the criminal proceedings are stayed as being an abuse of process. Trials which are an abuse of process may well breach Article 6 of the European Convention on Human Rights, which concerns the right to a fair trial.

The same rule applies to a reliance on a judicial decision which is later overruled: *Younger* (1793) 101 ER 253 (by inference). There is also no defence where the accused relies on *ultra vires* delegated legislation. No doubt with increasing EU legislation and judgments, reliance on UK law which is later found to be in conflict with EU norms will afford no defence. Such people are not at fault. Judges make mistakes of law: why do we have the doctrine of *per incuriam*, the Court of Appeal and Supreme Court and the Practice Statement permitting the latter to overrule its previous authorities? Yet they are not guilty of an offence. In *Campbell* (1972) 1 CRNS 273 Kearns DCJ thought that the outcome that if citizens relying on judgments make an error they are guilty, but judges whose decisions are overturned on appeal are not, was 'amusing'. Surely it cannot really be the law that ordinary people should be expected to know the law better than the judiciary. The heavens will not fall if mistake of law in reliance on official advice is accepted as a defence. South Africa does not have the rule: *S v de Blom* (1977) 3 SA 513 (A), and Canada has such a defence (*MacDougall* (1983) 1 CCC (3d) 65 (SCC)), and some US states have such a defence. For example, the New York Penal Code, s 15.20(2), relying on the Model Penal Code, provides a defence. Some states do not give a defence: in the Maryland case of *Hopkins v State* (1950) 69 A 2d 456, reliance on the State Attorney's advice was no defence.

In summary P. Brett 'Mistake of law as a criminal defence' (1966) 5 Melb ULR 179 at 203, wrote:

> [i]f we are seeking to achieve respect for law, it is surely unwise to tell citizens that they must disregard the considered advice of the public officials whose duty it is to administer the law and who may therefore be expected to tell citizens in effect that the advice which they received bona fide from qualified lawyers is to be treated as worthless.

Brett called *Battersby* a 'glaring injustice'. It is unjust that the state through its courts can disregard the advice of its officials such as the Director of Public Prosecutions and convict defendants of offences on facts which the officials informed them were not offences.

It is not unknown for Parliament to afford a defence to a person who relies on official advice. In the Control of Pollution Act 1974, s 3(4), it is a defence to the offence of unlicensed waste disposal that the accused 'took care to inform himself from persons who were in a position to provide information'. The obvious illustration is s 2(1)(a) of the Theft Act 1968, which provides that the accused is not dishonest for the purposes of theft if he believes, whether on reasonable grounds or not, that he had a legal right to deprive the victim of his property. If he believes he did but was mistaken, he is not guilty. In *Secretary of State for Trade and Industry* v *Hart* [1982] 1 All ER 817, the Divisional Court in relation to an offence under the companies legislation of acting as an auditor, knowing oneself to be disqualified, held that the accused was not guilty because he did not know that he was disqualified. It was not sufficient that he knew the *facts* which made him disqualified. His ignorance of the law was a defence. He did not have the requisite *mens rea*. He ought not to have acted as auditor because he was a director of the companies he was auditing. (If he knew he was disqualified but not that acting as an auditor when disqualified was an offence, he would not have a defence: he would have made a mistake of law.) Present law is stated in **Smith** [1974] QB 354 (CA), where a tenant destroyed property which had become his landlord's as a result of civil law in the belief that it was still his. The accused did intend to damage property, but he did not intend to damage property belonging to another. Indeed, he intended to damage property belonging to himself. He made a mistake as regards to whom the property belonged. Current law is sometimes stated as a mistake of civil law excuses. **Hart** could be explained as being a case on mistake of civil law.

Where ignorance of the law is no defence, it may constitute a ground for mitigating sentence: **Rahman** [2008] EWCA Crim 1465.

One problem with having different effects depending on the type of mistake, civil or criminal, is that it may not be obvious whether the error is as to civil or criminal law, for example a mistake as to whether goods are 'stolen' for the purposes of handling is a mistake of criminal law. In **Grant** v **Borg** [1982] 1 WLR 638 the House of Lords held that an error as to whether leave has been granted to a visitor to remain in the UK was not a defence though 'leave' looks very much like a civil law concept. Either the Lords themselves made a mistake (and **Hart** is inconsistent with the decision) or **Smith** is a questionable decision if it lays down this rule that a mistake of civil law is a defence. Lord Bridge said: 'The principle that ignorance of the law is no defence in crime is so fundamental that to construe the word "knowingly" in a criminal statute as requiring merely knowledge of the facts material to the offender's guilt, but also knowledge of the relevant law, would be revolutionary and . . . wholly unacceptable.'

Mistake of fact

Introduction

English law draws a sharp line between mistake of law (guilty) and mistake of fact (usually not guilty), yet the line is not always clear. According to the House of Lords in **Brutus** v **Cozens** [1973] AC 854, a case on the meaning of 'insulting' within s 5 of the Public Order Act 1936, which has since been repealed, the construction of an ordinary word in a statute is a matter of fact, not of law, though the rule seems to have been honoured in the breach more than in the observance. Two cases which are hard to reconcile are **Norton** v **Knowles** [1967] 3 All ER 1061 and **Phekoo** [1981] 1 WLR 1117 (CA), both of which concerned the term 'residential occupier'. In the former case whether the accused believed his victim to be a residential occupier was an issue of law and therefore he had no defence; in the latter the term was held to be a question of fact and accordingly the accused had a defence where he believed that the victim was a squatter and not a residential occupier. It is postulated that mistake of fact is a defence because as with some other defences punishing the accused would not deter him. This rationale is said to derive from J. Bentham, *An Introduction to the Principles of Morals and Legislation* (Methuen, 1932, first published 1789) Chapter 13, Section 3, though it can be argued that while punishing a mistaken person would not deter him, it might deter others.

Logically mistake of fact should negate *mens rea*, that is, the prosecution has not proved this element. There is nothing special about mistake. In this sense mistake is not a defence. The courts have, however, developed special restrictive rules. Three reasons might be hypothesised to explain this development. First, in the nineteenth century the current theory of subjective *mens rea* had not been formulated; therefore, the courts missed the opportunity of stating that mistake was incompatible with the fault element. Secondly, the judges were anxious not to let off an accused who, though telling the truth, had formed his opinion negligently. Thirdly, judges were worried that juries would accept bogus defences. Accordingly they laid down the rule that mistakes had to be reasonable. More recently the courts have brought mistake generally speaking more in line with *mens rea*. It should be remembered that while the courts have moved away from the requirement that a mistake had to be made on reasonable grounds, Parliament can stipulate that a mistake must be a reasonable one.

'Irrelevant mistakes'

Since mistake is intertwined with *mens rea*, if the offence is a strict one, the accused will not have the defence if his mistake is one as to the strict element. In **Prince** (1875) LR 2 CCR 154, s 55 of the Offences Against the Person Act 1861 was at issue: 'Whosoever shall unlawfully take . . . any unmarried girl, being under the age of 16 years, out of the possession of her father . . .' shall be guilty of an offence. The accused believed that the girl was over 16. He had no intention of doing what the law forbade. The court held that he was guilty. The abductee was a girl; she was unmarried; she was under 16; she was taken out of the possession of her parents. He knew that she was a girl, that she was unmarried, and that he was taking her out of the possession of her parents. He did not have to know that she was under 16. He was guilty because his mistake was an irrelevant one in that he was mistaken as to her age. Mistake is relevant only where the mistake is as to a *mens rea* element. In **Hibbert** (1869) LR 1 CCR 184 the accused was charged with the same offence. His conviction was quashed. He did not know that the girl had any parents. His mistake was a relevant one, because it related to a *mens rea* element. Before he could be convicted, he had to know that she had parents. He did not know that fact. Therefore, his conviction was quashed. The rule in **Prince** is not affected by developments in the next three sections but, as we have seen in Chapter 4, the doctrine of strict liability is in retreat: the fewer strict offences there are, the less scope there is for 'irrelevant mistakes'.

Tolson

Where there is a relevant mistake, it was stated for many years that the accused did not have a defence unless his mistake was made reasonably. If he made a mistake unreasonably in that he was careless, he had no defence. The principal authority was **Tolson** (1889) 23 QBD 168 (CCR). The accused thought that her husband had been killed in a shipwreck. Six years after that event she went through a second ceremony of marriage. In fact her husband was alive though he had made no contact with her since the shipwreck. Because she thought her husband was dead, she did not intend 'being married, to marry again' as would be the case in bigamy. The court afforded her the defence of mistake. It argued thus. When Parliament gave a defence to bigamy that the spouse has been absent for seven years, it cannot have intended to penalise someone who believed on grounds other than seven years' absence that her spouse was dead. There was nothing in the statute about a defence for a person who believed on reasonable grounds that her spouse was dead. The reasonable grounds were that she thought he had been lost at sea.

Several comments may be made:

(a) Mrs Tolson did not intend to marry again; Mr Prince did not intend to elope with or abduct a girl under 16. She was not guilty; he was guilty. In legal terms she made a relevant mistake, he made an irrelevant one.

(b) The court decided that a mistaken belief was a defence only if reasonably held. Stephen J in *Tolson* had no doubt:

> It may be laid down as a general rule that an alleged offender is deemed to have acted under that state of facts which he in good faith and on reasonable grounds believed to exist when he did the act alleged to be an offence. I am unable to suggest any real exception to this rule, nor has one ever been suggested to me.

Saying that mistake is a defence only if reasonably made is equivalent to saying that the accused will not have the defence if he was careless. Bray CJ commented on the Australian law which is the same as *Tolson* that 'the criminal law is designed to punish the vicious, not the stupid or the credulous' (*Brown* (1975) 10 SASR 139) and that the rule was an 'anomalous and unwarrantable excrescence' (*Brambles Holdings Ltd* v *Carey* (1976) 15 SASR 270). In this respect the *Tolson* defence shifts the question from *mens rea* to negligence. Bigamy has in this sense become a crime of negligence. If the view is held that mistake ought to negate *mens rea*, what *Tolson* seems to have done is to mix up evidence and substantive law. A defendant who sets up a defence of unreasonable belief may well fail to put forward sufficient evidence to raise a reasonable doubt as to guilt in the minds of the triers of fact; yet even an unreasonable belief should as a matter of substance avail if the triers of fact accept the accused's evidence.

(c) The mistake in *Tolson* did not relate to a failure by the prosecution to prove an element of the offence of bigamy. The accused was given a defence. Her mistake related to that defence.

Diplock J followed *Tolson* in *Gould* [1968] 2 QB 65 (CA) where the accused believed that the first marriage had been dissolved. Only a reasonable mistake would afford a defence. Similarly, a belief that the first marriage was void exculpates the accused, provided that his mistake was reasonable: *King* [1964] 1 QB 285 (CCA). On the *Tolson* approach the 'being married' element in bigamy is satisfied by carelessness. If bigamy is viewed as a serious offence, it is strange that one can commit it carelessly.

The most important case in this area is *DPP* v *Morgan*.

DPP v *Morgan* [1976] AC 182 (HL)

One of the accused, a sergeant in the RAF, invited three men to have sexual intercourse with his wife. He told them that if she resisted or screamed, she was merely enjoying the sexual act. The men had intercourse with her by force. In fact she did not consent. The men were charged with rape as it was then defined. By a majority of three to two the House of Lords ruled that the men had a defence if they (honestly) believed that the woman was consenting. Their mistaken belief did not have to be reasonably held. (In fact the House of Lords determined that no reasonable jury would believe their story, and accordingly there was no miscarriage of justice. This procedure is called 'applying the proviso': on the law the men would not have been guilty had their evidence been believed, but it was not. By their verdict the jury believed the appellants' evidence to be 'a pack of lies' and that there was 'a multiple rape', not 'a sexual orgy' as Lord Cross put it.)

The Lords did not overrule *Tolson* but no good reason for retaining *Tolson* was provided by the majority. The House also had the opportunity to overrule *Tolson* in *B* v *DPP* [2000] 2 AC 428 but it did not take it. However, Lord Nicholls criticised the requirement of reasonableness found in *Tolson*. 'Considered as a matter of principle, the honest belief approach must be preferable. By definition the mental element in a crime is concerned with a subjective state of mind. . . . To the extent that an overriding objective limit ("on reasonable grounds") is introduced, the subjective element is displaced.' It could be that the element of the crime of bigamy, 'being married', has the *mens rea* of negligence attached to it. That is, if a person has the mental element of negligence as to the *actus reus* of being married, this element of the offence is satisfied. Since an unreasonable mistake demonstrates negligence, only a reasonable mistake will lead to an acquittal.

There are several ways of reconciling *Morgan* with *Tolson*.

(a) *Tolson* applies to statutory offences, *Morgan* to common law ones. This argument will not wash. *Morgan* has been applied to statutory offences and was itself put into statutory form for rape in the Sexual Offences (Amendment) Act 1976 which, however, was repealed by the Sexual Offences Act 2003. That statute provides for a test of belief in consent based on reasonable grounds.

(b) There may be a distinction between the mistake in *Tolson* which related to a defence and that in *Morgan* which related to the failure by the prosecution to prove part of the offence (or would have done so, had the men's evidence been believed). However, the line between offence and defence is hard if not impossible to draw, as can be argued from the discussion in Chapter 1 about the third exception to *Woolmington* (HL). Parliament could easily have created a defence to bigamy of belief in the spouse's death but formulated as part of the offence: 'anyone without belief in the spouse's death who was married marries again . . .'. It should, however, be recalled that mistake in duress and duress of circumstances must be reasonably made. Is the mistake as to the unlawfulness of the act or is it one as to the defence? If one believes one is being subjected to duress when one is not, is one acting lawfully because one does not have the *mens rea* of the offence charged, or does one have a defence? If the former, according to the distinction the mistake would exculpate, but under present law it does not because a reasonable mistake is needed.

(c) There is something peculiar about the layout of the offence of bigamy. The relevant section, the Offences Against the Person Act 1861, s 57, stipulates an offence followed by provisos. There is no such distinctiveness about the offence of rape. Lord Hailsham seemed to hint at this distinction when he held that *Tolson* was a narrow decision based on the interpretation of the statute.

(d) The Lords in *Morgan* said that it did not intend to upset the bigamy cases. Therefore, different rules apply to different offences. Obviously consistency was not seen as a virtue. However, in recent years the Lords has consistently taken a subjective view: *B* v *DPP* [2000] AC 428, *K* [2002] 1 AC 462 and *G* [2004] 1 AC 1034. It may nowadays be that *Tolson* would not survive challenge in the Supreme Court. Their Lordships did not state that there were any exceptions to the rule that an (honest) mistake exculpates: the rule in *Tolson* that a mistake (at least in the crime of bigamy) was not discussed. It may be that the case is to be relegated to the dustbin of history as coming from an era when the law as to mistake of fact was not settled.

(e) Lord Cross in *Morgan* apparently took the view that *Morgan* was confined to rape, but the others did not. Lord Cross did, however, draw another distinction: one between offences such as rape where the defining words expressly or impliedly provide that the accused is not guilty if he believes something to be true and ones such as bigamy where the definition is on its face one giving rise to strict liability.

(f) ***Tolson*** may apply beyond bigamy, but only to crimes of negligence. There may be other offences and defences of which this can be said. In relation to self-defence, for instance, take the situation of ***Pagett*** (1983) 76 Cr App R 279 (CA), discussed in Chapter 2. If the police had time to check what the victim was doing, surely only a reasonable mistake as to that conduct should exculpate: it is not far-fetched to expect the police to check before shooting, provided that there is no danger to themselves or others.

(g) In situations involving the prevention of crime, there must, of course, be a crime to prevent. In ***Baker*** (CA), above, Brooke LJ said:

> If a defendant honestly believes that somebody is eating fish and chips and that eating fish sand chips is a crime, the law will not permit him to rely on s 3 [of the Criminal Law Act 1967] as a defence to a charge of assaulting the person eating fish and chips because as a matter of law no crime . . . is committed.

In other words, a mistake of law is no defence.

It was argued that the law in ***Morgan*** was unsatisfactory in relation to rape: the accused could easily have checked whether the victim was consenting. His carelessness should not exonerate him. Parliament took this view in the Sexual Offences Act 2003. The principle in ***Morgan*** was abrogated for sex crimes but it still remains authoritative elsewhere.

'The retreat from *Morgan*' and the ascendency of *Morgan*

For some time it was thought that the Court of Appeal was restricting ***Morgan*** to rape. In ***Barrett*** (1981) 72 Cr App R 212 (CA) the defendants thought that the court order which sent in the bailiffs had been obtained by fraud, and they used force to repel them. The court held that a mistake of civil law availed only if it was based on reasonable grounds. In ***Phekoo*** [1981] 1 WLR 1117 (CA) it was said, *obiter*, that a mistake that a residential occupier was a squatter provided a defence only when it was reasonably made. ***Barrett*** could be justified as being a case not concerned with mistake of fact. However that may be, ***Morgan*** came to prevail.

It came to prevail because of what Lord Hailsham in ***Morgan*** called 'inexorable logic':

> Once one has accepted . . . that the prohibited act in rape is non-consensual sexual intercourse, and that the guilty state of mind is an intention to commit it, it seems . . . to follow as a matter of inexorable logic that there is no room either for a 'defence' of honest belief or mistake or a defence of honest and reasonable belief or mistake. Either the prosecution proves that the accused had the requisite intent or it does not. In the former case it succeeds, and in the latter it fails.

The Court of Appeal ruled in ***Kimber*** [1983] 1 WLR 1118 on the then existing crime of indecent assault that ***Morgan*** was not restricted to rape and that *dicta* to that effect in ***Phekoo*** were wrong. The accused was charged with indecent assault after he had sexually interfered with a mental patient. The court held that a mistaken belief that the woman was consenting was a defence, whether or not the mistake was based on reasonable grounds. It is now accepted that ***Morgan*** applies to all offences of subjective *mens rea*. The law is the same in Canada: ***Pappajohn v R*** (1980) 111 DLR (3d) 1 (SCC). It may be that ***Tolson*** is restricted to bigamy.

Morgan is also applied to some defences. In **Williams** [1987] 3 All ER 411 (CA) the accused believed that a person was being attacked by X. In fact X was arresting him lawfully. It was said by the Court of Appeal that the accused was to be judged on the facts as he believed them to be. He believed that an assault was taking place. Therefore, he was not guilty of assault occasioning actual bodily harm on X when he attacked X. The accused did not intend to use unlawful force. He intended to use lawful force; that is, force to prevent a crime or in self-defence. His mistake negated his *mens rea*. **Williams** is thus an application of *Morgan*. (The conviction was overturned because the trial judge had misdirected the jury as to the burden of proof, so the above was *obiter*.) The court stressed that it was not dealing with any mental element necessary for a defence and the case could be distinguished on this basis. **Williams** was approved by the Privy Council in the following case.

Beckford v R [1988] AC 130

> The accused, an armed police officer, was investigating a report that an armed man was terrorising his family. In fact the man was unarmed. The accused alleged that the man had been shooting and was killed when fire was returned. It was held that he had the defence of self-defence on the facts which he mistakenly thought existed.

The question to be asked in a case of mistaken self-defence is whether the accused's response was commensurate with the degree of risk which he believed to have been created by the attack under which he believed himself to be: *Oatridge* (1992) 94 Cr App R 367 (CA). The development of the law that in general both offences and defences require only an honest belief was approved by the Lords in **B v DPP** [2000] 2 AC 428. Lord Nicholls said:

> By definition the mental element in a crime is concerned with a subjective state of mind, such as intent or belief. To the extent that an overriding objective limit ('on reasonable grounds') is introduced, the subjective element is displaced. To that extent a person who lacks the necessary intent or belief may nevertheless commit the offence. When that occurs the defendant's 'fault' lies exclusively in falling short of an objective standard. His crime lies in his negligence. A statute may so provide expressly or by necessary implication. But this can have no place in a common law principle, of general application, which is concerned with the need for a mental element as an essential ingredient of a criminal offence.

B v DPP was followed by the Lords in **K** [2002] 1 AC 462. A mistake as to the victim's age in the then existing crime of indecent assault was a defence if the error was honestly made. The belief need not be on reasonable grounds.

The law is different in duress and presumably duress of circumstances. The accused must believe on reasonable grounds that he is under a threat. The line sometimes drawn between **Williams** and **Graham** [1982] 1 WLR 294 (CA) is that in the former case the mistake negated the mental element in respect of an element of the *actus reus* whereas in the latter the mistake related to a true defence, a concept separate from *actus reus* and *mens rea*. It is uncertain whether this distinction is the law. Certainly the mistake in duress does not negate the *mens rea*. A suggested reconciliation is that in respect of justificatory defences, such as prevention of crime, any mistake exculpates, but a reasonable mistake is needed in respect of excuses such as duress. Besides the line being difficult to draw it is hard to discern any reason for the distinction. Although the law is that outside bigamy and some defences a mistake, reasonable or not, as to a relevant element of an offence or defence grants a defence, the courts do not always apply the law correctly. Lord Nicholls in **B v DPP** did not advert to duress when he dealt with the common law presumption that an honest mistake exculpates. Lord Steyn spoke of the 'disharmony' which would occur if in respect of some offences only a reasonable mistake exculpated, but again he made no attempt to overrule inconsistent authorities. *Tolson* is one of those authorities.

Summary of *Morgan*

The rule in *Morgan* does not affect offences where Parliament provides a defence only where a mistake was reasonable. In relation to rape the Sexual Offences Act 2003 reversed *Morgan*: a defence is now available only if the accused believed on reasonable grounds that the victim consented. Similarly *Morgan* does not affect the defences of duress by threats and duress of circumstances where the accused had to believe something on reasonable grounds (e.g. the existence of serious threats). This rule was indeed laid down after *Morgan*. There seems to be no justification for treating duress and self-defence differently.

Mistake and crimes of recklessness and negligence

Cunningham recklessness is described on pp 107–9 (Chapter 3). Compare with Caldwell recklessness on pp 108–12.

A person who makes an unreasonable mistake behaves negligently. Therefore he can be convicted of an offence of negligence. Only a defence based on reasonable grounds would exculpate. Crimes of *Cunningham* recklessness are treated under the principle in *Morgan*.

Intoxication and mistake

This topic is dealt with in the section on intoxication.

(a) Evidence of drunkenness to support a mistaken belief in the woman's consent to sexual intercourse was not admitted in *Woods* (1982) 74 Cr App R 312 (CA). Intoxication does not explain a mistake as to consent. However, for other offences evidence of intoxication causing a mistake will be admitted when intoxication is a defence to the crime charged.

(b) In *Fotheringham* (1988) 88 Cr App R 206 (CA), drunken sexual intercourse with a 14-year-old babysitter in the matrimonial bed in the mistaken belief that it was his wife did not give rise to a defence. A drunken mistake as to identity was irrelevant.

(c) Generally speaking a mistake brought about by drunkenness is no defence.

O'Grady [1987] QB 995 (CA)

> The accused drank eight flagons of cider. He then killed his friend. He argued that if he had not killed his friend he would have been killed by him. The court held, seemingly by way of *dictum*, that where the defendant was mistaken in his belief that any force, or the force he used, was necessary, but that the mistake was caused by voluntary drunkenness, the defence failed. It did not matter whether the offence was one of basic or specific intent.

There was no drunkenness in *Williams*, above, so that case could be distinguished. Lord Lane CJ, who gave judgment in both authorities, said that the court was faced with two competing principles. The first was that the accused had acted only according to what he believed was necessary to protect himself. The second was that the victim was killed through the accused's drunken mistake and the public had to be protected. 'Reason recoils from the conclusion that in such circumstances a defendant is entitled to leave the court without a stain on his character.'

O'Grady was followed in *O'Connor* [1991] Crim LR 135 (CA). The accused had been drinking heavily. He got into an argument with the victim, whom he head-butted three times. It was held that where the defendant, due to self-induced intoxication, formed a mistaken belief that he was acting in self-defence, that plea failed. The trial judge was correct in not directing the jury how drunkenness affected self-defence. In *O'Connor* the court assumed that *O'Grady* was binding, but in fact the accused in *O'Grady* was convicted of manslaughter. Anything that court said about murder was *obiter*.

O'Grady is open to criticism. It creates an exception to the rule in *Williams* that a person has the defence of self-defence if he makes a mistake of fact. There is nothing in *Williams* to suggest that the court intended such an exception. One result of *O'Grady* is that if the accused is so drunk that he does not have the fault element, he will be acquitted of murder; however, if the accused was drunk and believed that the victim was attacking him, he cannot rely on self-defence. *O'Grady* is out of line with cases which give a defence to drunkenness for offences of specific intent.

In relation to mistaken self-defence where the mistake is induced by intoxication the legal position is now incorporated into statute: Criminal Justice and Immigration Act 2008, s 76(4)(b).

The Law Commission, Report No. 177, *A Criminal Code for England and Wales*, 1989, recommended in para. 8.42 that the *O'Grady* principle should be abolished because it was 'unthinkable to convict of murder a person who thought for whatever reason that he was acting to save his life and would have been acting reasonably if he had been right'. In the proposals drunkenness would be taken into account to determine whether the accused believed in the existence of exempting conditions such as self-defence. Another possibility suggested by J.C. Smith in [1994] CLP 101 is to convict the accused of gross negligence manslaughter.

Summary of the law of mistake of fact

If the accused makes a mistake of fact as to an element of the *actus reus*, the mistake is irrelevant if the offence is one of strict liability (*Prince*); if the offence is one of *mens rea*, the accused has a defence if he made the mistake honestly (*Morgan*), unless the offence is one of bigamy in which event the mistake must have been made on reasonable grounds (*Tolson*). Parliament can change any of these rules as it did in the Sexual Offences Act 2003.

Reform of mistake in rape

The Law Commission in its Policy Paper, *Consent in Sex Offences*, 2000, examined the arguments in favour of introducing the requirement of reasonable belief in the victim's consent. In favour of revising the law were the following:

(a) 'Belief in consent is an easy defence to raise but hard to disprove.'

(b) 'It encourages defences to run which pander to outmoded and offensive assumptions about the nature of sexual relationships. The more stupid and sexist the man and his attitudes, the better chance he has of being acquitted on this basis.'

(c) 'The damage is done to the woman [*sic*] by the act of rape. She is entitled to expect the protection of the criminal law where, on any view, the man has acted on an unreasonably held assumption about her consent.'

(d) 'The mistaken belief arises in a situation where the price of the man's (gross) neglect is very high, and paid by the woman, whereas the cost to him in time and effort of informing himself of the position is minimal by comparison.'

In favour of the subjective test are these arguments:

1 'A person should not be guilty of a serious sexual offence . . . on the basis of negligence.'
2 'The burden is on those who argue for a change . . . to demonstrate that persons are being inappropriately acquitted . . . No such evidence has been produced.'
3 Whose reasonableness would apply? Would it be that of the accused, that of the jury, that of the hypothetical reasonable person?
4 Juries can sort out fact from fiction.
5 It would be rare for an accused to contend that he has a belief for which he had no reasonable grounds.
6 The introduction of reasonableness might make juries convict of rape even less than they do now.

The Law Commission thought that the subjective approach should be retained. However, the accused would have no defence if he was intoxicated and in assessing whether the accused believed the victim did consent, the jury should take into account whether he availed himself of the opportunity to ascertain whether the victim was consenting or not. The government refused to accept the Commission's recommendations and in the Sexual Offences Act 2003 only a reasonable mistake provides a defence. The result is, in the Commission's words, 'a person [is now] guilty of a serious sexual offence . . . on the basis of negligence'.

Intoxication

Introduction

> We confess that the doctrine touching cases of this character is not placed upon the clearest ground in the books (*Bishop's Criminal Law*, Vol. 1, 9th edn (Little, Brown & Co., 1923) para. 320).

This section discusses **intoxication** as a defence, not as an offence. In relation to crimes involving intoxication such as being drunk and disorderly, the whole law discussed below does not apply: *Carroll v DPP* [2009] EWHC 554 (Admin). It concentrates on situations where the accused did the prohibited act, does not have the required mental element, but is responsible for the fact that he does not possess it because of his self-induced intoxication.

Drunkenness was a crime punishable by imprisonment in the stocks or a fine from 1607 (4 James 1, c 5) to 1828 (9 Geo 4, c 61, s 35) but the law seems not to have been enforced. There is now no offence of (simple) drunkenness, but some instances are punished, such as being drunk and disorderly and drink-driving. The connection between intoxication and criminality is not a causal one: being drunk does not mean that the accused will necessarily commit an offence. Some drugs such as alcohol do, however, release inhibitions, and many who commit crimes have taken drugs, whether dangerous ones or ones not classified in law as being dangerous, for example alcohol. It is thought that the majority of non-fatal offences are committed when the accused was drunk. The then Home Secretary, Jack Straw, was reported in *the Guardian*, 18 July 2000, as saying: 'Some 40 per cent of violent crimes are committed when the offender is under the influence of alcohol, as are 78 per cent of assaults and 88 per cent of criminal damage incidents.' Over 50 per cent of rapists are intoxicated, according to the website of Alcohol Concern, www.alcoholconcern.org.uk.

Intoxication is considered here as a defence whether complete or in part, but it should be noted that intoxication sometimes makes the crime more serious than it otherwise would have been, as in drink-driving.

Involuntary intoxication

This section is largely restricted to voluntary intoxication. Where intoxication was caused by a medically prescribed drug, the accused's mistaking an intoxicant for a non-intoxicant (such as thinking a recreational drug is a paracetamol), someone spiking the accused's drink (by, for example, putting LSD or Rohypnol into the accused's vodka), forcing him to drink alcohol, or perhaps an adult deceiving a young person into taking alcohol, the question whether the accused will be convicted of an offence was thought to depend on his state of mind. Authorities are rare but include *Pearson* (1835) 168 ER 131.

The sole modern authority is the controversial one of *Kingston* [1995] 2 AC 355 (HL). A man enticed a 15-year-old boy to his flat and gave him some soporific drugs. The boy fell asleep. In order to blackmail him the man invited the appellant to his flat. He apparently also drugged him. The appellant sexually abused the boy. The man photographed and taped him so doing. The appellant admitted that he was a homosexual paedophile. The trial judge directed the jury that if the accused was so drugged that he did not intend to commit the crime, he was not guilty but if he did despite the drugs intend to commit it, he was guilty because a drugged intent is nevertheless an intent. The jury convicted but the conviction was quashed. The Court of Appeal held that if alcohol or drugs were surreptitiously given to the accused, he was not guilty if because of his intoxication he forms an intention which he would not have formed had he been sober. 'The intent itself arose out of circumstances for which he bears no blame.' Therefore, he was acquitted even though he had the *mens rea* of the crime. He was morally blameless.

Kingston in the Court of Appeal was strongly criticised. The accused did intend to commit indecent assault. He had the *mens rea*. Accordingly, he should have been convicted. The fact that he could not resist his impulse is irrelevant (as in insanity), as is the fact that someone made him intoxicated. Contrary to the court's view his involuntary intoxication did not negate his *mens rea*. Certainly he was not responsible for getting into a drugged state, but he may be responsible for what he does in that state. If *Kingston* (CA) had been correct it would presumably apply where a rogue has forced alcohol down the accused's throat or threatened him or another with violence if he did not drink it, and perhaps when the accused has taken drugs by mistake. For an attempt to support *Kingston* (CA) if the accused was not a practising paedophile, see G.R. Sullivan 'Involuntary intoxication and beyond' [1994] Crim LR 272, who argues that: 'It is not a fair test of character to remove surreptitiously a person's inhibitions and confront him with a temptation he ordinarily seeks to avoid.'

On appeal [1995] 2 AC 355 Lord Mustill, with whom the other Lords agreed, said that there was no principle in English law, as the Court of Appeal thought there was, that if no blame was attached to the accused, he did not have the *mens rea* and therefore was not guilty of any offence. Moral judgments do not affect the criminality of the act though they may affect the sentence. '*Rea*' means criminally, not morally, wrong. Blame related to sentence, not to substantive law. It was no defence to argue that he would not have done what he did had he been sober, except for insanity where the accused did intend to commit the offence. Lord Mustill approved the views of academic commentators in relation to the Court of Appeal's ruling. If the defence existed on these facts, bogus claims as to involuntary intoxication might succeed. Whether the intoxication was voluntary or involuntary, 'a drunken intent is still an intent', as was stated in **Sheehan** [1975] 1 WLR 739 (CA). While the House was not bound by any authority, it considered that when the accused was so involuntarily intoxicated that he did not form an intent, there is a defence. However, in terms of principle there was no defence of irresistible impulse deriving from innate causes (an example might be kleptomania), and therefore there should be no defence for irresistible impulse arising from a mixture of innate forces and 'external disinhibition'. Accordingly, the appeal was allowed. It should be noted that the distinction between basic and specific intent offences does not apply to involuntary intoxication. In criticism of **Kingston** (HL) it can be said that excuse defences are not all predicated on the absence of *mens rea*.

Intoxication is not involuntary when the accused did not know that the wine drunk was of high alcohol content: **Allen** [1988] Crim LR 698 (CA). The outcome may be explained by saying that the effects of alcohol are in any case unpredictable. It is interesting to compare **Allen** with the law stated under preliminary point (e) below. Failure to foresee the consequences of wine led to guilt; failure to foresee the consequences of drugs led to acquittal! The law may be different where the accused thought that the wine was non-alcoholic, rather than low in alcohol. In **Shippam** [1971] Crim LR 434, it was held that spiking of drinks was a special reason not to disqualify a person for driving with a blood alcohol level above the prescribed limit, but the argument that he should not have been guilty at all does not appear to have been put. The successful argument in **Shippam** seems to have been that the accused was driving voluntarily. His involuntary drunkenness was irrelevant to that fact. It is uncertain whether intoxication is involuntary where the accused has a medical condition which he does not know about which predisposes him to becoming intoxicated more quickly than he otherwise would.

Voluntary intoxication

Intoxication which is self-induced is also not a defence where the accused did possess the relevant *mens rea*. If a drunken person forms an intention to kill and does kill, he will be convicted of murder. If the accused killed his wife in a fit of temper, alcohol may explain why he was easily provoked. His inhibitions have been removed but the relaxation of inhibitions is not a defence. He is guilty of murder. Similarly, the fact that the accused would not have acted in the way that he did if he had not been drunk is no defence. The contrasting situation is where the accused while drunk stumbles against his wife, knocking her under a train. Intoxication is relevant because he is claiming that he did not form malice aforethought. Intoxication is not a defence when the accused says that he did not foresee the consequence of his behaviour because of his intoxication.

Preliminary points

(a) The accused does not have this defence if he gets drunk to give himself Dutch courage. In **Attorney-General for Northern Ireland v Gallagher** [1963] AC 349 (HL) the accused formed the intent to kill his wife, drank most of a bottle of whiskey, and killed her. (See also Chapter 3 on contemporaneity.) He could not use drunkenness as a defence and was guilty of murder.

(b) Drunkenness must be 'very extreme' for the defence to apply: **Stubbs** (1989) 88 Cr App R 53. The Court of Appeal of New Zealand in **Kamipeli** [1975] 2 NZLR 610 seems to have approved the trial judge's direction that the accused must be 'blind drunk', though as that court held the prosecution need not go so far as to prove that the accused was 'acting as a sort of automaton without his mind functioning'. (If the evidence is not such that the accused's mind was not working because of alcohol, it may still be that the prosecution cannot prove that he intended to commit the offence.) The Supreme Court of Canada in *Daviault v R* (1995) 118 DLR (4th) 469 said that the accused had to be 'in such an extreme degree of intoxication that [he was] in a state akin to automatism or insanity'. Only rarely will a person be in such a condition. The court was relying on the judgment of Wilson J in *Bernard* [1988] 2 SCR 833. Accordingly, it is not enough to demonstrate that the accused has been drinking heavily for the effect of alcohol varies from person to person: *Broadhurst v R* [1964] AC 441 (PC). For example, in *Groark* [1999] Crim LR 669 (CA) the accused had drunk 10 pints of beer but was not drunk. Other English cases are to the effect that the accused must be so intoxicated that he did not form the requisite intent as laid down by the definition of the offence: see, for example, *McKnight*, *The Times*, 5 May 2000 (CA), relying on the advice of Lord Hope in *Sooklal v State of Trinidad and Tobago* [1999] 1 WLR 2011 (PC). In *McKnight* the accused said that while she was drunk, she was not 'legless'. She gave a complete account of the incident in which she had killed the victim. The Court of Appeal held that her perceptions had not been altered by the alcohol and therefore she had no defence to a charge of murder. The trial judge was correct in not leaving the defence of intoxication to the jury. There is no need for the accused to be so drunk as to be almost unconscious: *Brown* [1998] Crim LR 485 (CA). Lord Denning in *Gallagher* said that the accused must be 'rendered so stupid by drinking that he does not know what he is doing . . . as where . . . a drunken man thought his friend was a theatrical dummy and stabbed him to death'. As we shall see, even if the accused is so drunk, he does not have a defence to all offences but only specific intent ones. In fact the amount of intoxication needed to afford a defence does not seem to have caused difficulties: Law Reform Commission of Ireland's Report on *Intoxication*, LRC 51, 1995, 2.

(c) If the accused's acts look involuntary, the defence is one of intoxication, not automatism, if the involuntariness was due to drunkenness. In legal terms the accused is acting voluntarily, and is so doing even though the imbibing and the deed are separated in time. However, if the intoxication is such that it falls within the *M'Naghten* rules, the defence is insanity, not intoxication. Since alcohol and other drugs are 'external' causes only rarely will intoxication amount to insanity. Delirium tremens ('DTs') is an example of a disease of the mind within *M'Naghten*. Normally even though the intoxication causes delusions there will not be a disease of the mind. In automatism and insanity basically the accused could not avoid the condition; in drunkenness he could. For the law on insanity, see Chapter 9. One issue which has arisen dealing with the borderline between insanity and intoxication is the following. A person is not insane if he cannot resist an impulse. If his irresolution in the face of an impulse is exacerbated by alcohol, he still cannot have the defence of insanity: *Gallagher*.

(d) The burden of proof is on the prosecution. *Dicta* to the contrary in *DPP v Beard* [1920] AC 479 (HL) are wrong: *Sheehan*. The Privy Council in *Broadhurst* accepted that *Woolmington v DPP* [1935] AC 462 (HL) had altered the burden of proof.

(e) The rules on intoxication as a defence apply to both alcohol and those drugs which are liable to make the user aggressive, dangerous or unpredictable. The definition of 'intoxicant' has not been a problem for the courts. Sedative drugs, however, such as valium, are not to be classed with alcohol, according to *Bailey* [1983] 2 All ER 503 (CA) (see under automatism in Chapter 9) and *Hardie* [1984] 3 All ER 848 (CA). In *Hardie* the accused was charged with damaging property with intent to endanger life or being reckless as to whether life would be endangered. He had taken valium (it had not been prescribed for him) and set fire to a bedroom. It was held that the effect of sedative drugs was not the same as intoxicating drugs or alcohol, which can produce aggression and unpredictable behaviour. Therefore, the accused is not (subjectively) reckless in taking his tablets, if the accused does not appreciate the risk of volatile behaviour.

It may not be easy to decide which drugs have these dangerous effects and which do not. Presumably drugs like cocaine and LSD would be classified as dangerous ones; heroin, which is an opiate, should for that reason be categorised with valium, but it is doubtful whether a court would so hold. The court did, however, say that he would nevertheless be guilty of reckless driving. If so, he would nowadays be guilty of dangerous driving. Presumably the argument is that he should not take any drug not knowing of the consequences of so doing. If, however, he does realise that he might act aggressively, unpredictably or uncontrollably, his behaviour is reckless and he is liable for any crime of recklessness which he commits under the influence of the drug. He need not foresee the actual occurrence of any specific risk. These rules apply whether or not these drugs were medically prescribed. The line between drugs which sedate and drugs which cause aggression is not necessarily a clear-cut one. Indeed valium causes aggressive behaviour in some people. It is strange that the determination whether each drug is dangerous or not is left to the judge.

(f) Presumably the accused would have a defence if the alcohol were prescribed by a doctor. Alcohol given to a person after an accident would, it is thought, be treated similarly.

(g) Loss of memory caused by drunkenness does not excuse the accused's behaviour if he did what he did intentionally: *C* [1992] Crim LR 642 (CA).

The defence of intoxication is confused (Figure 8.1). There is no easy way of stating the law. One reason for this mess is that drunkenness provides an arena for two conflicting principles. The first is the need to punish people who have acted wrongly. The second is that an accused who is intoxicated may not realise what he is doing and is not therefore deserving of punishment.

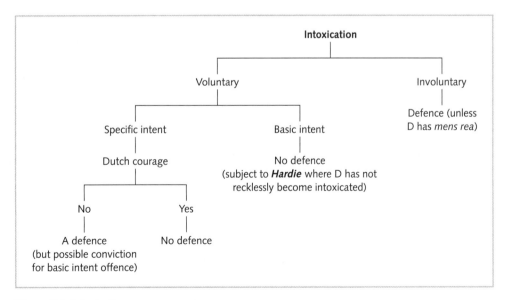

Figure 8.1 Intoxication

The special rules on intoxication

Example

Maurice, who is excessively drunk, attacks Norma with an axe. She is wounded but not killed. Is Maurice guilty of any non-fatal offence?

This is a question on drunkenness (note: in an exam mind your spelling, and if you're unsure, write 'intoxication'!). Here it is not stated whether the accused is voluntarily or involuntarily intoxicated. If the former, he is not guilty of specific intent crimes but is of basic intent crimes. The distinction between the two is not easily drawn, but s 18 of the Offences against the Person Act 1861, wounding or causing GBH with intent to do some GBH, is a specific intent crime, and drunkenness is therefore a defence, but s 20 of the same statute, wounding or inflicting GBH intending to do *some* harm ('some harm', not necessarily GBH) or being reckless as to whether *some* harm is caused, is a basic intent crime and therefore intoxication is a defence. See ***DPP v Majewski*** [1977] AC 443 (HL) for the distinction.

If, however, the intoxication was involuntary, Maurice's drunkenness is a defence to all offences, specific or basic intent, unless the accused had the *mens rea* for that offence: ***Kingston*** [1995] 2 AC 355 (HL).

Make sure you learn Table 8.1! (p 307)

The law is that if the jury accepts the evidence of intoxication, the accused will not be convicted if the crime is one of **'specific intent'**, but will if the offence is one of **'basic intent'**. For example, on a murder charge, murder being classified as a crime of specific intent, the accused's intoxication is relevant on the question whether he had malice aforethought. In other words, intention and intoxication are put together in a specific intent case. Where the accused is charged with murder and the accused either had direct intent or he did not, intoxication is taken into account at the point of determining whether he intended to kill or commit GBH. In an oblique intent case of murder, 'drink is relevant to the question whether the defendant appreciated that his actions were virtually certain to result in death or really serious bodily harm': ***Hayes*** [2002] EWCA Crim 1945.

Note that 'specific intent' and 'basic intent' are not to be confused with 'intention' as defined on pp 90–104 (Chapter 3).

Contrary to what was thought at the time of ***Beard*** – and contrary to what is still sometimes said by the Court of Appeal (see ***McKnight***, above) – one does not inquire whether the accused was capable of forming the specific intent but whether he did actually have the intent: ***Sheehan*** and other cases including ***O'Connor*** [1991] Crim LR 135 (CA). The law is the same in Australia: ***O'Connor*** (1980) 54 ALJR 349 (HCA).

If the accused did have the necessary fault element, he is guilty whether or not he was intoxicated, and it does not matter that the accused would not have done the act, had he been sober: ***Bowden*** among other cases. One looks at the accused's mind, not at what a reasonable person might have thought. The term 'basic intent' covers all offences to which intoxication is not a defence including those which can be committed recklessly or negligently. If the crime is a basic intent one, the accused is convicted even though he did not know what he was doing. He is guilty even though he did not intend or advert to the consequences of his behaviour. The difficulty is to distinguish between basic and specific intent offences. As Lord Mustill said in ***Kingston***, above: 'this area of law is controversial, as regards the content of the rules, their intellectual foundations, and their capacity to furnish a practical and just solution'.

The law was first authoritatively declared in ***DPP v Beard*** [1920] AC 479 (HL). To understand the law in this case one has to know the felony murder rule, which was abolished in

England and Wales in 1957 but continues to exist across much of the common law world. Before 1957 there was a rule that a killing in the course of a felony, a serious offence (a category abolished in 1967), was murder. This rule was called constructive murder or the felony/murder rule. Rape was a felony. The accused was committing a rape on a girl. He pressed his thumbs on her neck and killed her. Because of the doctrine of constructive murder, he was guilty of murder if the prosecution could show that he intended to rape and did kill. There was no need as nowadays to show that he intended to kill or commit grievous bodily harm. Lord Birkenhead stated that in those circumstances the accused had no defence unless he was so drunk as to be incapable of forming the intent to commit rape. (The question now is whether he did form the intent.) The accused could form this intent. Therefore, he was guilty of murder. Lord Birkenhead went on to utter *dicta* of high authority:

(1) If the accused is insane through drink, such as when he has delirium tremens, his defence is insanity, not intoxication.

The fact that the insanity was caused by drunkenness is irrelevant:

(2) Evidence of drunkenness which renders the accused incapable of forming the specific intent essential to constitute the crime should be taken into consideration with the other facts proved in order to determine whether or not he had this intent.

In **Beard** the accused did not make himself so drunk that he could not commit rape. The *dictum* is in terms of evidence. Therefore, the jury can reject the evidence and deal with the case in the usual fashion. Moreover, since intoxication relates to evidence in crimes of specific intent, it is a misnomer to call intoxication a defence; rather, it is a failure by the prosecution to prove all elements of the offence, namely the intent required is the definition of the offence. It should also be noted that intoxication does not negate *mens rea*; it is part of the evidence which is added to all the other evidence to determine whether the accused did have the *mens rea*:

(3) Evidence of drunkenness falling short of a proved incapacity to form the intent necessary to constitute the crime, and merely establishing that his mind was affected by drink so that he more readily gave way to some violent passion, does not rebut the presumption that a man intends the natural consequences of his conduct.

Section 8 of the Criminal Justice Act 1967 qualifies the third proposition. A court or jury is no longer bound to infer from the facts that a person intends the natural consequences of his action. The triers of fact must look at the whole evidence to decide whether the accused did have the requisite intent or foresight. Section 8 does not make drunkenness purely a matter of evidence whether the accused did or did not have *mens rea*. It is still treated as a matter of substantive law: **DPP v Majewski** [1977] AC 443 (HL).

The second proposition is the difficult one. There is no restriction to crimes of intention, though it is likely that Lord Birkenhead simply meant 'specific intent' to be 'intent'. The necessity is to distinguish between specific and basic intent offences, though the term 'basic intent' occurs nowhere in Lord Birkenhead's speech. As M. Goode put it in 'Some thoughts on the present state of the "defence" of intoxication' (1984) 8 Crim LJ 104 at 105: 'If there was no really coherent distinction, then the labels "specific" and "basic" intent were just that: labels. One might just as well have called murder a crime of "bacon" and manslaughter a crime of "eggs".' What has happened is that judges have thought that 'specific intent' bears a definite meaning in law different from 'intent' and they have sought to distinguish 'specific' from 'basic' intent. On the distinction rests English law.

The courts have struggled with defining the distinction. In **Gallagher**, Lord Denning followed **Beard** to hold that drunkenness was no defence unless it amounted to insanity or the crime was one of specific intent. He said that if drink impairs the accused's powers of perception so that he does not realise that what he is doing is dangerous, he has no defence if a sober and reasonable person in his place would appreciate the danger. This proposition does not occur in **Beard**, and if drunkenness is incompatible with specific intent, why is it not incompatible with foresight? Lord Denning stated that lack of self-control or moral sense induced by intoxication was no defence. In **Gallagher** the fact that the accused's psychomotor state was made worse by alcohol did not give him a defence of drunkenness if the effect of the alcohol made it harder for the accused to exercise self-control. Lord Denning relied on **Beard** and an anonymous case from 1748 (where a drunken nurse put a baby on a fire, thinking it was a log) to show that where the crime is one of specific intent, intoxication is a defence if the accused did not have that intent. It could be argued that the nurse's case is not one of specific intent because she had no *mens rea* at all. Lord Denning seems to have defined specific intent to mean crimes of ulterior intent (doing X with intent to do X or Y). Certainly all such crimes are specific intent ones, but the term 'specific intent' is wider. Lord Birkenhead may have meant 'specific intent' to mean the intent which forms part of the mental element in the offence. The mental element in murder is the intent to kill or commit grievous bodily harm. That intent is the 'specific' intent of murder. On this approach 'specific' adds nothing to 'intent'.

In **Gallagher** the earlier intention to kill was added to the *actus reus*, which took place after the accused had become drunk. This Dutch courage rule is at variance with the general principle of contemporaneity in criminal law. The argument is that such a breach is justified by catching dangerous people. **Lipman** [1970] 1 QB 152 (CA) exemplifies the continuing tendency of judges not to let defendants go free as they would if general principles of law were applied but to bend the law or create exceptions in order to convict 'manifestly guilty' persons of something, though it might be argued that the accused was not manifestly guilty.

Lipman [1970] 1 QB 152 (CA)

The accused and his girlfriend took some LSD. Under the influence of the drug he hallucinated that he was being attacked by giant snakes. He awoke the next morning to find his girlfriend dead, eight inches of sheet having been pushed down her throat. Lord Widgery CJ held that intoxication through drugs formed part of the defence of drunkenness. Applying **Gallagher** (HL) manslaughter was a crime of basic intent. Intoxication was no defence to basic intent offences. Therefore, the accused was guilty of manslaughter. The House of Lords refused leave to appeal.

Criticism of **Lipman** has been strong. In **Beard** the accused, who was guilty, intended to rape. In **Lipman** the defendant, who did not intend any offence, was guilty of manslaughter. The accused had no 'mind' because he was under the influence of drugs; how could he have a *mens rea*? At the time of the killing he had no *mens rea*. At the time of taking the drug he had committed no *actus reus*. The contemporaneity rule was broken. Lord Birkenhead did say in **Beard** that drunkenness was no defence to manslaughter but did not relate his remarks to a distinction between specific and basic intent. Even in manslaughter the accused is guilty only if he did have some type of *mens rea*. The type of manslaughter at issue in **Lipman** was constructive or unlawful act manslaughter. There has to be an unlawful act, but the accused did not commit one because his mind did not accompany his act. If the unlawful act was the stuffing of the sheet into the victim's mouth, he was unconscious at that time. If the unlawful act was the taking of the drugs, that consumption did not cause her death and anyway taking drugs is not an offence: it is possession which is the crime. Possessing drugs did not kill the girlfriend. Lord Widgery CJ did not tackle this objection. It might be argued that the court could have relied on a different form of manslaughter, manslaughter by gross negligence, but if the accused was unconscious at the time, how could he be careless? There is still the separation in time between the grossly negligent taking of the drugs and the death. *Lipman* looks like the Court of Appeal's response to drugs, as in part does the next case.

Both *Lipman* and *Majewski*, above, punish really the act of becoming intoxicated, but the punishment is based on the outcome of the actions of the accused, whether the accused was acting consciously or not. Lord Salmon in *Majewski* approved both *Lipman* and *Beard*.

DPP v *Majewski* [1977] AC 443 (HL)

A man spent 24 hours getting drugged and drunk. He smashed windows and attacked a police officer. The seven judgments in the Lords say different things but basically there was wide support for Lord Russell's analysis of Lord Birkenhead's speech in *Beard*.

Specific intent covered both:

(a) ulterior or further intent such as wounding with intent to do grievous bodily harm;
(b) where the *mens rea* extends beyond the intent to do the act. On this approach assault is a basic intent crime. The *actus reus* includes the apprehension of force. The *mens rea* is intending or being reckless as to the victim's apprehension of force. The *mens rea* does not extend beyond the *actus reus*.

Lord Simon considered that 'specific intent' meant the 'purposive element' (i.e. direct intent) in a crime. He did not further define purposive element, and the term is difficult to fit in with present law. Rape is a crime involving a purpose, but it is a crime of basic intent, to which drunkenness is not a defence. All Law Lords agreed that *Beard* should stand and that to depart from *Beard* would be contrary to public policy because the rule punished persons who got drunk and misbehaved. The community needs protection from drunken violence, and if violent drunks were not convicted, the public would have contempt for the law. Therefore, this area of law is not based on logic. Lord Salmon stated:

> I accept that there is a degree of illogicality in the rule that intoxication may excuse . . . one type of intention and not another. This illogicality is, however, acceptable because the benevolent part of the rule removes undue harshness without imperilling safety and the stricter part of the rule works without imperilling justice. It would be just as ridiculous to remove the benevolent part of the rule . . . as it would be to adopt the alternative of removing the stricter part of the rule for the sake of preserving absolute logic.

As Lord Edmund-Davies said: 'It is unethical to convict a man of a crime requiring a guilty state of mind when *ex hypothesis* he lacked it.' Another way of putting this is to say that drunkenness is not in conformity with criminal law principles. For example, intoxication is a defence to grievous bodily harm with intent, but not to maliciously inflicting grievous bodily harm. Yet, if intoxication negates the *mens rea* of the former offence, why does it prove it in the latter? To say as Lord Simon did that performing a prohibited act when insensible through drink is as wrongful as *mens rea* does not mean that the insensible accused has *mens rea*. Before a person can be convicted of an offence where the mental element is subjective recklessness, the prosecution should have to prove that state of mind. They do not have to prove it when the accused is intoxicated. If the accused contends that he thought because of intoxication there was no risk, *Majewski* will convict him automatically of a 'subjective recklessness' offence. The presumption of innocence is not applied. The outcome of *Majewski* was that the highest court had decided that there was a distinction between basic and specific intent, but could not say what that difference was.

The public policy concerns in *Majewski* have come in for criticism. A drunken person is hardly likely to be deterred by the law, even if he knew what it was. In countries where intoxication is taken into account with the other evidence in determining *mens rea* there is not proportionally more crime than in England. Indeed intoxication by stripping away inhibitions may well show that the accused did have the requisite fault element for the crime charged. It is also argued that it is morally wrong to convict people of an offence when the form of behaviour which the law should penalise is that of getting into the intoxicated state. At present people are convicted of offences when they did not have the required *mens rea*.

For a full explanation of recklessness, see pp 107–12 (Chapter 3).

The most authoritative case at present is *MPC v Caldwell* [1982] AC 341 (HL), which in relation to intoxication is unaffected by the overruling in *G* [2004] 1 AC 1034 (HL) of Lord Diplock's definition of recklessness.

MPC v Caldwell [1982] AC 341 (HL)

The accused did some work for the owner of a hotel. They quarrelled. The accused got drunk and set fire to the hotel. No one was injured, but there was some damage. He was charged, *inter alia*, with arson contrary to s 1(2) and (3) of the Criminal Damage Act 1971 in that he damaged property with intent to endanger life or being reckless whether life was endangered. He claimed he was so drunk that he never thought he was endangering life.

The majority's speech was delivered by Lord Diplock. He argued:

(a) 'If the only mental state capable of constituting the necessary *mens rea* for an offence under s 1(2) were that expressed in the words intending by the destruction or damage to endanger the life of another, it would have been necessary to consider whether the offence was to be classified as one of "specific" intent for the purposes of the rule of law which this House affirmed and applied in *DPP v Majewski* (1977); and plainly it is.' (That is, the *mens rea*, intent to endanger life, goes beyond the *actus reus*, criminal damage.)

(b) 'However, this is not . . . a relevant enquiry where "being reckless, as to whether the life of another should be thereby endangered" is an alternative mental state.'

(c) 'The speech of Lord Elwyn-Jones in *Majewski*, with which Lord Simon, Lord Kilbrandon and I agreed, is authority that self-induced intoxication is no defence to a crime in which recklessness is enough to constitute the necessary *mens rea*.'

(d) 'Reducing oneself by drink or drugs to a condition in which the restraints of reason and conscience are cast off was held to be a reckless course of conduct.' (There is a slippage in the reasoning between (c) and (d). 'Reckless' is used in two different senses. In (c) 'reckless' bears its *mens rea* meaning. In (d) it bears a non-criminal law meaning. By becoming drunk the accused does not become aware of the *actus reus* he may perform when he is drunk. The effect is that the accused is guilty of a crime of basic intent even though he did not have the *mens rea* of the crime.)

(e) 'In the instant case, the fact that the respondent was unaware of the risk of endangering the lives of residents in the hotel owing to his self-induced intoxication would be no defence if that risk would have been obvious to him had he been sober.'

The difference between the previous definition (*mens rea* goes beyond the *actus reus*) and the *Caldwell* recklessness one is seen from the crime charged in *Caldwell* itself. In s 1(2) of the 1971 Act the *mens rea* (intent to endanger life or recklessness thereto) goes beyond the *actus reus* (criminal damage). However, recklessness forms part of the *mens rea*, and therefore the crime is one of basic intent.

Accordingly where the defence was solely defined in terms of intention the distinction between basic and specific intent was relevant. If the offence were defined in terms of recklessness, getting drunk was reckless and the accused was guilty of the offence without the prosecution having to prove recklessness. Proof of intoxication amounted to proof of recklessness. The accused is deemed to be reckless. There is no need to show that at the time of getting intoxicated the accused foresaw the *actus reus* of the offence with which he is charged. In the words of the Law Commission in its Report No. 229, *Legislating the Criminal Code: Intoxication and Criminal Liability*, 1995, para. 1.19: 'The intentional taking of an intoxicant without regard to its possible consequences is properly treated as a substitute for the mental element normally required.' Lord Mustill spoke to this effect in *Kingston*, above. The accused cannot rely on the absence of *mens rea* when that is caused by his own act of getting intoxicated. This approach, however, takes no account of the principle of concurrence stated at the start of Chapter 1. Once the accused has got intoxicated, he should no longer be regarded as reckless. Therefore, he is not reckless at the time of the *actus reus*. In *Cullen* [1993] Crim LR 936 (CA) the court laid down English law: once the prosecution proved that the accused started a fire, he was guilty of (aggravated) arson if there was an obvious and serious risk of damage to property and of danger to life. He did not have to foresee either risk. The position is even stronger with regard to strict offences and crimes of negligence. The accused is guilty without proof of recklessness. Intoxication shows that the accused was negligent, and in strict offences no state of mind is relevant. The rule applies despite the separation in time between getting drunk and the forbidden conduct.

This 'constructive recklessness' is also impossible to justify from the viewpoint of the principle of legality, also discussed in Chapter 1. It is not the fault element stated in the crime which is relevant but the fact that the accused got drunk. After *Caldwell* all crimes of recklessness are basic intent offences, to which intoxication supplies the mental element of recklessness, for the prosecution do not have to prove recklessness, only intoxication. It is neither subjective nor objective recklessness. (What happened to the principle that the prosecution must prove all elements of the offence beyond reasonable doubt?) The result is a fiction. The accused is deemed to be reckless. As with all fictions current law is difficult to justify rationally. The House of Lords in *Caldwell* were adamant that whether there was recklessness was a matter for the jury, but that proposition is difficult to accept when intoxication is the recklessness element in an offence. The effect of *Caldwell* on intoxication is this: the prosecution has to show that the accused gave no thought to an obvious and serious risk. It is irrelevant why no thought was given. Therefore, it is immaterial that it was intoxication which caused the accused not to give any thought. Accordingly, *Majewski* is not in point. The risk of harm from getting intoxicated need not relate to the actual injury or damage caused. The test for the obviousness of the risk under *Caldwell* is whether or not the risk would have been obvious to a reasonable, prudent bystander. That paragon is not intoxicated by alcohol or drugs. The fact that the accused was intoxicated is irrelevant. That he was drunk merely explains why he gave no thought, but does not excuse him. His drunkenness supplies the *mens rea* of recklessness. He is guilty of a basic intent crime if he would have been aware of the risk but for his intoxication.

The Supreme Court of Canada in *Daviault v R* (1995) 118 DLR (4th) 469 by a majority rejected the *Caldwell* approach as being contrary to the fundamental principle of justice that each element of the offence has to be proved by the prosecution. The present English law by which proof of intoxication substitutes for proof of recklessness was in breach of this principle. The dissentients argued that a person who commits the *actus reus* of a general intent offence (in England a basic intent crime) when intoxicated deserves to be stigmatised as an offender and that the requirements of fundamental justice were satisfied by proof of intoxication without proof of *mens rea*. Sopinka J said that 'the rules of fundamental justice are satisfied by showing that the drunken state was attained through the accused's own blameworthy conduct'. The same rule applies to a person who puts himself into a state of automatism through his own fault. 'Society is entitled to punish those who of their own free will render themselves so intoxicated as to pose a threat to other members of the community.' Sopinka J added: 'to allow generally an accused . . . to plead absence of *mens rea* where he has voluntarily caused himself to be incapable of *mens rea* would be to undermine, indeed negate, that very principle of moral responsibility which the requirement of *mens rea* is intended to give effect to.' Besides intoxication being deemed to be recklessness for crimes where the *mens rea* includes recklessness, the usual connection between *actus reus* and *mens rea* is rendered unnecessary. For example, the accused is guilty of reckless criminal damage if he is drunk and damage happens to occur as a result of what he did when drunk: he need not recklessly cause criminal damage, yet he is guilty of that offence.

Outstanding problems

(a) One result of *Caldwell* is that the defence has been narrowed. Lord Birkenhead in *Beard* in one passage noted that specific intent was not exceptional. The minority in *Caldwell* saw that when *mens rea* is defined in terms of 'intentionally or recklessly', as modern statutes often are, there is no need for the prosecution to prove recklessness, only drunkenness. Only where intention alone is charged is intoxication possibly a defence.

Anomalies are created. Intoxication can be considered in a crime of attempted rape, but not in rape itself. Rape is a basic intent crime. After the Sexual Offences Act 2003 the *mens rea* includes negligence as to the victim's consent. All attempts are specific intent offences. It is conceded, however, that the position is unclear and some academics have argued that since some attempts may be committed recklessly, these are now basic intent offences. The argument runs that after *Khan* [1990] 1 WLR 815 (CA) the *mens rea* of rape and attempted rape is the same when the attempt is based on the failure of the accused to achieve penetration. Therefore, attempted rape based on this missing element is also a crime of basic intent. However, if the missing element in attempted rape is the victim's lack of consent, the *mens rea* of attempted rape is different from that of the full offence. An intent to have sexual intercourse without the consent of the victim is required and this form of attempted rape is a specific intent crime.

In *Fotheringham* (1988) 88 Cr App R 206 (CA), the accused made a drunken mistake that the person with whom he was having sexual intercourse was his wife, whereas it was a 14-year-old babysitter, whom his wife had told to sleep in the matrimonial bed.

He was guilty of the offence of rape as then defined. If, however, he had stopped just short of penetration, he would not have been guilty of attempted rape. The law looks the wrong way round. In rape the accused's *mens rea* is in part the intention to penetrate. Yet rape is always a basic intent offence.

Fotheringham may be criticised. On one view of *Majewski*, drunkenness supplies recklessness. Therefore, evidence other than that of intoxication, tending towards showing that the accused did not have the type of foresight required by the crime, is irrelevant: he is deemed to have the *mens rea* because he is intoxicated. In this case, however, the accused did not make a mistake as to a 'reckless' element, consent, but as to an element defined solely in terms of intent. The accused did not intend to have unlawful sexual intercourse, 'unlawful' being then understood as 'outside marriage'. He intended to have sexual intercourse with his wife. That was lawful. His mistake was as to the identity of the woman, and drunkenness explained why he made the error. Drunkenness does not supply intention. Another way of putting this proposition is to say that rape was a crime of basic intent as to consent (the accused was guilty at that time if he was reckless as to the woman's consent: after 2003 only negligence as to consent is required), but was a crime of specific intent in relation to the victim not being his wife. It is unlikely that the courts will hold that the answer to a question whether rape is a specific or basic intent crime depends on which element of the offence the accused has made a mistake. If *Fotheringham* is correct in stating that an offence is one of basic intent if any element of it may be committed recklessly, the list of specific offences in the section 'The present position' will have to be revised. For example, in burglary not all the elements of the *actus reus* need to be performed intentionally. The court stated: 'In rape self-induced intoxication is no defence, whether the issue be intention, consent or . . . mistake as to the identity of the victim.'

In *Woods* (1982) 74 Cr App R 312, the accused had drunk a lot and said that he was not aware that the woman was not consenting. The Court of Appeal held that the accused was guilty of rape as then defined when he made a mistake as to the woman's consent. Griffiths LJ said: 'The law, as a matter of social policy, has declared that self-induced intoxication is not a legally relevant matter to be taken into account when deciding as to whether or not a woman consents to intercourse.' This statement does not explain why the social policy does not apply to attempted rape and all specific intent offences. *Woods* is a decision to the effect that intoxication is not a legally relevant matter when the jury is considering whether the woman was consenting. By the law as it then existed, s 1(2) of the Sexual Offences (Amendment) Act 1976 as amended (now repealed), the jury had to judge the man's belief that the woman (or man) was consenting and could take into account the reasonableness of his belief and 'any other relevant matters'. Drunkenness was, however, held to be excluded. It was not one of the 'relevant matters'. Therefore, the jury is invited to inquire whether the accused believed the alleged victim was consenting but to exclude his intoxication. Since the intoxication led him to believe that the woman was consenting, he cannot explain why he thought that the woman (or the man) was consenting. That is, he was guilty of rape, since had he not been in a state of intoxication, he would have known that she (or he) did not consent. In other words, since the accused would have realised that the alleged victim was not consenting if he had been sober, he is automatically guilty of rape. He was reckless as to consent, even though the jury had not taken drunkenness into account.

There is a view that *Woods* is restricted to rape. In other offences being drunk takes away the requirement that the prosecution proves recklessness in offences of recklessness. In rape intoxication is excluded from consideration. Parliament surely did not have this distinction in mind when it enacted the 1976 Act. **Woods** is certainly inconsistent with the principle that in crimes of recklessness intoxication supplies recklessness, that is, once intoxication is proved, so is recklessness. In **Woods**, however, the court said that the accused is to be acquitted if he would not have had the *mens rea* of the offence had he been sober. In other words, evidence other than that of intoxication is relevant if it shows that the accused did not have the foresight required by the offence. This is inconsistent with **Majewski**. Perhaps the *ratio* of **Woods** is restricted to rape, for in other offences there is no such provision as s 1(2), and that sub-section was repealed by the Sexual Offences Act 2003. The difficulty with intoxication being proof of recklessness may have been resolved by **Heard** [2008] QB 43 (CA). Instead of intoxication supplying recklessness, the two states were said to be of broad equivalence in terms of culpability.

A case to compare with **Woods** is **Richardson** [1999] 1 Cr App R 392 (CA) – a non-rape case. The two defendants and the victim had been drinking. While indulging in horseplay the former inadvertently dropped the latter over a balcony: the injuries to the victim were serious. The court said that the defendants were guilty if they would have foreseen the risk of harm, had they been sober. However, the defendants could lead evidence of intoxication to show any absence of belief in consent. This is a surprising judgment. The charge was one of inflicting GBH, a basic intent offence, yet intoxication was relevant to the proof of law of consent. However, since the charge was one of s 20 of the Offences Against the Person Act 1861, a basic intent offence, the defendants' drunkenness proved that they had the *mens rea*, foresight of some harm. The court did not seek to reconcile its ruling with **O'Grady** [1987] QB 995 (CA) and the cases which followed that authority are noted in (d) below.

(b) It is sometimes said that drunkenness operates as a defence in relation to serious offences and there is a lesser 'fall-back' crime. This proposition is not true. Lord Salmon noted this point in **Majewski**, above, when he said that specific intent 'was not confined to cases in which, if the prosecution failed to prove [a specific] intent, the accused could still be convicted of a lesser offence'. One might have thought that rape would be a specific intent offence with indecent assault as the 'fall-back' crime but in fact rape is a crime of basic intent. The present law was best summarised and criticised on this point by C.M.V. Clarkson, *Understanding Criminal Law*, 4th edn (Thomson, 2005) 114–15:

> The whole concept of 'specific intent' was devised to enable drunkenness to operate as a substantive *mitigating* factor to certain crimes, particularly murder. But . . . drunkenness is sometimes a partial excuse (where there is a lesser included offence of basic intent) but sometimes a *complete defence* – as with theft where no lesser included offence exists. There is no rationale underlying such a distinction; the result is sheer chance. [Emphasis added.]

(c) It is sometimes thought that s 8 of the Criminal Justice Act 1967 creates a difficulty. By it the triers of fact are instructed to consider 'all the evidence'. It does not say 'all the evidence except drunkenness'. Lord Diplock did not mention s 8 in **Caldwell**. (In **Majewski** the House of Lords said that the law on intoxication was a substantive, not evidential, matter: s 8 deals only with legally relevant evidence. Drunkenness is not legally relevant.) **Caldwell** demonstrates that evidence of recklessness is not required if there is sufficient evidence of drunkenness. It looks as if the House of Lords has disobeyed Parliament by creating a presumption of recklessness.

(d) The law on intoxication in relation to other defences causes problems. In *O'Grady* the court said *obiter* that intoxication was not a defence where it induced a mistake. It does not matter whether the offence was basic (where *Majewski* would apply) or specific. In either event drunkenness is no defence. The accused is guilty of murder although he did not intend to kill or cause grievous bodily harm unlawfully, for he believed that he was acting to prevent a crime on himself. Compare *Williams* [1987] 3 All ER 411 (CA): the accused does have a defence of preventing crime when he makes a mistake which is not induced by intoxication. There is a failure to prove all the elements of the offence when a non-drunken error occurs. P. Seago, *Criminal Law*, 4th edn (Sweet & Maxwell, 1994) 178, commented:

> [a]lthough the case involved a manslaughter conviction, Lord Lane indicated *obiter* that the same [i.e. guilty] would be true of murder. If this is so, then it means that a man who, because of voluntary intoxication, mistakenly believes he is shooting at a gorilla will have a defence to murder if he kills a human being, whereas a defendant will have no defence if he mistakenly believes, because of voluntary intoxication, that he is about to be violently attacked by a man whom he consequently shoots. It is hard to justify such a distinction or see how you can keep the issues of mistake and intent apart since they are merely different ways of looking at the same issue.

For the use of the 'gorilla' example in the successor text, see A. Reed and B. Fitzpatrick, *Criminal Law*, 4th edn (Sweet & Maxwell, 2010) 213. See also the English case of *O'Connor*, above, where drunkenness was relevant to intent but not to self-defence. A reasonable juror may not be able to perform this mental contortion. The court also thought that the *dictum* in *O'Grady* was *ratio*. It was in fact *dictum* because the accused had been acquitted of murder. Anything said about specific intent offences such as murder was not *ratio*.

Despite criticism by academics of *O'Grady* it was followed by the Court of Appeal in *Hatton* [2006] 1 Cr App R 247. The accused, who had consumed over 20 pints of beer, killed the victim with a sledgehammer. He argued that he believed the accused was an SAS soldier armed with a sword. His appeal against a conviction for murder was dismissed. The court certified that a point of law of public importance was involved but refused leave to appeal. It is about time that this issue was resolved by the Lords. The policy argument against *O'Grady* is that if the reason for the rules on intoxication is that the public must be protected from the intoxicated, a conviction for manslaughter does that and there is no need to convict of murder. *O'Grady*, *Hatton* and *O'Connor* were given legislative backing by the Criminal Justice and Immigration Act 2008, s 76.

The contrasting case is the controversial one of *Jaggard v Dickinson* [1981] QB 527 (DC) (see Chapter 18). Under the Criminal Damage Act 1971, s 5(2)(a), evidence of drunkenness was used to establish what the accused believed. The accused believed she was entering a friend's house; in fact she was entering someone else's. She was intoxicated and would not have made this mistake had she been sober. She was not guilty of criminal damage contrary to s 1(1) of the 1971 Act, a basic intent offence. She had the lawful excuse that the person, her friend, entitled to consent to the damage, would have done so, had the friend known of the circumstances. The decision of Lord Donaldson MR was based on the language of the statute. Mustill LJ spoke more generally. Drunkenness on the facts did not negative intention or recklessness. It explained why the accused had the belief she did. By s 5(2) Parliament had isolated belief from the general law of recklessness. However that may be, to allow intoxication to a crime of belief but not to one of recklessness looks strange. This strangeness is exacerbated when one recalls s 8 of the Criminal Justice Act 1967 discussed in (c) above. Why is not s 5(2) of the 1971 Act read in the same way? If intoxication is not relevant in s 8, why is it in s 5(2)? *Jaggard* v *Dickinson* is a case where the court failed to apply the normal rules on intoxication.

The Courts-Martial Appeal Court in *Young* [1984] 1 WLR 654, 658, generalised *Jaggard* v *Dickinson*: 'Where there is an exculpatory statutory defence of honest belief, self-induced intoxication is a factor which must be considered in the context of a subjective consideration of the individual state of mind.' In *Young* it was held that self-induced intoxication was no defence where the accused, charged with possessing a controlled drug, seeks to prove within s 28(3)(b) of the Misuse of Drugs Act 1971 that he did not believe or suspect, nor had any reason to do so, that a substance or product was a controlled drug, when he would have done so when sober.

The outcome of the interrelation between *Caldwell* and *Jaggard* v *Dickinson* is amazing. If the accused damages another's property believing the property to be his own, that belief being induced by intoxication, he is guilty of criminal damage. If, however, he damages another's property believing that it belongs to a third party who would consent to the damage, if he knew of the circumstances, he is not guilty. The point can be taken further. *Jaggard* v *Dickinson* makes the drunken accused not guilty of criminal damage if he believed in consent; however, a drunken accused is guilty of rape if he believed mistakenly in the woman's consent. Lawyers have taken leave of their senses! One possible difference between *O'Grady* and *Jaggard* v *Dickinson* is that the former applies to common law offences, the latter to statutory ones. This distinction does not reflect any policy value and if true is an unfortunate one dependent on chance.

(e) What about intoxication in relation to other defences? In the former defence of provocation where the accused believed falsely because he was drunk that he was being provoked, a subjective view was taken. He was judged on the facts as he believed them to be: *Letenock* (1917) 12 Cr App R 221 (CCA). It is possible that *Letenock* would not be followed nowadays since the law on both intoxication and provocation (now loss of control) have moved on since the First World War. However, in relation to duress and duress of circumstances, the law is that only a mistake made on reasonable grounds exculpates: *Graham* [1982] 1 WLR 294 (CA). A mistake occasioned by alcohol is not one which has been made reasonably. Therefore, in relation to these defences a drunken mistake does not avail.

In respect of consent to assaults the Court of Appeal ruled in *Richardson*, above, that an erroneous belief that the victim is consenting to rough horseplay is a defence to the offence of inflicting GBH contrary to s 20 of the Offences Against the Person Act 1861, even though the mistake was caused by intoxication. The law contrasts strongly with that in *O'Grady* where it was held that a drunken mistake as to self-defence did not provide the accused with a defence. The Court did not consider *O'Grady* or cases such as *Woods* and *Fotheringham*, above. Moreover, *Richardson* is inconsistent with the rule that intoxication 'is no defence to a crime of basic intent.

(f) The serious problem remains that lawyers have failed to provide an adequate statement of which offences are specific intent ones.

(i) As we have seen, Lord Simon in *Majewski* said that specific intent crimes have a purposive element. This definition has already been criticised.

(ii) Sometimes it has been said that specific intent crimes are those in which intention alone is the sole mental element in respect of one or more elements of the *actus reus*. Murder, however, for many years was not defined solely in terms of intention, yet it was never doubted that murder was a specific intent crime. Handling is a crime of specific intent, yet intent is not part of the *mens rea*, which is dishonesty and knowledge or belief.

(iii) An accepted definition of specific intent is that the *mens rea* goes beyond the *actus reus*. This is a helpful tip but is not a definition. All ulterior intent offences are specific intent crimes, but the concept of specific intent crimes is not restricted to ulterior intent ones, as murder itself demonstrates. Another illustration is criminal damage with intent to endanger life or being reckless as to whether life is endangered. The crime is not solely defined in terms of intent but the *mens rea* does extend beyond the *actus reus*. One of the definitions must be wrong but it is unclear which one it is. Section 18 of the Offences Against the Person Act 1861 may be committed in several ways. One is by wounding with intent to do grievous bodily harm. On this definition this crime is one of specific intent. Another form is causing grievous bodily harm with intent to do grievous bodily harm. On this definition this crime is a basic intent one. *Davies* [1991] Crim LR 469 (CA), though not well reported, seems to hold that grievous bodily harm with intent to resist arrest is a specific intent crime. If this approach were correct, the defence of intoxication is dependent not on the distinction between basic and specific intent *crimes* but basic and specific intent *charges*. Some mental elements in offences such as s 18 are basic intent ones, some are specific intent ones. The problem is that offences have been held to be basic intent ones even though part of the *mens rea* is satisfied only by proof of intent. An example is rape. The accused must intend to penetrate the vagina, anus or mouth and must intend to do so with a woman or a man, yet rape is classified as a crime of basic intent: see the discussion of *Fotheringham* above.

One way of reconciling the authorities would be to say that rape is a crime of specific intent where the *charge* is one of rape knowing that the victim did not consent but one of basic intent where the *charge* is one of rape being negligent as to consent. The same reasoning could apply to all offences which are defined in terms of intentionally or recklessly misbehaving, such as criminal damage. The courts, however, classify by the *crime*, not by the *charge*, or at least that was the majority view until *Heard* [2008] QB 43, where Hughes LJ said: '. . . it should not be supposed that every offence can be categorised simply as either one of specific or of basic intent.' The accused was charged with sexual assault contrary to s 3 of the Sexual Offences Act 2003. Section 3(1) reads:

> A person (A) commits an offence if –
> (a) he intentionally touches author person (B),
> (b) the touching is sexual,
> (c) B does not consent to the touching, and
> (d) A does not reasonably believe that B consents.

The accused, who was extremely intoxicated, rubbed his penis on the thigh of a police officer. The court held that specific intent meant ulterior intent (as in burglary) or ulterior recklessness, a state of mind going beyond the act. Therefore, even though the touching had to be intentional, the crime was one of basic intent. Therefore, even crimes which can be committed only intentionally may be ones of basic intent. Where does that leave murder!?

Another criticism is that crimes of recklessness can be crimes of specific intent, contrary to all previous authorities including *Majewski*. For example, recklessly causing criminal damage being reckless as to whether someone's life is endangered is a crime of specific intent according to *Heard*. Furthermore, when Hughes LJ said that crimes of specific intent were ones where the accused had a purpose, that cannot be right because murder has always been a crime of specific intent but has never needed a purpose to kill or cause grievous bodily harm. **Heard** is *obiter* and more case law is needed before it can be seen whether it is an aberration or the start of a new understanding of the defence.

The most acceptable categorisation of specific intent offences was provided by Sopinka J (dissenting, but not on this point) in **Daviault v R**, above. 'In addition to the ulterior intent offences there are certain offences which by reason of their serious nature and importance of the mental element are classed as specific intent offences notwithstanding that they do not fit the criteria usually associated with ulterior intent offences. The outstanding example is murder.'

None of these three definitions gives full weight to the precedents. The operation of the basic/specific dichotomy looks capricious. For some offences such as murder there is a 'fall-back' basic intent crime, manslaughter; but for other crimes such as theft there is no 'fall-back' offence. There is no policy which rationalises this distinction. It is safe to say that Lord Birkenhead did not mean to create this dichotomy.

The present position

One way out of this difficulty, though unsatisfactory from the viewpoint of principle, is to list those precedents. Table 8.1 does that for the more important offences.

It seems that all offences of dishonesty are specific intent crimes. Despite intoxication's being a defence to theft, an accused will appropriate when he sobers up by assuming the rights of the owner such as hiding the item away. Therefore, the drunken taker does not avoid liability for theft.

It may be helpful at this point to give a concrete illustration. In relation to s 20 of the Offences Against the Person Act 1861 the judge would direct the jury that they are to convict if they are sure that the accused foresaw that he might cause some injury or would have foreseen that his act might cause some injury had he not been intoxicated.

Criticisms of the law of voluntary intoxication in brief

- There is no logical way of distinguishing between specific and basic intent crimes.

- The distinction follows no line as to, for instance, the gravity of the offence; for example, the full crime may be an offence of basic intent but the attempt to commit that offence is a specific intent crime. These are the wrong way round in terms of seriousness. Similarly, the distinction does not track public policy rationales such as the protection of the public or general deterrence.

- If intoxication negates the mental element in specific intent crimes, surely it also negates it in basic intent offences?

- Intoxication leads to the unsustainable doctrine of 'constructive recklessness' whereby the intoxicated accused is deemed to have the fault element for crimes of recklessness. Proof of intoxication is not proof of foresight of, for example, some harm for the purposes of s 20 of the Offences Against the Person Act 1861.

- On a practical point juries must find real difficulty in understanding and applying the law when several offences are charged, some of which are specific intent offences (and intoxication is to be taken into account) and some are basic intent ones (to which intoxication is no defence).

Table 8.1 Basic and specific intent – precedents

Basic intent	Authority (there are often others)
Manslaughter	*Lipman*
Rape	*Majewski* (Commonwealth courts are divided on this issue)
Sexual assault	*Heard* (but see below)
Section 20, Offences Against the Person Act	*Majewski*
Section 47, Offences Against the Person Act	*Bolton* v *Crawley* [1972] Crim LR 222 (DC)
Assault on constable	*Majewski*
Assault	
Joy-riding (s 12, Theft Act)	*MacPherson* [1973] RTR 157 (CA)
Presumably removing articles from an exhibition is also a basic intent crime, though a precedent does not exist	
Reckless criminal damage	*Caldwell*
False imprisonment and kidnapping	*Hutchins* [1988] Crim LR 379
Allowing pitbull terrier to be in a public place without a muzzle and a lead	*DPP* v *Kellet* [1994] Crim LR 916 (DC), but see the commentary, which is to the effect that a sober accused is not guilty of this offence unless he knows and consents to ('allows') a dangerous dog to be in a public place, whereas an intoxicated accused is guilty even though he or she does not permit the dog to be in such a place. How can one allow something if through drink or drugs one knows nothing about it?

Specific intent	Authority
Murder	*Beard*
Section 18, Offences Against the Person Act	*Pordage* [1975] Crim LR 575 (CA) (but see text)
Theft	*Ruse* v *Read* [1949] 1 KB 377 (DC)
Robbery	(Follows from theft)
Burglary with intent to steal	*Durante* [1972] 3 All ER 962 (CA)
Handling	Same case (though there is no mention of 'intent' in the definition)
Intentional criminal damage	*Caldwell*
Attempt	(Intention is sole *mens rea* subject to statement in text about reckless attempts in rape and possibly other offences)

For sexual assault, see *Heard*, above, where Hughes LJ said: 'sexual touching must be intentional . . . but voluntary intoxication cannot be relied upon as negating the necessary intention.'

Suggestions for the reform of drunkenness

The difficulty in reforming the law was well stated by the Scottish Law Commission in its Discussion Paper, *Insanity and Diminished Responsibility*, No. 122, 2003: 'The problem . . . is that of reconciling the basic principle of *mens rea* . . . with conditions in which persons can hardly be said to have any mental capacity at all. At the same time the social consequences of recognising . . . intoxication as [a] complete defence . . . in all circumstances would be extremely serious.'

Courts are reluctant to allow intoxicated persons to escape the consequences of their actions. *Lipman* and *Majewski* may be instanced. There is a feeling that these men should have been found guilty of something. There are few redeeming features of intoxication and drunkenness is the state in which many offences are committed. It could be said that in England and Wales people know the kind of events which can happen when a person becomes drunk or takes drugs. Nevertheless, as the High Court of Australia in *O'Connor*, above, demonstrated, the distinction between basic and specific intent makes no logical sense in *mens rea* terms. This breach of the fundamental principle of *mens rea*, the illogicality of the basic/specific intent distinction, and the lack of empirical support for the public policy concerns behind *Majewski* led to Australia's rejection of English law. If the accused had no *mens rea* because of intoxication, he cannot be guilty. This rule even applies to murder: *Martin* (1984) 58 ALJR 217, also a decision of the High Court of Australia. It does not matter that the lack of *mens rea* was caused by intoxication. An accused is guilty only if he had the mental element of the offence charged at the time of the *actus reus*. The fact that the accused got drunk recklessly does not prove that he had the fault element later. (Despite the logic of the situation the Australian Criminal Code Bill 1994 did revert to the specific/basic intent distinction, New South Wales, having accepted *O'Connor*, reverted to the *Majewski* position and Queensland did not adopt the *O'Connor* rule but applied English law.) On this approach there are no special rules applying to drunkenness. The normal principles of criminal law govern.

The Criminal Law Reform Committee recommended in its Report on Intoxication, 1984, that New Zealand should adopt the Australian subjectivist approach and should also not enact a special offence dealing with intoxicated persons who commit the *actus reus* of crimes, as has been proposed for England (see below). See also *Kamipeli*, above. South Africa follows the *O'Connor* doctrine: *Chretien* 1981 (1) SA 1097 (AD). Empirical research by Judge G. Smith in 'Footnote to *O'Connor*'s case' (1981) 5 Crim LJ 270 has shown that the Australian approach has not led to the breakdown of law. The Australian approach should be contrasted with the former Canadian authorities which followed *Majewski*. In *Leary* (1977) 74 DLR (3rd) 103 (by a majority), which was overruled in *Daviault v R*, above, and *Bernard* [1988] 2 SCR 833, the Supreme Court approved the policy behind *Majewski*. That policy was expressed by P. Healy '*R v Bernard*: difficulties with "voluntary intoxication"' (1990) 35 McGill LJ 610 at 612–613: 'Sodden people who do bad things deserve punishment.' A similar point was made over a century ago by Stephen J: 'It is almost trivial for me to observe that a man is not excused from crime by reason of his drunkenness. If it were so, you might as well shut up the criminal courts, because drink is the occasion of a large proportion of the crime which is committed' (*Doherty* (1887) 16 Cox CC 306). The contrary view is that endorsed by the majority in *Daviault v R*: 'The mental aspect of an offence, or *mens rea*, has long been recognised as an integral part of crime. The concept is fundamental to our criminal law. . . . However, the substituted *mens rea* cannot establish the *mens rea* to commit the offence' (*per* Cory J). The court rejected the Australian approach and retained the basic/specific intent distinction, but said that a person would be guilty of a basic intent offence if he had the minimum intent to do the prohibited act.

The *Report of the Committee on Mentally Abnormal Offenders* (Butler Committee), Cmnd 6244, 1975, paras 18.51–18.59, suggested the creation of a new offence, being drunk and dangerous. The accused could be convicted of this offence if charged with a sexual assault, an offence against the person, and criminal damage endangering life. There are advantages in this proposal. The problem of distinguishing between basic and specific intent would disappear. Persons would not be totally acquitted, as now happens when they are charged with a specific intent crime and there is no 'fall-back' basic intent offence. Moreover, if the mischief is truly one of intoxication, this proposed crime would focus on that mischief unlike present law. Three Lords in **Majewski** rejected this recommendation. One of its drawbacks is that it would be a status offence with little or no *mens rea* attached to it. Other proposals have included the creation of a crime of negligently causing injury, reforming offences so that there is always a 'fall-back' basic intent offence, and treating drunken offenders outside the criminal law system. The present law is out of line with what judges thought was social policy in earlier years. In **Reniger v Fogossa** (1551) 75 ER 1 (KB), the court stated that drunkenness was no defence, and a drunken killer was sentenced to be hanged. This attitude seemed to be based on the thought that, since many crimes were committed when the accused was drunk, to provide a defence would mean that few would be convicted. If intoxication was a defence to murder (as it is now), 'there would be no safety for human life' (**Carroll** (1835) 173 ER 64 (NP)). There is some evidence for the view that in the seventeenth and eighteenth centuries drunkenness aggravated the crime, unlike nowadays where it mitigates the offence or provides exculpation.

Present reform proposals are largely based on the Criminal Law Revision Committee's Fourteenth Report, *Offences Against the Person*, Cmnd 7844, 1980. The recommendations were:

(a) The abolition of the basic/specific dichotomy and of the 'constructive recklessness' in **Majewski**.

(b) Intoxication which did not totally exclude *mens rea* should not be a defence.

(c) Involuntary drunkenness should remain a defence but only 'if it negates the mental element', and not if it loosens inhibitions.

(d) Self-induced intoxication was to be defined, as the Butler Committee did, as 'intoxication resulting from the intentional taking of drink or drugs knowing that it is capable in sufficient quantity of having an intoxicating effect, provided that intoxication is not voluntary if it results from a fact unknown to the accused that increases his sensibility to the drink or drug'.

(e) The majority advocated that evidence of voluntary intoxication should be capable of negating the mental element in murder (which at that time was wider than intent) and the intention required for the commission of other offences. In offences where recklessness was an element, if the accused did not appreciate a risk which he would have appreciated when sober, he would not have a defence. These recommendations would largely enact the common law. The minority would allow the defence where the accused was not aware of the risk of causing the *actus reus*, but would have been, were he sober. The dissentients comprised the two law professors on the Criminal Law Revision Committee.

(f) There should be no offence of being dangerously intoxicated, as the Butler Committee had proposed. That crime would lump together the drunken child-killer and the inebriated brawler. The Committee's majority thought that an offence in the area of intoxication should refer to the degree of harm so that, for instance, a drunken killer would still be convicted of manslaughter. The accused should not be labelled incorrectly. The majority opined that a drunken rapist should be guilty of rape, not of some general offence. The minority recommended a special verdict that the offence was committed while the defendant was intoxicated. He would be liable to the same potential penalty (except murder, where the penalty would be equivalent to manslaughter) as he would have been, had he been convicted. The sentence would reflect the harm. In this way the present 'constructive recklessness' rule would be abrogated.

The Law Commission's 1993 and 1995 proposals

In 1993 the Law Commission issued a Consultation Paper, *Intoxication and Criminal Liability*, LCCP No. 127. The Consultation Paper investigated the present law on intoxication and various alternatives. The issue was seen to be an arena for the conflict of two policies: the policy of not convicting persons who did not know what they were doing and the policy of safeguarding citizens from violence which resulted from drink or drugs. The current resolution of this clash of policies is the House of Lords decision in *Majewski*. However, *Majewski* is dependent on the distinction between basic and specific intent crimes. 'The differences between these two types of offence, the policy reasons for the distinction, and the basis on which the distinction is made, are all obscure' (LCCP No. 127, 3). The law is complex and it is possible that it is ignored by the triers of fact. It does not advance the policy of criminalising intoxicated individuals in a straightforward manner but through technical rules which do not always reflect that policy. English law is also out of step with that in other jurisdictions which have abolished the special rules on intoxication.

There are also difficulties in knowing what *Majewski* decided. Is it that all offences are either basic or specific intent ones? On this view the offence found in s 18 of the Offences Against the Person Act 1861 is a specific intent crime. Or is the question whether an allegation is a specific or basic intent one? On this approach the charge that the accused caused grievous bodily harm with intent to do so contrary to s 18 is a basic intent offence, but causing such harm with intent to resist or prevent apprehension is a specific intent crime. Whichever rule is adopted there is the difficulty of crimes which have intent as to one element but recklessness as to another one. Leaving aside intoxication the accused must intend to commit one of the offences listed in s 9(2) of the Theft Act 1968 if he is charged with a s 9(1)(a) type of burglary, but recklessness suffices in relation to the trespass. Applying *Majewski* intoxication is not to be taken into account in determining whether the accused knew he was entering as a trespasser, but is considered with regard to the question whether he intended to commit an offence listed in s 9(2). Another question which arises in relation to *Majewski* is to say that the rule applies in relation to allegations of intent; that is, 'basic intent offences' is a concept which is wider than crimes of recklessness for it covers some crimes of intention.

The Law Commission noted that most crimes have been allocated to the basic or specific intent category. However, there is difficulty with offences which have not been allocated, for the width of *Majewski* is uncertain. Moreover, the treatment of the distinction between the courts 'means that there is no necessary connection between the seriousness of the offence involved and its categorisation . . .'. Murder is a specific intent crime but manslaughter is a basic intent one, yet both are serious offences. Manslaughter is more serious than the crime of grievous bodily harm with intent, yet the former crime is a basic intent one, the latter is a specific intent one. Furthermore, there are problems in applying *Majewski* to some offences, as we have seen with respect to burglary. Some serious specific intent offences have a 'fall-back' basic intent offence attached to them. For example, s 18 is a specific intent crime; an accused can be convicted of the s 20 crime, which is a basic intent offence. However, the same is not true of all serious offences. Intoxication is a defence to burglary and theft; the accused is not guilty, however, of some lesser crime if he was intoxicated. The Law Commission also adverted to the problem of *O'Grady* [1987] QB 995. The defendant is guilty of an offence where he makes a mistake as to an element of it whether that offence is a basic or a specific intent one. The Law Commission in its 1995 Report noted below disagreed with the Consultation Paper's main recommendation but it did repeat these criticisms.

In the Consultation Paper, the Law Commission examined the options for reform of the defence. The first option is to leave the law as it is. The Law Commission rejected this proposal as failing to achieve the policy objectives of a law which was not complex, a law which was certain, and a law which fully implemented the aims of upholding public order while permitting intoxicated defendants to be acquitted of serious offences. A second option was to codify the *Majewski* approach but rectify inconsistencies. This approach would of course ensure that the law was certain but would otherwise meet none of the other policy objectives just mentioned. The Law Commission also rejected the 1980 recommendation of the Criminal Law Revision Committee that an accused should not have a defence of intoxication in relation to an element of a crime which was defined in terms of recklessness if he would have appreciated the risk had he been sober. The effect of that proposal would be that, for example in rape, intoxication would be relevant to the intent to have sexual intercourse but not to recklessness as to consent. Why should the accused be exculpated on the first ground but not on the second? Moreover, it is thought that many believe that intoxication should not on policy grounds be a defence to rape at all. The Law Commission thought that the Criminal Law Revision Committee's proposal would be confusing to juries: they could for instance consider drunkenness in relation to the intent to have sexual intercourse but not in relation to recklessness as to consent. Moreover, the recommendation would lead to difficulties in sentencing. The drunken accused is to be treated as reckless. Should he be punished on the basis that he is reckless? The Law Commission opined that the offender should be penalised for what he was, not for what he was not, that is, for being a reckless but sober individual.

The third option considered by the Law Commission was to disregard the effect of intoxication in any offence. The specific/basic intent rule would be abolished and the accused would not be able to rely on intoxication as negating the fault element in any offence – even ones nowadays categorised as specific intent ones. This option would be an undeniable deterrent, for drunken defendants would have no defence. The Law Commission considered that such a result would be 'draconian' in a society which tolerated alcohol. The effect would also be inappropriate in some crimes. In the type of burglary found in s 9(1)(a) of the Theft Act 1968 intoxication would not be relevant to the further or ulterior intent, the intent to commit one of the four offences listed in s 9(2). The result would be that the prosecution would have to prove only that the accused entered a building as a trespasser, but such an entry is not a crime: 'where the entrant's drunkenness prevents the formation of an ulterior intent, it is simply impossible to characterise the entry as a burglary, and thus similarly impossible to use a conviction for burglary as a sanction against such an entry.'

The fourth option outlined by the Law Commission was the same as the third but with the proviso that the accused would not be convicted if he could demonstrate that he did not have the *mens rea* required for the offence because he was voluntarily intoxicated. The Law Commission considered, however, that someone who caused harm in a drunken state should not go free, which would be the result if the accused established this defence.

The fifth option would be simply to abolish the *Majewski* approach. Intoxication would merely be part of the evidence of *mens rea*. The law would be simple. In view of jurisdictions such as the common law states of Australia which have adopted this solution, there is no need for special rules for drunken defendants. The *mens rea* principle should be supreme. The argument that *Majewski* deters the intoxicated is not supported by the facts. Victoria, which abolished the specific/basic intent rule, does not have a more serious problem with drunks who cause harm than states which have retained *Majewski*. The Law Commission, however, thought that public safety would suffer and respect for the law would diminish if a drunken accused would be completely acquitted. The Irish Law Reform Commission in its Report on *Intoxication* commented thus: 'the traditional *mens rea* doctrine is an appropriate one for the sane and sober criminal, but to adhere to it in an unbending and inflexible fashion enables the offender himself, voluntarily, not just to "move the goalposts" but to remove them altogether! The point was, neatly, couched in more traditional terms by Lord Mustill . . . in **Kingston**, when he held, first, that the intentional taking of an intoxicant without regard to its possible consequences is a substitute for the mental element normally required; and, secondly, that the defendant is "estopped". . . from relying on the absence of a mental element if it is absent *because of his own acts*.' The Irish Law Reform Commission wanted voluntary intoxication never to be a defence.

The sixth option would be to abolish **Majewski** but replace it with a new offence of criminal intoxication. Criminal law should protect against drunken defendants. Such persons are at fault for committing harm. To acquit them would, it may be thought, be morally wrong and give an incorrect message to them, for they must be deterred. 'A new offence can be tailored by legislation to achieve more precisely the objective of the **Majewski's** approach without the faults of **Majewski** itself, and in particular without the practical difficulties that attend its present operation. A new offence can implement directly and overtly . . . policy considerations . . . by laying down clear rules in the light of that policy.' The Law Commission rejected the Butler Committee's proposal of an offence of dangerous intoxication and the idea of the minority of the Criminal Law Revision Committee of an offence of 'doing the act while in a state of voluntary intoxication', partly because in regard to the latter recommendation it required the jury to answer the hypo- thetical question: would this defendant have done what he did, had he been sober? The Law Commission proposed, first, that intoxication should be taken into account in determining whether the accused had the *mens rea* of an offence, whether he had made a mistake as to whether he was in a state of automatism; secondly, the creation of a new offence of criminal intoxication. The crime would be committed by an accused who, while substantially intoxicated, caused the harm proscribed by a so-called 'listed' offence. It would not be relevant that the accused did not have the mental element of the listed offence or that he was in a state of automatism. The Butler Committee's proposed offence would have applied only if the accused did not form the *mens rea* of an offence. A 'listed' offence is just that: one listed by the Law Commission. These were expressed as: homicide, bodily harm, criminal damage, rape, indecent assault, buggery, assaulting or obstructing a constable in the execution of his duty, violent disorder, affray, putting a person in fear of or provoking violence, and causing danger to road users. The offence would, therefore, not apply to other offences such as attempts, battery, theft and burglary. The maximum penalty would be less than for the substantive offence because a drunken defendant is less culpable than a person who intentionally or recklessly committed a crime. There should be no special maximum for the offence because having one maximum would not cater for punishment for the harm caused by an intoxicated accused. The Law Commission thought that there should be a maximum of two-thirds the maximum for the 'listed' offence but with a maximum of 10 years where the maximum for such offence was life. The Law Commission also recommended the abolition of the **O'Grady** principle, with the proviso that a drunken defendant would have the defence of mistake in a self-defence situation where a sober individual would have reasonably made the same mistake.

The Commission summarised the advantages of the proposed offence:

(i) Defendants will not be liable to be convicted of offences when, in law, they did not have the required mental state for guilt of that offence.

(ii) At the same time, the criminal law will be able to intervene in cases where the defendant, although not fulfilling the requirements for conviction of a specific crime, committed socially dangerous acts in a state of substantial intoxication.

(iii) This objective will be achieved by allowing the court and jury to apply a set of clear rules that require them to consider factual and not abstract or hypothetical questions; that clearly identify where the defendant has been convicted on grounds of intoxication rather than of actual intention or recklessness; and which accordingly give positive guidance to the sentencing tribunal as to the ground of his conviction. (LCCP No. 127, 93)

The Law Commission concluded by stating that the new offence could straightforwardly implement the policy of restraining intoxicated defendants, would concentrate on the damage or injury caused by them, and would abolish the complicated yet uncertain law found in *Majewski*.

One concern of commentators related to the sixth and favoured option. If the accused commits a listed offence when substantially intoxicated he has a defence. What, however, if despite his intoxication he intended to commit the offence? Surely as in *Kingston*, above, he should be liable for the (listed) offence, not just for the proposed offence. As *Kingston* confirmed, a drunken intent is nevertheless an intent.

The Law Commission published Report No. 229, *Intoxication and Criminal Liability*, 1995, which is noted below and which adopts a position very similar to that of the US Model Penal Code 1962, s 2.08(1), as the follow-up to LCCP No. 127. In the meantime it issued its Report No. 218, *Legislating the Criminal Code – Offences against the Person and General Principles*, 1993. Report No. 218 was restricted to non-fatal offences and three general defences. With regard to non-fatal offences, cl 21(1) provides that:

a person who was voluntarily intoxicated at any material time shall be treated
(a) as having been aware of any risk of which he would have been aware had he not been intoxicated, and
(b) as not having believed in any circumstances which he would have believed in had he not been intoxicated.

The Home Office Consultation Document, *Violence: Reforming the Offences Against the Person Act 1861*, 1998, accepted this definition for the purposes of its draft Offences against the Person Bill. What should be noted is that the accused will no longer be deemed to be reckless if he is intoxicated. He can adduce evidence to show that despite being intoxicated he did not have the requisite *mens rea*. For purposes of the revised offences, 'a person who was voluntarily intoxicated at any material time shall be treated as not having believed in any circumstance which he would not then have believed in had he not been intoxicated' (cl 33).

The Commission opined that the current distinction between basic and specific intent crimes could not be 'expressed in statutory terms, because its limits are almost impossible to specify'. For convenience, the law was to be reformulated to apply 'only to allegations of or cognate to recklessness'. In other words *Majewski* was for the purposes of the Criminal Law Bill attached to Report No. 218 restricted to offences of recklessness, just as Lord Elwyn-Jones thought in *Majewski* and Lord Diplock did in *Caldwell*. Evidence of intoxication can, however, be considered in respect of intention crimes such as the proposed one of intentionally causing serious injury. The retention of the law on intoxication is not consonant with the Law Commission's insistence on subjective fault.

Clause 33 of the Criminal Law Bill was directed at preserving the rule in *O'Grady* pending the full Report on intoxication. It will be remembered that the Law Commission had previously called the effect of *O'Grady* 'unthinkable'. Schedule 3, para 13(3) to the Bill would revise s 5(2)(b) (protection of property) of the Criminal Damage Act 1971 to make it consistent with the restatement in cl 33. *Jaggard v Dickinson*, a case in s 5(2)(a), would not be affected.

The Commission surprisingly resiled from the chief recommendation contained in its Consultation Paper when it published *Legislating the Criminal Code: Intoxication and Criminal Liability*, Report No. 229, 1995. The Commission considered that 'prudent social policy' (para. 1.14) overrode the general principle of criminal law that defendants were guilty only when as a minimum they were aware of the risk that their conduct might cause harm. They should not escape liability because they were intoxicated, for the public must be protected from violence. It is reasonable to hold them liable for misbehaviour when drunk. Consultees responded to the recommendations in the Consultation Paper that the abolition of the rule in *Majewski* without replacement (option 5) was unacceptable because it would result in the acquittal of drunken defendants and that the creation of a new offence (option 6) was also unacceptable on the ground that more trials would take place, expert evidence would be needed as to whether the accused was substantially impaired, more police time would be spent on uncovering the extent of his intoxication and the prosecution would not know in advance of trial whether the proposed offence should be included in the indictment. Options 3 and 4 were not supported on consultation.

That left option 1, doing nothing, and option 2, codifying and amending current law. These options were supported by the consultees: 'juries do not in fact experience as much difficulty with the present law as we had previously thought' (para. 1.28). Option 1 was rejected because it did not deal with the problems of the law such as whether a crime was one of basic or specific intent. That left option 2. Among the recommendations flowing from that decision were, first, that in respect of allegations of purpose, intent, knowledge, belief, fraud and dishonesty evidence of intoxication should be considered along with all the other evidence to determine whether that allegation was proved; secondly, in respect of other mental elements such as recklessness the accused should be deemed to be aware of anything he would have been aware of, had he not been intoxicated; and thirdly, if the accused when intoxicated whether involuntarily or voluntarily held a belief which would have exculpated him if he had been sober, the belief will not exculpate him if he would not have held it but for his intoxication and the crime is not one of purpose, intent, knowledge, belief, fraud or dishonesty: cf. *Jaggard v Dickinson*, above. An example of the first two propositions is attempt. The accused to be guilty must intend the full offence and intoxication would be taken into account; however, recklessness as to the circumstances suffices for the attempt if it suffices for the full crime: the accused will not be able to rely on intoxication in relation to recklessness such as recklessness as to the victim's consent in rape. At least this is how the provision is expected to work. A court might say that where a crime consists of both allegations of intent and of recklessness, it is in fact a crime of recklessness. Therefore, the accused is guilty if sufficiently intoxicated. 'Intoxicated' would be defined as occurring when awareness, understanding or control was impaired by an intoxicant, which would be defined as 'alcohol, a drug or any other substance (of whatever nature) which, once taken into the body, has the capacity to impair awareness, understanding or control'. Involuntary intoxication would cover situations where the accused took the substance not knowing that it was an intoxicant, he was given it without consent, he took it under duress or had some other defence, he was particularly susceptible to it and did not know, or finally he took it solely for a medical reason and either did not know of its propensity to give rise to aggressive or uncontrollable behaviour or (if he was aware) he took it with medical advice. If in spite of the voluntary intoxication he did have the requisite mental element he would be guilty: *Kingston*, above, would be unaffected.

The proposals would abolish the basic/specific intent divide and replace it with one based on the mental element alleged (though the difference in practice may be minimal and the distinction seems to exist already: see above), would abrogate the rule in *Hardie*, above, and replace it with a rule about medical advice, would abolish the *O'Grady* principle and would tidy up the law of involuntary intoxication.

The proposals have been criticised for failing to conform with the general principles espoused in the draft Criminal Code. The recommendations are based on the workability, but they would lead to a complicated law.

The Home Office issued a Consultation Paper *Violence: Reforming the Offences against the Person Act 1861* in 1998. In it the government returned to the approach of the 1989 draft Criminal Code. Because of the nature of the document intoxication was restated only in relation to non-fatal offences but in its 2000 Consultation Paper on involuntary manslaughter the Home Office took the same view with regard to this offence. There has been no movement since by any government.

The Law Commission's 2006 recommendations

The Law Commission issued its Report No. 304, *Murder, Manslaughter and Infanticide*, in November 2006. In it the Commission proposed a three-tier structure for fatal offences: first degree murder, second degree murder and manslaughter: see Chapter 11 for details. In respect of intoxication the Commission proposed that it should be a defence to first and second degree murder but not to manslaughter. The specific and basic intent formula would thus be mapped onto the new law. However, it should be noted that one form of the proposed mental element in first degree murder is 'intent to cause serious injury being aware that there is a serious risk of death'. This is therefore a crime partly defined in terms of (subjective) recklessness: awareness of a serious risk of death. Nevertheless, this type of murder will remain a crime of specific intent. Similar points may be made about second degree murder. In 2011 the government decided not to proceed with degrees of murder.

The Law Commission's 2009 proposals

The Commission returned to the subject of reform in its Report No. 314, *Intoxication and Criminal Liability*. The Report follows the main 1995 recommendations in that it proposes to codify the law but unlike the 1995 Report not all the law on intoxication would be put in statutory form.

1 The law of basic and specific intent is preserved but the terminology is dropped.

2 Five subjective states of mind are set out and in respect of these intoxication is to be taken into account to determine whether or not the accused had the *mens rea* for the crime: intent, knowledge of something other than a risk, belief, acting fraudulently or dishonestly, and being reckless for certain purposes within the Serious Crime Act 2007 (encouraging or assisting crime).

3 In all other instances of subjective fault the accused 'is to be treated as having been aware at the material time of anything which [he] would then be aware but for his

intoxication' (cl. 3(3) of the draft bill attached to the Report). In other words, becoming intoxicated is the functional equivalent of the *mens rea* with regard to these offences.

4 The rule on intoxicated mistake in self-defence is retained. However, the rule in *Jaggard v Dickinson*, above, would be reversed.

5 Also retained is the present scope of involuntary intoxication. There is to be no defence of loss of inhibitions or a reduction in moral sense caused by alcohol.

6 Insanity and automatism would not be affected.

Self-defence and the prevention of crime

Example

Armed police are called to a pub where the landlady has seen a man sitting in the pub carrying a parcel wrapped in brown paper. She tells the police that the shape of the parcel is that of a rifle. The police shout at the man to throw down his weapon. In fact he is deaf and cannot hear them, and he does nothing. He is shot dead by the police. The parcel contains a chair leg, not a rifle. Are the police guilty of murder?

These facts are based on real-life events.

The police did kill and did intend to kill; therefore, they are guilty of murder, unless they have a defence. The police may use such force as is reasonable in the prevention of crime and they are judged on the facts they (even if unreasonably) believe: see s 76 of the Criminal Justice and Immigration Act 2008, enacting case law. Later parts of the section instruct the jury on how to determine whether the force used was excessive. If it was, the police are guilty of murder; if it was not, they are completely acquitted, and there is no 'halfway house' of manslaughter.

However, even if the defence would seemingly apply, one should inquire into the possibility of a charge of gross negligence manslaughter if what the police did was so bad as to constitute a crime (in the eyes of the jury). Contrariwise, if the accused is seemingly guilty because the force used was excessive, one should look at the Coroners and Justice Act 2009 in relation to the defence of loss of control, which partly replaced provocation: one of the 'qualifying triggers' for loss of control is 'fear of serious violence' (see ss 54–55). There are details of these two defences in Chapter 12 on manslaughter.

Introduction

This section deals with the statutory defence of **prevention of crime** and effecting or assisting in an arrest, found in s 3(1) of the Criminal Law Act 1967 and the common law defence of **self-defence** insofar as it survives the enactment of s 3(1). The Criminal Justice and Immigration Act 2008, s 76, came into force on 14 July 2008. It was presented by the then Minister of Justice, Jack Straw, as a measure which would protect those charged with crimes who were seeking to prevent the commission of offences against themselves, others or property, particularly householders who used force against burglars, but in fact it is an enactment of the previous statutory and case law authorities. It does not completely supersede previous law. For example, the Act does not state that the attack has to be imminent.

Section 76 may be outlined thus:

1 'The question whether the degree of force used by D [the accused] was reasonable in the circumstances is to be decided by reference to the circumstances as D believed them to be . . .' (s 76(3)).

This subjective test of mistaken defence is, like the other parts of s 76, discussed below.

2 Section 76(4) provides:

If D claims to have held a particular belief as regards the existence of any circumstances –
   (a) the reasonableness or otherwise of that belief is relevant to the question whether D genuinely held it; but
   (b) if it is determined that D did genuinely hold it, D is entitled to rely on it for the purposes of subsection (3), whether or not –
       (i) it was mistaken, or
       (ii) (if it was mistaken) the mistake was a reasonable one to have made.

3 Section 76(5) stipulates: 'But subsection (4)(b) does not enable D to rely on any mistaken belief that was voluntarily induced.'

4 'The degree of force used by D is not to be regarded as having been reasonable in the circumstances as D believed them to be if it was disproportionate in the circumstances' (s 76(6)). Shooting a fleeing burglar in the back is, it is suggested, disproportionate. Whether s 76(6) complies with Article 2 of the European Convention on Human Rights is discussed below.

5 Section 76(7) provides that:

In deciding the question mentioned in subsection (3) the following considerations are to be taken into account (so far as relevant in the circumstances of the case) –
   (a) that a person acting for a legitimate purpose may not be able to weigh to a nicety the exact measure of any necessary action; and
   (b) that evidence of a person's having done what the person instinctively thought was necessary for a legitimate purpose constitutes strong evidence that only reasonable action was taken by that person for that purpose.

Whether the accused has a legitimate purpose is determined by s 76(10)(a): common law self-defence and statutory prevention of crime and effecting or assisting in arrest under the 1967 Act. The concept of 'strong evidence' is novel and is not defined in the Act.

6 The triers of fact are not restricted to these two pieces of evidence (s 76(8)). Perhaps s 76(8) will be interpreted so as to bring the accused's characteristics into account. If so, which traits may be relevant? Under the pre-2008 law the Court of Appeal hinted in the controversial case of *Martin* [2003] QB 1 that physical characteristics could be taken into account but ruled out psychiatric evidence that the accused perceived threats to be greater than they really were because of his mental condition: see further below. It is uncertain whether s 76(8) preserves the pre-existing law.

7 Subsection (10) provides in part: '. . . (b) references to self-defence include acting in defence of another person; and (c) references to the degree of force used are to the type and amount of force used.'

All these points are dealt with below. For example, the point in s 76(5) about drunken mistakes is considered below in section (g) *Mistake of fact*. The reader will quickly find that the 2008 statute does not enact new law but codifies case law. Even the term 'weigh to a nicety' in s 76(7)(a) is taken from case precedents. However, s 76 is only a partial codification of self-defence and prevention of crime; moreover, to understand s 76 one needs to understand the law which it puts into statutory form.

The boundaries of self-defence and prevention of crime

It might be said that self-defence and the prevention of crime are not true defences but, like the defence of consent, are failures to prove that the accused did the act unlawfully. His act was justified and there is no *actus reus*. Therefore, there was no crime. The policy basis of the defence is to inhibit aggressive behaviour. The Court of Appeal in *Abraham* [1973] 1 WLR 1270 emphasised that a judge should point out to the jury that while a plea of self-defence is called a defence, the burden remains on the prosecution to disprove it. Other authorities are to similar effect, such as *Khan* [1995] Crim LR 78 (CA). A Privy Council authority is *Chan Kau* v *R* [1955] AC 206. For Australia see *Viro* (1978) 52 ALJR 418 (HCA). The judge must direct the jury on this defence if the facts raise it, even though the accused did not seek to rely on it: *DPP* v *Bailey* [1995] 1 Cr App R 257 (PC).

By s 3(1) of the Criminal Law Act 1967:

> A person may use such force as is reasonable in the circumstances in the prevention of crime, or in effecting or in assisting in the lawful arrest of offenders or suspected offenders or of persons unlawfully at large.

This rule replaced the common law. The defence of one's own person and others and of property is also a defence, this time at common law. This defence probably has the same bounds as s 3 except that possibly the common law defence is restricted to defence against the use of force whereas s 3 is not. The degree of force lawful in self-defence is the same as that under the Act: *McInnes* (1971) 55 Cr App R 551 (CA) and *Clegg* [1995] 1 AC 482 (HL). In the latter case Lord Lloyd rejected the view of Lord Diplock in *Reference under s 48A of the Criminal Appeal (Northern Ireland) Act 1968 (No. 1 of 1975)* [1977] AC 105 (HL) that a person who uses force in self-defence is more blameworthy than he who uses it to prevent crime. Self-defence could in many circumstances fall within s 3, and both defences are available on the same facts: *Cousins* [1982] QB 526 (CA) and *Clegg*. This is another reason for rejecting Lord Diplock's view. If the force used is not in the prevention of crime, such as where the accused is defending himself against an attack by a child under 10 or an insane person, s 3 cannot be used. Accordingly there is not a total overlap. It should be noted that to have a defence of self-defence the attack against which the accused defended himself need not be an unlawful one: *per* Ward LJ in *Re A (Children) (Conjoined Twins: Medical Treatment)* [2001] Fam 147 (CA), a civil case. The Court of Appeal (Criminal Division) in *Kelleher* [2003] EWCA Crim 3525 did say that there had to be an unlawful or criminal act against which the defendants were defending themselves, but it did not consider the position, for example, of children under 10. Since the planting of genetically modified maize seed was lawful, the defendants did not have the defence. ('Unlawful' here means tortious.)

The jury is entitled to take into account the physical characteristics of the accused in assessing whether his reaction was reasonable: *Martin* [2003] QB 1 (CA), the case of the Norfolk former who shot a fleeing burglar in the back, killing him. For example, the fact that the accused was weak or small or both when the victim was strong or tall or both can be taken into consideration. The court added that psychiatric conditions can 'in exceptional circumstances' be considered. What those circumstances are was left undefined. The accused in *Martin* suffered from paranoia but that psychiatric condition was not to be used. Therefore, the law is uncertain. Moreover, in a different *Martin* case [2000] 2 Cr App R 42 (CA) psychiatric evidence was admitted to show that the accused suffered a mental condition which made him more likely than others to believe that he was under threat and that the threats would be carried out.

(a) *The interpretation of s 3*. The force must be used for the purposes specified. An example is **Renouf** [1986] 2 All ER 449 (CA). The accused was charged with reckless driving. He had forced a vehicle off the road and rammed it after the occupants had assaulted him and damaged his car. He was held to have been acting in order to assist in the lawful arrest of offenders. Whether the force was reasonable was a question for the jury.

Another point of construction is that s 3 is limited to the use of force: **Renouf**. There is no definition of 'force'. The term seems to require some sort of violent behaviour. Therefore, writing with a felt-tip on a concrete pillar is not force within s 3: **Blake v DPP** [1993] Crim LR 586 (DC). What about using something less than force? One answer is that such conduct falls within the common law and in principle if force is permitted, something less should be allowed too. An example given by Jeremy Horder in 'Self-defence, necessity and duress: understanding the relationship' (1998) 11 *Canadian Journal of Law and Jurisprudence* 143 at 144 is this: 'If the only way I can stop a would-be attacker killing me is to release a poisonous gas into a room through which he will pass to reach me, then I am entitled to have such a step considered as potentially necessary and proportionate, even though it does not involve the use of force.' In **Cousins**, above, Milmo J said: 'If force is permissible, something less, for example, a threat, must also be permissible . . .' In **DPP v Bayer** [2004] 1 WLR 2856 (DC) the defendants chained themselves to tractors to prevent genetically modified maize being drilled. The court suggested *obiter* that they might have had a defence if the other elements of defence of property had been satisfied. However, it cannot be said that the law is settled.

Section 3 also applies only when there is a crime to prevent. In **Burns** [2010] EWCA Crim 1023 the accused drove a prostitute to a secluded place for them to engage in a sexual activity. He then changed his mind and told her to get out of the car. She refused. He forcibly removed her, causing her minor injuries. The court held that he was not acting in prevention of crime when he ejected her from the car. If there had been an offence but at the time of the accused's seeking to rely on the defence he was not acting in self-defence, then he is not afforded the defence: **Attwater** [2010] EWCA Crim 2399.

(b) *The interpretation of self-defence*. Self-defence includes the protection of others: **Duffy** [1967] 1 QB 63 (CCA). It also covers protection of property: **Hussey** (1924) 18 Cr App R 160 (CCA): a trespasser may be killed in defence of one's home (but the force must be reasonable). The accused shot and wounded two of his landlady's friends, who were trying to break into his room to evict him illegally. Hewart CJ said that the law on defence of a home was different from the ordinary rules of self-defence. Had the facts occurred today, the friends would have been guilty of at least two offences and therefore the accused would be acting in prevention of crime. For example, one may kill another's dog which is threatening other people or property. In **Workman v Cowper** [1961] 2 QB 143 (DC) the accused killed a foxhound which was running wild on common land where there were sheep. The dog was not worrying the sheep, but it was lambing season. In **Faraj** [2007] EWCA Crim 1033 it was held that a householder could rely on reasonable force in self-defence in order to detain a burglar. In fact the alleged burglar was a gas repair man. See (g) below for mistake of fact. Also included are preventing a trespass, breach of the peace and escaping from unlawful imprisonment. Any other purpose such as retaliation does not suffice.

An act of self-defence need not be spontaneous: **Attorney-General's Reference (No. 2 of 1983)** [1984] QB 456 (CA), approved in **Beckford v R** [1998] AC 130 (PC). The accused therefore can prepare to repel an attack if that attack is about to start, at least provided that the police cannot offer protection. This proposition could give a defence to a battered woman who is in fear of further violence provided, it is thought, that the attack is imminent. If, however, the abuser is asleep, no attack is imminent. Lord Griffiths in *Beckford* stressed the necessity for imminence. Northern Ireland law is the same. The requirement of imminence (or immediacy) means that people can 'get their blow in first' far in advance of any attack.

The accused will not be acting in self-defence if he creates the dangerous situation for which he wished to use the defence. In other words, the defence is ruled out when the accused induces the victim to attack him. In *Malnik v DPP* [1989] Crim LR 451 (DC) the defendant was going to see a person who he believed had stolen cars belonging to his friend. Because the alleged thief was violent, the accused took with him a rice-flail, which is a weapon used in oriental martial arts. He was arrested before he reached the alleged thief's house. The court rejected his contention that he was justified in carrying the weapon because he feared being attacked. It was he who had created the situation of danger. This case was approved in *Salih* [2007] EWCA Crim 2750. Hooper LJ agreed with Bingham LJ in *Malnik v DPP* that 'the policy of the law' was against arming oneself with offensive weapons and that the exceptions were narrow. The requirement of imminence is one reason why battered wives may find difficulty in having this defence. Stabbing a sleeping partner does not suggest a situation of imminent danger. Another difficulty for such persons is that the degree of force may be excessive. This issue is discussed in (c) below.

(c) *The person attacked is under no duty to retreat: Julien* [1969] 1 WLR 839 (CA). In *Bird* [1985] 2 All ER 513, the Court of Appeal said that it was not necessary for the accused to have demonstrated an unwillingness to fight to have this defence. Whether the accused did retreat or show an unwillingness to fight is one factor to be taken into account: *Reference under s 48A of the Criminal Appeal (Northern Ireland) Act 1968 (No. 1 of 1975)*, above, and *Duffy v Chief Constable of Cleveland Police* [2007] EWHC 3169 (Admin), following the Privy Council in *Palmer v R* [1971] AC 814. Trying to withdraw is therefore evidence of the accused's acting reasonably. There is no reference in the 2008 Act to this rule.

(d) *The burden of proof is on the prosecution: Lobell* [1957] 1 QB 547 (CCA). The accused shoulders the evidential burden. Even if the accused does not rely on the defence, if the facts raise it the judge must put it to the jury.

(e) *The degree of force.* Under both s 3 and the common law the force used must (in fact) be reasonable in the circumstances. What is reasonable depends on the nature of the threat. It is common to say that the force used must be both necessary and proportionate. There is no need for exact proportionality: *Palmer v R* [1971] AC 814 (PC). The Court of Appeal in *Rivolta* [1994] Crim LR 694 followed *Palmer*. In *Oatridge* (1992) 94 Cr App R 367 the Court of Appeal stated that one of the questions to be answered was whether the accused's response was 'commensurate with the degree of danger created by the attack'. What the accused instinctively believed was necessary is evidence of the reasonableness of the force: *Whyte* [1987] 3 All ER 416 (CA). If the accused uses excessive force and kills when no reasonable person would have done so, he is guilty of murder (if he has malice aforethought): *Palmer v R*, above.

A killing in excessive self-defence is sometimes thought not to be as serious as a true murder, but the outcome is not manslaughter but murder. There have been several calls for the reform of this law. The Lords in *Clegg* rejected the opportunity to declare that a killing in self-defence was manslaughter. The question of reasonableness is for the jury: *Reference under s 48A; Cousins*, above. In *Cousins* it was said that a threat of force may be reasonable, when force would not be. As was held in *Clegg*, once the danger is over there is no necessity to use force. Therefore, force used then is not in self-defence or in the prevention of crime but is illegal. On the facts of *Clegg* the danger had passed and the accused was not acting in defence of another or to prevent the crime of death by dangerous driving. Provided that the accused did use reasonable force, it does not matter whether the accused was in a state of funk or was calm.

See also the discussion of Article 2 of the European Convention on Human Rights in the 'Conclusion' below.

(f) *Self-defence and duress of circumstances*. Both defences are based on threats. If the accused grabs a knife and uses it to prevent himself being killed, he is acting in self-defence and under the influence of duress of circumstances. Self-defence is limited to the use of force, whereas duress is available for most offences. Therefore, if the accused does not use force, duress of circumstances is a possible defence. Self-defence is a defence to all crimes, though the Court of Appeal in *Symonds* [1998] Crim LR 280 had difficulty with the concept of self-defence applying beyond the realms of offences against the person (here, driving offences), but duress of circumstances is not a defence to murder. In duress the harm threatened must be of death or serious injury. In self-defence the accused has to use only reasonable force, whereas the test may be higher in duress of circumstances: did this accused fall short of the standard of a person of reasonable firmness? It is strange that the test where the accused need not use force (duress) is stricter than the test where he does use force (self-defence). This proposition applies also to the next point. The tests for mistake also differ. Duress of circumstances requires reasonable belief. This difference can give rise to different verdicts. Take a variation on the facts of *Symonds*. Assume that the accused was mistaken as to what the victim was doing and to escape he drove his car at the victim. The defence is one of self-defence. The mistake, if honest, gives rise to a defence. If, however, in order to escape the accused drove away dangerously, the defence is one of duress of circumstances. An unreasonable mistake is not a defence. The outcome does differ depending on the defence. The Court of Appeal said that self-defence and duress of circumstances shared the same elements, but in relation to a mistaken belief they do not (though the law seems to be changing). Moreover, duress is no defence to murder, attempted murder, being an accessory to murder and some forms of treason; the threat in duress must be of death or serious injury; and there is no defence of duress when the accused has voluntarily put himself in a position where a criminal gang may exert violent pressure on him. Mistake in self-defence is discussed next.

See Chapter 7 for an explanation of duress of circumstances.

(g) *Mistake of fact*. The accused is to be judged on the facts as he perceives them to be. The test is subjective. To omit this part of the law constitutes a misdirection: *Duffy*, above. If the accused used excessive force because he made a mistake of fact, he has a defence if he would have had a defence on the facts as he believed them to be. There is no need for a reasonable mistake: *Williams* [1987] 3 All ER 411 (CA), *Jackson* [1984] Crim LR 674, *Fisher* [1987] Crim LR 334 (CA), *Beckford*, above, *Morrow* [1994] Crim LR 58, where the cases on self-defence were applied to the statutory defence of prevention of crime, *Dewar v DPP* [2010] All ER (D) 83 (Jan) (Administrative Division), where the defence was applied to a father who thought he was protecting his son from a person on the opposing football team who was about to kick his son, and *Faraj*, above, where the law on mistake of fact was applied to the defence of property. Lord Griffiths in *Beckford* emphasised that basing the law of mistaken self-defence on honest belief rather than reasonable belief would not allow bogus defences to succeed, for juries were adept at distinguishing truth from falsity. The Court of Appeal ruled in *Oatridge*, above, that in cases of honest mistake of fact in self-defence (in this case the fact that the accused believed her partner was going to kill her – he had abused her previously) the judge should direct the jury on whether the victim's response was commensurate with the attack which he believed he faced.

The force must still be (objectively) reasonable in the circumstances which the accused (subjectively) believed existed: *Owino* [1996] 2 Cr App R 128 (CA). Anything said by the Court of Appeal in *Scarlett* [1993] 4 All ER 629 to the effect that the accused was entitled to use such force as he believed reasonable was incorrect. *Owino* was followed in *Hughes* [1995] Crim LR 957 (CA). The court held that the trial judge must explain to the jury the effect of a mistaken belief. The law is that an accused who is mistaken that he is about to be attacked is entitled to be judged on the facts as he believed existed but he must use no more than reasonable force, reasonableness being assessed in the light of the circumstances the accused thought existed. Since Beldam LJ gave the judgment in *Scarlett* and in *Hughes*, *Scarlett* is now to be taken as incorrect. The Court of Appeal spoke to similar effect in *DPP* v *Armstrong-Braun* (1998) 163 JP 271. While the *facts* are to be judged as the accused honestly believed them to exist, the Court of Appeal in *Martin* [2003] QB 1 stated that his perception of the *danger* was to be assessed objectively. The fact that this accused because he had a paranoid personality saw danger when it did not exist was irrelevant. The court certified a question of law of general importance: 'Whether expert psychiatric evidence is admissible on the issue of a defendant's perception of the danger he faced . . . ?' Unfortunately leave to appeal was refused. However, the Privy Council advised in *Shaw* v *R* [2001] 1 WLR 1519 that the jury must take into account 'the circumstances and the danger as the [accused] honestly believed them to be . . .'. This was followed by the Court of Appeal in *Harvey* [2009] EWCA Crim 469. There is a clash of authority. It is suggested that the Privy Council is correct, for there is no distinction between 'facts' and 'danger'.

The contrast between *Williams* and *Clegg* should be noted. If the accused is mistaken as to whether there is a need for self-defence, he is acquitted: *Williams*. If, however, the accused is mistaken as to the degree of force, he is guilty, even of murder: *Clegg*. In respect of the latter situation, a comparison with provocation is instructive. In self-defence an overreaction leads to guilt, not an acquittal, whereas in provocation overreaction leads to acquittal on a charge of murder. Since a successful defence of provocation leads to a conviction for manslaughter, it is arguable that when the accused kills in defence of self or others but uses excessive force, this too should be manslaughter. However, it may well be that any killing in defence of property cannot be justified.

Four final points on mistake of fact should be made. First, 'If a defendant applies force to a police or court officer, which would be reasonable if that person were not a police or court officer, and the defendant believes that he is not, then even if his belief is unreasonable, he has a good plea of self-defence': *Blackburn* v *Bowering* [1994] 3 All ER 380 (CA, Civil Division).

Secondly, if the mistake is caused by intoxication, the accused has no defence: *O'Grady* [1987] 3 All ER 420 (CA), which was approved in *Hatton* [2006] 1 Cr App R 247 (CA). Thirdly, if the accused does not believe that he is acting reasonably in preventing crime or in self-defence but circumstances in fact exist which would have given him a defence, had he known of them, he has no defence, for the principle in *Dadson* (1850) 4 Cox CC 358 (CCR) explained in Chapter 2 applies.

Fourthly, while the point has not been conclusively settled by the European Court of Human Rights, current English law laid down in **Williams** may be inconsistent with Article 2 of the European Convention, which the Court has surprisingly interpreted as requiring the accused's belief to be based on reasonable grounds: see **McCann v UK** (1995) 21 EHRR 97, **Andronicou v Cyprus** (1998) 25 EHRR 491 and **Gul v Turkey** (2002) 34 EHRR 28. The European Court in **Brady v UK** (2001) 3 April had the opportunity to consider this issue but it seems that the Court failed to realise that a difference exists. The same must be said of **Caraher v UK** (2000) 11 January, an admissibility decision, and **Bubbins v UK** (2005) 41 EHRR 458, where the requirement that force used by the police be 'absolutely necessary' was satisfied by a constable's honest belief that there was 'a real and immediate risk to his life and the lives of his colleagues'. Collins J in the Administrative Court said that English law and Article 2 were the same when it came to assessing the reasonableness of the force, despite the difference in the language used: **R (on the Application of Bennett) v H.M. Coroner for Inner South London** (2006) 170 JP 109 (Collins J in the Administrative Court). Absolute necessity, the touchstone of the Convention, was made the equivalent of reasonable force in English law. He added that Article 2 applies to both intentional and non-intentional killings. It should be noted that Article 2 is restricted to the use of fatal force in self-defence. It would be absurd if different rules applied to the use of non-fatal force, but we await authority. It may be that reasonable grounds for the belief are needed because it is 'the very minimum required by law' (Joint Committee on Human Rights, *Legislative Scrutiny: Fifteenth Report of Session 2007–08*, para. 2.35).

(h) The same rules as apply to ordinary citizens govern the conduct of the security forces: *Clegg*. Lord Lloyd noted that there was no defence of superior orders in criminal law and that to create an exception for the armed services would be to make new law. Similarly, the High Court in **R (Bennett) v HM Coroner for Inner South London**, above, held that Article 2 of the European Convention on Human Rights applied not just to agents of the state such as police officers but also to members of the public. Section 76 does not distinguish between the two even in the context of mistake: one might have expected trained marksmen to take more care than the general public. Collins J suggested that the test of reasonableness in the English law of self-defence was the same as that found in Article 2 but as stated in (g), this *dictum* is questionable.

(i) The Court of Appeal held in **Jones v Gloucestershire Crown Prosecution Service** [2005] QB 259 that 'crime' in s 3 meant an act, omission or state of affairs and the mental element which constituted a crime in English domestic law. Therefore, the term did not include something which was a crime elsewhere or in international law but was not a crime in England and Wales. The international crime of aggression against a foreign country is not an offence in English law. Accordingly, aggression was not a 'crime' for the purposes of s 3, and the appellants could not use the defence against charges arising out of attempts to stop UK and US attacks on Iraq. The Lords dismissed the appeal on the same grounds [2006] UKHL 16. *Obiter* it was suggested that even if the crime of aggression existed in English domestic law, the defendants would not have been able to rely on the defence of prevention of crime because using force to obstruct military vehicles would not prevent the crime of aggression.

(j) In Australia a person, it seems, may defend himself, others and property against a lawful attack: **Zecevic** (1987) 71 ALR 641 (HCA). English law remains to be made definitely. The major authority is now **Hitchens** [2011] 2 Cr App R 26 (CA) where it was held that force may be used against an innocent person to stop him committing an offence.

Previously in *Re A* [2001] Fam 147, a civil case, Ward LJ held that it was lawful to kill one of conjoined twins when her existence was dragging the other twin towards death: obviously the other twin's 'attack' was lawful. Ward LJ compared her with killing a six-year-old boy who was shooting people in the school playground. If English law were to demand an unlawful (here meaning criminal or tortious) attack, one would not have a defence of self-defence against the type of persons mentioned earlier, the insane, automatons and those under 10. However, *DPP* v *Bayer*, above, is to contrary effect. The defendants' claim of defence of property failed because they were not defending against unlawful behaviour. There was nothing criminal or tortious about drilling seeds of genetically modified maize.

(k) *Zecevic* also provided Australian authority for the proposition that an accused 'may not create a continuing situation of emergency and provoke a lawful attack upon himself and yet claim . . . the right to defend himself against that attack'. The law is different in the defence of loss of control. Northern Irish law is the same as that stated in *Zecevic*: *Browne* [1983] NI 96. However, if the accused kills the victim in the course of a violent quarrel he (the accused) may rely on the defence if the victim's reaction was disproportionate to the accused's conduct: *Rashford* [2006] Crim LR 528 (CA). It is not certain whether *Rashford* has settled English law on this point but it seems to have done, and was approved in *Harvey* [2009] EWCA Crim 469. The latest authority, *Keane* [2010] EWCA Crim 2514, is to similar effect: where the accused starts a fight, she can use this defence when the victim fights back with excessive force. What is excluded, however, is where the accused sets out deliberately to engineer a defence of self-defence for himself, and this proposition was endorsed in *Harvey*.

(l) The fact that an accused has a defence of self-defence does not prevent his losing a civil claim for damages in respect of the same act. See *Revill* v *Newbery* [1996] QB 567(CA, Civil Division).

(m) The defendant's defence terminates when his victim is no longer threatening him. If there is a road rage incident, both drivers get out of their cars and one threatens the other with violence, the accused is entitled to use self-defence. If the first then drives off, the accused is not acting in self-defence if he follows him in order to drive him off the road.

(n) It does not matter whether the accused was acting calmly or in abject terror. The issue remains one of whether his action was reasonable.

(o) Section 3(1) affected both civil and criminal law. However, civil law is different not just as to the standard of proof but also the burden of proof. The defendant in civil law must prove that he has the defence: *Ashley* v *Chief Constable of Sussex Police* [2008] 1 AC 962 (HL). The House also held, in distinction to criminal law, that a mistake as to whether the defendant had to act in prevention of crime had to be made on reasonable grounds. It is suggested that the civil law of mistake in self-defence is closer to the European Convention on Human Rights as interpreted in *McCann* than is the criminal law!

The present law and proposed reform of mistake of fact and intoxication are discussed under those headings.

As in necessity, statutory words may conceal self-defence. By s 16 of the Firearms Act 1968: '[I]t is an offence for a person to have in his possession any firearm . . . with intent . . . to endanger life . . .' While there is no express mention, counsel for the prosecution conceded in *Georgiades* [1989] 1 WLR 759 (CA) that it would be a defence for the accused to act to endanger life for a lawful purpose as when the accused raised a shortened shotgun to waist level thinking he was about to be attacked. Note that force which causes the simple offence of criminal damage falls within the defence noted in Chapter 18, that of lawful excuse, whereas force causing the aggravated offence falls within self-defence.

Reform

The Law Commission's 1993 proposals

In its Report No. 218, *Legislating the Criminal Code – Offences Against the Person and General Principles*, 1993, the Law Commission recommended a statutory restatement as to when the use of force is justified. Clause 27(1) of the Criminal Law Bill attached to the Report is in these terms:

> The use of force by a person for any of the following purposes, if only such as is reasonable in the circumstances as he believes them to be, does not constitute an offence:
> (a) to protect himself or another from injury, assault or detention caused by a criminal act;
> (b) to protect himself or (with the authority of that other) another from trespass to the person;
> (c) to protect his property from appropriation, destruction or damage caused by a criminal act or from trespass or infringement;
> (d) to protect property belonging to another from appropriation, destruction or damage caused by a criminal act or (with the authority of the other) from trespass or infringement; or
> (e) to prevent crime or a breach of the peace.

This clause incorporated the law in **Williams** [1987] 3 All ER 411 (CA), stated expressly for the first time that force may be used against the property to protect the person, and revised s 5 of the Criminal Damage Act 1971 to bring it into line with the present s 3 of the Criminal Law Act 1967 with the effect that the force must be objectively reasonable and not merely reasonable from the accused's viewpoint. Clause 27(1)(a)–(e) listed the purposes for which the use of force is justifiable. It restates cl 44(1)(a)–(f) of the draft Criminal Code in slightly different words. It should be noted that the same act may fall within more than one of the categories, for example an accused who defends himself is preventing the commission of an offence and protecting against an assault. Clause 27(1)(e) is worth mentioning. The example given by the Commission is one where 'D restrains P, who is clearly dangerously intoxicated, from driving P's motor vehicle'. Here D is not protecting the person or property of himself or another but is preventing crime. There is special provision permitting defence against non-criminal acts done by persons under 10, acting under duress (of both kinds), acting involuntarily or in a state of intoxication and who are insane (cl 27(3)). This provision is needed only where the accused *knows* of the condition, for otherwise he is judged on the facts he believes to exist. There is another special provision dealing with the situation where the accused knows of the facts which make the other's acts non-criminal where the other has made a mistake. For example, the accused is making a lawful citizen's arrest; the other does not know this and thinks that the accused is attacking the victim; he intervenes; the accused uses force to resist the other; however, the accused knows that the other has made an error. By cl 27(6) the accused's reaction is lawful. The Commission argued that: 'P's act is lawful only because of a mistake or suspicion on the part of P that is in fact incorrect. D is nonetheless put in a position of potential peril that is not in any way lessened by P's error, and the fact that D knows of the error should not shut him out from the defence.'

There was no (separate) requirement that the accused was subject to or feared an immediate attack. The effect would be that more battered women who kill their sleeping or drunken abusers will have this defence. Clause 29(2) exempted from liability acts done immediately preparatory to the use of force such as the possession of firearms. Clause 27(7) took away the defence from one who deliberately provokes an attack; however, an accused does have the defence where he is going about his lawful business as illustrated by **Beatty v Gillbanks** (1882) 9 QBD 308, the case of the Skeleton Army. As at present there is no rule that the accused is under a duty to retreat: cl 29(4). The **Dadson** (1850) 169 ER 407 (CCR) principle is preserved by the Bill. In the words of the Law Commission:

> It follows from the requirement that the defendant be judged according to circumstances as he believes them to be that he cannot rely on circumstances unknown to him that would in fact have justified acts on his part that were unreasonable on the facts as he perceived them. . . . Citizens who react unreasonably to circumstances should not be exculpated by the accident of facts of which they were unaware.

Force to effect or assist in a lawful arrest receives separate treatment (cl 28). 'Force' in cll 27–29 is not defined. The restatement of the law of the justifiable use of force does not affect the defences of duress of circumstances or necessity. Therefore injury to a dog that is attacking one's children, and making a firebreak, will remain lawful.

Just as the defence of provocation came in for criticism for being based on the male psyche with the result that few women are afforded it because they do not react in the same way as men, so too has the defence of self-defence been criticised. The Australian Law Reform Commission in its Report No. 69, *Equality before the Law: Justice for Women*, 1994, paras 12.2–12.3 put it this way:

> What is 'reasonable' has traditionally been assessed on men's experiences of a reasonable response to the circumstances. For example, in establishing self-defence, there must be an immediate threat and a proportionate response. The typical scenario is that of an isolated incident in a public place between two strangers of relatively equal size, strength and fighting ability, that is, a 'bar-room brawl' model. . . . The 'bar-room brawl' model bears little relation to the situation of a woman who has been subjected to prolonged physical, mental and emotional abuse within her home by her male partner. In her terrorised state and usually inferior physical size and strength, her only reasonable option may be to take action some time later when it is safe for her to do so. This may be during a lull in the violence, for example, when the aggressor is asleep or incapacitated by alcohol. However, the law may construct her act as a premeditated one arising out of a long held grudge rather than as a defensive response triggered by a particular incident. For this reason it is argued that defences should be revised to reflect women's experiences of violence and acts of self-preservation.
>
> . . . Where juries and judges lack an understanding of the dynamics and effect of violence in the home, they may not see the woman's response as 'reasonable'. They may see her use of a gun or knife as excessive force in relation to the physical assaults inflicted on her by her unarmed partner . . . They may ask why she did not simply leave. This approach ignores the disempowering effect of the violence on the woman, her practical difficulties, such as where to go and how to support herself and her children, and her fear of retaliation if she were to leave, particularly where police assistance has not been adequate in the past. [footnotes omitted]

Excessive force in self-defence: the Law Commission's 2004 Report

The Law Commission in its Report No. 290, *Partial Defences to Murder*, 2004, considered whether excessive force should reduce murder to manslaughter in the same way as diminished responsibility and provocation (now loss of control) do. Currently self-defence operates as an 'all-or-nothing' defence; that is, either the accused succeeds in his defence, in which case he is acquitted, or he fails, in which case he is convicted of murder. Excessive force when some force would be reasonable in the context of the Report means that the accused is convicted of murder. This conclusion is to some degree mitigated by trial judges directing juries that they are to take all circumstances into account, including, for example, the size of the accused and victim, that they are not to use hindsight, and that where there is evidence of provocation, they should consider whether or not that defence succeeds with the effect that a verdict of voluntary manslaughter is reached.

The Commission rejected the provision of a defence of excessive force. In respect of householders who kill intruders, it considered that they could have a defence of provocation (see now the defence of loss of control discussed in Chapter 12) under the revised formula if these conditions were satisfied: if a person of ordinary tolerance and self-restraint acting in fear of serious physical violence to himself or another might have killed and the accused does kill, he will have a defence. In respect of battered adults or children who kill, fearing further abuse and not perceiving any route of escape and being aware of the mismatch in physique so that 'to respond directly and proportionately to an attack or an imminent attack will be futile and dangerous' (para 4.18), should they have a defence of self-defence if they use excessive force when, for example, their abuser is drunk or asleep? Again the Commission thought that such facts could fall within the revised definition of provocation: was the accused genuinely in fear of serious violence and might a person of ordinary tolerance and self-restraint have acted in the same or a similar way? In para. 4.29 the Commission said that the revised definition of provocation will work 'through the acknowledgement that even a person of ordinary tolerance and self-restraint might, on occasion, respond in fear by using an excessive amount of force'.

In conclusion the Law Commission was strongly of the view that there should not be a defence of excessive self-defence because in situations where that defence might arise, householders and the abused, the reformulated defence of provocation would be available. However, the Commission in its Report No. 304, *Murder, Manslaughter and Infanticide*, 2006, concluded that there should be such a defence but that since self-defence was a general defence, it would not consider it further in this Report.

The government did enact a revised provocation defence in the Coroners and Justice Act 2009 by means of the law of loss of control, which incorporates a defence of excessive force in relation to murder only (see Chapter 12), but its enactment of the law of self-defence by the Criminal Justice and Immigration Act 2008 simply put previous law into a statute with no attempt made to reform the law.

Conclusion: police, *Martin* and the ECHR

The Home Secretary announced in 1995 that, after the unsuccessful appeal of Private Lee Clegg, a Home Office group would review the law on excessive self-defence by members of the armed forces and the police. The Interdepartmental Steering Group on the Law on the Use of Lethal Force in Self-Defence or the Prevention of Crime did not come down firmly for any change in the law, including the creation of a partial defence available on a charge of murder of excessive self-defence and amendment to s 3 of the Criminal Law Act 1967 to flesh out the meaning of reasonable force, when it reported in 1996 because it favoured finer distinctions than murder or manslaughter and manslaughter or acquittal, but it rejected any difference between the armed forces and the police on the one hand and other citizens on the other. There is, however, an argument to the contrary. Experienced police marksmen should be judged against a higher standard than ordinary citizens because they are experts. Such an argument might lead to the law that members of the police force and the armed forces should have a defence only when they have made a reasonable mistake as to the amount of force. Furthermore, the use of force is a matter of political controversy, which it rarely is when force is used by private individuals. Since Parliament shows no inclination to define murder or to change the sentence for murder, any change to bring in a defence of excessive self-defence is just not going to happen.

The outcome in *Martin*, above, where a Norfolk farmer shot a burglar in the back, killing him, led to outcry in favour of the accused; listeners to the *Today* programme on Radio 4 voted the reform of self-defence as their top priority for a bill, and in 2005 the Conservatives pushed for a change to the law whereby force would be lawful unless it was 'grossly dispro-portionate', a higher threshold than 'unreasonable' or 'excessive'. Such strong feelings culminated in a bland (in the writer's view) and short Joint Statement from the Crown Prosecution Service and the Association of Chief Police Officers 'Householders and the Use of Force against Intruders', in February 2005. Among the statements are: 'So long as you only do what you honestly and instinctively believe is necessary in the heat of the moment, that would be the strongest evidence of you acting lawfully and in selfdefence [*sic*!]. This is still the case if you use something to hand as a weapon. As a general rule, the more extreme the circumstances and the fear felt, the more force you can lawfully use in self-defence' and '. . . if, for example: having knocked someone unconscious, you then decided to further hurt or kill them to punish them . . . you would be acting with very excessive and gratuitous force and could be prosecuted'. Interestingly, there is no mention of defence of property. It is suggested that the use of deadly force against burglars just because they are burglars is excessive, whether or not the European Convention on Human Rights, Article 2, prohibits killings in defence of property. For an Irish case see *DPP* v *Barnes* [2006] IECCA 165, relying in part on the right to life protected by the Irish Constitution and noting that a burglar can protect himself against force.

The European Convention on Human Rights does not permit the use of force to prevent harm to property. Therefore, a householder who killed a burglar in defence of property would not be able to rely on self-defence and the prevention of crime, unless he was also protecting himself or another. However, the Convention provides an exception to the right to life only when 'the use of force . . . is no more than absolutely necessary'. See the decision of the European Court of Human Rights in *Andronicou* v *Cyprus* (1998) 25 EHRR 491 where it was held that force had to be strictly proportionate to the threat posed by the victim. On the facts police officers were justified in using sub-machine guns in an attempt to rescue a hostage. This is a more stringent test than current English law, which speaks of 'reasonable' force (see s 76(6) of the 2008 statute, quoted above, which puts previous law into statutory form). Both statute and common law will have to be restricted to situations where only necessary force is used. The jurisprudence of the European Court of Human Rights may also lead to change. Present English law permits a defence based on mistaken belief. However, the European Court seems to look for an honest belief that is well founded ('good reason'), as it did in *McCann*, *Andronicou, Gul* and *Bubbins*. The reduction in scope of self-defence may lead to calls for the introduction of the defence of excessive self-defence.

Another distinction is that the Convention, Article 2, applies only when the victim was using 'unlawful violence'. English law applies whether the victim was using unlawful or lawful violence. One would hope that two sets of rules would not emerge depending on whether the force was lawful or not. Finally, English law permits the use of force to prevent crime but no such purpose exists in Article 2(2), and Article 2(1) is restricted to the use of force to kill whereas English law is not: it includes situations where the victim is not killed.

The Joint Parliamentary Committee on Human Rights, *Legislative Scrutiny: Fifteenth Report of Session 2007–08*, HL Paper 81/HC Paper 440, said that: 'the failure to require reasonable grounds for an "honest belief" as part of the defence risks putting the UK in breach of its positive obligation under Article 2 ECHR to ensure that its criminal law provides adequate protection for the right to life.' It is also thought that having the same law applying to ordinary citizens and 'state agents such as trained police agents' was of particular concern.

Summary

- *Mistake*: The basic rule is that mistake as to law is no defence but that Parliament may create such a defence. Mistakes of fact may provide a defence but not if they are to the strict element (one to which no *mens rea* is attached) of an offence. The mistake of fact need usually only be one honestly made but bigamy provides the exception: the mistake must be one made on reasonable grounds. For mistakes caused by intoxication, see below.

- *Intoxication*: Involuntary intoxication is a defence to all offences but is no defence where the accused nevertheless had the *mens rea* for the offence; voluntary intoxication is a defence only to offences of specific intent (e.g. murder) but not to crimes of basic intent (e.g. manslaughter); and drunken mistake is no defence to all offences including ones of specific intent. Debate rages as to the definition of 'specific intent' and the position of soporific drugs is not crystal clear. In relation to specific intent any suggested definition has a counterfactual argument, for example if a specific intent offence is one which involves a 'purposive element', why is rape a basic intent offence?; if specific intent means crimes which can be committed only intentionally (and not either intentionally or recklessly), why when malice aforethought in murder was defined wider than it is now because it included foresight of a highly probable consequence, was murder still a specific intent offence? While the law is not pellucid, it seems to be that a person does not have a defence of intoxication if she or he knew that soporific drugs would make her or him aggressive or violent.

- *Self-defence and the prevention of crime*: Section 3 of the Criminal Law Act 1967 provides a defence to any offence where the accused uses reasonable force to prevent a crime; where that defence is not available, the common law provides a defence, self-defence, to all offences subject again to the force being reasonable. For example, if a child under 10 is proposing to kill the accused's child, and the accused kills the threatener, there is no crime to prevent because a child under 10 cannot be guilty of any offence; however, the common law steps in to provide a defence. For both defences the force used must be reasonable; that is, it must be necessary and proportionate. Excessive force does not provide a defence. If the accused honestly believes that he or she is under attack or others are, the defences apply on the facts as the accused believes to exist. If the accused's mistake is, however, occasioned by alcohol, there is no defence. These rules are now encapsulated in, but not altered by, the Criminal Justice and Immigration Act 2008.

  It should be noted that 'self-defence' is something of a misnomer because it applies to the defence of self, others and property.

343

References

Reports

Australian Law Reform Commission Report no. 69, *Equality before the Law: Justice for Women* (1994)

Criminal Law Revision Committee 14th Report, *Offences against the Person*, Cmnd 7844 (1980)

Home Office Consultation Document, *Violence: Reforming the Offences Against the Person Act 1861* (1998)

Interdepartmental Steering Group on the Law on the Use of Lethal Force in Self-Defence or the Prevention of Crime (1995)

Joint Committee on Human Rights, *Legislative Scrutiny: Fifteenth Report of Session 2007–08*, HL Paper 81/HC Paper 440 (2008)

Law Commission Consultation Paper no. 127, *Intoxication and Criminal Liability* (1993)

Law Commission Policy Paper, *Consent in Sex Offences* (2000)

Law Commission Report no. 177, *A Criminal Code for England and Wales* (1989)

Law Commission Report no. 218, *Legislating the Criminal Code – Offences against the Person and General Principles* (1993)

Law Commission Report no. 229, *Legislating the Criminal Code: Intoxication and Criminal Liability* (1995)

Law Commission Report no. 290, *Partial Defences to Murder* (2004)

Law Commission Report no. 304, *Murder, Manslaughter and Infanticide* (2006)

Law Commission Report no. 314, *Intoxication and Criminal Liability* (2009)

Law Reform Commission of Ireland Report no. 51, *Intoxication* (1995)

Model Penal Code (US) (1962)

Report of the Committee on Mentally Abnormal Offenders (Butler), Cmnd 6244 (1975)

Scottish Law Commission Discussion Paper no. 122, *Insanity and Diminished Responsibility* (2003)

Books

Bentham, J. *An Introduction to the Principles of Morals and Legislation* (Methuen, 1932) (first published 1789)

Bishop's Criminal Law Vol. 1, 9th edn (Little, Brown & Co., 1923)

Clarkson, C.M.V. *Understanding Criminal Law*, 4th edn (Thomson, 2005)

Reed, A. and Fitzpatrick, B. *Criminal Law*, 4th edn (Sweet & Maxwell, 2010)

Seago, P. *Criminal Law*, 4th edn (Sweet & Maxwell, 1994)

Journals

Brett, P. 'Mistake of law as a criminal defence' (1966) 5 Melb ULR 179

Goode, M. 'Some thoughts on the present state of the "defence" of intoxication' (1984) 8 Crim LJ 104

Healy, P. '*R v Bernard*: difficulties with "voluntary intoxication"' (1990) 35 McGill LJ 610

Horder, J. 'Self-defence, necessity and duress: understanding the relationship' (1998) 11 *Canadian Journal of Law and Jurisprudence* 143

Smith, G. 'Footnote to *O'Connor*'s case' (1981) 5 Crim LJ 270

Sullivan, G.R. 'Involuntary intoxication and beyond' [1994] Crim LR 272

Further reading

Amirthalingam, K. 'Ignorance of law, criminal culpability and moral innocence: Striking a balance between blame and excuse' [2002] *Singapore Journal of Legal Studies* 302

Ashworth, A. 'Testing fidelity to legal values: official involvement in criminal justice' (2000) 63 MLR 63

Ashworth, A. 'Ignorance of the criminal law, and duties to avoid it' (2011) 74 MLR 1

Ashworth, A. Case comment on *Keane* [2011] Crim LR 393

Ayyildiz, E. 'When battered women's syndrome does not go far enough: the battered woman as vigilante' (1995) 4 Am U J Gender & L 141

Boyle, C. 'The battered wife syndrome and self-defence' (1990) 9 *Canadian Journal of Family Law* 171

Callaghan, A.R. 'Will the "real" battered woman please stand up?' (1994) 3 Am U J Gender & L 117

Child, J. 'Drink, drugs and law reform: a review of Law Commission Report No. 314' [2009] Crim LR 488

Clark, M. 'Self-defence against the innocent' (2000) 17 J of Applied Phil 145

Crosby, C. 'Culpability, *Kingston* and the Law Commission' (2010) 74 JCL 434

Dennis, I. 'What should be done about the law of self-defence?' [2000] Crim LR 417

Dimock, S. 'The responsibility of intoxicated offenders' (2009) 43 J Value Inquiry 339

Faigman, D.L. and Wright, A.J. 'The battered woman syndrome in the age of science' (1997) 39 Ariz LR 67

Gardner, S. 'The importance of *Majewski*' (1994) 14 OJLS 279

Getzler, J. 'Use of force in protecting property' (2006) Theoretic Inquiries L131

Gough, S. 'Intoxication and criminal liability' (1996) 112 LQR 335

Gough, S. 'Surviving without *Majewski*' [2000] Crim LR 719

Harlow, C. 'Self-defence: public right or private privilege' [1974] Crim LR 528

Horder, J. 'Sobering up: the Law Commission on criminal intoxication' (1995) 58 MLR 534

Husak, H. 'Intoxication and culpability' (2012) 6 Crim and Philos 363

Jefferson, M. 'Householders and the use of force against intruders' (2005) 69 JCL 405

Kaufman, W.R.P. 'Self-defense, imminence, and the battered woman' (2007) 10 New Crim L Rev 342

Lanham, D. 'Offensive weapons and self-defence' [2005] Crim LR 85

Leverick, F. 'Is English self-defence law incompatible with Article 2 of the ECHR?' [2002] Crim LR 347

Leverick, F. 'The use of force in public or private defence and Article 2' [2002] Crim LR 963

Leverick, F. *Killing in Self-Defence* (Oxford University Press, 2006)

Leverick, F. 'Defending self-defence' (2007) 27 OJLS 563

McAuley, F. 'The grammar of mistake in criminal law' (1996) xxxi *Irish Jurist* 56

McCord, D. 'The English and American history of voluntary intoxication to negate *mens rea*' (1990) 11 JLH 372

Martinson, D. *et al*. '*Lavallee* v *R* 1 SCR 852 – the Supreme Court of Canada addresses the issue of gender bias in the court: women and self-defence' (1991) 25 UBCLR 23

Norrie, A. 'Killing in self-defence' (book review of Leverick, above) (2009) 12 New Crim LR 326

O'Leary, J. 'Lament for the intoxication defence' (1997) 48 NILQ 152

Orchard, G. 'Surviving without *Majewski*: a view from down under' [1993] Crim LR 426

Ormerod, D. 'Voluntary intoxication: whether voluntary intoxication available on a charge of sexual assault' [2007] Crim LR 654

Parsons, S. and Andoh, B. 'Private defence and public defence in the criminal law and the law of tort – A comparison' (2012) 76 JCL 22

Polsby, D.D. 'Reflections on violence, guns and the defensive use of reasonable force' (1986) 49 L & CP 89

Rogers, J. 'Justifying the use of firearms by policemen and soldiers' (1998) 18 LS 486

Rosman, J.B. 'The battered woman syndrome in Florida: junk science or admissible evidence?' (2003) 15 St Thomas L Rev 107

Sangero, B. *Self-defence in Criminal Law* (Hart Publishing, 2006)

Segev, R. 'Justification, rationality and mistake' (2006) 25 *Law and Philosophy* 31

Shaffer, M. 'The battered woman syndrome revisited' (1997) 47 UTLJ 1

Simester, A.P. 'Intoxication is never a defence' [2009] Crim LR 3

Slater, J. 'Making sense of self-defence' (1996) 5 Nott LJ 140

Smith, J.C. 'The use of force in public or private defence and Article 2' [2002] Crim LR 958

Spencer, J.R. 'Drunken defence' [2006] CLJ 267

Uniacke, S. 'Proportionality and self-defense' (2011) 30 Law & Phil 253

Virgo, G. 'Reconciling principle and policy' [1993] Crim LR 415

Wallerstein, S. 'Justifying the right to self-defense: a theory of forced consequences' (2005) 91 Virg LR 999

White, S. 'Offences of basic and specific intent' [1989] Crim LR 271

Williams, R. 'Voluntary intoxication, sexual assault and the future of *Majewski*' [2007] CLJ 260

Yeo, S. 'Killing in defence of property' [2000] NLJ 730

Yeo, S. 'Revisiting excessive self-defence' (2000) 12 *Current Issues in Criminal Justice* 39

For an essay, see J. Horder in A.P. Simester and S. Shute (eds.), *Criminal Law: Doctrines of the General Part* (Oxford University Press, 2002), Chapter 12.

For a full-length study of self-defence, see S. Uniacke, *Permissible Killing: The Self-Defence Justification of Homicide* (Cambridge University Press, 1996). The principal English survey of excuses is J. Horder, *Excusing Crime* (Oxford University Press, 2003).

For Commonwealth reform proposals, see Tasmania Law Reform Institute, *Intoxication and Criminal Responsibility*, Issues Paper no. 7 (2005) and the Final Report no. 7 of the same name (2006), the principal recommendation being that intoxication should be relevant to all mental elements.

For a recent Irish approach, see Law Reform Commission, Commission Paper No. 41, *Legitimate Defence*, 2006.

For US law, which in general is similar to the law of intoxication in England and Wales, see M. Keiter, 'Just say no excuse' (1997) 87 JCL & Crim 482.

Visit **www.mylawchamber.co.uk** to access tools to help
you develop and test your knowledge of criminal law,
including interactive multiple choice questions, practice
exam questions with guidance, annotated weblinks,
glossary flashcards, legal newsfeed and legal updates.

Use Case Navigator to read in full some of the key cases referenced
in this chapter with commentary and questions:

DPP v Majewski [1976] UKHL 2
R v G and Another [2003] UKHL 50
R v Kingston [1995] 2 AC 355 (HL)
R v Williams (Gladstone) [1987] 3 All ER 411 (CA)

9

Defences of mental disorder

After reading this chapter you will understand and be able to critique:

- the definition and application of the defence of unfitness to plead
- the definition and application of the defence of insanity
- the definition and application of the defence of diminished responsibility
- the definition and application of the defence of automatism

Introduction

The accused does not necessarily have a defence if he is mentally disturbed through schizophrenia, paranoia, dementia or a myriad of other upsets affecting the mind. To have a defence the defendant must fall within one of the recognised excuses: insanity, diminished responsibility, automatism. Each of these defences has a different definition from the others including burden of proof and outcome. They should not be confused. Moreover, the defences are legal ones: they should not be confused with medical diagnosis.

These defences, however, may overlap. When they do, the accused will be seeking the defence which is most favourable to him. For example, he will be acquitted on the grounds of automatism; however, if he successfully pleads insanity, until 1991 he would, under the Criminal Procedure (Insanity) Act 1964, s 5, be detained in a hospital until the Home Secretary approved his release ('hospital order with restrictions'). This provision meant that he would be detained for a period longer than the norm for murderers, the 'life' sentence now being about 15 years' imprisonment plus the threat of recall. The result may have been that the accused would be kept longer away from the public if he was acquitted on the grounds of insanity than if he were guilty of murder. This way of thinking applies with even greater force to lesser offences. The effect is that the accused may be seeking to avoid succeeding on the defence! The accused may want to go to prison where he will not receive treatment for his ills. The interests of society, however, demand that mentally imbalanced persons who are 'dangerous' should be restrained and if possible treated. One major problem is to determine which people should be detained in hospital, which in prison, and which released. The law does not at present in all cases draw the most appropriate distinctions, as we shall see. The Criminal Procedure (Insanity and Unfitness to Plead) Act 1991 gives the judge discretion as to sentence. The outcome could be an absolute discharge, except for murder where the sentence must be a hospital order with restrictions on discharge.

Two principles may collide: individual responsibility for crime and the protection of society. A disordered person may not have the free will to control his actions and cannot be reformed by punishment. The law's commands are addressed to those who have the capacity to reason.

This chapter investigates mental aberration at the time of the offence or, in the case of unfitness to plead, at the time of trial. There are other ways of dealing with offenders, for example a person guilty of manslaughter may be given a hospital order under s 37 of the Mental Health Act 1983, if such is the most suitable way of disposing of his case.

Unfitness to plead

To stand trial the accused must be:

> . . . of sufficient intellect to comprehend the course of the proceedings in the trial so as to make a proper defence, to challenge a juror to whom he might wish to object and comprehend the details of the evidence.

So said Alderson B in *Pritchard* (1836) 173 ER 135, a case involving a deaf mute. This case is an illustration that the defence of **unfitness to plead** is available not just to the mentally incapable but also to others who cannot follow the proceedings. However, it must be stressed that the accused may be mentally ill (e.g. suffering from delusions) but still fit to stand trial according to the rules in *Pritchard*: see for example *Moyle* [2008] EWCA Crim 3059 (paranoid schizophrenic who believed that he would be convicted of witchcraft and that the court and jury were under Satan's influence, but still fit to plead because he could, for example, instruct lawyers and follow proceedings). This test is the one still used as *Patel*, unreported, 7 August 1991 (CA), *M* [2003] EWCA Crim 3452, *Norman* [2008] EWCA Crim 810, and *Erskine* [2009] EWCA Crim 1425 demonstrate. The accused must also be able to plead to the indictment. He must be able to instruct counsel.

A modern statement of the rule was given by Otton LJ in *Friend* [1997] 2 All ER 1012: 'The test of unfitness is whether the accused will be able to comprehend the course of the proceedings so as to make a proper defence. Whether he can understand and reply rationally to the indictment is obviously a relevant factor, but the jury must also consider whether he would be able to exercise his right to challenge juries, understand the details of the evidence as it is given, instruct his legal advisers and give evidence himself if he so desires.' *M* provides a handy summary: the accused is unfit to plead if any of the following is beyond his capability:

(1) understanding the charges;
(2) deciding whether to plead guilty or not;
(3) exercising his right to challenge jurors;
(4) instructing solicitors and counsel;
(5) following the course of proceedings;
(6) giving evidence in his own defence.

It is, however, irrelevant that the accused has a low mental age: *SC v UK* [2005] 1 FCR 347 (ECHR) (boy of 11 with the intellectual capacity of a six- or eight-year-old). The Court said: 'The defendant should be able to follow what is said by prosecution witnesses and, if represented, to explain to his own lawyers his version of events, point out any statements with which he disagrees and make them aware of any facts which should be put forward in his defence.' There is a breach of Article 6(1) of the European Convention on Human Rights in relation to children if these criteria are not met.

The conditions are generalisable. It is inhuman to try people who cannot understand anything of a trial, and it would reflect badly on the law if such persons were tried. The fact that he acts abnormally and cannot act in his own best interests is irrelevant, as is the fact that he can communicate with others on non-legal matters. Before 1992, if he could not perform these tasks, he was under the Criminal Procedure (Insanity) Act 1964 found unfit to plead at a Crown Court (i.e. this procedure does not apply to summary trial) by a specially empanelled jury (s 4(4)) and was hospitalised at a place specified by the Home Secretary (s 5(1)) for an indefinite period, a rather severe restriction when the charge was a petty one. The post-1991 procedure, which specifically retained the specially empanelled jury, was amended by the Domestic Violence Crime and Victims Act 2004, s 22, which placed the duty of determining fitness to plead on the judge alone.

The procedure remains inapplicable to summary trials, as does the whole law of unfitness to plead. Magistrates instead have the power to make a hospital order. There is no jurisdiction to commit to the Crown Court for a jury to rule on fitness to stand trial.

It should be noted that the courts are becoming adept at using devices such as the use of intermediaries to help defendants who may be unfit to plead. Such devices have received the approval of the Court of Appeal: **Walls** [2011] EWCA Crim 443.

The issue may be raised by the defendant, prosecution or judge. Where the accused raises the issue, the burden of proof is on him on the balance of probabilities: **Podola** [1960] 1 QB 325 (CCA). This has been criticised on the ground that when the accused pleads unfitness to plead he is simply saying that the prosecution cannot prove all the elements of the crime alleged and it is for the prosecution to do so beyond reasonable doubt. If, however, the issue is raised by the prosecution, or presumably if it is raised by the judge, the burden is on the prosecution to show that the defendant is unfit beyond reasonable doubt: **Robertson** [1968] 1 WLR 1767 (CA). The judge could postpone the issue of unfitness to plead until the close of the prosecution case, so allowing the accused to submit that there was no case to answer. This discretion should be exercised if there is a decent chance that the prosecution case will not convince.

Empirical research

R.D. Mackay examined the statistics for 1979–89 in 'The decline of disability in relation to the trial' [1991] Crim LR 87. There were 229 findings of unfitness to plead. Most of the accused were male, and most were aged between 20 and 39; 71 per cent had criminal records and 81 per cent had a psychiatric history. The number of trials for unfitness per year declined by half from the early to late 1980s (e.g. 28 in 1981, 13 in 1988). Offences against the person accounted for almost a quarter. Some defendants were back for up to their fourth unfitness-to-plead determination. Contrary to expectation the plea did not always involve serious crimes such as rape and murder. 'This was found to be particularly true of Theft Act offences which in many cases were accounted for by destitute and mentally ill defendants being unable to pay for meals or services' (at 90). A similar phrase occurs in his book (Mackay, *Mental Condition Defences in the Criminal Law* (Clarendon, 1995) 223). In 2001 there were 76 successful pleas.

Over half of the accused were diagnosed as schizophrenic, with a small number suffering from other mental illnesses such as dementia and psychosis. The Court of Criminal

Appeal in *Podola*, above, held that hysterical amnesia was not within the definition of unfitness to plead because the accused was normal at the time of the hearing, but three of the defendants in the sample were suffering from amnesia. Moreover, the criteria in *Pritchard* were not always fulfilled: each aspect seems to be treated individually, not cumulatively, with emphasis being placed on the ability to instruct a lawyer and follow proceedings.

A second study by D. Grubin for 1975–88 found 285 persons dealt with under the unfitness to plead provisions. About one-quarter of the crimes alleged were minor, such as shoplifting. He noted that as a result of Home Office policy about 15 per cent of those found unfit were later tried in the early years of the survey but in the later years the percentage went up to 60 per cent ('Unfit to plead in England and Wales 1976–88: A survey' (1991) 158 BJ Psych 540). He considered that the law worked only because psychiatrists and judges sometimes disregard *Pritchard*. The effect, however, is arbitrary: some persons suffering from the same disorder are found unfit, some are found fit ('What constitutes fitness to plead?' [1993] Crim LR 748). This finding is worrying.

A third survey published in 'An upturn in unfitness to plead?' [2000] Crim LR 532 by R.D. Mackay and Gerry Kearns found that in the five years after the coming into force of the 1991 Act the number of successful pleas of unfitness to plead had doubled. The largest proportion of those who were successful comprised schizophrenics. Those suffering from dementia, psychosis, brain damage and depressive states featured among the diagnostic groups. Two persons had 'deafness/communication difficulties'. Some 90 per cent of those found unfit to plead were male.

Criminal Procedure (Insanity and Unfitness to Plead) Act 1991

This Act, the first to be promoted by the Law Society, was directed at abolishing the mandatory commitment to a psychiatric hospital even though the accused had not been convicted of an offence. The procedure under the Act, as amended by the Domestic Violence, Crime and Victims Act 2004, is:

(a) A judge decides whether the accused is unfit to plead: s 4A of the Criminal Procedure (Insanity) Act 1964 as amended. The judge must hear two doctors, one of whom was approved by the Home Secretary as experienced in this field, before so determining. If, however, she decides that he is fit to plead, there is no need to hear the medical evidence: *Ghulam* [2010] 1 WLR 891 (CA). If an accused previously unfit to plead becomes in the opinion of the judge after a hearing fit to plead, he is arraigned in the normal way: *Hasani* v *Blackfriars Crown Court* [2006] 1 WLR 1992 (DC).

(b) If the judge determines that the accused was unfit on his arraignment a jury decides whether he committed the *actus reus* of the offence. Where the issue falls for consideration after arraignment it may be tried by the same or a different jury. This process is sometimes known as 'trial of the facts'. The prosecution must prove that the accused committed the *actus reus* beyond reasonable doubt. Section 4A(2) of the Criminal Procedure (Insanity) Act 1964, as inserted by the 1991 Act, does not say this expressly but it is consistent with criminal law principles. If the accused did not do the act alleged, there is no reason to subject him to the rigours of the criminal law. There is support in *Attorney-General's Reference (No. 3 of 1998)* [1999] 2 Cr App R 214 (CA) for the view that any defence, such as prevention of crime, must be considered by the jury. The mental element would not be considered according to the generally accepted view, but the Court of Appeal in *Egan* [1997] Crim LR 225 said that the *mens rea* must be proved too, and counsel did not argue the point. *Egan* had some support, for the Butler Committee on Mentally Abnormal Offenders referred to proof of the mental state (Cmnd 6244, 1975, para. 10.24).

The Court of Appeal held in *Attorney-General's Reference (No. 3 of 1998)* that *Egan* was wrongly decided. The determination was in the context of insanity where the jury has to say whether the accused 'did the act or made the omission charged' (Trial of Lunatics Act 1883, s 2). What was said about unfitness to plead was *obiter*, but the court stated that *Egan* was decided *per incuriam*. If the court was wrong on this point, *Egan* was restricted to unfitness to plead. The House of Lords ruled in *Antoine* [2001] 1 AC 340 that *Egan* was incorrect even in relation to unfitness to plead. *Antoine* also held that 'act' in s 4A(2) of the 1964 Act includes complete defences such as self-defence (it is often said that self-defence negates the *actus reus*). It left open the position as to provocation (now the defence of loss of control). However, in *Grant* [2002] 1 Cr App R 528 (CA) it was held that provocation, which depends on the accused's state of mind, does not fall within s 4A. Therefore, that defence (now loss of control) cannot be raised at this stage. (If the issue of unfitness to plead arises during the trial, the same jury which determined fitness determines whether the accused performed the *actus reus*.) If the jury finds that the accused did not commit the *actus reus*, he is acquitted. The Court of Appeal laid down these steps in *O'Donnell* [1996] 1 Cr App R 286. There is one situation where *mens rea* is investigated and that is where the accused is charged as an accomplice. He will have to know of the acts of the principal before it can be said that he did 'the act or omission charged': *Martin* [2003] EWCA Crim 357.

Courts continue to struggle with the phrase 'the act . . . charged . . . as the offence'. For example, it was held in *B* [2012] EWCA Crim 770 that in the crime of voyeurism contrary to s 67(1) of the Sexual Offences Act 2003 that the 'act' included 'the purpose of obtaining sexual gratification', which is very much a state of mind. It was this state of mind which made the 'act' of voyeurism 'injurious'. Deliberately observing someone doing an act in public did not capture the essence of the crime.

After the 1991 Act, which in turn has been amended, the judge must make one of these orders: a hospital order, a supervision order or an absolute discharge, but when the charge is murder, the judge must make a hospital order only, and in that event the order is without limit of time. The same law applies to the defence of insanity, discussed below. The Domestic Violence, Crime and Victims Act 2004 provides that such hospitalisation may take place only when the medical evidence as to the accused's mental state justifies a hospital order. The same applies to a restriction order. (After the 1991 Act the likelihood is that persons who would otherwise have pleaded unfitness to plead or insanity on a charge of murder are now opting for diminished responsibility as the defence because, if successful, they may receive a determinate sentence.)

The Home Secretary may (not must) remit for trial when the accused has recovered. On conviction all the usual sentences including probation are available. Because of the broader range of disposal options, it is likely that more people will plead unfitness to plead and insanity than previously, and this seems to be happening. With this broadened range of sentences comes a new sentence of a supervision and treatment order, whereby a person found insane can be placed under the supervision of a social worker or probation officer for not more than two years and subject to medical treatment. The possibility of a guardianship order was abolished by the 2004 Act. Research is demonstrating that judges are alert to the sentencing options under the 1991 Act. If the accused has been found unfit to plead, the trial even for murder ends. Therefore, an accused found unfit to plead cannot use the defence of diminished responsibility to avoid the mandatory commitment for murder on a successful plea of unfitness to plead: *Antoine*.

It may be thought that a trial on the facts breaches Article 6 of the European Convention on Human Rights. Article 6 guarantees the right to a fair trial. It would seem not to be a fair trial if the accused cannot fully participate in it, as occurs when he cannot understand the charges against him. As the European Court of Human Rights held in *Winterwerp* v *The Netherlands* (1979) 2 EHRR 387 the person who is of unsound mind must not be deprived of the right to a fair trial, including the right to defend oneself and the right 'to be informed . . . in a language which he understands and in detail, of the nature and cause of the accusation against him'. However, the House of Lords held in *H* [2003] 1 WLR 411 that there was no incompatibility between s 4A and Article 6, because the determination of fitness to plead does not involve a criminal trial with the possibility of punishment: instead the trial is to protect the public. For comment on *H* and its compatibility with Strasbourg jurisprudence see Andrew Ashworth in his case comment on *H* [2003] Crim LR 818. It is certainly possible that the criteria for assessing unfitness to plead do not conflict with Article 6, which relates in this respect to criminal law trials. See also the discussion of *Grant* below in relation to Article 5(1).

Appeal lies in both instances to the Court of Appeal under the Criminal Appeal Act 1968. If the appeal is allowed, an acquittal is recorded. There is no power to order a retrial.

Criticism

D. Grubin wrote in 'What constitutes fitness to plead?' [1993] Crim LR 748 at 755: '[T]here is a story, perhaps apocryphal, of a High Court judge who observed that if comprehension of court proceedings was a prerequisite for participation in a trial, then most of those in court, including members of the legal profession, would be considered unfit to plead.'

(a) In the words of the Butler Committee, *Report of the Committee on Mentally Abnormal Offenders*, Cmnd 6244, 1975, para. 10.18:

> It is not in the interests of the defendant to seek the protection of a disability plea unless the charge is very serious. If the trial went ahead he might be acquitted altogether.

(b) The definition in *Pritchard* focuses on the accused's intellectual ability at quite a low level. It does not take into account whether he possesses an understanding of the consequences of conviction, or even why he is on trial. It is arguable that the trial is unfair if he cannot grasp the significance of the proceedings.

(c) There is no statutory definition of unfitness to plead.

(d) The criterion of being able to instruct counsel, which was not found in *Pritchard* but has come to be accepted, should be included.

(e) The definition of unfitness to plead covers deaf mutes, as *Pritchard* illustrates. This is inconsistent with Article 5 of the European Convention on Human Rights. The European Court in *Winterwerp* demanded 'objective medical expertise' before a person could be detained as being 'of unsound mind', but deaf mutes are not of unsound mind as a matter of objective medical expertise. The court emphasised that the term 'of unsound mind' could not be given a definitive interpretation because its meaning is 'continually evolving as research in psychiatry progresses . . .'.

(f) If the accused is found to have committed the act but the conviction is for whatever reason overruled, no retrial may be ordered: *Norman* [2008] EWCA Crim 1810. Thomas LJ said that: '. . . serious public concern could arise where this court considered a verdict unsafe and was compelled to enter an acquittal, but nothing further could be done. We would hope that Parliament might give consideration to this lacuna in the statutory provisions and consider granting this court power to order a re-trial of the issue as whether the defendant did the act with which he is charged.' No government has heeded this call.

Reform

The Law Commission issued Consultation Paper No. 197 *Unfitness to Plead* in 2010. This Paper is part of the Commission's treatment of what may be called mental condition defences, which in turn forms part of the investigation of both civil and criminal law surrounding mentally vulnerable people. The defence of diminished responsibility was amended by the Coroners and Justice Act 2009, which from late 2010 substituted a revised definition into the Homicide Act 1957. Insanity is on the Commission's list. Unfitness to plead forms the sole body of law dealt with in this substantial Paper. There is a helpful and informative statistical analysis of unfitness to plead in Appendix C. This Appendix, written by Professor Ronnie Mackay, updates the articles by him on this topic. There is also a perceptive and hard-hitting passage (para. 8.56ff) on the defence of infancy rather hidden in the midst of unfitness to plead. While the Paper is lengthy, its recommendations are (fortunately) not. Please remember that this area of law deals with someone who is 'insane' at the time of the trial. Someone who is insane at the time of the offence but fit to plead at the time of the trial may have the defence of insanity. The Commission issued a 'Scoping Paper', *Insanity and Automatism*, in summer 2012 and the call for evidence ended in autumn 2012.

Why is reform needed?

The law stems from *Pritchard* (1836) 173 ER 135 as expanded in later common law authorities. The criteria are the abilities to:

- understand the proceedings at trial so as to be able to advance a proper defence;
- understand the gist of the evidence;
- give instructions to legal advisers; and
- 'plead with understanding to the indictment', as para. 2.49 puts it.

That law is based on outdated psychiatry, excludes other trial elements such as the ability to give evidence (for a summary of the research evidence underpinning criticism of the current test, see para. 2.65), and is not in line with other aspects of the law found in places such as the Mental Health Act 1983 as amended and the Mental Capacity Act 2005 (see in particular para. 3.46). 'The principal problem with *Pritchard* is that it represents a determination to focus on the intellectual abilities of the accused as opposed to his or her capacity to make decisions' (para. 2.69). For example, someone who suffers from delusions may still be fit to plead despite the severity of her mental illness; however, that mental illness does severely impair the ability to make decisions. In other words, the emphasis at present is on the intellectual ability to understand but the law should concentrate on the ability to do something, such as taking part in the trial by making a specific decision on a specific point.

Therefore, the test should relate to the ability to *participate* in the trial. The procedure for finding unfitness to plead has been amended in a piecemeal fashion by Parliament, most recently by the Domestic Violence, Crime and Victims Act 2004, but at no point has the substantive definition been changed. Case law on the European Convention on Human Rights, Article 6, demands that a person on trial is able to take an active part in the proceedings. That position is not attained by current law, which permits people to be tried who should not be, because the **Pritchard** criteria do not lead to the exclusion from the trial process of all persons who should be excluded. This is amply backed up by figures quoted by the Commission including that over 3,000 people found guilty each year have to be immediately transferred from prison to the NHS!

What is proposed?

The Commission wishes to reflect in the law the basis of the defence, namely that a person being tried should be able to understand why she is being tried (including being able to put forward any defence she may have) and if found guilty why she is being punished: otherwise a trial is a travesty of justice; and it proposes to change the definition to one based on decision-making reasoning supplemented by special measures such as diagrams, other visual aids, and simple language designed to assist the accused. The term used by the Commission is 'decision making capacity', defined as the ability to make the various decisions demanded of her during the trial. The test's application will therefore vary depending on the level of complexity of the case but, as stated, there may be special measures which assist the accused to understand the nature of the process. There will be no requirement that the decision made is a sensible one: the test is one of process, not of content. This proposed test of the ability to make decisions in respect of matters which arise during trial is grounded in psychiatric research, unlike the current test.

As well as redefining the legal test for unfitness to plead, the Commission proposes to revise the procedure outlined on pp 000–00 of this book ('trial of the facts': s 4A of the Criminal Procedure (Insanity) Act 1964, as inserted by the Criminal Procedure (Insanity and Unfitness to Plead) Act 1991, as amended by the 2004 statute mentioned above). The special verdict of unfitness to plead would be retained.

For a comment on the Consultation Paper see H. Howard, 'Unfitness to plead and the vulnerable defendant: An examination of the Law Commission's proposals for a new capacity test' (2011) 75 JCL 194. The Law Reform Committee of the Bar Council and the Criminal Bar Association of England and Wales have jointly produced a paper *Unfitness to Plead: A response to Law Commission C.P. 197*, 2011, which contains criticisms of the proposals.

Mental Health Act 1983, ss 47–48

There is a second way in which the Home Secretary can order an accused to be detained in a hospital. The power is found in the Mental Health Act 1983, ss 47–48 as amended, and is available only if the Home Secretary thinks it expedient to send a person who is committed in custody for trial to a hospital in the public interest. This order is called a 'transfer direction'. He must be satisfied by reports from two or more medical practitioners that the accused is suffering from mental illness or severe mental impairment and the accused must be in urgent need of treatment. Section 1(1) of the 1983 Act defines the latter term as:

> A state of arrested or incomplete development of mind which includes severe impairment of intelligence and social functioning and is associated with abnormally aggressive or seriously irresponsible conduct . . .

The accused is remitted for trial when he has recovered. It should be noted that this definition is by no means the same as that of insanity. A person can fall within s (1) but still not have the defence of insanity.

The 1983 Act applies where the accused is committed in custody for trial. Unfitness to plead arises when he is brought up for trial.

Insanity

In the defence of **insanity** (which applies only in the Crown Court; in a magistrates' court insanity results in a total acquittal, not a verdict of 'not guilty by reason of insanity', though there exist post-acquittal procedures) the accused was insane at the time of the offence but is fit to plead at the time of the trial. It is not often raised today. For example, there were two successful pleas in 1974, none in 1988, one in 1990, 1992 and 11 in 1996. Comparable figures for the companion defence of diminished responsibility (as defined in its original incarnation) were 78 in 1978 and 50 in 1988. Figures for the revised post-2010 definition of diminished responsibility are not yet available. It is suggested that many more people are legally insane than these figures suggest. Reasons why insanity is rarely used include:

(a) The accused is contending that he was insane, but now is sane: the defence may look hard to prove to a jury.

(b) Some people who formerly might have used this defence are now charged with infanticide or have the defence of diminished responsibility where the charge is one of murder. For example, in *Tickell* (1958) *The Times*, 24 January, the accused, a schizophrenic, successfully pleaded diminished responsibility but was sentenced to life imprisonment. Before the defence was instituted, he would have had a defence of insanity.

(c) If the punishment is less than life imprisonment it is better for the accused to spend time in prison for a few years than to go to a psychiatric hospital for a longer time. Therefore, if the defence realises that the judge is going to rule that the defence is one of insanity, it is better for the accused to plead guilty than to be acquitted on the grounds of insanity. The effect may be that the public are not protected. Doctors may believe the accused to be legally insane but knowing the consequences of a verdict of insanity, may not tell the court of their view. Moreover, the accused may succeed on diminished responsibility when the argument for it may not be very strong, in order to avoid the life sentence for murder.

In practice, therefore, insanity is not important in terms of numbers, but it bulks large in lawyerly writing because of the need to distinguish insanity (where the outcome may be that the accused is sent to a secure hospital) and automatism (where the outcome is a complete acquittal). The insane person was detained until the Home Secretary or a Mental Health Review Tribunal ordered release. Some were released swiftly, some were not: R.D. Mackay 'Fact and fiction about the insanity defence' [1990] Crim LR 247. The Criminal Procedure (Insanity and Unfitness to Plead) Act 1991 gives the judge the same powers of disposal as he has when the accused is found unfit to plead (see above). As with unfitness to plead, no hospital or restriction order may be made except when medical evidence justifies such an order. The possibility of a guardianship order, supervision and treatment order or absolute discharge makes insanity a more attractive plea than previously. The new methods of disposal undermine the argument in (c) above.

The definition of insanity is not laid down by statute but has to be gathered from the cases. The law was laid down in 1843 and according to the Lords in *Sullivan* [1984] AC 156 it is not necessary to go further back. Lord Diplock in that case said that the law on insanity was 'to protect society against recurrence of the dangerous conduct'. He argued that the purpose of the test for insanity was to identify the dangerous. Unfortunately he did not explain why on that test epileptics were dangerous but some diabetics not. The result in *Sullivan* is not affected by the 1991 Act.

The discussion below is concerned with insanity pleas in the Crown Court. Insanity pleas in the magistrates' courts bear the same definition but the outcome is a complete acquittal, but is subject to a hospital or guardianship order made under the Mental Health Act 1983, s 37(3), if the offence is one which may lead to imprisonment, in order to protect the public or the accused himself.

Evidence of mental condition may also be used elsewhere in the criminal law. For example, a person who has a mental illness may not intend to kill or be reckless as to killing, whereas a person lacking that illness may well be found to have intended or been reckless as to that consequence. The distinction is there because intent and recklessness both bear a subjective meaning: what did this accused intend? What did this accused foresee? Similarly, mental conditions may explain why the accused did as she did. In the terrorism case of *G* [2009] UKHL 13 Lord Rodger said: 'For example, if someone says that he had found a disk on a train and intended to take it to the police but forgot, in deciding whether to believe the defendant and to accept his excuse as reasonable, the jury might well take into account the fact that he was suffering from a condition which tended to make for memory lapses.' On the facts the accused was a paranoid schizophrenic and was insane within the *M'Naghten* Rules, discussed below, but nevertheless he did not have a defence of reasonable excuse to a charge of possessing information likely to be of use to a person committing or preparing an act of terrorism contrary to s 58 of the Terrorism Act 2000: his illness did not make it reasonable for him to acquire such information. His insanity could, however, be considered when determining the sentence.

The test for insanity

Example

How can sleepwalking/epilepsy be insanity? Insanity is a defence to all offences, provided, according to the *M'Naghten* Rules:

the accused had a 'disease of the mind' (the author suggests thinking of 'disease' as being 'dis-ease', a lack of ease);

the disease of the mind causes a 'defect of reason'; and

EITHER the accused did not know the 'nature and quality' of his act, OR he did not know that what he had done was (legally) 'wrong'.

A somnambulist or epileptic suffers from a disease of the mind: see especially *Sullivan* [1984] AC 156 (HL) and *Burgess* [1991] 2 QB 425 (CA) respectively. He has, secondly, a 'defect of reason', that is, he is deprived of the powers of rational thought (temporarily). While, thirdly, he knows for example killing people is (legally) wrong, that is, it is an offence to kill someone, he does not know the 'nature and quality' of his act while undergoing an epileptic seizure or sleepwalking. The phrase 'nature and quality' is interpreted as meaning that the accused did not know what he was physically doing: see *Codere* (1916) 12 Cr App R 21 (CCA).

In the discussion in this section it must be remembered that the definition of insanity (Figure 9.1) is a legal, not a medical one, as was shown by **Sullivan**, above, and confirmed by the Court of Appeal in **Hennessy** [1989] 1 WLR 287. The fact that someone is suffering from a medical condition, even a serious one, does not necessarily mean that she is legally insane.

It should also be noted that this section is limited to discussion of insanity on indictment. It was said in **DPP v H** [1997] 1 WLR 1406 by the Divisional Court that insanity is available in magistrates' courts only if the offence is one of *mens rea*. This proposition is criticised below. Lord Hutton, delivering the sole speech in **Antoine**, above, said that when insanity is successfully pleaded, the accused does not have the *mens rea* of the offence charged.

The principle governing insanity was laid down in **M'Naghten's Case** (1843) [1843–60] All ER Rep 229. The accused, believing he was being persecuted by the Tories, fired his gun at the Prime Minister, Peel, but killed Peel's secretary, Edward Drummond. Medical opinion showed that M'Naghten was suffering from morbid delusions which might have affected his perceptions of right and wrong. The jury returned a verdict of not guilty by reason of insanity. The case came to the House of Lords, who asked a series of questions to the judges of England. The main response was delivered by Tindal CJ, who seems to have striven to state the law so that an accused would not be blamed for what he had done through lack of intelligence or reasoning power or the ability to foresee consequences where punishment would deter neither the accused nor others.

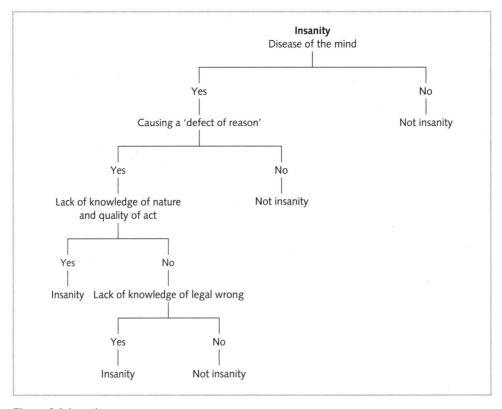

Figure 9.1 Insanity

The main part of Tindal CJ's statement in response to the hypothetical questions is:

> the jurors ought to be told in all cases that every man is presumed to be sane and [to] possess a sufficient degree of reason to be responsible for his crimes, until the contrary is proved to their satisfaction; and that to establish a defence on the grounds of insanity it must clearly be proved that, at the time of the committing of the offence, the accused was labouring under such a defect of reason from disease of the mind as not to know the nature and quality of the act he was doing; or if he did know it, he did not know he was doing what was wrong.

This definition is not affected by the Criminal Procedure (Insanity and Unfitness to Plead) Act 1991.

From the viewpoint of precedent it must be remembered that these words were not spoken in a 'live' case; however, the words, while not *ratio*, have come to be accepted as stating the law. Moreover, as Tindal CJ said himself, one should not make 'minute application' of the quoted words, but those words have been treated as if they appeared in a statute. The procedure for summoning judges to the House of Lords to give answers to questions was last used in 1898 and will presumably not be used again because since the mid-nineteenth century there is a lot more expertise in the Lords. Despite the above it should be said that when all the judges of England state that the law is so-and-so (the exception in *M'Naghten* was Maule J) their opinion is entitled to respect even if it is not authoritative for the purposes of the doctrine of precedent. The argument from precedent is not overwhelming because the *M'Naghten* Rules have been applied in cases of the highest authority. Despite the criticism that the Rules should not be read like a statute, the words have been used as if they were and the following discussion looks at the concepts in the definition.

(a) Disease of the mind

Lord Denning in *Bratty* v *Attorney-General for Northern Ireland* [1963] AC 386 (HL) said that a disease of the mind was 'any mental disorder which has manifested itself in violence and is prone to recur'. The definition is quite broad and gives effect to the policy that dangerous people should not be on the street. It would be strange that insanity should be restricted to violence, and the courts have not so restricted it. The principal judgment of the High Court of Australia in *Falconer* (1990) 65 ALJR 20 ran that a temporary mental disorder had to be prone to recur if it was to be classified as a disease of the mind. The likelihood of recurrence showed 'an underlying pathological infirmity'. This criterion was emphasised by Lord Lane CJ in *Hennessy*, above. Stress, anxiety and depression can be diseases of the mind even if caused by external factors, if they were prone to recur. The element of likelihood of recurrence is a frail basis for distinguishing between insanity and automatism. However, the Court of Appeal somewhat tentatively placed less emphasis on the possibility of recurrence in *Burgess* [1991] 2 QB 92. Lord Lane CJ said that the danger of recurrence was an extra reason for categorising the condition as a disease of the mind but 'the absence of the danger of recurrence is not a reason for saying that it cannot be a disease of the mind'. (It should be noted that the danger of recurrence of criminal behaviour in sane people is arguably not a reason for imprisoning them for a lengthy period.) That court otherwise accepted Lord Denning's proposition. In criticism of Lord Lane CJ's statement it may be said that the recurrence of a disease of the mind does not necessarily signify that the accused is dangerous. He may have been *very* dangerous at the time of the offences.

One criticism of the definition is that it is dependent on the nature of the accused's conduct and not on the nature of the disease. For this reason epilepsy as in *Bratty* and

Sullivan, both above, is a disease of the mind, yet not all epileptics should be detained. In *Sullivan* the defendant suffered from a rare form of epilepsy which manifested itself in violence. The House of Lords investigated the cause, thereby demonstrating at the highest judicial level that Lord Denning's *dictum* is not fully accepted, but the Court of Appeal in *Burgess* breathed new life into it. There are at present two streams of authority, though the courts do not seem to have noticed the definitional issue. Lord Diplock noted that it might seem harsh to call epileptics insane, but any reform was for Parliament.

Another problem with 'disease of the mind' is its uncertainty. Two cases are always contrasted. In *Charlson* [1955] 1 All ER 859 (CCA) a father invited his son to look out of the window at the river below to see a rat swimming in it. When the boy did so the father hit the boy over the head with a mallet and threw him out of the window. The father said that he knew that he was killing the boy but did not know why. He was suffering from a brain tumour. Barry J directed the jury that the tumour was a physical disease, not a disease of the mind within *M'Naghten*. Lord Denning considered in *Bratty* that *Charlson* was wrongly decided. The companion case to *Charlson* is *Kemp* [1957] 1 QB 399 at Bristol Assizes. The accused suffered from hardening of the arteries (arteriosclerosis) which led to a congestion of blood in the brain, causing a temporary loss of consciousness. While in this state he hit his wife over the head with a hammer. Devlin J said that the 'mind' in the definition covered the faculties of reason, memory and understanding, a phrase which gained Lord Diplock's approval in *Sullivan*, and that, while arteriosclerosis was a physical disease, the condition of the mind may be affected by it and if the mind is affected, there is a disease of the mind. Therefore, the physical cause of the mental disorder is not relevant. The general view is that *Charlson* and *Kemp* are indistinguishable, but *Kemp* is to be preferred because violent people should be detained. If *Kemp* is correct, insanity is defined broadly and covers forms of automatism which would not be included if *Charlson* were correct. If one wished, one could distinguish those cases by saying that in *Charlson* there was no medical evidence, whereas in *Kemp* there was. Nevertheless, the width of *Kemp* remains unclear. Would it cover a heart attack? The cause is the same as in arteriosclerosis: the brain's supply of blood is cut. In criticism of *Kemp*, one might inquire what the cause of the arteriosclerosis was. If the answer is high cholesterol food, the food is external, and the defence should not have been insanity but automatism. Cases such as *Kemp* illustrate that 'physical' diseases are included, and this is so despite such causes of 'disease of the mind' not being the concern of psychiatrists. The same may be said of diabetes and epilepsy.

Among the diseases which insanity would seem to cover are senility, traumatic brain injury, organic psychosis (as, for example, caused by syphilis), drug-induced psychosis, post-traumatic stress disorder, some forms of epilepsy, melancholia, manic depression and schizophrenia. 'Disease of the mind' can be read widely. Indeed, no 'disease' is required. In *Bell* [1984] 3 All ER 842 (CA) voices from God were said to be a disease of the mind. In practice about half of those held to be insane are schizophrenics. However, disease of the mind does not cover a temporary malfunction caused by something external: *Quick* [1973] QB 910 (CA) where Lawton CJ criticised Lord Denning's definition as leading to a diabetic being classified as insane. *Quick* demonstrates that though the accused has a mental aberration which manifests itself in violence, the accused is not always insane. The defendant in *Quick* had the defence of automatism. (The main accused in *Quick* had in fact been admitted to hospital on a dozen occasions in a semi-conscious or unconscious state: automatism as a defence is a complete one, yet surely he needed help with the containment of his diabetes.) In Australia it has been held that a temporary malfunctioning of the mind caused by an external factor such as a blow to the head or alcohol is not a disease of the mind: *Carter* [1959] VR 105. The same position is taken in New Zealand: *Cottle* [1958]

NZLR 999 (CA). Such factors, and the court added hypnotism in *Cottle*, cannot be called 'diseases'. In *Bailey* [1983] 2 All ER 503 (CA), a failure to take food to counteract the effect of insulin was categorised as an external factor and accordingly the resulting coma was not a disease of the mind. (For more on this see automatism, below.) Similarly, it was said by the House of Lords in *Attorney-General for Northern Ireland* v *Gallagher* [1963] AC 349 that a psychopathic state exacerbated by alcohol was not a disease of the mind.

The cases are not always easy to reconcile, especially those which lead to different results for epileptics and diabetics. Is it true that epileptics are more of a social danger than diabetics in a hypoglycaemic condition? Certainly there was no reason for keeping epileptics in psychiatric hospitals in the era before additional methods of disposal were given in 1992. Moreover, very rarely do epileptics perform the sort of act which occurred in *Sullivan*. What should be borne in mind is that, as Lord Diplock said in *Sullivan*, the cause, if internal, of the disease is irrelevant, as is whether it is permanent or transient. Similarly the fact that the medical profession would not call something a disease of the mind is immaterial. The difficulty is one of distinguishing in the light of policy if the *M'Naghten* Rules are to be retained. In the Australian High Court case of *Porter* (1933) 55 CLR 182, Dixon CJ said that disease of the mind did not include 'mere excitability of a normal man, passion, even stupidity, obtuseness, lack of self-control, and impulsiveness'. He emphasised that there need be no physical deterioration to the brain cells. Two recent cases throw the subject into relief by showing the width of the term.

In *Sullivan* the accused kicked a friend's head and body while he was recovering from an epileptic fit. The Lords held that despite his state of mind being temporary, he was insane. His defence was not automatism because the cause of his mental aberration was not external, but internal. This decision has been severely criticised. C.M.V. Clarkson, *Understanding Criminal Law* (Fontana, 1987) 44–5, wrote:

> One can, perhaps, understand the thinking behind the judgment. If the involuntary conduct has an internal cause then it is likely to recur; society needs protection against the recurrence of such dangerous conduct . . . ; the insanity verdict allows control to be maintained over the defendant. However, it seems absurd as well as highly insulting to utilise the insanity verdict here.

The fourth edition (Thomson, 2005) makes the same points but in slightly different words (pp. 39–42). He adds (p. 42 in the 4th edition) that: 'Nothing can be achieved by any of the orders that can be imposed pursuant to a finding of "not guilty by reason of insanity".' The reality is that most such persons will simply plead guilty to the charge, as Sullivan did, and will often receive a non-custodial sentence.

If, as Lord Diplock suggested, the *M'Naghten* Rules are meant to differentiate between dangerous and non-dangerous individuals, why are epileptics dangerous but some diabetics not? The line between internal and external causes does not divide dangerous from non-dangerous people. Moreover, even if the accused is insane, he can change his plea to guilty, yet he is still dangerous; after serving perhaps a short sentence, he is released on to the streets. Indeed, a custodial sentence need not be given. The classification of some epileptics as insane led a Crown Court judge in *McFarlane* (1990) *Guardian*, 11 September, to refuse to follow *Sullivan*. The brief report does not give the reason for not following precedent. But the judge seems to have directed the jury that the accused was not guilty if she was undergoing a fit when she occasioned actual bodily harm on a police constable searching her home for stolen goods. (He said that psychiatrists did not consider epilepsy to be a disease of the mind and therefore epilepsy is not part of the law of insanity. Once it is realised that whether a condition amounts to a disease of the mind is a question of law, one can appreciate the fallacy of this argument.) Furthermore as Lawton LJ put it in *Quick*, above, the law of 'disease of the mind' should not cause incredulity to laypeople.

An important case is *Burgess*, above. The accused attacked a friend with a video recorder and tried to strangle her. He had been sleepwalking. Lord Lane CJ said that the accused's 'mind was to some extent controlling his actions rather than the result simply of muscular spasm, but without his being consciously aware of what he was doing'. He rejected earlier authorities which had consistently held that sleepwalking was automatism. There was no external cause. Lord Lane applied part of Lord Denning's definition ('any mental disorder which has manifested itself in violence') but said that the latter part ('and was prone to recur') was simply an added reason for classifying the disease as one of the mind. On the facts, sleepwalking demonstrated 'an abnormality or disorder, albeit transitory, due to an internal factor, whether functional or organic, which had manifested itself in violence'. Therefore, the accused, the sleepwalker, was legally insane, since 'a purely temporary and intermittent suspension of the mental faculties of reason, memory and understanding' could be insanity. Any reform was for Parliament. It seems strange that a person who is sleepwalking should be treated in the same way as if he were a psychopath or otherwise mentally disturbed. This comment is underlined by the fact that the accused's violent behaviour was likely to recur. It can hardly be said that the public needed protection from him. On the other hand, it can be argued that a somnambulist can be treated in hospital and so an acquittal pure and simple would be inappropriate. Certainly labelling a sleepwalker as 'insane' is even more inappropriate. And it is sometimes said that a sleepwalker does only acts as he would like to do when conscious. He can avoid objects and climb stairs even though he does not have full consciousness. In criticism of *Burgess* it can be said that sleep is a natural condition. Sleepwalking is a consequence of that natural condition; therefore, sleepwalking is not a disease of the mind. Furthermore, as F. Boland put it in *Anglo-American Insanity Defence Reform: The War between Law and Medicine* (Ashgate, 1999) 11: 'If caused by cheese [sleepwalking] will qualify for the defence of automatism as cheese would probably be considered to be an external cause' [footnotes omitted]. The Supreme Court of Canada decided in *Parks* (1993) 95 DLR (4th) 27 that sleepwalking was not a disease of the mind. Sleepwalking arose from sleep, a socially acceptable cause. The 'internal cause' theory in *Quick* was rejected.

The draft Criminal Code, 1989, would have classified sleepwalking as automatism. This outcome would be better than the current one, insanity, but a successful plea of automatism means that the accused is acquitted, and no treatment is provided. A better solution would be to acquit the accused but then to oblige him to undergo an appropriate form of medical treatment such as a course of drugs.

(b) Defect of reason

This term is defined as a complete deprivation of the powers of reason, as distinguished from the failure to exercise those powers to the full, as the Court of Appeal held in *Clarke* [1972] 1 All ER 219. A depressed woman entered a supermarket and absentmindedly put goods into her basket. She was charged with theft. Her counsel counselled her to plead insanity – bad advice! A doctor in evidence said that depression was a (minor) mental illness. She had previously done things like putting sugar into her refrigerator. Thankfully for her, the court held her not to have a defect of reason. Failure to concentrate did not constitute a defect of reason. Looking at the *M'Naghten* Rules it might be said that her failure to understand what she was doing was a defect of reason. Even though the defect was only temporary, applying *Kemp*, above, her true 'defence' was insanity, and looking at *Burgess*, above, her movements were not simply muscular spasms. In fact the accused's appeal was allowed because she lacked *mens rea* in that she was not dishonest. An alternative way of reaching the same result is to hold that she did not have a disease of the mind. Non-severe depression is not such a disease. The defect of reason may be temporary or permanent, as the cases on epilepsy demonstrate. A defect of reason does not cover stupidity: *Kemp*.

(c)(i) Knowledge of the nature and quality of the act

Codere (1916) 12 Cr App R 21 (CCA) held that this phrase refers to the act's physical elements and not to the legal or moral constitution, that is, the accused must not know that he was doing the act at all, that he was incapable of foreseeing the result, or that he was incapable of appreciating the circumstances. In *Cottle*, above, Gresson P in the New Zealand Court of Appeal stated that: 'not to know at all is not to understand the nature and quality of the act'. A famous example is where a madman cuts a woman's throat under the delusion that he is cutting a loaf of bread. He may know that he is using a knife but he does not know the effect of using it and therefore does not know the nature and quality of his act. The accused in *Sullivan* did not know the nature of what he was doing. It is possible for the accused to fall under both this heading and the next. An irresistible impulse is not a lack of knowledge of the nature and quality of the act.

(c)(ii) Knowledge that the act was wrong

This phrase is the alternative to knowledge of the nature and quality of the act. It inquires of the accused whether he knew that what he was doing was contrary to law: *Windle* [1952] 2 QB 826, (CCA) contrary to previous authorities. As Lord Goddard CJ put it: 'courts of law can only distinguish between that which is in accordance with law and that which is contrary to law . . . it would be an unfortunate thing if it were left to juries to consider whether some particular act was morally right or wrong.' It is irrelevant whether he thought that what he did was morally wrong. The wife in *Windle* was certifiably insane. The husband had, as it were, caught a mental illness from her (*folie à deux*, a form of communicated mental disorder). He fed her 100 aspirins. When arrested he said: 'I suppose they will hang me for this?' The Court of Criminal Appeal ruled that his words meant that he knew that what he did was legally wrong, and he was indeed hanged. It should be noted that the sane adult has no defence of lack of knowledge that the act was legally wrong, at least if the act was criminally wrong (see the opening section of Chapter 8). A psychopath may well know that what he is doing is legally wrong and, therefore, he is not insane. In *Bell*, above, the accused heard what he thought were voices from God, which told him to ram the gates of a holiday camp with his van. He knew that what he did was legally wrong. It was irrelevant that he thought he was acting in a morally right way. An authority confirming that *Windle* remains good law is *Johnson* [2007] EWCA Crim 1978, though the judges thought that without *Windle* there was an argument that an accused ought to have the defence if he thought that what he was doing was morally justified, though illegal.

It appears that the judges in *M'Naghten* intended 'wrong' to mean morally wrong. In *Codere*, above, the test was said to be that of 'the ordinary standard adopted by reasonable men', a moral not legal test. For those reasons *Windle* was not followed by the High Court of Australia in *Stapleton v R* (1952) 86 CLR 358. If the Australian courts are correct, the accused in *Windle* may have had a defence. If he thought that mercy killing was morally proper, he did not know that his act was (morally) wrong. Canada has adopted the Australian approach: *Chaulk* (1990) 2 CR (4th) 1 (SCC). The accused is insane even though he knows that his act was illegal if he believes he was acting in a morally acceptable way. However, the Court of Appeal in *Johnson*, above, rejected *Stapleton* as being part of English law.

Summarising the effect of **Windle**, one may say that if the accused thought that what he did was right and believed that the law and public opinion agreed with him, he has a defence under this part of the **M'Naghten** Rules. (He may still know the nature and quality of his act.) If one of these beliefs is missing, he has no defence under this limb of the Rules – and let it not be forgotten that the question whether he knew that his act was legally wrong is being asked of a person who has suffered from a defect of reason from disease of the mind! Most murderers know that murder is a crime. **Windle** narrows the defence and under this limb of the Rules only those who are severely affected by a lack of intelligence fall within it. **Windle** may also be criticised because the accused was in such a state that even though he did know the law, he was not in a position to obey its dictates. Despite the above, research by Mackay demonstrates that Crown Court judges were not adhering to the principle in **Windle** but were instructing juries that an accused had the defence even though he thought he was doing something morally right but legally wrong. Psychiatrists giving evidence of insanity often took the same approach. **Johnson** recognised that this was happening.

The court in **Johnson** certified questions for the Lords: (i) Are the **M'Naghten** Rules still appropriate ones for determining insanity? (ii) Does 'wrong' mean legally or morally wrong? It is a pity that these questions have not been definitively answered.

Five procedural matters

(a) Since under the **M'Naghten** Rules every person is presumed to be sane, the accused bears the burden of disproving that he is sane. The burden, however, is the civil law one of the balance of probabilities: **Sodeman v R** [1936] 2 All ER 1138 (PC). See, however, point (c) below. The fact that the burden of proof is on the accused may be contrary to the European Convention on Human Rights. The Court of Appeal rejected the application of this Convention in **M** [2002] Crim LR 57, holding that findings that defendants are insane do not constitute criminal proceedings within Article 6(2) of the Convention. No one is convicted and no punishment is imposed. (This case is also called **Moore**.) For further discussion of the Convention see the next section.

(b) If the defence is successful, the verdict is 'not guilty by reason of insanity'. Formerly the verdict was 'guilty but insane'. Technically nowadays the outcome is an acquittal but there is an appeal against this verdict under the Criminal Procedure (Insanity) Act 1964, s 2.

(c) It is sometimes said the prosecution cannot raise the insanity issue. But in **Bratty**, above, the decision of highest authority, Lord Denning said that it was the prosecution's duty to raise the issue of insanity in order to prevent a dangerous person being free to roam the streets. It must, however, make available to the defence evidence supporting insanity: **Dickie** [1984] 3 All ER 173 (CA). The prosecution may, however, definitely raise the issue where the accused has led evidence of diminished responsibility (Criminal Procedure (Insanity) Act 1964, s 6), and where he has adduced evidence of mental incapacity. There is conflict whether in these circumstances the prosecution bears the burden of proof and, if so, how high that onus is. It is thought that the burden is on the prosecution, and the standard of proof is beyond reasonable doubt. However, with regard to cases where the accused has adduced evidence of mental capacity there is a *dictum* of Lord Denning in **Bratty** that the standard is on the balance of probabilities. This *dictum* seems incorrect. Only in exceptional cases such as on a charge of murder the accused raises the defence of diminished responsibility may the judge *sua sponte* (of his or her own accord) raise the issue of insanity: *Dickie*, above, and *Thomas* [1995] Crim LR 314 (CA). An exceptional case, for example, occurs when all the medical evidence is in favour of insanity, but the defence does not raise the issue.

(d) Under the Criminal Procedure (Insanity and Unfitness to Plead) Act 1991, s 1, a jury cannot return a verdict of not guilty by reason of insanity unless evidence of two medical practitioners, one of whom has been approved by the Home Secretary as having experience in mental disorder, has been adduced. It would seem that if the medical evidence is all one way, the jury must rely on it; if, however, the evidence is not all to the same effect, the jury has to choose which testimony is to be believed.

(e) Usually evidence of insanity is undisputed and both the Crown and the defence psychiatrists agree on the 'disease of the mind'. Nevertheless, a judge cannot dispose of the accused until the jury has delivered the special verdict of not guilty by reason of insanity.

Criticisms of the *M'Naghten* Rules

(a) An old criticism of the *M'Naghten* Rules is that no one is mad enough to be legally insane and have this defence. However, after the cases on epilepsy and sleepwalking, the force of this criticism has been reduced. A psychotic may not have this defence as the definition may not be satisfied. For example, the Yorkshire Ripper, Peter Sutcliffe, knew both the nature of his acts and the wrongfulness of them. This criticism should nowadays be phrased as this: in some respects the Rules are too narrow, while in others they are too wide.

(b) Key phrases in the definition are unclear: what is a disease of the mind? Until recently sleepwalking was not such an illness but was treated as an illustration of the defence of automatism. The width of this phrase, therefore, needs clarification.

(c) Under the Rules there is no defence for irresistible impulse: *True* (1922) 27 Cox CC 287 (CCA), *Kopsch* (1925) 19 Cr App R 50 (CCA), *Sodeman v R*, above, and *Attorney-General for South Australia v Brown* [1960] AC 432 (PC), though it is evidence towards showing both of the third 'limbs' of the *M'Naghten* test. The test ignores self-control. Similarly the defence does not cater for emotional factors. The accused is guilty if he knew what he was doing and that what he was doing was legally wrong, even if he did not have the emotional development to give meaning to this knowledge. Some of this criticism has been mitigated by the introduction of diminished responsibility. See below.

(d) It is immaterial whether the insanity was permanent or temporary, and even whether the disease of the mind is curable.

(e) The test is unscientific. The jury is the body which decides whether a person is insane, not the doctors, after the judge has ruled where there is evidence of insanity. Juries may find difficulty in applying the law to the facts, and there is some anecdotal evidence that the *M'Naghten* Rules are disregarded: juries ask themselves whether or not the accused is mad. The jury may reject medical evidence, as occurred for instance in *True*, above. It has been suggested that this law is in breach of Article 5 of the European Convention on Human Rights which provides that the mentally ill can be detained only after medical evidence has been used. Under the Criminal Procedure (Insanity and Unfitness to Plead) Act 1991, evidence of at least two medical practitioners, one of whom has been approved by the Home Secretary, is needed before a jury can return a verdict of not guilty by reason of insanity. One anomaly is that though the definition of insanity is a *legal* one, the accused may be committed to an institution which deals with conditions that are medical. Article 5(1) requires 'objective medical evidence' according to *Winterwerp* v *Netherlands* (1979) 2 EHRR 387. Since the jury has to apply a legal, not a medical, definition, it looks likely that Article 5(1) is breached. Hyperglycaemia, epilepsy and sleepwalking would not appear to make the sufferers of them 'persons of unsound mind' within Article 5(1). Moreover, *Winterwerp* demanded that the mental disorder must be of a type which warrants compulsory confinement; however, English law is that a person who is acquitted of murder by reason of insanity must be detained in a hospital. The Court of Appeal in *Grant* [2002] 1 Cr App R 528 said that it was a point 'of some difficulty' that 'no-one is required specifically to address, prior to the person's detention, the question whether he suffers from a mental disorder sufficiently serious to warrant detention'. The detention may be 'arbitrary' and fall foul of Article 5(1)(e), which, however, did not happen on the facts of *Grant* because the accused was mentally impaired in any case. She was therefore 'of unsound mind'. She also had the right to apply to the Mental Health Review Tribunal. *Grant* was itself a case of unfitness to plead but it applies generally.

Mental illnesses and disabilities are not the proper subject for criminal law courts. In murder such commitment remains mandatory, yet the offender may not be medically mentally ill. Many of the illnesses discussed in this section are ones which can be controlled by drugs. It is inappropriate to label such conditions as 'insanity'. If the accused has not taken the drugs prescribed, the issue should perhaps be whether he was forgetful on one occasion or whether he was for some reason against taking drugs. Current law does not take into account such issues.

The issue was well put by the Scottish Law Commission in its Discussion Paper No. 122, *Insanity and Diminished Responsibility*, 2003. The *M'Naghten* Rules may be incompatible with:

> the *Winterwerp* criteria (that there must be (i) a mental condition *at the time of disposal* [emphasis in original], (ii) established by medical evidence, which (iii) requires compulsory detention). The *M'Naghten* Rules do not necessarily fulfil these criteria, as they are concerned with insanity at the time of the offence . . . , and use a specialised definition of disease of the mind which does not coincide with the approach of medical science. . . . However it is far from obvious that a breach of the Convention is the result of the test used to establish insanity. If anything any breach is brought about by the provisions which deal with the disposal consequences of the defence. Article 5(1)(e) and the *Winterwerp* decision are not concerned with insanity as an issue of criminal responsibility but about limits on the power of the state to detain people on the basis of their mental disorder . . . It follows, as far as the Convention is concerned, that the test for the defence can be drawn up widely or narrowly and can take into account a whole range of policy considerations.

(f) The application of the Rules may cause problems. An old illustration is that a deluded person will not escape liability if his delusions do not relate to legal guilt. Accordingly if a person believes himself to be Napoleon, he will not have this defence because Napoleon was not allowed to kill.

(g) The burden of proof is anomalous. Insanity forms the sole common law defence where the burden is on the accused, and the position is hard to justify except historically. There may be a clash with the prosecutor's duty to prove *mens rea*. Proof of *mens rea* means that the accused knew the nature and quality of his act. However, the special rule for insanity means that he must prove that he did not know the nature and quality of his act. If the prosecution has proved *mens rea*, insanity calls for the accused to disprove what has been proved! This issue awaits judicial resolution. This conflict does not occur when the accused seeks to show that he did not know that what he was doing was wrong. The relationship between insanity and *mens rea* has not been satisfactorily resolved. In *DPP v H* [1997] 1 WLR 1406 the Divisional Court held that insanity, on the facts manic depression coupled with distorted judgment and impairments to the accused's moral sense and understanding of time, was not a defence to strict liability offences because insanity meant that the accused did not have the *mens rea* of the offence charged, whereas by definition strict liability offences lack *mens rea* as to one or more elements of the *actus reus*. *DPP v H* would appear to be incorrect. *Mens rea* is not inconsistent with insanity. A person may intend to kill, for example, but still be insane. Indeed, the part of the *M'Naghten* Rules which deals with the accused's knowledge that he has acted wrongly in law concerns persons who have *mens rea*. If the accused does not appreciate the nature and quality of his act, it could be said that the accused is not acting voluntarily and, therefore, there is no *actus reus*. The lack of *mens rea* is irrelevant in these circumstances. (*DPP v H* is also known as *DPP v Harper*.) There have been cases where insanity had been a defence to strict offence. A well-known example is *Hennessy* [1989] 1 WLR 287 (CA), a case of driving while disqualified. This case was not referred to in *DPP v H*.

(h) The defence of insanity is the sole defence where the judge cannot accept the accused's plea. He or she can do so in the 'partner' defence of diminished responsibility.

(i) Psychiatrists lack reliable means of telling whether a person was insane at the time of the offence. They can rely only on what the accused said and did. A shrewd accused might lie. On this basis he might escape punishment for his crimes.

(j) It is apparently difficult to persuade an 'insane' person to plead insanity.

(k) The test is all-or-nothing. Either the accused is insane or he is not. There is no verdict of 'partially insane'.

(l) Some persons put into psychiatric hospitals may be more dangerous when they come out than when they go in.

(m) Why should answers to hypothetical questions be legally binding? The judges in *M'Naghten* never intended their Rules to be read as if they were words in a statute.

(n) As stated above, it may be better to plead guilty than to attempt to prove insanity because of the problem of disposal. It may be more acceptable except in murder for the accused to take the punishment than to go to a hospital specified by the Home Secretary, as occurred before 1992. Even now a guilty verdict may be more to the accused's liking than one of insanity.

(o) A disease of the mind is partly defined in terms of the likelihood of recurrence. This prediction may be wrong, but people are classified as insane because of it.

(p) It cannot be said that arguments about a person's sanity are best heard in the criminal courts.

Summarising, perhaps the principal criticisms are the first and third. The Rules are too wide in that they cover epilepsy (*Sullivan*, above) but too narrow in that they do not cover lack of control arising out of a mental condition. If the Rules were based on a sound theory, application to the facts would not be difficult. The present quick release of some persons does not justify the law.

Reform

The Royal Commission on Capital Punishment, Cmd 8932, 1953, recommended that the whole set of *M'Naghten* Rules should be abolished. The jury (not, it should be noted, the doctors) should inquire whether the accused was suffering from a disease of the mind 'to such a degree that he ought not to be held responsible'. If that policy was not acceptable, the members wanted two new defences, irresistible impulse and diminished responsibility. Only the last proposal was partly put into effect in the Homicide Act 1957 (see below). The question of insanity was to remain in the hands of the jurors because it was seen as a matter of morality, not of medicine.

The Criminal Law Revision Committee proposed in its Eleventh Report, *Evidence (General)*, Cmnd 4991, 1972, 88, to place the legal burden of proof on the prosecution, leaving only the evidential burden on the accused. The Butler Committee (*Report of the Committee on Mentally Abnormal Offenders*, Cmnd 6244, 1975) also proposed that the burden of proof should lie on the prosecution and recommended that mentally disordered persons should continue to be exempt from criminal liability. The question was 'whether the offender, as a result of insanity . . . , is so much less responsible than a normal person that it is just to treat him as wholly irresponsible'. Irrational people should not be criminally liable. There would not need to be a link between the mental disorder and the crime. The *M'Naghten* Rules were unsatisfactory and should be abrogated. A new verdict of 'not guilty on evidence of mental disorder' was proposed. The accused would have this defence if he either did not know what he was doing or was suffering from severe mental illness or severe subnormality. On the first limb the burden of proof would be on the prosecution, and the defence would not include transient states arising from intoxication or physical injury. The Butler Committee thought that their definition would be wider than the *M'Naghten* Rules in that it would cover persons such as the mentally subnormal who at present have no defence. On the second limb:

A mental illness is severe when it has one or more of the following characteristics:
(a) lasting impairment of intellectual functions shown by failure of memory, orientation, comprehension and learning capacity;
(b) lasting alteration of mood of such degree as to give rise to delusional appraisal of the patient's situation, his past or his future, or that of others or to lack of any appraisal;
(c) delusional beliefs, persecutory, jealous or grandiose;
(d) abnormal perceptions associated with delusional misinterpretation of events;
(e) thinking so disordered as to prevent reasonable appraisal of the patient's situation or reasonable communication with others.

The definition of mental disorder would therefore not include diabetics, sleepwalkers and epileptics as the present law does. The verdict would not automatically lead to the accused's being committed to hospital: the judge would have full powers of disposal, including the grant of an absolute discharge. The Butler Committee, as stated above, proposed that the burden of proof should lie on the prosecution but cl 35 of the draft Criminal Code provides that either the prosecution or the defence should be permitted to prove mental disorder on the balance of probabilities.

These proposals remain unimplemented. The Criminal Law Revision Committee in 1980, Fourteenth Report, *Offences against the Person*, Cmnd 7844, recommended their adoption. They received a new lease of life in 1985 when the draft Criminal Code contained them (Report. No. 143) and in 1989 when the Law Commission proposed their enactment in Report No. 177, *A Criminal Code for England and Wales*. Clauses 35–36 would abolish the insanity defence, thereby removing the stigma of being labelled insane, an appellation that the Law Commission found 'offensive', replace it by a defence of not guilty on evidence of mental disorder if the mental disorder negated the *mens rea* and by a verdict of 'mental disorder' whether it did negate the *mens rea* or not (in other words even though the accused did not have the mental element for the offence charged, he could still be subject to restraint by the criminal justice system), and to have this defence the accused would have to suffer from 'severe mental illness or severe mental handicap'. Uncontrollable impulses would not fall within the term 'severe mental illness'. There need be no causal link between the mental disorder and the crime. Either the prosecution or the defence could prove that the accused was suffering from mental disorder. However, the Law Commission did not propose the full implementation of the Butler Report. 'Mental disorder' would no longer cover temporary depression, but would cover a diabetic who did not take insulin and an epileptic, and a person with a 'severe mental disorder' would be punished whether or not the crime is ascribable to the illness. The outcome for an epileptic, for example, would be that he would be subject to a mental disorder verdict but not of an insanity verdict. The Yorkshire Ripper would no doubt have a defence if these proposals were implemented. The 1991 Act retains mandatory commitment where the accused has committed murder. The Commission's view on this is not known. Either the prosecution or the defence would be entitled to raise this defence, whereas the Butler Report placed the burden of proof firmly on the prosecution.

The enactment of the Criminal Procedure (Insanity and Unfitness to Plead) Act 1991 may have reduced pressure for reform. That Act reforms procedure and sentencing but not the substance. It would be a pity if the reforms prevented the amendment of the law to prevent persons like the accused in *Burgess* being stigmatised as insane.

Many other reforms have been suggested especially in the USA after the acquittal of John Hinckley of the attempted assassination of the then President, Ronald Reagan. Some states totally abolished the insanity defence.

Enforcement of the Human Rights Act 1998 will lead to changes in the law. One suggested is that the application of the *M'Naghten* Rules in cases such as *Burgess* can no longer be justified. *Burgess* was decided, at least in part, in the way that it was because the accused was dangerous. The European Convention on Human Rights provides for the lawful detention of those 'of unsound mind' but it does not allow that detention on grounds of dangerousness. See also the discussion of *Winterwerp* and *Grant*, above.

The Law Commission is currently undertaking a review of insanity, and any proposals during the currency of this book will be added to the website.

Diminished responsibility

Example

The defence changed on 4 October 2010. What changes were made?

The Coroners and Justice Act 2009 substituted a new s 2(1) into the Homicide Act 1957 but did not, for example, amend s 2(2), which expressly places the burden of proof on the accused. Similarly, no change was made to the law that it is a defence only to murder and being a party to killing. The changes were: no longer must there be an abnormality of mind arising from one or more of five specified causes which substantially impaired the accused's mental responsibility, but instead:

- there must be 'an abnormality of mental functioning' (this simply updates the previous phrase in light of psychological terminology);
- which arose from 'a recognised medical condition' (this is new but is wider than the previous five grounds);
- and 'substantially impaired' the defendant's 'ability' to do one of three things: understand the nature of his conduct; form a rational judgment; or exercise self-control (this is a substantial change from previous law where 'substantial impairment' governed something completely different, the accused's so-called 'mental responsibility'; the excision of 'mental responsibility' is to take the issue out of the realm of morality and make it one of fact and law);
- and which 'provides an explanation' for the accused's conduct in killing or being a party to the killing. (This again is new: there has to be a causal nexus between the abnormality of the mental functioning and what happened. Previously to have this defence, it was sufficient to suffer from diminished responsibility as originally defined but without its providing an explanation for the killing or being a party to the killing.)

The defence of **diminished responsibility** has been reformulated and the new law came into force in 2010. However, much of the previous law remains in force, for example it remains a defence only to murder, the outcome of a successful plea is manslaughter, and the burden of proof remains on the accused. It is the *definition* of the defence which has been changed.

Why was the law changed? Certainly one aim was to modernise the law, using up-to-date terminology, and another was to clarify the concepts, but the principal government intention was to narrow the scope of the defence so that fewer would qualify. One might have thought that with fewer than 20 successful pleas per year this was not an important legal area for reform.

This defence 'does something to compensate for the lack of an insanity defence that can be used' (E. Griew 'The future of diminished responsibility' [1988] Crim LR 75 at 87). Certainly pressure to reform the law of insanity declined after 1957. One statistic after the Homicide Act's enactment demonstrates the justness of the quote: in 1990 there were 49 successful diminished responsibility pleas but only one of insanity. Similar figures occurred throughout the 1990s. There were 46 in 1997 but only 15 in 2001–02. Most pleas are successful. The main pre-2010 treatment is S. Dell, *Murder into Manslaughter* (Oxford University Press, 1984). She noted that in most cases the judge accepted the accused's plea (and the position remains the same today with fewer than 15 per cent of pleas leading to a trial). If the judge did not, most defendants were convicted of murder.

It is arguable that a person whose mental responsibility is impaired should not be found guilty at all and that he should have a defence to all crimes, but a special defence applying only to murder (Figure 9.2) has been created by s 2(1) of the Homicide Act 1957 as amended by the Coroners and Justice Act 2009, s 52(1):

A person ('D') who kills or is party to the killing of another is not to be convicted of murder if D was suffering from an abnormality of mental functioning which –

(a) arose from a recognised medical condition,

(b) substantially impaired D's ability to do one or more of the things mentioned in subsection (1A), and

(c) provides an explanation for D's acts and omissions in doing or being a party to the killing.

'Abnormality of mental functioning' replaced 'abnormality of mind' in the previous law. The hope is that psychiatrists will find the phrase easier to use. Perhaps also Parliament wanted to exclude bogus pleas of diminished responsibility.

'Recognised' means 'recognised either under the World Health Organisation's *International Classification of Diseases* or under the American Psychiatric Association's *Diagnostic and Statistical Manual of Mental Disorders*'. It was thought by the then government (see Hansard, col. 413, 3 March 2009) that the law would work in this way. 'If a qualified medical expert gives evidence that, at the time of the killing, a defendant was suffering from a condition included on one of these lists, and the jury accepts that, that part of the test will be met.' The first major case on the new law took a different line. In **Dowds** [2012] 1 Cr App R 34 the Court of Appeal took the view that Parliament could not have intended that the new definition should cover acute intoxication not amounting to a disease when the unamended law did not, even though the condition fell within both lists. The government also intended that the definition should cover conditions not (yet) included on the list if the work of the recognised specialist had been peer-reviewed or validated in some other way.

'Substantially' means 'more than trivially': see **Brown** [2011] EWCA Crim 2796, where it was said that when Parliament enacted the 2009 statute, it did so against the background of the phrase 'substantially impaired' in the original 1957 Act; therefore, 'substantially' in the revised Act meant the same as 'substantially' in the original version. Complete impairment is, therefore, not required. Present law also excludes the requirement from previous law of the substantial impairment to the defendant's 'mental responsibility'. There is no reference in current law to mental responsibility.

Subsection (1A) reads:

> Those things are:
> (a) to understand the nature of D's conduct;
> (b) to form a rational judgment;
> (c) to exercise self-control.

Therefore, it is only if these aspects of the accused's mental functioning are affected that he may be afforded the defence. Note that loss of self-control may also give rise to the defence of loss of control discussed in Chapter 12, and that a failure to understand the nature of the conduct closely resembles the first limb ('nature and quality') of the **M'Naghten** Rules discussed above.

Subsection (1B) explains a phrase in the new s 2(1):

> For the purposes of subsection (1)(c), an abnormality of mental functioning provides an explanation for D's conduct if it causes, or is a significant contributory factor in causing, D to carry out that conduct.

A link between the abnormality of mental functioning and the killing is therefore required. The position is otherwise with regard to insanity.

Diminished responsibility is, as the opening words in s 2(1) state, a specific defence: that is, it applies only to murder or being a secondary party (aider, etc.: see Chapter 5) to murder. It is not even a defence to attempted murder: **Campbell** [1997] Crim LR 495 (Crown Court). Therefore, if the victim dies, the accused will be guilty of manslaughter but if the victim lives, the accused will be guilty of attempted murder, provided that he had the mental element for this crime, the intent to kill. In this regard it is different from insanity which potentially applies to all offences. In respect of other offences, diminished responsibility can be taken into account in the sentencing.

Furthermore, diminished responsibility applies even though the accused knew the nature and quality of the act and knew that what he was doing was legally wrong: compare the defence of insanity which is dealt with above.

Like insanity, however, the burden of proof is on the accused: s 2(2). This sub-section was not changed by the 2009 Act. The judge must direct the jury that this is so: **Dunbar** [1958] 1 QB 1 (CCA). He must also tell them that the burden is on the balance of probabilities. The reverse onus found in s 2(2) is not incompatible with Article 6 of the European Convention because the defence is not an element in the crime of murder: **Lambert** [2002] 2 AC 545 (HL), discussed in Chapter 1. If the accused is represented by counsel, only the defence may raise this defence: **Campbell** (1987) 84 Cr App R 255 (CA, *obiter*). The court said that this ruling followed from s 2(2).

If there is evidence of diminished responsibility, the judge can only point out the evidence to the defendant's counsel: the defence is in this sense optional. If the defence contends that the accused is suffering from diminished responsibility, the prosecution may lead evidence that he is insane: Criminal Procedure (Insanity) Act 1964, s 6.

Discussion of the width of the defence

The 2010 revamped definition both updates and amends the definition in the previous law:

(a) 'Abnormality of mind' in the original version of s 2(1) is replaced by 'abnormality of mental functioning', a more modern term.

(b) The original version restricted the abnormality of mind to five causes but the current law is not so restricted. However, the abnormality must be a recognised one. It need not be a mental condition but can be a physical one. Diabetes and epilepsy are, for

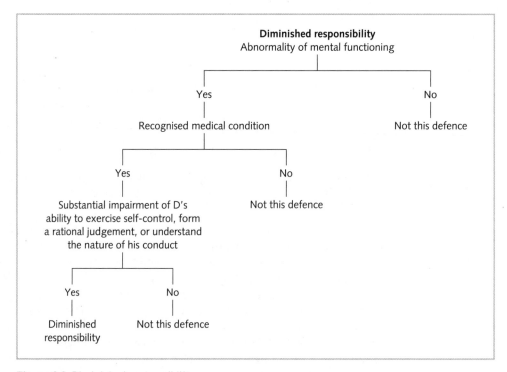

Figure 9.2 Diminished responsibility

example, covered. Depression is covered and therefore the defence is open to battered women who suffer depression as a result of their being abused.

(c) Unlike the original law the abnormality must cause the killing, a substantial narrowing of previous law. This means that if the accused would have killed despite his suffering from a recognised medical condition, he will not have a defence. The law of causation discussed in Chapter 2 applies here. For example, the mental condition need not be the sole or principal reason why the accused killed; it is sufficient that it was a more than trivial cause. Note that such a causal link is not required in the defence of insanity.

(d) Diminished responsibility is only a defence to murder or being an accessory to murder. It acts as a defence even when there is evidence of planning: *Matheson* [1958] 2 All ER 87 (CCA). It gets round the mandatory sentence by giving the judge discretion as to sentence. The effect, of course, is that irresistible impulse is no defence to other charges such as theft. Though there is a discretion it is not extraordinary for a judge to sentence the accused to life imprisonment when he succeeds in his plea, as occurred in *Byrne* [1960] 2 QB 396 (CCA). It will be recalled that even after the Criminal Procedure (Insanity and Unfitness to Plead) Act 1991, commitment is mandatory for insanity in a murder case and that diminished responsibility is a defence (only) to murder; therefore, an accused is more likely to rely on diminished responsibility than insanity when murder is charged.

(e) Diminished responsibility is not a complete defence but only a partial one. It reduces murder to manslaughter. A person may be sentenced to life imprisonment for manslaughter, and just as for murder he must receive that sentence. Accordingly for some defendants the effect of succeeding on this defence is nil, as occurred in *Gittens* [1984] QB 698 (CA). The court may make a hospital order under s 37 of the Mental Health Act 1983.

(f) If the accused seeks to prove that he is insane, the prosecution may put forward evidence that his defence is one of diminished responsibility. In that event the prosecution have to prove diminished responsibility beyond reasonable doubt.

(g) A judge may, not must, accept a plea of diminished responsibility where medical evidence is unchallenged: *Cox* [1968] 1 All ER 386. Pleas should not be accepted without clear evidence of an abnormality of mind: *Vinagre* (1979) 69 Cr App R 104 (CA). Dell (above) found that in only 13 per cent of her sample did the doctors disagree, but that if they did, the defence was likely to fail. The effect of *Cox* is to avoid a trial for murder, perhaps saving the public from the details of particularly savage murders. However, this did not happen in the case of the Yorkshire Ripper. In most cases pleas of diminished responsibility are accepted.

(h) All the evidence relating to abnormality, not simply the medical evidence, must be looked at by the jury, at least if the medical evidence is disputed: *Walton v R* [1977] AC 788 (PC), *Kiszko* (1978) 68 Cr App R 62 (CA). As Lawton LJ put it in *Robinson* (1979) 1 Cr App R (S) 108: 'these cases are to be tried by judges and juries and not by psychiatrists.' The jury can reject the medical evidence if there is other evidence: *Byrne* and *Walton v R* above, and *Tandy* [1989] 1 All ER 267 (CA). If there is only medical evidence, the jury must accept it: *Matheson*, above and *Sanders* (1991) 93 Cr App R 245 (CA), *obiter*, which also approved the previous sentence's statement of the law. Medical evidence normally consists of a history of mental breakdown such as a series of attempts at suicide. Evidence may be given of the nature of the killing and the accused's conduct before, at the time of, and after the *actus reus*. As in insanity any medical evidence will not take place until some time after the killing. Psychiatrists have to try to reconstruct the accused's state of mind at an earlier time. The fact that the accused has killed may, of course, affect his state of mind. In **Sanders** two psychiatrists gave evidence that the accused was suffering from an abnormality of mind, depression, and the prosecution accepted that he was. However, the Crown contended that the abnormality did not substantially impair his mental responsibility. He had made preparations as if he was about to commit suicide but he did not include his victim, his long-term mistress, among the beneficiaries and while he wrote letters to three or four people in anticipation of his death, he did not write to her. The jury evidently thought the killing premeditated. The court held that the will and the letters demonstrated that there was evidence other than that given by psychiatrists which the jury could use to reject the defence.

(i) Sometimes under the pre-2010 law flimsy evidence was used to get the accused off a charge of murder, for example **Price** (1971) *The Times*, 22 December: a father killing his severely disabled son. This looks like a mercy killing, which is murder. The law has no category, of 'not guilty by reason of mercy killing'. The accused was suffering from a dissociative state. It may have been that his mental condition was brought about by an external cause, the disabled boy. However, this cause would not fall within the defence. Therefore, the court had to concentrate on the dissociation, not the cause of the dissociation. Some people argued that some battered wives cases are also examples of flimsy evidence because the accused has, after all, killed, and killing is not permitted, and that counsel know that juries are likely to be sympathetic to abused women. Again the court has to concentrate on the mental state, say depression, not on the cause of that abnormality of mind, the beatings. Lawton LJ commented in **Vinagre**, above, thus: 'There was clear evidence of a killing by a jealous husband which, until modern times, no one would have thought was anything else but murder.' It may be that because the 2010 revision demands a link between the abnormality and the killing that fewer sympathetic verdicts will be reached under the new law than under the old.

(j) Where the defendant has taken alcohol or drugs, the jury must disregard them: **Gittens**, above (CA), which disapproved **Turnbull** (1977) 65 Cr App R 242. Therefore, the accused has to prove on the balance of probabilities that the murder resulted from an abnormality of mind and not from the intoxication. **Gittens**, which the House of Lords approved in **Dietschmann** [2003] 1 AC 1209, was applied in **Egan**, above. In that case the accused, who was described as bordering on the subnormal, killed an elderly widow after breaking into her home. He had been drinking heavily. The court in a reserved judgment held that intoxication was to be ignored by the jury when considering whether the abnormality substantially impaired the accused's mental responsibility and considering the cause of the abnormality. Such disregard may be difficult for the jury. One effect of the authorities is that the accused, to have the defence, has to prove that he would have had the defence, had he not been drunk! In **Dietschmann** the accused killed his victim while both very drunk and suffering from an adjustment disorder consequent on the death of his girlfriend. The prosecution case was that he would not have killed, had he been sober. He was convicted of murder and his appeal dismissed by the Court of Appeal. However, the Lords allowed his appeal. Lord Hutton provided a model direction which restates the law:

> drink cannot be taken into account as something which contributed to his mental abnormality and to any impairment of his mental responsibility . . . but you [the jury] may take the view that both [the accused's] mental abnormality and drink played a part in impairing his mental responsibility . . . and that he might not have killed if he had not

taken drink. If you take that view, then the question . . . is: has [the accused] satisfied you that, despite the drink, his mental abnormality substantially impaired his mental responsibility for his fatal acts . . . ?

Cases to the contrary are to be overruled: *Hendy* [2006] EWCA Crim 819 and *Robson* [2006] EWCA Crim 2749.

(k) The Royal Commission on Capital Punishment, the Report of which led to the creation of this defence (Cmd 8932, 1953), stated that there were degrees of insanity: sanity and insanity shaded into each other. Similarly, there was no clear line between responsibility and irresponsibility. The defence of diminished responsibility was introduced to bring the law into line with these perceptions.

(l) Current law falls short of the European Convention on Human Rights. First, where the accused is charged with murder, the court does not have an opportunity to determine whether the mental incapacity is of such a kind as to warrant mandatory commitment. Secondly, the law must not be too far out of line with medical opinion, but as we have seen the decision whether the defence applies is one for the jury, not the psychiatrists. Thirdly, in relation to Article 6 the burden of proof remains challengeable in the opinion of the author.

Comment

It is important to realise that a person having the defence of diminished responsibility is convicted of manslaughter and is often imprisoned. Some, perhaps one-seventh, receive life sentences. This result makes the public safe. It does not necessarily cure the accused's problems. Moreover, the original justification of the defence has gone. It started as a defence to murder when the penalty for that offence was death. Death is no longer the sentence for murder, mandatory life imprisonment is. The modern rationalisation is that diminished responsibility serves to mitigate the sole remaining fixed imprisonment penalty in English law by allowing the court to be flexible in sentencing. If murder at some time lost its mandatory punishment, there would be little or no need for this defence. The trouble with this argument is that if diminished responsibility were abolished, a mentally disabled defendant might not be able to come within the defence of insanity because of its narrowness, and he would be convicted of murder: yet, surely mentally ill defendants should not be convicted of murder. Alternatively, diminished responsibility could be extended to all offences. Why should a partly excused criminal have a defence if he killed but not if, for example, he stole or raped? The accused by definition is not fully responsible for his actions. Probably the main effect of this defence is to put persons into prison who before the Homicide Act would have been sent to a secure hospital. What has occurred is that diminished responsibility was meant to provide a defence to persons who were not legally insane. Instead it has been used for persons who before 1957 would have been classified as insane, as well as those 'on the borderline of insanity'.

Automatism

Introduction

Lawton CJ in *Quick*, above, called the defence of **automatism**, which seems to have originated in *Chetwynd* (1912) 76 JP 544, 'a quagmire of law seldom entered into nowadays save by those in desperate need of some kind of defence'. It is a narrow defence, made narrower by the rule that insane automatism is insanity, not automatism. A decision which determines that some mental aberration such as epilepsy and sleepwalking is insanity narrows the potential scope of automatism. It is a question of law whether the cause of the accused's mental condition is a disorder of the mind within the rules of insanity: *Sullivan*, above.

A reminder of the law which distinguishes insanity and automatism is *Roach* [2001] EWCA Crim 2700. The Court of Appeal *per* Potter LJ held that no matter what the doctors called the defendant's illness, the issue of whether the accused was suffering from insanity or automatism was a matter for the jury. The court said that 'the legal definition of automatism allows for the fact that, if external factors are operative upon an underlying condition which would not otherwise produce a state of automatism, then a defence of non-insane automatism should be left to the jury'. Here alcohol or drugs or both (external factors) had acted on the accused's 'mixed personality disorder' (a disease of the mind) to produce violence. The defence was one of automatism, not insanity.

When allowed, it is a defence to all crimes, including strict offences. Therefore automatism cannot be simply a denial of *mens rea*, as some judges have said, for strict offences do not require *mens rea* in relation to one or more elements of their *actus reus*. Therefore, the defence is not one where the accused is saying just that he was not at fault (Figure 9.3).

Whether recklessly getting into a state of automatism is inconsistent with automatism is discussed below. It is sometimes said that automatism negates *actus reus*. If so, it should not matter how the accused came to be suffering from automatism, but the law is that he has no defence if he was at fault in getting into a state of automatism. It is suggested again that *actus reus* and *mens rea* are sometimes but not always useful tools of analysis. The accused is really saying that what he did cannot be ascribed to him. He was not the author of the misdeed. Unlike insanity and diminished responsibility, the burden of proof is on the prosecution and the standard of proof is beyond reasonable doubt.

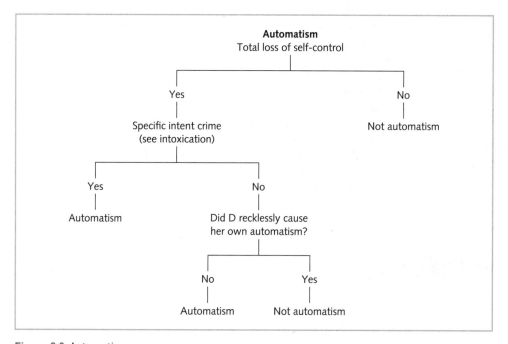

Figure 9.3 Automatism

Criticism has been directed at the outcome of a successful plea of automatism, total acquittal, because the public may be unprotected from a second attack. Lamer CJC in the Canadian Supreme Court case of *Parks* (1993) 95 DLR (4th) 27 desired 'some minimally intrusive conditions which seek to assure the safety of the community', perhaps an order that the accused should see a sleep disorder specialist. Yet the accused was not found to have a mental disorder and how can the court make an order when the defendant has been acquitted? The fact that the outcome of a successful plea of automatism is an acquittal may have influenced the courts to keep the defence within narrow bounds.

The basic rule: complete loss of control

The law is not completely clear. Contrary to the view of Neill J in *Roberts v Ramsbottom* [1980] 1 All ER 7, the defence extends beyond complete unconsciousness. The Court of Appeal in both *Quick* and *Isitt* [1978] Crim LR 159 referred to semi-conscious states falling within the definition. There is no clear line between consciousness and unconsciousness. The Court of Appeal in *Attorney-General's Reference (No. 2 of 1992)* [1994] QB 91, however, said that automatism denoted a total destruction of voluntary control. Impaired, reduced or partial control was insufficient. 'Driving without awareness', that is, in a trance-like state, did not amount to a total loss of control. Therefore, the accused should have been found guilty of causing death by reckless driving when he drove his lorry 700 yards along the hard shoulder of a motorway before crashing into a stationary van, killing two people. The trance-like state could be stopped by stimuli such as flashing lights. This case has been criticised for holding that a person in such a state is criminally liable, but the decision seems correct. It is acceptable to punish those who have allowed themselves to get into a trance-like state on a motorway. *Charlson*, above, would seem to be incorrect if this case is rightly decided for in *Charlson* the accused could not have hit his son with a mallet and defenestrated him without having some control over his bodily movements. *Broome v Perkins* (1987) 85 Cr App R 361 (DC), discussed below, is to the same effect as *Attorney-General's Reference (No. 2 of 1992)*: there had to be a total loss of control. Lord Taylor CJ said: '. . . the defence of automatism requires that there was a total destruction of voluntary control on the defendant's part. Impaired, reduced or partial control is not enough.' The Crown Court, however, held in *T* [1990] Crim LR 256 that a woman who had been raped was suffering from post-traumatic stress syndrome when she stabbed a victim during a robbery. She obviously did have some control over her movements but she acted as if in a 'dream', and accordingly had the defence. There have been suggestions by academics that the requirement of a total loss of consciousness is restricted to driving offences or offences of strict liability but the judiciary has not so held.

It should be noted that in automatism involuntary behaviour means conduct which is *physically* involuntary; *morally* involuntary behaviour does not fall within the rules of automatism but may form part of other defences such as the two types of duress.

Which mental states give rise to automatism?

Non-insane automatism is a defence when the accused has not got control over his movements because of an external cause. His actions are involuntary. He is not guilty unless his movements were willed (though there may be problems with crimes of omissions, where the accused is guilty without bodily movements). A legally relevant act or omission occurs only when the accused's will has led to it. If there is muscular movement without volition, without will, the act is involuntary and is classified as automatism. It covers abnormal states of mind which are not insanity. It covers dissociations and psychological trauma if not prone to recur, according to the High Court of Australia in *Falconer* (1990) 65 ALJR 20, while Lord Diplock in *Sullivan* [1984] AC 156 (HL) spoke of 'concussion or the administration of an anaesthetic for therapeutic purposes'. For an Australian case involving a blow to the head see *Cooper v McKenna* [1960] Qd R 406. In *King* (1962) 35 DLR (2d) 386 a Canadian court held that delirium caused by an organism which originated outside the body was automatism. In *Hill v Baxter* [1958] 1 QB 277, the Divisional Court referred to confusions, delusions and strokes as well as 'a blow from a stone or an attack by a swarm of bees' (per Lord Goddard CJ), while *Charlson* was concerned with a brain tumour. In *Bell* [1984] 3 All ER 842 (CA), Goff LJ referred to a driver's being attacked by 'a swarm of bees or a malevolent passenger', his being 'affected by a sudden blinding pain' and his becoming 'suddenly unconscious by reason of a blackout'. It may cover hypnotism, according to *Quick and Paddison* [1973] QB 910 (CA). Because of the requirement of an external cause *Charlson* and some other cases seem incorrect. A brain tumour is a disease of the mind within the rules on insanity.

Lord Denning in *Bratty v Attorney-General for Northern Ireland* [1963] AC 386 (HL) mentioned spasms, reflex actions and convulsions. Some of these holdings may need revision in the light of *Sullivan*, above, and *Hennessy* [1989] 1 WLR 287 (CA). Sleepwalking was thought to give rise to automatism for many years: see *Bratty*, relying on Stephen J in *Tolson* (1889) 23 QBD 168 (CCR); Toohey J did not question in *Falconer* that sleepwalking, like hypoglycaemia, amounted to automatism; and in *Lillienfield* (1985) *The Times*, 12 October, where a sleepwalker had stabbed a friend 20 times, a Crown Court judge held the defence to be automatism. In *Burgess*, above, the Court of Appeal held the defence to be insanity. Somnambulism was not an external factor such as a blow to the head, but an internal factor, which may result in violence. (See also under insanity.) The court held further that 'external cause' did not cover the ordinary stresses and disappointments of everyday life such as unrequited love (unless the outburst reveals a previously hidden disease of the mind). Automatism is the defence where the accused is suffering traumatic stress after a rape because it was held that the cause, rape, was an external factor: *T*, above (Crown Court). Any normal person would have been severely affected by rape. *T* has been criticised on the grounds that the accused was conscious of what she was doing. She was capable of choosing not to take part in a robbery. The law in relation to post-traumatic stress syndrome is in a flux. In *White* [1995] Crim LR 393 the Court of Appeal held that the accused, a bouncer, who had earlier been stabbed, was not to be convicted of grievous bodily harm with intent when he stamped on the victim's head but of inflicting grievous bodily harm since because of his disorder he did not intend to commit grievous bodily harm. The court did not consider whether he should have been totally acquitted on account of automatism. If driving without awareness had given rise to a state of automatism in *Attorney-General's Reference (No. 2 of 1992)* the external cause would have been the motorway conditions. An irresistible impulse is not automatism: *Bratty*. The US *Model Penal Code* (Official Draft 1985), s 2.01(a), states that:

The following are not voluntary acts . . . :
(a) a reflex or convulsion;
(b) a bodily movement during unconsciousness or sleep;
(c) conduct during hypnosis or resulting from hypnotic suggestion;
(d) a bodily movement that otherwise is not a product of the effort or determination of the actor, either conscious or habitual.

The Model Penal Code seeks to restate the best American criminal law. This definition is similar to the law in England and Wales, but a statutory definition would be helpful.

It is not automatism where the accused's mind was not 'in top gear': *Isitt*, above, where the accused's act of driving was purposeful (see also below). He drove away after an accident. The Court of Appeal held that: 'because of panic or stress or alcohol, the appellant's mind was shut to the moral inhibitions which control the lives of most of us. But the fact that his moral inhibitions were not working properly . . . does not mean that the mind was not working at all.' If the automatism is caused by drunkenness, the defence is one of intoxication, and the rules on automatism do not apply. A Scottish case to that effect is *Finegan* v *Heywood* 2000 SCCR 460.

These different forms of behaviour giving rise to automatism show that it is difficult to find one basis for this defence. According to Gresson P in *Cottle* [1958] NZLR 999 in the Court of Appeal of New Zealand lack of consciousness is the essence. In *Bratty* Lord Kilmuir said that automatism is 'a defence because the mind does not go with what is being done'. It is also difficult to fit automatism into the category of 'defence'. Sometimes the accused is treated as if he did not commit the *actus reus* because his act was not voluntary or was not willed; alternatively, he did not possess the *mens rea* for the offence because his mind was blank. Whichever approach is adopted, there is no offence because the prosecution has failed to prove an element of the offence. Accordingly automatism is not a defence in the sense that the accused did the *actus reus* and had the *mens rea* but is excused or acted justifiably.

There is doubt whether automatism fits into the traditional *actus reus*/*mens rea* dichotomy. It may be that, before the prosecution reaches the stage of *actus reus* and *mens rea*, they have to show that the accused acted voluntarily. The accused does not act voluntarily if he injures someone as a result of a muscular spasm. Therefore, he is not guilty and the stage of *actus reus* and *mens rea* is not reached. A Scottish case to that effect is *Finegan* v *Heywood*, above. If this is so one must be careful in distinguishing involuntary from voluntary acts. As Lord Denning noted in *Bratty*, on this approach an act is not involuntary simply because the actor could not resist the impulse or did not intend the consequences. However, to get the accused within the definition of automatism, the definition of involuntary behaviour must be stretched to accommodate the facts of *Charlson*. If the accused picks up a child, beats him and throws him through the window, the facts hardly present a picture of ordinary-language involuntarism; his conduct looked purposeful. In this context *Charlson* should be compared with *Broome* v *Perkins* (1987) 85 Cr App R 361 (DC). The accused drove home very erratically from his workplace. He collided with at least one other car and did not appear to have all his faculties. He said that he could recall only the start of his journey and his wife giving him a Mars bar to counteract his hypoglycaemia. There was evidence that people in such states could drive along familiar roads without being conscious of having done so. He was charged with careless driving. The Divisional Court allowed the prosecution's appeal by way of case stated. The defendant was not entitled to the defence of automatism because his actions were voluntary. His mind was in control of his movements, his driving, enabling him to steer his vehicle along the roads. He had driven for six miles and had avoided crashing into lorries.

This decision throws doubt on *Charlson*, where the father hit his son over the head and threw him out of the window. Surely he ought to be guilty when the accused in *Broome* v *Perkins* was? In both cases the acts were 'purposeful' as the Divisional Court put it. The verdict in *Charlson* might be supported, not by saying that the accused acted automatically, but that he had no *mens rea*. The alternative view is to hold that the true defence in *Charlson* was insanity. *Broome* v *Perkins* has been criticised as punishing someone who did his best. He was held to a very strict standard especially when another fact is added. He went to the police to tell them that he thought he had had an accident. Should we penalise such responsible behaviour?

Special rules in automatism

At least when the offence is one of strict liability or negligence and can be interpreted as occurring over a period of time, the accused will not be acquitted when the automatism is caused by his fault, such as occurred in **Kay v Butterworth** (1945) 173 LT 191 (CCA) where the accused had fallen asleep. The accused was convicted of careless driving, a crime of negligence, for not stopping his car before he fell asleep. His fault constituted the carelessness necessary for the offence. The doctrine by which the accused was convicted is sometimes known as 'prior fault'. This doctrine is inconsistent with the rules on contemporaneity of *actus reus* and *mens rea* discussed in Chapter 3. It may be that the Divisional Court found that the accused had also fallen asleep at the wheel in **Hill v Baxter**, cited above. This rule applies even though the automatic state was induced by hypoglycaemia (see below) induced by the defendant's negligent failure to counteract the deficiency of sugar, as occurred in **Marison** [1996] Crim LR 909 (CA). The accused knew that he was liable to hypoglycaemic episodes. He had an attack; his car crashed into an oncoming vehicle, and the driver was killed. He did not have a defence of automatism because he knew that his driving was dangerous when he was undergoing a diabetic attack. This rule is sometimes phrased that the accused has no defence if he was reckless in getting into the state of automatism. Driving for many hours without a break would be the epitome of this rule. If a defendant 'drives without awareness', that is, as if in a trance because he has not taken a rest, no defence is afforded him. **Marison** was distinguished in **G** [2006] EWCA Crim 3276, where the accused was charged with causing death by dangerous driving. She was suffering from hypoglycaemia at the time of the accident and was not at fault for getting into such a state.

Self-induced automatism, it used to be said, was no defence unless the accused's act was 'proper': **Quick and Paddison**, above. The term was undefined but it suggested that the defendant was not at fault. Possibly he was at fault, however, because he failed to prevent his diabetic coma, perhaps knowing what happened if he did not eat food. In **Quick**, the cause of automatism was the drug, insulin, prescribed by a doctor. It might be argued, however, that this rule should not exist. If this defence negatives *mens rea*, how can that be revived by fault? It may be that the case is inconsistent with previous authorities. In **Bailey** [1983] 2 All ER 503, the Court of Appeal cast grave doubt on this exception. See below for a full explanation of the relationship between **Quick** and **Bailey**.

Another rule is that according to Lord Morris in **Bratty**, 'It is not every facile mouthing of some easy phrase of excuse that can amount to an explanation.' It is not enough to say 'I had a blackout'. Voluntary conduct is assumed: the accused has therefore to bring forward some evidence of involuntary behaviour. The accused must show the nature of the incapability such as psychomotor epilepsy (**Bratty**) or abnormal consciousness (**Hill v Baxter**, above). Since the accused in the latter case could not point to medical evidence which would have founded his defence, the court directed the justices to convict. The usual way to show automatism is to adduce medical evidence: **Moses v Winder** [1983] Crim LR 233. The burden of proof, however, remains on the prosecution: **Stripp** (1978) 69 Cr App R 318 (CA) and **Bratty**. The contrary *dictum* of Lord Goddard CJ in **Hill v Baxter** is incorrect.

Lord Justice-General Hope in the Scottish High Court of Justiciary case of **Ross v HM Advocate** 1991 SLT 564 said: 'The requirement that the external factor must not be self-induced, that it must be one which the accused was not bound to foresee, and that it must have resulted in a total alienation of reason amounting to a complete absence of self-control, provide adequate safeguards against abuse.' English judges would no doubt express similar sentiments.

Automatism and diabetes

One somewhat uncertain point about automatism is whether diabetes gives rise to this defence. The first major authority is *Quick*, above. The accused, a male nurse at a psychiatric hospital, was charged with assault occasioning actual bodily harm to a paraplegic spastic patient. He led medical evidence to show that he was a diabetic. He had taken insulin but had not eaten properly. He had been hospitalised on several occasions because he had not eaten. He contended that at the time of the alleged assault he was suffering from hypogly-caemia (deficiency of sugar in the blood – the attack need not be caused by diabetes: fasting can lead to it) caused by taking insulin and not eating, making him not know what he was doing, and that this disorder gave him this defence. The trial judge, however, ruled that the disorder was a disease of the mind within the *M'Naghten* Rules. On appeal, the defence argued that a temporary and reversible condition was not a disease of the mind. Lawton LJ criticised the definition of disease of the mind given by Lord Denning in *Bratty*: 'any mental disorder which has manifested itself in violence and is prone to recur'. If that definition were correct, the accused would have to be detained in a psychiatric hospital. Lawton LJ said:

> Common sense is affronted by the prospect of a diabetic being sent to such a hospital when in most cases the disordered mental condition can be rectified quickly by pushing a lump of sugar . . . into the patient's mouth.

Against this argument from common sense (and the Court was strongly of the view that whether mental aberration constituted a disease of the mind had to be approached 'in a common-sense way', a way which is contradicted by more recent authorities on epilepsy, hyperglycaemia and sleepwalking) is the law that a disease of the mind need not be incurable or permanent (see Devlin J in *Kemp* [1957] 1 QB 399, see above). However, the law went further. In *Hill v Baxter* Lord Goddard CJ did not equate unconsciousness due to a sudden injury with disease of the mind. Lawton LJ held:

> A malfunctioning of the mind of transitory effect, caused by the application to the body of some external factor, such as violence, drugs, including anaesthetics, alcohol and hypnotic influences cannot fairly be said to be due to disease . . . A self-induced incapacity will not excuse . . . nor will one which could have been reasonably foreseen as a result of either doing or omitting to do something, as for example, taking alcohol against medical advice after using certain prescribed drugs, or failing to have regular meals whilst taking insulin.

In *Quick* there was held to be an external factor. The malfunction was caused not by diabetes, but by his use of insulin. Therefore, the accused should have had his defence of automatism put to the jury. The defence was not insanity but automatism. In medical terms, however, the cause of hypoglycaemic comas may be internal when the pancreas produces too much insulin. Moreover, the reason for the accused's taking insulin is an internal one, for diabetes is an internal matter.

Quick was explained in *Bailey*. The accused, while suffering a hypoglycaemic episode, hit his girlfriend's lover with an iron bar. The Court of Appeal said *obiter* that even though his mental failure was due to his own act, that is, was self-induced, in the sense that he could have avoided blacking out by having a meal:

(a) Self-induced automatism exculpated the accused from a crime of specific intent. Therefore, the accused could not be convicted of wounding with intent. This rule is the same as that in intoxication. The jury decides whether the defendant was acting as an automaton.

(b) In crimes of basic intent the rule relating to self-induced incapacity was a rule of drunkenness as a defence, not of automatism. Therefore, it does not apply to insulin. The jury is asked whether the accused was reckless and therefore had the mental element for a crime of recklessness.

The rule in *Quick* that the accused could have no defence where he was at fault was incorrect. However, the court said that the accused could not have this defence if he was subjectively reckless. Whether he was reckless or not was a question for the jury. The jury has to investigate whether the accused himself knew that having no meal meant that he would act dangerously. Some diabetics, including the accused in *Quick*, apparently do not know the effect of their illness. It is suggested that in the years since *Quick* the effects of insulin have become more widely known and fewer people will nowadays be able to rely on their lack of knowledge than 35 years ago. Perhaps *Quick* would be decided differently nowadays: did he know of the consequences of failing to take insulin? From the wording of the judgment the test is subjective but in *Quick* Lawton LJ said that incapacity 'which could have been *reasonably* foreseen' (emphasis supplied) did not excuse, an objective formula. In *Hardie* [1984] 3 All ER 848 the Court of Appeal said that the correct direction on recklessness was not clear and it unfortunately did not rule one way or another. The reason for the distinction between the law on intoxication and automatism is hard to understand. Why should an intoxicated person have no defence to a basic intent offence, but an automaton in some circumstances have one? The court in *Bailey* emphasised that diabetes was not a disease of the mind. It was not a basis for insanity. As we have seen, the House of Lords in *Sullivan* held that epilepsy can be a disease of the mind. Accordingly, epileptics, or some of them at least, cannot rely on this defence. *Sullivan* approved the 'external factor' rule laid down in *Quick*.

The outcome in *Bailey* is open to the criticism that in reality the risk of dangerous behaviour if a diabetic does not take sufficient food after an insulin dose may be common knowledge. It certainly would be if the risk is published on the packet in which the drug comes. As an empirical matter, however, the answer is not clear. In fact the accused's appeal was dismissed because insufficient evidence had been adduced that he was in a state of automatism.

A case, one on hyperglycaemia (an excess of sugar in the blood) which leads to confusion and then a coma, is *Hennessy*, above. The Court of Appeal also approved the external/internal dichotomy. The accused was charged with driving while disqualified and taking a vehicle without consent. He was a diabetic, who had not taken food or insulin as prescribed. The court agreed with the trial judge that the true defence was insanity. *Hennessy* is one of several authorities which over the last 40 years have been extending the law of insanity and thereby reducing the law of automatism. Lord Lane CJ said: 'Stress, anxiety and depression can no doubt be the result of external factors, but they are not . . . external factors of the kind capable in law of causing or contributing to a state of automatism . . . They lack the feature of novelty or accident.' They were not like an anaesthetic or a blow to the head. Therefore, on the facts they were not factors causing automatism. Similarly, marital problems were not external factors. As N.J. Reville commented ('Automatism and diabetes' [1989] 86 LSG 19):

[t]he implications of the external/internal factors distinction are disturbing, because it creates arbitrary rules. Should a diabetic, such as Mr. Hennessy, suffer a hyperglycaemic episode merely because he failed to eat enough, then any injury that he inflicts will result in an insanity verdict because his mental condition is not caused by an external factor. On the other hand, if the diabetic produced his state of automatism by taking insulin (and thereafter failing to eat), he would be regarded as being in a state of non-insane automatism.

One distinction between the two forms is that hyperglycaemia can come on slowly, whereas hypoglycaemia may come on quickly, but the two states are similar in effect: disorientation followed by loss of consciousness and death. It is strange therefore that one form leads to the stigma of being labelled insane whereas the other leads to a complete acquittal.

Certainly, the external/internal division does not necessarily differentiate between those who ought to be acquitted and those who ought to be treated or imprisoned. Yet the distinction between hypoglycaemia and hyperglycaemia was confirmed in **Bingham** [1991] Crim LR 433 (CA). The accused said that because of hypoglycaemia he was unaware of what he was doing, taking sandwiches and cola from a shop. The defence of automatism was available.

Summarising, taking too much insulin is an external factor. Automatism is a possible defence. Taking no insulin is an internal factor, which means that automatism is not available. Not enough sugar (hypoglycaemia) is automatism; hyperglycaemia (too much) is insanity, yet both involve the blood-sugar level and the difference in outcome is tremendous. In insanity the accused may be sent to a secure hospital even after the 1991 Act; in automatism the verdict is acquittal. The law should distinguish between dangerous persons and others: it does not.

The law in Australia is different. An accused suffering from an 'underlying mental infirmity' is insane but a temporary mental infirmity is automatism: see **Falconer**, above. One effect is that the defendant in **Hennessy** would be acquitted because of automatism if the Australian rule was imported into England.

Insanity and automatism

The previous section has shown the difficulty of distinguishing these defences in the context of automatism. **Quick** illustrates the problem. The accused's condition was due to the injection of insulin. The malfunction of the mind was held to be an external factor, not a disease. However, a high blood-sugar level, hyperglycaemia, is a disease and the **M'Naghten** Rules apply. In **Quick** the Court of Appeal said that a blow to the head was an external factor and therefore the defence was automatism. However, if the blow caused brain damage, then the defence is one of insanity provided that there is no other external blow. In **T**, above, if traumatic stress after a disease had been held to be a disease of the mind, the outcome was insanity quite possibly; if it was an illness caused by an external factor, the defence was automatism. Insane automatism is a rare defence in terms of successful pleas.

The basic distinction is that automatism stems from a 'temporary loss of consciousness arising accidentally', as Devlin J put it in **Hill v Baxter**, while insanity is founded on mental disease. In **Falconer**, above, where the High Court of Australia rejected the internal/external distinction, automatism was said to come from 'a transient non-recurrent mental malfunction caused by external forces which produces an incapacity' to control actions, whereas insanity was based on 'an underlying mental infirmity'. If the alleged automatism is a disease of the mind the plea really is one of insanity, and the burden of proof is on the accused, whereas if the automatism is of the non-insane variety the onus is on the prosecution to disprove beyond reasonable doubt that the accused has this defence. Therefore, the wider is 'disease of the mind', the narrower is automatism. It is arguable that if the accused's mental disorder is not likely to recur, there is little point in putting him into a secure hospital.

Even if a jury rejects evidence of insanity, they are entitled to consider automatism: *Burns* (1973) 58 Cr App R 364 (DC). As *Burns* also held, the jury must be directed separately on the differing burdens of proof. The cases stress that the burden in automatism is on the prosecution: *Budd* [1962] Crim LR 49 and *Bratty*, above.

One practical point remains. Counsel has the duty of choosing between advising the accused (a) to plead guilty and possibly get a light sentence or (b) plead automatism and so open the route to insanity. For example, in *Sullivan*, above, because the accused raised the plea of automatism, the prosecution could adduce evidence of insanity (which they had to prove beyond reasonable doubt).

The Criminal Procedure (Insanity and Unfitness to Plead) Act 1991, which was not in force at the time of *Sullivan* and *Hennessy*, means that commitment is not mandatory except in murder cases and the plea of insanity in theory ought to become more popular than before.

Reform

The Law Commission in its Report No. 177, *A Criminal Code for England and Wales*, 1989, cl 33(1), proposed to enact a large part of the Butler *Report of the Committee on Mentally Abnormal Offenders*, above:

> A person is not guilty of an offence if –
> (a) he acts in a state of automatism, that is, his act
>   (i) is a spasm or convulsion; or
>   (ii) occurs while he is in a condition (whether of sleep, unconsciousness, impaired consciousness or otherwise) depriving him of effective control of the act; and
> (b) the act or condition is the result neither of anything done or omitted with the fault required for the offence nor of voluntary intoxication.

This proposal has been criticised for failing to define what 'effective control' is. Still excluded from the defence are epileptics and diabetics, though sleepwalkers would be included, reversing *Burgess*, above.

However, under cl 34 a defendant who was in a state of automatism (not resulting only from intoxication) which is a feature of a disorder, whether organic or functional and whether continuing or recurring, that may cause a similar state on another occasion would be subject to a mental disorder verdict, and by cl 39 the court would have wide powers of sentence. The present law of automatism has been criticised for permitting persons who ought to be treated to roam the streets.

The effect of cl 33(1) could be to get rid of the present internal/external debate: there would also be no need to speak of will, voluntary behaviour or volition. Since cl 33(1)(a) speaks of deprivation of 'effective control', *Broome v Perkins* and *Attorney-General's Reference (No. 2 of 1992)*, above, would presumably be reversed. However, phrases such as 'impaired consciousness' and 'effective control' could be read widely or narrowly, and outcomes may be different on the same facts, because what is 'effective' is a question of degree. The 1985 draft Criminal Code required that the accused was totally deprived of control of his movements. In criticism of that draft it may be said that to deprive defendants of this defence when they are not totally deprived of control seems severe. Certainly on this draft **Broome v Perkins** would have survived. Sleepwalking would again be part of automatism. Note also that sub-cl (b) takes away much of what is given in sub-cl (a). Sub-cl (b) also means that the principle of contemporaneity does not apply when cl 33(1) does.

Tabular summary of the defences

Table 9.1 Insanity, diminished responsibility, automatism: a brief comparison

	Insanity	*Diminished responsibility*	*Automatism*
Defence to	All offences	Murder	All offences
Cause	Must be internal	Internal or external	Must be external
Definition requires	Disease of the mind	Abnormality of mind	Loss of consciousness
Burden of proof	On the accused	On the accused	On the prosecution
Standard of proof	Balance of probabilities	Balance of probabilities	Beyond reasonable doubt
Outcome if successful plea	Not guilty by reason of insanity	(Voluntary) manslaughter	Acquittal

Loss of control over a car

In **Spurge** [1961] 2 QB 205 the court held that a sudden and total loss of control over a car is a defence, provided that the accused did not know nor should he have known of the defect. Similarly in **Burns v Bidder** [1967] 2 QB 227 (DC) the accused was not guilty of failing to accord precedence to a pedestrian at a crossing when the brakes failed. The analogy with automatism is close and indeed the court used the hackneyed automatism example of a driver being attacked by a swarm of bees when exculpating the driver. Similarly, in **Bell**, above, Goff LJ mentioned an attack by a swarm of bees and loss of control caused, for example, by a blowout or a brake failure. The position may be different if a pedestrian jumps out. According to **Neal v Reynolds** [1966] Crim LR 393 (DC) the accused is guilty, but that case may be wrong. The courts have not been consistent in their use of terminology. If an accused has a defence of automatism because he is, for instance, attacked by a swarm of bees, the courts might say that the accused is not driving and is therefore not guilty of any offence involving the *actus reus* of driving. The act was involuntary; accordingly, there was no act. However, the court might say in different circumstances that the accused's act was voluntary even though he did not know of the circumstances of the activity. If an accused is driving with above the limit of alcohol in his blood because his drinks have been spiked, the court held in **Shippam** [1971] Crim LR 434 that he was guilty, under what is now s 5 of the Road Traffic Act 1988, because his driving was voluntary. (See the section on intoxication for the law on involuntary intoxication.) The point is this: be careful how the courts use the terms 'voluntary' and 'involuntary'. The terminology is inconsistent.

Automatism and the philosophy of criminal law

Automatism is based on the voluntary act requirement in criminal law. Just as merely thinking about committing an offence is not a crime, so too it is not a crime for the accused to commit the *actus reus* of an offence when he was acting in a physically involuntary manner.

Summary

- *Unfitness to plead*: This defence is open to an accused who at the time of the trial cannot understand the trial process to make a proper defence. Except for murder the Criminal Procedure (Insanity and Unfitness to Plead) Act 1991 as amended provides a range of orders.

- *Insanity*: This common law defence affords a defence to persons who are 'insane' at the time of the offence but are fit to plead at the time of the trial. The burden of proof lies on the accused and the standard of proof is on the balance of probabilities. He must prove:
  1 he was suffering from a 'disease of the mind';
  2 which caused a defect of reason and EITHER:
    3(a) which was such that the accused did not know the nature and quality of the act; OR
    3(b) which was such that the accused did not know that what he was doing was legally wrong (even if he knew that he or she had acted in a morally wrong way).
  Trenchant criticism of the rules on insanity has been made for many years, particularly of 'disease of the mind', a concept which covers epilepsy, sleepwalking and hypoglycaemia.

  The jury decides whether a person is insane or not, but two medical practitioners must testify as to the accused's mental state. The same orders after a finding of insanity as are made after a finding of unfitness to plead may be made except in respect of murder when only one order is possible.

  Despite insanity's being a defence the accused may appeal against the verdict of 'not guilty by reason of insanity'.

- *Diminished responsibility*: Section 2(1) of the Homicide Act 1957 as revised provides a defence to an accused who proves on the balance of probabilities that he or she is suffering from an abnormality of mental functioning which substantially impaired his or her ability (i) to understand the nature of his or her conduct, (ii) to form a rational judgment or (iii) to exercise self-control and which provides an explanation for his or her committing the killing or being a party to it.

- *Automatism*: Automatism, a defence to all crimes, is based on either unconscious (as may be caused by diabetes) or reflex bodily actions or the external application of something, for example force, to the accused which causes him or her completely to lose control over bodily movements, to act involuntarily. If the accused felt himself moving into a state of unconsciousness, there is no defence if he was at fault. Where the automatism was caused by insanity, the defence is one of insanity, not automatism. The burden of proving automatism lies on the prosecution, which must disprove it beyond reasonable doubt.

References

Reports

Criminal Law Revision Committee 11th Report, *Evidence (General)*, Cmnd 4991 (1972)

Criminal Law Revision Committee 14th Report, *Offences against the Person*, Cmnd 7844 (1980)

Law Commission Consultation Paper no. 177, *A New Homicide Act for England and Wales* (2005)

Law Commission Consultation Paper no. 197, *Unfitness to Plead* (2010)

Law Commission Report no. 143, *Criminal Law: Codification of the Criminal Law – A Report to the Law Commission* (1985)

Law Commission Report no. 177, *A Criminal Code for England and Wales* (1989)

Law Commission Scoping Paper, *Insanity and Automatism* (2012)

Law Reform Committee of the Bar Council and the Criminal Bar Association of England and Wales, *Unfitness to Plead: A response to Law Commission C.P. 197*, 2011

Model Penal Code (US), Official Draft (1985)

Report of the Committee on Mentally Abnormal Offenders (Butler) Cmnd 6244 (1975)

Scottish Law Commission Discussion Paper no. 122, *Insanity and Diminished Responsibility* (2003)

Books

Boland, F. *Anglo-American Insanity Defence Reform: The War between Law and Medicine* (Ashgate, 1999)

Clarkson, C.M.V. *Understanding Criminal Law*, 1st edn (Fontana, 1987)

Clarkson, C.M.V. *Understanding Criminal Law*, 4th edn (Thomson, 2005)

Dell, S. *Murder into Manslaughter* (Oxford University Press, 1984)

Mackay, R.D. *Mental Condition Defences in the Criminal Law* (Clarendon, 1995)

Journals

Ashworth, A. Comment on *H* [2003] Crim LR 818

Griew, E. 'The future of diminished responsibility' [1988] Crim LR 75

Grubin, D. 'Unfit to plead in England and Wales 1976–88: A survey' (1991) 158 BJ Psych 540

Grubin, D. 'What constitutes fitness to plead?' [1993] Crim LR 748

Howard, H. 'Unfitness to plead and the vulnerable defendant: An examination of the Law Commission's proposals for a new capacity test' (2011) 75 JCL 194

Mackay, R.D. 'Fact and fiction about the insanity defence' [1990] Crim LR 247

Mackay, R.D. 'The decline of disability in relation to the trial' [1991] Crim LR 87

Mackay, R.D. and Kearns, G. 'An upturn in unfitness to plead?' [2000] Crim LR 532

Reville, N. 'Automatism and diabetes' [1989] 86 LSG 19

Further reading

Bynoe, I. 'Unfitness to plead' [1991] SJ 984

Claydon, L. 'Are there lessons to be learned from a more scientific approach to mental condition defences?' (2012) 35 IJ of Law & Psychiatry 88

Dell, S. 'Wanted: an insanity defence that can be used' [1983] Crim LR 431

Duff, R.A. 'Fitness to plead and fair trials' [1994] Crim LR 419

Exworthy, T. 'Commentary: UK perspective on competency to stand trial' (2006) J Am Acad Psychiatry Law 466

Fennell, P. and Khaliq. U. 'Conflicting or complementary obligations? The UN Disability Rights Convention on human rights and English law' [2011] EHRLR 662 (on *Winterwerp*)

Gibson, M. 'Intoxicants and diminished responsibility: The impact of the Coroners and Justice Act 2009' [2011] Crim LR 909

Griew, E. 'Reducing murder to manslaughter: whose job?' (1986) 12 *Journal of Medical Ethics* 18

Grubin, D.R. 'What constitutes unfitness to plead?' [1993] Crim LR 748

Grubin, D.R. 'Fitness to plead and fair trials – (2) A reply' [1994] Crim LR 423

Grubin, D.R. *Fitness to Plead in England & Wales* (Psychology Press, 1996)

Howard, H. 'Unfitness to plead and the trial of facts' (2012) JC 421

Howard, H. and Bowen, M. 'Unfitness to plead and the overlap with doli incapax: An examination of the Law Commission's proposals for a new capacity test' (2011) 75 JCL 380

Jones, T.H. 'Insanity, automatism and the burden of proof on the accused' (1995) 111 LQR 475

Keating, H. and Bridgman, J. 'Compassionate Killing: The case for a partial defence' (2012) 75 MLR 697

Kennefick, L. 'Introducing a new diminished responsibility defence for England and Wales' (2011) 74 MLR 750

Loughnan, A. '"Manifest madness": towards a new understanding of the insanity defence' (2007) 70 MLR 379

Loughnan, A. 'Mental incapacity doctrines in criminal law' (2012) 15 New Crim LR 1

Mackay, R.D. 'The automatism defence' (1983) 34 NILQ 81

Mackay, R.D. 'Fact and fiction about the insanity defence' [1990] Crim LR 247

Mackay, R.D. 'Righting the wrong? Some observations on the second limb of the *M'Naghten* Rules' [2009] Crim LR 80

Mackay, R.D. 'The Coroners and Justice Act 2009 – partial defence to murder (2): The new diminished responsibility plea' [2010] Crim LR 290

Mackay, R.D. and Kearns, G. 'The continued underuse of unfitness to plead and the insanity defence' [1999] Crim LR 714

Mackay, R.D. and Mitchell, B.J. 'Sleepwalking, automatism and insanity' [2006] Crim LR 901

Mackay, R.D., Mitchell, B.J. and Howe, L. 'Yet more facts about the insanity defence' [2006] Crim LR 399

Mackay, R.D., Mitchell, B.J. and Howe, L. 'A continued upturn in unfitness to plead – more disability in relation to the trial under the 1991 Act' [2007] Crim LR 530

Ormerod, D. Case comment on *Ghulam* [2010] Crim LR 796

Peay, J. 'Fitness to plead and core competencies: Problems and possibilities' LSE Working Papers 2/2012

Ridgway, P. 'Sleep walking – insanity or automatism' (1996) 3 *eLaw: Murdoch University Electronic Journal of Law*

Virgo, G. 'Sanitising insanity – sleepwalking and statutory reform' (1991) 50(3) CLJ 386

Wake, N. 'Recognising acute intoxication as diminished responsibility? A comparative analysis' (2012) 76 JCL 71

Ward, T. 'Magistrates, insanity and the common law' [1997] Crim LR 790

Wells, C. 'Whither insanity?' [1983] Crim LR 787

Wilson, W. *et al.* 'Violence, sleepwalking and the criminal law (2): The legal aspects' [2005] Crim LR 614

Yannoulidis, S.Y. 'Mental illness, rationality and criminal responsibility' [2003] Syd LR 10

Yeo, S. 'The insanity defence in the criminal laws of the Commonwealth of Nations' [2008] *Singapore Journal of Legal Studies* 241

For a Scottish view, see the Scottish Law Commission, *Discussion Paper on Insanity and Diminished Responsibility*, no. 122, 2003.

For an American approach, see R.F. Schopp, *Automatism, Insanity and the Psychology of Criminal Responsibility* (Cambridge University Press, 1991). The author provides a useful critique of English law.

Visit **www.mylawchamber.co.uk** to access tools to help you develop and test your knowledge of criminal law, including interactive multiple choice questions, practice exam questions with guidance, annotated weblinks, glossary flashcards, legal newsfeed and legal updates.

Use Case Navigator to read in full some of the key cases referenced in this chapter with commentary and questions:

R v Sullivan [1984] AC 156

10

Inchoate offences

Aims and objectives

After reading this chapter you will understand and be able to critique:

- the definition of 'inchoate'
- the offence of encouraging or assisting another offence
- the offence of conspiring to commit another offence
- the offence of attempting to commit another offence

Introduction

English law intervenes to punish persons who have not (yet) committed an offence. The crimes which penalise conduct before the commission of the (full or substantive) crime are called **inchoate offences**. Having these charges available is to deter offending. The exception to this rule is conspiracy to defraud: the result to be achieved need not be a crime. Conspiracy to defraud cannot be described as a true inchoate offence. Unlike secondary offences, the full crime need not have taken place before the accused is guilty of an inchoate offence. If the principal offence is committed, the accused may also be liable as a secondary party. Inchoate offences are criminal only in relation to the full offence, that is, one is not guilty of attempt but, for example, of attempted murder.

There are three inchoate offences: assisting and encouraging, conspiracy, and attempt. This chapter deals with these offences. There are also specific offences. For example, there is an offence of inciting a person to commit murder contrary to s 4 of the Offences Against the Person Act 1861 (see below). Some other offences partake of the nature of inchoate offences. Two examples suffice: s 3 of the Criminal Damage Act 1971 deals with possessing anything with intent to damage property; s 1 of the Prevention of Crime Act 1953 penalises the carrying of offensive weapons. In neither crime need the accused have harmed any property or person. When assault was seen as attempted battery (which it no longer is), it was an inchoate offence. One form of burglary, entry into a building as a trespasser with intent to commit criminal damage, steal or commit grievous bodily harm, is also an inchoate offence. The offences are discussed in the order encouraging and assisting, conspiracy and attempt because generally speaking that sequence shows the movement towards the completion of the principal offence. For example, the crime of conspiracy is committed at an earlier stage than attempt and accordingly the police can intervene at an earlier time.

Encouraging and assisting

 Introduction

The Serious Crime Act 2007 replaced the common law offence of inciting crimes (which is abolished: s 59) with a statutory one of **encouraging and assisting**. The crimes of encouraging and assisting, which like the offence of incitement they replace, are inchoate offences (s 49(1)). The statute rectified a common law anomaly. If one encouraged or assisted another to commit a crime, the encourager or assister would be guilty of a secondary offence if the principal offence took place (see Chapter 5); if one encouraged or assisted what would have been a crime, had it taken place, but it did not occur, then the encourager would have been liable for incitement but the assister would not.

It should be noted that 'encouraging or assisting' are to be read as covering situations where the accused put pressure on another to commit an offence (s 65(2)), a strange partial definition of 'encouraging or assisting' but one fully in line with the common law offence of incitement. It does not matter how the offence is encouraged or assisted. In *Blackshaw* [2012] 1 WLR 1126, the main Court of Appeal authority on the English riots of 2011, the mode of instigation was Facebook. As Lord Judge CJ put it, '. . . modern technology has done away with the need for . . . direct personal communication'.

Section 44(1) creates the crime of 'intentionally encouraging or assisting an offence'. It reads:

A person commits an offence if –
(a) he does an act capable of encouraging or assisting the commission of an offence; and
(b) he intends to encourage or assist its commission.

It is suggested that 'intends' is to be given its narrower meaning, direct intention or purpose. See Chapter 3 for direct and indirect/oblique intent.

Section 44(2) makes the perhaps obvious point that:

. . . he is not to be taken to have intended to encourage or assist the commission of an offence merely because such encouragement or assistance was a foreseeable consequence of his act.

For example, if the accused suggests to a contract killer that the latter murders her husband for £5,000, the offence is complete. The contract killer need do nothing towards committing the murder.

Section 45 creates a second offence, that of 'encouraging or assisting an offence believing that it will be committed'. Section 45(1) provides:

A person commits an offence if –
(a) he does an act capable of encouraging or assisting the commission of an offence; and
(b) he believes –
   (i) that the offence will be committed; and
   (ii) that his act will encourage or assist its commission.

Section 46 deals with what are sometimes called 'laundry list' instances of encouraging or assisting, that is, where the accused believes that one or more offences may be committed but is unsure as to which one will in fact be committed. On these facts the person who encourages or assists is guilty when he does an act capable of assisting or encouraging and he believes that 'his act will encourage or assist the commission of one or more' of the potential offences. The Court of Appeal held in **Sadique** [2012] 1 Cr App R 19 (also known as **S**) that the s 46 offence did not breach Article 7 of the European Convention on Human Rights. It was not too vague and uncertain. Nevertheless, s 46 is 'very complex', and Hooper LJ thought that simplicity would have been obtained by adding a defence to s 45 that the accused would be guilty if he contemplated two or more offences but did not know which would take place. The statutory provisions use the word 'would', and not the word 'might'; therefore, belief that a certain crime *might* take place is insufficient. In the words of s 46(2) in relation to the s 44 offence the defendant must have 'intended to encourage or assist the doing of an act which would amount to the commission of that offence'. Hooper LJ added that it is irrelevant that ss 44–46 may penalise lawful trade: that has always happened, as **NCB v Gamble** [1959] 1 QB 11 (DC), discussed in Chapter 5, illustrates.

'Encouraging or assisting' also covers the following situation (s 66): 'If a person (D1) arranges for a person (D2) to do an act that is capable of encouraging or assisting the commission of an offence, and D2 does the act, D1 is also to be treated . . . as having done it.'

The definition of 'believes' in s 45(1)(b) is found partly in s 47(3):

> . . . it is sufficient to prove that he believed –
> (a) that an act would be done which would amount to the commission of that offence; and
> (b) that his act would encourage or assist the doing of that act.

There is a further explanation of the mental element in s 47(5):

> In proving for the purposes of this section whether an act is one which, if done, would amount to the commission of an offence –
> (a) if the offence is one requiring proof of fault, it must be proved that –
> (i) D [the accused] believed that, were the act to be done, it would be done with that fault;
> (ii) D was reckless as to whether or not it would be done with that fault; or
> (iii) D's state of mind was such that, were he to do it, it would be done with that fault.
> (b) if the offence is one requiring proof of particular circumstances or consequences (or both), it must be proved that –
> (i) D believed that, were the act to be done, it would be done in those circumstances or with those consequences; or
> (ii) D was reckless as to whether or not it would be done in those circumstances or with those consequences.

Section 47(5)(b) ensures that the accused is not guilty of encouraging or assisting an offence without any *mens rea*.

For the avoidance of doubt, s 47(8) provides that an 'act' includes an omission and the continuation of an act. Impossibility is not a defence: s 47(6). Section 49 provides in part that a person may commit more than one offence under ss 44–46 on the same facts.

There is a special defence to these offences found in s 50, the defence of acting reasonably. It is a defence for the accused to prove (sub-s (1)) that he knew that certain circumstances existed and it was reasonable for him to act in the way that he did in those circumstances; or (sub-s (2)) 'that he believed certain circumstances to exist; that his belief was reasonable; and that it was reasonable for him to act as he did in the circumstances as he believed them to be'. Subsection (3) goes on to provide:

> Factors to be considered in determining whether it was reasonable for a person to act as he did include –
> (a) the seriousness of the anticipated offence . . . ;
> (b) any purpose for which he claims to have been acting;
> (c) any authority by which he claims to have been acting.

It is uncertain whether the list of the factors is exhaustive but from the wording it appears not. It is difficult to envisage circumstances in which s 50 provides a defence to a s 44 charge but the Law Commission provided an example. The accused, a motorist, changes motorway lanes to allow a following driver through even though the accused knows that the overtaker is speeding. The burden of proof in respect of s 50 is on the accused but that could be read down so as to impose only an evidential burden, as dealt with in Chapter 1.

Section 51 exempts so-called protected persons from conviction for these offences. A protected person is one who is protected by a 'protective offence', which is one which exists 'for the protection of a particular category of persons' (s 51(2)). This provision is an enactment of the rule in *Tyrrell* [1894] 1 QB 710 (CCR), discussed below in the context of conspiracy.

The maximum sentence is that of the crime being encouraged or assisted, for example for encouraging burglary in a dwelling house the maximum is 14 years.

Criticisms

(a) The law is complex and is stated in a prolix fashion: 3,458 words are used not including the Schedule to the Act.

(b) The law is too complicated to meet the problem, which as stated above was the non-liability of the person who assists when the principal offence does not take place.

(c) Why are three offences used? Sections 44–45 do not spell out the differences; one has to read s 49 closely for the differences in the *actus reus* and *mens rea*.

(d) There is much overlap with the secondary offences dealt with in Chapter 5.

Statutory offences of incitement

The Offences Against the Person Act 1861, s 4 (as amended by the Criminal Law Act 1977), created the crime of incitement to murder. The accused is guilty if he acts to 'solicit, encourage, persuade or endeavour to persuade or . . . propose to any person to murder any other person'. The offence adds nothing to the general offence of encouraging or assisting in terms of substantive law. The Court of Appeal in *Winter* [2008] Crim LR 821 ruled that soliciting a person to be a secondary party to a killing fell within s 4. Section 4 includes inciting foreign nationals in England and Wales to commit murder abroad: *Abu Hamza* [2006] EWCA Crim 2918. It was not restricted to the solicitation of British subjects to commit murder. Parliament has created other incitement offences in, for instance, the Sexual Offences Act 2003 (there are several such offences in the statute), the Incitement to Mutiny Act 1797 and the Incitement to Disaffection Act 1934.

Conspiracy

Introduction

Lord Diplock in *DPP v Bhagwan* [1972] AC 60 (HL) said that common law **conspiracy** was 'the least systematic, the most irrational branch of English penal law'. Common law conspiracy has been largely abolished by s 5(1) of the Criminal Law Act 1977. The defendants as usual do not have to know that what they have agreed on is an offence.

When the full offence is committed conspiracy can still be charged, and will be if the charge is needed to give the full flavour of the criminal behaviour. The result is to make proceedings complex. However, the prosecution will not be allowed to proceed with both charges if the conspiracy count is prejudicial to the accused: *Practice Direction* [1977] 1 WLR 537.

For those offences which remain common law conspiracies the famous definition in *Mulcahy* v *R* (1868) LR 3 HL 306 remains the touchstone: 'an agreement by two or more to do an unlawful act or do a lawful act in an unlawful way.' Statutory conspiracy is defined in s 1(1) of the 1977 Act, a new s 1(1) being substituted by the Criminal Attempts Act 1981, s 5(1):

> Subject to the following provisions of this Part of this Act, if a person agrees with any other person or persons that a course of conduct shall be pursued which if the agreement is carried out in accordance with their intentions, either –
> (a) will necessarily amount to or involve the commission of any offence or offences by one or more of the parties to the agreement, or
> (b) would do so but for the existence of facts which render the commission of the offence or offences impossible,
> he is guilty of conspiracy to commit the offence or offences in question.

The effect of the 1981 amendment was to bring the law on impossibility in statutory conspiracy into line with impossibility in attempt (see later in this chapter). However, for conspiracies which remain ones at common law, the pre-1981 law applies and impossibility is a defence in certain circumstances.

An example of s 1(1) is *Mulligan* [1990] STC 220 (CA). There is a common law offence of cheating the public revenue. If two persons commit this crime together, there is a conspiracy. In *Drew* [2000] 1 Cr App R 91 (CA) it was held that an accused is guilty of conspiracy even when he is the intended victim of the conspiracy, as when he is to be supplied with drugs. For exceptional cases relating to 'victims', see below.

In s 1(1) the 'other person' need not be identified: *Phillips* (1987) 86 Cr App R 18.

A difficult authority on s 1(1) is *Anderson* [1986] AC 27 (HL). The accused, a person on remand in custody, was charged with conspiracy to effect a prisoner's escape. He contended that he never intended to go through with the plan; that is, he had no *mens rea*. The House of Lords dismissed his appeal. He had agreed with other persons that a course of conduct would be pursued which, when carried out 'in accordance with their intentions' – i.e. the others' intentions – would necessarily amount to or involve the commission of a crime. It was held that the accused had to play some part in the agreed course of conduct. The accused did not intend to let the prisoner escape but that was held to be irrelevant because it did not have to be proved that the individual accused intended that the agreement should be carried out. This reasoning leads to a problem if there is only one other person in the agreement. In that event the agreement will not be carried out in accordance with *their* intentions but only in accordance with one of their intentions. To say the least, the interpretation of s 1(1) is strained and *Anderson* is contrary to the intention of Parliament. On the wording at least two of the accused have to have the *mens rea*. The accused could have been convicted of being a secondary party, an aider and abettor, to the conspiracy.

In the much-criticised authority of *Yip Chiu-Cheung* v *R* [1995] 1 AC 111 (PC) a US drugs enforcement officer agreed to act as a courier of heroin from Hong Kong to Australia for the accused. The accused was arrested in Hong Kong and charged with conspiring with the officer to traffic in heroin. He contended that the officer could not be a conspirator because he did not have the *mens rea* for that offence; therefore, there was no conspiracy to which he could be a party for a conspiracy requires two participants. It was held that on the facts the officer did intend to commit the crime of trafficking in drugs: he did have the *actus reus* and *mens rea* for conspiracy. He too could be convicted of conspiracy. His motive and courage did not exculpate him. It was immaterial that he did not expect to be prosecuted: 'the fact that . . . the authorities would not prosecute the undercover agent does not mean that he did not commit the crime . . .' The position would have been different if he did not intend to commit the crime. He would have no *mens rea* and there would be no conspiracy: *Anderson*, above. The *ratio* of *Yip Chiu-Cheung* is contrary to *Anderson* in that it requires two parties to intend and agree to commit an unlawful act.

The Law Commission's draft Criminal Code, *A Criminal Code for England and Wales*, Report No. 177, 1989, rejected *Anderson* and preferred the plain meaning of the 1977 statute, which was based on the Law Commission's Report No. 76, *Conspiracy and Criminal Law Reform*, 1976. One recommendation was: 'Both must intend that any consequence in the definition of the offence will result.' Certainly the House of Lords ruling is contrary to the wishes of Parliament. The Court of Appeal in *Edwards* [1991] Crim LR 45 did not follow *Anderson* though they may not have realised what they were doing. The accused agreed to supply amphetamines but he may have intended to supply a drug called ephedrine. Since it was uncertain that he intended to supply amphetamines, he was not guilty of conspiracy to supply that type of controlled drug. In any case the decision in *Anderson* does not apply to the common law offence of conspiracy to defraud, for *Anderson* is based on the interpretation of the statute.

There is support in *Hollinshead* reported in [1985] AC 975 (CA) for the proposition that the phrase 'the commission of any offence . . . by one or more of the parties' should be read as requiring the involvement of one (or more) of them as the principal. Accordingly, if two secondary parties agree to assist the principal in killing the victim, they are not guilty of conspiracy to murder if the principal was not party to the agreement. (Presumably they could be convicted of conspiracy to incite the principal.) The Court of Appeal's judgment may be summarised as being that there is no statutory conspiracy to be a secondary party to an offence. One cannot therefore conspire to aid a murderer. One must conspire to commit the full offence, murder, as a principal. On appeal the Lords did not discuss the issue and did not approve or disapprove the Court of Appeal's decision. The ordinary meaning of the words in the statutory definition gives support to the Court of Appeal's proposition of law. If correct, when two parties agree to help a third party who is not part of the agreement between the first two, they are not guilty of conspiracy to commit whatever offence the third party committed.

The Court in *Kenning* [2008] EWCA Crim 1534 said that whether the reasoning of the same court in *Hollinshead* was binding was a matter of debate but that there was no crime of conspiracy to be a secondary party (aid, abet, counsel or procure) to a principal offence. The defendants ran a shop which sold cannabis seeds and they provided information on how to grow them. They could not be guilty of the crime of aiding and abetting a conspiracy to produce controlled drugs because no such crime exists. This ruling is in line with s 1(4)(b) of the Criminal Attempts Act 1981, which states that there is no offence of attempting to be a secondary party. Note, however, they may now be guilty of encouraging or assisting a crime contrary to ss 44–46 of the Serious Crime Act 2007, discussed earlier in this chapter.

Hollinshead applies only to statutory conspiracies and not to common law ones such as conspiracy to defraud.

Section 1(1) of the 1977 Act defines the *actus reus* of conspiracy. One might have expected s 1(2) to define the *mens rea*, but it seems to apply only when the crime agreed on is a strict offence:

Where liability for any offence may be incurred without knowledge on the part of the person committing it of any particular fact or circumstance necessary for the commission of the offence, a person shall nevertheless not be guilty of conspiracy to commit that offence by virtue of subsection (1) above unless he and at least one other party to the agreement intend or know that fact or circumstance shall or will exist at the time when the conduct constituting the offence is to take place.

However, as we shall see in the discussion of the *mens rea* of statutory conspiracy, this provision is read as applying whatever the *mens rea* of the crime to be committed and not just to strict offences.

An agreement to commit a summary offence is a conspiracy but cannot be charged without the consent of the Crown Prosecution Service (s 4(1) of the 1977 Act and the Prosecution of Offences Act 1985, s 1(7)). In attempt, however, there is no offence of attempting to commit a summary offence.

Actus reus

General

One element of the *actus reus* is an agreement, which is manifested in some way such as by words, action or writing. Agreement, which to lawyers is often seen as a meeting of the minds, is without an external manifestation a mental state, and English law does not penalise people for entertaining wicked thoughts. Nevertheless, 'agreement' is a low threshold for a crime: compare the offence of attempt where an act more than merely preparatory to the commission of the offence is needed. The agreement must be communicated to the other party: *Scott* (1979) 68 Cr App R 164. It must have reached a definite conclusion and the parties must be beyond the stage of considering the possibility of committing a crime: *King* [1966] Crim LR 280. In *O'Brien* (1974) 59 Cr App R 222 (CA) the accused had talked about effecting the escape of three Irish nationalist prisoners from Winson Green Prison, Birmingham, but he had not reached the stage of agreement. Therefore, there was at that stage no conspiracy to effect an escape. In *Barnard* (1979) 70 Cr App R 28 the accused was talking with others about stealing from a jeweller's. The others had decided to rob the jeweller and were guilty of conspiracy to rob. He found out that the jeweller took the best pieces home at night. He decided to proceed no further because his way of stealing was to come through the ceiling at night. The others robbed the jeweller in the daytime. The accused was not guilty of conspiracy to rob. He had not agreed to join in that offence. A more modern case is *Goddard* [2012] EWCA Crim 1756. The two accused had sent each other text messages in which, the court held, they fantasised about raping a six-year-old boy and after messages they masturbated. There was no agreement to rape a child under 13. Instead the parties were indulging their fantasies.

The parties need not have met previously provided that they acted in pursuance of a common purpose which was notified to at least one other party to the conspiracy: *Meyrick* (1929) 21 Cr App R 94 (CCA). This case has come in for criticism because it was not proved that each of the parties, night-club owners, knew that the other was paying a bribe to the same constable so that the police would turn a blind eye to breaches of the licensing laws, and it was suggested in *Griffiths* [1966] 1 QB 78 (CCA) that each knew what the other was doing because the premises were close, but that last fact does not explain why the court could say that there was an agreement. *Griffiths* holds that an accused can be guilty of conspiracy even though he did not know of all of its details. It is the common purpose, the agreement, which is the point to concentrate on. If there is no agreement and the parties are still negotiating, the situation looks like an attempted conspiracy, but there is no such offence: Criminal Law Act 1977, s 5(7).

There is no need for the accused to play an active part in the conspiracy: *Siracusa* (1990) 90 Cr App R 340 (CA), not agreeing with the House of Lords in *Anderson* that the accused was guilty only if the accused played an active part in furthering the crime. *Siracusa* is an important authority, one assumed to represent the law, but *Hollinshead* is unfortunately a decision of the Lords. Since the focus is on the agreement, it does not matter that the parties have done something different from what they agreed. As Woolf LJ put it in *Bolton* (1992) 94 Cr App R 74 (CA): '. . . it is what was agreed to be done and not what was in fact done which is all important.' On the facts of the case it was irrelevant that mortgage fraudsters expected to be paid by cheque but the money was actually transferred electronically.

Sometimes the courts have used the analogy of contract to determine whether an agreement existed. In *Walker* [1962] Crim LR 458 (CCA), there was no conspiracy where there were negotiations, not an agreement, to steal wages. It should be noted that the analogy with contract is inexact. There is less certainty needed for an agreement in conspiracy than for a contract. Unlike in contract no consideration need have passed. Conspiracies are not, unlike contracts, enforceable in the courts.

Once there is agreement, that is sufficient. The conspiracy need not be put into effect. Since conspiracy is a continuing offence, the defendants are guilty even though they were not all parties to the same agreement at the same time. Provided that all the other elements exist, the conspiracy is complete at the time of the making of the agreement. If, for example, two friends agree to steal a car on the next day, they are guilty, even though before that day one of them wins a car and they decide not to go ahead with their plan. Under the statute the agreement must necessarily amount to or involve the commission of a crime, if carried out. Donaldson LJ, as he then was, gave this example in *Reed* [1982] Crim LR 819 (CA): 'A and B agree to drive from London to Edinburgh in a time which can be achieved without breaking the speed limit, but only if the traffic which they encounter is exceptionally light . . . Accordingly the agreement does not constitute . . . conspiracy.' This passage was approved in *Jackson* [1985] Crim LR 442 (CA). In that case A, B and C agreed that C would be shot in the leg if he was convicted of the offence for which he was being tried in order that the court would feel sympathetic towards him and give him a light sentence. They were guilty of conspiracy to pervert the course of justice. Therefore, a conditional agreement ('We will shoot you if you are convicted') is a conspiracy. The men were guilty even though the trial was continuing. The person on trial might have been acquitted of burglary but the execution of the agreement would still be necessary in s 1(1) terms, for 'necessarily' does not mean 'inevitably' but 'if the agreement is carried out in accordance with the plan, an offence would take place'.

In *Reed*, A and B agreed that A would visit persons who wished to commit suicide and either help or discourage them, depending on what he thought was the better approach. He was guilty of conspiring to abet suicide. Similarly, an agreement to make bombs during the IRA ceasefire in the early 1990s to be used after the ceasefire, if it ended, was a conspiracy to cause explosions. After all, the IRA did break that ceasefire by exploding the Canary Wharf bomb. In *Jackson* and *Reed* the objects of the agreements were unlawful whereas in the London–Edinburgh example the breaking of the speed limit was incidental to the agreement. The line may be hard to draw. An agreement to rob a bank when it is safe to do so is a conspiracy (*Reed*, *obiter*). There is no need that the full offence will necessarily be committed: the point is that the defendants must so intend (*mens rea*).

Under the statute the term 'course of conduct' limits what the defendants can be convicted of conspiring to do. The facts of *Siracusa*, above, illustrate this proposition.

O'Connor LJ said: 'If the prosecution charge a conspiracy to contravene s 170(2) of the Customs and Excise Management Act 1979 by the importation of heroin, then the prosecution must prove that the agreed course of conduct was the importation of heroin. This is because the essence of the crime of conspiracy is the agreement and, in simple terms, you do not prove an agreement to import heroin by proving an agreement to import cannabis.' Therefore the defendants cannot in this way be guilty of conspiracy though they would be guilty of the full offence of importing heroin when they believed that the substance was cannabis. To clarify the point O'Connor LJ added that the accused would not be guilty of a conspiracy to murder unless they intended to kill, yet they are guilty of murder itself if they intended only grievous bodily harm. (The law on this point in conspiracy is the same as that for attempt.)

The requirement of two parties

Conspiracy is based on agreement. It does not matter that the accused does not know the identity of his partner or partners, and he need not be in contact with all of them. One person cannot conspire with himself. In *McDonnell* [1966] 1 QB 233 it was held at Bristol Assizes that a person was not guilty of conspiracy when he was the sole director of a company, the other alleged party to the agreement, even though in law companies have separate legal personalities from the directors. This issue of liability for conspiring with a company with which one is identified is unaffected by the 1977 Act.

Spouses and civil partners also cause difficulty. In *Mawji v R* [1957] AC 126 the Privy Council said, without the point being argued, that a husband could not conspire with his wife because she was assumed not to have a will independent from that of her husband. Oliver J accepted this *obiter dictum* as being the law in *Midland Bank Trust Co Ltd v Green (No. 3)* [1979] Ch 496 (CA), a civil law decision. It is uncertain whether the rule applies to actually or potentially polygamous marriages. The rule is preserved for statutory conspiracies in s 2(2)(a) of the Criminal Law Act 1977 as amended. The Law Commission's Report No. 76, *Conspiracy and Criminal Law Reform*, 1976, on which the Act was based, recommended that the rule should be preserved in order to maintain the stability of marriage and in accordance with the then policy of keeping the law out of marriage. If there is a third party, all become guilty of conspiracy. The wife is therefore guilty if she makes an agreement with her husband, knowing that he is conspiring with others: *Chrastny* [1991] 1 WLR 1381 (CA). There is no need to show that she herself came to an agreement with the third party. If the parties married after the agreement, they are liable. It should be noted that this rule is applicable only to conspiracy and not to incitement or secondary participation. It is also of course not applicable to all principal offences such as murder and theft which the husband and wife have agreed upon. No doubt it will be abrogated at some time in the future just as the husband's immunity in rape was in the early 1990s. There seems nowadays to be no good reason for keeping it. The fact that the accused is married has no bearing on the wrongfulness of criminal behaviour towards a victim. The previous exception for married partners alone was extended to civil partners by the Civil Partnership Act 2004, Sch 27.

An accused is not guilty of conspiracy if the sole other party is below the age of criminal responsibility: s 2(2)(b) of the 1977 Act. By s 2(3) a child is under the age of criminal responsibility when, by reason of the Children and Young Persons Act 1933, s 50, he cannot be guilty of any offence. The reference to the non-liability of the child means that s 2(2)(b) applies only to children under 10. Section 2(2) provides for exemptions from the general principle of liability where there are two parties and if Parliament wished to exempt parties not expressly mentioned it should have said so. The statute says nothing about agreements with mentally abnormal persons (who cannot form the intent necessary for conspiracy) but whether the same rule should apply as for infants under 10 is moot. Section 2 applies only to statutory conspiracies. It is suggested that the same rules apply at common law.

Section 2(2) goes on to provide that the accused cannot be convicted of conspiracy with the intended victim of the offence. Therefore if the accused elopes with a girl under 16, she is the intended victim. By s 2(2) the accused is not liable for conspiracy – perhaps he should be. The intended victim also is not guilty (s 2(1)). If two defendants agree with the underage girl to have sexual intercourse with her they are guilty of conspiracy; the girl is not because of s 2(1). The 1977 Act gives no definition of 'intended victim'. One wide meaning is to read the term as covering anyone who will be harmed by the offence when committed. It may, however, be that the term is restricted to members of a class protected by Parliament such as girls under 16 in relation to unlawful sexual intercourse. Lord Phillips P, Lord Judge CJ, and Lord Wilson in *Gnango* [2012] 1 AC 827 (SC) thought that this was so; otherwise if two persons agreed that one of them should be a suicide bomber, neither of them would be guilty of conspiracy. If this argument is correct, the law would be consistent with accomplice liability: see *Tyrrell*, above. On this approach the intended victim who is not a member of a specially protected class would be guilty, as would be the co-conspirator. A suggested illustration is where one party agrees with another that the latter will inflict harm on him or her in pursuance of sexual pleasure. Both would be guilty despite one being in ordinary language the intended victim. An accused to whom drugs are supplied is not a 'victim' within s 2 and can therefore be guilty of conspiracy: *Drew* [2000] 1 Cr App R 91 (CA).

There is no common law authority on infants and victims. For those agreements which remain conspiracies at common law (see later) the accused may be guilty. An example would be conspiring to defraud an infant or victim. It is, however, hard to envisage a victim agreeing to be defrauded. It has been suggested that the term 'intended victim' covers only a person who cannot perpetrate the full offence or be convicted as an accessory. On this approach a person aged 15 should be convicted of conspiring to commit homosexual offences even if he is the victim of the offence because he can be guilty of the full offence.

If one of the defendants does not fall within one of these exceptions, he is guilty of conspiracy even though he cannot commit the offence agreed upon. The crime of rape provides the best illustration. If a woman agrees with a man that he will rape a third party, she is guilty of conspiracy to rape despite her not being able to commit rape as a principal offender.

Immunity and acquittal of the other offender

May a person be convicted of conspiracy when the other is acquitted or immune from prosecution?

(a) *Immunity*. In *Duguid* (1906) 21 Cox CC 200 (CCR), the accused agreed with a woman to remove the woman's child from the custody of the lawful guardian, contrary to s 56 of the Offences Against the Person Act 1861 (now repealed). By that section the mother is immune from prosecution. It was held that the accused could be found guilty of conspiracy. The Court for Crown Cases Reserved did not investigate the liability of the mother for conspiracy. It may be that she is liable, for in *Whitchurch* (1890) 24 QBD 420 (CCR) a person was found guilty of conspiring to commit an offence which she could not have been convicted of as the principal. A woman who is not pregnant cannot be convicted of procuring her own abortion, but she is guilty of the conspiracy (though she is apparently never prosecuted nowadays), while in *Burns* (1984) 79 Cr App R 175 (CA) a father was found guilty of conspiring to steal his own child when he could not have been found guilty as the principal offender. (The exemption has since been abrogated.) The rule is not affected by s 2(2) of the 1977 Act. Contrary to the recommendation of the Law Commission, Parliament refused to overturn **Whitchurch**, and since the Act there is also **Burns**. The Court of Appeal looked at the purpose of the statute to see whether the exemption from the principal offence should apply to the conspiracy to commit that offence. Certainly on the facts of **Burns**, where the father and a 'posse of men' broke into his former wife's home to snatch the child, the husband would seem to have been justifiably convicted.

(b) *Acquittal.* Where one of two conspirators is acquitted, the old view was that, if both were tried together, the other could not be found guilty of conspiracy. However, the House of Lords held differently in **DPP v Shannon** [1975] AC 717. Two Law Lords said that the acquittal of one was not a bar to the conviction of the other (Viscount Dilhorne and Lord Simon); Lords Reid and Morris said that the traditional rule should apply; the casting vote was held by Lord Salmon who said that the orthodox rule should apply except in special circumstances. The common law therefore was confused. If the two accused were tried separately, the acquittal of one was not a bar to the conviction of another. (There might for instance have been a confession from one party but not from another, and the prosecution could not prove the case.)

In relation to statutory conspiracies, the 1977 Act, s 5(8), states:

> The fact that the person or persons who, so far as appears from the indictment on which any person has been convicted of conspiracy, were the only other parties to the agreement on which his conviction was based have been acquitted of conspiracy by reference to that agreement (whether after being tried with the person convicted or separately) shall not be a ground for quashing his conviction unless under all the circumstances of the case his conviction is inconsistent with the acquittal of the other person or persons in question.

The next subsection, s 5(9), abolishes inconsistent 'law or practice'. While not so stating expressly, s 5(9) abolishes the common law on this topic. Therefore, s 5(8) applies to both statutory and common law conspiracies.

According to **Merrick** (1980) 71 Cr App R 130 (CA), **Longman** (1980) 72 Cr App R 121 (DC) and **Roberts** (1983) 78 Cr App R 41 (DC), a judge may tell the jury to acquit both if to convict one and let the other go would be inconsistent. If the evidence is the same against each member, the judge should direct the jury to convict all or acquit all. If the evidence is substantially stronger against one accused than against the other, the judge should instruct the jury to consider each party separately. The result may be that the jury accepts that the first accused conspired with the second accused but that the second did not conspire with the first!

Unlawful object of the conspiracy

Section 1(1) of the 1977 Act, as substituted by the Criminal Attempts Act 1981, s 5(1), quoted above, begins: 'Subject to the following provisions . . .' That is a reference to s 5 of the 1977 Act, which states that certain conspiracies remain crimes at common law. By s 5(2) an agreement to defraud remains a common law crime. By s 5(3) conspiracies to corrupt public morals and outrage public decency remain common law offences if they would not necessarily amount to or result in a crime when performed by one person. If when done by one the behaviour does constitute a crime, the offence must be charged as a statutory conspiracy. For discussion see below. Unlike statutory conspiracies, impossibility in some forms is a defence in common law conspiracies.

Conspiracy to defraud

This offence, which is unhelpfully defined as an agreement to practise a fraud on someone, is useful in financial and economic affairs. An agreement to occasion loss by dishonest means is a conspiracy to defraud. For a contrary recent illustration, see *Norris* v *The Government of the United States of America* [2008] UKHL 9, which involved a cartel with dishonest agreement to fix prices by representatives of companies. Their Lordships held, disapproving earlier authorities, that this did not constitute a conspiracy to defraud. 'Dishonest' is of the normal *Ghosh* [1982] QB 1053 (CA) definition: see Chapter 15. A second form of this type of conspiracy is an agreement to persuade by dishonest means a person to act contrary to his or her duty. The former variety is very wide and has been criticised on this basis. For example, it is not theft to deprive the victim of an article temporarily. However, if two persons agree to do so, there is the offence of conspiracy to defraud. Similarly it is not the crime of theft if a person makes a secret profit from another's property (*Attorney-General's Reference (No. 1 of 1985)* [1986] QB 491 (CA) though the latest Privy Council authority (*Attorney-General of Hong Kong* v *Reid* [1994] 1 AC 324) is *contra*, see the discussion of 'Belonging to another' in Chapter 15), but it is a conspiracy to defraud if two persons agree to do so. The principal criticism of this offence is precisely that it makes unlawful something done by two which would have been lawful if done by one. A second criticism is that the offence is of uncertain width. The advantages to the prosecution are the reverse of these criticisms, and there is support for the view that a charge of conspiracy to defraud can reflect the overall criminality of the defendants' misconduct. Interrelated acts can be linked in one charge.

The Criminal Justice Act 1987, s 12(1), provides that this common law offence and the statutory conspiracy offence are not mutually exclusive. An agreement to commit a fraud can be both. The effect is that only conspiracies to defraud which do not involve the commission of an offence need to be charged as conspiracy at common law. By s 12(3) the maximum sentence is 10 years' imprisonment. (It should be noted that the law is different with regard to conspiracies to corrupt public morals and outrage public decency. If there are substantive offences of corrupting public morals and outraging public decency, charges of conspiracies to commit them must be brought under the 1977 Act.)

Until recently the definition of this offence given by Lord Diplock in *Scott* v *MPC* [1975] AC 819 (HL) was considered to be correct: one in which the defendants either intend to cause (or are reckless as to causing) economic loss to another (or injure a proprietary interest) or to induce another to act dishonestly contrary to his public duty. The latter half of this definition comes from *Welham* v *DPP* [1961] AC 103 (HL) and was used in *Moses* [1991] Crim LR 617 (CA). There was a conspiracy when the parties agreed to facilitate the obtaining of work permits by immigrants who were prohibited from working by a stamp in their passport, by deceiving the National Insurance Department into believing that the passports did not carry the stamp. The members of the department had acted contrary to their public duty. There was no need for the victim, the Crown, to suffer loss. Lord Denning in *Welham* rejected the contention that an intent to cause economic loss was required. The intent to defraud meant the intent to practise a fraud or to act to someone's prejudice. In this form of conspiracy to defraud there never existed a need to prove an intent to cause economic loss. It remains uncertain whether the public duty sub-head is indeed restricted to officials performing such obligations, but as stated in the next paragraph this type of conspiracy to defraud is now seen as merely an illustration of the general principle.

In the former part of the definition there must be depriving by dishonesty and it was thought there had to be an intention to cause or recklessness as to causing economic loss:

Scott, above, *Attorney-General's Reference (No. 1 of 1982)* [1983] QB 751 (CA) and *Wai Yu-Tsang v R* [1992] 1 AC 269 (PC). Viscount Dilhorne in *Scott* defined this version of the offence as 'an agreement by two or more by dishonesty to deprive a person of something which is his or to which he is or would be or might be entitled and an agreement by two or more by dishonesty to injure some proprietary right'. In *Attorney-General's Reference (No. 1 of 1982)*, the accused agreed to sell in the Lebanon whisky which was to be falsely labelled as made by a well-known firm. The court held that the true object of the conspiracy was to defraud the purchasers. There was no conspiracy to defraud in relation to the firm because their loss would have been incidental to the main object of the agreement. The case seems inconsistent with *Scott* where the principal object was to gain money for the defendants, yet they were guilty of conspiracy to defraud the copyright owners. Moreover, in most conspiracies to defraud the true object is to gain money, yet the agreement is still a conspiracy to defraud. The House of Lords in *Scott* did not distinguish between the true object of the agreement and the incidental effects.

An oblique intention (see Chapter 3) is sufficient as in *Scott*, *Hollinshead* and *Cooke* [1986] AC 909 (HL), where rail stewards were guilty of conspiring to defraud British Rail when their object was to make money for themselves. *Allsop* (1976) 63 Cr App R 29 (CA) held that recklessness was sufficient. Accordingly, the accused is guilty if he thought he could make good securities he had taken by striking a good deal on a different matter. The Privy Council in *Wai Yu-Tsang v R* said that the defendants were guilty if they realised that they had agreed to bring about a state of affairs which would or might deceive the victim into acting or failing to act in such a way that he would suffer economic loss or his economic interests would be imperilled. *Allsop* is to the same effect. Lord Diplock's division in *Scott* was incorrect. The public duty form of the offence was not a distinct category but merely an illustration of the general law. In neither type was economic loss necessary: it was sufficient that the defendants deprived the accused of something, actual or prospective, dishonestly. The Lords approved this formulation in *GG* [2009] 1 AC 92. In *Adams v R* [1995] 1 WLR 52 the Privy Council emphasised this criterion: 'there must exist some right or interest in the victim which is capable of being prejudiced whether by actual loss or by being put at risk.' Therefore, the accused is not guilty when he makes it more difficult for the victim to find out whether he had an interest in a sum of money. On the facts of the case the Judicial Committee held that a dishonest agreement by directors to impede a company in the exercise of its right to recover secret profits made by them constituted a conspiracy to defraud. The accused himself had taken part in setting up a structure of over-seas companies through which he had dishonestly concealed information, namely secret profits, in relation to which he had been under a legal duty to disclose to the company of which he was a director. Accordingly the company had a right or interest which could be prejudiced. Note that the accused's behaviour now falls within the Fraud Act 2006. Dishonesty must be proved. It bears the same definition as in theft (see Chapter 15).

Adams v R was followed by the Court of Appeal in *Fussell* [1997] Crim LR 812. The fact that the conspirators did not wish to harm the victim was irrelevant: *Wai Yu-Tsang v R*. The fact that the fraudsters did not desire to cause loss was motive, as *Allsop* had also held. In *Wai Yu-Tsang v R* the defendant's desire, to stop a run on the bank, was a good one but irrelevant. It could be said that his true object was to stop the run on the bank, yet he was guilty. This authority is inconsistent with *Attorney-General's Reference (No. 1 of 1982)*, above, which should be taken to be overruled.

Scott v MPC [1975] AC 819 (HL), discussed above, exemplifies the non-public duty part of the definition. There was an agreement to bribe cinema employees to make films available to be copied in breach of copyright. The Lords held this agreement to be a conspiracy to defraud. There was no need for deception. In **Hollinshead**, above, an agreement to make black boxes for others to get free electricity was a conspiracy to defraud. The conduct would probably amount to a fraud or some other offence against property by a third party who bought the equipment. Where the fraud agreed on amounts to a crime there is also a conspiracy under the 1977 Act. The Act states that a person is guilty of conspiracy under the Act only if at least one of the parties intends to perpetrate the offence. **Hollinshead**, as we have seen, held differently for conspiracy to defraud. The parties themselves need not carry out the fraud. An agreement to have the fraud committed by others is sufficient. In **Dearlove** (1989) 88 Cr App R 280 (CA), the dishonest purchase of goods (Oxo cubes) at the lower export price intending to sell them at a higher price on the domestic market amounted to obtaining property by deception, an offence since abolished but now incorporated within that of fraud contrary to the Fraud Act 2006.

The Law Commission and conspiracy to defraud

The Law Commission published its Working Paper on *Conspiracy to Defraud* (No. 104) as long ago as 1988. It listed four options: (a) do nothing; (b) put the law into a statute; (c) abolish the law and adjust offences to cover the gaps; (d) abolish present law and put into its place a wide fraud crime. Contrary to (a) are the policy arguments that judges should not make law and that Parliament is a better body than the courts to change the law. Contrary to (b) is the principle in the 1977 Act that agreements should not be conspiracies if they would not amount to a crime when carried out by one person. Contrary to (c) is the difficulty in seeing all the gaps. Contrary to (d) is the principle that the law should be clearly stated and not vague in its width. The Commission proposed a wide offence of dishonestly causing another to suffer economic prejudice or a risk of prejudice, or dishonestly making a gain for himself or another.

The Law Commission published its Report No. 228, *Criminal Law: Conspiracy to Defraud*, in 1994. At para. 1.17 it averred that it wished 'to reduce the length and complexity of trials by simplifying the law, while always ensuring that the defendant is fully protected'. It summarised its conclusion in para. 1.20: 'for practical reasons conspiracy to defraud performs a useful role in the present law of dishonesty, and we have concluded that it should remain intact pending our comprehensive review of the law. We have resolved that it would be inappropriate, at a time when we are about to re-examine the whole scheme of dishonesty offences, to make piecemeal recommendations for reform of other aspects of the law of dishonesty.' Defendants can be convicted of a crime appropriate to their conduct.

The Law Commission criticised the uncertainty surrounding the width of the offence and the fact that a conspiracy to defraud is lawful if done by one person. However, it referred to undesirable gaps in the law which would open up if the crime were abolished, such as a conspiracy to acquire confidential information and one to evade liability or to delay payment without intending to make permanent default. These lacunae were adjudged so substantial that the offence could not be abolished without replacement. An illustration from the case law after the publication of the Report is **Preddy** [1996] AC 815 (HL). A mortgage fraudster could not be convicted of the now repealed offence of obtaining property by deception, but had there been two of them acting in concert, they could have been convicted of conspiracy to defraud.

The Commission returned to the issue in its Report No. 276, *Fraud*, 2002. The Home Office issued the Consultation Paper *Fraud Law Reform* in 2004. The government in *Fraud Law Reform* (2005) rejected the abolition of the offence pending the settling in of the Fraud Act 2006. It stated that it was unclear whether the new offences in the 2006 statute would cover all the gaps in the law which conspiracy to defraud currently fills (para. 4).

It does not cover the facts of **Scott v MPC**, above, because in that case there was no false representation. The Attorney-General issued *Guidance on the Use of the Common Law Offence of Conspiracy to Defraud*, 2007. Paragraph 15 gives examples of agreements which are conspiracies to defraud but do not in themselves constitute conspiracies contrary to the statute. Illustrations are agreements dishonestly to obtain land or other property which could not be the subject of a theft charge, such as trade secrets or other confidential information, and agreements dishonestly to infringe another's rights, such as to exploit a patent.

Conspiracy to defraud and the European Convention on Human Rights

A contention that conspiracy to defraud was contrary to Article 7 of the European Convention on Human Rights was rejected at the Divisional Court in **Norris**, above. The court agreed that conspiracy to defraud: 'has long contained the clarity and precision required by the Convention and the common law, namely proof that two or more conspirators intended dishonestly to defraud another or others as explained in **Welham**, **Scott** and **Wai Yu-Tsang**.'

Nevertheless, the possibility of a successful Article 7 challenge should not be totally discounted. It is not always clear that what the accused had done does meet the requirements of reasonable foreseeability that the conduct amounts to a crime.

Conspiracy to corrupt public morals and outrage public decency

Example

Amir and Beth are artists. They agree to make earrings out of frozen embryos. Are they guilty of conspiracy to outrage public decency?

At the time of the Criminal Law Act 1977 the common law crime of conspiracy to corrupt public decency was deliberately not covered by the statute; the legislators did not know whether there was a crime of corrupting public decency (i.e. when done by one person); therefore, they did not know whether the crime was a conspiracy under the statute, which requires that the agreement 'will necessarily amount to or involve the commission of any offence . . .' (what is now s 1(1)(a) of the 1977 Act). Furthermore, in 1977 Parliament was awaiting the publication of a report on obscenity. The report in fact did not lead to any changes but what has led to a change is the courts' rulings that outraging public decency is a crime when done by one person. There are several CA authorities to this effect but for the purposes of this answer **Gibson** [1990] 2QB 619 is the most helpful (the alert may wish to discover the facts of the case). The effect is that since there is a crime of conspiring to outrage public decency, if two or more agree to do so, then the offence is one contrary to the 1977 statute and not one of the common law crime of conspiring to outrage public decency. Therefore, the crime which Amir and Beth are guilty of is conspiracy under the statute and not one of conspiring to outrage public decency at common law.

For a recent case on 'upskirting', one of the modern instances of outraging public decency, see **Hamilton** [2007] EWCA Crim 2062. It may be that corrupting public morals is also a crime if done by one person; if so, it too falls under the 1977 Act. However, conspiracy to defraud remains a common law offence even after the Fraud Act 2006, but if the conspiracy to defraud does not involve the commission of an offence if done by one person, only then should it be charged as a common law conspiracy: see s 12(1) of the Criminal Justice Act 1987.

In *Shaw* v *DPP* [1962] AC 220, the defendants published *The Ladies' Directory*, a 28-page book advertising prostitutes' names, telephone numbers, addresses and services. The House of Lords held, Lord Reid dissenting, that there was an offence at common law of conspiracy to corrupt public morals. No proof was needed that anyone was in fact corrupted. It was for the jury to say whether on the facts the crime was committed, which leads to uncertainty in the law. There was no need for a conspiracy charge because the defendants could have been convicted of publishing an obscene article, a crime under s 2(4) of the Obscene Publications Act 1959. Since Parliament had spoken so recently on the topic it seems strange that the House of Lords should create a novel crime.

There was a retreat from *Shaw* in *Knuller (Publishing, Printing and Promotions) Ltd* v *DPP* [1973] AC 435 (HL). Two Law Lords, Morris and Kilbrandon, thought that *Shaw* was correctly decided. Two Lords, Reid and Morris, thought it was wrong. Lord Simon was unwilling to overrule *Shaw*. Therefore, *Shaw* remains part of the law. However, the test for corrupting public morals was changed from that in *Shaw*, leading astray, to corrupting public morals.

Lords Simon and Kilbrandon and probably Morris thought in *Knuller* that there was a common law offence of conspiracy to outrage public decency. If there is an offence when committed by one person and *Gibson* [1990] 2 QB 619 (CA) held that there was a substantive crime of outraging public decency, as did, among other cases, *Rowley* [1991] 1 WLR 1020 (CA) *obiter* and *Hamilton* [2008] 1 All ER 1103 (CA) (which involved the practice of 'upskirting', videoing up skirts, as did *Ching Choi* [1999] EWCA Crim 1279), the charge is conspiracy contrary to s 1 of the 1977 Act. Therefore, the former common law offence of conspiracy to outrage public decency is now a statutory offence in accordance with s 5(3). An offence of conspiring to outrage *public* decency cannot take place in a private home. To 'outrage' means to disgust. No one actually needs to be outraged; it is sufficient that an ordinary person would be likely to be outraged if he saw the conduct. It is difficult to see which types of behaviour would be a conspiracy to outrage public decency if done by two people but not the crime of outraging public decency if done by one person. It should be added that 'decency' is not restricted to sexual matters: *Ching Choi*.

If conspiracy to corrupt public morals would amount to a crime when done by one person, the conspiracy is statutory, not common law: s 5(3)(b). There is doubt whether there is an offence of corrupting public morals. The Court of Criminal Appeal in *Shaw* thought that there was, but the Lords considered only conspiracy and not whether a substantive offence existed.

The Law Commission's Consultation Paper No. 193, *Simplification of Criminal Law: Public Nuisance and Outraging Public Decency*, 2010, proposed to put the crime of outraging public decency onto a statutory footing and to replace the element of strict liability with that of intent or recklessness as to whether ordinary people would be outraged, shocked or disgusted.

Like conspiracy to defraud in s 5(2), the retention of the conspiracy in s 5(3) was meant to be temporary only, pending reform of the law on obscenity. The government had the opportunity to abolish these crimes when it enacted the 1977 statute but it postponed changes until the Committee on Obscenity and Film Censorship chaired by Bernard Williams had reported, but when it did in 1979 the law remained unchanged. In relation to these common law conspiracies impossibility is a defence unless the means to be used were inadequate to effectuate the plan, in which case the accused are guilty. The obvious tip to prosecutors is that where the facts give rise both to common law and statutory conspiracy the latter should be charged, for impossibility has been abolished in respect of it. What may be called subsequent impossibility is no defence because conspiracy is complete on agreement. If the parties agree on 1 May to steal a gem on 1 July but another group steals it on 1 June, the original parties are guilty of conspiracy.

Because the law is not clear, it is not always clear in advance of trial whether a certain form of behaviour is one of these common law conspiracies. It is unsatisfactory that people do not know whether their acts are illegal, and it is costly and inefficient to find out by instigating prosecutions.

Conspiracy to trespass contrary to the 1977 Act

There was a crime at common law of conspiracy to trespass, provided that the execution of the agreement would invade the public domain or would inflict more than nominal damage. This type of conspiracy was abolished by the Criminal Law Act 1977. Sections 6–10 of that Act created five new offences of criminal trespass. An agreement by two or more persons to do any of these offences will be a statutory conspiracy. These crimes are:

(a) using violence to secure entry unless one is the displaced residential occupier or a person acting on his behalf (s 6(1)); there is a defence of lawful authority so that a police constable may use violence to secure entry in pursuance of a power granted by statute;

(b) remaining on premises, having entered as a trespasser and having been requested to leave by the displaced residential occupier or the protected intending occupier (s 7(1), as amended);

(c) trespassing while having with one a weapon of offence without lawful authority or reasonable excuse (s 8(1));

(d) trespassing on premises of diplomatic missions, or consular premises or private residences of diplomats. There is a list of the types of protected premises, s 9(2), which was amended by the Diplomatic and Consular Premises Act 1987 (s 9(1));

(e) obstructing a court officer who is executing a judgment for possession of any premises (s 10(1)).

There is also an offence of aggravated trespass in the Criminal Justice and Public Order Act 1994 aimed at hunt saboteurs.

Overseas conspiracies

The courts have treated the *actus reus* of conspiracy as a continuing matter. The principal authority is **DPP v Doot** [1973] AC 807 (HL). None of the five defendants was British, and the agreement to break UK drugs laws by importing cannabis was made outside the UK. Their Lordships held that conspiracy, being a continuing offence, was not complete at the moment the agreement was made. When one of the defendants arrived in England, he and his friends could be charged with conspiracy, even though originally English courts had no jurisdiction to try the offence. Viscount Dilhorne said: 'A conspiracy does not end with the making of the agreement. It will continue so long as there are two or more parties to it intending to carry out the design.' **Doot** involved conspiracy before the 1977 Act. That Act did not deal with the issue, but it is considered that the law remains the same.

In **Doot** there was an act in England. What if there was no such act? Lord Salmon in **Doot** considered that there was a conspiracy, as did Lord Diplock in **DPP v Stonehouse** [1978] AC 55 (HL), though Lord Keith spoke to the contrary. The position was in doubt until **Liangsiriprasert v Government of the USA** [1991] 1 AC 255 (PC), on appeal from Hong Kong, where the law on this point is the same as in England. Lord Griffiths said:

Why should an overt act be necessary to found jurisdiction? In the case of conspiracy in England the crime is complete once the agreement is made and no further overt act need be proved as an ingredient of the crime. The only purpose of looking for an overt act in England in the case of a conspiracy entered into abroad can be to establish the link between the conspiracy and England or possibly to show the conspiracy is continuing. But, if this can be established by other evidence, for example the taping of conversations between the conspirators showing a firm agreement to commit the crime at some future date, it defeats the preventative purpose of the crime of conspiracy to have to wait until some overt act is performed in pursuance of the conspiracy.

Inchoate offences were aimed at frustrating the completion of crimes. 'If evidence is obtained that a terrorist cell operating abroad is planning a bombing campaign in London what sense can there be in the authorities . . . not acting until the cell comes to England to plant their bombs with the risk that the terrorists may slip through the net?' He continued:

> [t]heir Lordships can find nothing in precedent, comity or good sense that should inhibit the common law from regarding as justiciable in England inchoate crimes committed abroad which are intended to result in the commission of criminal offences in England. Accordingly a conspiracy entered into in Thailand with the intention of committing the criminal offence of trafficking in drugs in Hong Kong is justiciable in Hong Kong even if no overt act pursuant to the conspiracy has yet occurred in Hong Kong.

The result is in line with the recommendations of the Law Commission's Report No. 180, *Jurisdiction over Offences of Fraud and Dishonesty with a Foreign Element*, 1989, para. 4.4. Defendants charged with a 'listed offence' would be triable in England and Wales if any part of the conspiracy took place there.

The Privy Council decision in *Liangsiriprasert* was followed by the Court of Appeal in *Sansom* [1991] 2 QB 130. The accused were charged with conspiring to evade the prohibition on the importation of a controlled drug, cannabis, into England. The agreement was made in Morocco, and no act pursuant to that agreement had been performed in England. Taylor LJ in a reserved judgment rejected the contention that *Liangsiriprasert* applied only to common law conspiracies. There was nothing in the 1977 Act which indicated that common law and statutory conspiracies were to be treated differently in relation to this point. It would be 'absurd' if *Liangsiriprasert* applied only to conspiracies to defraud, and the Privy Council would have restricted their opinions to the common law, if their advice had been only concerned with the common law. On the facts, moreover, there was an overt act in England, the hire of a fishing vessel to import the drugs from Morocco. Therefore, *Sansom* is like *DPP v Doot*. Although the endorsement of *Liangsiriprasert* is *obiter*, there is no doubt that it represents the law.

It should be noted that by s 1(4) of the 1977 Act an agreement for conduct to take place outside England and Wales is not a conspiracy unless the crime would constitute an offence triable in England and Wales. Therefore, an agreement to break foreign criminal law is not a conspiracy indictable in England and Wales unless it would amount to an offence if done in England and Wales. If there is an agreement made in England to commit abroad what would be an offence of conspiracy to defraud if committed in England, English courts have no jurisdiction: *Attorney-General's Reference (No. 1 of 1982)* [1983] QB 751 (CA). Exceptionally a conspiracy to murder is triable in England and Wales even though it would not otherwise 'be so triable if committed in accordance with the intentions of the parties to the agreement'.

By virtue of the Criminal Justice Act 1993, which came into force in 1999 (and see the Criminal Justice (Terrorism and Conspiracy) Act 1998 and the Coroners and Justice Act

2010, s 72, which amends the law), a conspiracy to commit a 'group A' offence in England or abroad is triable in England whether the accused became a party to the conspiracy in England or abroad and whether 'any act or omission or other event in relation to the conspiracy occurred in England . . .' or not. This provision confirms **Liangsiriprasert** and **Sansom**, which, however, are not confined to listed offences. A 'group A' offence is one of those listed in the 1993 Act as amended. The list includes theft, fraud contrary to the Fraud Act 2006, blackmail, handling and evading liability by deception. The Act also inserts a new s 1A into the Criminal Law Act 1977. In relation to conspiracies to commit a 'group A' offence, whether or not the offence if committed would be an offence triable in England, the accused is now triable in England if he did 'anything' in England in relation to the agreement before its formation, or became a party to it in England, or did or omitted to do 'anything' in England in pursuance of it. Another provision deals with conspiracies where no element required to be proved for the commission of the offence occurred in England. An example is if the accused in England conspired with another in France to steal the *Mona Lisa* from the Louvre in Paris. Both defendants may be tried in England, even though the group A offence itself cannot be tried in England. The provisions apply also where the accused abroad has duped an innocent agent in England to start a conspiracy to purloin the *Mona Lisa*. If, however, everything took place abroad, there is no conspiracy justiciable here. An example is a purely French operation to steal the painting. In this eventuality the English courts have no jurisdiction.

Mens rea in statutory conspiracies

The mental element in conspiracy is the intention to play a part in the agreed course of conduct: **Anderson**, above. Recent cases, particularly ones involving drugs, have re-emphasised that recklessness is insufficient: **Harmer** [2005] 2 Cr App R 23 (CA), **Ali** [2005] Crim LR 864 (CA), and in particular **Saik** [2007] 1 AC 18 (HL). The accused must also intend to carry out the agreement and have the *mens rea* required for the offence he intends to commit. For example, in a conspiracy to steal, the defendants must intend permanently to deprive and be dishonest. In conspiracy to murder the defendant must intend to kill; an intention to cause grievous bodily harm is insufficient: **Siracusa**, above. In a conspiracy to import heroin, there must be an agreement to import heroin, not just any drug. The reason is that according to s 1(1) the agreed course of conduct must necessarily amount to a crime if carried out, and an agreement to commit grievous bodily harm will not necessarily result in the death of their victim when carried out. A person is guilty even though he intended to take part in only a portion of the unlawful conduct. He must know that at least one of the conspirators intends to commit the full offence, but it need not be shown that he intended to carry it out, no matter that s 1 of the Criminal Law Act 1977 states 'in accordance with *their* intentions' (emphasis added). In **Anderson**, the facts of which are given above, the accused was held to be guilty. If he was guilty despite his not intending the agreed plan to be carried out, all of the other conspirators should also be guilty, even if those too did not intend the agreement to be carried out! The *ratio* of **Anderson** is inconsistent with s 1(1). Section 1(1) states when paraphrased that a person is guilty of conspiracy only when two or more of the defendants intended to carry out their agreement. This part of **Anderson** survives the clarification which another part of **Anderson** received in **Siracusa**, which is discussed below.

The Lords in **Churchill v Walton** [1967] 2 AC 224 held at common law that in relation to strict offences the accused is guilty only if he knows of the circumstances. Accordingly, an agreement to commit a strict offence requires *mens rea*. In relation to statutory conspiracies s 1(2) of the 1977 Act adopts the same position. The same applies where the *mens* *rea* of the substantive offence is satisfied by something less than knowledge. The principal authority is *Saik*, above. Suspicion was the relevant mental element but it was not for the crime of conspiring to commit that offence. Lord Nicholls said that 'know' meant true belief; suspicion did not constitute knowledge. Section 1(2) applies to all offences where at issue is the existence of a fact or circumstance. It is not restrictive to strict offences.

> Where liability for any offence may be incurred without knowledge on the part of the person committing it of any particular fact or circumstance necessary for the commission of the offence, a person shall nevertheless be guilty of conspiracy to commit that offence . . . unless he and at least one other party to the agreement intend or know that that fact or circumstance will exist at the time when the conduct constituting the offence is to take place.

On its face s 1(2) applies only when the agreement is one to commit an offence of strict liability but it was meant to be, and is, read as applying to all statutory conspiracies: see *Saik* for confirmation.

It is suggested that s 1(2) is at base inconsistent with *Anderson*. If intention as to circumstances is required (s 1(2)) then, contrary to *Anderson*, intention as to consequence ought also to be required. The contrary view is that while intent as to circumstances is needed, recklessness as to consequences suffices. If so, two men who agree to rape, being reckless as to consent, are guilty of conspiracy to rape. It should also be pointed out that one cannot 'know' that something 'will exist' in the future. What is meant is that the accused must believe that a fact or circumstance will exist.

In *Anderson* Lord Bridge said that the accused had the mental element 'if, and only if . . . the accused, when he entered into the agreement intended to play some part in the agreed course of conduct in furtherance of the criminal purpose which the agreed course of conduct was intended to achieve'. On this view the defendant would not be guilty of conspiracy if he incited the principal to kill the third party but intended doing nothing else. (What about IRA 'Godfathers'? Can one see the House of Lords letting them go?) To state the proposition is to see how silly it is. This view was confirmed by the Court of Appeal in *Siracusa*, above. Contrary to what Lord Bridge said, there is no rule of law that the accused had to intend to play an active part in the agreed course of conduct. It was sufficient that the accused intended to continue to agree that the criminal behaviour of the other parties should continue. It must also be said that Lord Bridge's *dictum* is inconsistent with the thrust of his speech that intention is irrelevant, and the *dictum* is inconsistent with his efforts to secure the acquittal of the law-abiding citizen who joins the conspiracy to entrap the co-conspirators. He is now liable if he does intend to play some part in the execution of the agreement. The Lords could have found the defendant guilty of being an accessory to the conspiracy to effect the escape.

In *Allsop*, above, a *dictum* of Lord Diplock in *Hyam* v *DPP* [1975] AC 55 (HL) that intention includes knowledge of the likelihood of consequences occurring was applied to conspiracy to defraud. The 1977 Act requires intent, and if *Allsop* is correct it is restricted to common law offences. It has, however, been argued that, as in attempt, recklessness as to circumstances should be enough. If two men agree to have sexual intercourse with a woman and believe that she may consent, under present law they are not guilty of conspiring to rape. If s 1(2) is applied not just to strict offences but generally, they do not 'intend or know that that fact or circumstance [lack of consent] will exist at the time when the conduct constituting the offence is to take place'. The accused is guilty of conspiracy only if he knew she did not consent. Recklessness as to the existence of circumstances, lack of consent, is not sufficient *mens rea* for statutory conspiracies, though it suffices for the full offence of rape. It also suffices for the crime of attempted rape (see below). The issue was discussed in **Mir** (1994) *Independent*, 23 May (CA). Applying s 1(2) generally the court held that an accused is guilty of conspiracy only when he knows that a circumstance exists or intends that a consequence shall ensue. Recklessness is insufficient. Therefore, defendants are not guilty of conspiring to commit aggravated criminal damage if they are reckless as to a serious risk to life. This ruling should be contrasted with the law in attempt where recklessness as to endangering life is sufficient *mens rea*. The court in **Mir** made no effort to reconcile its ruling with the law of attempt. The decision is inconsistent with the rule that the accused must have the *mens rea* of the full offence. Recklessness as to danger to life is one of the fault elements for aggravated criminal damage. Yet the Court of Appeal held that the accused was guilty only if he intended to endanger life.

General comments on conspiracy

Under present law there remains the difficulty that three types of conspiracies remain common law offences. Two of them, corrupting public morals and outraging public decency, are vague. These offences continue to exist, it is thought, because prosecutions are rarely brought. If more prosecutions were brought, liberal thinkers would have a field day criticising the potential width of those offences. The width of conspiracy to defraud is also uncertain. It is wider than conspiracies to commit fraud offences (**Scott v MPC**, above) but is an agreement to damage property or to handle stolen goods a conspiracy to defraud? That is not to say that conspiracies under statute are perfect. If the width of the crime to be committed is uncertain, so is the conspiracy to commit it.

At common law and under the statute there is no maximum fine which a court may impose. In the common law conspiracies to corrupt public morals and outrage public decency there is no maximum sentence of imprisonment. By s 12 of the Criminal Justice Act 1987 the maximum sentence for conspiracy to defraud is 10 years. The maximum for statutory conspiracies is the maximum for the offence. If the offence is one triable either way, the maximum is that for trial on indictment. Conspiracy is an indictable offence even though the crime agreed on is only summary. There are special rules of evidence for conspiracy cases, by which prejudicial evidence against a conspirator may be adduced which would be forbidden for all other offences.

Ian Dennis in 'The rationale of criminal conspiracy' (1977) 93 LQR 39 gave five reasons for having a law of criminal conspiracy. (a) It is evidence of criminal intent, just as a 'more than merely preparatory' act is an attempt. (b) It allows intervention to prevent persons committing offences. Unless prevented, a conspiracy may lead to many organised crimes, not just one. (c) It gets the organisers of crimes before the courts. The Godfathers of crime, who do not soil their hands with carrying out crimes such as terrorism and robbery, can be caught by this offence. (d) Conspiracies constitute injurious combinations and persons joining such agreements ought to be punished. (e) The law provides a means of stopping partnerships in crime. It is possible that two persons egging each other on are more likely to commit an offence than one person by himself. The fact that two people are involved increases the dangerousness of their behaviour. A terrorist gang is more difficult to stop than one terrorist. (Incitement can be seen in a similar light.) In law a conspiracy applies even though the parties have not reached the stage of an attempt. The same activity may be a conspiracy if done by two persons, but not an attempt if done by one: the crime prevention rationale seems to apply much more strongly to conspiracy than to attempt. Indeed, in **Board of Trade v Owen** [1957] AC 602 (HL), Lord Tucker saw this as the rationale of conspiracy. 'The whole object of making such agreements punishable is to prevent the commission of the substantive offence before it has even reached the stage of an attempt.'

It may be argued why the law applies more against two or more persons (who are guilty of conspiracy) than against one person (who is not guilty either of conspiracy or attempt). G. Fletcher, *Rethinking Criminal Law* (Little, Brown & Co., 1978) 133, thought that: '[T]he phenomenon of people forming criminal bands might be regarded as sufficiently unnerving to be prohibited for its own sake.' Nevertheless, one person can create just as much harm as two, and one gorilla-sized person may create as much alarm as two persons of restricted growth.

Reform

The Law Commission issued its Consultation Paper No. 183, *Conspiracy and Attempts*, in 2007. In it were the following proposals. First, and contrary to the current law in **Saik**, above, it was recommended that recklessness should suffice as to any circumstance element in the substantive offence. Secondly, and widening the law found in s 1(2), if knowledge or belief suffices for the full offence, it should also suffice for the conspiracy to commit that offence; s 1(2) demands that knowledge alone suffices at present. Thirdly, two parts of the law in **Anderson** – that the accused to be guilty of conspiracy must intend 'to play some part in the agreed course of conduct' and that conspiracy does not require that the accused intends that the agreement is to be carried through to completion – are to be abolished. Paragraph 1.39 expresses the Commission's concerns:

> First, there is no reason, in terms of statutory language or policy, for insisting that D must intend to play some part in implementing the agreement. If D1 and D2 agree to murder V, D1 ought to be convicted of conspiracy to murder even if it was not his or her intention to play any party in V's murder. Secondly, an agreement to commit an offence implies an intention that it should be committed, as section 1(1) of the 1977 Act seems to make clear. The idea of a conspiracy that the conspirators agree to take part in but which none intends to see carried out is very unsatisfactory.

Thirdly, the spousal immunity is recommended for abolition. Fourthly, the law that exempts both parties when a non-victim and his victim agree to commit a crime will be abolished with the result that the non-victim is to be liable for conspiracy; however, a defence will be given to the victim. The obvious example is when a man of mature years persuades an underage person to have sexual intercourse with him. Currently, both the man, the 'non-victim', and the other party, the victim, whose interests are protected by the law of sexual offences (now s 9 of the Sexual Offences Act 2003), have a defence. The proposal is that only the victim should have a defence. Fifthly, however, the law on conspiracy with a child under 10 is preserved, a recommendation which is hard to square with the previous one, especially when it is recalled that current law protects an adult who targets a vulnerable young child to enter into what would otherwise be a conspiracy. The Commission's argument (para. 1.47) is that when an adult agrees with a child to commit an offence, 'there can be no meeting of "criminal" minds of a kind at the heart of any criminal conspiracy'. It then notes that the adult should unless excluded be guilty of the crimes of attempt or criminal preparation, as it proposes in the same Consultation Paper (see later in this chapter). Sixthly, and in line with the Serious Crime Act 2007 in respect of assisting or encouraging crime (see earlier in this chapter), there should be a defence of acting reasonably. This defence would reverse the law in **Yip Chiu-Cheung**, above, so that for example an undercover officer would not be guilty of conspiracy. Finally, at present conspiracies to commit summary offences are, like other conspiracies, triable only on indictment; and the Director of Public Prosecutions' consent is required. The proposal is that such conspiracies should be triable summarily; one result is that the consent of the DPP would no longer be needed.

The Law Commission followed up its Consultation Paper with its Report No. 318, 2009, also called *Conspiracy and Attempt*. The following sums up its recommendations:

(a) Conspiracy's *actus reus* will be an agreement by two or more to engage in the conduct element of a crime and (if the offence is a result one) to bring about that result.

(b) The *mens rea* will be intent that the conduct element of the crime should be engaged in and if the principal offence is a conduct crime, to bring about the result.

(c) The accused must be reckless as to a circumstance where the full crime is one of negligence or strict liability.

(d) Where the full offence is one other than one of negligence, the accused will be guilty of conspiracy if he had the fault element of the full offence.

(e) Intoxication should be a defence even if the fault element of the full offence is one of recklessness.

(f) The Director of Public Prosecutions' consent should be abolished for conspiracies to commit summary offences.

(g) The exemption for married couple and civil partners should be abolished.

(h) The exemption for the conspirator who conspires with a 'victim' should be abolished, but that for the victim should be retained.

(i) The exemption for the adult who conspires with a child under the age of criminal responsibility should be retained.

(j) The defence of 'acting reasonably' to the offence of assisting or encouraging crime (see s 50 of the Serious Crime Act 2007, discussed above) should be also made available in conspiracy.

Attempt

Introduction

Attempt originated in the Star Chamber in the early seventeenth century. Its purpose was to criminalise conduct before the full offence had taken place. Attempt is a crime under statute, the Criminal Attempts Act 1981. Section 6(1) abolished attempt at common law. It is punishable in general to the same extent as the complete or full offence: s 4(1). A person may be convicted of an attempt even though he is guilty of the full offence: *Webley v Buxton* [1977] QB 481 (DC) in relation to summary trials and s 6(4) of the Criminal Law Act 1967 in relation to trials on indictment. Where there are two counts in the indictment, attempt and the full offence, the accused may be convicted of the full offence but found not guilty of the attempt. One way of explaining this rule is to say that the attempt is merged with the full offence when the attempt is successful. However, a person convicted on one indictment of attempt cannot later be charged with the full offence: *Velasquez* [1996] 1 Cr App R 155.

Attempt is a crime where principles of criminal law collide. First, people who are dangerous should be restrained. A person who shoots and misses is just as culpable as one who shoots and hits. His actions demonstrate a criminal intent. The law should prevent future misconduct as well as punish past misbehaviour. Both are dangerous. Moreover, the line between success and failure may be slight. In both eventualities the accused must be deterred. Secondly, people should not be penalised for simply thinking about committing crimes. Balancing these principles leaves the police in an invidious position. They have to hold back until the moment when the accused is well on his way towards committing the offence, even though it is certain that a crime will be performed. The Law Commission Report No. 102, *Attempt, and Impossibility in Relation to Attempt, Conspiracy and Incitement*, 1980, said that the rationale of the offence was to stop persons from committing the full offence. The law adopts the view that attempt is an offence where the accused both has the intent of carrying out the full offence and has put that intention partly into effect: in the words of the Act he must have done a 'more than merely preparatory' act. Both firmness of purpose and antisocial behaviour are looked at.

Each time a new indictable offence is created the crime of attempting to commit that offence is automatically created. Since, however, there is no offence of attempting to commit a summary offence, changing the category of an offence to make it summary means that the attempt is abolished unless Parliament expressly provides for the attempt. Accordingly because of ss 39 and 37 respectively of the Criminal Justice Act 1988 there are no longer crimes of attempting to assault or to take a vehicle without consent. Perhaps there should be. This law is laid down in s 1(4) of the 1981 Act, which also provides that one cannot attempt to aid, abet, counsel or procure a crime. One can, however, be a secondary party to attempting to commit an offence: ***Dunnington*** [1984] QB 472 (CA). Section 1(4) further states that one cannot attempt to conspire, assist offenders, or conceal information about arrestable offences. (Attempt to conspire is at least covered by the crime of encouraging or assisting: see above.)

It may be that one cannot be convicted of at least some forms of attempted manslaughter. The Criminal Attempts Act 1981, s 1(1), provides that the *mens rea* of attempt is intent. The test of gross negligence manslaughter is that the accused fell short, grossly, of a certain standard of care and thereby killed the victim; he does not have to intend a certain consequence. How can one intend to be grossly negligent? It was said by the Court of Criminal Appeal in ***Creamer*** [1966] 1 QB 72 that attempted (involuntary) manslaughter was not a crime known to law. This argument does not, however, hold true of voluntary manslaughter. If a person attempts to kill and would have had the defence of provocation (now loss of control) or diminished responsibility if he had killed, surely he may be convicted of attempted manslaughter if the victim does not die. In ***Bruzas*** [1972] Crim LR 367 the Crown Court did not accept the existence of such a crime. If the draft Criminal Code were enacted, cl 61 would permit the charge in relation to diminished responsibility and provocation (now loss of control). It is thought that one cannot attempt to attempt the full offence. If it were a crime, the accused would be guilty before he had reached the stage of a more than merely preparatory act, which the 1981 Act requires.

Where Parliament changes the law relating to the substantive offence, the width of the attempt to commit that offence may be affected. A good illustration is the new crime of fraud contrary to the Fraud Act 2006. If the accused sent an email to a person who unbeknown to him was dead, begging for money though he was already a rich man, there would before the 2006 Act have been the offence of attempting to obtain property (money) by deception. Here, amending the substantive law has changed the offence from one of attempt (attempted deception) to one of the full offence (fraud, not merely attempted fraud). Similarly, the crime of arranging or facilitating the commission of a child sex offence contrary to s 14 of the Sexual Offences Act 2003 is in itself a preparatory offence but it too can be attempted: ***R*** [2008] EWCA Crim 619 (***R*** is also known as ***Robson***). See also the former defence of impossibility discussed below.

Criminal Attempts Act 1981

Parliament substantially implemented the recommendations of the Law Commission in the 1981 Act, the main difference being that there is no crime of attempting to commit a summary offence unless Parliament says differently. The principal provisions of the Act are:

(a) the definition of the *mens rea*;

(b) the establishment of a new test of the *actus reus*;

(c) the abolition of the defence of impossibility, reversing ***Haughton* v *Smith*** [1975] AC 476 (HL);

(d) the abolition of 'sus' (see below) and the creation of an offence of interference with vehicles;

(e) the abolition of the offence of procuring materials for crime, though other preparatory offences continue to exist, such as those found in s 25 of the Theft Act 1968 (see Chapter 17) and s 3 of the Criminal Damage Act 1971 (see Chapter 18).

The Act was meant to remedy several defects in the law and to codify the law in preparation for the general codification of criminal law.

The definition of the *mens rea*

Section 1(1) of the Criminal Attempts Act 1981 provides that the mental element for attempt is 'intent'. There is no definition of this term in the Act. The government rejected a clause stating that recklessness as to circumstances sufficed if it sufficed for the full offence. In view of the legislative history one might have expected that intent meant intent with regard to every element of the *actus reus*. ***Mohan*** [1976] QB 1 is the main pre-Act authority and it is reasonable to assume that since Parliament provided no definition, it wished this definition to be adopted. The Court of Appeal had defined intent in attempt as 'a decision to bring about . . . the commission of the offence . . . no matter whether the accused desired that consequence or not'. The second part was meant to cover oblique intent, such as putting a bomb on a plane to claim the insurance on freight without desiring the death of the passengers and crew according to Stuart-Smith J in ***Pearman*** (1985) 80 Cr App R 259 (CA). Therefore, the accused is guilty when his intention cannot be achieved without the occurring of another consequence first. It will, using an example from ***Pearman***, not be difficult to find that the accused intended to injure a constable if he drove straight at him. Section 6 of the 1981 Act abolished the common law of attempt but s 1(1) still requires 'intent' and in ***Pearman*** the Court of Appeal said that the definition in ***Mohan*** applied to the Act. No case has as yet discussed the effect of ***Woollin*** [1999] AC 82 (HL) on attempt. ***Woollin*** was expressly restricted by the Lords to murder. If it applies generally throughout the criminal law, foresight of a consequence as virtually certain coupled with that consequence actually being virtually certain to occur *is only evidence of* intent. However, attempt may be restricted to direct intent: how can one attempt something without having the achievement of that result as one's purpose?

See pp 90–104 (Chapter 3), for an explanation of intent.

The requirement of intent continues to apply as to the *consequences* of conduct. The accused is not guilty of attempting to cause grievous bodily harm by driving so recklessly that he foresaw harm as likely. On usual principles the higher degree of foresight, the more likely it is that the accused intended the result. However, in relation to *circumstances* the requirement of intent has been watered down. In ***Pigg*** [1982] 1 WLR 762, a case decided on the common law, the Court of Appeal, seemingly without reflecting on the matter, held that recklessness as to circumstances was sufficient if it sufficed for the substantive offence.

Recklessness as to the woman's consent in rape was therefore sufficient for attempted rape. (The law of rape was subsequently amended by the Sexual Offences Act 2003 but the principle stands.) In *Millard* [1987] Crim LR 393, the Court of Appeal saw the problem about attempted rape but did not resolve it. It did state that it was wrong to say that attempted criminal damage could be committed recklessly. In *O'Toole* [1987] Crim LR 759, the Court of Appeal confirmed that recklessness as to criminal damage was insufficient for attempting to damage property by fire being reckless as to whether life was endangered. He had tried to set fire to a pub in which there was a barmaid. The courts appeared to be drawing a line between consequences (recklessness insufficient) and circumstances (recklessness sufficient), though s 1(1) of the Act is not so phrased; it speaks only of 'intent'.

The principal authority on circumstances is now *Khan* [1990] 1 WLR 815 (CA). The defendants tried but failed to have sexual intercourse with a 16-year-old girl, whom they had met at a daytime disco. Russell LJ argued thus. The then *mens rea* in rape, the full offence, was the intention to have sexual intercourse with a woman, knowing that she was not consenting or being reckless whether she consented. (Nowadays men as well as women can be raped.) The same applied to attempted rape. The difference between rape and attempted rape lay in the *actus reus*: in attempt, the sexual intercourse had not taken place. The difference therefore related to a physical matter, but the state of mind was the same. 'The words "with intent to commit an offence" . . . in s 1 of the Act of 1981 mean when applied to rape, "with intent to have sexual intercourse with a woman in circumstances where she does not consent" and the defendant knows or could not care less about her absence of consent. The only "intent" . . . of the rapist is to have sexual intercourse.' Therefore, the accused is guilty of attempted rape, even though he does not know that the victim was not consenting. He is guilty of attempted rape if he is reckless as to consent. Yet, according to *Millard*, one is not guilty of attempted criminal damage if one is reckless as to who owns the damaged property. Ownership, a circumstance, is not an element to which one can be reckless. The distinction between being reckless as to ownership (not guilty) and being reckless as to consent (guilty) is not easily acceptable.

Khan stated that recklessness as to circumstances (such as consent in rape) is sufficient to convict of the attempt but intent as to consequences (the intention to have sexual intercourse in rape) is needed. The rule still stands that intention as to consequences is necessary for the attempt even if recklessness as to consequences is sufficient for the full offence. *Khan* presumably applies to all 'circumstances' crimes, though it is in fact an authority on attempting to commit the crime of rape as defined in a since-repealed statute. Presumably the law applies to attempts to commit strict offences.

The width of *Khan* remains uncertain. The Court of Appeal said: 'our reasoning cannot apply to all offences and all attempts. Where for example, as in . . . reckless arson, no state of mind other than recklessness is involved in the offence, there can be no attempt to commit it.' In the first draft Criminal Code, Report No. 143, 1985, the academic drafters thought that the distinction between circumstances and conduct was not workable and, indeed, used rape as their example. On consultation their formulation of the mental element in attempted rape was criticised as being too narrow. The present draft Criminal Code, Report No. 177, 1989, which predated *Khan*, is consistent with the ruling, despite the fact that the draft Criminal Code team and the Law Commission itself in Report No. 102 on *Attempt*, 1980, para. 2.18, on which the Act was based, had previously rejected it. Indeed, if the Court of Appeal in *Khan* had looked at the Report (and under current law expressed in *Pepper* v *Hart* [1993] AC 593 (HL) it was entitled to do so), it would have discovered that it was wrong. Clause 49(2) of the 1989 version stipulates that for all attempts:

> An intention to commit an offence is an intention with respect to all the elements of the offence other than fault elements, except that recklessness with respect to circumstances suffices where it suffices for the offence itself.

The Law Commission did not define the line between circumstances and consequences, which was to be left for the courts. The Commission opined that in rape (as it was then defined) the distinction was easy in that absence of the victim's consent was a circumstance. But what about the former requirement that the victim was a woman? It looks like a circumstance but the Court of Appeal in *Millard* said that it was a consequence. It is thought that judges may require guidance if the draft Criminal Code is enacted.

Graham Virgo wrote in 'Reckless attempts – rape and circumstance' [1990] CLJ 390 that *Khan* is: 'justifiable because "intention" cannot relate to circumstances; whether a woman is consenting or not cannot be intended, but can be known or believed. No provision for circumstances was made in the Criminal Attempts Act 1981, so allowing the Court of Appeal's interpretation here.' On the other hand, the statute does say 'intent' not 'intent as to consequences and recklessness as to circumstances'. Certainly Parliament could have expressed itself more clearly but it did not do so. Furthermore, the term 'attempt' may imply intent: how can the accused attempt to do something unless one does intend it? Such was the view of Edmund-Davies LJ in *Easom* [1971] 2 QB 315 (CA). One might even argue that, accepting the circumstances/consequences split, the consequences in rape could be defined as sexual intercourse with a woman who does not consent. All the elements are consequences; therefore, intent is required throughout: therefore, recklessness as to consent is insufficient, and *Khan* is wrong. Whatever is said about statutory construction it would have been strange in principle to convict a person who had just achieved penetration, being reckless as to the victim's consent, and not convict the accused of attempted rape in a similar situation where he was stopped just before penetration. For a criticism of the circumstance/consequence dichotomy and a proposed solution, see Glanville Williams 'Intents in the alternative' [1991] CLJ 120.

Khan was approved in *Attorney-General's Reference (No. 3 of 1992)* [1994] 2 All ER 121 (CA). Schiemann J speaking for the court said in a reserved judgment that *Khan* was in accord with policy and common sense and did no violence to the words of the statute. *Khan* was not restricted to rape. He extended *Khan* from recklessness as to circumstances to recklessness as to endangering life in aggravated criminal damage. This element, it is suggested, is neither consequence nor circumstance but a further part of the mental element. Accordingly the mental element in the offence of attempted aggravated criminal damage is, at its lowest, intending to cause criminal damage, being reckless as to whether life would be endangered by the damage, a state of mind which on the facts of the case covered throwing a petrol bomb at the complainant's property but missing, being reckless as to endangering life. In the present case damage was missing, in *Khan* sexual intercourse had not taken place. With regard to that missing element intent was needed, but with regard to the other constituents of the attempt the same state of mind which sufficed for the substantive crime sufficed for the attempt. On the facts of the case what was missing was damage. Therefore, to be guilty of the attempt the accused had to intend to cause damage. However, the element of endangering life existed. Therefore, it was sufficient that the accused was reckless as to this element. Accordingly the *mens rea* for the attempt was intending to cause criminal damage, being reckless as to whether life would be endangered. If the accused does not intend to cause criminal damage he is not guilty of the attempt even though he is reckless as to endangering life.

In criticism of this *dictum* may be instanced the crime of attempted sexual intercourse with a girl under 16. Surely the accused is not guilty of this offence if the accused believes the victim to be over 16. The full crime is strict as to the age of the girl. It cannot be that the attempt is also strict. If it were, one might have expected the courts (and Parliament) to have said so in their analysis of attempt. Nevertheless, the missing-element point would make the accused guilty of the attempt. Another problem with current law is this: for the crime of attempted criminal damage it must be proved in the basic offence that the accused intended to damage property belonging to another; in attempted rape the prosecution must prove that the accused intended to have sexual intercourse but it is sufficient that the accused was reckless as to the victim's consent. It seems strange that 'belonging to another' is central to the crime of attempted (basic) criminal damage but 'without the consent of the victim' is not central to the crime of attempted rape, especially when both elements constitute circumstances of the crime. This proposition is preferred by Professor Paul Dobson in his commentary on the *Reference* case (1994) 11 Student LR 17 thus: 'ask "if the accused had succeeded in carrying out his intention, would the full offence have been committed?" If the answer is yes, then the accused had sufficient *mens rea* for the attempt.'

One issue which was not discussed in *Attorney-General's Reference (No. 3 of 1992)* was whether the type of recklessness mentioned was subjective or objective. From the phrasing of the judgment, objective recklessness was presumably meant. The court said that once the Crown had proved the intent to cause criminal damage, the sole other mental element is the remaining state of mind required for the offence of aggravated arson, that is, objective recklessness. The result was that an accused is guilty of attempted aggravated criminal damage if he sets light to a house, intending to do so, and does not realise that anyone is in the house, provided that there was an obvious and serious risk of endangering the life of any person who was in fact in the house. The court did not seem to have considered this issue. In any case the abolition of *Caldwell* recklessness in criminal damage in **G** [2004] 1 AC 1034 (HL) now means that subjective recklessness is the appropriate test. It should be noted that the definition of intention in *Khan* and *Attorney-General's Reference (No. 3 of 1992)* is restricted to attempt and does not extend throughout criminal law. For the definition of intent elsewhere, see Chapter 3.

Two further matters relating to intent in s 1(1)

In attempted murder the accused must intend to kill. It is not sufficient if he intended only to cause grievous bodily harm. Therefore, the more serious crime, murder, has a wider mental element than the lesser, attempted murder. In *Whybrow* (1951) 35 Cr App R 141 (CCA), the accused wired up the bath in an attempt to kill his wife. In *Walker and Hayles*, above, the victim was dropped by the accused from a third-floor window. In both cases the Court of Criminal Appeal and the Court of Appeal respectively held that intention to commit grievous bodily harm was insufficient.

The case of *Walker and Hayles*, which was discussed in Chapter 3, demonstrates how simple questions can become difficult. When the accused did what they did, did they intend to kill? The trial judge might have directed the jury that the accused were guilty if they intended to kill; in the event of any difficulty the jury might have been instructed in accordance with *Mohan* that the accused were guilty if they had made up their minds to kill or decided to kill. The case was one of direct intent or nothing. There was no oblique intent problem. The judge, however, directed the jury in terms of foreseeing death as a high probability. The Court of Appeal preferred the term 'virtual certainty' to a high probability of death but did not quash the conviction on the basis that a high probability of death was sufficient. On the facts the probability or certainty of death was in truth irrelevant if the accused did (directly) intend to kill. It is only when there is doubt about what the accused did intend to do that one need look at virtual certainties or high degrees of probability as matters of evidence. In those circumstances the jury could infer intention to kill from the accused's foresight of death as a virtually certain consequence.

Section 1(3) and intent

Section 1(3) of the 1981 Act provides:

> In any case where –
> (a) apart from this subsection a person's intention would not be regarded as having amounted to an intent to commit an offence; but
> (b) if the facts of the case had been as he believed them to be his intention would be so regarded,
> then, for the purposes of subsection (1) above, he shall be regarded as having had an intent to commit that offence.

What s 1(3) seems to mean is this. The common law rule as to impossibility in attempt was laid down by the House of Lords in *Haughton* v *Smith*, above. That case decided, *inter alia*, that the accused was not guilty of an attempt if he had done everything he wished to do but contrary to his belief his actions did not amount to a crime. In the case itself the accused had done all he intended to do in relation to the property, but he did not know that in law the goods were no longer stolen. Contrary to his belief what he did did not constitute the offence of handling stolen goods. Section 1(3) is designed to reverse this common law rule. By s 1(3) the accused is deemed to have the necessary intent for handling stolen goods on the facts as he believed to exist. He intended to handle goods which were stolen; he believed he was handling goods which were stolen; applying s 1(3) the *mens rea* of attempted handling is satisfied.

The establishment of a new test for the *actus reus*

Example

Don is a paedophile. On this occasion he seeks to lure away a boy from his school. He enters the boys' toilet with a large knife, rope and masking tape (to put over the boy's mouth). Is he guilty of attempted false imprisonment? (No knowledge is needed of the full offence.)

Section 1(1) of the Criminal Attempts Act 1981 defines the *actus reus* of attempt (there is no difficulty with the *mens rea*) as 'an act which is more than preparatory to the commission of the offence'. Here the offence is false imprisonment. The question resolves itself into whether what Don has done is '*more* than merely preparatory' within s 1(1). It is certainly 'preparatory'.

Authorities are fact-sensitive, but on the same facts the Court of Appeal in *Geddes* [1996] Crim LR 894 found the accused not guilty. As the author writes in this book in his discussion of the case: 'The Court of Appeal held ("with the gravest unease") that [the accused] was still at the preparation stage and therefore not guilty of attempted false imprisonment. Presumably he would have been found guilty if he had contacted the boy. The court felt uneasy about its decision, but no doubt parents feel much more uneasy. The decision does not encourage the disinhibition of the conduct of dangerous people. The reader may also think that the accused was deserving of punishment.'

Note that the accused could now be found guilty of a substantive offence, trespassing with intent to commit a sexual offence contrary to s 63 of the Sexual Offences Act 2003.

The *actus reus* is defined in s 1(1) of the 1981 Act as doing 'an act which is more than merely preparatory to the commission of the offence'. There is no such requirement in conspiracy.

'An act' is wide. It need not be a dangerous act. It is the *mens rea* which converts the act into a crime. I may be driving my car towards you. Only if the jurors know that I intend to run you down can they convict me of an offence.

By s 4(3) the question whether the accused committed an attempt is for the jury, provided that there is sufficient evidence in law to support that finding: that is, the judge can rule that the act may be an attempt but it is for the jury to determine that it was so. The judge cannot instruct the jury that a situation amounts to a more than merely preparatory act. However, he or she may tell the jury that there is no evidence that what the accused has done amounts to a more than merely preparatory act, and the issue can be withdrawn from the jury: *Campbell* (1991) 93 Cr App R 350 (CA). On the facts the accused was not guilty of attempted robbery even though he had reconnoitred a sub-post office he had intended to rob and he had an imitation gun (and he was convicted of possessing an imitation firearm) and a threatening note. He was arrested near to the office door. He said he was going back to his motorcycle, having decided not to rob. Presumably he would not on this approach have been guilty until he had crossed the threshold of the sub-post office – not a helpful decision in the prevention of crime. If the facts had been left to the jury a conviction might well have been secured, and presumably he could have been convicted of a different attempted crime, attempted burglary, for he had performed a more than merely preparatory act on his way towards entering the building as a trespasser with intent to steal. The Court of Appeal said that cases had to be decided on a case-by-case approach, which is not a help to juries. A contrasting case is *Griffin* [1993] Crim LR 515 (CA). A mother was guilty of attempting to abduct her children and take them out of the UK when she had bought ferry tickets for Ireland and told her children's teacher that she was taking them to the dentist's. She had not yet taken charge of the children, never mind set off for the port. She was found guilty, despite the fact that she was nowhere near removing them from the jurisdiction.

The rationale behind cases such as *Campbell* is that the accused is not guilty until he has gone through the psychological barrier on the way towards committing the offence. The accused is within striking distance of committing the offence. It is not sufficient that the accused merely thought about committing the offence. The line at present is between preparatory activities and others.

In *Qadir* [1997] EWCA Crim 1970 Potter LJ stated, as has been said before, that *actus reus* of attempt as laid down in the Act seeks to steer 'a midway course . . . [t]he attempt begins at the moment when the defendant embarks on the crime proper, as opposed to taking steps rightly regarded as merely preparatory'. Potter LJ continued: 'Whether or not an act crosses the threshold between preparation and embarkation on the commission of the crime will always depend on an examination of the scope or substance of the crime aimed at.' He gave several examples: 'in a case of [killing], wounding or causing [*sic*] actual bodily harm, it would be likely that any act leading up to the commission . . . of the crime but substantially anterior to it in time will be an act merely preparatory. In a case of deception . . . , since the *actus reus* of the crime itself may take place over an extended period of time, the moment of embarkation upon it may be quite remote in time from the point of its anticipated successful outcome.'

Present law does little to encourage the prevention of crime, for preparations to commit offences are not attempts, though there is the possibility that other crimes may have been committed (including conspiracy if there were two or more parties). In *Sidaway*, unreported, 11 June 1993, the Court of Appeal held that making an imitation bomb and taking it to London *en route* for Ramsgate did not amount to attempting to commit a bomb hoax in Ramsgate. In *Gullefer* [1990] 3 All ER 882 (CA), which has come to be seen as the leading authority, the accused backed a greyhound which was going to lose. He jumped onto the track trying to distract the dogs so that the stewards would call 'no race' and book-makers would return stake money. He failed. The Court of Appeal held that he was not guilty of attempt. There was no evidence to go to the jury. His acts were preparatory. The position would have been different if the stewards had called 'no race'. In that eventuality there would have been evidence for the jury. The jury might, however, have held that the accused was guilty only when he had presented his betting slip, or perhaps when he joined the queue. The court said that the accused was guilty only when he had embarked on the 'crime proper'. On the facts juries might have different views as to when the accused did that. After all, he did not have to do anything more. It was for the stewards to declare the race void. The Court of Appeal in *Tosti* [1997] Crim LR 746 held that the two defendants were guilty of attempted burglary of a barn when they had brought oxyacetelene equipment to the scene, hidden it in a hedge and examined the padlock because they were 'evidentially the first steps in the commission of the offence', and not merely preparatory steps.

Gullefer was applied in *Attorney-General's Reference (No. 1 of 1992)* [1993] 1 WLR 274 (CA). The accused was guilty of attempted rape when he had embarked on committing rape itself. 'The evidence of the young woman's distress, of the state of her clothing, and the position in which she was seen, together with the respondent's acts of dragging her up the steps, lowering his trousers and interfering with her private parts . . . left it open to a jury to conclude that the respondent had the necessary intent and had done acts which were more than merely preparatory.' There was no need to show that he had tried to penetrate the vagina. However, since rape requires penetration and the accused's penis was flaccid, it is perhaps strange that he was convicted of attempted rape. This case does not seem distinguishable from *Campbell*, yet there the accused was acquitted. Similarly in *Patnaik*, unreported, 5 November 2000 (CA), the accused had threatened the victim, attempted to kiss her and straddled her, but had not removed any of her or his own clothing and he had not touched her intimately. It was held that there was sufficient evidence of attempted rape to be left to the jury. In criticism it may be questioned whether the accused had embarked on the crime of rape. He had completed several offences of the then existing crime of indecent assault but the facts are far from as convincing as *Attorney-General's Reference (No. 1 of 1992)*. *Dagnall* [2003] EWCA Crim 2441 is similar as far as can be seen from the facts given. The accused had followed the victim, put his arms around her, told her that he wanted sexual intercourse, said that no one would hear her if he took her onto a dark road, pulled her backwards by her hair, put her into an arm-lock, covered her mouth and dragged her to a bus stop. The court rejected his argument that because he had not touched her in a sexual way, his actions were no more than merely preparatory.

Under present law intervention seems in many cases to come too late in the interests of crime prevention. For example, 'casing the joint', as in *Campbell*, is too early in the train of events leading to the crime and the judge withdraws the issue from the jury. In *Geddes* [1996] Crim LR 894 (CA), a case more distinguished than followed, the accused intended to kidnap a boy from a school. He ran away when he was discovered in the boys' toilets in which, of course, he was a trespasser. In his rucksack were a large knife, masking tape and rope. The Court of Appeal held ('with the gravest unease') that he was still at the preparation stage and therefore not guilty of attempted false imprisonment. Presumably he would have been guilty if he had made contact with the boy. The court felt uneasy about its decision, but no doubt parents feel much more uneasy. The decision does not encourage the inhibition of the conduct of dangerous people. The reader may also think that the accused was deserving of punishment. (Since the case Parliament has created the offence of trespass with intent to commit a sexual offence while on any premises where he is a trespasser, contrary to s 63 of the Sexual Offences Act 2003, and the accused would be guilty of this offence. Note, however, as the title of the crime shows, the accused must be a trespasser.) Similar is *Nash* [1999] Crim LR 308 (CA). The accused appealed against a conviction of attempting to procure an act of gross indecency. He had written three letters addressed to 'paper boy'. The first two contained invitations to indulge in mutual masturbation or oral sex or both. The third offered work with a security company. In respect of the third letter it was held that the accused had not gone beyond the stage of mere preparation. *Geddes* was approved.

A quite recent case is *Bowles & Bowles* [2004] EWCA Crim 1608. The two accused had set out on a plan to get hold of an old woman's money on her death. They had already received large sums from her. They drafted her last will and testament, which named them as beneficiaries. The unexecuted will was then put into the victim's bedside drawer and left for several months. The court held that they were not guilty of attempting to make a false instrument, the will, because they had performed only preparatory acts. Similarly in *Mason v DPP* [2009] EWHC 2198 (Admin) the accused had not attempted to drive a car with excess alcohol when he was at the stage of opening the door. *Campbell* was applied. He was not embarking on the crime proper until he had done something which was part of the process of putting the car into motion. It is suggested that in such cases crime prevention, a major rationale for the law of attempt, is undermined. The Northern Ireland Court of Appeal has distinguished *Geddes*. In *Stone* [2011] NICA 11 the accused, a Protestant terrorist, was found guilty of attempting to murder two Sinn Fein leaders when he had entered the Stormont building and set light to the fuse of an explosive, while in *Kerr* [2011] NICA 20 the accused was guilty of attempted murder when he attempted to set fire to the house of a family who were going to give evidence against him for handling stolen goods belonging to them.

Glanville Williams 'Wrong turnings on the law of attempt' [1991] Crim LR 416 wished the law to be that a judge would rule when preparation became an attempt. 'What the judges have lost is their power to protect the public by telling the jury firmly that the defendant's act, if proved, . . . did amount to an attempt' (at 425). There is nothing to prevent two juries reaching different conclusions on the same facts. This means that juries may reach their verdicts by taking into account non-legal matters. Even the judges are inconsistent, as this section has showed, as to when the accused moves to a 'more than merely preparatory' stage.

May judges refer to common law authorities?

At law the judges had several tests to which they could refer:

(a) The last act test inquired whether the defendant did the last act dependent on him. A modern phrasing of that test was to ask whether the accused had 'crossed the Rubicon and burnt his boats', as Lord Diplock put it in *DPP v Stonehouse* [1978] AC 55 (HL). This test was not always adopted at common law. In *White* [1910] 2 KB 124 (CCA), the accused was guilty of attempted murder despite the fact that he needed to put more doses of potassium cyanide into his mother's drink before he killed her. This last act test was approved in *Widdowson* (1985) 82 Cr App R 314 (CA) after the Act but rejected in *Gullefer*.

(b) The any-act-carrying-the-*mens-rea*-into-effect test was laid down in *Gurmit Singh* [1966] 2 QB 53 but overruled by s 6(1) of the 1981 Act: see below.

(c) The equivocality test, laid down in cases such as *Davey v Lee* [1968] 1 QB 366 (DC), asked whether the accused's conduct had any purpose other than the commission of the full offence.

(d) The test most often used was the proximity test. Parke B in **Eagleton** (1855) [1843–60] All ER Rep 363 said that: 'Acts remotely leading towards the commission of the full offence are not to be considered as attempts to commit it, but acts immediately connected with it are.' Three Law Lords approved the **Eagleton** test in **Stonehouse**. Despite having the approval of the highest court, the test did give rise to cases such as **Robinson** [1915] 2 KB 342 (CCA), in which the accused was not guilty of attempting to obtain money from his insurance company when he faked a robbery at his jeweller's shop because he had not sent in the claim form. The argument was that the accused (as also in **Gullefer**) was not yet engaged in the business of fraud. He had prepared the way but not reached the stage where deceit could be practised. Yet in both **Robinson** and **Gullefer** the accused did not have himself to do very much else. In **Gullefer** the only act for him to do was to collect his stake. The Law Commission's Report No. 102, 1980, on which the Criminal Attempts Act 1981 was based, wished to consign this case to the dustbin of history (paras 2.30, 2.42 and 2.48) but the same result could be reached on analogy with **Gullefer** and **Campbell** after the 1981 Act. Any resurgence of the proximity test would be contrary to the wishes of the Law Commission, the words of the statute and, it is suggested, common sense.

In **Ilyas** (1983) 78 Cr App R 17 (CA), a case decided at common law but after the enactment of the statute, the court used the statute's terminology. It said that it was acceptable under the new law to look at the old cases. In **Boyle** (1987) 84 Cr App R 270, the Court of Appeal held similarly in a case on the 1981 Act. The same occurred in **Widdowson**, above. In these cases it did not matter which of the two main pre-Act tests, last act or proximity, were used because the facts satisfied both tests. Later cases have taken a different view.

In **Gullefer**, however, the court determined that the 1981 Act did not enact previous law. The draftsmen could have done that but did not. Instead a middle course was steered. That midway course was the natural meaning of s 1(1). In **Jones** [1990] 1 WLR 1057 the Court of Appeal held that the Act did not incorporate any of the common law tests and judges should not refer to the previous law. It is the words in the Act which count. Taylor LJ said that the accused's: 'actions in obtaining the gun, in shortening it, in loading it, in putting on his disguise, and in going into the school could only be regarded as preparatory acts. But . . . once he had got into the car, taken out the loaded gun and pointed it at the victim with the intention of killing him, there was sufficient evidence for the consideration of the jury on the charge of attempted murder.' There was no need to wait until the accused had done the last act. There was evidence of a more than merely preparatory act even though the safety catch was on. There was no need to wait until the accused had released the catch, put his finger on the trigger, and started to squeeze it. The prosecution had to prove only that the accused's actions were 'more than merely preparatory' and those words bore their ordinary meaning. In **Campbell** the court held that the judge should not refer to the common law but direct the jury in terms of the 1981 Act.

Despite these strong authorities the Court of Appeal in **Rowley** above referred to **Ransford** (1874) 13 Cox CC 9 when asking whether notes passed to boys to lure them away for immoral purposes constituted the offence of attempting to incite a child under 14 to commit gross indecency. The notes were passed to set up meetings. They contained no express sexual invitation. The court ruled that they constituted preparation, not more than merely preparatory acts. Yet the question remains: what else did he have to do to be guilty? If he had actually met the boys and made lewd suggestions, he would have been guilty of incitement. Presumably attempted incitement occurs when he meets them but before making any proposition.

In at least one way the new law is better for students than the old. There is only one test of the *actus reus*, not several. The form of words is bound to lead to uncertainty, with juries disagreeing whether a more than merely preparatory act has been performed. Whatever happens juries without express provision will come to inconsistent verdicts as to at which point, to use an old example, an accused is guilty when he approaches a haystack intending to set light to it.

Three other points of interpretation

(a) It is cumbersome to speak of a 'more than merely preparatory' act. Unfortunately, to escape from the old law of proximity a different term had to be picked. Now that the courts have eschewed reference to the old law 'proximate' could be reinstated as an adjective which encapsulates the law.

(b) The adverb 'merely' seems to add nothing to 'more than preparatory'. It could mean that only 'merely preparatory' acts are not attempts, whereas 'preparatory' ones are, but such interpretation is inconsistent with the cases. What it seems to mean is that people such as the accused in **Robinson** would now be guilty: they went beyond mere preparation. Therefore, some preparatory acts are attempts.

(c) Section 1(1) refers to 'acts'. Does the term cover omissions? There is a division among commentators, and there is little case law. The government meant 'act' to cover omissions so that it would, for example, be a crime for a parent to fail to give food to her child but the infant is saved before death. An amendment that crimes of omission could not be attempted was defeated. However, if a statute says the accused is guilty if he does an 'act', an omission does not suffice (unless the omission can also be interpreted as an act). The Act could have been better drafted. If 'act' does include omissions, it may well be difficult to say when the accused commits a 'more than merely preparatory' omission. When, for example, does a father commit a more than merely preparatory omission when he is starving his daughter to death? The sole case is **Nevard** [2006] EWCA Crim 2896 where the accused attacked his wife with an axe and a knife. She tried to phone 999 but he stopped her. The emergency operator phoned back and he said that his grandchildren must have been messing about with the phone. The police nonetheless came to the house. One issue was whether the accused by failing to call the emergency services was guilty of attempted murder. The court said that the failure to summon help was evidence of intention but not decisive. The fact that this was an omission was not considered.

An alternative to 'more than merely preparatory'

The Law Commission's Working Party published a Paper, No. 50, *Codification of the Criminal Law: General Principles, Parties, Complicity and Liability for the Acts of Another*, 1973, which recommended the 'substantial step' test as adopted in the US *Model Penal Code*, 1962, s 5.01. The *Model Penal Code* in para (2) had a list of illustrations:

> The following, if strongly corroborative of the actor's criminal purpose, shall not be held insufficient as a matter of law:
> (a) lying in wait, searching for or following the contemplated victim . . . ;
> (b) enticing or seeking to entice the contemplated victim of the crime to go to the place contemplated for its commission;
> (c) reconnoitring the place contemplated for the commission of the crime;
> (d) unlawful entry of a structure, vehicle or enclosure in which it is contemplated that the crime will be committed;

(e) possession of materials to be employed in the commission of the crime which are specially designed for such unlawful use or which can serve no lawful purpose of the actor under the circumstances;

(f) possession, collection or fabrication of materials to be employed in the commission of the offence, at or near the place contemplated for its commission, where such possession, collection or fabrication serves no lawful purpose in the circumstances;

(g) soliciting an innocent agent to engage in conduct constituting an element of the crime.

The commentary found in the Proposed Official Draft 1985 stated that in each of these instances the accused had broken the psychological barrier and would be unlikely to desist. The US National Commission on Federal Criminal Laws, Final Report upon *A Proposed New Federal Criminal Code*, 1971, omitted these illustrations but only because the list could be extended.

One reason for the rejection of the substantial step test by the Law Commission in its Report No. 102, 1980, was that it was imprecise. After two decades it can be said that the 1981 Act's 'more than merely preparatory' test is just as imprecise, if not more so. The Court of Appeal recognised the difficulty in *Geddes* (above): 'There is no rule of thumb test. There must always be an exercise of judgment based on the particular facts of the case.' As A. Ashworth wrote: 'If the protection of individual rights and the confining of police discretion are regarded as important goals, does not its imprecision count against the test?' ('Criminal attempts and the role of resulting harm under the Code and in the common law' (1988) 19 Rutgers LJ 725 at 752). He was in favour of the list of authoritative examples as in the *Model Penal Code*, for without them the law is unsettled. Since there is no doubt that if two or more persons agreed to do one of the acts mentioned in the list, they would be guilty of conspiracy, surely if done by one person, a crime – attempt – should be committed.

The abolition of the defence of impossibility

Haughton v Smith [1975] AC 476 (HL) and *DPP v Nock* [1978] AC 979 (HL) were taken to have laid down a rule that a person was not guilty of attempt or conspiracy respectively where the facts were such that it was impossible to commit the full offence. For instance, if the accused put his hand into a pocket, having made up his mind to steal, he was not guilty of attempted theft if there was nothing in the pocket. Though this statement of law, which has been simplified for present purposes, had its defenders, most commentators thought it ludicrous, and the Law Commission and Parliament agreed. After all, the accused had demonstrated an intent to break the law. The law is now stated in s 1(2) of the Criminal Attempts Act 1981:

> A person may be guilty of attempting to commit an offence to which this section applies even though the facts are such that the commission of the offence is impossible.

Section 1(2) states 'may be'. 'Is' was meant. The Court of Appeal in *Shivpuri* [1985] QB 1029 thought that 'may be' was used to emphasise the requirements of *actus reus* and *mens rea*. On the pickpocket facts, the accused is now guilty. In an illustration based on *Partington v Williams* (1975) 62 Cr App R 225, the accused is guilty if he tried to take money from a wallet in a drawer but there was no money there. In an example based on *Farrance* [1978] RTR 225 (CA), the accused is guilty where he attempts to take a car but it is impossible to drive away because the clutch has burnt out.

The House of Lords applied s 1(2) in **Shivpuri** [1987] AC 1. The accused was charged with attempting to be knowingly concerned in dealing with a controlled drug, heroin. He was found carrying a package containing a powdered substance and more was found in his flat. He thought the substance was heroin, but in fact it was not. The House of Lords dismissed his appeal. Lord Bridge said that the accused had intended to commit the offence and he had performed a more than merely preparatory act. Though he could not have committed the full offence, s 1(2) deems him to be guilty. The Lords stated that the accused should also have been guilty in **Anderton v Ryan** [1985] AC 560 (HL) for attempting to handle a video which he believed to have been stolen. The law is plainly stated in s 1(2). To argue differently is to go against the words of the statute, which represent the intention of Parliament. One can nowadays be guilty of attempting to steal property which one already owns. Whether one should be guilty is a matter of policy, and should not be left to the discretion of the prosecution.

Cases since **Shivpuri** on impossible attempts have been rare but an example is **Brown**, unreported, 2 March 2004. The accused was convicted of attempting to pervert the course of justice when he made allegations of sexual and physical abuse by a person who was dead at the time to which the allegations related. Another example is **Jones** [2007] EWCA Crim 1118. The accused was found guilty of attempting to incite a child under 13 to engage in penetrative sexual activity contrary to s 8 of the Sexual Offences Act 2003. He had sought girls between 8 and 13 for sex by writing on a train lavatory. A police officer pretended to be such a girl but of course she was over 13. The accused contended that he did not intend to incite this person aged under 13 to engage in penetrative sexual activity because there was no such girl. The fact that the police officer was not under 13 was held to be irrelevant, and therefore the fact that it was impossible on the facts to commit the crime was also irrelevant.

The law has, however, not always been applied. In **Galvin** (1987) 88 Cr App R 85 (CA), the accused was charged under s 2(2) of the Official Secrets Act 1911, since repealed, with unlawfully receiving a government document. The court held that his conviction should be quashed because the government had disclosed the document so widely that the accused believed that he could use it. Perhaps he should have been convicted of attempting to receive the document unlawfully, which is what he believed was happening. Perhaps the accused in **DPP v Huskinson** [1988] Crim LR 620 (DC) should have been convicted of attempt too. He was given money by the Housing Services Department. He thought he was under a legal duty to use that money to pay off his rent arrears; in fact he was not. In those circumstances he could not be convicted of theft, which by s 5(3) of the Theft Act 1968 requires a legal obligation to exist in such circumstances (see Chapter 15). Perhaps **Shivpuri** does not apply to mistakes of law, which was the issue in **Huskinson**. He thought mistakenly he was breaking the law: he did not understand the legal nature of the money he was given. In **Shivpuri** there was a mistake of fact, the nature of the substance, and in **Anderton v Ryan** the mistake was as to the nature of the goods: were they stolen or were they not? The answer to **Huskinson** in terms of statutory interpretation is whether 'facts' in s 1(2) can cover a mistake of civil law – it may do. This construction would also cover this example. The accused agrees to buy a car and takes possession. He believes that he does not become the owner until he has paid for it. In fact by the Sale of Goods Act 1979, s 18, he does become owner. If he kicks the boot, damaging it, he is guilty of attempted criminal damage if 'facts' include mistakes of civil law. (Under the pre-Act law he would not have been guilty.)

Many cases will not give rise to problems. If the accused fires a gun at a pillow intending to kill someone, he is guilty of attempted murder. If the accused puts potassium cyanide into his mother's drink, intending to kill her, but the dose is too weak, he is guilty of attempted murder. If the accused tries to open a safe with the wrong tools, intending to steal, he is guilty of attempted theft. A slightly more difficult case is the well-known example of the accused who takes an umbrella from a London club, believing he has stolen it from another member. In fact it belongs to him. Because it does not belong to another, he is not guilty of theft. He is, however, guilty of attempting theft. It does not matter that the property in fact belongs to him. Leaving the solution to the discretion not to prosecute seems weak, but the law is clear.

The exceptional case of the imaginary crime

In *Taaffe* [1984] AC 539 (HL) the accused believed he was importing foreign currency into the UK in breach of the law. There is no such law. The accused was not guilty despite his state of mind. He could not be convicted of attempting to commit an imaginary offence. If someone does an act which he believes to be illegal but which is not, he is not guilty of attempt. Therefore, in this area there still is a law of impossible attempts.

A couple of illustrations make the point. If the accused believes adultery to be an offence, he is not guilty of attempted adultery when he has an affair with a married woman. Adultery is no offence. Therefore, attempted adultery is no offence. If the accused mistakenly believes that he is guilty of having sexual intercourse with a consenting girl of 17, he is not guilty, because there is no such crime. The position is different when the accused has sexual intercourse with a girl of 17, thinking her to be 15. There is a crime of sexual intercourse with a girl under 16. The crime is not imaginary, and the accused will be convicted of the attempt.

Christopher Ryan, *Criminal Law*, 4th edn (Blackstone, 1995) 143, commented:

> What distinguishes Mr Taaffe (who was not found guilty) from Mr Shivpuri (who was)? Both are morally reprehensible, both think they are engaged in committing a crime . . . If social danger is to be the governing factor then surely each of these men has evidenced that he is a danger, that he is prepared to break laws (or what he perceives to be laws) although it is impossible for either actually to do so.

Abolition of 'sus' and the creation of the offence of interference with vehicles

Section 9 of the Criminal Attempts Act 1981 repealed s 4 of the Vagrancy Act 1824, as amended, which contained the offence which came to be known as 'sus', suspected person loitering with intent to commit an arrestable offence. This crime had acquired a bad reputation because it was alleged that the police had used it selectively. In place of 'sus' there was instituted the crime of interference with vehicles in s 9. Besides being narrower and therefore more acceptable than 'sus', it got rid of a troublesome difficulty in the law. If a person was seen tampering with a car door, with which offence was he charged? Attempted theft of the car contrary to s 1 of the Theft Act 1968 would fail if he pleaded that he was going to joy-ride under s 12 of that Act; the same problems arose with the crimes vice versa; or the accused might contend that he wanted to steal the contents, not the car itself. Section 9 of the 1981 Act remedies this difficulty:

(1) A person is guilty of the offence of vehicle interference if he interferes with a motor vehicle or trailer or with anything carried in or on the motor vehicle or trailer with the intention that an offence specified in sub-section (2) below shall be committed by himself or some other person.

(2) The offences mentioned in sub-section (1) above are –
   (a) theft of the motor vehicle or trailer or part of it;
   (b) theft of anything carried in or on the motor vehicle or trailer; and
   (c) an offence under s 12 of the Theft Act 1968 (taking and driving away without consent): and, if it is shown that a person accused of an offence under this section intended that one of these offences should be committed, it is immaterial that it cannot be shown which it was.

A 'motor vehicle' is defined as a mechanically propelled vehicle intended or adapted for use on roads. This definition is narrower than that of 'conveyance' in the offence of taking without consent.

Points of interpretation

(a) One act of interference is enough. The accused need not be a suspected person.

(b) One of the intents specified in s 9 must be proved. There is no offence under this section if, for instance, the accused intends to commit criminal damage.

(c) 'Interference' seems to require some kind of meddling. Touching a vehicle or leaning against it may not suffice. In **Reynolds v Metropolitan Police** [1982] Crim LR 831, a judge in the Crown Court thought *obiter* that opening the door or applying pressure to the handle would amount to interference. Opening a door would not normally be called an interference but it is for the purposes of this offence.

(d) The long title of the Act speaks of 'unauthorised interference with vehicles'. Moving a car to create a space may be an authorised interference. However, s 9 does not speak of 'unauthorised interference', but only of 'interference', though the intention specified in sub-s (2) must be proved.

(e) The intents in sub-s (2) refer to Theft Act offences. The accused has a defence to s 9(1) if he has a defence under that statute. Belief in the owner's consent is a defence to taking a conveyance without consent. The accused has a defence to s 9(1) if he interferes but believes that the owner would have consented, had he or she known about it.

(f) This offence is a summary one. By s 1(4) of the Criminal Attempts Act 1981 there is no offence of attempting to commit summary offences. Therefore, there is no such crime as attempting to interfere with vehicles.

The abolition of the common law offence of preparation

Section 6 of the 1981 Act abolished the offence of procuring materials to commit a crime. It could be that there still exists at law a more general offence of preparing where the stage of a 'more than merely preparatory' act has not been reached. It is thought, however, that no such offence exists.

Withdrawal

In all three offences there is no defence of withdrawal. Lord Hailsham said so in relation to attempt in **Haughton v Smith**, above. Wright J in **Toothill** [1998] Crim LR 876 (CA) called it 'trite law' that withdrawal was no defence to attempts. Repentance can be taken into account in sentencing, and the Crown Prosecution Service may decline to prosecute. It could be argued that such a defence would accord with the policy of the law which is to encourage people to desist from offending. That argument is weakened where the reason for not committing the full offence is the presence of the police! In other words, if a defence were afforded, it should be restricted to the voluntary abandonment of purpose.

Reform

Proposals from the Law Commission are found in Consultation Paper No. 183, *Conspiracy and Attempts*, 2007. (The Report of the same name is noted below.) In respect of attempts the Commission proposes to abolish the current offence found in s 1(1) of the Criminal Attempts Act 1981 and to replace it with two offences, one of 'attempt', which would be restricted to the accused's last acts, and 'criminal preparation', which would cover behaviour which was part of the execution of his plan: the accused was still only preparing to commit the substantive offence but had proceeded beyond the stage of mere preparation. The mental element for both offences would be intent to commit the full offence and with regard to consequences (if any) but recklessness as to circumstances. The aim is not to extend liability but to clarify the law.

The proposals may be encapsulated thus. First, in respect of the *actus reus*, the Commission was concerned that the courts had struggled to draw the line between 'merely preparatory' and 'more than merely preparatory' conduct and instanced *Geddes*, above, as an example of where the courts had gone wrong. The Commission puts the result down to the wording of s 1(1) in that 'attempt' seems to imply 'trying' – the accused is not to be convicted unless the attempt is 'complete or all-but complete' (para. 1.77). Having two offences would get round the problem of definition found in cases such as *Geddes*. There should be a list of examples in the forthcoming Report which would fall within the proposed offence of criminal preparation but these would not appear in the legislation: see para. 12.39 for the illustrations and para. 16.40 for the proposal not to include the list in the legislation, though the Commission was open to persuasion (para. 16.47) as to whether the legislation should include a list of examples. Secondly, it should be made clear that if the substantive offence may be committed by an omission, so can the attempt to omit that offence. Thirdly, in respect of the fault element there should be intent (defined as in *Woollin* [1999] 1 AC 82) as to conduct and consequences but (subjective) recklessness as to circumstances. Similar fault elements are proposed for conspiracy. Fourthly, under the Criminal Attempts Act 1981, s 4(3), see above, the judge has to rule whether the accused did commit a 'more than merely preparatory' act but then the jury has to be instructed to answer the same question! The Commission proposes to revise the law so that the judge in the normal fashion rules whether the accused's behaviour could in law constitute an attempt but the jury holds whether or not that conduct did in fact constitute an attempt. Fifthly, the rule that there is no offence of attempting to commit a summary offence is seen as an 'anomaly' (para. 1.87) to be abrogated. This proposal would apply not just to the proposed attempt crime but also the proposed offence of criminal preparation. Sixthly, in relation of crimes of double inchoateness (e.g. attempting to conspire and conspiring to attempt) the Commission recommends the reversal of s 1(4)(a) of the 1981 Act: there should be a crime of attempting or criminally preparing to commit a statutory conspiracy. However, since the law would catch activities 'very remote' (para. 1.98) from the commission of offences, the Commission is open to consultees' proposing a defence of 'acting reasonably'.

The Consultation Paper was followed by Report No. 318 of 2009, also called *Conspiracy and Attempt*. The Commission abandoned its proposals for two crimes, criminal preparation and attempt, adopting the view of the majority of its consultees that the law was being interpreted in accord with Parliament's intention and that to create two crimes would make the law unnecessarily complicated. It also dropped its recommendation that there should be a list of examples. Instead it proposed that facts like *Geddes* above should be dealt with by specific offences. In relation to the mental element the Commission proposes that it should be recklessness as to circumstances when the full crime is one of negligence or strict liability; but it proposes that the same fault element for the attempt when the fault element for the full offence is higher than negligence such as knowledge or belief or recklessness as to a circumstance. This proposal is in line with that for conspiracy. Two other recommendations are that the accused can be found guilty of attempted murder if he omitted to perform a duty of care and can be guilty of an attempt if his intent was conditional on an event. The former partly gets round the problem that the statute on its face requires an act, and therefore a parent who intends to starve his child to death but is prevented from doing so by the intervention of a third party is on enactment of the proposal to be guilty of attempted murder.

To the author the Report is one of missed opportunities in relation to the *actus reus*. The examples would have led to more consistency than at present (see the discussion of the cases, above), and would have the allowed the police to intervene at an earlier stage to prevent all kinds of crimes such as drunk-driving and abduction, as the facts of those cases show.

Summary

- *Encouraging or assisting* is a crime contrary to the Serious Crime Act 2007. There are three offences: (i) intentionally encouraging or assisting an offence; (ii) encouraging or assisting an offence believing that it will be committed; and (iii) encouraging or assisting offences believing that one of more of them will be committed.

- *Conspiracy*: almost all conspiracies are statutory ones contrary to s 1(1) of the Criminal Law Act 1977 as amended. The principal exception is conspiracy to defraud. Impossibility is not a defence to statutory conspiracy, but is to the common law variety. The *actus reus* is an agreement to commit an offence and the *mens rea* is the intent to play a part in the prohibited conduct (according to **Anderson** [1986] AC 27 (HL)), intention to carry out the crime and the mental element specified in the crime agreed on. The need for two parties leads to non-liability for conspiracy where the accused has reached an agreement to commit an offence with the company he controls, with a spouse and with a person such as a child or one who is insane.

- *Attempt*: the law is laid down in the Criminal Attempts Act 1981. The *actus reus* is a more than merely preparatory act; the *mens rea* is the intent to commit the full offence. There is no crime of attempting to commit a summary offence unless Parliament has stated otherwise. Impossibility is not a defence.

References

Reports

Attorney-General, *Guidance on the Use of the Common Law Offence of Conspiracy to Defraud* (2007)

Home Office Consultation Paper, *Fraud Law Reform* (2005)

Law Commission Consultation Paper no. 183, *Conspiracy and Attempts* (2007)

Law Commission Consultation Paper no. 193, *Simplification of Criminal Law: Public Nuisance and Outraging Public Decency* (2010)

Law Commission Report no. 76, *Conspiracy and Criminal Law Reform* (1976)

Law Commission Report no. 102, *Attempt, and Impossibility in Relation to Attempt, Conspiracy and Incitement* (1980)

Law Commission Report no. 143, *Criminal Law: Codification of the Criminal Law – A Report to the Law Commission* (1985)

Law Commission Report no. 177, *A Criminal Code for England and Wales* (1989)

Law Commission Report no. 180, *Jurisdiction over Offences of Fraud and Dishonesty with a Foreign Element* (1989)

Law Commission Report no. 228, *Criminal Law: Conspiracy to Defraud* (1994)

Law Commission Report no. 276, *Fraud* (2002)

Law Commission Report no. 318, *Conspiracy and Attempt* (2009)

Law Commission Working Paper no. 50, *Codification of the Criminal Law: General Principles, Parties, Complicity, and Liability for the Acts of Another* (1973)

Law Commission Working Paper no. 104, *Conspiracy to Defraud* (1988)

US Model Penal Code (1962) American Law Institute

US National Commission on Federal Criminal Laws, *A Proposed New Federal Criminal Code* (1971) Presidential Advisory Committee

Books

Fletcher, G. *Rethinking Criminal Law* (Little, Brown & Co., 1978)

Ryan, C. *Criminal Law*, 4th edn (Blackstone, 1995)

Journals

Ashworth, A. 'Criminal attempts and the role of resulting harm under the Code and in the common law' (1988) 19 Rutgers LJ 725

Dennis, I. 'The rationale of criminal conspiracy' (1977) 93 LQR 39

Virgo, G. 'Reckless attempts – rape and circumstance' [1990] CLJ 390

Williams, G. 'Intents in the alternative' [1991] CLJ 120

Williams, G. 'Wrong turnings on the law of attempt' [1991] Crim LR 416

Further reading

Arenson, K.J. 'The pitfalls in the law of attempt: a new perspective' (2005) 69 JCL 146

Baker, D.J. 'Complicity, proportionality, and the Serious Crime Act' (2011) 14 New Crim LR 403

Clarkson, C. 'Attempt: the conduct requirement' (2009) 29 OJLS 25

Duff, R.A. 'Attempts and the problem of the missing circumstance' (1991) 42 NILQ 87

Duff, R.A. 'The circumstances of an attempt' [1991] CLJ 100

Duff, R.A., *Criminal Attempts* (Oxford University Press, 1996)

Duff, R.A. 'Guiding commitments and criminal liability' (2012) 6 Crim Law & Philos 411

Fortson, R. 'Inchoate liability and the Serious Crime Act 2007' http://www.rudifortson4law.co.uk/legaltexts/Lecture_S&M_R.Fortson_INCHOATE_ LIABILITY_and_the_SCA2007.pdf

Fortson, R. '*R v S and H*: Assisting and encouraging – trial – indictment' [2012] Crim LR 449

Husak, D. 'The nature and justifiability of nonconsummate offenses' (1995) 37 Ariz LR 151

Husak, D. 'Why punish attempts at all? Yaffe on "The Transfer Principle"' (2012) 6 Crim Law & Philos 399

Johnson, P.E. 'The unnecessary crime of complicity' (1973) 61 Col LR 1137

Katyal, N.K. 'Complicity theory' (2003) 112 Yale LJ 1307

Ormerod, D. and Fortson, R. 'Serious Crime Act 2007: the Part 2 offences' [2009] Crim LR 389

Robbins, I.P. 'Double inchoate crimes' (1989) 26 Harv JL 1

Rogers, J. 'The codification of attempts and the case for "preparation"' [2008] Crim LR 937

Smith, J.C. 'Conspiracy to defraud: some comments on the Law Commission's Report' [1995] Crim LR 209

Spencer, J. and Virgo, G. 'Encouraging and assisting crime: legislate in haste, repent at leisure' [2008] *Archbold News* 7

Stannard, J. 'Making up for the missing element: a sideways look at attempts' (1987) 7 LS 194

Sullivan, G.R. 'Inchoate liability for assisting and encouraging crime' – the Law Commission Report [2006] Crim LR 1047

Virgo, G. 'Encouraging or assisting more than one offence' [2012] *Archbold Review* 6

Westen, P. 'Impossible attempts: a speculative theory' (2008) 5 Ohio St LJ 523

For conspiracy to defraud, see A.T.H. Smith, *Property Offences* (Sweet & Maxwell, 1994), ch. 19

For an Irish view, see Law Reform Commission Consultation Paper No. 48, *Inchoate Offences* (2008)

Visit **www.mylawchamber.co.uk** to access tools to help you develop and test your knowledge of criminal law, including interactive multiple choice questions, practice exam questions with guidance, annotated weblinks, glossary flashcards, legal newsfeed and legal updates.

Use Case Navigator to read in full some of the key cases referenced in this chapter with commentary and questions:

R v *G and Another* [2003] UK HL 50
R v *Woollin* [1999] AC 82

Part 3

Particular offences

11

Murder

After reading this chapter you will understand and be able to critique:

- the definition of murder
- the sentence for murder
- the definition of death
- the mental element in murder

General introduction

> . . . the gradations of culpability in the crime of murder are almost as infinite as the variations in the human psyche itself. (Keane CJ 'Murder – the mental element' (2002) 53 NILQ 1 at 8)

If the accused kills someone who has been born alive, one or more of the following crimes may occur: **murder**, manslaughter, causing death by dangerous driving, **infanticide** or genocide. These offences are generally called **'homicide'**, but that word is not a term of art in English law. People are charged with murder, not with homicide. A killing may not always constitute a crime, and one must be careful that not too much is swept up into manslaughter, especially the gross negligence form, discussed later. Murder and manslaughter are distinguished by a difference in the state of mind of the accused at the time of killing (Figure 11.1). In both offences he has caused someone's death. Murder is a more serious crime than manslaughter because to be guilty of it he must have intended to kill or commit grievous bodily harm, whereas a lesser (which means 'less blameworthy') state of mind suffices for manslaughter. The difference resides in morality: the murderer is more morally culpable than a person guilty of manslaughter.

Most murders arise out of quarrels, jealousy, arguments over money and robbery. Many murders are committed against persons from the accused's family or friends and the killing often takes place in the home of the victim or killer. Indeed, the age category into which more victims fall than any other is being aged under one: C. Flood-Page and J. Turner (eds), *Crime in England and Wales 2001/2002* (Home Office, 2003). Most, perhaps 90 per cent, are committed by men, but victims are more or less evenly divided among males and females. In 2008–09 73 per cent of female victims knew their killer. See Flood-Page and Turner,

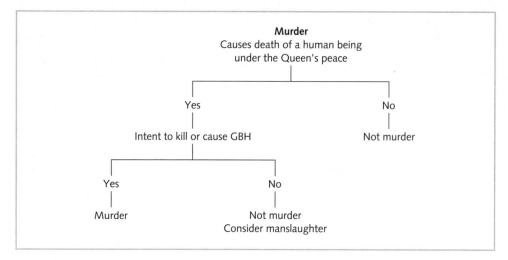

Figure 11.1 Murder

above, at p. 3. The number of homicides per annum did not vary much throughout the 1990s, being around 600 per year. In 1999–2000 there were 761. The figures for 2002–03 were 1,048 homicides, an increase of 18 per cent on the previous year, but including 172 killings by Dr Harold Shipman. Similarly figures for homicide can be distorted by other mass killings such as the murder of 52 in the 7/7 London bombings, which affected the 2004–05 figures, the death of 20 or more Chinese cockle pickers in Morecambe Bay in 2002–03, and the suffocation of 51 Chinese nationals in the back of a lorry en route to England in 2000–01. In 2008–09 there were 648 recorded homicides and this figure was not distorted by mass killings such as those by terrorists. There were, for comparison, 151 killed at work in 2008–09 according to the Health and Safety Executive.

The risk to the general population in 2001 was 15 per million, rising to 82 per million for children under one: see the Home Office's annual *Criminal Statistics*. That is, children under one run the most risk of being killed, usually by a parent (and very rarely by a stranger). Overseas readers, especially those in US cities, may wish to compare this level with that in their home towns.

The definition of murder

Example

Dave deliberately infects Pauline with HIV. She dies 20 years later from HIV. Is Dave guilty of murder?

There may be a problem with causation: did Dave's infecting her cause her death? Causation in murder is no different from causation in other areas of criminal law, and indeed the majority of causation cases are homicide ones. If 'but for' his infecting her, she would have lived, we have factual causation. If so, then we look at legal causation: was it reasonably foreseeable that she would die from his infecting her? If so, he has caused her death. As ever, causation is a question for the jury and they have to apply the law to the facts.

With regard to the *mens rea* of murder, malice aforethought, the accused must intend to kill or cause grievous bodily harm to the victim: see especially *Cunningham* [1982] AC 566 (HL). Intent is always judged subjectively (did Dave himself intend?) and is a question of fact for the jury. As always too the golden rule with regard to the definition of intent is that it bears its ordinary meaning and therefore there is normally no need to explain the definition to the jury: *Moloney* [1985] AC 905 (HL). Only exceptionally is a *Woollin* [1999] 1 AC 82 (HL) direction (see Chapter 3) needed.

Note that, until the modern era, before a killing could be murder death had to take place within a year and a day of the attack. This rule was abolished by the aptly named Law Reform (Year and a Day Rule) Act 1996. However, the Attorney-General's consent is required where death occurs more than three years after the assault and consent will be refused if, for example, prosecution would be oppressive (but when prosecution would be oppressive does not form part of a course on substantive criminal law).

Parliament has not defined murder. There have been several calls for placing murder on a statutory footing. For example, the (Nathan) *Report of the Select Committee of the House of Lords on Murder and Life Imprisonment* (HL Paper 78–1) made such a call in 1989. Despite such calls, the definition is left to the common law. The task is left for judges, who mostly adopt and adapt the definition of Chief Justice Coke from the early seventeenth century (3 Co Inst 47):

> Murder is when a man of sound memory and of the age of discretion unlawfully killeth . . . any reasonable creature *in rerum natura* under the King's peace, with malice aforethought, either expressed by the party or implied by law, so as the party wounded or hurt etc., die of the wound or hurt etc. . . . .

(a) The phrase 'any reasonable creature' means a human being. It is thought that persons born without heads are protected.

(b) '*In rerum natura*' is translated as 'in being'. Accordingly one cannot murder an unborn person, even if that foetus could have survived had it been born naturally; one can murder only a child who is born alive and fully extruded from the mother, though the law, being based on nineteenth-century cases, is not pellucid. Apparently there is no need for the child to breathe, and the umbilical cord need not be cut or the afterbirth expelled. The principal English authorities are pre-Victorian and may require reconsideration in the light of modern science. Nevertheless, they were followed by the New South Wales Court of Criminal Appeal in *Iby* [2005] NSWCCA 178. The accused drove a stolen car at excessive speed and collided head-on with a woman who was 38 weeks pregnant. An emergency caesarean was performed and the baby had a heartbeat and was put on the ventilator but he had no (or little) electrical activity in the brain and by two hours after birth there was no heartbeat; the court held that the baby had been born alive and therefore could be the subject of a manslaughter charge. The child had an existence independent of its mother, both as to breathing and as to heartbeat, and it was irrelevant that the heartbeat had been sustained mechanically. The case examines and applies the English authorities. The protection in Article 2 of the European Convention on Human Rights, the right to life, also does not extend to the foetus: *Vo v France* (2005) 40 EHRR 259.

The Infant Life (Preservation) Act 1929 created the offence of child destruction to deal with killing before the definition of murder could be satisfied. It is an offence wilfully to cause the death of a child who is capable of being born alive at any time before he obtains an independent existence. It is a defence to prove that the act was done in good faith for the preservation of the mother's life. The Fourteenth Report of the Criminal Law Revision Committee, *Offences Against the Person*, Cmnd 7844, 1980, adopted the test that 'the victim should have been born and have an existence independent of its mother' (para. 35). Before that the 1929 Act would apply; after that the law of homicide would.

In *Attorney-General's Reference (No. 3 of 1994)* [1998] AC 245 (HL) the accused was charged with the murder of a child. While the child was a foetus, the accused had stabbed the mother in the abdomen. He knew that the woman was pregnant. The child was born prematurely because of the injury and died six months after birth. The trial judge ruled that there was no *actus reus* for murder (or manslaughter) because a foetus was not a live person protected by the law of murder, and that there was no *mens rea* towards the foetus: the defendant intended to wound the mother, and malice towards her could not be transferred to the foetus because it was not a live person protected by the homicide law. Therefore, according to the trial judge, there was no crime. The Court of Appeal disagreed and would have convicted of murder. The House of Lords in turn disagreed with the Court of Appeal and would have found the accused guilty of manslaughter. Lord Mustill said that the Court of Appeal was wrong to hold that a foetus is part of the mother and therefore that an intent to injure the mother is an intent to injure the foetus. 'The mother and the foetus were two distinct organisms living symbiotically, not a single organism with two aspects.' Moreover, a foetus does not share human personality with its mother: it is an organism in and of itself, not part of the mother. Accordingly, when the accused acts without intent to injure the foetus, the intent to injure the mother seriously cannot be transferred from the mother to the foetus, and then from the foetus to the child, who is born alive but later dies as a result of the attack on the mother. Therefore, the accused could not be guilty of murder. He was, however, guilty of constructive manslaughter (see Chapter 12), because for that crime the unlawful and dangerous act can be a risk to anyone including a woman carrying a foetus, and that law applies whether or not the accused knew that she was pregnant.

See Figure 12.3 on p 472 (Chapter 12) for a diagram illustrating constructive (unlawful act) manslaughter.

There are difficulties integrating the offences of child destruction (and procuring a miscarriage contrary to s 58 of the Offences Against the Person Act 1861) with murder and manslaughter. If, as in the *Reference* case, the accused tries to kill the foetus, the child is born but then dies from its injuries, he may be guilty of murder or manslaughter. However, if the foetus is killed in the womb, murder and manslaughter are not applicable and the charge is one of child destruction (or procuring a miscarriage).

A conjoined twin is a human being even though he has 'a useless brain, a useless heart and useless lungs': *Re A* [2001] Fam 147 (CA), a civil law authority.

A human clone would presumably be a creature *in rerum natura*.

(c) 'Under the King's peace' exempts from liability those who kill active enemy aliens in time of war; it remains murder, however, to kill prisoners of war. It may well be that killing rebels against the Crown is also not murder.

(d) **Malice aforethought** is the mental element in murder and is dealt with separately below.

(e) For both murder and manslaughter it was until recently a rule of English law (though not of Scotland, of European Union member states, or of some parts of the Commonwealth) that the death must occur within a year and a day, even though it could otherwise be said that the accused caused the victim's death. This rule was abrogated by the Law Reform (Year and a Day Rule) Act 1996. For discussion see below.

(f) Murder or manslaughter by a citizen of the UK or colonies is triable in England and Wales, even if the crime was committed outside England, and a killing by a non-British citizen on a British ship or aircraft is triable in England. One effect of this rule should be noted. Because of it, the rule about killing persons not under the Queen's peace is needed; otherwise UK citizens who killed enemy aliens in battle abroad would be guilty of murder in England and Wales.

(g) Coke's definition has the term 'unlawfully' in it. For that reason the law of murder demonstrates that the sanctity of life is not always upheld and the following are not murder:

   (i) execution carried out by the person whose duty it is and in the manner appointed;

   (ii) killing by an officer of justice in the execution of his duty to arrest, search or seize property, provided that the force was necessary to protect himself and execute his duty; a private person helping such an officer will also not be guilty;

   (iii) killing by a citizen effecting a lawful arrest and using reasonable force;

   (iv) killing by a person using force to prevent a crime;

   (v) killing by a person using reasonable force to prevent trespass to land or goods (this is questionable because in the modern era it is difficult to justify or excuse the killing of a human being in order to preserve property);

   (vi) killing as a result of lawful chastisement;

   (vii) killing as a result of a lawful operation.

(h) The width of the definition should be noted. It covers, for example, both terrorists who set out to kill as many people as possible and mercy-killers. Mercy-killers are murderers, but those who drive recklessly and cause a crash in which many people die are not: reasonable people may disagree as to who is more blameworthy. So-called 'honour killings' are murder.

The sentence for murder

The sentence for murder must be life imprisonment. Figures show that the average time served for those released in 1992 was 12.5 years, a substantial increase on 1988 when it was 10.1 years. These are averages. The actual time spent in prison varies tremendously. The Moors murderers served over 30 years in prison before Myra Hindley died in November 2002. Her lover, Ian Brady, has served over 40 years. He is on a 'whole life' tariff.

The House of Lords in *Lichniak* [2003] 1 AC 903 held that the indeterminate life sentence was not contrary to Article 3 (inhuman or degrading treatment) or Article 5 (right to liberty) of the European Convention on Human Rights. This was because the sentence was not in fact indeterminate but was subject to the tariff period, which varied with the requirements of retribution and deterrence to the individual accused.

In a parliamentary debate on the subject, on 25 June 1991, the House of Commons overturned a House of Lords majority in favour of giving the judges discretion as to sentence. The then Home Secretary supported the life sentence on the ground that the seriousness of murder had to be marked out, while gradations in the type of killing could be dealt with by varying the amount of time actually spent in prison serving the mandatory life sentence: a mercy-killer would serve less than a sadistic murderer. The Opposition thought that the sentence should be determined by the judge, not by the Executive, which after all is what happens in other offences; the judge has seen the demeanour of the accused during the trial but the Executive has not; and sentences should not be determined and given behind closed doors. Giving judges discretion would also alleviate one problem: duress is not a defence to murder, but if a life sentence was no longer compulsory, duress could be taken into account in the sentence. Similarly, the battered spouse whose reaction is not quick enough for provocation could have a determinate sentence. Moreover, the difference between murder and another offence may depend on fortuitous circumstances such as a doctor being at hand; and in respect of attempted murder only an intent to kill will suffice, yet in murder itself the mental element also covers an intent to commit grievous bodily harm; in terms of *mens rea* attempted murder can be more serious than murder, but only the latter crime attracts a mandatory sentence. As Lord Hailsham, the former Lord Chancellor put it in **Howe** [1987] AC 417 in the Lords:

> [m]urder . . . , though often described as one of the [crimes of] utmost heinousness, is not in fact necessarily so, but consists in a whole bundle of offences of vastly differing degrees of culpability, ranging from brutal, cynical and repeated offences like the so-called Moors murders to the almost venial, if objectively immoral, 'mercy killing' of a beloved partner.

A survey of public attitudes about the mandatory life sentence was conducted by Professor Barry Mitchell and published by the Law Commission as part of its Report No. 290, *Partial Defences to Murder*, 2004. Paragraph 2.35 states: 'The notion that all murders, as the law is presently framed, represent instances of a uniquely heinous offence for which a single uniquely severe penalty is justified does not reflect the views of a cross-section of the public when asked to reflect on particular cases.' The abolition of the mandatory sentence would lead to the simplification and perhaps abolition of voluntary manslaughter: see the next chapter. This survey of public opinion is reflected in the views of consultees on the Consultation Paper No. 173, also called *Partial Defences to Murder*, 2003. However, some groups such as Support after Murder and Manslaughter support the mandatory sentence.

The Nathan Report, *Report of the Select Committee of the House of Lords on Murder and Life Imprisonment*, 1989, recommended that the mandatory life sentence for murder should be abolished. The judge should have a discretion in order that he can take into account the many forms of murder. The then government rejected this proposal. An amendment to a Bill which would have made the sentence discretionary failed in 1991. No change is likely for the next few years, despite the Human Rights Act 1998. The then Home Secretary said that arguments of deterrence and retribution supported the mandatory sentence and by murdering, the accused had forfeited his liberty to the state and it should therefore be the state which decided on release. The Labour government said in 1997 that it would not abolish the mandatory sentence. However, in a leaked memo reported in *the Guardian*, 11 July 2000, the then Prime Minister is reported as suggesting that a senior judge should report on whether the life sentence should remain mandatory in the light of the conviction for murder of Tony Martin who shot a teenage burglar dead at his isolated farm. However, nothing was done. Pressure for reform has been expressed elsewhere and Lord Mustill said in **Powell; English** [1998] AC 147 (HL) that England and Wales 'need a new law of homicide, or a new law of punishment for homicide, or preferably both'. Since the judges could not alter the law, he called for parliamentary intervention, but noted that a change in the law may not be popular. However, one straw in the wind was a prematurely released Home Office press release in 2004 which said that a revised law of murder had to be 'clear, comprehensive and fair', and surely it is not fair to sentence terrorists and mercy-killers to the same length of imprisonment.

The death sentence for murder was completely abolished in 1965. In 1998 the UK ratified the Sixth Protocol to the European Convention, by which execution in peacetime is prohibited and the Crime and Disorder Act 1998 abolished the death penalty for piracy and treason. The only way of restoring the death penalty would be to revise the Human Rights Act 1998.

Death

There is no legally accepted definition of death in homicide cases: is it when the heart and breathing stop or is it brain-death? Certainly people whose heart has stopped and whose breathing has ceased have been revived. Probably, if the judges had to choose, they would select brain-death, which is in accord with the doctors' Code of Practice for the Diagnosis and Confirmation of Death. This definition means that the brain stem has ceased to function with the result that reflex actions, in particular circulation of the blood and breathing, have ceased to function. If so, an accused who decapitated a brain-dead person would not be guilty of murder, even though the victim is 'breathing' by means of a ventilator. Three Law Lords, Keith, Goff and Browne-Wilkinson, accepted the following definition (apparently) *obiter* in *Airedale NHS Trust* v *Bland* [1993] AC 789, a civil case: a person in a persistent vegetative state is alive if there is brain activity. There is authority from a lower civil court to the same effect: *Re A (a Minor)* [1992] 3 Med LR 303. A person in a persistent vegetative state (PVS), is not brain-dead. Presumably therefore someone in a deep coma is also not dead. One who is not brain-dead but who is on a ventilator can be the subject of homicide, as *Malcherek* [1981] 2 All ER 422 (CA) demonstrates.

The Criminal Law Revision Committee in its Fourteenth Report, *Offences Against the Person*, Cmnd 7844, 1980, recommended that there should not be a statutory definition of death because it might become out of date through improvements in medical technology. The draft Criminal Code 1989 recommended that the lack of functioning of the brain stem should be the definition, with the effect that those in a PVS would not be dead for legal purposes even though their cortex was no longer working. No government has attempted to put any definition on to a statutory footing.

For an explanation of causation, see Chapter 2. This is illustrated in Figure 2.1 on p 00.

For causation, see Chapter 2.

Abolition of the year-and-a-day rule

The Law Commission in 1995 recommended the abolition of the year-and-a-day rule, which was arbitrary in its effect (Report No. 230, *The Year and a Day Rule in Homicide*). A Bill was attached to the Report, and it was enacted as the Law Reform (Year and a Day Rule) Act 1996. The Act applies to cases where the act or omission causing death occurred on or after 17 June 1996. The year-and-a-day rule came increasingly under attack both for not being in accord with modern medical science and for reducing the nature of the crime in a fortuitous way. If the victim died within a year, the crime was one of the homicide offences. If he died a year and two days after the attack, it was not, yet the survival for slightly longer in the second instance than the first may be dependent on factors such as the use of a ventilator, outside the control both of victim and accused. The Commission opined (at para. 3.19) that 'it is wrong that a defendant should be charged with an offence which does not properly reflect the consequences of his conduct merely because his victim happens to survive for more than 366 days'. Sentences lower than would otherwise be the case are imposed. The law also meant that offenders were incorrectly labelled and sentenced. The Law Commission received a petition requesting abolition of the rule and noted a case from Darlington: the attacker could be convicted only of inflicting grievous bodily harm and was sentenced to two years' imprisonment.

Another problem was that the rule permitted the accused to escape liability where he had infected the victim with a long-term illness such as AIDS. Furthermore, if the victim of what would otherwise be manslaughter by gross negligence survived for longer than a year and a day, the accused could not be found guilty of any crime because there is no non-fatal gross negligence offence. Various Australian states such as Victoria have abolished the rule: Crimes (Year-and-a-Day Rule) Act 1991, s 3. The sole Australian state to preserve the rule is Queensland, but the Criminal Code Review Committee recommended its abolition.

The argument that the rule prevented prosecutions long after the attack is ill-founded. Persons are prosecuted many years after they have killed, an obvious instance being Frederick West, the Gloucester builder, who killed at least 11 women. If there is no time limit for homicide in this sense, why should there have been one in relation to the gap between the attack and the killing? Where the victim dies before conviction of a non-fatal offence, there is no problem with trying the accused for murder. The difficulty lies with an accused who is convicted of a non-fatal offence and then the victim dies. There can only be a new trial where there is 'new and compelling evidence', and there is no such evidence when the sole additional fact is that the victim has died. The judge may stop the trial if there is an abuse of process, which there might be if the trial is many years after the events giving rise to the offence.

In light of these criticisms, the Law Reform (Year and a Day Rule) Act 1996 abolished the rule for all offences. The Attorney-General's consent (which will be refused if the prosecution is oppressive) is required when the death occurred more than three years after the injury or when the accused had been convicted of another offence alleged to be connected to the injury. The offence will normally be a non-fatal offence but could, for example, be burglary. The Law Commission in Report No. 230 proposed that the first exception, which relates to death more than three years after the injury, is to protect the accused in situations where his memory may not be reliable or where evidence has disappeared, but this exception does not apply to other offences where memory may have become defective or evidence may have disappeared. It is unclear why the consent of the Attorney-General is required under the Act when it is not usually required for other offences.

Malice aforethought

> In human affairs we are always concerned with probabilities rather than certainties. The difference between intention and recklessness is the difference between a virtual (or moral) certainty and a high probability (Lord Edmund-Davies in **MPC v Caldwell** [1982] AC 341 at 359).

The mental element in murder is:

(a) the intention to kill;

(b) the intention to cause grievous bodily harm.

The Lords in **Cunningham** [1982] AC 566 settled a dispute as to whether the second form was indeed an alternative mental element. To say that intent is the fault element for murder is, therefore, only partly true, for an intent to frighten, say, is insufficient. In respect of both intention and recklessness, the harm required for the offence to be consummated must be stated. One can extend the formulation of the mental element, also known as malice aforethought, in this way: the accused must intend to kill, or cause grievous bodily harm to, a human being, knowing or perhaps only foreseeing that the victim is under the

Queen's Peace. As is general in criminal law, motive is no defence, but there may be a defence such as loss of control. Malice aforethought is a legal term of art. It is not necessary that the accused acted spitefully or gave much thought to the killing. Intention does not require a plan. A fleeting state of mind suffices.

That these two forms of *mens rea* were the sole ones was affirmed by the House of Lords in *Moloney*.

Moloney [1985] AC 905 (HL)

The accused and victim had been celebrating the ruby wedding anniversary of the accused's grandparents. The victim was the accused's stepfather. They had both been drinking heavily. The victim claimed that, even with his crippled arm, he could outload, outdraw and outshoot the accused. They put the claim to the test. Unfortunately for the victim the accused won, and blew off the victim's head with a twelve-bore shotgun. The accused said that he had no idea that by shooting the gun, he would injure his stepfather. He was convicted of murder. The Lords allowed his appeal but substituted a conviction for manslaughter (on the grounds of gross negligence or recklessness) for there was no doubt in the mind of Lord Bridge that the accused acted with 'a high degree of recklessness'. The case was remitted for sentence to the Court of Appeal, and an immediate release was ordered.

Morally conduct committed intentionally should be punished more severely than recklessly committed behaviour. For this reason a sharp line should be drawn between intention and recklessness.

The European Convention on Human Rights, Article 2(1), protects persons from being intentionally deprived of life. Brooke and Walker LJJ in *Re A* [2001] Fam 147 (CA), a civil case concerning surgical separation of conjoined twins, said that doctors did not kill 'intentionally' when they knew that the separation would cause the death of one of the twins within minutes, because they acted to save the life of the other twin, her life before separation being shortened by her twin. 'Intentionally' therefore covers only 'direct intent' (see Chapter 3), not oblique intent.

See pp 90–104 (Chapter 3) for a definition of intent.

The intention to cause grievous bodily harm

As stated above, the present law holds that this head of malice aforethought exists, and the Lords said in *Moloney* and *Attorney-General's Reference (No. 3 of 1994)* that any amendment was for Parliament. The law was laid down in *Cunningham* [1982] AC 566 (HL), see 'Malice aforethought' above, where the accused hit his victim, who was lying defenceless on the floor, over the head with a chair. He argued that he had only 'implied malice', that is, he only intended to cause grievous bodily harm, and that the head of malice aforethought no longer existed. Lord Hailsham stated:

(a) The Homicide Act 1957 did not abolish implied malice. Two cases to that effect, *Vickers* [1957] 2 QB 664 (CCA) and *Hyam v DPP* [1975] AC 55 (HL) were approved.

(b) The test for proving intent is subjective, as the Criminal Justice Act 1967, s 8, laid down. On this point also *Hyam* was approved.

(c) 'Grievous bodily harm' meant 'really serious bodily harm', as the House of Lords had held in *DPP v Smith* [1961] AC 290, above, and the Court of Criminal Appeal had determined in *Metharam* [1961] 3 All ER 200 (though the modern approach is to drop 'really' where there is no doubt that the injury was serious (see *Janjua* [1999] 1 Cr App R 91 (CA) where it was said that 'really' might be required in some cases but normally it was not and it was definitely not required when the accused had used a $5^1/_2$-inch sharp knife with which the victim had been killed); *Saunders* [1985] Crim LR 230 (CA) where the victim suffered a broken nose and cuts).

(d) *Vickers* as endorsed by *Smith* was correct as to the definition of grievous bodily harm. It did not mean endangering life as the dissentients had stated in *Hyam*. Moreover, the test of intent to cause serious harm was not too difficult for a jury, and changing it to intent to endanger life would not facilitate the jury's task.

The Lords refused to use their *Practice Statement* on precedent to overrule *Smith* on this point, for (a) their power to overrule their previous cases must be used sparingly, especially in the criminal law; (b) to rule otherwise would mean that some people including Vickers had been wrongfully hanged; (c) such a change is too great for the judges and should be left for Parliament. Accordingly, murder remains what might be called a crime of 'half *mens rea*': the defendant's *actus reus* is killing, but his *mens rea* need not be that. He is guilty if he intended to commit grievous bodily harm. For example, in *Middleton*, unreported, 11 March 1999, the defendants attacked their victim with their fists and feet. The Court of Appeal held that the jury was entitled to find that they intended (at least) serious harm.

The arguments in favour of the rule are that whether death results when the accused intended to commit grievous bodily harm may depend on chance (such as proximity of an accident and emergency unit) and that there is insufficient moral distinction between one who intends to kill and one who intends to cause grievous bodily harm. Lord Edmund-Davies said that the result of causing serious harm was so unpredictable that the person who inflicted it deserved to be called a murderer if the victim died because he had acted 'wickedly'. Lord Bingham spoke to similar effect in *Rahman* [2008] UKHL 45. He said that the law 'may lack logical purity but it is underpinned by a quality of earthy realism.'

The minority in *Cunningham* strongly criticised this result. Lord Edmund-Davies thought it 'strange that a person can be convicted of murder if death results from, say, his intentional breaking of another's arm, an action which . . . would in most cases be unlikely to kill'. There is also the argument contrary to the one noted above, that there is a moral difference between the two forms of intent. Lord Mustill in *Attorney-General's Reference (No. 3 of 1994)* [1998] AC 245 (HL) criticised the fact that intent to cause grievous bodily harm was part of malice aforethought. The Law Commission in one of its first reports, *Imputed Criminal Intent (DPP v Smith)*, No. 10, 1967, argued in favour of changing current law:

(a) Murder is commonly understood to mean the intentional killing of another human being; and, unless there are strong reasons which justify a contrary course, it is generally desirable that legal terms should correspond with their popular meaning.

(b) To limit intent in murder to the intent to kill is not to disregard the very serious nature of causing death by the infliction of grievous bodily harm, but . . . if such an offence were to be treated as manslaughter only, it could nevertheless be punished by a maximum penalty as severe as the penalty prescribed for murder . . .

(d) . . . [A] man should not be regarded as a murderer if he does not *know* that the bodily harm which he intends to inflict is likely to kill.

The proposed reform dealt with in the previous section would not abolish this head of *mens rea*, but narrow it slightly.

It may be noted that this head of *mens rea* may not always be correctly applied. Barry Mitchell found a case where the accused had gagged a victim, who died. The accused was convicted of murder, but doubt must remain whether the defendant did intend to cause serious harm. The intent seems to have been to incapacitate: 'Distinguishing between murder and manslaughter' [1991] NLJ 935. Accordingly, even if the law were tightly defined, the jurors might let their feelings lead to the conviction of the 'bad' person and acquit the 'good'. The same point can be made in relation to provocation and the prosecution of terrorists for murder.

One point of interest is that when Parliament overrode *DPP v Smith* in relation to the presumption that a person intends the natural consequences of his conduct so that he is no longer taken to have the intention to commit murder when he killed someone, it was given the opportunity to abolish another part of *DPP v Smith*, namely that implied malice had survived the enactment of the Homicide Act 1957. The Law Commission Report No. 10, *Imputed Criminal Intent (DPP v Smith)*, 1967, was partly enacted in the Criminal Justice Act 1967, s 8. Another part was not. The Commission recommended (para. 18): 'So long as a distinction between murder and manslaughter is to be maintained, there must be a defensible criterion for distinguishing between them. In our view the essential element in murder should be willingness to kill, thereby evincing a total lack of respect for human life.' But Parliament's rejection of the proposal shows that it did not wish to remove the intent to commit grievous bodily harm from malice aforethought.

The Fourteenth Report of the Criminal Law Revision Committee, *Offences Against the Person*, Cmnd 7844, 1980, para 31, supported the Law Commission's 1967 proposal, as did the draft Criminal Code, Law Com. Report No. 177, 1989. Clause 54(1) is quoted above.

The Northern Ireland Court of Appeal in *Anderson* [2003] NICA 12 ruled that current law does not breach Article 3 of the European Convention on Human Rights (no 'inhuman or degrading . . . punishment') because imprisonment is not such and does not breach Article 7, the principle of legality, because the concept of grievous bodily harm is no harder for a jury to apply than any other term in criminal law.

Retaining the offence of murder

Lord Kilbrandon in *Hyam v DPP* [1975] AC 55 (HL) was the main proponent of the view that murder and manslaughter should be amalgamated to form a crime of unlawful homicide in respect of which the judge would have discretion as to sentencing. Only on the most heinous facts would the accused receive life imprisonment. This reform would receive the support of those involved in or supporting euthanasia. The defences of loss of control, diminished responsibility and killing in pursuance of a suicide pact, which reduce murder to manslaughter, could be abolished. The argument against is that there should be marked a category for those particularly serious killers, and the crime of murder, perhaps with the deletion of the intent to cause grievous bodily harm, reflects that moral distinction. This principle is sometimes known as 'fair labelling'. Murder is a well-established term with moral connotations, and the public accepts that murderers should be distinguished from those who are guilty of less blameworthy homicides. There is a vast difference between the contract-killer and a person who kills through gross negligence. The former deserves to be called a murderer and be stigmatised, whereas the latter does not. Decisions on issues such as whether the killing was grave or not should be for juries, not for judges.

Murder, manslaughter and infanticide

The Law Commission Report No. 304, *Murder, Manslaughter and Infanticide*, November 2006, was a follow-up to the Consultation Paper (CP) No. 177, *A New Homicide Act for England and Wales?*, December 2005.

'The law governing homicide . . . is a rickety structure set upon shaky foundations . . .' (para. 1.8). Therefore, '. . . for the first time, the general law of homicide [must be] rationalised through legislation. Offences and defences specific to murder must take their place within a readily comprehensible and fair legal structure' (para. 1.10). 'Although twentieth century legislation on murder brought many valuable reforms, the definitions of murder and the partial defences remain misleading, out-of-date, unfit for purpose, or all of these' (para. 1.70). There should be a new Homicide Act, replacing the 1957 version, with 'clear and comprehensive definitions of the homicide offences and the partial defences' (para. 1.63). Murder would be retained but divided into two degrees. The government wrote to the Law Commission in 2011 that it would not take the proposals forward. It said that the time was not right for a substantial reform of homicide.

The main difficulties with the current definition of murder

The following are the major problems:

1   The 'serious harm' rule in murder.
    Example: 'D intentionally punches V in the face. The punch breaks V's nose and causes V to fall to the ground. In falling, V hits his or her head on the kerb causing a massive and fatal brain haemorrhage.'
    Parliament in passing the Homicide Act 1957 did not expect that the courts would construe malice aforethought so widely: see *Vickers* (1957) CCA.
    Recommendation: where D intends serious harm and was aware that the conduct posed a serious risk of death, that should be top-tier (first degree) homicide; however, where D intends serious harm but was not aware of a serious risk of death, that would be second tier homicide.

2   'The law is too generous in treating all those who realise that their conduct poses a risk of causing death but press on regardless as guilty only of manslaughter.' These killers should be guilty of top-tier homicide.

The first problem stems from murder being too wide, the second from murder being too narrow.

The principal recommendations of the Law Commission's Report, *Murder, Manslaughter and Infanticide*

The outcome is a three-tier structure with the terms 'murder' and 'manslaughter' preserved. This structure is 'clearer and more intelligible, as well as being morally more defensible' (para. 2.4).

1   'First degree murder':
    (a) intentional killing, for example contract killers: there is an intention to kill;
    (b) killing through an intention to do serious injury with an awareness of a serious risk of causing death.
    There would be a mandatory life sentence.
        This proposal differs from that in the CP where first degree murder was restricted to intentional killing. The recommendation is based on morality: some reckless killings are as heinous as intentional killings (para. 2.60).

2   'Second degree murder':
    (a) killing through an intention to cause serious injury (even without an awareness of a serious risk of causing death);

(b) killing where D was aware of a serious risk of causing death coupled with an intent to cause some injury, or fear of injury or a risk of injury (this would cover the terrorist who gave insufficient warning of a bomb);

(c) provocation (now loss of control);

(d) diminished responsibility;

(e) suicide pact.

The concept of second degree murder would be new to Anglo-Welsh law. There would not be a mandatory life sentence for this second rank of murder: the maximum sentence would be life imprisonment. However, it must be noted that second degree murder is still 'murder' with the result for example that a successful plea of provocation (now loss of control) would lead to a verdict of murder, admittedly in the second degree, and not as now manslaughter. In this respect second degree murder covers some who now are murderers, some who are guilty of manslaughter and some who have a successful partial defence to manslaughter. The current partial defences to murder would not lead to a verdict of manslaughter because D did kill intending to kill: such killers fall within the label of first degree murderers except for the defence (para. 2.156).

The term 'injury' would replace 'bodily harm' to ensure that psychiatric harm is covered. However, there would be no definition of 'serious' injury (para. 2.94) and whether injury is serious or not would be left to the jury.

The term 'reckless indifference' used in the CP would be replaced by (b) above.

It should be noted that to be guilty of second degree murder, an accused who kills being aware that his or her conduct involved a serious risk of death would also have to intend to cause injury, fear of injury or risk of injury. Without that intent, D would be guilty of manslaughter. For example, an electrician who believes that she can cut corners may be aware of the risk of death but would not be guilty of second degree murder but of manslaughter because she did not intend injury or fear of injury or the risk of injury (para. 2.110).

It should be added that provocation (now loss of control), diminished responsibility and suicide pacts will not provide defences to second degree murder. They are to be taken into account in the sentence.

3 'Manslaughter':

(a) death caused by a criminal act intended to cause injury;

(b) death when D was aware that the criminal act involved a serious risk of causing injury;

(c) death where D was grossly negligent as to causing death.

The remit of the Commission did not allow it to make recommendations as to manslaughter but (a) and (b) are very similar to the Government's proposals for replacing unlawful act (or constructive) manslaughter found in the Home Office's *Reforming the Law on Involuntary Manslaughter: The Government's Proposals* (2000).

In this way there would be a 'ladder' (para. 1.64) of offences.

Additional proposal

There should be a defence of excessive self-defence when D overreacts to a threat of serious violence from an aggressor. This recommendation is dealt with in Chapter 8. The defence of loss of control now provides a defence to an accused who uses excessive force to kill but it is restricted to murder and the outcome is (voluntary) manslaughter, not an acquittal: see Chapter 12.

Summary

- *Murder*: Murder is the unlawful killing of a human being under the Queen's peace with malice aforethought. 'Malice aforethought' is simply the *mens rea* of murder and comprises the intent to kill and the intent to cause grievous bodily harm (GBH). Intention is considered in Chapter 3. Death means the non-functioning of the brain-stem; GBH means (really) serious bodily harm.

References

Reports

Criminal Law Revision Committee 14th Report, *Offences Against the Person*, Cmnd 7844 (1980)

Home Office *Reforming the Law on Involuntary Manslaughter: The Government's Proposals* (2000)

Law Commission Consultation Paper no. 173, *Partial Defences to Murder* (2003)

Law Commission Consultation Paper no. 177, *A new Homicide Act for England and Wales?* (2005)

Law Commission Report no. 10, *Imputed Criminal Intent* (*DPP v Smith*) (1967)

Law Commission Report no. 177, *A Criminal Code for England and Wales* (1989)

Law Commission Report no. 230, *The Year and a Day Rule in Homicide* (1995)

Law Commission Report no. 290, *Partial Defences to Murder* (2004)

Law Commission Report no. 304, *Murder, Manslaughter and Infanticide* (2006)

Report of the Select Committee of the House of Lords on Murder and Life Imprisonment (Nathan), HL Paper 78–1 (1989)

Books

Flood-Page, C. and Turner, J. (eds.), *Crime in England and Wales 2001/2002* (Home Office, 2003)

Journals

Keane, C.J. 'Murder – the mental element' (2002) 53 NILQ 1

Mitchell, B. 'Distinguishing between murder and manslaughter' [1991] NLJ 935

Further reading

Ashworth, A. 'Principles, pragmatism and the Law Commission's recommendations on homicide law reform' [2007] Crim LR 333

Davis, C. 'Conjoined twins as persons that can be victims of homicide' (2011) 19 Medical LR 430

Elliott, C. and de Than, C. 'Restructuring the homicide offences to tackle violence, discrimination and drugs in a modern society' (2009) 20 KLJ 69

Homicide Review Advisory Group, *Public Opinion and the Penalty for Murder* (Waterside Press, 2011)

Horder, J. 'Two histories and four hidden principles of mens rea' (1997) 113 LQR 95

Horder, J. (ed.), *Homicide Law in Comparative Perspective* (Hart Publishing, 2007)

Justice 'Response to Law Commission Consultation Paper No. 177, *A New Homicide Act for England and Wales?*' (2006) (written by Sally Ireland)

Mitchell, B. 'Further evidence of the relationship between legal and public opinion on the homicide law' [2000] Crim LR 814

Mitchell, B. 'Distinguishing between murder and manslaughter in practice' (2007) 71 JCL 318

Mitchell, B. and Roberts, J.V., *Public Opinion and Sentencing for Murder: An Empirical Investigation of Public Knowledge and Attitudes in England and Wales* (Nuffield Foundation, 2010)

Mitchell, B. and Roberts, J.V. 'Sentencing for murder: Exploring public knowledge and public opinion in England and Wales' (2012) 52 BJ Crim 141

Morris, T. and Blom-Cooper L., *Fine Lines and Distinctions: Murder, Manslaughter and the Unlawful Taking of Human Life* (Waterside Press, 2011)

Phillips, Lord, 'Issues in criminal justice – Murder' University of Birmingham, 8 March 2007

Reddy, R. 'Gender, culture and the law: Approaches to "honour crimes" in the UK' (2008) 16 *Feminist Legal Studies* 305

Rogers, J. 'The homicide ladder' (2007) 157 NLJ 48

Smith, J.C. 'A note on intention' [1990] Crim LR 85

Spencer, J.R. 'Juries and the life sentence' (2009) 173 JPN 165

Stannard, J. 'Murder and the reckless risk-taker' [2008] Oxford University Commonwealth LJ 137

Tadros, V. 'The homicide ladder' (2006) 69 MLR 601

Taylor, R. 'The nature of "partial defences" and the coherence of (second degree) murder' [2007] Crim LR 345

Tur, R.H.S. 'The doctor's defence and professional ethics' (2002) 13 *King's College Law Journal* 75

For an Irish approach, see Law Reform Commission Report No. 87, *Homicide: Murder and Involuntary Manslaughter*, 2008.

Visit **www.mylawchamber.co.uk** to access tools to help you develop and test your knowledge of criminal law, including interactive multiple choice questions, practice exam questions with guidance, annotated weblinks, glossary flashcards, legal newsfeed and legal updates.

12

Manslaughter

Aims and objectives

After reading this chapter you will understand and be able to critique:

- the distinction between voluntary and involuntary manslaughter
- the defence to murder of loss of control
- the defence to murder of killing in pursuance of a suicide pact
- the offence of (subjectively) reckless manslaughter
- the offence of gross negligence manslaughter
- the offence of unlawful act or constructive manslaughter

Introduction

Manslaughter is not defined in a statute. In **Church** [1966] 1 QB 59 (CCA), Edmund Davies J was driven to say that 'there has never been a complete and satisfactory definition of manslaughter'. It acts as a catch-all offence where the accused has caused death but did not have malice aforethought or has a defence to murder. Since 'murder' is a strong term and some killings are not seen to be as heinous as the archetypal murder case, the retention of a second form of criminal killing is probably a good idea. One difficulty, however, is that this offence covers a wide range of situations from killings just short of murder to carelessly causing death (Figure 12.1). In some instances death is caused fortuitously. It is unfair to

---

Types of manslaughter

Voluntary	*Involuntary*
(both Homicide Act 1957)	(all common law)
Diminished responsibility (s 2)	Constructive (or unlawful acts)
Killing in pursuance of a	Gross negligence
suicide pact (s 4) and	(Subjectively) reckless
Loss of control (Coroners and	
Justice Act 2009)	

Figure 12.1 Types of manslaughter

use the same label for those who kill accidentally and those whose conduct is just short of murder. The *actus reus*, death, is very serious, but the accused is guilty though his *mens rea* is substantially less than intending or foreseeing death. There is therefore no gradation in the types of manslaughter, though there is in the sentence. The maximum is life imprisonment, but the average in the 1980s was four and a half years. The average crept up in the 1990s and is now about six years. The law is not easy to state and is obscure in places.

The old classification of manslaughter was into **voluntary** and **involuntary**, the former being when the accused had the *mens rea* for murder but there is some mitigating factor, which could be provocation, diminished responsibility or killing in pursuance of a suicide pact. Involuntary manslaughter is unlawful homicide without malice aforethought. The accused has acted unlawfully and the consequence is that someone has died. He is guilty even though he did not foresee that his activity might cause death or even serious bodily harm. A person does not need to be acting involuntarily (see Chapter 2) to be guilty of this form of manslaughter. As can be seen, there is a conceptual difference between voluntary manslaughter (the accused had malice aforethought) and involuntary manslaughter (the accused did not have malice aforethought). A person cannot be charged with voluntary manslaughter. The charge is one of murder, but if one of the three mitigations applies, the verdict is (voluntary) manslaughter.

The order in this chapter is that voluntary manslaughter is treated before involuntary manslaughter because the former, but not the latter, requires the *mens rea* of murder, the subject of the previous chapter. A modern categorisation is this:

(a) killing by gross negligence, including omission to act;

(b) killing by an unlawful act, also called constructive manslaughter;

(c) killing by (subjective) recklessness;

(d) killing where there is loss of control (see later in this chapter), diminished responsibility (see Chapter 9), or a suicide pact (see below).

'Involuntary' therefore bears a meaning different from elsewhere in criminal law: for example, in mental condition defences the act of the accused may be involuntary because he suffers from a disease of the mind or an abnormality of mind; in duress the accused may act involuntarily because of pressure placed on him (e.g. 'Kneecap her or I will kill you').

Because these forms of manslaughter have very different requirements, it may be a good idea to think of each of them as a separate offence. The Court of Appeal, as noted below, twice in 1993 called for reform of involuntary manslaughter, and a head of steam is developing in favour of radical change. For proposals for reform of involuntary manslaughter see the end of this chapter.

It seems very likely but it is not yet quite clear that there is a defence of (subjectively) reckless manslaughter. This is, as it were, a companion offence to murder. It occurs where the accused foresees (subjectively) that death or serious injury may occur as a highly probable consequence. It would seem that facts falling within subjectively reckless manslaughter also always fall within unlawful act manslaughter. The Court of Appeal in **Lidar** [1999] 11 November, unreported, seems to confirm this crime's existence. See below for further discussion.

Voluntary manslaughter

There are three types of voluntary manslaughter: loss of control, diminished responsibility, and killing in pursuance of a suicide pact. All are defences to murder. Therefore, for these defences to come into play, the accused must be guilty of murder. All the elements, both *actus reus* and *mens rea*, must be proved.

Loss of control

Introduction

The Coroners and Justice Act 2009 is an oddly named statute to find the replacement of provocation by a new defence. Section 56 abolished that defence; the abolition expressly includes s 3 of the Homicide Act 1957 and the law that issues of provocation are left to the jury. All references to the 'reasonable man' and to 'characteristics' are expunged. In *Clinton* [2012] 1 Cr App R 362 the Court of Appeal stated that interpretation of the new law should not be based on the old law of provocation. As we shall see, that is not exactly what they did!

Provocation was replaced by a new defence, 'loss of control', which like provocation is a defence only to murder. Because it applies to murder only, the accused must have the conduct and fault elements for murder first. Since the accused must have malice aforethought, the intent to kill or commit grievous bodily harm, if aware, for example through anger, is not aware of what he is doing, there is no *mens rea* for murder and therefore no need for this defence.

The law

The three requirements for the defence are, according to s 54(1):

- a loss of self-control; and
- 'a qualifying trigger' for the loss of self-control; and
- 'a person of D's sex and age, with a normal degree of tolerance and self-restraint and in the circumstances of D, might have reacted in the same or similar way to D'. ['D' is the accused.]

The later sub-sections in s 54 elucidate the requirements:

1 The loss of self-control need not be 'sudden': s 54(2). Cf. provocation where there had to be a 'sudden and temporary' loss of self-control. This is a large shift in the law and opens the defence to those who kill their abusers while the latter are drunk or asleep. However, the judge may draw the issue of delay to the attention of the jury. There must, however, be 'a loss of self-control'. This requirement means that some so-called 'honour' killings and killings of abusers by those abused such as battered women do not attract the defence. It need hardly be added that almost by definition a killing which takes place when there is a loss of self-control also takes place suddenly. If there is a cooling-off period, a delay, there may be no loss of self-control. And since there must be a loss of control, a mercy-killer remains liable for murder unless there is a loss of control.

2 '. . . the reference to "the circumstances of D" is a reference to all of D's circumstances other than those whose only relevance to D's conduct is that they bear on D's general capacity for tolerance or self-restraint': s 54(3). This resembles the previous law of provocation after *A-G for Jersey* v *Holley* [2005] AC 580 (PC). For example, D's history of being abused may be taken into account but not D's short-temperedness, intoxication,

or aggressive nature. The reference to 'circumstances', rather than 'characteristics' in the previous law, means that the history such as years of abuse between the parties may be looked at to see whether the loss of control stemmed from an accumulation of matters over time. Similarly, 'circumstances' include matters such as the physical strength of the parties. It is possible for someone who does not fall within the third part of the loss of control defence to fall within the defence of diminished responsibility, which is discussed in Chapter 9.

3 The reference to 'age and sex' means that, for example, young people are permitted some leeway because one cannot expect old heads on young bodies, and perhaps similarly it may be expected that men and women would react differently to being called a 'whore'.

4 The accused is expected not to kill in, for instance, a sadistic way: he must kill in a manner in which a person of the accused's age and sex, exercising that hypothetical person's powers of tolerance and self-control, may have killed.

5 There is no defence if the accused acts out of 'a considered desire for revenge' (s 55(4)), and this happens even if D loses control as a result of a qualifying trigger. This encapsulates the now abolished law of provocation. In particular, some people who react slowly to the trigger lose out on this defence. So-called 'honour' killings fall foul of this rule if there is premeditation. Killings in cold blood do not meet this requirement and they do not meet the requirement of a loss of self-control. In **Clinton**, above, the Court of Appeal said that 'considered desire for revenge' are ordinary English words and therefore whether the accused did have such a state of mind is an issue for the jury. The trial judge should give no instruction as to their meaning.

6 The burden of proof is on the prosecution, which must disprove the defence beyond reasonable doubt: s 54(5).

7 Contrary to the position with regard to provocation, the judge must allow the issue to go to the jury only when a properly directed jury could reasonably conclude that the defence might apply: s 54(6).

8 The outcome of a successful plea of loss of control is the same as for provocation: namely manslaughter: see s 54(7).

The phrase 'qualifying trigger' in the second bullet point above is elucidated in s 55:

- D's loss of control must be 'attributable' to 'fear of serious violence from V [the victim] against D or another identified person'; or
- 'D's loss of self-control was attributable to a thing or things done or said (or both) – which:

    constituted circumstances of an extremely grave character, and
    caused D to have a justifiable sense of being seriously wronged'; or

- both of these together.

One point to make is that in relation to the first part, fear of serious violence, it must be the victim who gave rise to the fear and not a third party. Provocation could come from a third party. The term 'attributable to' may mean that something less than causation as discussed in Chapter 2 is required. In the law of provocation anything 'said or done' potentially gave rise to the defence; s 55 narrows the defence so that only matters specifically mentioned may be relied on.

The first bullet point is new and is a disguised defence of self-defence and could provide a defence where the accused has used excessive force. Note that this part of the defence is limited to threats from the deceased and that no violence need be used – a threat suffices. The threat must be of serious violence to the accused or an identified person (the obvious example being the accused's child); therefore, a threat to property is insufficient. Both this defence and self-defence may be run together by the accused, and a person may lose on one but win on the other. For example, if the accused kills and uses excessive force, there can be no defence of self-defence but there may be a defence of loss of control.

In the second limb, 'things said and done' excludes circumstances of life such as a traffic jam on the M25. 'Extremely grave' is undefined. What this phrase excludes are the normal vicissitudes of life. Also undefined is 'seriously wronged'. This term excludes, for example, minor irritations of life, insults at least of an everyday nature, and a baby's crying (which could constitute the former defence of provocation). An example of circumstances of an 'extremely grave character' in the second bullet point is given by the Law Commission's Report: a parent comes home to find his or her child raped, and kills the escaping offender. It is irrelevant that the accused thought that the matter was extremely grave. This is one way by which honour killings are supposed to be excluded from the defence. The 'justifiable' requirement was also thought by the government to exclude so-called 'honour' killings, because it was not justifiable to kill out of feelings of perceived dishonour to the family. It might have been better to exclude such killings expressly. A controversial issue is that of homeowners killing burglars. To fit within the defence the 'circumstances', burglary in a dwelling, have to be of 'extremely grave character' and as a result of that the accused had a justifiable sense of 'being seriously wronged.'

The Act, s 55(6), adds that:

in determining whether a loss of self-control had a qualifying trigger –
(a) D's fear of serious violence is to be disregarded to the extent that it was caused by a thing which D incited to be done or said for the purpose of providing an excuse to use violence;
(b) a sense of being seriously wronged by a thing done or said is not justifiable if D incited the thing to be done or said for the purpose of providing an excuse to use violence;
(c) the fact that a thing done or said constituted sexual infidelity is to be disregarded.

The defence is not barred, for example, when the accused is a member of a criminal gang: cf. duress.

The exception in (c) has attracted the most attention, and by no means solely because of its drafting: how can sexual infidelity be a 'thing said'? Law pre-the Homicide Act 1957 was that only certain matters could constitute provocation, one of which was the accused catching his wife *in flagrante delicto*. There were cases which, for instance, said that a man catching his fiancée in the same position could not amount to provocation; and being told about the unfaithfulness could constitute provocation, even though generally speaking pre-1957 words alone could not constitute provocation. The Act allowed potentially everything to count, such as, famously, a crying baby: see the words of s 3. The 2009 Act goes completely the other way from the pre-1957 law: not even catching one's spouse in bed with someone else can constitute provocation. If there are two or more causes, one of which is sexual infidelity, that is not to be taken to be a trigger for the defence. For example, a wife sees her husband having sexual intercourse with their child; the infidelity is to be disregarded but the abuse is a trigger. The rest of this section considers this change to the law.

Clinton [2012] EWCA Crim 2

> This is the first (and a highly important) case law authority to examine this thorny issue. Section 55(6)(c) of the Coroners and Justice Act 2009 states that 'the fact that a thing done or said constituted sexual infidelity is to be disregarded' when considering the 'qualifying trigger' stage. Differently put, sexual infidelity *per se* could not be a qualifying trigger for the purposes of this defence. However, the Court of Appeal stressed that that paragraph did not prevent the jury from taking sexual infidelity into consideration in all situations. When determining the accused's 'circumstances' for the purposes of s 54(1)(c) of the Act, the jury may take sexual infidelity into account. Furthermore, '. . . where sexual infidelity is integral to and forms an essential part of the context in which to make a just evaluation whether a qualifying trigger properly falls within the ambit of subsections 55(3) and (4), the prohibition in section 55(6)(c) does not operate to exclude it.' Therefore, only when sexual infidelity stands alone as the sole qualifying trigger is it to be disregarded. This result is certainly in line with (at least male) academic commentators and does draw support from statements by ministers in Parliament. Furthermore, sexual infidelity is not excluded at the third stage, that of the reasonableness of the reaction. At that stage 'all' circumstances except those bearing on 'D's general capacity for tolerance or self-restraint' must be considered by the jury. 'All' therefore includes sexual infidelity. It will be difficult for a jury to disregard sexual infidelity at the second stage and to consider it at the third.
>
> On the facts of *Clinton* sexual infidelity with five men was part of the evidence bearing on the totality of the facts, including that the victim had told her husband that he did not have 'the fucking bollocks' to kill himself. It could not be disregarded by the jury. A retrial was ordered.

The arguments in favour of excluding the jury's consideration of sexual infidelity at the 'qualifying trigger' stage and the counter-arguments are considered next.

Sexual fidelity and the new defence of loss of control: the arguments

The arguments in favour of abolition

1 The abolition makes the law less gender-biased. Provocation, it is usually agreed, was predicated on typical male reactions, the instant response to a slight, whereas women generally react more slowly, partly through physiology and partly though social conditioning (for example as a whole, they are weaker than their male partners and tend to wait for the latter to fall asleep or get drunk before killing him or her). If defendants do not have a defence if they kill on seeing or being told of sexual unfaithfulness, then by far the greater proportion of these defendants will be male. The result is to make the new defence less sexist than its predecessor.

2 The Justice Minister responsible in the House of Commons, Claire Ward, said, 'Frankly, we do not think it is appropriate, in this day and age, for a man to be able to say that he killed his wife as a result of sexual infidelity' (Hansard, 9 November 2009, col. 79). The law is meant to demonstrate society's values. This, moreover, is not the sole limitation on the new defence. Similarly, if the accused acts out of a 'considered desire for revenge', there is also no possibility of a defence of loss of self-control.

3 If the change in the law is publicised, fewer men will kill their former sexual partners. Around 100 women a year are killed by their ex-partners. In comparison some 20–25 men are killed by their ex-partners.

The arguments against abolition

1 It is absurd to single out one source of loss of self-control and exclude that. What is so unique about sexual infidelity? Why should a jury be instructed to disregard a relevant factor?

2 While sexual infidelity cannot be a trigger, it can be a background factor in the scenario which led to the loss of self-control. A feat of mental gymnastics may be needed to distinguish when it may and when it may not be taken into account.

3 It is also absurd to jettison hundreds, if not thousands, of years of human experience.

4 People may disagree about behaviour which constitutes sexual infidelity, just as President Clinton argued that he did not have sexual intercourse with Monica Lewinsky because there was no penetration. What about unmarried couples? Or those in an 'open' marriage? Does sexual infidelity cover sexual jealousy?

5 The jury will face an impossible task if there are more than one 'trigger', one of which is not a 'qualifying trigger'. An example given by the shadow Home Secretary, Dominic Grieve (who is also the shadow Attorney-General), on 9 November 2009 in the HC Hansard at col. 80, is this:

> A woman is abused by her husband over a long period, at the end of which they are reconciled. He says that he will moderate his behaviour and promises to be faithful to her in future. She comes home the following weekend to find him *in flagrante* with his lover. He tells her that the marriage is now at an end, and she kills him. How is the jury going to be invited to disentangle the elements that went into causing that act? How is it supposed to disentangle the abuse, which it will be entitled to take into account, from sexual infidelity . . . ?

How can a jury put out of its mind that sexual infidelity led to the killing?

6 Juries should be trusted to reach common-sense decisions.

7 The Law Commission did not propose to exclude sexual infidelity in its Report No. 290, *Partial Defences to Murder*, 2004.

8 Public opinion may well support killing in response to sexual infidelity as constituting a partial defence to murder. Passions may run very high on these occasions.

9 The effect of the abolition may well be gendered: women who kill after years of abuse no longer need to act suddenly, but men who kill in response to sexual infidelity no longer have a defence.

Example

Can you establish a defence of loss of control in the following scenarios?

1 Norman catches his wife Olive *in flagrante delicto* with her lesbian lover Poppy. He immediately stabs Olive to death.

  While the other requirements of the defence of loss of control may be satisfied (e.g. killing, loss of control, no considered desire for revenge, a normal person of the accused's age and sex in relation to tolerance and self-restraint might have reacted in a similar way), Parliament has expressly excluded killing because of sexual infidelity: s 55(6)(c) of the Coroners and Justice Act 2009, in force 4 October 2010. Unfaithfulness is deemed not to be a 'qualifying trigger' for the purposes of the new defence. This exclusion marks a value which a majority in Parliament wanted to endorse.

2 Queenie has been severely beaten over the years by her husband Ronnie. She finally becomes exasperated and kills him by crashing an iron down onto his sleeping head.

This is a case of cumulative provocation (used in a non-legal sense: the defence of provocation was abolished in 2010) and slow-burn reaction. The accused has lost self-control but it is debatable whether or not she is acting out of a considered desire for revenge (s 54(4)) because Ronnie is asleep. She must also react to a 'qualifying trigger' (s 55): 'a fear of serious violence' from the victim to the accused OR something done or said or both which (a) constitutes circumstances of an 'extremely grave' character and (b) causes the accused to have a 'justifiable sense of being seriously wronged'. The student should work her way through these qualifications.

On your own, consider this scenario: does a so-called 'honour killing' give rise to a defence of loss of control?

Killing in pursuance of a suicide pact

Like loss of control, this form of manslaughter is applied to someone who has malice aforethought. By s 4(1) of the Homicide Act 1957 if the accused kills in pursuance of a suicide agreement by two or more persons, the crime is manslaughter. Unlike the normal rule, the consent of the victim to being killed is significant. The burden of proof demonstrating this mitigating factor is on the accused: s 4(2). By s 4(3) a suicide pact is defined as:

A common agreement between two or more persons having for its object the death of all of them, whether or not each is to take his own life, but nothing shall be treated as done by him in pursuance of the pact unless it is done while he has the settled intention of dying in pursuance of the pact.

If each individual intends to take his or her own life, there is obviously no liability for murder or manslaughter.

Placing the burden of proof on the accused is not incompatible with Article 6(2) of the European Convention on Human Rights: *A-G's Reference (No. 1 of 2004)* [2004] I WLR 2111 (CA). The rationale is that the reverse burden of proof makes it more difficult than otherwise for the accused to hide a murder behind a plea of a suicide pact.

In its Report No. 304, *Murder, Manslaughter and Infanticide*, 2006, the Law Commission proposed to retain the defence pending reform of the law on mercy and consensual killings. This is a change from their previous recommendations that the defence should be abolished but that some killings in these circumstances would fall within a revised defence of diminished responsibility: Consultation Paper No. 177, *A New Homicide Act for England and Wales?*, 2005.

Involuntary manslaughter

There are two, perhaps three, types of involuntary manslaughter.

Subjectively reckless manslaughter

Before **Seymour** [1983] 2 AC 493 (HL) there was a type of manslaughter where the accused, being aware of the possibility of injury (i.e. subjectively reckless), killed someone. It is a pity that this type does not have a snappy title. **Pike** [1961] Crim LR 547 (CCA) illustrated this form. The accused gave his mistress carbon tetrachloride to increase sexual satisfaction. He had administered the fumes to a number of women over several years with no side-effects. However, on this occasion the victim died. It was held that the trial judge was correct to direct the jury that the accused was guilty of manslaughter if he was aware of the risk that some physical harm might occur. This test is less than that in manslaughter by gross negligence, which requires a risk as to life (see the next section). It is suggested that this form of (subjectively) reckless manslaughter survives the abolition of (objectively) reckless manslaughter discussed next. In the Crown Court case of **Smith** [1979] Crim LR 547 the judge referred to a civil case where it had been said that 'to do a lawful act which is dangerous with reckless disregard whether or not it injures another is also manslaughter'. Griffiths J read 'reckless disregard' as meaning 'fully appreciating that there was a real risk to her health'. Both this formula and that in **Pike** are ones of 'subjective recklessness'.

The Court of Appeal in **Lidar**, unreported, 11 November 1999, where the accused drove off with the victim's foot caught in the wheel, the victim fell off and was run over and killed, said that manslaughter could be committed by consciously taking a risk of serious injury and that 'to some extent' this form of manslaughter survives the revival of gross negligence manslaughter. It is not absolutely certain whether the court considered subjectively reckless manslaughter to be a separate offence or whether it was part of gross negligence manslaughter. While the existence is admitted, it is uncertain whether the formulation is correct. Perhaps there must be a high probability of serious injury foreseen by the accused, as **Lidar** suggested, and not just foresight of a risk of serious harm as possibly occurring. The formulations in **Pike** and **Lidar** differ: harm or serious harm? In conformity with murder, it should be 'serious harm'.

At present it seems that facts giving rise to this form of manslaughter are treated as ones which fall within constructive and gross negligence manslaughter, which are easier to prove than subjectively reckless manslaughter. If constructive manslaughter were abolished, there would be a need for (subjectively) reckless manslaughter, and pressure would develop for an exact definition of its elements. The existence of this offence has simply not been discussed in the cases noted elsewhere in this section.

Killing by gross negligence

Example

Donna is an electrician who faultily rewires a Victorian house. Victor is killed when he touches a live wire (which would not have been live, had Donna not done such a bad job). Is Donna guilty of manslaughter?

She cannot be guilty of voluntary manslaughter because she does not have the *mens rea* for murder. There are two main forms of involuntary manslaughter, unlawful act (or constructive) and gross negligence. If there is no unlawful act, here meaning a criminal offence, there is no unlawful act manslaughter. For manslaughter by gross negligence according to **Adomako** [1995] 1 AC 171 (HL):

the accused must be under a (tortious) duty of care;

she must have breached that duty;

the breach must have been grossly negligent (the issue of grossness being left to the jury);

the breach must have caused death; and

(the issue sometimes omitted by students) there must have been a risk of death: authorities confirm that a risk of harm, even serious harm, is insufficient.

Certainly there is no difficulty with any of these elements except perhaps the grossness of the conduct but the facts do state that the victim would not have died, but for the 'bad' rewiring job. Therefore, there is at least some evidence of gross negligence. If all the elements are proved beyond reasonable doubt, the accused is guilty of this form of manslaughter.

There is a form of manslaughter where the accused had killed the victim in a grossly negligent fashion (Figure 12.2). Anybody may be convicted of the offence of **gross negligence**, though often the defendants occupy professional jobs. With the development of the form of recklessness found in ***MPC v Caldwell*** [1982] AC 341 (HL), which applied in this area (***Seymour*** [1983] 2 AC 493 (HL)) there were authorities to the effect that manslaughter by gross negligence had been totally swallowed up by objectively reckless manslaughter: ***Kong Cheuk Kwan v R*** (1985) 82 Cr App R 18 (PC) and ***Goodfellow*** (1986) 83 Cr App R 23 (CA).

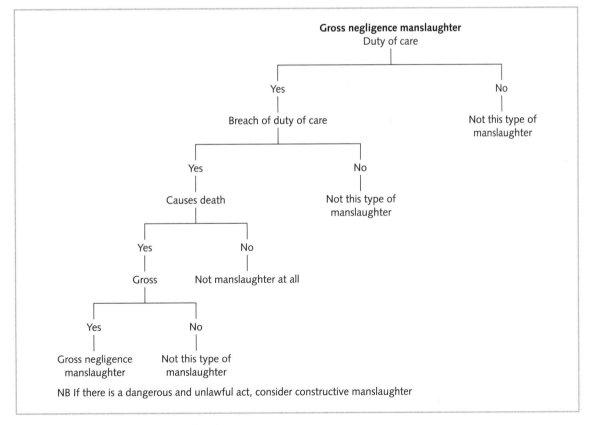

Figure 12.2 Gross negligence manslaughter

The basic rule of liability for reckless manslaughter was stated in *Goodfellow*: has the accused acted in such a way as to create an obvious and serious risk of causing physical harm and, having recognised it, gone ahead, or not given any thought to that risk? The accused need not realise that he is putting someone at risk: *Seymour*. As a result of *Seymour*, an accused was guilty if he did not realise that there was an obvious risk of some personal injury to another.

In *Reid* [1992] 1 WLR 793 (HL) Lord Ackner used the illustration of a diver jumping off a springboard into a pool and colliding with a swimmer without having considered whether anyone might be harmed. If the swimmer died, the crime would be reckless manslaughter if the ordinary prudent bystander would consider that the risk was obvious and serious. If, however, the swimmer survived, the accused would not be guilty of any non-fatal offence because all of them are defined in terms of subjective recklessness. In modern post-*Caldwell* terms if an accused kills by gross negligence, he is killing in this type of manslaughter. If the victim survives (perhaps through the fortuitous intervention of a paramedic), the accused is not guilty of any non-fatal offence, because non-fatal offences cannot be committed by gross negligence, only intentionally or in a subjectively reckless manner.

Although the *Caldwell* formulation is no longer to be used, only by looking at history can one understand present law.

A risk of what?

Before the irruption of reckless manslaughter Fenton Atkinson LJ in *Stone and Dobinson* [1977] QB 354 (CA) rejected the view that the accused had to be grossly negligent as to the likelihood of death or serious injury. He said that gross negligence signified a high degree of negligence and 'indifference to an obvious risk to health and welfare [or] an appreciation of such risk coupled with a determination to run it'. After *Caldwell* Lord Roskill in *Seymour* spoke of a very high risk of death, but he said that in the context of manslaughter caused by a car ('motor manslaughter') in order to distinguish that offence from causing death by reckless driving, or at least such is the construction put on his words in *Kong Cheuk Kwan* v *R*, and Lord Roskill did uphold the trial judge's direction which included a reference to an obvious and serious risk of physical injury. There was no need for the recklessness to be gross. Both *Goodfellow* and *Kong Cheuk Kwan* v *R* demanded only a risk of physical injury. Therefore, it can be said that there need not be an obvious and serious risk of death or even serious injury in reckless manslaughter. *Stone and Dobinson*'s test of 'obvious risk to health or welfare' would broaden manslaughter perhaps unacceptably, and the position until 1993 was that accepted by the Privy Council and Court of Appeal. Manslaughter is a serious crime, for which the maximum sentence is life imprisonment; yet the requirement of only a risk as to some physical injury is not commensurate with the gravity of the offence.

In *Lawrence* [1982] AC 510 (HL) Lord Diplock said that there had to be an obvious and serious risk of some physical harm or substantial damage to property in relation to reckless driving and causing death by reckless driving. Omitting the reference to property this decision was extended to manslaughter involving cars in *Seymour*, though the Crown wished to reserve the question whether a risk to property was sufficient: on the facts it was not relevant. In *Kong Cheuk Kwan* v *R*, Lord Roskill referred to a risk of causing damage but on the facts that was a relevant risk because a collision between two hydrofoils did create such a risk. It is not certain whether he realised that his reference to 'physical damage' was different from 'substantial damage to property' in *Caldwell*. In *Goodfellow* the Court of

Appeal ruled that there should be no reference to the risk of damage to property. These cases illustrate that *Seymour* was not restricted to manslaughter through the use of a car. In *ex parte Jennings* [1983] 1 AC 624, the House of Lords decided that in both causing death by reckless driving and reckless manslaughter there had to be 'an obvious and serious risk of causing physical injury'. Since *Lawrence* had held that a risk of substantial damage to property was sufficient in causing death by reckless driving, the effect of *ex parte Jennings* was that the same was true of manslaughter. The point was not discussed in cases such as *Goodfellow*. Lord Roskill in *Seymour* simply stated that on the facts there was no need to refer to damage to property. He did not say that it was never relevant. If it was relevant, the law had been extended, for previous law required gross negligence as to life or safety and no reference was made to property.

Lord Goff in *Reid*, above, reformulated the test in *Caldwell* and *Lawrence* in relation to causing death by reckless driving. The law on recklessness in that offence, criminal damage, and subject to the 'property' point above reckless manslaughter, was to the same effect. Reckless manslaughter was in the normal run of cases defined thus: did the accused create a serious risk of causing physical injury to some other person and either (a) did he recognise that there was some risk of that kind involved but nevertheless did he go on to take it, or (b) did he not address his mind to the possibility of there being any such risk, the risk being obvious to the reasonable person? This reformulation changed the law (and reversed the second part of Lord Diplock's speech in *Caldwell*). In (a) the risk need not be obvious to the reasonable bystander. Lord Browne-Wilkinson supported Lord Goff's formula. Lords Ackner and Keith did not mention it and Lord Roskill agreed with all the speeches. Accordingly it could not be said that the law on 'obviousness' was settled. If the formula was correct, in (a) there had to be a serious risk but it need not be a risk obvious to the reasonable individual. In the words of the Court of Appeal in *Reid*, 'serious' meant 'to be taken seriously'. A risk which is one to be taken seriously is one which is dependent on the inverse proportionality between the harm which would occur if the risk of injury eventuated and the degree of probability of harm occurring. The greater the harm, the less the degree of occurrence is the test postulated. On the facts of the Zeebrugge ferry disaster case the chance of harm was thought to be small enough to be disregarded, but if the bow doors did take water in, the results would be disastrous. If the reasonable person would classify the risk as serious, then if the accused knew of the risk, he would be reckless on the reformulation in (a).

The survival of gross negligence manslaughter

While most of the cases which were decided under the heading of gross negligence would have been decided the same way under objectively reckless manslaughter, apart from cases such as *Lamb* [1967] 2 QB 981 (CA) where the accused was guilty of gross negligence manslaughter but would not have been guilty of objectively reckless manslaughter because he, mistakenly, thought about the risk and thought there was none, manslaughter by gross negligence does survive, despite Lord Roskill's statement in *Kong Cheuk Kwan v R* that the term was not to be used.

The term gross negligence was never clearly defined in the cases. The criminal law, however, did recognise that an accused could be guilty only if he acted in a grossly negligent fashion. Acting carelessly was insufficient. As was said in the classic authority, *Andrews v DPP* [1937] AC 576 (HL), 'simple lack of care as will constitute civil liability is insufficient'. The accused must break a duty he owed the victim, the victim must die, and the accused's carelessness must be gross, taking into account all the circumstances of the case. In

Bateman [1925] All ER Rep 45 (CCA), Lord Hewart CJ said that a person was guilty only if he demonstrated 'such disregard for the life and safety of others as to amount to a crime against the State and conduct deserving of punishment', a circular definition (the judges have accepted that this is so) but one which gives a flavour of the topic. (He talked of the negligence being 'criminal', 'culpable', 'wicked', 'clear' and 'complete' as synonyms for 'gross'. None of these terms is of much help to a jury. Indeed, different juries may convict or acquit on the same facts, one finding the carelessness not gross, the other disagreeing.) This formula has also been criticised for leaving a question of law to the jury. See below for further criticism of juries and the grossness of the accused's behaviour.

In the Zeebrugge case, *Stanley*, unreported, 10 October 1990, Turner J at the Old Bailey said that gross negligence manslaughter no longer existed (if it had done at that time, quite possibly the jury would have convicted). Yet in *Ball* (1990) 90 Cr App R 378 the Court of Appeal did refer to negligence but the mention was *obiter*. The former Lord Chief Justice said in *Goodfellow*, above, that the face of *Kong Cheuk Kwan* raised the issue whether the accused was 'guilty of recklessness (or gross negligence)'. Yet in *Kong Cheuk Kwan* the Privy Council made no reference to gross negligence. Accordingly, the cases were equivocal whether this form of manslaughter survived.

Gross negligence manslaughter in the modern era

The Court of Appeal blew fresh life into manslaughter by gross negligence in *Prentice* [1994] QB 302, which on appeal to the House of Lords is known as *Adomako* [1995] 1 AC 171. The accused, an anaesthetist who had been working long hours, failed to notice that a tube carrying oxygen to a patient had become disconnected and the patient died. The case was joined with others in the Court of Appeal and all appeals were allowed there except for this accused's. The prosecution alleged that the appellant, who conceded that he had been negligent, had been grossly negligent for not noting the obvious signs of disconnection, for example the chest was not moving, the dials on the ventilator were not moving, the patient was turning blue, and the pulse and blood pressure were dropping. He had also failed to see that the alarm on the ventilator was not switched on. Only when the alarm on the machine monitoring blood pressure went off did he check that machine and only after the patient had had a heart attack and was undergoing resuscitation was the disconnection discovered. Lord Mackay stated that the law in *Bateman* and *Andrews*, above, was correct and 'satisfactory'. He approved the classic if circular definition of Lord Hewart CJ in *Bateman*: '. . . the facts must be such that, in the opinion of the jury, the negligence of the accused went beyond a mere matter of compensation between subjects'. He also approved the opinion of Lord Atkin in *Andrews* that '. . . a very high degree of negligence is required, and that the crime's mental element covers both an indifference to a risk and the situation where the accused appreciated the risk and intended to avoid it and yet [showed] such a high degree of negligence in the manner adopted to avoid the risk as would justify a conviction'. The jury has to assess whether 'the conduct of the defendant was so bad in all the circumstances as to amount . . . to a criminal act or omission'. Lord Mackay in a highly important passage summarised the offence thus:

> [t]he ordinary principles of the law of negligence apply to ascertain whether or not the defendant has been in breach of a duty of care towards the victim who has died. If such a breach of duty is established the next question is whether that breach of duty caused the death of the victim. If so, the jury must go on to consider whether the breach of the duty caused the death of the victim. If so, the jury must go on to consider whether the breach of

the duty should be characterised as gross negligence and therefore as a crime. This will depend on the seriousness of the breach of duty . . . in all the circumstances in which the defendant was placed. The jury will have to consider whether the extent to which the defendant's conduct departed from the proper standard of care incumbent upon him, involving as it must have done a risk of death . . . , was such that it should be judged criminal.

It will in the normal run of cases not be difficult to demonstrate that a duty of care existed. There must be a reasonable foreseeability of death, a relationship of 'proximity', and the situation must be 'one which the Court considers it fair, just and reasonable that the law should impose a duty . . .'. These three factors constitute standard tort law requirements laid down by Lord Bridge in *Caparo Industries Ltd v Dickman* [1990] 2 AC 605 (HL). The Court of Appeal approved of the trial judge's use of these three principles in *Winter* [2010] EWCA Crim 1474. If death is reasonably foreseeable, it will be rare that there is no relationship of proximity. Surely all neighbours must take care not to endanger the lives of others. So, for example, a car driver owes a duty of care to his passengers during the journey. Doctors and other similar professionals owe such a duty, but the duty is not restricted to professional persons. It is uncertain how far one can take the tort analogy into criminal law, despite Lord Mackay's words quoted above. Kennedy LJ in *R (on the application of Lewin) v DPP* [2002] EWHC 1049 (Admin) (DC) spoke of applying the ordinary principles of negligence, but it is by no means certain that he was correct. The tortious duty of care is explicitly founded on public policy and serves the function of shifting financial loss from one person to another, but criminal law does not promote this aim.

There are differences too in relation to omissions. Surely the Lords did not intend to overrule *Stone and Dobinson*, which they would have done if the narrower tort law on omissions had replaced the quite possibly wider criminal liability for omissions? See Chapter 2 for examples of situations in which the criminal law imposes a duty to act. *Adomako* itself was a case on omissions. It cannot be stated for certain if this is the case; indeed, there may be areas of tort law on omissions which are broader than criminal law. Furthermore, if tort law is to be incorporated into gross negligence manslaughter, there may be instances where there is no duty of care in tort but there should be one in criminal law. Surely everyone is under a duty not to do anything which causes danger to the lives of others, even though no duty of care arises in tort law. If this is the law, the duty of care issue which occurs in the tort of negligence is irrelevant. The contrary argument is that the former Lord Chancellor was very definite that 'the ordinary principles of the law of negligence apply'. If so, changes in tort, such as whether a duty exists, will affect criminal law, an unexpected development. For more on the position in relation to omissions, see below. One other issue is problematical. If the accused did foresee the risk of death, why should it matter that in applying the law of negligence a reasonable person would not?

For an explanation of the law on omissions, see Chapter 2.

Cases from *Adomako* onwards exemplify situations where the accused owed a duty of care to his victim:

Adomako: doctor to patient;

Prentice, which was one of the cases joined with *Adomako* at the Court of Appeal stage: electrician to customer;

Litchfield [1998] Crim LR 507 (CA): captain of ship to sailors (for facts see below).

Adomako brings up an issue of who should be criminally liable. In this case the doctor was tired after working long hours, and it seems that his training had been deficient. Should not the National Health Service have been on trial? Prosecuting the anaesthetist will not *per se* improve the system.

Evans [2009] EWCA Crim 650

A half-sister and half-sister. The accused bought heroin which she handed over to her half-sister, who injected herself. Neither the accused nor their mother sought medical attention. They put her to bed and checked on her on occasion. She died. The court held that the accused was under a duty arising from **Miller** [1983] 2 AC 161 (HL), discussed in Chapter 2: she had caused a state of affairs which she did know or ought reasonably to have known had become a threat to life; those facts put her under a duty of care to the victim, and she was therefore obliged to take reasonable steps to save her life. For more on the causation aspect of this case, see Chapter 3 with regard to the victim's free, deliberate and informed decision to take the drugs.

The statement by Lord Mackay LC in **Adomako** that 'the ordinary principles of the law of negligence' govern whether or not there has been a breach of the duty of care must, therefore, not be read as a definitive outline of the law. The Law Commission in its Consultation Paper No. 135, *Involuntary Manslaughter*, 1994, said that 'negligence' meant 'carelessness'; it did not mean duty/breach/damage as found in tort. In **Wacker** [2003] QB 1207 (CA) the accused drove a lorry from the Netherlands to the UK. At Dover 58 illegal immigrants were found dead in the back of the lorry. The accused had closed a vent and the victims suffocated. He argued that he was not guilty of manslaughter because *ex turpi causa non oritur actio* (that is, no legal action may be founded on an unlawful event). In other words, the joint unlawful conduct, the smuggling of immigrants, prevented any duty of care arising between claimants and defendants in tort. The Court of Appeal held that civil law and criminal law served different purposes. The fact that the civil law of compensation for wrongs was disapplied did not mean that the criminal law was also disapplied. Accordingly, the *ex turpi* doctrine was inapplicable to gross negligence manslaughter. Thus it is true to say, as the Commission did in its Report No. 237, *Legislating the Criminal Code: Involuntary Manslaughter*, 1996, that the concepts of tort law are best avoided. **Wacker** also illustrates the point that an accused can be grossly negligent even though the victims have consented to the activity.

The law in **Caldwell** no longer applied to involuntary manslaughter even before the expurgation on **Caldwell** from criminal law in **G** [2004] 1 AC 1034 (HL). The abolition of causing death by reckless driving in the Road Traffic Act 1991 was said to justify this approach. This *dictum* cannot be right, for the statute did not affect the common law of manslaughter. The Court of Appeal in **Prentice** had, as they were obliged to do by the doctrine of precedent, stated that **Seymour** still governed motor manslaughter. Lord Mackay said, however, that manslaughter by gross negligence now included motor manslaughter. If the exception had been retained the law would have been unnecessarily complex. 'For example, in **Kong Cheuk Kwan v R** it would give rise to unnecessary differences in the law applicable to those navigating vessels and the lookouts on the vessels.' It should be noted that **Andrews** itself is a case of motor manslaughter.

The term 'reckless' can still be used in manslaughter, but not in its **Caldwell** sense, which in any case has since been abolished throughout criminal law. There was, in Lord Mackay's view, no need to use it. The Court of Appeal used it in **Lidar**, above, applying the *dictum* of Lord Mackay. It would have been elegant if the use of the term 'recklessness' had been wiped out in this context.

Elaborate directions such as those laid down in **Prentice** were to be avoided because of the manifold circumstances in which this form of manslaughter applies. Professionals were to be judged against the standard of their 'reasonably competent' colleagues. On the facts the trial judge had given a correct instruction and the Court of Appeal had been right to dismiss the appeal, though their approach had been over-elaborate.

It is suggested that while elaborate directions are likely to confuse juries, there are two points which need elucidation, and enlightenment is not found in Lord Mackay's speech. First, which kind of risk must the accused have failed to notice? The Lord Chancellor approved specifically the *Bateman* test of 'life and safety' and he speaks of 'the risk of death' (that is a risk of death foreseeable by a reasonably prudent person) in a passing comment on the issue of grossness being supremely a jury question, and he did not specifically overrule the test in *Stone and Dobinson* [1977] QB 354 (CA) of 'injury to health and welfare' (indeed he said that this case defined gross negligence 'with complete accuracy') or Lord Taylor's test in *Prentice* of 'injury to health'. Perhaps *Stone* is impliedly overruled on this point. (The House of Lords expressly approved another part of *Stone and Dobinson*, the proposition that gross negligence covers indifference.) The fact that someone has died shows that there was a risk of death. The requirement must mean something other than this, otherwise it serves no purpose. In the light of the difficulty which this issue caused after *Seymour*, one might have hoped that it would have been addressed by the Lords. It is suggested that the law is that risk of death has to exist. In *Singh* [1999] Crim LR 582, the Court of Appeal held that only a risk of death sufficed, though the issue was not fully aired, and the Court of Appeal in *Lewin v Crown Prosecution Service* [2002] EWHC (Admin) 1049 cited this passage approvingly (as did the Court of Appeal in *Yaqoob* [2005] EWCA Crim 1269), though later that year the same court in *Lidar*, above, spoke *obiter* of a risk of death or injury, where the accused had managed properties owned by his father and a gas fitter had grossly negligently installed a fire.

If confirmation is needed that only a risk of death suffices, it is found in Judge LJ's judgment in *Misra* [2005] 1 WLR 1. The Court of Appeal approved the statement in *Singh* that: 'The circumstances must be such that a reasonably prudent person would have foreseen a serious and obvious risk not merely of injury, even serious injury, but of death.' This passage was also approved by the same court in *Yaqoob*. The requirement of a risk of death or perhaps a risk of serious injury should be compared with the requirement of a risk of (only) injury in unlawful act manslaughter. Secondly, which type of level of risk is needed? Would a risk suffice or is a substantial risk needed? Lord Mackay's speech provides no assistance. Lord Taylor CJ mentioned in separate places an 'obvious' risk and a 'serious' risk. Perhaps he was under the influence of objective recklessness. It is a pity that further cases (and time and expense) will be needed to settle this point. Furthermore, since the Lords in *Adomako* got rid of the 'elaborate' directions of the Court of Appeal in *Prentice*, there is little law for the judge to direct the jury to consider.

Because the issue of grossness is one for the jury and the issue is one whether or not the accused's act of omission was 'bad', the criticism is easy to make that juries may be sympathetic to one accused and find him not guilty but unsympathetic to another and find him guilty. Moreover, how is a jury to assess whether what the accused did was so gross as to be deserving of punishment? There is a possibility of two juries holding one accused to be guilty and another not guilty, on exactly the same facts, and the Court of Appeal would be powerless to intervene. If they say that the negligence was not gross, there is no criminal liability though the defendant may be liable in tort.

The grossness of the conduct will vary with regard to the facts of each case. This point was adopted by a majority of the Supreme Court of Canada in *Creighton* (1993) 105 DLR (4th) 432. For example, a surgeon may justifiably run the risk of killing the patient if the operation is necessary to save life, whereas employers may not take a substantial risk with the lives of their workers in order to increase profits. Even a bad mistake need not be the result of gross negligence but the jury may be instructed to take into account the 'badness' of the accused's behaviour: *R* (*on the application of Rowley*) v *DPP* [2003] EWHC 693 (Admin). Grossness is a question for the jury.

Litchfield [1998] Crim LR 507 (CA)

The accused asserted that he was not guilty of gross negligence manslaughter when he both sailed his sailing ship too close to land and knew that the fuel in the engines was contaminated. He contended that **Adomako** required the jury to ask whether his behaviour was so bad that it demonstrated a lack of regard for the lives of others such that it amounted to a crime, but he was already guilty of a crime, one under the merchant shipping laws; therefore, **Adomako** was irrelevant. The Court of Appeal dismissed his appeal. **Adomako** applied generally and it was immaterial that the accused was also guilty of another offence. The accused's conduct was grossly negligent.

Litchfield also demonstrates that the accused has to be judged against the standards of a reasonably competent person undertaking the task he was performing, for example a reasonably competent driver, a reasonably competent doctor. In **Litchfield** the standard to be measured against was that of a reasonably competent sailor. **Litchfield** furthermore shows that the **Adomako** test applies whether the accused failed to act or did not, omission or commission. The trial judge said that the behaviour was grossly negligent when it was 'so bad, so obviously wrong . . . that it can be properly considered as criminal . . . in the ordinary language of men and women of the world'.

The facts in **Litchfield** look like ones which could give rise to a charge of (subjectively) reckless manslaughter. The accused knowingly took the risk of death. He was advertent. **Adomako** by contrast is a case of carelessness: the accused did not know of any risk of death to his patient. He was inadvertent.

The Court of Appeal in **Attorney-General's Reference (No. 2 of 1999)** [2000] QB 796 stated: 'Although there may be cases where the defendant's state of mind is relevant to the jury's consideration when assessing the grossness and criminality of his conduct, evidence of his state of mind is not a prerequisite to a conviction for manslaughter by gross negligence.' The accused himself therefore need not foresee the risk of death. If, however, he did do so, that is evidence going towards proving that his behaviour was *grossly* negligent. The Divisional Court approved this passage in **DPP ex p Jones** [2000] IRLR 373. The test for negligence is an objective one. The Court of Appeal spoke to similar effect in **Misra**, above, rejecting the application of the subjective test for recklessness found in *G* [2004] AC 1034 (HL).

Because the test for grossness is left to the jury there is a possibility that the offence contravenes Article 5, the right to liberty, and Article 7, the right not to be punished without law, of the European Convention on Human Rights. The Court of Appeal in **Misra**, above, a case where two doctors failed to diagnose a serious infection after a routine knee operation, held that the definition did not infringe Article 7. Judge LJ stated that a law achieved the standard laid down in that Article if it was sufficiently certain; it need not be absolutely certain in its scope. Moreover, Article 7 did not apply to situations where juries had to evaluate an accused's conduct. Furthermore, the jurors were not deciding an issue of law. All that was meant by saying that they had to determine whether the accused was 'criminal' was that his conduct or omission had to be grossly negligent as to the risk of death. There was no extra requirement of *criminal* negligence. The jury was simply applying the law to the facts, as it does for example with intent and dishonesty. Therefore, a crime did not infringe Article 7 if its ambit was not entirely clear: the court did not say when a crime was of sufficient certainty to pass the test. There was also no breach of Article 6, the right to a fair hearing, because the jury was not deciding an issue of law. 'The question for the jury is not whether the defendant's negligence was gross, and whether, *additionally*, it was a crime, but whether his behaviour was grossly negligent and *consequently* negligent. This is not a question of law, but one of fact, for decision in the individual case.' The court refused permission to appeal.

Examples involving medical facts help to show the distinction between carelessness and gross negligence. In *Akerele* v *R* [1943] AC 255 (PC), which approved the law in *Bateman*, a doctor's careless mixing of a powder with the result that five children died was not manslaughter. The fact that someone died is not by itself gross negligence, and one cannot multiply the carelessness by the five deaths to create gross negligence. Grossness was a question of degree for the jury, and it would be rare to find a professional person so negligent. A jury should look at the quality of the accused's behaviour, not at the quantity of it. In *Bateman* itself the accused took part of the victim's uterus away during childbirth and did not remove her to hospital for five days. She died. On appeal he was found not guilty because he was carrying out a normal procedure approved by the medical profession. It was merely that the procedure had gone wrong. *Bateman* emphasises that the accused's behaviour is to be judged against the current standards of the industry or profession. An error, even one with grave consequences, is not necessarily gross negligence. In *Long* (1830) 172 ER 756, a person who was not a doctor killed two patients by applying corrosive plasters to their chests. There was 'gross and improper rashness and want of caution'. He was convicted (but fined £250). Cases such as these demonstrate how far the assessment of whether the accused was grossly negligent is a question for the jury.

It should be noted that the crime of gross negligence manslaughter has been superseded by corporate manslaughter in respect of organisations covered by the Corporate Manslaughter and Corporate Homicide Act 2007.

Recklessness as a synonym for gross negligence

One difficulty in knowing whether gross negligence manslaughter did survive is the use in older cases of recklessness as a synonym for gross negligence. The Court of Oyer and Terminer, Dublin, required 'gross negligence' or 'recklessly negligent conduct': *Elliott* (1889) 16 Cox CC 710. The accused was not guilty of manslaughter of 76 passengers when he separated a train on an incline, causing coaches to run backwards into another train. The court said in a phrase which academics today could still use: '. . . the degree of care to be expected from a person, the want of which would be gross negligence or less than that, must in the necessity of things . . . have some relation to the subject and the consequences . . . [T]here must be a certain moral quality carried into the act for which [the accused] is made criminally responsible.' In *Andrews* v *DPP* [1937] AC 576 (HL) Lord Atkin defined gross negligence as 'a very high degree of negligence' or recklessness. Gross negligence was thought to be more appropriate because it covered the situation where the accused appreciated the risk but was grossly negligent as to how he sought to avoid it, whereas recklessness did not. Recklessness was therefore either a synonym for gross negligence or only one form of it. In *Cato* [1976] 1 WLR 110 gross negligence and recklessness were used synonymously. Even after *Seymour*, gross negligence and recklessness were used interchangeably. In *Sargent* (1990) *Guardian*, 3 July, Boreham J at Leeds Crown Court is reported as saying: 'You were so negligent as to be reckless as to this woman's welfare', by pumping so much oxygen into her during an operation that she swelled up like a Michelin man. Note the reference to 'welfare', a low test which was below that required for reckless manslaughter. It is uncertain what is meant by 'welfare'. In the cases it is something separate from and less serious than recklessness as to injury. The obvious comment is that manslaughter, being a serious crime, should not be founded on gross negligence as to welfare. It would appear that when the Court of Appeal referred to 'health and welfare' in *Stone and Dobinson* it did not realise that it was departing from the *Andrews* test.

Summary of gross negligence manslaughter

In summary, gross negligence manslaughter is wider than objectively reckless manslaughter when it existed because, provided that the carelessness was gross, the lacuna case is covered. However, according to *Reid* [1992] 1 WLR 793 (HL) the accused was, it seems, guilty of reckless manslaughter if he did not advert to a risk which ought to have been taken seriously and someone died. Inadvertence is another way of saying 'negligence'. Accordingly (simple) carelessness fell within reckless, but not gross negligence, manslaughter. Another distinction is that in objectively reckless manslaughter recklessness as to physical injury was needed; in gross negligence the criterion has usually been gross negligence as to death. Such tests are also low thresholds for such a serious crime as manslaughter. The point about gross negligence has already been made, but consider too the nature of the risk in reckless manslaughter. The accused did not need to be objectively reckless as to serious harm. *Caldwell* recklessness as to any physical harm sufficed. In another respect reckless manslaughter is narrower than the gross negligence variety, for in it the accused must have caused the risk.

Manslaughter by omission

The general issue of omissions in the criminal law was discussed in Chapter 2, though it should be noted that in *Adomako* itself there was no reference to the general rule on omissions. Manslaughter by omission occurs where the accused, in breach of a duty imposed by law, fails to carry out an undertaking, whether contractual or otherwise, and the victim dies as a result: *Khan* [1998] Crim LR 830 (CA). The court ruled that the jury should be left four questions: '(1) Was there in the circumstances a duty of care owed by the defendants to the deceased . . . ? (2) Was there a breach of that duty? (3) Did the breach cause the death of the deceased? (4) Should the breach of duty be characterised as gross negligence . . . ?' The rule in gross negligence that the duty of care's existence is determined by the tort law of negligence is somewhat controversial but in respect of omissions the position is plain: if in respect of omissions there is a duty of care in tort, there is also a duty of care in criminal law.

It is suggested that the issue whether a duty of care exists is really a matter of law for the judge, not a matter of fact for the jury, and *Singh* [1999] Crim LR 582 (CA) and *Evans*, above, so held. See also *Willoughby* [2005] 1 WLR 1880 where the Court of Appeal rejected a contention that the accused owed a duty to the victim of arson because he was the owner of the premises he had set alight. However, there was on the facts a duty because he had enlisted the victim's help in committing the arson. Controversially the court said that whether a duty existed was a matter for the jury contrary to the general principle that whether a duty exists is a decision for the judge but it is the jury's task to apply the law to the facts. It would seem that after *Evans*, *Willoughby* is wrong.

There are several case law examples across the years of gross negligence manslaughter, many nowadays being concerned with drugs and professional workers. In *Pittwood* (1902) 19 TLR 37, a level-crossing keeper failed to close a gate. A person crossing the line was killed. The court held that the keeper was guilty of gross negligence manslaughter, even though he did not owe the contractual duty to open and close the gate to the victim.

(This and other cases are given in Chapter 2.) If there is no legal duty to act, this form of manslaughter is not committed. In *Khan* the defendants supplied the victim with heroin. She snorted it and overdosed. They failed to summon medical assistance and she died. Drug dealers did not on the facts owe a duty to their customer. *Khan* makes plain that there is no separate category of manslaughter by omission, but it is one way in which gross negligence manslaughter is committed. (There is in fact a way of making the drug dealers in this case criminally liable: they created a dangerous situation and failed to rectify it. *Evans*, noted above, exemplifies this area of law.)

Sinclair [1998] NLJ 1353

The Court of Appeal applied the law and held that the accused was under a duty of care when he was a close friend of the victim, a drug addict, had previously supplied him with methadone, had helped to obtain the fatal dose, and had stayed with him until he died.

See the further discussion of omissions in Chapter 2.

Singh exemplifies this area of law. Tenants told the accused that gas fires in their flats were not working properly. The accused did not have an expert to check the fires. The victim died. It was held that the accused did owe a duty of care; that duty was broken by his not bringing in an expert; his negligence caused the victim's death.

The mental element is that laid down in *Adomako* (above). The test is objective pure and simple, which is objectionable from the viewpoint of subjectivists for such a serious crime.

It should be noted that an omission is not sufficient for unlawful act manslaughter. The lack of liability in unlawful act manslaughter for an omission which caused death has been criticised on the grounds that an omission, especially a deliberate one, is blameworthy, and it can cause death. Subjectively reckless manslaughter may be committed by omission.

The Law Commission's Report No. 237, *Legislating the Criminal Code: Involuntary Manslaughter*, 1996, does not affect the occasions when a duty of care arises. The Law Commission considered that the topic of omissions should be separately reviewed.

Unlawful act or constructive manslaughter

Example

Duncan and his girlfriend Erica have just sat down in a pub. Near them is Valentino, who is looking around. His eye happens to settle on Erica, who is very attractive. Duncan sees this and says: 'Are you looking at my bird?' The words lead inexorably to a fight in the pub carpark. Duncan punches Valentino hard on the cheek. He falls down, hits his head on a half-brick, has a brain haemorrhage, and shortly afterwards dies. Assuming Duncan did not intend to kill or cause grievous bodily harm, the mental element for murder, is Duncan guilty of manslaughter?

These facts, which constitute what is sometimes known as 'one punch manslaughter', may constitute unlawful act manslaughter. Duncan has, following the HL in both *A-G's Ref. (No. 3 of 1994)* [1998] AC 245 and *Kennedy (No. 2)* [2008] 1 AC 269:

● committed an unlawful act, here meaning a crime (with the *actus reus* and *mens rea* of that offence) such as a battery;
● performed an act (as distinguished from an omission: *Lowe* [1973] QB 702 (CA));

- performed an act which reasonable (and sober) people would recognise as likely to cause some harm, not necessarily serious harm (see, e.g., *DPP* v *Newbury* [1977] AC 500 (HL)); and
- caused death (cf. *Carey* [2006] EWCA Crim 17).

Therefore, he is guilty of unlawful act manslaughter, a serious crime punishable with a maximum sentence of life imprisonment.

This type of manslaughter gets its name from the requirement that the victim must have died as a result of an unlawful criminal act and liability is **constructive** because the accused is guilty even though he did not foresee death. A similar doctrine in relation to murder was abolished in 1957. Both doctrines are harsh in the effect on the accused. They might however represent current opinion which focuses on results, death, and there is correspondingly a reduced emphasis on the accused's fault. In the Australian case of *Creighton*, above, McLachlin J endorsed this proposition. 'To tell people that if they embark on dangerous conduct which foreseeably may cause bodily harm which is neither trivial nor transient, and which in fact results in death, that they will not be held responsible for the death but only for aggravated assault, is less likely to deter such conduct than a message that they will be held responsible for the death . . . Given the finality of death and the absolute unacceptability of killing another human being, it is not amiss to preserve the test which promises the greatest measure of deterrence, provided the penal consequences of the offence are not disproportionate.'

The same act could be both this form of manslaughter and gross negligence manslaughter. In *Goodfellow* above, the accused set fire to a house so that he could be rehoused. Three died. The unlawful act was arson, and he was grossly negligent as to the risk of injury.

This type of manslaughter occurs when death is caused by an unlawful act intentionally or recklessly committed by the accused which reasonable persons would foresee as liable to cause some injury, though not necessarily serious injury: *Church* [1966] 1 QB 59 (CCA), as approved in *DPP* v *Newbury* [1977] AC 500 (HL) and *Goodfellow*. Lord Hope in *Attorney-General's Reference (No. 3 of 1994)* [1998] AC 245 (HL) stated:

The only questions which need to be addressed are (1) whether the act was done intentionally, (2) whether it was unlawful, (3) whether it was dangerous because it was likely to cause harm to somebody and (4) whether that unlawful and dangerous act caused the death.

A similar definition was laid down by the Lords in *Kennedy (No. 2)* [2008] 1 AC 269. Some of these phrases need lengthy exposition in the light of the unclear case law but some issues can be dealt with quickly. The fact that death ensues converts the crime from a lesser offence to manslaughter. The accused is guilty even though he personally foresaw no risk of injury. An example occurs when the accused punches the victim, who loses his balance, falls to the ground, bangs his head on a kerbstone and dies. If the victim had not died, the accused might have been guilty only of a battery. By mischance he is, however, guilty of manslaughter. This bad luck has converted a minor offence against the person into a major crime of homicide. Furthermore, not even the reasonable bystander need foresee serious injury, never mind death. 'Injury' covers shock causing physical injury, but not emotional disturbance: *Dawson* (1985) 81 Cr App R 150 (CA). It is only where a reasonable person might foresee physical harm resulting from an emotional disturbance that frightening someone to death amounts to this type of manslaughter.

A recent case gives a flavour of this offence.

R v A [2005] All ER (D) 38 (July) (CA)

The two 16-year-old defendants and the victim were celebrating finishing their exams. Some drink having been taken, the accused hoisted the victim over a railing and he fell into the river and drowned. The act of the defendants was dangerous within the definition used in this form of manslaughter and it had caused death. The defendants argued that what they did was horseplay and therefore since the victim had consented to the horseplay, there was no 'unlawful' act, here the crime of battery. The Court of Appeal held that the victim had not in fact consented. The accused were guilty of manslaughter.

The accused's unlawful act must of course cause the death of the victim. Where the accused hits the victim, it is only if that act caused her death that the accused is guilty. In *Carey* [2006] EWCA Crim 17 it was said that the accused's blow did not cause the death and therefore he could not be guilty of manslaughter. For a good case comment see D. Ormerod 'Manslaughter: unlawful act – affray – dangerous act' [2006] Crim LR 843.

It was said at one time that the act had to be directed or aimed at the victim. In *Dalby* [1982] 1 WLR 425 (CA), the accused was found not guilty because the unlawful act, the supply of a dangerous drug, did not cause the victim's death. (Both the accused and the victim had injected themselves. There was no argument run that the victim's self-injection was an unlawful act.) *Obiter* the court said that the supply of the drug was not directed at the person of the accused. The drug, which was obtained on a prescription, was taken by the accused and the victim together, but each individual injected himself. The act of the accused was not aimed at the victim but at herself. This was a novel requirement and appeared inconsistent with the decision of the Lords in *Newbury*, where the defendants did not aim at the victim the stone which killed him. They aimed at the train. Nevertheless, the House of Lords refused leave to appeal in *Dalby*. A comparison case is *Cato*, above. The accused was guilty when he injected heroin into his friend. It could thus be said that the accused aimed the act at the victim. In *Dalby* the victim injected herself. In *Mitchell* [1983] QB 741 the Court of Appeal held that there was a *novus actus interveniens* in *Dalby*. The chain of causation had been broken. In this way the result in *Dalby* can be reconciled with earlier law. Even at the time when *Dalby* was taken to represent the law, it was not quite true to say that the act had to be directed at the victim, since the doctrine of transferred malice applies. In *Mitchell* the accused pushed a man who fell against an 89-year-old woman in a queue at a post office. She suffered a broken leg, developed thrombosis and died. The accused was guilty of manslaughter even though he did not direct his attack at the victim. The chain of causation had not been broken. It should be noted that the accused was guilty of manslaughter, even though he intended only a battery. In *Pagett* (1983) 76 Cr App R 279 (CA), where a girl was used as a shield by the accused (see Chapter 2), the court did not deal with the point that under *Dalby* the act had to be directed at the victim. The court said *obiter* that the accused would have been guilty even if the police had shot dead an innocent bystander, though the actual victim was innocent too. The point is that the accused did not direct his act at her. *Mitchell* followed *Pagett* and did not make any special rule for constructive manslaughter, but instead applied general rules on causation, and did not refer to *Dalby* or the principle there stated.

The Court of Appeal finally gave the 'aimed at' rule its quietus in *Goodfellow*. *Dalby* was held to have been decided in the way that it was because a direction was needed whether or not there was an intervening act, that is, the words in *Dalby* did not mean what they said. The result in *Dalby* is preserved. The accused did not (now) cause the victim's death. On the facts of *Goodfellow* where the accused set fire to his dwelling, there was no break in the chain of causation which led to the death of his wife, son and son's girlfriend. He did not aim his arson at the victims. In **Ball**, above, the court mentioned the 'aimed at' doctrine but did not treat it as a separate element. It *obiter* referred to both the **Dalby** test and the **Goodfellow** test of no *novus actus interveniens*. This may signify a return to **Dalby**. The court instanced a pub landlord who sold alcohol to an underage drinker. The alcohol contained poison but the landlord did not know it. If the drinker imbibed the poison, the landlord would not be guilty of this type of manslaughter because he did not direct the unlawful act, sale of alcohol to a person under age, at the victim. The law was clarified by the House of Lords in **Attorney-General's Reference (No. 3 of 1994)**, above, in which Lord Hope *per curiam* stated that the 'aimed at' rule was not a requirement of constructive manslaughter. **Goodfellow** is therefore correct. Unfortunately **Dalby** was not overruled.

The argument in favour of the 'aimed at' doctrine is that it is a limit on the very wide ambit of constructive manslaughter. If a person drops some chips on the floor, the victim happens to slip on them, falls to the ground banging her head and dies, he is guilty of manslaughter, a serious offence. A contrary argument is that since the harm need not be foreseen by the accused for him to be guilty of this type of manslaughter, why should the accused have to aim his act at the victim?

The elements of the offence

(a) *Lawful acts done carelessly are not lawful acts for this purpose.* This type of manslaughter is different from gross negligence manslaughter, as Figure 12.3 illustrates. A lawful act which is performed carelessly does not automatically become an unlawful act for this purpose, even if a lawful act done carelessly amounts to an offence (e.g. careless

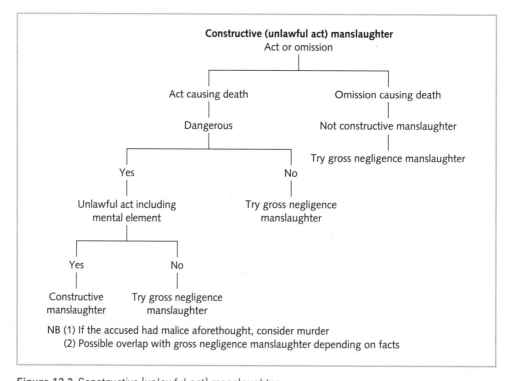

Figure 12.3 Constructive (unlawful act) manslaughter

driving): *Andrews* v *DPP*, above, where the crime was that of dangerous driving in that the accused knocked down and killed a pedestrian while overtaking. Therefore a person who kills while driving carelessly is not guilty of this form of manslaughter, but may be guilty of manslaughter by gross negligence. It should be said that the width of this exception is uncertain.

(b) *The unlawful act must be 'dangerous'.* The unlawful act need not be a violent act but it must be 'a dangerous act, that is, an act which is likely to injure another person': *Larkin* [1943] 1 All ER 217. Previous law did not require this element. The Court of Criminal Appeal held that brandishing a razor was an assault, a dangerous act. When a woman inadvertently fell against the razor, cut her throat and died, the person holding the razor was guilty of manslaughter. *Church* adopted a like definition. In some cases, as Lord Hope put it in *Attorney-General's Reference (No. 3 of 1994)*, 'dangerousness in this context is not a high standard' and in others the danger is obvious. In *Mahal* [1991] Crim LR 632 (CA), it was held that a jury could find that pushing someone through an open window 22 feet from the ground could lead to 'the risk of some harm'. In *Attorney-General's Reference (No. 3 of 1994)* the accused's attack on the child's mother was a dangerous act likely to injure her. The death of the child, therefore, was constructive manslaughter. A risk of danger to anyone, therefore, suffices. The attacker need not even know that the woman attacked was pregnant. There is no need to foresee death or serious harm. The element of dangerousness must be proved: *Scarlett* [1993] 4 All ER 629 (CA).

(c) *The act must be criminal.* There must be an act which must be unlawful: see Lord Hope in *Attorney-General's Reference (No. 3 of 1994)*, above. Both an *act* and an *unlawful* act are needed. An omission, even a deliberate one, which causes death, cannot be a wrongful act: *Lowe* [1973] QB 702 (CA), not following *Senior* [1899] 1 QB 283 (Court for Crown Cases Reserved). The fact that the accused was guilty of wilful neglect of his child who died as a result did not mean that he was guilty of this type of manslaughter. The court drew a line between an act which was likely to cause harm and an omission which was likely to do the same. But in both instances the accused caused the death of the child. Starving a child to death does not seem morally less reprehensible than beating it to death. In this context the drawing of a distinction between act and omission has been strongly criticised. It seems strange that murder can be committed by an omission (*Gibbins and Proctor* (1918) 13 Cr App R 134 (CCA)) but unlawful act manslaughter cannot. Both gross negligence and subjectively reckless manslaughter may be committed by omissions.

Normally the unlawful act, which must be a crime, is a non-fatal offence such as battery but it could, for example, be arson, as in *Goodfellow*, above. Other examples include attempted robbery in *Dawson*, above, and burglary in *Watson* [1989] 1 WLR 684 (CA). In *Andrews* [2003] Crim LR 477 the Court of Appeal held that if the underlying crime (here, supplying a prescription-only drug without a prescription) is one of strict liability, no *mens rea* as to that crime need be proved for the accused to be convicted of unlawful act manslaughter. However, *Andrews* is a weak case. The court did not discuss the issue, and if a careless act is not an unlawful act for this purpose (see (a) above), *a fortiori* a strict offence is not. *Andrews* is also contrary to the statement in *Lamb* that *mens rea* is 'an essential ingredient in manslaughter'. Furthermore, there in fact was a *mens rea* offence which could have formed the basis of the charge: s 23 of the Offences against the Person Act 1861, administering a noxious thing. An act which is a tort only and not a crime is not an unlawful act for the purposes of unlawful act manslaughter: *Franklin* (1883) 15 Cox CC 163, where the tort was one of trespass to goods when the accused threw a box from one of the piers in Brighton and it struck and killed a swimmer. (In *Franklin* there was a crime, larceny (nowadays theft), but that crime was not mentioned and it was not in itself dangerous.) Civil liability remains immaterial today: *Lamb*, above, *per* Sachs LJ. It seems strange to reduce the width of unlawful act manslaughter in *Franklin* because manslaughter is a serious crime, yet in *Andrews* to hold that no *mens rea* as to the underlying offence need be established, even though manslaughter is a serious crime.

Jennings [1990] Crim LR 588 (CA) confirmed the need for there to be a crime and for the unlawful act to be identified. Possessing a knife was not *per se* an unlawful act under the Prevention of Crime Act 1953, s 1. The accused's intention had to be considered to determine whether he wished to use it to inflict injury. Whether the accused had that intent had to be left to the jury. Without that state of mind there was no unlawful act manslaughter when the accused stabbed his brother who was trying to restrain him. There must, therefore, be a mental element in the 'unlawful act', though this proposition is not always stated in the cases. (See, for instance, *Newbury*, where it is difficult to state what the unlawful act was: the Lords did not refer to this point, counsel having conceded that there was an unlawful act. One possible crime is endangering the safety of passengers conveyed by rail. Other possibilities include criminal damage and assault occasioning actual bodily harm. It is unclear whether a property offence can be an unlawful act.) See also *Lamb*, below, which clearly demonstrates the condition that there must be *mens rea* as to the unlawful act.

It has to be said that this point about the necessity for *mens rea* in the unlawful act is not always clearly stated in the cases. For example, in *A-G's Reference (No. 3 of 1994)* [1998] AC 245 (HL) Lord Hope said: 'All that need be proved is that he intentionally did what he did.' Here, 'intentionally' means 'voluntarily', that is, Lord Hope expressed what is already understood. It is suggested that Lord Hope should have said that the accused must have the mental element for the basic offence in line with a good number of Court of Appeal authorities such as *Lamb*.

The requirement of *mens rea* for unlawful act manslaughter may be easily satisfied. If the accused kills by fire, the unlawful act is arson as in *Goodfellow*. That offence can be committed by a person who was reckless. Therefore, he is guilty of manslaughter, even though he gave no thought to an obvious (and serious) risk of criminal damage. The *actus reus* and *mens rea* are totally out of step. A lawful act, such as a killing in self-defence, or a minor harm committed with the victim's consent, such as a tackle in a game of football, is not an unlawful act for this purpose. If, however, the force used was excessive, the act is a crime and unlawful for this purpose. *Jennings* demonstrates that the unlawful act need not in fact be an act but can be a state of affairs crime, in this case possessing an offensive weapon. If the crime is one of specific intent and the accused was intoxicated, he is not guilty of unlawful act manslaughter based on that offence: *O'Driscoll* (1977) 65 Cr App R 50 (CA). However, if there is a basic intent crime as a fall-back to the specific intent one, he is guilty because intoxication is no defence to such an offence.

In two cases the 'unlawful act' is hard if not impossible to find despite the requirement of an unlawful act. The courts suggested that the unlawful act need not be a recognised crime. It is sufficient that the accused acted voluntarily; in other words, there need be no *mens rea*. In *Cato*, above, the victim produced heroin and syringes and invited the accused to have a fix. Several times during the night they injected one another with heroin and water. In the morning the victim died. The accused's conviction for manslaughter was upheld. There was a crime, administering a noxious thing. Lord Widgery CJ went on, however, to say that injecting the victim irrespective of this crime was an unlawful act for the purposes of constructive manslaughter. Yet injecting someone with heroin at his request is not a crime. Lord Widgery CJ's suggestion was *obiter*, for as he noted there already was an offence, administering a noxious thing.

In the second troubling case, ***Lipman*** [1970] 1 QB 152 (CA), the defendant was also convicted of manslaughter (for facts see Chapter 8). In these cases the taking of drugs was not a crime. Possession is the offence but possession did not cause the death. The defendants in ***Cato*** and ***Lipman*** at the time of the victims' deaths were presumably unconscious and it is accordingly difficult to attribute to them any *mens rea*. Getting into a state as a result of which someone died may have been reckless in ordinary language but there was a gap in time, a lack of contemporaneity, between the getting into the state and the victim's death. The House of Lords refused leave to appeal in ***Lipman***, and it was approved by the Lords in ***DPP v Majewski*** [1977] AC 443. The issue whether the act had to be unlawful was not addressed in ***Newbury***, above, though as a minimum criminal damage existed, as did the more esoteric offence of endangering the safety of any person conveyed upon a railway, but Lord Hope did require it in ***Attorney-General's Reference (No. 3 of 1994)***, quoted above. It is suggested that cases such as ***Cato*** are incorrect. Surely it cannot be the law that a person who commits the *actus reus* only of battery can be convicted of manslaughter, but not of battery itself? Moreover, if the act need not be criminal, the courts spent a long time in cases such as ***Lamb*** overruling the first instance judgment, considering whether an offence existed. The accused need not know that the act is unlawful: ***Newbury***, ***DPP v Daley*** [1980] AC 237 (PC). However, his state of mind must be investigated to see whether he intended to commit an *actus reus*.

As we have seen, the unlawful act need not be an offence against the person. Stanley Yeo criticised this law in *Fault in Homicide* (Federation Press, 1997) 188: 'To convict a person of manslaughter on the basis of a property offence seems almost as objectionable as convicting her or him on account of a tort.'

A final point is this. As we have seen, the rule is that the unlawful act must be a crime. This means that mere psychological harm or making one's life a misery is by itself insufficient: ***Dhaliwal*** [2006] EWCA Crim 1139 (CA). The victim committed suicide after years of abuse by her husband. On the evening before her suicide he had hit her, causing a cut from his bracelet to her forehead. This amounted to a crime contrary to s 20 of the Offences Against the Person Act 1861. However, the court held that her suicide could not be attributed to that blow: the non-fatal offence had not caused the death and therefore was not the underlying offence for unlawful act manslaughter. Similar is ***Carey*** [2006] EWCA Crim 17, noted above. Emotional disturbance was insufficient. There had to be a risk of physical harm, which can arise from shock.

(d) *The reasonable person assesses whether the unlawful act was dangerous.* Whether the unlawful act was a dangerous one is judged not by the accused's state of mind, but by a sober and reasonable person in the defendant's position. It is the act which has to be dangerous, not whether the accused believed it to be dangerous. The test is objective: ***Church***, ***Lipman***, ***Newbury***, ***Dawson*** and ***Ball***, above. In ***Newbury***, two teenagers pushed part of a paving stone from the parapet of a railway bridge as a train was approaching. The stone passed through the window of the cab and killed a guard. The Lords held that the boys were guilty even though they did not realise that what they were doing might harm others. They were guilty if they did an act which was unlawful and which 'all sober and reasonable people' would recognise as being dangerous. Accordingly, whether the boys recognised that there was a risk or not was irrelevant (cf. the law of objective recklessness). It has to be questioned why the boys should be guilty of such a serious offence as manslaughter when they did not realise that any harm may be caused by what they did. In *Church* the accused did not know that there was 'a risk of harm' to his victim when he threw her into the river, because he believed her to be dead. His mistaken belief was immaterial: reasonable people would have recognised that there was such a risk. As the next paragraph demonstrates, the test is not a purely objective one. In *Carey*, above, the Court of Appeal said that despite the principle in *Church* being wide, it is 'clear and now well-established as part of our law . . . This principle must . . . be loyally applied and without reservation'. Any formulation of the law such as that in *Larkin* that the act had to be likely to injure another is incorrect.

The jury must place themselves in the accused's position with the accused's knowledge. In *Dawson* it was held that a reasonable person robbing a petrol station would not know of the attendant's bad heart. A sober and reasonable person would foresee that an attack by several persons, one of whom was clad in a balaclava, would cause fear through their pointing a replica gun at the attendant, banging a pick-axe handle on the counter and demanding money but he or she would not foresee physical harm resulting from the fear. Therefore, there was no dangerous act. However, the accused would be guilty if he became aware of the condition during the robbery. One effect of *Dawson* is that frightening someone, even when that act constitutes an assault, will rarely amount to this type of manslaughter because reasonable people would not foresee the risk of physical harm, generally speaking, on the facts. A contrasting case is *Watson*, above (CA): the jury were to take into account the burglar's knowledge of the victim's age and (frail) condition, which he had acquired after he had broken into her house. The accused was guilty even though his intent was only to steal. Theft or burglary is an unlawful act; on the facts it was a dangerous act because of the victim's physical state; and the victim died from a heart attack caused by the burglar. The reasonable person was fixed with the accused's knowledge acquired during the burglary.

If the accused had not become aware of the victim's frailty, the reasonable person in this context knows the facts which are obvious to a reasonable person, but not those facts which are not obvious. On the facts of *Watson*, however, the prosecution could not prove that the accused's acts caused the victim's death.

The reasonable person, while imbued with the knowledge the accused acquired throughout the crime, is not imbued with the mistaken beliefs he had. In *Ball*, above, the accused killed his neighbour with a shotgun. He said he thought the gun contained blanks. He had grabbed a handful of cartridges from his pocket, which as he knew contained both blank and live cartridges. The court held that it did not matter whether the accused thought about dangerousness. Whether the act was dangerous was to be judged by what the reasonable person would have appreciated. The reasonable person would have realised that he was inserting live cartridges because they were heavier than blanks: he would by definition not have made an unreasonable mistake. The accused's own 'intention, foresight or knowledge is irrelevant', said Lord Lane CJ. Therefore, the accused is not to be judged on the facts which he believed existed, but on the reasonable person's assessment of the facts. Accordingly, the reasonable person is imbued with the accused's knowledge, including expert knowledge, but not his mistaken beliefs. *Dawson* was distinguished as being an authority on the victim's vulnerability, whereas *Ball* was about the dangerousness of the accused's act. In a situation like *Ball* the jury is to look at all the facts, not just at the facts known to the accused. In actual fact **Ball** is similar to **Dawson** and there is no need to talk about mistake. The reasonable person with the accused's knowledge that his pocket contained both live and blank cartridges would have realised that what was done was dangerous.

In other areas of law, in particular loss of control and duress, the reasonable person standard is modified by at least some of the accused's personal characteristics. No English case has discussed this eventuality in the context of manslaughter, but the possibility is there. The ruling as to the objective test is not affected by s 8 of the Criminal Justice Act 1967, which relates to proof: **Newbury**. Section 8 concerns the accused's intent or foresight: neither state of mind constitutes an element in the objective test of whether the accused's act was a dangerous one.

(e) *Death must be caused by the unlawful and dangerous act.* The unlawful and dangerous act must cause the death of the victim. In **Carey**, above, one of the defendants punched the victim, who ran away. She died: she had a severely damaged heart which no one knew about. The harm to the victim caused by the defendant did not bring about her death. The punch was an unlawful and dangerous act but it did not cause her death. Similarly, the affray was unlawful but the threats issued during it were not dangerous in the sense here used, likely to cause some physical injury.

Further examples of unlawful act manslaughter

Hayward (1908) 21 Cox CC 692: 'death from fright alone, caused by an illegal act, such as threats of violence, would be sufficient' (Ridley J).

Larkin, above: brandishing an open razor, intending to frighten the victim's man and inadvertently killing the victim.

Hall (1961) 45 Cr App R 366 (CCA): producing a knife, intending to terrify his wife. **Larkin** was applied.

Mackie (1973) 57 Cr App R 453 (CA): using excessive violence on a child. This case was approved by the Privy Council in **DPP v Daley**, above. A similar case on chastisement is **Conner** (1835) 173 ER 194. (For more on the 'escape cases', see Chapter 2.)

Buck and Buck (1960) 44 Cr App R 213: illegal abortion.

Mahal, above: pushing the victim through an open window 22 feet above ground.

Where there is no unlawful act, there is no unlawful act manslaughter. In **Lamb**, above, the accused pulled the trigger of a gun and killed his best friend, but there was no assault because both did not expect a bullet to come out of the barrel. Sachs J said that *mens rea* was an essential part of this type of manslaughter. In **Jennings**, above, the accused had a sheathknife to protect himself from a person with whom he had been quarrelling. He was told by his brother that the person was looking for him. He got out his knife but stabbed to death his brother, who was attempting to restrain him. Since the possession of the knife was not in itself illegal, the jury should have been directed to look at the accused's intent. He might have had it with him to protect himself against 'an imminent and particular threat'. It was not sufficient that any bystander would on those facts have realised that some injury was inevitable.

Summary of unlawful act manslaughter

Goodfellow sums up this area of law. The accused is guilty of unlawful act manslaughter if the responses to these questions are in the affirmative: '(1) was the act intentional? (2) was it unlawful? (3) was it an act which any reasonable person would realise was bound to subject some other human being to the risk of physical harm, albeit not necessarily serious harm? (4) was the act the cause of death?' (This summary may be too favourable to the accused. There is debate whether the unlawful act must be intentionally committed. For example, in *Scarlett*, above, the Court of Appeal assumed that a reckless battery was an unlawful act.) The Court of Appeal took a similar view in *Watson*, above, when it approved the trial judge's direction:

> Manslaughter is the offence committed when one person causes the death of another by an act which is unlawful and which is also dangerous, dangerous in the sense that it is an act which all sober and reasonable people would inevitably realise must subject the victim to the risk of some harm resulting whether the defendant realised that or not.

The same scenario can give rise to both gross negligence and unlawful act manslaughter, as the facts of *Goodfellow* demonstrate, but need not. The differences are, first, that the former requires 'grossness' whereas the latter does not and, secondly, the former requires foresight of death whereas the latter requires only reasonable foreseeability of some harm however slight. For a case where the Court of Appeal said that on the facts the prosecution should have pursued unlawful act manslaughter and not gross negligence manslaughter, see *Willoughby* above. Since criminal damages had been proved, the prosecution had only one element of unlawful act manslaughter to prove: did the accused cause the victim's death?

Reform of manslaughter

The main criticism of unlawful act manslaughter is that it is a serious crime, yet a person is guilty of it if a reasonable person might foresee that some harm might occur: it is not necessary that some reasonable person might have foreseen death or GBH. Subjectivists are of course most unhappy that the accused is not being judged by what he foresaw but by what a reasonable person might have foreseen. Subjectivists also think that gross negligence manslaughter is unsupportable because again a jury does not consider what the accused intended or foresaw but uses the tort test of reasonable foreseeability.

The 1996 recommendations on involuntary manslaughter

Other reform proposals emanate from the Law Commission in its Report No. 237, *Legislating the Criminal Code: Involuntary Manslaughter*, 1996. There are four major recommendations in relation to the liability of natural persons. The Commission was concerned that the current law of manslaughter is too all-encompassing, ranging from a person who commits arson knowing that his family is in the burning house to a very careless electrician. It thought that juries may be reluctant to find incompetent doctors guilty of manslaughter, which has stigma attached to it. Two principal forms of unlawful killing, (a) and (d) below, are proposed.

(a) The crime should be reckless killing when the accused kills, being subjectively reckless as to death or serious injury. The risk must be one which in all the circumstances which he knows or believes to exist it is unreasonable for him to take. The Law Commission expressed some doubt about whether recklessness as to serious injury was sufficient *mens rea* for such a serious crime in its Consultation Paper No. 135,

Involuntary Manslaughter, 1994, which preceded the Report, but wished the law to be in line with murder; moreover, 'there is a very thin line between behaviour that risks serious injury and behaviour which risks death, because it is frequently a matter of chance, depending on such factors as the availability of medical treatment, whether serious injury leads to death' (para 4.19). The maximum sentence should be life imprisonment. This offence covers killings only a little short of murder (and pre-*Moloney* [1985] AC 905 (HL), discussed in Chapter 3, such killings may have amounted to murder). Recklessness is defined as in the draft Criminal Code 1989 and the Law Commission Report No. 218, *Legislating the Criminal Code – Offences against the Person and General Principles*, 1993. As in that Report no definition is given of 'serious injury'.

(b) Unlawful act manslaughter should be abolished. The mishap that a person kills when he had the fault element for a crime less than causing serious injury is unfortunate, and the crime should not be manslaughter. The Law Commission has generally opposed constructive liability. In its opinion manslaughter is a crime about causing death when there is a significant risk of death or serious injury. Causing death by accident was not appropriately called manslaughter. Present law was also thought to be confused and uncertain. In its words, 'unlawful act manslaughter is . . . unprincipled because it requires only that a foreseeable risk of causing some harm should have been inherent in the accused's conduct, whereas he is actually convicted of causing death'. This recommendation is consonant with the proposed abolition of constructive liability in ss 18 and 20 of the Offences Against the Person Act 1861: see Law Commission Report No. 218. The accused should be punished for what he did and thought – reckless injury or assault – not for the unexpected outcome of his act. The effect of the abolition of this form of manslaughter would not be that the accused would escape liability. He could be convicted of the types of manslaughter noted in (a) or (d) or of a non-fatal offence.

(c) The special category of motor manslaughter which received the sanction of the Court of Appeal in *Prentice* should be abolished on the basis that the law of manslaughter should apply generally, and not become divided into several crimes dependent on the accused's activity. There already is the offence of causing death by dangerous driving which since 1993 has been punishable by 10 years' imprisonment, and the new offence in (a) would cover the most heinous instances of killing through the use of a vehicle. Other fact situations would fall within (d).

(d) There should be an offence called killing by gross carelessness where the accused did not subjectively act recklessly as to death or serious injury. The Commission wished to avoid references to negligence and the duty of care, which are concepts of uncertain scope, as well as to recklessness, and so formulated a new crime penalising the accused who has killed and reasonably ought to have been aware of a risk, which would have been obvious to a reasonable person in his position, that his act might result in death or in serious injury and whose conduct fell far below that which could reasonably have been demanded *of him* in preventing the occurrence of the risk (or in preventing the risk that had arisen from resulting in death). The bracketed phrase is where the liability of doctors will arise. The accused must also have been capable of appreciating that the risk of death or serious injury would have been obvious to a person in his position. As an alternative to the test of the accused's conduct falling far below what could reasonably be expected of him in the circumstances, the Commission proposed a test whereby the accused would be guilty if he intends to cause some injury or realises and unreasonably takes the risk that injury may be caused and the conduct causing the injury is an offence. If the risk was apparent to the accused, he will be guilty of reckless manslaughter, as defined in (a) above. The term 'of him' means that the accused will not be guilty if, for example, he does his best to give assistance at a car crash, but means too that practice in the relevant field of activity could be investigated: the defendant may still be guilty even though he followed normal procedure in the sphere of action concerned. The Law Commission phrases liability for this possible offence as serious negligence and considers that the main application will be in relation to public services such as transport. While the Commission was of the view that the maximum sentence should be a determinate one of less than life imprisonment, it made no recommendation as to length. In Consultation Paper No. 135, *Involuntary Manslaughter*, which preceded the Report, the suggestion of the Commission was 10 years' imprisonment as the maximum. This offence would replace the crime of manslaughter by gross negligence. The Commission thought that an accused should be liable for a result he had not foreseen when the risk of harm was high and the failure to notice that risk was blameworthy. For recommendations as to corporate manslaughter, see Chapter 6.

(e) There is no proposal relating to omissions. The Law Commission recommended that the topic form the subject of another law reform project.

The Court of Appeal has twice called for an urgent and full review of the law of manslaughter: *Prentice* and *Scarlett* [1993] 4 All ER 629. The overruling of *Scarlett* does not affect this call for reform. The Law Commission's proposals are complex in that the jury would have to answer more questions than exist in present law.

The government's proposals

In its Consultation Paper, *Reforming the Law of Involuntary Manslaughter: The Government's Proposals*, 2000, the Home Office accepted most but not all of the recommendations of the Law Commission in its Report No. 237. In particular, it welcomed the new offences of (subjectively) reckless killing and killing by gross carelessness. However, it did not support the abolition of constructive manslaughter. On public consultation there was a strong response that constructive manslaughter in some form should be retained. In para. 2.10 it stated: 'The Government is concerned that the Law Commission's approach would mean that behaviour which may be regarded as seriously culpable because it involves intentional or reckless criminal behaviour which results in death would no longer attract an appropriate charge. It might be viewed as unacceptable if the law permitted only a charge of assault where that assault had in fact resulted in death. The Government considers that there is an argument that anyone who embarks on a course of illegal violence has to accept the consequences of his act, even if the final consequences are unforeseeable.' Accordingly, another homicide offence was needed when the accused killed intending to injure or being reckless as to some injury and 'the conduct causing, or intended to cause, the injury constitutes an offence'. This crime would differ from constructive manslaughter because the objective test of dangerousness would be replaced by a subjective *mens rea* test. Excluded from this offence would be death caused by normally minor diseases which were fatal to susceptible persons (para. 4.14). In respect of the transmission of fatal diseases, those who recklessly or by gross carelessness pass on a disease which results in death would be liable except where there is direct transmission from one person to another as by sexual contact. To this exception there is engrafted another exception: where a person owed a professional duty to the victim, he would be liable (para. 4.12). The government has since announced that it does not intend to legislate on the basis of the Home Office's paper. Its focus currently is on corporate manslaughter. However, the Law Commission has returned to the fray, as is discussed in the next section of the book.

The Law Commission's 2006 proposals on involuntary manslaughter

The Law Commission in its Report No. 304 of November 2006, *Murder, Manslaughter and Infanticide*, recommended a three-tier structure for fatal offences: first degree murder, second degree murder and manslaughter. The terms of reference did not permit it to examine involuntary manslaughter in depth, particularly as it had made proposals for reform in its 1996 Report, noted in the previous section of this book, and the Home Office had given the government's response, also noted there. What the Commission did do, however, was to redefine unlawful act manslaughter and gross negligence manslaughter. The former has come in for much criticism because (para. 3.42): '. . . a person can be convicted of a very serious offence even though he or she was not aware that their criminal act posed a risk of any harm occurring. It suffices if a reasonable person would have been aware.' Nevertheless, the consultees to the Consultation Paper No. 177, *A New Homicide Act for England and Wales?*, 2005, supported the continued existence of both offences.

The government wrote to the Commission in 2011 stating that it would not take forward the proposals for a three-tier 'ladder' of homicide.

Unlawful act manslaughter would be defined as: killing another through a criminal act intended to cause injury or through a criminal act being aware that it involved a serious risk of causing injury. The Law Commission rejected a suggestion that there should be awareness of a risk of *serious* injury because that would overcomplicate the law: there should not be debate before the jury whether the injury was serious or not.

Gross negligence manslaughter differs somewhat from that found in the Home Office's 2000 proposals. First, there would be no separate category of (subjectively) reckless manslaughter. Some scenarios falling within that category would become second degree murder (intent to cause injury or fear of injury or risk of injury coupled with awareness that the conduct may cause death); the remainder would fall within gross negligence manslaughter. If this proposal were enacted, 'recklessness' could disappear from fatal offences. Secondly, the gross negligence must be as to death; gross negligence as to serious injury would not suffice. This would restate the common law as it has developed after *Adomako* above.

Conclusion

Lord Mustill in *Attorney-General's Reference (No. 3 of 1994)* [1998] AC 245 (HL) stated that 'the offence of manslaughter unites a group of crimes which have nothing in common except their name'. One might add that they also share the same *actus reus* and maximum sentence, but there is much sense in what Lord Mustill said, and that good sense is reflected in this book: diminished responsibility is akin to insanity and both are discussed in Chapter 9, while provocation (see earlier in this chapter) is a defence only to murder, discussed in Chapter 11. In such, bar the name, *actus reus* and sentence, voluntary and involuntary manslaughter are really separate offences, and the fact that they have the same name is apt to mislead.

Summary

In this chapter voluntary and involuntary manslaughter are considered. 'Voluntary' in this context means that the accused had malice aforethought, the *mens rea* of murder, but has a defence. Loss of control is one of the two principal forms of voluntary manslaughter (the other being diminished responsibility, which is considered in Chapter 9). Besides loss of control and diminished responsibility there is a third form of voluntary manslaughter, killing in pursuance of a suicide pact. The standard example is when the accused and his victim, lovers, decide that they cannot live in an unforgiving world. The victim agrees to be killed by the accused; the accused kills the victim; but the accused then decides not to kill himself.

Involuntary manslaughter is where the accused kills but does not have the *mens rea* of murder, but does fall within two (or almost certainly three) definitions. One form of involuntary manslaughter is manslaughter by gross negligence; the second form is constructive manslaughter, which also goes by the name of unlawful act manslaughter, a name preferred by the author because it reminds the reader that there must be both an act (an omission will not suffice) and an act which is unlawful, that is, criminal in its own right (though not all the cases are to that effect). The third form, which does seem to exist, is that of (subjectively) reckless manslaughter, a type of killing which only just falls short of murder.

- *Loss of control*: This defence, which is available only to murder, was introduced by the Coroners and Justice Act 2009. There has to be (1) a loss of self-control and (2) a qualifying trigger for the attack, and sexual infidelity and a '"considered" desire for revenge' are ruled out. However, there is no requirement that the accused has a 'sudden' loss of control, thereby bringing some abused persons who kill within the defence. Finally, (3) 'A person of D's sex and age, with a normal degree of tolerance and self-restraint and in the circumstances of D, might have reacted in the same or a similar way to D' (s 54(1)(c)).

- *Gross negligence manslaughter*: This form of involuntary manslaughter occurs when the accused kills and does so in breach of a duty of care he or she owes to the victim, and that breach falls far short of the standard to be expected, and there is a risk of death. Where the accused is an expert such as a doctor performing his or her job, the standard is that of a reasonably competent person in that work.

- *Unlawful act manslaughter* (also known as constructive manslaughter): This is where the accused kills as a result of a crime (for which he or she performed the *actus reus* and usually at least had the *mens rea*), what he or she did was an act (not an omission), and the act was dangerous in the sense that all sober and reasonable people would say that what the accused did was likely to cause some harm.

   While the same act may give rise to both of these forms of involuntary manslaughter, they have different rules attached to them. For example, gross negligence manslaughter may be committed by an omission but unlawful act manslaughter may not; and in gross negligence manslaughter there must have been a risk of death but in unlawful act manslaughter it is sufficient that there was a risk of some injury, not even serious injury, never mind death.

- *(Subjectively) reckless manslaughter*: While no case definitively so rules, it is thought that there is an offence of (subjectively) reckless manslaughter when the accused foresees death or GBH as a possible consequence but nonetheless goes on and kills.

References

Reports

Home Office Consultation Paper, *Reforming the Law of Involuntary Manslaughter*: The Government's Proposals (2000)

Law Commission Consultation Paper No. 135, *Involuntary Manslaughter* (1994)

Law Commission Consultation Paper No. 177, *A New Homicide Act for England and Wales?* (2005)

Law Commission Report No. 218, *Legislating the Criminal Code – Offences against the Person and General Principles* (1993)

Law Commission Report No. 237, *Legislating the Criminal Code: Involuntary Manslaughter* (1996)

Law Commission Report No. 290, *Partial Defences to Murder* (2004)

Law Commission Report No. 304, *Murder, Manslaughter and Infanticide* (2006)

Books

Yeo, S. *Fault in Homicide* (Federation Press, 1997)

Journals

Omerod, D. 'Manslaughter: unlawful act – affray – dangerous act' [2006] Crim LR 843

Further reading

Ashworth, A. and Mitchell, B. *Rethinking English Homicide Law* (Oxford University Press, 2000)

Baker, D. and Zhao, L.X. 'Contributory and non-contributory triggers in the loss of control defence: A wrong turn on sexual infidelity' (2012) 76 JCL 254

Brazier, M. and Alghrani, A. 'Fatal medical malpractice and criminal liability' [2009] PN 51

Busuttil, A. and McCall Smith, A. 'Flight, stress and homicide' (1990) 54 JCL 257

Buxton, R.J. 'By any unlawful act' (1966) 81 LQR 174

Cherkassy, L. '*Kennedy* and unlawful act manslaughter: an unorthodox application of the doctrine of causation' (2008) 72 JCL 387

Clarkson, C. and Cunningham, S. (eds) *Criminal Liability for Non-Aggressive Death* (Ashgate, 2008)

Clough, A. 'Loss of self-control as a defence: The key to replacing provocation' (2010) 74 JCL 118

Criminal Law Revision Committee 14th Report, *Offences Against the Person*, Cmnd 7844 (1980)

Docherty, P. 'Unlawful act manslaughter and causation' (2010) 174 JPN 549

Dressler, J. 'Why keep the provocation defense? Some reflections on a difficult subject' (2002) 86 Minn LR 959

Fitz-Gibbon, K. and Pickering, S. 'From provocation to defensive homicide' (2012) 52 BJ Crim 159

Freckleton, I. 'When plight makes right: the forensic abuse syndrome' (1994) 18 Crim LJ 29

Gardner, S. 'Manslaughter by gross negligence' (1995) 111 LQR 22

Golder, B. 'The homosexual advance defence and the law/body nexus' (2004) 11 *eLaw: Murdoch University Electronic Journal of Law*, Pt I

Herring, J. and Palser, E. 'The duty of care in gross negligence manslaughter' [2007] Crim LR 24

Keating, H. 'The Law Commission's Report on Involuntary Manslaughter: the restoration of a serious crime' [1996] Crim LR 535

Law Commission (of New Zealand), *Some Criminal Defences with Particular Reference to Battered Defendants*, Report No. 73 (2004)

Leigh, L.H. 'Loss of control: The significance of sexual infidelity and other matters' [2012] *Archbold Review* 4

Mitchell, B. 'Minding the gap in unlawful and dangerous act manslaughter: a moral defence of one-punch killers' (2008) 72 JCL 537

Mitchell, B. 'More thoughts about unlawful and dangerous act manslaughter and one-punch killers' [2009] Crim LR 661

Mitchell, B. and Mackay, R.D. 'Investigating involuntary manslaughter: an empirical study of 127 cases' (2011) 31 OJLS 165

Mousourakis, C. *Criminal Responsibility and Partial Excuses* (Ashgate, 1998)

Mytton, L. and Webley, L. 'Families and violence: making difference(s) visible' (2000) 7 *International Journal of the Legal Profession* 273

Norrie, A. 'The Coroners and Justice Act 2009 – partial defences to murder (1): Loss of control' [2010] Crim LR 275

Ormerod, D.C. Case comment on *Evans* [2010] CLJ 186

Peiris, G.L. 'Involuntary manslaughter in the Commonwealth' (1985) 5 LS 21

Quick, O. 'Prosecuting "gross" medical negligence: manslaughter, discretion and the Crown Prosecution Service' (2006) JLS 421

Quick, O. 'Medicine, mistakes and manslaughter: a criminal combination' [2010] CLJ 186

Reed, A. and Bohlander, M. (eds), *Loss of control and diminished responsibility* (Ashgate, 2011)

Reilly, A. 'The heart of the matter' (1997–98) 29 Ottawa LR 117

Spencer, J.R. 'Manslaughter by gross negligence' [1983] CLJ 187

Sullivan, G.R. 'Anger and excuse' (1993) 13 OJLS 421

Tyson, D. 'Victoria's new homicide laws: Provocative reforms or more stories of women "asking for it"?' (2011) 23 *Current Issues in Criminal Justice* 203

Wake, N. 'Recognising acute intoxication as diminished responsibility? A comparative analysis' (2012) 76 JCL 71

Withey, C. 'Loss of control, loss of opportunity?' [2011] Crim LR 263

Williams, R. 'Policy and principle in drugs manslaughter cases' (2005) CLJ 66

Wilson, W. 'The structure of criminal homicide' [2006] Crim LR 471

Yeo, S. 'Resolving gender bias in criminal defences' (1993) 19 Monash ULR 104

Yeo, S. *Unrestrained Killings and the Law* (Oxford University Press, Delhi, 1998)

Yeo, S. 'English reform of partial defences to murder: Lessons for New South Wales' (2010–11) 22 *Current Issues in Criminal Justice* 1

Yeo, S. 'English reform of provocation and diminished responsibility: Whither Singapore?' [2010] *Singapore Journal of Legal Studies* 177

There are a number of feminist writings on this topic. They include S. Lees in J. Radford and D.E.H. Russell (eds.), *Femicide: The Politics of Woman Killing* (Oxford University Press, 1992) and S.S.M. Edwards, *Sex and Gender in the Legal Process* (Blackstone Press, 1996), ch. 6. For a book which includes gendered killings, see F. Brookman, *Understanding Homicide* (Sage, 2005).

The latest Australian law reform proposals are contained in Victoria Law Reform Commission, *Defences to Homicide: Final Report*, 2004. For the Irish approach see Law Reform Commission, *Homicide: Murder and Involuntary Manslaughter*, Report no. 87, 2008.

For a discussion of 'homosexual advance defence' see A. Howe in C. Stychin and D. Hermann (eds), *Sexuality in the Legal Arena* (Athlone Press, 2000). For a US view see R.B. Mison 'Homophobia in manslaughter: the homosexual advance as insufficient provocation' (1992) 80 *California Law Review* 133. For a contrary view see J. Dressler, 'When "heterosexual" men kill "homosexual" men: reflections on provocation law, sexual advances, and the "reasonable man" standard' (1995) 85 JCL & Crim 726.

There is an overwhelming number of American law review articles on battered woman syndrome. One way into the literature is A.M. Coughlin 'Excusing women' (1994) 82 Cal LR 1. Her views, that the syndrome categorises women as lacking the self-control which men possess and therefore that it demeans women, have been criticised on the grounds that the syndrome is founded not on a distinction of gender but on society's response to the predicament in which women find themselves.

An exposition of the work of Lenore Walker appears in N.Z. Hilton (ed.), *Legal Responses to Wife Assault* (Sage, 1993) ch. 9. Her books include *The Battered Woman* (Harper & Row, 1979); *The Battered Woman Syndrome*, 2nd edn (Springer, 2000); and *Terrifying Love* (Harper & Row, 1989). Interestingly, she was a defence witness in the O.J. Simpson trial. For a criticism of battered persons' syndrome, see A.M. Dershowitz, *The Abuse Excuse and Other Cop-outs, Sob Stories and Evasions of Responsibility* (Little, Brown & Co., 1994). For a less polemic critique, see R.A. Schuller and N. Vidmar 'Battered woman syndrome, evidence in the courtroom' (1992) 16 *Law and Human Behavior* 273. For criticism of battered woman syndrome in the context of self-defence, see J. Dressler 'Battered women, sleeping abusers, and criminal responsibility' (1997) 2 *Chicago Policy Review* 1.

Visit **www.mylawchamber.co.uk** to access tools to help you develop and test your knowledge of criminal law, including interactive multiple choice questions, practice exam questions with guidance, annotated weblinks, glossary flashcards, legal newsfeed and legal updates.

Use Case Navigator to read in full some of the key cases referenced in this chapter with commentary and questions:

DPP v *Majewski* [1976] UK HL 2
R v *Adomako* [1994] 3 WLR 288
B v *Church* [1966] 1 QB 59, [1965] 2 WLR 1220
R v *Evans* [2009] EWCA Crim 650

13

Non-fatal offences

Aims and objectives

After reading this chapter you will understand and be able to critique:

- the two definitions of 'assault'
- assault as a separate offence
- the offence of battery
- the defence of consent: the rule and its exceptions
- the offence of assault occasioning actual bodily harm
- the two offences of wounding and inflicting or causing grievous bodily harm

Introduction

> The history of our law upon personal injuries is certainly not creditable to the legislature, and the result at which we have at present arrived is extremely clumsy. (Sir James Fitzjames Stephen, *A History of the Criminal Law of England*, vol. 3, 1883, 118.)

The same may be said at the present day.

This chapter considers crimes against the person which do not result in death. Many but not all appear in the Offences Against the Person Act 1861 (hereinafter OAPA), a consolidation statute with no attempt made to bring order to the terminology, level of seriousness, mental element, or sentencing. Famously described by Sir John Smith in [1991] Crim LR 43 as a 'ragbag', it covers for example non-fatal offences, bigamy, illegal abortion, assaults on clergymen in the execution of their duty. Lord Steyn in ***Ireland; Burstow*** [1998] AC 147 (HL) stated that: 'The interpretation and approach [to non-fatal offences] should so far as possible be adopted which treats the ladder of offences as a coherent body of law.' As we shall see, it is not always possible to do that. Those offences which are considered are those most likely to be reviewed on a criminal law course. Assault on a constable in the execution of his duty, it is argued, properly belongs in constitutional law. This chapter also deals with the issue of consent. Two points to bear in mind throughout the discussion are that the same facts can give rise to more than one offence and that the crimes are defined in terms both of the fault element of the accused and the harmful consequences, but the relationship is not perfect. One is guilty of assault occasioning actual bodily harm even though one does not intend to do so and one is not reckless as to that result: *Savage* [1992] 1 AC 699 (HL). The law is predicated on the right not to be touched without consent.

Recorded offences of violence, including murder, totalled 93,000 in the 12 months ending June 2012. This is a decline of some 13,000. The figure for unreported violent attacks must be many times higher.

Assault

Example

Adrian steps out of the shadows in a dark alleyway and scares Bettany by shouting 'Yah, boo, sucks!' at her. Does he have the *actus reus* of assault?

For many years words alone could not constitute an assault (though they could negate them: *Tuberville* **v** *Savage* (1669) 86 ER 684: 'If it were not assize time, I would not take such language' [impliedly, 'but would run you through with my sword']. In the famous words of Holroyd J in *Meade & Belt* (1823) 168 ER 1006: 'no words or singing are equivalent to an assault.' However, more recently words and even silent phone calls have been held to be an assault if the other elements are satisfied: see especially *Ireland; Burstow* [1998] AC 147 (HL). The definition of assault was best laid down by James J in *Fagan* **v** *MPC* [1969] 1 QB 439 (DC): 'any act which intentionally or . . . recklessly causes another person to apprehend immediate and unlawful violence.' There seems to be no problem with the other conduct elements of the crime. Therefore, Adrian does have the *actus reus* of assault.

'**Assault**' is used in two different senses: first as a generic term for the separate offences of assault and battery (this usage occurs in s 47 of the OAPA: see below); and secondly as a term denoting the crime of assault. The second use is sometimes called 'psychic assault' or 'technical assault'. Since there can be an assault without a battery, this section of this book uses the second meaning.

Both assault and battery have been held, contrary to earlier views, to be statutory offences: *DPP* v *Little* [1992] 1 QB 645 (DC), though this case was criticised for so holding in *Cross* v *DPP*, unreported, 20 June 1995 (CA). The Divisional Court thought in *Haystead* v *Chief Constable of Derbyshire* [2000] 3 All ER 890 that assault and battery remained common law offences, but *DPP* v *Little* was not referred to. If *DPP* v *Little* is correct, this is the position. The charge should be one of assault (or battery) contrary to s 39 of the Criminal Justice Act 1988. Section 39 reads: 'Common assault and battery shall be summary offences and a person guilty of either of them shall be liable to a fine not exceeding level 5 on the standard scale, to imprisonment for a term not exceeding six months, or to both.' Currently, level 5 is up to £5,000. The allegation in the information should not be 'assault and battery', which is bad for duplicity (the legal phrase for saying that two separate offences cannot be contained in one charge), but 'assault and beat' or preferably 'assault by beating', both forms constituting only one offence.

The outcome in *Little* is surprising. It had been thought that only the penalty was prescribed by statute, just as the penalty for murder is laid down by Parliament. The court said that assault and battery had been statutory offences since the enactment of s 47 of the OAPA, but that section simply stated the punishment. When Parliament abolished the common law penalty for murder (hanging) and substituted a different one (life imprisonment), it did not make it a statutory offence. *DPP v Little* does confirm that assault and battery are two separate offences. It was sometimes thought that assault had no separate existence: it was simply an attempted battery. The ruling by the Court of Appeal in *Notman* [1994] Crim LR 518 that assault is one offence committable either through (psychic) assault or (physical) battery is incorrect. The phrase 'common assault' is sometimes used. It means both (psychic) assault *and* battery, though sometimes it means only (psychic) assault.

James J defined assault in *Fagan v MPC* [1969] 1 QB 439 (CA) as 'any act which intentionally or possibly recklessly causes another person to apprehend immediate and unlawful violence'. The mental element now definitely includes recklessness. *Savage* (HL) confirmed this proposition. Robert Goff J used this definition of the *actus reus* in *Collins v Wilcock* [1984] 1 WLR 1172 (DC): 'an act which causes another person to apprehend the infliction of immediate, unlawful force on his person.' Whichever definition is used, the gist of the offence is the creation of fear in another's mind. If there is fear, there can be an assault. Examples include pointing a gun which may be loaded (*St George* (1840) 173 ER 921). As long as there is fear, it does not matter that the gun was in fact unloaded, or as in *Logdon* [1976] Crim LR 121 (DC), the weapon was an imitation firearm. The accused is therefore guilty even though he could not carry out the threat in the way that the victim feared. *Logdon* demonstrates also that the accused is guilty even though he did not intend to execute the threat. Shaking a fist at the victim (*Stephens v Myers* (1830) 172 ER 735) and threatening physical harm (*Mackie* [1973] Crim LR 54) were assaults. If there is no apprehension of immediate harm, there is no assault. Examples would be: where the act is not seen, as when the victim is asleep; where the victim believes that the gun was unloaded (*Lamb* [1967] 2 QB 981 (CA)); where the victim knows by the accused's words that the threat will not take place (*Tuberville v Savage* (1669) 86 ER 684, a civil case); or where the accused could not put his threat into effect for some time: the usual illustrations are shaking a fist while on a non-stop train at a person standing on the platform and doing the same to a person standing on the opposite bank of a fast-flowing and wide river where there is no bridge. Merely looking for a person is not an assault. The victim need fear only a battery, an offence which is committed by an accused who touches the victim and the victim does not consent. The victim need not fear serious injury.

The threat must be one which can be carried out immediately, though 'immediately' is read broadly. See also *Ireland; Burstow* in which Lord Steyn said that the immediacy requirement was satisfied by the accused's saying that, 'I will be at your door in a minute or two'. Therefore, this requirement is satisfied if the victim fears that he may be attacked imminently. Frightening a woman by looking into her bedsit at 11 at night causing her to fear violence was held to be immediate (it was open to the Justices to convict on these facts), despite the fact that the victim was behind a locked door and that she could have escaped in the time it would have taken for the accused to get to her: *Smith v Chief Superintendent, Woking Police Station* (1983) 76 Cr App R 234 (DC). Kerr LJ said that his remarks were limited to a case where the accused was 'immediately adjacent, albeit on the other side of a window'. It might also be doubted whether the accused intended to apply any force, whether immediately or otherwise. Surprisingly, Kerr LJ said that it would not be assault if the accused threatened someone in a locked car. Surely it should be an assault in both fact situations or neither? Possibly the case is explained that there was at that time no crime specifically directed against voyeurs (a specific offence of voyeurism was created by the Sexual Offences Act 2003), and the offence of assault had to be stretched to cover the accused's conduct. In *Lewis* [1970] Crim LR 647 (CA), a case of assault occasioning actual bodily harm, the accused was guilty even though the victim, his wife, was on the other side of a locked door. The *Smith* case also demonstrates that the prosecution need not show exactly what the victim was afraid of. The requirement of immediate fear means that a threat to carry out violence a long time in the future does not amount to an assault, even though fear is present. There is, however, an offence of threatening to kill (OAPA, s 16: see below).

It must be said that the law is unclear as to how immediate the threat must be. The established rule was that the victim had to be put in fear of an immediate attack. Lord Steyn in *Ireland; Burstow* extended the requirement to causing the victim to apprehend that he possibly could be attacked in the immediate future. He spoke of a threat that violence would occur 'within a minute or two' but did not specify the width accorded to the requirement of a threat of imminent harm. The effect is that whether, for example, phone calls amount to assaults depends on the facts. The Court of Appeal in *Constanza* [1997] 2 Cr App R 492, which involved some 800 letters and numerous silent phone calls, spoke of 'fear of violence at some time not excluding the immediate future'. On the facts it is difficult to see that the victim was put in fear of *immediate violence* when she received many silent telephone calls and many letters from the accused. Rather she was put in *immediate fear* of violence, but that is not what the definition demands. It was only the last two letters which made the victim afraid. She was afraid when she received them but she did not fear that she would be immediately attacked. The accused might have been in a country far, far away. This scenario now falls within the Protection from Harassment Act 1997 and the Communications Act 2003. Two offences specifically called stalking came into force towards the end of 2012.

While no case so holds as *ratio*, a threat to set one's dog on the victim suffices. This was assumed in *Dume* (1986) *The Times*, 16 October (CA). It follows that asking one's boyfriend to beat up one's enemy in the latter's presence may constitute an assault.

The threat must be an unlawful one. Therefore, a threat in self-defence, preventing crime, furthering arrest or lawful discipline is not an assault. Consent is dealt with below. It is often said that an assault and a battery can be committed only by an act and that an omission is not sufficient. However, in *Fagan* v *MPC* the court held the accused to be guilty when he inadvertently parked his car on a police officer's foot, realised what he had done, and refused to drive off. His omission was converted into an act by the means stated in Chapter 2. The continuing act of his sitting in the car which rested on the foot, coupled with his *mens rea*, rendered him liable. There was a series of events which were all part of one transaction. Nowadays *Fagan* v *MPC* could also be justified on the principle that the accused created a dangerous situation which he deliberately did not rectify. Since grievous bodily harm can be committed by an omission, it would be strange if assault and battery could not be. It is thought that a deliberate refusal to put a victim's mind at rest when the accused has unwittingly frightened him is an assault.

Ireland; Burstow [1998] AC 147 (HL)

These two cases involving stalkers were heard together. In *Ireland* the accused made many telephone calls to three women. He remained silent when they answered the phone. They suffered psychological harm. He was charged with assault occasioning actual bodily harm. In *Burstow* the accused harassed a woman. As part of his campaign he too made silent phone calls. She suffered severe depression. He was charged with maliciously inflicting grievous bodily harm. Both were convicted and their appeals were dismissed. On further appeal, the Lords dismissed both appeals.

One issue raised in *Ireland* was whether verbally abusive or silent phone calls could constitute assault. *Constanza*, above, which was cited but not referred to by the House of Lords, held that written words could amount to an assault. As long as the victim apprehended fear, it did not matter how he came to apprehend fear. Words, letters and faxes were instanced. Famously in **Meade and Belt** (1823) 168 ER 1006 Holroyd J had said: 'no words or singing are equivalent to an assault'. Lord Steyn ruled to the contrary. 'The proposition that a gesture may amount to an assault, but that words can never suffice, is unrealistic and indefensible. There is no reason why something said should be incapable of causing an apprehension of immediate personal violence, e.g. a man accosting a woman in a dark alley saying "Come with me or I will stab you." I would, therefore, reject the proposition that an assault can never be committed by words.' Indeed, if words could not constitute an assault, there would be no assault if the accused made threats to a blind person. That disposed of the question of whether an assault could be committed by words.

In relation to silence, Lord Steyn stated that silence could constitute an assault, but whether it did so was a question of fact. 'As a matter of law the caller may be guilty of an assault: whether he is or not will depend on the circumstance and in particular on the impact of the caller's potentially menacing call or calls on the victim.' Accordingly, silence *may* constitute an assault but does not necessarily do so. This statement also resolved the issue whether the victim feared immediate personal violence: it was sufficient that she feared the possibility of immediate personal violence. There was no requirement that the victim feared an instantaneous attack. The Lords stressed that they were not ruling on the width of the concept of immediacy. What this case and **Constanza** seem to have done is to make the accused guilty if the victim fears that he may be attacked soon. This is a departure from earlier law which required a threat causing 'immediate' fear. Like **Constanza** the facts of **Ireland; Burstow** now fall within the Protection from Harassment Act 1997.

As stated above, words can negative (that is, render non-criminal) what would otherwise be an assault. In **Tuberville v Savage**, the accused laid his hand on his sword and said: 'If it were not assize time, I would not take such language.' The accused's words showed that he did not intend violence and the victim did not apprehend immediate personal violence. The same principle was applied in **Blake v Barnard** (1840) 173 ER 485. The accused said that he would blow the victim's brains out if he was not quiet. It may be that **Blake v Barnard** is incorrect. The threat was not as it was in **Tuberville** an extraneous condition ('assize time'), but was a conditional restraint on the victim's freedom of behaviour: that is an assault. Restraining the victim from doing what she wants may be an assault because she may apprehend immediate and unlawful personal violence. One suggestion is that **Blake v Barnard** is badly reported and should not be followed in respect of there being no assault when there is a condition. Certainly in **Light** (1857) [1843–60] All ER Rep 934, the accused was seemingly guilty of an assault when he said: 'Were it not for the bloody policeman outside, I would split your head open.' **Light** is inconsistent with **Tuberville v Savage**. An alternative view is to say that the effect of the words is rendered nugatory by the overwhelming threat of violence of the situation. In **Light** the accused was holding a shovel over his wife's head at the time. The problem with the attempted reconciliation is that the accused in **Tuberville v Savage** had his hand on the sword. An alternative approach is to say that in **Light** the words did not negate the assault because the strength of them was such that the victim did fear immediate personal violence but surely the same was true (or not true, as the case may be) in **Tuberville**?

The accused must cause the victim to apprehend immediate and unlawful personal violence. The principles of causation were discussed in Chapter 2.

The *mens rea* in assault is intention or recklessness, as stated by Lord Simon (dissenting) in **DPP v Morgan** [1976] AC 182 (HL), approved by Lord Elwyn-Jones CJ in **DPP v Majewski** [1977] AC 443 (HL). The Lords in **Savage**, above, confirmed that recklessness is of the **Cunningham** variety.

For a review of these concepts, see pp 49–67 (Chapter 2), on causation and pp 107–112 (Chapter 3), on recklessness.

In **Williams** (1983) [1987] 3 All ER 411 (CA), Lord Lane CJ held that 'the mental element necessary to constitute guilt is the intent to apply unlawful force to the victim. We do not believe that the mental element can be substantiated by simply showing an intent to apply force and no more.' It is sometimes said that assault is committed only when the accused has a hostile intention. There is, however, no need for any anger, spite or incivility. What hostility means in this context is that the accused must act without lawful excuse.

Threat to kill

Section 16 of the OAPA as amended creates the offence of threatening to kill without lawful excuse. An illustration is provided by a sentencing case. A threat to kill a foetus does not fall within s 16 because it is not a person in being for the purpose of murder. A threat to kill the foetus when it had been born, it is suggested, does fall within s 16. See **Tait** [1990] QB 290 (CA) where it was said, wrongly it is thought, that the threat to kill the foetus would not constitute this offence. It covers a threat to kill in the future. The threat may be implied as it was in **Solanke** [1970] 1 WLR 1 (CA): 'I do not wish to take her life but . . . I hope my children will be looked after.' The history between the parties may also be taken into account. **Williams** (1986) 84 Cr App R 299 (CA): the accused had repeatedly harassed and been violent to his ex-girlfriend.

Since assault requires an apprehension of immediate violence, a threat to injure in the future is not a criminal offence. Perhaps in the nineteenth century a threat to injure was not something which would be regarded as sufficiently serious to merit criminalisation. A modern view is that the victim of such a threat can seek official protection before the menace is executed. This lacuna in the law will be filled if the draft Criminal Code is enacted (see below). It is certainly anomalous that a threat to destroy or damage property is a crime but a threat to injure is not, and the proposed reform would cover only a threat to cause serious injury: a threat to impose less serious injury at some time in the future would remain non-criminal. At least the change would catch an accused who threatened to kneecap his victim if the latter did not do some act in the future.

The *mens rea* is the intention to cause the victim to apprehend that the threat will be carried out. A lawful excuse would occur when a person threatens to kill the man raping him or her.

The maximum penalty is 10 years' imprisonment, twice the length of assault occasioning actual bodily harm and maliciously inflicting grievous bodily harm or wounding.

Battery

Example

May the following constitute battery?

1 Touching someone's clothes.
2 Shouting 'fire' in a theatre with the result that the theatre-goers rush out and are trampled underfoot as they leave.
3 Silently phoning someone.
4 Not telling a constable that one has needles in one's pockets when specifically asked about having sharp objects there and she pricks her finger on a needle.

> A battery is an intentional or reckless touching of another without consent (or of course another defence).
>
> 1 Yes, skin need not be touched: **Day** (1845) 173 ER 1042 actually involved touching the victim's clothes.
> 2 Yes, a battery may be indirectly inflicted as the facts of **Martin** (1881) 8 QBD 54 (CCR), which resemble our facts, demonstrate.
> 3 No, a silent phone call cannot be a battery because no one is touched: **Ireland; Burstow** [1998] AC 147 (HL).
> 4 Yes, these are the facts of **Santana-Bermudez** [2004] Crim LR 471 (DC), applying **Miller** [1983] 2 AC 161 (HL): creating a dangerous situation and not remedying it. For further details, see Chapter 2.

The old definition of **battery** was that used in *Cole* v *Turner* (1705) 87 ER 907, 'the least touching of someone in anger'. Three more recent definitions are:

(a) 'The actual intended use of unlawful force to another person without his consent' (since then recklessness has been added to the *mens rea*), *per* Jones LJ in *Fagan* v *MPC*, above. The court in *Attorney-General's Reference (No. 6 of 1980)* [1981] 1 QB 715 (CA) added 'or any other lawful excuse' to that definition. 'Excuse' covers exceptions such as properly conducted games, lawful chastisement, reasonable surgery and the like. (It is uncertain what properly conducted games are: what about a wall of death?)

(b) 'The actual infliction of unlawful force on another person': Robert Goff J in *Collins* v *Wilcock*, above. Touching a woman on her shoulder was a battery.

(c) Apparently the most authoritative: 'Any intentional touching without the consent of that person and without lawful excuse. It need not necessarily be hostile or rude or aggressive, as some of the cases seem to indicate', *per* Lord Lane CJ in *Faulkner* v *Talbot* [1981] 1 WLR 1528 at 1536 (DC), which was approved by Lord Ackner in *Court* [1989] AC 28 at 41–42 (HL). Again, the mental element of recklessness should be added. (In fact, as Lord Goff, dissenting, said in *Court*, *Faulkner* v *Talbot* was a case on indecent assault, in which in most cases the sole mental element was intention: did the accused intend to assault in indecent circumstances? Indecent assault has since been abolished but the 'assault' part continues to apply.)

Statute has not defined battery, and cases do not give a single definition.

The requirement of force means that a threat is not a battery. For example, causing psychiatric harm by a threat is not a battery because there is no touching. Using force to pull away from the victim is not a battery because it is not used *on* the victim. Whether the accused did cause unlawful force is governed by the law of causation discussed in Chapter 2.

There is some debate whether hostility is a requirement. For example, in *Brown* [1994] AC 212 (HL) Lords Jauncey and Lowry spoke of hostility being a necessary ingredient. *Faulkner* v *Talbot*, *Collins* v *Wilcock* (a civil case) and Lord Goff in *Re F* [1990] 2 AC 1 (HL, a civil law authority) do not require hostility. Perhaps the reference to hostility is another way of saying that touching is only a battery if it is unlawful. The *dicta* in *Brown* can be interpreted in this way. In that case the victims, masochists, had willingly consented to being sexually tortured by the defendants, sadists. It is difficult to demonstrate hostility on the facts. If the interpretation is correct, where there is consent to the causing of harm but the consent is not for an approved purpose, here sadomasochism, there is hostility, that is, hostility is not a separate requirement. In *Collins* v *Wilcock* the touching was unlawful because a police constable has no power to restrain a person temporarily. Her powers in this regard do not exceed those of an ordinary citizen. The tort of trespass to the person does seem to require hostile contact, but the difference of hostility from unlawfulness is not clear. There is no need for hostility in the offence of indecent assault. In this context 'assault' includes battery. Accordingly, there should be no need for hostility in the crime of battery.

There is no need for an assault. One may batter an unconscious, sleeping or unsuspecting victim. Examples include: touching, throwing a stone which hits someone, tripping up, kicking, spitting on the victim, and throwing beer over the victim (*Savage* (1990) 91 Cr App R 317 (CA), which decision the Lords approved). Force may also be applied by setting a dog on the victim. In other words, the accused need not himself touch the victim. There must, however, be some form of contact. As Lord Steyn said in *Ireland; Burstow*, a silent phone call cannot amount to a battery because no force is applied.

Though the law is not entirely clear, it seems that the violence need not be directly inflicted. An old illustration deriving from civil law is digging a pit into which the victim falls. Another one is putting a bucket of water on top of a door which the victim will push open. The escape cases provide another example: the accused frightens the victim so much that she jumps out the window and is injured by coming into contact with the ground. In *Martin* (1881) 8 QBD 54 (CCR) the accused called 'fire' in a theatre, causing the victims to be crushed against an iron bar into which they dashed. There are problems with this case discussed later, but it is thought, though some commentators disagree, that the accused would still be guilty nowadays. The Court of Appeal in *Spratt* did not hold *DPP* v *K* [1990] 1 WLR 1067 (DC) to be incorrect on the point that the injury was indirectly caused (for the facts see later). The injury, actual bodily harm occasioned by a battery, in *DPP* v *K* was indirectly caused, but the accused was guilty.

The contrary view, that a battery must be directly inflicted, has the support of some commentators. They point out that while injury may be directly or indirectly caused or inflicted within ss 20 and 18 of the OAPA, there is little support in the cases for indirect causing being a battery. It would, however, be strange that a less serious offence could not be committed indirectly when more serious ones could be. If the accused tied a rope between two trees intending to decapitate the next cyclist who rode along a path, it would be absurd if he was guilty of an offence if the victim was killed or injured but not if she merely ran into the rope. The latest authority, *Haystead* v *Chief Constable of Derbyshire* [2000] 3 All ER 890 (DC), does not resolve the issue. The accused punched the complainant who dropped the child she was holding. It was held that he was guilty of battery on the child. The Divisional Court said that, even if a battery could be committed only by the direct application of force, the accused had had direct physical contact with the complainant which caused her to drop the child, which was the direct and immediate result of his punching her. *Obiter* it was suggested that force could be indirectly inflicted. The Court said: 'there is no difference in logic or good sense between the facts of this case and one where the defendant might have used a weapon to fell the child to the floor.'

The force need not be applied on the victim's body: it can be on the clothes he is wearing: *Day* (1845) 173 ER 1042 and *Thomas* (1985) 81 Cr App R 331 (CA) *obiter*. There is from these cases no requirement that the victim feels that he is being touched. It was suggested in *Thomas*, which involved touching the hem of the victim's skirt, that cutting the victim's clothes would be a battery even though he did not feel the snip. In *Fagan* v

MPC (see above and Chapter 2), it was held to be a battery when the accused inadvertently applied force and wrongfully decided not to stop using it. The effect is that an accused can be found guilty of battery if the *Miller* [1983] 2 AC 161 (HL) principle applies. See the next paragraph for further details.

If there is no violence, there is no battery. In *Walkden* (1845) 1 Cox CC 282, the accused put 'Spanish fly', an aphrodisiac, into the beer at a wedding reception. Since no force was applied, there was no battery. (The offence would be one of administering a noxious thing with intent to injure or annoy contrary to s 24 of the OAPA.) Similarly, putting out poison for a person to take is not a battery, again because no force is applied.

There was doubt whether an omission sufficed, even when there was a duty to act. In *Fagan* v *MPC*, above, the court said that a defendant was guilty when the whole conduct was considered, but he would not have been guilty if he had merely omitted to act. For example, if I fail to remove my body from the path of a blind person, I do not occasion a battery when she bumps into me. However, the law has developed since 1968. The facts of *DPP* v *K*, however, show that a battery can be committed by an omission, a failure to remove sulphuric acid from a hand dryer. The situation constituted a knowing failure to correct a dangerous situation which the accused has created, the area of law governed by *Miller* [1983] 2 AC 161 (HL). The Court of Appeal in *Spratt* did not criticise this part of *DPP* v *K* and both *Miller* and *DPP* v *K* were applied in *DPP* v *Santana-Bermudez* [2004] Crim LR 471 (DC) (see Chapter 2). The court said that if the accused creates a danger which exposes another to a reasonably foreseeable risk of injury and does cause actual bodily harm, there is an assault (i.e. battery) occasioning actual bodily harm. The law now is that a battery can be committed by omission but it still remains the law that a 'mere' omission does not suffice. It would certainly be strange that an accused could be convicted of murder if the victim died but not of battery if she lived. The issue is whether all the ways in which an accused can be found guilty by omission as outlined in Chapter 2 apply, or whether only *Miller* does. The cases have not discussed this matter but it is suggested that the law is that a defendant is guilty only when *Miller* applies and not otherwise.

See p 76 (Chapter 2) for a discussion of the *Miller* principle as applied in *DPP* v *Santana-Bermudez*.

Consent is a defence to battery. It may be implied from the circumstances. For example, in a crowd one impliedly consents to some jostling. Whether the touching went beyond what is acceptable is a question of fact. One can tap a person to gain attention without being charged with battery: *Rawlings* v *Till* (1837) 150 ER 1042. A police officer who taps a suspect on the shoulder does not commit battery: *Donnelly* v *Jackman* [1970] 1 WLR 562 (DC). However, it was said in *Rawlings* v *Till* that physical restraint was a battery. Accordingly, if the accused takes hold of the victim's arm to restrain him there is a battery: *Collins* v *Wilcock*, above. It is not entirely clear whether touching is a battery, where the victim has indicated that he does not wish to be touched. There are other exceptions besides consent: lawful chastisement of a child, force used to effect an arrest, reasonable force in self-defence or to prevent crime.

The *mens rea* is intention to apply unlawful force or recklessness as to unlawful force: *Venna* [1976] QB 421 (CA). The House of Lords in *Savage* adopted the *Cunningham* approach to the definition of recklessness.

One question involving *mens rea* is this. The accused intends to commit a battery on the victim but does not get as far as touching her; instead she is made afraid and the accused commits the *actus reus* of assault. Can the *mens rea* of battery be added to create an offence? It is thought not because assault and battery are two separate crimes (*DPP* v *Little*, above) and one cannot aggregate one crime's *actus reus* with another's *mens rea* to create one offence.

Consent

Example

Has the accused caused any crime when while boxing he knocks his victim out or he, a sadist, inflicts harm on a masochist victim?

These two scenarios may be taken at the same time. The general rule is that an alleged victim may consent to any non-fatal offence below the level of assault occasioning actual bodily harm (s 47 of the OAPA). However, there are exceptions, such as ear piercing, religious flagellation and horseplay, and one of these is 'manly sports' such as boxing. That is so despite the fact that the aim of boxing is to achieve a knock-out, which is grievous bodily harm within the 1861 statute, and may incidentally cause bleeding, a wound within the 1861 Act. There is also the possibility of death, and no one can consent to being killed, not even to a mercy killing, never mind a duel or letting oneself be eaten, as occurred recently in Germany.

Sado-masochism does not constitute an exception. Students may wish to consider why whipping for religious purposes is acceptable but not whipping for sexual reasons. The landmark authority is **Brown** [1994] AC 212 (HL), a case readers may have come across before. This is the classic case on the rule and the attempt to make sexual practices behind closed doors lawful as one of the exceptions to that rule. Readers may wish to make a comparison between boxing, where medical assistance may be required, and the sado-masochism in **Brown**, where it was not.

The law does not prohibit all force on the person, but only the unlawful use of force. For example, parents may punish their children moderately. Surgeons may perform operations on their patients. Consent is often implied and certainly it need not always be expressly given. For example, in **H v CPS** [2010] EWHC 1374 (Admin) the accused argued that the victim of an attack implicitly consented to being violently assaulted because he was a teacher in a special school. The Divisional Court had no difficulty rejecting that contention. Teachers could not reasonably be expected to put up with such behaviour, and the facts did not fall within any of the exceptions discussed below.

The law is based on reasonableness, yet it may well not reflect public opinion. Swift J in **Donovan** [1934] 2 KB 498 (CCA) said that with some exceptions: 'It is an unlawful act to beat another person with such a degree of force that the infliction of bodily harm is a probable consequence and when such an act is proved, **consent** is immaterial.' The victim suffered bruising, which constitutes actual bodily harm. The basic rule was stated by Lord Lane CJ in **Attorney-General's Reference (No. 6 of 1980)** [1981] QB 715 (CA), where the victim suffered actual bodily harm in the form of a bloody nose: the accused is guilty of a crime even though the victim has consented 'if actual bodily harm is intended and/or caused'. This principle was approved by the Lords in the landmark case of **Brown** [1994] AC 212. It should be noted that Lord Lane CJ's proposition covered a situation where the accused does *not* intend and is *not* reckless as to occasioning actual bodily harm. It is sufficient that such harm occurs. The use of 'and/or' is a strange one. If correct, it means that an accused will not be able to rely on the victim's consent if he intends actual bodily harm but such injury does not occur. In principle, consent is a defence to assault and battery, as indeed the Lords held in **Brown** and, therefore, if no actual bodily harm is occasioned, the accused should not be guilty of assault occasioning actual bodily harm.

Intending an offence is not committing an offence. A second criticism of 'and/or' looks at the words from the accused's *mens rea*. If actual bodily harm is occasioned, the phrase means that he is guilty even though he does not foresee an assault or a battery; in other words, he does not have the *mens rea* of the crime. This cannot be right!

To this rule there are exceptions. Those exceptions are difficult to state. Boxing is permissible, even though the aim is to knock someone out, while spanking, at issue in **Donovan**, is unlawful. Contrary to what has been suggested, the presence of a referee hardly explains the distinction.

The relevance of consent is best dealt with by answering three questions: (a) What is the meaning of full or true consent? (b) Are there limitations on the classes of person who may give consent? (c) Are there any forms of behaviour to which the law provides that consent cannot be given? If the alleged consent falls foul of any of these principles, a crime is committed. Therefore, for example, medical treatment is illegal if a mentally capable adult refuses it.

Whether there is consent or not is a question of fact, as is illustrated by **DPP v Shabbir** [2009] 1 All ER (D) 221. CCTV footage showed 'a prolonged and vicious attack' with 'an appalling level and degree of violence'. The Divisional Court held that lack of consent to the assault could be inferred from the evidence.

What is the meaning of true or full consent?

Consent may be express, but is usually implied. As we have seen in battery, consent may arise through custom. Consent to being tapped on the shoulder in the street, consent to jostling in a rugby match (rugby is the most dangerous sport played in the UK: a participant is four times more likely to be injured in rugby than in Association Football) or on the football terraces, are implied. William Hardy was tried at the Old Bailey in 1994 for the manslaughter of an opponent in a rugby union match. The victim did not consent to the accused's alleged punching him in an off-the-ball incident. Canadian courts have been building up a jurisprudence based on a division between unintentional, instinctive or incidental to the game and other assaults. The former are permitted. There is also something of a line between professionals and amateurs. The former are taken to consent to more than the latter. In **Collins v Wilcock**, above, the court preferred to base such instances as those occurring in sport, on 'a general exception embracing all physical contact which is generally acceptable in the ordinary conduct of daily life', not on implied consent. The same judge when he became Lord Goff said in the civil case of **Re F**, above, that the implied consent approach led to difficulties when the 'victim' was young or mentally disordered. In all cases consent goes up to a certain point only. For example, if one consents to sexual intercourse, one does not consent to being strangled: **Sharmpal Singh** [1962] AC 188 (PC). Submission is not consent, nor is consent obtained when the victim is drugged or drunk.

The old law was that only where there was deception as to the nature of the act or as to the identity of the accused was there consent. Accordingly, in **Clarence** (1888) 22 QBD 23 (CCR), a woman's agreement to sexual intercourse with her husband meant that, surprising as it is to modern ears, he was not guilty of inflicting grievous bodily harm when he infected her with VD. She had consented to intercourse with him and would not have done so had she known of the disease, yet her consent was not vitiated by his omission to tell her of his bodily condition. (It may be inquired whether, if the wife knew of the VD, the law permitted the husband to infect her with it on the ground that she consented to his occasioning actual bodily harm to her. It is thought that the husband would be guilty under s 47 and consent would not be a defence, the argument being that there is no social benefit in the spread of VD.) The House of Lords discussed *Clarence* in *Ireland; Burstow*, above. Lord Steyn said that since that case was not about psychiatric injury, it was not useful in respect of s 20 of the OAPA. Since the facts the House of Lords was dealing with concerned psychiatric harm, anything said about inflicting physical harm was *obiter*. However, the Lords did hold that s 20 can be committed when no physical violence is applied directly or indirectly to the body of the victim. That is what occurred in *Clarence*. Accordingly, the Law Lords should not just have distinguished *Clarence*, but overruled it. Neither a wife nor anyone else can consent to the reckless infliction of serious harm. This was the strong view of the Court of Appeal in *Dica* [2004] QB 1257. The court held that where the victim is unaware of the fact that the accused is infected with a disease, here HIV/AIDS, and the latter had unprotected sexual intercourse with the former, the victim did not impliedly consent to the risk of being infected. If the victim was aware of the accused's condition, then the consent to sexual intercourse would be consent to the risk of infection and therefore a defence to s 20. *Dica* was explained in *Konzani* [2005] 2 Cr App R 198 (CA). Consent will only be effective if the victim gives informed consent. It is not informed consent if the victim does not know that the accused has the disease. Even where the victim knows that the accused is HIV positive, and thereby consents to the risk of being infected, the latter is guilty of GBH with intent to commit GBH contrary to s 18 of the OAPA.

There was a second appeal in *Dica* [2005] All ER (D) 405 (July) after a retrial. The Court of Appeal dismissed the appeal and refused leave to appeal but did certify a point of law of general public importance: 'in what circumstances, if any, might a defendant who knows or believes that he is infected with a serious sexually transmitted infection and recklessly transmits it to another through consensual sexual activity be convicted of inflicting grievous bodily harm, contrary to s 20 of the Offences against the Person Act 1861?' It would have been useful for the highest court to have resolved the issue.

Another authority is *Richardson* [1998] 2 Cr App R 200 (CA). Patients did not know that the accused, a dentist, had been suspended from her duties. The patients knew her identity and were mistaken only as to her attributes, whether she was disqualified or not. Accordingly, their consent to dental treatment was valid. Fraud as to identity did not include a mistake as to attributes or qualifications. If the accused was not afforded the defence, she would have been guilty of assault occasioning actual bodily harm. The court, however, said that the dental treatment was reasonable. If so, where was the harm? Reasonable treatment, medical or dental, is not harm. *Richardson* is a doubtful decision. Surely, however, consent to treatment by a dentist does not cover consent to treatment by a disqualified dentist. Similar to *Richardson* is *Bolduc and Bird* (1967) 63 DLR (2nd) 82, a decision of the Supreme Court of Canada. A doctor brought a friend to a vaginal examination. It was held that there was no indecent assault. The patient was mistaken as to the identity of the friend, who was introduced as a trainee doctor, but not as to the nature of the examination. The accused was not guilty. The case of *Harms* [1944] 2 DLR 61 was distinguished. In that case the accused falsely represented sexual intercourse as a medical examination. He was guilty. There are English authorities similar to *Harms*. The dissent in *Bolduc and Bird* repays study: if consent is to a doctor and student, it is not to a doctor and friend. The case was distinguished by the majority of the Court of Appeal in *Maurantonio* (1968) 65 DLR (2nd) 674 on the grounds that one must take into account the circumstances which give meaning to the physical acts (such as the fact that the accused was not a doctor when he examined the victim). For more on consent in the context of rape, see Chapter 14.

Are there limitations on the classes of persons who can give consent?

Persons who do not understand the nature of the act cannot give consent. An example is the case of **Burrell v Harmer** [1967] Crim LR 169 (DC): boys of 12 and 13 could not consent to being tattooed. The Tattooing of Minors Act 1969 prohibits the tattooing of persons under 18. Mentally abnormal people cannot consent. Boys and girls cannot consent to indecent (now sexual) assault, no matter how willing they are: **McCormack** [1969] 2 QB 442. One effect of this area of law is that an accused is guilty even though he believed that the victim had consented to the activity. Another is that, although a boy cannot consent to his genitals being touched, he can consent to being touched on the arms and legs in order to pose for pornographic photographs. A person under 16 cannot consent to surgery, but the parent can on his behalf.

Are there any forms of behaviour to which the law provides that consent is no defence?

The law does not allow even an adult to do with his body as he wishes. It was said in **McShane** (1977) 66 Cr App R 97 (CA) that no consent can render a dangerous act innocent, but that statement is too broad. A person can consent to dangerous activities such as sport and surgery. There are some offences to which no matter how full the consent is, there is no defence.

(a) *Murder and serious non-fatal offences including sexual practices resulting in serious harm* (except for organised games, chastisement, etc.): a person cannot consent to being killed, nor can one consent to grievous bodily harm, such as when one person was crucified – though not unto death – by the defendants driving six-inch nails through his palms. The House of Lords in **Brown** [1994] AC 212 held that consent was no defence to *sado-masochists* charged under ss 20 and 47 of the OAPA. The activities of the defendants, who were male homosexuals, included nailing a penis to a board and taping lighted matches to nipples. Any instruments were sterilised and wounds were dressed. The acts were videotaped and the videos were circulated. There were no permanent injuries, medical treatment was not needed, no one had complained of harm and the acts had been committed in private. There is some dispute as to whether the participants were truly consenting. The 'victims' were at times drugged, and the voyeurs watching the performances egged on the parties. It is not clear whether the 'victims' could freely refuse to engage in the activities.

Their Lordships relied both on precedent and policy. The majority held that consent was not a defence to deeds which caused harm except in recognised circumstances such as boxing. Public health was at stake. Lord Jauncey thought that it was not in the public interest that a defence should be allowed to ss 20 and 47. Young men were likely to be corrupted. He said: 'It would appear to be good luck rather than good judgment which has prevented serious injury from occurring. Wounds can easily become septic if not properly treated, the free flow of blood from a person who is HIV positive or who has AIDS can infect another and an inflictor who is carried away by sexual excitement or by drink and drugs could very easily inflict pain and injury beyond the level to which the receiver had consented . . . when considering the public interest potential for harm is just as relevant as actual harm.' Lord Lowry refused to permit sado-masochism as a defence. Violence could get out of hand. Lord Templeman said that no defence should be afforded to persons who indulged in sado-masochism, which bred and glorified cruelty. Degradation was not a good reason to excuse such behaviour. Society (which partly comprises male homosexuals) was entitled to protection against such conduct. Violence in sex was violence. The sexual preferences of the participants did not affect that equation. The minority stressed that sexual behaviour was a sphere of private life in which the state should not intervene without good cause. Consent was presumed to be valid unless there was a good reason to the contrary. Paternalism was to be rejected in favour of liberty. People should be able to determine the satisfaction of their sexual needs. Before the criminal law intervened harm had to exist. There was no danger to life or limb. Public health was not affected. Young men were not corrupted. Reform was for Parliament.

The starting-points of the majority and minority are so different that compromise is impossible. The men do not seem to have tried to recruit outsiders, but what they did was violent and it is possible that not all masochists consented with full knowledge of everything which was done to them. Vulnerable persons require protection whether or not they think they do. The alternative view is to say that private sexual behaviour among consenting adults is lawful, provided that it does not cause serious injury. *Brown* penalises people for expressing their sexuality in a certain way, sado-masochism, and unless the injuries are trifling, all such conduct is illegal. The outcome of *Brown* is that sado-masochists who intend to cause more than actual bodily harm must not give way to their urges; differently put, they must be celibate. Boxing can likewise be seen as a game of skill or as conduct, the aim of which is to cause serious harm. Yet boxing, a 'manly diversion', is lawful. The European Court of Human Rights ruled that on the facts of *Brown* the state was pursuing a lawful aim, the protection of health and morals, and that the law was necessary in a democratic society within Article 8 of the European Convention on Human Rights: *Laskey* (1997) 24 EHRR 39 (the name is that of one of the accused in *Brown*). The Court stated that: 'The State is unquestionably entitled to . . . seek to regulate, through the operation of the criminal law, activities which involve the infliction of physical harm. This is so whether the activities in question occur in the course of sexual conduct or otherwise.'

A final comment on *Brown* is this. Under present law if the House of Lords had accepted that consent was a defence to non-serious injury, there is a problem with s 20. That section covers both grievous bodily harm and wounding. Wounding may or may not be serious injury, depending on the facts. If a person could consent to woundings which were not serious, then the line between offences to which consent is a defence and the others would be drawn in the middle of s 20! This result demonstrates the need for revision of s 20 to take out non-serious woundings, for as it stands it covers both serious and non-serious injuries.

In *Wilson* [1997] QB 47, which was approved in *Dica*, above, the Court of Appeal held that a person could consent to the *branding* of her husband's initials onto her buttocks. The reasoning was that the rule that there could be no consent to serious offences was subject to exceptions; one of those exceptions and one which had been recognised in *Brown* was tattooing; what the accused had done was no more dangerous than tattooing, therefore he was not guilty. The court considered what he had done equivalent to nose and tongue piercing, and was totally dissimilar from the activities in *Brown*. There was no reason of public policy to forbid this type of behaviour. The court considered that public policy did not demand that the accused's conduct should be criminalised. *Donovan*, above, was also distinguished. It is hard to distinguish the two cases; indeed, branding would appear to be worse than caning, yet the branding was lawful, the caning unlawful. If the distinction resides in the purpose of the activity, adornment of the body and sexual gratification, then contrary to the normal pronouncement of the courts, motive is an element in criminal law in this respect. The accused did not have an aggressive intent – but neither did the defendants in *Brown* – and it was his wife who instigated the branding. The court could just as easily have held that the consent was invalid because there was no good reason for what the husband did. Instead it seems that the court preferred to adopt what the minority had said in *Brown*. The court also based its decision on the privacy between married partners ('[c]onsensual activity between husband and wife, in the privacy of the matrimonial home, is not . . . normally a proper matter for criminal investigation, let alone criminal prosecution' (*per* Russell LJ)), but it is strange in modern times that the law is limited to such relationships. In the case next discussed, *Emmett*, the court rejected this analysis. Moreover, it is strange too that the victim required medical treatment in *Wilson* but the accused was acquitted, whereas the victims in *Brown* did not require treatment but the defendants were convicted. The defendants in *Brown* intended to inflict pain, whereas the accused in *Wilson* did not but the court did not use this reason to distinguish the cases.

One of the latest cases on consent to *sexual practices* is *Emmett*, unreported, 18 June 1999, (CA) which was approved in *Dica* on the basis that what happened transgressed the boundary laid down in *Wilson*. The male accused semi-asphyxiated and poured lighter fuel onto the breast of his female partner, whom he later married. The Court of Appeal held that the accused did not have the defence of consent to a charge of assault occasioning actual bodily harm. *Brown* was applied, although it should be added that in *Brown* the violence was intended (the same is true of *Wilson*) whereas it was not in *Emmett*. There was no difference between homosexual and heterosexual sado-masochism. *Wilson* was distinguished on the grounds that the injury, actual or potential, was less serious in that case than in *Emmett*. Where the line was to be drawn was not always easy to see but there was no doubt in *Emmett* that what the accused did went beyond the boundary of reasonable behaviour. Partial asphyxiation can lead to brain damage and even death; the burn was serious and painful and it became infected. *Brown* was applied as to the effect of the European Convention on Human Rights. Article 8 does not apply where the accused has gone beyond the permitted limit of consent. The court in *Emmett* said that *Wilson* and *Brown* were to be distinguished on the ground that in *Wilson* the facts were analogous to the recognised exception of tattooing whereas *Brown* did not fall within any exception and neither did *Emmett* itself.

The latest major case on consent in *sport* is *Barnes* [2005] 1 WLR 910 (CA). In a football match the accused made a late and high tackle on the victim, who was seriously injured. The tackler was found guilty under s 20. Lord Woolf CJ said that a prosecution should be brought only when the accused's conduct was intentional or was so reckless that it went beyond what the victim could reasonably have consented to. Only in those circumstances could injuries be accounted as so grave as to constitute crimes. If the accused's behaviour was within the explicit or implicit rules of the game being played, that was a strong indication that the injury was not to be characterised as criminal. Whether the injury exceeded the threshold for being a crime depended on all the factors including whether the injury occurred during play or 'off the ball', the extent of the risk of injury, the type of sport, the level at which it was being played (such as amateur, as in *Barnes* itself, or professional) and (perhaps surprisingly) the accused's state of mind. Therefore, a foul can be consented to because it can be expected to occur in a football match; however, a bad foul may be conduct which one could not reasonably expect to occur on a soccer pitch. The court applied *Brown* when it held that sports were on public policy grounds an exception to the rule that no one could consent to the actual or more serious bodily harm.

A *prize-fight* is at least a battery: *Coney* (1882) 8 QBD 534 (CCR). It is not an activity to which one can consent (even though at times more serious injuries are caused by boxing under the Queensberry Rules). One view of *Coney* is that it decided that prize-fighting was illegal and no one can consent to illegal acts. An alternative view is that *Coney* held that consent is no defence to acts which are intended or likely to cause injury, unless there was a good reason for them. The latter approach has been adopted in recent cases including *Brown*.

In *Leach* (1969) *The Times*, 13 January, a man had himself crucified (though not to death). He could not consent to the wounds. In *Donovan* a girl could not consent to the infliction of six or seven weals on her bottom. It may be that the case is out of line with modern mores. Certainly the judges adopted a paternalistic attitude towards the victim, a 17-year-old girl. It might be thought that she understood what she was doing, and there was no permanent harm (cf. boxing where there may be). If *Donovan* is correct a bite during love-making would appear to be actual bodily harm. In *Boyea* [1992] Crim LR 574 the Court of Appeal stated, however, that the change in social attitudes since *Donovan* should be taken into account in determining whether or not injury during sexual activity was so trifling or transient that the victim could consent to it. The accused's twisting his hand in his victim's vagina went beyond behaviour to which she could consent. One modern view of *Donovan* is that the law was correctly stated but wrongly applied. Consent is a defence to battery, but not to assault occasioning actual bodily harm, yet the accused was convicted of common assault as well as indecent assault.

In *Jones* (1986) 83 Cr App R 375, the Court of Appeal held that victims, even ones trying to run away, could consent to *horseplay* including throwing them nine or ten feet into the air, which resulted in a ruptured spleen and a broken arm, though the position would be different if the accused intended to cause harm. It may be wondered whether the risk of harm outweighed the public policy behind horseplay – boys will be boys. The harm was more serious than in *Donovan*, yet the accused was not guilty. Moreover, did the boys in *Jones* truly consent to such rough play? *Jones* looks like a case on bullying. Whether *Jones* is correct on its facts or not, this exception is well established and would cover, for example, paintballing.

A summary of the law on consent to sexual practices can be stated thus:

(i)   one cannot consent to the intentional infliction of serious harm: *Brown*;

(ii) one can consent to being branded on the buttocks: *Wilson*;

(iii) however, *Emmett* shows that *Wilson* is restricted to activities in the nature of tattooing;

(iv) *Dica* holds that one can consent to the reckless infecting of oneself provided one knows of the risk but one cannot consent if one does not know the nature of the risk.

These propositions are subject to caveats.

(b) It used to be thought that *sterilisation* (perhaps only of a man) for a non-therapeutic reason without just cause was unlawful as being contrary to the public interest. Denning LJ said so in the civil case of *Bravery v Bravery* [1954] 3 All ER 59 (CA). The two Lord Justices with him dissociated themselves from his remarks. This possible restraint seems to have disappeared. In **Dica** [2004] QB 1257 the Court of Appeal said *obiter* that Denning LJ's view was outdated. Certainly one can consent to wounds in the course of surgery, at least it is thought to be so if there is a sound benefit such as sex change. It is thought that both non-therapeutic (such as cosmetic surgery and sex changes) and therapeutic operations provide such a social benefit because of the psychological benefit. In this sense there is, it might be said, no harm and therefore no grievous or actual bodily harm. Presumably maiming oneself to avoid conscription in wartime remains a crime, as does an operation to change facial features to evade arrest. Ritual mutilation is a difficult issue. It is suggested that it is unlawful in England despite its legality in the 'victim's' country of origin: cf. the Prohibition of Female Circumcision Act 1985 and the Female Genital Mutilation Act 2003. Section 1(5) of the latter statute provides that custom or ritual does not give rise to a defence. It is suggested that flagellation for religious purposes may be consented to, whereas flagellation for sexual purposes may not. It is strange that the law may depend on the nature of the defendant's motive.

(c) *Incest,* which is now called sexual activity with a child family member and sex with an adult relative.

(d) *Administration of drugs* except for medical purposes: **Cato** [1976] 1 WLR 110 (CA).

Consent and the law in the twenty-first century

The law on the issue of consent continues to change because it is based on public policy. In **Boyea**, above, the Court of Appeal said that more vigour was permissible nowadays than in the time of **Donovan**, and in **Wilson** it was stated that: 'the law should develop upon a case by case basis rather than upon general propositions to which, in the changing times in which we live, exceptions may arise from time to time not expressly covered by authority.' If so, it is difficult to predict outcomes and uncertainty in law is not conducive to people knowing in advance whether what they are doing is illegal or not. For example, is **Wilson** itself a decision on body adornment (like tattooing) or is it an exception to **Brown** in the area of consensual sex? Is branding an exception like boxing or is **Wilson** part of a movement outflanking **Brown** by restricting it to its own facts? Would the law be different if the 'victim' was a homosexual? The court stated that public interest did not require what the husband did to be criminalised. On the other hand, there are indications that that *male circumcision* may become illegal in time despite Lord Templeman's saying in **Brown** that it was lawful. In July 2012 a district court in Cologne, Germany, ruled that circumcision of a four year old Muslim boy was illegal. There is much recent academic debate, some centring on male circumcision's usefulness as a preventive measure against AIDS, and it is becoming harder to justify the excision of perfectly good human tissue. There are of course contrary religious arguments put forward by Jewish and Muslim scholars. The Jewish one is that circumcision is the expression of the Covenant between God and Jews.

The Court of Appeal in **Attorney-General's Reference (No. 6 of 1980)**, above, said: 'It is not in the public interest that people should try to cause or should cause each other actual bodily harm for no good reason. Minor struggles are another matter. So . . . it is immaterial whether the act occurs in private or in public.' The question is not just whether the victim consented but also whether there was nothing contrary to the public interest in what the accused did. The phrase 'no good reason' is vague and unhelpful to citizens and advisers. Reasonable people may differ as to whether one type of behaviour, such as smacking a child or tattooing, is good or not. In *Brown* the majority apparently started from the proposition that all harm was criminal unless there was a good reason, whereas the minority proceeded from the basis that harm to which the victim consented was lawful unless there was a good reason for punishing the accused. It would be interesting to see how the same Lords of Appeal would approach boxing. If rough horseplay is permitted where true consent does not exist, why is not wounding where there is true consent? The court listed activities where consent was a defence, especially properly conducted sports, lawful chastisement (though how punishment can truly be said to be consented to is not explained), dangerous exhibitions (though why does public policy allow them? Is titillation a good reason?) and surgery. The court in *Jones* added *horseplay*. After *DPP v Smith* [2006] 1 WLR 1571 (Administrative Court), hairdressing must be added to the list.

In *Aitken* [1992] 1 WLR 1006 the Court of Appeal extended horseplay between boys to setting light to white spirit poured over a colleague by RAF officers, causing severe burns – what a jolly jape! The acts were dangerous and the victim did not consent to the burns. Nevertheless, the court held that the victim did consent to this very rough horseplay. If such horseplay is acceptable, why is not sado-masochism? Moreover, these horseplay cases look like ones on bullying. *Aitken* was followed by the Court of Appeal in *Richardson* [1999] 1 Cr App R 392. The defendants and their victim were students who had been drinking. The former dropped the latter over a balcony. He suffered serious injuries. The court held that the defendants' drunken belief that the victim was consenting to the risk of harm provided them with a defence, a decision at odds with the usual rules on drunken mistakes. An authority which rejected consent as a defence is *H v CPS* [2010] EWHC 1374 (Admin) where the court held that a teacher in a special school did not impliedly consent to the use of violence against them by pupils, including those with behavioural difficulties.

A major authority is *Dica* [2004] QB 1257 (CA). It was held that women who knew that the accused was suffering from HIV/AIDS could validly consent to the risk of infection and therefore to the risk of GBH or death. (Similarly, they could consent to the risk of getting pregnant.) However, if the accused had concealed his infectious condition, the women had not consented. It would have been different if the accused had deliberately spread infection: he would have been guilty under s 18 of the OAPA. The same applies to violence above actual bodily harm. The court in *Attorney-General's Reference (No. 6 of 1980)*, above, did not lay down a closed list: the public interest was the governing consideration. The House of Lords in *Brown* also thought that these exceptions depended on public policy and policy was a matter for Parliament, not for the courts. The open nature of the lists permits judges to control the infliction of harm for what they see as improper purposes. Yet the victims in *Jones* did not consent to their injuries and it is hard to believe that bullying serves a socially useful function, whereas the men in *Brown* allegedly did consent fully to the injuries, and the boys in *Jones* were taken to have consented to grievous bodily harm, whereas the men had no defence to the legal charge of actual bodily harm. It may be added that the victim in *Aitken* would not have been permitted by the law to consent to having others pour white spirit over his body and set it alight. Moreover, dangerous exhibitions such as bungee-jumping are permitted, but not dangerous sexual practices: boxing is permitted, but not fights with fists. The law is in a mess. Why can one consent to rough horseplay but not masochism?

The position where the accused thinks the victim is consenting but in fact there is no consent was discussed in *Jones*, above, and the Court of Appeal held that the accused had a defence. It did not matter whether the accused's belief was formed unreasonably. As we have seen, the same surprisingly applies even though the accused was drunk: *Richardson*, above, an authority which, it is suggested, is wrong.

It is uncertain whether consent is no defence when the injury is *intentionally* caused or whether it is not also a defence when the harm is caused, but not intentionally. *Dicta* in *Brown* and *Attorney-General's Reference (No. 6 of 1980)* suggest the latter. *Dica* supports the former interpretation: consent is irrelevant where the actual bodily harm was both intended *and* caused.

The burden of proof of lack of consent lies on the prosecution: *Donovan, Attorney-General's Reference (No. 6 of 1980)*. A mistaken belief in consent is a defence, whether or not the belief was reasonably held: *Jones*, applying *Kimber* (on the then existing crime of indecent assault) and *Williams*, both above. See also under mistake.

If the accused lacked the *mens rea* for the offence, he is not guilty even though the victim has consented in fact to behaviour she could not in law consent to. In *Slingsby* [1995] Crim LR 570 (Crown Court) the accused was not guilty of constructive manslaughter because he gave no thought to any risk of injury when he penetrated the victim's anus and vagina with his hand and his ring cut her. He had no *mens rea* for the offence of wounding on which the charge was based. Therefore, he was not guilty of manslaughter. The issue of consent was irrelevant. This decision seems irreconcilable with the *dicta* noted two paragraphs above about harm caused unintentionally.

Reform of consent and other defences to assault and battery

In *Richardson* [1998] 2 Cr App R 200, referred to above, the Court of Appeal said: 'For the best part of a century the common law concept of consent in criminal law has been certain and clearly delineated. It is not for this Court to unwrite the law which has been settled for so long. This is an area in which it is to be hoped that the proposals of the Law Commission will be given an early opportunity for implementation.' Reform proposals from the Law Commission are contained in its Consultation Papers No. 134, *Consent and Offences Against the Person*, 1994, and No. 139, *Consent in the Criminal Law*, 1995. These Papers are the outcome of comments on the Consultation Paper which led to *Legislating the Criminal Code: Offences Against the Person and General Principles*, Law Com. No. 218, 1993, and of the House of Lords decision in *Brown*. The Law Commission had previously thought that defences to non-fatal offences could be left to common law development. These defences include surgery, dangerous exhibitions, properly conducted games and so on.

In Law Com. No. 218 the Law Commission put into cl 6(1) of the Criminal Law Bill its thinking that consent should be a defence to assault, when it consists of intentionally or recklessly applying force to or causing an impact on the body of another, but not to assault where the act is intended or likely to cause injury. This distinction encapsulates *Brown*.

In the first of the Papers the Law Commission also considered that a line should be drawn between offences to which the 'victim', whether a willing participant or not, may consent and those to which he may not and that the line should be drawn between acts which are not intended or likely to cause injury ('actual bodily harm' in current terminology) and those which are. If the drawing of the line at this place is not supported, the Law Commission recommended drawing it between injury and serious injury, with the provisos: (a) the defence would not be available when the accused intended to cause serious injury; (b) it would be available if the victim had consented to serious injury but the accused had inflicted only non-serious harm; but (c) it would not be available if the accused knows that the victim is consenting to serious injury.

In the 1994 Paper, the Law Commission proposed that as at present 'consent' should be given its ordinary-language meaning but that, unlike current law, fraud as to any part of the deed (cf. the current law of rape) should be ineffective (with the effect that *Bolduc and Bird*, above, would be decided differently), as should consent obtained by force, threat of force, other threats (such as to demote the victim) and the exercise of authority (perhaps where a police constable tells his victim that he is entitled by reason of his office to punch the victim's face). Consent would not be available where the victim made a mistake and the accused knew of the error. The Law Commission suggested that young persons should be able to consent provided both that they did consent and they had 'sufficient understanding and intelligence to be capable of giving consent': for instance, a child might be able to decide to have her ears pierced but not to be tattooed because she may understand the significance of the former but not of the latter. The different attitude of the Law Commission to some of these recommendations is noted below in the discussion of the 1995 Paper.

Besides consent the Commission looked also at matters which are often dealt with alongside consent. It proposed that if the rule is retained that consent is not a defence to acts intended or likely to cause injury, there should be exceptions only for ritual (male) circumcision, ear piercing (perhaps body piercing is meant, though there is no discussion of nose and nipple piercing, for example) and tattooing. Tribal scarring is not mentioned. Comment was invited about religious flagellation (though only the accused's motive in *Donovan* distinguishes his guilt from non-liability for religiously motivated beatings) and dangerous exhibitions, such as shooting a cigarette out of a victim's mouth and throwing knives around her body. After all, there is a risk of death in the William Tell scenario. The Commission noted that the current law on sport was unclear. With regard to properly organised sports and games except boxing and martial arts, the Commission considered that the intentional or reckless infliction of injury should be criminal. In cricket, bowling bouncers may therefore become illegal in circumstances where the batsman is ill-equipped to deal with them. The present law which permits rough horseplay should be abolished because it is not distinguishable from fighting. See *Aitken*, above. If, however, the law were amended to permit consent to injury, the sole exceptions should be sports and games.

The recommendations can be criticised from perspectives both of paternalism and personal autonomy, and there are instances where argument is conspicuously lacking: why is it obvious that ear piercing and tattooing are lawful? Both may lead to infection. The Law Commission left boxing to a special category. The purpose of boxing is to cause grievous bodily harm, and if the victim dies, the assailant would be guilty of murder. The Commission thought that boxing (and presumably kick-boxing, full-contact karate and the like), if it is to be non-criminal, should be placed in a special category based on public policy, but it did note that between 1945 and 1992, 361 deaths had been caused worldwide by legal boxing. (The World Medical Association has called for a ban on boxing.) In the 1994 Paper there was no investigation into chastisement and medical treatment, both of which were said to 'raise complex issues of policy that go very far beyond the issues that we address. . . .'. These omissions detracted from the force of the Paper. Perhaps the Law Commission shied away from these areas in order to have its proposals on the other matters accepted.

The 1995 Paper, unlike the 1994 one, included sections on lawful correction (though the Law Commission recognised that consent has very little to do with this issue and it made no recommendations), surgery, whether therapeutic or cosmetic (on the ground that it looks odd to omit this topic while including cosmetic body piercing), and boxing (recognising that it would similarly be strange to deal with martial arts while disregarding boxing). It did not consider consent in relation to other offences, such as theft and burglary, but the Law Commission proposed that the revisions should apply throughout criminal law. One theme of the 1995 Paper is that the Commission did not wish to be out of line with the wishes of Parliament whether expressed in statutes, in debates or in committee reports. For example, there should be no relaxation of the prohibition of euthanasia or female circumcision (on which now see the Female Genital Mutilation Act 2003), and boxing should not be outlawed. The Commission realised that this approach may result in 'what our critics may believe to be attitudes on related issues that are mutually inconsistent'. It sought ways of remedying these inconsistencies provided that they 'do not cut across prevailing Parliamentary culture, although we recognise that in the last resort we may simply have to live with them' (para. 2.17). Boxing in particular could have been banned on several occasions but Parliament has chosen not to.

In brief, consent is to be lawful to any harm short of a seriously disabling injury. **Brown** would prospectively be overruled because the injuries were not seriously disabling. The purpose of the injury would be irrelevant. The 1994 Paper proposed to raise the level of the harm to which consent would provide a defence but did not clearly define that level. The 1995 Paper adopted the definition of Glanville Williams in 'Force, injury and serious injury' [1990] NLJ 1227, though his was a definition of 'serious injury' made in response to the failure of the draft Criminal Code to define that concept: a seriously disabling injury is one which:

(a) causes serious distress, and

(b) involves loss of a bodily member or organ, or permanent bodily injury or permanent functional impairment, or serious or permanent disfigurement, or severe or prolonged pain, or serious impairment of mental health, or prolonged unconsciousness. . . .

The Law Commission proposed that if a seriously disabling injury resulted, consent should be invalid on the ground that the victim had not truly consented to it because such harm is contrary to his interests. A major criticism of this proposal is that the level of harm to which the 'victim' can consent is high. A seriously disabling injury is not minor harm. No account is to be taken of whether the injury was remediable by surgery or not. Consent to lesser injuries would be allowed, provided that it was valid and was consent to the type of injury caused. The Commission invited views on where the burden of proof should lie in relation to this defence.

The Law Commission sought to render ineffective any consent which was not given voluntarily. In respect of children, minors (i.e. persons who are under 18) must be able to understand what consent means. They should not be permitted to give consent if they were unable because of age or immaturity to make a decision on consent. The finder of fact would take into account the implications of the decision and the seriousness of the matter to which the minor allegedly gave consent. Children under 18 would not be allowed to consent to the infliction of pain on them for sexual or spiritual purposes. This would be in line with the law on anal intercourse. In respect of the mentally disabled, they would not be able to give consent if their disability rendered it impossible for them to make a decision on consent. Those who could not communicate consent, for instance because they were unconscious or asleep, would also be incapable of consent. In criticism it may be said that consent even in other instances is not an unproblematic concept. In a relationship of power, such as a lecturer/student one, true consent may be lacking.

The Law Commission proposed to extend the law to cover a person who did not realise that the victim was not consenting when the lack of consent would have been obvious to a reasonable person and the accused was capable of appreciating that fact: 'it does not seem unreasonable to expect a person, before subjecting another to what will be a serious invasion of his or her bodily integrity if he or she does not consent to it, to make sure that he or she *does* consent to it' (para. 7.25). The same rule would apply to sex crimes but not to property offences, which do not violate the victim's rights as much as non-fatal and sexual offences do. The distinction may be open to dispute, and the extension itself is not justified on a purely subjectivist approach. The proposed rule would also apply when a sexual offence was defined in terms of age. The defendant is to be guilty if it was obvious to a reasonable person that the victim was under the relevant age and the accused was capable of realising that fact if he had given any thought to it.

Consent should not be valid if there is deception as to the nature of the act or the identity of the other person. Possibly fraud should render consent invalid when the deception was as to freedom from sexually transmitted diseases and the Commission invited views on whether any other deception should nullify consent. A self-induced mistake as to the nature of the act or the identity (or perhaps freedom from a sexually transmitted disease and so on) would not provide a defence if the accused knew of the error. Non-disclosure of relevant facts would negate consent. Consent would exclude 'consent' given as a result of a threat to use force if the threat was to be carried out immediately or before the victim could free himself of the menace. There should be a crime of procuring consent by deception and the Law Commission invited views on whether there should be a crime of procuring consent by threats. It resiled from its proposition in its 1994 Paper that any fraud should negate consent because that law 'would be disproportionate', a phrase which it does not explain; instead the proposed offences would come into play. The accused would have a defence if he believed the victim to be consenting even though this was not the case, provided that the rule stated above did not apply.

Some issues of consent relate to the intentional causing of harm. Examples are surgery, tattooing, flagellation for religious reasons, male circumcision and ear piercing. Other aspects of the law are concerned with the risk of danger, not with the intentional causing of injury, for example dangerous exhibitions and some sports injuries. The risk must be one which is reasonable in the circumstances in which the accused acts.

The Law Commission invited views on whether the present age limit on tattooing, 18, should be retained and whether there should be any age limit for body piercing below the neck, branding and scarification when done for cultural or cosmetic reasons. Certainly hygiene controls should be tightened up. Male circumcision would continue to be lawful, and female circumcision unlawful.

In respect of boxing, the Commission was of the opinion that the question whether it should be legal was one for Parliament. It noted that Parliament had recently voted not to criminalise it. Clarkson, Keating and Cunningham, *Criminal Law: Text and Materials*, 7th edn (Sweet & Maxwell, 2010) pointedly comment (at p 15): '... by not allowing people to consent to seriously disabling injuries in the course of sadomasochism while not criminalising the same injuries in the course of, say, boxing, it is possible to assert that in reality the Law Commission has adopted a stance of paternalism hardened at the edges by legal moralism.' For other sports the Law Commission thought that 'a person should not be guilty of causing injury in the course of playing or practising a recognised sport *in accordance with the rules*' (emphasis added). This provision would, for example, cover fast bowlers in cricket and the playing of rugby football. Head-butting would obviously fall out with this stipulation. However, care will have to be taken in drafting the law because as stated, the mere fact that the accused was offside in football would make a non-criminal act into a criminal one. Dangerous exhibitions such as knife throwing would remain lawful but possibly there should be a lower age limit for victims.

The risk of harm to others is a factor which may render some activities unlawful even though there is consent. The Commission suggested that fighting should remain illegal. Horse-play, however, should not be unlawful unless a seriously disabling injury was caused. Presumably *Aitken*, above, would be overruled.

The Law Commission was of the view that consent to activities such as sport and surgery, which are normally seen as beneficial, should be accepted, provided that the rules are appropriately controlled, even though a seriously disabling injury occurs. Surgery is seen to occupy a special category. The 1994 Paper did not discuss the issue because it thought that surgery was not related to consent, but the 1995 Paper did because 'except in emergencies, the common law has never granted the medical profession the unqualified *legal right* to perform medical or surgical procedures irrespective of the patient's consent, even when the procedures are in the patient's best interests' (para. 8.5). The Commission proposed to restate the medical exception thus: 'a person should not be guilty of an offence, notwithstanding that he or she causes injury to another, of whatever degree of seriousness, if such injury is caused during the course of proper medical treatment or care administered with the consent of that other person' (para. 8.50). Medical treatment would cover, *inter alia*: sterilisation, sex reassignment surgery, lawful abortions and cosmetic surgery. Treatment would be improper, for instance, when fingers are amputated to facilitate an insurance claim. Medical treatment would also cover properly approved medical research.

In the Home Office's Consultation Document, *Violence: Reforming the Offences against the Person Act 1861*, 1998, the government left the issue of consent to the common law. Once the Law Commission concluded its work on consent, there would be reform. There has been no government move since 1998.

Assault occasioning actual bodily harm

The OAPA consolidated several statutes dealing with non-fatal offences. The draftsman did not make the crimes formerly contained in those statutes consistent or create a hierarchy of offences. It is very much of a hotchpotch. Section 47 creates the offence of assault occasioning **actual bodily harm** (Figure 13.1).

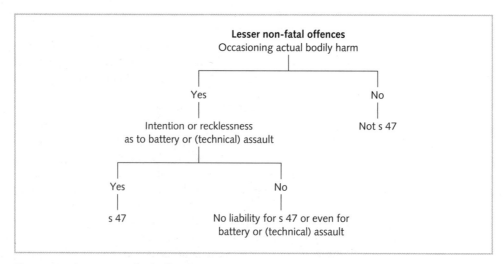

Figure 13.1 Lesser non-fatal offences

Actus reus

There is no definition of 'actual bodily harm' – surely all harm is actual! The term 'assault' covers both assault and battery, as was assumed in *DPP v Little*, above. An example from the cases is *Lewis* [1970] Crim LR 647 (CA). The accused threatened his wife, who was injured while escaping. 'Occasioning' means 'causing', a concept which is discussed in Chapter 2. A somewhat out-of-the-ordinary actual bodily harm was occasioned in *Savage*, above. The accused threw a glass of beer at the victim, the glass slipped from the accused's hand, hit the bar table and broke; a fragment of it flew off and cut the victim on the wrist. Throwing the beer was a battery and that battery had occasioned the actual bodily harm that the victim suffered.

According to *Saunders* [1985] Crim LR 230 (CA) grievous bodily harm means 'serious harm'. Actual bodily harm must mean something less than serious harm. In *Miller* [1954] 2 QB 282 (DC), Lynskey J said that the term 'includes any hurt or injury calculated [likely] to interfere with the health or comfort' of the victim. Hysterics fell within this definition. 'Hurt' alone is insufficient. A head-lock is painful but not actual bodily harm.

'Actual' seems to mean 'more than trivial' though *Taylor v Granville* [1978] Crim LR 482 said that it covered any harm, however slight. It covers bruises, grazes, black eyes and burns. In *Chan-Fook* [1994] 2 All ER 552 (CA) the accused suspected the victim of theft of his fiancée's ring. The victim felt humiliated and abused. The accused dragged him upstairs and locked him in a room. The victim, in fear of being assaulted, climbed out of a window and down a rope of knotted sheets. He fell, fracturing his wrist and dislocating his pelvis. Surprisingly the prosecution was based on the victim's fright, humiliation and distress, not on his physical injuries. The trial judge said, applying *Miller*, that a nervous and hysterical condition was actual bodily harm. The Court of Appeal allowed the appeal. 'Actual' meant not so trivial as to be wholly insignificant. 'Harm' was injury which goes beyond interference with the health or comfort of the victim while including injury to health such as infection with a disease. In other words, harm requires injury.

'Bodily' is not limited to harm to skin, flesh and bones, but includes injury to the nervous system and brain such as recognised and identifiable psychiatric harm, but not 'mere emotions or states of mind which are not themselves evidence of an identifiable clinical condition'. An hysterical condition, which according to *Miller* fell within the definition of actual bodily harm, no longer does. It did not cover fear, distress or panic. These are regarded as emotions, not harms. *Chan-Fook* was followed in *Dhaliwal* [2006] 2 Cr App R 348 (CA). Psychological injury which was not a clinically recognised psychiatric condition was not 'bodily harm'. *Dhaliwal* is also known as *D*: see [2006] EWCA Crim 1139. This is a narrow interpretation of *Chan-Fook*, which did not restrict the definition to clinically recognised states of mind but to 'identifiable' ones. *Dhaliwal* also provides a great contrast to the next case discussed. If cutting off a ponytail may be actual bodily harm so too surely is serious psychological harm?

In *DPP v Smith* [2006] 1 WLR 1571 it was held in the Administrative Court that magistrates were entitled to find that cutting off a substantial amount of hair, a ponytail, could constitute actual bodily harm. The court rejected contentions that 'harm' could apply only to living material, that 'harm' requires pain, and that 'harm' applies only when the part injured will not regrow. The arguments against the ruling that cutting hair is actual bodily harm are these: (1) there is no 'hurt or injury' within *Miller*; (2) distress does not constitute actual bodily harm. It should be noted that the court held that cutting hair *could* constitute actual bodily harm, not that it always did.

In *Morris* [1998] 1 Cr App R 386 (CA) it was held that sleeplessness, tearfulness, tension, and anxiety were not actual bodily harm. The court stated that fear of unlawful violence was the crime of assault, not of assault occasioning actual bodily harm; otherwise there was no difference between the two. It added that if psychiatric injury is relied on and is not admitted by the defence, expert evidence should be admitted. One of the issues raised in *Ireland*; *Burstow*, above, was whether 'bodily harm' in the OAPA included psychiatric illness. Lord Steyn said that, when drafting the OAPA: 'the Victorian legislator . . . would not have had in his mind psychiatric illness . . . But the subjective intention of the draftsman is immaterial. The only relevant inquiry is as to the sense of the words in the context in which they are used. Moreover, the Act of 1861 . . . must be interpreted in the light of the best current scientific application of the link between the body and the psychiatric injury.' He approved the ruling of the Court of Appeal in *Chan-Fook* noted above that 'bodily' in the phrase 'bodily harm' does not restrict the definition to 'the skin, flesh and bones of the victim'. In the words of Hobhouse LJ: 'the body of the victim includes all parts of his body, including his organs, his nervous system and his brain. Bodily injury therefore may include injury to any of those parts of the body responsible for his mental and other faculties.' Accordingly, psychiatric illnesses were included, provided that they constituted 'some indentifiable clinical condition'. However, 'bodily harm' does not cover 'mere emotions such as fear or distress or panic'.

The Court of Appeal in *Morris* held that psychiatric evidence of the nature of the victim's symptoms should be led when there was a non-physical assault which caused tension and sleeplessness. That type of evidence is needed to distinguish between the 'mere emotions' and psychiatric illnesses, such as 'a chronic anxiety state or depressive disorder'. Injuries can be aggregated to make the harm 'actual'. In *Smith* [1985] LSG Rep 198, four or five bruises caused by a belt were sufficient. In *Jones* [1981] Crim LR 119 (CA) minor abrasions and a bruise were held to be actual bodily harm, though the case was thought to be on the margins. Pain caused by a kick to the stomach with tenderness afterwards, but leaving no visible injury, was sufficient: *Reigate JJ, ex parte Counsell* (1983) 148 JP 193. In *Miller*, an injury to the state of a person's mind was enough (cf. *Dawson* (1985) 81 Cr App R 150 (CA) on manslaughter in the previous chapter: shock is not harm unless physical injury is caused). *Chan-Fook* reminds us that there must be harm, even when the assault is on the victim's mind. Where there is a psychic assault, for the accused to be guilty that assault must cause the bodily harm: the apprehension of violence must cause the harm.

A quite recent authority is *T v DPP* [2003] Crim LR 622, which is also called *R (on the application of T) v DPP* at [2003] EWHC 886 (Admin). The accused kicked the victim momentarily unconscious. There were no contusions or other marks. The trial judge directed the jury according to the words of Swift J in *Donovan*, above: '. . . "bodily harm" has its ordinary meaning and includes any hurt or injury calculated [i.e. likely] to interfere with the health or comfort of the [victim]. Such hurt or injury need not be permanent, but must . . . be more than merely transient or trifling.' The jury convicted. The Divisional Court dismissed his appeal. Maurice Kay J, as he then was, said that Swift J's words were not to be treated as a statute but, in any case, while the injury here was 'transient' it was not 'trifling'. In other words, not to be actual bodily harm the injury had to be, as Swift J said, both transient *and* trifling. However, the main authority is *Chan-Fook*. The words in s 47 were ordinary ones. On the facts of the case loss of consciousness was 'harm'; the harm was 'bodily' because the victim's senses were impaired; and the harm was most definitely 'actual'. Therefore, the accused was rightly convicted.

Criticism of s 47 comes from academics. Glanville Williams wrote in 'Force, injury and serious injury' (1990) 140 NLJ 1227:

> What the Victorian draftsman intended by 'actual' is anyone's guess. He was evidently searching, unsuccessfully, for something between 'trivial' and 'serious'. The courts have not helped him by sensible pronouncements. They might have said that harm is not 'actual' unless it is something beyond the trivial, for which a charge of common assault is adequate; but they have not imposed even this degree of control. The question is held to be one for the unrestricted discretion of the jury or magistrates who are allowed to find that even a bruise is enough. In the scale of harms, a bruise is trivial. The offence under s 47 is relatively serious, carrying a possible sentence of five years. If only a bruise is caused, s 47 is an overcharge.

The penalty for s 18 is life imprisonment, substantially more than that for s 20, yet the harm may be the same: indeed, it could be less serious.

Mens rea

No mental element is expressly stated in s 47. In *Roberts* (1971) 56 Cr App R 95 (CA), an important case which was approved by the House of Lords in *Savage*, the court seems to have held that the *mens rea* is the same as for common law assault. After *Venna* [1976] QB 421 (CA), where the victim suffered a broken finger, that means that the accused is guilty if he intended to create or is reckless as to creating fear or as to touching and the outcome is actual bodily harm. On this approach the accused need not intend or be reckless as to actual bodily harm. On the facts of *Roberts* a person who assaults with the result that the victim tries to escape and suffers actual bodily harm is guilty of this offence, even though the accused did not foresee actual bodily harm. This issue is dealt with below.

The meaning of recklessness in s 47

In *DPP v K* [1990] 1 WLR 1067 (DC), the accused, a 15-year-old schoolboy, was using sulphuric acid in an experiment at school. Some splashed onto his hand. He washed it off in the lavatory. Unknown to the teacher he had taken with him a test tube of the acid to test its reaction with lavatory paper. While in the lavatory he heard footsteps, panicked and poured the acid into a dryer, intending to come back later to wash it out. Unfortunately another pupil came in, turned on the dryer and the acid splashed over his face, causing a scar. The Divisional Court directed the magistrates to convict. It held that s 47 could be committed indirectly: 'A defendant who pours a dangerous substance into a machine just as truly assaults the next user of the machine as if he himself switched the machine on.' Controversially the court held that *Caldwell* [1982] AC 341 (HL) applied to the mental element in s 47. *Cunningham* [1957] 2 QB 396 (CCA) was not cited. The main criticism of *DPP v K* was in the words of Bennett and Hogan, 'Criminal law, criminal procedure and sentencing' [1990] All ER Rev 69, that it brought the 'thoughtlessly stupid' into the criminal law.

The Court of Appeal in *Spratt* overruled *DPP v K* on this point.

Spratt [1990] 1 WLR 1073 (CA)

The accused fired shots from an air pistol from his flat. Two pellets hit a seven-year-old girl playing outside. He had not realised that there were people in the area, that is, he gave no thought to the risk. The Court of Appeal quashed his conviction.

McCowan LJ held that:

> The history of the interpretation of the 1861 Act shows that, whether or not the word 'maliciously' appears in the section in question, the Courts have consistently held that the *mens rea* of every type of offence against the person covers both actual intent and recklessness, in the sense of taking the risk of harm ensuing with foresight that it might happen.

Venna was approved in *DPP* v *Majewski* [1977] AC 443 (HL) and seemingly by Lord Diplock himself in *Caldwell. Savage* (HL) confirms that *Cunningham* applies. *Caldwell* does not apply because 'maliciously' is a term of art with 'a special restricted meaning'. Any doubt as to the position was resolved by *G* [2004] 1 AC 1034 (HL), which held that *Caldwell* was wrong.

Does the accused have to intend to cause or be reckless as to causing actual bodily harm or is intention to recklessness as to battery sufficient?

In *Spratt*, though interpretations vary, the Court of Appeal seems to have required intentionally or recklessly occasioning actual bodily harm. In *Savage* (1990) 91 Cr App R 317, the same court (but a different division) on the same day said that intentionally or recklessly causing a battery was sufficient, as long as actual bodily harm occurred. In *Savage* the accused threw beer on the victim in a pub. She let go of the glass (whether deliberately or not is unknown) and the victim was cut by broken glass. She was held guilty under s 47. The battery was the consequence of her deliberate throwing of the beer as a result of which the victim was injured. There was no need to show that she foresaw the possibility of some harm. The stress was on causation, not recklessness: did the accused commit the assault which caused the actual bodily harm? The result is in line with *Roberts*, and is consistent with the decision if not the reasoning in *Spratt*, where the court seems to have been discussing the nature of recklessness, not whether there had to be *mens rea* as to the occasioning of actual bodily harm. Since *Roberts* was not mentioned in *Spratt* or in the next case, *DPP* v *Parmenter* [1992] 1 AC 699 (HL), those cases are *per incuriam*. The House of Lords in *Savage* approved *Roberts*.

In *Parmenter*, the Court of Appeal chose *Spratt* in preference to *Savage*. The court thought that the law was 'impenetrable' and called for the Lords to review it. The House in *Savage* approved the *Savage* (CA) approach. Lord Ackner said in *Savage*:

> The Court of Appeal in *Parmenter* was wrong in preferring the decision in *Spratt*. The decision in *Roberts* was correct. The verdict of assault occasioning actual bodily harm may be returned upon proof of an assault together with proof of the fact that actual bodily harm was occasioned by the assault. The prosecution are not obliged to prove that the defendant intended to cause some actual bodily harm or was reckless as to whether such harm would be caused.

'Occasioning' is an objective issue not dependent on the accused's state of mind. The law was made complex partly by *Mowatt* [1968] 1 QB 421 (CA). A person is guilty under s 20 of the OAPA (see later) when he does not foresee grievous bodily harm but does foresee some harm. According to *Savage; DPP* v *Parmenter* [1992] 1 AC 699 (HL) this definition applies to both ss 20 and 47. Mustill LJ said in *DPP* v *Parmenter* that, although the two offences are seen as different by defendants and lawyers, the *mens rea* is the same:

> If the *Cunningham* subjective test combined with the low level of intent prescribed by *Mowatt* is applied to s 47 in the same way as s 20, the moral overtones of the two offences become indistinguishable, and the differences between the two depend upon variations between the levels of physical injury which may often be the result of chance.

Both sections have the same maximum punishment, five years' imprisonment, yet s 20, which deals with maliciously inflicting grievous bodily harm, is seen as the more serious offence, yet that gravity may now depend on chance. Mustill LJ continued:

> The authorities can no longer live together and . . . the reason lies in a collision between two ideas, logically and morally sustainable in themselves, but mutually inconsistent, about whether the unforeseen consequences of a wrongful act should be punished according to the intent [*Cunningham*] or the consequences [*Mowatt*].

In other words, the accused is guilty not for what he intended to do or was reckless as to doing but for the result of his actions. This is a form of constructive liability in the same sense that liability for unlawful act manslaughter is constructive. Such liability is frowned upon by those people, sometimes called subjectivists, who hold that people should be punished according to their states of mind. The doctrine of constructive murder, by which an accused who killed in the course of a violent felony was guilty of murder, was abolished in 1957 and the Law Commission would like to abolish all forms of constructive criminality. In *Savage* it mattered whether the mental element was the intent to batter or assault rather than intent to cause actual bodily harm. The victim apprehended a battery and the accused foresaw such apprehension. She had the mental element of battery but did not foresee actual bodily harm. Such harm occurred through the accused's careless or accidental dropping of the glass. Nevertheless, she was guilty. She would also have been guilty if the harm had been done through the purely fortuitous circumstance that the glass had a defect in it which made it break easily. No wonder the House of Lords thought that the law was irrational.

Included offences

If the accused is charged with s 47, he cannot be convicted of common assault: *Mearns* (1990) 91 Cr App R 312 (CA) and *Savage* (HL). Assault and battery are summary offences (Criminal Justice Act 1988, s 39). A separate count for common assault must be added, and often is. The position was different before the statute. In all but exceptional cases, wounding will involve a battery. Therefore, on a charge of wounding (OAPA, s 20), one can convict of s 47 (*Savage* (CA) among other cases). Similarly, on a charge of inflicting grievous bodily harm, one can convict of s 47. The law is unsatisfactory.

Wounding and grievous bodily harm

Example

Read ss 18 and 20 below. Without reading any further, answer the following:

1 Alphonse attacks Bessie with a knife, wounding her severely. Has he committed a s 18 offence?
2 He attacks her with a knife and causes superficial injuries. Has he committed a s 20 offence?

Answers:

1 He commits a s 18 offence only if he wounds or commits GBH with intent to do some GBH. A mistake often made is that in both s 18 and s 20 the *mens rea* includes intention to wound (or recklessness as to wounding). Neither of them does so. In s 18 there must

> be an intent to do some GBH; an intent therefore to wound (even one to wound griev-
> ously unless it amounts to GBH too) is insufficient. On the facts if Alphonse intends to
> do some harm, only then will he be guilty of one form of the s 18 offence, wounding
> with intent to do some GBH. There is of course no problem with the *actus reus*: the
> facts tell us that there is a wound.
>
> 2 Section 20's *mens rea* is again often got wrong, and it is a very bad error to err on this
> point. The *mens rea* is exactly this: with intent to cause some harm (not necessarily GBH)
> or recklessness as to some harm. Again, note that there is no 'wound' on the *mens rea*
> side. The other tricky point should now be obvious: the *mens rea* is *not* intent to do GBH
> or being reckless as to whether GBH is caused. On the facts the accused may have the
> mental element for s 20 but the issue then becomes one of the conduct element. Does
> he wound or 'inflict' GBH? There is no GBH ('superficial injuries') but there may be a
> wound provided that the layers of the skin are broken. If there is no wound, then s 47,
> assault occasioning actual bodily harm, comes into play.

Section 18 of the OAPA as amended reads:

> [w]hosoever shall unlawfully and maliciously by any means whatsoever wound or cause
> any grievous bodily harm to any person . . . with intent . . . to do some grievous bodily harm
> to any person or with intent to resist or prevent the lawful apprehension or detainer of any
> person shall be guilty . . .

Section 20 reads in part:

> [w]hosoever shall unlawfully and maliciously wound or inflict any grievous bodily harm upon
> any person, either with or without any weapon or instrument shall be guilty . . .

Section 18 is the most serious non-fatal offence against the person, and differs from
s 20 in the need for the ulterior intent ('with intent to') and in the different verbs for
committing the **grievous bodily harm** (hereinafter GBH): 'cause' in s 18, 'inflict' in s 20
(Figure 13.2). It should be noted that in s 18 the ulterior intent does not relate to wounding: the offence is not satisfied by wounding (or causing GBH) with intent to wound. Such
facts fall within s 20 (if the GBH was inflicted). The phrase 'either with or without any
weapon' makes s 20 pleonastic. Section 18 speaks of 'lawful' apprehension or detention.
If the arrest is wrongful, the accused is not guilty. If the arrest is lawful but the accused
believes it to be unlawful, he is guilty because he has made a mistake of law: *Bentley* (1850)
4 Cox CC 406. It might, however, be argued to the contrary that the mistake is really one
as to civil law, which does afford a defence, or that if the mistake is a factual one (e.g. was
he a constable?) he should also not be convicted. (See Chapter 8 for discussion of mistake.)
One result of the wording of s 18 should be noted. It is an offence to cause GBH with intent
to prevent lawful apprehension. If the accused hits a constable while resisting arrest and
the constable bangs his head on a kerbstone causing serious injury, he is guilty of GBH with
intent. He need not intend GBH, yet he may be sentenced to any period of imprisonment,
including for life.

The term 'unlawfully' in both sections exonerates a person who acts in self-defence or
where there is consent or lawful chastisement. If the accused acts in defence of property,
he is entitled to use reasonable force, force which would otherwise amount to GBH. It is
hard to see how 'unlawfully' can operate with regard to some forms of s 18. One difference
should be noted. Section 20 refers to 'upon any other person'; s 18 says 'to any person'.
Section 18 could be interpreted as holding it to be illegal to wound or cause GBH to the

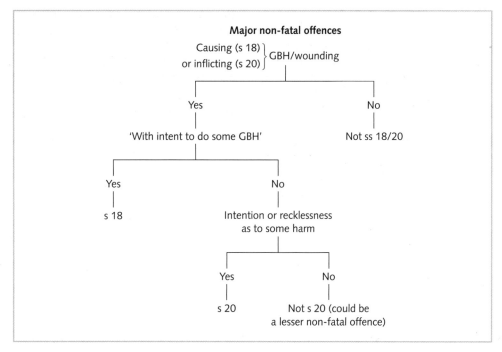

Figure 13.2 Major non-fatal offences

accused himself, provided the ulterior intent is satisfied. Maiming oneself to avoid conscription in wartime, the example used above in relation to consent, would therefore be an offence contrary to s 18, but not to s 20. It seems the prosecutions for self-harm are not brought. The criminal law would not seem to be the appropriate mechanism for dealing with self-harmers.

Actus reus

A **wound** is a breach in the whole skin, a phrase which includes the internal lining of the mouth and the vagina and penis. It was so held in, among other cases, *JCC (A Minor) v Eisenhower* [1984] QB 331 (DC), where a ruptured blood vessel was held not to be a wound. A bruise is not a wound. It was thought that a wound requires a battery: *Taylor* (1869) LR 1 CCR 194 among other cases, except perhaps in 'extraordinary' circumstances: *Savage* (CA), above, which the Lords approved. Their Lordships did not give illustrations of these extraordinary circumstances. Perhaps an illustration of extraordinary facts would be a knife which is sent into the victim as a result of her touching a tripwire. Since, as we shall shortly see, 'inflict' does not require an assault or battery, it might be expected that the same rule should apply to 'wound'. It is suggested that should the issue arise in the Lords, they would overrule this line of cases. The force is not directly applied by the person who set the trap but force is applied to the victim with the result that she is wounded. It is suggested that the rule that wounding requires a battery would not survive scrutiny nowadays in the Supreme Court. There is no longer a condition that GBH must be caused by a battery, and the law should be the same for both.

It has been argued by William Wilson, *Criminal Law*, 4th edn (Longman, 2011), 280, that 'wound' necessitates the accused to inflict a wound on the victim directly as with a knife; if so, causing the victim to run into a broken window on which he cut himself would not be a 'wound'. There is no judicial authority on this point. It is also uncertain whether a wound may be caused by an omission.

In the context of murder the Lords held in **DPP v Smith** [1961] AC 290 that GBH meant 'really serious bodily harm'. This statement was applied to these offences in **Metharam** [1961] 3 All ER 200 (CCA). However, the Court of Appeal in **Saunders**, above, held that 'really' did not add anything to 'serious'. That is, there were not three types of harm, 'really serious', 'serious' and 'non-serious', but just two, 'serious' and 'non-serious'. 'Really' meant 'actually', not 'very'. On the facts of **Saunders**, a broken nose was grievous harm.

Whether harm is grievous is judged by an objective test according to standards of usage and experience, not subjectively dependent on whether the jury would call it grievous if done to them: **Brown** [1998] Crim LR 485 (CA). Similarly, as **Brown** states, it is irrelevant what the victim thought about the injuries. In that case the accumulation of gross facial swelling, missing teeth, fracture of the nose, widespread lacerations and bruising was serious harm. However, what is grievous to one victim may not be grievous to another: **Bollom** [2004] 2 Cr App R 50 (CA) – a 17-month-old baby. The court said that there was no requirement that the injuries be permanent, dangerous or life-threatening, but that injuries should be seen in the context of the victim. Injuries to a child or an elderly person may be more serious than the same injuries to 'a six-foot adult in the fullness of health'. On the facts, bruises which are harm to soft tissue, were capable of being grievous within the definition. They were superficial and would heal spontaneously, but whether the harm had lasting consequences or needed treatment was irrelevant to whether the harm was grievous. Extensive bruising and abrasions on a 17-month-old were therefore capable of being grievous.

The jury should not ask whether each individual harm is very serious; instead the injuries should be added together to see whether as a whole they constitute GBH: **Grundy** [1989] Crim LR 502 (CA) and **Birmingham** [2002] EWCA Crim 2608 (11 knife wounds, not individually grievous but the aggregation made the harm grievous). The same law applies to *actual* bodily harm. 'Bodily' and 'harm' presumably bear the same meaning as in the crime of assault occasioning actual bodily harm (see discussion). One effect is that 'bodily harm' covers psychiatric harm. In **Bullerton**, unreported, 1992 (CA), mentioned by R. Burns in 'GBH of the earhole' [1992] NLJ 1725, the accused, in order to stop obscene phone calls from the victim, attached a 'screech-box' to his phone. When the victim phoned, he was partly deafened and suffered tinnitus. The court seems not to have doubted that the results were grievous harm. In **Gelder** (1994) *The Times*, 25 May a man was convicted when the victim suffered sickness and diarrhoea as a result of his obscene phone calls. The Court of Appeal allowed the appeal (1994) *The Times*, 16 December, but only on the ground that the judge had wrongly instructed the jury on the mental element. The court did not rule whether GBH could be inflicted by phone.

It is a question of fact whether harm is serious. GBH covers situations where the skin is not broken as in **Wood** (1830) 172 ER 749, where a collar bone was broken. Conversely a wound is not necessarily GBH. An example is a pinprick. Sometimes the same facts are both GBH and wounding, such as when the accused chops off the victim's arm. It should be noted that a wound need not be a serious wound, yet the harm must be serious. It is difficult to accept that the law should treat a pinprick in the same way as a ruptured spleen.

The House of Lords in **Wilson** [1984] AC 242 overturned earlier authorities which held that 'inflict' in s 20 required an assault. 'Assault' is here used in the sense of battery. The House in **Savage** also thought that there can be infliction of GBH without a battery, as where the accused tampers with car brakes with the result that someone is seriously injured. An example, suggested in *Savage* by Lord Ackner, is inflicting GBH by creating panic. (Usually, however, there is a battery.) Most inflicting will involve an assault. For many years there has been debate as to the width of 'inflict' in s 20. These issues were raised in *Ireland; Burstow*, above. The first issue was whether or not s 20 required an assault (in the sense of a battery). The authorities were divided. Lord Steyn stated that s 20 does not require an assault on the basis that, if it did, words would have to be read into s 20 ('inflict *by assault* any grievous bodily harm'), whereas s 20 'works perfectly satisfactorily without any such implication'.

There is a problem arising from *Wilson*. Lord Roskill apparently believed that 'inflict' required the direct application of force to the victim or the doing of an act which directly resulted in force being applied to the victim's body. What is said is *dictum*. On this approach, to take an old example, if one dug a pit for the victim to fall into, one would be guilty under s 20 because, although one has not directly applied force to the victim, one has done an act which directly resulted in force being applied. One will have caused GBH within s 18, because 'cause' does not require the direct application of force. On the facts of *Martin*, above, the accused would be guilty of the more serious offence, s 18, and guilty of the less serious offence, s 20, for the same reason, but one is not guilty in the poisoning example because no force is used. The result is absurd. It would appear that the *dictum* is wrong. It could have been avoided by having the same verb in ss 18 and 20 or by the House of Lords in *Wilson* deciding that 'cause' and 'inflict' covered the same ground. The Lords took the point further: 'inflict' did not require direct application of force, but assault occasioning actual bodily harm and common assault did. Therefore, a person could be guilty of the most serious non-fatal assault but not of the lesser assaults! It is about time that the meaning of 'inflict' was settled. There are also problems with this definition of 'inflict' in s 20 with regard to s 23 of the OAPA, which creates the offence of administering a noxious thing '. . . so as thereby to inflict . . . any grievous bodily harm . . .'. Administering poison requires neither a battery nor the application of force. Therefore 'inflict' in s 23 must be wider than 'inflict' in s 20. The OAPA is a mess but surely it is not such a mess. There seems to be little difference between the lack of a requirement of assault and the necessity for a direct application of force.

Another issue was whether s 20 required the direct or indirect application of force. The Lords held that no direct physical violence was necessary. Lord Steyn said:

> The problem is one of construction. The question is whether as a matter of current usage the contextual interpretation of 'inflict' can embrace the idea of one person inflicting psychiatric injury on another. One can without straining the language in any way answer that question in the affirmative. I am not saying that the words cause and inflict are exactly synonymous. They are not. What I am saying is that in the context of the Act of 1861 one can nowadays quite naturally speak of inflicting psychiatric injury.

In this way 'inflict' in s 20 and 'cause' in s 18 are of similar width, at least where psychiatric harm results. Lord Steyn thought it would be 'absurd' if 'cause' and 'inflict' were of different width. This interpretation was consistent with the hierarchy of non-fatal offences. As Lord Steyn said, 'the . . . approach should, so far as possible, be adopted which treats the ladder of offences as a coherent body of law'. One difference may be that 'cause' may be committed by omission, but 'inflict' cannot.

'Cause' in s 18 also does not require an assault: *Austin* (1973) 58 Cr App R 163 (CA). Perhaps 'cause' covers poisoning where the poison is left for the victim to take, whereas 'inflict' does not. 'Cause' thus does not require violence but 'inflict' does. A possible difference was suggested by Lord Hope in *Ireland; Burstow*. He said that 'inflict' denotes: 'that the consequence of the act is something which the victim is likely to find unpleasant or harmful. The relationship between cause and effect, when the word "cause" is used, is neutral. It may embrace pleasure as well as pain.' If this statement is correct, the defendants in *Brown*, the sado-masochists, should not have been found guilty of a s 20 offence, but could have been convicted of a s 18 offence! It is suggested that whatever Lord Hope did mean by his comment, he did not intend to say that *Brown* was wrong. Lord Steyn said that 'inflict' and 'cause' were not 'exactly synonymous' but he did not advert to what those differences were. The law therefore remains uncertain as to whether there is a difference between 'cause' in s 18 and 'conflict' in s 20. The reader is reminded that the 1861 Act is a consolidation statute, bringing together laws from different Acts passed at different times and that no attempt was made to make the definitions consistent across the statute.

Mens rea

In both ss 18 and 20 the mental element is stated to be 'maliciously'. Section 18 requires proof of a further state of mind: 'with intent to do some grievous bodily harm'. Coleridge CJ said in *Martin* that 'maliciously' did not mean spitefully. It normally means in a statute 'intentionally or recklessly'. Negligence is insufficient. Yet one can be guilty of a more serious offence, manslaughter by gross negligence, by acting in a seriously careless fashion. As we have seen (Chapter 3), *Cunningham* [1957] 2 QB 396 (CCA) held that on a charge of administering a noxious thing under s 23 of the OAPA recklessness was defined as: did the accused himself foresee the consequence? Though there is a *dictum* to the contrary in *Seymour*, above, this definition still applies to ss 18 and 20: **W v Dolbey** (1983) 88 Cr App R 1 (CA) (a case where the accused would not have been guilty under a test of objective recklessness because he considered whether there were pellets in his air rifle and decided that there were none), *Lynch* (1985) LEXIS, 14 January (CA), *Morrison* (1989) 89 Cr App R 17 (CA), and *Rainbird* [1989] Crim LR 505 (CA). Though the Court of Appeal in *Dume* (1986) *The Times*, 16 October, refused to say whether **W v Dolbey** was correct, there is now the Lords' decision in *Savage* to the effect that it is.

The following cases exemplify this area of law.

See Chapter 3 for a review of *Cunningham* recklessness.

Lynch (1985) LEXIS, 14 January (CA)

During the night the accused fired his air gun out of the window of his first-floor flat. He was hoping to hit bottles he had placed on the roof of the garage opposite. A person standing in the garage was hit. The defendant contended that he thought that he was a good enough shot to hit only the bottles. He had put them in a place where the risk would be minimal and he had not pumped the gun the maximum number of times. It was held that the accused was aware of the probable consequences of firing the gun as he did.

Morrison (1989) 89 Cr App R 17 (CA)

The victim, a detective constable, tried to arrest the accused. She grabbed his clothes. The accused dived through a window. The victim was brought into contact with the glass and serious lacerations were caused. The accused was charged with one form of s 18, wounding with intent to resist arrest. The court corrected the trial judge by holding that *Cunningham* applied. It expressed regret that English law recognised two forms of recklessness at that time.

Rainbird [1989] Crim LR 505 (CA)

The accused, a school caretaker, fired an air gun at some boys who were trespassing. He hit one of them. The trial judge seems to have mixed up the objective and **Cunningham** versions of recklessness. The Court of Appeal quashed the conviction, declaring that the subjective definition was necessary.

Brady [2006] EWCA Crim 2413

The accused, while having consumed alcohol and Ecstasy tablets, sat on a 44 inch high railing on a balcony above a dance floor. On the assumed facts, he fell on to one of the dancers, rendering her a paraplegic. The court held, applying **G** [2004] 1 AC 1034 (HL), that the accused was reckless for the purposes of s 20 if he foresaw some risk of harm. There was no need to prove that the risk of injury was significant and obvious.

Though Diplock LJ said in **Mowatt**, above, that the accused was guilty when he should have foreseen harm, the foresight must be that of the accused, not of a reasonable person: **Grimshaw** [1984] Crim LR 108, **Parmenter** (CA) and **Savage** (HL), both above. In **Parmenter** the accused confessed to causing injuries to his three-month-old son, but said that he did not realise that what he was doing would injure him. Mustill LJ held that the accused himself must foresee some harm. The Court of Appeal in **Rushworth** (1992) 95 Cr App R 252 confirmed that the correct direction is to ask whether the accused might have foreseen some physical harm, not whether he *would* have foreseen harm. In **Savage**, above, Lord Ackner had used both concepts – the accused is guilty if he foresaw some harm might result and if he foresaw that some harm would result. **Rushworth** clarifies the law. On the facts the accused knew that some physical harm might result from his act of pushing a vibrator into a woman's vagina. The law was not that the accused had to foresee that some harm must result from what he did. The court in **Pearson** [1994] Crim LR 534 (CA) purported to follow **Rushworth** but at one point used the word 'would', as did the rial court in **DPP v A** [2001] Crim LR 140 (DC). If that were correct, the definition would constitute intent on one of the views of **Woollin** [1999] AC 82 (HL), discussed in Chapter 3. Professor Smith's comment on **Mowatt** at [1990] Crim LR 711 (case comment on **Savage**) is: 'We need some system of stamping a judicial health warning across certain pages of the law reports which have an unending capacity to mislead.' Though the *actus reus* comprises GBH or wounding, the *mens rea* for both is intention or recklessness as to physical harm.

Diplock LJ's statement in **Mowatt** that the harm foreseen need not be GBH so long as he foresaw some physical harm, however minor, was approved in **Sullivan** [1981] Crim LR 46 (CA), followed in **Jones**, above, and approved again in **Savage**; **DPP v Parmenter**. It is sufficient that the accused intends or is reckless as to causing some harm and GBH in fact results. The result is sometimes known as 'half *mens rea*'. The accused is guilty even though he did not intend, nor was he reckless as to the full *actus reus*, GBH. Whether the law should be this is a moot point. Commentators often say that the *actus reus* and *mens rea* should correspond, and they do not in s 20.

An intention to frighten is not by itself sufficient *mens rea* for s 20: **Sullivan**, above. For this reason it may be difficult to convict stalkers of the s 20 offence. Section 47 is, however, a possible charge provided that a recognised psychiatric illness is occasioned. Another possibility is a charge of s 20 where the accused intends to scare but foresees some psychiatric harm.

In s 18 the prosecution must prove that the accused acted with intent to do some GBH or resist arrest or prevent apprehension or detainer. In **Belfon** [1976] 3 All ER 46, the Court of Appeal held that this mental element was not satisfied by recklessness. In **Bryson** [1985] Crim LR 669 (CA), it was decided that the fact that harm was probable did not mean that the accused intended that harm. Intention bears the same meaning as in murder: **Bryson** and **Purcell** (1986) 83 Cr App R 45 (CA): see Chapter 3. As with regard to murder, the jury should not be directed as to the definition of intent save in exceptional situations. In **Belfon**, a *dictum* of Lord Diplock in **Hyam v DPP** [1975] AC 55 (HL) that intent covered both desiring a consequence and knowing that a result was likely to happen was disapproved. Section 18 in summary requires intention. Foresight is insufficient. The different forms of the ulterior intent do not sit happily together in s 18: causing GBH with intent to do GBH may be more serious than causing GBH with intent to resist arrest yet the crime and punishment are the same.

Because s 18 is expressed in terms of 'cause GBH with intent to do GBH', the Court of Appeal in **Mowatt** opined that the term 'maliciously' was superfluous. The thinking is that if one intends GBH, one must foresee GBH as a probable or possible outcome. If, however, the indictment is based on GBH with intent to resist arrest, 'maliciously' is not superfluous. If the accused seriously harms an arresting officer, without 'maliciously' he would be guilty if he did not foresee any harm at all. By retaining 'maliciously' in the definition, the accused is not guilty unless he foresaw some harm. It has to be admitted that the law is in a mess.

Included offences

A person found not guilty under s 20 may be convicted under s 47: **Wilson**, approved by the House of Lords in **Savage**. While it is not possible to convict of a s 20 wounding, a s 47 actual bodily harm or common assault on a charge of s 18 (**Austin**, above), one may convict of a s 20 inflicting GBH: **Mandair** [1995] 1 AC 208 (HL). 'Causing' in s 18 covers all forms of 'inflicting' in s 20. A jury's verdict of causing GBH contrary to s 20, which the Court of Appeal had on this and previous occasions thought was a crime unknown to law, was to be read as meaning that causing GBH was contrary to s 20 because it consisted of inflicting GBH. The Lords emphasised that it was 'highly desirable' to use the actual words of the statute in the count and that if necessary alternative counts could be included in the indictment. **Mandair** has apparently been superseded by the ruling in **Ireland; Burstow** that there is little, if any, difference between 'cause' and 'inflict'.

Possessing anything with intent to commit an offence under the OAPA

Section 64 of the OAPA penalises any person who has 'in his possession . . . any . . . thing, with intent thereof' to commit an offence under the Act. The Law Commission's draft Criminal Code, Law Com. No. 177, 1989, does not include this crime. All remaining portions of the 1861 Act would be included in the Criminal Code. Therefore, s 64 would no longer serve a useful purpose. It does nevertheless seem a useful offence to catch persons who have not reached the stage of an attempt. An alternative view is that s 64 is restricted to explosives because it falls within the part of the Act dealing with explosives. On a literal reading, however, it is not so restricted.

Reform of ss 18, 20 and 47

Criminal law should work in practice. Clarkson and Keating 'Codification: offences against the person under the draft Criminal Code' (1986) 50 JCL 405, at 415, wrote:

> Each of the non-fatal offences against the person is, to varying degrees, confused and uncertain . . . [I]n relation to each other, they are incoherent and fail to represent a hierarchy of seriousness.

Reading such parts of the OAPA is more likely to confuse the student than enlighten him or her. It is possible to substitute all the terms in the sections and thereby produce an authoritative modern version of the crimes which gets rid of all the difficult and case-encrusted phraseology. The definition of concepts such as 'wound', 'cause', 'inflict', 'actual bodily harm' and 'grievous bodily harm' have to be gathered from the cases. The OAPA was a consolidation statute with no attempt made to grade the offences or fit them together. That said, since the Act dates from 1861 and, as stated, that was simply a consolidation Act, it is easy to see why modern judges find difficulty fitting modern methods into the 1861 statute. The telephone, email, fax were not invented then. Similarly, HIV infection was unknown.

A Police–Crown Prosecution Service Working Group has drafted guidelines to distinguish among non-fatal offences including battery and attempted murder in an endeavour to ensure consistency of charges across the country. The first version was published in [1994] NLJ 1168 as *Charging Standards: Offences Against the Person*. A second version, *Offences Against the Person: Charging Standard Agreed by the Police and the Crown Prosecution Service*, was issued in 1996. An interesting point is that the guidelines at times adopt a charge below that stated in the texts. They classify, for instance, a graze as a battery, not as actual bodily harm, and put an undisplaced broken nose on the borderline between the two. Examples of actual bodily harm include broken teeth, extensive bruising, minor cuts which require stitching and minor bone fractures. The guidelines give as examples of GBH those injuries which require extensive surgery or a transfusion, permanent disabilities and significant visible disfigurement, and broken limb, skull, cheekbone and jaw injuries requiring lengthy treatment. There is a handy list of alternative verdicts, a topic which often creates difficulties in the courts. The aims of the Working Group are the choice of charges to reflect the nature of the attack, the provision of sufficient sentencing power and the facilitation of simple presentation of the case. Good administration of criminal justice is promoted. The guidelines have been criticised for channelling non-fatal offences into the magistrates' court where the chances of conviction are higher than in the Crown Court. The contrary argument is that the guidelines help to prevent a serious charge from being brought in the expectation that, as a result of plea bargaining, the accused will plead guilty to a lesser offence. Moreover, since Parliament has provided a hierarchy of offences, it is not legitimate that some other body should seek to lay down rules.

In its Fourteenth Report, *Offences Against the Person*, Cmnd 7844, 1980, the Criminal Law Revision Committee proposed replacing s 18 by 'intentionally' causing serious injury, s 20 by recklessly causing serious injury, and s 47 by intentionally or recklessly causing serious injury. The Criminal Code team adopted these proposals in the draft Criminal Code of 1985 (*Codification of the Criminal Law: A Report to the Law Commission* Law Com. No. 147). The 1989 version substitutes 'personal harm' for 'injury' (cll 70–72). By cl 6 'personal harm means harm to body or mind and includes pain and unconsciousness'. It covers cuts and bruises. There is no definition of 'serious', which is left to the triers of fact. No doubt there will be inconsistent decisions. Wounding is not dealt with separately. The crime will depend on whether the wound was serious harm or not.

Of the other offences adverted to in this chapter, the crime of threatening to kill would be extended to threats to cause serious personal harm (cl 65); administering a substance without consent (cl 73) and assault to resist arrest (cl 77) would be redrafted. The crime of assault with intent to rob, found in s 8 of the Theft Act 1968, would be taken out of property offences and placed with offences against the person (cl 78).

In a roundabout way the defence of consent is preserved by cll 14(4) and 45(c). The exception of consent is expressly mentioned in assault (cl 75). No list of when consent is a defence was provided in relation to cll 70, 71, 72 and 75 because 'it is impossible to provide a comprehensive and closed list', a rather lame sentiment.

As the Court of Appeal said in *Lynsey* [1995] 2 Cr App R 667, 'Most, if not all, practitioners and commentators agree that the law concerning non-fatal offences against the person is in urgent need of comprehensive reform to simplify it, rationalise it, and make it trap-free . . . [B]ad laws cost money and clog up courts with better things to do.' Reform is a long time coming, even though the proposed changes would save money. This value-for-money approach was developed by the Commission in its proposals discussed in the next section.

The 1993 recommendations on assaults

The Law Commission made proposals for reforming crimes of violence in its Report No. 218, *Legislating the Criminal Code – Offences against the Person and General Principles*, 1993, which is based on the Criminal Law Revision Committee's Fourteenth Report, *Offences Against the Person*, Cmnd 7844, 1980, and the draft Criminal Code, Law Com. No. 177, 1989. The intention is to enact the draft Criminal Code in tranches, the first one being this area which was selected as being the one most in need of reform. The revised portions will be brought together into a Code.

The Law Commission followed its predecessors in noting that the law was inconsistent in substance and form and 'inefficient as a vehicle for controlling violence'; for example even after *Savage* 'many aspects of the law are still obscure, and its application erratic'. Money was wasted in an attempt to find out the law and correct errors. The Law Commission estimated the costs of the trial and appeal in *Scarlett* [1993] 4 All ER 629 (CA) at £42,170 and the financial cost of the accused's imprisonment at some £7,000.

The proposals are as follows:

(a) Intent is defined as covering both 'purpose' and knowledge that a result 'would occur in the ordinary course of events if he [the defendant] were to succeed in his purpose of causing some other result'. The latter part of the definition catches the bomb-in-the-aeroplane scenario. The accused will not intend something which he wishes to avoid; for example, a defendant will not intend to hurt a child when he throws her out of a window to escape a fire.

(b) Recklessness is defined in the subjective sense, awareness of a risk that a result will occur or awareness of a risk that a circumstance exists or will exist.

(c) Sections 18, 20 and 47 of the OAPA are to be repealed as unjust, ineffective, illogical, and seriously defective in terms of the hierarchy of harms and penalties, and incomprehensible to juries. A few illustrations will suffice. A person is guilty of s 18, a crime with a maximum sentence of life imprisonment, if his sole intention is to resist arrest. An accused is guilty of s 20 if he is reckless as to the risk of minor harm: *Mowatt* and *Savage*. The distinction between 'inflicting' in s 18 and 'causing' in s 20 is problematic. And the maximum punishment is the same for both s 20 and s 47 despite the difference in harm caused.

(d) In para. 12.34 the Law Commission states: 'The interests both of justice and social protection would be much better served by a law that was (i) clearly and briefly stated; (ii) based on the injury intended or contemplated by the accused, and not on what he happened to cause; and (iii) governed by clear distinctions, expressed in modern and comprehensible language, between serious and less serious cases.' The new structure is based on (1) the abolition of the distinction between wounding and actual or GBH; (2) a distinction between serious and other injuries; and (3) a division between intentionally and recklessly causing injury. The effect, therefore, is the creation of three offences:

(i) intentionally causing serious injury – maximum sentence life;

(ii) recklessly causing serious injury – five years;

(iii) intentionally or recklessly causing injury – three years. This would be the replacement for assault occasioning actual bodily harm. It could be used, for example, against stalkers when it is difficult to prove which of a series of acts caused the victim to be made afraid.

The Law Commission assures readers that these crimes would be 'just, simple, workable and effective in at least the great majority of cases' and that juries should have no difficulty understanding the wording. The enactment of these proposals would deal with the problems noted in the previous paragraph.

Only intentionally causing serious injury could be committed by an omission to act.

(e) The term 'injury' is preferred to 'personal harm' in the draft Criminal Code as being apt to describe both physical and mental interference. 'Injury' is a term in ordinary use and juries should find no difficulty with it. In criticism it might be said that 'harm' is more apt than 'injury' to cover mental interference. The proposed law has been criticised for subsuming too broad a range of injuries within its definition of 'injury', on the ground that there is a moral difference between causing a slight injury and causing one just short of a serious injury.

(f) The law should continue to cover non-serious injuries.

(g) 'Serious' is not to be defined but left to the jury as in current law.

(h) Pain and unconsciousness are expressly mentioned as 'injury'. Wounding as a separate head of liability is abolished. Depending on the character of the wound it will be either a serious injury or an injury. This reform would remove the criticism that wounding is treated in the same fashion as grievous harm even when it does not amount to such harm.

(i) The transmission of diseases, such as AIDS, can be caught by the phrase 'impairment of a person's physical condition' in the definition of injury found in cl 18 of the Criminal Law Bill attached to the Report.

(j) Assault is defined in cl 6 of the Bill.

(1) A person is guilty of the offence of assault if –

(a) he intentionally or recklessly applies force to or causes an impact on the body of another –

(i) without the consent of the other, or

(ii) where the act is intended or likely to cause injury, with or without the consent of the other; or

(b) he intentionally or recklessly, without the consent of the other, causes the other to believe that any such force or impact is imminent.

(2) No such offence is committed if the force or impact, not being intended or likely to cause injury, is in the circumstances such as is generally acceptable in the ordinary conduct of daily life and the defendant does not know or believe that it is in fact unacceptable to the other person.

The term 'assault' thus covers both (psychic) assault and battery. Despite the Criminal Law Revision Committee's recommendation that assault did not need to be defined by Parliament, the Commission considered that it should be put on a statutory footing.

(k) Section 16 of the OAPA, threats to kill, is extended to threats to cause serious injury. One criticism is that the maximum penalty for this offence is 10 years' imprisonment, whereas the maximum for recklessly causing serious injury is only five.

The issue of consent to violent non-sexual crimes is dealt with separately by the Law Commission in its Consultation Papers noted above.

The 1998 Home Office proposals

The Home Office issued a Consultation Document, *Violence: Reforming the Offences against the Person Act 1861*, in 1998. Attached was a draft Offences against the Person Bill. The principal non-fatal offences provisions are the following:

1(1) A person is guilty of an offence if he intentionally causes serious injury to another. . . .

2(1) A person is guilty of an offence if he recklessly causes serious injury to another. . . .

3(1) A person is guilty of an offence if he intentionally or recklessly causes injury to another. . . .

4(1) A person is guilty of an offence if –
(a) he intentionally or recklessly applies force to or causes an impact on the body of another, or
(b) he intentionally or recklessly causes the other to believe that any such force or impact is imminent.

(2) No such offence is committed if the force or impact, not being intended or likely to cause injury, is in the circumstances such as is generally acceptable in the ordinary conduct of daily life and the defendant does not know or believe that it is in fact unacceptable to the other person. . . .

10(1) A person is guilty of an offence if he makes to another a threat to cause the death of, or serious injury to, that other or a third person, intending that other to believe that it will be carried out. . . .

15(1) In this Act 'injury' means –
(a) physical injury, or
(b) mental injury.

(2) Physical injury does not include anything caused by disease but (subject to that) it includes pain, unconsciousness and any other impairment of a person's physical condition.

(3) Mental injury does not include anything caused by disease but (subject to that) it includes any impairment of a person's mental health.

(4) In its application to section 1 this section applies without the exceptions relating to things caused by disease.

The effect of cl 15(4) is that intentional transmission of disease resulting in serious injury will be a crime, but the intentional or reckless transmission of disease causing injury will not. Clause 10(1) extends the present offence of threat to kill to threat to cause serious injury. In relation to omissions, it should be noted that the offence of intentionally causing serious injury will be committable by omission, but there will be no liability for recklessly causing serious injury or for intentionally or recklessly causing injury. Intent and recklessness are defined as in the 1993 Recommendations. Clause 18 provides that the offences are subject to any defence, lawful authority, justification or excuse. What these defences are is left to the common law.

As can easily be seen, the Home Office proposals are those of the Law Commission outlined in the previous section of this book. The then Home Secretary, Jack Straw, in his Foreword to the Consultation Document, stated that the aim was to reform 'outmoded and unclear Victorian legislation', thereby demonstrating 'this Government's commitment to modernising and improving the law'. This commitment awaits enactment.

The proposals have also come under criticism. First, there is what is sometimes called moral vacuity at the heart of the proposals; that is, ordinary people do not just take into account the *actus reus* and *mens rea* of the accused when they are assessing the gravity of his conduct. They also inquire into matters such as the way in which the injury was caused. For example, the weapon may be important or the fact that the accused tortured the victim. Secondly, there is the strange distinction between cll 1 and 2, on the one hand, and 3 and 4, on the other. If, as the Commission thought, there is a moral distinction between intent and recklessness, why are the two combined in the lesser non-fatal offences? Thirdly, 'serious injury' is undefined. How serious is 'serious'? Moreover, it may be said that there is a vast difference between, say, a broken cheekbone and the loss of an arm, but both constitute serious injury. In that light, perhaps there should be several grades of serious injury. Fourthly, cl 10(3) excludes anxiety and distress from the ambit of 'impairment of a person's mental health'. However, minor physical harms remain within the definition of physical injury. So, minor mental injuries are not to be criminal, but minor physical ones are. For the sake of consistency the two should be brought into line. A fifth issue is that the revised definition of battery does not by its words ('force or impact') cover the situation where the accused's conduct is an omission, such as leaving one's hand on a knee on which it has rested accidentally, and where the accused's behaviour is unacceptable, but there is no force or impact, as when he strokes the victim's hair without consent.

Nevertheless, as the Conclusion to the Consultation Document states, the enactment of the draft Bill would create a more consistent hierarchy of offences than that which exists at present, and 'making the law more accessible in this way will help to smooth the passage of thousands of cases each year, enabling the citizen to understand the criminal offences more easily. . . . It should also make the task of judges, magistrates and juries more straightforward in the day to day administration of justice'. Unfortunately, work at the Home Office on reform of non-fatal offences appears to have stopped.

Summary

Non-fatal, non-sexual offences constitute the subject of this Chapter. The sequence is from the least serious, assault, up the 'ladder' of seriousness, through battery to assault occasioning actual bodily harm contrary to s 47 of the Offences Against the Person Act 1861 (OAPA) to malicious wounding or inflicting grievous bodily harm (GBH) contrary to s 20 of the OAPA to malicious wounding or causing GBH with intent to do some GBH contrary to s 18 of the OAPA. The defence of consent, both to assault and battery and exceptionally to more serious offences (cf. boxing), is considered. There is discussion of the case of the sado-masochists, *Brown* (1994), and the cases in which this authority has been applied and distinguished. Emphasis is placed on problems which students face, for example the two definitions of assault, the constructive nature of liability in ss 20 and 47, the possible distinction between 'inflicting' and 'causing' GBH. The chapter concludes with a consideration of reform proposals.

- *Assault*: Assault is the least serious non-fatal offence but care must be taken when reading the cases. This is because the term is used in two different but overlapping senses: first, as a separate offence concerned with making the victim afraid (in this sense assault is sometimes known as 'psychic' or 'technical' assault); secondly, as a generic term covering assault in the first sense and the discrete offence of battery. Assault is used here to mean the separate offence. The *actus reus* is causing another to apprehend immediate and unlawful personal violence and the *mens rea* is intentionally or (subjectively) recklessly causing another to apprehend immediate and unlawful personal violence. In relation to the *mens rea* the word 'subjectively' is put in brackets because even when objective recklessness existed, the law was always that the accused himself or herself had to foresee the relevant consequence.

  For many years it was said that one could not commit the crime by words alone but that rule has now gone; indeed, silent phone calls have in the quite recent past been classified as assaults (and therefore some instances of stalking are caught by this offence). The timescale of 'immediate' has been widened too recently and it now includes 'making someone afraid at some time not excluding the immediate future'; in this way phone calls are covered because the victim may not know where the caller is. However, words may negate what would otherwise be an assault. Modernising the words of the most famous authority on this point, 'I would shoot you dead if armed police weren't next to you', is not an assault. The word 'unlawful' is a reminder that some threats of immediate personal violence are not unlawful, for example a threat to hit someone may be a lawful threat in preventing crime.

- *Threats to kill*: Section 16 of the OAPA creates a specific offence dealing with threats to kill without a lawful excuse. The *mens rea* is intentionally causing the victim to apprehend that the threat to kill will be carried out.

- *Battery*: A battery is the intended or (subjectively) reckless use of force on a person without consent or other lawful excuse. There is no need for the direct infliction of force and an omission suffices as the *actus reus* where there is a duty to act. Hostility, it would seem, is not a requirement. The exception of lawful excuses covers for example lawful chastisement of children. Consent, which is noted next, is a defence.

- *Consent*: The basic rule is that consent is no defence to crimes more serious than a battery (e.g. to assault occasioning actual bodily harm) but there are several exceptions, including:

Boxing	Sports, within the rules of the particular sport
Cosmetic surgery	Sterilisation
Flagellation for religious purposes	Surgery
Horseplay	Tattooing
Scarification	

- *Assault occasioning actual bodily harm*: This is an offence contrary to s 47 of the OAPA. 'Assault' bears its wider meaning of 'technical' or 'psychic' assault and the separate crime of battery.

'Actual' means 'more than trivial'.

'Bodily' does not just cover flesh and bones but also the psyche. It does not, however, include emotions such as distress or panic.

'Harm' means 'injury'.

More difficult is the *mens rea*, which is intention or recklessness as to assault (in its narrow sense of being an independent crime) or battery. There is no need for intent or recklessness as to actual bodily harm. As we have seen, murder's *mens rea* is somewhat similar: an intent to cause GBH suffices; and as we shall see, in s 20 of the 1861 statute intention or recklessness as to actual bodily harm constitutes the *mens rea*.

- *Malicious wounding or inflicting grievous bodily harm*: Section 20 of the OAPA creates the crime of malicious wounding or inflicting GBH. 'Bodily' and 'harm' have been defined above. 'Grievous' means 'really serious'. A 'wound' is a breach in all the layers of the skin. The *mens rea* is a trap for the unwary: it is intent or recklessness as to actual bodily harm: intent or recklessness as to GBH is not needed. It should be noted that both for the wounding and for the inflicting GBH versions of this offence, the *mens rea* is the same.

- *Malicious wounding or causing GBH with intent to do some GBH* (etc.): This crime is laid down in s 18 of the OAPA. Its main versions may be expanded as 'wounding with intent to do some GBH' and 'causing GBH with intent to do some GBH'. Therefore, s 18 does not include 'wounding with intent to wound'. One difference from s 20 is that the verb used in s 18 is 'cause' (GBH) whereas in s 20 it is 'inflict' (GBH). For many years it was thought that there was a distinction: if one left something for the victim to take, one might have caused GBH but not inflicted it. Modern thinking, however, is that the two verbs cover the same activities.

References

Reports

Criminal Law Revision Committee 14th Report, *Offences Against the Person*, Cmnd 7844 (1980)

Home Office Consultation Document, *Violence: Reforming the Offences against the Person Act 1861* (1998)

Law Commission Consultation Paper no. 134, *Consent and Offences against the Person* (1994)

Law Commission Consultation Paper no. 139, *Consent in the Criminal Law* (1995)

Law Commission Report no. 177, *A Criminal Code for England and Wales* (1989)

Law Commission Report no. 218, *Legislating the Criminal Code: Offences Against the Person and General Principles* (1993)

Police–Crown Prosecution Service Working Group, *Charging Standards: Offences Against the Person* [1994] NLJ 1168

Police–Crown Prosecution Service Working Group, *Offences Against the Person: Charging Standard Agreed by the Police and the Crown Prosecution Service* [1996]

Books

Clarkson, C.M.V., Keating, H. and Cunningham, S.R. *Criminal Law: Text and Materials*, 7th edn (Sweet & Maxwell, 2010)

Stephen, J.F. *A History of the Criminal Law of England*, vol. 3 (MacMillan, 1883)

Wilson, W. *Criminal Law*, 4th edn (Longman, 2011)

Journals

Bennett, G. and Hogan, B. 'Criminal law, criminal procedure and sentencing' [1990] All ER Rev 69

Burns, R. 'GBH of the earhole' [1992] NLJ 1725

Clarkson, C.M.V. and Keating, H. 'Codification: offences against the person under the draft Criminal Code' (1986) 50 JCL 405

Smith, J.C. 'Comment on *Savage*' [1990] Crim LR 711

Williams, G. 'Force, injury and serious injury' [1990] NLJ 1227

Further reading

Allen, M.J. 'Consent and assault' (1994) 58 JCL 183

Anderson, J. 'The business of hurting people: A historical, social and legal analysis of professional boxing' (2007) 7 Oxford U Commonw LJ 35

Anderson, J. 'No licence for thuggery: violence, sport and the criminal law' [2008] Crim LR 751

Bergelson, V. 'Consent to harm' (2007–8) 28 Pace LR 683

Clarkson, C.M.V. 'Law Commission Report on offences against the person and general principles: (1) Violence and the Law Commission' [1994] Crim LR 324

Cooper, S. and James, M. 'Entertainment – the painful process of rethinking consent' [2012] Crim LR 188

Fox, M. and Thomson, M. 'Short changed? The law and ethics of male circumcision' (2005) 13 IJ of Children's Rights 161

Fox, M. and Thomson, M. 'The new politics of male circumcision: HIV/AIDS, health law and social justice' (2012) 32 LS 255

Francis, L.P. and Francis, J.G. 'Criminalizing health-related behaviors dangerous to others? Disease transmission, transmission-facilitation, and the importance of trust' (2011) 6 Crim Law and Philos 47

Gardner, J. 'Rationality and the rule of law in offences against the person' [1994] CLJ 502

Gunn, M.J. and Ormerod, D.C. 'The legality of boxing' (1995) 15 LS 181

Horder, J. 'Rethinking non-fatal offences against the person' (1994) 14 OJLS 335

Horder, J. 'Reconsidering psychic assault' [1998] Crim LR 392

Jefferson, M. 'Offences against the person: Into the 21st Century' (2012) 76 JCL 471

Livings, B. 'Legitimate sport or criminal assault' (2006) 70 JCL 495

McCutcheon, J.P. 'Sports violence, consent and the criminal law' (1994) 45 NILQ 267

Munro, V.E. 'An unholy Trinity? Non-consent, coercion and exploitation in contemporary legal responses to sexual violence in England and Wales' [2011] CLP 45

Murphy, P. 'Flogging live complainants and dead horses: We may no longer need to be in bondage to Brown' [2011] Crim LR 758

Ormerod, D.C. 'Criminalising HIV transmission' (2001) 30 *Common Law World Review* 135

Ormerod, D.C. and Gunn, M.J. 'The legality of boxing' [1996] Crim LR 694

Reed, D. 'Court of Appeal: offences against the person: reckless transmission of HIV' (2005) 69 JCL 389

Roberts, P. 'Consent to injury: how far can you go?' (1997) 113 LQR 27

Roberts, P. 'The philosophical foundations of consent in the criminal law' (1997) 17 OJLS 389

Ryan, S. 'Reckless transmission of HIV: knowledge and culpability' [2006] Crim LR 981

Schueklenk, U. 'Should we use the criminal law to punish HIV transmission?' (2008) 4 IJ Law in Context 277

Shute, S. 'The Law Commission's second consultation paper on consent' [1996] Crim LR 685

Slater, J., 'HIV, trust and the criminal law' (2011) 75 JCL 309

Spencer, J. 'Retrial for reckless infection' (2005) 154 NLJ 762

Smith, J.C. 'Case comment on *Mandair*' [1994] Crim LR 667

Smith, J.C. 'Offences against the person: the Home Office Consultation Paper' [1998] Crim LR 317

Stannard, J. 'Sticks, stones and words: Emotional harm and the English criminal law' (2010) 74 JCL 533

Tolmie, J. 'Consent to harmful assaults: The case for moving away from category-based decision making' [2012] Crim LR 656

TOP website, http://oldestprof.com/index.php/sexlaws/86-hiv ('TOP' stands for 'The Oldest Profession')

Weait, M. 'Harm, consent and the limits of privacy' (2005) 13 *Feminist Legal Studies* 97

Weait, M. 'Knowledge, autonomy and consent: *R v Konzani*' [2005] Crim LR 763

Weait, M. 'Criminal liability for sexually transmitted infections' (2009) 173 JPN 45

Wilson, W. 'Consenting to personal injury: how far can you go?' (1995) 1 *Contemporary Issues in Law* 45

For a book on assaults and HIV, see M. Weait, *Intimacy and Responsibility: The Criminalisation of HIV Transmission* (Routledge-Cavendish, 2008)

Visit **www.mylawchamber.co.uk** to access tools to help you develop and test your knowledge of criminal law, including interactive multiple choice questions, practice exam questions with guidance, annotated weblinks, glossary flashcards, legal newsfeed and legal updates.

Use Case Navigator to read in full some of the key cases referenced in this chapter with commentary and questions:

DPP v *Majewski* [1976] UKHL 2
R v *Brown* [1994] AC 212 (HL)
R v *G and Another* [2003] UKHL 50
R v *Ireland; Burstow* [1998] AC 147
R v *Woollin* [1999] AC 82

14

Rape and other sexual offences

Aims and objectives

After reading this chapter you will understand and be able to critique:

- the research into rape as an offence
- the definition of rape
- the definition of consent
- the crimes in ss 2–4 of the Sexual Offences Act 2003

Introduction to rape

In 2008–09 there were 12,165 reported rapes of women and 968 of men, and in 2009–2010 there were approximately 45,000 serious sexual assaults excluding rapes. The 2000 British Crime Survey (BCS) estimated that there had been some 61,000 rapes in the previous year and that some three-quarters of women had been raped in their lifetime. The BCS deals not with crimes reported to the police but with figures derived from interviews. BCS figures are usually some four times greater than reported crimes. The Home Office sees the BCS figures as more accurate than totals reported to the police. It is unclear whether the rise in reported rapes over the last 30 years, a twentyfold increase, represents an actual rise in the number of rapes or whether the figure represents a rise in the number of rapes reported to the police.

Although reports of **rape** increased steadily after the Second World War, a belief remained among victims that they would not be believed and would be treated unsympathetically; reporting levels of rape did not approach the actual figures (L.J.F. Smith, *Concerns About Rape*, Home Office Research Study No. 106, 1989). Changes initiated in the 1980s, such as police use of trained female officers, provision of victim examination suites, and liaison with victim support schemes, had apparently gone some way towards reassuring victims that their complaints would be taken seriously and pursued, but reporting levels, while increasing, remained low. Nevertheless, there are myths surrounding rape and the work of Liz Kelly, Jennifer Temkin and Sue Griffiths in *Section 41: An Evaluation of the New Legislation Limiting Sexual History Evidence in Rape Trials*, 2006, Home Office, is of great assistance in debunking myths and stereotypes, for example most rapes are committed not by strangers but by men known to the victim; often the victim does not resist; and contrary to myth, most rapes take place indoors. L.J.F. Smith's detailed 1989 study revealed that in half of the cases there was actual or threatened violence, half of the victims were aged 16-24, and 60 per cent of offenders were aged 16–29. Only one-third of the perpetrators were total strangers, and 40 per cent were well known to the victims. There was some indication that rape by the husband was the most common form. This survey may exaggerate the percentage of stranger rapes in light of later reports.

The research report *The Nature of Rape of Females in the Metropolitan Police District*, by Chandni Ruparel (Home Office Research Study No. 247, 2004), reports that 16 per cent of victims were under 16, and more than one-third were under 21. Some 6 per cent were rapes in which drugs were used, but in over 90 per cent of cases no weapon was involved. Of rapes by 'intimates', 64 per cent took place in the victim's home.

The Government's Response to the Stern Review: An Independent Review into how Rape Complaints are Handled by Public Authorities in England and Wales, March 2011, is focused on the issues raised by Baroness Stern's 2010 Report and therefore does not discuss substantive criminal law issues, but readers may like to know the following:

- 89 per cent of rapes go unreported;
- 38 per cent of all rapes recorded by the police are on children aged under 16;
- the average cost of an adult rape (including the emotional impact on the victim) is £96,000;
- the most common perpetrators of serious sexual offences including rape are current or ex-partners (54 per cent);
- some degree of physical force was used in 64 per cent of rapes;
- the attrition rate for rape as widely publicised is the subject of a report from the Ministry of Justice's Chief Statistician (CS). The first stage was the publication of a report by that person (Jill Matheson), *Consultation on Improvements to Ministry of Justice Statistics*, 2010, CP15/10. One thing the CS did write in her report was that rape should not be singled out and her report was therefore on how to improve the whole of Ministry of Justice statistics.

Although reporting rates have risen, there is great concern that the conviction rate for rape is low and falling. J. Harris and S. Grace, *A Question of Evidence? Investigating and Prosecuting Rape in the 1990s*, Home Office, 1999, found that fewer than 10 per cent of recorded rapes resulted in a successful prosecution. Home Office figures from 2003 reported the same proportion; in early 2005, they reported a conviction rate as low as 7 per cent; it is now below 6 per cent (L. Kelly, J. Lovett and L. Regan, *A Gap or a Chasm? Attrition in Reported Rape Cases*, Home Office Research Study No. 293, 2005). The Fawcett Society has a map on their website (www.fawcettsociety.org.uk) showing conviction rates for recorded rapes in 2006. Examples are Surrey, 3.2 per cent and South Yorkshire 9.6 per cent. The lowest was Leicestershire, 2.8 per cent, the highest Cleveland, 13.2 per cent: a fivefold difference. However, once the cases reach the Crown Court the conviction rate approaches 60 per cent, which is higher than for some other crimes. It should be noted that in modern times it is rare for an accused to contend that he did not penetrate the victim, because of DNA and other evidence, and all turns on whether the alleged victim consented, which may be a matter known only to them. With the male arguing that the alleged victim did consent, the burden of proof being on the Crown, and the standard of proof being beyond reasonable doubt, it would seem difficult to push the conviction rate much above 60 per cent unless the law was fundamentally changed, for instance by placing the burden of proof on the accused, which may be contrary to Article 6 of the European Convention on Human Rights.

The basic definition of rape

Example

Norbert plies Olivia with alcoholic drink. They have sexual intercourse. Is this rape?

Rape, which is contrary to s 1(1) of the Sexual Offences Act 2003, requires (a) the intentional penetration of one or more of three orifices, (b) without consent and (c) the accused must not reasonably believe that the victim is consenting. There is an explanation of (c) in s 1(2), whereby in brief all the circumstances must be taken into account. The first requirement is clearly satisfied. The second and third may be taken together. If the victim consents there is no rape. 'Consent' for the purposes of rape is defined in ss 74–76 of the Act. It is recommended that the sections are tackled in reverse order because if s 76 is fulfilled there is no consent; if it is not, but s 75 is, then the accused bears the evidential burden of showing that the victim was not consenting; only if the facts do not fall within ss 76 or 75 need the general definition in s 74 be looked at. On the facts s 76 does not apply; s 75 may apply if the accused gives the victim a stupefying drug, and alcohol is a stupefying drug; however, it does not take much for the accused to shoulder the evidential burden and switch the onus to the prosecution, in which case they must disprove consent beyond reasonable doubt. Section 74 comes into play where the basic definition of consent is: the victim 'agrees by choice, and has the freedom and capacity to make that choice'. Whether he or she does or not is fact-sensitive, but for a major case see **Bree** [2008] QB 131 (CA). The final part is whether the accused believed on reasonable grounds that the victim was consenting. Again this is a fact-sensitive issue and the jury is instructed by s 1(2) to take into account 'any steps A has taken to ascertain whether B consents'. On the facts we do not know.

Section 1 of the Sexual Offences Act 2003 defines rape in this way:

(1) A person (A) commits an offence if –
   (a) he intentionally penetrates the vagina, anus or mouth of another person (B) with his penis,
   (b) B does not consent to the penetration, and
   (c) A does not reasonably believe that B consents.
(2) Whether a belief is reasonable is to be determined having regard to all the circumstances, including any steps A has taken to ascertain whether B consents.

This definition replaces that found in the Sexual Offences Act 1956, s 1, as amended, and s 1(1)(c) and (2) replace s 1(2) of the Sexual Offences (Amendment) Act 1976. The principal changes are that rape can now by committed by the penetration of the mouth by the penis (sometimes called 'oral rape') and that the *mens rea* is extended to include situations where the accused had an unreasonable belief in the victim's consent (overruling *DPP* v *Morgan* [1976] AC 182 (HL) for the purposes of rape). It may come as a surprise that rape may take place via the mouth. The extension of the law raises issues of fair labelling, that is, is it fair to call this behaviour rape when many would not consider it to be so as a matter of ordinary language? The Home Offence 2000 Report said that oral rape was just as demeaning and as traumatising as any other type of rape (para. 2.8.5).

Section 2 of the 2003 Act creates the offence of assault by penetration and s 3 creates the offence of sexual assault, the replacement for indecent assault, and the mental element in both offences includes an unreasonable belief in the victim's consent. Section 4 creates the offence of causing a person to engage in sexual activity without consent. Sections 2–4 are discussed below.

Expanding rape's definition

The Act is based on, but not the same as, the Law Commission's Consultation Paper No. 139 on *Consent in the Criminal Law*, 1995, the Home Office Consultation Paper, *Setting the Boundaries: Reforming the Law on Sex Offences*, 2000, and the White Paper, *Protecting the Public*, 2002. The government was concerned with finding the correct label for each offence it created so that an appropriate amount of stigma attached. The 2003 Act is the culmination of several changes in the law: in *R* v *R* [1992] 1 AC 599 (HL) it was held that husbands could rape their wives, even when they were cohabiting; since the Sexual Offences Act 1993 boys aged 10–14 can be guilty of rape; and by the Criminal Justice and Public Order Act 1994 rape was extended to include 'anal rape' of men and women as we have seen. The 2003 Act reversed *Morgan* and added mouths to the list of orifices. The latter extension was justified by the Home Office in its Report *Setting the Boundaries*, 2000, as being 'as horrible, as demeaning and as traumatising as other forms of forced penile penetration'. There are arguments in restricting rape to penetration of the vagina: that may accord with ordinary language, the stigma of rape may be reduced by extending the law to the anus and the mouth, and there is no possibility of pregnancy if the penetration is of an orifice other than the vagina.

Penetration

The Act is restricted to penetration by the penis. Therefore, it can still only be committed by men. 'Penis' includes a surgically constructed penis and 'vagina' includes a surgically constructed vagina (s 79(3)). By s 79(9) 'vagina includes vulva', thereby confirming that the slightest penetration suffices. Rape is complete on penetration; however, if the victim consents to penetration but withdraws consent after penetration, the accused must in turn withdraw his penis, as s 79(2) makes clear ('penetration is a continuing act from entry to withdrawal'). It is uncertain how much time a man has to withdraw: the government's view was that he would have a reasonable time and whether or not the time he took was reasonable would be left to the jury's good sense. However, that is not what the statute says: there is on the face no defence of withdrawal within a reasonable time. Under the old law it did not have to be proved that the hymen was broken or that semen was ejaculated. The 2003 Act does not mention these rules but since the offence is complete on penetration, both rules apply under the new law.

Consent

Consent is a 'defence' to rape. If the prosecution cannot prove this element beyond reasonable doubt, then there is no rape. Proof is particularly problematic when as is usual there are only two persons present when sexual intercourse takes place. Section 74 states in part: 'a person consents if he agrees by choice, and has freedom and capacity to make that choice.' The words 'choice', 'freedom' and 'capacity', which are surprisingly not defined in the statute, are open-textured and reasonable juries may disagree as to their application to the facts. 'Capacity' to choose in particular may give rise to difficulties. Does it cover only the nature of the penetration or include the consequence, for example STDs, pregnancy? Consent is very much person-specific and situation-specific: one can agree to sexual intercourse with one person but not agree to it with another. One may agree to intercourse in one scenario but not another. Article 8 of the European Convention on Human Rights protects the freedom to have a private life and the definition of consent should be read in light of the jurisprudence on Article 8. There is no need to prove active resistance. Similarly there is no requirement that the victim communicates his non-consent to the accused. The difference between consent, even consent given reluctantly especially in a long-term relationship, and submission is one for the jury to decide on the facts. See for an illustration *Doyle* [2010] EWCA Crim 119, where the jury had to decide between the facts as given by the accused and those presented by the victim and they preferred the victim's account (the accused held her head under water, tied her up, then untied her, and said he wanted sex; the victim refused and protested; he removed her underwear, forced her legs apart, and penetrated her).

By s 76 it is *conclusively* presumed that the victim did not consent and that the accused did not reasonably believe that he or she consented if: '(a) the defendant intentionally deceived the complainant as to the nature or purpose of the relevant act; or (b) the defendant intentionally induced the complainant to consent to the relevant act by impersonating a person known personally to the complainant.' If there is no deception or inducement, s 76 does not apply. Strangely s 76 would seem to apply even though the victim was not deceived. For example, the alleged victim may be mistaken as to 'the nature or purpose of the relevant act', but if the mistake was not brought about by the defendant's deception, the scenario does not fall within s 76. Compare a scenario where the accused persuades the victim to agree to intercourse as an expression of their undying love; however, the accused does not love the victim; if intercourse does take place, these facts fall within s 76 and constitute rape. Whether Parliament so intended may be doubtful. An illustrative case is *Jheeta* [2008] 1 WLR 2582 (CA). The accused lied to the victim, telling her that she must have sexual intercourse with him or she would be fined by the police. She was not deceived as to the nature or purpose of the activities. Therefore, the facts did not fall within s 76. However, the accused was guilty of rape because under s 74 there was no agreement by choice. Note that to fall within s 76 the accused's deception or inducement must have been intentional. It remains to be seen whether s 76 complies with Article 6 of the European Convention on Human Rights: 'Everyone charged with a criminal offence shall be presumed innocent until proven guilty according to law.' It may be that it would survive challenge on the basis that it is a proportional response to a social problem.

Another recent case is *Devonald* [2008] EWCA Crim 527. The offence was one contrary to s 4, discussed below, causing sexual activity without consent, but s 76 applies to that offence too. The accused, the father of a girl whom he believed the victim had treated badly, decided to humiliate him and inveigled him into masturbating in front of a webcam. He deceived him into thinking that he was doing it for the pleasure of a young woman whose persona the accused had taken on. The court held that he had deceived the victim as to the purpose of the sexual activity.

By s 75 there is a *rebuttable* (evidential) presumption that the victim did not consent and that the accused did not reasonably believe in the victim's consent if the accused was using or threatening to use violence whether against the victim or some other person; if the complainant was being unlawfully detained; if he or she was 'asleep or otherwise unconscious'; if he or she was because of 'physical disability' unable to communicate consent; or if he or she had been administered a stupefying or overpowering substance. It should be noted that the complainant's voluntary intoxication does not give rise to a rebuttable presumption of lack of consent. Instead the general provision in s 74 applies. It is for the accused to rebut the presumption of lack of consent by leading sufficient evidence. Once that is done the legal burden is on the accused. It has to be said that not much evidence needs to be adduced. If s 75 is irrelevant on the facts, no direction should be given about it: *White* [2010] EWCA Crim 1929, a case on assault by penetration. This crime is discussed below but ss 74–76 apply to it in the same way as they apply to rape. Goldring LJ stressed that there had to be some foundation in the evidence before s 75 applied. On the facts the accused digitally penetrated the victim and sent photographs to the victim. The question was concerned with consent pure and simple, not with any of the facts situations in s 75.

A case on s 75 in the context of sexual assault is *Ciccarelli* [2011] EWCA Crim 2665. The accused sexually touched the victim who was either asleep or unconscious through alcohol. The Court held that s 75 does not reverse the burden of proof, but that the accused must put forward some evidence that there was consent and/or reasonable belief in consent. The case simply restates what is obvious from a reading of the statute but is welcome for stating the law clearly.

It is not always clear why some matters are one of conclusive presumption (s 76) and some only of the evidential presumption. For example, surely if the accused gave the victim a stupefying drug in order to have intercourse with him or her, these facts should amount to a conclusive presumption that the victim did not consent. At present, furthermore, it is uncertain whether alcohol is a 'substance . . . which . . . was capable of causing or enabling the complainant to be stupefied or overpowered . . .'. Similarly is the use of violence really not as bad as impersonating the victim's boyfriend? Section 75 provides for only a rebuttable presumption in the former case but s 76 states that the latter event falls within the irrebuttable presumption.

Accordingly there are three situations involving consent: the conclusive presumption in s 76; the rebuttable presumption in s 75; and the general rule, the default position, in s 74. There is no minimum age at which children can agree by choice to penetration but, as s 74 states, they must have 'capacity' to give agreement. If a child aged under 16 does freely agree, the crime is not one of rape itself but, for example, of rape of a child under 14 (s 5 of the 2003 Act; see also ss 6–15 of that statute, all of which deal with sexual offences against children). A mentally ill or mentally disabled person can consent if he or she does so within s 74. The problem again is one of 'capacity', and presumably he or she must be *Gillick*-competent (see the civil case of *Gillick* v *West Norfolk and Wisbech AHA* [1986] AC 112 (HL)). The issue of whether there was consent or not is very much one for the jury: *H* [2007] EWCA Crim 2056. (This case is also known as *Hysa*.) This is so perhaps especially when the victim was intoxicated, as the facts of *H* demonstrate. She was 16, alone at night and drunk and was picked up by a stranger who very quickly had sexual intercourse with her. This case also demonstrates that a person can at the time of the intercourse not be consenting, even though she later cannot remember what happened.

Further criticism of the distinction drawn in ss 75 and 76 may be made. For example, why is there a conclusive presumption against consent where the victim is deceived or there is impersonation, but only an evidential presumption where the victim has been drugged or is asleep?

Section 74 also applies in this situation: the victim is not so drunk that he or she is 'asleep or otherwise unconscious' (s 75(2)(d)) and is not voluntarily intoxicated (s 75(2)(f)) but is, say, loudly demanding sexual intercourse, that is, he or she would not have been so acting, had he or she been sober; in other words, his or her inhibitions have been loosened by alcohol. In that event the jury must decide whether there is an agreement by choice to penetration and whether the victim had the freedom and capacity to make that choice. For example, in *Bree* [2008] QB 131 (CA), it was held that where the alleged victim was drunk but still capable of choosing whether to have intercourse or not, there was no rape. The state of mind of each victim must be looked into. It may be difficult for a jury to decide these issues and it would not be surprising if juries came to different decisions. Such an outcome, however, is antithetical to justice for in one instance the accused is guilty of an offence with a maximum sentence of life imprisonment and in the other is not guilty of that offence. Section 74, however, does not prevent consent to sexual intercourse occurring when the accused does not reveal his HIV status: *B* [2007] 1 WLR 1567 (CA). However, these facts will not provide him with a defence to a grievous bodily harm offence.

Section 75 is largely self-explanatory but note that the paragraph dealing with violence does not apply if the accused makes a threat to destroy or damage property. Similarly, the provision does not apply if the threat is to inflict violence in the non-immediate future.

Section 76 is based on the common law, but the first point to make is that even if the facts do not fall within s 76, there can still be a lack of agreement within s 74. For example, to fall within s 76(2)(a) the accused must intentionally deceive the victim as to the nature or purpose of the penetration. If the victim is mistaken as to the nature or purpose but not because of the accused's deception, s 76(2)(c) does not apply but s 74 does. The application of s 76 may be illustrated by the facts of the following cases, all dating from before the 2003 statute.

Williams [1923] 1 KB 340 (CCA): the accused persuaded the victim into agreeing to sexual intercourse by saying that the penetration would improve her breathing. Under both the old and the new law the accused is guilty of rape. He has intentionally, as s 76 requires, deceived her as to the 'nature' of the act. If the victim knew what sexual intercourse was but she was told by the accused that engaging in such conduct would improve her singing, there is deception as to the 'purpose' within s 76, though not as to the 'nature'.

Linekar [1995] 2 Cr App R 49 (CA): the victim, a prostitute, consented to sex with the accused for £25. The Court of Appeal held that the facts did not constitute rape: the accused's deception that he would pay her, but in fact he did not, did not invalidate her consent. She was deceived and thereby consented to the intercourse but she was not deceived as to the fact that what the parties did was sexual intercourse. There was no deception under the old law as to the nature of the act or the identity of the accused; similarly under the new law there is no deception as to the 'purpose' or as to the 'nature' of the act. This is at least what the Court of Appeal thought in *Jheeta*, above. Note, however, that if s 76 does not apply on the facts, s 74, the general definition of consent, comes into play. However, there is a contrary argument. If it may be said that the nature of the act is 'paid-for sex', there is a conclusive presumption of lack of consent and the accused is guilty of rape. Presumably sex with a condom is different from sex without a condom too. Is sexual intercourse with an HIV positive person different from that with one who is not?

The facts of *Linekar* at the time would have fallen within s 3 of the Sexual Offences Act 1956. Section 4 of the 2003 Act, discussed below, is the replacement provision but it is so worded that the same definition of consent applies to it as to rape. Therefore, the difficulty with the current definition of rape also affects s 4.

Tabassum [2000] 2 Cr App R 328 (CA): this was a case on indecent assault. The Sexual Offences Act 2003 replaced this crime with the offence of sexual assault (s 3). In respect of the old and the new crime the law as to consent is the same as in the old and the new (respectively) offence of rape. The accused touched women's breasts, allegedly to show them how to conduct self-examinations. He had no medical training but he lied that he was a breast cancer specialist undertaking a breast cancer survey. The Court of Appeal held that the women consented to the nature of the act but not as to the quality; therefore, the accused was guilty. *Tabassum* was much criticised for drawing a distinction between nature and quality. Under the new law, however, the conviction is more securely grounded. The victims did not consent to the 'purpose' of the touching. Their consent was negated by the accused's deception as to the purpose of the act.

Section 76 also deals with the conclusive presumption of the lack of consent where there is a mistake as to identity. The person impersonated must be one 'known personally to the complainant'. Therefore, s 76 does not apply when the accused deceives the victim into believing that he is a rock star. Similarly, s 76 does not apply when the accused deceives the victim as to his wealth in order to achieve penetration. As with s 75, if s 76 does not apply, the general rule in s 74 applies. To use a pre-Act case as an example: in *Elbekkay* [1995] Crim LR 163 (CA) the victim thought that the accused was her boyfriend; he (the accused) did not impersonate him. Under the new law s 76 does not apply because there was no impersonation; however, s 74 does apply and a jury may well hold that the victim consented to sex with her boyfriend, not with the accused, and that therefore there was no agreement by choice within s 74.

It is worth stating that consent to sex in one orifice does not extend to consent in any other. For example, if one consents to vaginal intercourse, one does not consent to anal intercourse.

It should be noted that the presumptions do not apply to the inchoate offences of assisting or encouraging, attempt to commit and conspiracy to commit crimes to which ss 75 and 76 apply.

And finally one should also note the difference between consent in sexual offences and consent in non-fatal non-sexual offences. Knowing consent in one area of law may be positively misleading when it comes to the other one. For instance, the evidential and irrebuttable presumptions discussed above do not apply to non-fatal offences.

Mens rea

The mental element consists of intentional penetration and the accused's lack of a reasonable belief that the victim is consenting. In relation to the first aspect, the phrase 'intentionally penetrates the vagina, anus or mouth' in s 1(1)(a) seems to require intention as to the penetration of an orifice which the accused intends to penetrate. If so, negligently penetrating the anus when one intended to penetrate the vagina does not give rise to rape. In *Heard* [2008] QB 43 the Court of Appeal said that intentional penetration means deliberate penetration and not reckless or accidental penetration.

In relation to the second aspect the accused will have the mental element if he knows that the victim is not consenting, if he gives no thought as to whether or not he or she is consenting, and if he has no reasonable grounds for believing that he or she is consenting. *Morgan*, above, is overruled: the men did not believe on reasonable grounds that the woman was consenting. Sections 75 and 76, quoted above, apply to the lack of reasonable belief in consent. For example, there is a rebuttable presumption (s 75) that the accused does not have a reasonable belief in consent when the victim is asleep; and there is a conclusive presumption (s 76) when the accused deceives the victim as to the nature or purpose of the penetration or impersonates a person known personally to the complainant.

Section 1(2), quoted above, instructs the jury to take into account all the circumstances, which include, presumably, nods and winks indicating a willingness to engage in sexual congress. 'Circumstances' is undefined, but includes matters such as deafness, immaturity and learning difficulties. It is uncertain, for example, whether the accused can rely on previous occasions when the victim did consent. What about a culture where women are subservient to men's sexual demands? Are they to be treated as consenting and are the men to be deemed to have reasonable belief in the women's consent? It is suggested that the accused's sexual proclivities such as the fact that he finds women in low-cut dresses sexually attractive are excluded from 'circumstances'. Arguably too circumstances individual to the accused should also be excluded because they would subjectivise the objective standard. It has to be said that this area of law is ripe for judicial development. The jury has to decide the s 1(2) issues in each case.

The former requirement of the unlawful nature of the sexual intercourse

Until 1994 (see the Criminal Justice and Public Order Act 1994, Part XI) the statutory definition of rape included the element that the intercourse was 'unlawful'. Until quite recently the sexual intercourse was unlawful if it took place outside marriage: *Chapman* [1959] 1 QB 100 (CA). However, in *R* [1992] 1 AC 599 the Lords ruled that the law no longer was that the husband was incapable in law of raping his wife. In the light of existing law it was surprising that the accused was even prosecuted, never mind convicted, for no crime seemed to exist. The principal speech was delivered by Lord Keith.

(a) The institutional writer Hale may have been correct to write in his *History of the Pleas of the Crown*, 1736, Vol. 1, 629, published by E. & R. Nutt and R. Gosling, that 'the husband cannot be guilty of a rape committed by himself upon his lawful wife, for by their mutual matrimonial consent and contract the wife hath given herself up in this kind unto her husband which she cannot retract'. However, the common law developed in accord with social, economic and cultural shifts. Marriage was now a partnership, and the wife was no longer a chattel. In the light of these changes, the idea that a woman had to have sexual intercourse with her husband, no matter how she felt or how her health was, was unacceptable. Accordingly, there was no justification for the marital exemption.

(b) The former state of the law had been undermined by the case law. In *Miller* [1954] 2 QB 282 (DC), it was held that the husband, while not guilty of rape, could be guilty of assault occasioning actual bodily harm. It was unrealistic, in Lord Keith's view, to separate the acts leading up to the sexual intercourse from the intercourse, and then find the husband guilty of the minor crime but not of the major one. Moreover, exceptions had been created which had cut into Hale's hard-and-fast rule. In *O'Brien* [1974] 3 All ER 663, the Court of Appeal held that the husband was guilty of rape when there was a decree nisi of divorce. In *Steele* (1976) 65 Cr App R 22 (CA), the husband was guilty when he had given an undertaking not to molest his wife. In *Roberts* [1986] Crim LR 188 (CA), the husband was guilty where there was a formal separation order.

(c) The undermining of the marital exemption was, however, a common law development. In the statute there was the word 'unlawful'. To say that sexual intercourse outside marriage was unlawful was not the natural meaning of the word. The word was otiose, mere surplusage. The view that Parliament kept the word 'unlawful' in the 1976 Act to preserve the marital exemption with its exceptions was rejected. (This approach had been upheld by Rougier J in *J* [1991] 1 All ER 759 (Crown Court).) If Parliament had been asked in 1991, it might not have wished to preserve the exemption.

R may be criticised

(a) When it enacted the Sexual Offences (Amendment) Act 1976 Parliament rejected a clause which would have made rape within marriage illegal. *R* is therefore contrary to Parliament's intention. Law-making is for Parliament, not the judges, especially in controversial matters.

(b) Since Parliament did not change the law in 1976 the Lords have created an offence, something which they vowed they would not do (see Chapter 1).

(c) The offence of rape has been widened retrospectively. It has been applied to an accused who before this case would not have been guilty of rape. The European Court of Human Rights, however, ruled in *CR v UK* [1996] 1 FLR 434 (a case also called *SW v UK*) that the decision in *R* was not inconsistent with Article 7 of the European Convention on Human Rights, which prohibits retroactive criminal law. The Convention's purpose was to impose dignity and freedom, both of which were promoted by the case of *R*.

(d) The Law Commission issued a Working Paper, *Rape within Marriage*, Law Com. No. 116, 1989, where the options for reform were discussed. At the time of the decision in *R* the full Report was expected. The proposals of the Commission could have been enacted by Parliament, which through the Report would have seen the whole of the problem and not just the part at issue in *R*.

(e) Many cases have proceeded on the basis that 'unlawful' in the pre-1994 definition meant outside marriage. *Chapman*, a case on abducting girls contrary to s 19 of the Sexual Offences Act 1956 (since repealed), is one, as is *Jones* [1973] Crim LR 710 (CA) on abducting women contrary to s 17 of the same Act (also since repealed). The cases on the exceptions to the marital rape exemption assume that the rule exists. Some of those authorities are noted above. Others include *Clarke* [1949] 2 All ER 448, where the judge held that the marital exemption did not apply when the wife had obtained a non-cohabitation order in a separation order, and *Sharples* [1990] Crim LR 198 (Crown Court), where there was an undertaking not to have sexual intercourse. Another case showing that the courts recognised the marital exemption is *Cogan and Leak* [1976] QB 217 (CA), discussed in Chapter 5. The husband made his wife consent to sexual intercourse with a man who believed that the wife was consenting. That man was acquitted of rape on the grounds of honest mistake. The husband was convicted as principal to rape, with the other man being the innocent agent, i.e. in law he raped through the genitals of someone else! One difficulty in accepting that the husband was the principal party was the marital exemption rule. If the husband could in law rape his wife, criticism of *Cogan and Leak* would have been substantially less. As it was, the court found a way round the marital exemption. Hale's proposition has been cut back by the exceptions to the marital exemption and in *Clarence* (1888) 22 QBD 23 (CCR) the judges were *obiter* split on the crime, but it was accepted for 250 years.

(f) The word 'unlawful' must have meant something. It is not included in the crime of incest because a husband cannot commit that offence with his wife. Section 6 of the Sexual Offences Act 1956 (since repealed) dealt with unlawful sexual intercourse with a girl under 16. What if the accused is married by foreign law to a girl under 16? If 'unlawful' does not mean outside marriage, the husband is guilty of this offence if he has sexual intercourse in England with his wife. Surely that outcome is incorrect. A perhaps more contentious issue occurred in s 7 of the same Act (since repealed). It is a crime for a man to have unlawful sexual intercourse with a woman who is mentally defective. What if they are married? If 'unlawful' is surplusage, the husband is guilty.

Policy arguments against the marital exemption

(a) It is wholly unjust and contrary to common sense that a husband could go away for a lengthy period, come back, commit an act which would otherwise be rape on his wife, yet be found not guilty of rape.

(b) The Court of Appeal in *R* [1991] 2 All ER 257 thought it 'repugnant and illogical' that a husband could be punished for violence against the wife in the course of sexual intercourse to which she did not consent but could not be guilty of rape itself, especially when rape can be seen as a heinous form of violence. Whether the sexual intercourse without consent is by the husband, an acquaintance or a stranger, there may be a fear of sexually transmitted disease or pregnancy.

(c) The court also said that the law should not be based on fictions. It was a fiction that by marrying her husband the wife had consented to intercourse whenever he wanted it. That fiction was 'anachronistic and offensive'.

(d) It should not matter who the victim of the rape is: 'a rapist remains a rapist . . . irrespective of his relationship with the victim' (*per* Lord Lane CJ in *R* in the Court of Appeal). A husband can frighten and humiliate his wife just as much as a stranger can do to the same woman. Indeed it may be that marital rape is the most common form of rape.

(e) It is a fiction to say that at the wedding ceremony the wife surrenders her right to choose when and with whom to have sexual intercourse. Moreover, a woman who is cohabiting without marriage receives the protection of the law. Why should it make any difference that she is married?

(f) In the civil law the wife may refuse sexual intercourse when, for example, her health would be endangered. It would be strange if criminal law were out of line.

(g) It could be argued that one effect of the marital immunity was that criminal law protected property more than persons. A husband can steal from his wife but could not rape her. Moreover, a husband can kidnap and falsely imprison his wife. It seems strange if he cannot rape her.

(h) The law is made consistent with Scottish law, which abolished the marital immunity in *S* v *HM Advocate* 1989 SLT 469. The court held, *inter alia*, that on marriage the wife does not irrevocably consent to sexual intercourse, that since she cannot in law consent to a major battery, she could not consent at one time to non-consensual battery by intercourse at some time in the future, and that a charge of rape against the husband would not undermine domestic relations more than, for instance, a charge of indecent assault based on facts other than vaginal penetration. By late 1991 of the seven husbands tried for raping their wives in Scotland none had been convicted.

As J.A. Scutt commented, 'Consent in rape: the problem of the marriage contract' (1977) 3 Monash ULR 255 at 288:

> Public policy surely requires protection of citizens, married or unmarried, from aggressive sexual acts; it also requires that potential defendants be treated alike . . . Again, public policy in upholding the marital relationship must be directed toward upholding those relationships wherein criminal acts are not committed by one spouse upon the other.

Indeed, the fact that the husband has foisted himself on his wife may demonstrate that the marriage has irretrievably broken down. The irretrievable breakdown of a marriage is the ground for divorce. There seems little point in using the very blunt instrument of marital immunity to patch up such a marriage. One problem which has not been addressed, however, is where does the victim go, whether married, cohabiting or otherwise, when she is a non-earner?

Boys and women as rapists and accessories

With effect from 20 September 1993 the Sexual Offences Act 1993 abolished the irrebuttable presumption that a boy under 14 was incapable of committing an offence involving sexual intercourse, whether anal or vaginal. A boy over 10 but under 14 can rely on the defence of infancy if he lacks mischievous discretion. A boy can be convicted of being a secondary party to rape: *Eldershaw* (1828) 172 ER 472.

A woman may be a secondary party to rape: *Ram and Ram* (1893) 17 Cox CC 609. She cannot commit rape.

Sexual offences other than rape

The Sexual Offences Act 2003 establishes three offences which are in some respects drafted similarly to rape: assault by penetration, sexual assault and causing a person to engage in sexual activity without consent. These offences are considered next. There may be overlaps among them, and the alert reader should be able to construct scenarios where two, three or even four of the offences found in ss 1–4 of the 2003 Act occur. The 2003 Act also defines many other **sexual offences** including crimes against family members, children and those suffering from learning difficulties, zoophilia, necrophilia, voyeurism and others, but these are not dealt with here.

Assault by penetration

Section 2(1) of the 2003 Act reads:

> A person (A) commits an offence if –
> (a) he intentionally penetrates the vagina or anus of another person (B) with a part of his body or anything else,
> (b) the penetration is sexual,
> (c) B does not consent to the penetration, and
> (d) A does not reasonably believe that B consents.

The maximum sentence on indictment is imprisonment for life: s 2(4). This offence is a partial replacement for the crime of indecent assault. The Home Office in *Setting the Boundaries*, 2000, concluded that 10 years, the maximum sentence for indecent assault, was not long enough for the most serious sexual assaults. In terms of the maximum this crime is equivalent to rape. The phrase 'part of his body' includes the penis, so some facts may constitute both rape and this offence. In this sense s 2 is useful where it is uncertain with what the victim has been penetrated.

The reasonableness of the belief as in rape 'is to be determined having regard to all the circumstances, including any steps A has taken to ascertain whether B consents': s 2(2). Also as in rape, the provisions in ss 75 (the rebuttable presumption of lack of consent) and 76 (irrebuttable presumption of lack of consent) apply. One effect is that if a doctor performs, say, a vaginal examination not for the purpose of medical treatment but for the purpose of sexual gratification, deception as to purpose falls within s 76. Indeed, the same activity such as penetration of the anus without consent falls within both the crime of rape and this offence. However, there are also differences: rape includes penetration of the mouth whereas this offence does not; this offence must be committed via a penetration which is sexual in nature, whereas rape need not be (though penetration by the penis is presumably sexual); rape turns on penetration by a penis whereas this offence does not (for example, penetration by fingers, bottle or brush handle suffices). This last point demonstrates that unlike rape this offence is not restricted to male defendants. It should be noted that the maximum sentence for both offences is life imprisonment. *Whitta* [2006] EWCA Crim 2626 held that liability is strict as to the identity of the victim. If the accused intends to penetrate one person digitally but makes a mistake as to the identity of the complainant, the fact that the intended victim would have consented to the penetration is irrelevant.

However, unlike rape the offence of assault by penetration (and the offences contrary to ss 3(1) and 4(1), below) is committed only when the assault was 'sexual'. By s 78:

> . . . penetration, touching or any other activity is sexual if a reasonable person would consider that –
>
> (a) whatever its circumstances or any person's purpose in relation to it, it is because of its nature sexual, or
> (b) because of its nature it may be sexual and because of its circumstances or the purpose of any person in relation to it (or both) it is sexual.

These words are largely self-explanatory. One effect of s 78 is to exclude medical examinations from being 'sexual'. Where the penetration is not sexual in nature within either (a) or (b), the accused's purpose or the surrounding circumstances cannot make it 'sexual' within s 78. Therefore, the fact that the accused has a shoe fetish does not make the act of removing a shoe from a girl's foot into a sexual assault (see below) despite the sexual satisfaction the accused obtained from doing so. Similarly, touching the hem of a girl's skirt is not sexual despite the accused deriving sexual gratification in doing so. Telling a young girl to strip may be sexual but need not be, as when a mother tells her daughter to get undressed for the bath. See *H* [2005] Crim LR 735 (CA) on the post-2003 law: saying 'Do you fancy a shag?', touching the victim's tracksuit bottoms and trying to put a hand over her mouth were held to be 'sexual'. The court said that fetishes may be 'sexual' within s 78 but was not 'of its nature sexual' within s 78(a). The position remains unclear. Presumably the accused need not know that what she did was 'sexual'. Certainly it is immaterial whether or not the accused thought his conduct was 'sexual'.

Sexual assault

Section 3(1) of the 2003 Act creates the offence of sexual assault. By s 3(1):

> A person (A) commits an offence if –
> (a) he intentionally touches another person (B),
> (b) the touching is sexual,
> (c) B does not consent to the touching, and
> (d) A does not reasonably believe that B consents.

The definition covers all kinds of sexual assaults from frottage to forcible penetration.

As in rape and assault by penetration the reasonableness of A's belief is determined by considering all the circumstances including any steps A took to ascertain whether B did consent; and as in rape and assault by penetration ss 75 and 76 apply. The definition of 'sexual' found in s 78, discussed above in relation to assault by penetration, applies. Section 3(1) applies to 'touching', which is defined in s 79(8) as including 'touching (a) with any part of the body, (b) with anything else, (c) through anything, and in particular includes touching amounting to penetration.' 'Assault' in s 3(1) really means 'battery'. 'Assault' in its technical or psychic sense (see Chapter 13) does not fall within s 3. Therefore, the same acts which constitute rape and assault by penetration can also constitute sexual assault. The maximum sentence, however, for this offence, on indictment, is 10 years' imprisonment, whereas that for rape and assault by penetration is life imprisonment. The overlap is particularly acute in terms of sentence when it is known that the maximum sentence on summary conviction is six months' imprisonment or a fine not exceeding the statutory maximum, currently £5,000.

For an explanation of assault, see pp 488–91 (Chapter 13).

Reported cases on this offence as yet are rare and the main authority is *H*, above, where the Court of Appeal dismissed the accused's appeal. It held that since s 79(8) did not define 'touching' but merely stated that certain activities constituted 'touching', a person who touched the victim's clothes, here tracksuit bottoms near the right-hand pocket, fell within the boundaries of the offence. The Court also rejected an argument that the touching was not sexual. Since the touching was not unequivocally sexual, s 78(b) applied. The jury had to consider whether the touching might be sexual; and, if so, whether the jury considered the touching to be sexual, taking into account the accused's (or any other person's) purpose and the circumstances.

Causing a person to engage in sexual activity without consent

Section 4(1) of the Sexual Offences Act 2003 creates the offence of causing a person to engage in sexual activity without consent. By it:

A person (A) commits an offence if –
(a) he intentionally causes another person (B) to engage in an activity,
(b) the activity is sexual,
(c) B does not consent to engaging in the activity, and
(d) A does not reasonably believe that B consents.

'Causes' bears it usual meaning, as discussed in Chapter 2. It therefore includes any contribution which is more than minimal. It includes causing by threats of violence and actual violence and by inducements. For case facts falling within s 4(1) see *Devonald*, above. Another example is forcing two people to engage in sexual acts for the accused's lewd pleasure.

Unlike s 3(1), there is no need for a touching. As may be expected, whether the belief is reasonable depends on all the circumstances including any steps taken by A to determine whether B consents; ss 75 and 76 apply; and the definition of 'sexual' noted above applies. The sexual activity may be one not between A and B but between B and someone else or something else. An example is forcing B to masturbate. The section is also satisfied where a woman forces a man to have sexual intercourse with her. Section 4 may be seen as some compensation for the law that a woman cannot be guilty of rape, though the maximum sentence for a s 4(1) offence is less than that for rape.

It should be noted that s 4(1) may on the facts cover behaviour also caught by s 1(1), rape, s 2(1), assault by penetration, and s 3(1), sexual assault. For this reason there are complicated provisions as to sentence. By s 4(4):

A person guilty of an offence under this section, if the activity caused involved –
(a) penetration of B's anus or vagina,
(b) penetration of B's mouth with a person's penis,
(c) penetration of a person's anus or vagina with a part of B's body or by B with anything else, or
(d) penetration of a person's mouth with B's penis,
is liable, on conviction on indictment, to imprisonment for life.

Otherwise the maximum term is 10 years on indictment and six months or a fine not exceeding the statutory maximum, currently £5,000, or both. One perhaps surprising effect of s 4(4) is that if the accused forces the victim to submit to penetration of the anus or vagina by a dog, the maximum sentence is life, but if the penetration is of the mouth, the maximum is 10 years.

Summary

This chapter deals with some of the more important sex crimes, all of which were revised in the Sexual Offences Act 2003. The main focus is on rape but other linked offences such as sexual assault are considered. With regard to these crimes there is not just the problem of the *actus reus* (e.g. does sexual penetration cover penetration of an artificial vagina?) but also of the *mens rea*, which was changed in 2003, to include the state of mind of a man who decided on unreasonable grounds that the victim was consenting. Section 1(1) of the 2003 Act defines rape thus:

A person (A) commits an offence if –
(a) he intentionally penetrates the vagina, anus or mouth of another person (B) with his penis,
(b) B does not consent to the penetration, and
(c) A does not reasonably believe that B consents.

Sub-section (2) adds: 'Whether a belief is reasonable is to be determined having regard to all the circumstances, including any steps A has taken to ascertain whether B consents.'

Despite the difficulties of interpretation of the *actus reus* words, there is an even greater problem, that of consent. The current law revolves around three situations: in some situations lack of consent is irrebuttably presumed (s 76 of the Act); in other circumstances there is a rebuttable presumption of lack of consent (s 75 of the Act); and thirdly, there exist situations in which there is a lack of consent where neither s 76 nor s 75 applies. In this third scenario s 74 defines consent thus: 'a person consents if he agrees by choice, and has freedom and capacity to make that choice.'

References

Reports

Home Office Consultation Paper, *Setting the Boundaries: Reforming the Law on Sex Offences* (2000)

Home Office White Paper, *Protecting the Public*, Cm 5668 (2002)

Law Commission Consultation Paper no. 139, *Consent in the Criminal Law* (1995)

Law Commission Report no. 177, *A Criminal Code for England & Wales* (1989)

Law Commission Working Paper no. 116, *Rape within Marriage* (1989)

Books

Hale, M. *History of the Pleas of the Crown* (E. & R. Nutt and R. Gosling, 1736)

Harris, J. and Grace, S. *A Question of Evidence? Investigating and Prosecuting Rape in the 1990s* (Home Office, 1999)

Kelly, L., Lovett, J. and Regan, L. *A Gap or Chasm? Attrition in Reported Rape*, Home Office Research Study no. 293 (2005)

Kelly, L., Temkin, J. and Griffiths, S. *Section 41: An Evaluation of the New Legislation Limiting Sexual History Evidence in Rape Trials* (Home Office, 2006)

Ruparel, C. *The Nature of Rape of Females in the Metropolitan Police District*, Home Office Research Study no. 247 (2004)

Smith, L.J.F. *Concerns about Rape*, Home Office Research Study no. 106 (1989)

Journals

Scutt, J.A. 'Consent in rape: the problem of the marriage contract' (1977) 3 Monash ULR 255

Further reading

Amnesty International ICM opinion poll, *Stop Violence against Women* (2005)

Athanassoulis, N. 'The role of consent in sado-masochistic practices' (2002) 8 *Res Publica* 141

Bryden, D.P. and Lengnick, S. 'Rape in the criminal justice system' (1996–97) 87 J Crim L & Criminology 1194

Card, R. *Sexual Offences: The New Law* (Jordans, 2004)

Cowan, S. 'The trouble with drink: intoxication, (in)capacity and the evaporation of consent to sex' (2008) 41 Akron LR 899

Crowe, J. 'Consent, power and mistake of fact in Queensland rape law' (2011) 33 Bond LR 21

Dingwall, G. 'Addressing the boundaries of consent in rape' (2002) 13 *King's College Law Journal* 71

Elliott, C. and de Than, C. 'The case for a rational reconstruction of consent in criminal law' (2007) 70 MLR 225

Elvin, J. 'The consent of consent under the Sexual Offences Act 2003' (2008) 72 JCL 519

Finch, E. and Munro, V.E. 'Breaking boundaries? Sexual consent in the jury room' (2006) 26 LS 303

Finch, E. and Munro, V.E. 'The demon drink and the demonized woman' (2007) 16 SLS 591

Finney, A. *Alcohol and Sexual Violence: Key Findings from the Research*, Home Office Research Findings 215, 2004

Gallavin, C. 'Fraud vitiating consent to sexual activity' (2008) 23 NZULR 87

Gardner, J. and Shute, S. 'The wrongness of rape', in J. Horder (ed.), *Oxford Essays in Jurisprudence*, 4th edn (Oxford University Press, 2000)

Gardner, S. 'Appreciating *Olugboja*' (1996) 16 LS 275

Gross, H. 'Rape, moralism and human rights' [2007] Crim LR 220

Gunby, C., Carline, A. and Beynon, C. 'Alcohol-related rape cases: Barristers' perspectives on the Sexual Offences Act 2003 and its impact on practice' (2010) 74 JCL 579

Henderson, N.H. 'Review essay: What makes rape a crime?' (1987–8) 3 Berkeley Women's LJ 193

Her Majesty's Crown Prosecution Service and Her Majesty's Inspectorate of Constabulary, *Without Consent – a Report on the Joint Review of the Investigation and Prosecution of Rape Offences* (2007)

Horder, J. 'How culpability can, and cannot, be denied in under-age sex crimes' [2001] Crim LR 15

Lacey, N. 'Beset by boundaries: the Home Office Review of sex offences' [2001] Crim LR 3

Larcombe, W. 'Falling rape convictions: (some) feminist aims and measures for rape law' (2011) 19 *Feminist Legal Studies* 27

McGlynn, C. 'Feminism, rape and the search for justice' (2011) 31 OJLS 825

McGlynn, C. and V. Munro (eds), *Rethinking rape law: International and comparative perspectives* (Routledge, 2010)

McGregor, J. *Is it Rape?* (Ashgate, 2005)

Matravers, M. Review of Gardner's *Offences and Defences: Selected Essays in the Philosophy of Criminal Law* (OUP, 2007) (2011) 5 Crim Law and Philos 231

Munro, V.E. 'Concerning consent: standards of permissibility in sexual relations' (2005) 25 OJLS 335

Munro, V.E. 'Constructing consent: legislating freedom and legitimizing constraint in the exercise of sexual autonomy' (2008) 41 Akron LR 923

Mumsnet, 'We believe you – rape myths we're challenging' www.mumsnet.com/campaigns/we-believe-you-mumsner-rape-awareness-campaign

Power, H. 'Towards a redefinition of the *mens rea* in rape' (2003) 23 OJLS 379

Powlesland, P. 'Male rape and the quest for gender neutrality in the Sexual Offences Act 2003' [2005] Cambridge Student LR 11

Rapecrisis England and Wales, 'Myths and facts', www.rapecrisis.org.uk/mythsampfacts2.php [last accessed 22 August 2012]

Rumney, P. 'The review of sex offences and rape law reform: another false dawn?' (2001) 64 MLR 890

Rumney, P. and Morgan-Taylor, M. 'Recognising the male victim: gender neutrality and the law of rape' (1997) 26 A-A LR 330

Schulhofer, S. 'Taking sexual autonomy seriously: rape law and beyond' (1992) 11 *Law and Philosophy* 35

Tadros, V. 'Rape without consent' (2006) 26 OJLS 449

Temkin, J. *Rape and the Legal Process*, 2nd edn (Oxford University Press, 2002)

Temkin, J. and Ashworth, A. 'The Sexual Offences Act 2003: (1) Rape, sexual assaults and the problems of consent' [2004] Crim LR 328

Temkin, J. and Krahé, B. *Sexual Assault and the Justice Gap: A Question of Attitude* (Hart, 2008)

Wallerstein, S. '"A drunken consent is still consent" – or is it?' (2009) 73 JCL 318

Warburton, D. 'The rape of a label – why it would be wrong to follow Canada in having a single offence of unlawful sexual assault' (2004) 68 JCL 533

Wells, C. 'Law reform, rape and ideology' (1985) 12 JLS 63

For a symposium on consent, see (1996) 2 *Legal Theory* 89–164

For the proposals for reform which led to the 2003 Act, see the Sex Offences Review Committee, *Setting the Boundaries*, 2 vols (Home Office, 2000). Volume 2 includes the Law Commission's Policy Paper, *Consent in Sex Offences*

For current proposals for reform see Office for Criminal Justice Reform, *Convicting Rapists and Protecting Victims – Justice for Victims of Rape*, 2006, and HM Crown Prosecution Service Inspectorate and HM Inspectorate of Constabulary, *Without Consent* (2007)

For the view of the Scottish Law Commission see Report 209, *Rape and Other Sexual Offences* (2007)

Visit **www.mylawchamber.co.uk** to access tools to help you develop and test your knowledge of criminal law, including interactive multiple choice questions, practice exam questions with guidance, annotated weblinks, glossary flashcards, legal newsfeed and legal updates.

Use Case Navigator to read in full some of the key cases referenced in this chapter with commentary and questions:

R v Bree [2007] EWCA Crim 256
R v Jheeta [2007] EWCA Crim 1699

Theft and robbery

Aims and objectives

After reading this chapter you will understand and be able to critique:

- the crime of theft
- the mental elements: dishonesty and intent permanently to deprive
- the conduct elements: appropriation, property, belonging to another
- the crime of robbery

Introduction to the Theft Act 1968

The Theft Act 1968 was based on the Eighth Report of the Criminal Law Revision Committee, *Theft and Related Offences*, Cmnd 2977, 1966. The Committee decided that the law required thorough overhauling because it was complex and failed to tackle several instances of dishonest dealing with property. The 1968 Act was to be a short, simple measure, a fresh start, free from technicalities and the first step towards codification of the criminal law. Old terminology such as larceny, larceny by a trick, false pretences and embezzlement were replaced by modern terms. The Committee replaced 'fraudulently converts' in the old law of larceny with 'dishonestly appropriates' in the new law of **theft** (para. 35). No change in the meaning was intended. It is partly for this reason that *Gomez* [1993] AC 442 (HL) has been trenchantly criticised: it adopted a much wider meaning of appropriation than did the pre-1968 law. It may be argued that in simplifying Parliament left too much of the law to be worked out by the judges. Some words which had a fixed meaning under the old law were retained, such as 'receive' in handling, and 'menaces' in blackmail. Some parts of the new law are best explained by reference to the defects of the old, for example s 5(4) is difficult to understand without reference to *Moynes v Coopper* [1956] 1 QB 439 (DC). The court called for reform of the law to convict the accused and Parliament obliged.

Unfortunately the 1968 Act has not turned out in the way that its progenitors hoped. Interpretation of the Act has led to difficulties even in simple situations. For example, does one appropriate property for the purposes of theft when one touches it, takes it, or puts it in one's bag? Part of the Act, since repealed, was called by the Court of Appeal in *Royle*

[1971] 1 WLR 1764 a 'judicial nightmare'. In *Hallam* [1995] Crim LR 323 the Court of Appeal said that the 1968 Act was in urgent need of simplification and modernisation because juries should not have to 'grapple with concepts couched in the arcane Franglais of "chose in action"' and public money should not be spent on 'hours of semantic argument divorced from the real merits of the case'. (Interestingly, the term 'chose in action' does not appear in the statute.) Offences overlap, and there are problems with key concepts such as dishonesty. Where the statute looks as if it does not cover certain forms of conduct the courts have sometimes read the statute widely to convict the 'manifestly guilty'. The phenomenon is especially common in theft when a charge would have been more appropriately brought under s 15, obtaining property by deception (since repealed). Time is ripe for a thorough review of the Act.

There are also difficulties in seeing how the Theft Act offences relate to civil law concepts, such as restitution and equity on which they are based. Despite criticism it is confidently asserted that criminal law judges cannot jettison civil law notions. Only by knowing when property belongs to another can one say that a person is or is not guilty of theft, and these concepts are civil law ones, not ones created *ad hoc*. As Lord Hobhouse put it in *Hinks* [2001] 2 AC 241 (HL): 'Section 5 and, particularly, s 5(4), demonstrates that the 1968 Act has been drafted so as to take account of and require reference to the civil law of property, contract and restitution.' Lord Diplock in *Treacy* v *DPP* [1971] AC 537 (HL) said that the Act was 'expressed in simple language as used and understood by ordinary literate men and women'. Interpretation of the statute has, however, been technical. Since some terms such as 'trust' are technical, a technical interpretation cannot always be avoided. For example, even a literate person may not know the meaning of 'equitable interest' in s 5(1). It is a question of law whether a certain legal relationship existed between the parties such as a trust: *Clowes (No. 2)* [1994] 2 All ER 316 (CA). It has to be said that much of the law of theft is complex simply because the civil law on which it is based is complicated.

Moreover, changes in what constitutes property in civil law will have unforeseen consequences in criminal law. One debatable issue is that of property purchased with bribes, discussed below: see the consideration of *Attorney-General of Hong Kong* v *Reid* [1994] 1 AC 324 (PC) below. A simpler illustration is the consequential effect which would occur if trade secrets were held to be property in civil law. They would presumably also be property for the purpose of criminal law including the Theft Act 1968. The case of *Hinks*, discussed below in the context of whether property belongs to another, demonstrates, however, that even the House of Lords is willing to permit civil and criminal law to diverge.

The 2000 British Crime Survey estimated that in 1999 there were a little over 14.7 million crimes, of which some 1,284,000 were burglaries or attempted burglaries. There were about 1.7 million thefts. The authors, C. Kershaw *et al.* (Home Office Statistical Bulletin, 2000), estimated that only 23 per cent of offences are reported to the police. Some 95 per cent of all offences in England and Wales are property-related. S. Nicholas, D. Povey, A. Walker and C. Kershaw *Crime in England and Wales 2004–2005* (Home Office, 2005) said at 58 that there were 3,324,000 thefts. Thefts vary in magnitude. The latest British Crime Survey *Crime in England and Wales: Quarterly Update to September 2011* (2012) estimates 599,000 thefts from the person, 1,224,000 thefts relating to vehicles, 458,000 thefts of bicycles, and 1,100,000 other domestic thefts. At the time of writing (summer 2012) Asil Nadir was found guilty of stealing £29 million from Polly Peck International, whereas a son who steals a cigarette from his mother is also guilty of theft but the value is substantially less.

Theft

Basic definition

> **Example**
>
> If a Law student reads an exam paper which has not yet been sat in an attempt to cheat, is she guilty of theft?
>
> 'No!' The accused has not within s 1(1) of the Theft Act 1968 dishonestly appropriated property belonging to another with the intention of permanently depriving the other of it. The problem is one concerned with 'property'. There is no independent definition of property in criminal law. Only that which is property within civil law is protected by the law of theft. Civil law excludes, for example, human corpses and electricity from its definition and a further exception is confidential information, which an exam paper is. Therefore, taking of the Boardroom table can amount to theft because a table is property, but taking the Boardroom's confidential information, on which the business depends and may be worth millions and worth much more than any table ever made, is not theft: see the Law Commission's Consultation Paper No. 150, *Misuse of Trade Secrets*, 1997. For a case with similar facts to ours (but not involving a Law student), see ***Oxford v Moss*** (1978) 68 Cr App R 183 (DC).

Section 1(1) of the 1968 Theft Act contains a basic definition of theft: 'the appropriation of property belonging to another with the intention of permanently depriving [him] of it.' The *mens rea* is 'dishonesty' and 'the intention permanently to deprive'. The *actus reus* is 'appropriates', 'property' and 'belonging to another' (Figure 15.1). Sections 2–6 offer partial or sometimes complete explanations of these concepts. The penalty is seven years' maximum imprisonment: Criminal Justice Act 1991, s 26(1), amending the Theft Act 1968, s 7. The alteration is the result of a recommendation in the White Paper, *Crime, Justice and Protecting the Public*, Cm 965, 1990, para. 3.14. Previously the maximum had been 10 years.

Lack of consent to the appropriation by the owner need not be proved: ***Lawrence v MPC*** [1972] AC 626 (HL). Lack of consent is therefore not a constituent element in theft. It is, however, relevant to the other elements. If the owner agrees to the appropriation, the accused may not be dishonest. Moreover, once the elements of theft are satisfied, it does not matter that the victim has no civil law remedy. Because an appropriation of property belonging to another may be done by an honest person as well as a dishonest one, it is the *mens rea* of theft which is of great importance. The *actus reus* is 'neutral', contrary, it is suggested, to what Parliament intended. Performing the *actus reus* does not distinguish the thief from an innocent person. Dishonesty is now the crux of theft. For this reason it is considered before the *actus reus*, an arrangement which would normally be strange but one which is appropriate in the light of its importance.

It should be noted that theft forms part of the definition of the crimes of robbery, burglary and handling.

Dishonesty

Dishonesty replaced the concept of fraud in the previous law. Fraud was a legal concept, but dishonesty is largely a matter for the jury. It seems that the framers of the Theft Act 1968

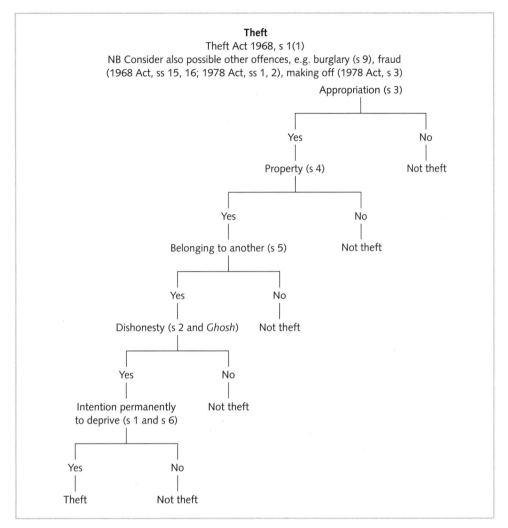

Figure 15.1 Theft

wanted to update the terminology, but not to change the concept. Many of the offences under the Theft Act 1968 and all of those in the Theft Act 1978 require dishonesty. Even when dishonesty is not expressly mentioned, it may be an ingredient. For example, robbery requires a theft, which in turn requires dishonesty. One form of burglary consists of entering a building as a trespasser with intent to steal; again theft with its element of dishonesty is needed. A similar point can be made about going equipped, a crime contrary to s 25 of the 1968 Act. Perhaps half of all cases tried at the Crown Court involve dishonesty: the importance of this concept cannot be exaggerated.

The Act states in s 1(2): 'It is immaterial whether the appropriation is made with a view to gain or is made for the thief's own benefit.' A person can therefore steal property by destroying it and it is irrelevant that the item is of no use to the thief. In one case, **Welsh** [1974] RTR 478 (CA), the accused poured a sample of his own urine down a sink; the sample would have been tested. He was guilty of theft despite the fact he had poured it away. The Criminal Law Revision Committee's Eighth Report, *Theft and Related Offences*, Cmnd 2977, 1966, gave another example. The accused can be guilty of theft even though the property appropriated is useless to him. Section 1(2) also has the effect that, while in the general run of events the victim will have been made poorer by the accused's theft, there is no requirement for the victim to become poorer as a result of the theft: *Wheatley* **v *Commissioner of Police of the British Virgin Islands*** [2006] 1 WLR 1683 (PC), dealing with legislation identical to the Theft Act 1968. The appellant argued that the government had lost nothing when he made a contract with companies to re-erect a wall which had fallen down. The Privy Council advised that there could be dishonesty when a contract had been agreed on at an appropriate price.

(a) Section 2(1)

Dishonesty is partly defined in the statute. The Criminal Law Revision Committee did not totally define dishonesty because 'dishonesty is something which laymen can easily recognise when they see it' (at 20). By s 2(1) the accused is not dishonest if he:

s 2(1)(a) believes he has a legal right to deprive the victim of the property;

s 2(1)(b) believes that the victim would have consented to the appropriation of the property, if he had known of the circumstances;

s 2(1)(c) finds or otherwise appropriates property, when he believes that the owner, posessor or controller cannot reasonably be found.

Section 2(1)(a) gives the accused a defence if he makes a mistake of civil law. (If the accused does in fact have the right in law to deprive the owner of the property, there is no need to consider the effect of s 2(1)(a) because there is no *actus reus* of theft.) There is no need for the mistake to be a reasonable one. A mistake of criminal law does not bring s 2(1)(a) into play. Examples of (a) are a belief that the accused was allowed to borrow the item (*Kell* [1985] Crim LR 239 (CA)) and where the accused took pottery in lieu of wages (*Wootton* [1990] Crim LR 201 (CA)). A belief that the owner has consented to the appropriation falls within (a) above. A claim of a moral right to the asset does not fall within s 2(1)(a), but may be not dishonest within the principles to be discussed shortly. In *Forrester* [1992] Crim LR 793 (CA) the accused burst into a house in which he formerly had a tenancy. The landlord had retained his £200 deposit. The accused thought that the deposit was withheld unfairly because the landlord had no justification for asking him to leave. He took various items, intending to keep ones to the amount of over £200 in order to force the landlord to hand back the deposit. He would sell the items if the deposit was not returned, paying over the excess. Since he did not believe that he had a legal right, s 2(1)(a) did not apply. An example of (b) is *Flynn* [1970] Crim LR 118, where a cinema manager took £6 as an advance on his salary. Section 2(1)(b) provided that the accused is not guilty only when he believes the owner would have consented to the appropriation in the particular circumstances of the appropriation. A belief that a neighbour would have consented to your using her lawnmower to cut your lawn does not allow you to use it to mow the whole estate's verges. A person can be convicted of stealing from a company of which he is the controller. The company is separate from the controller and would not have consented to being divested of its property: *Attorney-General's Reference (No. 2 of 1982)* [1984] QB 624 (CA). As for (c), there will be an appropriation for the purposes of theft if the accused cannot at first discover the owner but later finds out the identity. In those circumstances whether the accused is dishonest falls outwith s 2(1) but within the principles discussed below.

An example of s 2(1)(c) is where clothing is left in a locker at a swimming pool. The local authority cannot readily trace the owner normally. It is not dishonest when it sells the clothes to defray expenses. It should also be noted that for the purposes of theft property may belong to more than one party. A lost golf ball may be owned by the golfer but possessed or controlled by the landowner. The golfer's name may not easily be discovered, but it may be easy to determine the landowner's identity. Section 2(1)(c) extends beyond people who find things to anyone who assumed one or more of the rights of the owner. If a cobbler repairs shoes and the owner does not reclaim them he is not dishonest if he sells them to recoup his expenses provided that he believes that 'the person to whom the property belongs cannot be discovered by taking reasonable steps'. The word 'cannot' has not been considered by the courts. It is suggested that it means 'cannot in the ordinary run of things'. It is often possible to find the owner by taking some steps, though what is reasonable is a matter for the jury. In any event if the accused does not fall within (c), he may fall within the general test, below.

Throughout s 2(1) an honest belief suffices. The accused does not, for instance, need to have reasonable grounds for his belief that the owner would have consented, had he known of the circumstances. An illustration is **Holden** [1991] Crim LR 478 (CA). The accused claimed that he had been granted permission by a supervisor to take scrap tyres from a certain firm. He had previously worked for the firm and was due to go back to it. He believed on those grounds that he had a legal right to the tyres.

This partial definition of dishonesty applies to theft and other Theft Act offences where theft is an ingredient. It does not, for example, apply to the offence of abstracting electricity. The different definitions open up the possibility of divergent interpretations. Furthermore, in the Theft Act 1968 as enacted seven offences expressly mentioned dishonesty, but six do not. In blackmail the equivalent of dishonesty is an unwarranted demand. The Act has a further provision on dishonesty in theft. By s 2(2): 'A person's appropriation of property may be dishonest notwithstanding that he is willing to pay for the property.' Therefore, an individual can be guilty of theft even though he had £1,000 in his purse and said on arrest that he would pay for the items shoplifted. The Act states 'may be' because there may be circumstances in which an accused is otherwise honest, for example because the facts fall within s 2(1).

(b) Ghosh

Even if the accused does not fall within s 2(1), he may still be not dishonest for the purposes of the Act. The first major case in this area was **Feely** [1973] QB 530. The accused took money from his employers, intending to repay. The Court of Appeal ruled that outside s 2(1) the question of dishonesty was for the jury applying 'the current standards of ordinary decent people'. The jury does not consider whether the accused thought that what he had done was dishonest or not. For example, even if a person of high moral standards thought that what he was doing was dishonest, that state of mind is irrelevant. One looks to see whether ordinary decent people would consider it dishonest. The court said that dishonesty can be equated with immorality. The case itself was concerned with the substitution of money but was applied generally to other instances of dishonest conduct. With regard to the taking of money, the accused has the intention permanently to deprive the victim of the coins and notes actually taken, even though he means to replace them with an equivalent amount. The law was simple to state and was in accordance with **Brutus v Cozens** [1973] AC 854, where the House of Lords held that ordinary English words such as 'insulting' should be left for the jury. It is also in accord with the Eighth Report of the Criminal Law Revision Committee, *Theft and Related Offences*, Cmnd 2977, 1966, which was the basis of the Theft Act 1968. As stated at the start of this chapter, the Committee wished to substitute 'dishonestly' for 'fraudulently' because the former concept would be understood more easily by juries than the latter.

Feely was applied to since repealed offences of obtaining by deception in *Greenstein* [1975] 1 WLR 1353 (CA). The same test applies now throughout the Theft Acts and in conspiracy to defraud and fraudulent trading. It is that stated in *Ghosh* [1982] QB 1053 (CA). The accused is dishonest if his conduct is dishonest according to the current standards of ordinary decent people and if the accused knows that his conduct is regarded as dishonest according to those standards. In *Ghosh*, the accused, a surgeon acting as a locum in a hospital, claimed fees for performing operations. Those fees were not owing to him. He was charged with dishonestly obtaining money by deception, contrary to s 15(1) of the Theft Act 1968. This offence has since been abolished but the law on dishonesty remains. He was found guilty and the Court of Appeal in a reserved judgment dismissed his appeal.

The twofold test is:

(a) The jury are to apply the 'ordinary standards of reasonable and honest people': if the accused is not dishonest by those standards he is not guilty.

(b) If he is dishonest by the first test: 'The jury must consider whether the defendant himself must have realised that what he was doing was by those standards dishonest.' The accused is dishonest if he acts in a way which he knows ordinary people would regard as dishonest. A juror should not ask whether what the accused did was dishonest by that juror's standards but by the standards of reasonable and honest people. A person who is fervently anti-vivisection should not use his own standards to judge an accused who broke into a laboratory to release rabbits. The court gave illustrations of ardent anti-vivisectionists who raided laboratories, and Robin Hood. The court thought that these people were dishonest, though reasonable jurors may disagree. On the *Ghosh* approach an accused who steals from the rich to give to the poor must be acquitted if he believes that reasonable people would regard what he did as not dishonest. Before *Ghosh* and its precursors the judge could rule that the evidence adduced was insufficient to negate dishonesty and Robin Hood would have been dishonest. The test should be put to the jury in the order stated: *Green* [1992] Crim LR 292 (CA). If the accused knows that what he is doing is illegal, he may still be acting honestly. Assume that there is an express or implied term in his contract of employment as a shop assistant that he will not take money from the till for his own purposes. He does so. He is liable for breach of contract and for the tort of conversion. Nevertheless, a jury might find that he was not acting dishonestly because ordinary decent people might so regard his behaviour. Some defendants may believe that using the contents of the stationery cupboard at work for their own purposes is not dishonest and may argue that they believe that ordinary decent people think the way they do. The fact that a witness believed the accused to be acting dishonestly is not conclusive: *Green*. While 'dishonesty' is an ordinary word, it is inappropriate to consider whether the accused himself thought that he was acting dishonestly. The jury does not, for example, ask whether the defendant knew that he was acting recklessly when he is charged with a crime of recklessness. The standard should be an objective one.

The *Ghosh* definition applies to fraud offences: *Lockwood* [1986] Crim LR 244 (CA). The court said that the *Ghosh* test of 'reasonable and honest people' applied to businesspersons. There was no test of: how would a businessperson have reacted? The difference between *Feely* and *Ghosh* should be noted. In *Feely* the test of dishonesty was objective. In *Ghosh* the state of the mind of the accused is relevant. The court did not say why the test changed from 'ordinary decent people' to 'reasonable and honest people': are honest people different from ordinary ones? The test for dishonesty of 'reasonable and honest people' is circular. The test lays down a criterion of what might be called 'objective morality'. The jury looks both at the objective nature of the act and at the accused's own state of mind.

The same facts may fall within both s 2(1) and *Ghosh*. If the accused believes that the property he has appropriated is his own or if he believes that he is legally entitled to do as he did ('claim of right'), he is not dishonest under both. A *Ghosh* direction is sufficient: no reference need be made to s 2(1). If, however, he realised that what he was doing was dishonest by the standards of reasonable people, it seems he is honest within s 2(1) but dishonest under *Ghosh*. Such a scenario is unlikely to arise in practice.

An example of the application of *Ghosh* is *Atkinson* [2003] EWCA Crim 3031, [2004] Crim LR 226. The accused was charged with false accounting, an offence to which *Ghosh* applies. It was argued that she had submitted false claims relating to prescription forms. The first instance judge directed the jury that the accused would not be guilty if she was careless or acting under stress but would be if she 'knew that what she was doing would result in her submitting prescription forms containing false information'. The jury convicted and the Court of Appeal upheld the direction.

(c) Application and criticism of *Ghosh*

The *Ghosh* test may be quite difficult to explain to a jury. The jury embodies in one sense community values. The further away from those values the accused's beliefs are, the more likely he is to be acquitted. An accused who believes it is socially acceptable to eat a supermarket's food in the store and leave without paying for it is more likely to be acquitted than one who does not. Similarly, a person who believes it socially acceptable to keep overpayments from bookmakers or to take his employers' stationery home is entitled to be judged on his beliefs.

Ghosh appears to be contrary to what the Criminal Law Revision Committee and Parliament intended when they established 'dishonesty' in the 1968 Act. There is a linked issue. If the law of theft exists to protect property, it is strange that it does not do so when the jury decides that the accused was not dishonest.

Judges have the duty of interpreting the law and juries apply the law so interpreted to the facts but the *Ghosh* test places them in control of the former function as well as the latter. Furthermore, juries can reach inconsistent verdicts. What is dishonest in York may not be dishonest in London, and since dishonesty is judged by current standards, what was not dishonest in 1995 may be dishonest in 2012. There is evidence that women find more behaviour dishonest than men do, although men are more likely to convict of dishonesty offences than women, and that older people consider more conduct to be dishonest than younger ones: see the work of Stefan Fafinski mentioned in 'Sexes differ over dishonesty, says new study', *Independent*, 7 September 2009, 17. Moreover, the *Ghosh* approach downgrades respect for property. There seems to be little evidence to support the view that 12 persons chosen at random can decide what is dishonest better than could Parliament or the judges.

The decision creates a distinction between dishonesty in s 2(1) and dishonesty outside of it. Section 2(1) looks at the genuineness of the belief, not at the reasonableness of it. Under *Ghosh* the test is partly objective. In *Small* (1988) 86 Cr App R 170, the Court of Appeal held that unreasonable belief could be an honest belief, but reasonableness of the belief was 'a strong factor' in determining the honesty of the belief. With regard to blackmail the Criminal Law Revision Committee did not want a test that the accused's belief had to be reasonable because such could be out of line with the rest of the 1968 Act, yet *Feely* and *Ghosh* do just that in relation to dishonesty falling outside of s 2(1). Furthermore, some ordinary-language terms in the Act are matters of law, such as 'makes any . . . demand' in blackmail (*Treacy v DPP*, above). It may well be that when Parliament enacted the three exemptions from dishonesty, it intended there to be no others, but *Ghosh* creates an exception of undefined width. Countries which have adopted the English Theft Act as their model have not applied *Ghosh*. For example, in **Williams** [1985] NZLR 294 the New Zealand Court of Appeal held that the test in New Zealand was subjective. An accused's belief in the morality of his conduct is a defence. The House of Lords has not had the opportunity of considering *Ghosh*.

The courts have held that if there is no evidence that the accused believed that he was not dishonest by the standards of ordinary people, the judge need not give a direction in *Ghosh* terms: **Roberts** (1987) 84 Cr App R 117 on handling; **Price** (1989) 90 Cr App R 409 on deception; **Wheelhouse** [1994] Crim LR 756 (CA) on burglary; and **Squire** [1990] Crim LR 341 on conspiracy to defraud. The same is also true of theft. In a more recent authority, **Wood** [2002] EWCA Crim 832, the court stated that: 'the **Ghosh** direction . . . is best left only for that kind of case where there is a dispute about whether ordinary people would have different views from a defendant as to whether what he was doing was honest or not.' In other words, the whole *Ghosh* instruction is only needed where the accused asserts that what he did was not dishonest, no matter what others thought. After all, shoplifting is dishonest according to current standards of ordinary decent people. It need not be decided in every case. Indeed in **Price** Lord Lane CJ said that in a majority of cases a *Ghosh* direction was inappropriate. In **O'Connell** (1992) 94 Cr App R 39, the accused had obtained several mortgage advances on houses. He said that he intended to repay the sums by renting out the dwellings or by selling them. He gave evidence that he did not regard the giving of a false name on an application form as being dishonest. The Court of Appeal held that the trial judge was incorrect to hold that such evidence should be excluded. By stating that he intended to fulfil his contractual obligations by repaying the loan, there arose the question whether he was dishonest in giving a false name. While the fulfilling of the obligations or the intention to repay is *per se* not dishonest it is evidence that the accused was not dishonest under *Ghosh*. **O'Connell** was applied in **Clarke**, unreported, 2 April 1996. The accused falsely represented that he had been a member of the Fraud Squad and a court bailiff, in order to secure work as a private investigator. The trial judge excluded evidence that the accused believed that he could do the work. The Court of Appeal held that such evidence was relevant to dishonesty. If the accused admits that his conduct was dishonest according to current standards of decent people, there is no need for a direction on this first part of the *Ghosh* test: **Thompson**, unreported, 1988 (CA).

Where the case is apt for a *Ghosh* direction, the whole test must be given, not just the first part: **Ravenshad** [1990] Crim LR 398 (CA) and **Brennan** [1990] Crim LR 118 (CA) (on handling). The fact that the accused was suspicious that barrels of lager were stolen was not sufficient. The exact words should preferably be given: **Ravenshad**, **Vosper** (1990) *The Times*, 16 February and **Hyam** [1997] Crim LR 419 (CA). To do so will as a minimum reduce appeals. The court in **Gohill v DPP** [2006] EWCA Crim 2894 held that no reasonable person would say that the manager of a tool hire shop was not dishonest when he allowed customers to borrow items for short periods of time without payment and he would alter the records to show that the items had been faulty or wrongly chosen. The case was remitted to determine whether he himself thought that what he did was dishonest by the ordinary standards of reasonable and honest people.

It should be noted that (a) where the accused's behaviour falls within s 2(1), **Ghosh** is irrelevant (**Wootton**, above) and no *Ghosh* direction should be given; (b) the accused may act dishonestly even though he did something which the civil law allows him to do, such as retain the overpayment of a bet (**Gilks** [1972] 1 WLR 1341 (CA)); and (c) as a result of **Lawrence v MPC**, above, and later cases a person may be dishonest despite the fact that the owner has consented to the appropriation.

In *Forrester*, above, the Court of Appeal left open the point whether an accused was not dishonest when he knew that what he was doing was unlawful. The general view of commentators is that under s 2(1)(a) and *Ghosh* it is the accused's belief that matters, not whether it is illegal in fact.

There was discussion of dishonesty in *Hinks* [2001] 2 AC 241 (HL), which is noted below under 'Appropriation'. Lord Hutton dissented on the correct direction on dishonesty. The case involved an accused who induced a man with learning difficulties to transfer some £60,000 to her. She contended that he had given her the money of his own free will. Lord Hutton said that if her contention was correct, she was not dishonest. In cases with such facts he stated that the judge should instruct the jurors that they could not convict unless the donor lacked the mental capacity to make the gift and the donee knew of that incapacity. The direction is more specific than *Ghosh* and is tailored to the facts. It is suggested that Lord Hutton's speech is the way forward out of one of the uncertainties into which *Ghosh* put the law. It may take some time for precedents to build up, but in time the law will become more certain than it is at present, avoiding the charge that English law is inconsistent with the European Convention on Human Rights. See below for more on the Convention. However, it must be emphasised that Lord Hutton was dissenting and that the majority view in *Hinks* was that the issue of dishonesty when the issue does not fall within s 2(1) is resolved by *Ghosh*. The appellant's attempt to rely on Lord Hutton's remarks in *Wheatley* v *Commissioner of Police of the British Virgin Islands*, above, was firmly rejected by the Privy Council. Indeed, the Privy Council extended *Hinks* by applying it beyond gifts to contracts. On the facts *Ghosh* was applied, and the appellant was dishonest despite the fact that he, a government employee, had entered into a contract for a fair price for the re-erecting of a wall.

One academic point in *Ghosh* deserves consideration. Two problematical areas in modern-day criminal law are dishonesty and intention. With regard to the latter the House of Lords has stated that intention is an ordinary English word which in most eventualities the judge should leave undefined. The jury, however, does not ask whether the accused believed he was acting with the relevant state of mind, but under the Theft Acts as well as offences of fraud the jury must acquit if the accused believed that what he did was not dishonest by the standards of ordinary decent people. If the accused falls below that standard, it seems strange to inquire whether he knew that he fell below it. Both intention and dishonesty are questions for the jury, but are treated in different ways. What the Court of Appeal wanted to do in *Ghosh* was to punish only those people to whom 'moral obloquy' was attached. To illustrate this proposition the court took the example of a person who comes to England and Wales from a country where public transport is free. In England and Wales public transport is not free but the foreigner believes it is. The court said that he was dishonest by the standards of ordinary decent people: 'His conduct, judged objectively by what he has done, is dishonest.' To exonerate him the court invented the second stage: did he believe that reasonable people would regard his behaviour as not dishonest? Surely, however, the court dealt with the first stage wrongly. The accused was not dishonest, judged objectively as well as subjectively. The question might be phrased as: do you believe it dishonest for a person not to pay a fare which he believes he does not owe? Unlike the Robin Hood example, the answer should be straightforward. If the foreigner is not dishonest at this first stage there is no need to ask the second question. Moreover, the hypothetical situation presented by the court is really one of mistake of fact. The foreigner thought that fares were not paid, whereas in truth they were. On the facts as he believed them to be he was not dishonest. The facts are not ones involving different beliefs about what is honest and what is not.

A more practical point is this. While it is often simple to say whether or not an accused is dishonest under the *Ghosh* test (e.g. it would not be difficult to hold that when he puts a frozen chicken into a large pocket on the inside of his coat he is dishonest), there are occasions where not all ordinary people would say that the accused was acting dishonestly. If he proposes to buy shares in an offer, has not enough money, but expects that the number of shares he will be allocated will be fewer than he asked for because of oversubscriptions, it is not self-evident to all that he is dishonest. Similarly, some people may think it dishonest to conceal the fact that a book is a valuable one whereas others may consider it honest. Certainly some people think it not dishonest to keep overpayments from shops and bookmakers, but others disagree.

A five-person Court of Appeal was assembled in *Cornelius* [2012] EWCA Crim 500 to determine whether *Ghosh* was correct. The case went off on a different point but does illustrate that the judiciary is willing to consider arguments against *Ghosh*.

(d) *Ghosh* and human rights

The law in *Ghosh* may come under attack as a result of the ECHR. Article 7, the rule against retroactivity, may come into play, because an accused may not be able to foresee when his behaviour will break the law: according to the European Court of Human Rights an offence cannot be defined by reference to moral obloquy, only by reference to the effect of the accused's behaviour. A Crown Court thought it was not incompatible in *Pattni* [2001] Crim LR 570 but that decision lacks authority and is concerned not with the Theft Acts offences but with another crime, cheating the Revenue. Possibly, the law in *Ghosh* may infringe Article 5(1), the right to liberty, because an accused may not foresee the possibility that what he did is dishonest for the purposes of English law. The European Court of Human Rights said *obiter* in *Hashman* v *UK* [2000] Crim LR 185 that the concept of dishonesty in the Theft Acts did not breach Article 5 because dishonesty was only one element in theft, but its mind was not on this issue. The law it was actually looking at was binding over to keep the peace, a long way from dishonesty.

(e) Reform of dishonesty

The Supreme Court could overrule *Ghosh*. For the Law Commission's proposal to abolish dishonesty as a separate element in deception offences, see Chapter 16, below, which discusses Consultation Paper No. 155, *Legislating the Criminal Code: Fraud and Deception*, 1999. The Law Commission also agreed with the point made at the end of the previous paragraph, that the law in *Ghosh* is incompatible with Article 7 of the ECHR. However, in its Report No. 276, *Fraud*, 2002, the Law Commission resiled from its 1999 position. In para. 5.18 it said: 'The fact that *Ghosh* dishonesty leaves open a possibility of variance between cases with essentially similar facts is . . . a theoretical risk. Many years after its adoption, the *Ghosh* test remains, in practice, unproblematic. We also recognise the fact that the concept of dishonesty is now required in a very large number of criminal cases, so to reject it at this stage would have a far-reaching effect on the criminal justice system.'

Intention permanently to deprive

(a) Theft and borrowing

The second element of the *mens rea* in theft is the intention permanently to deprive. An intention to return sooner or later is not such an intent: *Warner* (1970) 55 Cr App R 93. As the Court of Appeal said, s 6 gives illustrations of 'intention permanently to deprive';

it does not water down the basic definition of theft found in s 1(1). Similar but more modern is **Mitchell** [2008] EWCA Crim 1351. There was no intent permanently to deprive when the accused abandoned the victim's car. Within the second part of s 6(1) the 'borrowing or lending' could be deemed to be an intent permanently to deprive when the accused's intent was to return the property in such a state that all the value had got out of it. On the facts that was not so. Therefore, there was no intent permanently to deprive and in turn no theft.

'Intention' and 'intention permanently to deprive' are not defined in the Act. Presumably 'intention' bears the same meaning as it does after **Woollin** [1999] AC 82 (HL). Section 6 merely gives three extensions to the concept of intent permanently to deprive: it does not define it. The word 'permanently' prevents most unauthorised borrowings being theft. Dishonest borrowings, even for a long time, are not theft. The Criminal Law Revision Committee justified non-liability in para. 56 of *Theft and Related Offences*, Cmnd 2977, 1966. The moral considerations of dishonest borrowings were different from those of theft. Usually a borrowing is not as serious as a permanent taking. Such borrowings were not very common. Criminalising them would cover trivial matters, such as neighbours quarrelling over a lawnmower. To create a law would waste police time on minor matters. It would be especially hard on students. Additionally, it can nowadays be said (i.e. after the case of **Gomez**, above) that making dishonest borrowing into theft would place even more weight on the somewhat fragile concept of dishonesty than exists at present. Two instances of dishonest borrowing, removal of articles from buildings (s 11) and cars (s 12), are offences. The contrary arguments are these:

(a) If the crux of theft is the dishonest appropriation of another's property, the intention permanently to deprive seems otiose.

(b) The social importance of the accused's conduct does not depend on such an intention. After all there are many trivial thefts.

(c) If the victim wants the property during the time when the accused has dishonestly borrowed it, he cannot use it, whether or not the accused intends permanently to deprive. If a student wants this textbook for an exam in January, it is not to the point that he will get it back in February.

(d) Such an intent is not needed in most other Theft Acts offences such as obtaining a pecuniary advantage by deception (s 16).

(e) As we have seen, an intention to repay or substitute may be dishonest because the defendant cannot replace the very thing taken, yet if he intends to return the property itself, he is not guilty of theft because he does not have the intention permanently to deprive.

(f) Some items such as puffball skirts or gypsy tops are fashionable at one time but not trendy after; appropriating a child's toy and handing it back after its popularity has plummeted exemplifies the situation.

(g) It is not thought that the courts would be overwhelmed with cases.

The main argument to the contrary is that in respect of many items their value lies in the ability to use them at a particular time. Returning a lawnmower in February is no use when one wished to cut the grass over the previous summer.

Where there is no intent *permanently* to deprive, a conspiracy to defraud charge may lie. There may be one situation where an intention temporarily to deprive is caught by s 6(1). This possibility occurs where the victim has only an interest limited in time in the item and the accused intends to borrow it for longer than that person. For example, if the victim hires a skip from its owner for a week and the accused takes it away for longer than a week intending to return it, he has intended to deprive the victim of his whole interest. Towards him there is an intent permanently to deprive, and there is theft from him (though not from the owner).

(b) Section 6(1)

The concept is explained in s 6(1):

> A person appropriating property belonging to another without meaning the other permanently to lose the thing itself is nevertheless to be regarded as having the intention of permanently depriving the other of it if his intention is to treat the thing as his own to dispose of regardless of the other's rights; and a borrowing or lending of it may amount to so treating it if, but only if, the borrowing or lending is for a period and in circumstances making it equivalent to an outright taking or disposal.

The Court of Appeal in **Lloyd** [1985] QB 829 said that s 6 'sprouts obscurities at every phrase'. It certainly could be better worded. The basic thrust of it is that it should be looked at only exceptionally: **Lloyd**. Section 6(1) does not define intention permanently to deprive; instead it is a statutory extension of that concept. Most cases fall simply within s 1(1)'s basic definition of theft, which includes the phrase 'intention of permanently depriving', and there is no need to consider s 6. If I burn your £10 note, I do intend permanently to deprive you of it: one need not look to s 6(1) for guidance. Only in cases when the accused intends to return the property or it is not clear whether or not there is an intention permanently to deprive, where the accused acts 'without meaning the other permanently to lose the thing', need one look at s 6. Only if the accused intends the victim to get the property back, s 6(1) is relevant. Thus, s 6(1) is a deeming provision: it deems something to be so when it is not.

Lord Lane CJ thought that s 6(1) applied in only two circumstances, as can be seen from the wording of s 6(1): where the accused takes property and then offers it back to the owner (the so-called 'ransom' principle) and where the accused borrows or lends out the victim's property in circumstances 'equivalent to an outright taking or disposal'. It is also relevant where the accused deals with property in such a way that he knows that he is risking its loss: **Fernandes** [1996] 1 Cr App R 175 (CA), where the accused, a solicitor, invested money belonging to his clients in a firm of moneylenders, knowing the investment not to be a safe one. Otherwise only s 1(1) needs to be referred to. Therefore, s 6 is a deeming provision. According to **Warner**, s 6 clarifies and gives explanations of the requisite state of mind. In **Warner** the accused took a box of tools, intending to return them shortly. He was not guilty of theft because he had an intention to return, even though the handing back might be an indefinite period later. The Court of Appeal in **Fernandes** more recently said that the thrust of s 6 is the issue of whether the accused did intend 'to treat the thing as his own to dispose of regardless of the other's rights'. The rest of s 6(1) and (2) consists of illustrations of that issue. Auld LJ thought that Lord Lane CJ was wrong to restrict s 6(1) to the two situations he mentioned. Accordingly s 6(1) offers only a partial definition of 'intention of permanently depriving'.

(c) The interpretation of s 6(1)

Section 6 has been interpreted in the following ways. It speaks of intention permanently to deprive. There is no need for actual permanent deprivation; that is, s 6 belongs to *mens rea*, not *actus reus*. A person can be guilty of theft even though the owner gets the property back at some time. In the latter part of s 6(1) 'borrowing' is not restricted to a lender loaning something to a borrower. It covers a taking to which the victim has not agreed. In the first part selling the item back to the owner is treating it as one's own to dispose of regardless of the owner's rights.

The phrase 'equivalent to an outright taking' is obscure. It would seem to cover the situation where the accused takes the victim's umbrella dishonestly and the victim buys back the umbrella, not realising that it is his own. In ordinary language the accused does not intend to deprive the victim permanently of his umbrella, but s 6 deems there to be an intention permanently to deprive. The accused has appropriated one of the rights of the owner, the right to sell the article. This principle seems to have been applied in *Johnstone* [1982] Crim LR 454 (Crown Court). Two defendants were lorry drivers for a soft drinks company. They collected more bottles than they had accounted for. There was a deposit on each bottle. The bottles were dishonestly delivered to a shopkeeper, the third defendant, who was to get the deposits on the bottles from the company and share the money with the first two defendants. The bottles would therefore go back to the company, which would only pay one deposit on each bottle but the deposit would end up in the hands, not of the purchasers of the soft drinks, but of the defendants. The Recorder held that since the bottles would be returned to the company, the defendants did not intend to treat the bottles as their own to dispose of regardless of the company's rights. Therefore, there was no theft. If the accused takes the umbrella and leaves it on a bus, the victim is unlikely to get it back. The accused may have the requisite intent; if not s 6 can supply it. Another example may be a stolen cheque. In the ordinary course of banking the victim gets the cheque back but after encashment. It is no longer a valid cheque. The accused intends permanently to deprive the victim of a thing in action, the right to be paid the sum stated. The accused is deemed to have the intention permanently to deprive (see *Mulligan*, below).

The words 'to dispose of' are important. In *Cahill* [1993] Crim LR 141 (CA) one accused early one morning picked a newspaper out of a bundle outside a newsagent's. The second defendant had then picked it up. When a police car came level with them, the second accused dropped it. The first defendant said that the second was taking it to the police station because it was lost. (They had been drinking.) The court held that 'to dispose of' meant 'to get rid of', not 'to use'. The phrase must not be omitted when dealing with s 6(1). This issue is also noted in the next section of this book. If the accused intends to keep the thing until all the goodness or virtue has gone out of it that is equivalent to an outright taking. In *Lloyd* the accused had cinema films copied to be sold as videos and returned them. It was held that the virtue had not gone out of the films as films. The public would still pay to see them at the cinema. The accused intended to cause loss to the cinema owners but that is not an intention permanently to deprive. To intend to use the property does not constitute an intent to deprive permanently. The position is different where the accused takes the victim's season ticket, uses it up and then hands it back. In those circumstances the accused has the intention permanently to deprive because of s 6(1).

In *Bagshaw* [1988] Crim LR 321, the accused intended to return gas cylinders when he had finished with them. The court hinted that the accused was guilty of theft of the cylinders even though not all of the goodness had gone out of the property. They could on return have been refilled. (He should have been charged with theft of the gas.) There is debate whether in these circumstances s 6(1) is fulfilled. 'Equivalent to an outright taking' may cover a situation where the season ticket is almost used up, but not where only one of the journeys is made or operas attended. The difficult, totally unresolved issue involves the situations in between. Lord Widgery CJ in *Lloyd* took a stronger view: '*all* its goodness or virtue' must go for s 6(1) to apply (emphasis added). The Court of Appeal, as stated above, held in *Fernandes* that s 6(1) was not restricted to two of the situations noted in this paragraph, attempting to sell the item back to the owner and giving it back when its value had been extinguished. The Court of Appeal had earlier spoken to similar effect in *Bagshaw*.

An example of intending to treat the thing as one's own to dispose of regardless of the other's rights is ***Chan Man-sin v Attorney-General of Hong Kong*** [1988] 1 All ER 1 (PC). The accused, an accountant, forged 10 cheques on two companies' bank accounts. He was charged with theft of the debt owed by the bank to its customers, the companies. The Privy Council rejected the argument that there was no theft because the companies had not been deprived of anything. He knew that the fraud would be uncovered. The companies stood to lose nothing. Their bank balances would not be affected. The Judicial Committee held that the accused purported to deal with the companies' property (the companies' accounts, things in action) regardless of their rights. Accordingly, the Hong Kong version of s 6(1) was satisfied. As a criticism it may be said that the Judicial Committee gave no weight to the words 'to dispose of' in s 6(1). See the next section in this book.

(d) Some examples of s 6(1) and its relationship with s 1(1)

Velumyl [1989] Crim LR 299 (CA)

> The accused took £1,050 from a safe at work to lend to a friend. He expected to get the money back after the weekend. It was held that since the accused did not intend to return the particular banknotes, he had the intention permanently to deprive. His intention to repay the equivalent amount was relevant to dishonesty, not to the intention permanently to deprive. The same result will apply to petrol. You borrow my car, intending to replace the petrol you have used. You have the intention permanently to deprive me of the petrol. There is also nothing to stop this argument applying to things in action (see below for the definition of things in action). For example, if the accused obtains a mortgage loan by deception but intends to repay, since he cannot return the same thing in action, there is an intent permanently to deprive. Lord Goff in *Preddy* [1996] AC 815 (HL) declined to rule on this point.

Coffey [1987] Crim LR 498 (CA)

> The accused obtained possession of machinery by a worthless cheque. He was charged with obtaining property by deception contrary to s 15 of the Theft Act 1968 (since repealed), which also requires an intention permanently to deprive. He claimed he intended to keep the machinery until a dispute with its owner had been settled. The court said that these facts gave rise to one of those rare cases where a direction on s 6(1) was needed. Did the accused intend that the period of his keeping the machinery would be so long as to amount to an outright taking? Was the accused treating the goods as his own to dispose of regardless of the owner's rights because the owner could get the machinery back only by giving in to the demands? The conviction was quashed because no such direction was given.

Scott [1987] Crim LR 235

> The accused took a pair of curtains from a store. He returned them the next day, asking for a refund. It was held that he was treating the property as his own to dispose of regardless of the shop's rights contrary to s 6(1).

Mulligan [1990] STC 220 (CA)

Stolen Inland Revenue certificates about payment of tax were found in the accused's sock. It was alleged that the accused had stolen some of the vouchers in the book and sold them. The accused contended that the vouchers were worthless because their essential character had been destroyed. It was held that he had an intention permanently to deprive because he intended to sell them irrespective of the Revenue's rights, despite the fact that the vouchers would come back to the Revenue.

DPP v Lavender [1994] Crim LR 297 (DC)

The accused's conduct fell within s 6(1) when he removed doors from a council house which was being repaired and used them to replace doors on another council house where his girlfriend was the tenant. The court said that he intended to treat the doors as his own regardless of the owner's rights. A disposal covered dealing with property as in **Chan Man-sin v R**, above. The accused had done so. If this is correct, any moving of property is a disposal of it. One moot point is the meaning of 'to dispose of'. If the phrase means 'to get rid of', such as by burning or selling the doors, he did not do so. See **Cahill**, above, which is inconsistent with **Lavender**. In **Cahill** the Court of Appeal accepted that 'to dispose of' meant 'to get rid of'. The accused did not get rid of the doors in **Lavender**. The point is aptly put by A.T.H. Smith, *Property Offences* (Sweet & Maxwell, 1994) para. 6–33: 'one would not ordinarily say that a pianist disposes of his piano by playing it.' Yet such is the meaning attributed to the phrase in **DPP v Lavender**. Smith continued: '"dispose" as used in section 6 was fairly evidently used as the verb corresponding to "disposal", not disposition; indeed, sub-section (1) expressly links it with disposal ("equivalent to an outright disposal").' On the view taken in **Lavender**, s 6(1) is otiose. By s 3(1) an intent to treat property as one's own is an appropriation.

Marshall [1998] 2 Cr App R 282 (CA)

The defendants obtained London Underground tickets or Travelcards which had not expired. They argued that there was no intention permanently to deprive because London Underground would in due course get the items back. The tickets and cards remained the property of London Transport. The acquisition and resale of that property was an 'intention to treat the thing as his own to dispose of regardless of the other's rights', the rights being London Transport's exclusive right to sell tickets and Travelcards. It was irrelevant that the tickets and cards would come back to London Transport. Whether a jury would have found the defendants dishonest is debatable. The Court of Appeal did not discuss the logically prior question: to whom did this property belong at the time of the alleged appropriation? Whether the tickets and Travelcards belonged to London Underground is a matter of civil law. Who the owner is depends on the conditions of issue and whether these conditions were brought reasonably to the attention of the defendants. For further discussion see the 'ticket cases' in contract textbooks or Sir John Smith's article 'Stealing tickets' [1998] Crim LR 723.

Raphael [2008] EWCA Crim 1014

The defendants drove away with the victim's car. They then offered to sell it back to him. The court had no doubt that s 6(1) applied, no matter how restrictively it was to be read: see the discussion of **Fernandes**, above. There was an intention to treat the thing as the defendant's own to dispose of regardless of the other's rights.

Vinall [2012] Crim LR 386

The victim's bicycle was abandoned at a bus shelter 50 yards from where the defendants had taken it from him. Did they intend permanently to deprive him of the bike? The Court of Appeal held that the leaving of the bicycle was evidence of an intent permanently to deprive at the time of the first taking of the bicycle within s 1(1) or the extended definition in s 6(1) but the trial judge had not so instructed the jury. Whether abandonment is such evidence depends on the facts of each case. For example, in **Mitchell**, above, leaving a car with its hazard lights flashing was not inconsistent with the accused's using the vehicle as a getaway car without intending the victim permanently to lose it.

(e) 'Intention', 'meaning' and 'the thing'

While no case has been discussed, 'intention' in the concept 'intention permanently to deprive' presumably bears that meaning which was discussed in Chapter 3. Section 6(1) also includes the term 'meaning'. That term is another way of saying 'intending'.

The phrase 'the thing' means 'the property' mentioned in the opening words of s 6(1) and defined in s 4. If something is not property, the accused cannot have an intention permanently to deprive the owner of that property. In **Oxford v Moss** (1978) 68 Cr App R 183 (DC), an engineering student at a university read the contents of an examination paper. All the goodness and virtue went out of the paper by his action. The court held, however, that confidential information, that is, the questions on the paper, was not property for the purpose of the Theft Act. Accordingly, the accused's behaviour did not amount to an intention permanently to deprive the owner of the information. If the accused had taken the paper itself, he would have been found guilty of theft of that piece of paper if he did not intend to return it, but that charge does not reflect the nub of what the accused did, namely cheat.

(f) Section 6(2)

Section 6(2) states:

> . . . where a person, having possession or control (lawfully or not) of property belonging to another, parts with the property under a condition as to its return which he may not be able to perform this (if done for purposes of his own and without the other's authority) amounts to treating the property as his own to dispose of regardless of the other's rights.

This subsection covers pawning property, intending to redeem it, without being able to guarantee that it will be returned, and gambling with the item. An alternative view is that the accused is guilty only if he foresaw that he might not be able to redeem the article, a proposition supported in **Fernandes**, above. This point awaits discussion. In either event the accused is guilty even though he does not *intend* permanently to deprive. This makes theft by virtue of s 6(2) an offence which can be committed by negligence. It is in truth simply an example of the first part of s 6(1).

One point of fundamental importance with regard to s 6(2) is that it deems a person to have a fault element when he does something ('parts with the property'). Proving the *actus reus* does not necessarily mean that the *mens rea* of, say, intent is proved, but s 6(2) breaches this basic principle.

(g) The problem of conditional intention

Does the accused have the intention permanently to deprive when he has not made up his mind to keep the thing permanently? In *Easom* [1971] 2 QB 315 (CA), there was a spate of handbag-snatching in cinemas. A policewoman sat in a cinema with her bag attached to her wrist by cotton. A man sat next to her, took the bag and walked away. He opened the bag and found no money or other valuables. He discarded the bag and its contents. Edmund-Davies LJ said that conditional appropriation was not theft. The accused did not have the intention permanently to deprive at the relevant time. The charge nowadays would be one of attempted theft where the accused intended to steal anything of value or anything in a container such as a pocket, holdall or room. In criticism of *Easom* it might be said that the accused did intend permanently to deprive the owner at the time when he appropriated. This point was emphasised by the Full Court of the Supreme Court of Victoria in *Sharp* v *McCormick* [1986] VR 869, when it distinguished *Easom*. The accused was found with an item of apparatus for a car engine. The part belonged to his employers and he admitted dishonesty. His defence was that he intended to return it, should it have been the wrong size. Murray J said: 'If the facts in the present case establish that the defendant intended to keep the coil unless he *later* decided to return it then his intention *at the time of the appropriation* is sufficient to establish theft . . .' The same might be said of the contents of the bag in *Easom*. It should be noted that certainly after *Gomez*, above, touching a handbag is an appropriation even though the accused has a conditional intent.

(h) Reform

The Law Commission, in its Consultation Paper No. 155, *Legislating the Criminal Code: Fraud and Deception*, 1999, provisionally proposed in the context of deception offences that temporary deprivations should be criminal unless, in its words, 'there is a significant countervailing argument'. The Commission's Report No. 276, *Fraud*, 2002, also proposed that obtaining property by deception (now repealed) should no longer require an intent permanently to deceive but no recommendation was made as to theft.

Appropriation

Under the old law of larceny the thing had to be carried away (asportation). Accordingly land could not be stolen. Now it can be, subject to the rules in s 4 (see below). The new word was 'appropriation', which it was hoped would be easily understood by the triers of fact. That hope has been dashed. Under present law an article can be stolen without being taken away. For example, if the accused puts his hand into the victim's pocket and grabs hold of a watch, there is an appropriation because of the definition found in s 3(1) of the Theft Act 1968: 'any assumption by a person of the rights of an owner amounts to an appropriation . . .'. The House of Lords in *Morris* [1984] AC 320 said that s 3 contained only a partial definition, as indeed did the Criminal Law Revision Committee in para 34 of the Eighth Report, *Theft and Related Offences*, Cmnd 2977, 1966. Therefore, a person may appropriate despite his actions not falling within s 3(1). Note also s 4(2)(d) noted below which states that severance of something forming part of land is an appropriation. One must, however, know that one is appropriating. An accused does not appropriate if his young son slips sweets into his shopping trolley at a supermarket.

(a) *Lawrence*

In *Lawrence* the Lords held that the accused can steal even though the victim consents to the taking. One can assume the rights of the owner even though the owner permitted one to do so. The House's decision in *Lawrence*, that there may be theft despite the owner's consent, is applied generally to all forms of consent. In *Lawrence* the appropriation took place because an Italian student handed over extra money to a taxi-driver who had deceived him as to the taxi fare, but *Lawrence* is not restricted to instances where the accused appropriated by deception. Within the Theft Act there is an appropriation even though the owner consented to it. In *Rader* [1992] Crim LR 663 the Court of Appeal said that *Lawrence* applied even when the accused had taken the victim's money with his full consent. The victim gave him almost £10,000 on the latter's promise that he would return it on the due date with some sort of profit. The accused said that he was investing the money via an acquaintance in Miami, but that person had not repaid the money. His appeal was dismissed. The victim had consented to the taking but the facts constituted an appropriation.

(b) *Morris*

In *Morris* the accused took goods from the shelves of a self-service supermarket. He substituted lower price labels for those on the goods. He paid the lower price at the checkout but was then arrested and charged with theft. It should be noted that the accused would have had no defence to a charge of fraud by false representation by switching the price labels. The question for the House of Lords was whether the swapping of the labels amounted to an appropriation. The principal speech was delivered by Lord Roskill. He said that the accused is guilty if he assumes *any* of the rights of the owner. He need not assume all of the rights. (Section 3(1) actually says 'any assumption . . . of the rights . . .', not 'any assumption of any right among the rights', is an appropriation. The construction of the phrase by the Lords is not the obvious interpretation. Only by knowing that this part of *Morris* represents the law can full weight be given to s 3(1).) The courts do not normally discuss which particular right has been assumed. The destruction of property or the accused's putting his hand over money in the victim's pocket will be a usurpation of one of the rights of the owner. This *dictum* was approved by the Lords in *Gomez* [1992] AC 442.

Academic criticism has been strong. Sir John Smith commented in 'Reforming the Theft Acts' (1996) 28 *Bracton Law Journal* 27 at 37, that in relation to this interpretation of s 3(1): 'Lord Keith thought this was obviously right. I think that, as a matter of statutory construction, it is obviously wrong . . .' Leigh in 'Some remarks on appropriation in the law of theft after *Morris*' (1985) 48 MLR 167 used the example of the accused's kicking a camel. He wrote that this act cannot be an appropriation. The law after *Morris* and *Gomez* is different. The camel-kicker is assuming one of the rights of the owner and therefore appropriates. There is no need for the accused to ride the camel into the sunset before an appropriation takes place.

This part of *Morris* was in turn approved in *Chan Man-sin v Attorney-General of Hong Kong*, above. The Privy Council held that a person who drew on someone's bank account was assuming the rights of the owner, and to be guilty the accused did not have to assume all rights of the owner. Presenting a cheque which was forged or otherwise not authorised constituted an appropriation, even though in law the transaction was a nullity and had no effect on the account holder's bank account because the bank would reimburse the loss. *Wille* (1988) 86 Cr App R 296 (CA) is to the same effect. A bank account was opened by a company. Each cheque had to be signed and countersigned. However, from the start the bank honoured cheques signed by one party only, the accused. It was held that by drawing on the company's bank account, the defendant had assumed the rights of an owner.

Morris also illustrates the proposition that the act by which the accused appropriates need not be the act by which he intends permanently to deprive. If an accused switches price labels on two items intending to pay a lower price for the higher priced item, he appropriates at that stage, even though he does not intend permanently to deprive until he reaches the cash till.

(c) *Gomez*

The principal authority on the definition of appropriation is *Gomez*.

Gomez [1992] AC 442 (HL)

The accused, assistant manager of an electrical goods shop, agreed to supply items costing over £16,000 to a person in exchange for two stolen building society cheques. The accused and that person were acting together in a dishonest enterprise. The shop manager agreed to the transaction provided that the bank agreed that the cheques were acceptable. The accused later told the manager that the cheques were as good as cash, that is, there was a fraudulent misrepresentation. The manager would not have agreed, had he known of the truth. The cheques were later dishonoured. The Court of Appeal held that there was no theft because the accused had not appropriated the property. The contract for the sale of goods was voidable not void, and had not been avoided when the goods were delivered. The manager had expressly authorised the goods to be removed. Accordingly, there was no misappropriation, and the conviction was quashed.

The Lords by a four to one majority reversed. The majority held that Lord Roskill had been incorrect to say *obiter* in *Morris*, above, that there was an appropriation only when the accused adversely interfered with or usurped one of the owner's rights. While adverse interference with or usurpation of the rights constituted one mode by which an appropriation may take place, the concept did not fully comprehend the situations in which an accused appropriated. Therefore, although the decision in *Morris* was correct, the reasoning was wrong: the law was wider than that stated in *Morris*. Applying *Lawrence*, above, the fact that the owner consented to the taking was irrelevant to the question whether or not there was an appropriation. Therefore, it did not matter that consent was induced by deception. Consent is not vitiated by fraud. Similarly, and contrary to Lord Roskill's *dictum*, the fact that the victim had expressly or impliedly authorised the accused to take an item was immaterial. Authorities which applied *Morris* were incorrect and those cases after *Morris* which sought to reconcile *Lawrence* and *Morris* were rejected. Therefore, an alleged fraudster did appropriate even though the victim consented to or authorised the transaction, and the Lords had been correct in *Lawrence* to hold that a conviction for theft was not dependent on the accused's appropriating without the consent of the owner. The Theft Act expressly noted where consent was relevant (e.g. in s 2(1)(b)). In the words of Lord Browne-Wilkinson 'appropriation' is 'an objective description of the act done irrespective of the mental state of either the owner or the accused'.

The dissenting Lord of Appeal in Ordinary, Lord Lowry, delivered a strong speech trenchantly criticising the decision of the majority. His criticisms were not answered by the majority. He said that as a matter of ordinary language appropriation meant 'take possession of, take to oneself, especially without authority'. It was a unilateral, not a consensual act. The majority had adopted the view that appropriation was a neutral term: a neutral act such as taking a can of beans from a supermarket shelf was converted into theft through the accused's state of mind. For them the lack of consent or authorisation by the owner was relevant only to *mens rea*, to dishonesty. For Lord Lowry it was by dictionary definition a constituent of appropriation. If he was wrong in his view that appropriation was not a neutral word, he said that if a meaning of a word in a statute was unclear, the report on which the statute was based would be looked at. In this instance the Theft Act 1968 was largely the work of the Criminal Law Revision Committee (Eighth Report, *Theft and Related Offences*, see above). The Report was to the effect that 'appropriation' was to bear its ordinary-language meaning. If the accused deceived the victim into handing over property, the proper charge was obtaining by deception, not theft. It was not theft because the definition of appropriation did not cover a situation where the victim consented to the taking. In other words property passed when the owner consented to the transfer and there was therefore no property to appropriate after the moment of transfer. Lord Lowry also said that *Lawrence* had been correct in holding that lack of consent was an extra element which the prosecution had to prove in theft but, while it was not an additional part of the *actus reus*, it was part and parcel of the definition of appropriation. Lord Lowry in summary may be said to have been protecting the honest shopper. Not until he did something wrongful with the goods did he appropriate. The majority said that both the honest shopper and the shoplifter appropriate. Innocence or guilt depends on their state of mind.

In Lord Lowry's view if the accused by deception induces the victim to transfer his entire right of ownership to him, he is not guilty of theft. If, however, the accused induces the owner to transfer (only) possession, he is. This distinction was the one drawn by the Criminal Law Revision Committee and endorsed by Parliament. The offence of obtaining property by deception was designed to cover situations where the accused had fraudulently obtained ownership. In most instances where there is deception the accused as buyer becomes the owner of the goods. For example, if there is a misrepresentation that the accused will pay for the item but in fact he will not, property nevertheless passes to him. It is only if there is a fundamental mistake of fact that property does not pass. The contractual effect of a non-fundamental mistake induced by deception is to render the contract not void but voidable. *Gomez* makes the accused into a thief even though he is the owner in civil law.

To summarise the criticism of *Gomez*, the accused should not have been convicted of theft because the words in the statute should have been construed in a case of ambiguity in favour of the accused; Parliament has enacted the Report of the Criminal Law Revision Committee, which was contrary to *Gomez*; and the House of Lords in *Morris* has decided differently from *Gomez*.

The implications of *Gomez* are profound:

(a) Since appropriation is a neutral term, the guilt of the accused depends on his state of mind. The emphasis is on his dishonesty or lack of it. In theft the *mens rea* is of more importance than the *actus reus* and for that reason *mens rea* has been considered first in these pages. Unfortunately current law does not enable one to say that a certain form of conduct is dishonest in advance of trial. It may be that the law after *Gomez* is inconsistent with the European Convention on Human Rights. The concept of appropriation is very wide and that of dishonesty is uncertain at the margins. A person may not be able in advance to judge whether or not his conduct constitutes theft.

(b) While the facts of *Gomez* involved deception, the case is not limited to such facts. Appropriation occurs whether or not the accused has deceived the victim into transferring his property. An accused appropriates if he buys or hires property.

(c) Since neutral facts may constitute an appropriation and since appropriation need involve the assumption of only one of the rights of the owner, appropriation after *Gomez* occurs at an earlier stage than it did under *Morris*. If the accused touches the can of beans mentioned above he appropriates. Under *Morris* he would not have appropriated until he did something inconsistent with the rights of the owner such as hiding the tin among other items in his own bag – simply taking the beans off the shelf would not have been an appropriation because the removal would have been impliedly authorised by the shopkeeper. This example illustrates how *Gomez* and *Morris* differ and how only the mental element in theft distinguishes the innocent from the guilty, the point made in (a) above. The example also demonstrates how far the law has been extended since 1968. Under the previous law, that of larceny, there had to be a taking away ('asportation') which was performed without the consent of the owner. Neither element is required in theft. The accused appropriates before he takes away and does so even though the owner consents. Facts which pre-1969 would have perhaps been attempted larceny are now definitely the full offence of theft. *Gomez* ensures that acts amount to appropriation when under the law prevailing previously they would at most be attempted theft and quite possibly not even that. If an East Midlands Trains train manager puts a suitcase in a rack intending to steal it later, he nowadays appropriates it. Previously he was guilty of attempted theft and only then if the jury decided he had done a more than merely preparatory act. This outcome is sanctioned by reading 'the rights' as 'any of the rights', which is not what s 3(1) states. Theft is concerned with stealing property, not with stealing one of the rights in that property.

(d) It may be that the police and store detectives will not arrest until the accused walks past the till or out of the shop without paying or puts the item into his pocket, but these actions are part of the proof of appropriation, not appropriation itself. They constitute evidence, not substantive law.

(e) *Gomez* led to an almost total overlap between theft and the former offence of obtaining property by deception where the accused has obtained the item by fraud. In these offences there are four common elements: property, belonging to another, dishonesty, and intention permanently to deprive. One element is similar: appropriation can cover the same facts as obtaining. One difference is that obtaining requires a deception whereas theft does not, but there is nothing to stop the bringing of a charge of theft where there is a deception. If there is any problem with proving deception, a theft charge will lie. An exception to this statement is that, in general, land cannot be stolen (see below) but it can be obtained by deception, the usual example being the accused's moving the boundary fence. The land gained is not stolen but the accused has gained it by deception. Though the same facts can give rise to both crimes it should be noted that the current maximum for theft is seven years' imprisonment, whereas that for obtaining property by deception before its repeal was 10 years. Lord Lowry has a strong point when he states that obtaining property by deception fulfils little or no function when almost all instances of the offence fall within theft. The practical effect of this point is that theft is now an 'included offence' so that if the prosecution cannot prove a deception, the accused may still be convicted of theft. In terms of statutory construction, it cannot be right that one major offence was intended by Parliament to swallow another. It is also argued that theft and deception are different concepts. Deception is concerned with the accused's doing something which affects the victim's mind: the latter is deceived. In theft the accused, to use a paradigm example, takes something from the victim. Since the rationales are different, the coverage of the crimes should be different too.

Contracts are voidable for fraud. In cases like **Lawrence**, **Gomez** and **Hinks** the contracts have not been avoided. Therefore, the property belongs to the defendant, who cannot by definition be guilty of theft of their own property. That is why the crime of obtaining property by deception was put into the Theft Act 1968. **Lawrence**, **Gomez** and **Hinks** destroyed the aim behind having two different offences.

(f) Because consent is irrelevant, it no longer matters whether the effect of fraud on consent to the passing of property is to render a contract void or voidable.

(g) One aspect of **Morris**, minor in comparison with the others, is that Lord Roskill said that a person who switched price labels in a shop out of mischief did not appropriate. This *dictum* was criticised because, applying Lord Roskill's *dictum*, he did interfere with or usurp the rights of the owner. Changing price tags was a right of the owner. Commentators said that the reason why the mischievous label-switcher was not guilty of the theft was not because he did not appropriate but because he was not dishonest. This reasoning was accepted in **Gomez**. A final comment is that the accused in **Morris** was after all convicted. By swapping the price labels and removing the items from the shelves he did appropriate. *A fortiori* he appropriates if one applies **Gomez**.

In **Gomez** the charge was theft but should have been obtaining property by deception. In order to convict the accused the concept of appropriation had to be stretched. Sir John Smith's comment that appropriation is now much wider than Parliament intended is a weighty one and his comment is yet weightier when it is noted that he was a member of the Criminal Law Revision Committee, the Report of which underlies the 1968 Act. The Committee's view is summarised in para. 38a. 'Obtaining by false pretences is ordinarily thought of as different from theft, because in the former the owner in fact consents to part with his ownership; a bogus beggar is regarded as a rogue but not as a thief . . . To create a new offence of theft to include conduct which ordinary people would find difficult to regard as theft would be a mistake.' **Gomez** draws no distinction between a rogue and a thief, the accused who obtains fraudulently and the accused who appropriates by stealth. The crimes which an accused commits should be fairly labelled so that he can be appropriately punished. A taking by stealth is different from a taking with consent, even when consent is vitiated by fraud. The majority in **Gomez** refused to refer to the Report because there was clear Lords' authority for the proposition that consent was irrelevant. The contrary argument is that **Lawrence** was not pellucid, that there was another House of Lords' authority which seemed to decide differently, there was a string of Court of Appeal cases which sought to reconcile **Lawrence** and **Gomez**, and that anyway the Lords did not in **Lawrence** consider the Report. Only the dissentient, Lord Lowry, looked at the Report and by doing so he persuasively demonstrated that the majority ruling was inconsistent with the will of Parliament. Despite this criticism **Gomez** is wonderfully clear in its ruling. Its effect on appropriation from companies is discussed later. It will be seen that **Gomez** has also clarified the law in that area.

The argument from principle was pithily put by P.R. Glazebrook in 'Revising the Theft Acts' [1993] CLJ 191. 'Holding swindlers to be thieves does no injustice, will save much inconvenience in cases where it transpires only late in the day that a crook has resorted to deception, and avoids the extreme absurdity of denying the name of thief to those who misappropriate property received as a result of a mistake that they have induced while awarding it to those who had done nothing to bring about the mistaken transfer.' (The last phrase is a reference to s 5(4): see below.)

(h) In *Gomez* there was a contract to sell the goods. Since the contract was voidable, the shopkeeper could have elected to treat the contract as subsisting and sue for the price. The buyer would then have the sole proprietary interest in the goods. In this scenario the purchaser's title to the goods would not have been disputable by anyone. Nevertheless this is presumably theft because all the elements are present at the moment of the purchase.

(i) One consequence of *Gomez* is that the trial judge is saved from instructing the jury on civil law concepts such as the difference between void and voidable contracts. This point was made by Lord Steyn in *Hinks* [2001] 2 AC 241 (HL).

(d) *Gallasso*

On the day on which the speeches were delivered in *Gomez* the Court of Appeal heard argument in *Gallasso* (1994) 98 Cr App R 284. The accused, a nurse, became the house leader for a group of mentally handicapped adults. She opened trust accounts for each patient. She was the sole signatory and spent the money on various living expenses of the patients. Having opened three trust accounts for one patient, she, *inter alia*, withdrew sums over time from the third account. She was charged with theft of £1,800.32, the amount of a cheque she had deposited on opening the account. The jury convicted but the court allowed her appeal. Lloyd LJ giving the judgment said that if she had placed the cheque into her own account, she would have appropriated, but held that by paying a cheque for the patient into his account, she was not appropriating, no matter how dishonest she was. The court accepted the defence's contention that: 'by paying in the cheques, the applicant was not assuming the rights of the owner. On the contrary, she was affirming those rights, by placing the cheque in trust accounts of which he was the named beneficiary.' The court either did not like *Gomez* or did not understand its implications.

Gallasso may be criticised for not applying *Gomez*:

(a) Lloyd LJ said that he was giving appropriation its ordinary meaning. Only the dissentient in *Gomez* gave that concept its dictionary meaning. The majority adopted what has come to be known as a 'neutral' definition.

(b) Lloyd LJ said that Lord Keith did not mean to say in *Gomez* that every touching was an appropriation. Lloyd LJ instanced a shopper who knocked an item from a shelf and then replaced it and a passer-by who picked up a lady's purse. He considered that such examples were not ones of appropriation. In the latter case he said that the passer-by would, however, appropriate if he ran away with the purse. Clarkson, Keating and Cunningham, *Criminal Law: Text and Materials*, 7th edn (Sweet & Maxwell, 2010) 753 comment: 'It is absurd to assert that picking up a dropped purse to hand it back to the owner is assuming the rights of the owner.' In criticism it may be said that appropriation does occur at the moment of the touching. It is suggested that Lord Keith meant to say exactly that. A person does assume the rights of the owner when he puts his hand on a tin of beans on the supermarket shelves. It is for this reason that dishonesty has to bear the weight which it does after *Gomez*. Dishonesty, not lack of appropriation, distinguished the passer-by who hands back the purse from the one who decamps with it. The external elements, the *actus reus*, are exactly the same whether the accused was an innocent shopper or a shoplifter. On the facts of *Gallasso* she appropriated the cheque by removing it from the envelope which it came in. Her *mens rea* makes her guilty of theft. Even though her action was impliedly authorised by the patient, even though it was only a preliminary stage in her withdrawing money from the account for her own purposes, she did appropriate for within s 3(1) she assumed (one of) the rights of the owner. Applying *Gomez* to *Gallasso* the accused appropriated by paying in the cheque.

(c) Lloyd LJ said that the accused was affirming the rights of the owner by paying the cheque into his account. However, if one applies *Gomez*, one appropriates goods by putting them into a basket provided by the shop. One is on these facts affirming the rights of the shop to the goods but one does assume one of the rights of the owner.

(d) There is a suggestion in the judgment ('the paying in was not a taking at all') that one can appropriate only if one takes the item, though Lloyd LJ did say that he was not incorporating the requirement of asportation (see above) into theft. However that may be, there exist some illustrations of appropriation which do not require a taking. If I sell your furniture, I appropriate even though I do not take or touch the property. Lord Keith in *Gomez* said that a person appropriates by switching price labels even when the item to be taken is not moved.

(e) The accused had possession of the victim's property at the time when she paid in the cheque. She did not need to 'take' it for she already had it. To use pre-Theft Act terminology, she converted the cheque. Since appropriation is the modern term for conversion, she appropriates the cheque by paying it in.

(f) The result which Lloyd LJ desired would have been obtained under *Morris*. The accused would not have adversely interfered with or usurped the rights of the owner before she withdrew cash for her own purposes. Her conduct until then would have been impliedly authorised by the patient. Only when she deviated from the authorisation did she appropriate under *Morris*. *Morris* has, however, gone and the reasoning in it is no longer applicable. Applying *Gomez* she appropriates.

In summary, *Gallasso* is wrong (and should not be followed) because an appropriation is simply a dealing with another's property. There need not be a nonconsensual dealing. For this reason it is suggested that Lloyd LJ was wrong to say that a hall-porter did not appropriate when he placed a suitcase under his desk, preliminarily to stealing it, in breach of hotel regulations which provided for the porter to lock it away. The accused in *Gallasso* did not just break the rules of the health authority which employed her, she also appropriated for the purposes of the law of theft. And if one were to consider *Gallasso* wrong, as from the viewpoint of precedent it is, the outcome exemplifies a point made above. The accused is guilty of theft at the point of paying in the cheque. She has not yet taken anything out of the account. Applying a combination of the law of attempt and *Morris* it is doubtful whether she would be guilty of attempted theft. After *Gomez*, however, she is guilty not merely of attempted theft but of the full offence of theft when she places the patient's cheque into his account.

(e) *Briggs*

The Court of Appeal in *Briggs* [2004] 1 Cr App R 34 held that appropriation required the accused to perform a physical act; deceiving the victim into transferring property was not an appropriation. As in *Gallasso* the court was seeking to restrict *Gomez*. Certainly it may be argued that in *Gomez* there was a physical appropriation. Possession of the goods was taken. (Similarly in *Hinks* the accused received the money: see below for a discussion of

Hinks.) However, *Gomez* is not restricted to physical takings. Indeed, if it were, how would one be able to appropriate those intangibles which are property for the purposes of theft? The contention that theft was restricted to physical takings might have been arguable when the Theft Act 1968 came into force, but not in the twenty-first century, one might have thought. Amazingly the court did not refer to *Gomez* or *Hinks*; and Silber J said: 'it is not easy to see why an act of deceiving an owner to do something would fall within the meaning of "appropriation"', yet that is what *Gomez* holds.

(f) *Mazo* and *Kendrick*

The Court of Appeal also found difficulty in applying *Gomez* in *Mazo* [1997] 2 Cr App R 518. A lady's maid was given various items including £37,000 in cheques by her mistress, who was mentally incapable. The court allowed her appeal. The cheques were property, they belonged to another, the maid intended permanently to deprive, and the jury found that she was dishonest. Did she appropriate? By receiving the gifts she assumed all of the rights of the owner: she became the owner. Therefore, she ought to have been found guilty of theft. The actual outcome of the case raised the possibility that *Gomez* does not apply when in civil law the accused has a good title. The absurdity in the situation is that an accused can be found guilty of theft after *Gomez* despite the fact that he retains ownership even after a conviction for theft. Sir John Smith commented thus in his case comment on *Mazo* [1996] Crim LR 437: 'However all-embracing *Gomez* may seem, a line must be drawn where conviction of theft would cause a conflict with the civil law. . . . If the effect of the transaction is that [the accused] gets an absolute, indefeasible right to the property in question, it would be unacceptable for a criminal court to hold that the transaction amounted to a theft of the property by him. If [he] has a right to retain the property, or even to recover it from the alleged victim, it can hardly be held to be theft for him to take and keep it. Otherwise the civil law would be assisting [him] to recover or to retain the fruits of his crime.' There were two possible *ratios* to *Mazo*. First, a valid gift cannot constitute an appropriation. The cases in the next paragraph held that this proposition was wrong. Secondly, consent is relevant where the appropriation is not induced by fraud (deception). There is nothing in *Gomez* that supports this restriction, and the cases mentioned in the next paragraph do not support it.

Mazo was distinguished in *Kendrick* [1997] 2 Cr App R 524 (CA). The court stated that it was not being called upon to decide whether *Mazo* was correct in holding that a gift *inter vivos* could not constitute an appropriation (but it did call this ruling an 'apparent gloss' on *Gomez*, demonstrating that it thought *Mazo* to be incorrect). It held that the consent of the owner did not negate an appropriation. *Mazo* was distinguished as a case involving a person with reduced mental capacity, whereas *Kendrick* involved a person incapable of managing her own affairs.

(g) *Hinks*

The Court of Appeal in *Hinks* [2000] 1 Cr App R 1 ruled that a gift could be an appropriation. The concession by counsel in *Mazo* that it could not be an appropriation was wrong. Therefore, the act by which the accused gets ownership is an appropriation. The Criminal Law Revision Committee did not so intend. Contrary to the view of Sir John Smith, civil unlawfulness was not an element of theft. Whether the gift was validly made was irrelevant. Pitt LJ said: 'In relation to theft, one of the ingredients for a jury to consider is not whether there has been a gift, valid or otherwise, but whether there has been an appropriation.' As he earlier noted, the consent of the owner, the donor, is immaterial when determining appropriation. The court specifically rejected the analysis of Sir John Smith [1997] Crim LR 359 in his commentary on *Gomez* that the speech of Lord Browne-Wilkinson in *Gomez* has seen off all challenges to its authority. There is, however, a difference between *Hinks* and *Gomez*. In the former case the accused would not have been guilty of any offence, had the accused not been guilty of theft.

By a majority of three to two the House of Lords upheld the Court of Appeal decision in *Hinks* [2001] 2 AC 241. It applied *Lawrence* and *Gomez* to the following facts. The victim was a man of limited intelligence. He 'gave' his principal carer some £60,000 over a period in 1996. Her argument was that she received the money as gifts. Lord Steyn delivered the leading speech. He said that a person appropriates property belonging to another even though the victim transfers an indefeasible title to it and does not retain any interest in it. Therefore, the donee of a gift appropriates it by receiving it, and this is so despite the fact that in civil law the donor cannot get it back. The majority in *Gomez* had already held that an appropriation occurred even though the entire proprietary interest passed to the accused. Lord Steyn noted that *Gomez* was not restricted to situations in which an alleged fraud took place. He approved the statement of Rose LJ in the Court of Appeal that: 'Belief or lack of belief that the owner consented to the appropriation is relevant to dishonesty. But appropriation may occur even though the owner has consented to the property being taken.' He also rejected counsel's argument that an appropriation had to be an unlawful one. To accept it would be to interpolate a concept into the definition of theft, which had been 'carefully drafted'. In other words Parliament did not intend that the appropriation had to be an unlawful one. He furthermore rejected the contention that it was absurd that civil law and criminal law should reach different conclusions for they served different purposes. Counsel provided illustrations where the application of *Gomez* might be said to lead to unsettling outcomes: the accused was guilty of theft when he should not have been. An example is where the buyer of a painting believes it to be by a major artist when it is not and the seller knows of the mistake. Providing dishonesty can be proved, there is theft, even though in civil law there is an enforceable contract and if the buyer does not pay, the seller can sue for the price.

Lord Steyn thought that the difficulties could be obviated by using the concept of dishonesty. On the facts the accused was dishonest. No one was likely to prosecute in marginal cases; and 'at the extremity of the application of legal rules there are sometimes results which may seem strange'. In his view, if a narrower conception of appropriation were adopted, 'the outcome is likely to place beyond the reach of the criminal law dishonest persons who should be found guilty of theft'. He was happy to reach the conclusion that appropriation bore a wide meaning for there was as a result no need to explain to juries civil law concepts such as indefeasibility and civil law unlawfulness. Finally he stated that *Gomez* does not lead to injustice in practice. 'The mental requirements of theft are an adequate protection against injustice.'

The minority forcefully dissented on the basis that where there was a valid gift, there was no dishonesty and therefore no theft, as *Mazo* had held. However, in *Kendrick* there was dishonesty because the accused knew that the donor was mentally incapable. Lord Hutton said that the judge should have directed the jury on whether the victim in *Hinks* was mentally capable. If he was, 'the defendant could not be found to be dishonest no matter how much they thought her conduct morally reprehensible'. If the victim was mentally incapable of making a valid gift, the *Ghosh* test applied. Similarly, if there was alleged to be undue influence or coercion, there would have to be a specific direction; if the gift was invalid for either reason, again *Ghosh* had to be applied. Lord Hobhouse said that: 'the reasoning of the Court of Appeal . . . depends upon the disturbing acceptance that a criminal conviction and the imposition of custodial sanctions may be based upon conduct which involves no inherent illegality and may only be capable of being criticised on grounds of lack of morality.' One purpose of criminal law, however, was to define the boundary between criminality and immorality. Once the item had been given, there is no property belonging to another; 'the donee is not "assuming the rights of an owner": she already has them' and therefore there is no appropriation; even if the acceptance of the gift constitutes an appropriation, the accused is not dishonest because of s 2(1)(a); the accused does not intend to act regardless of the donor's rights within s 6(1) because he has relinquished those rights. 'The person who accepts a valid gift is simply conforming to the wishes of the owner.' There is no appropriation. On this approach, taking an article to the check-out in order to buy it is not an appropriation; it is merely complying with the implied request of the supermarket. In Lord Hobhouse's view *Mazo* was correct and *Kendrick* was wrong. He was strongly of the opinion that 'dishonestly appropriates' was one concept. There were not two, dishonesty and appropriation. A person does not 'dishonestly appropriate' if acts are done in relation to the property which are performed in accordance with the actual wishes or actual authority of the owner. Either there is no assumption of rights or there is no dishonesty. (Assuredly the accused may also be able to rely on s 2(1)(a): if he believes that he is legally entitled to the gift, he is not dishonest.) The position is different when there is fraud, misrepresentation, undue influence, cases falling within s 5(4) (where the victim has made a mistake and the accused is under a duty to restore) and cases falling within s 5(1) (where the victim retains an equitable interest).

Other problems with *Hinks* should be noted:

- First, the accused may not have been dishonest and accordingly could not have been guilty of theft.

- Secondly, if the gift was valid in civil law, then the owner could not recover it; if the owner used self-help to get it back, he could be sued by the alleged thief. It is unsatisfactory that the person who in civil law owns the property is in criminal law guilty of theft. Since civil law does not allow the owner to bring an action in respect of the gift, why should criminal law say that acceptance of a gift is an appropriation?

- Thirdly, in the law of handling, goods are no longer stolen when the owner loses the right to restitution. Therefore, there are no stolen goods and the crime of handling cannot take place. If on the facts of *Hinks* the owner never had such a right, how can it be said that the property is 'stolen'?

- Fourthly, Lord Steyn said that if criminal law and civil law were inconsistent, it may be that civil law was incorrect. However, the criminal law of theft exists to protect the civil law of property. If it is not, what exactly is the criminal law protecting? Coverage must be the same.

- Fifthly, if the victim took the property back dishonestly intending to keep it, he would be guilty of theft from the accused!

- Sixthly, the accused did not assume the rights of the owner: she *was* the owner.

- Seventhly, the accused was ordered to pay a substantial amount of compensation to the victim. It is arguable that this order was in breach of Article 1 of Protocol 1 to the European Convention on Human Rights, the right to peaceful enjoyment of property.

- Eighthly, there is the difficulty with the moral basis of the law of theft. Theft is concerned with protecting civil law rights to property, whereas the basis for fraud is the prevention of exploitation of the victim. *Hinks* extended theft into the field also covered by fraud, thereby undermining the moral basis of theft.

- Finally, the Criminal Law Revision Committee, the Eighth Report, *Theft and Related Offences*, Cmnd 2977, 1966, which forms the basis of the Theft Act 1968, did not intend the law to be as stated by the majority in *Hinks*.

Academic criticism of *Hinks* reached its acme in E. Philips, C. Walsh and P. Dobson, *Law Relating to Theft* (Cavendish, 2001) 43, who called the outcome of the case a 'horror'. They suggest (at 50) that *Hinks* breaches Article 6 of the ECHR, what may in US terms be called the 'void for vagueness' provision, because whether an accused is guilty of theft or not depends on his dishonesty or lack of it.

(h) *Atakpu*

One might have thought that *Gomez* would have widened the law in all respects. In one matter, however, it has narrowed it. The facts of *Atakpu* [1994] QB 69 (CA) exemplify this proposition. The defendants planned to hire expensive cars abroad, bring them to England, modify them and then sell them. English courts have no jurisdiction to try accused persons for thefts committed abroad. Where did the appropriation take place? The court held that appropriation occurred when the cars were hired. Therefore, there was no appropriation in England and the English courts lacked jurisdiction. Ward J said that it was incorrect to say that there could be one theft abroad and another in England (unless the defendants had lost possession abroad and then resumed it in England). The court was willing to consider the argument that theft was a continuing act (see below) but on the facts the theft was complete and did not continue for days after the appropriation. Since the issue did not arise on the facts, the court was unwilling to give a decided view on this point but did note that applying *Gomez* strictly, there was little scope for the doctrine of continuing appropriation. It is suggested that *Gomez* did not affect the law whether appropriation could be a continuing act. See the discussion of this point in robbery later in this chapter. The statements in *Atakpu* are *obiter*. Ward J said that the defendants were rogues but their conviction had to be quashed. It should be noted that under *Morris* the English courts would have had jurisdiction. A modification to a car would be an adverse interference with the owner's rights, and the modification would have taken place in England. Under *Gomez*, however, there was only one appropriation (there was no appropriation each time the accused touched the car), and that occurred abroad. Unlike the judges in its sister division in *Gallasso*, the Court of Appeal in *Atakpu* loyally followed, as it was obliged to, the decision in *Gomez*, despite doubts as to its effects. Incidentally, a charge of conspiring to steal money from buyers in England would have succeeded.

On the jurisdiction point, the English courts if *Atakpu*'s *ratio* is correct could still not try the offence of theft after the coming into force of the Criminal Justice Act 1993, s 2: no 'relevant event' occurred in England. No element to be proved before theft is committed occurred in England. However, the appellants were also charged with conspiracy to steal. By virtue of s 1A of the Criminal Law Act 1977, as inserted by s 5(1) of the 1993 Act, the courts have jurisdiction provided that what the men did was an offence under the law of the foreign law district. For criticism of *Atakpu*, see G.R. Sullivan and C. Warbrick 'Territoriality, theft and *Atakpu*' [1994] Crim LR 650 and 'Current developments: private international law' (1994) 43 ICLQ 464–465. They argue that the cars were not stolen abroad because stolen means 'stolen according to English domestic law'. Therefore the cars were stolen only when they were imported. In terms of the later part of s 3(1) the defendants came by the property (abroad) and kept or dealt with it (in England). The court therefore did have jurisdiction.

(i) Other examples of appropriation

As these examples illustrate, appropriation occurs when the accused deals in any way with the property. Damaging property belonging to another will amount to criminal damage but it is also an appropriation. As always, the reader should take care to consider that more than one crime can arise on the same facts.

1　Taking the goods: *Stapylton* v *O'Callaghan* [1973] 2 All ER 782 (DC).

2　Putting goods into the accused's shopping bag: *McPherson* [1973] Crim LR 191 (CA). After *Gomez* simply taking hold of the goods is an appropriation, even if the owner agrees to that. One cannot appropriate without assuming possession or control. As *Gomez* demonstrates it is irrelevant whether or not the accused deceived the victim. There is even an appropriation when the accused buys an item.

3　Grabbing a handbag is an appropriation, even though the accused dropped the bag immediately and did not get away with it: *Corcoran* v *Anderton* (1980) 71 Cr App R 104 (DC).

4　Taking money from a customer and not ringing up the price on the till: *Monaghan* [1979] Crim LR 673 (CA). (She is also guilty of false accounting, contrary to s 17 of the Theft Act 1968.) It should be noted that the shop assistant was guilty of theft, and not just of attempted theft. She may never have decided to remove the money, and she did exactly what the shop had instructed her to do: put the money in the till. Her dishonesty was used to prove her appropriation. Under the old law of larceny she may not even have been guilty of attempted larceny. Indeed, it could be argued that there was only a preparatory step towards the full offence, and not a more than merely preparatory step, in which event she would not even have been guilty of the attempt. The law has been extended so that she is now guilty of theft. If it could not be proved that she intended to exercise control over those banknotes and coins the customer had given her but intended to take an equivalent amount, it is suggested that the offence is not theft but the attempt because she did not appropriate identifiable money. Again, a charge of false accounting appears to meet the facts better than theft does.

5　Deceiving the victim into handing over an extra £6 for a taxi-ride: *Lawrence* v *MPC* [1972] AC 626 (HL), discussed above.

6　Deceiving a shop assistant into charging less: *Bhachu* (1977) 65 Cr App R 261 (CA). The assistant will also be guilty of theft if she was in league with the customer, for example *Pilgram* v *Rice-Smith* [1977] 1 WLR 671 (DC). A supermarket assistant, in cahoots with a customer, wrapped goods and deliberately understated the price. It was held that there was an appropriation by the assistant because she had no authority to deal with the goods in this way. She had assumed one of the rights of the owner, the right to put the price on items for sale. Within s 3(1) she had come by property, bacon and corned beef, innocently but she had assumed 'a right to it by keeping or dealing with [the property] as an owner'.

7　Getting a shopkeeper to cash a cheque sent to the accused by mistake: *Davis* (1989) 88 Cr App R 347 (CA).

8　Transferring export licences from one firm to another: *Attorney-General of Hong Kong* v *Chan Nai-Keung* [1987] 1 WLR 1339 (PC).

9　Presenting another's cheque, forging a cheque, or getting funds transferred from another's bank account into one's own: *Kohn* (1979) 69 Cr App R 395 (CA), discussed below, and *Wille*, above, even though the bank had no mandate to honour the cheque, and *Chan Man-sin* v *Attorney-General of Hong Kong* [1988] 1 All ER 1, where the cheques were not binding on the company because they were forged. Yet compare the civil law. In *Tai Hing Cotton Mill Ltd* v *Liu Chong Hing Bank Ltd* [1986] AC 80 (PC) an account was debited because of a forged cheque. The debit was void because the bank had authority to pay only against valid cheques. Honouring a forged cheque is a nullity. The bank had to pay for the account-holder's loss. Therefore, the account-holder lost nothing. The Privy Council in *Chan Man-sin*, where a company's accountant wrote unauthorised cheques to withdraw money from the bank accounts of two companies, advised that the owner of a credit at the bank or of a right to draw on an account: 'has, clearly, the right as owner to draw by means of a properly completed negotiable instrument or order to pay and it is . . . beyond argument that one who draws, presents and negotiates a cheque on a particular bank account is assuming the rights of the owner . . . It is . . . entirely immaterial that the end result of the transaction may be a legal nullity, for it is not possible to read into [the Hong Kong version of s 3(1)] any requirement that the assumption of rights there envisaged should have a legally efficacious result.' In other words, the accused appropriates even though the owner's rights against the bank are not reduced. He is doing something which only the owner is permitted to do. Since only the account-holder has the right to draw a cheque, the accused appropriates by doing so: *ex parte Osman* [1990] 1 WLR 277 (DC) and *Ngan* [1998] 1 Cr App R 331 (CA).

To the contrary is *Hilton* [1997] 2 Cr App R 445 (CA) where it was held that there had to be a transfer of funds for the accused to be guilty. The Court said that the transfer had to be complete before there could be an appropriation. In the words of Evans LJ: '. . . where property consists of a credit balance . . . then the defendant appropriates it by assuming the rights of the owner of the balance and so causing the transfer to be made out of the account. His instructions to the bank to make the transfer, whether given by cheque or otherwise, are the key which sets the relevant inter-bank (or inter-account) machinery in motion. The fact that the transfer is made is enough to complete the offence . . .' This is inconsistent with the earlier authority of *ex parte Osman* and the later one of *Ngan*. It is suggested that *Hilton* is wrong on this point. The rest of *Hilton*, in particular the court's ruling that the chair of a charity appropriated when he sent faxes to a bank asking it to transfer money from the charity account to another one and when he presented a cheque on the charity's account to move money into the other account is correct. The Court of Appeal held that he had appropriated a thing in action, the right of the charity to sue the bank. It does not matter that the owner's property is not affected by the accused's assumption of one of his rights. Simply signing a cheque is not theft, but attempted theft: *Ngan*.

This situation, where the accused has his account credited and the victim's debited, should be contrasted with the situation where he uses a bank card to debit his account, knowing that he does not have enough money to meet the price. In this situation the bank is obliged to honour the cheque if the accused goes through the correct procedure. Since there is no money in the account, there is no property, no debt (a thing in action) to steal (see *Kohn*, discussed below). Moreover, there is no appropriation. The bank was legally obliged to meet the cheque; therefore, no right of an owner had been assumed: *Navvabi* [1986] 1 WLR 1311 (CA), which illustrates a very important principle. See (10) next.

10 Sending a telex to a bank asking it to transfer funds: *ex parte Osman*. There was not merely an attempt to appropriate, but an appropriation. The accused had assumed the

rights of a customer to have the cheque met. A contrasting case is **Navvabi** [1986] 1 WLR 1311 (CA), where **Kohn** was applied. The accused drew by cheque card on a bank balance which he knew had insufficient funds to meet the sum. It was held that there was no appropriation because there was no identifiable property, merely a contractual right against the bank. There was no thing in action. Therefore, the accused had not assumed any of the rights of the owner, the bank. There was no appropriation. This is an important principle. The correct charge is one of fraud contrary to the Fraud Act 2006.

11 Assuming rights over property which one has previously taken but then abandoned: **Starling** [1969] Crim LR 556 (CA), a case on larceny but the law is unchanged.

12 Destroying property is appropriation.

Even if the accused is not in possession there may be an appropriation, as indeed was the case in **ex parte Osman**. It did not matter whether the bank complied with the demand; it sufficed that the accused pretended to be exercising one of the rights of the owner. That right was one to have cheques or instructions as to his account met.

Section 3(1) does not mention possession and therefore it is not restricted to situations where the accused becomes possessed of property. An illustration is **Pitham and Hehl** (1976) 65 Cr App R 45 (CA). An acquaintance of the victim offered to sell furniture to third parties. The furniture belonged to a man in prison, and the acquaintance was not in possession. It was held (the court seemingly assuming that the acquaintance held himself out as owner, though the actual facts tell a different story, which is one of joint theft by the acquaintance and the third parties) that by the offer to sell, the acquaintance was assuming one of the rights of the owner, the right to sell. If the intended buyer has refused to purchase, the owner of the furniture would not have lost any property but, according to the *ratio*, the accused would still have been guilty. The victim is still the owner and the purported sale interferes with his proprietary rights. In **Pitham** the acquaintance was at the scene of the sale but presumably he would still have been guilty, had he been 100 miles away and the owner was in possession of the goods. (If another person dishonestly agreed to buy, he will be guilty of handling stolen goods.) There is debate whether there is an appropriation in such circumstances. Glanville Williams, *Textbook of Criminal Law*, 3rd edn, ed. D. Baker (Sweet & Maxwell, 2012) 1027 criticised **Pitham**: if a butler invites the maid to join him in stealing the Duke's silver when he has found the key to the safe, surely he has not at that time appropriated the silver. It is very strange that one of the attributes of property is that a non-owner has the right to sell it!

The civil case of **Dobson v General Accident Fire and Life Assurance Corp plc** [1990] QB 274 (CA) illustrates the proposition that the defendant assumes one of the rights of the owner by acquiring ownership. The owner of a watch and a ring sold them to a rogue over the telephone. The next day the rogue paid for the articles by a bad cheque. Therefore, at the time of acquiring ownership he did not have possession. Nevertheless, he had assumed one of the rights of the owner, ownership. Alternatively, if by civil law ownership did not pass at that moment but only on payment, the rogue appropriated then.

(j) 'Come by the property'

Section 3(1) deems there to be an appropriation where the accused 'has come by the property (innocently or not) without stealing it'. (If the accused does come by the property by stealing it, these later words in s 3(1) do not apply and any later assumption will not be an appropriation. This phrase prevents a thief from becoming a thief again each time he deals with an item.) There is an appropriation where in those circumstances he later assumes 'a right to it by keeping or dealing with it as owner'. The use of the phrase 'later assumption' demonstrates that when the accused 'comes by' property, he appropriates it, that is, there are two appropriations. If the accused hired a car and then sold it, the later words of s 3(1) apply. Another example is when a drunken student takes a flashing yellow light from a road excavation, puts it into his bedroom, wakes up to discover it there, and decides to keep it. He has come by the property without stealing it and has later assumed a right to it by keeping it. In *Rader* [1992] Crim LR 663 (CA), discussed above, the accused was given money, that is, he 'came by' it. Then he used it for his own purposes. It is likely that most of the situations where s 3(1) applies are ones where the accused has been overpaid. An example where the latter part of s 3(1) did not apply is *Broom v Crowther* (1984) 148 JP 592 (DC). The accused bought a theodolite, suspecting that it was stolen. He then found out that it was indeed stolen. He left it in his bedroom while he decided what to do with it. It was held that there was no appropriation while he was making up his mind. There would be an appropriation once he had decided to keep it. Therefore, one can appropriate by making up one's mind – a far cry from asportation. *Broom v Crowther* shows that one can appropriate by an omission, though as Leggatt LJ said in *Ngan* [1998] 1 Cr App R 331 (CA), it may be difficult to prove that the accused did intend to keep property as owner when he simply refrained from doing anything. If the accused kept the item he has appropriated it even though he has not done anything physically with it. Within s 3(1) he has assumed a right to it 'by keeping . . . it as owner'. The case also demonstrates the purpose of s 3(1). An innocent first appropriation would have become an unlawful second appropriation if the accused has exercised any of the owner's rights. (The facts of *Broom v Crowther* actually fall within s 3(2), which is discussed next, because the accused was a bona fide purchaser.) The cases are not helpful as to the last words in s 3(1): 'dealing with it as owner.' It is suggested that this phrase includes a situation where the accused sells the item, swaps it, spends it, eats it and the like.

(k) The bona fide purchaser for value without notice

One person who would otherwise appropriate is exempted by s 3(2):

> Where property or a right or interest in property is or purports to be transferred for value to a person acting in good faith, no later assumption by him of rights which he believed himself to be acquiring shall, by reason of any defect in the transferor's title, amount to theft of the property.

An example of the application of s 3(2) is *Adams* [1993] Crim LR 72 (CA). The accused, a motorcycle enthusiast, bought for £350 parts which had been stolen. He was told they came from a motorcycle written off in a crash. He did not begin to suspect that the parts had been stolen until two or three days after acquisition. There was no *actus reus* at the moment of acquiring the parts. Another illustration is *Wheeler* (1991) 92 Cr App R 279 (CA). The stallholder received the medal in the course of sale. His later sale of it was protected by s 3(2). Protection is given only to Equity's Darling. A person who is given property cannot rely on s 3(2) if he later discovers that the property was stolen. Similarly a person who is not dishonest when he acquires goods is guilty of theft if he later discovers the identity of the owner and then he keeps or alienates the property. Protection is not given by s 3(2) to honest finders who turn dishonest. If the accused was a bona fide purchaser for value without notice, finds out about the defect in title and then sells the item, he will be guilty of obtaining the price by deception and of theft under *Gomez* because he is not entitled to sell the goods.

(l) Appropriation as a continuing act

Appropriation may be a continuing act. In *Hale* (1978) 68 Cr App R 415 (CA), the accused, wearing stocking masks, went into the victim's house, took her jewellery box, and tied her up. The court held that the theft was not over by the time the lady was tied up. They were therefore guilty of robbery when they used force seconds after seizing the property. Because the courts have held that appropriation does not occur instantaneously they have been able to expand and contract the term to catch those who are 'manifestly guilty'. *Hale* was a case on robbery. The accused is not guilty of that offence if force or threat of force is not used at the time of the theft. Therefore, to catch the accused the appropriation must be read as a continuing act to include situations where the taking is not by force but there is a struggle afterwards. However, the accused is not guilty of the offence of handling if the *actus reus* is committed otherwise than 'in the course of the stealing'. That phrase is read narrowly to convict the accused of handling rather than theft, handling being a more serious offence than theft. Such a construction explains *Pitham*. The accused appropriated property by offering the furniture for sale. At that moment it became stolen property. When his confederates took delivery of it, they received it for the purposes of the crime of handling because their handling was not in the course of stealing. The theft was already, as it were, completed. (See Chapter 17 for explanation of handling.) What is certain is that the theft is over at some point: *Atakpu*, above. Importing or selling the cars did not constitute an appropriation because they had been appropriated when the defendant hired them abroad.

(m) Theft by partners, co-owners, directors and sole controllers of companies

Where the director or directors is or are not in sole control of the company, there is no difficulty in holding that he or they can appropriate from the company and the property belong to another. For example, in *R (on the Application of R)* v *Snaresbrook Crown Court* (2001), *The Times*, 12 July, the Administrative Court rejected an application for a judicial review of the decision of a Crown Court judge that a director could dishonestly appropriate corporate property with the intention of permanently depriving the company of it even though he was the directing mind and will of the company and therefore the company had consented to the appropriation. He assumed the rights of the owner when the company's money was transferred from its bank account into another account; the company's consent was, applying *Gomez*, irrelevant. Similarly a partner can appropriate partnership property (*Bonner* [1970] 1 WLR 838 (CA), rejecting an argument that since one partner is not liable in tort for conversion, he cannot be guilty of theft), and a co-owner such as a member of a club can appropriate property from the other co-owners as occurs when he sells the item. In these instances the company, the other partners and co-owners have a proprietary right to the property within s 5(1). *Gomez*, above, confirms *obiter* the view taken in *Philippou* (1989) 89 Cr App R 290 (CA) that despite persons being the sole directors and sole shareholders of a company they could appropriate from it by misusing corporate assets. It does not matter that they, through their being sole controllers of the company, did give the company's assent to the misappropriation. Accordingly when the accused used their company's money to buy a Spanish building, they did appropriate. If the approach of the dissentient were adopted, sole controllers would not be guilty because the persons entitled to consent to the transfer of the asset did consent. Sole controllers may, however, not be guilty of theft because they may not be dishonest. (The *ratio* of **Philippou** is incorrect because **Morris** was applied, but the principle in it that sole controllers can appropriate is correct.) Since owners can be found guilty of stealing their own property (see the discussion of 'Belonging to another' below), policy dictates that partners, other co-owners and sole controllers should also be liable.

Property

The second element of the *actus reus* of theft is **property**. Section 4(1) gives a broad definition of property: 'money and all other property, real or personal, including things in action and other intangible property.' Whether something is property is determined by the civil law: criminal law has no separate definition. 'Money' includes foreign money but it excludes out-of-date currency. A thing in action is property without physical existence (and therefore cannot be seen or touched) which can, however, be enforced by legal action, such as the right to sue to recover a debt. Cheques, direct debits and credit cards give rise to things in action. Copyright is a thing in action and therefore if the accused purports to sell copyright in this book, appropriation occurs. (However, infringement is not theft because there is no appropriation of the copyright.) A right by contract to overdraw a bank account is also a thing in action. Rights of way are property which can be stolen by dishonestly conveying the property to another.

In **Marshall** [1998] 2 Cr App R 282 (discussed above in the context of intent permanently to deprive) the Court of Appeal thought that London Underground, which they held had an exclusive right to sell tickets, had a right of action over its tickets to prevent their being used by persons who did not buy them. If so, people who pass on unexpired bus tickets or parking tickets will, depending on their *mens rea*, be guilty of theft. It should be noted that the court did not discuss whether London Underground retained ownership of the tickets, an issue which depends on civil law, in particular the so-called 'ticket' cases in the law of contract. Intangible property, which by definition cannot be touched, can be appropriated by the accused's assuming any of the owner's rights. (See also (c) below.)

Some forms of intellectual property such as patents (and applications for patents) are also covered. A patent is in civil law not a thing in action but personal property. An invention over which there is no patent is intangible property and therefore can be stolen. Therefore, *in this respect*, confidential information is property. However, **Oxford v Moss** (1978) 68 Cr App R 183 (DC), above, held that confidential information such as exam questions is not property for the purposes of the Theft Act. Information such as trade secrets does contain at least some constituents of property. For example, they can be bequeathed and sold. Nevertheless, because a trade secret is not property for the purposes of civil law, it cannot be stolen. Other offences, in particular conspiracy to defraud and fraud within the Fraud Act 2006, ss 1 and 4, may be committed. (The Law Commission proposed a specific separate offence to deal with the use or disclosure of trade secrets: see Consultation Paper No. 150, *Misuse of Trade Secrets*, 1997. However, in 2005 the Commission decided not to continue with the work.)

Services are not property. Therefore, a ride in a taxi cannot be stolen. However, s 11 of the Fraud Act 2006 covers dishonest obtaining of services. The Criminal Law Revision Committee's Eighth Report, *Theft and Related Offences*, Cmnd 2977, 1966, 39, said that electricity could not be stolen because it was not a substance and the Divisional Court held so in **Low v Blease** [1975] Crim LR 513 where the accused was not guilty of theft when he used a telephone; instead a separate offence, s 13, abstracting electricity, was created. One effect of the law should be noted. A person who having entered part of a building as a trespasser and then steals is a burglar, but one who turns on an electric fire is not, despite electricity's being a valuable commodity. A battery can be stolen but not the electricity it contains despite the battery's uselessness without electricity. Water flowing freely whether underground or overground cannot be stolen.

At common law a human corpse and body parts could not be stolen because there was no 'property' in them, but anatomical specimens can be stolen: *Kelly* [1999] QB 621 (CA). The distinction is that such specimens 'have acquired different attributes by virtue of skill, such as dissection or preservation techniques, for exhibition or teaching purposes'. These uncertainties should be cleared up. Certainly a sample of blood (*Rothery* [1976] RTR 550 (CA)) and of urine (*Welsh* [1974] RTR 478 (CA), a sentencing appeal, where the issue was not discussed) can be stolen. In fact, in *Rothery* the accused was found guilty of theft of the container which held the blood, but if urine can be stolen, so can blood. Presumably also sperm in a sperm bank, human eggs and human organs for transplant can be stolen. Whether a body kept in a store for medical students' use is property is debatable. Burke and Hare and other 'resurrection men' would not be guilty of theft if the events took place on English soil at the present time. It is suggested that the common law rule that a human body cannot be stolen will over time become so encrusted with exceptions that Parliament will abolish it. Whatever the position with corpses, live human beings cannot be stolen.

Items such as illegal drugs are property despite its being unlawful to possess them: *Smith* [2011] EWCA Crim 66 (heroin).

Some examples

As the trade secrets example above demonstrates, if there is no property in civil law there is no property for the purposes of the law of theft. Some examples as to what constitutes property follow:

(a) Property covers export quotas: *Attorney-General of Hong Kong* v *Chan Nai-Keung*, above. They are intangible property, not a thing in action.

(b) If a first person owes the victim a sum of money, the accused forges an assignment from the victim to him, and the first person pays the accused, the accused has stolen property (and obtained it by deception).

(c) A patent is not a thing in action (Patents Act 1977, s 30(1)) but it is intangible property. The same is true of an unpatented invention (s 7(2)(b) of that Act).

(d) A difficult topic is cheques. If a company secretary uses company cheques to settle his own debts, he has stolen the company's credit balance as well as the cheque itself. While there has been development, the principal authority remains *Kohn*.

Kohn (1979) 69 Cr App R 395 (CA)

The accused, an accountant, drew cheques on his employer's account. He was guilty of theft. The causing of the bank account to be reduced was appropriation, and the account was property.

The court held that debiting an account which is not overdrawn or one where the overdrawing is within the agreed limit (a credit facility) is theft because the bank has an obligation to meet the drawing. That obligation is enforceable by action. Therefore, it is a debt, a thing in action, which is property. Causing a bank to transfer money out of one account into another, for example by drawing a cheque on the first account, was theft of a credit balance, as where the chair of a charity caused its account to be debited and his to be credited. (In ***Chan Man-sin*** v ***Attorney-General of Hong Kong***, above, the thing in action was said to be the benefit of the contract with the bank.) However, drawing on an overdrawn account or an account overdrawn beyond the agreed credit limit does not amount to the appropriation of property because the bank has no obligation to meet the drawing. The accused has not appropriated a thing in action, because the bank did not owe the money to anyone. The charge should be attempted theft or obtaining a pecuniary advantage by deception.

The problem is, however, this. If the accused gets a transfer of funds from the victim, it is a thing in action but it never existed before it was drawn up. Therefore, it never belonged to anyone but the accused. It was not property belonging to another. In ***Preddy*** [1996] AC 815 (HL) it was held that cheques cannot be stolen where the accused induces the victim to write a cheque in his favour, though it remains to be seen whether the courts would accept Sir John Smith's suggestion that a cheque is a valuable security, which can be stolen: 'Obtaining cheques by deception' [1997] Crim LR 396. Cases have, however, distinguished ***Preddy*** as being an authority on the now repealed law of obtaining. In ***Williams*** [2001] 1 Cr App R 362, the accused dishonestly overcharged for building work. The victims sent cheques to him. He paid them into his bank account. The Court of Appeal held that he was guilty of theft of the thing in action, the right to sue on the cheque, belonging to the person who had signed the cheque. The court said that appropriation occurred when the accused by presenting the cheque reduced the victim's account. The accused has extinguished the victim's rights. The court stressed that ***Preddy*** had not affected ***Kohn***. If the victim's account is in credit, the accused's reducing of the credit constitutes an appropriation. It should be noted that the victims' bank accounts were in credit. If they had been in the red, there would have been no thing in action to steal, as ***Kohn*** demonstrates. It is different if the accused gets a cheque drawn by another for the victim's benefit. In this example the thing in action did exist before the appropriation. It did belong to another and so could be stolen. The obvious charge in these situations is that of obtaining a money transfer by deception.

One possible way round these difficulties is to say that a cheque is not just a piece of paper (which is property), but is also a valuable security, which can be stolen too.

Cheques, telexes and appropriation

Kohn was approved in ***Thompson*** [1984] 1 WLR 962(CA), ***Doole*** [1985] Crim LR 450, ***Chan Man-sin***, above, and ***ex parte Osman***, above. An alternative view is found in ***Wille***, above. The accused, a company director, drew cheques on the company's account and used the money for his own purposes. The cheques had not been countersigned, and it was arguable that the bank had no authority to honour them. The Court of Appeal, however, held that the lack of authority was irrelevant, and the accused had appropriated the credit balance, which was a thing in action, by drawing the cheques. This case was approved in ***Chan Man-sin***. One problem with cheques is: when does the appropriation take place? Does it occur on withdrawal or when the entry is made in the bank's books, i.e. when the account is debited? What happens when the account is in the black at the time of presentation but in the red when the bank honours the withdrawal? If the latter applies, there is no thing in action and so no property to steal. ***Kohn***, ***Tomsett*** [1985] Crim LR 369 (CA) and ***Doole*** support that view. For example, in ***Tomsett***, the accused, a telex operator employed by a bank in England, diverted money sent by his bank to New York. The court held that the money was appropriated only when the telex took effect. Since the telex did not take effect in England, the English courts had no jurisdiction at the time. Jurisdiction is now available under the Criminal Justice Act 1993. ***Navvabi*** [1986] 1 WLR 1311 (CA) said that ***Kohn*** was *obiter* on this point. The Privy Council refused to decide this point in **Chan Man-sin**, where the accused assumed the rights of the owner by drawing on the account. **Ex parte Osman** held that the sending of a telex amounted to an appropriation. (See also **Ngan**, above.) Therefore, theft was complete at that moment, contrary to **Tomsett**. The Divisional Court in **ex parte Osman** refused to follow **Tomsett**, where it was held that the bank had to comply with the instruction to debit one account and credit another. (It was thought in **Tomsett** that there can be an appropriation only when the accused's act affected the property but the concept bears a wider meaning than that.) **Tomsett** was said not to be binding because the prosecution did not wish to argue the view accepted in **ex parte Osman**, even though the court had invited counsel to do so. See also the section on **Atakpu**, above. In point of interpretation the line taken in **ex parte Osman** looks correct. Under **Morris** and **Gomez** any assumption of any of the rights of the owner suffices, and there is no need to prove that the accused deprived the owner of anything. The appropriation need not have any legal effect. Accordingly a preparatory act can be an appropriation (cf. the law of attempt)!

If an accused steals a cheque, he might appear to be guilty of theft of a piece of paper, though that is not the gist of what he did. The difficulty here is that the accused may not have an intent permanently to deprive. It is certainly arguable that when the cheque is returned, its virtue or value remains. It is still a piece of paper, both before and after the bank stamped it as having been accepted. Lord Goff accepted this argument in **Preddy**. Surprisingly the Court of Appeal in **Graham** [1997] 1 Cr App R 302 treated this *dictum* as *ratio* and in **Clark** [2001] Crim LR 572 the same court somewhat reluctantly held that it was bound by **Graham**, which held that there was no offence of obtaining a cheque by deception. See the next chapter for a discussion of cheques as 'property belonging to another'.

Prosecutors should be aware of the offence of procuring the execution of a valuable security. Cheques are valuable securities, whether they constitute consideration in contract law or not. Since they are, they are property. If the accused acquires a cheque and uses it to obtain money from the victim's account, he has appropriated the cheque. This argument has not yet been adopted by the courts in relation either to theft or to fraud, though in **Graham** the judges thought that it was highly persuasive.

Land, flora and fauna

By s 4(2) of the Theft Act 1968:

> A person cannot steal land, or things forming part of land and severed from it by him or by his direction, except . . .
>
> (a) when he is a trustee or personal representative, or is authorised by power of attorney, or as a liquidator of a company, or otherwise, to sell or dispose of land belonging to another, and he appropriates the land or anything forming part of it by dealing with it in breach of the confidence reposed in him; or
> (b) when he is not in possession of the land and appropriates anything forming part of the land by severing it or causing it to be severed, or after it has been severed; or
> (c) when, being in possession of the land under a tenancy, he appropriates the whole or part of any fixture or structure let to be used with the land . . .

The basic rule is therefore that land cannot be stolen, but there are exceptions. An example of (a) is where a trustee sells a plot of land for his own purposes. The Act is not limited to express trustees. Constructive trustees are presumably covered. An example of (b) is where one farmer grazes cattle on the victim's land without the latter's consent. The farmer has caused to be severed something which forms part of the land. Lead on a church roof is property for this purpose. Soil is land. Manure spread on land is land; manure in a dung heap is personal property. A person who trespasses on land to pick fruit falls under (b) but may have a defence under s 4(3); if, however, the accused gains possession of the land and then picks fruit, there is no theft since he is in possession of the land and (b) demands that he is not in possession.

There may be difficulties knowing what forms part of the land and what does not. Before the 1968 Act a hut that was bolted onto a concrete base was held not to be part of the land, whereas the concrete base, *obiter*, was. A fixed caravan may be part of the land but a mobile one is not, even though mains water and electricity are supplied. Grazing cattle on land will cause the grass, part of the land, to be severed. Under (b) the extension of a boundary fence does not steal the land enclosed because there is no severance. Taking bricks from a wall or fallen apples falls within s 4(2)(b).

Under (c) an accused will be guilty of theft (provided all the other ingredients of theft are satisfied) if he, the tenant, hacks out an Adam fireplace for whatever purpose. There is no need for severance. If, however, the person in possession of the house is not a tenant but a licensee or squatter, s 4(2)(c) does not apply and he will not be guilty of theft of the fireplace! And by being in possession, s 4(2)(b) does not apply. The law is in need of reform to bring about consistency between tenants and licensees and squatters (provided squatters are held to be in possession of the land). Section 4(2)(c) applies only to the person in possession under a tenancy. Therefore, the tenant's partner does not fall under this paragraph if he appropriates a fixture. Section 4(2)(b) is, however, applicable but only when the fixture has been severed from the land. Accordingly under (c) the tenant is guilty at the time of appropriation, the partner is guilty under (b) only on severance. A tenant who picks fruit does not commit theft because fruit is not a 'fixture or structure'. A 'structure' includes a shed and a garage; a 'fixture' includes bathroom ware and central heating radiators.

Under a later part of s 4(2) land does not include incorporeal hereditaments such as easements and profits, which can therefore be stolen because these are property falling within s 4(1).

> A person who picks mushrooms growing wild on any land, or who picks flowers, fruit or foliage from a plant growing wild on any land, does not (although not in possession of the land), steal what he picks, unless he does it for reward or for sale or other commercial purpose.
>
> For purposes of this subsection 'mushroom' includes any fungus, and 'plant' includes any shrub or tree (s 4(3)).

Under s 4(3) the accused is guilty only if he has a commercial purpose. If the accused picks mistletoe to sell in the streets at Christmas, he is guilty, provided the other elements of theft are satisfied. The commercial purpose assuredly must exist at the time of the picking. If the accused picks wild strawberries and later decides to sell them to the Ritz, he is not appropriating property within s 4(3). Possibly a one-off sale cannot be described as being 'for a commercial purpose'. With regard to plants s 4(3) will be satisfied if they are picked for a commercial purpose. If, however, a whole plant is dug out, s 4(2) comes into play because the plant forms part of the land and is stolen by severing it (s 4(2)(b)). Moreover, one does not 'pick . . . from a plant' if one picks the whole plant or if one lops and tops a tree.

> Wild creatures, tamed or untamed, shall be regarded as property; but a person cannot steal a wild creature not tamed nor ordinarily kept in captivity, or the carcase of any such creature, unless either it has been reduced into possession by or on behalf of another person and possession of it has not since been lost or abandoned, or another person is in course of reducing it into possession (s 4(4)).

In s 4(4) there is no need for a commercial purpose. An example is the taking of animals kept in captivity in a wild life safari park. The animal is one normally kept in captivity and remains so even though it has escaped from the park. The accused who appropriates a grouse hidden by a poacher to be collected later will be guilty of theft (provided the other elements exist), even though he does not intend to sell it in a pub. The accused steals the grouse from both the poacher and the landowner. Under the law of larceny before the Theft Act 1968 it was held that a person was not in possession of mussels growing naturally when he raked them over. Therefore, when a second person took the mussels he did not steal them. Such is also the law after 1968.

Belonging to another

By s 5(1) of the Theft Act 1968:

> [p]roperty shall be regarded as belonging to any person having possession or control of it, or having in it any proprietary right or interest (not being an equitable interest arising only from an agreement to transfer or grant an interest).

This subsection needs careful consideration. For some reason students sometimes miss that a person 'having in it any proprietary right or interest' is the owner (whether legal or equitable or both) and they talk about theft from the possessor or controller, but in all likelihood theft will be from the owner. Note too (i) that a person may be the owner, possessor and controller at the same time, or ownership, possession, and control may be split among two or even three people (for more, see below) and (ii) it is difficult to find property which in law does not belong to another.

R (on the Application of Ricketts) v Basildon Magistrates' Court [2011] 1 Cr App R 15 (DC)

The Court was faced with two scenarios involving a suitcase left on the pavement outside a charity shop and bags put in bins provided by a charity shop; in both cases the bags belonged to unknown people. The accused drove off with the contents of the suitcase at 02:15. He was seen by a constable monitoring CCTV. When he was stopped, the police also found a set of bags in his car. He said he was going to sell the items at a car boot sale. With regard to the first items the Court held that the charity had not yet acquired a proprietary interest and were not in possession or control of them. However, the original owner had not abandoned them but was intending to make a gift of them and to effect delivery of them to the charity. Therefore, that unknown person was no longer in possession or control but remained the owner, and the accused could be charged with theft of the bags belonging to a person or persons unknown. In respect of the second set of facts the bins belonged to or were in possession of the charity. Therefore, at the time of the appropriation the bags were possessed by the charity.

One effect of s 5(1) is that a thief may steal from several people: the owner, the possessor and the person in physical control. For this reason the owner may be guilty of theft from the possessor or controller. 'Belonging to' refers not just to ownership as it normally does, but extends beyond to possession and control. Property which is about to be destroyed nevertheless belongs to another. An example is misappropriating property which is on the point of being burnt in a municipal incinerator.

An example of the application of the term 'control' in s 5(1) is *Woodman*.

Woodman [1974] QB 754 (CA)

A company sold off all the scrap metal on the site of its disused factory but retained control of the site. It did not know that the purchaser of the scrap had left some behind. The accused removed some of the metal. It was held that he was properly indicted with stealing from the company because a person or company in control of the site is deemed *prima facie* to have control over things on the land. The company retained control because it intended to exclude others by surrounding the site with barbed wire and erecting warning notices. (The presumption that the owner had control over items on the land would, however, be rebutted where a third party had hidden drugs or explosives on the land.) *Woodman* demonstrates that the owner need not know he owns the property and that the owner need not even know that he possesses it.

The same argument applies to lost golf balls. The balls belong to the club. It seems that rubbish left in a skip belongs to the skip-owner and rubbish in dustbins belongs to the local authority. Property buried in the soil belongs to the occupier. Items abandoned and not owned by anyone no longer belong to another and so cannot be stolen. An illustration would be a newspaper left in the street. Section 5(1) does not, however, cover the following facts. The accused purchases goods from the victim without dishonesty. He now has ownership and possession. At that point he decides to keep the goods but not to pay for them. The items are now his, not property belonging to another. Therefore, he is not guilty of theft despite his dishonesty, his intent permanently to deprive and his appropriation.

Gomez, above, exemplifies another situation covered by s 5(1). If an accused gets hold of property by misrepresentation, in contract law the transaction is voidable for fraud. In criminal law terms the property still 'belongs to another' and can therefore be stolen despite the accused's having a (voidable) title.

The phrase in brackets in s 5(1) excludes from 'belonging to another' the following situation. The accused agrees to transfer shares to the victim but before doing so he transfers them to a third party. The victim has only an equitable interest, and the accused is not guilty of theft of the shares. The accused may, however, be guilty of theft of the money or of obtaining the money by deception. The principal equitable interest referred to arises under an agreement to buy and sell land. The seller retains the legal interests, the buyer acquires an equitable interest. If the vendor then sells to a third party, he is not guilty of theft.

There is a *dictum* in *Edwards* v *Ddin* [1976] 1 WLR 942 (DC) that s 5 offers only a partial definition of 'belonging to another', but the statement is probably incorrect. Section 5(1) has been interpreted in the following ways:

(a) It does not cover cases where under the civil law the entire proprietary interest in the goods has passed. If there is a contract and the seller has delivered to the buyer, the latter obtains ownership even though he has not paid for the item. The principal case is *Edwards* v *Ddin*. A driver had his tank filled with petrol. He then (the facts are not clear – perhaps he all the time intended to drive out without paying) decided not to pay and drove away. By virtue of the Sale of Goods Act 1979, s 18, at the moment of driving off the petrol no longer belonged to the garage. Therefore, it was not property 'belonging to another', and so could not be subject to theft. (If, however, the accused intended all along to drive off without paying, he has obtained the petrol by deception: *McHugh* (1977) 64 Cr App R 92 (CA). There is no doubt nowadays that there is an appropriation despite the garage owner's desire that a motorist put the petrol into the tank.) At a self-service petrol station it is suggested that the same principle applies.

The property passes and therefore the accused is not guilty of theft. *McHugh* is *contra*, but seems incorrect. The same principle applies to the accused who eats a meal in a restaurant and then decides to leave without paying: *Corcoran v Whent* [1977] Crim LR 52 (DC). As well as there being no theft, the accused has not obtained property, the petrol or the food, *by* deception because he obtained the property before the deception. Parliament has filled this gap by creating the offence of making off without payment in s 3 of the Theft Act 1978. It should be remembered that the position is different in a shop, whether self-service or otherwise, where ownership does not pass to the alleged thief, the buyer, until the goods have been paid for even if the buyer obtains possession before payment. In this case the seller retains ownership, the 'proprietary right' within s 5(1), and so the goods belong to another and can be stolen.

An easier case is *Walker* [1984] Crim LR 112 (CA). The victim bought a video recorder from the accused. It was defective and he took it for repair to the accused, who sold it. The accused's conviction was quashed because the judge had not explained to the jury that the sale amounted to theft only if the victim had a 'proprietary right or interest' in the recorder. The victim had served on the accused a summons for return of the purchase price. Doing so rescinded the contract of sale, and the accused regained full ownership of the video recorder. A charge of attempted theft would have succeeded.

(b) The interests under s 5(1) include liens and bailments at will: *Turner (No. 2)* [1971] 1 WLR 901 (CA). In *Turner (No. 2)* the accused left his car at the victim's garage for repair. After it had been repaired, he drove away without paying. In civil law the victim had a 'lien' over the car, which meant that he was entitled to keep the car until the repairs had been paid for. (The same rule applies to cobblers and ship repairers.) The trial judge instructed the jury to ignore the concept of a lien. On that approach the repairer was a bailee at will. The Court of Appeal, upholding the judge's direction and expressly stating that its decision was not based on the existence of a lien, held that the owner had stolen his own car because the victim had been deprived of 'possession or control of it' within the terms of the statute. The jury had only to see whether the accused had in fact deprived the other of possession. Therefore, even though in civil law the bailee at will's right was inferior to that of the owner, the latter could steal from the former. Therefore, the owner, the person with the right to immediate possession, is guilty of theft when he exercises that right! A bailee at will cannot prevent a bailor from getting the item back, yet doing so is theft. Accordingly, in civil law the bailor may recapture the property but his doing so is appropriating property belonging to another. This means that if a person lends the next-door neighbour his lawn mower, then depending on his state of mind he may be guilty of theft when he takes it back without telling the owner what he has done. Moreover, the bailor may well not be dishonest, and it cannot be said that he intends permanently to deprive the bailee of his property in the item because a bailee does not have any interest in it. The case has been heavily criticised on these grounds. Had there been a lien, the position would have been different, because the car repairer would have had a right to the property. It was unfortunate that the Court of Appeal had to work on the basis that the garage had only a bailment at will because of the trial judge's instruction. It is suggested that rather than use civil law terms such as liens and bailments at will judges should refer to the words used in s 5(1): did the victim have 'possession or control' of the property? On the facts of *Turner (No. 2)* there was no doubt on that score.

It is thought that there is no theft where the owner recovers an impounded car because the police have no legal right to retain it: *Meredith* [1973] Crim LR 253, *per*

Judge Da Cunha in the Crown Court. (The accused was also not dishonest.) The police's power lawfully to remove obstructions did not include a power to keep the car from the owner. However, the judge should surely have said that for the purposes of theft, as indeed s 5(1) states, property can be stolen from people who have possession or control over it such as the police had on these facts.

There is no theft where the accused induces a testatrix to revoke her will and make another, for there is no proprietary interest in the executors: *Tillings* [1985] Crim LR 393. The intended beneficiaries did not at the time of the revocation have property in the items which they would have received under the former will. In *Hancock* [1990] 2 QB 242 it had not been decided whether coins were treasure trove or not under law which was abolished in 1996. The answer to that question would mean that they belonged either to the Crown or not. The accused, the finder, was not guilty of theft because at the moment of appropriation the coins were not property belonging to another. The Crown's right had not been proved. It is therefore not such property where there is only in the alleged owners a claim to a proprietary interest. There is also authority for the proposition that for the purposes of s 5(1) a copyright owner does not have a proprietary interest in the item copied: *Storrow* [1983] Crim LR 332 (Crown Court).

(c) In *Shadrokh-Cigari* [1988] Crim LR 465 (CA), a bank made a mistake of fact and the accused received money. The bank retained an equitable right to the money. Therefore, it belonged to them within s 5(1). Presumably the reason why the bank has an equitable proprietary interest is that the law imposes a constructive trust. There is, however, the contrary authority of *Attorney-General's Reference (No. 1 of 1985)* [1986] QB 491 (CA), where the manager of a tied pub sold beer as that of the brewery when he had purchased it elsewhere. The court held that, even if there was a constructive trust of the secret profit, such did not create an equitable interest in the brewery. It thought that in any case there was no constructive trust because the making of a secret profit by a fiduciary, as the manager was, did not give rise to any trust. Furthermore, trusts cannot exist without there existing property to which the trust attaches, and no separate property was to be found in the profit. The case has been criticised for deciding that there is no constructive trust where the accused uses the victim's facilities to make a secret profit and for holding that a constructive trust is not a proprietary right or interest within s 5(1). Civil law developments since 1985 tend towards showing that there is a constructive trust when property is obtained by fraud. The profit made from selling cheaper alcoholic drinks at the normal suppliers' price was surely property which could be the subject of a trust. Whether *Shadrokh-Cigari* is correct on the equitable interest point, the decision does point up the fact that there is no need to refer to s 5(4), on which see below, where the owner retains ownership but has transferred possession to the alleged thief. The property still belongs to another within s 5(1) and accordingly can be stolen by him. If the owner makes a mistake as to the identity of the accused and that error is fundamental at civil law, ownership of the property is not transferred and the owner retains the proprietary right. See also below.

The *Reference* case was distinguished in *Re Holmes* [2005] 1 WLR 1857 (DC) as being a case on secret profits, whereas *Re Holmes* concerned the fraudulent acquisition of property.

(d) A thief has 'possession or control' within s 5(1). 'Possession or control' need not be lawful possession or control: *Turner (No. 2)*, above, and *Kelly* [1999] QB 621 (CA). By parity of reasoning the accused can steal heroin, an illegal drug: *Smith* [2011] EWCA

Crim 66. It is irrelevant that the victim could not lawfully possess the heroin. Therefore, a second thief can steal from the first: *Meech* [1974] QB 549 (CA). (Another aspect of *Meech* was impliedly overruled in *Gomez*, above, but the point stands.) It does not matter that the owner has a better right to possession than either of the thieves.

(e) In *Clowes (No. 2)* [1994] 2 All ER 316, one of the accused mixed his own money with that of investors. The Court of Appeal said that there was a trust between him and them. They were in civil law entitled to a first charge on the mixed fund. When he removed £14,000 from the fund, he appropriated a sum in which they had an equitable interest. Accordingly, he had appropriated an interest in property. The definition in s 5(1) was satisfied. The court rejected the contention that there was a presumption that he had withdrawn his own money first from the mixed fund.

(f) If the accused takes property which previously was owned by a dead person, that property belongs to those entitled under the will or on intestacy (or if none, the Crown).

Trusts

Section 5(2)–(4) deals with cases where property belongs to the accused before he dishonestly appropriates it. By s 5(2):

> [w]here property is subject to a trust, the persons to whom it belongs shall be regarded as including any person having a right to enforce the trust, and an intention to defeat the trust shall be regarded accordingly as an intention to deprive of the property any person having that right.

Normally theft by a trustee from a trust will fall within s 5(1). The trustee has a legal interest in the property; the beneficiaries have an equitable interest. Section 5(2) deems the property to belong to the beneficiaries. (Similarly appropriation by an executor will be theft because the legatees have an equitable proprietary interest within s 5(1).) Where the trust does not have identified beneficiaries, such as a charitable trust, s 5(2) applies. The Attorney-General is the person who enforces charitable trusts, and by s 5(2) a theft by a trustee of such a trust is a theft from him. Section 5(2) covers constructive trusts. If Lord Browne-Wilkinson was correct to say in *Westdeutsche Landesbank Girozentrale* v *Islington Borough Council* [1996] AC 669 (HL), a civil case, that if property is obtained by deception, there is a constructive trust imposed on the recipient, the victim has an equitable interest, and s 5(2) applies.

Where a trustee is charged, not with theft from the intended beneficiaries, but with theft from the public who gave them the money, the public have parted with the whole proprietary interest; therefore, it no longer belongs to them but to the trustees. They are the legal owners. Therefore, the trustees do not steal from the public when they appropriate the money for themselves: *Dyke* [2002] 1 Cr App R 404 (CA). What the court missed, however, was s 5(2). The Attorney-General is the person charged with enforcing charitable trusts. Therefore, he is the owner for the purposes of s 5(2) and the money, again by s 5(2), was stolen from him.

Receipt of property and duty to retain and deal

By s 5(3):

> [w]here a person receives property from or on account of another, and is under an obligation to the other to retain and deal with that property or its proceeds in a particular way, the property or proceeds shall be regarded (as against him) as belonging to the other.

The first point to make about s 5(3) is that it is really a fall-back (and a deeming) provision. If the victim has a legal or equitable interest in the property or its proceeds, s 5(1) applies too. If a person obtains property under a trust, it belongs to the beneficiary and s 5(1) applies. The same is true of a bailment. The bailor retains property in the item and again s 5(1) governs. Whether the victim has a legal or equitable interest may turn on whether a constructive trust occurs. There is also an overlap between s 5(1) and s 5(3) when a fiduciary has a legal interest in the property. In other words, the same facts can fall within both s 5(1) and s 5(3). If it is uncertain whether the victim had a proprietary interest, s 5(3) comes into play. *A fortiori* it applies where there is no legal or equitable interest. The main point about s 5(3) and s 5(4) is that the accused has got the property such as money and should use it for a particular purpose or should morally hand it back because she has got it in error.

Section 5(3) requires the jury under the judge's instruction to consider questions of civil law. There has to be an obligation to retain and deal as laid down by civil law: *Breaks* [1998] Crim LR 349 (CA). The trial judge was wrong to rule that s 5(3) avoided civil law. There is no criminal rule which determines whether or not the accused 'is under an obligation . . . to . . . deal, with that property . . . in a particular way.'

Section 5(3) has been interpreted in the following ways:

(a) The accused himself must know of the obligation. It is insufficient that his agent knew: *Wills* (1991) 92 Cr App R 297 (CA).

(b) The principal problem is understanding the need for particular arrangements. The basic rule is that s 5(3) applies only where the victim has imposed particular arrangements on the accused. The main authority is *Hall*.

Hall [1973] QB 126 (CA)

> The accused, a travel agent, received money from clients. He did not arrange trips and could not repay the money. It was held that he was not guilty of theft because there was no such special arrangement as would give rise to the obligation in s 5(3).

Hall looks surprising. One might expect one's money to be used to buy holidays, but that is not what happens. The money can be mixed with other money, for instance to pay the electricity bill. The money is not kept separate. It is not those coins and notes which are to be handed over. Accordingly, the mere fact that there is a contractual obligation does not mean that the accused is under a duty to retain and deal with the property. (If the accused is dishonest from the start, he will appropriate on receiving the money and therefore be guilty of theft at that moment; in these circumstances there is no need to rely on s 5(3).)

The same position has been held to apply to an insurance agent, who was under no duty to hand those notes and coins to the company (*Robinson* [1977] Crim LR 173 (CA)), to a person who received premia to buy insurance (*Breaks* [1998] Crim LR 349 (CA)) and to a person in receipt of housing benefit, who was under no legal obligation to use the money to pay off rent arrears (*DPP v Huskinson* [1988] Crim LR 620), even though that was the purpose for which the accused received the benefit. In *Dyke*, above, the Court of Appeal held that where a person collects money on behalf of a charity, property passes from the donors to the charity. Therefore, if a trustee misappropriates that money, s 5(3) applies because he is under an obligation to deal with the money in a particular way, to hand it over to the charity. The court allowed the appeal because the accused had been charged with theft from the donors, and not with theft from the beneficiaries of the trust. However, circumstances alter cases. In *Re Kumar* [2000] Crim LR 504 (DC) the accused was also a travel agent, but he was subject to a trust that he would, after deducting commission, transfer money from the agency's account to another body. The Divisional Court held that he was under an obligation to retain and deal with the money in a particular way.

In *Attorney-General's Reference (No. 1 of 1985)*, above, the accused sold other beer than that of the brewery to which he was tied and made a profit for himself. It looks like s 5(3) should apply: the profit should be paid over to the brewery, because there was a constructive trust which created an equitable interest. He was accountable for the profit. It was held that he was not a trustee of the money for the brewers and therefore he was under no obligation to deal with it in a certain way. Section 5(3) was inapplicable. The same reasoning presumably applies to bribes.

The law may, however, be on the point of turning. In *Attorney-General of Hong Kong* v *Reid* [1994] 1 AC 324, a civil case, the Privy Council was faced with a defendant, a New Zealander, who was the acting DPP for Hong Kong. It was conceded that he was a fiduciary. He had been taking bribes to obstruct prosecutions. The Crown sought to exercise proprietary rights over property which the defendant had bought in New Zealand with the proceeds. English civil law provides that breaches of fiduciary duty which involve misapplication of existing trust property result in the property acquired being held on trust, whereas other breaches result in the property not being held on trust: the remedy is an account, a personal remedy not a proprietary one, and the relationship is treated as one of debtor and creditor: *Lister* v *Stubbs* (1890) 45 Ch D 1 (CA). For example in *Lister* the actual banknotes of the bribe belonged to the bribee; he had to account for the amount of the bribe. In a criminal case a bribe to a turnstile-operator at Wembley was held not to give rise to a charge of theft of the bribe. He was not a fiduciary. There is no property which can be stolen. (The defendant may be liable for breach of contract.) The Privy Council held that *Lister* v *Stubbs* was incorrect. Reid was such a senior employee that he was a fiduciary and as such was a constructive trustee, holding the property for the Crown, the beneficiary. The effect on criminal law is this. If *Lister* is correct and subsequent English law is not certain, a person who has been bribed is not guilty of theft, no matter how dishonest he is. If it is wrong, an employee, say, who is bribed is guilty of theft of that sum from his employers provided that in civil law he is a fiduciary. There is property which can be stolen. *Attorney-General's Reference (No. 1 of 1985)*, above, which relied on *Lister* v *Stubbs*, will be overruled. There will now be a resulting trust where the salaried manager of a tied house sells his own beer. One difficulty with this argument may be that, as *Attorney-General's Reference (No. 1 of 1985)* held, a constructive trust does not create a 'proprietary right or interest' within s 5(1). The profit is not a separate item of property. The contrary contention is that there is a notional (equitable) interest in the employers. A constructive trust creates an equitable proprietary interest. Section 5(1) applies to 'any proprietary . . . interest'. Therefore, a constructive trust falls within s 5(1).

A second difficulty is that Lord Wilberforce in *Tarling* v *Government of the Republic of Singapore* (1978) 70 Cr App R 77 (HL) said: 'The making of a secret profit is no criminal offence.' We await developments. It should be noted that even if the accused is not guilty of theft, he may be convicted of an offence of corruption. If *Reid* is followed, the decision would be an example of how changes to civil law affect criminal law. From the viewpoint of precedent, in cases on provocation the Court of Appeal held that it is bound by its own decisions and not by the advice of the Privy Council.

It is uncertain whether it would similarly rule in respect of this area of the law. It should be noted that the difficulty with *Lister* v *Stubbs* has been reduced by the Fraud Act 2006, ss 1 and 4, because a person who receives a bribe or makes a secret profit can be guilty of fraud.

The position is different where there are particular arrangements. The law is illustrated by the pre-Theft Act case of *Hassall* (1861) 169 ER 1302 where the treasurer of a Christmas club did not spend the money on Christmas treats. In *Wain* [1995] 2 Cr App R 660 (CA) the accused organised events which raised nearly £3,000 for charity. He put the money into his own bank account and withdrew money from that account. The court held that the accused was under a duty to retain the money in his bank account, the proceeds of the specific notes and coins raised for charity, because s 5(3) applied. (Indeed, there might have been a duty to retain the specific notes and coins for the benefit of the charity.) The case of *Lewis* v *Lethbridge* [1987] Crim LR 59 where the Divisional Court had held that sponsorship money did not belong to the charity by virtue of s 5(3) was overruled. The court held that there is an obligation because the donors impose a trust on the recipient to give the money to the charity. It does not matter that there is no rule imposed by the charity that recipients hand over the specific notes and coins. Note that the money is also the subject of a trust and s 5(1) applies.

In *Klineberg* [1999] 1 Cr App R 427 (CA) there was similarly an obligation imposing particular arrangements when purchasers of timeshares paid money into a trust which was charged with the duty of safeguarding moneys. *Klineberg* was applied in *Floyd* v *DPP* [2000] Crim 411 (DC). An agent for a firm supplying hampers was under a duty to send the money she had collected from her colleagues to the firm. The court held that the prosecution did not have to prove that the firm as victim had a legal or equitable interest in the money collected by the accused. However, what the court did not inquire into was the source of the obligation to deal with the money in a particular way. There was no express or implied contract between the accused and the victim that she should transmit the money to the company. If contract was not the source of the duty, it is difficult to see how the duty arose.

In *Davidge* v *Bunnett* [1984] Crim LR 297 (DC), which was approved in *Wain*, the accused was given money by her flatmates to pay the gas bill. She spent it on other things. She was held to be guilty of theft. She was under a duty to use the money to pay the gas bills (cf. *Hall*, where the accused was not under a duty to use that money for that holiday). On the facts of *Rader* given above the accused was under a duty to invest the money in a way that would yield a profit for the victim. The court distinguished *Hall*. The Court of Appeal in *McHugh* (1993) 97 Cr App R 335 spoke of s 5(3) applying where there was a legal arrangement whereby the victim's money was to be kept separate from the accused's. It should be noted that s 5(3) does, however, apply where the accused has put the money he received into his own bank account, as *Wain* demonstrates. In *Brewster* (1979) 69 Cr App R 375 (CA), an insurance agent was guilty of theft of the premiums because the money had to be handed over to the companies he worked for under the terms of his contract.

Therefore, he was under an obligation to deal with the money in a particular way, that obligation being constituted by the contract. The fact that the firms allowed him to use the money for his own purposes and replace it was merely an indulgence. *Robinson*, above, also concerned an insurance agent, but there was no such obligation. In *Crown Prosecution Service, ex parte Judd*, unreported, 1 November 1999, the Divisional Court held that money received in weekly instalments from five colleagues at work belonged to the mail order company for which the accused had collected. There was no need for an express contract to that effect. In *Wakeman v Farrar* [1974] Crim LR 136 (DC), the accused received a warning that he must return a lost cheque after he had received an over-the-counter payment from the Department of Health and Social Security. The cheque was thereby subject to a legal obligation within s 5(3). In *Hallam* [1995] Crim LR 323 the Court of Appeal held that two defendants, financial advisers, who did not invest money on behalf of investors, fell within s 5(3) because the victims retained an equitable interest in the cheques they drew and the proceeds of the cheques.

(c) On analogy with *Gilks* [1972] 1 WLR 1341(CA) on s 5(4) the obligation in s 5(3) must be a legally enforceable one, and this proposition was apparently accepted in *Meech* [1974] QB 549 (CA) and *Mainwaring* (1981) 74 Cr App R 99 (CA). That the obligation had to be legally enforceable was accepted in *Williams* [1995] Crim LR 77 (CA). An example of a non-legally enforceable obligation is a gambling debt. (However, a bet on the Tote is legally enforceable because the Tote can neither win nor lose, and there is accordingly no wager.) *Cullen*, unreported, 1974, seems to be contrary to cases such as *Mainwaring*. A mistress was given money to buy food. The court thought that there was a legal obligation, which she breached by spending the money on herself. As a matter of contract law, however, the outcome would have been different. There would have been no contract but a non-binding domestic arrangement. She therefore would not have been liable for breach of contract. The result looks odd: she is guilty in criminal law but not liable in civil law. Whether there is a legal obligation is a question for the judge: *Mainwaring* and *Dubar* [1994] 1 WLR 1484 *obiter* (Courts-Martial Appeal Court), among other cases. Cases which state that the question whether there is an obligation is one for the jury are incorrect, as are ones which state that there is no need for the jury to consider matters of civil law. The jury's task is to see whether the duty arose on the facts.

(d) *Meech* held that the accused was under an obligation to retain and deal with a cheque if he believed that he was under such a duty, though in fact he was not. In the light of the need for a legal obligation *Meech* looks incorrect on this point. In *Meech* the victim obtained a cheque by fraud. The accused cashed it for him. The accused and a couple of friends staged a false robbery of the accused in order not to have to pay over the money. The Court of Appeal held that the accused was under an obligation despite the victim's inability to enforce the obligation because he had obtained the cheque fraudulently. Section 5(3) says 'is under an obligation', not 'believes himself to be under an obligation'. A charge of attempted theft should have been brought.

(e) Where there is a trust, s 5(3) will apply (as well as s 5(2)). In *Arnold* [1997] 4 All ER 1 the Court of Appeal held that s 5(3) applied to relationships falling short of trusteeship. It covered the relationship of a franchisor and franchisee where the former had received from the latter bills of exchange and he had then discounted them. The bills of exchange were property which belonged to another within s 5(3). It did not matter that they had only temporarily been in the hands of the franchisees or that the relationship between the parties was a contractual one. The court held that s 5(3) applied, even though the accused retained the property throughout the dealings. For comment, see Sir John Smith in his casenote on *Malone* [1998] Crim LR 834.

(f) Section 5(3) applies when there is an obligation in respect of 'that property or its proceeds'. In *Klineberg*, above, the court held that when the purchasers of timeshare apartments paid by cash or by cheques, the defendants were under an obligation to retain the funds; in the case of bank transfers from the purchasers to the defendants, the latter had come by the property and were also under the same obligation. The new credit was 'proceeds' of property. However, this analysis fails to take account of *Preddy* [1996] AC 815 (HL). Bank transfers create a new thing in action. There is no transfer.

Receiving by mistake and obligation to restore

By s 5(4):

> [w]here a person gets property by another's mistake and is under an obligation to make restoration (in whole or in part) of the property or its proceeds or the value thereof, then to the extent of that obligation the property or proceeds shall be regarded (as against him) as belonging to the person entitled to restoration, and an intention not to make restoration shall be regarded accordingly as an intention to deprive that person of the property or proceeds.

Section s 5(4) applies where the victim has made a mistake. The mistake need not have been induced by the accused. Section 5(4) comes into play only if the accused is under a legal duty to restore. If there is no such obligation, but, say, a duty to pay the price of an article, s 5(4) does not apply. One way of approaching s 5(4) is to hold that ownership of goods is not transferred to the alleged thief in situations where under civil law it would not have passed. Therefore, s 5(4) does not apply where under civil law ownership would not have been transferred. Ownership would not have been transferred where the mistake is so fundamental that the transaction is void, such as when there is a mistake caused by fraud as to the relevant identity of the recipient. In this event, s 5(1) applies.

In *Williams* [1980] Crim LR 589 (CA) it was held that there was a fundamental mistake in the mind of a cashier at a bureau de change when the accused proffered obsolete foreign currency, knowing it to be obsolete, and the cashier took it, not knowing it was obsolete. When the cashier handed over money in exchange, no property passed to the accused. That money remained property belonging to another within s 5(1). If s 5(4) does not apply to such mistakes, what is left? Therefore, s 5(4) applies to voidable contracts; that is, where the mistake is not so fundamental that the contract is void. Ownership passes to the alleged thief under a voidable contract and remains with him until the contract is avoided by the innocent party. Section 5(4) deems ownership to remain with the victim. Section 5(4) is not needed for void contracts because ownership remains with the victim and s 5(1) applies. Therefore, although s 5(1) does not expressly apply when mistakes are made, it does apply to them when the property still belongs to the victim as a matter of civil law.

This reading derives support from the legislative history of the provision. The aim was to reverse the decision in *Moynes v Cooper*, above. The employee received a pay packet which contained an overpayment. The amount should have been reduced because he had received an advance on his wages. He later discovered the overpayment and spent the money. He was not guilty of the offence, which is now theft, but would now be so because of s 5(4) where the innocent party's belief is classified as a non-fundamental one. Under civil law the accused is under a duty to make restitution ('an obligation to make restitution'). Section 5(4) is applicable and the accused is guilty of theft of the excess. This effect of s 5(4) can be seen from *Attorney-General's Reference (No. 1 of 1983)* [1985] QB 182. The accused was overpaid, the money going into her current account. The Court of Appeal held that she had acquired something, a right of action against the bank, by mistake and she was under a duty to make restoration of the value of the property she had received. The case demonstrates that s 5(4) applies to intangible property (the debt) as well as tangible property. The court considered, however, that the criminal law should not normally be used in such situations. Possibly she did not appropriate. The Court of Appeal did not discuss this issue. If she kept her account above the sum wrongly paid to her, by civil law she would be deemed to have spent her own money when withdrawing from the account. Her omission to inform the authorities that she had been overpaid was not an act and on general principles a failure to act does not normally constitute the *actus reus* of an offence. The concept of theft by omission seems strange but this case illustrates that it can occur.

Another approach to s 5(4) is to argue thus: s 5(4) applies only if the contract is void. If the contract is voidable, there is no 'obligation to make restoration' because the obligation does not arise until the innocent party elects to avoid the contract. There is only a potential, not an actual, obligation. The accused *is* not under an obligation. The contrary contention is that there is a legal obligation even though it depends on the innocent party's making the election.

Certainly s 5(4) applies where property does pass. There is deemed to be property still owned by the victim, and the accused is under a duty to restore.

In *Chase Manhattan Bank NA v Israel-British Bank NA* [1981] Ch 105, a civil case, it was held by Goulding J that the innocent party to an overpayment retains an equitable right where the overpayment was brought about by a mistake of fact. Therefore, s 5(1) applies and there is no need to rely on s 5(4). The case has been criticised in the House of Lords but not overruled. The Court of Appeal in its criminal guise adopted this understanding of the law in *Shadrokh-Cigari*, above, but also held that s 5(4) was another way to the same result since there was also an obligation to make restoration. In *Shadrokh-Cigari* a bank erroneously transferred money to an account of a child, whose guardian the accused was. He knew that the bank had made a mistake. He persuaded the child to sign mandates authorising the bank to issue drafts in his favour. Either the bank retained an equitable interest in the drafts within s 5(1) or the accused was under a duty to restore within s 5(4). It must be said that as a matter of civil law the existence of an equitable proprietary interest is unclear. If, however, *Shadrokh-Cigari* is correct, there is no problem with instances of overpayment such as *Stalham* [1993] Crim LR 310. The debt owed by the bank to the accused belongs in equity to the employers. The accused appropriated her employers' equitable interest. If *Chase Manhattan* is wrong, as seems to be the view after *Westdeutsche Landesbank Girozentrale* v *Islington Borough Council* [1996] AC 669 (HL), at least where the recipient does not know of the error, there is still a route to conviction via s 5(4). The reasoning behind *Shadrokh-Cigari* was applied in *Webster* [2006] EWCA Crim 2894. A soldier erroneously received a second medal for service in Iraq. He gave it to the accused, who sold it on an internet auction site. The court held that because of the fundamental error in sending the second medal, the Crown retained an equitable interest, therefore s 5(1) applied with the result that there was no need to rely on s 5(4). If *Shadrokh-Cigari* is correct, then the purpose behind s 5(4), the deeming of overpaid money to belong to the giver, has been destroyed, for s 5(4) is not needed when the facts fall within s 5(1). The Court of Appeal in *Ngan* [1998] 1 Cr App R 331 relied on s 5(4) where the accused's account had been credited with the victim's cheques because the bank made a mistake. It did not discuss whether or not a constructive trust existed.

Under s 5(4) the obligation must be a legally enforceable one: *Gilks*, above. A gambling debt is not legally enforceable. Therefore, if a bookmaker pays out money in the mistaken belief that a certain horse has won, s 5(4) is inappropriate. Ownership of the money, it was then thought, did not pass. Therefore, the money remained property belonging to another. (Civil law appears to be, however, that property does pass to the winner of a bet.)

Under *Gomez* the accused nowadays appropriated when he took the money from the bookmaker's even though the clerk gave it to him. If it was not until later that the accused discovered that he had been overpaid, it is suggested that the money no longer belongs to another because ownership of it passes on payment. On the understanding that *Shadrokh-Cigari* is correct, the bookmaker in *Gilks* retained an equitable interest in the money which the assistant manager mistakenly overpaid, and s 5(1) applied.

'Proceeds' in s 5(4) covers money received from a third party who had cashed a cheque for the accused.

Davis (1989) 88 Cr App R 347 (CA)

The accused received cheques for housing benefit from his local authority. He was not entitled to that benefit. He cashed the cheques. The court held that he had obtained the paper on which the cheques were written by mistake. He was under a legal duty to make restoration. He did not do so but converted the cheques into money, which constituted the proceeds of the property. By s 5(4) the money belonged to another.

The accused had also for a time received two housing benefit cheques for the same period. It was uncertain to which of the cheques he was or was not entitled. The court held that the accused was under an obligation to restore such of the proceeds as belonged to another. Section 5(4) covers property, proceeds and 'the value thereof' whereas s 5(3) refers only to 'property or its proceeds'. In *Dubar*, above, the accused received money from a fellow member of the armed forces. The obligation was to find a second-hand car for him. If the accused did not become dishonest until all the money had been spent and no proceeds of that money survived, s 5(3) could not apply.

Robbery

Introduction

This offence may be seen as a crime against both property and the person. By s 8(1) of the Theft Act 1968:

> [a] person is guilty of **robbery** if he steals, and immediately before or at the time of doing so, and in order to do so, he uses any force on any person or puts or seeks to put any person in fear of being then and there subjected to force.

The maximum sentence is life imprisonment (s 8(2)). Robbery covers both serious crimes and facts which are not as serious as some thefts. There is also a separate crime of assault with intent to rob. 'Assault' covers both psychic (for definition see Chapter 13) assault and battery. There is no requirement that the victim is in fact put in fear of force: *R v DPP* [2007] EWHC 739 (Admin), a case with facts which are concerned with what is nowadays the most common form of robbery, that of a mobile phone. Robbery covers a wide spectrum of cases from armed bank robbery to snatching a purse forcibly from the victim's hand.

For an explanation of assault, see pp 487–91 (Chapter 13).

Robbery is essentially an aggravated form of theft. All the elements of theft must be proved before a conviction may be secured for this offence. An accused is therefore not guilty of robbery if he believes that he has a legal right to deprive the victim of the property. In *Robinson* [1977] Crim LR 173 (CA), the accused with his friends demanded that the victim repay a debt owed by the victim's wife to him. He had a knife to reinforce his demand. The court held that the facts did not constitute robbery because the accused was not dishonest, because he thought he had a legal right to the money (see the discussion of s 2(1)(a) above). In *Forrester* [1992] Crim LR 793 (CA), the accused had no claim of right and applying *Ghosh* he was dishonest. All the other elements of theft were present. He used force by knocking off balance his victim, who was also kept under restraint, and the force was used immediately before stealing and in order to do so. There is a *dictum* that 'steals' does not mean the same as it does in theft (ss 1–7 of the 1968 statute, with robbery being s 8) but it would be very strange if it did not, and later cases have assumed that 'steals' in s 8 means 'steals contrary to s 1 of the Theft Act 1968'. The *Ghosh* test of dishonesty and the *Gomez* test of appropriation apply.

V. Harrington and P. Mayhew, *Mobile Phone Thefts*, Home Office Research Study No. 235, 2001, stated that 28 per cent of robberies involved the appropriation of mobiles. In 2007–08, 85,000 robberies were reported, two-thirds of the number in 2001–02, and this declined to 77,500 in the year ending September 2011. Certainly the number of robberies has fallen more or less every year since 1995.

The *actus reus*

'Force' is an ordinary English word, apparently chosen because it is comprehensible to lay people. It is for the jury to determine its meaning: *Dawson* (1976) 64 Cr App R 170 (CA). The victim was a sailor. Two of the accused placed themselves on either side of him and nudged him on his shoulder, causing him to lose his balance. A third man then picked his pocket, stealing his wallet. Lawson LJ said that 'force' was an ordinary English word and one whose meaning was for the jury to decide when applying the term to the facts of each case. Therefore, whether jostling is force is for the jury. The Court of Appeal approved this approach in *Clouden* [1987] Crim LR 56. The victim was carrying a shopping basket. The accused pulled the basket down and out of her grasp. The Court followed *Dawson* and held that the question whether force on the person was being used was a question of fact for the jury.

The latest authority is *RP v DPP* [2012] EWHC 1657 (Admin). The accused snatched a cigarette from between the victim's fingers, making no contact with her hand. The issue was whether the snatching constituted 'force'. Mitting J, allowing the appeal, held that force had not been used on the person of the victim (or someone else), as required by s 8. The case was similar to that of a pickpocket, and that was theft, not robbery. In both scenarios no force was used on the person: there was no contact between the accused's fingers and those of the victim. Force on the property alone is insufficient. It would have been different if for instance the accused had grabbed the cigarette from the victim's closed hand and the latter had struggled to keep it. The Court substituted a conviction for theft. It is suggested, first, that rather than concentrating on 'force', the jury should consider whether 'force' was used 'on any person', and, secondly, it would be better if this term were defined by law, rather than leaving the matter for the jury as a matter of fact and degree in each individual case.

The force must be used *in order to* steal, as s 8(1) states. In *Donaghy* [1981] Crim LR 644 (Crown Court), the accused ordered a taxi-driver to take him from Newmarket to London and made threats to his life. Once in London he stole £22 from the driver. He was held not guilty of robbery because the threats were not made in order to take the money. If a person is engaged in a fight, knocks down the victim, and then decides to take her purse, he has not used force in order to steal. The force enables him to steal, but the definition of robbery is not satisfied because the force is not used *in order to* steal.

The force must be used 'on' the person. An example is putting a hand over the victim's mouth to stop her screaming: *Hale* (1978) 68 Cr App R 415 (CA). It should also be noted that this action amounted to 'force'. It has been suggested that 'on' means 'against' and therefore it is not robbery if the accused snatches the victim's bag unless the victim retains hold or recovers it and there is a fight. Perhaps this distinction is too little to bear the weight placed on it. The section states 'on any person' not 'against'. In *Corcoran v Anderton* (1980) 71 Cr App R 104 (DC), there was robbery where a handbag was tugged away from the victim, even though she did not lose control. This case exemplifies that an accused is guilty of robbery even though he has not succeeded in his purpose. In *Clouden* snatching a basket out of the victim's hands was robbery. It is certain that the Criminal Law Revision Committee, the Report of which formed the basis of the Theft Act (*Theft and Related Offences*, Cmnd 2977, 1966), would not have wanted such a result but would have preferred the outcome to be theft (see para. 65). The Court of Appeal did not resort to the Report in *Clouden* despite the provision's being ambiguous. Simple pickpocketing or slipping one's hand into a bag and removing a purse is theft because no force is used on the victim. Nevertheless, since the meaning of 'force' is left to the jury, it is possible that some juries might conclude that force has been used on a person. A maximum sentence of life imprisonment for pulling a handbag from a victim's grasp would seem to be excessive.

The force must be used 'immediately before or at the time of' the theft. It is not robbery, wrote the Criminal Law Revision Committee in the same paragraph, where the accused uses force to escape. If, however, 'appropriation' in the definition of theft is a continuing act, the accused may be convicted of robbery if there is a force during a struggle to escape: *Hale*, approved in *Gregory* (1982) 77 Cr App R 41 (CA). Therefore, robbery is seen as a continuing act. It seems that whether the accused is guilty of robbery if he uses force when escaping is a question for the jury: *Hale* (unreported on this point). In *Lockley* [1995] 2 Cr App R 554 the Court of Appeal held that *Gomez* had not affected *Hale*. Appropriation was not over at the moment when the accused took cans of beer but was continuing when at a later stage he used violence against the off-licence shopkeeper who had challenged him. *Gomez* related to the issue whether there was an appropriation when the victim consented to the accused's assumption of his rights, not whether appropriation was a continuing act. The accused's conviction was upheld. Accordingly whether there is a robbery depends on whether the force or threat of force is used while the accused is still 'on the job'.

It is immaterial that the accused uses force on some person other than the one from whom he takes the item. If the accused uses force on a railway signalman to make him stop a train, it is robbery if the accused steals from the train.

Section 8(1) covers not only force but the threat of force. The threat must be one which puts the victim 'then and there' in fear of force. A threat of future force is not sufficient. In those circumstances a charge of blackmail is appropriate. The subsection also covers where the accused 'seeks to put' a person in fear of force. An example is threatening a deaf person. The victim need not actually be made afraid. An example of this type of robbery was briefly noted in the *Guardian*, 1 March 1994, where a Mr Muldownie was jailed by the Southwark Crown Court for brandishing a syringe which he said contained his blood contaminated with HIV.

Mens rea

Besides the mental element required for theft, it is probable that the force must be applied intentionally or at least recklessly and that the accused must be aware that the force is being used on a person. The force or threat of force must be done 'in order to' steal. This is a *mens rea* term. As stated above in the discussion of *Robinson*, if the *mens rea* of theft does not exist robbery is not committed, even though the accused in that case used a knife to get the money he was owed.

Summary

- *Theft* – the basic definition: Section 1(1) of the Theft Act 1968 prohibits the (i) dishonest (ii) appropriation of (iii) property (iv) belonging to another (v) with the intention of permanently depriving the other of it. Sections 2–6 treat of those concepts in order. There is no need for the accused to act with a view to gain, and there is no need for the thief to receive any benefit from the theft: s 1(2).

- *Dishonesty*: Unlike in the rest of this book the *mens rea* is dealt with before the *actus reus*. This is because it is the *mens rea* which converts an otherwise innocuous *actus reus* into the crime of theft. If you take a can of beans from your local supermarket, you have committed the *actus reus* of theft, the appropriation ('take') of property ('a can of beans') belonging to another (the 'local supermarket'). Indeed, even one of the elements of the *mens rea*, intent permanently to deprive, does not distinguish the thief from the honest shopper, for presumably both intend to eat the beans. The distinction lies in the 'dishonesty' element. Section 2(1) gives a partial definition of when the accused is NOT dishonest:
    belief in a legal right to deprive the other;
    belief that the victim would have consented, had he or she known of the true circumstances; and
    belief that the owner cannot be found by taking reasonable steps.
  Even outside s 2(1), however, an accused will be not dishonest if he or she was not dishonest by the standards of ordinary decent people, or if he or she was so dishonest, he or she did not know that what he or she was doing was dishonest by those standards.

- *Intention permanently to deprive (IPD)*: An error often committed by students is to think that s 6(1) defines IPD – it does not! Section 6(1) is used only where the accused intends that the victim should get the item back; otherwise the basic definition in s 1(1) is all that is needed. For example, if I take your coat and use it as the basis for a fire, I do intend to deprive you of it permanently. Indeed, s 6(1) does NOT apply because I do not mean you to get the coat back. In sum, s 6(1) applies only when it says it applies: 'without meaning the other permanently to lose the thing itself'. It governs two situations, both of which are ones in which the accused does intend that the victim gets the item back: 'his intention is to treat the thing as his own to dispose of regardless of the other's rights' and 'a borrowing or lending of it [the property] may amount to so treating it if, but only if, the borrowing or lending is for a period and in circumstances making it equivalent to an outright taking or disposal'.

- *Appropriation*: Section 3(1) of the Theft Act 1968 states that appropriation consists of 'any assumption by a person of the rights of an owner . . .'. 'The rights' has been construed as meaning 'any of the rights'; and appropriation covers not just taking but receiving, including receiving something as a gift, a far-fetched judicial construction one may think. If one deceives another into giving one an item of property, one also appropriates. Indeed, the stage has been reached where it can be said that any dealing with property (even honestly) is an appropriation. There is no need for a misappropriation.

  One person who would otherwise appropriate is exempted by s 3(2), the bona fide purchaser for value without notice.

- *Property*: Section 4(1) provides that 'money and all other property, real or personal, including things in action and other intangible property' constitutes property. The section may be read as 'property = property' but a better equation is: 'property for the purposes of the criminal law of theft = property for the purposes of civil law'; therefore anything which is property at civil law is also property for the purposes of theft, and the corollary is that what is not property at civil law is also not property for theft (e.g. confidential information such as that found on an exam paper). A thing in action is something which does not physically exist but which may be enforced by legal action, for example a debt. Intangible property includes patents and export quotas: they can be appropriated by the accused's transferring them from the victim to a third party. At common law a human body cannot be stolen but the exceptions are growing and include body parts which have had work done on them, for example anatomical specimens. There is much law on cheques but the basic rules are these: drawing a cheque on an account in credit or on an account which is within the agreed overdraft limit creates a debt, which is property, as we have seen; however, drawing a cheque on an account which is beyond the overdraft limit does not create a debt because the bank is not obliged in law to meet the cheque and therefore in this case there is no debt which may be the subject of a theft charge.

  Section 4(2)–(4) contains special rules about land, wild fungi, flowers, fruit, and foliage and wild animals.

- *Belonging to another*: The main provision is s 5(1), which states that property belongs to 'any person having possession or control of it, or having any proprietary right or interest (not being an equitable interest arising only from an agreement to transfer or grant an interest)'.

  Section 5(2) ensures that persons who appropriate assets subject to charitable trusts are deemed to be thieves, if all the other elements of the offence are satisfied. Section 5(3) is another deeming provision and concerns the obligation to deal with property in a particular way. Section 5(4) is also a deeming provision. This subsection is about situations where the accused has received the victim's property through the latter's mistake but it should be noted that most, if not all, such scenarios fall also within s 5(1); the other major noteworthy point concerns the interpretation of s 5(4) and may be put in this way: the fact that the accused has received property by mistake does not automatically mean that he or she is under a duty to restore; whether there is such an obligation depends on the civil law of restitution.

- *Robbery*: The offence of robbery, contrary to s 8(1) of the Theft Act 1968, may be seen as one of 'theft plus': that is, all the elements of theft must be proved plus either force or the threat of force. One of the points of interpretation that should be noted is that s 8(1) applies where the force or threat of force is on a person other than the victim of the theft.

References

Reports

Criminal Law Revision Committee, 8th Report, *Theft and Related Offences*, Cmnd 2977 (1966)

Home Office, *Crime in England and Wales: Quarterly Update to September 2011*, HOSB:01/12

Home Office White Paper, *Crime, Justice and Protecting the Public*, Cm 965 (1990)

Law Commission Consultation Paper No. 150, *Misuse of Trade Secrets* (1997)

Law Commission Consultation Paper No. 155, *Legislating the Criminal Code: Fraud and Deception* (1999)

Law Commission Report No. 276, *Fraud* (2002)

Books

Clarkson, C.M.V., Keating, H. and Cunningham, S.R. *Criminal Law: Text and Materials*, 7th edn (Sweet & Maxwell, 2010)

Harington, V. and Mayhew, P. *Mobile Phone Thefts*, Home Office Research Study No. 235 (2001)

Kershaw, C. *et al. The 2000 British Crime Survey* (Home Office Statistical Bulletin, 2000)

Nicholas, S., Povey, D., Walker, A. and Kershaw, C. *Crime in England & Wales 2004–2005* (Home Office, 2005)

Philips, E., Walsh, C. and Dobson, P. *Law Relating to Theft* (Cavendish, 2001)

Smith, A.T.H. *Property Offences* (Sweet & Maxwell, 1994)

Williams, G. *Textbook of Criminal Law*, 3rd edn, ed. D. Baker (Sweet & Maxwell, 2012)

Journals

Glazebrook, P.R. 'Revising the Theft Acts' [1993] CLJ 191

Leigh, L.H. 'Some remarks on appropriation in the law of theft after *Morris*' (1985) 48 MLR 167

Smith, J.C. Case comment on *Mazo* (1996) Crim LR 437

Smith, J.C. 'Reforming the Theft Acts' (1996) 28 *Bracton Law Journal* 27

Smith, J.C. Case comment on *Gomaz* (1997) Crim LR 359

Smith, J.C. 'Obtaining cheques by deception' [1997] Crim LR 396

Smith, J.C. Casenate on *Malone* [1998] Crim LR 834

Smith, J.C. 'Stealing tickets' [1998] Crim LR 723

Sullivan, G.R. and Warbrick, C. 'Current developments: private international law' (1994) 43 ICLQ 464

Sullivan, G.R. and Warbrick, C. 'Territoriality, theft and *Atakpu*' [1994] Crim LR 650

Wall, J. 'The legal status of body parts' (2011) 31 OJLS 783

Further reading

Ashworth, A. 'Robbery re-assessed' [2002] Crim LR 851

Bogg, A. and Stanton-Ife, J. 'Protecting the vulnerable: legality, harm and theft' (2003) 27 LS 402

Campbell, K. 'The test for dishonesty' in *R* v *Ghosh* [1984] CLJ 349

Elliott, D.W. 'Dishonesty in theft – a dispensable concept' [1982] Crim LR 395

Gardner, S. 'Property and theft' [1998] Crim LR 35

Green, S. and Kugler, M.B. 'Community perceptions of serious theft cases: a challenge to the Model Penal Code and the English Theft Act consolidation' (2009) Rutgers School of Law – Newark, Research Paper Series Paper No. 031 (2010) J Empirical Leg Studs 511

Griew, E. 'Dishonesty: the objections to *Feely* and *Ghosh*' [1985] Crim LR 341

Griew, E. 'Stealing and obtaining bank credits' [1986] Crim LR 356

Halpin, A. 'The test for dishonesty' [1996] Crim LR 283

Halpin, A. *Definition in the Criminal Law* (Hart Publishing, 2008)

Hammond, G. '*R* v *Stewart*: the final judgment?' (1989) 11 Sup Ct LR 21

Melissaris, E. 'The concept of appropriation and the law of theft' (2007) 70 MLR 581

Shute, S. 'Appropriation and the law of theft' [2002] Crim LR 445

Simester, A.P. and Sullivan, G.R. 'On the nature and rationale of property offences', in R.A. Duff and S. Green (eds), *Defining Crimes: Essays on the Special Part of Criminal Law* (Oxford University Press, 2005)

Smith, J.C. 'The sad fate of the Theft Act 1968', in W. Swadling and G. Jones (eds), *The Search for Principle* (Oxford University Press, 1999)

Smith, J.C. [2001] Crim LR 573 (for case comment on *Clark*)

Stannard, J. 'Fools rush in – the meaning of s 6 of the Theft Act' (1979) 30 NILQ 225

Steel, A. 'The harms and wrongdoings of stealing: the harm principle and dishonesty in theft' (2008) 31 UNSWLJ 712

Steel, A. 'The meanings of dishonesty in theft' (2009) 38 *Common Law World Review* 103

Williams, G. 'Temporary appropriation should be theft' [1981] Crim LR 129

Williams, G. 'Innocuously dipping into trust funds' (1985) 5 LS 183

The principal modern work on this and the next two chapters is A.T.H. Smith, '*Property Offences*' (Sweet & Maxwell, 1994). For a simpler and more modern work see E. Phillips, C. Walsh and P. Dobson, *Law Relating to Theft* (Cavendish, 2001).

J.C. Smith, *The Law of Theft*, has been updated by D. Ormerod and D. Williams (Oxford University Press, 9th edn, 2007). It is now published as *Smith's Law of Theft*.

Visit **www.mylawchamber.co.uk** to access tools to help you develop and test your knowledge of criminal law, including interactive multiple choice questions, practice exam questions with guidance, annotated weblinks, glossary flashcards, legal newsfeed and legal updates.

Use Case Navigator to read in full some of the key cases referenced in this chapter with commentary and questions:

R v *Ghosh* [1982] EWCA Crim 2
R v *Hinks* [2001] 2 AC 241
R v *Woollin* [1999] AC 82 (HL)

16

Fraud, making off without payment

◖◗ ## Aims and objectives

After reading this chapter you will understand and be able to critique:

- the offence of fraud and the three ways in which it may be committed
- the offence of making off and how it complements theft

Introduction

The Theft Act 1968 created several offences of obtaining by **deception**, of which the most important were obtaining property by deception (s 15) and obtaining a pecuniary advantage by deception (s 16). Section 15A was inserted into the 1968 Act by the Theft (Amendment) Act 1996. It created the offence of obtaining a money transfer by deception. Part of s 16 was abolished by the Theft Act 1978, which created three offences: obtaining services by deception (s 1), evading liability by deception (s 2), and making off without payment (s 3). The s 3 crime does not require deception and is treated separately. At no time has there been a generic offence of fraud.

The Fraud Act 2006 replaced all the deception offences, namely ss 15, 15A and 16 of the Theft Act 1968 and ss 1 and 2 of the Theft Act 1978. Because the crime of making off is not an offence of deception, s 3 of the Theft Act 1978 is unaffected. The Act creates one offence of fraud (s 1) but that is committed in three ways: by false representation (s 2), by failing to disclose information (s 3), and by abuse of position (s 4). The law has been both modernised and expanded. One aim was to make the law flexible enough to deal with increasingly sophisticated frauds including those perpetrated using new technology: Ministry of Justice, *Post-legislative Assessment of the Fraud Act 2006: Memorandum to the Justice Select Committee*, Cm 8372, 2012.

The policy of the law was explained by HHJ Miller QC in *McDevitt* [2012] NICC 16. 'Fraud is not a victimless crime. The monetary cost is significant, but fraud offences also cause considerable social and economic harm beyond their immediate financial impact. Fraud can be used to fund organised crime that may target vulnerable victims (drug and people smuggling, for example) and fraud offences can ruin lives, close businesses or take life savings.' An example of a fraud is provided by the facts of an Oldham magistrates' court case involving a shop-keeper who attempted to defraud an elderly couple of their

EuroMillions win of £1 million by telling them that their ticket had not won; he intended to claim the money for himself: *Nizzar* 20 August 2012 on the BBC website (http://www.bbc.co.uk/news/uk-england-manchester-19318742). This is an example of s 2 of the Fraud Act 2006, fraud by representation.

The Fraud Act 2006

The new offence of fraud

Example

Althea is a town hall official working in the planning office. She tells Bert that she can speed up his planning application if he pays her £500. Is she guilty of fraud?

Fraud is contrary to the Fraud Act 2006, s 1(1). This offence is committed in three ways. Most facts fall within s 2(1), as this one would easily seem to, but s 4(1) is perhaps more interesting on the facts given. This way of committing fraud comprises three elements:

- the accused 'occupies a position in which he is expected to safeguard, or not to act against, the financial interests of another': the question is whether a planning officer is expected to safeguard the *financial* interest of another, and maybe he does because house prices may be affected by, for example, an inappropriate extension, as perhaps are the facts here, though even then is it really part of his job to protect that neighbour's interests? While 'position' is not defined, a planning officer does surely occupy a position, namely that of planning officer;
- he must 'dishonestly abuse his position': again, there is no definition of 'abuse' but the facts fall solidly within its meaning; 'dishonestly' is defined in the normal way (see **Ghosh** [1982] QB 1053 (CA)); and
- he must intend by means of the abuse to make a gain for himself or another or to cause a loss to another or expose another to a risk of loss: there is no difficulty here.

Whether the method of committing fraud is via s 4(1) or s 2(1), there is no requirement that the accused actually does obtain any benefit or that the victim makes a loss. This is different from previous law where the accused had actually to obtain property by deception.

The Act creates the general offence of **fraud**, which is punishable on indictment to a maximum of 10 years' imprisonment or an unlimited fine or both; the maximum on summary conviction is 12 months' imprisonment or a fine not exceeding the current maximum (£5,000) or both. There is no definition of 'fraud': rather there are three ways in which the general offence of fraud may be committed. The offence may be committed in three ways, which are laid down in ss 2–4 of the Act. There is no need for the financial interests of the victim to be imperilled. The Home Office's Criminal Law Policy Unit in *Fraud Law Reform: Government Response to Consultations* (2006) at para. 12 stated that the offence did not breach Article 7 of the European Convention on Human Rights. Nevertheless, each of the ways in which fraud may be committed is widely drawn, partly to avoid the problems which bedevilled earlier law. The government's view was that the wording of the new offence reflected the ordinary meaning of the term 'fraud'.

The Home Office, *Crime in England and Wales 2008–09*, 2009, reported that there were 122,569 s 2 crimes, 305 s 3 ones, and 265 s 4 ones in that reporting year.

Fraud by false representation (s 2)

Section 2(1) states:

A person is in breach of this section if he –
(a) dishonestly makes a false representation, and
(b) intends, by making the representation –
    (i) to make a gain for himself or another, or
    (ii) to cause loss to another or to expose another to a risk of loss.

There is no need for the intended victim to be deceived. Unlike its predecessor, fraud is a conduct, not a result, crime. There is also no requirement, unlike the previous law, for anyone to be deceived. Neither need anyone's economic interests be imperilled. By s 2(3) a representation means 'any representation as to fact or as to law, including a representation as to the state of mind of – (a) the person making the representation, or (b) any other person.' An example of a representation to a person's present state of mind is when the accused promises that he will pay the victim tomorrow. A representation of opinion may be a misrepresentation as to fact: if the opinion was not the accused's real one, there is a misrepresentation. There is no actual definition of 'representation'. The representation may be express or implied: s 2(4). An example is the famous second-hand car dealer's 'it's a good little runner'. This is not just a statement of opinion but an implied representation as to fact: 'it is my honest opinion that this car is a good little runner'. Also covered are mortgage and insurance frauds. By s 2(2) a representation is false if: '(a) it is untrue or misleading, and (b) the person making it knows that it is, or might be, untrue or misleading.' 'Untrue' and 'misleading' are not defined. Section 2 goes on to cover deception of machines: '. . . a representation may be regarded as made if it (or anything implying it) is submitted in any form to any system or device designed to receive, convey or respond to communication (with or without human intervention).' This provision means that unlike earlier law a fraud may be committed where a machine is 'deceived'.

Gain and loss are defined in s 5, which also applies to ss 3 and 4 (see below). By s 5(2), which is very similar to s 34(2)(a) of the Theft Act 1968 discussed in the next chapter: '"Gain" and "loss" – (a) extend only to gain and loss in money or other property; (b) include any such gain whether temporary or permanent; and "property" means any property whether real or personal (including things in action and other tangible property).' For explanation of 'things in action' see Chapter 15; 'gain' is further defined as 'a gain by keeping what one has, as well as a gain by getting what one does not have.' (s 5(3)). 'Gain' covers getting what the victim legally owes to the accused. Similarly, by s 5(4) 'loss' includes 'a loss by not getting what one might get, as well as a loss by parting with what one has'. Because there need be no actual gain or loss, fraud can be seen as an inchoate offence. However, the exceptions to the definition of property found in s 4(2)–(4) of the 1968 Act do not apply. Therefore, land can be the subject of fraud but not of theft.

See p 582
(Chapter 15) for
an explanation of
'things in action'.

Throughout the 2006 Act 'dishonestly' bears its *Ghosh* [1982] QB 1053 (CA) definition: see Chapter 15, but note that s 2(1) of the Theft Act 1968 does not apply to the offence of fraud. It is suggested that it would have been better to have stated expressly that a claim of right defeats dishonesty. The other elements of the *mens rea* are intending to make a gain or lack a loss and knowledge that the representation is or may be false. There is no requirement that the accused acts with the intent that the victim is permanently deprived of the property. It is also sufficient that the accused intends to expose the victim to the risk of loss. It is suggested that intention bears its usual *Woollin* [1999] 1 AC 82 (HL) definition: see Chapter 3.

For more on the
Ghosh definition
of dishonesty,
see pp 553–58
(Chapter 15).

This revision to the previous law gets rid of the difficulty of proving that the deception operated on the mind of the victim and thereby resolves the difficulties posed by *MPC* v *Charles* [1977] AC 177 (HL) and *Lambie* [1981] 2 All ER 776 (HL) where the persons accepting the cheque card and credit card respectively were indifferent to the creditworthiness of the accused because the issuer of the cards would make up any loss. Making false applications, such as for mortgages, falls within s 2(1). There is no need for the victim to rely on the representation; the crime is complete once the false representation is made. Section 2(1) also deals with an increasingly common problem, that of 'phishing', that is, the accused sends out requests over the internet for victims to re-register their accounts at a replica website with a view to emptying the victim's account. Section 2(1) covers situations where the accused has obtained the entire proprietary interest before he makes a representation. For example, a driver put petrol into his tank. In civil law he owns it. He then falsely represents that his company will pay. Another charge possible on these facts is s 3 of the Theft Act 1978, making off.

In respect of the definition of 'property', which is similar to that laid down in s 4(1) of the Theft Act 1968, the government rejected an extension to 'confidential financial data', but where the accused intends to make a gain, for example through the exploitation of the information which he has accessed, the crime is committed.

In relation to the *mens rea* it should be noted that 'know that it . . . might be' in s 2(2) is the equivalent to subjective recklessness as discussed in Chapter 3 but there is no requirement that it was unreasonable for the accused to take the risk.

Most frauds fall under s 2. Reported cases on the specific offences of fraud are rare as yet but one is *Goldsmith* [2009] EWCA Crim 1840. The accused was guilty of dishonestly making a false representation for gain when he obtained the services of male prostitutes by paying cheques which he had stolen, knowing that the cheques would not be honoured. In *Greig* [2010] EWCA Crim 1183 the defendants were convicted when they did £300-worth of gardening but collected cheques worth over £6,000. The Court held that the jury could infer that the defendants had falsely represented that the work was worth over £6,000. Mortgage frauds fall straightforwardly into s 2: *Kausar* [2009] EWCA Crim 2242. In *McDevitt* [2012] NICC 16 the victims gave the accused £75,000 to hold for six months in connection with the purchase of more than 400 petrol stations in Bulgaria. The accused spent it. The Crown Court in Northern Ireland held that s 2 of the Fraud Act 2006 was satisfied. The accused had dishonestly made a false representation that he would hold the money on behalf of the victims and return it within six months with the intention to make a gain for himself or to cause loss to the victims or to expose the victims to a risk of loss.

A recent example of s 2 is *Reference by the Judge Advocate General under section 34 of the Court Martial Appeals Act 1968 as amended. Appeal against conviction by Timothy Twaite* [2010] EWCA Crim 2973. The Court Martial Appeals Court held that the accused's conduct did not fall within s 2 when he dishonestly made a false representation that he was about to be married in order to obtain service families' accommodation and did not withdraw his representation when he was not in fact married until a year after moving into married quarters. His silence did not suffice for s 2. However, the court emphasised that a charge under s 3, discussed next, might have succeeded.

Fraud by failing to disclose information (s 3)

The second way in which the offence of fraud may be committed is when the accused (s 3(1)):

(a) dishonestly fails to disclose to another person information which he is under a legal duty to disclose,

(b) intends, by failing to disclose the information –
 (i) to make a gain for himself or another, or
 (ii) to cause loss to another or to expose another to a risk of loss.

The matters covered by s 3 may also fall within s 2. It should be noted that there must be a legal duty to disclose and therefore a moral duty to disclose is insufficient. There is no definition of 'legal duty'. A duty imposed by statute is one example, for example statute imposes an obligation that company prospectuses are accurate. Similarly, insurance contracts with the implied duty of the utmost good faith fall within the definition. Legal duties may arise in other ways, such as through equity or trade practice. Liability seems to be strict as to the existence of the legal duty. In other words, the accused need not know that he is under a legal duty. Furthermore, there need be no deception. There is no definition of 'information'.

The *mens rea* besides dishonesty is the intent to make a gain or cause a loss or to expose to the risk of loss. 'Gain' and 'loss' bear the same definition as in s 2, noted above.

Fraud by abuse of position (s 4)

Section 4(1) provides the third manner in which fraud may be committed:

A person is in breach of this section if he –
(a) occupies a position in which he is expected to safeguard, or not to act against, the financial interests of another person,
(b) dishonestly abuses that position, and
(c) intends, by means of abuse of that position,
 (i) to make a gain for himself or another, or
 (ii) to cause loss to another or to expose another to a risk of loss.

It is expressly provided by s 4(2) that abuse of position includes an omission to act. There is, however, no definition of 'abuse'. There need be no deception. Among persons covered by s 4(1) are government officials and those taking care of the elderly. Fiduciaries such as directors are also covered, as when a secret profit is acquired. There is no restriction as there is in s 3(1) to persons who are under a legal duty to disclose information. There is no need for the abuse to be carried out secretly (contrary to the recommendation of the Law Commission). 'Position' and 'financial interests' are also not defined. There need be no gain or loss.

The *mens rea* is the same as in s 3.

Supplementary provisions to the offence of fraud

Sections 6 and 7 create the offences of possessing articles for use in frauds and making or supplying articles for use in frauds respectively. Section 6 replaces in part s 25 of the Theft Act 1968 (going equipped), discussed in Chapter 17, which is now restricted to going equipped for theft or burglary. Unlike s 25, s 6 applies whether or not the accused is at his 'place of abode'. Therefore, a home computer falls within s 6. Section 6(1) reads:

A person is guilty of an offence if he has in his possession or under his control any article for use in the course of or in connection with any fraud.

The maximum sentence is five years' imprisonment, whereas it is three years for going equipped. One example of an 'article' is a device used to record films in cinemas surreptitiously. Other examples include hard drives, name badges and cloned credit cards. The crime can be used against for example charity and wine scams (where the accused falsely holds out that he is collecting on behalf of a charity or he has fine wine for sale but the charity and wind do not exist), investment fraud, and deceiving victims into buying worthless pieces of land.

'Article' is not defined. A pen is an article for this purpose. Section 6(1) does not apply to any article which may be used for fraud but only to an article intended to be used for fraud. There is no need to prove that the article is to be used for any particular fraud, and the accused need not intend to use the item in a fraud committed by himself. It is arguable that the accused has control over information on the internet which he can download. An example of an article caught by s 6 is that of a blank plastic card which the accused intends to make into a false credit card. Section 6 has no express *mens rea*. However, 'possession' requires some mental element: one does not possess something one is unaware of; presumably also the accused must be aware of the nature of the article, that is, that it may be used 'in the course of or in connection with any fraud.' The government expected that by using the same words as in s 25 of the Theft Act 1968 the same *mens rea* as in s 25 would be implicitly incorporated. Express words would have avoided any possibility of erroneous interpretations.

Section 7(1) provides:

A person is guilty of an offence if he makes, adapts, supplies or offers to supply any article –
(a) knowing that it is designed or adapted for use in the course of or in connection with fraud, or
(b) intending it to be used to commit, or assist in the commission of, fraud.

By s 8(1), 'article' in ss 6 and 7 includes 'any program or data held in electronic form'. Therefore, an email system is covered. Also included are hard drives and PIN cloning devices. It is uncertain whether these sections are restricted to fraud under the 2006 Act. It is suggested that conspiracy to defraud is covered. One type of fraud is fraudulent trading by a non-corporate business contrary to s 9 of the Fraud Act 2006. If this offence is covered, it would be difficult to exclude fraudulent trading by a corporation contrary to the Companies Act 1985, s 458. If so, presumably all offences of fraud outside the Fraud Act are covered.

Obtaining services dishonestly

Section 11 of the 2006 Act creates the offence of obtaining services dishonestly. Unlike previous law there is no requirement of a deception, but unlike the general offence of fraud the services must actually be obtained. Section 11(1) reads:

A person is guilty of an offence . . . if he obtains services for himself or another –
(a) by a dishonest act, and
(b) in breach of subsection (2).

There is no definition of both 'obtain' and 'services'. It would seem that because of the reference to 'act' this offence cannot be committed by an omission.

Subsection (2) provides:

A person obtains services in breach of this subsection if –
(a) they were made available on the basis that payment has been, or is being or will be made for or in respect of them,
(b) he obtains them without any payment having been made for or in respect of them or without payment having been made in full, and

(c) when he obtains them, he knows –

    (i) that they are being made available on the basis described in paragraph (a), or

    (ii) that they might be,

but intends that payment will not be made, or will not be made in full.

The maximum sentence for this offence if tried on indictment is five years' imprisonment or an unlimited fine or both (s 11(3)).

One aim behind s 11(1) is that services made by automatic means are covered. Previous law was that machines could not be deceived. For example, giving false credit card details is covered. However, it is not restricted to machines. Therefore, both opening a bank account dishonestly through a bank official and downloading music dishonestly from the Web are covered. Similarly covered is using a device to watch pay-per-view TV free of charge. The obvious situation covered by this offence which was not covered by its predecessor, obtaining services by deception, is sneaking into a football ground to watch a match free of charge. The crime is restricted to the obtaining of services. If services are not obtained, a charge of attempting to obtain services may be available. There is no definition of 'services' except that they must be 'paid for' ones. Therefore, gratuitous services are not caught by s 11(1), though the general fraud offence may apply. It should be noted that s 11(1) applies only where there is no intent to pay either in full or partly. Accordingly, parents who lie about the religion of their child in order to get him or her into a fee-paying faith school are not guilty of this offence if they intend to pay. This example is that of the Law Commission in its Report No. 276, *Fraud*, 2002.

The *mens rea* besides dishonesty is knowledge that the services are to be paid for, and either an intent not to pay at all or an intent not to pay in full. It is unclear whether there must be an intent to avoid payment permanently but for consistency with making off (discussed below) there should be. Dishonesty is defined in the usual way: see *Ghosh*, above, discussed in the previous chapter.

Conclusion: conspiracy to defraud

The government refused to take the opportunity to repeal the common law crime of conspiracy to defraud (see Chapter 10 of this book). The Law Commission's original view was that on the passing of the Fraud Act 2006 conspiracy to defraud would be abolished because there would be no reason for it: any gaps in the law would be filled by the statute. Certainly there is less room for conspiracy to defraud now that we have the Fraud Act. A large minority of the consultees to the consultation exercise preferred to see the offence abolished because it was illogical that two people could be guilty of an offence when a single person doing the same act would not be; moreover, the crime is so broad that it covered potentially agreements to do things which ought not to be criminal, and the width of the offence is uncertain. The government, however, decided that (para. 40 of the government's *Fraud Law Reform*, noted above): '. . . at least until we have experience of how the new offences operate in practice, it would be rash to repeal conspiracy to defraud as it provides flexibility in dealing with a wide variety of frauds. . . . [I]t was not clear that the new offences could successfully replace it in every case, especially bearing in mind developing technology and possible new types of fraud.' The Labour government, however, was committed to the long-term repeal of the crime and promised to review it on publication of the Commission's Report on assisting and encouraging crime, which has since taken place, and after the Fraud Act 2006 has bedded down.

The latest report, Ministry of Justice, *Post-legislative Assessment of the Fraud Act 2006: Memorandum to the Justice Select Committee*, Cm 8372, 2012, stated in its final paragraph, 43, that: 'While it would be possible to consider codifying the common law offence in statute, the evidence strongly suggests that the current situation is working perfectly satisfactorily and therefore we have concluded that we should leave matters as they are.' The high hopes for reform of conspiracy which existed at the time of the reform of conspiracy by the Criminal Law Act 1977 have disappeared.

Making off without payment

Example

Shirley, a law student, has had a little bit to drink but is nowhere near drunk, and decides to finish off her evening at the world-renowned Indian restaurant, 'The Balti Queen'. She eats her meal and then decides not to pay. She saunters to the Ladies, where she leaves the building via a tiny window. Is she guilty of making off?

This is a straightforward case. All of the elements of the crime occur contemporaneously:

she knows that payment on the spot is expected or required;
she is dishonest within *Ghosh* [1982] QB 1053 (CA);
she intends to avoid payment (permanently); and
she 'makes off' by sauntering away from the spot where payment is expected or required.

Note that she is not guilty of theft of the meal because when she ate it she was not dishonest, and because one element of theft was missing, it cannot be theft.

Making off without payment is covered in Section 3 of the Theft Act 1978, which provides:

1 Subject to subsection (3) below, a person who, knowing that payment on the spot for any goods supplied or service done is required or expected from him, dishonestly makes off without having paid as required or expected and with intent to avoid payment of the amount due shall be guilty of an offence.
2 For purposes of this section 'payment on the spot' includes payment at the time of collecting goods on which work has been done or in respect of which service has been provided.
3 Subsection (1) above shall not apply where the supply of the goods or the doing of the service is contrary to law, or where the service done is such that payment is not legally enforceable.

The offence is triable either way and the maximum sentence is two years or a fine of £2,000.

Points of interpretation

'This is not an easy section to construe': *Allen* [1985] 1 WLR 50 (CA). The omission of a definition of 'service' in s 3 is inexplicable.

(a) The principal difference between this offence and the others in this chapter is that the accused is guilty of making off whether or not he deceived anyone. Where there is a deception, s 3 and the deception offences will both apply.

(b) Section 3 is restricted to legally enforceable payments (s 3(3)). The offence in s 3 will not be committed by an accused who walks away from a betting shop or brothel. The Criminal Law Revision Committee (Thirteenth Report, *Section 16 of the Theft Act 1968*, Cmnd 6733, 1977) considered that s 3 would not apply if the accused did not intend to pay from the start of the transaction. The last phrase in s 3(3) should be noted. Section 3(3) does not apply to goods. Therefore, if the victim supplies goods to the accused, a s 3 charge is available even though the contract between the parties is not enforceable. The provision of non-necessary items to a minor falls within this exception.

(c) The 'payment' need not be by money. If a restaurant accepts luncheon vouchers, 'payment on the spot' in s 3(1) applies.

(d) Dishonesty need not be present at the start of the transaction. It is sufficient that there exists dishonesty at the time of making off. Section 3 covers the situation where the accused goes into a restaurant or petrol station intending to pay but leaves without doing so.

(e) The phrase 'with intent to avoid payment' is read as meaning 'with intent never to pay': *Allen* [1985] AC 1029 (HL). On the facts the accused was not guilty if he intended merely to delay paying a hotel bill of £1,286. He told the hotel that he was in financial difficulties and surrendered his passport to it. The effect of *Allen* would appear to undermine the thrust of the crime. The accused will after *Allen* be guilty if he simply vanishes with no intent to repay. It is thought that *Allen* undermines the rationale behind s 3, and in any case the subsection does not include the word expressly, so why read it in? It may be hard to prove that the accused never intended to return to pay.

(f) It is uncertain whether s 3 covers the giving of worthless cheques. It is sometimes thought that it does. The accused has not paid as 'required or expected'. However, in *Hammond* [1982] Crim LR 611 (Crown Court), a judge ruled that if the victim accepts a cheque without a guarantee card, he knows that he is taking a risk. The accused is therefore not guilty of this offence if he drafts a worthless cheque. One argument is that payment by a worthless cheque does not satisfy the requirement in s 3(1) that the creditor is 'paid' because the victim takes it in conditional satisfaction of the debt. On the other hand, the creditor does expect a valuable cheque. Therefore, payment by a dud cheque is not payment as 'required or expected' within s 3(1). If the accused merely intends to defer paying, s 3 is inapplicable for the reason stated in (e).

(g) Section 3 does not cover the moonlighting tenant. The rent is payable 'then' but not 'there'.

(h) *Troughton v Metropolitan Police* [1987] Crim LR 138 (DC) illustrates a nice point. A very drunk accused did not give his name and address to the taxi-driver. The cab driver drove to a police station. The court held that the driver was in breach of contract through not completing the journey (in civil law terms there was an entire contract). Therefore, he could not legally demand the fare. The accused was never bound to pay on the spot for the service. He was not guilty. Accordingly, within s 3 it is not enough that the victim expects or requires the accused to pay. The payment must be legally due.

(i) Where is 'the spot'? In *Brooks* (1982) 76 Cr App R 66, the Court of Appeal determined that 'the spot' meant the place where payment was required. In a restaurant that place was the cash desk. There was no need for the accused to reach the restaurant door. In an underground system 'the spot' includes the gate at the exit. In *McDavitt* [1981]

Crim LR 843, it was held at Crown Court level that the accused was guilty of the attempt if he had not yet reached 'the spot'. In *Aziz* [1993] Crim LR 708 (CA) the defence argued that in relation to a taxi ride 'the spot' was at the end of the ride. The driver had reached that spot but had driven off to a police station when the defendants refused to pay. The court held that when they ran off from the cab, they had departed from the spot. Payment was expected when the taxi reached the destination specified. The court held that the trial judge had properly directed the jury that the driver continued to require payment after reaching the destination and driving off to the police station. The place of the spot could differ according to circumstances and it is a question of fact whether the accused has departed from the spot.

(j) Section 3 stipulates that the accused must make off. It is moot whether that phrase covers a situation where the accused departs with the victim's consent. For instance, if the defendant tells a taxi-driver that he must get money from his flat and the driver agrees, does he make off? In *Hammond*, above, it was said that there was no making off when the creditor allowed the accused to leave. In *Brooks* the Court of Appeal decided that there was no need for the accused to make off stealthily, and that the words 'dishonestly makes off' usually required no explanation because they bore their 'ordinary natural meaning', which covers making off with the consent of the victim. If so, *Hammond* would appear to be wrong. An accused does make off even when he has the creditor's consent to leave. Note that the accused in *Hammond* would now be guilty of fraud.

(k) A shoplifter in a shop where goods are served will be guilty of this offence and theft when the item is given to him. In a self-service shop, however, goods are, it is thought, not 'supplied' to him within s 3(1). He will in any event be guilty of theft. It had been suggested that 'supplied' means 'available for purchase' or is to be read as including 'supplied to himself'. If this interpretation is correct, the accused is guilty of this offence. If the accused receives ham from the meat stall in a supermarket he is guilty if he makes off before paying at the cash desk. Similarly, the accused is guilty where ownership passes on delivery such as when food is eaten or petrol put into the tank. However, the accused who sneaks out of a cinema which he has sneaked into is not guilty: no service has been 'done'.

(l) There is no definition of service. It is suggested that the ordinary language definition is the one to be used. The same point can be made about 'goods'. One might have expected an incorporation of the definition of 'goods' used for the purposes of the offence of handling.

(m) It is suggested that the accused who can be traced (for example he has put his real name and address on the back of a cheque) can still be guilty of making off. There is no restriction in the definition to persons who cannot easily be traced. The opposing argument is that the section applies only when the accused has done something which makes him harder to trace.

(n) The supplying or service need not take place before the payment is required. Payment is required on one-man buses before getting on the bus, but a s 3 offence can be committed if the accused stands by the driver, looking through his purse, and jumping off before paying.

If the accused obtains credit, even when the obtaining was dishonest and by deception, he is not guilty of this offence because 'payment on the spot . . . is [not] required or expected': *Vincent* [2001] 1 WLR 1172 (CA). The accused contended that two hotel proprietors had agreed that payment due could be postponed. The court held that 'payment on the spot' was not required even though the accused may have obtained the agreements by deception. The reason why payment was not required or expected was irrelevant. The court also said that 's 3(1) is . . . intended to create a simple and straightforward offence'. Therefore, any attempt to complicate matters should be eschewed. The correct charge now is that of false representation contrary to the Fraud Act 2006 s 2. There is an overlap between s 3(1) of the 1978 Act and s 2(1) of the 2006 Act. Section 2(1) can be committed even when the accused has received ownership of the property *before* making the false representation. For example, to use a common illustration, if the accused puts petrol into his tank, under civil law he has obtained the entire proprietary interest in it; if he then says that his company will pay for it by asking for it to be put on the company's account but the petrol is to be used for private purposes, and this is not contractually permitted, then both making off and fraud are committed.

References

Reports

Criminal Law Revision Committee, 13th Report, *Section 16 of the Theft Act 1968*, Cmnd 6733 (1977)

Home Office, *Crime in England and Wales 2008–09* (2009)

Home Office Criminal Law Policy Unit, *Fraud Law Reform: Government's Response to Consultations* (2006)

Law Commission Report No. 276, *Fraud* (2002)

Ministry of Justice, *Post-legislative Assessment of the Fraud Act 2006: Memorandum to the Justice Select Committee*, Cm 8372, 2012

Further reading

Allgrove, B. and Sellars, S. 'The Fraud Act 2006: Is breach of confidence now a crime?' (2009) 4 *Journal of Intellectual Property Law & Practice* 278

Attorney-General, *Guidance on the Use of the Common Law Offence of Conspiracy to Defraud* (2007)

Campbell, K. 'The Fraud Act 2006' (2007) 18 KCLJ 347

Collins, J. 'Fraud by abuse of position: Theorising section 4 of the Fraud Act 2006' [2011] Crim LR 513

Home Office, *Fraud Law Reform* (2004)

Home Office, *Fraud Law Reform: Government Response to Consultations* (2006)

Kiernan, P. and Scanlan, G. 'Fraud and the Law Commission: the future of dishonesty' (2003) 24 Co Law 4

Liberty, *Liberty's Response to the Home Office Consultation on Fraud Law Reform* (2004)

Ormerod, D. 'A bit of a con? The Law Commission's Consultation Paper on fraud' [1999] Crim LR 789

Ormerod, D. 'The Fraud Act 2006 – criminalising lying?' [2007] Crim LR 193

Ormerod, D. Case comment on GG [2009] Crim LR 433

Peck, M. *The Fraud Bill [HL]*, Research Paper 06/31, House of Commons Library (2006)

Sullivan, G.R. 'Framing an acceptable general offence of fraud' (1989) 53 JCL 92

Visit **www.mylawchamber.co.uk** to access tools to help
you develop and test your knowledge of criminal law,
including interactive multiple choice questions, practice
exam questions with guidance, annotated weblinks,
glossary flashcards, legal newsfeed and legal updates.

Use Case Navigator to read in full some of the key cases referenced
in this chapter with commentary and questions:

R v *Ghosh* [1982] EWCA Crim 2

17

Blackmail, burglary, going equipped, handling

Aims and objectives

After reading this chapter you will understand and be able to critique:

- the offence of blackmail
- the offences of burglary and aggravated burglary
- the offence of going equipped
- the offence of handling and the 18 ways in which it can be committed

Blackmail

Example

Arlene is a member of a student 'rag' committee. She visits shops in a local street near the university and says: 'If you don't put some money into this collecting box, we'll put stickers with "Rag Week – Not Exempt" on your window!' The implication is that the shopkeeper will be asked time and time again for money but won't be if he or she pays up now. Is this blackmail?

Blackmail is the making of an unwarranted demand with menaces with a view to gain (for the accused or another) or with intent to cause a loss: s 21(1), Theft Act 1968. 'Unwarranted' is defined in the same subsection as occurring *unless* the accused believed he had 'reasonable grounds for making the demand and believed that 'the use of the menaces [was] a proper means of reinforcing the demand'. It is not a problem that the demand was made implicitly. The demand is on the facts made within the definition, and there is also no problem that the accused has acted with 'a view to gain' for another. The issue is whether there were any 'menaces'. It is suggested that none existed because a trivial threat is not a menace; indeed, the word itself seems to be used when describing something worse than a threat. For a case on similar (but not identical) facts see *Harry* [1974] Crim LR 32.

Introduction

The term **blackmail** seems to derive from an old English word 'mail', meaning tribute or rents paid in work, goods, crops or base metal ('black'). If the threat is one of violence, blackmail may be classified both as a property offence and a crime against the person. By s 21(1) of the Theft Act 1968:

> [a] person is guilty of blackmail if, with a view to gain for himself or another or with intent to cause loss to another, he makes any unwarranted demand with menaces; and for this purpose a demand with menaces is unwarranted unless the person making it does so in the belief –
> (a) that he had reasonable grounds for making the demand; and
> (b) that the use of the menaces is a proper means of reinforcing the demand.

The framework is that a demand concerning an economic matter is blackmail, but there is an exception that it was warranted. This exception is the equivalent of lack of dishonesty in other parts of the Act.

Blackmail and theft may overlap. If the accused forces the victim to deliver property by threats, he has appropriated it within s 3(1) of the 1968 Act and he has also made an unwarranted demand with menaces. If, however, he does not just oblige the victim to hand over property but makes him act in such a way (e.g. makes him sell it) that in civil law the victim transfers to him the ownership of the item, the question whether he is guilty of theft depends on the present state of the civil law. If duress renders the contract voidable, the victim would transfer ownership and the property would belong to the accused. Therefore, he would not be guilty of theft. If the effect is to render it void, no property is transferred, and the accused is guilty. Because of the lack of clarity in the civil law, it is suggested that in this situation he should be charged with blackmail. In this offence the accused is guilty whether or not he has acquired the entire proprietary interests over the asset.

Getting property by threatening immediate force (for example, 'your money or your life') may be both blackmail and robbery. The usual charge is robbery. If the threat is to beat up the victim later, the facts do not constitute robbery because the victim was not put in fear of being 'then and there subjected to force'. In blackmail the demand must be to make a gain or loss, whereas in robbery the threat is made to get property. Blackmail occurs as soon as the demand is made, whereas robbery requires an appropriation. Blackmail requires menaces, whereas robbery is dependent on the threat or use of force. Accordingly, using force without threat is robbery, only because there must be menaces in blackmail. Menaces other than threats of immediate force cannot be robbery, only blackmail.

See pp 598–601 (Chapter 15) for an explanation of robbery.

The paradox of blackmail

If the accused asks his victim 'Will you give me money?', that is not a crime. If the accused said to his victim, 'I will tell your husband that you have been committing adultery', that too is no crime. If, however, the two are run together thus: 'Unless you give me money, I will tell your husband you are an adulteress', that is a crime. Two non-crimes added together create the offence of blackmail. This startling proposition is sometimes known as 'the paradox of blackmail'.

The *actus reus*

A major part of the *actus reus* is 'a demand with menaces'. Making the demand is sufficient. The prosecution need not prove that the victim complied or that the accused obtained anything by his threat.

Demand

The nature of the act or omission demanded is immaterial and it is also immaterial whether the menaces relate to action to be taken by the person making the demand. (s 21(2))

The word is defined as in ordinary language: ***Treacy* v *DPP*** [1971] AC 537 (HL). A demand couched in polite terms is still a demand. In ***Lambert*** [2010] 1 Cr App R 21 (CA) over the phone the accused said in the voice of the victim's grandson: 'They've got me tied up. They want £5,000, Nana.' Those words constitute a demand, illustrating that a demand may be made by words or impliedly. ***Lambert*** also illustrates that a person makes a demand even when it is not in his power to effectuate the threat, as when the accused could not harm the grandson because he was not in his power. Actions will suffice, at least if 'an ordinary reasonable man' would realise that a demand was being made: ***Collister*** (1955) 39 Cr App R 100 (CCA), a case which would probably be followed today. A demand is made when and where a letter containing it is posted (***Treacy***, by a three to two majority), and probably continues to be made until it is read by the victim (***Treacy*** five to zero, but *obiter*). A demand by fax will be made when the fax is sent.

It was once thought that blackmail could not be attempted because blackmail itself is in the nature of an offence of attempt, an attempt to obtain property. It seems absurd to charge attempting to attempt to obtain property. It is, however, suggested that such a charge does exist. In *The Theft Acts 1968–1978*, 7th edn (Sweet & Maxwell, 1995) 225, E. Griew wrote:

> [i]f a blackmailing demand is 'made' as soon as it is spoken or dispatched beyond recall, the possibility of a case of attempted blackmail is limited to fanciful situations such as where [the accused] is affected by a stammer or interrupted in the act of posting.

Blackmail is complete on the making of the demand. The offence is therefore committed when the accused makes the demand even though the victim is deaf.

Menaces

The term does not cover only threats of violence but anything detrimental or unpleasant, according to Lord Wright in the civil case of ***Thorne* v *MTA*** [1937] AC 797 (HL). Despite that wide definition, 'menaces' is stronger than 'threats'. It bears the meaning it has in ordinary language: ***Lawrence and Pomroy*** (1971) 57 Cr App R 64 (CA). By that, the court meant that there was no need for the judge to define the term to the jury, at least in the general run of cases. The Appeal Court was not saying that the ordinary-language meaning of 'menaces' was a detriment, for the term does seem restricted in ordinary language to threats of violence. In ***Garwood*** [1987] 1 All ER 1032, the accused, believing that the victim had burgled his house, aggressively demanded £10 'to make it quits'. The victim gave him the money. The Court of Appeal held that menaces did not exist unless they (a) would affect the mind of a reasonable person or (b) did affect the mind of the victim and the accused knew that his actions were likely to have such an effect. The accused, therefore, is guilty of blackmail against a timorous person, when a reasonable person would not have been frightened, only if the accused knew of the timidity. Trivial threats are not menaces: ***Harry*** [1974] Crim LR 32. A student who offered shopowners immunity from the activities of rag week in return for donations to charity was held by the trial judge not to have used menaces.

The Divisional Court ruled in ***Chambers* v *DPP*** [2012] EWHC 2157 (QB) that 'menace' in a statute had to be given an objective meaning: might the mind of an ordinary person of normal stability and courage be affected by the menace? The case involved a 'tweet': 'Crap! Robin Hood Airport is closed. You've got a week and a bit to get your shit together otherwise I am blowing the airport sky high.' The accused used his hashtag. The court held that on an objective assessment this was not a menace within s 127 of the Communications Act 2003. However, it stressed that the meaning of the word could differ from statute to statute and therefore the definition given does not necessarily apply to the Theft Act 1968, s 21(1).

Gain or loss

Gain and loss are to be construed as extending only to gain or loss in money or other property, but as extending to any such gain or loss whether temporary or permanent; and

(i) 'gain' includes a gain by keeping what one has, as well as a gain by getting what one has not; and

(ii) 'loss' includes a loss by not getting what one might get, as well as a loss by parting with what one had. (Theft Act 1968, s 34(2)(a))

'Gain' and 'loss' bear wide meanings. By s 21(1), above, the gain or loss need not be for the accused or to the victim. The gain or loss need not be permanent. It is sufficient that, for example, the accused is allowed to borrow something. However, this definition shows that blackmail protects economic interests. Accordingly, it is not blackmail where the accused extorts oral sex from the victim because that is not 'money or other property'. Similarly, it is not blackmail where the accused extorts a position of honour or release from lawful custody. English cases are few, but a threat to get back money owing to the accused falls within s 34(2)(a)(i) because it is a 'gain': *Parkes* [1973] Crim LR 358 (Crown Court); and a threat by a person suffering from osteoarthritis to a doctor that he would shoot him unless he was given a pain-killing injection was held to be blackmail in *Bevans* (1988) 87 Cr App R 64 (CA). The drug which the doctor used under threat was property. The outcome is somewhat stretched. What the accused really obtained was a pain-killing injection. While a demand for sex is not blackmail, a demand for money in return for not disclosing that the accused has indulged in such behaviour would be, because the gain would be money within s 34(2)(a). If the conduct falls within s 34(2) it does not matter that the accused's purpose was not economic gain. In *Bevans* the fact that he obtained relief from pain and not a financial advantage was irrelevant: there still was a 'gain' within the statute. Most cases involve gains to the accused but the definition extends to loss to others. A threat to the victim that she must throw away her wedding ring falls within (ii) above.

Permitted demands with menaces

It is not blackmail where the accused believes he has reasonable grounds for making the demand *and* believes the use of menaces is a proper means of reinforcing the demand. The requirement of belief relates to the accused's own belief. He does not have to believe on reasonable grounds that he has reasonable grounds for making the demand and so on: *Lambert* [1972] Crim LR 422 (Crown Court), where the accused threatened to tell the victim's employers of his affair with the accused's wife unless the victim paid him £250 for his rights to his wife. The jury acquitted him. As the 2010 *Lambert* case, above, shows, a demand can be unwarranted even though the victim owes the accused the money demanded.

In *Harvey* (1981) 72 Cr App R 139, the Court of Appeal ruled that 'proper' was wider than 'lawful' and held that whether a threat to kill, rape or maim (the accused not knowing that killing, raping and maiming are breaches of the criminal law) was a proper means of reinforcing the demand was a question for the jury, as was the question whether the accused believed that he had reasonable grounds. Bingham LJ said: 'It matters not what the reasonable man, or any man other than the defendant, would believe save in so far as that may throw light on what the defendant in fact believed.' However, the court held that the accused does not have this exception when he knows that what he proposes to do is a crime. Accordingly 'a fanatic or deranged idealist' has no defence when he knows or believes that what he is doing is a crime but is justified by the end to be achieved. The accused's own standards are not used to assess whether his means were 'proper'. Instead his standards are judged against those of society. The statute is not so worded, and *Harvey* may be incorrect on this point. It may be in respect of a petty offence that the accused believed that what he was doing was generally acceptable even though it was a crime. *Harvey* is inconsistent with *Lambert*'s thrust. If the accused is not guilty when he believes (whether on reasonable grounds or not) that he has reasonable grounds for making the demand, should he also not be guilty when he believes that the means of reinforcing the demand is proper? The Criminal Law Revision Committee, Eighth Report, *Theft and Related Offences*, Cmnd 2977, 1966, para. 123, goes against the 1972 case of *Lambert* in that it would have given a defence only when the accused's act was 'morally and socially acceptable'. The requirement of belief in social acceptability means in theory that if the accused has low standards of morality, he will not be convicted, but if he has high standards, he will be! The requirement of 'proper means' covers where the accused demands what he believes to be his: such would not be robbery but can be blackmail.

A case which might now be determined differently because of this exception is *Dymond* [1920] 2 KB 260. The victim of a sexual assault threatened to tell the town of the crime unless she was paid money. Before the Act she was guilty. After the Act she might have believed that she had reasonable grounds for making her demand and that her threat was a proper means of reinforcing the demand.

Mens rea

There are three elements:

(a) an intent to make a demand with menaces;

(b) a view to gain for himself or another, or intent to cause loss to another;

(c) either no belief that he has reasonable grounds for making the demand or no belief that the use of menaces is a proper form of reinforcing the demand.

'A view to' is a way of phrasing 'intent'.

Burglary

Introduction

This offence may be seen as one which is directed against 'criminal trespass' to the home and other buildings such as factories and shops. It applies even though the accused has not reached the stage of attempt for the purposes of theft. Mere preparation is not enough for attempted crimes but it may constitute **burglary**. At a deeper level it safeguards the feelings of those whose houses have been entered and one aim of the offence may be to prevent violence between householders and burglars. The *British Crime Survey* as reported in the *Home Office Statistical Bulletin*, HOSB 01/12, 2012, estimated that there were some 733,000 burglaries in the year ending September 2011, while there were 514,000 burglaries reported to the police.

By s 9 of the Theft Act 1968, as amended:

1 A person is guilty of burglary if –
   (a) he enters any building or part of a building as a trespasser and with intent to commit any such offence as is mentioned in subsection (2) below; or
   (b) having entered any building or part of a building as a trespasser he steals or attempts to steal anything in the building or that part of it or inflicts or attempts to inflict on any person therein any grievous bodily harm.

2 The offences referred to in subsection (1) above are offences of stealing anything in the building or part of a building in question, of inflicting on any person therein any grievous bodily harm therein, and of doing unlawful damage to the building or anything therein.

Until the coming into force of the Sexual Offences Act 2003, s 9(2) of the Theft Act, as amended by s 142 of the Criminal Justice and Public Order Act 1994, contained the words 'or raping any person' after 'grievous bodily harm'. The 2003 Act, s 63, replaced this form of burglary with a specific sex crime. The accused must be a trespasser on premises, he or she must intend to commit 'a relevant sexual offence on the premises'; and he or she must know, or be reckless as to whether, he or she is trespassing. A 'relevant sexual offence' includes rape.

The maximum penalty is 14 years' imprisonment in the case of burglary in a dwelling and 10 years elsewhere, such as a shop, after conviction on indictment. It is unclear whether the accused is guilty of the more serious offence only if he knows that what he entered was a dwelling. An aspect of the sentence is that an accused is guilty under s 9(1)(a) even though he has not yet even attempted to steal in a house and is liable to 14 years' imprisonment, yet if he does actually steal, the maximum sentence for theft is seven years. The difference between 'dwelling' and other buildings was introduced in 1991. There has not been a problem so far in distinguishing the two. A flat is undoubtedly a dwelling, but what of a house in the process of construction? It is uncertain whether the accused is subject to the higher penalty only if he knew that what he entered was a dwelling or whether it is sufficient that the building he entered was in fact a dwelling, whether he knew it to be so or not. Since, if the accused trespasses in a building and intends to steal (but has not yet stolen), he is guilty of burglary, a maximum sentence of 14 years looks excessive in relation to the harm.

In s 9(1)(a) it is not necessary to show that the accused intended to take a specific object or even that that object was in the building: *Attorney-General's References (Nos 1 and 2 of 1979)* [1980] QB 180 (CA). Section 9(1)(a) is really an inchoate offence. However, it seems that the accused must know or believe that the item or the person is in the building. In other words, at the time of the entry the accused must intend to commit the further offence against the person or thing who or which is therein. What is more certain is that an accused is guilty of burglary if he enters with intent to commit the relevant offence on a person or thing whom or which he will remove to another place where he will commit the offence.

Paragraphs (a) and (b) create separate offences. It was thought that a person charged under one paragraph may not be convicted under the other: *Hollis* [1971] Crim LR 525 (CA). However, the same fact situation may give rise to either offence: *Taylor* [1979] Crim LR 649 (CA). Therefore, a person only charged under s 9(1)(b) may be convicted under s 9(1)(a) because the former includes the latter when the accused is charged with entering with intent to steal or inflict grievous bodily harm: see *Whiting* (1987) 85 Cr App R 78. This ruling applies even though on the facts it very probably is that the accused did not intend the further offence until he was in the building. A person charged only under s 9(1)(a) cannot be convicted under s 9(1)(b).

For a definition of grievous bodily harm, see p 516 (Chapter 13).

In s 9(1)(a) the statute speaks of 'offence' of grievous bodily harm. It has been said that in s 9(1)(b), which does not mention the term 'offence', grievous bodily harm does not necessarily mean the offences found in ss 20 and 23 of the Offences Against the Person Act 1861: *Jenkins* [1983] 1 All ER 993, a Court of Appeal decision. (Section 18 requires the *causing* of grievous bodily harm. Presumably Parliament meant to include this offence but the paragraph is not well drafted.) It would certainly be strange if the accused could be guilty of this form of burglary if he accidentally or indeed lawfully inflicted the harm, for all other ulterior offences in burglary require intent. It was sufficient in *Jenkins* that the victim was so shocked by the accused's presence that the victim suffered a stroke. There was no need for an assault. The accused need not know that the victim was present. An alternative reading of *Jenkins* is to say that s 9(1)(b) does require an offence involving the infliction of grievous bodily harm but the prosecution need not specify the offence. The House of Lords reversed, but not on this point (***MPC v Wilson*** [1984] AC 242 (HL)). It is suggested that *Jenkins* should not be followed. If the accused inflicts grievous bodily harm on the victim without intending to do so and without being subjectively reckless, he is not guilty of a non-fatal offence. It would be strange if he were guilty of burglary on those facts. Moreover it seems to be a draftsman's error that the word 'offence' is omitted in s 9(1)(b), especially as it is found in s 9(1)(a). Finally, burglary is a serious offence but the ruling in *Jenkins* inappropriately makes it a strict one in respect of grievous bodily harm. The draft Criminal Code, 1989, cl 147, would clear up this difficulty by requiring an offence of grievous bodily harm.

A possible difficulty which requires resolution is whether the accused is guilty of burglary when he kills. Does 'inflicts' or 'inflicting' cover murder? A strict constructionalist would argue that the offence cannot be so read, but surely no court would so rule. A court might reason that the infliction of harm is a step on the way to killing and that the less (grievous bodily harm) includes the greater (murder).

Another difficulty is the omission of other offences. Fraud is not listed in s 9(2). Therefore, trespassory entry in order to obtain a watch by fraud is not burglary, though the likelihood is that the fraud may also be theft. This result is an unexpected outcome of *Gomez*. If there is no 'offence' there will, subject to the grievous bodily harm point, be no burglary. A simple illustration is where the accused enters a house as a trespasser with intent to resume possession of an item to which he has a lawful claim. There is no theft and thus no burglary.

The *actus reus*

(1) Building or part of one

By s 9(4) 'building' includes inhabited vehicles and vessels. The later part of sub-s (4) is to the effect that a vehicle or vessel remains inhabited even if no one is living there at the time of the burglary. An 'inhabited vehicle' includes a caravan. It is uncertain whether it covers a caravanette, a vehicle which can be used as an ordinary car or as a motorised caravan. It seems a little inept to consider the crime to be burglary when the caravanette is being used as a holiday home and theft when it is not. A Crown Court held in ***B & S v Leathley*** [1979] Crim LR 314 that a large freezer container resting on railway sleepers in a farmyard was a building. It does not include an articulated trailer used as a store despite its having electric power, steps up to it, and lockable shutters: ***Norfolk Constabulary v Seekings*** [1986] Crim LR 167 (Crown Court). Both the container and the trailer were being used as an extra store for shops. It does seem strange that burglary could be committed in the first instance but not the second. The accused would have been convicted had someone been living in the trailer, which would then have been an inhabited vehicle. A tent will not be a building, nor, it is thought, will a phone kiosk or a mobile shop or mobile library. A camper van is debatable. There may also be problems with buildings in the course of construction. Is a house being erected only a building when its roof is on?

'Part of a building' can also give rise to problems. In **Walkington** [1979] 2 All ER 716 (CA), the accused was guilty under s 9(1)(a) when he went into a three-sided partition in the middle of a shop where the till was. The area inside the partition was 'part of a building'. There need be no physical separation between one part of a building and another. A sign is sufficient. There may be difficulties in determining whether the accused has entered a part of a building. If he enters a shop, hides in a corner, comes out when the members of staff have gone home, and steals some items, is he a burglar? In the evening when he comes out, is his previously lawful presence converted into a trespassory entrance? Is he guilty only when he crosses some notional line?

(2) Entry

For both types of burglary the accused must enter a building or part of one as a trespasser. Edmund-Davies LJ in an extempore judgment said that the accused has to make 'an effective and substantial entry': **Collins** [1973] QB 100 (CA), the case of the 'socks maniac'. Fortunately or unfortunately this case, well known to generations of law students, has been deprived of some of its reasoning by the fact that entry into a building or part of one as a trespasser with intent to rape no longer is burglary. Nevertheless, its authoritativeness on the *actus reus* of trespass and the *mens rea* of the offence remains undiminished.

Collins [1973] QB 100 (CA)

The accused, having taken drink, determined upon sexual intercourse. He placed a ladder against an upper window, climbed up, and saw a naked woman on the bed. He climbed down and removed all his clothing except for his socks, which he left on in order to make a quick getaway. He climbed up and at some point he was beckoned in. Intercourse took place. The woman, who had earlier thought that the male was her boyfriend, discovered that it was not. The question was whether any part of his anatomy had made an effective and substantial entry (into the building) at the moment she beckoned him in. Until the Sexual Offences Act 2003 entry as a trespasser to commit rape was one form of burglary.

On the facts the answer was not certain.

The Court of Appeal in **Brown** [1985] Crim LR 212 widened the **Collins** definition by holding that the entry had to be effective, but need not be substantial. The question whether the entry was effective was for the jury. There was no need for the whole of the accused's body to be in the building: the top half was in a shop-front display, the bottom half outside. In **Ryan** [1996] Crim LR 320 the accused had his head and right arm inside a house but he was trapped by the neck by the window. The Court of Appeal applied **Brown**. There was evidence on which a jury could find that the accused had entered. The accused had entered a building even though only part of the body was within the building and even though he could not do anything 'effective' in the position in which he was caught. 'Effective' therefore does not mean 'effective to commit the ulterior offence'. This ruling seems right in principle. After all a person can be guilty of burglary with intent to rape when there is no person present in the building.

It is thought that 'effective' relates to the entry, not to the possibility of theft, etc. The problem is this: if the accused's intention is unlawful damage and he is in the same position as in *Brown* with the top half of his body in the building, is his entry therein effective for the purposes of the unlawful damage form of burglary? On the wording of the statute it would seem that an effective entry into the building is sufficient without the accused's going so far as to be in a position to effect his ulterior intent. *Ryan* confirmed this supposition. It may be that *Brown* and *Ryan* are leading to a position where entry need not be effective just as it need not be substantial.

It is questionable whether the accused has entered if he inserts a key into a lock or puts his hand through a window. Under the pre-Theft Act law it was sufficient if any part of the accused's body was inside. *Collins* and *Brown* scotch that notion (a charge of attempted burglary is available), but uncertainty remains whether inserting an implement into the premises is sufficient. It was under the old law if done in pursuance of the ulterior intent, not if done simply to gain access. Perhaps the same rule stands. The *Daily Telegraph*, 4 March 1979, notes a case where transvestites who hooked dresses through letter boxes pleaded guilty to burglary in a magistrates' court, even though no part of their bodies was through the letter boxes. This case may be inconsistent with *Collins* and *Brown*. The wording of the Act supports the view that the accused is not guilty: 'He enters' and 'having entered . . . *he*' (emphasis added). It must be the accused or at least some part of him who enters. It would be helpful if this point were resolved.

(3) As a trespasser

If an accused is pushed into a building, it is suggested that he does not enter as a trespasser because an involuntary entry is no trespass. Furthermore, one cannot 'enter' by an omission. Therefore, burglary is one of those offences which require an act.

Trespassing means entry without the consent of the owner, express or implied. The accused must enter as a trespasser. Stealing does not convert a lawful entry into trespass. On the facts of *Collins* the accused did not know that the woman had made a mistake and he was not entering as a trespasser. If the owner's daughter, as occurred in *Collins*, invites the accused into her bedroom for the purpose of sexual intercourse, he is not trespassing. The Court held that it was not only the occupier who could license entry but also her child. It will, however, be trespass if she had no authority to issue that invitation. In *Jones and Smith* [1976] 1 WLR 672 (CA), the occupier's son had general permission to enter the house but he did not have permission to come in with a friend to steal two televisions, despite the father's saying that his son would never be a trespasser in his house. The limits of permission were exceeded. The same rule applies in shops provided that the accused had the ulterior intent before entering the shop, it is thought. Therefore, many shoplifters are burglars. If the accused made his mind up to steal only on seeing the goods displayed in the shop, he is not guilty under s 9(1)(a) because he has not entered the shop, or a forbidden part of the shop, as a trespasser. However, it has for a long time been thought that the case was wrongly decided: for example, in *Taylor* [2004] VSCA 189 the Supreme Court of Victoria referred to the earlier decision of the High Court of Australia in *Barker v R* (1983) 153 CLR 338 as impliedly holding that *Jones and Smith* was wrongly decided and that the English court should have held that the boys' entry was not trespassory.

Jones and Smith may be inconsistent with *Collins*, where the accused should, applying the *ratio* of *Jones and Smith* (retrospectively), have been held to be a trespasser because he exceeded his permission to enter. (If so, it would not have mattered whether any part of his male anatomy had intruded into the daughter's bedroom before she invited him to engage in sexual congress. He had trespassed because he had exceeded the invitation to enter because he intended to rape (as the definition of burglary then provided) unless the victim consented.) Following *Jones and Smith* the accused in *Collins* intended to rape and should have been found guilty of burglary, no matter which side of the sill his naked male form was on at the time when the daughter invited him in. The point was not seen in *Collins*, which would seem to be incorrect on this issue. The son's friend could have been convicted of burglary with the son's being found guilty of being a secondary party to that crime. A possible reconciliation is to argue that in *Collins* the accused's intent was to rape, if necessary, whereas in *Jones and Smith* there was no 'if necessary' about the intent to steal. This definition is narrower than that in the tort of trespass. *Jones and Smith* looks like a simple theft case and the defendants should be so charged. This approach is supported by *Walkington* (above). The Court of Appeal would not have needed to debate whether the place the accused had entered was part of a building if all shoplifters are trespassers from their first entry into the building (if they have intent at that stage). The accused will be trespassing if he enters fraudulently, for example by falsely claiming that he is a police officer investigating crime. A person who would otherwise enter lawfully is a trespasser if he enters for an unauthorised purpose such as theft. Despite this criticism of *Jones and Smith* it remains authoritative.

It should be noted that permission to enter is usually impliedly given. One does not ask for permission to enter a shop in normal circumstances. One may also have implied permission from one's neighbour to enter his house to put out a fire or turn off taps when a thaw sets in.

Where the offence is of the s 9(1)(b) type, the attempt or full crime must be proved. Abstracting electricity is not theft. Therefore, the accused who enters a building as a trespasser and turns on the electric fire is not guilty of this form of burglary.

Mens rea

The accused must deliberately enter knowing that he is a trespasser: *Collins*; *Jones and Smith*. Perhaps recklessness is sufficient: *Collins*. The court in *Jones and Smith* was clear that recklessness was sufficient. Presumably recklessness means *Cunningham* recklessness [1957] 2 QB 396 (CCA). The conviction was quashed in *Collins* because the trial judge did not direct the jury as to the mental element in relation to trespass. Where the charge is under s 9(1)(a), there must also be the ulterior intent. No theft, GBH or criminal damage need occur. This further intent may be conditional. Under s 9(1)(b) the accused must have the *mens rea* of the completed crime, for example grievous bodily harm requires intention or recklessness in the *Cunningham* form as to the infliction of some harm, though see the discussion of *Jenkins*, above. The term 'with intent' in s 9(1)(a) would seem to require purpose, a narrower meaning than intent in murder (see Chapter 3). There is no explanation why s 9(1)(a) covers intent to commit criminal damage but s 9(1)(b) does not include the completed offences. Burglars often wreak havoc and one would have thought it prudent to include criminal damage in that paragraph.

Aggravated burglary (s 10)

This offence occurs when the accused has with him a firearm, imitation firearm, weapon of offence, or explosive. The time at which he must have it with him is the time when he stole, etc., if the burglary is the s 9(1)(b) type: *O'Leary* (1986) 82 Cr App R 341 (CA), which was applied in *Kelly* (1993) 157 JP 845 (CA). In the latter case the accused had a screwdriver with him which he used to gain entry and used it as a weapon of offence to threaten a young couple at the time of the theft of a video recorder. He was guilty. For criticism see J.C. Smith in his case comment [1993] Crim LR 765. In *Chevannes* [2009] EWCA Crim 2725 the weapon of offence was a squirtable bottle containing ammonia. In *Francis* [1982] Crim LR 363, the accused had a stick with him when he demanded entry into a house, but not when he was stealing from a room. He did not intend to steal when he entered the house. The Court of Appeal held that the crime was not aggravated burglary. For the purposes of the s 9(1)(a) type, the relevant time is that of entry. If the act of theft, etc. is over and the accused picks up a weapon in order to make good his getaway, it is suggested that the facts do not constitute burglary in its aggravated (or even simple) form. The burglary is complete once the underlying offence is complete. Nevertheless, it is possible that a court may hold that burglary is a continuing offence with the result that, contrary to what has been argued, the accused is guilty of this offence.

A weapon of offence is defined in s 10(1)(b) as 'any article made or adapted for use for causing injury to or incapacitating a person or intended by the person having it with him for such use'. A screwdriver falls within this definition, which is wider than that in s 1(4) of the Prevention of Crime Act 1953, in relation to offensive weapons, for it includes incapacitating articles such as handcuffs and rope (to tie up security guards) as suggested by the Criminal Law Revision Committee's Eighth Report, *Theft and Related Offences*, Cmnd 2977, 1966, 128. 'Firearm' includes an airgun: s 10(1)(a). An imitation firearm means 'anything which has the appearance of being a firearm' (s 10(1)(a)).

The prosecution does not have to show that the weapon of offence was intended to be used during the burglary. As Potts J said in *Kelly*, above, s 10 'is directed at the use of articles which aggravate the offence of simple burglary, so as to render the offender punishable with imprisonment for life'. In fact s 10 is not directed at the use of the article but at its presence. Section 10's aim is to prevent use by penalising a person who has a weapon on him. It is not directed at the spontaneous grabbing of a weapon. In *Stones* [1989] 1 WLR 156 (CA), Glidewell LJ said that: 'The mischief at which the section is clearly aimed is that if a burglar has a weapon which he intends to use to injure some person unconnected with the premises burgled, he may nevertheless be tempted to use it if challenged during the course of the burglary and put under sufficient pressure.' The court did not state why they thought this was the mischief, and the Criminal Law Revision Committee' Report considered aggravated burglary was aimed at instances where the accused intends to use or threaten the use of weapons in order to steal. The Committee also stated that this offence was aimed at deterring those whose activities frightened householders. Burglary with weapons can lead to violence and death. For these reasons the maximum sentence is life imprisonment. A conditional intent to use the firearm, etc., should the need arise, suffices for liability.

The accused is not guilty of s 10 if he uses a weapon to gain entry but does not take it in with him. In *Klass* [1998] 1 Cr App R 453 (CA) the accused smashed the window of a caravan with a pole; the occupier came outside and the accused beat him with the pole. These facts do not constitute aggravated burglary.

The accused must know that he has the prohibited article. If a knife is planted on him, he is not guilty. The outcome is the same if he has forgotten that he has a knife on him.

One last point on s 10: the prohibited articles form the mnemonic 'wife' – Weapon of offence, Imitation firearm, Firearm, Explosive!

Going equipped

Introduction

By s 25 of the Theft Act 1968 as amended by the Fraud Act 2006:

> [a] person shall be guilty of an offence if, when not at his place of abode, he has with him any article for use in the course of or in connection with any burglary or theft.

This offence is often known as **'going equipped'**. This term appears in the side-note. The crime is one aimed at stopping the accused from committing offences even before he has attempted to steal. Since one can attempt to go equipped, the range of s 25 together with its inchoate offence is broad. The crime could be called a 'double inchoate' or 'double preparatory' one. Moreover, there is no need for the accused to be on his way to a burglary or theft. If he has his bag marked 'swag' in the back of his car, he is guilty of this offence, even if, say, he is driving the car to the Channel Tunnel for a holiday.

Section 25 used to cover going equipped to cheat, but that offence is now governed by the Fraud Act 2006, which is discussed in the previous chapter.

Actus reus

The accused must have with him an article. Since the article need not be made or adapted for burglary or stealing it bears a wide meaning. The Criminal Law Revision Committee's Eighth Report, *Theft and Related Offences*, 1966, Cmnd 2977, which formed the basis of the Theft Act 1968, said that a getaway car was an 'article for use . . . in connection with any burglary, theft or cheat'. (As originally drafted s 25 included articles to be used for cheating. Many of the cases below involved cheating but their principles are not affected by the deletion of 'cheating' from s 25.) Where the accused had Kenyan five shilling pieces which were the same shape, size and weight as 50p pieces (but worth less) for use in slot machines, he was guilty of this offence: *Goodwin* [1996] Crim LR 262 (CA). (He would also be guilty of theft of any winnings.) A pair of pliers is an article: *Sekfall* [2008] EWHC 894 (Admin). A pair of gloves which a burglar uses to prevent his fingerprints getting onto panes of glass falls within the definition. A shirt is an article, so *In the matter of McAngus* [1994] Crim LR 602 (DC) one with a false label specifying wrongly that it was made in America was an article made for cheating. A bottle of wine was sufficient in *Doukas* [1978] 1 All ER 1061 (CA), which was approved in *Cook* (1988) 83 Cr App R 339. In *Minor v CPS* (1988) 86 Cr App R 378 (DC) a piece of tubing with which to syphon petrol was held by the Divisional Court to be an 'article'. In *Rashid* [1977] 2 All ER 237 (CA) a sliced loaf and some tomatoes fell within 'any article', though the court held the accused not to be guilty on the facts because train passengers would not care whether sandwiches were provided by British Rail or the steward personally, a questionable decision in the light of *Doukas* and *Cooke* [1986] AC 909 (HL). The question whether a customer knowing of the facts would have taken part in the fraud is one for the jury. It should not be assumed that people did not care whose sandwiches they were buying in a railway station buffet.

The phrase 'with him' may cover articles which the accused does not have on his person but does have under his control a short way off. The phrase 'has with him' seems to exclude articles picked up for immediate use. For example, if the accused was reconnoitring a home preparatory to burglary, he may not be guilty of this offence if he picks up some ladders which he has found in the garden. Nevertheless, the accused in *Minor v CPS* was guilty when he did not take the articles for syphoning petrol, a tube and two empty petrol cans, from his home but (apparently) found them near the car the petrol cap of which he was removing. It is suggested that the court did not give sufficient weight to the phrase 'has with him', which seems to require something more than picking up an article at or near the scene of the ulterior offence. He was not 'going equipped'. See also the previous section ('Aggravated burglary (s 10)') where the same phrase is discussed.

'Place of abode' means the accused's home and no doubt his garage.

The term 'theft' covers both theft and taking a conveyance (s 12). There is no need for any theft to occur. This definition is found in s 25(5).

The side-note says that the crime is 'going equipped' but there is no need for the accused to go anywhere with the article provided that he is not at his place of abode, as *McAngus*, above, demonstrates. The accused was in a bonded warehouse, selling shirts to two persons who happened to be undercover agents. *McAngus* also shows that the persons the accused intended to cheat need not in fact be deceived.

'In connection with' imports a requirement of proximity. In *Mansfield* [1975] Crim LR 101 (CA) it was held that having with one a driving licence in order to get a job in which one would have an opportunity to steal was too remote from the crime of theft. Thus one is not guilty under s 25(1). However, in *McAngus* showing shirts was proximate to cheating.

Mens rea

None is stated in the subsection, but it is assumed that the accused must intend to use the article in the course of or in connection with the burglary or theft, and he must know that he has the article with him. In *Hargreaves* [1985] Crim LR 243, the accused had a piece of wire adapted to clock up credits on gaming machines. The Court of Appeal held that he was not guilty when he had not decided whether to use it or not. The court did say that an intention to use the article, should a suitable opportunity arise, would be sufficient *mens rea*. A conditional intent is sufficient. If the accused intends to burgle only if he finds something worth stealing, this crime applies.

Perhaps the principal authority is *Ellames* [1974] 3 All ER 130 (CA). The accused had been involved in a robbery. He had with him masks, gloves and guns. It was held that he was not guilty. Section 25 deals with preparation for crime, not what occurs after crimes. The court said, however, *obiter*, that he would be guilty of the offence if he was storing the articles for use by others (i.e. 'use' need not be his use) or if the accused intended to use the article for any burglary. It did not have to be proved that the accused intended to use the article for a particular burglary, theft or cheat. The court said, moreover, that 'in connection with' covered using an article to escape from the scene of a crime.

Handling

Section 22(1) of the Theft Act 1968 stipulates:

> [a] person handles stolen goods if (otherwise than in the course of the stealing) knowing or believing them to be stolen goods he dishonestly receives the goods, or dishonestly undertakes or assists in their retention, removal, disposal or realisation by or for the benefit of another person, or if he arranges to do so.

This crime is aimed at making theft harder to carry out successfully and less profitable: *Tokeley-Parry* [1999] Crim LR 578 (CA). Before 1968 only 'receiving' was a crime. Now there are 18 ways in which the offence of **handling** may be committed: see *Nicklin* [1977] 2 All ER 444 (CA) – there is only one crime but several ways of committing it. A *dictum* to the contrary in *Bloxham* [1983] 1 AC 109 (HL) seems to be wrong.

The main division is that between receiving and the rest of the subsection: *per* Lord Bridge in *Bloxham*. The second part is often charged as a single count embodying such words of the subsection as are appropriate to the facts: *Deakin* [1972] 3 All ER 803 (CA), *Bloxham*. If one is charged under one part, one cannot be convicted under the other: *Nicklin*. The effect is that if it is unclear as to which form the handling took, the indictment should have separate counts for each possible form.

All the elements of the offence must be contemporaneous. In *Brook* [1993] Crim LR 455 (CA) a husband was given a bag containing stolen cheque books and cards by his wife. She said she had found the bag in a public lavatory. The accused left the bag in the back of the car until he decided what to do. The court in quashing his conviction held that he was guilty only if at the time of the handling he believed the goods to be stolen. A later handling could not be added to an earlier receipt. As ever, all the elements of the offence must be proved. If the prosecution cannot prove that the goods were stolen, there is no offence: *Defazio v DPP* [2007] EWHC 3529 (Admin). The victim had lost one of his credit cards. The accused alleged he had found it and put it into one of his drawers. He was not guilty of receiving the credit card because it could not be proven that the card was stolen.

The rationale of handling is that if handlers did not exist, there would be fewer thieves. Thieves would be less able to realise even part of the value of what they had stolen. In the words of the Criminal Law Revision Committee's Eighth Report, *Theft and Related Offences*, Cmnd 2977, 1966, para. 127, the aim behind the crime of handling is 'to combat theft by making it more difficult and less profitable to dispose of stolen property'. In some senses handling can be seen as a secondary offence to theft.

Actus reus

Handling is a term of art. There is no need for the accused actually to touch the goods, and he may touch the goods without being a handler. There is also no requirement that the accused makes a profit out of the transaction.

Section 34(2)(b)

By s 34(2)(b) of the Theft Act 1968:

> [g]oods, except insofar as the context otherwise requires, includes money and every other description of property except land, and includes things severed from the land by stealing.

The definition of 'goods' is very much like that of 'property' in theft except for land which cannot be handled unless severance has taken place. Things in action are covered: *Attorney-General's Reference (No. 4 of 1979)* [1981] 1 All ER 1193 (CA): balance in a bank account. They fall within 'every other description of property'. On the facts money taken from a bank account is 'proceeds' for the purposes of handling if the account derives (at least in part) from stolen money or other goods and if the money taken out is (again at least in part) derived from the proceeds of the stolen money or other goods. Accordingly if a thief pays money he has stolen into a bank account he has opened for this purpose and assigns the debt to the accused, the latter is guilty of handling if he has the *mens rea*. As will be seen, 'handling' covers retention, removal, disposal and realisation and any of these can happen to intangibles.

Section 24

By s 24 (as amended) of the Theft Act 1968 goods are stolen for the purposes of handling if any one of four conditions is fulfilled:

(a) they have been stolen contrary to s 1;

(b) they have been obtained by fraud contrary to the Fraud Act 2006;

(c) they have been obtained by blackmail contrary to s 21;

(d) they consist of money which has been dishonestly withdrawn from a wrongful credit (for the crime of dishonestly retaining a wrongful credit, see below);

(e) they have been subject to an act done in a foreign country which both was a crime in that country and, had it occurred in England, would have been theft, obtaining by deception (including obtaining a money transfer by deception) or blackmail in this country.

Goods which are stolen contrary to s 1 include those obtained by robbery and burglary provided that the robbery or burglary include a theft.

Condition (e) is aimed at preventing persons acting in England for goods stolen abroad. 'Country' is used in its conflict of laws sense. Therefore, Scotland is a foreign country because it forms a law district separate from England and Wales. The fact that the item was stolen within the meaning of the foreign law must be proved, even though theft, blackmail and fraud are probably crimes in every law district (the width may vary), especially within western Europe: *Ofori (No. 2)* (1994) 99 Cr App R 223 (CA). It is interesting to note that in a civil case where the parties do not plead foreign law, English domestic law is applied. It is uncertain why only these four crimes were chosen. One might have expected that the law would apply to the proceeds of any crime. If there is no theft within the s 24 definition such as occurs when the accused is insane, there is no offence of handling. (A charge of attempted handling is, however, possible.) The person who would otherwise be the handler is the thief. If the goods are not 'stolen' within the wide definition in s 24, there is no crime of handling. Other jurisdictions have a wider definition. For example, in New Zealand the goods which are the subject of handling need only be 'obtained by any crime'.

The offence of handling extends to the proceeds of the stolen goods: s 24(2). If the accused, a fence, sells an item, the money he receives is the proceeds of the sale, and he is the handler of that money. Similarly, if the thief steals a pig and slaughters it, the accused who receives the pork can be guilty of handling it. This means that the property the subject of the handling charge need not itself have been stolen.

The goods must actually have been stolen at the time of the offence. It is not enough that he believes them to have been stolen: *Haughton v Smith* [1975] AC 476 (HL). A person who mistakenly believes the goods to be stolen is therefore not guilty of handling – charge the attempt.

And see s 24(3):

[n]o goods shall be regarded as having continued to be stolen after they have been returned to the person from whom they were stolen or to other lawful possession or custody or after that person and any other person claiming through him have otherwise ceased as regards these goods to have any right to restitution in respect of the theft.

So goods once stolen cease to be so on restoration. They also cease to be stolen when taken into police possession: *Attorney-General's Reference (No. 1 of 1974)* [1976] QB 744 (CA). Possibly this was not the intention of Parliament, for 'restored' seems inappropriate to describe the situation where goods have come into the police's possession. The goods must have been reduced into the custody of the police.

Attorney-General's Reference (No. 1 of 1974) (CA)

> A constable reported that goods on the back seat of a car were stolen. He removed the rotor arm and kept watch on the car. The Court held that whether the officer had taken possession was a question for the jury, and that the answer depended on whether he had made his mind up to take possession so that they would not be removed, or whether he had an open mind and merely wanted to stop the driver getting away without being questioned. Accordingly, whether the property is reduced into possession depends on the intention of the person in control of it. (If the alleged handler is not guilty because the item has been reduced into the possession of the police, he may well be guilty of attempted handling or theft.)
>
> The case is to be distinguished from **Haughton v Smith** [1975] AC 476 (HL) on the ground that in that case the prosecution conceded, perhaps wrongly, that the goods had been reduced into the police's possession.

A similar case is *GLC Police Commissioner v Strecker* (1980) 71 Cr App R 113 (DC) – initialling goods to indicate that they had been stolen did not indicate possession.

Goods will cease to be stolen, for example, if the victim's property is sold to a bona fide purchaser for value without notice by the person who stole it.

'Handling'

Handling may be done in several distinct ways. It is easier to divide up s 22 than to look at it all at once. Handling means:

(a) receiving the goods (which was the form of this offence before the Theft Act 1968);

(b) undertaking the retention, removal, disposal or realisation of the goods by or for the benefit of another person;

(c) assisting in their retention, etc.; or

(d) arranging to do any of these things.

The phrase 'by or for the benefit of another person' applies to each preceding word denoting handling: that is, to retention, removal, disposal and revaluation (but not to receiving): *Sloggett* [1972] 1 QB 430 (CA). The other person must be someone who is not jointly charged with the handling.

'Receiving' means acquiring possession or control of the goods. The accused need not have physical possession of the goods. Finding stolen goods is not 'receiving' them: *Haider* (1985) LEXIS 22 March (CA). The accused must 'receive' them from another. One does not 'receive' when one is bargaining with a thief over the price. Receiving covers obtaining possession or control. One can control something without being in physical possession of it, as when one's employee has it. 'Retention' connotes a positive act such as concealment or misleading the police: *Kanwar* [1982] 2 All ER 528 (CA). It does not matter that the lies do not in fact deceive the police. It does not cover simply keeping goods after the accused has discovered that they have been stolen: *Broom v Crowther* (1984) 148 JP 592 (DC). It is thought, however, that receiving covers the situation where the accused has taken goods out of the thief's possession without consent.

'Disposal' covers dumping, giving away and destruction. It has been suggested that 'disposal' is limited to alienation of the asset but that is not the natural meaning. A buyer is not involved in the 'realisation' of stolen goods: *Bloxham*, above. The term does cover the sale or exchange of goods, according to *Bloxham*.

'Assisting' is based on a positive act of encouragement or helping. The fact that the accused's wife spent money on their flat does not mean that he assisted in the disposal of money stolen by the wife: *Coleman* [1986] Crim LR 56 (CA). He did not arrange or help in the disposal of the money. He would have been convicted, had he instructed his wife to use the money to buy certain items. 'Assisting' is thus a narrow term. In *Burroughes*, unreported, 29 November 2000, the Court of Appeal said that 'assisting' connoted concealing the goods, making them more difficult to identify, holding them pending disposal and doing some other act which was part of the chain of handling. It does not cover using stolen property, here a stolen heater, left in one's father's garage: *Sanders* (1982) 75 Cr App R 84 (CA). A mere refusal to answer police questions does not constitute 'assisting'. However, telling lies to the police is assisting in the retention of stolen goods: *Kanwar*, above.

Arranging to receive is really an inchoate offence. The accused is guilty of handling at an early stage. Before the Theft Act 1968 the accused would at most be found guilty of attempted receiving. Now he is guilty of the full offence of handling. Arranging to receive goods before they have been stolen does not amount to handling: *Park* (1988) 87 Cr App R 164 (CA), because 'guilty knowledge must exist at the time when the offence is committed'. The goods have to be stolen before the offence is committed. A charge of conspiracy to handle would succeed on these facts. Incitement and secondary participation (abetting) are other possible crimes. The court in *Park* also held that there must be specified goods which have been stolen before the crime of handling takes place. This holding means that a fence who has an arrangement with a thief to take whatever the latter brings along is not a handler. It is suggested that in the light of the policy of getting rid of fences *Park* is incorrect on this point.

May a person handle by an omission?

The words 'receiving', 'undertaking' and 'arranging' all seem to suggest a positive act, but 'assisting' covers omissions, provided that there is a legal duty to act: *Brown* [1970] 1 QB 105 (CA) – allowing another to place stolen goods on his property. The court ruled that '"retain" means "to keep possession of, not lose, continue to have"'. On the facts of *Brown* the accused was not guilty because he did not have a duty to reveal the fact that there were stolen goods on his premises. *Brown* was followed in *Pitchley* (1972) 57 Cr App R 30 (CA), where the accused was under a duty to withdraw money from his bank account and return it to the owner. He assisted in the retention of stolen money for the benefit of the thief, his son. The court held that 'retain' covers 'keep possession of'.

'Otherwise than in the course of stealing'

These words ensure that not every thief is also a handler but many will be. If the thief after having stolen assists another to sell the property, he will be a handler too. The phrase contemplates that the 'course of stealing' extends beyond the point and moment of theft. Only if the issue, whether the accused is really the thief or the handler, is live, need the phrase be proved by the prosecution: see *Cash* [1985] QB 801 (CA), approving *Griffiths* (1974) 60 Cr App R 14 (CA), and *Attorney-General of Hong Kong v Yip Kai-foon* [1988] AC 642 (PC). It is strange that Parliament's words are disregarded. In *Greaves* (1987) *The Times*, 11 July, it was held that it was a question for the jury whether a gap of 17 days between burglary and handling meant that the accused was not the burglar and so could be convicted of handling. Often a handler will also be a thief. If the accused sells stolen property, he appropriates it, and there is little difficulty in proving the *mens rea* of theft.

The phrase 'otherwise than in the course of stealing' does not solve every issue of the relationship between theft and handling. The problem is complex. In *Pitham and Hehl*

(1976) 65 Cr App R 45 (CA), a person took the two defendants to his friend's house and sold them the furniture of his friend who was in prison. Were the defendants guilty of handling? They could only be so if the seller had stolen the goods. The Court of Appeal held that he had appropriated the goods for the purposes of theft when he showed them the goods and invited them to buy. Accordingly, he was a thief. Therefore, the defendants could be convicted as handlers. The Court of Appeal in *Gregory* (1982) 77 Cr App R 41 considered this case to be one of 'instantaneous appropriation', yet *Pitham and Hehl* does look like a case where the course of stealing was not complete at the time when the defendants got their hands on the furniture. This case has come under much criticism. Cases concerning robbery suggest that stealing continues beyond the moment of appropriation but *Gomez* [1993] AC 442 (HL) seems to lay down the rule that appropriation is instantaneous. Another way of thinking is to say that even though appropriation is instantaneous, theft is not and can be a continuing activity. Therefore, 'in the course of stealing' extends beyond the moment of appropriation.

For a definition of bona fide purchaser, see p 580 (Chapter 15).

One difference between theft and handling is that the bona fide purchaser of goods is not guilty of theft when he later discovers that they were stolen (s 3(2)). However, if he gets the goods, finds out that they are stolen, and sells them, he is guilty of handling. When the accused handles, he appropriates for the purposes of theft, and so will be guilty of theft, but the phrase in brackets ensures that it is not this theft which matters for this purpose but the original theft.

Though not resolving all problems, the Court of Appeal in *Shelton* (1986) 83 Cr App R 379 held in accordance with previous practice: (a) if there is doubt as to whether the appropriate charge is theft or handling, both can be charged; (b) the jury should be directed that a handler may also be a thief but he cannot be convicted of both in relation to the same property at the same time; and (c) if the jury cannot agree whether theft or handling has been proved, the jury should be discharged. The Privy Council in *Yip Kai-foon* went a little further. If there are alternative theft and handling counts, the jurors should not be instructed to convict of the offence which it seems more probable to them that the accused committed. They should look first at theft. If theft is not proved beyond reasonable doubt, they should consider handling. If handling is not proved, the accused is not guilty of either, even though the jury thought that he was definitely guilty of one of them. *Yip Kai-foon* was applied by the Court of Appeal in *Foreman* [1991] Crim LR 702 and by the Divisional Court in *Ryan v DPP* (1994) 158 JP 485. The court in the latter case held that the prosecution does not have to disprove theft before the triers of fact can consider handling. Professor Smith's comments on the case [1991] Crim LR 704 are noteworthy:

> The jury may well be sure that the defendant is guilty either of theft or of handling but quite unable to decide which. In *Yip Kai-foon* the Privy Council rejected the solution which has been adopted in some jurisdictions of directing the jury to convict of the offence which they consider to be more probable. Such a solution 'detracts, or may be thought to detract, from the obligation of the jury to be satisfied beyond reasonable doubt that the accused is guilty of the particular offence, before they enter such a verdict'. But if that solution is objectionable, the one adopted is more so.
>
> Suppose that the jury, having been directed in accordance with the present decision, consider first the robbery charge, as instructed. They conclude that the defendant was probably guilty of robbery. But they are not satisfied beyond reasonable doubt so they decide, quite properly, to acquit of robbery. When they turn to the handling charge they must presume that he is not guilty of robbery; and, if they are quite satisfied that he must have been guilty of the one offence or the other, they are bound to conclude that he was guilty of handling. That is, they must convict him of the offence which they think he probably did not commit.

The result is entirely arbitrary. If the jury were to consider the handling count first they would reach the conclusion that he was guilty of the robbery. It is not clear why the theft or robbery count should be considered before that of handling except that the theft or robbery must have come first in time. The solution rejected in **Yip Kai-foon** of directing the jury to convict of the offence which they consider to be the more probable is, at least, rational and less potentially repugnant to the principle that the prosecution must prove its case.

(Of course since we do not know what happens in the jury room – and it is illegal to find out – the likelihood is that the jury will disregard the law and convict the accused of one offence or the other, hardly the best possible outcome.) Perhaps there should be a review of possible alternative verdicts under the Theft Acts. Professor A.T.H. Smith suggested the following in *Property Offences* (Sweet & Maxwell, 1994) paras 30–77: 'there can be no objection to a conviction of theft either on the basis that the defendant was the original thief, or that he stole when he acquired the goods as a handler. Where the jury is in doubt, therefore, they should convict of theft.'

Shelton points out that handling is a more serious offence than theft, which has a maximum penalty of seven years' imprisonment, and has a maximum of 14 years' imprisonment. Handling is a serious offence because handling encourages thieves. It is, in the words of the Criminal Law Revision Committee's Eighth Report, *Theft and Related Offences*, Cmnd 2977, 1966, para 127, 'to combat theft by making it more difficult and less profitable to dispose of stolen property'.

Mens rea

It must be proved that the accused handled the goods 'knowing or believing them to be stolen goods' and that he acted dishonestly. Knowledge must be proved at the time of the handling: **Atwal v Massey** [1971] 3 All ER 881 (DC). Finding out that the goods were stolen after receipt is not handling, but if the accused then, for example, sells them, he may have arranged for their disposal for the benefit of another and so handle. (It could also be theft, where there is no need for the disposal to be for the benefit of another.) The test of 'knowing or believing' is subjective: **Atwal**, **Stagg** [1978] Crim LR 227. Constructive knowledge, that is, that the accused ought to have known that goods were stolen, is insufficient: **Bellenie** [1980] Crim LR 137 (CA). The accused must know or believe that the goods are stolen, not that they may be stolen. Whether the accused did believe that the goods were stolen is a matter for the jury.

One of the leading authorities is **Hall** (1985) 81 Cr App R 160. The Court of Appeal held:

> [a] man may be said to know that goods are stolen when he is told by someone with first hand knowledge . . . that such is the case . . . Belief . . . may be said to be the state of mind of a person who says to himself: 'I cannot say I know for certain that these goods are stolen, but there can be no other reasonable conclusion in the light of circumstances . . .' What is not enough . . . is mere suspicion.

This definition of 'believing' appears narrow. Certainly suspicion is most definitely not belief. It does not include thinking that something is probably true, a state of mind which may be part of 'believing' in ordinary language. Thinking that something is more likely than not stolen is not 'believing': **Reader** (1978) 66 Cr App R 33 (CA). The test for belief is subjective. It is not to the point that a reasonable person might have believed that the goods were stolen: **Brook**, above. There is no need for this direction to be given if the issue is solely one of belief, for 'believing' is an ordinary word and its scope is a matter for the jury. Only if the distinction is between belief and suspicion is it 'prudent' to give it: **Toor** (1987) 85 Cr App R 116 (CA) following **Harris** (1987) 84 Cr App R 75 (CA). The point seems to be that 'knowing or believing' are simple words which do not in the ordinary run of things require an explanation.

As stated in **Hall**, suspicion is insufficient. **Grainge** [1974] 1 All ER 928 (CA) had so held previously. The Court of Appeal held in **Forsyth** [1997] 2 Cr App R 299 that judges should not instruct juries that 'mere suspicion' is insufficient *mens rea*, for doing so might lead them into thinking that 'great suspicion' is sufficient. Whatever the degree of suspicion, no amount of it constitutes 'believing'. 'Belief is the mental acceptance of a fact as true or existing.' 'Believing' is an ordinary English word which should be left to the jury. Nor is it enough if the accused acted with wilful blindness, even though in some areas of criminal law wilful blindness is treated as knowledge: **Griffiths** (1968) 49 Cr App R 279, above, **Pethick** [1980] Crim LR 242 (CA) and **Moys** (1984) 79 Cr App R 72 (CA). This ruling is contrary to the wishes of the Criminal Law Revision Committee's Eighth Report, *Theft and Related Offences*, Cmnd 2977, 1966, on which the 1968 Act is based. The members considered that an accused who bought items in a pub at a substantial undervalue ('ridiculously low price') did believe that they were stolen. In the words of the Criminal Law Revision Committee: 'the man . . . may not *know* [their emphasis] that the goods are stolen, and he may take the precaution of asking no questions. Yet it may be clear on the evidence that he believes that the goods were stolen.' In **McDonald** (1980) 70 Cr App R 288 (CA) it was held that a jury could infer that a TV set was known or believed to have been stolen when the accused paid a third of its shop price in a betting shop to an unnamed individual. The Court of Appeal in **Griffiths** said that a jury could infer knowledge or belief from suspicion. The cynic might say that the upshot of this law is that since the question of belief is one for the jury, there is nothing to stop a jury from inferring belief from suspicion.

It is handling if the accused knows or believes the goods to be stolen. He need not know the identity of the thief or of the owner or the nature of the goods: **McCullum** (1973) 57 Cr App R 645 (CA), where the goods were in a locked suitcase.

The question of dishonesty is settled by reference to **Ghosh** [1982] QB 1053 (see under 'Theft'). The three forms of 'not dishonesty' found in s 2(1) do not apply but they would presumably always be not dishonest under **Ghosh**. **Roberts** (1987) 84 Cr App R 117 (CA) held that the second stage of the **Ghosh** test does not have to be given in handling cases if there is no evidence that the accused did believe that he was not dishonest by the standards of ordinary decent people. On the facts **Roberts** looks incorrectly decided. His argument was that he was a businessperson who was trying to return two paintings for what he called a 'commission', and that this behaviour was not dishonest. The court held that no jury would find that selling back stolen items was not dishonest but it is suggested that the appellant's argument ought to be left to the jury. It will be rare for a person who is handling stolen goods, knowing or believing them to be stolen, not to be dishonest but if he is keeping stolen goods in readiness to hand them over to the police, he is not dishonest.

For more on the *Ghosh* definition of dishonesty, see pp 553–58 (Chapter 15).

Dishonestly retaining a wrongful credit

The Theft (Amendment) Act 1996 inserted s 24A into the Theft Act 1968 and in turn s 24A has been amended by the Fraud Act 2006. By it a person is guilty of a crime if 'a wrongful credit has been made to an account kept by him or in respect of which he has any right or interest, he knows or believes that the credit is wrongful, and he dishonestly fails to take such steps as are reasonable in the circumstances to secure that the credit is cancelled'. Section 24A(2A) as inserted by the Fraud Act 2006 reads:

> A credit to an account is wrongful to the extent that it derives from –
> (a) theft;
> (b) blackmail;
> (c) fraud (contrary to s 1 of the Fraud Act 2006); or
> (d) stolen goods.

It does not matter that the account was overdrawn before or indeed after the credit arrived in it.

The principal situation covered by s 24A is where one accused has procured the crediting of another accused's account, but it also covers the situation where one accused has procured the victim to credit his account. In the latter scenario, if the accused does not take the steps mentioned, he is guilty of this offence. In both scenarios the accused is guilty even though he has done nothing in respect of his account. Presumably he will avoid liability if he tells the police about the credit. It is suggested, however, that simply spending the money on wine, women (or men) and song does not amount to steps securing that the credit is cancelled. It is a pity that this interpretation is not expressly stated in s 24A.

The maximum sentence is 10 years' imprisonment.

Summary

- *Blackmail*: Blackmail contrary to s 21(1) of the Theft Act 1968 is based on a demand with menaces: 'a person is guilty of blackmail if, with a view to gain for himself or another or with intent to cause loss to another, he makes any unwarranted demand with menaces; and for this purpose a demand with menaces is unwarranted unless the person making it does so in the belief –
  (a) that he had reasonable grounds for making the demand; and
  (b) that the use of the menaces is a proper means of reinforcing the demand.'

- *Burglary*: Burglary contrary to s 9 of the Theft Act 1968 comprises two offences: entering a building or part of one with intent to steal, commit grievous bodily harm or cause criminal damage; and having entered a building or part of one, the accused steals, attempts to steal, commits criminal damage or attempts to cause criminal damage. A building must, it seems, have some sort of permanence.

- *Going equipped*: This is the crime of having with one 'any article for use in the course of or in connection with any burglary or theft' provided that the accused is not 'at his place of abode'. It is a crime contrary to s 25 of the Theft Act 1968 as amended by the Fraud Act 2006. It resembles inchoate crimes discussed in Chapter 10: the defendant is guilty even though she has not (as yet) burgled, stolen or committed an offence of cheating.

- *Handling*: Handling is contrary to s 22(1) of the Theft Act 1968. There are 18 ways of committing this offence, as close reading of s 22(1) reveals. 'Handling' is a term of art: one can handle stolen goods without touching them. 'Goods' are defined in s 34(2)(b) as including 'money and every other description of property except land, and includes things severed from the land by stealing'. 'Stolen' is wider than theft and covers obtained by fraud and by blackmail. The phrase 'otherwise than in the course of stealing' exempts the thief during theft from the crime of handling.

References

Reports

Criminal Law Revision Committee, 8th Report, *Theft and Related Offences*, Cmnd 2977 (1966)

Home Office Statistical Bulletin, *Crime in England and Wales: Quarterly Update to September 2011*, HOSB 01/12 (2012)

Books

Griew, E. *The Theft Acts 1968–1978*, 7th edn (Sweet & Maxwell, 1995)

Smith, A.T.H. *Property Offences* (Sweet & Maxwell, 1994)

Journals

Smith, J.C. Case comment on *Ryan* [1991] Crim LR 704

Smith, J.C. Casenote on *Kelly* [1993] Crim LR 765

Further reading

Green, S.P. 'Thieving and receiving: Overcriminalizing the possession of stolen property' (2011) 14 New Crim LR 35

Lamond, G. 'Coercion, threats and the puzzle of blackmail', in D.P. Simester and A.T.H. Smith (eds.), *Harm and Culpability* (Oxford University Press, 1996)

Reville, N.J. 'Mischief of aggravated burglary' [1989] NLJ 835

Spencer, J.R. 'Handling, theft and the mala fide purchaser' [1985] Crim LR 92 and 440

Williams, G. 'Handling, theft and the purchaser who takes a chance' [1985] Crim LR 432

There is a symposium on blackmail in (1993) 41 UPaLR.

Visit **www.mylawchamber.co.uk** to access tools to help you develop and test your knowledge of criminal law, including interactive multiple choice questions, practice exam questions with guidance, annotated weblinks, glossary flashcards, legal newsfeed and legal updates.

Use Case Navigator to read in full some of the key cases referenced in this chapter with commentary and questions:

R v *Ghosh* [1982] EWCA Crim 2

18

Criminal damage

Aims and objectives

After reading this chapter you will understand and be able to critique:

- the 'simple' and 'aggravated' offence of criminal damage
- arson: criminal damage by fire
- the definitions of damage, destruction, property and belonging to another
- the lawful excuse defence
- the mental element
- the *Miller* principle
- the offence of custody or control of anything with intent to destroy or damage
- the offence of threatening to destroy or damage property

Introduction

Criminal damage is based on the 1971 Act of the same name, by which Parliament simplified the law. It is normally seen as an offence against property dealing with vandalism and suchlike, but it is in part a crime which deals with the protection of people and can deal with the maintenance of public order, as occurs when rioters burn down American-owned coffee shops. There were 661,000 criminal damage offences reported to the police in the year ending September 2011, a year which included the riots in various English cities, a decline nevertheless of 11 per cent on the previous year.

The 'simple' and 'aggravated' forms

It is an offence for a person without lawful excuse to destroy or damage property belonging to another with intent to destroy or damage the property or being reckless as to whether that property is destroyed or damaged: s 1(1). The maximum sentence is 10 years' imprisonment. This type of crime is sometimes known as the 'simple' form of criminal damage. The 'aggravated' form, with a maximum of life imprisonment, is the simple form of the offence without the restriction on who owns the property (the defendant may own it or he may damage the victim's property with the latter's consent, as in *Merrick* [1996] 1 Cr App R 130

(CA)) but with the addition of a further *mens rea*: the accused must also intend by the destruction or damage to endanger another's life or he must be reckless as to whether life is endangered thereby: s 1(2). There is no need to show that life was in fact endangered: *Parker* [1993] Crim LR 856 (CA). This aggravated form could be seen as an offence against the person, rather than an offence against property. Recklessness as to whether life is endangered is sufficient.

Furthermore the defence of lawful excuse, s 5, does not apply to the aggravated form (including arson contrary to s 1(2)). Nevertheless, though s 5 does not apply to s 1(2), that subsection still provides for a defence of lawful excuse. The sort of happening which would be covered by s 1(2)'s 'lawful excuse' provision would be where the accused uses a weapon in self-defence against the victim, whose life he thereby intends to endanger. There would be a lawful excuse if the accused damaged the article. No doubt this behaviour would rarely be charged as criminal damage. (A man the author once met on holiday had been tried at the Old Bailey for murder when he killed a burglar with a spear he had grabbed off his wall. If the spear had been broken, he could nowadays be charged under s 1(2), but he would have this defence.) It should be noted that while there is no general defence of endangering life, s 1(2) creates an offence when the endangering is caused by criminal damage.

Arson

If the destruction or damage is caused by fire, the offence is **arson**: s 1(3). The fire need not be a major one: it suffices that the slightest damage is caused by the fire. The maximum penalty is life imprisonment. Section 1(3) reads: 'An offence committed under this section by destroying or damaging property by fire shall be charged as arson.' Section 1(3) applies to both s 1(1) and s 1(2). The charge is arson contrary to s 1(1) (or s 1(2)) and s 1(3) of the Criminal Damage Act 1971). The restrictions in s 1(1) and s 1(2) also apply where the cause of the damage is fire, for instance if the property belongs to the accused, there is no charge possible under s 1(1) and s 1(3). It should be noted that the maximum sentence in s 1(3) applies even though the sole difference between the 'simple' offence and s 1(3) is that the damage was caused by fire. Presumably the accused must intend to cause, or be reckless as to causing, damage by fire. If, for instance, he intends a bomb to explode, but the damage is in fact occasioned by fire, he is not guilty under s 1(3). This point, however, is not settled. The Law Commission in its Report No. 29, *Offences of Damage to Property*, 1970, recommended the abolition of the separate offence of arson, but Parliament disagreed. The charge of arson was retained because of the public's desire to stigmatise the defendant who set light to property. Another reason was given by the Commission, the Report of which led to the 1971 statute. Fires were often started by the mentally ill. Finding them guilty of an offence for which the maximum sentence was life imprisonment could result in safeguarding the public. The contrary argument on this point is easily put: pyromaniacs by definition cannot stop themselves causing fires and prison is unlikely to cure them.

Despite the mandatory words in s 1(7) ('shall be charged as arson'), according to the Court in *Drayton* [2005] EWCA Crim 2013 there is no need to charge criminal damage by fire as 'arson'. It is sufficient that the charge is one of criminal damage by fire.

Steer

In the aggravated form the prosecution must show that the destruction of or damage to property caused the danger to life; it is not sufficient to show that the danger to life resulted from the act which caused the damage or destruction.

Steer [1988] AC 111 (HL)

> The accused went to the home of his former business partner, against whom he had a grudge, and fired several shots at the house, breaking the bedroom window. No injuries were caused. He was held not guilty of s 1(2). That subsection applies only if the property damage caused life to be endangered. Danger came from the shots, not from the damage to property. The subsection applies only if it is 'by the . . . damage' that the danger is caused.

The result would have been different if flying glass had been proved to be dangerous to life. Lord Bridge said: 'It is not the match, the flaming firebrand or other inflammatory material which the arsonist uses to start the fire which causes danger to life; it is the ensuing conflagration which occurs as the property which has been set on fire is damaged or destroyed.' A similar case is *Asquith* [1995] 1 Cr App R 492 (CA), which is called *Webster* in [1995] 2 All ER 168. The defendants pushed a very heavy stone off a bridge on to a train. The stone caused bits of the roof to fall on the passengers but did not itself come through the roof. In the words of Lord Taylor CJ:

> The effect of the statute may be thought strange. If the defendant's intention is that the stone itself should crash through the roof of a train or motor vehicle and thereby directly injure a passenger or if he was reckless only as to that outcome, the section would not bite . . . If, however, the defendant intended or was reckless that the stone would smash the roof of the train or vehicle so that metal or wood struts from the roof would or obviously might descend upon a passenger, endangering life, he would surely be guilty. This may seem to many a dismal distinction.

On the facts if the defendants intended to endanger the lives of the passengers by the stone, they were not guilty of intending to endanger life but they were reckless as to endangering life by bringing down the roof.

Steer was distinguished in *Dudley* [1989] Crim LR 57 (CA). The accused threw a fire-bomb at the victim's house. The fire was quickly extinguished, with only trivial damage caused. The accused was found to be guilty of the aggravated offence. It did not matter that only minor damage was caused. The defendant did act with the intention to endanger life. That is, indeed, how this offence is defined: by reference to intent or recklessness, not by reference to the harm caused. *Steer* was a case where the actual and intended damage were the same, and the accused did not have the further or ulterior intent specified in s 1(2).

Wenton [2010] EWCA Crim 2361 is a case with unusual facts and gives rise to a demonstration in the art of construing statutes. D smashed the window of a house with a brick and then threw a canister of petrol and a piece of burning paper through. Five people were in the house. The 'petrol-like fluid' in the canister did not catch fire. He was charged with damaging property with intent to endanger life or being reckless as to whether life was endangered contrary to s 1(2) of the Criminal Damage Act 1971. On the indictment it was stated that the criminal damage 'simple' offence on which the danger to life was based was the breaking of the glass through the throwing of the stone. It was held that the accused could not be guilty of the 'aggravated' offence through his throwing of the stone because the act of throwing it did not threaten the inhabitants of the house: it was the throwing of the petrol canister and the lighted taper which did, but that was not the charge. The risk to life was from the fire, not the stone.

The outcome would have been different if the accused's two acts of throwing were inseparable, part of the same transaction. The Court accepted this law in principle but said that on the facts the principle did not apply because 'the incident of damage [by the stone] was unrelated to the incident that gave rise to the risk of endangerment to life'.

So, on the facts D broke the window to facilitate the danger to life (by throwing the canister through the broken window) but did not break it in order to endanger life. Cf. **Dudley**. There the accused damaged a window by throwing a petrol bomb through it; he was guilty because he damaged property in order to endanger life. The distinction in the facts, seemingly narrow, leads to different results, guilty in **Dudley**, not guilty in **Wenton**; and that result is because of the wording in s 1(2). As Leveson LJ said: '. . . whoever was responsible for drafting the indictment in this case failed to pay proper attention to the terms of the Act.'

Actus reus

In both the simple and aggravated forms, part of the *actus reus* is destruction or damage to property of a tangible nature. In the 'simple' form the property must belong to another. 'Belonging to another' is defined in such a way that, although the accused may own and possess the property, it belongs to someone else for the purposes of this offence. Accordingly, the accused can be guilty of the 'simple' offence in some situations, even though he owns the property. When property belongs to another is defined in s 10(2):

(a) Where another has custody or control. An example is **Pike v Morrison** [1981] Crim LR 492. A person who ran his mother's home could be said to have custody of it (*obiter*). It is not certain whether 'custody' is preferred to 'possession' which appeared in the 1968 Theft Act. It is suggested that 'custody' means that the accused has physical control over the item, whereas 'control' means that he has the right to tell others what to do with it.

(b) Where a person has a proprietary right or interest over the property (but not where that right or interest arose from a contract for the sale of land).

(c) Where a person has a charge over the property. (A charge is a proprietary right or interest such as a mortgagor has: this exception falls within the second one.) Presumably restrictive covenants and equitable easements are included.

(d) By s 10(3), property subject to a trust belongs to any person having a right to enforce the trust.

(e) Subsections 5(3) and (4) of the Theft Act 1968 do not apply to criminal damage.

Points (b), (c) and (d) relate to civil law, to which the reader is referred.

If damage is to property which falls outside these circumstances, the accused will not be guilty of the 'simple' offence if he destroys or damages his own property. For example, he smashes a bottle of wine he has just bought: not guilty. Similarly, if he crashes his own car to claim the insurance – not guilty of this offence: the charge would be obtaining property by deception. The accused is not guilty because the insurers have no proprietary interest in the car. He would, however, be guilty of the more serious offence under s 1(2), (3), if he set light to his own car intending to endanger the life of a joy-rider: the restriction to 'belonging to another' applies to s 1(1), not s 1(2). It should be realised that a person's dishonesty is irrelevant in criminal damage.

What is **property**? There is a wide definition in s 10(1). The following should be noted:

(a) unlike the Theft Act 1968, there is no difference between land and other property with the result that agricultural land which the accused has incorporated into his garden has been criminally damaged;

(b) intangible property is excluded – the essence of criminal damage is damage to a physical thing, though the damage itself need not be tangible (but see below for computer programs);

(c) also excluded are wild mushrooms and wild flowers, fruit and foliage – one can squash wild mushrooms as much as one likes: there is no test of commercial purpose as exists in the Theft Act;

(d) the same rules apply to wild animals as occur in the Theft Act (badgers are not property within the 1971 Act when they are lured into traps: *Cresswell* **v** *DPP* [2006] EWHC 3379 (Admin) (DC));

(e) it would seem that water flowing naturally over or under land cannot be criminally damaged, but it can be if reduced into possession, for example, in a reservoir;

(f) confidential information such as trade secrets cannot be damaged. It is not property.

A simple illustration is the printed circuit card in *Cox* **v** *Riley* (1986) 83 Cr App R 291 (DC). Other examples occur in the following paragraphs dealing with destruction and damage. Neither of those terms is defined in the Criminal Damage Act or in the Law Commission Report No. 29, *Offences of Damage to Property*, 1970, on which the statute is based.

Destroy

This term does not add anything to 'damage'. If one destroys property, one damages it. It may have been included to forestall the argument that 'damage' does not cover 'destroy'. The Divisional Court in *Barnet LBC* **v** *Eastern Electricity Board* [1973] 2 All ER 319, a case on town and country planning legislation, stated that: 'The act of destruction must be one having at least the elements of finality and totality about it.' Killing a pet is destruction of it.

Damage

Property is damaged if it is rendered imperfect or inoperative, or if the harm impairs its usefulness or value: *A (A Juvenile)* **v** *R* [1978] Crim LR 689 (Crown Court) Spitting on the back of a police sergeant's uniform was not criminal damage because the saliva could be wiped off. The raincoat was service issue, designed not to be affected by the British weather. (No doubt it would be different with a silk coat or if dry-cleaning were needed.) However, the Divisional Court in *Roe* **v** *Kingerlee* [1986] Crim LR 735 disagreed with the reasoning in *A* **v** *R*. The court held that magistrates were wrong to hold that graffiti made from mud smeared on the walls of a police cell could not amount to damage, even though the mud could be removed easily. In *Morphitis* **v** *Salmon* [1990] Crim LR 48, the Divisional Court held *obiter* that damage included 'not only permanent or temporary physical harm but also permanent or temporary impairment of value or usefulness'. Scratching a scaffolding bar was not criminal damage but merely an incident of normal use of scaffolding components. The accused could have been charged with damage through dismantling the barrier of which the bar formed a part. Some examples are:

Faik [2005] EWCA Crim 2381 – stuffing a blanket down the lavatory and flushing the cistern. The blanket was wet and had to be dried and cleaned; the police cell and two adjoining cells had to be cleaned. The accused was guilty of criminal damage.

Henderson, unreported, 29 November 1984 (CA) – rubbish dumped on a building site. The court applied the *Concise Oxford Dictionary* definition of damage as 'injury impairing value or usefulness'. The value and usefulness of the land were both impaired, even though the land beneath was not harmed by the rubbish.

Cox v *Riley* (above) – damaging a plastic circuit card thereby erasing a computer program (the program was intangible and not covered by the Act). D. Ormerod, *Smith and Hogan's Criminal Law*, 13th edn (Oxford University Press, 2011) 1013, states: 'what is contemplated . . . is some *physical* harm, impairment or deterioration. This will usually be capable of being perceived by the senses' (emphasis in original).

Whiteley (1991) 93 Cr App R 25(CA): a computer hacker gained access to a system called JANET, the Joint Academic Network, which links institutions of higher education. He got to know his way around the files which were stored on large metal magnetic disks. He added and deleted files and changed the password of authorised users. He wiped the files containing his use of the system and even deleted the program designed to catch him. He was charged with, among other things, damaging the disks by altering their magnetic particles. He contended that the functions of the disks were not altered by him; they did not suffer physical damage; any destruction or damage was to information on the disk; such damage did not damage or impair the usefulness of the disk. Lord Lane CJ in a reserved judgment in the Court of Appeal held:

> [w]hat the Act requires . . . is that tangible property has been damaged, not necessarily that the damage itself should be tangible . . . [T]he magnetic particles upon the metal discs [*sic*] were a part of the discs and if the appellant was proved to have intentionally and without lawful excuse altered the particles in such a way as to cause impairment of the value or usefulness of the disc to the owner, there would be damage . . .

He continued by summarising the law:

> Any alteration to the physical nature of the property concerned may amount to damage. Whether it does so or not will depend upon the effect that the alteration has had upon the legitimate operator . . . If the hacker's actions do not go beyond, for example, mere tinkering with an otherwise empty disc, no damage would be established. Where, on the other hand, the interference with the disc amounts to an impairment of the value or usefulness of the disc to the owner, then the necessary damage is established.

Note the emphasis on the effect of the alleged damage to the operator.

The difficulties which arose in *Cox* v *Riley* and *Whiteley* are in part dealt with by s 10(5) as amended:

> For the purpose of the this Act a modification of the contents of a computer shall not be regarded as damaging any computer or computer storage medium unless its effect on that computer or computer storage medium impairs its physical condition.

The effect on *Cox* v *Riley* was to make the accused now guilty under this Act and not the 1971 one, if the damage did not impair the physical condition of the circuit card. The offence under the 1990 Act can only be committed intentionally, whereas criminal damage may be committed recklessly. In the event of both charges being possible, there is a higher penalty for criminal damage on indictment than for conviction of computer misuse. It might have been more sensible to amend the Criminal Damage Act 1971 directly than to declare in a different statute that the accused is not guilty under that Act. *Cox* v *Riley* and *Whiteley* are now crimes under the revised s 3 of the Computer Misuse Act 1990: 'unauthorised acts with intent to impair or recklessness as to impairing, operation of computer etc.' If the effect of the act of the accused is to change a program which leads to physical damage, that damage can be prosecuted against under the 1971 Act.

The court in *Whiteley* approved *Tacey* (1821) 168 ER 893 and *Fisher* (1865) LR 1 CCR 7 from before the 1971 Act. *Fisher* was also approved in *Cox* v *Riley*: tampering with part of a machine was malicious damage and would now be criminal damage. In **Lloyd v DPP** [1992] 1 All ER 982 (DC) the cutting of two padlocks which secured a wheel-clamp to his car, which he had parked in a private car park which had notices stating that clamps were in use and removable only on payment of a fine of £25, was criminal damage. Could it be argued that by attaching the clamp to the wheel the clampers had rendered the car unusable and thus criminally damaged it? It is thought not. The accused has been deprived of use of his car, and that is not criminal damage. If the accused threw away the key to a shop door, one would not say that the shop has been criminally damaged. There was no damage to the car in **Lloyd v DPP** despite the fact that it could not immediately be driven away. The case from this viewpoint resembles the next case. Had there been damage, the question would then be: did the clampers have a lawful excuse? See below. The same principles apply to the situation where the landowner arranges for a sticker to be placed on a trespassing driver's windscreen. In fact this also happened in **Lloyd v DPP**. The sticker cannot be removed without considerable time and effort. The court held that this was not criminal damage. In **Drake v DPP** [1994] Crim LR 855 the Divisional Court justified this holding by saying that the use of stickers and wheel-clamps did not interfere with the integrity of the car.

In **Tacey** removing an essential part from a machine was sufficient even though the part, an iron bar, could easily be put back in position. Also amounting to criminal damage would be so running a machine that impairment results (**Norris** (1840) 173 ER 819) and trampling on grass (**Gayford v Chouler** [1898] 1 QB 316 (DC)). However, simply trespassing on land will not amount to criminal damage: **Eley v Lytle** (1885) 2 TLR 44. In the case of arson, it is presumably sufficient that, for example, wood is charred, but it will not be criminal damage if it is blackened, though after **Whiteley** (above) the result may be different depending on the owner's use for the wood. Perhaps the result in **Henderson** (above) would have been different if the land was not about to be used for building but was waste.

Six other matters should be noted:

(a) Damage need not be permanent, nor need it result in a loss which can be quantified in monetary terms. In **Hardman v Chief Constable of Avon** [1986] Crim LR 330, a Crown Court held that there was damage even though the pavement on which CND members had painted human silhouettes on Hiroshima Day could be restored to its original condition. A high pressure hose was needed to remove the silhouettes.

(b) **Hardman** also demonstrates that a good motive does not excuse.

(c) The question whether property is damaged or not is one for the triers of fact. Whitewashing over National Front slogans does not necessarily amount to damage: **Fancy** [1980] Crim LR 171 (DC), which was approved in **Seray-Wurie v DPP** [2012] EWHC 208 (Admin). Another court could, however, rule that it was. The wall was already white and it is arguable that there was no intent to cause criminal damage, but the accused's *mens rea* does even then depend on the uncertain scope of 'damage'. It is uncertain also how far **Fancy** extends. If the accused improves something, can it be said that he has criminally damaged it?

(d) **Seray-Wurie** held that it was irrelevant that the accused thought he was improving and not damaging the property. Banksy's graffiti are criminal damage, even if he and others think that they are life-enhancing and even though value is added to the wall.

(e) The method of destruction or damage does not matter. It could for instance be chemical, as in dissolving something in an acid bath, or it could be by fire, as in burning a house down.

(f) The same fact situation can give rise to both theft and criminal damage, as when the accused takes the victim's car and sets fire to it.

The defence of lawful excuse (s 5)

Apart from any other defence the accused may have, such as mistake, he may have a lawful excuse. For the purpose of the 'simple' offence, s 1(1), s 5 grants him a defence if:

(a) he believed that the person whom he believed entitled to consent to the destruction or damage of the property would have consented, had he known of the circumstances (s 5(2)(a)); *or*

(b) he acted 'in order to protect' the property of himself or another, or a right or interest in property and he believed that:
(i) the property, right, or interest was in immediate need of protection; and
(ii) the means adopted were reasonable, having regard to all the circumstances (s 5(2)(b)).

An example of s 5(2)(a) is **Denton** [1982] 1 All ER 65 (CA). The accused set fire to a cotton mill on the request of his employer, who wished to claim the insurance money. His conviction was quashed. He believed the person entitled to consent did consent. (A possible charge here is conspiracy to defraud.) If the accused burns his own property in order to claim insurance money, he is not guilty under s 1(1) because he has not destroyed property belonging to another.

An example of how s 5(2)(b) is used is **Mitchell** [2004] Crim LR 139 (CA). The accused had his car wheel-clamped. He cut through the clamp. He could not rely on s 5(2)(b) because his car was not in immediate need of protection. Similarly in *Cresswell v DPP*, above, the accused could not rely on s 5(2) because the badgers did not belong to himself or another.

In s 5(2) 'right' covers a right of way: **Chamberlain v Lindon** [1998] 2 All ER 538 (DC). The accused was held to be protecting it when he demolished a wall and that right was in immediate need of protection because it was being obstructed. Whether what he was doing was lawful in civil law was irrelevant: if the facts fell within s 5(2), he had a defence.

Points to note

(a) It is immaterial whether or not the belief was justified, as long as it was honestly held (s 5(3)). The test, therefore, is subjective.

(b) As stated, the defence in s 5 does not apply to s 1(2), the aggravated offence. There is, however, a defence of lawful excuse to s 1(2), but it is not defined by reference to s 5. An example is smashing a coal shovel over the head of a person who is attempting to burgle one's house. One intends to damage property with intent to endanger life but, provided the force used in self-defence is reasonable, one has a s 5 defence.

(c) The burden of proof lies on the prosecution, which must disprove the lawful excuse.

(d) The difficult principle to understand in this topic is this: s 5 is construed to give a defence to persons intoxicated. In **Jaggard v Dickinson** [1981] QB 527 (DC) (well discussed by Glanville Williams 'Two nocturnal blunders' (1990) 140 NLJ 1564, who ably contrasted the instant case with **Gannon** (1987) 87 Cr App R 254 (CA)), a magistrates' court held that the accused could not rely on the defence of lawful excuse because her belief that the person entitled to consent to the damage would have consented was brought about by alcohol. Since the crime was one of basic intent (see the section on intoxication), she had no defence. The Divisional Court reversed the magistrates'

See Chapter 8 for
an explanation
of intoxication.
There is a diagram
illustrating this
on p 307.

court's decision. It held that her defence was based on her state of belief, *not* upon her drunkenness. The intoxication merely explained her belief. The Act does not provide that the accused's belief must be a sober one. Therefore, drunkenness giving rise to a belief in the owner's consent establishes this defence.

The contrasting position is where the accused puts forward evidence that he did not have the *mens rea* of recklessness because he was drunk. *MPC* v *Caldwell* [1982] AC 341 (HL) decided that intoxication not merely does not negative recklessness, it supplies it. Therefore, he has no defence to a charge of criminal damage if while drunk he sets light to a hotel. Accordingly, while drunkenness can explain why the accused believed as he did and so provide the basis for a lawful excuse, it leads to a conviction for recklessly causing criminal damage. The prosecution has shown recklessness, but he may have a lawful excuse.

(e) If the accused who is not drunk destroys property, believing it to be his own, the defence is not lawful excuse but is a failure to prove part of the offence: *Smith* [1974] QB 354 (CA). (See also Chapter 8 on mistake.)

(f) Section 5 is not exhaustive of lawful defences. Any other defence, such as self-defence, remains: s 5(5). Section 5(2) notes that there can be a lawful excuse as a defence in areas falling outside the terms of s 5(2). The Divisional Court in *Stear* v *Scott* (1984) LEXIS, 28 March, rejected the contention that breaking off a wheel clamp was such an excuse.

(g) It is not a lawful excuse for defendants to cut the wire at an airforce base in order to show their opposition to nuclear weapons, even if they subjectively believed that their actions fitted within s 5: *Ashford* [1988] Crim LR 682 (CA). They argued that the reduction of the risk of the use of nuclear weapons would protect property in England because the risk of retaliation would be reduced. The court held that the test of whether the accused was acting 'in order to protect property' was objective. *Ashford* was followed in *Kelleher*, unreported, 20 November 2003. The accused knocked the head off a statue of Baroness Thatcher in a protest against the influence multinational companies had over the policies of democratic governments and over the policies of the governments of the USA and UK, which he believed made the world a more dangerous place to live in and which would lead to the destruction of this planet. The accused was not acting 'in order to protect property' within s 5(2)(b); whether he subjectively believed he was was irrelevant; instead he was acting to secure publicity for what he believed. This ruling is inconsistent with the wording of s 5, which looks at the accused's own (subjective) belief. In *Hill* (1989) 89 Cr App R 74, the Court of Appeal held that the act of cutting the perimeter wire of a US base with a hacksaw was too remote from the prevention of nuclear war. The property, nearby houses, was not 'in immediate need of protection'. Therefore, it did not matter that the defendants believed they were acting 'in order to protect property belonging to another'. In *Chamberlain* v *Lindon* (above) the right of way was in immediate need of protection because the obstruction would otherwise continue until litigation had resolved the matter several years in the future. *Hill* also confirmed that the test was objective. The Divisional Court in *Chamberlain* v *Lindon* applied *Hill*.

This interpretation is contrary to the recommendation of the Law Commission (above), which proposed a subjective test. The phrase 'in order to' looks at the mind of the accused. It is interesting to note that the Court of Appeal has here made a subjective test into an objective one, whereas in self-defence it once made an objective test into a subjective one: *Scarlett* [1993] 4 All ER 629, though it later recanted and reinstated the objective test. A belief that God ordered the accused, a vicar, to write words from the Bible on a concrete pillar to protest against the use of force by the coalition against Iraq was not a lawful excuse: **Blake v DPP** (1992) 93 Cr App R 169 (DC). The law of England overrode the law of God. Belief in the consent of God to damage did not constitute a valid excuse. (Section 5(2)(a) requires a person to consent and it is moot whether God, if He exists, is a person.) The act, moreover, was not objectively capable of protecting property. It was too remote from protecting property in the Gulf States. The subjective belief that he was acting within s 5(2)(b) was irrelevant. A similar ruling was made in **Jones v Gloucestershire Crown Prosecution Service** [2005] QB 259 (CA). The defendants contended that they had a defence within s 5(2)(b) when they damaged property at RAF Fairford in order to demonstrate their belief that the war in Iraq was illegal. They argued that they had acted to preserve their homes and the homes of friends. The court held that none of the defendants could reasonably believe that cutting wire around the base could reasonably protect those houses. This is an objective test. The court held that the sole objective test was: 'could the act be said to be done in order to protect property?' All the other tests in s 5(2)(b) were subjective. In criticism it must be said that the paragraph is phrased in subjective terms. The courts have read in an objective limitation, a limitation impossible to square with the requirement that the accused acts 'in order to' protect property. There is, of course, nothing to prevent a Crown Court jury from not following a judge's direction and applying a subjective test.

The court in the **Jones** case summarised the law as follows. The accused has a defence if:

(i)   he acted in order to prevent damage to property, whether his own or another's. This test requires an answer to the question: 'could the act done be said to be done in order to protect property? . . .';

(ii) at the time he acted, he believed that the property was in immediate need of protection; and

(iii) he believed that the means adopted or proposed to be adopted were or would be reasonable having regard to all the circumstances;

(iv) in determining the answers to (ii) and (iii), it is immaterial whether the belief was justified, provided that it was honestly held.

The first test alone is objective.

(h) The act must be done in order to protect property. In **Hunt** (1977) 66 Cr App R 105 (CA), the accused, husband of the deputy warden of a block of flats, set fire to bedding in order to show that the alarm system was inadequate. He did show that the alarms did not work. His appeal was dismissed. His intention was not to protect property, but to reveal defects in the alarm system. His subjective belief was irrelevant. The Act must not be too remote from the protection of property. **Hunt** was applied in **Blake v DPP**, above. A belief that property may at some time in the future be damaged does not constitute a belief that it is in immediate need of protection: **Johnson v DPP** [1994] Crim LR 673 (DC). It is irrelevant though the accused believed that a certain date in the future is immediate. The court also held that the purpose of the accused in breaking locks was to bring in his furniture, not to protect it, when he was squatting. The phrase 'in order to . . .' in s 5(2)(b) means 'purpose': his purpose must have been to protect property to give rise to this defence. This objective reading of 'in order to' is criticised in (g) above.

(i) As stated above, s 5(2) is restricted to the protection of property. Therefore, it does not apply to the protection of a person, even a child: **Baker** [1997] Crim LR 497 (CA).

(j) The Court of Appeal in *Jones*, the facts of which are outlined above, rejected the argument that the accused must act to prevent *unlawful* damage. He is allowed to act to prevent lawful damage. This issue was not the subject of the appeal to the Lords [2006] UKHL 16.

The draft Criminal Code 1989, cl 185(1)(a), would extend the present s 5 to cover 'doing an act which . . . is immediately necessary and reasonable to protect himself or another from unlawful force or injury'. This recommendation would give consistency of treatment to the protection of persons and property: *Baker*. The Law Commission would revise s 5(2)(b) so that the force used is objectively reasonable as in the current law on self-defence: Report No. 218, *Legislating the Criminal Code – Offences against the Person and General Principles*, 1993. This recommendation would bring the law into line with that of the protection of people in the law of self-defence.

Mens rea

Example

In *G* [2004] 1 AC 1034 the House of Lords were faced with the following facts. Two boys, one of 11, one of 12, set fire to papers under a wheelie bin in the yard of a Co-op store. The bin caught fire and the fire spread to the Co-op, causing £1 million-worth of damage. Were the boys guilty of arson?

Arson is when criminal damage is caused by fire: Criminal Damage Act 1971, s 1(3). One form, the 'simple' form, of criminal damage (s 1(1)) occurs when the accused without lawful excuse destroyed or damaged property belonging to another with the intent to destroy or damage that property or being reckless as to whether it was destroyed or damaged. On the facts:

the Co-op is 'property';
it belongs to another;
there is no lawful excuse; and
there is damage to, if not destruction of, that property.

The boys did not intend criminal damage. The sole issue is whether they were reckless. *G* held that to be reckless a person had to foresee the possibility that damage may be caused. If because of their age (or tiredness or any other reason for failing to advert to a risk) they did not foresee damage, they are not guilty of criminal damage, even though had they been older, they would have foreseen the risk.

MPC v *Caldwell*, which has been mentioned in relation to recklessness (see Chapter 3) and intoxication (see Chapter 8), was for a decade thought to be the most important case in modern English criminal law. In relation to intoxication, the Lords held that where the charge was one of recklessly causing criminal damage the mental element of recklessness existed when the accused was drunk. In relation to recklessness, the accused had this mental element in criminal damage not just when he himself foresaw an unjustifiable obvious risk of damage occurring, but also when a reasonable person would have foreseen that risk. The former state of mind is sometimes called 'subjective recklessness', the latter 'objective recklessness'. Subjective recklessness is often called '*Cunningham* recklessness' after the CCA case which is the classic authority. Objective recklessness is often called '*Caldwell* recklessness'. What the Lords said is stated in the next paragraph. It should be remembered that in criminal damage there is an alternative mental state, intention, which was dealt with above. Since in both the aggravated and the simple forms, recklessness is sufficient, the definition of intent is not as important in criminal damage as in murder, where the sole requisite *mens rea* is intention. Besides intention or recklessness as to the destruction or damage, in the simple offence the accused must know that the property belongs to another. In criminal damage, the mental element (omitting knowledge that the property belongs to another in the simple offence) can be stated thus:

For a review of *Caldwell*, see pp 108–19 .

(a) 'simple offence' (s 1(1)):
   (i) intentionally causing criminal damage; and
   (ii) recklessly causing criminal damage;

(b) 'aggravated offence' (s 1(2)):
   (i) intentionally causing criminal damage with intent to endanger life;
   (ii) intentionally causing criminal damage being reckless as to whether life is endangered;
   (iii) recklessly causing criminal damage with intent to endanger life; and
   (iv) recklessly causing criminal damage being reckless as to whether life is endangered.

Form (b)(iii) must be rare.

The facts of *Caldwell* were simple. The accused, who bore a grudge against the victim, set fire to the victim's hotel. The accused was drunk. Lord Diplock in a model direction gave what he himself described as an appropriate instruction, that recklessness throughout criminal damage was to be defined as follows. The accused was guilty if:

1 he does an act which in fact creates an obvious risk that property will be destroyed or damaged; and

2 when he does the act he either has not given any thought to the possibility of there being any such risk or has recognised that there was some risk involved and has nonetheless gone on to do it.

Lord Diplock considered that the two states of mind in (2) were not practically distinguishable, yet the difference has marked criminal law over many years. Indeed Lord Goff in *Reid* [1992] 1 WLR 793 (HL) went further and said that in many situations a driver who failed to think was more blameworthy than one who considered the existence of a risk but disregarded it. This direction came under severe criticism (see previous editions of this book) and was 'departed from', in other words overruled, by the Lords in *G* [2004] 1 AC 1034. For further details of recklessness in modern law see Chapter 3. Not surprisingly Rose LJ said in *Cooper* [2004] EWCA Crim 1382: 'It is now, in the light of *G*, incumbent on a trial judge to direct a jury, in a case of this kind [criminal damage], that the risk of danger to life was significant to the defendant.' The accused, who had learning difficulties, lived in a hostel for those with mental health problems. He set light to the underside of a mattress in his room, using lighter fuel as accelerant. His conviction was quashed because the trial judge had directed the jury in *Caldwell* terms. In *Castle* [2004] EWCA Crim 2758 in which the court held that in respect of aggravated criminal damage being reckless as to whether life was endangered (1) that the accused was reckless as to a consequence when he was aware of a risk that it might occur and (2) that an accused was reckless as to a circumstance when he was aware of a risk that it existed or would exist.

Transferred malice

An issue of transferred malice (see Chapter 3) may arise in the crime of intentionally or recklessly causing criminal damage. The intention or recklessness need not be directed at a particular piece of property which was damaged as long as the accused intended to damage some property or was reckless as to the damage. For example, if the accused threw a stone at a car, intending to damage it, but missed and broke a shop window, he is guilty of criminal damage. He has the intent necessary in relation to the window as he intended to damage another's property. However, he will not necessarily be guilty under s 1(1) if he threw a stone at his own car intending to damage it but broke the window. His intention is not transferred: he has no 'malice' to transfer. Whether he is guilty of criminal damage depends now on whether he acted recklessly.

See pp 121–3 (Chapter 3) for an explanation of the doctrine of transferred malice.

Creating a dangerous situation and not dealing with it

In *Miller* [1983] 2 AC 161 (HL), the accused, a squatter, lit a cigarette, lay down on a mattress, and fell asleep. The cigarette fell onto the mattress. He woke up and saw it smouldering. He went into another room and fell asleep again. The house caught fire. He was charged with arson. He contended that all he had done amounted to an omission, a failure to put the fire out, and that did not constitute the *actus reus* of criminal damage. (See Chapter 2 for more about omissions.) The Lords held that the accused was guilty. Lord Diplock criticised the use of the term '*actus reus*' because that phrase made one believe that in the criminal law the accused was guilty only if he had *acted*. He said that he was guilty if his *conduct* had caused the damage. In this instance it had. The defendant had failed to take measures to stop the danger he had created. Since he also had the required mental element in that he was aware that the fire presented an obvious risk of damaging the house, he was under a responsibility to put out the fire: since he did not do so, he was guilty.

As in *Caldwell*, Lord Diplock gave a model direction:

> The accused is guilty of the offence under s 1(1) of the 1971 Act if, when he does become aware that the events in question have happened as a result of his own act, he does not try to prevent or reduce the risk of damage by his own efforts or if necessary by sending for help from the fire brigade and the reason why he does not is either because he has not given any thought to the possibility of there being any such risk or, because having recognised that there was some risk involved, he has decided not to try to prevent or reduce it.

Accordingly, the accused must be aware of the circumstances, but he need not realise that he ought to do something. Applying *Miller* the accused would not be guilty if he watched a fire which someone else had started. The width of *Miller* is a little uncertain, but presumably it would cover the 'hit-and-run' driver who leaves his victim unconscious at the side of the road.

The effect of intoxication in a *Miller* situation was discussed in *Cullen* [1993] Crim LR 936 (CA). The accused had taken a large dose of sedatives and a large amount of alcohol. He set fire to material in his room in a hostel. The court applied *Miller* and *Caldwell*. He had caused criminal damage. If he did not appreciate the risk because he was drunk, he was guilty because he was to be judged on how he would have reacted to the fire, had he been sober. If he had been sober, he would immediately have put the fire out. He was thus guilty.

Custody or control of anything with intent to destroy or damage

Section 3 of the Criminal Damage Act 1971 reads:

A person who has anything in his custody or under his control intending without lawful excuse to use it or cause or permit another to use it –

(a) to destroy or damage any property belonging to some other person; or

(b) to destroy or damage his own or the user's property in a way which he knows is likely to endanger the life of some other person

shall be guilty of an offence.

It is sufficient that the accused intends to use the thing at some future time. There is no need for an intent to make immediate use. 'Anything', which is not defined in the Act, would seem to be just that, anything. The Law Commission gave two examples: a hammer and a box of matches. In *Hill* (1989) 89 Cr App R 74 (CA) a hacksaw blade fell within 'anything'. The lawful excuse defence in s 5 does not apply to s 3 if the offence falls within (b); it does if it falls within (a). Section 3 is a preliminary offence. It covers a situation where the crime of attempted criminal damage does not apply because of the narrowness of the definition of attempt. This offence enables the police to intervene at an early stage to prevent criminal damage. As was seen in Chapter 10, the trial judge has power to withdraw the issue of attempt from the jury and may do so in circumstances where most juries would convict, such as when the accused is near the entrance of the Post Office he intended to steal from. Section 3 would catch the accused at this stage if he intended to cause criminal damage as a preliminary to the theft or robbery. Surprisingly there is no equivalent offence in the area of non-fatal offences: the accused would not be liable until he had done a more than merely preparatory act. In the interests of crime prevention it is suggested that s 3 could be generalised to apply beyond criminal damage, thereby protecting the public more than the law of attempts does at present. The mental element is 'intending'. In this context only direct intent (see the previous chapter) is included because it must be the accused's purpose to destroy or damage. The accused is guilty of this offence if he intended to use the 'thing' should it prove necessary: *Buckingham* (1976) 63 Cr App R 159 (CA). This ruling is in line with the law on possessing explosives.

Threats to destroy or damage property

This offence is created by s 2 of the Criminal Damage Act 1971. The *mens rea* is the intent to make the threat; there is no need to intend to carry it out. It need not be shown that the victim was made afraid. Section 2(1) reads:

A person who without lawful excuse makes to another a threat, intending that the other would fear it would be carried out –

(a) to destroy or damage any property belonging to that other or a third person; or

(b) to destroy or damage his own property in a way which he knows is likely to endanger the life of that other or a third person

shall be guilty . . .

There is no restriction of the form of the threat. It may be made orally or in writing, expressly or impliedly. A threat is made when it is uttered. There is no need for the victim to receive or understand the threat. The threat need not be one of immediate harm.

The threat must be one to do an act which falls within s 1. If it falls within s 1(1), the 'simple' offence, the s 5 defence of 'lawful excuse' applies (see above). If it is one to do a s 1(2) offence, that definition does not apply.

Cases are rare but a recent one is **Cakmak** [2002] Crim LR 581. Six defendants threatened to set fire to themselves if an attempt was made to storm the two pods of the 'London Eye' which they had taken over in a protest against human rights abuses in Turkey. The Court of Appeal quashed the convictions because the trial judge had not properly directed the jury that there had to be a threat to destroy or damage the property of another. On the facts there was a threat to another, the controller of the 'Eye', and the defendants intended to damage the attraction.

Summary

- There are two types of criminal damage crime: 'simple' criminal damage, which is where the accused intentionally or recklessly destroys or damages property belonging to another, a crime contrary to s 1(1) of the Act; and 'aggravated' criminal damage where the accused intentionally or recklessly destroys or damages any property (including property belonging to the accused herself) with intent to endanger life or being reckless as to whether life will be endangered contrary to s 1(2) of the Act. When either form of criminal damage is caused by fire, it should be charged as arson: s 1(3).

- To the 'simple' form of the offence there is a defence of lawful excuse: see s 5(1).

- The chapter concludes with the crimes of custody or control of anything with intent to destroy or damage, an offence contrary to s 3 of the 1971 Act, and threats to destroy or damage property contrary to s 2(1) of the Act.

References

Reports

Home Office, *Crime in England and Wales: Quarterly Update to September 2011*, HOSB 01/12, 2012

Law Commission Report no. 29, *Offences of Damage to Property* (1970)

Law Commission Report no. 218, *Legislating the Criminal Code – Offences against the Person and General Principles* (1993)

Books

Ormerod, D., *Smith and Hogan's Criminal Law*, 13th edn (Oxford University Press, 2011)

Journals

Williams, G. 'Two nocturnal blunders' (1990) 140 NLJ 1564

Further reading

Edwards, I. 'Banksy's graffiti: a not-so-simple case of criminal damage?' (2009) 73 JCL 345

Elliott, D.W. 'Endangering life by destroying or damaging property' [1988] Crim LR 403

Visit **www.mylawchamber.co.uk** to access tools to help
you develop and test your knowledge of criminal law,
including interactive multiple choice questions, practice
exam questions with guidance, annotated weblinks,
glossary flashcards, legal newsfeed and legal updates.

Use Case Navigator to read in full some of the key cases referenced
in this chapter with commentary and questions:

R v G and Another [2003] UKHL 50

Glossary

actual bodily harm injury which is more serious than a touching but less serious than grievous bodily harm (q.v.). 'Bodily' is read widely to cover not just the flesh and bones but also psychiatric matters. The crime of assault occasioning actual bodily harm is contrary to s 47 of the Offences Against the Person Act 1861.

actus reus this Latin term means the act, omission or state of affairs required by the offence. It is distinguished from the **mens rea** or mental element of the crime. The *actus reus* differs from crime to crime. For example, in theft it comprises three elements: appropriation, property and belonging to another.

age the age of criminal responsibility is 10 in England and Wales. The Crime and Disorder Act 1998, s 34, abolished the previous law of mischievous discretion which applied to those above 10 and below 14.

aiding and abetting helping or encouraging.

arson this is the crime of criminal damage by fire. It is contrary to s 1(1) and s 1(3) of the Criminal Damage Act 1971 when the accused did not intend to endanger life or was reckless as to endangering life and contrary to s 1(2) and s 1(3) when he did.

assault in criminal law this word bears two meanings. The first, narrower definition is the intentional or reckless causing of the victim to apprehend immediate and unlawful violence. This type of assault is sometimes known as psychic or technical assault. The second, wider meaning covers both the first type of assault and the crime of battery (q.v.). It is in this second sense that 'assault' is used in the offence of assault occasioning actual bodily harm contrary to s 47 of the Offences Against the Person Act 1861. The offence of 'psychic' or 'technical' assault is, the Divisional Court has ruled, contrary to s 36 of the Criminal Justice Act 1988.

attempts most indictable offences (i.e. those triable in the Crown Court) are committable as attempted crimes when the accused intends to commit the offence and performs a 'more than merely preparatory' step on the way towards committing the offence. For example, I, having made my mind up to kill you, am stopped from shooting you dead just before I pull the trigger. I intend to kill you and I have performed a more than merely preparatory step on the way towards killing you. Similarly, if I shoot to kill but miss, I can be found guilty of attempted murder. It should be noted that the crime of attempted murder's *mens rea* is intent to kill even though murder itself may be committed by either an intent to kill or an intent to cause grievous bodily harm. All attempts are contrary to the Criminal Attempts Act 1981.

automatism this is a defence to all offences and occurs where the accused is not in control of his or her bodily actions: the defendant has acted involuntarily. There is debate as to whether the accused does not have the *actus reus* for the offence or does not have the *mens rea* or has a defence; or (and this is the view taken by the writer) whether there is something preliminary to *actus reus*, *mens rea* and any defence, namely that the prosecution has to prove that the defendant acted voluntarily: if the accused has not so acted, he or she is not guilty at that point, i.e. before there is any need to prove the *actus reus* and *mens rea*. Whichever theory is preferred, the outcome is the same: the accused is not guilty.

basic intent offences crimes to which **intoxication** is not a defence, e.g. manslaughter.

battery this crime occurs when the accused intentionally or recklessly touches another person without consent. The Divisional Court has held, it would seem incorrectly, that battery is contrary to the Criminal Justice Act 1988, s 36.

beyond reasonable doubt this phrase represents the criminal law burden of proof. The prosecution must prove each element of the offence in such a manner that the jury (in the Crown Court) or the magistrates (Justices of the Peace) or District Judge Magistrates' Court, formerly a stipendiary, in the magistates' courts are sure that the accused committed the offence.

blackmail this is defined in s 21(1) of the Theft Act 1968 as taking place when: 'with a view to gain for himself or another or with intent to cause loss to another, he [the accused] makes any unwarranted demand with menaces; and for this purpose a demand with menaces is unwarranted unless the person making it does so in the belief – (a) that he had reasonable grounds for making the demand; and (b) that the use of the menaces is a proper means of reinforcing the demand.'

burden of proof in criminal law it is normally the prosecution which has to establish that the offence took place. This principle extends even to most defences. For example, the prosecution has to prove that the accused is not afforded the defence of loss of control. The exceptions to the rule about defences are insanity (because every person is according to the law of insanity presumed to be sane) and diminished responsibility (because Parliament has so ruled: see s 2(2) of the Homicide Act 1957). The third exception, found in s 101 of the Magistrates' Courts Act 1980, is where the crime is defined in terms of an offence followed by an exception. Where the burden of proof is on the defendant, the standard of proof is the civil law one of 'on the balance of probabilities'. The current controversy is whether these so-called 'reverse onus' of proof exceptions are justifiable under Article 6 of the European Convention on Human Rights.

burglary an offence contrary to s 9 of the Theft Act 1968. Better put, s 9 is divided into two ways of committing the crime and there are two crimes, dependent where the accused is in relation to the building or part of one she wishes to enter or has entered. The two ways of committing burglary are:

1 entering a building or part of a building as a trespasser with intent to commit one of three crimes: theft, grievous bodily harm and criminal damage;

2 having entered a building or part of one as a trespasser, stealing or attempting to steal or committing grievous bodily harm or attempting to do so.

If the building is a dwelling place, the maximum sentence is 14 years' imprisonment; if it is not a dwelling place, the maximum is 10 years.

The case which generations of law students loved for its facts, *Collins* (1973) CA, involved the crime of burglary as it then existed: it then covered entry as a trespasser with intent to rape. This crime was abolished and replaced by a wider crime with the Sexual Offences Act 2003.

Aggravated burglary is contrary to s 10 of the same statute. It is committed when the accused is guilty under s 9 and in sum enters with a weapon of offence, an imitation firearm, a firearm, or explosive (the mnemonic is 'wife'!)

causation in criminal law it is usual to state that whether the accused caused a certain consequence depends on two issues, causation in fact (also known as factual causation and 'but for' causation) and causation in law (sometimes called legal causation). The prosecution must prove both beyond reasonable doubt. See also **eggshell skull rule**.

children see **age**.

coercion see **marital coercion**.

conduct crimes offences where only the forbidden behaviour is to be proved such as the offence of dangerous driving: no result of the accused's conduct has to be proved, cf. **result crimes**.

consent the basic rule is that consent is a defence to assault and battery but not to more serious offences such as wounding with intent to cause grievous bodily harm. The leading authority is *Brown* [1994] HL. To this rule there are several exceptions including 'manly sports' such as boxing, horseplay, flagellation for religious purposes, male circumcision, and branding one's initials onto one's wife's buttocks (!).

conspiracy this offence is known as an 'inchoate' one, i.e. it occurs before the principal offence takes place. For example, there may be a conspiracy to murder at a time before the murder itself takes place. Conspiracy is based on an agreement to do an unlawful act. If the unlawful act is a crime, the offence is one contrary to the Criminal Law Act 1977, s 1(1), as amended. There are one or two common law conspiracy offences, the main one being conspiracy to defraud: one can be guilty of this offence even though the object is not in itself criminal.

constructive manslaughter a person is guilty of this form of **manslaughter** if she kills as a result of committing a crime which is seen objectively as being dangerous. The term 'dangerous' in this context means: one which 'all sober and reasonable people would inevitably recognise must subject the other person to, at least, the risk of some harm resulting therefrom, albeit not serious harm' (per Edmund Davies LJ, *Church* [1966] 1 QB 59 (CCA). This crime is also known as unlawful act manslaughter, a term which is helpful because it reminds us that it can be committed only by an act and not by an omission.

contributory negligence is not a defence in Criminal Law.

corporate liability at times a company may be responsible for the crimes of others. The controversial method of so doing is via the doctrine of identification, i.e. the company is criminally liable for the acts and omissions of high-ranking officers of the company. Those officers are identified as being the company; in other words, they are the company. Corporate criminal liability for manslaughter is contrary to the Corporate Manslaughter and Corporate Homicide Act 2007, which has its own rules of attributing liability to the company or other undertaking.

counselling advising on the commission of an offence.

criminal damage this offence occurs when the accused destroys or damages property. It comprises two different offences. The first is contrary to s 1(1) of the Criminal Damage Act 1971: the accused intentionally or recklessly destroys or damages property *belonging to another*. This crime is sometimes known as 'simple' criminal damage. Section 1(2) creates what may be called 'aggravated' criminal damage. This crime occurs when the accused intentionally or recklessly

destroys or damages property *whether belonging to another or not*, intending to destroy or damage property or being reckless as to whether property is destroyed or damaged. Criminal damage by fire should be charged as **arson**: see s 1(3) of the 1971 Act.

deception misrepresentation, fraud, telling lies. See also **fraud**.

diminished responsibility this defence found in s 2(1) of the Homicide Act 1957 as inserted by the Coroners and Justice Act 2009 has the effect of reducing murder to (voluntary) manslaughter. It comprises three elements: (i) an abnormality of mental functioning, which arises from 'a recognised medical condition'; (ii) this must substantially impair the accused's ability to do one of three things (understand the nature of her conduct; to form a rational judgment; or to exercise self-control); and (iii) these must provide an 'explanation' for the killing. Note that this defence is a defence only to murder and that the burden of proof is on the accused (s 2(2)); however, the standard of proof is the civil law one of 'on the balance of probabilities'.

drunkenness as a defence see **intoxication**.

duress this is a defence to all offences except murder, attempted murder and 'some forms of treason', as the authorities put it. The width of the defence has recently been tightened by *Hasan* [2005] 2 AC 467 (HL). This defence is sometimes called **duress *per minas*** (by threats) to distinguish it from the next entry where the threat is not caused by a human being. It takes the form of 'do this or else' and has a human source, e.g. 'I will seriously harm your mother unless you take part in a bank robbery'.

duress of circumstances a defence with similar boundaries to that of **duress** but the foundation for the defence is an emergency (e.g. 'drive through red lights to escape armed robbers') rather than 'unless you break the law, I will kill your children', which is the form duress (by threats) takes.

'eggshell skull' rule this is one of the 'rules' of causation. It is also known as 'you must take your victim as you find him'. It means that if the victim is physically or psychologically 'weak', the accused is responsible in criminal law just as in tort law for the injuries or death caused by a blow to him or her, even though the victim would not otherwise have suffered death or injury. For instance, assume that I am attacking you. Unknown to me, your skull is weak and when I hit you there with a brick, you die, then even though you would have lived, had you not had a thin skull, I have caused your death; and I have done so whether or not I (or anyone else including the victim) knew of the thinness of your skull.

encouraging and assisting a statutory offence contrary to the Serious Crime Act 2007 whereby the accused seeks to persuade in whatever manner the main offender to commit a crime. It replaced incitement, a common law offence.

excuse a type of defence where the accused is not justified in doing as she did but has a defence personal to her, e.g. 'at the time of the killing, I was insane'.

fitness to plead see **unfitness to plead**.

fraud there were several offences of fraud in criminal law. The main ones are contrary to the Fraud Act 2006. One still surviving common law offence of fraud is conspiracy to defraud.

going equipped this crime, contrary to s 25 of the Theft Act 1968, as amended by the Fraud Act 2006, takes place when the accused has with him otherwise than at his 'place of abode' 'any article for use in the course of or in connection with any burglary or theft'.

grievous bodily harm (GBH) injury to the person, whether to the body or to the psyche, which is more serious than 'actual' bodily harm (but which does not result in death). Examples include the effects of chopping someone's arm off, gouging out the victim's eye, and shooting someone in a vital organ. The Offences Against the Person Act 1861 contains two GBH offences: in brief, maliciously causing GBH with intent to do some GBH (s 18) and maliciously inflicting GBH (s 20).

gross negligence carelessness which is so bad that it deserves being called criminal. See *Adomako* [1995] 1 AC 171 (HL).

handling is a crime contrary to s 22(1) of the Theft Act 1968, which reads: 'A person handles stolen goods if (otherwise than in the course of the stealing) knowing or believing them to be stolen goods he dishonestly receives the goods, or dishonestly undertakes or assists in their retention, removal, disposal or realisation by or for the benefit of another person, or if he arranges to do so.' 'Goods' according to s 34(1) 'includes money and every other description of property except land, and includes things severed from the land by stealing'. The word 'stolen' in this definition is not restricted to goods which have been stolen contrary to s 1(1) of the 1968 Theft Act but extends e.g. to goods obtained by fraud and by blackmail. Whether the accused is dishonest is determined by the *Ghosh* [1982] QB 1053 (CA) test.

homicide the generic term for killing a human being. The main homicide offences are murder and manslaughter but there are others such as genocide and **infanticide**.

inchoate offences these crimes are ones in which the principal offence has not (yet) been committed. An example is the crime of **attempt** (q.v.). The other two inchoate offences are **encouraging and assisting** and **conspiracy**. It should be noted that other offences take the form of inchoate offences. For example, **burglary** contrary to s 9(1) of the Theft Act 1968 includes entry as a trespasser with intent to steal. The accused is guilty of this offence even though she has not yet stolen any property.

infanticide this offence is where a woman causes the death of her child who is aged under 12 months 'but at the time of the act or omission the balance of her mind was disturbed by reason of her not having fully recovered from the effect of giving birth to the child or by reason of the effect of lactation consequent upon the birth of the child'. In those circumstances the crime is infanticide, a form of manslaughter, and not murder.

insanity an accused has the defence of insanity to any offence if she proves on the balance of probabilities that at the time of the offence she (i) was suffering from a disease of the mind, (ii) which caused a defence of reason and (iii) either (a) did not know the nature and quality of the act or (b) did not know that what she was doing was wrong. This statement of the law derives from *M'Naghten* (1843) 8 ER 718. Note that the burden of proof is on the accused and that the standard of proof is on the balance of probabilities. For insanity at the time of the trial see **unfitness to plead**.

intent(ion) in criminal law this term bears two different meanings depending on the crime charged. The narrow meaning is 'aim' or 'purpose'. This definition is sometimes known as direct intent. The other meaning both covers the first meaning and may cover the situation where the accused foresees a consequence as virtually certain and that consequence is in fact virtually certain, as occurs when the accused explodes a bomb on a plane at 30,000 feet, wishing to claim on the insurance. Here she would be very happy if the plane victims survived – it is not her aim to kill them – but she knows that it is virtually certain that they will be killed and that outcome is virtually certain to occur. The definition says 'may cover' because it is a question for the jury looking at all the facts in deciding whether the accused did intend to kill. The principal authority on intent in this second, wider meaning is *Woollin* [1999] 1 AC 82 (HL), which is a case on **murder**. The term sometimes used for the scenario where the accused foresees a situation as virtually certain and that outcome is in fact virtually certain is 'oblique intent'.

intoxication whether it is caused by alcohol or drugs, intoxication is a defence to specific intent offences such as murder but not to basic intent offences such as manslaughter. The distinction between basic and specific intent offences is controversial. See this textbook for details.

involuntary manslaughter see **manslaughter**.

joint enterprise an agreement by two or more to carry out a common purpose. For example, Alf and Beth agree to burgle Connie's house. The phrase is not used when one party goes beyond what has been agreed, e.g. Beth kills Connie while performing the burglary.

justification in criminal legal theory this term denotes a defence where the accused's conduct was praiseworthy or at least permissible. An example is the defence of the use of reasonable force in self-defence.

loss of control a defence, partly replacing provocation, set out in the Coroners and Justice Act 2009. See text for discussion.

making off without payment this offence, contrary to s 3 of the Theft Act 1978, occurs when the accused, 'knowing that payment on the spot for any goods supplied or service done is required or expected from him, dishonestly makes off without having paid as required or expected and with intent to avoid payment of the amount due'. An example is where the defendant drives into a petrol station, intending to pay, changes her mind about paying after the petrol is put into the tank and drives off. Where the spot is will vary with the facts but in a restaurant it may be the point where the accused is to pay, often nowadays the table where the meal was eaten. Dishonesty bears its *Ghosh* [1982] QB 1053 (CA) definition. The HL in *Allen* [1985] AC 1029 held that the accused must intend to deprive *permanently*.

malice aforethought the *mens rea* of murder. It comprises the intent to kill and the intent to commit grievous bodily harm. It should be noted that no 'aforethought', i.e. premeditation, is needed and no malice, i.e. spite or ill-will, is needed.

manslaughter this is best seen as two different offences. The first type, voluntary manslaughter, occurs when the accused has **malice aforethought** and kills but has one of the defences found in ss 2 and 4 of the Homicide Act 1957: **diminished responsibility** and killing in pursuance of a suicide pact respectively or when the accused has the defence of **loss of control** contrary to the Coroners and Justice Act 2009. The second type, involuntary manslaughter, takes place when the accused kills either by an unlawful act ('**constructive manslaughter**') or when the accused kills through his or her **gross negligence**. There is also almost certainly a crime of (subjectively) reckless manslaughter.

marital coercion a defence available to wives only who commit an offence under the domination of their husband. The boundaries of the defence are similar to but seemingly wider than **duress**.

mens rea this Latin term, sometimes translated as 'guilty mind', is the mental element required by the crime. The mental element varies from crime to crime. For example, the accused is guilty of theft if she appropriates property belonging to another only when she does so dishonestly and with the intention permanently to deprive. The concepts of 'dishonesty' and 'with the intention permanently to deprive' form the *mens rea* of theft. When added to the *actus reus* of the offence, there is the crime of theft. Where an offence is defined in such a way that there is no *mens rea* as to one or more elements of the *actus reus*, that is a crime of **strict liability**.

mistake the general rules are that a mistake as to law is no defence but a mistake as to an element of the crime is a defence; however, the mistake, to be a defence, must be one as to a relevant element. Take the following illustration. Parliament has created an offence of selling 'bad' meat; the accused sells a piece of lamb, not knowing that it is 'bad'; therefore, she has made a mistake as to whether the meat is of the correct quality; if, however, the offence is a **strict liability** one as to the badness or otherwise of the meat, then the accused is guilty because it is irrelevant whether she knew the meat to be 'bad' or not.

murder often thought to be the most serious crime, murder is committed when the accused causes the death of the victim with **malice aforethought**. The victim must be alive at the time of the killing and not an enemy alien in time of battle. The former rule that the victim had to die within a year and a day of the attack was abolished in 1996. There are several defences to murder, both those which are defences only to murder such as **loss of control** and **diminished responsibility** and those which apply to all defences including murder such as **self-defence**. The defences of **duress** (by threats) and **duress of circumstances** do not apply to murder.

necessity there is debate in English law as to whether necessity exists as a defence and, if so, what its boundaries are. One view is that there is no defence at all; another is that there is a defence but it is restricted in its application in that it does not apply to murder, attempted murder and 'some forms of treason' (i.e. the same crimes to which **duress** is not a defence); and a third view is that it is a defence to all offences. This debate in part turns on the definition of necessity. If necessity is seen as a **justification**, it is defined as having a choice between committing a less serious crime and a more serious one and choosing to commit the less serious one. For example, the accused is faced with the choice between shooting dead a bomber (murder unless there is a defence) or letting the terrorist explode the bomb on public transport. The difficulties underlying this defence are exacerbated by the inconsistent use of terminology by the courts: sometimes, for instance, necessity is seen as a synonym for **duress of circumstances**.

novus actus interveniens there may be an act supervening between what the accused has done and the injury or damage. Where that act breaks the chain of **causation**, it is known as '*novus actus interveniens*'.

obtaining by deception see **fraud**.

omissions sometimes an accused is criminally liable for not doing something. An example is murder: if one deliberately starves one's victim, one is guilty of murder.

prevention of crime by s 3(1) of the Criminal Law Act 1967 the use of force is justified if done in the prevention of crime. There is a large overlap with the common law defence of **self-defence**. In both defences the force must be necessary and proportionate.

procuring instigating an offence.

property for the purposes of the Theft Act 1968 property is defined in s 4(1) of the Act as 'money and all other property, real or personal, including things in action or other intangible property'. This definition applies to both the offence of theft itself and to the crime of fraud. For the purposes of criminal damage property is defined in s 10(1) of the Criminal Damage Act 1971 as: 'property of a tangible nature, whether real or personal, including money and – (a) including wild creatures which have been tamed or are ordinarily kept in captivity, and any other wild creature or their carcasses if, but only if, they have been reduced into possession which has not been lost or abandoned or are in the course of being reduced into possession; but (b) not including mushrooms growing wild on any land or flowers, fruit or foliage of a plant growing wild on any land.'

rape this crime, which can be committed only by men, consists according to s 1(1) of the Sexual

Offences Act 2003 in the intentional penile penetration of the vagina, anus or mouth of the victim (whether male or female) without consent. The mental element as to consent is that the accused did not have reasonable belief in the victim's consent.

recklessness the definition of recklessness in criminal law was settled by the House of Lords in *G* (2004). It means that the accused has foreseen that a consequence may occur but has nonetheless gone on with his or her conduct. The risk of that consequence's occurring must be an unjustifiable one.

result crimes offences which the accused is not guilty of unless the prosecution can prove that her act or omission caused the consequence stated in the definition of the offence. For example, the result in murder is the death of the victim. If there is no death, murder is not committed (though attempted murder is a possible crime).

robbery an offence committed where the accused, while stealing, uses force on any person (whether the victim of the theft or not) or puts or seeks to put any person (similarly) in fear of force. See s 8 of the Theft Act 1968 for the full definition.

secondary participation not only is the perpetrator guilty of an offence (as the principal offender) but also those who help and encourage may be guilty as secondary parties. These accused are liable as aiders, abettors, counsellors, and procurers.

self-defence this is a defence to all offences. It covers the defence of oneself, of others and of property. The force used must be necessary and proportionate. It largely overlaps with **prevention of crime**. One difference is that in the defence of prevention of crime the force must, as may be evident, be used to prevent an offence; if the victim of the alleged defence would not be a criminal, e.g. because she is an infant (under the age of 10: see **age** above) or has the defence of **insanity**, then the user of force, the accused, cannot be acting to prevent crime but may have the defence of self-defence.

sexual offences these crimes are almost all contrary to the Sexual Offences Act 2003. The most serious one is **rape**.

specific intent offences crimes to which **intoxication** is a defence, e.g. murder and theft.

spouses and civil partners husbands and wives and civil partners may be guilty of most offences but not conspiracy; however, if the agreement to commit an offence is made by the wife, husband, or civil partner and a third party, all may be criminally liable.

status offences crimes where the *actus reus* consists of no voluntary action on the part of the accused. The most famous case involving such an offence is ***Larsonneur*** (1933) 24 Cr App R 74 (CCA).

stealing the offence of **theft**.

strict liability many offences in English law are ones where the prosecution does not have to prove *mens rea* as to one or more elements of the *actus reus*. An example is a butcher who is charged with the crime of 'selling bad meat'. If she is guilty of the crime even when she does not know that the meat she is selling is 'bad', the part of the *actus reus* of 'bad' in the crime of selling bad meat has no *mens rea* attached to it: this element of the offence is 'strict' and the offence is one of strict liability. Note that all the other elements of the *actus reus* have *mens rea* attached to them: the butcher must know that what she is doing is 'selling' and must know that she is selling 'meat'; nevertheless, because one element is 'strict', the whole crime is known as an offence of strict liability.

theft an offence, contrary to s 1(1) of the Theft Act 1968, which occurs when the accused dishonestly appropriates property belonging to another with the intention of permanently depriving the other of it. The maximum sentence is seven years' imprisonment (s 7 of the 1968 Act).

transferred malice this so-called doctrine applies where in simple terms the accused attacks one human being (or thing), misses him, and hits another (or another thing). For example, I shoot at you intending to kill you but I miss and kill your friend standing at your side. My intent ('malice') against you is transferred from you to your friend. The crime will be one of murder: I intended to kill and I did kill. Note that the doctrine does not apply between people and things (or vice versa). For instance, I intend to shoot you dead, but miss and my bullet breaks a window. My 'malice' against you, a human being, cannot be transferred against a thing, the window, to make me guilty of criminal damage. I may, however, be guilty of attempted murder and reckless criminal damage.

unfitness to plead this is a defence to all offences and applies when the accused is insane at the time of the trial. Note that insanity at the time of the offence constitutes the defence of **insanity**.

unlawful act manslaughter see **constructive manslaughter**.

vicarious liability rarely in criminal law may one person be responsible for the criminal acts and omissions of another person or of an organisation, but when he or she is, he or she is said to be vicariously liable. For readers who know the tort doctrine of vicarious liability, it must be emphasised that the criminal law doctrine is much narrower.

voluntary manslaughter see **manslaughter**.

wounding is defined as a breach of both layers of the skin. There are two offences of wounding: one contrary to s 18 of the Offences Against the Person Act 1861 (wounding with intent) and one contrary to s 20 (malicious wounding).

Index